Abnormal Psychology and Modern Life

James C. Coleman

UNIVERSITY OF CALIFORNIA AT LOS ANGELES

Abnormal Psychology and Modern Life

5th edition

Scott, Foresman and Company GLENVIEW, ILLINOIS

DALLAS, TEX. OAKLAND, N.J. PALO ALTO, CAL. TUCKER, GA. BRIGHTON, ENGLAND

Library of Congress Cataloging in Publication Data
Coleman, James Covington.
    Abnormal psychology and modern life.
Bibliography: p. 755
Includes indexes.
    1. Psychiatry. I. Title. [DNLM: 1. Mental disorders.
2. Psychopathology. WM100 C692a]
RC454.C6 1976   616.8′9   75-26876
ISBN 0-673-07889-2

1 2 3 4 5 6 7 8 9 10-RRW-82 81 80 79 78 77 76 75

Preface

During the past few years, it has become increasingly clear to scientists and world leaders alike that abnormal behavior has become a crucial social problem, involving not only the maladaptive behaviors of individuals and families but also of larger groups, including entire societies; it is also clear that such behavior is often the result of interactions between individuals or groups and aversive environments. The Fifth Edition of *Abnormal Psychology and Modern Life* is designed to clarify and elaborate on abnormal behavior from this broader perspective: to show the effects of social conditions and social change on the nature and incidence of maladaptive behaviors, and from this standpoint to help the reader better understand abnormal behavior both on a scientific level and on a compassionate, human level.

In our complex and rapidly changing world, human beings are confronted with three crucial problems, all interrelated and all having vitally important implications for our mental health both as individuals and as a society: first, there is *unfinished business*, including poverty, prejudice and discrimination, and the social stresses and maladaptive behaviors associated with them; second, *new business*, including the alarming rise in drug abuse and violent crime, energy and ecological crises, and accelerating and often uncontrolled social change; and third, *future business*, focusing on building a better world for all human beings.

Many people feel that these problems defy solution—that the human race is quite simply doomed. At the same time, however, new hope has been engendered by our changed perspective of the world resulting from the landing of human beings on the moon and from the possibility of an international community in outer space. From this new vantage point we have come to see ourselves as "astronauts" on a spaceship hurtling through the universe; it has become obvious that all people must join together to "shape up our spaceship" if we are to survive. This new hope has been nurtured by the realization that we do have the resources for coping with our problems and that the kind of future world we as human beings will have depends on our own decisions and actions as well as on our dedication to the "human enterprise."

All this is not to say that this revision pays less attention to the biological and psychological bases of maladaptive behavior or to individual mental disorders; rather, the Fifth Edition has been reorganized and extensively updated with respect to abnormal behavior on the part of both individuals and groups. Throughout, relevant new scientific findings, case materials, and summary charts have been introduced. A new illustration program has been designed to convey the reality of the many unusual forms of human experience and behavior being described. Overall, the attempt has been made to present in a clear and interesting manner the major concepts, issues, and trends in our contemporary views of abnormal behavior.

The general sequence of the Fifth Edition may be summarized as follows:

Part I sets the stage with an overview of abnormal behavior. It begins by defining the concept of *abnormal*, or *maladaptive*, behavior and describing the tremendous toll it exacts in human resources and suffering. A brief historical discussion traces the changing views of mental disorders from ancient to modern times, along with the development of contemporary medical, psychosocial, and sociocultural approaches. The differing emphases of these various viewpoints show the need for an interdisciplinary approach to understanding and dealing with abnormal behavior.

Completing Part I is a review of the basic principles of human development and adjustment, both normal and abnormal. Behavior is seen as a function of (a) our biological and psychological makeup; (b) the stress situations, both internal and external, with which we are confronted; and (c) the resources and limitations of our environments. The crucial roles of both learning and stress in the development and maintenance of abnormal behavior have been emphasized throughout. Within this general context, maladaptive behavior is viewed as involving not only individuals but the physical, interpersonal, and sociocultural environments in which they live.

Part II details the clinical pictures, causal factors, and treatment and outcomes of the major maladaptive patterns included in the DSM-II—the current classification of mental disorders worked out jointly by the American Psychiatric Association and the World Health Organization. Included here are transient situational disorders, neuroses, psychosomatic disorders, schizophrenia, depression, alcoholism and drug abuse, sociopathic disorders (including delinquency and crime), autism and other behavior disorders of childhood, and mental disorders associated with acute or chronic brain pathology.

Part III goes beyond the traditional and established classification syndromes to anticipate the shifting scene in maladaptive behaviors, specifically reflecting the changing attitudes and interest in the areas of sexual "deviations," suicide, and maladaptive behavior of groups. In dealing with sexual deviations, the Fifth Edition distinguishes between those which are clearly maladaptive—and are included in the DSM-II—such as pedophilia and forcible rape, and those which represent dysfunctions or alternative patterns or life-styles, such as prostitution and homosexuality. In discussing the problem of suicide, this edition examines the motives and issues involved in taking one's own life and investigates available resources for prevention. And in dealing with the maladaptive behavior of groups, it examines the crucial problems of war and violence, group discrimination, over-population, ecological violations, and uncontrolled technological and social change.

Part IV deals with the areas of assessment, therapy, and prevention. The chapter on assessment not only describes modern techniques but also examines the major issues involved in assessing and "labeling" people. The chapter on therapy covers contemporary biological, psychosocial, and sociocultural approaches in some detail. In the final chapter of the text, "Action for Mental Health and a Better World," attention is devoted to possibilities for preventing maladaptive behavior, to national and international efforts toward fulfilling the dream of comprehensive health, to the challenge of building a good future for human beings on our "spaceship," and to the role that the individual can play in these crucial endeavors.

Finally, in the present edition, the Glossary has been refined in an effort to make it of maximal use to the reader. Not only does it include those possibly unfamiliar terms that appear in the text itself, but also some additional terms that the student may encounter in lectures or supplementary reading. Also, as in the previous edition, the back endsheets are printed with the currently accepted classification of mental disorders, although certain modifications have been made in the text presentation for purposes of instruction.

For simplicity of presentation, the words "he" and "his" are used when referring to patients or therapists where the individual's sex is not specified. However, the author and editors are well aware of the sexual bias of the English language and have attempted to follow the "Guidelines for Nonsexist Use of Language," established by the Task Force of the American Psychological Association (1975), whenever practicable.

While this text provides the reader with a comprehensive and coherent picture of the field of abnormal psychology, it is also designed to provide maximum flexibility in the use of content materials. For example, even though each chapter ties in with the others, all are relatively independent in their own right. Thus a particular combination of chapters can be used in accordance with the needs and goals of given students, classes, and instructors. In short, this text can be used effectively with classes which differ markedly in student background, length of course, and educational objectives.

Several ancillary publications are available to provide additional flexibility and depth in the planning of the course in abnormal psychology: first, a student guide prepared by Dr. Joel D. West of Northern Michigan University which can be used to focus and extend the student's understanding of the material of each chapter through review, analysis, and personal involvement; second, two sets of tapes—the Six Diagnostic Interviews, prepared by Dr. Rudolph Novick of Forest Hospital, Des Plaines, Illinois, and Six Modern Therapies, prepared by Dr. Stewart Shapiro of the University of California at Santa Barbara; and, third, an instructor's resource book, including suggestions for organizing the course, possible lecture topics, activities for student involvement, provocative discussion questions, an up-to-date list of films in the mental health field, and multiple-choice and essay-type test items.

An author of a text such as this is greatly indebted to many pioneers in the study of human behavior—from Plato and Shakespeare to Sigmund Freud—and to his many colleagues in the biological and social sciences whose research is helping to conquer the frontier of "inner space" and of abnormal behavior. The author would like to express his particular appreciation to several of his contemporaries, including Dr. Albert Bandura of Stanford University, Dr. Karl Menninger of the Menninger Foundation in Topeka, Kansas, Dr. Carl Rogers of the Center for Studies of the Person, in La Jolla, California, and Dr. B. F. Skinner of Harvard University.

In addition, acknowledgment is due to the many concerned students whose critical evaluations, helpful suggestions, and creative ideas have added greatly to the readability and relevance of each chapter. Special thanks also go to Dr. Andrew Comrey, Dr. Elliot Rodnick, and Dr. Joseph Sheehan of the University of California at Los Angeles for their many contributions; to Dr. Irving Maltzman, Chairman of the Department of Psychology at UCLA for his active support and help; to George Erdmann of the State of Illinois Department of Mental Health; to John Heiken, M.D., of the Malibu Medical Group; to Dr.

Matthew Maibaum of the Veterans Administration; to John Harris of Ventura College; to James Moss of the University of Southern California; and to Dr. Ira Iscoe of the University of Texas.

Many other people made valuable contributions to the book. For the illustration program, special thanks are due to Sandy Schneider; for design, to Mary Ann Lea; and for editorial-production coordination, to Meredith Whipple. Finally, the author's grateful thanks go to Joanne Tinsley and Amanda Clark of the Scott, Foresman editorial staff for both highly competent assistance and dedication "far beyond the call of duty"; and to Mrs. Marguerite Clark of the same staff, who worked on the First Edition of this text and has continued to make valuable contributions over the years. Particularly, the author would like to express his profound appreciation to Azalea, his esteemed colleague and loving wife, whose encouragement and assistance were crucial during the three years of sustained pressure required to complete this Fifth Edition.

At the close of his journeys Tennyson's Ulysses says, "I am a part of all that I have met." It is the author's hope that the readers of this book, at the end of their journey through it, will see what they have learned as a meaningful part of their life experience—and that it will contribute to their understanding of and empathetic concern for those for whom the problems of living create severe stress and perhaps become too great.

James C. Coleman

Contents

II

Patterns of Abnormal (Maladaptive) Behavior

Dorothea Lange Collection, The Oakland Museum

III
Other Key Areas of Problem Behavior

Abnormal Psychology and Modern Life

I
Perspectives on Abnormal Behavior

1

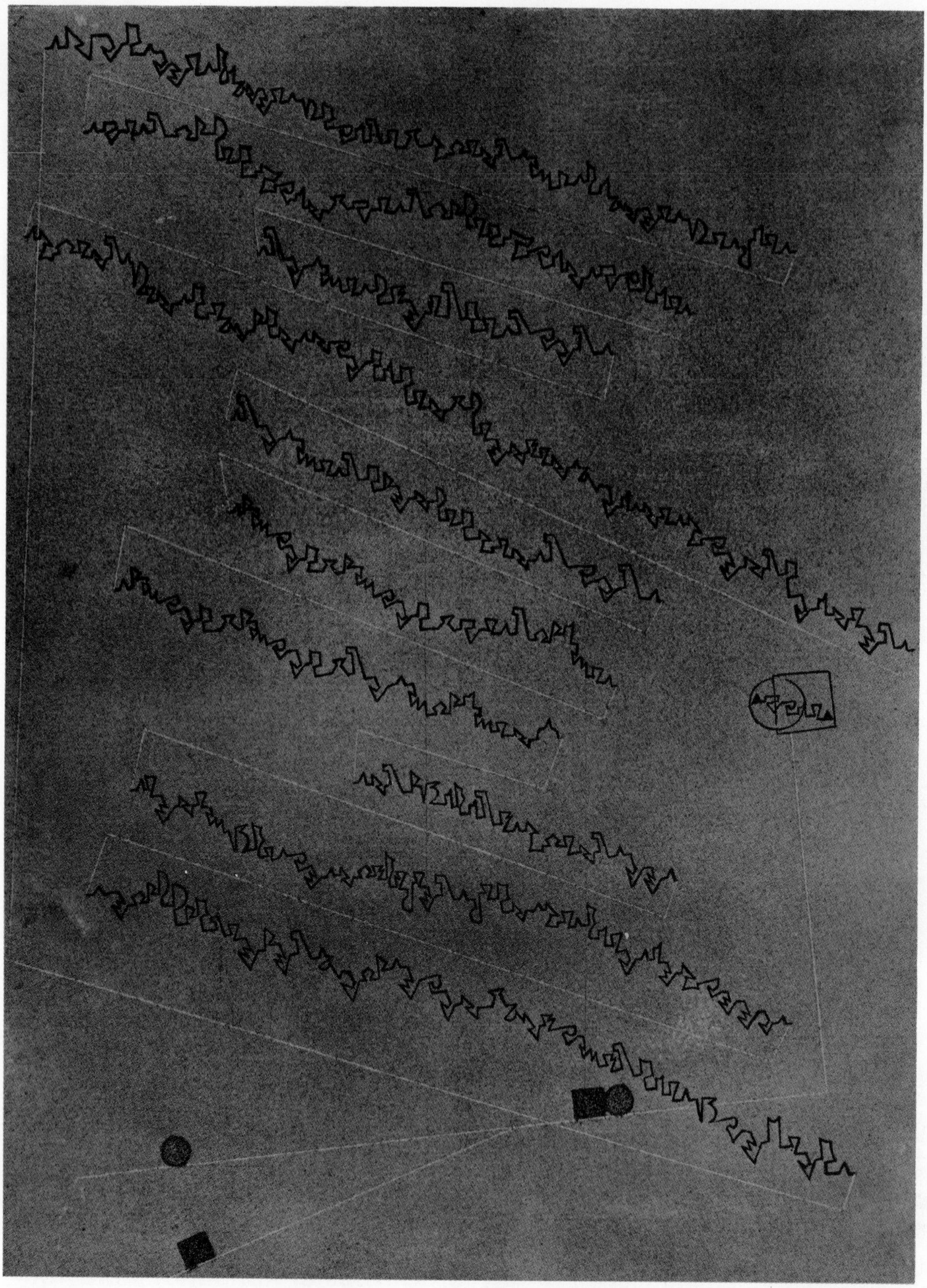

Abnormal Behavior in Our Times

The seventeenth century has been called the Age of Enlightenment; the eighteenth, the Age of Reason; the nineteenth, the Age of Progress; and the twentieth, the Age of Anxiety. Although the path to a meaningful and satisfying way of life has probably never been an easy one, it seems to have become increasingly difficult in modern times.

Wars have disrupted both personal and national life, leaving in their wake grief, destruction, and social unrest. Economic fluctuations and inflation have taken their toll in unemployment, dislocation, and poverty for millions of people. Racial prejudice, with its unreasoned feelings of superiority, hatred, and resentment, hurts both the individual and the community. Urban society, with its high mobility, disrupted friendships, and loss of extended family bonds, places increasing stress on the home. Unhappy marriages and homes broken by divorce bring hurt and disillusionment and leave emotional scars on parents and children alike. Excessive competition and impersonal bureaucracy tend to "dehumanize" the individual and lead to a loss of meaning in human existence. The human population explosion increases widespread hunger and starvation, canceling out the advances of the "green revolution" and creating difficult social problems and tensions. Grinding poverty and discrimination exist side by side with abundance and opportunity—leading to social pressures that periodically erupt in violence. The wasteful use of our natural resources, coupled with the pollution of air, water, and soil, threatens the life-support system of all who travel on the spaceship Earth. And the ever-present threat of global atomic war further aggravates our anxieties.

Ours is an age of tremendous growth of knowledge and of rapid social change. More scientific and technological advances have been made in the past fifty years than in all previous recorded time; for many people, the pace of change is simply too fast, resulting in what has been termed "future shock." Modern science and technology affect all phases of our lives. Innovations in transportation and communication have broadened our horizons and shown the interdependence of peoples, so that

Popular Views of Abnormal Behavior

Abnormal Behavior as the Scientist Sees It

The Orientation of This Book

3

daily we face international as well as national and local problems. The landing of men on the moon has inevitably placed the earth and its inhabitants in a new perspective; and as we venture farther into the universe, we are increasingly and inescapably confronted with our own finiteness and with questions concerning the meaning of human existence.

At the same time, traditional values and beliefs no longer seem self-evident; we lack the comforting religious and social absolutes that provided security for our forebears. Today we are increasingly questioning long-accepted assumptions about religion, education, sex, marriage, and social and political institutions and processes. And often we seem unable to anticipate and prepare for the problems that confront our society or to foresee the consequences of group decisions and actions until the results approach catastrophic proportions.

Unfortunately, advances in our understanding of human nature and behavior have lagged far behind our advances in the physical and biological sciences. We know much about the atom and the gene but not nearly enough about love or the values needed for achieving a meaningful and fulfilling life, or for constructing a better world for us all. As a consequence, many of us tend to stumble around seeking answers among diverse religions, philosophies, and social programs that we hope will provide direction and meaning for living in our contemporary world.

Small wonder that on every side we see anxious, unhappy, bewildered people who miss the realization of their potentialities because they cannot find satisfactory answers to problems that seem just too great. The stress of modern life is indicated by the incredible amount of tranquilizers, sleeping pills, and alcoholic

---

ESTIMATED INCIDENCE OF MAJOR MALADAPTIVE BEHAVIOR PATTERNS IN THE UNITED STATES IN 1975

20,000,000 or more labeled as neurotics

20,000,000 or more suffer from chronic high blood pressure (typically associated with stress)

3,000,000 or more labeled as psychotics

5,000,000 or more labeled as psychopathic (antisocial) personalities

12,000,000 or more labeled as alcoholics

2,000,000 or more dependent on heroin, barbiturates, and other dangerous psychoactive drugs

6,500,000 or more labeled as mentally retarded

200,000 or more attempt suicide*

6,000,000 or more emotionally disturbed children and teen-agers

1,000,000 or more students withdraw from college each year as a result of emotional problems

10,000,000 or more juveniles and adults arrested in connection with serious crimes*

*The incidence of suicide attempts and serious crimes may be much higher due to the large number which are not officially reported.

4 Chapter One / Abnormal Behavior in Our Times

beverages consumed in our society; by the emergence of heart attacks as the leading cause of death in our society; by the marked increase in suicide among our youth; and by the alarming increase in delinquency and crime, particularly crimes of violence. In an equally dramatic way, it is reflected in the widespread preoccupation with altered states of consciousness and parapsychology as well as the ample literature on dehumanization and alienation.

Despite the stress of modern life, most people still manage to "muddle through," worrying along and solving their problems after a fashion. But for many people, the stress proves too great. It is startling to note that emotional disturbances incapacitate more people than all other health problems combined. If present trends continue, it is estimated that one person in ten now living in the United States will at some time require professional treatment for such emotional disturbances. Furthermore, this figure says nothing of the many kinds of organic illness brought on and aggravated by emotional conflict and tension.

Abnormal behavior has for good reason been designated the country's number-one health problem. This does not mean that effective personality adjustment is impossible in modern life. It does mean, however, that many of us encounter serious difficulties in dealing with life's problems—particularly problems centering around intimate personal relationships and the search for values contributing to a meaningful and fulfilling way of life. Thus the study of abnormal behavior may be of great help in fostering personal adjustment and growth and in reducing the great toll of misery and lost productivity that mental disorders are exacting in our society.

Popular Views of Abnormal Behavior

When we think of abnormal behavior, we are likely to think of extreme, spectacular examples because, as in other fields, it is the bizarre and the sensational that command attention. Examples of mental disorders that we have heard or read about are apt to be extreme cases that, isolated and lumped together, give us a "chamber-of-horrors" picture of abnormal behavior rather than the truer picture, in which less spectacular minor maladjustments are far more common. Popular present-day beliefs about abnormal behavior thus tend to be based on atypical and unscientific descriptions. Partly this has been inevitable, because it is only recently that scientific research methods have been turned to an understanding of abnormal behavior.

A brief review of a few cases of mental disorders from history and literature will be of value in giving us a broader perspective, for most of the forms of severe mental disorder that we see today have been observed and reported in other ages too.

Views carried over from history

Some of the earliest historical writings— Chinese, Egyptian, Hebrew, and Greek—provide striking "case histories" of disturbed individuals.[1] Saul, King of Israel in the eleventh century B.C., suffered from recurrent manic-depressive episodes. During an attack of mania (excitement) he stripped off all his clothes in a public place. On another occasion he tried to kill his son Jonathan.

[1]Sources on which this section is based include the following: Bluemel (1948), Born (1946), Lombroso (1891), Marks (1925), Martindale (1972), Sewell (1943), Whitwell (1936), and Zilboorg & Henry (1941).

William Blake's eighteenth-century depiction of Nebuchadnezzar, king of Babylon, based on a biblical description: ". . . he was driven from men, and did eat grass as oxen, and his body was wet with the dew of heaven, till his hairs were grown like eagles' feathers, and his nails like birds' claws" (Daniel 4:33).

Greek mythology contains many descriptions of mentally disturbed persons that afford some insight into the nature of the real-life cases from which the descriptions must have been drawn. For example, Hercules seems to have been afflicted with convulsive seizures accompanied by a homicidal fugue-type reaction. His attacks are graphically described by Euripides in the "phrenzy of Hercules": his eyes rolled, his consciousness clouded, he frothed at the mouth, showed violent fury, and attacked persons in his way, then fell, writhed, and finally fell into a deep sleep. Upon awakening, he had complete amnesia for the seizure. During the course of several attacks, Hercules killed two of his own children, two of his brother's children, his best friend, and his teacher. Ajax, too, became mentally disordered and slew a flock of sheep under the impression that he was attacking his enemies. On regaining his senses, he was so overcome with remorse that he committed suicide by throwing himself on his sword.

Many of the notables of later Greece and Rome, including Socrates, Alexander the Great, and Julius Caesar, apparently suffered from mental disorders of one kind or another, and the ensuing period of the Middle Ages contains innumerable instances of abnormal behavior. The great Oriental conqueror, Tamerlane (1336–1405), for example, was particularly fond of building pyramids of human skulls. One of his architectural achievements is reported to have contained some forty thousand of them.

In more recent times, George III of England—known as the "mad monarch"—showed a variety of symptoms, including periods of intense excitement and overactivity. During these periods of mania he shifted rapidly from one topic to another, asked precipitate questions without waiting for an answer, ate his food so rapidly that the members of his court had to bolt their food or leave the table hungry, raced up and down stairs, rode his horse to death, indulged in obscene language, and displayed the tireless energy typical of the manic who is just too busy to sleep.

The French philosopher Jean Jacques Rousseau (1712–1778) developed marked paranoid symptoms during the latter part of his life. He was obsessed with fears of secret enemies and

Cambyses, King of Persia in the sixth century B.C., was one of the first alcoholics on record. His alcoholic excesses were apparently associated with periods of uncontrollable rage during which he behaved "as a madman not in possession of his senses" (Whitwell, 1936, p. 38). On one occasion, without making any provision for the feeding of his army, he set out against the Ethiopians, who had greatly enraged him by calling the Persians "dung eaters." He was shortly forced to return to Memphis, where he found the people celebrating the feast of Apis. Furious at what he took to be rejoicing at his failure, he ordered that all the people taking part in the feast be killed. Cambyses also defied Persian law by marrying one of his sisters, and later he killed his other sister by kicking her during pregnancy. On another occasion he used his friend's son as a target for his arrows to demonstrate that his excessive drinking had not affected his skill. His aim was true and he killed the boy, proving his point, at least to his own satisfaction.

thought that Prussia, England, France, the king, priests, and others were waging a terrible war against him. He believed that these enemies caused him to suffer indigestion, diarrhea, and other internal troubles, but their chief trick was to torture him by overwhelming him with benefits and praise, even going so far as to corrupt vegetable peddlers so that they would sell him better vegetables more cheaply. According to Rousseau, this was undoubtedly designed to prove his baseness and their generosity. It would be interesting here to know whether this behavior was related to the fact that he and his wife had left each of their five children at a foundling hospital.

Rousseau became panicky during a visit to London and fled, leaving all his luggage and money at the hotel. On his arrival at the coast, the winds were not favorable for his departure, and in this he saw another indication of the plot against him. After his return to France, his invisible enemies apparently stepped up their persecution. They corrupted his coffee merchant, his hairdresser, and his landlord; the shoeblack had no more blacking when Rousseau needed him; the boatman had no boats when this unfortunate man wished to cross the Seine; his enemies even prevented his front door from opening. He demanded to be put in prison, but even this was prevented by his imaginary foes. No longer able to trust people, he turned to God, to whom he addressed a very tender and familiar letter. To ensure the arrival of the letter at its proper destination, he tried to place it on the altar of Notre Dame at Paris. Finding the railing closed, he believed that Heaven, too, was conspiring against him. Finally he even came to distrust his dog.

The names of other philosophers, painters, writers, musicians, and celebrities who suffered emotional disturbances would make a long list. Mozart, for example, during the time he was composing the Requiem, thought that he was being poisoned. Beethoven, although miserably poor, was constantly changing his living quarters and sometimes had to pay for lodgings at three or four different places at once. Keats was a hypochondriac who suffered from chronic tension and was subject to spells of uncontrollable laughter and crying.

A fifteenth-century interpretation of the "tormenting of St. Anthony," the founder of Christian monasticism. He was said to engage in strange conflicts with demons during the many periods of his life he spent in solitude.

On one occasion van Gogh cut off his ear and sent it to a prostitute, an action apparently performed in a state of clouded consciousness resulting from his epileptic condition. Schopenhauer, Chopin, and John Stuart Mill suffered from attacks of depression. Rabelais, Samuel Butler, Burns, Byron, and Poe used alcohol excessively. Coleridge acknowledged using opiates before writing "Kubla Khan."

Many rulers and conquerors have been able to indulge seemingly sadistic inclinations. Attila the Hun is remembered mainly for the ruthlessness and barbarity of his conquests. Queen Mary I of England, better known as "Bloody Mary," was responsible for the Marian persecution—the wholesale burning of

Protestants as heretics during the years 1553 to 1558.

In reviewing these historical instances of abnormal behavior, it should be made clear that we are to some extent evaluating this behavior in the light of present-day concepts of mental disorder. In their own day, some of these people were looked on as perfectly normal, and others as only eccentric or unusual. We may also take note of the fact that, although many individuals with mental disorders have made significant contributions to society and the shaping of history, it has been those men and women of more effective personality adjustment who have carried the major burden in the achievement of social progress.

Ideas carried over from literature and drama

Long before abnormal psychology became an area of scientific study, the masters of fiction and drama developed many brilliant and moving characterizations of abnormal behavior, based on their keen observations of human behavior. Such literary classics, in their descriptions of human abnormality in all of its infinite subtleties of degree and variety, often achieve a lifelike vividness and an emotional force that science cannot achieve. *Othello*, for example, provides an unforgettable insight into the subjective quality of obsessive, violent jealousy.

Of course, literature cannot provide either the theoretical or practical basis for understanding and treating specific cases of abnormal behavior, but it does complement psychology in giving a different kind of understanding of such behavior. Literature yields valuable information, for example, about personality dynamics, about mental disorders prevalent during a particular historical period, and about the inner experiences of those who have undergone such disorders.

The writings of the Greek poets and dramatists contain many allusions to abnormal behavior. In his play *Medea*, Euripides (480–406 B.C.) described and analyzed the emotions of jealousy and revenge as displayed by a mother who murders her children. Sophocles (495–

406 B.C.) in *Oedipus Rex* and *Electra* has given us the first intimation of incest motives in the shaping of human behavior. And in the *Oresteia* trilogy, Aeschylus clearly described delusional and hallucinatory symptoms arising out of severe feelings of remorse and guilt.

Many of the characters in the plays of William Shakespeare portray the development of abnormal behavior with clinical accuracy. The intense guilt reaction of Lady Macbeth, after planning and participating in the bloody murder of King Duncan, is well brought out in her uneasy sleepwalking and symbolic handwashing:

Diana Rigg, contemporary actress, as Lady Macbeth examining her "blood-stained" hands.

"It is an accustomed action with her, to seem thus washing her hands: I have known her continue in this a quarter of an hour." (*Macbeth*, Act V, Scene i)

That her compulsive handwashing has failed, however, to "cleanse" her of her feelings of guilt is shown in her admission that

"Here's the smell of the blood still: all the perfumes of Arabia will not sweeten this little hand. Oh, oh, oh!" (Act V, Scene i)

Consider the humor as well as the pathos in the adventures of Don Quixote. Cervantes' hero becomes so overwhelmed by reading the most famous books of chivalry that he believes them to be true. How natural it seems for him to accept his "mission" as a knight errant and to sally forth into the world to defend the oppressed and to fight injustice like the heroes of his romances. Even when his excited imagination turns windmills into giants, solitary inns into castles, and galley slaves into oppressed gentlemen, the reader can feel a part of his adventuring. And finally when he is restored to his "right" mind through a severe illness and is made to renounce the follies of knight errantry, most of us probably feel a tinge of disappointment that the hero must give up his dreams and his noble "mission."

De Quincey (1821) revealed something of the "world within" in his description of his opium dreams:

". . . I brought together all creatures, birds, beasts, reptiles, all trees and plants, usages and appearances, that are found in all tropical regions, and assembled them together in China or Indostan. From kindred feelings, I soon brought Egypt and all her gods under the same law. I was stared at, hooted at, grinned at, chattered at, ran into pagodas: and was fixed for centuries at the summit, or in secret rooms; I was the idol; I was the priest; I was worshipped; I was sacrificed. I fled from the wrath of Brama through all the forests of Asia: Vishnu hated me: Seeva laid wait for me. I came suddenly upon Isis and Osiris: I had done a deed, they said, which the ibis and the crocodile trembled at. I was buried for a thousand years in stone coffins; with mummies and sphinxes, in narrow chambers at the heart of external pyramids. I was kissed, with cancerous kisses, by crocodiles: and laid, confounded with all unutterable slimy things, amongst reeds and Nilotic mud." (*Confessions of an English Opium Eater*)

Don Quixote, the noble but deluded idealist, sits in his library surrounded by some of the figures he saw during his various hallucinations.

It is interesting to speculate concerning the motivation that prompted other writings. For example, was a sort of vicarious sadism behind the fantasies of Jonathan Edwards when he pictured the brutal torturings in hell of those he considered to be sinners? When he preached on "Sinners in the Hands of an Angry God," his congregation received a terrifying warning:

"The God that holds you over the pit of hell, much as one holds a spider or some loathsome insect over the fire, abhors you, and is dreadfully provoked; His wrath towards you burns like fire; He looks upon you as worthy of nothing else, but to be cast into the fire; He is of purer eyes than to bear to have you in His sight; you are ten times so abominable in His eyes, as the most hateful and venomous serpent is in ours. . . .

"If we knew that there was one person, and but one, in the whole congregation, that was to be the subject of this misery, what an awful thing it would be to think of! . . . But alas! instead of one, how many is it likely will remember this discourse in hell! . . . And it would be no wonder if some persons that now sit here . . . should be there before tomorrow morning. These of you . . . that shall keep out of hell longest, will be there in a little time!" (Edwards, 1809, pp. 489–502)

Many modern writers have attempted to capture, often from their own experience, the pattern of thought processes underlying various types of abnormal behavior. Themes so treated have included schizophrenia, depression, suicide, alcoholism, drug dependence, mental retardation, sexual sadism, and homicide—in fact, almost the entire gamut of behaviors considered to be abnormal.

Even the biographer, historian, and political scientist have inevitably become interested in abnormal psychology. The biographer tries to explain the personality development and the odd or peculiar behavior of historical persons in the light of present psychological knowledge. And the historian cannot afford to ignore psychological principles in an attempt to understand historical events. For example, psychiatric evaluations of Nazi leaders have added much to our insight into events that shocked the world during and after their period of power. In 1960 the World Health Organization expressed the opinion that the stresses on persons in high positions are often too great for normal people. It suggested that, as a consequence, individuals with psychopathic personality makeup, who tend to exploit power for selfish purposes and have little concern for ethical values or social progress, often become leaders (WHO, 1960). Such a possibility obviously has profound social implications, especially since the stresses on world leaders are even greater today.

Some popular misconceptions

Throughout most of history, as we shall see in Chapter 2, beliefs about mental disorders have been generally characterized by superstition, ignorance, and fear. Although successive advances in the scientific understanding of abnormal behavior have dispelled many false ideas, there remain a number of popular misconceptions that merit brief discussion.

The belief that abnormal behavior is bizarre. The instances of abnormal behavior reported in the mass media, like those recorded in history and literature, are likely to be extreme ones involving murder, sexual assault, airplane hijacking, or other striking deviations from accepted social norms. Patients in mental hospitals and clinics are often pictured as a weird lot who spend their time ranting and raving, posing as Napoleon, or engaging in other bizarre behavior. In fact, most hospitalized patients are quite aware of what is going on around them, and only a small percentage exhibit behavior that might be labeled as bizarre. The behavior of most mental patients, whether in a clinical setting or not, is indistinguishable in many respects from that of "normal" people.

Actually, the term "abnormal" covers a wide range of behaviors. Some types of abnormal behavior are bizarre; but in the great majority of cases, abnormal behavior is so labeled because it is self-defeating and maladaptive. Such self-defeating patterns are a cause of concern, but they are well within the bounds of ordinary, understandable human experience. Included here would be the college student who for no apparent reason is so anxious that she can't concentrate on her studies and has to drop out of school, or the youth who creates serious difficulties in his social relationships by telling trivial lies. On a more serious level would be the young husband who mistreats his wife and then attempts suicide when she leaves him, or the adolescent girl who turns to prostitution to pay for her drug habit.

Finally, there are behaviors that are recognized generally as severely abnormal—the adolescent who pours gasoline over an old man and sets him on fire; the indignant youth who insists that his enemies have set up an electronic device that "pours filth into his mind"; the mother who abuses and eventually kills her baby; the alcoholic who cringes in terror before an imaginary invasion of cockroaches; or the paranoid who murders several innocent people he believes are plotting against him.

Cases like these are unusual, however, and not typical of abnormal behavior in general.

The view that "normal" and "abnormal" behavior are different in kind. Clearly, a sharp dividing line between "normal" and "abnormal" behavior simply does not exist. There are not "normal" people on the one hand and "abnormal" people on the other—two different and distinct kinds of beings. Rather, adjustment seems to follow what is called a normal distribution, with most people clustering around a central point or average, and the rest spreading out toward the two extremes. Most people are moderately well adjusted, with minor maladaptive patterns; a few at one extreme enter mental hospitals or clinics; and a few at the other extreme lead unusually satisfying and effective lives.

We have probably all known and sympathized with someone who became severely depressed after an unhappy love affair, or someone who began to drink excessively following a serious business failure. These people were showing behavior that differed only in degree from that of patients in mental hospitals or clinics, on the one hand, and from that of "normal, well-adjusted" people on the other.

Not only does the behavior of different individuals range by imperceptible degrees from normal to abnormal, but most of us shift our position somewhat along the continuum from time to time. For example, we may be coping adequately with our problems when some change in our life—perhaps a hurtful divorce, a prolonged illness, a serious financial loss, or several problems at once—may increase the severity of the demands made on us to the point where we can no longer cope with them satisfactorily.

Both normal and abnormal behavior patterns are now seen as attempts to cope with life problems as the individual perceives them. Although people have different adaptive resources, use different methods of coping, and have differing degrees of success, the same general principles apply to understanding both normal and abnormal behavior, however unusual the latter may be.

The view of former mental patients as unstable and dangerous. The common misconception persists that mental disorders are essentially "incurable." As a consequence, persons who have been discharged from mental hospitals or clinics are often viewed with suspicion as being unstable and possibly dangerous. Commonly they are discriminated against in employment or job advancement as well as in the political arena. While it is true that persons with certain forms of mental disorders—such as those associated with severe senile brain damage—will never recover completely, most mental patients respond well to treatment and later meet their responsibilities satisfactorily. Indeed, many achieve a higher level of personality adjustment than before their breakdowns.

Moreover, the great majority of persons who recover from serious mental disorders do not engage in violent or socially disruptive behavior after completing treatment. While it is apparent that care should be taken in releasing patients with a history of violence, less than 1 percent of all patients released from mental hospitals or clinics can be regarded as dangerous, and they are much more likely to be a threat to themselves than to others. In fact, mental patients with no history of arrests before their hospitalization have a strikingly low rate of arrests after release, and are *less* likely than the general population to engage in violent behaviors, such as assault, rape, and homicide (NIMH, 1969).

**PATIENTS IN STATE AND COUNTY
MENTAL HOSPITALS FROM 1880 TO 1973**
(Approximate figures)

The year 1973 represented the eighteenth consecutive
year in which the resident population of state and
county mental hospitals showed a decline, and this
trend is continuing into the mid-1970s. This decline
is considered to be due to a number of factors, including (a) introduction of major tranquilizing and antidepressant drugs; (b) increased availability of alternate
care facilities for the aged (for example, nursing
homes); (c) reduction in length and stay of first admissions; (d) more effective aftercare facilities; and (e) introduction of outpatient clinics, day hospitals, and
related community health facilities.

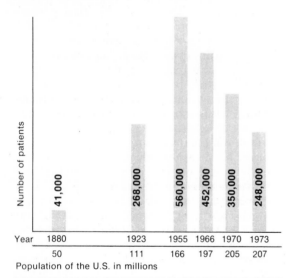

Year	1880	1923	1955	1966	1970	1973
	41,000	268,000	560,000	452,000	350,000	248,000
Population of the U.S. in millions	50	111	166	197	205	207

Number of patients (y-axis label)

**The belief that mental disorder is something to
be ashamed of.** Many people who do not hesitate to consult a dentist, a lawyer, or other
professional person for assistance with various types of problems are reluctant to go to a
psychologist or a psychiatrist with their emotional problems. Actually, a mental disorder
should be considered no more disgraceful
than a physical disorder. Both are adaptive
failures.

Nevertheless, there is still a tendency in our
society to reject the emotionally disturbed.
Whereas most people are sympathetic toward
a crippled child or an adult with cancer, they
may turn away from the person suffering
from an incapacitating mental disorder. Even
many psychologists and medical personnel are
both uninformed and unsympathetic when
they are confronted with persons evidencing
mental disorders (Rabkin, 1972; Langer &
Abelson, 1974). Yet the great majority of persons suffering mental disorders are doing the
best they know how and desperately need
understanding and help.

Fortunately, treatment of mental disorders
is becoming an integral part of total social and
community health programs. But the stigma
that has traditionally been attached to mental
disorders still lingers in the minds of many
people in our society.

**An exaggerated fear of one's own susceptibility
to mental disorder.** Fears of possible mental
disorder are quite common and cause much
needless unhappiness. "Other people seem so
self-assured and capable. They cannot possibly have the irrational impulses and fantasies
I do, or feel the hostility or anxiety or despair
that plagues me." Probably most people feel
anxious and discouraged during difficult periods in their lives, and may notice with alarm
that they are irritable, have difficulty in concentrating or remembering, or even feel that
they are "going to pieces." In one study, a representative sample of Americans were asked
if they had ever felt they were going to have a
"nervous breakdown." Almost one out of five
people interviewed replied "yes" (U.S. Department of Health, Education, and Welfare, 1971).

We should not be misled by the apparent
self-confidence and competence of other people into thinking that we alone are unhappy

and having difficulty with life's problems. Often we are surprised, when we are going through a particularly difficult period, to find that other people do not notice our distress. By the same token, we often fail to recognize the unhappiness of others. The fact that even the seemingly most successful person may be experiencing serious inner difficulties is dramatically illustrated in E. A. Robinson's poem "Richard Cory" (1943):

Whenever Richard Cory went down town,
We people on the pavement looked at him:
He was a gentleman from sole to crown,
Clean favored, and imperially slim.

And he was always quietly arrayed,
And he was always human when he talked;
But still he fluttered pulses when he said,
"Good morning," and he glittered when he walked.

And he was rich—yes, richer than a king—
And admirably schooled in every grace:
In fine, we thought that he was everything
To make us wish that we were in his place.

So on we worked and waited for the light,
And went without the meat, and cursed the bread;
And Richard Cory, one calm summer night,
Went home and put a bullet through his head.

Of course, any of us may experience serious emotional difficulties, especially when problems seem to pile up. In such instances we can avoid unnecessary mistakes and suffering by obtaining competent psychological assistance instead of worrying it out alone. However, a realization that our difficulties are not unique and that most people have many "loose ends" does help reduce the feelings of isolation and of being different that often play a large part in personal fears of mental disorder.

In this connection, it should perhaps be mentioned that medical students, in reading about various physical disorders, are likely to imagine that they have many of the symptoms described; the same reaction is likely among those reading about mental disorders. However, by gaining a better understanding of abnormal behavior and of the factors that can interfere with or foster mental health, students can become increasingly confident of their own ability to function effectively.

Abnormal Behavior as the Scientist Sees It

In order to conceptualize abnormal behavior and to assess, treat, and eventually prevent such behavior, the scientist must work out clear definitions of "normal" and "abnormal," and develop criteria for distinguishing one from the other in actual clinical cases. Unfortunately, this has not proven an easy task.

What do we mean by "abnormal behavior"?

Since the word *abnormal* literally means "away from the normal," it implies deviation from some clearly defined norm. In the case of physical illness, the norm is the structural and functional integrity of the body; here the boundary lines between normality and pathology can usually be clearly delineated. On a psychological level, however, we have no "ideal model" or even "normal model" of human nature to use as a base of comparison. Thus we suffer considerable confusion and disagreement as to just what is or is not *normal,* a confusion aggravated by the rapid change and rejection of old, established norms.

In part, too, our difficulty stems from clinicians' preoccupation with abnormal behavior and consequent neglect of the concept of the normal. The philosopher Kaplan (1967) has formulated a principle called the "Law of the Instrument," which he finds operative throughout the behavioral sciences. He illustrates it this way: "If you give a small boy a hammer, it will turn out that everything he runs into needs pounding" (p. 325). Inevitably, clinical psychologists and other "helping personnel," because of the job they are doing, tend to focus on personality difficulties rather than on normal functioning.

Different approaches used in defining "normal" and "abnormal"

Because we have no "ideal model" of human behavior, various approaches have been taken to distinguish between what is meant by "normal" and "abnormal." These approaches are by no means mutually exclusive but tend to overlap. Briefly they may be summarized as follows:

Frontal attack. Formulating general definitions of what constitutes mental health. The eminent psychiatrist Karl Menninger (1945) said, "Let us define mental health as the adjustment of human beings to the world and to each other with a maximum of effectiveness and happiness." Failure to conform to such definitions would presumably constitute maladjustment or abnormal behavior.

Multiple traits. Listing traits which most investigators would consider essential for mental health. After an extensive review of the literature, for example, Jahoda (1958) listed such traits as a realistic view of oneself and one's world, adequate self-acceptance and self-identity, and the development of essential competencies for coping with the problems of living. Failure to develop or maintain such traits would constitute abnormality.

Specific criteria. Establishing specific criteria for labeling behavior as abnormal. For example, two criteria which have been extensively used are (a) personal distress, such as chronic feelings of anxiety, depression, or guilt, and (b) deviation in behavior from established social norms. Presumably freedom from personal distress and/or conformity to social norms would constitute normal behavior.

"Models" of human nature and behavior. Basing concepts of normal and abnormal behavior on a particular "model" or set of assumptions about human nature and behavior, such as the psychoanalytic, behavioristic, humanistic, or interpersonal model.

For example, the behavioristic model strongly emphasizes the role of faulty learning in abnormal behavior. We shall review these various models and their implications in Chapter 3.

Various approaches, as described in the illustration on the left, have been used in distinguishing between normal and abnormal behavior. From the diversity of these approaches there emerge two basic and conflicting views. One maintains that the concepts of "normal" and "abnormal" are meaningful only with reference to a given culture: abnormal behavior is behavior that *deviates* from society's norms. The other view maintains that behavior is abnormal if it interferes with the well-being of the individual and/or the group. Let us examine each of these perspectives.

Abnormal as deviation from social norms. A number of social scientists have argued for the concept of "abnormal" as deviation from societal norms. This position has been well formulated by Ullmann and Krasner (1969), who maintain that *abnormal* is simply a label given to behavior that is deviant from social expectations. Conversely they maintain that behavior cannot be considered abnormal so long as society accepts it. As *cultural relativists*, they reject the concept of a "sick society" in which the social norms themselves might be viewed as pathological.

"A critical example is whether an obedient Nazi concentration-camp commander would be considered normal or abnormal. To the extent that he was responding accurately and successfully to his environment and not breaking its rules, much less coming to the professional attention of psychiatrists, he would not be labeled abnormal. Repulsive as his behavior is to mid-twentieth-century Americans, such repulsion is based on a particular set of values. Although such a person may be made liable for his acts—as Nazi war criminals were—the concept of abnormality as a special entity does not seem necessary or justified. If it is, the problem arises as to who selects the values, and this, in turn, implies that one group may select values that are applied to others. This situation of one group's values being dominant over others is the fascistic background from which the Nazi camp commander sprang." (Ullmann & Krasner, 1969, p. 15)

The acceptance of complete cultural relativism obviously simplifies the task of defining abnormality: behavior is abnormal if—and only if—the society labels it as such. But serious questions may be raised about the validity of this definition. It rests on the questionable assumption that socially accepted behavior is not abnormal and that normality is nothing more than conformity to social norms. It then follows that the task of the psychotherapist is to ensure that patients conform to the norms their society views as appropriate, regardless of the values on which these norms are based.

Thus, viewing abnormal behavior as culturally relative implies that one set of values is as "good" as another for human beings to follow. However, this viewpoint was dealt a heavy blow following World War II when a number of Nazi leaders were convicted of genocide and other "crimes against humanity." The Nuremberg trials were based on the assumption that a whole society can develop maladaptive patterns and that there are standards which groups as well as individuals must follow for human survival and well-being.

Abnormal as maladaptive. Some degree of social conformity is clearly essential to group life, and some kinds of deviance are clearly harmful not only to society but to the individual. *However, the present text maintains that the best criterion for determining the normality of behavior is not whether society accepts it but rather whether it fosters the well-being of the individual and, ultimately, of the group.* By *well-being* is meant not simply maintenance or survival but also growth and fulfillment—the actualization of potentialities. According to this criterion, even conforming behavior is abnormal if it is *maladaptive*, that is, if it interferes with optimal functioning and growth.

So defined, abnormal behavior includes the more traditional categories of mental disorders—alcoholism, neuroses, and psychoses, for example—as well as prejudice and discrimination against persons because of race or sex, wasteful use of our natural resources, pollution of our air and water, irrational violence and political corruption—regardless of whether such patterns are condemned or condoned by a given society. All represent maladaptive behavior that impair individual and/or group well-being. Typically they lead to personal distress, and often they bring destructive group conflict.

Increasingly, the definition of abnormal behavior as behavior that is maladaptive has solid scientific support. For in much the same way that the biological sciences are identifying conditions that are conducive or detrimental to physical health, such as an adequate or inadequate diet, the social sciences are delineating conditions that foster or impede psychological and social well-being. For example, research has made it clear that parental neglect, rejection, and lack of love are likely to have serious detrimental effects on a child's early development and later capacity for self-acceptance and coping. Similarly, there is ample evidence of the detrimental effects of racial discrimination on both individuals and groups. As research findings reveal more about the conditions that are detrimental to or foster individual and group well-being and fulfillment, our scientific base will be broadened accordingly.

In defining abnormal behavior as *maladaptive* and in basing our evaluation of given behaviors on available scientific evidence, we are making two value assumptions: (a) that survival and actualization are worth striving for on both individual and group levels; and (b) that human behavior can be evaluated in terms of its consequences for these objectives. As with the assumption of "cultural relativism," such value assumptions are open to criticism on the grounds that they are arbitrary. But unless we value the survival and actualization of the human race, there seems little point in trying to identify abnormal behavior or do anything about it.

Thus mental health personnel are increasingly adopting the concept of abnormal as *maladaptive.* And in assessing, treating, and preventing abnormal behavior—on both individual and group levels—they are concerned not only with the individual but also with the family, community, and general societal setting. Increasingly, the goal of therapy is defined not solely in terms of helping individuals adjust to their personal situations—no matter how frustrating or abnormal—but also in terms of the alleviation of group and societal conditions that may have brought about the maladaptive behavior or may be maintaining it.

The term *maladaptive* itself has an advantage over the term *abnormal* in shifting the focus to the behavior rather than the person and implying more possibility of change. A person once seen as "abnormal" may forever thereafter be seen that way, whereas maladaptive behavior today can usually be changed to more adaptive behavior tomorrow. Thus for a variety of reasons the term *abnormal* is less used than formerly.

The traditional term *patient*, too, is less often used than formerly, especially in cases of less severe disorder. Many clinicians feel that the term *client* is preferable because it implies more responsibility on the part of the individual for bringing about his or her own recovery; it also carries an implication of therapy as a relearning process rather than as the curing of a disease.

The problem of classification

Classification involves the delineation of various types, or categories, of abnormal behavior. Thus it is a first step toward introducing some order into our discussion of the nature, causes, and treatment of abnormal behavior—and in communicating about such behavior in agreed-upon and meaningful ways.

None of the various classification schemes developed so far, however, has been completely satisfactory. In 1952 the APA (American Psychiatric Association) adopted a classification of mental disorders that was based largely on a scheme worked out by the United States Army during World War II. In 1968 the APA adopted a modified classification worked out in conjunction with the World Health Organization.[2] This international classification permits mental health workers to compare incidence, types of disorders, treatment procedures, and other relevant data concerning mental disorders throughout the world. However, as we shall see, it has certain serious limitations.

Current classification of mental disorders. A complete outline of the current APA classifi-

cation—with its ten categories of mental disorders—appears on the endsheets at the back of this book. These ten categories may be regarded for purposes of clarity as fitting into three broader categories:

a) *Organic brain disorders*, including brain injuries, drug intoxication, and a wide range of other conditions based on brain pathology;

b) *Disorders of psychological or sociocultural origin*, in which no known brain pathology is involved as a primary causal factor, such as neuroses, psychosomatic disorders, sociopathic disorders, severe depression, schizophrenia, and other "functional" psychoses; and

c) *Mental retardation*, involving subnormal intellectual and adaptive functioning that originates during early development as a result of biological and/or psychosocial factors.

The new APA classification also includes a special category for the behavior disorders of childhood and adolescence. Although most mental disorders can occur at any time during a person's life cycle, there are special problems that may occur in children, such as autism, which warrant separate categorization.

In referring to mental disorders, several qualifying terms are commonly used: *acute* refers to the relatively short duration of a disorder, while *chronic* refers to long-standing and usually permanent disorders. *Mild, moderate,* and *severe* are used, as might be expected, to refer to the severity of the disorder. *Episodic* refers to recurrent disorders, such as the repeated occurrence of depressive patterns.

In recent years, the APA classification has undergone some slight changes—for example, homosexuality is no longer classified as an abnormal sexual pattern or mental disorder—and these changes are incorporated in this text. In addition, the text makes some modifications in the APA classification for instructional purposes. It also includes a chapter on the maladaptive behavior of groups, which is not covered in the APA classification.

Limitations of classification. The presently accepted classification of mental disorders suffers from a number of serious limitations—some of which would characterize any classification scheme.

---

[2]Diagnostic and Statistical Manual of Mental Disorders. American Psychiatric Association: Washington, D.C., 1968.

Terms used in referring to abnormal behavior

The comprehensive terms *abnormal behavior, maladaptive behavior, mental disorder,* and *psychopathology* will be used more or less interchangeably in this book. There are, however, some important distinctions to be noted concerning the use of these terms. The following descriptions not only indicate how they and other key terms are used in the present text, but also allude to differences in usage within the field.

Abnormal behavior	Used in a variety of ways to refer to a person's inner personality makeup or outer behavior or both; to refer to specific behavior like phobias or more pervasive patterns like schizophrenia; to mean chronic, long-lasting problems or those — such as drug intoxication — in which symptoms are acute and temporary. Roughly synonymous with *mental disorder* as so defined; however, in a broader context is synonymous with *maladaptive behavior.*
Maladaptive behavior	As used in this book, a term that widens the conceptual framework of *abnormal behavior* to include any behavior that has undesirable consequences for the individual and/or the group — e.g., includes not only disorders like psychoses and neuroses but also such individual or group patterns as unethical business practices, racial prejudice, alienation, and apathy.
Mental disorder	As indicated above, applies to abnormal behavior patterns, covering the whole range from mild to crippling. Although criticized by some on the grounds that it seems to imply not only a mind-body dualism but also a severe disturbance of normal functioning, *mental disorder* nevertheless is a well-established term and is integral to the only comprehensive (APA) classification system yet to be developed in the field.
Psychopathology	Refers to the study of *abnormal behavior* or *mental disorder;* also used as synonymous with those terms.
Emotional disturbance	Refers to inadequate personality integration and personal distress. Commonly used in referring to maladaptive behavior of children.
Behavior disorder	Used especially in referring to disorders that stem from faulty learning — either the failure to learn needed competencies or the learning of maladaptive coping patterns. May be used more broadly as roughly synonymous with *abnormal behavior.*
Mental illness	Once used as synonymous with *mental disorder* but now ordinarily restricted to disorders involving brain pathology or severe personality disorganization. The label *illness,* although it seems justified when referring to disorders that are severely incapacitating, is hardly appropriate in cases which apparently stem largely from faulty learning.
Mental disease	Formerly used to refer to disorders associated with brain pathology, but rarely used today.
Insanity	Legal term, indicating mental incompetence for managing one's affairs or foreseeing the consequences of one's actions. Denotes serious mental disorder.

In the course of this text, we shall try to clarify these distinctions further. As is the case with most attempts at labeling, none of these terms is completely satisfactory, and professional usage varies a great deal both from person to person and from one school of thought to another.

While the present system attempts to delineate maladaptive behavior and also to point to certain causal patterns and appropriate treatment procedures, some of its most important categories—such as the functional psychoses and the personality disorders—are mainly descriptive. Consequently, one must guard against the tendency to think something has been explained when in fact it has only been named. This limitation is not exclusive to the APA classification, but rather reflects the fact that scientific understanding of psychopathology is still far from complete.

A second limitation involves the failure to take into consideration the group setting or the pathological behavior of groups. Disturbed families, delinquent subcultures, and even pathological societies represent maladaptive patterns that do not fit into the classification scheme. Classifying only individual behavior as abnormal implies that a lack of harmony between individuals and their social milieu represents maladjustment on their part, and that they are the ones who must change. But this attitude casts the mental health profession in the role of a force for the preservation of the establishment or status quo. We shall deal further with this point in the course of the text; in our own discussion, however, we will deal with pathogenic families and maladaptive group behavior as well as with the maladaptive behavior of individuals. In addition, we will attempt to show the interaction and the vicious circles that may result from such behaviors.

A third limitation of the current classification system is its failure to provide for changing patterns of maladaptive behavior. Not adequately covered are maladaptive patterns that are emerging in our rapidly changing society, such as the dehumanization and alienation of individuals in an impersonal mass bureaucracy—as well as the effects of the tremendous stress imposed on individuals by the accelerating rate of technological and social change. In short, we need to be able to describe the disorders that are occurring now as well as predict trends in mental disorders and the problems we are likely to encounter in the future.

In defense of the present APA classification, it should be noted that it does provide an idea of the range of behaviors considered to be abnormal in major societies throughout the world. Familiarity with it helps teachers, researchers, clinicians, and students to be sure they are talking about the same thing when they are communicating about abnormal behavior patterns. Also, it is useful to know what a label like *schizophrenia* is intended to mean, since labels—for better or for worse—do influence the way we perceive and react to other persons as well as how we communicate about them. Nevertheless, it should be emphasized that classification is a human activity that is influenced by time, place, and culture—and therefore subject to change.

Assessing and treating maladaptive behavior

What is involved in helping people overcome maladaptive behaviors? With disorders so diverse and still not always understood, it is inevitable that conflicting views of the nature, causes, treatment, and prevention of abnormal behavior should have developed. And these conflicting views often influence both assessment and treatment. Consequently, it is useful to point up some of the limitations—summarized in the illustration on p. 19—as well as the general nature of assessment and treatment.

The problem of assessing abnormal behavior. Before maladaptive behavior patterns can be treated, they must first be identified. Sometimes assessment is undertaken at the individual's own request—for example, because of feelings of anxiety, depression, and personal distress. In other cases, mental health personnel may make an assessment at the request of courts or other public agencies. In the case of children, parents or teachers may take the initiative in requesting that an assessment be made.

Many assessment methods are available to the clinician, including medical, psychological, and sociological procedures. On a psychological level, the clinician can use interviews, psychological tests, rating scales, observations of the individual's behavior in actual situations, and a variety of other techniques de-

Feelings of loneliness and despair can happen to anyone. Often these feelings are associated with life stresses that can require professional assistance.

scribed in Chapter 19. Usually, psychological findings are combined with medical data and sociological data concerning the individual's family and general life situation to provide an overall clinical picture.

Assuming no relevant organic pathology is found, the clinician or clinical team usually makes an overall evaluation of the patient's behavior in terms of such factors as meeting daily demands, meeting overall needs, and social responsibility. Included here also would be information about possible depressive,

Limitations of psychological assessment

There are a number of serious problems to be considered in the psychological assessment of abnormal behavior, including these:

1. Cultural bias of the instrument or the clinician. For example, psychological tests may not elicit valid information from a patient of an ethnic minority,* or a clinician from one sociocultural background may have trouble assessing objectively the behavior of a patient from another background.

2. Theoretical orientation of the clinician. Closely related to cultural bias is the theoretical orientation of the clinician. For example, a psychoanalyst may assess given behaviors quite differently than would a behaviorist. In essence, assessment is inevitably influenced by the assumptions and perception of the clinician.

3. Overemphasis on internal traits. There is a tendency to assume that personality traits are the cause of the patient's problems without due attention to the possible role of stresses in the person's life situation.

4. Inaccurate assessment data and labels. There is the possibility that assessment data, as well as diagnostic labels based on such data, may be inaccurate. On page 20 we note the harm which a diagnostic label may inflict on the individual; where the label is inaccurate, this harm may be even more serious.

5. Difficulty of maintaining confidentiality. If assessment data—including possible labels—get into a computerized data system or are otherwise made available to the public, they may adversely affect an individual's opportunities for employment and political office as well as many other aspects of that person's life.

Attempts to minimize these problems of assessment are discussed in Chapter 19, but it is useful to be aware of the nature and limitations of psychological assessment before dealing with patterns of abnormal behavior.

*Useful references here are Cleary, Humphreys, Kendrick, and Wesman (1975) and Schmidt and Hunter (1974).

A young therapist makes a game out of helping an autistic boy learn to imitate adults, a normal response that autistic children lack but which is all-important in training them. The child is rewarded with food (from the tray in the background) every time he imitates the therapist. It is hoped that eventually this will help the child to develop more normal responses as he progresses with the therapist.

schizophrenic, or other maladaptive tendencies that the individual may be manifesting—as well as any conditions in the patient's life situation which may be exacerbating or maintaining such behavior. And although the trend is away from using assessment data for labeling behavior, a label—such as *acute schizophrenia*—may be assigned at this time.

Here we should emphasize that assigning a label such as "mentally retarded," "alcoholic,"

or "schizophrenic" may have unfortunate effects on the persons labeled. The label may devaluate their self-concept; it may adversely influence their personal relationships and occupational and other opportunities; and it may provide them with a "sick role" which they think they are expected to play, and hence tend to be a self-fulfilling prophecy.

In addition, a diagnostic label may be misleading. Although individuals labeled as schizophrenic, for example, do tend to share certain characteristics in common—serious thought disturbances and loss of contact with reality, for example—this category includes a wide range of maladaptive behaviors. Thus, knowing the diagnostic category to which certain patients have been assigned may tell little about them or their behavior; in fact, it may tend to obscure their uniqueness as individuals.

Possible adverse effects such as these are largely responsible for the trend away from rigid labeling and classification. Further, it becomes apparent that those charged with deciding when a person's behavior is abnormal—and how abnormal it is—have an awesome responsibility to the individual and to society.

Helping fields and personnel. At the present time, there are several distinct but closely related professional fields concerned with the study of abnormal behavior and with mental health. The distinction among them is often hard to draw precisely, for even though each has its own functions and areas of work, the contributions in one field are constantly influencing the thinking and work in others.

Abnormal psychology has long been referred to as that part of the field of psychology concerned with the understanding, treatment, and prevention of abnormal behavior. However, the term is now relegated largely to titles of courses in colleges and universities that cover the subject matter of abnormal behavior. In other contexts it has generally been replaced by the term *clinical psychology*, the professional field broadly concerned with the study, assessment, treatment, and prevention of abnormal behavior. *Psychiatry* is the corresponding field of medicine, and is thus closely related to clinical psychology. *Social work*, an offshoot of sociology, is concerned with the analysis of social environments and with providing services which assist the adjustment of the patient in both family and community settings.

Personnel in these and related fields concerned with emotional problems and psychotherapy are described briefly in the illustration on the right.

As in the case of assessment, treatment may

Personnel in psychotherapy

Clinical psychologist
Ph.D. in psychology plus internship in a mental hospital or clinic setting

Psychiatrist
M.D. degree (medicine) plus residency training in mental hospital or clinic setting

Social worker
M.A. degree in social work plus supervised training in clinical or social service agencies

Counseling psychologist
Ph.D. in psychology plus internship training in marital, family, and other areas of counseling

Psychoanalyst
M.D. or Ph.D. degree plus intensive training in theory and practice of psychoanalysis

Psychiatric nurse
R.N. in nursing plus specialized training in care and treatment of mental patients

Occupational therapist
B.S. in occupational therapy plus internship training with the physically handicapped helping them to make the most of their resources

Paraprofessional
Capable person with limited professional training who works under supervision, especially in crisis intervention

In both mental health clinics and hospitals, personnel from several fields may function as an *interdisciplinary team* in therapy—for example, psychiatrist, clinical psychologist, social worker, psychiatric nurse, and occupational therapist. And of course, other mental health personnel may be utilized depending upon their availability and the needs of the particular patient.

be requested by the individual—as is usually the case—or by a court or other public agency. In any given case, a wide range of medical, psychological, and sociological procedures may be used. Such procedures range from the use of drugs through individual or group psychotherapy and encounter groups to sociotherapy aimed at modifying adverse conditions in the patient's life situation. Often the latter— as in helping an employer become more understanding and supportive of the patient's needs—is as important as treatment directed toward modifying the patient's personality makeup and/or behavior.

Of growing importance in helping the maladjusted is the *team approach* to assessment and treatment. This approach involves the coordinated efforts of medical, psychological, social work, and other mental health personnel working together as the needs of each case warrant. Also of key importance is the trend toward providing treatment facilities in the community. Instead of considering maladjustment as a private misery of the individual, which in the past often required one's confinement in a distant mental hospital, this approach integrates family and community resources in the treatment program.

In the chapters that follow we shall note many examples of specific therapeutic procedures and their outcomes; in Chapter 20, we shall deal in some detail with the goals, procedures, and outcomes—as well as the problems and limitations—of contemporary approaches to therapy.

The Orientation of This Book

Throughout this book we shall be attempting to acquire a perspective on abnormal behavior and its place in contemporary society. Although we shall deal with all the major categories of mental disorders, we shall not attempt an encyclopedic coverage, but rather shall focus on those patterns that seem most relevant to an understanding of abnormal behavior on both individual and group levels. And while we shall not hesitate to include the unusual or bizarre, our emphasis will be on the unity of human behavior, ranging from the normal to the abnormal ends of the continuum.

This text is predicated on the assumption that a sound and comprehensive study of abnormal behavior should be based on the following concepts:

1. *A scientific approach to abnormal behavior.* Any comprehensive view of human behavior must draw upon concepts and research findings from a variety of scientific fields. Of particular relevance are genetics, neurophysiology, sociology, and anthropology, as well as psychology. Such common scientific concepts as causal processes, control groups, dependent variables, placebos, and models and theories will figure prominently in our discussion. Emphasis will also be placed on the application of learning principles to the understanding and treatment of mental disorders.

In this general context, students are encouraged to take a critical and evaluative attitude toward research findings presented in this text and in other available sources. Scientific research, when properly conducted, does provide us with information having a high probability of being accurate, but many research findings are subject to bias and open to serious question.

2. *An awareness of our existential problems.* There are many experiences and prob-

lems common to human existence about which science as yet has had little to say. Included are such vital experiences as hope, faith, courage, love, grief, despair, death, and the quest for values and meaning. Authentic insights into such experiences can often be gained from literature, drama, and autobiographical accounts that strike a common chord and relate directly to an understanding of human behavior. In addition, material from such fields as art, history, religion, and parapsychology can also provide useful insights into certain aspects of abnormal behavior. However, information from the preceding sources will be distinguished from that obtained through scientific observation.

3. *Respect for the dignity, integrity, and growth potential of the individual.* A basic orientation of this book is well described in the opening statement of the *Ethical Standards of Psychologists*, formulated by the American Psychological Association:

"The psychologist believes in the dignity and worth of the individual human being." (1972, p. 1)

Implicit in this statement is a view of individuals not merely as products of their past conditioning and present situation but as potentially active agents as well—persons who can develop and use their capacities for building the kind of life they choose and a better future world for humankind.

In attempting throughout this volume to provide a perspective for viewing abnormal behavior, we shall focus not only on how maladaptive patterns such as schizophrenia are perceived by clinical psychologists and other mental health personnel, but also on how such disorders feel and are perceived by the individuals experiencing them. In dealing with the major patterns of abnormal behavior, we shall focus on four significant aspects of each: clinical picture, causes, treatment, and outcome. And in each case we shall examine the evidence for biological, psychological and interpersonal, and sociocultural factors.

Most of this volume will be devoted to well-established patterns of abnormal behavior and to special problem behaviors of our time that are more controversial but directly relevant to any discussion of maladaptive be-

havior. Initially, however, we shall trace the development of our contemporary views of abnormal behavior from early beliefs and practices, sketch several attempts to explain what makes human beings "tick," and review briefly the basic principles of adjustive behavior and the general causes of abnormal behavior.

Finally, after our discussion of the various problem behaviors, we shall devote two chapters to modern methods of assessment and treatment, and one to the potentialities of modern psychology and allied sciences for preventing mental disorders and for helping humankind achieve a more sane and harmonious world.

At the close of his journeys, Tennyson's Ulysses says, "I am part of all that I have met." It is the author's hope that readers of this book, at the end of their journey through it, will have a better understanding of human experience and behavior—and that they will consider what they have learned as a meaningful part of their own life experience.

In this introduction we have briefly reviewed the nature and scope of abnormal behavior; we have surveyed some examples of mental disorders from history, literature, and drama; we have noted some popular misconceptions of mental disorders; we have dealt with the scientific problem of what we mean by "abnormal"; we presented a brief summary of the current APA listing of mental disorders; and we have briefly touched on the problem of assessment and treatment.

In the course of our discussion, we have emphasized that (a) *abnormal behavior* may be defined as behavior that is *maladaptive;* (b) human behavior falls along a continuum extending from highly adaptive behavior at one extreme to highly maladaptive behavior at the other; (c) a person's position on this continuum of adjustment may shift over time; and (d) the same principles that are used to conceptualize and understand normal behavior are also applicable to abnormal or maladaptive behavior.

Having presented this brief orientation to the study of abnormal behavior, let us now trace the progress that has been made in understanding psychopathology from ancient times to the present.

2

Historical Background and the Organic Viewpoint

With the development of modern research methods, psychotherapeutic drugs, techniques of psychotherapy, and community mental health concepts and facilities, we feel that we have come a long way from the superstitious and often cruel treatment of persons with mental disorders characteristic of earlier times. The story of this journey is a fascinating one, and one that will help us understand how modern views of abnormal behavior have come about.

Not only do many popular misconceptions about mental disorders have roots in the dim historical past, but even many of our modern scientific concepts are the result of a long developmental process. For example, modern brain surgery, as we shall shortly see, had its early precursor many thousands of years ago, and electroshock treatment for severe depression is antedated by flogging, immersing a person in cold water, and other crude "shock" treatments. Even the method of "free association" — a cornerstone of psychoanalytic therapy, designed to allow repressed conflicts and emotions to enter conscious awareness — is described by the Greek playwright Aristophanes in his play *The Clouds*. Interestingly enough, the scene in which Socrates tries to calm and bring self-knowledge to Strepsiades is complete with a couch.

In this chapter we shall trace the evolution of views on psychopathology from ancient times to the turn of the present century, from the generally ignorant ideas and often inhumane treatment given those who suffered from mental disorders, to the development of the organic viewpoint and the medical model, with its emphasis on the biological aspects of mental "illness." For it's only recently, as we shall see, that mental disorders have been generally recognized as having natural causes. The great advances that have come about during the twentieth century in the understanding and treatment of abnormal behavior become all the more remarkable when viewed against the long background of ignorance, superstition, and fear.

Abnormal Behavior in Ancient Times

Demonology in the Middle Ages

Emergence of Humanitarian Approaches

Development of the Organic Viewpoint and the Medical Model

Abnormal Behavior in Ancient Times

Although human life presumably appeared on earth some three million or more years ago, written records extend back only a few thousand years. Thus our knowledge of "primitive man" is very limited and often based on extrapolation from so-called primitive peoples who remained isolated and relatively static into modern times. Beginning with the Egyptian and other ancient civilizations, historical information becomes more reliable, although far from complete.

Demonology among the ancients

The earliest treatment of mental disorders of which we have any knowledge was that practiced by Stone Age cave dwellers some half million years ago. For certain forms of mental disorders, probably those in which the individual complained of severe headaches and developed convulsive attacks, the early shaman, or medicine man, treated the disorder by means of an operation now called *trephining*. This operation was performed with crude stone instruments and consisted of chipping away one area of the skull in the form of a circle until the skull was cut through. This opening, called a *trephine*, presumably permitted the evil spirit that supposedly was causing all the trouble to escape—and incidentally may have relieved a certain amount of pressure on the brain. In some cases trephined skulls of primitive people show healing around the opening, indicating that the patient survived the operation and lived for many years afterward (Selling, 1943).

References to mental disorders in the early writings of the Chinese, Egyptians, Hebrews, and Greeks show that they generally attributed such disorders to demons that had taken possession of the individual. This is not surprising when we remember that "good" and "bad" spirits were widely used to explain lightning, thunder, earthquakes, storms, fires, sickness, and many other events that otherwise seemed incomprehensible. It was probably a very simple and logical step to extend this theory to peculiar and incomprehensible behavior in their fellows.

The decision as to whether the "possession" involved good spirits or evil spirits usually depended on the individual's symptoms. If speech or behavior appeared to have a religious or mystical significance, it was usually thought that the person was possessed by a good spirit or god. Such individuals were often treated with considerable awe and respect, for it was thought that they had supernatural powers. In the Bible story, David took advantage of this popular belief when he simulated "madness" in order to escape from Achish, the king of Gath (1 Samuel 21:12–14).

Most possessions, however, were considered to be the work of evil spirits, particularly when the individual became excited and overactive and engaged in behavior contrary to religious teachings. Among the ancient Hebrews, such possessions were thought to represent the wrath and punishment of God. Moses is quoted in the Bible as saying, "The Lord shall smite thee with madness. . . ." Apparently this was thought to involve primarily the withdrawal of God's protection, and the abandonment of the individual to the forces of evil. For example, Saul presumably disobeyed God, so that the spirit of the Lord left him and an evil spirit was thereby permitted to enter. In such cases every effort was made to rid the person of the evil spirit. Christ reportedly cured a man with an "unclean spirit" by transferring the devils that plagued him to a herd of swine who, in turn, became possessed and "ran violently down a steep place into the sea" (Mark 5:1–13).

The primary type of treatment for demoniacal possession was exorcism, which included various techniques for casting the evil spirit out of the body of the afflicted one. These varied considerably but typically included prayer, incantation, noisemaking, and the use of various horrible-tasting concoctions, such as pur-

38 T Satan

This 15th-century German engraving emphasizes the belief held by medieval Christians that God could protect them from possession by demons.

gatives made from sheep's dung and wine. In extreme cases flogging, starving, and other more severe measures were often used in an attempt to make the body of the possessed person such an unpleasant place that the evil spirit would be driven out.

Such treatment was originally in the hands of shamans, but was eventually taken over in Greece and Egypt by the priests, who were apparently a curious mixture of priest, physician, psychologist, and magician. Although these priests were dominated in the main by beliefs in demonology and established exorcistic practices, they did make a beginning in the more humane and scientific treatment of mental disturbances. For example, as early as

860 B.C. in the temples of Asclepius in Greece, the priests supplemented the usual prayer and incantation with kindness, suggestion, and recreational measures, such as theatricals, riding, walking, and harmonious music. However, starving, flogging, and chains were still advocated for recalcitrant patients.

Early philosophical and medical concepts

During the Golden Age of Greece considerable progress was made in the understanding and treatment of mental disorders. Originally, membership in the medical priesthood of the Greek temples of healing was hereditary, but gradually outsiders were admitted and various "schools" began to form. It was in one of these groups that Hippocrates received his early training.

Hippocrates. The great Greek physician Hippocrates (460–377 B.C.) has been called the "father of modern medicine." He denied the intervention of deities and demons in the development of disease, and insisted that mental disorders had natural causes and required treatment like other diseases. His position was unequivocal: "For my own part, I do not believe that the human body is ever befouled by a God" (Lewis, 1941, p. 37). Hippocrates emphasized the view, earlier set forth by Pythagoras, that the brain was the central organ of intellectual activity and that mental disorders were due to brain pathology. Hippocrates also emphasized the importance of heredity and predisposition and pointed out that injuries to the head could cause sensory and motor disorders.

Hippocrates classified all the varieties of mental disorder into three general categories—mania, melancholia, and phrenitis—and gave detailed clinical descriptions of the specific disorders included in each category, such as alcoholic delirium and epilepsy. Hippocrates relied heavily on clinical observation, and his descriptions, which were based on the daily clinical records of his patients, were surprisingly thorough. It is interesting to note that Hippocrates realized the clinical importance of dreams for understanding the personality of the patient. On this point he anticipated one of the concepts basic to several forms of contemporary psychotherapy.

The methods of treatment advocated by Hippocrates were far in advance of the exorcistic practices then prevalent. For the treatment of melancholia, for example, he prescribed a regular and tranquil life, sobriety and abstinence from all excesses, a vegetable diet, continence, exercise short of fatigue, and bleeding if indicated. But for hysteria,[1] which was thought to be restricted to women and caused by the wandering of the uterus to various parts of the body because of its pining for children, Hippocrates recommended marriage as the best remedy. He also believed in the importance of environment, and not infrequently removed his patients from their families.

Hippocrates' emphasis on natural causes, clinical observations, and brain pathology in relation to mental disorders was truly revolutionary. Like his contemporaries, however, Hippocrates had very little knowledge of physiology. (Greek physicians were poor physiologists and anatomists because they deified the human body and dared not dissect it.) Thus in his concept of the "four humors"—blood, black bile, yellow bile, and phlegm—Hippocrates apparently conceived the notion of a balance of physiological processes as essential to normal brain functioning and mental health. In his work *On Sacred Disease*, he stated that when the humors were adversely mixed or otherwise disturbed, physical or mental disease resulted: "depravement of the brain arises from phlegm and bile; those mad from phlegm are quiet, depressed and oblivious; those from bile excited, noisy and mischievous." Although this concept went far beyond demonology, it was too crude physiologically to be of any great value. Medical treatment based on such inadequate anatomical and physiological knowledge was to continue for many centuries, often proving both humorous and tragic.

---

[1]The appearance of symptoms of physical illness in the absence of organic pathology.

Plato and Aristotle. The problem of dealing with mentally disturbed individuals who committed criminal acts was studied by the great philosopher Plato (429–347 B.C.). He made it clear that such persons were obviously not responsible for their acts and should not receive punishment in the same way as normal persons: ". . . someone may commit an act when mad or afflicted with disease . . . [if so,] let him pay simply for the damage; and let him be exempt from other punishment." Plato also made provision for mental cases to be cared for in the community as follows: "If anyone is insane, let him not be seen openly in the city, but let the relatives of such a person watch over him in the best manner they know of; and if they are negligent, let them pay a fine . . ." (Plato, n.d., p. 56). In addition to this emphasis on the more humane treatment of the mentally disturbed, Plato contributed to a better understanding of human behavior by pointing out that all forms of life, human included, were motivated by physiologic needs or "natural appetites." He also seems to have anticipated Freud's insight into the functions of fantasies and dreams as substitutive satisfactions, concluding that in dreams, desire tended to satisfy itself in imagery when the higher faculties no longer inhibited the "passions." In his *Republic*, Plato emphasized the importance of individual differences in intellectual and other abilities, and pointed out the role of sociocultural influences in shaping the thinking and behavior of the individual. Despite these modern ideas, however, Plato shared the belief of his time that mental disorders were partly organic, partly moral, and partly divine.

The question of whether mental disorders could be caused by psychological factors like frustration and conflict was discussed and rejected by the celebrated systematist Aristotle (384–322 B.C.), who was a pupil but not a follower of Plato. In his extensive writings on mental disorders, Aristotle generally followed the Hippocratic theory of disturbances in the bile. For example, he believed that very hot bile generated amorous desires and loquacity, and was also responsible for suicidal impulses.

Tseng (1973) traced the development of concepts of mental disorders in China by reviewing the descriptions of the disorders and their recommended treatment in Chinese medical documents. For example, the following is taken from an ancient Chinese medical text supposedly written by Huang Ti (c. 2674 B.C.), the third legendary emperor, but now considered by historians to have been written at a later date, possibly during the seventh century B.C.:

"The person suffering from excited insanity initially feels sad, eating and sleeping less; he then becomes grandiose, feeling that he is very smart and noble, talking and scolding day and night, singing, behaving strangely, seeing strange things, hearing strange voices, believing that he can see the devil or gods. . . ." (p. 570)

Even at this early date, Chinese medicine was based on natural rather than supernatural causes. For example, in the concept of Ying and Yang the human body, like the cosmos, is divided into a positive and a negative force which are both complementary and contradictory to each other. If the two forces are balanced, the result is physical and mental health; if they are not, illness will result. Consequently:

"As treatment for such an excited condition withholding food was suggested, since food was considered to be the source of positive force and the patient was thought to be in need of a decrease in such force." (p. 570)

Chinese medicine apparently reached a relatively sophisticated level during the second century, and Chung Ching, who has been called the Hippocrates of China, wrote two well-known medical works around A.D. 200. Like Hippocrates, he based his views of both physical and mental disorders on clinical observations and implicated organ pathology as the primary cause. However, he also believed that stressful psychological conditions could cause the organ pathology, and

his treatment, like that of Hippocrates, utilized both drugs and the regaining of emotional balance through appropriate activities. During this period, for example, the following treatment for excited insanity was recommended:

"If a patient wants to go, let him go; if he wants to stay, let him stay; do not deny him what he wants and do not suppress him. If we comply to his wishes and let him satisfy his needs, then all of his excessive positive force will be appropriately discharged and he will consequently get well." (p. 571)

Here it may be noted that the excessive positive force —again involving the concept of Ying and Yang— was based on the idea that some vital organ had lost its essential stability, thus interrupting the normal rhythm of life. And while seemingly a rather passive method of treatment, it was both humane and socially oriented.

As in the West, however, Chinese views of mental disorders were to regress to the belief in supernatural forces as causal agents. From the later part of the second century through the early part of the ninth century, ghosts and devils were implicated in "Ghost-evil" insanity, which presumably resulted from bewitchment by evil spirits. However, the "Dark Ages" in China were not so severe—in terms of the treatment of mental patients—nor did they last so long as in the West. And a return to somatic views as well as the emphasis on psychosocial factors were to occur in the centuries which followed.

In this context, it is interesting to note the conclusion of Tseng that ". . . concepts of how mental illness is perceived and pathology explained have gone through the sequence of supernatural, natural, somatic, and psychological stages in both the East and the West" (p. 573). And in both East and West, there were setbacks—"Dark Ages"—involving a return to prehistoric views of evil spirits and related supernatural causal forces.

Later Greek and Roman thought. Work along the lines that had been established by Hippocrates was continued by some of the later Greek and Roman physicians. Particularly in Alexandria, Egypt (which after its founding in 332 B.C. by Alexander the Great became the center of Greek culture), medical practices developed to a high level, and the temples dedicated to Saturn were first-rate sanatoriums. Pleasant surroundings were considered of great therapeutic value for the mental patients, who were provided with constant activities including parties, dances, walks in the temple gardens, rowing along the Nile, and musical concerts. The later Greek and Roman physicians also employed a wide range of other kinds of therapeutic measures, including dieting, massage, hydrotherapy, gymnastics, hypnotism, and education, as well as certain less desirable measures, such as bleeding, purging, and mechanical restraints (R. W. Menninger, 1944).

Among the Greek and Roman physicians who continued in the Hippocratic tradition were Asclepiades, Aretaeus, and Galen. Asclepiades (born *c.* 124 B.C.) was the first to note the difference between acute and chronic mental disorders, and to distinguish between illusions, delusions, and hallucinations. In addition, he invented various ingenious devices designed to make patients more comfortable. One of these was a suspended hammock-like bed whose swaying was considered very beneficial for disturbed patients. Asclepiades' progressive approach to mental disorders was also evidenced by his opposition to bleeding, mechanical restraints, and dungeons.

The first hint that certain mental disorders were but an extension of normal psychological processes was put forth by Aretaeus near the end of the first century A.D. People who were irritable, violent, and easily given to joy and pleasurable pursuits were thought to be prone to the development of manic excitement, while those who tended to be serious were thought to be more apt to develop melancholia. Aretaeus was the first to describe the various phases of mania and melancholia, and to consider these two pathological states as expressions of the same illness. His insight into the importance of emotional factors and of the pre-psychotic personality of the patient was quite an achievement for his day.

Galen (A.D. 130–200) did not contribute much that was new to the therapy or clinical description of mental disorders, although he did make many original contributions concerning the anatomy of the nervous system and maintained a scientific approach to mental disorders, performing a major service in compiling and integrating the existing material in this field (Guthrie, 1946). In the latter connection, he divided the causes of mental disorders into physical and mental. Among the causes he named were injuries to the head, alcoholic excess, shock, fear, adolescence, menstrual changes, economic reverses, and disappointment in love.

Although historians consider the fall of Rome to the barbarians toward the end of the fifth century to be the dividing line between ancient and medieval times, the Dark Ages in the history of abnormal psychology began with Galen's death in A.D. 200. The contributions of Hippocrates and the later Greek and Roman physicians were shortly lost in the welter of popular superstition, and most of the physicians of later Rome returned to some sort of demonology. One notable exception to this trend, however, was Alexander Trallianus (A.D. 525–605), who followed the works of Galen rather closely but placed a great deal of emphasis on constitutional factors—stating, for example, that people with dark hair and a slim build were more likely to be affected by melancholia than persons with light hair and a heavy build. Worthy of note also are some of the clinical cases he recorded (Whitwell, 1936), such as that of a woman who had the delusion that her middle finger was fixed in such a way that it held the whole world within its power. This caused her great distress for fear she should bend her finger, thus overthrowing the world and destroying everything. Another interesting case was that of a man who was greatly depressed because he was convinced that his head had been amputated. Trallianus reported that he cured this case by suddenly placing a close-fitting leaden cap on the patient's head so that he was able to feel the weight and thought his head had been replaced.

Survival of Greek thought in Arabia. During medieval times it was only in Arabia that the more scientific aspects of Greek medicine survived. The first mental hospital was established in Baghdad in A.D. 792; it was soon followed by others in Damascus and Aleppo (Polvan, 1969). In these hospitals the mentally disturbed received much more humane treatment than they did in Christian lands.

The outstanding figure in Arabian medicine was Avicenna (c. A.D. 980–1037), called the "prince of physicians" (Campbell, 1926). In his writings Avicenna frequently referred to hysteria, epilepsy, manic reactions, and melancholia. The following case shows his unique approach to the treatment of a young prince suffering from a mental disorder:

"A certain prince . . . was afflicted with melancholia, and suffered from the delusion that he was a cow . . . he would low like a cow, causing annoyance to everyone, . . . crying, 'Kill me so that a good stew may be made of my flesh,' finally . . . he would eat nothing. . . . Avicenna was persuaded to take the case. . . . First of all he sent a message to the patient bidding him be of good cheer because the butcher was coming to slaughter him, whereat . . . the sick man rejoiced. Some time afterwards Avicenna, holding a knife in his hand, entered the sickroom saying, 'Where is this cow that I may kill it?' The patient lowed like a cow to indicate where he was. By Avicenna's orders he was laid on the ground, bound hand and foot. Avicenna then felt him all over and said, 'He is too lean, and not ready to be killed; he must be fattened.' Then they offered him suitable food of which he now partook eagerly, and gradually he gained strength, got rid of his delusion, and was completely cured." (Browne, 1921, pp. 88–89)

Unfortunately, most medical men of Avicenna's time were dealing with mental patients in a very different way.

Demonology in the Middle Ages

With the collapse of Greek and Roman civilization, medicine as well as other scientific pursuits suffered an almost complete eclipse in Europe. There was a tremendous revival of the most ancient superstition and demonology, with only a slight modification to conform to current theological demands. Human beings now became the battleground of demons and spirits who waged eternal war for the possession of their souls. Mental disorders were apparently quite frequent throughout the Middle Ages, and toward the end of the period, when medieval institutions began to collapse, their incidence seems to have increased. As Rosen (1967) has described it:

"The medieval world began to come apart in the 14th century, and the process of disintegration continued inexorably through the succeeding centuries. Fundamental changes took place in its institutions, its social structure, its beliefs and outlook. It was a period of peasant revolts and urban uprisings, of wars and plagues, and thus an age in which many felt acutely insecure and discontented. An emotional malaise was abroad." (p. 775)

"Mass madness"

The last half of the Middle Ages saw a peculiar trend in abnormal behavior, involving the widespread occurrence of group mental disorders that were apparently mainly cases of hysteria. Whole groups of people were affected simultaneously.

Dance manias, taking the form of epidemics of raving, jumping, dancing, and convulsions, were reported as early as the tenth century. One such episode, occurring in Italy early in the thirteenth century, was recorded by physicians of the time whose records have been reviewed by the medical historian H. E. Sigerist. He has written:

An engraving based on a painting by Pieter Brueghel (1525–1569) shows peasant women overcome by St. Vitus's dance.

"The disease occurred at the height of the summer heat. . . . People, asleep or awake, would suddenly jump up, feeling an acute pain like the sting of a bee. Some saw the spider, others did not, but they knew that it must be the tarantula. They ran out of the house into the street, to the market place, dancing in great excitement. Soon they were joined by others who like them had been bitten, or by people who had been stung in previous years. . . .

"Thus groups of patients would gather, dancing wildly in the queerest attire. . . . Others would tear their clothes and show their nakedness, losing all sense of modesty. . . . Some called for swords and acted like fencers, others for whips and beat each other. . . . Some of them had still stranger fancies, liked to be tossed in the air, dug holes in the ground, and rolled themselves into the dirt like swine. They all drank wine plentifully and sang and talked like drunken people. . . ." (1943, pp. 103, 106–107)

Actually, the behavior was very similar to the ancient orgiastic rites by which people had worshiped the Greek gods. These had been banned with the advent of Christianity, but were deeply embedded in the culture and were apparently kept alive by secret gatherings. Probably considerable guilt and conflict were engendered; then, with time, the meaning of the dances changed, and the old rites appeared as symptoms of disease. The participants were no longer sinners but the poor victims of the tarantula (Gloyne, 1950).

Known as *tarantism* in Italy, the dancing mania later spread to Germany and the rest of Europe, where it was known as *St. Vitus's dance*. Other peculiar manifestations also appeared. In the fifteenth century, a member of a German convent was overcome with a desire to bite her fellow nuns. The practice was taken up by her companions, and the mania spread to other convents in Germany, Holland, and Italy (A. D. White, 1896).

Isolated rural areas were also afflicted with outbreaks of *lycanthropy*—a form of mental disorder in which the patient imagined himself a wolf and imitated its actions. In 1541 a case was reported in which the lycanthrope told his captors, in confidence, that he was really a wolf but that his skin was smooth on the surface because all the hairs were on the inside (Stone, 1937). To cure him of his delusions, his extremities were amputated, following which he died, still unconvinced.

These epidemics continued into the seventeenth century, but apparently reached their peak during the fifteenth and sixteenth centuries—a period noted for oppression, famine, and pestilence. During this period, Europe was ravaged by an epidemic known as the "Black Death," which spread across the continent, destroying millions of human lives and severely disrupting social organization. Undoubtedly many of the peculiar manifestations during this period, including the Children's Crusade, in which thousands of children left their homes to liberate the Holy Sepulcher, were related to the depression, fear, and wild mysticism engendered by the terrible events of the time. People did not dream that such frightening catastrophes were attributable to natural causes and thus would some day be within our power to control, prevent, or even create.

Exorcism in medieval times

In the Middle Ages treatment of the mentally disturbed was left largely to the clergy. Monasteries served as refuges and places of confinement. During the early part of the medieval period, the mentally disturbed for the most part were treated with considerable kindliness. Much store was set by prayer, holy water, sanctified ointments, the breath or spittle of the priests, the touching of relics, visits to holy places, and mild forms of exorcism. In some monasteries and shrines exorcism was performed by the gentle "laying on of hands." Such methods were often intermixed with vague ideas of medical treatment derived mainly from Galen, which gave rise to such prescriptions as the following: "For a fiend-sick man: When a devil possesses a man, or controls him from within with disease, a spew-drink of lupin, bishopswort, henbane,

garlic. Pound these together, add ale and holy water" (Cockayne, 1864–1866).

As exorcistic techniques became more fully developed, it was emphasized that it was Satan's pride which had led to his original downfall. Hence, in treating persons possessed by a devil, the first thing to do was to strike a fatal blow at the devil's pride—to insult him. This involved calling the devil some of the most obscene epithets that imagination could devise, and the insults were usually supplemented by long litanies of cursing:

". . . May all the devils that are thy foes rush forth upon thee, and drag thee down to hell! . . . May God set a nail to your skull, and pound it in with a hammer, as Jael did unto Sisera! . . . May . . . Sother break thy head and cut off thy hands, as was done to the cursed Dagon! . . . May God hang thee in a hellish yoke, as seven men were hanged by the sons of Saul!" (From *Thesaurus Exorcismorum*)

This illustration showing a physician curing fantasy and folly may be an exaggeration of the treatments used during the 1600s, but there's no doubt that drastic—and often fatal—methods were used to treat many disorders which were poorly understood.

This procedure was considered highly successful in the treatment of possessed persons. A certain bishop of Beauvais claimed to have rid a person of five devils, all of whom signed an agreement stating that they and their subordinate imps would no longer persecute the possessed individual (A. D. White, 1896).

As theological beliefs concerning abnormal behavior became more fully developed and were endorsed by the secular world, treatment of the mentally disturbed became more harsh. It was generally believed that cruelty to people afflicted with "madness" was punishment of the devil residing within them, and when "scourging" proved ineffective, the authorities felt justified in driving out the demons by more unpleasant methods. Flogging, starving, chains, immersion in hot water, and other torturous methods were devised in order to make the body such an unpleasant place of residence that no self-respecting devil would remain in it. Undoubtedly many men and women who might have been restored to health by more gentle and humane measures were driven into hopeless derangement by such brutal treatment.

Witchcraft

During the latter part of the fifteenth century, it became the accepted theological belief that demoniacal possessions were of two general types: (a) possessions in which the victim was unwillingly seized by the devil as a punishment by God for past sins, and (b) possessions in which the individual was actually in league with the devil. The latter persons were supposed to have made a pact with the devil, consummated by signing in blood a book presented to them by Satan which gave them certain supernatural powers. They could cause pestilence, storms, floods, sexual impotence, injuries to their enemies, and ruination of crops, and could rise through the air, cause milk to sour, and turn themselves into animals. In short, they were witches.

These beliefs were not confined to simple serfs but were held and elaborated upon by most of the important clergymen of this period. No less a man than Martin Luther (1483–1546) came to the following conclusions:

"The greatest punishment God can inflict on the wicked . . . is to deliver them over to Satan, who with God's permission, kills them or makes them to undergo great calamities. Many devils are in woods, water, wildernesses, etc., ready to hurt and prejudice people. When these things happen, then the philosophers and physicians say it is natural, ascribing it to the planets.

"In cases of melancholy . . . I conclude it is merely the work of the devil. Men are possessed by the devil in two ways; corporally or spiritually. Those whom he possesses corporally, as mad people, he has permission from God to vex and agitate, but he has no power over their souls." *(Colloquia Mensalia)*

Those who were judged to have been unwillingly seized by the devil as punishment by God were treated initially in accordance with the established exorcistic practices of the time. As time went on, however, the distinction between the two types of possessions became somewhat obscured, and by the close of the fifteenth century, the mentally ill were generally considered heretics and witches.

More and more concern was expressed in official quarters over the number of witches roaming around and the great damage they were doing by pestilences, storms, sexual depravity, and other heinous crimes. Consequently, on December 7, 1484, Pope Innocent VIII sent forth his bull *Summis Desiderantes Affectibus,* in which he exhorted the clergy of Europe, especially Germany, to leave no means untried in the detection of witches. This papal bull was theologically based on the scriptural command "Thou shalt not suffer a witch to live" (Exodus 22:18).

To assist in this great work, a manual, *Malleus maleficarum (The Witches' Hammer),* was prepared by two Dominican monks, Johann Sprenger and Heinrich Kraemer, both Inquisitors appointed by the pope to act in northern Germany and territories along the Rhine. This manual, revered for centuries in both Catholic and Protestant countries as being almost divinely inspired, was complete in every detail concerning witchcraft and was of great value in witch-hunting. It was divided into three parts. The first confirmed the existence of witches and pointed out that those who did not believe in them were either in honest error or polluted with heresy. The second part contained a description of the clinical symptoms by which witches could be detected, such as red spots or areas of anesthesia on the skin, which were thought to resemble the claw of the devil ("devil's claw") and were presumably left by the devil to denote the sealing of the pact with him. The third part dealt with the legal forms of examining and sentencing a witch.

In accordance with the precepts laid down in the *Malleus*, the accepted way to gain sure proof of witchcraft was to torture the person until a confession was obtained. This method was eminently effective. The victims of these inhuman tortures—writhing in agony and viewed with horror by those they loved—confessed to anything and everything. Frequently they were forced to give the names of alleged accomplices in their evildoing, and these unfortunate persons were in turn tortured until they, too, confessed.

Witch-burning, 16th-century copper engraving.

Confessions were often weird, but this seldom deterred the learned judges. For example, James I of England proved, through the skillful use of unlimited torture, that witches were to blame for the tempests that beset his bride on her voyage from Denmark. A Dr. Fian, whose legs were being crushed in the "boots" and who had wedges driven under his fingernails, confessed that more than a hundred witches had put to sea in a sieve to produce the storms (A. D. White, 1896).

Further impetus to these persecutions was undoubtedly given by many of the suspects themselves, who, although mentally disordered by present standards, participated so actively in the beliefs of the time that they often freely "confessed" their transactions with the devil, almost gleefully pointed out the "marks" he had left on their bodies, and claimed great powers as a result of their evildoing. Others, suffering from severe depressions, elaborated on their terrible sins and admitted themselves to be beyond redemption. (Even today many psychotics are convinced of their hopeless guilt and damnation.) This sort of basis for the iron-bound logic of the Inquisitors is well illustrated in the following case of a woman who was probably suffering from involutional melancholia.

"A certain woman was taken and finally burned, who for six years had an incubus devil even when she was lying in bed at the side of her husband . . . the homage she has given to the devil was of such a sort that she was bound to dedicate herself body and soul to him forever, after seven years. But God provided mercifully for she was taken in the sixth year and condemned to the fire, and having truly and completely confessed is believed to have obtained pardon from God. For she went most willingly to her death, saying that she would gladly suffer an even more terrible death if only she would be set free and escape the power of the devil." (Stone, 1937, p. 146)

To be convicted of witchcraft was a most serious matter. The penalty usually followed one of three general forms. There were those who were beheaded or strangled before being burned, those who were burned alive, and those who were mutilated before being burned. The treatment accorded a mentally disordered man caught in the wrong period of history is illustrated in the following case:

"In Königsberg in 1636 a man thought he was God the Father; he claimed that all the angels and the devil and the Son of God recognized his power. He was convicted. His tongue was cut out, his head cut off, and his body burned." (Zilboorg & Henry, 1941, p. 259)

There seems to have been little distinction between the Roman and the Reformed churches in their attitudes toward witchcraft, and large numbers of people were put to death in this period.

"A French judge boasted that he had burned 800 women in sixteen years on the bench; 600 were burned during the administration of a bishop in Bamberg. The Inquisition, originally started by the Church of Rome, was carried along by protestant churches in Great Britain and Germany. In protestant Geneva 500 persons were burned in the year 1515. In Trèves some 7000 people were reported burned during a period of several years." (Bromberg, 1937, p. 61)

The full horror of the witch mania and its enthusiastic adoption by other countries, including some American colonies, took place during the sixteenth and seventeenth centuries. And though religious and scientific thought began to change gradually, the basic ideas of mental disorder as representing punishment by God or deliberate association with the devil continued to dominate popular thought until well into the nineteenth century.

Emergence of Humanitarian Approaches

Any criticism or questioning of the theological doctrine of demonology during the Middle Ages was made at the risk of life itself. Yet even during the early part of the sixteenth century we find the beginnings again of more scientific intellectual activity. The concepts of demonology and witchcraft, which had long acted to retard the understanding and treatment of mental disorders, began to be challenged and attacked by men greater than their time—men from the fields of religion, physics, medicine, and philosophy.

Reappearance of scientific questioning in Europe

In the early part of the sixteenth century Paracelsus (1490–1541) insisted that the "dancing mania" was not a possession but a form of disease, and that it should be treated as such (Zilboorg & Henry, 1941). He also postulated a conflict between the instinctual and spiritual nature of human beings, formulated the idea of psychic causes for mental illness, and advocated treatment by "bodily magnetism," later recognized as hypnosis (Mora, 1967). Although Paracelsus thus rejected demonology, his view of abnormal behavior was colored by belief in astral influences (*lunatic* is derived from the Latin word "luna" or moon): he was convinced that the moon exercised a supernatural influence over the brain. Nevertheless, Paracelsus stood clearly in defiance of both medical and theological tradition, and he was hounded and persecuted until his death.

Johann Weyer (1515–1588), a physician and man of letters who wrote under the Latin name of Joannus Wierus, was so deeply impressed by the scenes of imprisonment, torture, and burning of persons accused of witchcraft that he made a careful study of the entire problem of witchcraft and about 1563 published a book on the subject. In it he argued that a considerable number, if not all, of those imprisoned, tortured, and burned for witchcraft were really sick mentally or bodily, and consequently that great wrongs were being committed against innocent people. Weyer's work received the approval of a few outstanding physicians and theologians of his time. In the main, however, it met with vehement protest and condemnation. Father Spina, the author of a polemical book against Weyer, stated: "Recently Satan went to a Sabbath[2] attired as a great prince, and told the assembled witches that they need not worry since, thanks to Weyer and his followers, the affairs of the Devil were brilliantly progressing" (in Castiglioni, 1946, p. 253).

Weyer was one of the first physicians to specialize in mental disorders, and his wide experience and progressive views justify his being regarded as the true founder of modern psychopathology. Unfortunately, however, he was too far ahead of his time. His works were banned by the Church and remained so until the twentieth century.

Perhaps there is no better illustration of the spirit of scientific skepticism that was developing in the sixteenth century than the works of the Oxford-educated Reginald Scot (1538–1599), who devoted his life to exposing the fallacies of witchcraft and demonology. In his book *Discovery of Witchcraft*, published in 1584, he convincingly and daringly denied the existence of demons, devils, and evil spirits as the cause of mental disorders.

"These women are but diseased wretches suffering from melancholy, and their words, actions, reasoning, and gestures show that sickness has affected their brains and impaired their powers of judgment. You must know that the effects of sickness on men, and still more on women, are almost unbelievable. Some of these persons imagine, confess, and maintain that they are witches and are capable of performing extraordinary miracles through the arts of witchcraft; others, due to the same mental disorder, imagine strange and impossible things which they claim to have witnessed." (in Castiglioni, 1946, p. 253)

King James I of England, however, came to the rescue of demonology, personally refuted Scot's thesis, and ordered his book seized and burned. But churchmen also were beginning to question the practices of the time. The wise and far-seeing St. Vincent de Paul (1576–1660), surrounded by every opposing influence and at the risk of his life, declared: "Mental disease is no different to bodily disease and Christianity demands of the humane and powerful to protect, and the skilful to relieve the one as well as the other."

In the face of such attacks, which continued through the next two centuries, demonology was forced to give ground, and the way was gradually paved for the triumph of observation and reason, culminating in the development of modern experimental science and psychopathology.

Title page of Reginald Scot's *Discovery of Witchcraft* (1584), which denied the common belief that demons caused mental disorders.

THE
Diſcovery of Witchcraft:
PROVING,
That the Compacts and Contracts of WITCHES with *Devils* and all *Infernal Spirits* or *Familiars*, are but Erroneous Novelties and Imaginary Conceptions.

Alſo diſcovering, How far their Power extendeth in Killing, Tormenting, Conſuming, or Curing the bodies of Men, Women, Children, or Animals, by Charms, Philtres, Periapts, Pentacles, Curſes, and Conjurations.

WHEREIN LIKE WISE

The Unchriſtian Practices and Inhumane Dealings of *Searchers* and *Witch-tryers* upon *Aged*, *Melancholly*, and *Superſtitious* people, in extorting Confeſſions by Terrors and Tortures, and in deviſing falſe Marks and Symptoms, are notably Detected.

And the Knavery of *Juglers*, *Conjurers*, *Charmers*, *Soothſayers*, *Figure-Caſters*, *Dreamers*, *Alchymiſts* and *Philterers*; with many other things that have long lain hidden, fully Opened and Deciphered.

ALL WHICH

Are very neceſſary to be known for the undeceiving of *Judges*, *Juſtices*, and *Jurors*, before they paſs Sentence upon Poor, Miſerable and Ignorant People; who are frequently Arraigned, Condemned, and Executed for *Witches* and *Wizzards*.

IN SIXTEEN BOOKS.

By REGINALD SCOT *Eſquire*.

---

[2]The word *Sabbath* has no relation to the Biblical Sabbath, but refers to witches' gatherings in which orders were supposedly received from Satan.

Two 18th-century views of "Bedlam," exterior and interior. It was customary to allow the public to see the lunatics, as the two "ladies of fashion" are doing here. One of the common sights was patients chained to the walls (opposite page).

Establishment of early asylums and shrines

From the sixteenth century on, monasteries and prisons gradually relinquished the care of persons suffering from mental disorders to special institutions that were being established in increasing numbers. The care received by patients, however, left much to be desired.

Early asylums. In 1547 the monastery of St. Mary of Bethlehem at London was officially made into a mental hospital by Henry VIII. Its name soon became contracted to "Bedlam," and it became widely known for the deplorable conditions and practices that prevailed. The more violent patients were exhibited to the public for one penny a look, and the more harmless inmates were forced to seek charity on the streets of London in the manner described by Shakespeare:

". . . Bedlam beggars, who, with roaring voices . . . Sometime with lunatic bans, sometime with prayers Enforce their charity." (*King Lear*, Act II, Scene iii)

Such hospitals, or "asylums" as they were called, were gradually established in other countries (Lewis, 1941). The San Hipolito, established in Mexico in 1566 by the philanthropist Bernardino Alvares, was the first hospital for the care and study of mental disorders to be established in the Americas. The first mental hospital in France, La Maison de Charenton, was founded in 1641 in the suburbs of Paris. A mental hospital was established in Moscow in 1764, and the notorious Lunatics' Tower in Vienna was constructed in 1784. This was a showplace in Old Vienna, and the description of the structure and its practices makes interesting reading. It was an ornately decorated round tower within which were square rooms. The doctors and "keepers" lived in the square rooms, while the patients were confined in the spaces between the walls of the square rooms and the outside of the tower. The patients were put on exhibit to the public for a small fee, and were, in general, treated like animals and criminals.

The Pennsylvania Hospital at Philadelphia, completed under the guidance of Benjamin Franklin in 1756, provided some cells or wards for the mental patients, but the first hospital in the United States devoted exclusively to mental patients was constructed in Williamsburg, Virginia, in 1773.

These early asylums, or hospitals, were primarily modifications of penal institutions, and the inmates were treated more like beasts than like human beings. Selling gives a striking account of the treatment of the chronic insane in La Bicêtre Hospital in Paris. This treatment was typical of the asylums of this period and continued through most of the eighteenth century.

The patients were ordinarily shackled to the walls of their dark, unlighted cells by iron collars which held them flat against the wall and permitted little movement. Ofttimes there were also iron hoops around the waists of the patients and both their hands and feet were chained. Although these chains usually permitted enough movement that the patients could feed themselves out of bowls, they often kept them from being able to lie down at night.

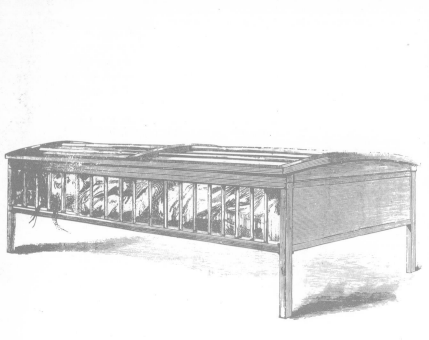

Since little was known about dietetics, and the patients were presumed to be animals anyway, little attention was paid to whether they were adequately fed or to whether the food was good or bad. The cells were furnished only with straw and were never swept or cleaned; the patient was permitted to remain in the midst of all the accumulated ordure. No one visited the cells except at feeding time, no provision was made for warmth, and even the most elementary gestures of humanity were lacking. (Modified from Selling, 1943, pp. 54–55)

Treatment of mental patients in the United States was little, if any, better. The following is a vivid description of their plight in this country during colonial times:

"The mentally ill were hanged, imprisoned, tortured, and otherwise persecuted as agents of Satan. Regarded as sub-human beings, they were chained in specially devised kennels and cages like wild beasts, and thrown into prisons, bridewells and jails like criminals. They were incarcerated in workhouse dungeons or made to slave as able-bodied paupers, unclassified from the rest. They were left to wander about stark naked, driven from place to place like mad dogs, subjected to whippings as vagrants and rogues. Even the well-to-do were not spared confinement in strong rooms and cellar dungeons, while legislation usually concerned itself more with their property than their persons." (Deutsch, 1946, p. 53)

Some insight into the prevalent forms of treatment in the early American hospitals may be gained from a thesis on "Chronic Mania," written by a medical student in 1796 at the New York Hospital, in which cells or wards were provided in the cellar for the mentally ill patients. He considered that restraint should be avoided as long as possible, "lest the strait jackets, and chains and cells should induce a depression of spirits seldom surmounted." He also doubted the propriety of "unexpected plunging into cold water," of "two to six hours in spring water or still colder," of the "refrigerant plan," of bleeding, purging, vomiting, streams of cold water on the head, blisters, and similar procedures (Russell, 1941, p. 230).

Even as late as 1830, new patients had their heads shaved, were dressed in straitjackets, put on a low diet, compelled to swallow some active purgative, and placed in a dark cell. If these measures did not serve to quiet unruly or excited patients, more severe measures, such as starvation, solitary confinement, cold baths, and other torturelike methods, were used (Bennett, 1947).

The Gheel shrine. There were a few bright spots in this otherwise tragic situation. Out of the more humane Christian tradition of

Even after reform of mental institutions had begun, various devices were used to control unmanageable patients: (from the left) the crib, used as late as 1882 to restrain violent patients; the "tranquillizing chair" of Benjamin Rush; and the circulating swing, used in the early 19th century to bring the mentally disordered back to sound reasoning. It was said that "no well-regulated institution should be without one."

prayer, the laying on of hands, or holy touch, and visits to shrines for cure of illness, there arose several great shrines where treatment by kindness and love stood out in marked contrast to generally prevailing conditions. The one at Gheel in Belgium, visited since the thirteenth century, is probably most famous—and the story of its founding is a most interesting one.

"Somewhere in the dim past there lived a king in Ireland who was married to a most beautiful woman and who sired an equally beautiful daughter. The good queen developed a fatal illness, and at her death bed the daughter dedicated herself to a life of purity and service to the poor and the mentally bereft. The widowed king was beside himself with grief and announced to his subjects that he must at once be assuaged of sorrow by marrying the woman in his kingdom who most resembled the dead queen. No such paragon was found. But the devil came and whispered to the king that there was such a woman—his own daughter. The devil spurred the king to propose marriage to the girl, but she was appropriately outraged by this incestuous overture and fled across the English Channel to Belgium. There the king overtook her and with Satan at his elbow, slew the girl and her faithful attendants. In the night the angels came, recapitated the body and concealed it in the forest near the village of Gheel. Years later five lunatics chained together spent the night with their keepers at a small wayside shrine

near this Belgian village. Overnight all the victims recovered. Here indeed must be the place where the dead girl, reincarnated as St. Dymphna, was buried, and here was the sacred spot where her cures of the insane are effected. In the 15th century pilgrimages to Gheel from every part of the civilized world were organized for the mentally sick. Many of the pilgrims remained in Gheel to live with the inhabitants of the locality, and in the passing years it became the natural thing to accept them into the homes and thus the first 'colony' was formed and for that matter the only one which has been consistently successful." (Karnosh & Zucker, 1945, p. 15)

The colony of Gheel has continued its work into modern times (Aring, 1974, 1975; Belgian Consulate, 1975). In the mid-1970s more than two thousand certified mental patients lived in private homes, worked with the inhabitants, and suffered few restrictions other than not using alcohol. Many types of mental disorders are represented, including schizophrenia, manic-depressive psychoses, psychopathic personality, and mental retardation. Ordinarily patients remain in Gheel until they are considered recovered by a supervising therapist. It is unfortunate that the great humanitarian work of this colony—and the opportunity Gheel affords to study the treatment of mental patients in a family and community setting—has received so little recognition.

Humanitarian reform

Although scientific skepticism had undermined the belief that mental disturbance was the devil's work, most early asylums were no better than concentration camps. The unfortunate inmates lived and died amid conditions of incredible filth and cruelty. Humanitarian reform of mental hospitals received its first great impetus from the work of Philippe Pinel (1745–1826) in France.

Pinel's experiment. In 1792, shortly after the first phase of the French Revolution came to a close, Pinel was placed in charge of La Bicêtre (the hospital for the insane in Paris to which we have previously referred). In this capacity he received the grudging permission of the Revolutionary Commune to remove the chains from some of the inmates as an experiment to test his views that mental patients should be treated with kindness and consideration—as sick people and not as vicious beasts or criminals. Had his experiment proved a failure, Pinel might well have lost his head, but, fortunately for all, it proved to be a great success. Chains were removed, sunny rooms were provided instead of dungeons, patients were permitted to exercise on the hospital grounds, and kindliness was extended to these poor creatures, some of whom had been chained in dungeons for thirty years or more. The effect was almost miraculous. The previous noise, filth, and abuse were replaced by order and peace. As Pinel said: "The whole discipline was marked with regularity and kindness which had the most favorable effect on the insane themselves, rendering even the most furious more tractable" (Selling, 1943, p. 65).

The reactions of these patients when all their chains were removed for the first time is a pathetic story. One patient, an English officer who had years before killed a guard in an attack of fury, tottered outside on legs weak from lack of use, and for the first time in some forty years saw the sun and sky. With tears in his eyes he exclaimed, "Oh, how beautiful!" (Zilboorg & Henry, 1941, p. 323). Finally, when night came, he voluntarily returned to his cell, which had been cleaned during his absence, to fall peacefully asleep on his new bed. After two years of orderly behavior, in-

cluding helping to handle other patients, he was pronounced recovered and permitted to leave the hospital. It is a curious and satisfying fact of history that Pinel was saved from the hands of a mob who suspected him of antirevolutionary activities by a soldier whom he had freed from asylum chains.

Pinel was later given charge of the Salpêtrière Hospital, where the same reorganization in treatment was instituted with similarly gratifying results. The Bicêtre and Salpêtrière hospitals thus became the first modern hospitals for the care of the insane. Pinel's successor, Jean Esquirol (1772–1840), continued his good work at the Salpêtrière and, in addition, helped in the establishment of some ten new mental hospitals, which helped put France in the forefront of humane treatment for the mentally disturbed.

Tuke's work in England. At about the same time that Pinel was reforming the Bicêtre Hospital, an English Quaker named William Tuke established the "York Retreat," a pleasant country house where mental patients lived, worked, and rested in a kindly religious atmosphere. This represented the culmination of a noble battle against the brutality, ignorance, and indifference of his time. Some insight into the

Philippe Pinel (opposite page), French physician best known for his work leading to more humane treatment of institutionalized mental patients. The painting depicts him releasing the shackles from the inmates at Salpêtrière Hospital.

difficulties and discouragements he encountered in the establishment of the York Retreat may be gleaned from a simple statement he made in a letter regarding his early efforts: "All men seem to desert me." This is not surprising when we remember that demonology was still widespread, and that as late as 1768 we find the Protestant John Wesley's famous declaration that "The giving up of witchcraft is in effect the giving up of the Bible." The belief in demonology was too strong to be conquered overnight.

As word of the amazing results obtained by Pinel spread to England, Tuke's small force of Quakers gradually gained support from John Connolly, Samuel Hitch, and other great English medical psychologists. In 1841 Hitch introduced trained women nurses into the wards at the Gloucester Asylum and put trained supervisors at the head of the nursing staffs. These innovations, regarded as quite revolutionary at the time, were of great importance not only in improving the care of mental patients but also in changing public attitudes toward the mentally disturbed. As mental disorders came to be put on somewhat the same footing as physical illness, the mystery, ignorance, and fear that had always surrounded them began gradually to give way.

Rush and Dix in America. The success of Pinel's and Tuke's experiments in more humanitarian methods revolutionized the treatment of mental patients throughout the civilized world. In the United States, this was reflected in the work of Benjamin Rush (1745–1813), the founder of American psychiatry. Becoming associated with the Pennsylvania Hospital in 1783, Rush encouraged more humane treatment of the mentally ill, wrote the first systematic treatise on psychiatry in America, *Medical Inquiries and Observations upon the Diseases of the Mind* (1812), and was the first American to organize a course in psychiatry. But even he did not escape entirely from the established beliefs of his time. His medical theory was tainted with astrology, and his principal remedies were bloodletting and purgatives. In addition, he invented and used a torturous device called "the tranquillizer." Despite these limitations, however, we may consider Rush an important transitional figure between the old era and the new.

The early work of Benjamin Rush was followed through by an energetic New England schoolteacher, Dorothea Dix (1802–1887). Dix was retired early from her teaching because of recurring attacks of tuberculosis, and in 1841 she began to teach in a Sunday school for female prisoners. Through this contact she soon became acquainted with the deplorable conditions prevalent in jails, almshouses, and asylums. In a "Memorial" submitted to the Congress of the United States in 1848, she stated that she had seen "more than 9000 idiots, epileptics and insane in the United States, destitute of appropriate care and protection . . . bound with galling chains, bowed beneath fetters and heavy iron balls attached to drag-chains, lacerated with ropes, scourged with rods and terrified beneath storms of execration and cruel blows; now subject to jibes and scorn and torturing tricks; now abandoned to the most outrageous violations" (Zilboorg & Henry, 1941, pp. 583–584).

As a result of her findings, Dix carried on a zealous campaign between 1841 and 1881 which aroused the people and the legislatures to an awareness of the inhuman treatment accorded the mentally ill. Through her efforts many millions of dollars were raised to build suitable hospitals, and some twenty states responded directly to her appeals. Not only was she instrumental in improving conditions in the United States, but she directed the opening of two large institutions in Canada, and completely reformed the asylum system in Scotland and several other countries. She is credited with the establishment of some thirty-two modern mental hospitals, an astonishing record considering the ignorance and su-

A common 19th-century view of the face of "madness" is shown in this drawing (left) by Charles Bell. Dorothea Dix (above) did much to challenge this view; she was one of the most important forces in the world for the improvement of conditions in insitutions and asylums during the last half of the 19th century.

perstition that still prevailed in the field of mental health. She rounded out her amazing career by organizing the nursing forces of the Northern armies during the Civil War. A resolution presented by the United States Congress in 1901 characterized her as "among the noblest examples of humanity in all history" (Karnosh & Zucker, 1945, p. 18).

Moral therapy. During the early part of this period of humanitarian reform, the use of moral therapy in mental hospitals was relatively widespread. This approach stemmed largely from the work of Pinel and Tuke and was based on the view that most of the people labeled as *insane* were essentially normal people who could profit from a favorable environment and help with their personal problems. As Rees (1957) has described it:

"The insane came to be regarded as normal people who had lost their reason as a result of having been exposed to severe psychological and social stresses. These stresses were called the moral causes of insanity, and moral treatment aimed at relieving the patient by friendly association, discussion of his difficulties, and the daily pursuit of purposeful activity; in other words, social therapy, individual therapy, and occupational therapy." (pp. 306–307)

There seems little doubt that moral therapy was remarkably effective, however "unscientific" it may have been. Records indicate that during the first half of the nineteenth century, when moral therapy apparently reached its peak as the sole method of treatment, at least 70 percent of mental patients who had been hospitalized for less than one year were discharged as recovered or improved. Some recovery rates were reported to be as high as 80 to 90 percent (Tourney, 1967).

Despite these impressive results, moral therapy declined in the latter half of the nineteenth century—in part, paradoxically, because of the acceptance of the view that the insane were ill people. Though those who suffered from mental disorders were no longer seen as "possessed," neither were they seen as able to meet expectations, carry out tasks, or make decisions. Rather, it was assumed that they were helpless, sick persons, and that the application of new techniques of physical

medicine would be more "scientific" than any psychological therapy. This approach gained strength as the superintendence of mental hospitals was taken out of the hands of wardens or stewards and placed under the auspices of medical superintendents.[3]

The attempt to provide hospital facilities for larger numbers of patients seems to have contributed also to the decline of moral therapy, since its procedures were practical only when the patient population was relatively small in relation to treatment personnel. In any event, hospital statistics show that recovery and discharge rates declined as moral therapy was given up in favor of medical approaches and mental hospitals became huge custodial warehouses (Rabkin, 1972).

Only in recent years has the trend been reversed as remote state mental hospitals have given way to community mental health centers and facilities, and the view has come to be accepted that people with mental disorders can best be helped if they are treated as nearly as possible like normal human beings.

The beginning of the mental health movement. In the last half of the nineteenth century the mental hospital or asylum—"the big house on the hill"—with its high turrets and fortress-like appearance, became a familiar landmark in America. In it mental patients lived under semiadequate conditions of comfort and freedom from abuse. To the general public, however, the asylum was an eerie place, and its occupants a strange and frightening lot.

Little was done by the resident psychiatrists[4] to educate the public along lines that would reduce the general fear and horror of insanity. One principal reason for this, of course, was that the early psychiatrist had very little actual information to impart. Even as late as 1840 no clear-cut classification of mental disorders had been worked out, and a German teacher, Dr. Heinroth, was still advancing the

[3]The present American Psychiatric Association developed out of an organization originally formed in 1844 by thirteen superintendents of mental hospitals, the Association of Medical Superintendents of American Institutions for the Insane (Lowry, 1946).

[4]It is of interest to note that psychiatrists were formerly called *alienists*—and in some places still are—referring to persons who treat the "alienated" or insane.

These men were all pioneers in various ways in laying the groundwork for modern psychiatric thought: (from top) **Johann Weyer** (1515–1588) wrote against the prevalent beliefs in witchcraft and decried the persecution of the mentally ill; **Benjamin Rush** (1745–1813) was the first American to write a systematic treatise on psychiatry and to organize a course in the subject; and **Emil Kraepelin** (1856–1926), by integrating clinical data, worked out the first systematic classification of mental disorders.

theory that sin produced insanity and repentance a cure, and that piety was conducive to mental health (Lewis, 1941).

With the beginnings of the mental health movement, however, important strides were made toward changing the attitude of the general public toward mental patients. In America, the pioneering work of Dorothea Dix in educating the public about mental disorders was followed up by that of Clifford Beers, whose now-famous book, *A Mind that Found Itself,* was published in 1908. Beers, a Yale graduate, described his own mental collapse and told of the bad treatment he received in three typical institutions of the day, and of his eventual recovery in the home of a friendly attendant. Although chains and other torture devices had long since been given up, the straitjacket was still widely used as a means of "quieting" excited patients. Beers experienced this treatment and supplied a vivid description of what such painful immobilization of the arms means to an overwrought mental patient in terms of intensification of inner excitement. He began a campaign to make people realize that this was no way to handle the sick, winning the interest and support of many public-spirited individuals, including the eminent psychologist William James and the "dean of American psychiatry," Adolf Meyer.

Thus through the combined efforts of many dedicated people our contemporary mental health movement had its start. And with the development of modern scientific views of psychopathology, it was to receive great impetus—contributing greatly to better public understanding of mental disorders, to the development of community mental health programs and facilities, and to the concept of comprehensive health.

Development of the Organic Viewpoint and the Medical Model

With the emergence of modern experimental science in the early part of the eighteenth century, knowledge of anatomy, physiology, neurology, chemistry, and general medicine increased rapidly. These advances led to the gradual identification of the organic pathology underlying many physical ailments, and it was only another step for these early workers to look upon mental disorder as an illness based on organic brain pathology.

As early as 1757, Albrecht von Haller (1708–1777) in his *Elements of Physiology* emphasized the importance of the brain in psychic functions and advocated studying the brains of the insane by postmortem dissection. The first systematic presentation of the organic viewpoint, however, was made by the German psychiatrist William Griesinger (1817–1868). In his textbook *The Pathology and Therapy of Psychic Disorders*, published in 1845, Griesinger insisted that psychiatry should proceed on a physiological and clinical basis and emphasized his belief that all mental disorders could be explained in terms of brain pathology.

This concept of mental disorders is called the *organic viewpoint* or *medical model*. Although this model was too broadly used before limitations of its applicability were recognized, it represents the first great advance of modern science toward the understanding and treatment of mental disorders.

Systematic classification of mental disorders

Although the work of Griesinger received considerable attention, it was his follower, Emil Kraepelin (1856–1926) who played the dominant role in the early development of the organic viewpoint. Kraepelin, whose textbook *Lehrbuch der Psychiatrie* was published in 1883, not only emphasized the importance of brain pathology in mental disorders but also made several related contributions that helped establish this viewpoint. The most important of these was his system of classification. Kraepelin noted that certain symptom patterns occurred with sufficient regularity to be regarded as specific types of mental disease—each with a predictable course—in much the same way that we think of measles, smallpox, and other physical ailments. He then proceeded to describe and clarify these types of mental disorders, working out the scheme of classification that is the basis of our present categories. The integration of the clinical material underlying this classification was a herculean task and represented a major contribution to the field of psychopathology.

Kraepelin looked upon each type of mental disorder as separate and distinct from the others, and thought that its course was as predetermined and predictable as the course of measles. Such conclusions led to widespread interest in the accurate description and classification of mental disorders, for by this means the outcome of a given type of disorder could presumably be predicted even if it could not yet be controlled. The subsequent period in psychopathology, during which description and classification were so heavily emphasized, has been referred to as the "descriptive era."

Establishment of brain pathology as a causal factor

During this "descriptive" period, tremendous strides were being made in the study of the nervous system by such now-famous scientists as Golgi, Ramón y Cajal, Broca, Jackson, and Head, and the brain pathology underlying many mental disorders was gradually being uncovered. For example, the syphilitic basis of general *paresis* (syphilis of the brain) was finally established as the result of the brilliant contributions of a series of medical scientists. Similarly, the brain pathology in cerebral arteriosclerosis and in the senile psychoses was established by Alzheimer and other investigators. One success was followed by another, and eventually the organic pathology underlying the toxic psychoses, certain types of mental retardation, and other "organically" caused mental disorders was discovered.

These discoveries were not made overnight but resulted from the combined efforts of many scientists. As an example, at least ten different steps can be traced in the discovery of the organic pathology underlying general paresis—one of the most serious of all mental illnesses, which produced paralysis and insanity and typically brought about the death of the afflicted subject in from two to five years. Prior to this discovery, organic pathology had been suspected in many mental disorders but had not been demonstrated systematically and completely enough to allow for effective therapy. The sequence of events in this long search shows graphically the way in which scientists working independently can utilize research by others in the field in advancing knowledge bit by bit and developing a model that will fit all the known facts. The major steps involved in the conquest of general paresis and the development of appropriate treatment were:

1. Differentiation of general paresis as a specific type of mental disorder by the French physician A. L. J. Bayle in 1825. Bayle gave a very complete and accurate description of the symptom pattern of paresis and convincingly presented his reasons for believing paresis to be a distinct disorder.

2. Report by Esmarch and Jessen in 1857 of cases of paresis who were known to have had syphilis and their conclusion that the syphilis caused the paresis.

3. Description by the Scot Argyll-Robertson in 1869 of the failure of the pupillary reflex to light (failure of the pupil of the eye to narrow under bright light) as diagnostic of the involvement of the central nervous system in syphilis.

4. Experiment by the Viennese psychiatrist Richard Krafft-Ebing in 1897, involving the inoculation of paretic patients with matter from syphilitic sores. None of the patients developed the secondary symptoms of syphilis, which led to the conclusion that they must previously have been infected. This was a crucial experiment that definitely established the relationship of general paresis to syphilis.

5. Discovery of the *Spirochaeta pallida* by Schaudinn in 1905 as the cause of syphilis.

6. Development by von Wassermann in 1906 of a blood test for syphilis. Now it became possible to check for the presence of the deadly spirochetes in the bloodstream of individuals who would not otherwise realize they were infected.

7. Application by Plant in 1908 of the Wassermann test to the cerebrospinal fluid, to indicate whether or not the spirochete had invaded the patient's central nervous system.

8. Development by Paul Ehrlich in 1909, after 605 failures, of the arsenical compound arsphenamine (which he thereupon called "606") for the treatment of syphilis. Although "606" proved effective in killing the syphilitic spirochetes in the bloodstream, it was not effective against the spirochetes that had penetrated the central nervous system.

9. Verification by Noguchi and Moore in 1913 of the syphilitic spirochete as the brain-damaging agent in general paresis. They discovered these spirochetes in the postmortem study of the brains of patients who had suffered from paresis.

10. Introduction in 1917 by Julius Wagner-Jauregg, chief of the psychiatric clinic of the University of Vienna, of the malarial fever treatment of syphilis and paresis. He inoculated nine of the paretic patients in his clinic with the blood of a soldier who was ill with malaria, and found marked improvement in three patients and apparent recovery in three of the others.

Thus the organic brain pathology underlying one of the most serious mental disorders was uncovered and scientific measures for its treatment developed. True, the complete understanding of paresis—why one patient becomes euphoric and another depressed with the same general organic brain pathology—involves an understanding of certain psychological concepts yet to be discussed. Also, of course, progress in treatment has continued, and penicillin has become the preferred method of treatment, avoiding the complications of malaria. But the steps outlined above show the way in which, *for the first time in all history, a clear-cut conquest of a mental disorder was made by medical science.*

Advances achieved by the medical model

Let us take a moment here to examine the important advances that had been made in psychopathology up to the turn of the twentieth century, which represented the end of the period during which the medical viewpoint almost completely dominated psychopathology.

1. The early concepts of demonology had finally been destroyed, and the organic viewpoint of mental disorder as based on brain pathology was well established.

2. For general paresis and certain other mental disorders, definite underlying brain pathology had been discovered and appropriate methods of treatment developed.

3. A workable, though not yet completely satisfactory, scheme of classification had been set up.

4. Mental disorders had finally been put on an equal footing with physical illness, at least in medical circles, and for the first time mental patients were receiving humane treatment based on scientific findings.

5. A great deal of research was under way in anatomy, physiology, biochemistry, and other allied medical sciences, in an attempt to ascertain the brain pathology (or other bodily pathology that might be affecting the brain) in other types of mental disorders and to clarify the role of organic processes in all behavior.

These were truly remarkable achievements, and they helped pave the way for some of the great advances that have come about in the present century in clarifying the causal role of genetic, biochemical, and other biological factors in various mental disorders.

One of the most dramatic and far-reaching advances achieved by the medical model came about in the 1950s with the introduction of tranquilizing and antidepressant drugs. Although these drugs have undergone refinement over the years, and new ones have been introduced, they cannot "cure" mental disorders. But they have made it possible for more mental patients to remain in their family and community settings; they have led to the earlier discharge of patients who do require hospitalization; and they have reduced the severity of symptoms and the need for restraints and locked wards. As R. W. White (1959) predicted, chemotherapy would make Pinel's mission in striking the chains from mental patients come close to its ultimate fulfillment.

Contemporary progress in the understanding and treatment of mental disorders cannot be wholly explained, however, in terms of advances in the medical sciences. At least equally important has been the belated recognition that psychosocial and sociocultural factors are key elements in the causation of both normal and abnormal behavior. But during the early years of the twentieth century, most students of abnormal behavior became convinced that organic pathology of the brain or nervous system must be at the root of *all* mental disorders, as they had been shown to be in the case of paresis.

In this chapter we have traced the development of our views of psychopathology from ancient times to the beginning of the twentieth century. We noted the belief in demonology and exorcism followed by the emergence of early medical concepts during the Golden Age of Greece, and the elaboration of many of these concepts by Roman physicians. With the fall of Rome toward the end of the fifth century and the beginning of the Dark Ages, there was a return to the most primitive concepts of demonology, which continued to dominate views of mental disorders for over a thousand years. However, by the beginning of the sixteenth century, there was a reappearance of scientific questioning in Europe followed by more humanitarian approaches and the eventual development of the basic medical model of mental disorders.

Understanding this developmental sequence, with its forward steps and reverses, helps us understand the emergence of modern psychopathology and provides us with a perspective for understanding the advances still to come.

Psychosocial and Sociocultural Viewpoints

Despite the great advances in the understanding and treatment of mental disorders achieved by the organic viewpoint and medical model, many puzzling and important questions remained unanswered.

For one thing, repeated clinical examinations and research studies failed to reveal any organic pathology in most patients with mental disorders. True, a given patient might show some minor deviation in bodily chemistry, but then, so did a great many normal people; furthermore, many patients with the same symptoms of mental disorder did not show the same organic deviation.

To some scientists these discrepancies were a challenge to intensify research, for they felt certain that organic pathology must be there, and that the refinement of their laboratory techniques would make it clear. But there was also a new school of thought emerging that questioned the dominant belief that brain pathology was the sole cause of mental disorders. This was the "revolutionary" view that certain types of mental disorders might be caused by *psychological* rather than organic factors.

Although one might assume that the role of psychological factors in mental disorders would have been recognized long before 1900, such was not the case. Psychology as a science was still in its infancy in 1900, its inception dating back only twenty-one years to the establishment of the first experimental psychology laboratory at the University of Leipzig in 1879 by Wilhelm Wundt. In addition, early psychology was rather naive in its approach to understanding human behavior, consisting primarily of experimental studies of sense perception. True, in 1890 William James had published his monumental work, *Principles of Psychology*, in which he attempted to explain emotion, memory, reasoning, habits, consciousness of self, hysteria, and other aspects of human behavior. However, he was handicapped because little experimental work had been done in these areas, and his brief allusions to abnormal behavior were mainly descriptive and speculative.

This is not to disparage the contributions of the early investigators who helped psychology through its infant period or to minimize the

Development of the Psychosocial Viewpoint and Models
Emergence of the Sociocultural Viewpoint
Toward a Unified Viewpoint

importance of physiological studies as a foundation for what came next. The fact remains, however, that psychology was still in its early stages, and there was little systematic knowledge regarding the role of psychological factors in maladaptive behavior.

The usefulness of models in science

A model is essentially an analogy that helps scientists order their findings and see important relationships among them. The computer model of the brain, for example, has made it commonplace to utilize the concepts of input, information processing, and feedback in conceptualizing human thought processes. Unlike formal theories, which purportedly account for all relevant data, models are not intended to be entirely accurate explanations of reality. Rather, they are conceptual tools that can help investigators organize and interpret masses of data that might otherwise prove meaningless and unwieldy.

A model may be very comprehensive or relatively limited in scope. Thus, in psychology, we have comprehensive models of human behavior, such as the psychoanalytic model, and more specific models, such as the various models of schizophrenia. Models also differ in terms of completeness and degree of detail. Some of the psychosocial models examined in this chapter actually represent more of a perspective, or point of view, than a clearly formulated model with a systematized and agreed-upon structure. This is particularly true of the humanistic, existential, and interpersonal models.

Although the models we will be discussing in this book are commonly referred to as "theories" of normal and abnormal behavior, the concept of "models" seems more appropriate in view of our present limited knowledge and the need for maintaining flexibility in our thinking about human behavior. Theories, once formalized, tend to seem like final explanations and are often adhered to long after new research findings cast them in doubt. Models, on the other hand, follow a strategy of successive approximations, and they can be readily modified—or, if necessary, abandoned—to accommodate new evidence. It is this ability of science to be "self-correcting" that makes scientific progress possible.

In reviewing the development of contemporary psychological thought, we shall examine five systematic models of human nature and behavior—the psychoanalytic, behavioristic, humanistic, existential, and interpersonal. Although these various models represent distinct and sometimes conflicting orientations, they are also, as we shall see, in many ways complementary. All of them take some cognizance of social influences as well as of psychological processes within the individual—hence the term *psychosocial* as a general descriptive label.

The psychoanalytic model

The first systematic steps toward understanding psychological factors in mental disorders came about through the astounding contributions of one man—Sigmund Freud (1856–1939). Freud developed his psychoanalytic model over a period of five decades of observing and writing. The major principles of his model were based on the clinical study of individual patients—mostly neurotic—who were undergoing treatment for their problems.

In reviewing the psychoanalytic model, it is useful to divide our discussion into an examination of (a) the roots of psychoanalysis, (b) Freud and the beginnings of psychoanalysis, (c) the basic principles of the model, including its concept of psychopathology, and (d) the impact of the psychoanalytic model on our views of human nature and human behavior.

Roots of psychoanalytic thought. We find the early roots of the psychological viewpoint and of psychoanalysis in a somewhat unexpected place—in the study of hypnosis, especially in its relation to hysteria.

1. *Mesmerism.* Our story starts out with one of the most notorious figures in psychiatry, Anton Mesmer (1734–1815), who further developed Paracelsus' notion of the influence of the planets on the human body. Their influence was believed to be caused by a universal magnetic fluid, and it was presumably the distribution of this fluid in the body that determined health or disease. In attempting to find a cure for mental disorders, Mesmer came to the conclusion that all persons possess magnetic forces that can be used to influence the distribution of the magnetic fluid in other persons, thus effecting cures.

Mesmer attempted to put his views into practice in Vienna and in various other towns, but it was not until he came to Paris in 1778 that he achieved success. Here he opened a clinic in which he treated all kinds of diseases by "animal magnetism." The patients were seated around a tub (a *baquet*) containing various chemicals and from which protruded iron rods that were applied to the affected portions of the body; the room was darkened, appropriate music was played, and Mesmer appeared in a lilac robe, passing from one patient to another and touching each one with his hands or his wand. By this means Mesmer was apparently able to remove hysterical anesthesias and paralyses and to demonstrate most of the phenomena discovered later by the use of hypnosis.

Eventually branded as a charlatan by his medical colleagues, Mesmer was forced to leave Paris, and he shortly faded into obscurity. However, his methods and results were the center of controversy in scientific circles for many years—in fact, mesmerism in the early part of the nineteenth century was as much a source of heated discussion as psychoanalysis was to be in the early part of the twentieth century. This discussion eventually led to a revival of interest in the hypnotic phenomenon as itself an explanation of the "cures" that took place.

2. *"The Nancy school."* One of the physicians who used hypnosis successfully in his practice was the Frenchman Liébeault (1823–1904), who practiced at Nancy. Also in Nancy at this time was a professor of medicine, Bernheim (1840–1919), who became interested in the relationship between hysteria and hypnosis primarily as a result of Liébeault's success in curing by hypnosis a patient whom Bernheim had been treating unsuccessfully by more conventional methods for some four years (Selling, 1943). Bernheim and Liébeault worked together on the problem

A contemporary engraving of a mesmeric *baquet*. The protruding rods, charged with "animal magnetism," were applied to the affected part of the body to cure it, as the man on the left of the tub is doing.

and developed the concept that hypnotism and hysteria were related and that both were due to suggestion (Brown & Menninger, 1940). Their view was based on two lines of evidence: (a) phenomena observed in hysteria, such as paralysis of an arm, inability to hear, or anesthetic areas in which the individual could be stuck with a pin without feeling pain—all of which occurred when there was apparently nothing organically wrong—could be produced in normal subjects by means of hypnosis; and (b) symptoms such as these in hysterical subjects could be removed by means of hypnosis so that the patient could use the formerly paralyzed arm, or hear, or feel in the previously anesthetized areas. Thus it seemed likely that hysteria was a sort of self-hypnosis. The physicians who accepted this view were known as "the Nancy school."

Meanwhile, Jean Charcot (1825–1893), who was head of the Salpêtrière Hospital in Paris and the leading neurologist of his time, had been experimentally investigating some of the phenomena described by the old mesmerists. As a result of his research, Charcot disagreed with the findings of Bernheim and Liébeault and insisted that there were degenerative brain changes in hysteria. In this Charcot proved to be wrong, but work on the problem by so outstanding a scientist did much to awaken medical and scientific interest in hysteria.

In one of the major medical debates of history, in which many harsh words were spoken on both sides, the adherents of the Nancy school finally triumphed. The recognition of one psychologically caused mental disorder spurred research, and it soon became apparent that psychological factors were involved in morbid anxiety, phobias, and other psychopathology. Eventually Charcot himself, a man of great scientific honesty, was won over to the new point of view and did much to promote an interest in the study of psychological factors in various mental disorders.

Toward the end of the nineteenth century, then, it was clear to many that there were mental disorders with a psychological basis as well as those with an organic basis. But one major question remained to be answered: How do these psychologically caused mental disorders actually come about?

Freud and the beginnings of psychoanalysis. The first systematic attempt to answer this question was made by Sigmund Freud. Freud was a brilliant young Viennese physician who at first specialized in neurology and received an appointment as lecturer on nervous diseases at the University of Vienna. On one occasion, however, he introduced to his audience a neurotic patient suffering from a persistent headache, and mistakenly diagnosed the case as chronic localized meningitis. As a result of this error in diagnosis, he lost his job—although, as he pointed out in his autobiography, greater authorities than he were in the habit of diagnosing similar cases as cerebral tumor. Freud went to Paris in 1885 to study under Charcot and later became acquainted with the work of Liébeault and Bernheim at Nancy. He was impressed by their use of hypnosis on hysterical patients and came away convinced that powerful mental processes may remain hidden from consciousness.

On his return to Vienna, Freud worked in collaboration with an older physician, Joseph Breuer, who had introduced an interesting innovation in the use of hypnosis on his neurotic patients, chiefly women. He let the patient under hypnosis talk about her problems and about what bothered her. Under these circumstances the patient usually spoke rather freely, displayed considerable emotion, and on awakening from the hypnotic state felt considerably relieved. Because of the emotional release involved, this method was called the "cathartic method." This simple innovation in the use of hypnosis proved to be of great significance, for not only did it help the patient discharge her emotional tensions by discussion of her problems, but it revealed the nature of the difficulties that had brought about her neurotic symptoms. The patient saw no relationship between her problems and her hysterical symptoms, but the therapist could usually see it quite readily.

Thus was made the discovery of the "unconscious"—the realization of the important role played by unconscious processes in the determination of behavior. In 1893, Freud and Breuer published their joint paper *On the Psychical Mechanisms of Hysterical Phenomena*, which constituted one of the great milestones of psychodynamics.

Freud soon discovered, moreover, that he could dispense with the hypnotic state entirely. By encouraging the patient to say freely whatever came into her mind without regard to logic or decency, Freud found that she would eventually overcome inner obstacles to remembering and would discuss her problem freely. The new method was called *free association*, and the term *psychoanalysis* was given to the principles involved in analyzing and interpreting what the patient said and did, and in helping her gain insight and achieve a more adequate adjustment.

Freud devoted the remainder of his long and energetic life to the development and elaboration of the psychoanalytic model. His views were formally introduced to American scientists in 1909, when he delivered a now-famous series of lectures at Clark University at the invitation of G. Stanley Hall, the eminent American psychologist who was then president of the university. These *Introductory Lectures on Psychoanalysis* led to a great deal of controversy that helped publicize the concepts of psychoanalysis to both scientists and the general public.

Basic principles of the psychoanalytic model. The psychoanalytic model is both highly systematized and complex, and we shall not attempt to deal with it in detail. Its general principles, however, may be sketched as follows:

1. *Id, ego, and superego.* Basically the individual's behavior is assumed to result from the interaction of three key subsystems within the personality: the id, ego, and superego.

The *id* is the source of instinctual drives which are considered to be of two types: (a) constructive drives, primarily of a sexual nature, which constitute the *libido*, or basic energy of life, and (b) destructive drives which tend toward aggression, destruction, and eventual death. Thus *life*, or constructive, instincts are opposed by *death*, or destructive, instincts. Here it may be noted that Freud used the term *sex* in a broad sense to refer to almost anything pleasurable, from eating to creativity. The id is completely selfish, concerned only with the immediate gratification of instinctual needs without reference to reality or moral considerations. Hence it is said to operate in terms of the *pleasure principle*.

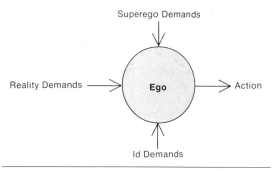

While the id can generate mental images and wish-fulfilling fantasies, referred to as the *primary process*, it cannot undertake the action needed to meet instinctual demands.

Consequently a second key subsystem develops—the *ego*—which mediates between the demands of the id and the realities of the external world. The basic purpose of the ego is to meet id demands, but in such a way as to ensure the well-being and survival of the individual. This requires the use of reason and other intellectual resources in dealing with the external world, as well as the exercise of control over id demands. Such adaptive measures of the ego are referred to as the *secondary process*, and the ego is said to operate in terms of the *reality principle*. Freud viewed id demands, especially sexual and aggressive strivings, as inherently in conflict with rules and prohibitions imposed by society.

Since the id-ego relationship is merely one of expediency, Freud introduced a third key subsystem—the *superego*—which is the outgrowth of learning the taboos and moral values of society. The superego is essentially what we refer to as *conscience*, and is concerned with right and wrong. As the superego develops, we find an additional inner control system coming into operation to cope with the uninhibited desires of the id. However, the superego also operates through the ego system and strives to compel the ego to inhibit desires that are considered wrong or immoral.

The interplay between these intrapsychic subsystems of id, ego, and superego is of crucial significance in determining behavior. Often inner conflicts arise because each subsystem is striving for somewhat different goals. Neuroses and other mental disorders result when the individual is unable to resolve these conflicts.

2. *Anxiety, defense mechanisms, and the unconscious.* The concept of anxiety is prominent in the psychoanalytic model. Freud distinguished among three types of anxiety, or "psychic pain," that people can suffer: (a) *reality* anxiety, arising from dangers or threats in the external world; (b) *neurotic* anxiety, caused by the id's impulses threatening to break through ego controls, resulting in behavior that will be punished in some way; and (c) *moral* anxiety, arising from a real or contemplated action in conflict with the individual's superego or moral values, and arousing feelings of guilt.

Anxiety is a warning of impending danger as well as a painful experience, so it forces the individual to undertake corrective action. Often the ego can cope with the anxiety by rational measures; if these do not suffice, however, the ego resorts to irrational protective measures—such as rationalization or repression—which are referred to as *ego-defense mechanisms* and will be examined in Chapter 4. These defense mechanisms alleviate the painful anxiety, but they do so by distorting reality instead of dealing directly with the problem. This creates an undesirable schism between actual reality and the way the individual sees reality.

Another important concept in the psychoanalytic model is that of the *unconscious.* Freud thought that the conscious represents a relatively small area of the mind while the unconscious part, like the submerged part of an iceberg, is the much larger portion. In the depths of the unconscious are the hurtful memories, forbidden desires, and other experiences that have been pushed out of the conscious. Although the individual is unaware of such unconscious material, it continues to seek expression and may be reflected in fantasies

and dreams when ego controls are temporarily lowered. Until such unconscious material is brought to awareness and integrated into the ego structure—for example, via psychoanalysis—it presumably leads to irrational and maladaptive behavior.

3. *Psychosexual development.* Freud viewed personality development as a succession of stages, each characterized by a dominant mode of achieving libidinal (sexual) pleasure. The five stages as he outlined them were:

a) *Oral stage.* During the first two years of life the mouth is the principal erogenous zone; the infant's greatest source of gratification is assumed to be sucking.

b) *Anal stage.* From age 2 to age 3, the membranes of the anal region presumably provide the major source of pleasurable stimulation.

c) *Phallic stage.* From age 3 to age 5 or 6, self-manipulation of the genitals provides the major source of pleasurable sensation.

d) *Latency stage.* In the years from 6 to 12, sexual motivations presumably recede in importance as the child becomes preoccupied with developing skills and other activities.

e) *Genital stage.* After puberty the deepest feelings of pleasure presumably come from heterosexual relations.

Freud believed that gratification during each stage is important if the individual is not to be *fixated* at that level. For example, an individual who does not receive adequate oral gratification during infancy may be prone to excessive eating or drinking in adult life.

In general, each stage of development places demands on the individual that must be met, and arouses conflicts that must be resolved. One of the most important conflicts occurs during the phallic stage, when the pleasures of masturbation and accompanying fantasies pave the way for the Oedipus complex. Oedipus, according to Greek mythology, unknowingly killed his father and married his mother. Each young boy, Freud thought, symbolically relives the Oedipus drama. He has incestuous cravings for his mother and views his father as a hated rival; however, he also dreads the wrath of his dominant male parent and fears especially that his father may harm him by removing his penis. This *castration anxiety* forces the boy to repress his sexual desires for his mother as well as his hostility toward his father. Eventually, if all goes well, the boy identifies with his father and comes to have only harmless tender affection for his mother.

The female Oedipus (Electra) complex is more intricate, but it is based essentially on the view that the girl wants to possess her father and replace her mother. For either sex, resolution of the Oedipal conflict is considered essential if the young adult is to develop satisfactory heterosexual relationships.

Impact on our views of psychopathology. According to the psychoanalytic model, people are dominated by instinctual biological drives, as well as by unconscious desires and motives. Although there is a constructive libidinal side in each individual, there are also the darker forces of aggression leading toward destruction and death. And although the ego tends toward rationality, the counterforces of intrapsychic conflict, defense mechanisms, and the unconscious all tend toward a high degree of irrationality and maladaptive behavior. In addition, behavior is further determined through past learning, especially from early experiences. About the best we can hope for is a compromise from which we will realize as much instinctual gratification as possible with minimal punishment and guilt.

Thus the psychoanalytic model presents a negativistic and deterministic view of human behavior that minimizes rationality and freedom for self-determination. On a group level, it interprets violence, war, and related phenomena as the inevitable product of the aggressive and destructive instincts present in human nature.

Many of Freud's ideas have been revised or discarded as a result of subsequent research findings, and the psychoanalytic model is no longer widely used as the principal framework for organizing and interpreting scientific observations about psychopathology. However, two of Freud's contributions stand out as particularly noteworthy:

1. The development of psychoanalytical techniques—for example, free association and dream analysis—for becoming acquainted

Sigmund Freud   (1856–1939)

with both the conscious and unconscious aspects of the mental life of the individual. The data thus obtained led Freud to emphasize (a) the dynamic role of unconscious motives and ego-defense processes, (b) the importance of early childhood experiences in later personality adjustment and maladjustment, and (c) the importance of sexual factors in human behavior and mental disorders. Although, as we have said, Freud used the term *sex* in a much broader sense than it is ordinarily used, the idea caught the popular fancy, and the role of sexual factors in human behavior was finally brought out into the open as an appropriate topic for scientific investigation.

2. The demonstration that certain abnormal mental phenomena—such as the repression of traumatic experiences and irrational fears—occurred as a result of attempts to cope with difficult problems and were simply exaggera-

C. G. Jung (1875-1961)

Alfred Adler (1870-1937)

Karl Menninger (1893-   )

Sigmund Freud is generally regarded as the founder of the psychoanalytic viewpoint. As his work received recognition, he gained a number of students and supporters, among them C. G. Jung and Alfred Adler. Later, however, Jung and Adler found themselves in disagreement with various aspects of Freud's system, particularly what they felt was the undue emphasis placed on sex as a determinant of behavior. Jung founded the analytic school of psychology; two of his most valuable concepts are the "collective unconscious" and "inner self-experience." Not only does each individual have a personal unconscious, but also a collective unconscious consisting of memories established throughout human history and inherited in the brain structure as "primal images" or "archetypes." The importance of the "inner self-experience" is that the individual achieves true "wholeness" only as fantasies, images, and dreams from the personal and collective unconscious become accessible to the conscious self.

Adler differed from Freud and Jung in his emphasis on social rather than inherited determinants of behavior. He viewed people as inherently social beings whose most basic motivation is to belong to and participate in the group. Adler did not submerge the individual in the group, however; he emphasized an active, creative, conscious "self" that plays a central role in the individual's attempts to organize his experiences and achieve fulfillment as a human being.

Karl Menninger has remained more within the general theoretical framework developed by Freud and has been a leading figure in the elaboration and dissemination of psychoanalytic thought in America. He has gathered data from his own clinic in support of Freud's principles and has written extensively about them.

tions of normal ego-defense mechanisms. With the realization that the same psychological principles apply to both normal and abnormal behavior, much of the mystery and fear surrounding mental disorders was dispelled and mental patients were helped to regain their dignity as human beings.

The psychoanalytic model has been criticized on a number of grounds: for overemphasis on the sex drive; for undue pessimism about basic human nature; for exaggerating the role of unconscious processes; for failing to consider motives toward personal growth and fulfillment; for neglect of cultural differences in shaping behavior; and for a lack of scientific evidence to support many of its assumptions. However, these criticisms should not obscure the fact that Freud greatly advanced our understanding of both normal and abnormal behavior, nor should they obscure the fact that many of the concepts formulated by Freud and his followers have become fundamental to our thinking about human nature and behavior.

In historical perspective, psychoanalysis can be seen as the first systematic model to show how human psychological processes may result in mental disorders. Much as the medical model replaced demons and witches with organic pathology as the cause of mental disorders, the psychoanalytic model replaced brain pathology with exaggerated ego defenses against anxiety as the cause of some—but not all—mental disorders.

The behavioristic model

While psychoanalysis largely dominated psychological thought about abnormal behavior in the early part of this century, a new school—behaviorism—was emerging to challenge its supremacy. Behavioristic psychologists felt that the study of subjective experience—via the techniques of free association and dream analysis—did not provide acceptable scientific data, since such observations were not open to verification by other investigators. In their view, only the study of directly observable behavior and the stimulus and reinforcing conditions that "control" it could serve as a basis for formulating scientific principles of human behavior.

As we shall see, the behavioristic model is organized around one central theme: the role of learning in human behavior. Although this model was initially developed through research in the laboratory rather than through clinical practice with disturbed individuals, its implications for explaining and treating maladaptive behavior soon became evident.

Roots of the behavioristic model. The origins of the behavioristic model can be traced to the work of the Russian physiologist Ivan Pavlov (1849–1936), but credit for its elaboration belongs largely to three distinguished American psychologists: J. B. Watson (1878–1958), E. L. Thorndike (1874–1949), and B. F. Skinner (1904–   ). We shall examine the contributions of each of these men in turn.

1. *Pavlov and the conditioned reflex.* While performing a series of studies on the salivary response in dogs, Pavlov discovered the phenomenon of the conditioned reflex. He found that stimuli regularly present just before food

was presented came to elicit salivation even in the absence of food. For example, even seeing the person who ordinarily brought the food, or hearing his footsteps, came to produce salivation on the part of the dogs. This simple method of learning came to be called *conditioning.* It was destined to become a key building block in the systematic study of learning.

In 1914, while pursuing the study of conditioned reflexes in dogs, one of Pavlov's students reported an unusual and dramatic incident. He had conditioned a dog to distinguish between a circle and an ellipse, as demonstrated by the fact that the dog had learned to salivate to the ellipse but not to the circle. The ellipse was then gradually altered in shape so that it became more and more like the circle, until the dog could no longer distinguish accurately between the two. During three weeks of subsequent experimentation, the dog's ability to discriminate between the two similar figures not only failed to improve, but became considerably worse, and finally disappeared altogether.

At the same time the behavior of the dog underwent an abrupt change. The previously quiet and cooperative animal squealed and squirmed in its stand and tore off the experimental apparatus with its teeth. In addition, when taken into the experimental room, the dog now barked violently, instead of going quietly as it had before. On testing, even the cruder differentiations between the circle and the ellipse that the dog had previously mastered could not be elicited. Pavlov considered this change in the dog's behavior to be equivalent to an "experimental neurosis."

Thus an unusual incident in laboratory routine, that might have been overlooked as merely trivial and annoying by an observer less astute than Pavlov, led to a whole new method of attack in the study of abnormal behavior. On the basis of subsequent experimental findings, Pavlov went on, after the age of eighty, to attempt a rather comprehensive formulation of human psychopathology (Pavlov, 1941). This formulation was based on the speculative assumption that the different reaction patterns shown by dogs to the conditioned-reflex techniques would also be reflected on the human level in reactions to life stresses. Among dogs Pavlov had found three general reaction, or constitutional, types: an *excitatory* group, an *inhibitory* group, and a *central* group. Each reaction type was found to develop a somewhat different kind of experimental neurosis. For example, when an animal of the excitatory type was forced beyond the limits of its discriminatory ability, it developed periods of depression or excitement comparable to manic-depressive reactions in humans. Under similar conditions, the inhibitory type developed schizophrenic-like reactions, whereas the central group developed what appeared to be mixed reactions.

In applying these findings to human beings, Pavlov distinguished two personality types: (a) an artistic type—intense, vivid, and highly responsive to external stimulation; and (b) a thinking type—quiet, comtemplative, and more responsive to verbal concepts and ideas. In the event of mental disorder, people of the artistic type presumably would be prone to hysterical or manic-depressive reactions, while those of the thinking type would be more prone to obsessive-compulsive and schizophrenic reactions.

Thus much of Pavlov's work was concerned with individual differences in types of nervous systems, which in turn presumably would provide the basis for different reactions to stimulation and different forms of mental disorders. While his formulations on the human level have not proven definitive, his conditioning techniques and production of "experimental neuroses" paved the way for a vast amount of research in psychopathology.

2. *Watson and "behaviorism."* Pavlov's discovery of conditioning was seized upon by the American psychologist J. B. Watson as a procedure for studying human behavior more objectively. If psychology were ever to become a science, Watson concluded, it must limit itself to the study of events that could be objectively observed.

Starting with this fundamental assumption, Watson changed the focus of psychology from

Ivan Pavlov (1846–1936), a pioneer in showing the part conditioning plays in behavior, shown here with his staff and some of the apparatus used to demonstrate the conditioned reflex in dogs.

the study of inner psychic process to the study of outer behavior, an approach he called "behaviorism." His book *Psychology from the Standpoint of a Behaviorist* was published in 1919. As we might expect, this approach placed heavy emphasis on the role of the social environment in "conditioning" personality development and behavior.

In their now-famous experiment with little Albert, an eleven-month-old boy who was fond of animals, Watson and Rayner (1920) dramatically demonstrated how an irrational fear, or phobia, could be readily learned through conditioning. The procedure was simple: the experimenter stood behind the boy and struck a steel bar with a hammer when Albert reached for a white rat. The loud noise elicited a fear response on the boy's part and made him cry. After several repetitions of this experience Albert became greatly disturbed at the sight of the animal even without the loud noise, and his fear generalized to include other furry animals and objects as well. This demonstration of the development and generalization of an irrational fear suggested that other types of abnormal behavior might also be the result of learning.

Later, Mary Cover Jones (1924) succeeded in eliminating such fears by presenting a white rabbit at a distance when a child, Peter, previously conditioned to fear it, was reacting positively to food—an anxiety inhibitor. By bringing the animal gradually closer, always avoiding overbalancing the positive tendency by the strength of the negative fear tendency, the experimenter finally eliminated the boy's fear and replaced it with pleasant feelings toward the white rabbit; these feelings, in turn, generalized to other furry animals.

3. *The contributions of Thorndike and Skinner.* The work of Pavlov and Watson convinced many investigators that all learning is based on conditioned reflexes, and that studying the lawful properties of such conditioned reflexes could explain human behavior—normal and abnormal.

However, the work of E. L. Thorndike was to provide the basis for the development of a second fundamental concept of the behavioristic model. In his formulation of the "law of effect," Thorndike (1913) made the observation that responses that have rewarding con-

sequences are strengthened or learned, whereas responses that have negative or aversive consequences are weakened or extinguished. Thus he emphasized the control of human behavior by reward and punishment.

Following this early lead, Skinner (1953) concluded that the most important, understandable, and manipulable determinants of behavior lie outside the organism in environmental events or stimuli; he further concluded that these stimuli can be manipulated to control the learning and behavior of the organism. As Skinner expressed it:

"The practice of looking inside the organism for an explanation of behavior has tended to obscure the variables which are immediately available for a scientific analysis. These variables lie outside the organism, in its immediate environment and in its environmental history." (1953, p. 31)

Skinner's emphasis on the use of stimuli to control behavior from outside the organism led to a second major concept of conditioned learning—operant conditioning. The concepts of respondent and operant conditioning have markedly influenced our views of adaptive and maladaptive behavior as well as the development of contemporary techniques of behavior modification and therapy.

Basic principles of the behavioristic model. As we have noted, *learning* provides the central theme of the behavioristic model. Since most human behavior *is* learned, the behaviorists have addressed themselves to the question of how learning comes about.[1] In trying to answer this question, they have focused on the effects of environmental conditions (stimuli) on the acquisition, modification, and elimination of given response patterns—both adaptive and maladaptive ones.

1. ~~Respondent~~ *(classical) and operant conditioning.* Even prior to learning, a specific stimulus may elicit a specific response. For example, food elicits salivation. Food is thus referred to as an *unconditioned* stimulus, and the salivation is called an *unconditioned* re-

---

[1] Distinguished American psychologists who contributed to the development and extension of learning theory include E. C. Tolman, E. R. Guthrie, Clark Hull, R. R. Sears, J. Dollard, N. E. Miller, O. H. Mowrer, K. W. Spence, W. K. Estes, and A. Bandura.

sponse. Through conditioning, the same response may come to be elicited by a wide range of other stimuli in the manner demonstrated by Pavlov. This form of conditioning is called *classical* or *respondent conditioning.*

The classic demonstration of respondent conditioning is the experiment cited previously in which little Albert was conditioned to fear a white rat, a fear that generalized to other furry objects. Much of our learning—particularly during infancy and childhood—is based on this kind of conditioning. It can be adaptive, as when we learn to fear and avoid aversive or hurtful stimuli, or it can be maladaptive, as when we learn irrational fears or phobias.

In *operant conditioning,* the individual makes a response in an attempt to achieve a desired goal. The individual "operates" on or modifies the environment; hence the term *operant.* The goal in question may be to obtain something that is rewarding or to avoid something that is aversive. As we grow up, operant learning becomes an important mechanism for discriminating between the desirable and the undesirable—between what will prove rewarding and what will prove unrewarding or aversive—and for acquiring the competencies essential for achieving our goals and coping with our world.

Unfortunately, however, there is no guarantee that what we learn will be accurate or effective. Thus we may learn to value things that will hurt us; we may fail to learn needed competencies for coping, or we may learn coping patterns such as helplessness, bullying, or other irresponsible behavior that is maladaptive rather than adaptive.

2. *Reinforcement.* Essential to both respondent and operant conditioning is *reinforcement*—the strengthening of a new response by its repeated association with some stimulus. Such a stimulus is called *a reinforcer* and may be either positive (pleasant) or negative (aversive). In the experiment with little Albert, the reinforcer was the loud noise; successive repetitions of the noise in association with the presentation of the rat strengthened—reinforced—Albert's conditioned fear.

In operant learning, the response may be strengthened because it is repeatedly associated with a reward or with avoiding some aver-

sive condition. For example, a child may learn some response either to receive a reward, such as candy, or to avoid a punishment, such as a spanking. In both "positive" and "negative" reinforcement, the learner is rewarded for making an appropriate response.

Initially a high rate of reinforcement may be necessary to establish a response, but lesser rates are usually sufficient to maintain it. In fact, learning appears to be especially persistent when reinforcement is intermittent—when the reinforcing stimulus does not invariably follow the response—as demonstrated in compulsive gambling when occasional wins seem to keep the response going. However, when reinforcement is consistently withheld over time, the conditioned response—whether classical or operant—eventually *extinguishes.* The subject stops making the response.

There is a special problem in extinguishing a learned response in *avoidance learning,* in which the subject has been conditioned to anticipate an aversive event and to respond in such a way as to avoid it. For example, a boy who has been bitten by a vicious dog may develop a conditioned avoidance response in which he consistently turns away from and avoids all dogs. When he sees a dog, he feels anxious; avoiding contact lessens his anxiety and is thus reinforcing. As a result, his avoidance response is highly resistant to extinction. In addition, it prevents him from having experiences with friendly dogs that could bring about reconditioning. We shall examine the significance of such conditioned avoidance responses in our later discussion of neuroses and other patterns of abnormal behavior.

3. *Generalization and discrimination.* We noted in the experiment conducted by Watson and Raynor that little Albert's fear generalized from white rats to other furry animals. This tendency for a response that has been conditioned to one stimulus to become associated with other similar stimuli is referred to as generalization. The greater the similarity of stimuli, the greater the likelihood of generalization.

A process complementary to generalization is *discrimination,* which occurs when the individual learns to distinguish between similar stimuli and to respond differently to each. The ability to discriminate may be brought about

Albert Bandura, b. 1925 *(left),* clarified and integrated learning principles in the causation and treatment of maladaptive behavior in his important book, *Principles of Behavior Modification* (1969), as well as later publications.

B. F. Skinner, b. 1904 *(right),* whose important contributions to the behavioristic viewpoint include the concept of *operant conditioning,* that is, the acquisition or elimination of a response as a consequence of reward or punishment.

through selective reinforcement. For example, since red strawberries taste good and green ones do not, a conditioned discrimination will occur if the individual has experience with both. According to the behavioristic model, complex processes like attending, perceiving, forming concepts, and solving problems are all based on an elaboration of this basic discriminative process.

The concepts of generalization and discrimination have many implications for the development of maladaptive behavior. While generalization enables us to profit from past experience in sizing up new situations, there is always the possibility of making inappropriate generalizations—as when a woman who has been deceived and emotionally hurt by a man concludes that men are not to be trusted. Similarly, faulty discriminations may lead to trouble, as when a delinquent youth fails to develop discriminations between "re-

sponsible" and "irresponsible" behavior, or a schizophrenic makes bizarre discriminations that other people would not. In some instances, a discrimination that is needed may be beyond the individual's capability—as we noted in the case of Pavlov's production of experimental neuroses in dogs—and may lead to psychological disorganization and inefficient coping behavior.

4. *Modeling, shaping, and learned drives.* The behavioristic model has been extended by the concepts of modeling, shaping, and primary and secondary drives.

Modeling involves precisely what the term implies—the demonstration of desired response patterns by parents or others and the systematic reinforcement of the subject's imitation of such responses. If the individual is capable of imitating the act modeled and is motivated to do so, new performances can be acquired very rapidly. Often, of course, a child spontaneously imitates parental behavior; hence parents are viewed as important models in a child's early development. Unfortunately, a child may imitate maladaptive as well as adaptive parental behavior or the behavior of undesirable models seen on television or in movies.

Often an appropriate response is not available in a person's behavior repertoire, a matter that presents problems for the behavior therapist, who cannot reinforce a response until it occurs. In such cases it is often possible to *shape* the response by reinforcing successive approximations of the desired behavior. Here behavior that is in the right direction—even though it does not represent the final performance to be achieved—is reinforced, while other responses are not reinforced and hence extinguish. For example, in getting a mute chronic schizophrenic to speak, slight movement of the lips may be reinforced first; later, when the individual starts to make sounds, they are reinforced. Thus behavior is gradually shaped until the final goal of coherent speech is achieved.

Behaviorists view motivation as being based on a limited number of primary biological drives, such as hunger and thirst, that are directly related to meeting bodily needs. The many different motives in everyday life are seen as learned extensions of these primary drives. For example, an infant soon learns that parental approval leads to the gratification of bodily needs and thus learns to seek parental approval. With time this seeking may generalize or come to be associated with academic achievement and other behavior valued by the parents. Thus motives for approval, achievement, and so on, regarded as "secondary drives," are seen as merely extensions of our more basic biological drives. And as in other learned behavior, motives which lead to maladaptive as well as adaptive behavior may be learned and reinforced.

Impact on our views of psychopathology. By means of these relatively few basic concepts, behaviorism attempts to explain the acquisition, modification, and extinguishing of all types of behavior. Maladaptive behavior is viewed as essentially the result of (a) a failure to learn necessary adaptive behaviors or com-petencies, such as how to establish satisfying personal relationships; (b) learning ineffective or maladaptive responses, as in the case of little Albert; (c) stress situations that the individual feels incapable of dealing with, as in the case of Pavlov's production of experimental neurosis. Maladaptive behavior is defined in terms of specific responses—undesirable reactions resulting from faulty learning and/or excessive stress.

The focus of therapy is on changing specific behaviors—eliminating undesirable ones and bringing about the learning of desirable ones. A number of *behavior-modification* techniques have been developed based on the systematic application of learning principles. Typical are the following: (a) the use of aversive conditioning or related procedures, such as withholding positive reinforcement, to eliminate undesirable behaviors; (b) the use of modeling, positive reinforcement, and other techniques to help the person acquire more effective behavior patterns; and (c) the change or removal of environmental conditions that may be serving to reinforce and maintain maladaptive behavior. The illustration on p. 65 contains a brief summary of some of the techniques—and the learning principles upon which they are based—commonly used in behavior therapy; many examples of the application of behavior-modification techniques will be given in later chapters.

We should emphasize, however, that the behavior therapist specifies the behavior to be changed, sets forth well-defined goals in terms of precise changes in behavior, and decides on the learning principles to be used. The effectiveness of behavior therapy can thus be evaluated objectively by the degree to which stated goals are achieved.

The behavioristic model has been heralded for its preciseness and objectivity, for the wealth of research it has generated, and for its demonstrated effectiveness in changing specific behaviors. On the other hand, it has been criticized on a number of grounds, including (a) failure to include the data of subjective experience—such as self-awareness—which are highly meaningful to the individual; (b) failure to tackle more complex dimensions of behavior, such as love, courage, faith, hope, and despair; (c) failure, in gen-

Some behavior-modification techniques based on learning principles

Learning principle	Technique	Example in treatment
Behavior patterns are developed and established through repeated association with positive reinforcers.	Use of positive reinforcement to establish desired behavior.	Wahler (1968) successfully modified extreme oppositional and negativistic behavior on the part of children by having parents reward cooperative behavior with approval and with tokens exchangeable for prized toys. Tokens were gradually eliminated, but dramatic improvement in cooperative behavior remained stable.
The repeated association of an established behavior pattern with negative reinforcers results in avoidance behavior.	Use of negative reinforcement to eliminate undesirable behavior (aversive conditioning).	Wolpe (1965) successfully treated drug addiction in a physician by having him use a portable apparatus to give himself an electric shock whenever he had a craving for the drug.
When an established behavior pattern is no longer reinforced, it tends to be extinguished.	Withdrawal of reinforcement for undesirable behavior.	Lovaas et al. (1965) found that self-injurious behavior of emotionally disturbed children could be reduced by cutting off social reinforcers—e.g., by having parents and others show less attention and concern when such behavior occurred.
Avoidance behavior will be inhibited or reduced if the conditions that provoke it are repeatedly paired with positive stimuli.	Desensitization to conditions that elicit unreasonable fear or anxiety.	In a classic experiment by Mary Cover Jones (1924), a boy's phobia for white rabbits and other furry animals was inhibited by feeding the boy his favorite food while the rabbit was in the background; the rabbit was gradually brought closer during feeding until the boy's fear of the animal was eliminated.
A specified behavior can gradually be established if successive approximations of the behavior are reinforced.	Shaping of desired behavior.	Isaacs, Thomas, and Goldiamond (1960) successfully reinstated speech in a schizophrenic subject who had been mute for 17 years by rewarding behavior that led in the direction of verbal communication. The initial objective was to have the subject focus his eyes on a stick of gum; when he did, he was given the gum. Next, the gum was withheld until the subject made a small mouth movement. By the end of the 4th week he made a croaking sound. Then, when a piece of gum was held up, the subject was told to pronounce the word *gum*. By the end of the 18th session he said "Gum, please," and subsequently he responded to questions in individual and group therapy sessions.

eral, to come to grips with the problem of values and meaning in human existence and the question of how human beings *should* relate to each other; and (d) failure to deal adequately with the problem of self-direction. Human beings are viewed as being completely at the mercy of previous learning and present environmental conditions that may shape behavior in ways that are good or evil, rational or irrational, and adaptive or maladaptive. "Freedom of choice" and "self-determination" are viewed as illusions.[2]

Paradoxically, however, the most ardent behaviorists, like Watson and Skinner, have repeatedly emphasized the potential use of modern science and technology for planning a better future world. In his famous didactic novel, *Walden Two* (1948), and its nonfiction version, *Beyond Freedom and Dignity* (1971), Skinner has depicted the utopian world he thinks would result from the systematic application of learning principles and behavior-modification procedures to our present world problems. In fact, Skinner (1974) has stated the matter very succinctly: "In the behavioristic view, man can now control his own destiny because he knows what must be done and how to do it" (p. 258). He does not explain how people who have no choice could choose to exert such control.

Whatever its limitations and paradoxes, the behavioristic model has had and continues to have a tremendous impact on our contemporary views of human nature and behavior in general and on psychopathology in particular.

The humanistic model

The humanistic perspective has been influenced by both the psychoanalytic and behavioristic models, but is in significant disagreement with both. The behavioristic model, with its focus on the stimulus situation and observable behavior, is seen as an over-simplification which neglects the psychological make-up, inner experiencing, and potential for self-direction of the individual. At the same time, humanistic psychologists disagree with the negative and pessimistic picture of human nature portrayed by the psychoanalytic model; rather, the humanistic model views our basic nature as "good," and places strong emphasis on our inherent capacity for responsible self-direction.

Roots of the humanistic approach. The humanistic model has been heavily influenced by such outstanding psychologists as William James, Gordon Allport, Abraham Maslow, Carl Rogers, and Fritz Perls. Although some of its roots extend deep into the history of psychology—as well as philosophy, literature, and education—others are of relatively recent origin. It appears to have emerged as a major perspective in the 1950s and 1960s when middle-class America realized its simultaneous material affluence and spiritual emptiness.

As an important new "third force" in contemporary psychology, the humanistic model is concerned not only with the characteristics we share in common as human beings but with the uniqueness of each individual. While it recognizes the importance of learning and other traditional subject matter of psychology, this model is also concerned with topics about which we have as yet little scientific information—topics such as love, hope, creativity, values, meaning, personal growth, and self-fulfillment. In essence, the humanistic psychologists feel that modern psychology has failed to address itself to many of the problems that are of crucial significance in the lives of all of us.

Basic principles of the humanistic model. The humanistic model is characterized as much or more by its general orientation toward human beings and their potentialities as by any coherent set of principles of personality development and functioning. There are, however, certain underlying themes and principles that humanistic psychologists hold in common.

1. *Self as a unifying theme.* As we noted at the beginning of this chapter, William James included consciousness of self in his early text

---

[2]Skinner (1974) has listed twenty criticisms of the behavioristic model, all of which he considers to be largely or totally unjustified. Nevertheless, the critical views mentioned here are widely held and appear to have merit. It may be noted, however, that Bandura (1974) has suggested that the behavioristic model be broadened to deal with such critical views. For example, he has stated that human beings do have "a capacity for self-direction" and that recognition of this capacity "represents a substantial departure from exclusive reliance upon environmental control" (pp. 861, 863).

written before the turn of the century, but this concept was later dropped by the behaviorists because the self could not be observed by an outsider. Eventually, however, the need for some kind of unifying principle of personality and some way of accounting for an individual's subjective experiences led to the reintroduction of the self-concept in the humanistic model.

Here it may be noted that the concept of the self is analogous to the psychoanalytic concept of the ego in that both represent inferred subsystems concerned with evaluating, problem solving, decision making, and coping. The humanistic viewpoint, however, extends the self-concept to include the individual's sense of identity and relation to the world and tendencies toward self-evaluation and self-fulfillment.

Among contemporary humanistic psychologists, Carl Rogers has developed the most systematic formulation of the self-concept, based largely on his pioneering research into the nature of the psychotherapeutic process. Rogers has stated his views in a series of propositions that may be summarized as follows:

a) Each individual exists in a private world of experience of which the I, me, or myself is the center.

b) The most basic striving of the individual is toward the maintenance, enhancement, and actualization of the self.

c) The individual reacts to situations in terms of the way he perceives them, in ways consistent with his self-concept and view of the world.

d) Perceived threat to the self is followed by defense—including the narrowing and rigidification of perception and behavior and the introduction of self-defense mechanisms.

e) The individual's inner tendencies are toward health and wholeness; under normal conditions he behaves in rational and constructive ways and chooses pathways toward personal growth and self-actualization.

In using the concept of self as a unifying theme, humanistic psychologists emphasize the importance of individuality. Because of our great potential for learning and the great diversity in our genetic endowments and backgrounds of experience, each one of us is unique. In studying "human nature," psychologists are thus faced with the dual task of describing both the uniqueness of each individual and the characteristics that all members of the human race have in common.

This does not mean, however, that humanistic psychologists discount the importance of interpersonal relations and the general life situation and sociocultural setting in which the individual functions; rather, these are recognized as factors that do influence development and behavior and bear significantly on the satisfactions and meaning one finds in living.

2. *Focus on values and personal growth.* Humanistic psychologists place strong emphasis on values and the process of value choices for guiding our behavior and achieving a meaningful and fulfilling way of life. At the same time, they consider it crucially important that each one of us develop values based on our own experience and evaluation rather than blindly accept values held by others; otherwise we deny our own experiences of value and become increasingly out of touch with our own real feelings.

To evaluate and choose requires a clear sense of our own self-identity—the discovery of who we are, of what sort of person we want to become, and why. Only in this way can we achieve the actualization of our potentialities and self-direction.

Here it may be emphasized that the humanistic model stresses the problem of values and fulfillment, not only as they apply to the individual, but to society as well. As Maslow (1969) has pointed out, it is essential that we develop a "good society" as well as a "good person," because the actualization of human potentialities on a mass basis is possible only under favorable social conditions.

3. *Positive view of human nature and potential.* We have seen that the psychoanalytic model takes an essentially negative view of human nature, while the behavioristic model takes the more neutral view that our nature may be good or evil, rational or irrational, depending on our conditioning history. According to both models, however, our behavior is seen as determined by forces beyond our control.

In contrast to the psychoanalytic and behavioristic models, the humanistic model takes a

Before the turn of the twentieth century, **William James,** 1842–1910 *(left),* set the stage for the humanistic model in a chapter on the concept of the self in his book *Principles of Psychology.*

Frederick Perls, 1893–1970 *(center),* was influential in the development of therapeutic procedures for enhancing human experiencing and functioning, particularly in the context of confrontation groups.

A. H. Maslow, 1908–1970 *(right),* devoted more than two decades to showing the potentialities of human beings for higher self-development and functioning.

much more positive view of human nature and potential. Despite the myriad instances of violence, war, and cruelty that have existed from ancient times, humanistically oriented psychologists conclude that under favorable circumstances, human propensities are in the direction of friendly, cooperative, and constructive behavior. They regard selfishness, aggression, and cruelty as pathological behavior resulting from the denial, frustration, or distortion of our basic nature. Similarly, they suggest that although we can be misled by inaccurate information, handicapped by social and economic deprivation, and overwhelmed by the number and complexity of issues we are expected to act upon, we still tend to be rational creatures. We try to find sense and meaning in our experience, to act and think in consistent ways, and to follow standards and

principles we believe are good. According to this view, we are not passive automatons but active participants in life with some measure of freedom for shaping both our personal destiny and that of our social group.

In fact, not only are we not automatons, but, in the view of humanistic psychologists, we actually have a natural inclination—an inner propensity—toward personal growth and the actualization of our potentialities. The realization of this propensity is considered especially important in a world of flux and change in which increasing emphasis is placed on inner processes of self-regulation and self-direction if we are to find our way.

Humanistic psychologists believe that as science discovers more about our inherent nature and effective functioning, it will become increasingly possible to make judg-

Carl R. Rogers, b. 1902 *(above),* has contributed significantly to the humanistic viewpoint with his theoretical formulations and his systematic studies on the therapeutic process and its outcomes.

Thomas S. Szasz, b. 1920 *(right),* a psychiatrist, has argued that *illness* is an inappropriate term for most maladaptive behavior, bècause it results from problems in living rather than from organic causes.

ments about what is good or bad for humankind, both for individuals and for societies. And as our techniques for modifying personality and behavior become increasingly powerful, psychologists—as well as other scientists—can no longer avoid concern with values or the ethical dilemmas that arise when value choices are made.

Impact on our views of psychopathology. According to the humanistic model, psychopathology is essentially the blocking or distortion of personal growth. This is generally the result of one or more of these causal factors: (a) the exaggerated use of ego defense mechanisms so that the individual becomes increasingly out of touch with reality; (b) unfavorable social conditions and faulty learning; and (c) excessive stress.

Thus humanistic approaches to therapy usually focus on helping individuals drop their defenses, acknowledge their actual experience, perceive themselves as they really are, achieve needed competencies, and find satis-

fying values—in essence, to increase their capabilities for personal choice, growth, and fulfillment. As might be expected, humanistic psychologists are keenly interested in encounter groups, awareness training, and other innovative techniques for fostering personal growth, more satisfying relationships with others, and more effective methods of coping.

It is too early to assess the ultimate impact of the humanistic model, but it has clearly introduced a new dimension to our thinking about abnormal behavior in its view of psychopathology as a blocking or distortion of the individual's natural tendencies toward health and personal growth rather than as abnormality or deviance per se. In fact, Maslow (1962, 1969) has even expressed concern about the "psychopathology of the normal"—that is, the disappointing and wasteful failure of so many "normal" people to realize their potentialities as human beings.

The humanistic model has been criticized for its diffuseness, for a lack of scientific rigor in its conceptualizations, and for expecting too much from psychology. But while some psychologists would view its goals as "grandiose," others would view them as a useful description of the challenging long-range task that confronts psychology today.

The existential model

The existential model emphasizes our uniqueness as individuals, our quest for values and meaning, and our freedom for self-direction and self-fulfillment. In these ways it is highly similar to the humanistic model, and, in fact, many humanistic psychologists are also referred to as *existentialists*. However, the existential model represents a somewhat less optimistic view of human beings and places more emphasis on the irrational tendencies in human nature and the difficulties inherent in self-fulfillment—particularly in our bureaucratic and dehumanizing mass society. And the existentialists place considerably less faith in modern science and more in the inner experience of the individual in their attempts to understand and deal with the deepest human problems.

Central themes and concepts. The existential model, like the humanistic model, is not a highly systematized school of thought, but it is unified by a central concern with the ultimate challenge of human existence—to find sound values, to grow as a person, and to build a meaningful and socially constructive life. Its basic concepts stem mainly from the writings of such European philosophers as Heidegger, Jaspers, Kierkegaard, and Sartre. Especially influential in the development of existential thought in the United States have been the theologian Paul Tillich and the psychologist Rollo May.

1. *Existence and essence.* A basic theme of existentialism is that our existence is given, but what we make of it—our essence—is up to us. The adolescent girl who defiantly blurts out, "Well, I didn't ask to be born" is stating a profound truth; but in existential terms, it is completely irrelevant. For whether she asked to be born or not, here she is in the world and answerable for herself—for one human life. What she makes of her essence is up to her. It is her responsibility to shape the kind of person she is to become and to live a meaningful and constructive life.

However, this is not an easy task in an age of profound social change in which many traditional values and beliefs are being questioned. For this is an age which tends to engender inner confusion and deep emotional and spiritual strain concerning the kind of person we should be and become, and the way of life we should try to build for ourselves.

Essentially, we can resolve this dilemma in one of two ways: (a) by giving up the quest and finding some satisfaction in blind conformity and submergence in the group; or (b) by striving for increased self-definition in the reality of our own existence. The existentialists view the first alternative as being unauthentic and the pathway to anxiety and despair.

2. *Choice, freedom, and courage.* Our essence is created by our *choices*, for our choices reflect the values on which we base and order our lives. As Sartre put it: "I am my choices."

In choosing what sort of person to become, we are seen as having absolute *freedom*; even refusing to choose represents a choice. Thus the locus of valuing is within each individual. We are inescapably the architects of our own lives. Morris (1966) has stated the situation in the form of three propositions:

"1. I am a *choosing* agent, unable to avoid choosing my way through life.

2. I am a *free* agent, absolutely free to set the goals of my own life.

3. I am a *responsible* agent, personally accountable for my free choices as they are revealed in how I live my life." (p. 135)

The problems of choice and responsibility often become an agonizing burden, for finding satisfying values is a lonely and difficult matter. It requires the *courage* to break away from old patterns if need be and to stand on one's own. In a very real sense, the freedom to shape one's essence is "both our agony and our glory."

Some people lack "the courage to be"—to seek and follow new paths that offer greater possibilities for self-fulfillment. Often they do not want their essence to be left up to them; rather they seek some outside authority such as religion or their social group to advise them on what to believe and how to act. But if blind conformity cuts the individual off from new possibilities for *being* and leads to a wasted life, the individual cannot blame anyone else or evade the consequences. For to flee from one's freedom and responsibility to life is to be *unauthentic, to show bad faith,* and *to live in despair.*

3. *Meaning, value, and obligation.* A central theme in the existential model is the *will-to-meaning.* This is considered a basic human characteristic and is primarily a matter of finding satisfying values and guiding one's life by them. As we have noted, this is a difficult and highly individual matter, for the values that give one life meaning may be quite different from those that provide meaning for another. Each of us must find his or her own pattern of values.

This emphasis on individual value patterns, however, is not to be construed as moral nihilism. For there is a basic unity to humankind, and all people are faced with the task of learning to live constructively with themselves and others. Hence, there will be an underlying continuity in the value patterns chosen by different individuals who are trying to live authentically.

Existentialism also places strong emphasis on our *obligations* to each other. The most important consideration is not what we can get out of life but what we can contribute to it. Our lives can be fulfilling only if they involve socially constructive values and choices.

4. *Existential anxiety and the encounter with nothingness.* A final existential theme that adds an urgent and painful note to the human situation is that of *nonbeing* or *nothingness.* In ultimate form it is death, which is the inescapable fate of all human beings.

This encounter with nothingness is unique to human beings: we are the only creatures who live with the constant awareness of the possibility of nonbeing. At each moment, we make our way along the sharp edge of possible annihilation; never can we escape the fact that death will come sometime, somewhere. This awareness is essential for a full grasp of what it means to *be,* but it adds a crucial dimension to our existence and immediate experiencing. It is this awareness of our inevitable

The social roots of psychopathology as emphasized by Laing

R. D. Laing, a British existential psychiatrist who has won widespread attention for his views of why people experience psychotic breakdowns and for his therapeutic approach as well, is vehement in his emphasis on the damaging effects of pathological social relationships upon the individual. Each of us, Laing says, is not a discrete entity but is part of our culture, or of the groups to which we belong, including the family group; thus we are shaped by significant others, just as we, for our part, shape others. In this never ending process an illimitable number of transactions may occur between people, with potentially destructive results.

In Laing's view, these social interactions typically are based on façades and "games" in which people are not encouraged to discover and be their true selves but rather to meet the expectations and demands of others. The end result is an elaborate charade which has highly destructive effects on those involved:

"By the time the new human being is 15 or so, we are left with a being like ourselves, a half-crazed creature more or less adjusted to a mad world. This is normality." (1967, p. 58)

Describing the so-called normal world as a place where all of us are "bemused and crazed creatures, strangers to our true selves, to one another, and to the spiritual and material world," Laing explains that a split arising between an individual's false outer self and true inner self is a consequence of intolerably confusing and conflicting social demands, sanctions, and life situations. And he sees the psychotic breakdown as occurring when the split can no longer be maintained; the processes involved in "madness" represent the individual's attempts to recover wholeness as a human being. The implications of this viewpoint for therapy are elaborated upon in Chapter 9.
Based on Gilluly (1971), Gordon (1971), and Laing (1967).

Soren Kierkegaard, 1813–1855 *(far left),* Danish theologian and philosopher, is generally regarded as the first major existential thinker. Those currently engaged in elaborating on the concepts of existentialism are focusing, as did Kierkegaard, on the individual's struggle to shape his "inner self" and find a meaningful, authentic, and fulfilling way of life.

Jean-Paul Sartre, b. 1905 *(left),* is one of the most influential modern existential thinkers, known for his novels and dramas as well as for his other works of existential philosophy.

death and its implications for our living that lead to *existential anxiety*—to deep concern over whether we are living a meaningful and fulfilling life.

We can overcome our existential anxiety and deny victory to nothingness by living a life that counts for something, that should not be lost. If we are perishable, we can at least perish resisting—living in such a way that nothingness will be an unjust fate.

Impact on our views of psychopathology. Existentialists are very much concerned with the social predicament of modern human beings. They emphasize the weakening of traditional values and the crisis of faith; the depersonalization of the individual in our bureaucratic mass society; and the loss of meaning in human existence. They see us as alienated and estranged—strangers to God, to other human beings, and to ourselves; they view the social context of contemporary life as forcing us to an awareness of our empty existence, to existential anxiety, and to psychopathology.

Thus the primary focus of the existential therapist is to help the individual clarify his or her values and work out a meaningful way of "being-in-the-world." In this therapy, the individual is assumed to be capable of rational, responsible choice.

From a broad perspective, the major impact

of both humanistic and existential models on our views of psychopathology has been their emphasis on our capacity for full functioning as human beings. "Abnormality" is failure to develop sufficiently our tremendous potentials as human beings, and therapy is not just to move the individual from maladjustment to adjustment but to foster personal growth toward a socially constructive and personally fulfilling way of life.

The existential model has been severely criticized for its lack of scientific grounding and its reliance on the unique experience of the individual in attempting to understand and deal with maladaptive behavior. It is, of course, flatly in contradiction to the view of the behaviorists that our behavior is determined and choice an illusion. Nevertheless, many of the concepts of the existential model—such as freedom, choice, courage, values, meaning, obligation, authenticity, nonbeing, and existential anxiety—have had a profound impact on contemporary thought.

The interpersonal model

We are social beings, and much of our behavior grows out of our attempts to establish meaningful and fulfilling relationships with other people. As yet, however, there is no sys-

Psychologist **Rollo May,** b. 1909 *(right),* is one of the leading exponents of the existential viewpoint in America.

The concepts of the existentialist **R. D. Laing,** b. 1927 *(far right),* also fit under the interpersonal model. He is sometimes considered a radical because he has rejected the idea of psychosis as abnormal. Instead, he asserts that the psychotic state is simply a different way of looking at reality.

tematic model of human nature and behavior based entirely on interpersonal relationships or the social context in which human beings function. Perhaps the closest approximation is the interpersonal viewpoint developed by the psychiatrist Harry Stack Sullivan (1953) and elaborated on by many later psychiatrists, psychologists, and sociologists.[3]

Basic principles of the interpersonal view. While the interpersonal model is not highly systematized, there are certain principles and concepts that are heavily emphasized. Among the most important of these are the following.

1. *Interpersonal relationships and personality development.* According to Sullivan, one's personality development proceeds through various stages involving different patterns of interpersonal relationships. At first, for example, interactions are mainly with parents, who begin the socialization of the child. Later, with adolescence and a gradual emancipation from parents, peer relationships become increasingly important; and in young adulthood, intimate relationships are established, culminating typically in a marital set-

ting. Failure to progress satisfactorily through the various stages of development paves the way for later maladaptive behavior.

In this developmental context, Sullivan was intensely concerned with the anxiety-arousing aspects of interpersonal relationships during early development. Since the infant is completely dependent on "significant others" for meeting all physical and psychological needs, lack of love and care lead to an insecure and anxious human being. Sullivan emphasized the role of early childhood relationships in shaping the self-concept, which he saw as constructed largely out of the reflected appraisals of significant others. For example, if a little boy perceives others as rejecting him or treating him as being of little or no worth, he is likely to view himself in a similar light and to develop a negative self-image that almost inevitably leads to maladjustment.

The pressures of the socialization process and the continual appraisal by others leads a child to label some personal tendencies as the "good-me" and others as the "bad-me." It is the bad-me that is associated with anxiety. With time, the individual develops a *self-system* that serves to protect him or her from such anxiety through the use of ego-defense mechanisms. Often, if an anxiety-arousing tendency is too severe, the individual perceives it as the "not-me," totally screening it

---

[3]It may be noted that G. H. Mead—whose *Mind, Self, and Society* was published in 1934—was an early pioneer in focusing attention on such concepts as communication, social roles, and interpersonal relationships in human behavior.

The interpersonal model is based largely on the work of **Harry Stack Sullivan,** 1892–1949 *(far left),* who thought it was pointless to speak of the individual personality, since the individual personality does not exist apart from interactions with others.

Eric Berne, 1910–1970 *(left),* who elaborated on the interpersonal views of Sullivan, is probably best known for his book *Games People Play* (1964) and for the development of the system of therapy known as *transactional analysis.*

out of consciousness or even attributing it to someone else. However, such actions lead to an incongruity between the individual's perceptions and the world as it really is, and may therefore result in maladaptive behavior. Here we can readily see a similarity between Sullivan's views and those of both Freud and Rogers.

2. *Social exchange, roles, and games.* Three ways of viewing our relationships with other people are helpful in understanding both satisfying and hurtful interactions.

The *social-exchange* view, largely developed by Thibault and Kelley (1959) and Homans (1961), is based on the premise that we form relationships with each other for the purpose of satisfying our needs. Each person in the relationship wants something from the other, and the exchange that results is essentially a trading or bargaining one. For example, when a person feels that he has entered into a bad bargain—that the rewards are not worth the costs—he may attempt to work out some compromise or simply terminate the relationship.

A second way of viewing interpersonal relationships is in terms of social *roles.* Society prescribes role behavior for teachers, generals, and others occupying given positions designed to facilitate the functioning of the group. While each individual lends a personal

interpretation to the role, there usually are limits to the "script" beyond which the person is not expected to go. Similarly, in intimate personal relationships, each person holds certain role expectations—in terms of obligations, rights, duties, and so on—that the other person in the relationship is expected to meet. If one spouse fails to live up to the other's role expectations or finds them uncomfortable, or if husband and wife have different conceptions of what a "wife" or "husband" should be or do, serious complications in the relationship are likely to occur.

Another view of interpersonal relationships focuses on the *"games* people play." Eric Berne (1964, 1972) has pointed out that such games are not consciously planned but rather involve a sort of role playing of which the persons are either entirely or partially unaware. For example, a woman who lacks self-confidence may marry a man who is very domineering and then complain that she could do all sorts of outstanding things "if it weren't for you."

Such games presumably serve two useful functions: (a) as substitutes for or defenses against true intimacy in daily life, intimacy for which many people are unprepared; and (b) as stabilizers to help maintain a relationship. Such games, however, are likely to prove a poor substitute for an authentic relationship. Though called "games" in the sense of being ploys, they are often deadly serious.

3. *Interpersonal accommodation.* Interpersonal accommodation is the process whereby two persons evolve patterns of communication and interaction that enable them to attain common goals, meet mutual needs, and build a satisfying relationship.

People communicate in many verbal and nonverbal ways, and the individuals in a relationship use many cues in their attempts to interpret what is really being said to them. Sullivan believed that faulty communication is far more common than most people realize, especially in family interactions on an emotional level. Koestler (1954) has underscored the unique nature of communication difficulties among family members:

"Family relations pertain to a plane where the ordinary rules of judgment and conduct do not apply. They are a labyrinth of tensions, quarrels and reconciliations, whose logic is self-contradictory, whose ethics stem from a cozy jungle, and whose values and criteria are distorted like the curved space of a self-contained universe. It is a universe saturated with memories—but memories from which no lessons are drawn; saturated with a past which provides no guidance to the future. For in this universe, after each crisis and reconciliation, time always starts afresh and history is always in the year zero." (p. 218)

If individuals in a close relationship have a tangle of unresolved misunderstandings and conflicts, they will likely have trouble communicating clearly and openly with each other. In fact, the final phase of a failing marriage is often marked by almost complete inability of the couple to communicate, or the closing of communication channels altogether.

In addition to establishing and maintaining effective communication, interpersonal accommodation involves meeting a number of other adjustive demands. Among these are role relationships, methods of resolving disagreements and conflicts, and meeting situational demands which may markedly influence the relationship—for better or for worse. Sullivan thought that interpersonal accommodation is facilitated when the motives of the persons in the relationship are complementary, as when both persons are strongly moti-

vated to give and receive affection. When interpersonal accommodation fails and the relationship does not meet the needs of one or both partners, it is likely to be characterized by conflict and dissension and eventually to be ended.

In Chapter 5, we will examine some disordered interpersonal relationships and observe the detrimental effects on one or both of the partners involved—particularly in intimate relationships. In fact, it has been shown that certain interpersonal patterns can literally drive another person "crazy"; conversely, some interpersonal patterns are "disorder reducing" or therapeutic in their effects.

Impact on our views of psychopathology. The interpersonal model places strong emphasis on unsatisfactory interpersonal relationships as the primary causal factor in many forms of maladaptive behavior. Such relationships may extend back to childhood, as when a boy's self-concept was distorted by significant others who appraised him as being worthless or when rigid socialization measures made it difficult for a young girl to accept and integrate the bad-me into her self-concept. However, it is the individual's current interpersonal relationships and their effects on behavior that are of primary concern.

Thus the focus of therapy is on the alleviation of current pathogenic relationships and on helping the individual achieve more satisfactory relationships. Such therapy is concerned with verbal and nonverbal communication, social roles, processes of accommodation, and the general interpersonal context of behavior. And, as might be expected, strong emphasis is placed on the use of the therapy situation itself as a vehicle for new learning of interpersonal skills.

The interpersonal model is handicapped by incomplete information concerning most aspects of interpersonal relationships. As a result, many of Sullivan's concepts and those of later investigators lack adequate scientific grounding. Despite such limitations, however, the interpersonal model has served to focus attention on the quality of the individual's close personal relationships as a key factor in determining whether behavior will be effective or maladaptive.

In reviewing these psychosocial models of human behavior—the psychoanalytic, behavioristic, humanistic, existential, and interpersonal—we have seen that each contributes to our understanding of psychopathology, but that none alone seems to account for the complex types of maladaptive behavior exhibited by human beings. Each has a substantial amount of research evidence to support it, yet each model also depends on generalizations from limited kinds of events and observations. In attempting to explain a complex disorder such as schizophrenia, for example, the behavioristic model focuses on faulty learning and on environmental conditions that may exacerbate or maintain such maladaptive behavior, while the humanistic model focuses on problems relating to values, meaning, and personal growth.

Thus it becomes apparent that adopting one model or another has important consequences: it influences our perception of maladaptive behavior as well as the types of evidence we look for and how we are likely to interpret the data. In later chapters we shall utilize concepts from all these viewpoints when they seem relevant, and in many instances we shall find it useful to contrast different possible ways of explaining the same behavior.

Emergence of the Sociocultural Viewpoint

By the beginning of the twentieth century, sociology and anthropology had emerged as independent scientific disciplines and were making rapid strides toward understanding the role of sociocultural factors in human development and behavior.[4] Soon it became apparent that human beings are almost infinitely malleable and that personality development reflects the larger society—its institutions, norms, values, ideas, and technology—as well as the immediate family and other interpersonal relationships to which individuals are exposed. Eventually, too, it became clear that there is a relationship between sociocultural conditions and mental disorders—for example, between the particular stresses in a society and the frequency and types of mental disorders that occur in it. And it was also observed that the patterns of both physical and mental disorders in a given society may change over time as sociocultural conditions change. These sociocultural discoveries have added another dimension to modern thinking concerning abnormal behavior.

Findings from cross-cultural studies

With the publication of Malinowski's *Sex and Repression in Savage Society* in 1927, it became apparent that the then dominant psychoanalytic model had certain definite limitations in its applicability to different cultures. Malinowski found little evidence among the Trobriand Islanders of any Oedipal conflict, as described by Freud, and he concluded that the phenomenon was not a universal one but rath-

[4]Prominent early contributors to this field were Ruth Benedict, Ralph Linton, Abram Kardiner, Margaret Mead, and Franz Boas.

In prescribing and rewarding certain behavior, a culture is an important determiner of what is seen as normal or abnormal. For example, to a tribe of headhunters and cannibals in New Guinea, life is a "nightmare of fear," and an appropriate way of warding off supernatural foes is by displaying bones of the dead—the man above wears his mother's skull, not for ornamentation but as a protection against her ghost. From another point of view, the beauty of the girl of the Korongo tribe (right) is enhanced by the scar-tissue design on her chest and the facial rings; evidently the results are considered worth the pain it took to achieve them.

er a product of the patriarchal family in Western society. Shortly thereafter, a paper by Ruth Benedict (1934) dealing with anthropology and abnormal behavior suggested that such limitations extended to the definition of "abnormality" itself. Citing various ethnographic reports, she pointed out that what is considered abnormal in one society may be considered normal in another. For example, she noted that cataleptic and trancelike states were often valued by "simpler" peoples. Thus she concluded that normality is a culturally defined concept.

Not only were differences found among cultures with regard to what each considered abnormal, but some types of abnormal behavior appeared to occur only in given cultures. Thus, various "ethnic" psychoses were delineated. One was *amok*, found among the Malays and involving a sudden, wild outburst of homicidal aggression during which an individual might kill or injure anyone standing in his or her way. The phrase "to run amok" stems from early observations of this behavior. Other patterns included the *windigo* psychosis found among the Algonquin Indian

The great love felt by these Caribou Eskimo parents for their infant is typical of a culture characterized by warm family and community life. The social structure is simple, with several families making up a camp in which the good will of neighbors is more highly prized than possessions, and community disapproval in the form of ostracism is the punishment reserved for the gravest crimes.

hunters, in which the hunter became extremely anxious and agitated, convinced that he was bewitched and being turned into a windigo, or cannibal, by the power of a supernatural monster with an insatiable craving for human flesh.

These early anthropological findings led many investigators to take a position of *cultural relativism* concerning abnormal behavior. According to this view, each culture is more or less an island unto itself, and there are no universal standards that can be applied to all societies. As we noted in Chapter 1, however, the concept of cultural relativism underwent considerable modification following the Nuremberg trials in Germany after World War II, in which a number of Nazi leaders were convicted of genocide and other "crimes against humanity," and it became evident that certain standards of group as well as individual behavior are essential for human survival and well-being.

A strictly relativistic view of abnormal behavior was dealt a further blow as it gradually became apparent that the more severe types of mental disorders delineated in Western society were, in fact, found among peoples throughout the world. For example, although the relative incidence and specific symptoms varied, schizophrenia was found among all peoples, from the most primitive to the most technologically advanced. And, finally, it was noted that when individuals became so mentally disordered that they could no longer control their behavior, perform their expected role in the group, or even survive without the special care of others, their behavior was considered abnormal in any society.

Cross-cultural studies have helped clarify the role of sociocultural conditions in abnormal behavior—in our own society as well as in others. This point has been well summarized by Draguns and Phillips:

". . . the features of one's own culture often escape notice unless they are highlighted by comparison with other cultures, and the role that social and cultural factors play in causing psychopathology and in shaping its manifestations can only be brought to the fore by the systematic comparison of social and psychopathological variables in several cultures." (1972, p. 3)

Sociocultural influences in our own society

As we narrow our focus to our own society, we find a number of early studies dealing with the relation of social class and other subgroup factors to the nature and incidence of mental disorders. For example, a pioneering study in this area was that reported by Faris and Dunham (1939), who discovered that a disproportionate number of the schizophrenics admitted to mental hospitals came from the lower socioeconomic areas of a large city. The rate of admission decreased with distance of residence from these disorganized and deteriorating sections of the city.

These early studies concerning social class were gradually augmented by studies dealing with urban-rural, ethnic, religious, occupational, and other subgroups in relation to mental disorders. In one of these—an extensive study of mental disorders in Texas—Jaco (1960) found the incidence of psychoses as a group to be three times higher in urban than in rural areas, and higher among the divorced and separated than among the married or widowed. And according to a more recent study by Levy and Rowitz (1974), it was the areas of large cities that were undergoing rapid and drastic social change that appeared to produce the highest rates of mental disorders.

The study of the incidence and distribution of physical and mental disorders in a population, such as the studies just cited, is referred to as *epidemiology*. The epidemiological approach serves to indicate both "high-risk" areas and groups and the social conditions that are correlated with a high incidence of given disorders. For example, in our later discussion we shall deal with high-risk groups with respect to heart attacks, suicide, drug dependence, and other maladaptive patterns.

This information provides a basis for formulating prevention and treatment programs; the effectiveness of these programs, in turn, can be evaluated by means of further epidemiological studies.

Social pathology and community mental health

With the gradual recognition of sociocultural influences, the almost exclusive concern with the individual patient broadened to include a concern with societal, communal, familial, and other group settings as contributors to mental disorders. It had become apparent that an individual's maladaptive behavior might be caused not by faulty internal processes but by abnormal conditions in the surrounding social environment. As Lennard and Bernstein (1969) put it, "Therapeutic or damaging potentials often inhere in social contexts rather than in individuals . . ." (p. 205).

This concept has led to the community mental health movement, which calls for an assessment of the sociocultural environment as well as of the individual in relation to the causation, treatment, and prevention of mental disorders. Smith (1968) has referred to the community mental health movement as "the third mental health revolution."

"The first mental-health revolution unshackled the insane. By calling them sick, it managed to treat them as human. Its monuments and symbols are the great, usually isolated, state mental hospitals. The second revolution came from the spread of dynamic psychiatry (mainly Freud's) and was characterized by individual, one-to-one psychotherapy. Now the third revolution throws off the constraints of the doctor-patient medical model—the idea that mental disorder is a private misery—and relates the trouble, and the cure, to the entire web of social and personal relationships in which the individual is caught." (p. 19)

Here it may be noted that the sociocultural viewpoint is concerned not only with the relationship of existing social conditions to mental disorders but also with the nature and incidence of mental disorders that may be anticipated as a consequence of the profound changes taking place in our society and in other countries of the world.

In later chapters we shall deal with the clinic facilities and other programs—both governmental and private—that have been established on the basis of the community mental health movement. Suffice to note that this viewpoint has led to the introduction of programs designed to alleviate social conditions that foster maladaptive behavior and to the provision of community facilities for the early detection, treatment, and long-range prevention of mental disorders.

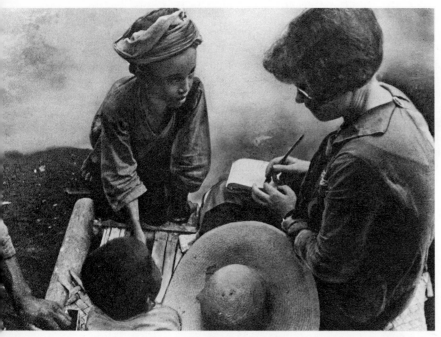

Margaret Mead, b. 1901, the world-famous anthropologist, has spent years studying primitive peoples and amassing cross-cultural data. She has contributed greatly to our understanding of variations in individual and group behavior patterns—both normal and abnormal. Here she is pictured learning the language of Bali from Balinese children.

Toward a Unified Viewpoint

As the research engendered by the organic, psychosocial, and sociocultural perspectives gradually led to a better understanding of the role of all these factors in mental disorders, it became increasingly apparent that explanation on any one of the three levels was incomplete in itself. Even in the mental disorder *paresis*, the pride and joy of the organicists, it was observed that some patients became depressed and others expansive and happy with approximately the same underlying organic brain pathology. Similarly, in psychoses associated with senile and arteriosclerotic brain damage, it was found that some patients became severely disordered mentally with only a small amount of brain damage, whereas others showed only mild symptoms despite relatively extensive brain damage.

Gradually investigators came to realize that the patient's psychological reaction to the brain damage and to the resulting change in his or her life were of vital importance in determining the overall clinical picture. It also became apparent that the emotional support of family members as well as the general nature of the patient's life situation—for example, the kind of situation to which the patient would be returning after discharge from the hospital—were significant factors in determining the prognosis. On the other hand, in certain functional psychoses in which the patient's disorder was apparently the result of psychological rather than organic factors, it was nevertheless found that the use of organic therapies—such as antidepressant drugs or electroshock—produced dramatic results. And, finally, it was found that the symptoms, prognosis, and reaction to a given treatment might all vary somewhat for individuals from different cultural backgrounds.

The interdisciplinary approach

Such considerations have led to the emergence of the *interdisciplinary* approach, which calls for the integration of biological, psychosocial, and sociocultural factors into a comprehensive clinical picture. In dealing with a particular case, of course, we may be primarily concerned with one set of determinants or another. For example, one case of homicidal behavior may be closely associated with drug intoxication, another with pent-up frustration and hostility, and still another with the learning of criminal values in a faulty environment. Thus the problem becomes one of assessing and dealing with the particular interaction of these three sets of determinants—biological, psychosocial, and sociocultural—as they affect a particular patient or group.

The interdisciplinary approach has led to the integration of research findings from such varied disciplines as genetics, biochemistry, neurophysiology, psychology, sociology, anthropology, and ecology in efforts to understand and cope with abnormal behavior. On a practical level, it has led to the meaningful coordination of medical, psychological, and other mental health personnel in the assessment, treatment, and prevention of mental disorders. It has become increasingly apparent to workers in these fields that maladaptive behavior can only be fully understood and effectively dealt with in this comprehensive way.

The general systems approach

Related to the interdisciplinary approach is the *general systems theory* developed by physical and biological scientists, who have long thought in terms of energy systems. An increasing number of behavioral scientists have also found it helpful to view the human organism as an energy system, comparable in many ways to other living systems but also possessing certain unique characteristics.[5]

[5]Among the scientists who have been prominent in the development of general systems theory and its application to the behavioral sciences have been J. G. Miller (1965a, 1965b), L. von Bertalanffy (1967, 1968), W. Buckley (1968), and E. Laszlo (1972).

Properties of living systems

All living systems have three kinds of properties: structural, integrative, and field properties.

1. Structural properties

Each living system contains parts or subsystems—including a "central decider" subsystem—which are interdependent and whose combined action enables the system to function as an integrated unit. Some of the subsystems, such as the nervous system, can be observed; others, such as the self-system, are inferred on the basis of the functioning of the system. Structural properties vary greatly from one type of living system to another, leading to widely differing potentials for behavior. The structure of a fish—and the behavior it makes possible—is obviously very different from that of a human being. That is why it is important to understand the structure of a system if we are to understand its behavior.

2. Integrative properties

Living systems have built-in tendencies to maintain their organization and functional integrity and to develop in accordance with their potentialities. If a system's equilibrium is disturbed beyond a certain point, the system automatically takes action necessary to restore it. Functional integrity is maintained by means of transactions with the surrounding environment as well as by changes within the system itself. These transactions and changes involve *matter-energy processing,* as in the assimilation of food, and *information processing,* as in the recognition of danger.

3. Field properties

Each lower-level system is part of a higher-level system. For example, an organ is a subsystem of an individual, an individual of a group, and a group of a society. The total field, of course, includes the physical as well as the sociocultural environment. Living systems are "open systems"—that is, they are not self-sufficient but can continue to exist only if they can maintain favorable transactions with their surroundings. Thus each living system is in continual transaction with its field, and this constant interaction modifies both system and field. Our ecological crisis is largely the result of our failure to recognize that we were upsetting a complex ecosystem that not only surrounds us but includes us.

Special characteristics of human systems. As we go up the scale from simple to complex living systems, we find that new structural and functional properties begin to appear. Often properties present in rudimentary form at lower levels of living things become further refined and more influential at higher levels. The evolution of the nervous system, for example, can be traced from a very simple segmental apparatus in a worm to the highly complex human brain.

While sharing many characteristics with lower-level systems, human beings reveal many characteristics that are different and some that are unique. Some of the most significant human characteristics are self-awareness, a great capacity for learning and change, ability to use symbols (including languages and abstractions), and concern with information, values, and meanings. These in turn provide a potential for far greater planned self-direction and for more complex transactions with our environment than are possible for members of any other species.

System characteristics change with time. Living creatures develop in accordance with their inherited potentials throughout a life cycle characteristic for each species. In human beings, as in other living creatures, changes in early phases of the life cycle are toward increased size, complexity, and competence. Changes in the later phases are toward entropy—in the direction of decreasing ability, deterioration, and eventual disintegration of the system.

Not all change is genetically determined. Changes in both structural and integrative properties may be brought about in the course of the system's transactions with its field. Accidents, deficiencies, or disease may disrupt or erode the system's potentials for effective action; favorable events may strengthen them. We all are changed by the experiences we have, the people we interact with, the ideas we encounter.

In human beings particularly, a tremendous amount of change comes through learning: besides acquiring new skills and knowledge, we develop a fairly consistent structure of beliefs and assumptions about ourselves and our world that guide our behavior.

An energy system can be described as an assemblage of parts held together by some form of interaction or interdependence. There are nonliving systems—like our solar system—and living systems—like plants and animals. These living systems can be arranged in a hierarchy, extending from cells to organs, individuals, groups, organizations, societies, and supranational bodies like the United Nations. Each higher-level system is composed of lower-level ones and provides the environment for systems on the level directly below. For example, a group made up of individuals also provides the social environment in which these individuals function. Thus the general systems theory does not view individuals as distinct from their environment but rather as integral and interacting parts of it.

As we go from one level of system to a higher one, new behavioral capabilities emerge that were not apparent on the level below. Thus an organism has structural and behavioral characteristics that individual body organs do not, and a group has characteristics and behavioral capabilities beyond those of an individual. To explain the behavior of groups, it is necessary to introduce principles of group behavior that go beyond those necessary for explaining individual behavior. Cohesion, morale, social power, and communication structure are examples of group characteristics. They are not present in the individuals in isolation but are important in shaping the behavior of the group.

The general systems approach gives us a tool that is equally useful whether the "system" we are considering is a malfunctioning organ, a disturbed individual, or a pathological group. In each case, we look for structural and integrative properties of the system itself and also for properties *in* its field or faulty patterns of transaction *with* its field that may be responsible for the malfunctioning of the system under analysis. Only with such a broad perspective are we likely to identify all the interacting causal factors on various levels that may be involved and undertake a treatment program broad enough to encompass them all.

Whereas each of the models we have described emphasizes certain characteristics of human nature and behavior but ignores others, the general systems approach can encompass both our overt behavior and our inner experiencing, both our biological and our psychological propensities, and both our individuality and the mutual interdependence of individual and society. In addition, it goes beyond other models in recognizing both our uniqueness as human beings and the characteristics we share with other living things.

In this chapter we have reviewed the development of (a) the psychological viewpoint and psychosocial models—the psychoanalytic, behavioristic, humanistic, existential, and interpersonal; (b) the sociocultural approach, including the nature and significance of cross-cultural studies, epidemiological studies, and social pathology; and (c) the interdisciplinary and general systems approaches, integrating the biological, psychosocial, and sociocultural viewpoints into a unified view of human behavior.

In our review we have seen that no one general viewpoint or specific psychosocial model alone seems to account for the myriad types of maladaptive behaviors exhibited by human beings. In dealing with particular types of disorders or specific cases, we may find one viewpoint or model most useful. In general, however, the problem focuses on assessing and dealing with the interaction of biological, psychosocial, and sociocultural factors involved in the total clinical picture.

Finally, we noted that this comprehensive view, as represented by the interdisciplinary and general systems approaches, must not only encompass the maladaptive behavior of individuals and groups with which we are confronted today but also the nature and incidence of maladaptive behaviors that may be anticipated in the future as a consequence of the profound social changes taking place in our society and in the world.

4

Personality Development and Adjustment: An Overview

Why are some people alcoholics and others teetotalers, some criminals and others law-abiding citizens, some schizophrenics and others happy and productive individuals? Why are some children autistic and others open and loving, some runaways and others adjusted to their home situations? The task of trying to explain such variations in behavior necessarily begins with a consideration of the broad principles underlying human development and functioning.[1]

Our initial focus in this chapter will be on the developmental process itself. We shall consider not only the basic determinants of development—the individual's genetic endowment, environment, and emerging self-structure—but also the general patterning of development. Here we shall note the orderly sequencing and cumulative nature of the growth process, and the interplay of maturation and learning in producing both likenesses and differences among individuals.

Turning next to adjustment and human behavior, we shall consider the key role of motivation in directing the individual's actions toward the satisfaction of basic needs and strivings; the kinds of adjustive demands or stresses that commonly interfere with efforts to achieve need satisfaction; and the behavior patterns that may be brought into play as the individual attempts to cope with such demands.

We shall see that the biological and psychological traits built into the human system during the process of development are basic resources within each individual for coping with each new adjustive demand. We shall also see that characteristics of the environment—the groups and subgroups each individual belongs to, as well as the actual physical environment—influence the way these resources are used. With both normal and abnormal behavior, we are dealing with an interaction of inner and outer determinants.

The Determinants of Development

The Patterning of Development

Motivation: Human Needs and Strivings

Adjustive Demands (Stress)

Reactions to Life Stress

---

[1]This chapter is intended as an overview of the basic principles of personality development and adjustment based on well-established research findings. While research from investigators adhering to each of the models of human behavior we have discussed is represented, a sizeable portion of the research findings stem from scientists who owe allegiance to no particular model but take an eclectic view—as we have done in this text.

The Determinants of Development

The basic sources of personality development are heredity and environment. However, as a person's genetic inheritance interacts with and is shaped by environmental factors, there emerges a self-structure that becomes an important influence in shaping further development and behavior.

Heredity

Although there are about two million different kinds of plants and animals on our planet, each kind breeds true. Oak trees have acorns that grow into more oak trees and never into elms; deer give birth to fawns and never to lambs. It thus becomes apparent that each type of living thing transmits specific hereditary information from one generation to the next. With the breaking of the genetic code (see illustration on page 89), we have learned a great deal about this genetic information: how it is transmitted and how it operates in guiding our development.

At conception—when the egg cell of the female is fertilized by the sperm cell of the male—each new human being receives a genetic inheritance that provides potentialities for development and behavior throughout a lifetime. This inheritance influences the development of some traits more than others. Its influence is perhaps most noticeable in physical features, such as eye color and physique, but it also appears to play an influential role in "primary reaction tendencies," such as activity level, sensitivity to stimuli, and adaptability. Even very young babies reveal differences in their reactions to particular kinds of stimuli. Some of them are startled at even slight sounds, or cry if sunlight hits their faces; others are seemingly insensitive to such stimulation. Thus, conditions that one baby can tolerate may be quite upsetting to another.

Although such constitutional differences may be influenced by environmental as well as genetic factors, longitudinal (long-term) studies have shown certain of these differences to be relatively stable from infancy to young adulthood. By virtue of such constitutional reaction tendencies, individuals may interact quite differently with and be affected in diverse ways by similar environmental conditions.

Probably the most unique aspect of our human inheritance is a superior brain. It has been described as the most highly organized apparatus in the universe, consisting of some ten billion nerve cells, or neurons, with countless interconnecting pathways as well as myriad connections with other parts of the body. Thus the human brain provides a fantastic communication and computing network with tremendous capabilities for learning and "storing" experience; for reasoning, imagining, and problem solving; and for integrating the overall functioning of the organism.

It would appear that the essential characteristics of human inheritance are basically the same for persons of all racial and ethnic groups; however, the specific features of this endowment vary considerably from one person to another. Thus heredity not only provides the potentialities for development and behavior typical of the species but also is an important source of individual differences.

Environment

In much the same sense that we receive a genetic inheritance that is the end product of millions of years of biological evolution, we also receive a sociocultural inheritance that is the end product of many thousands of years of social evolution—the significance of which was well pointed up by Huxley (1965):

"The native or genetic capacities of today's bright city child are no better than the native capacities of a bright child born into a family of Upper Paleolithic cave-dwellers. But whereas the contemporary bright baby may grow up to become almost anything—a Presbyterian engineer, for example, a piano-playing Marxist, a professor of biochemistry who is a mystical agnostic and likes to paint in water colours—the paleolithic baby could not possibly

The various subgroups people belong to can influence the social roles they adopt. The self-identity of each of these young teen-age girls is probably reinforced by her feeling of group identity.

have grown into anything except a hunter or food-gatherer, using the crudest of stone tools and thinking about his narrow world of trees and swamps in terms of some hazy system of magic. Ancient and modern, the two babies are indistinguishable. . . . But the adults into whom the babies will grow are profoundly dissimilar; and they are dissimilar because in one of them very few, and in the other a good many, of the baby's inborn potentialities have been actualized." (p. 69)

Because each group fosters its own cultural patterns by systematically teaching its offspring, all its members tend to be somewhat alike—to conform to certain "basic personality types." Individuals reared among headhunters will become headhunters; individuals reared in societies that do not sanction violence will learn to settle their differences in nonviolent ways. In New Guinea, for example, Margaret Mead (1949) found two tribes—of similar racial origin and living in the same general geographical area—whose members developed diametrically opposed characteristics. The Arapesh were a kindly, peaceful, cooperative people, while the Mundungumor were war-

like, suspicious, competitive, and vengeful. Such differences appear to be social in origin.

The more uniform and thorough the education of the younger members of a group, the more alike they will become. Thus, in a society characterized by a limited and consistent point of view, there are not the wide individual differences typical of a society like ours, where children have contact with many divergent beliefs. Even in our society, however, there are certain core values that we attempt to perpetuate as essential to our way of life.

Subgroups within a general sociocultural environment—such as family, sex, age, social class, occupational, and religious groups—also foster beliefs and norms of their own, largely by means of *social roles* that their members learn to adopt. Thus there are expected role behaviors for the student, the teacher, the army officer, the priest, the nurse, and persons occupying other specific positions. The extent to which role expectations can influence development is well illustrated by the assignment of sex roles among the Tchambuli, another New Guinea tribe studied by Mead

The Determinants of Development **87**

(1949); in this tribe, women are supposed to earn the living, handle business transactions, take the initiative in courtship, and head the family in general—while men are expected to be coquettish, prone to gossip, interested in dancing and theatricals, and good at housekeeping. Obviously the sex roles among the Tchambuli tend to channel personality development along lines quite different from those encouraged in our society.

The individual, being a member of various subgroups, is subject to various role demands. And, of course, social roles change as group memberships—or position in a given group—change. In fact, the life of the individual can be viewed as consisting of a succession of roles—child, student, worker, husband or wife, parent, and senior citizen. The group may allow the individual considerable leeway in role behavior, but there are limits. Conformity to role demands is induced by the use of positive and negative reinforcers—money, prestige, status, punishment, or loss of membership in the group—as well as through instruction in group norms and role behavior. When an individual's social roles are conflicting, unclear, or uncomfortable, or when he is unable to achieve a satisfactory role in the group, personality development and adjustment may be impaired.

Each individual is exposed to various interactions with other persons, typically beginning with family members and gradually extending to peer group members and "significant others" in his world. Much of an individual's personality development reflects experiences with these key people. For example, the child who is rejected and mistreated is likely to develop quite differently from one who is accepted and encouraged. Similarly, relationships in a Boy Scout troop will likely have quite different effects on development than will the relationships in a delinquent gang. The behavior patterns children learn depend heavily on models to which they are exposed.

Since each of us belongs to different subgroups and experiences different interpersonal relationships, we each participate in the sociocultural environment in a unique way. As a consequence of such "differential participation," no two of us grow up in quite the same world. Thus the sociocultural environment is the source of differences as well as commonalities in personality development.

In discussing environment and its effects in shaping development, it is important to note the effects of the physical as well as the sociocultural environment. Each physical setting is unique in the particular pattern of favorable and unfavorable conditions it provides and on the special demands it makes on the organisms living within it. As a result, different physical environments may foster somewhat different personality characteristics.

In summary so far, we may say that our genetic endowment provides our potentialities for both biological and psychological development, but the shaping of these potentialities—in terms of perceiving, thinking, feeling, and acting—depends heavily on our physical and sociocultural environment.

Self as a third determinant

As the infant grows and learns to distinguish between himself and other people and things, a part of his total perceptual field is gradually delineated as the "me," "I," or "self." As this self-structure develops, it becomes the integrating core of the personality—the reference point around which the individual's experiences and coping patterns are organized. When a problem arises, it is perceived, thought about, and acted upon in relation to the self;[2] that is, the individual comes to perceive himself as an active agent in determining his own behavior—as indicated by such statements as "I know," "I want," and "I will." In essence, the experience of self-direction involves the self as knower, striver, and doer; these are the three key functions of the self-structure as a centralized decider subsystem.[3]

---

[2]The self-structure, like gravity, cannot be observed directly, but is inferred from the finding that psychological functions operate in an integrated manner as part of a unified organism. As Hebb (1960) has pointed out, "The self is neither mythical nor mystical, but a complex mental process" (p. 743). It has a developmental course, is influenced by learning in both structure and degree of differentiation, and can be studied by various experimental procedures. In the present context we shall use the concepts of *ego* and *self* as roughly synonymous.

[3]Miller (1965) has inferred a "centralized decider subsystem" that controls the entire system in all living organisms. The self appears to function as such a decider subsystem in human beings.

Breaking the genetic code

One of nature's best-kept secrets has been how a single fertilized egg cell can develop into an adult human being with billions of highly differentiated cells and complex organ systems and functions. In a series of epic research studies, scientists have traced the secret to DNA (*deoxyribonucleic acid*), which contains the necessary genetic instructions.

The instructions carried in the DNA make provision for two main functions. The first is reproduction of cells by making exact copies. For example, a new liver cell or red blood cell can be formed, which, in turn, is capable of replicating itself. The second key function provided by the DNA instructions is direction of the activities in each cell, including the making of proteins. Proteins are the "building blocks" of life: structural proteins play a crucial role in the development of body tissues and organs, and protein enzymes regulate bodily processes. In fact, it is by means of proteins that the genetic instructions are carried out—that a living organism is created and its growth and functioning implemented.

The DNA molecule is a helix, a spiral that looks like a coiled ladder (illustration). The sides of this "ladder" are chains of alternating sugar and phosphate; the rungs are formed between the sugar groups by combinations of four basic control chemicals— adenine, thymine, guanine, and cytosine—a given rung being formed by a pair of these chemicals. It is in the sequence of the rungs (center) that the specific hereditary instructions of the growing organism are encoded. Each living thing resembles the stock from which it descended because of the DNA it inherits. In fact, the same four "letters" appear to be present in the DNA codes of all living creatures, demonstrating the oneness of the whole living world.

In breaking the genetic code, it was found that each base represented a letter in the genetic alphabet. Just as the uniqueness of each word in the dictionary depends on a specific arrangement of letters from the 26 in the alphabet, the uniqueness of each word in the DNA ladder depends on the sequencing of these chemical letters or bases. All DNA words are short, however—never more than three letters long. Each three-letter word stands for one of the twenty different varieties of amino acids which are used in the production of proteins. Each of the proteins is made up of a different sequencing of these amino acids, a given protein typically requiring a linear sequence of some 300 to 500 amino acids. The DNA *sentence* or *gene* specifies the sequence of amino acids for manufacturing one type of protein.*

Interestingly enough, each cell in the human body contains all the DNA information needed for producing a new human being; somehow "turn-off" mechanisms manage to delete all the DNA information except what is needed for the cell to duplicate itself or to produce a particular protein. If any detail of the DNA instructions is missing or garbled—as we might misspell *cat* as *cot*—the organism may be in for trouble. For example, people become ill and die with inherited sickle-cell anemia, in which a single amino acid is wrong out of the 574 that make up a hemoglobin molecule of the blood.

Some idea of the difficulties inherent in breaking the genetic code can be gleaned from noting that the vast information stored in the DNA is written in such a tiny script that all the DNA in all the fertilized egg cells that have given rise to the approximately three billion people on earth would fit into a ⅛-inch cube.

*The smallest segment of the DNA molecule which contains specific genetic information is called a *gene*. The gene, either singly or in combination with other genes, determines a given trait. A gene is located in a larger segment of a DNA molecule, called a chromosome; each species has a characteristic number of chromosomes. Diagrams redrawn, with permission from Sonnenborn (1962).

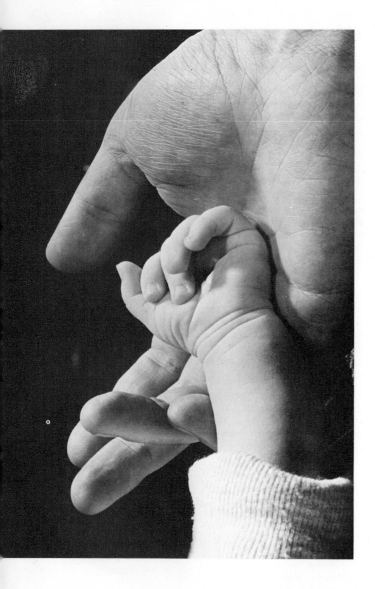

Fundamental to the functioning of the self-system are the assumptions that the individual makes about himself and his world. These assumptions are based on learning and are of three kinds: (a) *reality assumptions*—the view of things as the individual thinks they really are, of the kind of person he is, and of the nature of the surrounding world; (b) *possibility assumptions*—the view of how things could be, of possibilities for change, of opportunities for personal growth and social progress; and (c) *value assumptions*—the view of the way things should be, of right and wrong, good and bad, desirable and undesirable. These three sets of assumptions provide an individual with a *frame of reference*, or *cognitive map*—a consistent view of himself in relation to his environment, which is essential for guiding behavior.

Several aspects of an individual's frame of reference merit further mention. For one thing, the individual's assumptions about reality, possibility, and value afford him a sense of *self-identity*—a realization of who and what he is. They also provide him with a *self-ideal*—a picture of what he could and should be. As we shall see, an unclear self-identity or a marked discrepancy between "real" and "ideal" selves can lead to serious inner conflict. Second, an individual's pattern of assumptions contributes to consistency in perceiving, thinking, feeling, and acting—to the evolution of a characteristic *life-style*. Third, the individual's assumptions serve not only as guides to behavior but also as *inner controls*. For example, value assumptions may prevent the individual from stealing or behaving in other ways that he considers unethical. Such value assumptions are often referred to as the individual's *superego*, or *conscience*.

When inner controls are strong enough to direct behavior in accordance with the expectations and norms of the group, the individual is said to be *socialized*. In some cases, for reasons we shall examine later, these inner controls do not develop to an adequate degree; and under certain conditions—such as alcoholic or drug intoxication—they may give way. However, society does its best to see that such restraints are well developed and maintained, for without them, organized social life would be impossible.

Particular assumptions may be valid or invalid; they may be held with varying degrees of conviction; and they may be more or less explicit and conscious. Since they are learned, they are subject to modification, although new learning tends to be consistent with the individual's existing assumptions. In any event, the frame of reference that the individual develops provides the essential basis for evaluating new experience and for coping with his world. As a consequence, he tends to defend his existing assumptions and to reject or distort new information that is contradictory to them. And because the self is experienced as the very core of his existence, the individual tends to develop a system of *ego* or *self-defense mechanisms* to maintain the adequacy and worth of the self and to defend it from devaluation. We shall examine the operation of such mechanisms in the final section of this chapter.

As each of us develops a sense of selfhood, we become an increasingly important force in directing our own behavior. While much of our behavior—in many instances most of it—is determined by external demands and influences, each of us nevertheless typically perceives ourself as an active force in initiating our plans and actions. It is the *I* who is seen as wanting or needing some things while trying to avoid others, and it is the *I* who perceives and responds to new situations in light of our own motives, assumptions, and feelings. In the process, each of us achieves an increasing sense of identity and of *self-direction*.

Thus if we view each person as a striving, evaluating, adapting system in his or her own right—not simply as the passive result of heredity and environment—we may consider the "self" as the third and final determinant of personality.

When we consider the unique pattern of interacting determinants—genetic, environmental, and self—that shape a given individual, we can readily see that the potentialities for individual differences are beyond calculation. Yet as we have seen, these determinants produce commonalities as well as differences in development. On a *universal level*, we share an inheritance that distinguishes human beings from all other living things, and we are born into a sociocultural environment unlike that of any other species. On a *communal level*, members of a given society inherit the genetic legacy of their particular group, which tends to produce similar physical characteristics, and a sociocultural environment that tends to produce similarities among them. On an *individual level*, each of us has a unique genetic inheritance (except for identical twins), and a pattern of learning and experience different from anyone else's. Thus every person in some respects is *like all other human beings, like some other human beings, and like no other human being*. An understanding of both the uniqueness of each individual and the commonalities among all human beings is essential for an understanding of development and adjustment.

Characteristics of healthy development

While there are differences in emphasis, most investigators would consider the following personality characteristics essential for healthy personality development.

Adequate frame of reference—accurate reality, possibility, and value assumptions concerning oneself and one's world.

Essential competencies—the mastery of needed physical, intellectual, emotional, and social competencies.

Self-direction—adequate self-identity, independence from social influences, and stress tolerance to enable meaningful self-direction.

Personal growth and self-actualization—trends toward the development of one's potentials and self-fulfillment as a person.

These characteristics appear essential for effective coping behavior and for achieving a meaningful and fulfilling way of life.

The Patterning of Development

A key characteristic of the human life cycle is the relatively long period of infancy and childhood, during which the growing individual is expected to acquire the information and competencies essential for adult functioning. In contrast to animals lower on the phylogenetic scale, who have "built-in" patterns of behavior and who mature rapidly, the human infant begins life with few built-in patterns and a far greater capacity to learn from experience. But the price of such a high degree of modifiability is initial helplessness and the necessity of mastering the "know-how" and "know-why" of living. In our society, such learning is coming to require most of the life cycle.

The direction of development

In reviewing the patterning or sequencing of development, we shall focus on the formative period of the life cycle to see how growth is patterned under the combined influence of inner and outer determinants. Within limits, human development follows a predictable sequence and proceeds in a characteristic direction toward increasing differentiation, integration, and complexity. However, the maintenance of this overall pattern depends on a favorable environment and on the individual's learning essential information and competencies along the way.

Trends toward maturity. Although children's growth is shaped in different ways in different sociocultural settings, there are certain characteristic trends in development that are seen in any society, primitive or advanced. These trends lead the individual toward responsible self-direction and toward ability to participate in and contribute to society. Here we may briefly note seven of these specific but interrelated trends toward personal maturity:

1. *Dependence to self-direction.* One of the most obvious progressions toward maturity is from the dependency of fetus, infant, and child to the independence of adulthood. Bound up with this growth toward independence and self-direction is the development of a clear sense of personal identity and the acquiring of information, competencies, and values. In our society this includes sufficient emancipation from family and other social groups to be a person in one's own right.

2. *Pleasure to reality (self-control).* As we have seen, Freud postulated the *pleasure principle* – the tendency to seek pleasure and to avoid pain and discomfort – as fundamental in governing early behavior. However, he thought this principle was in time subordinated to the *reality principle* – the realization that the individual must learn to perceive and face reality in order to meet his needs. This means distinguishing between fantasy and reality, controlling impulse and desire, delaying immediate gratification in the interest of long-range goals, and learning to cope with the inevitable hurts, disappointments, and frustrations of living.

3. *Ignorance to knowledge.* The human infant is born in a state that might be called total ignorance, but he rapidly begins to acquire information about himself and his world. With time, this information is organized into a coherent pattern of assumptions concerning reality, possibility, and value that provides a stable frame of reference for guiding behavior. If this frame of reference is to prove adequate, it needs to be realistic, to be relevant to the kinds of problems that he must deal with, and to be one in which the individual has faith. Also, it needs to be flexible enough to be modified by new experience.

4. *Incompetence to competence.* The entire preadult period from infancy through adolescence is directed toward the mastery of intellectual, emotional, social, and other competencies essential for adulthood. The individual acquires skills in problem solving and decision making, learns to control his emotions and to use them for the enrichment of living, and learns to deal with others and to establish satisfying relationships. Included here, too, is preparation for sexual, marital, occupational, parental, and other roles and relationships associated with adult life.

5. *Diffuse to differentiated sexuality.* Initial expressions of sexuality, while relatively diffuse and generalized, are found at an early age; even infants may experience pleasure from genital stimulation, and childhood "crushes" often have a high degree of sexual involvement. With the onset of puberty, sexual differentiation progresses rapidly, usually eventuating in heterosexual patterns and marriage. Sexual maturity is a matter of psychological as well as physical development and is closely related to the individual's level of maturity in other life areas.

6. *Amoral to moral.* The newborn infant is amoral in the sense that he has no concept of "right" and "wrong." Very early, however, he learns that certain forms of behavior are approved, or "good," while other forms are disapproved, or "bad." Gradually he learns a pattern of value assumptions that operate as inner guides and controls of behavior, which we have referred to as the conscience or superego. Initially the individual accepts these value assumptions blindly, but with increasing maturity he learns to appraise them, and works out a value orientation that bears his own stamp.

7. *Self-centered to other-centered.* Infants are concerned almost exclusively with their own needs and wants, but with time there is normally an expanding understanding and concern for the needs of others as well. This includes the ability to give love in one's family setting, and to be concerned about and involved with people in one's community and with society as a whole.

There are widespread differences in the success with which individuals reach these goals, but all are important in the realization of one's growth potential and development into a productive, effective member of society.

Answering three key questions. As a child's awareness and understanding expand to include family, neighborhood, nation, world, and the particular time and place in history, he gradually formulates answers to three key questions: *Who am I? Where am I going? Why?* Finding satisfying answers is essential both for establishing an effective life pattern and for the individual's peace of mind and sense of fulfillment as a person.

General principles of development

The following general principles provide a useful perspective for viewing the overall nature and course of human development.

Development normally proceeds in an orderly sequence, although its rate is not constant but rather shows spurts as well as periods of slow growth; in addition, each part and subsystem has its own pattern and sequence of development.

Development can be viewed in terms of stages, each having its own characteristics; although there is an underlying continuity to the human life cycle, we can point to differing characteristics of development during infancy, childhood, and later life periods.

Each new stage of development builds on and is limited by previous development, and, in turn, provides the foundation for the stages that follow; what happens in childhood is influenced by the events of infancy and, in turn, helps codetermine the course of adolescence.

The pathway from infancy to maturity involves increasing differentiation, integration, and complexity of structure and behavior. On a psychological level, this is evidenced in the progression from dependence to self-direction.

There are both similarities and differences in the development of individuals; each person goes through the same stages, but there are differences in learning, growth patterns, and outcomes among the members of any age group.

Development may be normal or faulty depending on the quality and interaction of genetic and environmental factors.

Answers to these questions come easily in some societies, where values are clear and noncontradictory and roles are clearly prescribed for all members of the society. But in our society, where individuality and individual choice are stressed, where value conflicts are prevalent, and where there is so little continuity and so much change and fragmentation, it is often extremely difficult for young people to figure out who and what they want to be and how they want to invest their life energies in order to achieve a fulfilling way of life. Although there are more alternatives to choose from than ever before, the difficulties and uncertainties often seem to outweigh the expected benefits from any of them. Having to choose and take responsibility for one's choices is much more difficult and more risky than having a specific slot provided by the society, with guaranteed material security and public approval. It is perhaps not surprising that the kind of personal responsibility needed for self-direction may seem frightening to many people of all ages, or that some seek "escape from freedom" and find refuge in religious, political, or other groups who make their choices for them and tell them how to live.

To the extent that overall development follows the basic trends toward maturity discussed in the preceding section, an individual is likely to find satisfying answers to these three key life questions. Especially needed for adequate answers are (a) accurate basic assumptions about what is real, what is valuable, and what is possible; (b) development of basic physical, intellectual, emotional, and social competencies; and (c) self-acceptance and self-confidence. Self-acceptance and feelings of adequacy tend to be associated with personality integration and effective adjustment, whereas self-rejection and feelings of inadequacy are commonly associated with maladaptive behavior.

Development may be considered faulty to the extent that it does not follow these trends toward maturity and bring adequate answers to the questions "Who?" "Where?" and "Why?" Faulty development may take the form of (a) arrested development, as in mental retardation; (b) distorted development, as in learning criminal values; or (c) special vulnerabilities, as in low resistance to bronchial infections. Some of the frequent causes of faulty development, on biological, psychosocial, and sociocultural levels, are presented in the next chapter.

Developmental stages and tasks

Intensive studies of infants and children by Gesell (1953), Piaget (1970), and other investigators have shown that human development tends to follow a definite sequence, not only in physical and motor development but also in intellectual, emotional, and social development. Crawling and sitting up come before walking; early diffuse emotional reactions become differentiated into love, humor, grief, and other specific patterns; and language behavior progresses from random vocalizations to the words that eventually become vehicles for thinking.

In the present context, it is not necessary to review the stages of human development—prenatal, infancy, childhood, adolescence, adulthood, and old age—or to delineate the details of development in intellectual or other specific areas. But it is important for our purposes to know that at each stage of development there are certain tasks or competencies to be mastered if the individual is to maintain a normal schedule of development. For example, learning to walk and talk are major tasks of infancy; establishing a mature sense of identity and acquiring the intellectual, emotional, and interpersonal competencies needed for adulthood are key tasks of adolescence.

If developmental tasks are not mastered at the appropriate stage, the individual suffers from immaturities and incompetencies and is placed at a serious disadvantage in adjusting at later developmental levels. A young child who had not learned to walk or talk would be at a serious disadvantage in entering nursery school or kindergarten; the adolescent who does not date misses a major opportunity for acquiring the experience and skill in interpersonal relations and role behavior that will be needed later for establishing a satisfactory marriage or other intimate relationship. The demands of a given developmental period may be relatively easy or difficult to meet, depending on how well the tasks at prior developmental levels have been mastered and on what kind of guidance the individual receives.

Some developmental tasks are set by the individual's own needs, some by the physical and social environment. Members of different socioeconomic and sociocultural groups face somewhat different developmental tasks, and social and technological changes may create new developmental tasks for all of us.

The crucial roles of maturation and learning

Built-in maturational processes[4] provide the potentials for the orderly progression of development, but these potentials can be realized only under favorable environmental conditions.

Critical periods and stimulation. During early development, there are *critical periods*, when certain types of stimulation and learning are essential for normal development. For example, Hunt (1961) showed that if chicks were kept in darkness for up to five days after hatching, they showed no apparent defects in their pecking response; but if the perceptual restriction lasted eight or more days, they were unable to learn to peck. Similarly, Harlow and Harlow (1966) found that if infant monkeys were reared in isolation during the first six months after birth, they evidenced serious inadequacies in social and sexual behavior as adolescents and adults.

We know less about critical periods in human development, but some infants appear to be more severely affected than others by early deprivation; however, mental retardation, inability to form warm interpersonal relationships, and antisocial behavior have all been shown to be associated with extreme emotional, social, and intellectual deprivation in infancy. In this context, it is interesting to note the findings of Skeels (1966) on the adult intellectual status of two groups of individuals who had been placed in an orphanage as infants.

One group of 13 children, ranging from 7 months to 3 years of age, had been transferred from the orphanage to another institution where the adult inmates, though mentally retarded, provided more

---

[4]*Maturation* refers to growth of the organism following birth that is determined primarily by genetic factors and occurs more or less independently of learning.

stimulation and personal contact for the children. A follow-up study 21 years later showed an average gain of 31.6 IQ points for this group, as compared with an average loss of 20.6 IQ points for a matched (control) group who had stayed in the original orphanage.

The effects of maternal deprivation and of aversive stimulation on children's intellectual, emotional, and social development will be examined in Chapter 5. Here we may simply reemphasize the point that if needed stimulation and learning are lacking during early critical periods, the functions expected to develop at these times: (a) may not appear; (b) may be slower in making their appearance; or (c) may be only partially adequate. And once the critical period has passed, it may be difficult or impossible to correct the physiological and/or psychological deficiencies that have occurred.

Early and later learning. Simple conditioning, as described in Chapter 3, is common in infancy and early childhood, and provides many new response patterns—often without the child's awareness of such learning. However, as their perceptual and cognitive capabilities develop, children become increasingly active agents in pursuing their own interests and shaping their own learning. In fact, by the age of four most children have a fairly clear picture of themselves and their world, and their ability to discriminate, interpret, and evaluate experience makes them less susceptible to simple conditioning.

Although learning in later childhood and adolescence usually focuses on formal school instruction, much of the individual's most important learning takes place in the informal learning situations of everyday life. But while new learning may lead to marked changes in an individual's frame of reference and coping techniques, most psychologists emphasize the relatively enduring impact of a person's basic cognitive style. This cognitive style may be more or less efficient for facilitating further learning and personal growth.

Motivation: Human Needs and Strivings

Underlying the apparently limitless diversity of human behavior are certain basic strivings common to people the world over. This common motivational core enables us to understand such divergent behavior as that of the student cramming for an examination, the hate-monger fanning fear and prejudice, and the priest performing the last rites for a dying man. In our brief review of motivation, we shall emphasize its key role in determining both the *direction* and the *activation* of human behavior—the goals we pursue and the effort we expend in trying to attain them.

In attempting to understand human motivation, it is useful to distinguish between the terms *motive* and *need*. Motive refers to any inner condition of the individual that initiates or directs behavior toward a specific goal, while *need* refers to a requirement that must be met for healthy development and/or functioning. The motives an individual may develop are almost limitless, and may be in conflict with actual needs—as when greed, for example, interferes with a person's ability to form loving and meaningful interpersonal relationships.

For present purposes, we shall focus on the basic core of human needs that we all share in common. This basic core includes both biological and psychological needs, and it is strongly influenced by the needs and demands of society.

Tendencies toward maintenance and actualization

The motivation of all living organisms is based on their fundamental tendencies toward *maintenance* or survival and toward the *actualization* of their potentialities. The individual organism resists disintegration or decay[5] and tends to develop and behave in accordance with its genetic possibilities. Among human beings we see these tendencies operating on both biological and psychological levels.

Although we do not fully understand the processes involved, it is apparent that digestive, circulatory, and other body functions operate in such a way as to maintain the body's physiological equilibrium and integration. In the mechanisms for ensuring normal blood chemistry, for maintaining constant body temperature, and for combating invading microorganisms, we see this continuous endeavor of the body to preserve *steady states* —to maintain physiological variables within a range essential to survival—an endeavor generally referred to as *homeostasis*. The tendency toward actualization on the biological level can be seen in physical growth and in sexual and parental behavior that perpetuates the species.

If we do not fully understand the forces underlying biological maintenance, we understand still less the forces related to psychological maintenance. They appear, however, to be an extension of the strivings that operate on the biological plane. On the psychological level our maintenance strivings become an attempt to protect the self. For damage to the self—as through severe feelings of inadequacy and worthlessness—can disable a person just as surely as can failure of physiological homeostatic mechanisms. Thus we strive to maintain the functional integration of the self-system.

As Miller (1965) has pointed out, living organisms also strive to maintain steady states with their environment so as to prevent environmental variations from disrupting their functioning or perhaps even destroying them. Human beings generally attempt to maintain steady states with respect to safety, work, love, marriage, and other conditions that we consider important to our well-being. On the psychological level, actualization strivings may take various forms, such as improving one's capabilities and growing as a person, establishing more fulfilling relationships with others, and improving one's environment.

It is in relation to maintenance and actualization strivings that we use the terms *adjustment* and *maladjustment,* for they refer to the outcome of these strivings. The term *treatment,* too, becomes meaningful only in this context, where the goal of therapy— whatever its particular orientation—is to help the individual meet his needs in a socially constructive way.

Biological needs

The biological needs that appear most relevant to human behavior include visceral needs, the need for stimulation and activity, the need for safety and avoidance of pain, and the need for sexual gratification.

Visceral needs. The most basic of all human needs are those for food, water, sleep, the elimination of wastes, and for other conditions and substances necessary for life. In order to survive and meet adjustive demands, the organism must constantly renew itself through rest and the taking in of nutrients to replace materials used up in the process of living. Prolonged interference with such renewal weakens the organism's resources for coping with even normal adjustive demands and makes it highly vulnerable to special stresses. Prisoners have sometimes been "broken" by nothing more persuasive than the systematic prevention of sleep or deprivation of food over a period of several days.

Experimental studies of volunteers who have gone without sleep for periods of 72 to 98 hours show increasing psychological disorganization as the sleep loss progresses—including disorientation for time and place and feelings of depersonalization. As Berger (1970) has summarized it, "One thing is sure . . . we must sleep in order to stay sane" (p. 70).

---

[5]The tendency of living matter to preserve itself is dramatically illustrated in Wilson's (1925) classic experiment with a sponge. He reduced the sponge to a pulp, squeezed and rolled it flat, and centrifuged it so that no trace of its original form remained. He then allowed the remains to stand overnight. Slowly and in orderly fashion, the material reconstituted itself into the organized sponge it had been before its mistreatment. Similarly, later experiments have shown that completely scrambled cells taken from the liver or kidneys of chick embryos can reconstruct the same organ (Weiss & Taylor, 1960).

"The snowcapped Andes of South America are a cruel and unforgiving barrier. When storms are brewing, plane crashes are frequent; invariably after an aircraft goes down, mountain people remark that 'the Cordillera never gives anyone back.' Last week though, the Cordillera had been forced to give back 16 of the 45 people who had been aboard a Uruguayan air force plane that hit a mountain peak in mid-October. Incredibly, the survivors lasted for 73 days in deep snow and subfreezing temperatures. They took extremely grim measures in order to do so—they ate the bodies of those who had died in the crash."

From "Cannibalism on the Cordillera" from *Time* (January 8, 1973), p. 27. Reprinted by permission from *Time,* The Weekly Newsmagazine; Copyright Time Inc.

Those who survived were members, relatives, and friends of a rugby team called the "Old Christians." There was a great deal of controversy about their actions when the story became known, but a medical student who was among the survivors maintained that it was acceptable to eat the bodies of the dead in order to save the living, just as it is acceptable to transplant the heart of a dead person to sustain the life of another. The Rev. Gino Concetti, in the Vatican newspaper *L'Osservatore Romano,* also defended the actions of the survivors, concluding that "From a theological and ethical point of view, the action cannot be branded as cannibalism" (*Newsweek,* Jan. 8, 1973, p. 27). In its headline account of the incident, a Chilean newspaper asked, "WHAT WOULD YOU HAVE DONE?"

Studies of dietary deficiencies have pointed to marked changes in psychological functioning, the exact change depending largely on the type and extent of the deficiency. Some of these effects were demonstrated in a pioneering study of semistarvation carried out by Keys (1950) and his associates during World War II.

Thirty-two conscientious objectors served as volunteer subjects. The men were first placed on an adequate diet for three months, then placed on a very low calorie diet characteristic of European famine areas for a period of six months, and then provided with a three-month period of nutritional rehabilitation. Comparisons were then made of the subjects during the six-month period of semistarvation, which resulted in an average weight loss of 24 percent, and the other two periods.

Dramatic personality and behavioral changes were shown by the subjects during the period of semistarvation. They became irritable, unsociable, and increasingly unable to concentrate on anything but food. In some instances they resorted to stealing food from one another and lying in attempts to obtain additional food rations. Among other psychological changes were apathy, loss of pride in personal appearance, and feelings of inadequacy. By the close of the experiment, there was a marked reduction or disappearance of their interest in sex, and the predominant mood was one of gloom and depression. Food dominated the men's thoughts, conversation, and even daydreams. They even pinned up pictures of chocolate cake instead of pretty girls. In some cases, they went so far as to replan their lives in the light of their newly acquired respect for food. The investigators concluded that by the end of the twenty-fifth week, hunger had become the dominant influence in the behavior of their subjects.

In ordinary life chronic deprivation may result in lowered resistance to stress. Insufficient rest, inadequate diet, or attempts to carry a full work load under the handicap of a severe cold, fatigue, or emotional strain may deplete a person's adjustive resources and result in increased vulnerability to stress.

Stimulation and activity. Research studies, as well as personal accounts of explorers, have shown that psychological integration depends on adequate contact with the outside world.

"People confined to dark, quiet chambers—the traditional 'solitary confinement' of the prisoner or the soundproof room used for training astronauts—often display bizarre stress and anxiety symptoms, including hallucinations, delusions, apathy, and fear of losing sanity. Their performance deteriorates." (Haythorn & Altman, 1967, p. 19)

In addition, individuals become more receptive to information that is "fed-in"—a tendency that suggests why brainwashing may be effective after a long period of solitary confinement.

An unusual and dramatic account of the need for stimulation comes from the experience of Dr. Alain Bombard, who sailed alone across the Atlantic Ocean for sixty-five days on a life raft to prove that shipwrecked people could survive an indefinite length of time. He subsisted solely on the food he could get from the sea. During this period of isolation, Bombard stated, he "wanted terribly to have someone . . . who would confirm my impressions, or better still, argue about them. . . . I began to feel that I would be incapable of discerning between the false and the true" (Bombard, 1954, pp. 106–7).

On the other hand, too much input may lead to "overloading" and to lowered psychological integration and impaired performance. Miller (1965) found that when messages—in the form of information that had to be acted on—came in too fast, subjects could not handle even the usual number effectively; when such excessive input continued, psychological functioning became disorganized. Similarly, Gottschalk, Haer, and Bates (1972) exposed subjects to overwhelming sensory input in the form of high-intensity sound color movies; they found that such overloading resulted in serious personality disorganization similar to that found in organic brain disturbances.

In general, there appears to be for each individual an optimal level of stimulation and activity that varies over time but must be maintained within limits for normal psychological functioning. Under some conditions—such as boredom—we may strive to increase the level of stimulation by doing something different or engaging in an "exciting" activity. On the other hand, under excessive pressure, or "overload," we may strive to reduce the level of input and activity.

Possible role of sleep deprivation in psychopathology

Recordings of brain waves, eye movements, and other measures have shown that there are four stages of sleep, extending from light sleep to progressively deeper sleep. From such recordings we have learned that a normal adult spends about 20 percent of his sleep in Stage 1 (considered the main stage for dreaming, in which rapid eye movements — REM — occur), about 60 percent in intermediary Stages 2 and 3, and about 20 percent in the deep sleep of Stage 4. Although some dreaming may occur, the latter stages are referred to as non-REM, or NREM sleep. Typically, the individual goes through all four stages in cycles of about 90 minutes, from light through deep sleep and back again to light sleep.

A number of scientific studies have pointed to the importance of normal sleep patterns in mental health — particularly adequate REM and deep sleep. For example, Dement (1960) deprived 5 normal subjects of most of their REM sleep for 5 consecutive nights by awakening the subjects whenever their brain waves and eye movements indicated that they were entering a REM period. This procedure reduced REM time some 80 to 90 percent. Among the many interesting findings reported by Dement were: (1) An increasing number of awakenings were required to keep the subjects from having REM periods — from 4 to 5 the first night to 20 to 30 the fifth night. (2) In the daytime, during the deprivation period, the subjects were observed to be unusually tense and irritable; although they had slept 6 to 7 hours, they behaved as if they had been de-

prived of a great deal of sleep. (3) During the recovery period, the subjects showed a marked increase in REM time which often took up to 30 to 40 percent of their total sleeping time. In a later study, Dement (1963) subjected 3 human subjects to 15 nights of REM deprivation and found that these effects were accentuated. He concluded that the prevention of REM sleep may trigger a mental breakdown in a marginally adjusted individual.

In a study of three groups of poor sleepers — normal elderly persons, severe asthmatics, and patients suffering from insufficient thyroid hormones — it was found that all members of these groups had a marked lack of deep sleep and in some cases almost none. When the thyroid-deficient patients were treated with thyroid hormone, the percentage of sleep in Stage 4 rose significantly (Jacobson & Kales, 1967). It has also been shown that manic and depressed patients suffer a deficit of REM and of deep sleep, and following therapy these patients tend to show more REM and deep sleep than normal controls (Whybrow & Mendels, 1969; Wyatt, Fram, Kupfer, & Snyder; Hauri, Chernik, Hawkins, & Mendels, 1974).

Although we do not understand the precise role of REM and deep sleep in maintaining normal physiological and psychological functioning, it appears probable that disturbed sleep patterns in depression, schizophrenia, and other mental disorders may play an important interactive role in both the causal factors and clinical picture.

Safety and avoidance of pain. From early infancy on we tend to withdraw from painful stimuli and try to avoid objects that have brought us pain or discomfort in the past. The threat or experience of pain is acutely unpleasant and highly motivating.

Severe hunger, thirst, and fatigue can be extremely painful, as can most forms of intense stimulation such as heat, cold, and pressure. And certain emotions—particularly anxiety—are also painful and highly motivating. In fact, anxiety has been referred to as "psychic pain." In this sense, just as pain serves as a warning or indicator to protect us from bodily harm, it can serve also as a safeguard against psychological damage.

The precise influence of physical pain on behavior has never been fully delineated, although experience and observation indicate that it can be very great. Through the centuries, torture and pain have been used to elicit confessions as well as for punishment. When pain is severe and long-continued—as it is in certain types of disease—it may gradually wear down the sufferer's adjustive resources and lead to overwhelming feelings of hopelessness and despair.

Sex. Although the meaning and importance of sexual motives vary greatly from one person to another, sexual tensions, fantasies, and experiences, as well as problems centering around sexual gratification, usually are important facets of a person's life. Depending on our attitude toward sex and the part it plays in our own life plan, sex can be an important source of satisfaction and self-realization or else a source of anxiety and self-devaluation. In any case, sexual motivation is probably second only to the hunger motive in its far-reaching implications for both personal and social living.

Although the sex drive has a hormonal basis and stimulation of the genitals is innately pleasurable, the strength of an individual's sex drive depends heavily on past learning. A person indoctrinated with the view that sex is dirty and evil may develop little sexual motivation, and may even find sexual intercourse unpleasant or repugnant. Because of differences in age, cultural viewpoints, and individual life experiences, there are widespread differences in the strength of sexual motivation and the perceived significance of sexual behavior. Approved patterns of sexual gratification also vary considerably from one society to another and within particular societies over a period of time. In our own society sexual codes are being liberalized, but certain sexual patterns—such as incest and rape—are considered abnormal. We shall deal with these and other aspects of sexual behavior in Chapter 16.

Psychological needs

The psychological requirements for healthy human development and functioning are influenced by learning and social requirements to a greater degree than are biological requirements, and the goals relating to their gratification are capable of greater variation. A position of leadership, for example, so highly valued in our society as a means of meeting needs for adequacy and worth, was found by Mead (1949) to be a nuisance and burden to the Arapesh, who avoided leadership roles whenever possible.

Despite wide individual and group differences in human motives, however, there does appear to be a common core of psychological needs related to maintenance and actualization.

Psychological maintenance. Although psychological requirements are less readily identified than requirements for food, water, sleep, and the like, there is widespread agreement that the following basic core of psychological needs characterize all of us as human beings.

1. *Curiosity: understanding, order, predictability.* Human beings are inherently curious and strive to understand and achieve a meaningful picture of their world. Such a frame of reference is essential for evaluating new situations and guiding adjustive actions. Unless we can see order and predictability in our environment, we cannot work out an intelligent response to it. Social customs, rules, and laws are in part a reflection of this need for order and predictability.

People do not like ambiguity, lack of structuring, chaos, or events that seem beyond their understanding and control. Even the

"To love and to be loved are crucial to healthy personality development and adjustment."

most primitive people develop explanations for lightning, thunder, death, and other frightening phenomena. Accurate or not, such explanations tend to impose order and meaning on seemingly random events, thereby giving a sense of potential prediction and control. Modern science is simply a more sophisticated attempt in the same direction.

Our striving for understanding, order, and predictability is evidenced in our tendency to maintain the consistency and stability of our frame of reference. When new information contradicts existing assumptions, it is experienced as *cognitive dissonance*—an unpleasant state of tension—and the person is uncomfortable until the discrepancy can be reconciled. In fact, Aronson (1973) concluded that cognitive dissonance may result in such acute discomfort that an individual may risk his life in an effort to resolve it.

2. *Adequacy, competence, security.* Each of us needs to feel capable of dealing with life's problems. Seeing oneself as incapable of coping with a stressful situation is conducive to confusion and disorganization.

Feelings of adequacy are heavily dependent on the development of intellectual, social, and other competencies for dealing with adjustive demands. Several investigators have pointed out that even the early playful and investigatory behavior of children involves a process of "reality testing" which fosters the development of learning, reasoning, and other coping abilities which are greatly expanded by formal education.

The need for security develops with and is closely related to the need for adequacy. We soon learn that failure to meet biological or psychological needs leads to unpleasant results. Consequently we strive to maintain whatever conditions can be counted on to assure present and future need gratification. The need for security is reflected in the preference for jobs with tenure, in social security legislation, in insurance against disability and other contingencies, and in society's emphasis on law and order. Feelings of insecurity may have widely differing effects on behavior; but pervasive and chronic feelings of insecurity typically lead to fearfulness, apprehension, and failure to participate fully in one's world. The more adequate we feel and the greater our level of competence, the less aware we are of our need for security and the more we may value the exploration of unfamiliar paths and freedom for self-direction.

In this general context, it is interesting to note that one of the key functions of psychotherapy is to help patients achieve a sense of adequacy, competency, and mastery over their lives.

3. *Love, belonging, approval.* To love and to be loved are crucial to healthy personality development and adjustment. In their extensive study of patterns in child rearing, Sears, Maccoby, and Levin (1957) concluded that the most crucial and pervasive of all the influences exerted in the home were the love and warmth imparted by the parents. For the child who feels loved and accepted, many conditions that might otherwise impair development, such as a physical handicap, poverty, or harsh discipline, may be largely neutralized.

Evidence of our needs for love, belonging, and approval is provided in the illustration on page 104, which describes the nature and effects of the "silent treatment." The need for close ties to other people continues throughout life and becomes especially important in times of severe stress or crisis. In a study of terminal cancer patients, Bard (1966) concluded that the need for affiliation and human contact is never greater than it is as death approaches.

As Pierre Teilhard de Chardin has expressed it, "Love alone is capable of uniting living beings in such a way as to complete and fulfill them, for it alone takes them and joins them by what is deepest in themselves" (1961, p. 265).

4. *Self-esteem, worth, and identity.* Closely related to feelings of adequacy and social approval is the need to feel good about oneself and worthy of the respect of others.

Self-esteem has its early foundation in parental affirmation of worth and in mastery of early developmental tasks; it receives continual nourishment from the development of new competencies and from achievement in areas deemed important; and eventually it comes to depend heavily on the values and standards of significant others. If a person measures up to those standards—for example, in terms of physical appearance, achievement, or economic status—he can approve of himself and feel worthwhile.

Intermeshed with feelings of self-esteem and worth is one's sense of self-identity. This, too, is heavily influenced by significant others and by the person's status and role in the group. Here it is interesting to note that despite changes in physical appearance, in status, and in social roles, people tend to maintain continuity in their basic feelings of self-identity. That is, we each think of ourself as much the same *I* or *me* today that we were yesterday and will be tomorrow.

While many of us might like to make some change in our self-identity, it is doubtful that we would willingly give it up. In any event, when a person's sense of self-identity and continuity becomes disorganized—as happens sometimes in psychotic disorders—the experience is usually acutely painful. Sargent (1973) has reported on the loss of self-identity in prison and its consequences in terms of self-esteem, worth, and adequacy.

"The prisoners increasingly depend on authority, become susceptible to suggestion, tend toward magical thinking, and become more anxious and impulsive. In some cases the symptoms reach psychotic proportions." (p. 390)

5. *Values, meaning, hope.* We have previously commented on the need for values as a guide in making decisions and achieving a meaningful way of life. In the present context, we will simply reemphasize the central importance of values and meaning to our very existence:[6]

---

[6]As we noted in Chapter 3, existential psychologists consider the quest for values and meaning to be the *primary* human striving.

Eloquent testimony to our needs for love, belonging, and approval is provided by the experience of small groups of scientists, officers, and enlisted personnel who voluntarily subjected themselves to isolated antarctic living for the better part of a year. During this period troublesome individuals were occasionally given the "silent treatment" in which a man would be ignored by the group as if he did not exist.

This "isolation" procedure resulted in a syndrome called the "long eye," characterized by varying combinations of sleeplessness, outbursts of crying, hallucinations, a deterioration in habits of personal hygiene, and a tendency for the man to move aimlessly about or to lie on his bunk staring into space. These symptoms cleared up when he was again accepted by and permitted to interact with others in the group.

Based primarily on Rohrer (1961) and on Popkin, Stillner, Osborn, Pierce, and Shurley (1974).

"In the midst of the probabilities and uncertainties that surround them, people want some anchoring points, some certainties, some faith that will serve either as a beacon light to guide them or as a balm to assuage them during the inevitable frustrations and anxieties that living engenders." (Cantril, 1967, p. 17)

Closely related to our needs for values and meaning are our goals and plans, for we live in the future as well as in the past and present. Thus our goals and plans serve as a focus for both our strivings and our hopes. And when we feel uncertain and anxious about the future, personal adjustment and effectiveness are likely to be impaired.

In extreme cases, hope may give way to hopelessness and lead to apathy and even death. For example, reports from prisoner-of-war camps have told of cases in which prisoners who had lost hope simply pulled their blankets over their heads and waited for death to come (Nardini, 1952; *U.S. News and World Report*, 1973).

Surprisingly, there has been little research on the human need for values, meaning, and hope. But we can infer such needs, like the need for love, from observations of the typical

results when people are unable to find satisfying value patterns, are "planless," or lack hope. Values, meaning, and hope appear to act as catalysts; in their presence energy is mobilized, competencies are developed and used, and satisfactions are achieved. Without them life seems futile and the individual is bored and enervated.

The needs discussed above appear to represent the basic core of psychological requirements that emerge through normal interaction with the world and that contribute significantly to the direction of behavior. The strength of a given psychological need and the behaviors for meeting it may vary considerably, of course, from one person to another, and from one social group to the next. It is apparent, too, that biological and psychological needs are closely interrelated and that failure to meet particular needs may adversely influence our entire motivational structure as well as physical and psychological well-being.

Actualization strivings. Our views of motivation have long been dominated by the concepts of maintenance and homeostasis, according to which our energies are directed toward meeting any deficiency that arises and returning to a state of equilibrium. But although maintenance strivings represent the central core of human motivation, they do not tell the entire story. Maintenance strivings alone, for example, do not explain sexual and parental behavior that perpetuates the species nor do they explain the efforts expended by the mountain climber, the great artist, or the astronaut. We strive not only to maintain ourselves and survive but to express ourselves, to improve, to grow — to *actualize our potentialities*. Over two decades ago, Huxley (1953) made this point very eloquently:

"Human life is a struggle—against frustration, ignorance, suffering, evil, the maddening inertia of things in general; but it is also a struggle *for* something . . . And fulfillment seems to describe better than any other single word the positive side of human development and human evolution—the realization of inherent capacities by the individual and of new possibilities by the race; the satisfaction of needs, spiritual as well as material; the emergence of new qualities of experience to be enjoyed; the building of personalities." (pp. 162–63)

Strivings toward actualization take different forms with different people, depending on their abilities, values, and life situations. In general, however, we appear to share certain strivings as human beings: (a) toward developing and using our potentials in constructive and creative ways, as in art, music, writing, science, athletics, and other pursuits which foster creative self-expression; (b) toward the enrichment of living—toward enriching the range and quality of our experiences and satisfactions, as, for example, in travel; (c) toward increasing our relatedness to the world—forming warm and meaningful relationships with others and becoming involved in the "human enterprise"; and (d) toward "becoming a person"—answering the question "Who am I?" and becoming the "self" that one feels one should be. Here it may be noted that the various psychological needs we have discussed—considered maintenance needs in that they must be met for normal development and functioning—may also be considered routes to self-actualization. Many of our deepest satisfactions come through improving our understanding and competence, forming loving relationships with others, and acquiring values that contribute to a meaningful and fulfilling life.

Motivation and behavior

In the preceding discussion we have been concerned with the nature of our basic needs and strivings. Now let us broaden our perspective to include (a) activation—the mobilization of energy in order to pursue our goals and meet our needs; (b) motivational selectivity—the influence of needs and motives on other psychological processes; (c) the concept of a hierarchy of needs; (d) conscious and unconscious aspects of motives; and (e) the relation of motive patterns to life styles.

Then we shall conclude our review of motivation with a brief look at the needs of groups and the role of social forces in inhibiting and facilitating the development and expression of given motives.

Levels of activation. Motivation not only accounts for the direction but also for the activation of behavior—the energy mobilized in pursuit of our goals.

Activation can vary in degree from very low to very high, from deep sleep to intense excitement. At any moment a person's level of activation is influenced by a wide range of individual and situational factors. It is affected by the way one perceives the situation and evaluates its potential satisfaction and frustrations; it is affected by many inner conditions, including biological drives, emotions, and drugs; it is affected by sudden loud noises and strange or novel stimuli; and it is affected by fatigue, disease, and pain. Usually, efficient task performance requires a moderate level of activation. With too low a level, the person may fail to expend the energy and effort essential for task achievement, while very high levels tend to result in poorly coordinated functioning and impaired performance.

Although there are individual differences in personal tempo and sensitivity or excitability, most people learn to respond to familiar situations with appropriate levels of activation. However, an individual is likely to react with an overly high level of activation in the face of an unfamiliar challenge or under stress conditions to which he is particularly vulnerable. Similarly, conditions such as severe fatigue, intense inner conflict, or faulty assumptions and loss of hope may lead to extreme and inappropriate fluctuations in activation, as well as to slow recovery from the effects of prior activation and energy output.

Motivational selectivity. An individual's needs and motives influence perceiving, reasoning, learning, and other psychological processes. For example, people tend to perceive only those aspects of the environment which are related to the gratification of immediate or long-term needs. A person lost in the desert and suffering from intense thirst would likely ignore the vivid colors of the sunset and keep scanning his surroundings for some indication of water. This tendency of the organism to single out particular elements considered to be especially relevant to its purposes is called *selective vigilance*.

While motivation may sensitize the individual to particular stimuli, it may also have the opposite effect. Thus people tend to screen out information that is incompatible with their expectations, assumptions, and wishes. Proud parents may selectively perceive the desirable traits and behaviors of their children while tending not to perceive undesirable ones; people often do the same thing in evaluating themselves. This tendency to avoid perceiving unpleasant stimuli or undesired information is referred to as *perceptual defense*.[7]

Motivation also influences what the individual learns as well as how rapidly and how much. And despite our attempts to be logical, our motivation may influence our beliefs and subvert our thought processes in helping us justify our assumptions and behavior.

Hierarchy of needs. Maslow (1954, 1970, 1971) has suggested that human needs arrange themselves in a hierarchy from the most basic biological requirements to the need for self-actualization. According to this formulation, the level that commands the individual's attention and effort is ordinarily the lowest one on which there is an unmet need. For example, unless needs for food and safety are reasonably well met, behavior will be dominated by these needs. With their gratification, however, the individual is free to devote time and energy to meeting needs on higher levels.

Maslow used the term *deficiency motivation* to refer to motives aimed at meeting the needs on lower levels, since these motives are activated by deficiencies and force the individual to take action to restore equilibrium. He used the term *growth motivation* to refer to motives aimed at meeting the higher-level needs for self-actualization. Although meeting lower-level needs is clearly necessary for maintenance of the organism, Maslow considered a long-term preoccupation with *only* the maintenance needs to be unhealthy because of the resulting failure to develop the individual's uniquely human potentialities.

Maslow's hierarchy concept tends to be borne out by observations of behavior under extreme conditions. Friedman (1949) reported that: "In all survivors of the Nazi concentration camps, one might say the self-preserva-

tion instinct became so dominant that it blotted out all other instincts." Similarly, in the Japanese prisoner-of-war camps in World War II, it was a common pattern for those inmates who had been subjected to prolonged deprivation and torture to obtain food at the expense of their fellow prisoners and in other ways surrender the loyalties and values they had held under more normal conditions (Nardini, 1952, 1962).

Under conditions of extreme deprivation, most people do appear likely to sacrifice their higher-level actualization needs to meet more basic needs for survival; as Maslow acknowledged, however, there are many exceptions, as shown by the countless number of people who have remained faithful to ethical, social, or religious values despite severe deprivation, torture, and even certain death.

Conscious and unconscious aspects of motivation. We noted that the concept of unconscious motivation is basic to the psychoanalytic model; some three decades ago W. A. White (1947) concluded that the failure to take unconscious motivation into consideration was "probably the cause of more inadequacies in the understanding of human behavior than any other one thing." Although there is still considerable controversy among psychologists concerning the nature and importance of unconscious processes in human behavior, there is abundant evidence that the individual is often unaware or only partially aware of what his needs and goals really are.

Many of our biological needs operate on an unconscious level, and we may become aware of others—for example, via feelings of hunger and thirst—only when they become pressing. Psychological needs, such as those for security, adequacy, social approval, and self-esteem, may also operate on relatively unconscious levels. Thus a businessman may criticize his associates, join exclusive clubs, and even get married for reasons of which he is unaware. Of course, he may think of good reasons to justify his behavior, but they may not be the real reasons at all.

The degree to which individuals are aware of their motives varies considerably from one person to another. Usually individuals who

---

[7]An informative discussion of perceptual defense and vigilance may be found in Erdelyi (1974).

are seriously maladjusted lack insight into many key facets of their motivational patterns. The following now-classic illustration demonstrates the action of unconscious motivation and is especially revealing, because here we do know the individual's exact motivational pattern, which is not generally the case.

"During profound hypnosis the subject was instructed to feel that smoking was a bad habit, that he both loved and hated it, that he wanted to get over the habit but he felt it was too strong a habit to break, that he would be very reluctant to smoke and would give anything not to smoke, but that he would find himself compelled to smoke; and that after he was awakened he would experience all of these feelings.

"After he was awakened the subject was drawn into a casual conversation with the hypnotist who, lighting one himself, offered him a cigarette. The subject waved it aside with the explanation that he had his own and that he preferred Camels, and promptly began to reach for his own pack. Instead of looking in his customary pocket, however, he seemed to forget where he carried his cigarettes and searched fruitlessly through all of his other pockets with a gradually increasing concern. Finally, after having sought them repeatedly in all other pockets, he located his cigarettes in their usual place. He took them out, engaged in a brief conversation as he dallied with the pack, and then began to search for matches, which he failed to find. During his search for matches he replaced the cigarettes in his pocket and began using both hands, finally locating the matches too in their usual pocket. Having done this, he now began using both hands to search for his cigarettes. He finally located them but then found that he had once more misplaced his matches. This time however he kept his cigarettes in hand while attempting to locate the matches. He then placed a cigarette in his mouth and struck a match. As he struck it, however, he began a conversation which so engrossed him that he forgot the match and allowed it to burn his finger tips whereupon, with a grimace of pain, he tossed it in the ash tray. . . .

"This behavior continued with numerous variations. He tried lighting a cigarette with a split match, burned his fingers, got both ends of one cigarette wet, demonstrated how he could roll a cigarette, kept stopping to converse or tell a joke, and so on. Several cigarettes were ruined and discarded. When he finally got one going successfully, he took only a few good puffs with long pauses in between and discarded it before it was used up." (Erickson, 1939, pp. 342–45)

HIERARCHY OF NEEDS

According to Maslow, needs on the "lower" levels are prepotent as long as they are unsatisfied. When they are adequately satisfied, however, the "higher" needs occupy the individual's attention and effort.

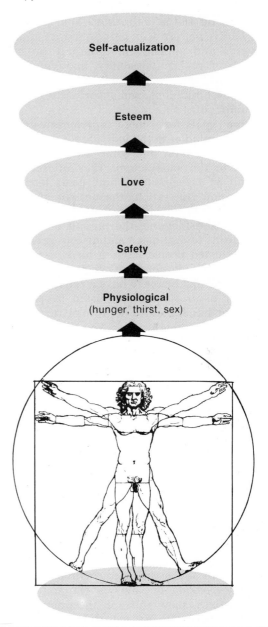

Motive patterns and life style. Each individual tends to develop a relatively consistent life style, an essential element of which is his *motive pattern* – the needs, goal objects, and means that characterize his strivings. Some persons are primarily concerned with love and relatedness, others with material possessions and power, and still others with personal growth and self-actualization. The individual's motive pattern is in part a product of past rewards and punishments; in part an outgrowth of reality, possibility, and value assumptions; and in part a reflection of the demands, limitations, and opportunities of the environment.

Some goals are more appropriate than others in relation to the individual's resources and opportunities, and some are superior to others in the satisfactions they afford. The pursuit of unrealistically high goals leads to failure and frustration; the pursuit of goals that are too low leads to wasted opportunities and lost satisfactions; the pursuit of "false" goals leads to disillusion and discouragement. Well-adjusted people tend to have a reasonably accurate view of themselves in relation to their world and hence to have a fairly realistic *level of aspiration.* Maladjusted people, on the other hand, tend to be unrealistic – to set their goals too high or too low or to pursue unrewarding goals. In many cases, maladjusted people seem unable to formulate meaningful life plans and goals and drift through life with little or no sense of direction. Usually such persons experience feelings of dissatisfaction, aimlessness, and being "lost."

Although each of us tends to show a relatively consistent pattern of motives, this pattern undergoes change over time. The key motives of the child are not those of the adolescent, nor are the motives of the adolescent those of the adult or older person. Similarly, changes in one's life situation may lead to the modification of motive patterns. For example, a person who is sentenced to twenty years in prison may find it necessary to make drastic changes in his established motive pattern. Broadly speaking, one may develop important new motives, show shifts in the priorities of existing motives, or discard motives that have formerly been of significance. Some of these changes emerge as the products of experience and learning; others seem to result from new requirements at different life stages; and still others are influenced by changed environmental conditions.

Social forces in motivation

Thus far we have viewed motivation primarily in terms of the needs and strivings of the individual. However, environmental factors are of great importance in facilitating or inhibiting given strivings, in the formulation of goals, and in determining the extent to which one's needs are met.

Social inhibition and facilitation of motives. By its system of values and by the manipulation of rewards and punishments, society encourages the gratification of certain needs while it attempts to inhibit or limit that of others. In most societies, for example, patterns of sexual gratification are strictly regulated by society; in general, unusual or aberrant expressions of such desires are inhibited. Conversely, the pursuit of other needs, such as the need for social approval, may be strongly encouraged.

The rewards and punishments supplied by the group also influence the goals its members seek and the means they learn to use in working toward these goals. In our society, for example, there are strong incentives to strive toward such goals as academic excellence, creative accomplishment, financial success, and leadership. And although a wide range of means for achieving these goals is approved, there nevertheless are limitations; if we use socially disapproved means, we may be punished.

Needs of groups and of society. Social groups have basic needs in much the same sense that individuals do. Their survival depends, for example, on the maintenance of orderly social relationships – which in turn requires the development of various "homeostatic" mechanisms, such as customs and laws and the means for enforcing them.

When normal group functioning or organizational structure is disrupted, groups strive to reestablish a state of equilibrium. This applies to small groups as well as larger ones. If a general is killed in battle, another officer moves up to take his place; if one member of a family dies, there are changes in relationships and responsibilities as other family members attempt to establish a new pattern of effective functioning.

The needs of groups and of society are important determinants of the behavior of individual members. Usually meeting the needs of one's family and other groups, as well as those of the larger society, tends to promote one's own welfare too. However, the needs of the group or the society may conflict with or eclipse the needs of the individual, as when a young mother must work long hours at a monotonous job to support her family or when a soldier is forced to risk his life in combat.

In concluding our brief review of human motivation, it may be reemphasized that motives and goals focus our energy and effort, help determine the competencies we need, and provide a basis for deciding between alternative courses of action. And while specific motives and goals may change during the course of our lives, it is equally relevant to note that the basic core of biological and psychological needs required for maintenance and actualization—needs that we share in common as human beings—remain essentially the same throughout our lives.

Adjustive Demands (Stress)

Life would be simple indeed if one's biological and psychological needs were automatically gratified. But as we know, there are many obstacles, both environmental and personal, that may interfere. Such obstacles place *adjustive demands* or *stress* on the individual.

In the present section, we shall be concerned with five aspects of stress: (a) types of stress; (b) factors influencing the severity of stress; (c) the role of key stresses and crises in adjustive demands; (d) the unique and changing stress patterns that characterize each person's life; and (e) the costs that may be exacted by severe stress.

Types of stress: frustration, conflict, pressure

Adjustive demands may be classified as frustrations, conflicts, and pressures. While we shall consider each type of adjustive demand separately, it will be apparent that they are all closely interrelated.

Frustration. Frustration occurs when one's strivings are thwarted, either by obstacles that block progress toward a desired goal or by absence of an appropriate goal.

A wide range of obstacles, both environmental and internal, can lead to frustration. Inflation, group prejudice and discrimination, and the death of loved ones are common frustrations stemming from the environment; physical handicaps, lack of needed competencies, and inadequate self-control are sources of frustration that can result from our own personal limitations. Often frustrations arise out of psychological barriers in the form of ethical or moral restraints. Many college students refrain from premarital sexual intercourse, for

Sources of adjustive demands

The response of an individual to a stress situation is significantly affected by the specific source of the adjustive demand: an individual will respond quite differently to hunger if he is on a diet, for example, than if he lacks money to buy food. Adjustive demands may be classified in a general way as imposed, assigned, chosen, or devised. As some of the following illustrations suggest, however, these categories aren't always discrete.

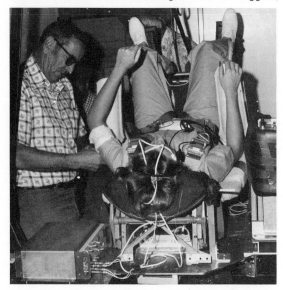

Devised: Stress may be devised in artificially controlled laboratory conditions. Here the effect of the low accelerator forces that will occur in the Space Shuttle are being tested on this flight nurse volunteer.

Chosen: An individual may choose a stressful situation for personally valid reasons; for example, Admiral Byrd preferred complete isolation in wintering over in Antarctica.

Assigned: People in hazardous and confined situations, ranging from astronauts to coalminers to submariners, may be subject to long periods of unusual stress.

Imposed: Draftees in the military service may be involuntarily subjected to rigid discipline and other stressful conditions. The picture illustrates marines training for combat conditions.

example, because their moral values make such behavior unacceptable. And, of course, faulty value assumptions, such as the belief that the world owes us a living, may lead to unnecessary frustrations as well as other types of stress.

The frustrations we face depend heavily on such factors as age and other personal characteristics, our specific life situation, and the society in which we live.

Conflict. In many instances stress results from the necessity of choosing between two needs or goals. Usually the choice of one alternative means frustration with regard to the other. An early marriage may mean foregoing or shortening one's college education; choosing one job may mean turning down another that seems equally desirable.

Although we are dealing with frustration and conflict as if they were distinct sources of stress, this differentiation is largely for convenience; the key element in conflict is often the frustration that arises when we must choose one alternative and give up the other. In addition, however, the necessity of making a choice commonly involves "cognitive strain": it is often difficult "to make up one's mind," especially when each alternative offers values that the other does not, and the choice is an important one.

Conflicts with which everyone has to cope may be conveniently classified as approach-avoidance, double-approach, and double-avoidance types.

1. *Approach-avoidance conflicts* involve strong tendencies both to approach and to avoid the same goal. A woman may want to marry for sexual, social, and security reasons, while at the same time fearing the responsibilities of married life and the loss of personal freedom. In a similar way, other desires may conflict with inner reality or ethical restraints or with fear of failure. Perhaps a man wants to join a high-status group but can do so only by endorsing views contrary to his values; or he may feel physically attracted to a woman and want to marry her while recognizing that he strongly disagrees with her scale of values.

Approach-avoidance conflicts are sometimes referred to as "mixed-blessing" dilemmas, because some negative and some positive features must be accepted regardless of which course of action is chosen.

2. *Double-approach conflicts* involve competition between two or more desirable goals. On a simple level the individual may have to decide between leather or vinyl upholstery, or between two dinner entrées, or between two invitations for a particular weekend. To a large extent, such simple "plus-plus" conflicts result from the inevitable limitations in one's time, space, energy, and personal and financial resources—and are handled in stride. In more complex cases, however, as when an individual is torn between two good career opportunities, or between present satisfactions and future ones, decision making may be very difficult and stressful.

3. *Double-avoidance conflicts* are those that completely hem us in—we are caught "between the devil and the deep blue sea." We may, for example, have to choose between finishing a job we intensely dislike or quitting and being called a failure. In wartime we may have to choose between fighting, with the possibility of killing or being killed, and refusing to fight, with the attendant social disapproval and possible punishment.

It can be seen that this classification of conflicts is somewhat arbitrary, and that various combinations among the different types are perhaps the rule rather than the exception. Thus a "plus-plus" conflict between alternative careers may also have its "plus-minus" aspects growing out of the responsibilities that either imposes. But regardless of how we categorize conflicts, they represent a major source of stress and can be overwhelming in their intensity.

Pressure as a type of stress. Stress may stem not only from frustrations and conflicts, but also from pressure to achieve particular goals or to behave in particular ways. Such pressures may originate from external or internal sources. A college student may feel under severe pressure to make good grades because her parents demand it, or she may submit herself to such pressure because she wants to gain admission to graduate school.

In general, pressures force a person to speed up, intensify, or change the direction of goal-oriented behavior. All of us encounter many different pressures in the course of everyday living, and often it is possible to handle them without undue difficulty. In some instances, however, pressures seriously tax our adjustive resources, and if they become excessive, they may lead to a breakdown of organized behavior.

It is apparent that a given stress situation may involve elements of all three types of stress—frustration, conflict, and pressure. For example, a serious financial loss not only may lead to lower living standards but also confront the person with evidence of poor judgment. If such evidence is contrary to the person's view of himself as a shrewd businessman, the resulting cognitive dissonance may add to the complexity of the stress situation. And although a particular stress may predominate in any situation, we rarely deal with an isolated situation, but rather with a continuously changing complex of interrelated and sometimes contradictory demands. Thus we usually speak of "stress patterns" rather than simply of a given stress situation.

Factors influencing the severity of stress

The severity of stress is gauged by the degree of disruption in the human system that will occur if the individual fails to cope with the adjustive demand. For example, lack of food over a sustained period is regarded as a severe stress because it causes serious disruption of both physiological and psychological functioning.

The actual degree of disruption that occurs depends partly on the characteristics of the adjustive demand, partly on the individual, and partly on the cultural and situational context in which the stress occurs. On a biological level, for example, the severity of stress created by invading viruses depends partly on the strength and number of the invaders, partly on the organism's ability to resist and destroy them, and partly on available medical resources for helping the body's defenses. On a psychological level, the severity of the stress depends not only on the nature of the stress and the individual's resources—both personal

and situational—but also on how the stress situation is perceived and evaluated. For example, a divorce may be highly stressful for one partner but not for the other.

Characteristics of the adjustive demand. Several objective factors influence stress severity. These are relatively independent of the individual involved or the situational context in which the demand occurs.

1. Importance, duration, and multiplicity of demands. In terms of importance, it has been shown that certain stresses—such as the death of a loved one, divorce, and serious personal illness—tend to be highly stressful for most people (Holmes & Rahe, 1967; Cochrane & Robertson, 1973). Ordinarily, the longer a stress operates, the more severe it becomes. Prolonged exhaustion imposes a more intense stress than does temporary fatigue. Often, too, stress appears to have a cumulative effect. A married couple may maintain amicable relations through a long series of minor irritations or frustrations only to "explode" and dissolve the relationship in the face of the "final straw."

Encountering a number of stresses at the same time makes a difference too. If a man has a heart attack, loses his job, and receives distressing news of his son or daughter's being arrested for drug abuse—all at the same time—the resulting stress will be more severe than if these events occurred separately.

2. Strength and equality of conflicting forces. Conflict between weak motives or between motives with little self-investment involves minimal stress, for neither alternative would lead to serious loss. On the other hand, conflicts between strong motives—such as one requiring a choice between self-esteem and social approval—are likely to subject the individual to considerable stress. In addition, the more nearly equal the strength of the opposing motives, the greater the stress.

The picture is complicated further by the fact that the strength of a given motive or the value of a goal does not remain static or unchanging. In approach-avoidance conflicts, for example, the strength of opposing motives is likely to increase as the goal draws near. For a young person ambivalent about getting married, both eagerness and fear will become greater as the wedding date approaches, and stress will mount accordingly. This probably helps explain why some people experience a feeling of near panic on their wedding day.

3. *Imminence of anticipated stress.* In most stress situations, including those involving conflict, the severity of stress increases as the anticipated stress approaches. For example, Mechanic (1962), observing graduate students, found that although the students thought about their examinations from time to time and experienced some anxiety during the prior three months, anxiety did not become intense until the examinations were nearly upon them. Similarly, persons anticipating other stress situations—such as major surgery—have found that the severity of stress increased as the time for the ordeal approached.

For individuals who repeatedly subject themselves to a particular stress situation—as in the sport of skydiving—a somewhat different pattern of severity may be involved. For novice jumpers, the peak of anxiety or avoidance does not come at the period of greatest danger—the free fall—but at the "ready" signal, when the individual can choose to go ahead or to cancel the jump. For experienced jumpers, on the other hand, the anxiety peaks earlier, during the morning of the scheduled jump, and once they have made the decision that they will jump that day, their fear and anxiety usually decrease (Fenz & Epstein, 1969).

4. *Unfamiliarity or suddenness of the problem.* Often new adjustive demands that have not been anticipated and for which no ready-made coping patterns are available will place an individual under severe stress. One reason major catastrophes are so overwhelming is that all one's knowledge and skills seem totally inadequate and irrelevant to the task at hand. By contrast, if a stressful event, even a potentially catastrophic one, can be prepared for, it loses some of its severity. The training of fire fighters, police officers, and soldiers for crisis situations makes it possible for them to function more effectively under extreme degrees of stress.

The same sense of adequacy and control may be achieved when the stress has been chosen voluntarily, rather than having been

At one time the human brain was thought of as a "switchboard" where stimuli and responses were connected. Present-day computer-simulation studies, however, support the notion that it is more like an elaborate communications, problem-solving, and decision-making center where incoming information is continuously evaluated, alternative responses are formulated and weighed, decisions are made and implemented, and feedback is checked with a view to correcting possible error.

1. Appraising the stress situation. When a new adjustive demand is perceived, it is quickly assigned to a particular category of problems based on its similarities to and differences from previous demands. At the same time, the degree of danger or threat posed by the adjustive demand is assessed. If the stress is evaluated as a serious threat, it is likely to elicit anxiety and to lead to the interruption of other ongoing activities in order to cope with it.

2. Problem solving and decision making. After the situation has been appraised, alternative courses of action are formulated. Often the categorization of the adjustive demand also provides possible ways of dealing with such stress situations, because they have been used in the past in similar situations. Next the individual must assess the relative merits of alternative solutions and make a choice. Influencing the decision will be the probabilities of success, the degree of satisfaction he is willing to accept, and the cost he is willing to pay—in short, he must balance probability, desirability, and cost.

3. Taking action and using feedback. Once a decision has been made, the next step is to implement it—to put the alternative chosen into action. And once a course of action has been embarked upon, the individual can keep checking on whatever feedback information is available to see if corrections or adjustments in ongoing actions are indicated and feasible. This may include abrupt termination of one course of action and the formulation and implementation of another that appears more likely to prove effective.

Although the human brain tends to be a highly efficient computer in processing stress, it is subject to error. For example, faulty assumptions, time pressures, emotional involvement, and many other factors may lead to wrong answers. And such errors may lead to seriously maladaptive behavior.

imposed by others or having come unexpectedly (Averill, 1973). Understanding the nature of a stressful situation, preparing for it, and knowing how long it will last, all lessen the severity of the stress when it does come.

Characteristics of the individual. The person's perception of the problem, the degree of threat it entails, and available resources for meeting it all influence the severity of stressful situations. Thus, situations that one person finds highly stressful may be only mildly stressful or even nonstressful for another.

1. *Perception of the problem.* One factor that is often crucial in determining the severity of stress is the individual's own evaluation of the stress situation. This point is particularly important in understanding abnormal behavior. As outsiders, we may see no stresses in a person's life situation severe enough to result in serious depression. Yet to the individual, the situation may be intolerable. We always react not simply to the situation, but *to the situation as we evaluate it*—especially in relation to our ability to cope with it.

2. *Degree of threat.* Threat is the anticipation of harm. Stress situations that are perceived as potentially damaging or threatening to survival—such as having a limb amputated or being given a diagnosis of cancer—carry a high degree of threat. Similarly, stress situations that threaten the adequacy and worth of the self—such as loss of social status, failure in one's chosen occupation, or desires incompatible with one's self-concept and self-ideal—involve a strong element of threat. We are also likely to feel threatened in situations that place demands on us that we see as important but beyond our power to meet. For this reason, if we doubt our general adequacy and worth, we are much more likely to experience threat than if we feel generally confident and secure. In general, any situation we see as threatening is much more stressful than one we see as presenting a difficult but manageable problem.

3. *Stress tolerance of the individual.* The severity of a given stress depends, too, on resources for withstanding stress in general and that stress in particular. If a person is marginally adjusted, the slightest frustration or pressure may be highly stressful. The term *stress tolerance* or *frustration tolerance* refers to

one's ability to withstand stress without having integrated functioning seriously impaired. Both biologically and psychologically, people vary greatly in general vulnerability to stress as well as in the types to which they are most vulnerable. Emergencies, disappointments, and other problems that one person can take in stride may prove incapacitating to another. Sometimes early traumatic experiences leave the individual especially vulnerable to certain kinds of stress.

External resources and supports. Lack of external supports—either personal or material—makes a given stress more severe and weakens an individual's capacity to cope with it. A divorce or the death of one's mate is more stressful if one is left feeling alone and unloved than if one is still surrounded by people one cares about and feels close to.

Pressures to violate one's principles or beliefs are less stressful and more easily withstood when one has an ally than when one is alone. It is hardly surprising that studies have found a tendency for individuals exposed to highly stressful situations to turn to others for support and reassurance.

Environmental supports are a complex matter, however, and behavior by one's family or friends that is intended to provide support may actually increase the stress. In his study of graduate students facing crucial examinations, Mechanic (1962) compared the effects of different types of behavior on the part of the spouses:

"In general, spouses do not provide blind support. They perceive the kinds of support the student wants and they provide it. The [spouse] who becomes worried about examinations also may provide more support than the spouse who says, 'I'm not worried, you will surely pass.' Indeed, since there is a chance that the student will not pass, the person who is supportive in a meaningful sense will not give blind assurance. . . . Often a statement to the effect, 'Do the best you can' is more supportive than, 'I'm sure you are going to do well.' The latter statement adds to the student's burden, for not only must he fear the disappointment of not passing, but also the loss of respect in the eyes of his spouse." (p. 158)

Often the culture provides for specific rituals or other courses of action that give support as the individual attempts to deal with certain types of stress. For example, most religions provide rituals that help the bereaved through their ordeal, and in some faiths, confession and atonement help people deal with stresses related to guilt and self-recrimination.

Despite the several subjective factors that help determine how severe a specific stress is for a given individual, accurate methods now exist for assessing the severity of stress in a person's life. The chart on page 117 summarizes one approach to such assessment.

Key stresses and crises

In the course of the days and years that create a lifetime, innumerable demands are made on us. For most of us, however, only a limited number of key stresses and crises have a major effect on our lives.

Continuing stresses in a person's life. Sometimes there are key stresses in a person's life that center around a continuing difficult life situation. A person may be stuck in a boring and unrewarding job from which there is seemingly no escape, suffer for years in an unhappy and conflictful marriage, or be severely frustrated by a physical handicap or a chronic health problem.

In other instances, the continuing stress derives from a traumatic experience from which the person has never fully recovered—as in the case of some prisoners of war who endured years of imprisonment, deprivation, and torture before being released. Similarly, the unexpected or violent death of a loved one—particularly a spouse or a child—may have a lasting effect on a person's life.

Crises. The term *crisis* refers to "a limited period in which an individual or group is exposed to threats or demands which are at or near the limits of their resources" (Lazarus, 1966, p. 407). As Langsley (1972) has pointed out, crises are often especially stressful because the coping techniques we are used to depending on do not work.

A crisis might center around a traumatic divorce, or an episode of depression in which

A little South Vietnamese boy weeps over the grave of his father, who was killed in combat.

the person seriously considers suicide, or the aftermath of a serious injury or disease that forces difficult readjustments in one's self-concept and way of life. The incidence of such crises in the life of the average person is unknown—estimates range from about once every ten years to about once every two years. However, in view of the complex and rapidly changing society in which we live, the latter estimate may be the more realistic one.

In any event, the outcome of such crises has profound significance for the person's subsequent adjustment. An effective new method of coping developed during a period of crisis may be added to the person's previous repertoire of coping behaviors; or inability to deal adequately with the crisis may impair one's ability to cope effectively with similar stresses in the future because of expectation of failure. For this reason "crisis intervention"—providing psychological help in times of severe and special stress—has become an important element in contemporary approaches to treatment and prevention of abnormal behavior.

Stress patterns are unique and changing

Each individual faces a unique pattern of adjustive demands. This is true partly because of differences in the way people perceive and interpret similar situations. But objectively, too, no two people are faced with exactly the same pattern of stress. An individual's age, sex, occupation, economic status, personality makeup, competencies, and family situation help determine the demands made on him. The stress pattern a child faces will differ in many ways from that of an older person, and the stress pattern faced by a carpenter will differ from that of a business executive.

Stress patterns change with time too—both predictably, as when the individual enters different life periods, and unpredictably, as when an accident, a death in the family, or a drastic social change makes new demands. Some of these changes bring only minor stress, while others place the individual under severe or excessive stress. But regardless of severity, the stress pattern the individual faces today is somewhat different from what it was a week ago; and it will be different in the future from what it is now.

Furthermore, stresses do not usually come singly or operate independently of one another. Not only is a multiplicity of demands more stressful than just one, as we have seen, but the total pattern at any time determines the part any one stress will play and how much difficulty we are likely to have coping with it. And it is the way that we cope with stress over time that shapes the course of our lives.

Stress can be expensive

Stress is a fact of life, and reactions to stress are one way in which needed competencies are developed. Stress can be damaging, however, if it is too severe for a person's coping resources or if he believes it is and acts as if it were. Severe stress can exact high cost in terms of lowered efficiency, the depletion of adaptive resources, wear and tear on the system, and, in extreme cases, disintegration and death.

Lowering of adaptive efficiency. On a physiological level, severe stress may result in alterations that impair the body's ability to fight off invading viruses. On a psychological level, perception of threat brings a narrowing of the perceptual field and increased rigidity of cognitive processes so that it becomes difficult or impossible for the individual to see the situation from a different perspective or to perceive the range of alternatives actually available. This process often appears to be operative in suicidal behavior.

Our adaptive efficiency may also be impaired by the intense emotions that commonly accompany severe stress. Acute stage fright may disrupt the performance of a public speaker; "examination jitters" may lead to a poor performance despite adequate preparation; in a sudden catastrophe, intense fear may cause the individual to panic or freeze. In fact, high levels of fear, anger, or anxiety may lead not only to impaired performance but to disorganization of behavior.

Lowering of resistance to other stresses. In using its resources to meet one severe stress, the organism may suffer a lowering of tolerance for other stresses. The Canadian physiologist Hans Selye (1956, 1969) has found that mice exposed to extremes of cold developed increased resistance to the cold but became unusually sensitive to X rays. Similarly, soldiers who develop resistance to combat may show a lowering of tolerance to other stresses, such as viral infections or bad news from home.

It appears that the coping resources of the system are limited; if they are already mobilized to capacity against one stress, they are not available for coping with others. This helps explain how sustained psychological stress can lower biological resistance to disease, and how sustained bodily disease can lower resistance to psychological stress. Interestingly, prolonged stress may lead to either pathological over-responsiveness to stress—as illustrated by the "last straw" response—or to pathological insensitivity to stress, as in loss of hope and extreme apathy.

In general, it would appear that severe and sustained stress on any level leads to a serious reduction in the overall adaptive capacity of the organism.

Wear and tear on the system. Probably most of us believe that even after a very stressful experience, rest can completely restore us. In his pioneering studies of stress, however, Selye has found evidence to the contrary:

"Experiments on animals have clearly shown that each exposure leaves an indelible scar, in that it uses up reserves of adaptability which cannot be replaced. It is true that immediately after some harassing experience, rest can restore us almost to the original level of fitness by eliminating acute fatigue. But the emphasis is on *almost*. Since we constantly go through periods of stress and rest during life, just a little deficit of adaptation energy every day adds up–it adds up to what we call *aging*." (1956, pp. 274–75)

Later studies have strongly supported Selye's findings and also indicate that, in general, symptom intensity is directly related to the severity of the adjustive demand placed on the organism (Coleman, 1973; Uhlenhuth & Paykel, 1973).

Measuring and relating life stress to physical and mental disorders

Holmes and his colleagues (1967, 1970) have developed the Social Readjustment Rating Scale (SRRS), an objective method for measuring the cumulative stress to which an individual has been exposed over a period of time. This scale measures life stress in terms of "life change units" (LCU) involving the following events.

Events	Scale of Impact
Death of spouse	100
Divorce	73
Marital separation	65
Jail term	63
Death of close family member	63
Personal injury or illness	53
Marriage	50
Fired at work	47
Marital reconciliation	45
Retirement	45
Change in health of family member	44
Pregnancy	40
Sex difficulties	39
Gain of new family member	39
Business readjustment	39
Change in financial state	38
Death of close friend	37
Change to different line of work	36
Change in number of arguments with spouse	35
Mortgage over $10,000	31
Foreclosure of mortgage or loan	30
Change in responsibilities at work	29
Son or daughter leaving home	29
Trouble with in-laws	29
Outstanding personal achievement	28
Wife begins or stops work	26
Begin or end school	26
Change in living conditions	25
Revision of personal habits	24
Trouble with boss	23
Change in work hours or conditions	20
Change in residence	20
Change in schools	20
Change in recreation	19
Change in church activities	19
Change in social activities	18
Mortgage or loan less than $10,000	17
Change in sleeping habits	16
Change in number of family get-togethers	15
Change in eating habits	15
Vacation	13
Christmas	12
Minor violations of the law	11

For persons who had been exposed in recent months to stressful events that added up to an LCU score of 300 or above, these investigators found the risk of developing a major illness within the next two years to be very high, approximately 80 percent.

When pressure is severe and long continued, physiological mobilization may become chronic and in time lead to irreversible pathology in bodily organs—ranging from peptic ulcers and high blood pressure to heart attacks or strokes. In some individuals sustained or very severe stress appears to lead to chemical changes in the blood that interfere with brain functioning and seriously impair the individual's ability to think, feel, and act in an integrated manner.

Later in this chapter we shall describe the stages of personality disorganization or decompensation that may occur under excessive stress. Suffice it to note here that severe stress can exact high costs indeed from the human system.

Reactions to Life Stress

Since stress—beyond a minimal level—threatens the well-being of the organism, it engenders automatic, persistent attempts at its resolution; it forces a person to do something about it. What is done depends on many factors, including one's frame of reference, motives, competencies, stress tolerance, environmental limitations and supports, prior mental set, and social demands and expectations. Sometimes inner factors play the dominant role in determining one's stress reactions; at other times environmental conditions are of primary importance. Any stress reaction, of course, reflects the interplay of a combination of *inner* and *outer determinants*—some more influential than others, but all working together to make the individual react as he does.

In this section we will begin by considering some general principles of adjustive behavior; then we will examine the particular characteristics of both task-oriented and defense-oriented coping patterns; and finally we will conclude this chapter with a brief review of the types and stages of decompensation under excessive stress.

General principles of adjustive behavior

In reviewing certain general principles that underlie stress reactions, we shall again find it convenient to utilize the concept of three interactional levels. Thus, on a biological level there are immunological defenses against disease, and damage-repair mechanisms; on a psychological and interpersonal level there are learned coping patterns and self-defenses; and on a sociocultural level there are group resources, such as labor unions, religious organizations, and law-enforcement agencies.

The failure of coping efforts on any of these levels may seriously impair an individual's adjustment on other levels. For example, a breakdown of immunological defenses against disease may impair not only bodily functioning but psychological functioning as well; chronic malfunctioning of psychological coping patterns may lead to peptic ulcers or other "diseases of adaptation"; and the failure of a group on which one depends may seriously interfere with ability to satisfy basic needs.

Reactions are holistic. We have seen that living organisms tend to maintain their integrity or "wholeness." Basic to this integration of behavior are the neural processes of *excitation* and *inhibition*.

Since all of an individual's adjustive behavior must use the same bodily equipment—sense organs, nervous system, glands, muscles, and so on—the overall adjustive demands of the moment will determine how it is used. If there are several competing demands, the one that is most important, or is perceived as most important, will commandeer the organism's adjustive resources, and some functions or actions will be inhibited while others are facilitated.

This coordination is well illustrated by emergency emotional reactions—for example, in a combat situation. Here, digestive and other bodily processes that are not immediately essential for survival are slowed down or stopped, while the organism's resources for increased activity and effort are mobilized—with the heightening of muscle tonus, the releasing of stored sugar into the bloodstream, and the secretion of adrenalin—a key agent in helping the body to tolerate stress.

In general, the processes of excitation and inhibition provide the organism with the flexibility it needs for dealing with stress. Only under unusual or pathological conditions does the organism function "segmentally" rather than as an integrated unit. Such segmental actions may occur as a consequence of interference with the integrating functions of the higher brain centers by alcohol, drugs, or brain damage; or it may occur as a consequence of excessive psychological stress which leads to behavior disorganization.

Reactions are economical. Not only does an individual react to stress as an integrated unit, but he responds in a way that entails a minimum expenditure of resources. This, of course, is what we might expect in view of the organism's tendencies toward self-maintenance. One's needs and goals are many, but one's resources, while impressive, are limited.

J. G. Miller (1965) has pointed out that organisms that survive—whether they are low or high on the evolutionary scale—tend to employ first those defenses that are least expensive; if these are ineffective, then additional and more expensive resources are brought into operation. If a continuously increasing amount of acid is injected into a dog's veins, for example, the first defense mechanism that appears is overbreathing. If this does not prove effective, more drastic protective mechanisms, such as biochemical changes in the blood, are employed. Similarly, if a general finds a squad too small to achieve a military objective, he may commit a company or a regiment, but at an increasing cost in resources.

The principle of economy is also relevant in a slightly different context. The individual tends to maintain his existing patterns of thought and action not only because they provide a basic source of security in dealing with the world but also because less effort is required to follow established patterns than to modify them or adopt new ones. This tendency to resist change in established ways of perceiving and acting has been referred to as *inertia* on the individual level and as *cultural lag* on the social level. These concepts help us understand the tendency of maladaptive behavior patterns to persist long after new, more effective patterns have become available.

Reactions may be automatic or planned. Reactions to stress situations may be undertaken with conscious planning, with only partial awareness, or with no conscious involvement at all. In general, an individual's potentials for conscious and automatic functioning represent complementary resources for meeting adjustive demands.

On a biological level, the repair of damaged tissue, immunological defenses against disease, and other corrective and defensive processes take place automatically. Some psychological tension-reducing and repair mechanisms such as crying and repetitive talking also take place automatically. Even if the individual is aware of what he is doing, such responses are not usually planned or consciously thought out. Seeing what one wants to see, screening out or distorting threatening information, and repressing painful experiences are other examples of automatic and mainly unconscious processes. Automatic functioning on a psychological level also commonly takes the form of habits, in which responses that were once conscious and planned no longer require the individual's attention.

Automatic functioning can be a boon in processing routine stresses, since it frees one's attention for problems that require careful thought. It is apparent, however, that automatic behavior can also impair effective adjustment. A person who unthinkingly employs habitual patterns of response in coping with a marital problem, for instance, is clearly reducing the chances that the problem will ever be satisfactorily resolved. In all but routine situations, the ability to adapt effectively depends on conscious effort and the flexibility to choose an appropriate response.

Reactions have emotional components. The particular emotional states accompanying reactions to stress may vary greatly from positive emotions, such as elation, to negative emotions, such as depression. Three emotional patterns are of special significance here: anger, fear, and anxiety.

1. *Frustration tends to elicit anger.* Frustrating conditions often elicit anger accompanied by a tendency to attack and remove the obstacle to one's goals. Where frustration continues, anger may blend into a more enduring attitude of hostility, characterized by feelings of wanting to hurt or destroy the person viewed as the source of frustration. Anger and aggressive feelings may or may not be carried out in aggressive action depending on past learning, probable consequences, and other factors. Where anger is intense, however, and the individual's inner controls are poorly developed or temporarily lowered by alcohol or other conditions, the result may be impulsive behavior of a destructive nature, such as assault or homicide.[8]

---

[8]The role of anger and aggression in human behavior has been ably presented by Bandura (1973) and Berkowitz (1974).

2. *Danger tends to elicit fear.* The perception of danger tends to arouse fear and to impel the individual toward withdrawal or flight. However, the nature of the stress situation and the degree of fear elicited have much to do with the direction and quality of resulting behavior. In the face of extreme danger, the individual may panic or "freeze" and become unable to function in an organized manner. Such behavior is commonly observed in fires and other disasters.

3. *Threat tends to elicit anxiety.* Although closely related to fear, anxiety is a feeling of impending threat in which the specific nature of the danger is often not clearly perceived. Many stress situations—such as the possibility that one's marriage will end in divorce—may give rise to both fear and anxiety. Stress situations inducing anxiety are often difficult to cope with since the precise nature of the threat is usually unclear to the individual, yet the anxiety or "psychic pain" demands some sort of protective action. As we shall see, the defenses mustered to cope with anxiety may run the entire gamut of abnormal behavior.

Anger, fear, and anxiety may be aroused singly or in various combinations. Where fear is aroused, anger often follows, for the things we fear are usually actual or potential sources of frustration. These so-called negative emotions may be intermeshed with more positive ones such as love, as when a person has *ambivalent* feelings toward a parent or mate. The specific emotions that occur are heavily influenced by past learning and by the perceived significance of the stress situation to the individual.

Reactions may be task-oriented or defense-oriented. In coping with stress, a person is confronted with two problems: (a) to meet the requirements of the adjustive demand, and (b) to protect the self from psychological damage and disorganization. When the person feels competent to handle a stress situation, his behavior tends to be *task-oriented*—that is, aimed primarily at dealing with the requirements of the adjustive demand. But when his feelings of adequacy are seriously threatened by the adjustive demand, his reactions tend to be *defense-oriented*—aimed primarily at protecting the self from hurt and disorganization.

Since the distinction between task-oriented and defense-oriented reactions is crucial to the understanding of abnormal behavior, we shall deal with these patterns in some detail in the following sections.

Task-oriented reaction patterns

Since task-oriented reactions are aimed at meeting the demands of the stress situation, they tend to be based on an objective appraisal of the situation, to be rational and constructive, and to be consciously directed. The typical steps in reacting to stress—whether the reaction turns out to be effective or ineffective—are generally flexible enough to enable the individual to change course.

Task-oriented reactions may involve making changes in one's self or one's surroundings or both, depending on the situation. The action may be overt—as in showing one's spouse more affection; or it may be covert—as in lowering one's level of aspiration. And the action may involve attacking the problem directly, withdrawing from it, or trying to find a workable compromise.

Attack. In attack behavior, the individual tries to remove or surmount obstacles to his goals. The possible ways of attacking a problem are legion; they range from obvious actions, such as physical assault or learning new skills, to subtle means, such as patience or passive resistance. The type of stress may influence the particular form that an attack reaction takes.

1. *Frustration and direct action.* In the face of frustration, a person often tries to take direct action in an effort to solve the problem and remove the obstacle. Such responses are apparently based on tendencies of living organisms toward increased activity and variation in mode of response when obstacles are encountered. For example, if someone is failing on a job, he may exert greater effort and go about systematically trying to improve his skills.

2. *Conflict and choice.* In conflict situations, the individual can attack the problem by analyzing the advantages and disadvantages of various options and making an objective, informed decision. Sometimes, however, when there are many unknowns, the best solution may come through keeping one's options open. Thus a woman trying to decide between several eligible partners may postpone the decision as long as possible in order to ascertain the best course of action and avoid a premature choice.

3. *Pressure and resistance.* Usually the individual resists undue pressure, especially when the pressure is seen as arbitrary and unwarranted. Children, for example, often develop highly effective techniques for coping with perfectionistic parents or teachers. Defiance and rebellion are active forms of resistance, but there are passive forms too, such as inattention, dawdling, helplessness, and deliberate underachievement. Resistance to pressure is an attempt by the organism to maintain its own integrity and to be in control of its own actions.

When appropriate to the situation and the resources of the individual, an attack approach usually offers the best channel for using and coordinating resources in constructive action. However, attack behavior may be destructive as well as constructive. With anger and hostility, there is a tendency to destroy as well as attack—a tendency that may lead to socially disapproved and self-defeating behavior.

Withdrawal. Simple withdrawal is a second type of task-oriented reaction to stress. Many animals seem capable of fairly well-coordinated withdrawal or flight reactions shortly after birth, but the human infant lacks such built-in patterns. However, the infant is able to withdraw a hand or foot from a painful stimulus, such as a hot object, and when subjected to sudden, unexpected stimuli may tend to curl up into a ball, apparently manifesting a primitive type of fear reaction.

In addition to withdrawing from danger physically, the individual may withdraw in various psychological ways—for example, by admitting defeat, avoiding certain types of adjustive demands, or reducing emotional involvement in a situation and becoming apathetic. In these ways the individual can exercise considerable control over the nature and degree of stress to which he is exposed and thus keep pressures and other stresses from becoming excessive.

Attack and withdrawal—fight and flight—are fundamental forms of coping with stress found in all animals. They appear to be part of the organism's built-in evolutionary heritage. Attack helps the organism to overcome obstacles and attain goals necessary to its survival; withdrawal serves to remove the organism from dangerous situations it cannot overcome. However, the most common emotion accompanying withdrawal is fear, which can lead to panic and other maladaptive behavior.

Compromise. Since most stress situations cannot be dealt with successfully by either direct attack or withdrawal, it usually becomes necessary to work out some sort of compromise solution. This approach may entail changing one's method of operation, accepting substitute goals, or working out some sort of accommodation in which one settles for part of what was initially wanted.

Individuals faced with starvation may compromise with their consciences and steal "just this one time"; or they may ignore their squeamishness and eat worms, bugs, spiders, or even human flesh. A related form of compromise is the acceptance of substitute goals under conditions of severe frustration. Thus a prisoner may gain some sexual satisfaction from pinup pictures or from wish-fulfilling daydreams. In fact, Masserman (1961) has shown that under sustained frustration individuals usually become increasingly willing to accept substitute goals—both symbolic and nonsymbolic ones.

When compromise reactions succeed in meeting the essential requirements of the stress situation, the problem is resolved and the person can go on to other activities. From time to time, however, each of us is likely to make compromises that we cannot fully accept and live with because important needs continue to go unmet. In such instances, additional adjustive action is required.

While a task-oriented approach usually offers the best chance of resolving the stress situation, it is by no means infallible. Inaccurate information, faulty values, and poor judgment can lead to unsuitable and maladaptive reactions. And even if we choose well and act

with skill, factors beyond our control may tip the balance against us. As the poet Burns put it so succinctly:

"The best-laid schemes o' mice an' men,
    Gang aft agley,
An' lea'e us nought but grief an' pain
    For promis'd joy!"

Task-oriented reactions of all three types—attack, withdrawal, and compromise—involve the same basic steps: (a) defining the problem, (b) working out alternative solutions and deciding on an appropriate course of action, and (c) taking action and evaluating the feedback. Perhaps the most difficult step in this sequence is that of decision making, or choice.

Even if the individual suffers a setback in dealing with severe stress or a crisis situation, the results may not be entirely negative if feedback is utilized in a task-oriented way. For example, the person who is going through a traumatic divorce may gain a better understanding of himself and improve on his competencies for the sake of future intimate relationships.

Defense-oriented reaction patterns

Defense-oriented reactions to stress, as we have noted, are aimed chiefly at protecting the self from hurt and disorganization.

Two types of defense-oriented reactions are commonly differentiated. The first consists of responses such as crying, repetitive talking, and mourning that seem to function as psychological damage-repair mechanisms. The second type consists of the so-called ego or self-defense mechanisms, such as denial and rationalization, that function to relieve tension and anxiety and to protect the self from hurt and devaluation.

In our present discussion, we shall focus on certain common ego-defense mechanisms in which learning ordinarily plays a key role. These defense reactions protect the individual from both external threats, such as devaluating failures, and internal threats, such as guilt-arousing desires or actions. They appear to protect the self in one or more of the following ways: (a) by denying, distorting, or restricting the individual's experience; (b) by reducing emotional or self-involvement; and (c) by counteracting threat or damage. Often, of course, a given defense mechanism may offer more than one kind of protection.

Each of us uses such defense mechanisms to some extent—singly and in various combinations—for coping with the problems of living. In fact, Gleser and Sacks (1973) have concluded that a person tends to be fairly consistent in the specific use of such mechanisms. While these reactions may serve useful defensive functions, they usually involve some measure of self-deception and reality distortion; they may be maladaptive in terms of realistically coping with adjustive demands. For these reasons, ego-defense mechanisms are considered maladaptive when they become the predominant means of coping with stress.

Ego-defense mechanisms. Since there are numerous ego-defense mechanisms, we shall review only those that seem immediately relevant to an understanding of abnormal behavior.

1. *Denial of reality.* Probably the simplest and most primitive of all self-defense mechanisms is denial of reality, in which an attempt is made to "screen out" disagreeable realities by ignoring or refusing to acknowledge them. The tendency toward perceptual defense, discussed earlier, is part of this inclination to deny or avoid reality. One may turn away from unpleasant sights, refuse to discuss unpleasant topics, faint when confronted with a traumatic situation, deny criticism, or become so preoccupied with work that there is no time to deal with marital, child-rearing, or other personal problems. Under extreme conditions, such as imprisonment, an individual may experience the feeling that "This isn't really happening to me." Here the defensive reaction appears, at least temporarily, to provide insulation from the full impact of the traumatic situation. Similarly, in a study of persons with severe illness, Hamburg and Adams (1967) reported that:

"At first there are efforts to minimize the impact of the event. During this acute phase there tends to be extensive denial of the nature of the illness, its seriousness, and its probable consequences." (p. 278)

2. *Fantasy.* By means of this mechanism, frustration is overcome by the imaginary achievement of goals and meeting of needs. Two common varieties of wish-fulfilling fantasy are the *conquering hero* and *suffering hero* patterns. In the first, one may picture oneself as a great world leader, a courageous astronaut, a celebrated athlete, a famous movie or television star, or other renowned figure who performs incredible feats and wins the admiration of all—the idea being that the individual is capable, powerful, and respected. Frequently hostility is dissipated safely through conquering-hero fantasies in which all who stand in one's way are destroyed or punished. Such fantasies act as safety valves and provide some measure of compensatory gratification for the individual.

In the *suffering hero* pattern, no admission of personal inferiority is necessary, since one is suffering from some dread disease, debilitating handicap, or visitation from unjust fate. When others find out about such difficulties and realize the bravery and courage it took to carry on under such conditions, they will be sympathetic and admiring. Thus, inferior performance or failures are explained away without any threat to one's feelings of adequacy and worth.

3. *Repression.* This is a defense mechanism by means of which threatening or painful thoughts and desires are excluded from consciousness.[9] Although it has often been referred to as "selective forgetting," it is more in the nature of selective remembering. For although the material that is repressed is denied admission to conscious awareness, it is not really forgotten. The soldier who has seen his best friend's head blown off by shrapnel may find the experience so terribly painful that he excludes it from consciousness and becomes "amnesic" with regard to the battle experience. When brought to an aid station, he may

---

[9]Repression may be distinguished from suppression in that it occurs without the awareness or conscious intent of the individual. In suppression, the individual *consciously* decides not to express a feeling or even think about a disturbing event. A critical review of the concept of repression may be found in Holmes (1974).

"Built-in" psychological coping and damage-repair mechanisms

There appear to be a number of coping and damage-repair mechanisms built into the human system which operate on a psychological level. While learning may influence these reaction patterns, they appear to operate automatically and to be part of the coping resources of human beings. Among the more common and important of these mechanisms are the following:

Crying.	"Crying it out" seems to be a common means of alleviating emotional tension and hurt. This reaction is commonly seen in children who have been frustrated or hurt, but it is not uncommon among adults. This pattern is particularly apparent as part of the "grief work" one goes through to regain emotional equilibrium after a period of bereavement for the loss of a loved one.
Talking it out.	This pattern is so widely used that its importance is often overlooked. Yet people who have undergone traumatic experiences seem to have a need to repetitively tell others about the experience as a means of alleviating tension and desensitizing themselves to the point where the experience can be accepted as something in the past and integrated into the self-structure.
Laughing it off.	Viewing setbacks and hurts with a sense of humor and trying to joke about them and laugh them off is another common damage-repair mechanism. In essence this pattern appears to both alleviate emotional tension and also help the individual see the experience in a broader perspective. Historically this reaction has been emphasized in the role of the clown who presumably laughs to cover his inner sadness; in fact, when this mechanism fails, the individual often bursts into tears.
Seeking support.	In times of stress, infants often put their arms around their mothers and cling to them for protection and support. On an adult level, we see the same pattern in more sophisticated form, as in the increased need of critically ill patients for affection and companionship. But even in less severe stress situations, many people turn to others for emotional support until they can regain their own equilibrium.
Dreaming and nightmares.	Individuals who have undergone highly traumatic experiences—for example, severe earthquakes, fires, airplane crashes, or other civilian catastrophes—often report repetitive dreams or nightmares in which they relive the traumatic experience. As in the case of repetitive talking, this pattern appears to desensitize the individual to the traumatic experience so that he can accept it as something in the past and integrate it into his self-structure without undue disruption.

These built-in reaction patterns may be used in varying degrees and combinations depending on the individual, the social setting, and the nature of the traumatic event which resulted in the psychological hurt or damage.

Adapted in part from Coleman and Hammen (1974).

be nervous and trembling, unable to recall his name or what has happened to him, and manifesting other signs of his ordeal. But the intolerable battle experience, screened from consciousness, may be brought into awareness by means of hypnosis or sodium pentothal interviews.

Repression is an extremely important self-defense mechanism in that it affords protection from sudden, traumatic experiences until time has somewhat desensitized the individual to the shock. Repression may also help the individual to control dangerous and unacceptable desires—and at the same time alleviate the anxiety associated with such desires. The reality of repression in freeing the individual from anxiety has been demonstrated in an interesting study by Sommerschield and Reyher (1973). They induced posthypnotic conflicts in their subjects and found that various symptoms, including gastric distress, tension, and anxiety, appeared as the hypnotically induced repression weakened and the conflict threatened to enter consciousness.

Repression, in varying degrees, enters into many other defense mechanisms. There is some evidence that it is only when repression fails that stronger, more maladaptive defenses are tried.

4. *Rationalization.* Rationalization is justifying maladaptive behavior by faulty logic or ascribing it to noble motives that did not in fact inspire it. Rationalization has two major defensive values: (a) it helps justify specific behaviors; and (b) it aids in softening the disappointment connected with unattainable goals.

Typically, rationalization involves thinking up logical, socially approved reasons for past, present, or proposed behaviors. With a little effort a person may be able to justify to himself spending money needed for essentials on lavish entertainment, neglecting work for cultural pursuits, or marrying someone whom he does not love. Even callous brutality can be rationalized as necessary or even praiseworthy. Adolf Hitler saw the extermination of the Jews as his patriotic duty.

Curiously enough, as Erich Fromm (1955) has pointed out:

"However unreasonable or immoral an action may be, man has an insuperable urge to rationalize it— that is, to prove to himself and to others that his action is determined by reason, common sense, or at least conventional morality." (p. 65)

Rationalization is also used to soften the disappointment of thwarted desires. A common example of such rationalization is the "sour grapes" reaction—stemming from Aesop's fable of the fox who, unable to reach a cluster of delicious grapes, decided he did not want them after all because they were probably sour. Similarly, students may justify their mediocre college performance on the grounds that they are refusing to get involved in the "competitive rat race" of modern society. One way of reducing the discrepancy embodied in failure to take action toward a desired goal is to decide that the goal is really not anything worth having anyway.

Frequently, of course, it is difficult to tell where an objective consideration of realities leaves off and rationalization begins. Behaviors that commonly indicate rationalization are (a) hunting for reasons to justify one's behavior or beliefs; (b) being unable to recognize inconsistencies or contradictory evidence; and (c) becoming upset when one's "reasons" are questioned. Such questioning is a threat to the defenses the individual has managed to construct against self-devaluation.

5. *Projection.* Projection is a defensive reaction by means of which (a) others are seen as responsible for one's own shortcomings, mistakes, and misdeeds; and (b) others are seen as responsible for one's unacceptable impulses, thoughts, and desires.

Projection is perhaps most commonly evidenced by the first tendency. The student who fails an examination may feel that the teacher was unfair; the delinquent teen-ager may blame her problems on a rejecting and nonunderstanding parent; and even the small boy being punished for fighting may protest, "It wasn't my fault—he hit me first." Fate and bad luck are particularly overworked objects of projection. Even inanimate objects are not exempt from blame. The three-year-old who falls off a hobby horse may attack it with blows and kicks; the basketball player who slips may return to inspect the alleged slippery spot. In extreme cases, an individual may become convinced that other persons or forces are systematically working against him. Such ideas may develop into delusions of persecution involving the supposed plots and conspiracies of "the enemy."

In other projective reactions, the individual attributes his own unacceptable desires and thoughts to others. This tendency appears to be particularly common among those with rigid moral values and strict conscience development. For example, a man who is sexually attracted to children may insist that a child is behaving seductively toward him. Consequently, the child becomes the offender, while the man remains conveniently "pure," unaware of his own unacceptable inclinations.

6. *Reaction formation.* Sometimes an individual protects himself from dangerous desires by not only repressing them, but actually developing conscious attitudes and behavior patterns that are just the opposite. Thus he may conceal hate with a facade of love, cruelty with kindness, or desires for sexual promiscuity with moralistic sexual attitudes and behavior. In this way the individual erects obstacles or barriers that reinforce his repression and keep his real desires and feelings from conscious awareness and from being carried out overtly.

On a simple level, reaction formation is illustrated by the old story about the spinster who looks hopefully under her bed each night for fear that a man may be lurking there. On a more complex level, reaction formation may be manifested by people who crusade against loose morals, alcohol, "pornography," gambling, and other real or alleged evils. Often such people have a background of earlier difficulties with these problems themselves, and their zealous crusading appears to be a means of safeguarding themselves against recurrence of their difficulties.

Self-appointed protectors of the public morals may gain vicarious satisfaction—for example, by reviewing "pornographic" materials—without endangering their self-concepts. In some cases reaction formation is more subtle, as when, say, a juror demands the severest penalty under the law for an infraction that he himself has been tempted to commit.

Reaction formation, like repression, may have adjustive value in helping the individual maintain socially approved behavior and avoid awareness of threatening and self-devaluating desires. But because this mechanism, too, is self-deceptive and not subject to conscious control, it often results in exaggerated and rigid fears or beliefs that may complicate an individual's adjustive reactions and lead to excessive harshness or severity in dealing with the lapses of others.

7. *Displacement.* In displacement there is a shift of emotion or symbolic meaning from a person or object toward which it was originally directed to another person or object. Often displacement involves difficult emotions, such as hostility and anxiety. A common subject for cartoons about displacement is the meek office clerk who has been refused a raise by his domineering boss. Instead of expressing his hostility toward his employer—which would be dangerous—he goes home and snaps irritably at his wife because dinner is a few minutes late.

In some instances the individual whose hostility has been aroused by an outside person or event may turn the hostility inward, engaging in exaggerated self-accusations and recriminations, and feel severe guilt and self-devaluation. Such intropunitive reactions do protect the individual from expressing dangerous hostility toward others, but may lead to depression and even to attempted or actual suicide.

Through a process of symbolic association, displacement may become extremely complex and deviant. Swearing is commonly used as a means of discharging pent-up feelings. Destructive criticism and vindictive gossip frequently are only disguised methods of expressing hostility. In a study of skydivers, Fenz and Epstein (1969) found that the fear and anxiety associated with skydiving was displaced onto other situations unrelated to parachuting. "It is as if the jumper were saying: 'This feeling of fear that I have, it is of other things, not parachuting'" (p. 28). This type of defensive reaction is referred to as "stimulus displacement": while the fear or anxiety remains, it is displaced to other situations.

8. *Emotional insulation.* Here the individual reduces his emotional involvement in situations that are viewed as disappointing and hurtful.

Since many disappointments are encountered in life, people usually learn to keep their anticipations within limits. Until a hoped-for event occurs, they are careful to avoid premature celebrations or to let their hopes run too high. The boy who looks foward to a date with a very attractive girl may not let himself get too excited or enthusiastic for fear she may not like him. Such reactions are well expressed in the common saying, "I didn't dare even hope."

In more extreme cases of long-continued frustration, as in chronic unemployment or prison confinement, many persons lose hope, become resigned and apathetic, and adapt themselves to a restricted way of life. Such "broken" individuals thus protect themselves from the bitter hurt of sustained frustration by becoming passive recipients of whatever life brings them. Similarly, in extreme forms of alienation the individual may become noninvolved and apathetic, feeling isolated, bewildered, and without hope. In certain mental disorders, too, such as chronic schizophrenia, there is often an extreme use of insulation that apparently protects the individual from emotional involvement in a life situation and world that have proved unbearably hurtful.

Up to a point, emotional insulation is an important means of defense against unnecessary disappointment and hurt. But life involves calculated risks, and most people are willing to take a chance on active participation. Emotional insulation provides a protective shell that prevents a repetition of previous pain, but it reduces the individual's healthy, vigorous participation in life.

9. *Intellectualization (isolation)*. This defense mechanism is related to both emotional insulation and rationalization. Here the emotional reaction that would normally accompany a painful event is avoided by a rational explanation that divests the event of personal significance and painful feeling. The hurt over a parent's death is reduced by saying that he or she lived a full life or died mercifully without pain. Failures and disappointments are softened by pointing out that "it could have been worse." Cynicism may become a convenient means of reducing guilt feelings over not living up to one's ideals. Even the verbalization of good intentions, as in a glib admission that "I should work harder" or that "I should be less selfish and more interested in the welfare of others," seems to cut off a good deal of guilt and relieve one of the necessity of positive action.

Intellectualization may be employed under extremely stressful conditions as well as in dealing with the milder stresses of everyday life. Bluestone and McGahee have found that this defense mechanism was often used by prisoners awaiting execution. They have described the pattern as follows: " 'So they'll kill me; and that's that'—this said with a shrug of the shoulders suggests that the affect appropriate to the thought has somehow been isolated" (1962, p. 395).

10. *Undoing (atonement)*. Undoing is designed to negate or annul some disapproved thought, impulse, or act. Apologizing for wrongs, repentance, doing penance, and undergoing punishment are all forms of undoing.

Undoing apparently develops out of early training in which the child learns that once he apologizes, makes some restitution, or is punished for disapproved behavior, his misdeed is negated and he can start over with a clean slate and with renewed parental approval. As a consequence of such early learning, people commonly develop methods of atoning for or undoing their misdeeds—methods to avoid or ameliorate the punishment and self-devaluation that would otherwise result. The unfaithful husband may bring his wife presents; the unethical executive may give huge sums of money to charity.

The opportunity for confession and the assurance of forgiveness in some religions appear to meet a deep human need to be able to get rid of guilt feelings and make a new beginning. As an ego-defense mechanism, however, undoing operates on an unconscious level. The individual assuages feelings of guilt by making some kind of reparation, but without conscious awareness of the intent of the action.

11. *Regression*. Regression is a defense mechanism in which one returns to the use of reaction patterns long since outgrown. When a new addition to the family has seemingly undermined his status, a little boy may revert to bed-wetting and other infantile behavior that once brought him parental attention; the

Summary chart of ego-defense mechanisms

Denial of reality. Protecting self from unpleasant reality by refusal to perceive or face it

Fantasy. Gratifying frustrated desires by imaginary achievements

Repression. Preventing painful or dangerous thoughts from entering consciousness

Rationalization. Attempting to prove that one's behavior is "rational" and justifiable and thus worthy of self and social approval

Projection. Placing blame for difficulties upon others or attributing one's own unethical desires to others

Reaction formation. Preventing dangerous desires from being expressed by exaggerating opposed attitudes and types of behavior and using them as "barriers"

Displacement. Discharging pent-up feelings, usually of hostility, on objects less dangerous than those which initially aroused the emotions

Emotional insulation. Reducing ego involvement and withdrawing into passivity to protect self from hurt

Intellectualization (isolation). Cutting off affective charge from hurtful situations or separating incompatible attitudes by logic-tight compartments

Undoing. Atoning for and thus counteracting immoral desires or acts

Regression. Retreating to earlier developmental level involving less mature responses and usually a lower level of aspiration

Identification. Increasing feelings of worth by identifying self with person or institution of illustrious standing

Introjection. Incorporating external values and standards into ego structure so individual is not at their mercy as external threats

Compensation. Covering up weakness by emphasizing desirable trait or making up for frustration in one area by overgratification in another

Acting-out. Reducing the anxiety aroused by forbidden or dangerous desires by permitting their expression.

young bride may return home to her mother at the first sign of trouble.

The developmental process from dependence to independence is by no means an easy one. Consequently, it is not surprising that in the face of severe stress or new challenges, an individual may retreat to a less mature level of adjustment. We might expect something akin to regression to occur merely on the basis of the frequent failure of newly learned reactions to bring satisfaction. In looking for other, more successful modes of adjustment, it would be only natural to try out discarded patterns that previously had brought satisfaction.

However, regression is a more comprehensive reaction than merely trying out older modes of response when new ones have failed. For in regression the individual retreats from reality to a less demanding personal status—one that involves lowered aspirations and more readily accomplished satisfactions. This point is well illustrated by Bettelheim's reference to a general "regression to infantile behavior" seen in nearly all the prisoners at the Nazi concentration camps of Dachau and Buchenwald.

"The prisoners lived, like children, only in the immediate present: . . . they became unable to plan for the future or to give up immediate pleasure satisfactions to gain greater ones in the near future. . . . They were boastful, telling tales about what they had accomplished in their former lives, or how they succeeded in cheating foremen or guards, and how they sabotaged the work. Like children, they felt not at all set back or ashamed when it became known that they had lied about their prowess." (1943, p. 443)

In our discussion of the psychoses, we shall describe patients whose regression is so extreme that they are no longer able to dress, feed, or otherwise take care of themselves.

12. *Identification.* Identification often takes place in imitative learning, as when a boy identifies with his father and uses him as a model. Identification may also operate as a defense mechanism in enhancing feelings of worth and protecting the individual against self-devaluation.

The growing child soon learns that the way in which he is evaluated by others depends heavily on his family and other group memberships. During adolescence and adulthood, the mechanism of identification is expanded to include a wide range of persons and groups. Not only does society evaluate the individual in the light of his group memberships, but he comes to evaluate himself in the light of them. Students may identify with the college they attend, and many employees identify with the power and prestige of the company for which they work. By doing so, they take as their own some of the desirable attributes of the groups to which they belong. Particularly for persons who feel basically inferior, such identifications may have important supportive and defensive value.

When feelings of adequacy and worth are based too heavily on identification with others, however, the individual becomes highly vulnerable to stress situations in which such identifications prove devaluating, for example, when the values and behavior of the group prove disillusioning, when the group suffers humiliation, or when the group is relegated to low social status. In such cases, the individual's identifications lead to self-devaluation rather than to self-enhancement. This is one reason it is difficult for an athletic coach to hold his job when his team loses consistently.

13. *Introjection.* Introjection is closely related to identification. As a defense reaction it involves the acceptance of others' values and norms as one's own even when they are contrary to one's previous assumptions. After revolutions leading to dictatorial forms of government, for example, many people introject the new values and beliefs as a protection for themselves. By internalizing the socially prescribed values and norms, they can then trust themselves to avoid behavior that would bring social retaliation and punishment.

In describing the use of introjection under extreme conditions, it is again useful to refer to the experiences of Bettelheim at the Nazi concentration camps of Dachau and Buchenwald. Under the cruel and insidious camp experiences, previous values and identifications were broken down and new norms were introjected—Nazi norms.

"A prisoner had reached the final stage of adjustment to the camp situation when he had changed his personality so as to accept as his own the values of the Gestapo. . . . old prisoners were sometimes instrumental in getting rid of the unfit, in this way making a feature of Gestapo ideology a feature of their own behavior." (1943, pp. 447–49)

Introjection has been referred to as "identification with the aggressor" and is a defensive reaction that seems to follow the principle, "If you can't beat 'em, join 'em." However, it is evident that introjection may lead to seriously distorted and maladaptive behavior.

14. *Compensation.* Compensatory reactions are defenses against feelings of inferiority and inadequacy growing out of real or imagined personal defects or weaknesses, as well as out of the individual's inevitable failures and setbacks. Such reactions may take many forms and may represent constructive, deliberate, task-oriented behavior, as in the case of an individual who attempts to overcome a physical handicap through increased effort and persistence. Demosthenes, the great orator, had to overcome early stuttering, and Wilma Rudolph, crippled and unable to walk until she was eight years old, became an Olympic track winner. Compensatory reactions of this type may be a deciding factor in success, as biographers are quick to point out.

More commonly, compensatory reactions are indirect; there is an attempt to substitute for the defect in some way or to draw attention away from it. The physically unattractive boy or girl may develop an exceptionally pleasing personality, the puny boy may turn from athletics to scholarship, and the mediocre nobody may become the Grand Imperial Potentate of some secret order. Much of the cosmetics industry has developed around minimizing undesirable facial features and emphasizing desirable ones.

Unfortunately, not all compensatory reactions are desirable. The child who feels insecure may show off to try to get more attention; the person who feels unloved and frustrated may eat too much. Some people brag about their illustrious ancestors and exaggerate their own accomplishments, while others resort to criticism or innuendoes in attempts to cut others down to their own size. In extreme cases, an individual may engage in antisocial behavior or develop eccentricities in an un-

 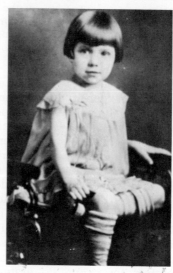 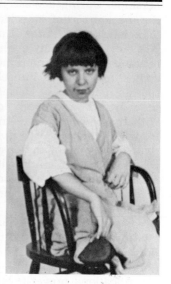

This young woman looked like an average 17-year-old girl (left) until she found the photograph of herself taken at the age of 5 (center). Thereafter, she tried to look as much as she could like the pictured child (right).

From her childhood, the girl had been the victim of an extremely contentious and unstable environment. She first showed neurotic symptoms about the age of 4, when her parents began to quarrel violently. When the girl was 7, the mother refused further sexual relations with the father, but the girl slept with the father until she was 13. The mother, suspecting incestuous seduction, obtained legal custody of the girl at this time and removed her to another home.

Resenting the separation from her father, the girl quarreled with her mother, became a disciplinary problem at school, and acquired a police record for delinquency. On the girl's insistence the mother and she visited the father after 3 years, and found him "living with a girl in questionable circumstances." A violent scene ensued, and again the mother took her daughter home, against her wishes.

After this the girl would not attend school, and she became sullen and withdrawn. In her mother's absence she would go on destructive forays of the house, and in one of these forays discovered the early picture of herself. In her subsequent behavior she "appeared to have regressed to a relatively desirable period in life antedating disruptive jealousies and other conflict; moreover, she acted out this regression in unconsciously determined but strikingly symbolic patterns of eliminating the mother as a rival and regaining the father she had lost in her childhood" (adapted from Masserman, 1961, pp. 70–71, case of Dr. John Romano).

conscious attempt to get some attention and evidence of interest and concern from others.

15. *Acting out.* Acting out is a reaction in which the individual reduces the anxiety and tension associated with dangerous desires by actually permitting their expression. For example, a person who feels mistreated and discriminated against may lash out in physical violence against those viewed as responsible. Often the damage or destruction of property, as in instances of vandalism, appears to be serving this function.

All of us have probably experienced times of acute conflict or stress when tension and anxiety have built up to such a level that almost any action that would "get it over with" is welcome. Soldiers under the stress of waiting have been known to leave their relatively safe shelter and blindly attack the enemy. But although such acting-out behavior may momentarily reduce tension and anxiety, it is obviously not well designed to deal effectively with the stress situation eliciting the anxiety. Under most circumstances acting out is not feasible except for those who have relatively weak reality and value controls; most people are deterred not only by their values but by the likelihood of social disapproval, punishment, personal injury, or other aversive results.

Evaluation of ego-defense mechanisms. These defense mechanisms are ordinarily used in combination, rather than singly, and often they are combined with task-oriented behavior. Because they are essential for softening failure, alleviating anxiety and hurt, and protecting one's feelings of adequacy and worth, we may consider them to be normal adjustive reactions unless they seriously interfere with the effective resolution of stress situations. Both the "positive" and "negative" functions of such defenses have been well illustrated in an investigation of the ego defenses used by thirty hospitalized women who were awaiting the outcome of breast tumor biopsy (Katz, et al., 1970). These researchers found the defense mechanisms of denial and rationalization to be highly effective in coping with anxiety, particularly when used in combination. They also found, however, that many of the women who allayed their anxieties with these defenses did not seek early enough medical help.

In summary, it may be emphasized that these defense mechanisms are, in the main, learned; they are designed to deal with inner hurt, anxiety, and self-devaluation; they operate on relatively automatic and habitual levels; and they typically involve some measure of self-deception and reality distortion.

Decompensation under excessive stress

When the individual's coping behavior fails to deal effectively with the stress situation, there is a lowering of integrated functioning and eventually a breakdown of the system. This lowering of integration is referred to as *decompensation.* Whether stress becomes "excessive" depends, of course, not only on the nature of the adjustive demand but also on the individual's available resources for coping with it. Decompensation has been observed on biological, psychological, and group levels.

Biological decompensation. A model that helps explain the course of biological decompensation under excessive stress has been advanced by Selye (1956, 1969) in his formulation of the general adaptation syndrome. Selye found that the body's reaction to sustained and excessive stress typically occurs in three major phases: (a) *alarm and mobilization*—representing a general call to arms of the body's defensive forces; (b) *stage of resistance*—in which biological adaptation is optimal in terms of bodily resources; and (c) *exhaustion and disintegration*—in which bodily resources are depleted and the organism loses its ability to resist so that further exposure to the stress can lead to disintegration and death.

Where decompensation does not run its entire course and result in the death of the organism, maintenance mechanisms attempt to repair damage and reorganize normal function. If the stress has resulted in extensive damage, this restorative process is often a matter of reorganizing "remaining parts and resources," but there is a permanent lowering of the previous level of integration and functioning.

Psychological decompensation. Personality decompensation under excessive stress appears to follow a course resembling that of biological decompensation.

1. *Alarm and mobilization.* At first there is an alerting of the organism and a mobilizing of resources for coping with the stress. Typically involved at this stage are emotional arousal and increased tension, heightened sensitivity and alertness (vigilance), and determined efforts at self-control. At the same time, the individual undertakes various coping measures—which may be task-oriented or defense-oriented or a combination of the two—in attempts to meet the emergency. During this stage, symptoms of maladjustment may appear, such as continuous anxiety and tension, gastrointestinal upset or other bodily manifestations, and lowered efficiency—indications that the mobilization of adaptive resources is not proving adequate.

2. *Stage of resistance.* If the stress continues, the individual is often able to find some means for dealing with it and thus to resist psychological disintegration. Resistance may be achieved temporarily by concerted task-oriented coping measures; the use of self-defense mechanisms may also be intensified during this period. Even in the stage of resistance, however, there may be indications of strain, including psychosomatic symptoms. During the stage of resistance the individual tends to become rigid and to cling to previously developed defenses rather than trying to reevaluate the stress situation and work out more adaptive coping patterns.

3. *Stage of exhaustion.* In the face of continued excessive stress, the individual's adaptive resources are depleted and the coping patterns called forth in the stage of resistance begin to fail. Now as the stage of exhaustion begins there is a lowering of integration and an introduction of exaggerated and inappropriate defensive measures. The latter reactions may be characterized by psychological disorganization and a "break with reality," involving delusions and hallucinations. These appear to represent increased disorganization in thought and perception along with a desperate effort to salvage some measure of psychological integration and self-integrity by restructuring reality. Metabolic changes that impair normal brain functioning may also be involved in delusional and hallucinatory behavior. Eventually, if the excessive stress continues, the process of decompensation proceeds to a stage of complete psychological disintegration—perhaps involving continuous uncontrolled violence, apathy, or stupor, and eventually death.

As we shall see, relatively severe psychological decompensation may be precipitated by sudden and extreme stress; but more often the decompensation is a gradual and long-range process. Typically, of course, treatment measures are instituted before decompensation runs its course. Such measures may increase the individual's adaptive capabilities or alleviate the stress situation so that the process of decompensation is reversed to *recompensation*. We shall illustrate the stress-decompensation model with case material in later chapters.

Decompensation in group life. Although science is just beginning to make inroads into the understanding of group pathology, it would appear that the concept of decompensation is just as applicable here as on biological and psychological levels. In the face of wars, economic problems, and other internal and external stresses that surpass their adjustive capabilities, societies may undergo varying degrees of decompensation, often resorting to extreme measures in their attempts to maintain their organization and resist disintegration. This process has been depicted by the historian Toynbee and other writers in their descriptions of the decline and fall of Greece, Rome, and other societies.

In completing our immediate discussion of decompensation, it may be emphasized that the outcome in a given situation—on biological and group as well as on psychological levels—depends on the extent to which any damage can be repaired and remaining resources reorganized. In some instances the functional level may be permanently lowered following excessive stress; in other cases the system may attain a higher level of integration and functioning than had existed previously.

Our primary purpose in reviewing personality development and adjustment in this chapter has been to lay the foundation for a better understanding of both normal and abnormal behavior. Toward this end, we have reviewed the primary determinants of human development; we have seen that development normally proceeds in an orderly manner through predictable stages; and we have noted that the quality of development at each stage is limited by what has gone before. We have stressed the crucial role of learning in shaping personality development and in determining the individual's resources for coping with the problems of living.

In our discussion of personality adjustment, we have dealt with our basic needs and strivings in relation to both maintenance and actualization; we have examined the nature of stress and the factors which determine its severity; and we have reviewed both task-oriented and defense-oriented coping reactions. In the final section of this chapter we noted the course of decompensation under excessive stress—on both individual and group levels.

In the chapter which follows, we shall see the application of these basic principles of personality development and adjustment to understanding the causes of abnormal behavior.

5

Causes of Abnormal Behavior

The causation of any particular behavior pattern is tremendously complex, and even with the information we do have it is all but impossible to predict how given circumstances will affect given individuals. In considering the life and achievements of Rousseau, for example, Will and Ariel Durant (1967) raise a provocative question:

"How did it come about that a man born poor, losing his mother at birth and soon deserted by his father, afflicted with a painful and humiliating disease, left to wander for twelve years among alien cities and conflicting faiths, repudiated by society and civilization, repudiating Voltaire, Diderot, the Encyclopedie and the Age of Reason, driven from place to place as a dangerous rebel, suspected of crime and insanity, and seeing, in his last months, the apotheosis of his greatest enemy—how did it come about that this man, after his death, triumphed over Voltaire, revived religion, transformed education, elevated the morals of France, inspired the Romantic movement and the French Revolution, influenced the philosophy of Kant and Schopenhauer, the plays of Schiller, the novels of Goethe, the poems of Wordsworth, Byron and Shelley, the socialism of Marx, the ethics of Tolstoi, and, altogether, had more effect on posterity than any other writer or thinker of that eighteenth century in which writers were more influential than they had ever been before?" (p. 3)

Whether or not one wholly agrees with the Durants' evaluation of Rousseau, his accomplishments seem truly remarkable when viewed against the developmental and stressful conditions of his life. Although he apparently suffered from serious emotional difficulties (see page 6), he nevertheless reached an unusually high level of achievement. His story makes clear the need for caution in interpreting the effects of given conditions in the etiology, or causal picture, of abnormal behavior. Psychology is still a long way from providing an adequate answer to the Durants' question, "How did it come about . . . ?"

Nevertheless, contemporary research findings in the biological and social sciences have greatly advanced our understanding of the causes of abnormal behavior. But before considering these causal factors, let us take a moment to broaden our perspective on causation.

Perspectives on Causation
Biological Factors
Psychosocial Factors
Sociocultural Factors

Perspectives on Causation

In our review of personality development and adjustment in Chapter 4, we established a framework for examining the causes of abnormal behavior; it can be regarded as the outcome of faulty development, severe stress, or a combination of both.

In some instances, as in the case of a child who learns criminal values and becomes a hired killer, it is faulty development that appears primarily responsible for the abnormal behavior; in other instances, as in combat fatigue, it is the overwhelming stress that ordinarily plays the dominant role. The type of adjustment we are achieving at any time is always a function of both our personality development and the level of stress we are facing. Anything that leads to either faulty development or increased stress may bring trouble.

In attempting to analyze the causal factors in abnormal behavior, we shall find it helpful to briefly review (a) differing viewpoints of causation, and (b) changing views of causal relationships.

Differing viewpoints of causation

In Chapters 2 and 3 we noted the concepts of psychopathology inherent in the medical, psychosocial, and sociocultural viewpoints. Here we shall see that each of these different viewpoints contributes to our overall picture of the etiology of abnormal behavior.

The view of causation underlying the medical model emphasizes the role of various organic conditions that can impair brain functioning and lead to psychopathology. Included here are a wide variety of conditions, ranging from syphilitic infection to drug intoxication and nutritional deficiencies. We also noted the possibility that constitutional factors may predispose some persons to specific metabolic alterations under severe stress, and that these changes may in turn impair brain functioning.

The psychoanalytic and humanistic models are concerned primarily with stress situations that involve a threat to the individual and therefore elicit anxiety, which in turn functions as both a warning of danger and an acutely unpleasant condition demanding alleviation. If the individual copes effectively with the stress situation, anxiety is eliminated; however, if the stress and anxiety continue, the individual typically resorts to various ego-defense mechanisms, such as denial and rationalization. This process of self-defense leads to an incongruence between reality and the individual's experiencing, and in extreme degree may result in lowered integration and maladaptive behavior.

Faulty learning is seen as the key cause of psychopathology in the behavioristic model, but it is also recognized as an important causal factor by all the major psychosocial models. Behaviorists assume that maladaptive behavior is the result of either (a) the failure to learn necessary adaptive behaviors or competencies, or (b) the learning of maladaptive behaviors. Delinquent behavior based on a failure to learn necessary social values and norms would be an example of the former; the phobia or fear response to the white rat learned by little Albert (page 61) would be an example of the latter.

As we have seen, the behaviorists not only emphasize failure to learn—together with aversive conditioning or other faulty learning—as causes of maladaptive behavior, but also place strong emphasis on conditions that reinforce and hence maintain the maladaptive behavior.

The humanistic and existential models believe blocked or distorted personal growth is a primary cause of psychopathology. Proponents of these models speak of maintenance vs. growth motivation, and the necessity of being and shaping one's self. If the individual is denied opportunities for personal growth and self-fulfillment, or if he fails to utilize the freedom he does have to shape his potentialities into the self he feels he should be, and to achieve a meaningful and fulfilling life, the inevitable consequences are anxiety, futility, and despair.

Included here also is the distortion of human nature—which presumably tends toward cooperative and constructive behavior—by unfavorable environmental conditions, resulting in aggression, cruelty, and other abnormal behavior.

The interpersonal model concentrates on unsatisfactory interpersonal relationships as being at the root of maladaptive behavior. Such roots may extend back to childhood, as when the child's self-concept was distorted by significant others who appraised him as being worthless, or when rigid socialization measures made it difficult to accept and integrate the "bad me" into his self-concept.

However, the primary focus of the interpersonal model is on unsatisfactory intimate relationships in adulthood. Such relationships are seen as causal factors in the development and maintenance of maladaptive behaviors on the part of one or both partners. In fact, certain pathogenic relationships are considered capable of "driving a person crazy."

The sociocultural viewpoint emphasizes the role of pathological social conditions such as poverty, racial prejudice and discrimination, and destructive violence in the development of abnormal behavior. The stresses to which an individual is exposed and the maladaptive behaviors which may develop are determined in no small part by the social context in which the individual lives.

Not only do immediate social conditions affect the nature and incidence of mental disorders in a given society, but the pattern of mental disorders changes over time as technological innovations and other conditions lead to profound alterations in society. In fact, the patterning of both physical and mental disorders changes with each major change in civilization.

Implicit in all the models is the process of psychological decompensation under excessive stress, which we discussed in the latter part of Chapter 4. We also noted there that such decompensation may occur in the face of sudden acute stress which is beyond the range of the individual's adjustive resources.

More typically, however, the process of decompensation is a gradual one that (a) is marked by the progressive depletion of an individual's adaptive resources, and (b) follows a predictable course from alarm and mobilization, through resistance, to eventual exhaustion and destruction of the organism if the process is not stopped or reversed. We also noted that such decompensation may take place on group and societal as well as biological and psychological levels.

It may be emphasized here that although we have dealt with these specific concepts of causation in terms of their distinctive features, several or all of them may be essential to understanding the etiology of a particular maladaptive pattern.

Changing views of causal relationships

In analyzing the causes of abnormal behavior it is helpful not only to keep the preceding models in mind but also to note certain more general ways of viewing causal relationships. As we shall see, these views reflect changes in contemporary scientific thought concerning causation.

Primary, predisposing, precipitating, and reinforcing causes. The *primary* cause is the condition without which the disorder would not have occurred—syphilis of the brain, in the case of general paresis. A *predisposing* cause is a condition that comes before and paves the way for later psychopathology; an example would be parental rejection. A *precipitating* cause is a condition that proves too much for the individual and "triggers" the maladaptive behavior, as in a severe disappointment in love. A *reinforcing* cause is a condition that tends to maintain maladaptive behavior already present, such as being provided with a "sick role" and being relieved of unwanted responsibility.

In a given case, the primary cause may be unknown, and the exact pattern of predisposing, precipitating, and reinforcing causes may be far from clear. And what precipitates today's "symptoms" may become a predisposing factor in tomorrow's maladaptive behavior. For example, the conditions that precipitate a

An example of the complexity of causal factors

Charles Whitman, a college student who in 1966 shot and killed 15 people—including his wife and his mother—and wounded over 30 more, presents a good example of the complexity of the causes of abnormal behavior. His childhood, while seemingly normal, was presided over by a strict, quick-tempered father whose violence eventually led to a marital separation; this separation of his parents evidently bothered Whitman, who blamed and hated his father for mistreating his mother.

A few months before his shooting rampage, Whitman had visited the school psychiatrist to discuss his feelings of violence and hostility and his fear that he would lose his temper and go "up on the tower [at the University of Texas] . . . and start shooting people." He also complained of suffering from painful headaches. After his death (he was killed by the police during the shootout), an autopsy revealed that he had a brain tumor about the size of a pecan. Some amphetamine tablets were also found among his belongings.

Exactly what precipitated Whitman's actions is not known; *Time* Magazine (August 12, 1966) predicted that "psychiatrists will undoubtedly debate the causes for years" (p. 19). But it seems possible that biological and psychosocial causes could have somehow combined so that primary and predisposing factors may, indeed, have left Charles Whitman vulnerable to whatever it was that triggered his extreme action.

schizophrenic episode today may serve as predisposing causes for a recurrence of such an episode at a later time.

In terms of our changing views of causation, however, it is the concept of reinforcing causes—conditions tending to maintain maladaptive behavior—that has received increasing emphasis.

Feedback and circularity ("vicious circles"). Traditionally in the sciences, the task of determining cause-and-effect relationships had entailed the isolation of a given condition X (cause) which leads to another condition Y (effect). For example, alcoholic intoxication occurs when the alcohol content of the blood reaches a certain level. Where more than one causal factor is involved, the term *causal pattern* is used. Here conditions A, B, C, etc., lead to condition Y. Thus, in essence, the concept of cause follows a simple linear model, in which a given variable or set of variables leads to an end result.

With the introduction of the concept of self-regulating systems, however, causation is often viewed as being more complex than a simple cause-and-effect relationship. For now the effects of *feedback* on the causal agent must also be taken into account. Consider, for example, the following situation:

A husband and wife are undergoing counseling for difficulties in their marriage. The husband accuses his wife of drinking excessively, while the wife accuses her husband of rejecting her and showing no affection. In explaining her frustrations to the therapist, the wife views the situation as "I drink because my husband rejects me"; while the husband sees the problem differently: "I reject my wife because she drinks too much."

Over time a vicious circle develops in which the husband increasingly withdraws as his wife increasingly drinks. Assuming that each contributes about equally to their mutual difficulties, it becomes extremely difficult, if not impossible, to differentiate cause from effect. Rather, the problem is one of circularity; A influences B in this interaction, and B influences A— and so on.

This hypothetical situation helps point out that new concepts of causal relationships must deal with the more complex factors of feedback loops, information exchange or communication, patterns of interaction, and circularity.

In the remainder of this chapter we shall attempt to delineate the role that several kinds of biological, psychosocial, and sociocultural factors can play in causing maladaptive behavior, either by producing faulty development (thus hampering our adjustive ability) or by increasing stress or both. This task can be approached in many ways with many different kinds of methods. In some instances, causal factors can be seen more clearly with an electron microscope; in others, with a chemical analysis; in still others, with a psychological test or a sociological survey. And although we will be discussing biological, psychosocial, and sociocultural factors separately in this chapter, we shall bear in mind that their interaction is critically important.

Biological Factors

Biological factors influence all aspects of our behavior, including our intellectual capabilities, basic temperament, primary reaction tendencies, stress tolerance, and adaptive resources. Thus a wide range of biological conditions, such as faulty genes, diseases, endocrine imbalances, malnutrition, injuries, and other conditions that interfere with normal development and functioning are potential causes of abnormal behavior.

In the present section we shall focus on five categories of biological factors that seem particularly relevant to an understanding of the development of maladaptive behavior: (a) genetic defects; (b) constitutional liabilities; (c) physical deprivations; (d) disruptive emotional processes; (e) brain pathology. Each of these categories encompasses a number of conditions that influence the quality and functional intactness of our bodily equipment.

These conditions may function in varying combinations, and they may serve as primary, predisposing, precipitating, or reinforcing causes of maladaptive behavior.

Genetic defects

Since our behavior is inevitably influenced by our biological inheritance, genetic defects are clearly a potential cause of psychopathology. The three defects of major concern are chromosomal aberrations, faulty genes, and inherited predispositions to mental disorders.

Chromosomal aberrations. Dramatic progress in the field of genetics during recent years has enabled us to detect chromosomal aberrations and to study their implications for development and behavior.

The first major breakthrough in this area was the identification of the complement of forty-six chromosomes in the nucleus of each normal living cell and the discovery that encoded in the chromosomes is the hereditary

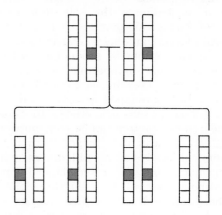

The wedding of "General" Tom Thumb and Miss Lavinia Bump in 1863 united two midgets. The groom was 38 inches tall, the bride 32 inches. Recessive genes probably caused their small stature, as suggested in the schematic drawing of chromosomes (McKusick & Rimoin, 1967). A recessive gene (color) in the paired chromosomes of both parents (top) could be combined in different ways in the paired chromosomes of their offspring (bottom). A combination of two recessive genes (third from left) would give rise to the recessive trait.

plan—the overall strategy or information for guiding development. When fertilization takes place, the normal inheritance of the new individual consists of twenty-three pairs of chromosomes—one of each pair being from the mother and one from the father. Twenty-two of these chromosome pairs are called *autosomes;* they determine body characteristics. The remaining pair, the *sex chromosomes,* determine the individual's sex and certain other characteristics. In the female, both of these sex chromosomes—one from each parent—are designated as *X chromosomes.* In the male, the sex chromosome from the mother is an X but that from the father is different and is called a *Y chromosome.*

Research in developmental genetics has shown that abnormalities in the structure or number of the chromosomes are associated with a wide range of congenital malformations and hereditary disorders. When the chromosome is deficient in specific genetic information, the result may be color blindness, hemophilia, or any of a wide range of other defects. For example, in mongolism, or *Down's syndrome*—a type of mental retardation in which the individual has slanting eyes, a flat face, and other characteristics that produce a superficial resemblance to Mongolians—investigators have discovered the presence of an extra chromosome, involving a trisomy (three instead of two) of one autosomal pair.

In a study of 2159 consecutively born babies, Sergovich et al. (1969) found a gross chromosomal abnormality rate of 0.48 percent. The exact causes of chromosomal anomalies are not yet fully understood. Some have evidently been passed on from one or both of the parents; some apparently occur in the combining of egg and sperm or from genetic mutations occurring after conception.

Females are less susceptible to defects from faulty sex chromosomes because they have two X chromosomes. Thus, if one proves faulty, the other member of the pair generally can handle the work of development. Since males have a single X chromosome paired with a single Y chromosome, a defect in either will mean trouble.

A search for chromosomal irregularities in schizophrenia and other psychoses has not proved fruitful, and none of the chromosomal anomalies thus far observed has appeared to be directly related to such disorders. Even in the case of Down's syndrome, where a trisomy in chromosome 21 has been identified, it has been estimated that 65 percent of the fetuses spontaneously abort (Creasy & Crolla, 1974). The potential effects of more gross chromosomal irregularities are largely unknown because they ordinarily result in the death of the embryo.

Faulty genes. A major breakthrough in modern genetics has been the development of ultramicroscopic techniques—for example, the combined use of the electron microscope and X-ray diffraction—which makes it possible to study the actual structure of the chromosomes. Each chromosome is made up of a long molecule of DNA (deoxyribonucleic acid) arranged in two strands linked together at regular intervals to form a double spiral, or helix, that looks like a ladder curving round and round (as shown in the illustration on p. 89). In a series of epic experiments, scientists have shown that our genetic instructions are stored in this DNA ladder, or "book."

The "sentences" in this DNA book of instructions are the genes, which follow one another like beads strung together to form a necklace. Genes carry the instructions for specific body traits, such as eye color and blood type;

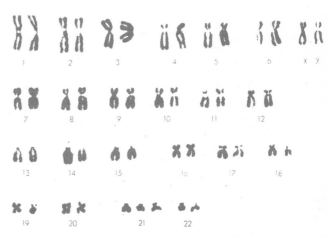

This picture of chromosomes shows an aberration involving the trisomy of chromosome 21. Most cases of Down's syndrome, a type of mental retardation, reveal 47 instead of the normal complement of 46 chromosomes.

thus, they are the specific units or bearers of an individual's genetic inheritance.

Some genes are called *dominant* genes: their instructions are followed even if the other member of the pair carries contradictory instructions. *Recessive* genes are genes whose instructions are not followed unless the individual has inherited two such genes, one from each parent.

The breaking of the genetic code has made it possible for the first time to study losses, gains, or changes of material in the gene itself, thus introducing a more precise approach to relating genetic factors to physical and mental disorders. As Dobzhansky (1960, 1972) has pointed out:

"Every one of the tens of thousands of genes inherited by the individual has a tiny probability of changing in some way during his generation. Among the small, and probably atypical, sample of human genes for which very rough estimates of the mutation frequencies are available, the rates of mutation vary from one in 10,000 to one in about 250,000. For example, it has been calculated that approximately one sex cell in every 50,000 produced by a normal person carries a new mutant gene that causes *retinoblastoma*, a cancer of the eye affecting children." (1960, p. 206)

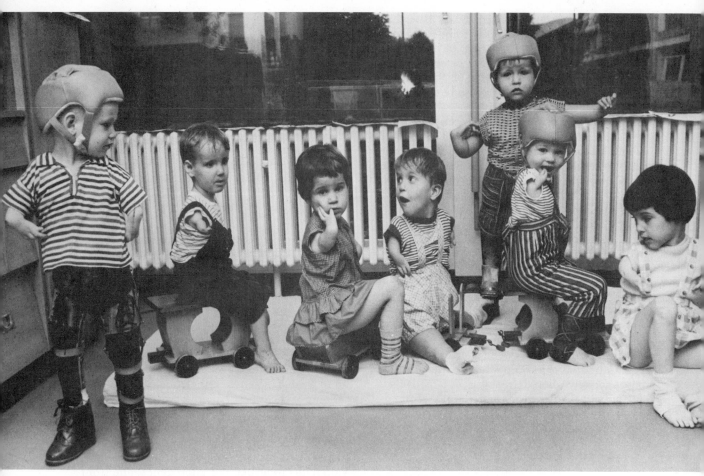

One of the most tragic examples of a mutagen-caused genetic defect in recent years is the case of the "thalidomide babies," children born to women who had taken the now-banned tranquilizing drug thalidomide during pregnancy. The defect was most commonly manifested in malformed arms and legs. The children in the picture above are being taught to use artificial limbs and their own limbs as well as possible; they wear head protection because their sense of balance may be faulty, and they cannot protect themselves if they fall.

As a consequence of such spontaneous changes, it has been estimated that the average person carries five to ten mutant genes—including more than one lethal recessive gene—along with thousands of normal ones (Levitan & Montagu, 1971; Lappe, 1973; Bergsma, 1974; Committee 17, 1975).

The incidence of gene mutations may be much higher if the individual has been exposed to special *mutagens*, such as ionizing radiation and certain drugs and chemicals, which are known to cause gene damage. Mutagens are particularly hazardous since their effects may not be immediately apparent, but may show up in future generations. For example, a higher incidence of mental retardation associated with small head circumference has been reported among the children of survivors of the nuclear bombings at Hiroshima and Nagasaki (Miller, 1969).

Although some kinds of gene mutations are relatively harmless, many are seriously detrimental to development—such as Tay-Sachs disease, sickle-cell anemia, and Huntington's chorea, described in the illustration on p. 143. There are more than 2000 known genetic defects, about one fourth of which are carried by dominant genes; they are estimated to affect about 1 percent of our population (Chapnick, 1973). The remainder are linked to recessive genes and are present in a far larger section of the population. Such genetic defects range from relatively minor ones such as red-green color blindness to serious congenital malformations, special vulnerabilities, and lethal conditions such as Tay-Sachs disease.

Genetic predisposition to specific mental disorders. Although marked advances have been made in the identification of faulty genes, most of the information we have concerning the role of genetic factors in mental disorders is based on family studies.

The family history method requires that the investigator observe a large sample of relatives of each *proband* or *index case* (the subject, or carrier of the trait in question, such as schizophrenia) in order to see whether the incidence increases in proportion to the degree of hereditary relationship. In addition, the incidence of the trait in a normal population is compared with its incidence among the relatives of index cases. This approach is well illustrated by Kallmann's (1953, 1958) statistics for schizophrenia, shown below, although his research has been challenged, and later studies have found considerably lower figures.

Degree of Relationship to Schizophrenic	Percent Who Develop Schizophrenia
Identical (one-egg) twins	86.2
Fraternal (two-egg) twins	14.5
Siblings	14.2
Half-siblings	7.1
General population	0.85

These figures indicate that the incidence of schizophrenia is much higher among all degrees of blood relationship to the schizophrenic than in the general population, and that with an increasing degree of blood relationship there is an increasing incidence—from 7.1 percent in half-siblings of schizophrenics to 86.2 percent in identical twins. Kallmann tentatively concluded from his findings that schizophrenia must be transmitted via recessive genes.

Three serious inherited disorders: Tay-Sachs disease, sickle cell anemia, and Huntington's chorea

Tay-Sachs disease is a hereditary disease of the nervous system. The afflicted infant may appear normal until about six months of age but then suffers progressive deterioration and death, usually before the age of 4. It is found mostly among Jews of Middle-European ancestry; about 1 in 30 is a carrier of this recessive gene. If two carriers have a baby, the chances are 1 in 4 that the baby will be a victim of this disease.

Sickle cell anemia is a hereditary disorder affecting the red blood cells which usually results in death between the ages of 20 and 40. It is largely confined in our society to blacks, and about 1 in 10 carries the recessive gene; about 1 in 500 actually has the disease.

Huntington's chorea is a progressive degenerative disease of the nervous system affecting involuntary movements and mental functioning. It usually appears between the ages of 30 and 50 with the classical features of the disease generally occurring at about age 38, often when the individual is at the peak of his productive life. Unlike Tay-Sachs disease and sickle cell anemia, Huntington's chorea is carried by a dominant gene: if either parent carries this gene, the child will inherit the disorder.

Fortunately, new methods of genetic detection make it possible to counsel parents concerning the risks they run in having defective children. Even after a mother is pregnant, a relatively simple test called *amniocentesis* can reveal quite accurately whether or not the fetus is normal, thus making possible the choice of an abortion. In rare instances, the genetic defect can be treated successfully in the uterus—by special dietary or other measures—before the baby is born.

Based on Dewhurst, Oliver, and McKnight (1971), Harmetz (1974), Jarvik, Yen, and Goldstein (1974), Lynch, Harlan, and Dyhrberg (1972), Nelson (1974b), and Spencer (1973).

While later studies—which we shall summarize in our discussion of schizophrenia—do not rule out the influence of genetic factors in schizophrenia, they indicate that such an influence is not as great as Kallmann's findings suggest, nor does it follow a simple recessive genetic pattern. This general viewpoint has also been extended to other mental disorders, with the exception of Huntington's chorea and a few other rare diseases of the central nervous system.

Here it may be noted that most genetic studies have failed to take into consideration the importance of early environmental conditions. In addition, it has been pointed out that even physical diseases may "run in families" without necessarily having a genetic basis. For example, what is apparently "inherited" by some children who develop beriberi—a vitamin deficiency disease accompanied by serious mental symptoms—is a preference for vitamin-poor foods, a preference acquired through learning and parental example rather than through genetic transmission.

As a consequence, most investigators now take the position that only a *predisposition* to mental disorders can be inherited. Many genes, rather than just one, may be involved in such a predisposition. Here it is presumed that certain individuals are especially prone to develop schizophrenia or some other mental disorder if placed under severe stress. Given a favorable life situation, the individual's inherent vulnerability may never show up. This position is bolstered by medical evidence concerning inherited predisposition to diabetes, high blood pressure, coronary heart disease, and some forms of cancer (Kaiser Foundation, 1970; Bergsma, 1974).

Constitutional liabilities

The term *constitution* is used to denote the relatively enduring biological makeup of the individual resulting from both genetic and environmental influences.[1] Physique, physical handicaps, and vulnerability to stress are among the many traits included in this cate-

---

[1]It may be noted that genetic defects are, in turn, translated into metabolic disorders and other constitutional liabilities.

gory. Here our focus will be on the role of these constitutional traits in the etiology of maladaptive behavior.

Physique. Since ancient times, attempts have been made to classify people into types in terms of physique and other constitutional factors and to use these classifications for predicting general personality and behavior patterns. When Shakespeare's Julius Caesar exclaims:

Let me have men about that are fat;
Sleek-headed men and such as sleep o'nights:
Yond Cassius has a lean and hungry look;
He thinks too much: such men are dangerous.
(*Act I, Scene ii*)

he expresses the age-old popular belief that plump people are more likely to be good-natured and reliable than lean ones.

Perhaps the best known of various scientific attempts to relate physique to personality and psychopathology is the early work of Sheldon and his associates (1954). As shown in the illustration on p. 145, Sheldon concluded that there are three types of body build, each associated with particular temperamental and other personality characteristics. While physique is not a primary cause of psychopathology, it does presumably influence the type of disorder the individual is likely to develop under stress. Although Sheldon's work has received limited support from later investigators—for example, Glueck and Glueck (1968) reported a higher incidence of individuals with muscular physiques among juvenile delinquents and adult criminals—most have been critical of his typology. It seems unlikely that the complexities of human development and behavior can be predicted on the basis of one relatively simple variable, especially a nonpsychological one such as physique.

However, we have only to look at everyday situations to realize that physique, including physical appearance as well as body build, does play an important role in personality development and adjustment. Beauty, for example, is highly valued in our society. One need only attend a social gathering, watch television, or note the billions of dollars spent each year on cosmetics to see the influence of beauty on people's behavior. In fact, Landy and

The influence of environment on human behavior

It is now generally agreed that human environments can be supportive or destructive; their physical characteristics can affect the way human beings behave, just as human beings can affect their environments. Even though we can't always choose or control our environments — who, for example, chooses to be caught in a traffic jam? — knowledge of the *importance* of environment can help us be more aware of destructive aspects and thus change them, and encourage development of environments that are supportive. Although most of us tend to think in terms of our own living, work, or school environments, this idea can also have ramifications for such diverse areas of environmental importance as therapeutic treatment centers and spaceship design.

An elementary but instructive picture of the difference environment makes is shown by the facial expressions on the people trapped in the car — obviously under stress — contrasted with the utter joy of the child playing in an open meadow. A different example of the importance of environment is illustrated by the urban street fair, in which people have used their surroundings to help foster a sense of community identity.

The environment of the office or factory relates not only to the type of work to be done but, equally important, also affects the state of mind of the individual worker. The worker's feelings influence his attitude toward his work, the quality of his work, and, of course, even his interpersonal relations outside of work.

The difficulty, of course, is in determining what *is* a supportive work environment, given the needs of the work to be done. Can an assembly line foster a sense of individual pride in a product, or a sense of cooperation and joint responsibility with fellow workers? Is a huge impersonal office arena indicative of a depersonalized attitude toward the workers, or does it give them a chance to confer informally, perhaps giving them a sense of control over what they do? And is cooperative teamwork, such as that evident in a rural "barn-raising," more or less conducive to a feeling of individual accomplishment and identity? Questions such as these cannot be answered simplistically, but asking them can open new ways of dealing with destructive patterns that may have been taken for granted.

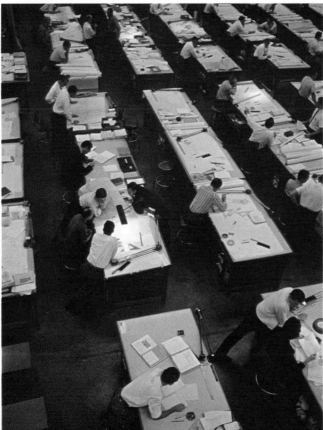

One of the most influential aspects of a child's life is the time spent in school; how the school environment is structured is bound to have an affect on the child's development and reality assumptions. For instance, the children in the formal Amish classroom will probably grow up with a different frame of reference than will the Navajo children shown watching an educational TV program. And the children in the more "typical" classroom will have yet a third viewpoint.

Again the question of value judgments is raised, and is still unanswerable. But it is hoped that experiments in classroom methods as well as insights into the needs of children will result in school environments that are conducive to the mental health and growth of each individual student.

Physique, temperament, and psychopathology

	Endomorphic	Mesomorphic	Ectomorphic
Physique	Soft, round	Strong, muscular, athletic	Slender, fragile
Temperament	Comfort-loving, sentimental, pleasure-seeking, socializing	Active, energetic, less religious, more achievement-oriented, aggressive	Sensitive, delicate, intellectual, more religious, withdrawing
Most likely psychopathology	Severe mood alternations involving extreme elation or depression (particularly the latter)	Delinquency, criminal behavior, mood alternations involving extreme elation or depression	Schizophrenia, anxiety neurosis, peptic ulcers

The work of Sheldon and his associates (1954) relating body type to personality type was widely criticized for over-simplification and for weaknesses in methodology. Subsequent studies have shown that physical characteristics may indeed be related to personality characteristics, but suggest that the relationship is much less direct than Sheldon first supposed. As Cortés and Gatti (1970) have emphasized, the fact that physique and temperament seem to be correlated does not necessarily mean that one determines the other.

Based on work of Cortés and Gatti (1970), Damon and Polednak (1967), Davidson, McInnes, and Parnell (1957), Glueck and Glueck (1962), and Sheldon et al. (1954).

Minde (1972) and his associates studied the psychological development of 41 physically handicapped children — 13 female and 28 male — during their early school years in a special school in Montreal, Canada. The following sequence and characteristics of development between the ages of 5 and 9 were highlighted:

1. The cognitive realization, triggered by separation from outside peer group members and exposure to other crippled children, that the "handicap was not going to suddenly disappear" (p. 108).

2. This realization was followed by a period of severe depression in 16 children which varied from 6 weeks to an entire year in duration. During this period, the children talked about the futility of their lives and would not do schoolwork. Some even wished not to have another birthday.

3. The gradual development of emotional readiness to see the physical handicap as part of the self, and a hesitant beginning on the part of the child to incorporate it into his self-image and life style.

During these early school years, the parents of the children appeared to be in a "continuous struggle between their wish to have a fully normal child . . . and their knowledge of the child's handicap" (p. 109). This struggle could not be described in terms of simple "acceptance" or "rejection," but appeared to be considerably more complex. "In facing this conflict of marginality, they chose either normalcy or deviance, but have not yet been able to create an identity for their children that embraces both concepts. They have either made their children into 'sick' people or else spent immense energies to give them a feeling of being 'like everyone else'" (p. 109). Unfortunately, the failure of the parents to resolve this conflict in a constructive way apparently took attention and care away from siblings of the handicapped children who showed a significant increase in behavior disorders during the period of this study.

Sigall (1974) found that judges even evaluated the quality of an essay as much higher if they thought it had been written by a physically attractive woman than if they thought it had been written by an unattractive one. Similarly, tallness, shortness, and other variations in physique influence the adjustive reactions of an individual as well as other people's reactions to him or her.

Perhaps of most significance is the view we take of our own physical appearance. A conception of one's body as being too different from the standards valued by one's group can be self-devaluating — as can dissatisfaction over changes in bodily proportions during adolescence and old age. As Hurlock (1968) has pointed out, "It is difficult for a pubescent to be self-acceptant when he is anxious and concerned about his changing body and when he is dissatisfied with the image of himself he sees reflected in the mirror" (p. 376). And in our youth-oriented culture, it is difficult for both men and women to accept the physical deterioration that comes with aging.

Physical handicaps. Robert Burton (1577–1640), in his *Anatomy of Melancholy*, wrote these poignant words: "Deformities and imperfections of our bodies, as lameness, crookedness, deafness, blindness, be they innate or accidental, torture many men. . . ." Such physical handicaps may result from genetic defects or from environmental conditions operating before or after birth.

In this country an estimated 7 out of every 100 babies are born with mental or physical defects (Solomon, 1973). About a third of these defects are considered to be hereditary; another sixth are due to drugs or disease; the rest — about half — result from unknown causes. Some of the aberrations are apparent at birth, while others — such as mental retardation, endocrine disturbances, and heart defects — may not be detected until months or years later. Often such anomalies are minor, but more serious congenital defects constitute one of the five leading causes of death during childhood, accounting for over half a million deaths annually.

Prenatal conditions that can lead to birth defects and to premature birth include nutritional deficiencies, disease, exposure to radiation, drugs, and emotional stress. The most common birth difficulty associated with later mental disorders—including mental retardation, hyperactivity, and emotional disturbances—is prematurity, which is defined as either an elapsed gestation time of less than 280 days or a birth weight of five and a half pounds or less. Mothers who are subjected to severe emotional stress during pregnancy appear to have a much higher incidence of premature deliveries. Even in the case of full-term babies, severe maternal stress appears to produce hyperactivity in the fetus during later pregnancy, and after birth to be reflected in feeding difficulties, sleep problems, irritability, and other difficulties in adjustment (Blau et al., 1963; Sontag, Steele, & Lewis, 1969). As might be expected, socioeconomic status has been found to be related to fetal and birth difficulties, the incidence being several times greater among mothers on lower socioeconomic levels.

As a consequence of such findings, it would appear that the fetus is not so well protected as many investigators formerly thought—that a variety of biological and psychological conditions affecting the mother during pregnancy can have profound effects on development and adjustment.

Accidents and disease also exact a high toll in our society. Each year accidents alone take the lives of over 100,000 persons and permanently disable approximately a million others. These figures suggest that accidental injuries are the "neglected disease" of modern civilization, often leaving in their wake physical mutilations, disrupted lives, and severe problems of adjustment.

In addition, over 20 million persons suffer from heart conditions or other serious physical impairments that may be both painful and debilitating; many of these victims are young people. In fact, figures projected by the U.S. Dept. of Health, Education, and Welfare for the 1970s indicate that one-fifth of this country's under-seventeen age group will suffer from at least one chronic physical condition that adversely affects their adjustment. When such conditions involve severe and long-continued pain, they may gradually wear down the individual's adjustive resources and lead to discouragement and even despair. Chronic dis-

ease may also reduce the individual's expected life span.

Except in the case of defects that seriously restrict one's activities, are severely disabling, or are chronically painful, however, the significance of a physical impairment depends primarily on the way the individual evaluates and adjusts to it. One of the obstacles that a handicapped person faces is the tendency to accept the role of a "cripple," which society often seems to expect and subtly encourage. This picture is often complicated by family members who either encourage such a sick role or expect performance beyond the individual's capabilities. Other common and undesirable reactions to physical handicaps are feelings of inferiority, self-pity, and hostility. As a consequence of such obstacles, the individual—whether child, adolescent, or adult—may develop psychological handicaps that are much more disabling than his physical impairment.

The effects of severe physical impairments on children are well described by Minde, Hackett, Killou, and Silver (1972), and are summarized in the box on page 146.

Vulnerability to stress. In discussing the role of heredity in development, we noted how primary reaction tendencies such as sensitivity, temperament, and activity level affect our interactions with the environment. Several investigators have attempted to relate such tendencies to stress vulnerability and maladaptive behavior.

Loving relationships may help offset a child's deficiencies, both personal and situational. Dark-haired Lisa, who is blind, lives in an atmosphere in which she is loved and encouraged to develop as fully as possible. At school she delights in participating in the same activities as the sighted children.

Shaw and Schelkun (1965) found that children and adolescents who seem most susceptible to suicide have been characterized as "highly sensitive." And in a longitudinal study of infant development, Chess and her associates (1965) found that a particular type of temperament, such as that of the "difficult baby," may predispose the individual to later maladjustment. According to this study, 7 to 10 percent of all babies are "difficult"—they evidence irregular patterns of eating, sleeping, and bowel movement; tend to cry a great deal and to show a predominantly negative mood; and are inclined to be irritable and have difficulty in adjusting to change. Since the mother does not gain the satisfactions she expected from having her baby, the temperamental difficulty becomes overlaid and complicated by an unsatisfactory mother-infant relationship, with undesirable consequences for both.

Primary reaction tendencies also include characteristic ways of reacting to stress. Some infants react to changes in routine or other stress by running a fever; others, by digestive disorders; still others, by sleeping disturbances. It would appear that a particular subsystem of the body is often especially vulnerable to stress and hence more likely to develop "symptoms" if the overall functioning of the organism is disturbed. In our discussion of hypertension and other psychosomatic disorders, we shall comment further on this tendency as well as on the vulnerability to disruption of various biochemical systems involved in brain functioning.

Physical deprivations

A wide range of physical deprivations may act as predisposing or precipitating causes in mental disorders. For our immediate purposes we shall focus briefly on two categories of these: (a) malnutrition and (b) sleep deprivation and fatigue.

Malnutrition. Severe malnutrition during infancy not only impairs physical development and lowers resistance to disease, but also stunts brain growth and results in markedly lowered intelligence (Bladeselee, 1967; Cravioto, 1975; Dobbing, 1967; Kaplan, 1972).

Often physical handicaps need not unduly curtail physical activity. These men developed enough skill in basketball to play in the 1972 Olympic Games of the Handicapped.

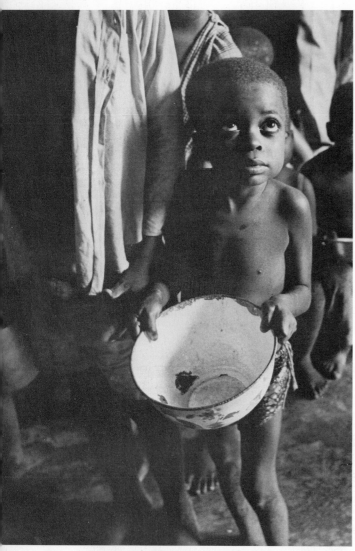

Malnutrition can affect not only the sufferer, but future generations as well. This child waits for his small allotment of food, not knowing if his condition will ever improve.

In a postmortem study of infants who died of malnutrition during their first year of life, Winick (1968) found a total brain cell content that was 60 percent below that of normal infants. Even in the case of babies who suffer severe malnutrition but survive, the stunting of brain growth is considered irreversible since the period of fastest growth of the brain is from about five months before until ten months after birth. In a random sample of areas where 75 to 80 percent of the resident families were living either in poverty or close to it, a preliminary study by the U.S. Dept. of Health, Education, and Welfare found that 15 percent of all children studied showed evidence of physical and mental growth retardation associated with malnutrition (Loyd, 1969). Malnutrition because of faulty diet is found even in families with incomes over $10,000 per year, resulting in a wide range of physical disorders and generally lowered resistance to stress (Reice, 1974). Similarly, Robinson and Winnik (1973) have reported on the relatively high incidence of psychoses and other mental disturbances among individuals who have been following a "crash diet" involving semi-starvation and rapid weight loss.

The broader social magnitude of the problem of malnutrition is indicated by estimates made in the late 1960s that some two thirds of the world's preschool children—more than 300 million—lacked sufficient protein food for minimum nutritional needs (Scrimshaw, 1969; Behar, 1968); since then conditions have not improved but have become more desperate (Brown, 1974; Sanderson, 1975). In fact, as we entered the mid-1970s it was estimated that over a fourth of the world's people suffered from malnutrition and the situation was expected to worsen in the years ahead (Knowles, 1974).[2]

One of the most sobering aspects of this world picture is the knowledge that the effects of malnutrition continue into later generations. Not only do malnourished children suffer lowered mental and physical capacity, but the children of malnourished mothers also show serious deficits.

[2]An extensive discussion of the world population explosion and of food and related problems may be found in *Scientific American*, September 1974, *231*(3).

Sleep deprivation and fatigue. In Chapter 4 we noted that symptoms of mental disorder can be produced by deprivation of sleep over a sustained period of time, and sleep disturbances are common in schizophrenia, anxiety states, and other psychopathology. In fact, two out of three hospitalized mental patients have suffered severe sleep disturbances before being hospitalized (Nelson, 1967; Adelson, 1974; Antrobus, 1974).

While sleep deprivation is a major cause of fatigue, it is by no means the only one. In order to survive and have the capacity for meeting adjustive demands, the organism must constantly renew itself not only through rest but through taking in the various nutrients needed to replace the materials being used up in the process of living. Prolonged interference with such renewal leads to physical and mental fatigue, to a reduction in the organism's resources for coping with even normal adjustive demands, and to a marked increase in vulnerability to special or severe stresses.

In everyday life we are rarely exposed to excessive and prolonged physical demands. But many of us lower our general resistance to stress through insufficient rest, inadequate diet, trying to carry a full work load under the handicap of a bad cold or other illness, and through sustained emotional mobilization. We deprive ourselves of needed adjustive resources and render ourselves more vulnerable to the stresses of life.

Disruptive emotional processes

We have noted that emotional processes like fear and anger represent the mobilization of body resources to meet emergency situations. Such a mobilization of resources enables a threatened organism either to fight or to flee more effectively. In modern civilization, however, we are rarely confronted with situations that can be met adequately by simple physical attack or flight. Yet we have not experienced a comparable reduction in our emotional excitability: we still become mobilized for physical flight or attack when we feel endangered or threatened, even though some reactions are now inappropriate and ineffective.

Mild emotions may be constructive in their overall effect by reinforcing our actions toward worthwhile goals. But as we get into the intermediate range of intensity, emotions are typically detrimental to problem solving and task performance, and, as the level of emotional tension increases, it becomes increasingly disruptive to organized behavior. For example, the typical effects of mild, intermediate, and intense levels of anxiety—a key emotion in maladaptive behavior—have been well summarized by Basowitz and his associates.

"At low levels of anxiety there is a general alerting of the organism, an increase in vigilance. . . . In this state there is an increased sensitization to outside events and an increased ability to cope with danger. The organism is in the state of preparedness. . . . The threshold for potentially noxious stimuli particularly is lowered as the alert and apprehensive organism seeks the sources of danger in its world. This sensitivity continues at higher levels of anxiety, but the ability to differentiate the dangerous from the trivial becomes reduced. . . .

"As stress increases . . . or anxiety mounts, the organism becomes less capable of mastery. Behavior loses its spontaneity and flexibility. There is a general rigidification and individuals respond in terms of the more habitual . . . response tendencies. Anything novel is threatening and the ability to improvise is reduced. . . .

"At high levels of free anxiety there is no longer the ability for effective action. The organization of behavior breaks down. . . . In this state the organism can no longer differentiate between dangerous and harmless stimuli, nor respond in a differentiated way. . . . It is as if the central control mechanisms were disordered." (1955, pp. 12–13)

Thus it would appear that severe emotional upheavals actually defeat their emergency function, and, as we have seen, the work of Selye (1956, 1969) and other investigators has shown that prolonged emotional mobilization produces physiological changes that are not only useless but actually harmful to the organism. In Chapter 8 we shall discuss psychosomatic disorders—peptic ulcers, hypertension, and coronary heart disease, for example—in which chronic emotional mobilization typically plays a major role.

Brain pathology

Another set of biological factors, whose role in psychopathology has been better delineated, are the more typical organic disturbances that directly affect the central nervous system. About one half of the patients in mental hospitals are suffering from mental disorders associated with toxic or organic brain pathology—that is, conditions that result in the destruction of brain tissue or otherwise interfere with normal functioning of the brain. Brain pathology may be temporary, as in the delirium of fever or drug intoxication, or it may be permanent, as in the case of syphilitic infection of the brain.

Another neurophysiological factor receiving intensive study is the way in which defects in the body's defenses against disease and other stresses may contribute to brain pathology. Normally the body produces antibodies to defend itself against invading viruses and other microorganisms, and faulty functioning of the antibody-producing system leaves the body vulnerable to certain diseases—possibly including degenerative diseases of the central nervous system. Similarly, the brain has special forms of reaction to stress in comparison with other organs, and stress may disrupt the delicate biochemistry of the brain, with adverse consequences for certain predisposed individuals. In fact, a disorganization of thought processes similar to that observed in various severe mental disorders can be induced temporarily in normal people by the injection of certain drugs, such as LSD or mescaline. In Chapter 13 we shall deal with the various mental disorders associated with demonstrable brain pathology.

Psychosocial Factors

Although we may assume that the same psychological principles underlie both normal and abnormal behavior, the problem still remains of delineating the specific conditions responsible for different outcomes.

In comparison with the variables associated with biological causes of maladaptive behavior, those associated with psychosocial causes are less understood and more elusive. However, a good deal has been learned about psychological and interpersonal factors that appear to play significant roles in maladaptive behavior: (a) maternal deprivation, (b) pathogenic family patterns, (c) early psychic trauma, (d) disordered interpersonal relationships, and (e) key stresses of modern life.

Again we shall see that these factors are by no means independent of each other and that a given condition may function as a primary, predisposing, precipitating, or reinforcing cause.

Maternal deprivation

Faulty development has often been observed in infants deprived of maternal stimulation (or "mothering") as a consequence of either (a) separation from the mother and placement in an institution, or (b) lack of adequate "mothering" in the home. Although the emphasis here is on maternal deprivation, we are essentially concerned with warmth and stimulation, whether it be supplied by the mother, father, or other persons responsible for the child's rearing.

Institutionalization. In an institution, as compared with an ordinary home, there is likely to be less warmth and physical contact, less intellectual, emotional, and social stimulation, and a lack of encouragement and help in positive learning.

A study by Provence and Lipton (1962) compared behavior of infants living in institutions with that of infants living with families. At one year of age, the institutionalized infants showed a general impairment in their relationship to people, rarely turning to adults for help, comfort, or pleasure and showing no signs of strong attachment to any person. These investigators also noted a marked retardation of speech and language development, emotional apathy, and impoverished and repetitive play activities. In contrast to the babies living in families, the institutionalized infants failed to show the personality differentiation and learning that "can be thought of both as accomplishments of the first year of life and as the foundation upon which later learning is built" (p. 161).

With more severe and pervasive deprivation, development may be even more retarded. For example, Dennis (1960) found that over 60 percent of the two-year-olds in a Teheran orphanage, where stimulation was minimal, were not yet sitting up alone, and 85 percent of the four-year-olds were not yet walking alone.

The long-range effects of severe early deprivation of maternal love and stimulation are suggested by the findings of Beres and Obers (1950) in their study of 38 adolescents who had been institutionalized between the ages of about 3 weeks and 3 years. At the time of the study, 16 to 18 years after discharge from the orphanage, 4 were diagnosed as psychotic, 21 as having a character disorder, 4 as mentally retarded, and 2 as neurotic. Only 7 were judged to have achieved a satisfactory personality adjustment.

In general, it would appear that "affectionless psychopathy"—characterized by inability to form close interpersonal relationships and often by antisocial behavior—is a syndrome commonly found among children who have been institutionalized at an early age, particularly before the age of one year; the long-range prognosis is considered unfavorable (Robins, 1970; Rutter, 1972; Wolkind, 1974; Tizard & Rees, 1975).

"Masked deprivation" in the home. By far the greatest number of infants subjected to maternal deprivation are not those separated from their mothers, but rather the ones who suffer from inadequate or distorted maternal care. Here the mother typically neglects the

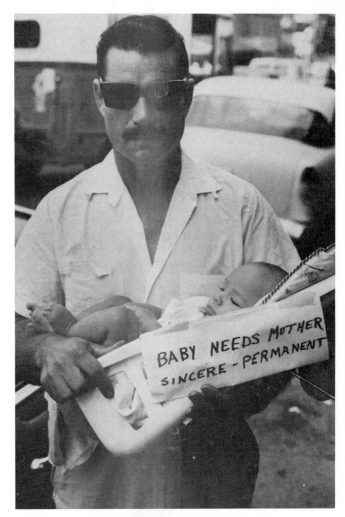

The reasons behind this case of "maternal deprivation" and the man's apparent desperation are not known, but the picture does show the emphasis we place on the mother's important role.

In Harlow's (1965, 1973) well-known experiments, monkeys separated from their mothers at birth and raised in isolation with artificial mothers (wire frames covered with terry cloth) treated them like real mothers, spent hours clinging to them, and apparently developed normally (left). At maturity, however, they failed to establish normal sexual relations, and those that bore young were helpless and dangerous mothers.

Another experiment involved raising four motherless monkeys together in one cage (center), permitting them 20 minutes each day in a playroom. Although they appeared normal at one year of age, they spent their early months huddled together.

When the young monkeys were raised under conditions of relatively complete social deprivation, they exhibited various symptoms of maladaptive behavior. The monkey huddling in a corner of a cage (right) has been taken out of isolation and is reacting with a typical response of fear and withdrawal.

child, devotes little attention to him, and is generally rejecting.

The effects of such masked deprivation may be devastating. The early work of Ribble (1944, 1945), for example, showed that rejecting, indifferent, or punishing mothers may cause tense, unsatisfied, and negativistic behavior among their infants even at a very early age. Such behavior may even take the form of a refusal to nurse, as a result of which the infant may fall into a semistuporous condition from which it is extremely difficult to arouse him. In fact, Bullard and his associates (1967) have delineated a "failure to thrive" syndrome that:

". . . is a serious disorder of growth and development frequently requiring admission to the hospital. In its acute phase it significantly compromises the health and sometimes endangers the life of the child. Investigations of social and psychological aspects of this syndrome have led to demonstrations of parental neglect and variable forms of 'maternal deprivation.' " (p. 689)

In a follow-up study conducted eight months to nine years after hospitalization of children for treatment, Bullard found that almost two-thirds of the subjects showed evidence "either of continued growth failure, emotional disorder, mental retardation, or some combination of these" (p. 681).

The effects of maternal deprivation vary considerably from infant to infant, and babies in other societies appear to thrive under widely differing conditions of maternal care. Also, the effects of unfavorable conditions during the first year of life are not always as irreversible as many investigators have thought. For example, Kagan (1973) found that Guatemalan Indian infants raised during their first year in a psychologically impoverished environment—due to the custom of the culture—were severely retarded in their development, as compared with American-raised infants. However, after the first year, the environment of these infants was enriched, and by the age of 11, they performed as well or better than American children on problem-solving and related intellectual tasks.

Despite such encouraging findings, available evidence leaves little doubt that severe and sustained maternal deprivation—whether it involves growing up in an institution with restricted stimulation or suffering masked deprivation in the home—can seriously retard intellectual, emotional, social, and even physical development. The actual nature and extent of the damage resulting from maternal deprivation appear to depend on: (a) the age at which deprivation first occurs; (b) the extent and duration of such deprivation; (c) the constitutional makeup of the infant; and (d) the substitute care, if any, that is provided. For example, mother surrogates or nursery schools may provide needed stimulation and loving care, thus preventing harmful effects to the infants of working mothers. However, in cases of early and prolonged deprivation, the damage to the infant may be irreversible or only partially reversible despite later corrective experiences.

Pathogenic family patterns

As the infant progresses into childhood, he must master new competencies, learn usable assumptions about himself and the world, and exert increasing inner control over his behavior.

During this period, the family unit remains the crucial guiding influence in the child's

---

Parental separation or loss as a traumatic experience

Bowlby (1960, 1973) has summarized the effects of parental separation on children from 2 to 5 years of age who were hospitalized for prolonged periods. He cited three stages of their separation experience:

1. Initial protest—characterized by increased crying, screaming, and general activity.

2. Despair—which included dejection, stupor, decreased activity, and general withdrawal from the environment.

3. Detachment—following the children's discharge from the hospital and reunion with their mothers—in which the children appeared indifferent and sometimes even hostile toward their mothers.

The effects of long-term or permanent separation from one or both parents are complex. When the separation occurs as early as 3 months after birth, the infant's emotional upset seems to be primarily a reaction to environmental change and strangeness, and he usually adapts readily to a surrogate mother figure. But once attachment behavior has developed, the emotional hurt of separation may be deeper and more sustained, and the child may go through a period of bereavement and have greater difficulty adjusting to the change. It would appear that the age at which the infant is most vulnerable to long-term separation or loss is from about 3 months to 3 years. The long-term consequences of such loss appear to depend not only on the time of its occurrence, but also on the child in question, his previous relationship with the parent, and the quality of subsequent parental care.

The magnitude of the problem of separation from parents is indicated by the statistic that well over 10 million children in the United States have had the experience of losing at least one parent through separation, divorce, or death.

Effects of early deprivation and trauma on adult behavior of animals

Early experience	Adult behavior—species
Raised in darkness or with restricted tactual stimulation	Permanent impairment of vision (birds, monkeys, other mammals); retarded use of limbs, abnormal sitting and walking posture (chimps)
Immobilization of movement in early infancy	Inability to fly (buzzards); impaired ability to swim (fish)
Partial starvation in early infancy	Increased hoarding tendency and faster eating rate (rats)
Total social isolation for six months or more after birth	Permanent deficiencies in exploratory, play, sexual, and maternal behaviors, and in grooming (monkeys)
Raised by humans	Preference for human company over own species (chimpanzees, lambs, wild sheep, birds, guinea pigs)
Subjected to aversive stimulation, such as electroshock or loud noise	Modification of emotional reactivity to later stress (rats); greater emotionality and possible timidity in wide range of situations (mice)
Raised in overcrowded environment	Many forms of abnormal behavior in rats, including infant mortality rate as high as 96 percent. Dogs raised in overcrowded conditions neither fought nor mated.
Trained to fight over food	Fighting over food even when not hungry (mice). In comparison, mice trained in noncompetitive or cooperative behavior were far less aggressive.

The material in this chart is based in part on the excellent summary of earlier literature in this field by Beach and Jaynes (1954), and also on Calhoun (1962), Calhoun and Marsden (1973), Davenport, Rogers, and Rumbaugh (1973), Denenberg et al. (1970), Dennis (1941), Harlow (1973), Harlow and Harlow (1966), Harlow and Suomi (1970), Hersher et al. (1962), Lessac and Solomon (1969), and Reisen (1947).

personality development; unfortunately, faulty family patterns are a fertile source of unhealthy development and maladjustment. In fact, the Joint Commission on Mental Health of Children (1970) estimated that the parents of one-fourth of the nation's children are inadequate.

In view of the incidence of pathogenic family patterns, we shall deal with this problem in some detail. It may be emphasized, however, that parent-child relationships and family interactions are extremely complex matters. Thus caution is considered essential in applying given patterns to the explanation of specific cases of maladaptive behavior.

Faulty parent-child relationships. Several types of specific parent-child patterns appear with great regularity in the background of children who show emotional disturbances and other types of faulty development. Seven of these patterns will be discussed here.

1. *Rejection.* Parental rejection of the child is closely related to "masked deprivation" and may be shown in various ways—by physical neglect, denial of love and affection, lack of interest in the child's activities and achievements, harsh or inconsistent punishment, failure to spend time with the child, and lack of respect for the child's rights and feelings as a person. In a minority of cases, it also involves cruel and abusive treatment, as described in the illustration on p. 166. Parental rejection may be partial or complete, passive or active, and subtly or overtly cruel.

In an early study of 379 mothers of five-year-olds, Sears, Maccoby, and Levin (1957) found that cold and rejecting mothers reported a background of feeding problems, persistent bed-wetting, aggressiveness, and slow conscience development in their children. Hurley (1965) found parental rejection to be associated with diminished intelligence during the early school years. He concluded that an unpleasant emotional climate and discouragement had a general inhibiting and suppressing effect on a child's intellectual development and functioning. Pringle (1965) found that many adults who had been rejected in childhood had serious difficulty in giving and receiving affection.

More recent studies have supported and extended these earlier findings. In a ten-year study of 427 children, Lefkowitz, Huesmann, Walder, and Eron (1973) found parental rejection to be a key predictor of aggression in young children; Poznanski (1973) found parental rejection to be a key factor among children suffering from excessive fears; Pemberton and Benady (1973) found an association between parental rejection and lying and stealing on the part of children; and Stierlin (1973) found parental rejection a major reason why adolescents decide to run away from home. In a study of a wide variety of psychological disorders among urban children, Langner et al. (1974) found parental coldness a causal factor. In general, research studies indicate that parental rejection tends to foster low self-esteem, feelings of insecurity and inadequacy, retarded conscience and general intellectual development, increased aggression, loneliness, and inability to give and receive love.

A consideration of why parents reject their children would take us too far afield, but it would appear that a large proportion of such parents have themselves been the victims of parental rejection. In this sense, lack of love has been referred to as a "communicable disease." And, of course, rejection is not a one-way street; the child may be unaccepting of his parents whether or not they reject him. This pattern sometimes occurs when the parents belong to a low-status minority group of which the child is ashamed. Although the results of such rejection have not been studied systematically, it would appear that children who reject their parents deny themselves needed models, loving relationships, and other essentials for healthy development.

2. *Overprotection and restrictiveness.* Maternal overprotection, or "momism," involves

---

One case of overprotection

I was a girl who had almost everything: a beautiful home; money for personal pleasures whenever I asked; nice clothes; and parents who coddled me, picked up after me, and chauffeured me wherever I wanted to go. What didn't I have? Well, I didn't have any knowledge of how to sort out laundry or run a washing machine. I didn't know how to discipline myself to use time properly, to make sure I got enough sleep, to feed myself the right foods. I didn't have the basics for coping with life on my own.

My parents — undoubtedly out of love, but with a mixture of guilt added — had, for some reason, overcompensated during my childhood. They had done too much for me. And when the time came for me to be on my own, I struggled for independence from this overprotective nest, stumbled over my new-found physical, moral, and social freedoms, and suffered a crushing fall. But by the time I hit bottom, I had learned one principle that I hope will guide me throughout the rest of my life: I can make it on my own. I learned this the hard way. I only hope that, by sharing my experience, I can help others become independent young adults without the physical and emotional trauma I endured.

Quoted from Traub (1974, p. 41).

---

the "smothering" of the child's growth. Overprotecting mothers may watch over their children constantly, protect them from the slightest risk, overly clothe and medicate them, and make up their mind for them at every opportunity. In the case of mother-son relationships, there is often excessive physical contact, in which the mother may sleep with the child for years and be subtly seductive in her relationships with him.

Different parental motivations may lead to overprotection. An early study by Levy (1945) found that in an experimental group of abnormally protective mothers, 75 percent had little in common with their husbands. Such maternal reactions appeared to represent a compensatory type of behavior in which the mother attempted, through her contact with the child, to gain satisfactions that normally should have been obtained in her marriage. It is not uncommon in such cases for the mother to call the child her "lover" and actually to encourage the child in behaviors somewhat typical of courting.

In a study of the family background of children referred to a child guidance clinic, Jenkins (1968) found that those youngsters characterized as "overanxious" were likely to have an infantilizing, overprotective mother. Similarly, in his study of children with excessive fears, Poznanski (1973) found a dependent relationship upon an overprotective mother to be one key reason for such fears. In shielding the child from every danger, this type of mother denies him needed opportunities for reality testing and the development of essential competencies. In addition, her overprotection implies that she regards the child as incapable of coping with everyday problems. It is not surprising that such children often reach adolescence and young adulthood feeling inadequate and threatened by a dangerous world.

As one eighteen-year-old girl expressed it, "Outside the protective walls of my parents' home, things don't seem to come so easy for me."

Closely related to overprotection is restrictiveness. Here the parents rigidly enforce restrictive rules and standards and give the child little autonomy or freedom for growing in his own way. Whether justified or not, parental restrictiveness is one of the most commonly heard complaints of adolescents. In a review of available literature, Becker (1964) concluded that while restrictiveness may foster well-controlled, socialized behavior, it also tends to nurture fear, dependency, submission, repressed hostility, and some dulling of intellectual striving. Often, too, extreme behavior on the part of the adolescent is a way of rebelling against severe restrictions. As we shall see, this conflict between rebellion and submission is not infrequently reflected in the sexual behavior of adolescent girls.

3. *Overpermissiveness and indulgence.* Although it happens less commonly than is popularly supposed, sometimes one or both parents cater to the child's slightest whims and in so doing fail to teach and reward desirable standards of behavior. In essence, the parent surrenders the running of the home to an uninhibited son or daughter. Pollack (1968), for example, has quoted a permissive father who finally rebelled at the tyranny of his nine-

year-old daughter, and in a near tantrum exploded with: "I want one thing clearly understood—I live here, too!" (p. 28).

Overly indulged children are characteristically spoiled, selfish, inconsiderate, and demanding. Sears (1961) found that high permissiveness and low punishment in the home were correlated positively with antisocial, aggressive behavior, particularly during middle and later childhood. Unlike rejected, emotionally deprived children, who often find it difficult to enter into warm interpersonal relationships, indulged children enter readily into such relationships but exploit people for their own purposes in the same way that they have learned to exploit their parents. In dealing with authority, such children are usually rebellious since, for so long, they have had their own way. Overly indulged children also tend to be impatient, to approach problems in an aggressive and demanding manner, and to find it difficult to accept present frustrations in the interests of long-range goals.

The fact that their important and pampered status in the home does not transfer automatically to the outside world may come as a great shock to indulged youngsters; confusion and adjustive difficulties may occur when "reality" forces them to reassess their assumptions about themselves and the world. As a 25-year-old woman in psychotherapy reflected:

"The worst mistake my parents made was giving me free rein. I was an only child, so my parents treated me like a queen. They made me think I could always have everything I wanted—not just money, but privileges. I wish they had set some limitations, because when I got out in the world I found things different." (Pollack, 1968, p. 28)

4. *Unrealistic demands.* Some parents place excessive pressures on their children to live up to unrealistically "high" standards. Thus they may be expected to excel in school and other activities. Where the child has the capacity for exceptionally high-level performance, things may work out; but even here the child may be under such sustained pressure that little room is left for spontaneity or development as an independent person.

Typically, however, the child is never able to quite live up to parental expectations and demands. If he improves his grade from a C to a B, he may be asked why he did not get an A. If he succeeds in getting an A, the next step is to attain the highest A in his class. The parents seem to be telling the child that he could do better if he tried, and that he is not good enough the way he is. But no matter how hard he tries, he seems to fail in the eyes of his parents and, ultimately, in his own eyes as well—a fact that results in painful frustration and self-devaluation. And in promoting failure by their excessive demands, parents also tend to discourage further effort on the child's part. Almost invariably he eventually comes to feel, "I can't do it, so why try?"

One need only observe a child's eager "Watch me, Mommy," as he demonstrates some new achievement, to understand how important the mastery of new competencies and parental recognition for such mastery are to healthy development. And research studies, such as the investigation of the antecedents of self-respect in children carried out by Coopersmith (1967), have shown that high parental expectations are both common and helpful for the child's development. Yet such expectations need to be realistic, and to take into consideration the capabilities and temperament of each child. Too often, such standards become a matter of what the parents value rather than what the child may need. Thus a professional football player may have his heart set on his son's following in his footsteps, when actually the son lacks both capability and interest. In some instances unrealistic demands may take the form of parental overdependence on the child. Parents who are unhappy with each other or in other ways are failing to find a meaningful and fulfilling life may focus on the child for meeting their own needs.

Not infrequently, unrealistic parental demands focus around moral standards—particularly with regard to sex, alcohol, and related matters. Thus the parents may instill in the child the view that masturbation or any other sexual activity is terribly sinful and can lead only to moral and physical degeneration. The child who accepts such rigid parental standards is likely to develop a rigid and restricted personality and to face many guilt-arousing and self-devaluating conflicts.

In still other instances, parental demands are unrealistically low, and the parents do not care what the child does as long as he stays out of trouble. Coopersmith (1967) found that the children of such parents were significantly lower in both achievement and self-esteem than were children whose parents had high but realistic expectations for them. Thus we can see that unrealistic expectations and demands—either too high, too low, or distorted and rigid—can be important causes of faulty development and maladjustment.

5. *Faulty discipline.* Parents have been particularly confused during recent years about appropriate forms of discipline. Sometimes a misinterpretation of psychological findings and theories has led to the view that all punishment and frustration should be avoided lest the child be "fixated" in his development. In other cases parents have resorted to excessively harsh discipline, convinced that if they "spare the rod" they will spoil the child. And in still other cases, the parents have seemed to lack general guidelines, punishing children one day and ignoring or even rewarding them the next for doing the same or similar things.

As we have noted, overpermissiveness and lack of discipline tend to produce a spoiled, inconsiderate, antisocially aggressive child—and an insecure one as well. On the other hand, overly severe or harsh discipline may have a variety of harmful effects, including fear and hatred of the punishing person, little initiative or spontaneity, and less friendly feelings toward others. When accompanied by rigid moral standards, overly severe discipline is likely to result in a seriously repressed child who lacks spontaneity and warmth and devotes much effort toward controlling his own unacceptable impulses. Such children often subject themselves to severe self-recrimination and self-punishment for real or imagined mistakes and misdeeds. Overly severe discipline, combined with restrictiveness, also tends to incite rebellion and socially deviant behavior as children grow older and are subjected increasingly to outside influences that may be incompatible with parental views and practices.

When severe discipline takes the form of physical punishment of the child for breaking

Summary chart of faulty parent-child relationships

Undesirable condition	Typical effect on child's personality development
Rejection	Feelings of anxiety, insecurity, low self-esteem, negativism, hostility, attention-seeking, loneliness, jealousy, and slowness in conscience development
Overprotection — domination	Submissiveness, lack of self-reliance, dependence in relations with others, low self-evaluation, some dulling of intellectual striving
Overpermissiveness — overindulgence	Selfishness, demanding attitude, inability to tolerate frustration, rebelliousness toward authority, excessive need of attention, lack of responsibility, inconsiderateness, exploitativeness in interpersonal relationships
Perfectionism, with unrealistic demands	Lack of spontaneity, rigid conscience development, severe conflicts, tendency toward guilt and self-condemnation if there is failure to live up to parental demands
Faulty discipline:	
Lack of discipline	Inconsiderateness, aggressiveness, and antisocial tendencies
Harsh, overly severe discipline	Fear, hatred of parent, little initiative or spontaneity, lack of friendly feelings toward others
Inconsistent discipline	Difficulty in establishing stable values for guiding behavior; tendency toward highly aggressive behavior
Contradictory demands and communications	As in case of "double bind" communications, the tendency toward confusion, lack of an integrated frame of reference, unclear self-identity, lack of initiative, self-devaluation
Undesirable parental models	The learning of faulty values, formulation of unrealistic goals, development of maladaptive coping patterns

The exact effects of faulty parent-child relationships on later behavior depends on many factors, including the age of the child, the constitutional and personality makeup of the child at the time, the duration and degree of the unhealthy relationship, his perception of the relationship, and the total family setting and life context, including the presence or absence of alleviating conditions and whether or not subsequent experiences tend to reinforce or correct early damage. There is no uniform pattern of pathogenic family relationship underlying the development of later psychopathology, but the conditions we have discussed often act as predisposing factors.

rules—rather than the withdrawal of approval and privileges—the result tends to be increased aggressive behavior on the part of the child (Lefkowitz, et al., 1973; Eron et al., 1974; Steinmetz & Straus, 1973). Apparently physical punishment provides a model of aggressive behavior that the child then tends to emulate.

Similarly, inconsistent discipline makes it difficult for the child to establish stable values for guiding his behavior. When the child is punished one time and ignored or rewarded the next for the same behavior, he is at a loss to know what behavior is appropriate. Deur and Parke (1970) found that children with a history of inconsistent reward and punishment for aggressive behavior were more resistant to punishment and to the extinction of their aggressive behavior than were children who had experienced more consistent discipline. The preceding study supports earlier findings showing a high correlation between inconsistent discipline and later delinquent and criminal behavior.

In the past, discipline was conceived both as a method for punishing undesirable behavior and for preventing such behavior in the future. At the present time discipline is thought of more positively as providing needed structure and guidance for promoting healthy growth on the part of the child. Where coercion or punishment is deemed necessary, it is considered important that the parent make it clear that it is the child's behavior which is disapproved and not the child as a person. In order to develop needed inner controls, it is also considered important that the child know what behavior is expected, and that positive and consistent methods of discipline be worked out for dealing with infractions. In general, it would appear that freedom should be commensurate with the child's maturity and ability to use it constructively.

6. *Communication failure.* Parents can discourage a child from asking questions and in other ways fail to foster the "information exchange" essential for healthy personality development, for example, helping the child develop a realistic frame of reference and essential competencies. Such limited and inadequate communication patterns have commonly been attributed to socially disadvan-

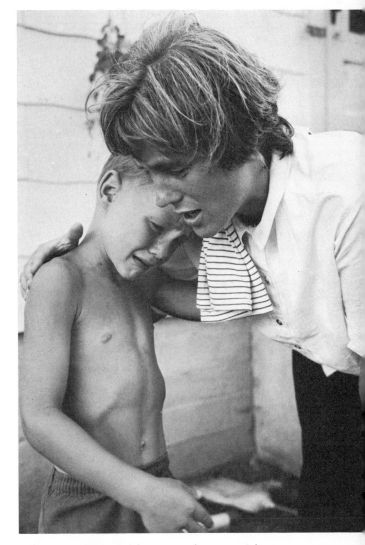

During periods of special stress or crises, parental support and assistance are of vital importance to children.

taged families, but these patterns are by no means restricted to any one socioeconomic level.

Such patterns may take a number of forms. Some parents are too busy with their own concerns to listen to their children and try to understand the conflicts and pressures they are facing. As a consequence, these parents often fail to give needed support and assistance during crisis periods. Other parents may have forgotten that the world often looks different to a child or adolescent and that rapid social change can lead to a very real communication gap between generations.

In other instances faulty communication may take more deviant forms. In their discussion of pathological communication, Watzlawick, Beavin, and Jackson (1967) cite a passage from *Through the Looking Glass* in which Alice's straightforward communication is corrupted by the "brainwashing" approach of the Red and White Queens; they accuse Alice of trying to deny something because of her "state of mind":

" 'I'm sure I didn't mean—' Alice was beginning but the Red Queen interrupted her impatiently.

" 'That's just what I complain of! You should have meant! What do you suppose is the use of a child without any meaning? Even a joke should have a meaning—and a child is more important than a joke, I hope. You couldn't deny that, even if you tried with both hands.'

" 'I don't deny things with my hands,' Alice objected.

" 'Nobody said you did,' said the Red Queen. 'I said you couldn't if you tried.'

" 'She is in that state of mind,' said the White Queen, 'that she wants to deny something—only she doesn't know what to deny!'

" 'A nasty, vicious temper,' the Red Queen remarked; and then there was an uncomfortable silence for a minute or two."

The author was apparently intuitively aware of the effects of this kind of illogical communication, for after some additional harassment, he mercifully has Alice faint.

Although the preceding illustration is an extreme example of pathological communication, some parents apparently follow similar patterns. One such pattern that conveys contradictory messages has been referred to by Bateson (1960) as the *double bind*. For example, a mother may complain of her son's lack of affection toward her, but when he tries to be demonstrative, she freezes up and shows strong disapproval. Similarly, parents may convey one message by their words and another by their behavior. Thus a father may deplore lying and admonish his son "never to tell a lie" while obviously lying a good deal himself.

An even more subtle and damaging communication pattern involves contradicting or undermining the child's statements and conclusions, so that he is left confused and devaluated as a person. The effects of this pattern have been vividly described by Laing and Esterson (1964):

"The ultimate of this is . . . when no matter how [a person] feels or how he acts, no matter what meaning he gives his situation, his feelings are denuded of validity, his acts are stripped of their motives, intentions, and consequences, the situation is robbed of its meaning for him, so that he is totally mystified and alienated." (pp. 135–36)

Faulty patterns of communication have been found to be more common in the backgrounds of emotionally disturbed adolescents and young adults than in those of young people more adequately adjusted. Normal families tend to show a much higher incidence of supportive interactions and communication, which tend to foster the unity of the family and well-being of the family members (Alexander, 1973).

7. *Undesirable parental models.* Since children tend to observe and imitate the behavior of their parents, it is apparent that parental behavior can have a highly beneficial or detrimental effect on the way a youngster learns to perceive, think, feel, and act. We may consider parents as undesirable models if they have faulty reality, possibility, and value assumptions, or if they depend excessively on defense mechanisms in coping with their problems—as when they consistently project the blame for their own mistakes on others, if they lie and cheat, if they refuse to face and deal realistically with family problems, or if there is a marked discrepancy between their proclaimed values and those reflected in actual behavior.

A parent who is emotionally disturbed, addicted to alcohol or drugs, or otherwise maladjusted may also serve as an undesirable model. In his extensive study of emotional dis-

Children tend to observe and imitate the maladaptive behavior of their parents.

turbances in children, Jenkins (1966) found that nearly half of a group of children diagnosed as "overanxious-neurotic" had mothers who were described as neurotic because of extreme anxiety, nervousness, and related symptoms. Concurrently, the children characterized by habitual delinquent behavior tended to come from a background combining poverty, parental neglect, a bad neighborhood, and an inadequate father figure. Similarly, Anthony (1969) found a much higher incidence of maladaptive behavior among children with psychotic parents than among a control group with nonpsychotic parents; and several investigators, including Green, Gaines, and Sandgrund (1974), found that child abusers tend to come from families in which they themselves had been rejected and mistreated.

Undesirable parental models are undoubtedly an important reason why mental disorders, delinquency, crime, and other forms of maladaptive behavior tend to run in families.

But it should be pointed out that there is nothing inevitable in the effects of parental pathology on the child's development. The pathology of one parent may be compensated for by the wisdom and concern of the other, or an alcoholic parent may perhaps serve as a "negative model," showing the child what *not* to be like. Kadushin (1967) has cited a number of studies in which children coming from homes with undesirable parental models have grown up to be successful and well-adjusted adults. As Chess, Thomas, and Birch (1965) have found:

"We see loving mothers whose children have problems. And we see very sick mothers with healthy and well-adjusted children who are apparently immune to the mother's pathology and the erratic patterns of care." (p. 13)

Although the reasons for such favorable outcomes are not clear, it is useful to emphasize that specific pathogenic parent-child pat-

Imitative learning of aggression from adult models

The extent to which children may imitate adult models is graphically illustrated in a study by Bandura et al. (1963). In this sequence, an adult model (top) throws, batters, and kicks a large inflated doll.

After viewing an adult model perform such actions, in person or on film, each child in the experimental group underwent mild frustration and was then observed in a playroom supplied with a variety of toys—including crayons, a tea set, a mallet, a dart gun, and an inflated doll—which could be used in aggressive or nonaggressive play. A control group (who saw no aggressive model) underwent the same mild frustration. Children who had seen the adult model were nearly twice as aggressive in their play activities as the control group. Some children, such as those depicted here, imitated the adult model almost exactly.

Social groups differ markedly in the extent to which aggressive behavior occurs and in the exposure of children to adult models of aggression. We shall elaborate on this point in our discussion of violence in Chapter 18.

terns usually take place in a broader social context. The latter may tend to minimize or exacerbate the influence of a particular condition.

Maladaptive family structures. In the previous section we considered particular patterns of faulty parent-child relationships; here we will focus on more comprehensive patterns of family pathology. The current research on families as group systems has revealed that maladjustive behavior on the part of the child may be fostered by the general family environment as well as by the child's relationships with one or both parents.

In reviewing the effects of the family system on development, we again encounter the problem of establishing criteria for differentiating between what is "healthy" and what is maladaptive; for, as in the case of the individual, we have no model of the "ideal" family. However, several investigators have attempted a typology of families that clearly have a detrimental influence on child development in our society. For present purposes, we shall briefly describe four such types of families.

1. *The inadequate family.* This type of family is characterized by inability to cope with the ordinary problems of family living. It lacks the resources, physical or psychological, for meeting demands with which most families can satisfactorily cope. Consequently, the inadequate family relies heavily on continued outside assistance and support in resolving its problems. The incompetencies of such a family may stem from immaturity, lack of education, mental retardation, or other shortcomings of the parents. Sometimes, of course, demands are so severe that they overtax the adjustive resources of even highly adequate families.

A family that is floundering against odds too great for its resources, for whatever reason, cannot give its children the feeling of safety and security they need, or adequately guide them in the development of essential competencies. Nor can financial or other outside assistance be counted on to meet the needs of such families, for families, like individuals, need to feel they are self-directing and in control of their own destinies.

2. *The disturbed family.* At all socioeconomic levels we find some parents who, because of personal instability, interact with other people in ways that are destructive to others as well as themselves. Parents with grossly eccentric and abnormal personalities may keep the home in constant emotional turmoil.

Disturbed homes may involve many pathological patterns, but such homes appear to have certain characteristics in common: (a) the presence of parents who are fighting to maintain their own equilibrium and who are unable to give the child needed love and guidance; (b) exposure of the child to irrationality and faulty parental models; and (c) almost inevitably, the enmeshment of the child in the emotional conflicts of the parents.

In general, disturbed homes have been found to be associated with a high incidence of psychological disorders among children and adolescents (Wolkind & Rutter, 1973; Langner et al., 1974). Parental quarreling, conflict, and general tension are unfortunate conditions for the growing child, representing a threat to his "base of operations" and the only security he knows. For this reason, it often appears that maladjusted parents who are able to establish a harmonious relationship to each other despite their individual problems are much less damaging to the child than are maladjusted parents who live in disharmony.

3. *The antisocial family.* Here the family espouses values not accepted by the wider community. In some families the parents are overtly or covertly engaged in behavior that violates the standards and interests of society, and they may be chronically in difficulty with the law. Such antisocial values usually handicap marital and other family relationships, as well as providing undesirable models for the child.

Children in such families may be encouraged in dishonesty, deceit, and other undesirable behavior patterns; or they may simply observe and imitate the undesirable behavior and attitudes of their parents. In some cases, children may develop a high degree of courage, self-discipline, and loyalty to the family group at the expense of identification with the society as a whole. More often, the models they see are immature and self-seeking, and

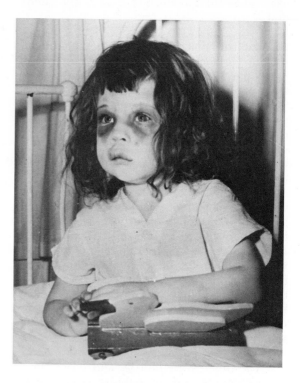

The child who is loved and respected as an individual in his own right develops a basic sense of security and trust, and a positive self-image. What vision of the world and himself does a battered child develop?

Unfortunately, a substantial number of parents in our society not only fail to provide adequate care for their infants; they actually subject the infants to cruel and brutal treatment. In the United States each year an estimated 50,000 to 70,000 infants and young children are subjected to cruel and inhuman treatment by their parents; more than 300,000 children are in foster homes as a result. Hundreds of victims die each year from abusive treatment, and many others are paralyzed, physically deformed, or rendered mentally retarded by their injuries. Earl (1965) reported the following cases:

The mother of a 29-month-old boy claimed he was a behavior problem, beat him with a stick and screwdriver handle, dropped him on the floor, beat his head on the wall or threw him against it, choked him to force his mouth open to eat, and burned him on the face and hands. After she had severely beaten him, the mother found the child dead.

Because her 2½-year-old daughter did not respond readily enough to toilet training, the mother became in-

dignant and in a fit of temper over the child's inability to control a bowel movement gave her an enema with near scalding water. To save the child's life a doctor was forced to perform a colostomy.

In a study of 140 cases of child abuse, Helfer and Kempe (1968) reported that 74 percent suffered bruises and welts, 25 percent abrasions and lacerations, 14 percent punctures, and 11 percent burns and scalds. The figures add up to more than 100 percent, since many of the children suffered multiple injuries.

As might be expected, the parents most commonly involved in such behavior appear to be emotionally unstable or mentally disordered. Alcoholic fathers are commonly found in the group, particularly in cases of rape and child-beating, but disturbed mothers appear to be worse offenders, in that more mothers than fathers kill their infants. Some of the abused children are illegitimate, but most are not. Usually the parents are between 20 and 40 years of age, and most live in poverty. A large percentage, having themselves been reared with neglect and brutality, showed little or no remorse for their cruel behavior; thus brutality tends to breed brutality.

Based on Earl (1965), Flynn (1970), Gardner (1967), Gil (1975), Helfer and Kempe (1968), Loper (1970), and Terr (1970).

the social interactions they observe and take part in are shallow and manipulative—a poor preparation for mature, responsible adulthood. Here it is of interest to note that Langner and Michael (1963), in an extensive study of mental health and mental disorder in a congested urban area, found a higher mental health risk for children who disapproved of their parents' character than for those who experienced a broken home.

4. *The disrupted family.* Disrupted families are incomplete, whether as a result of death, divorce, separation, or some other condition. According to the U.S. Census Bureau, over 2.5 million families were headed by mothers alone in 1972 due to divorce or separation; by 1980, the figure is expected to go well beyond the 3 million mark (*U.S. News & World Report,* July 16, 1973; April 22, 1974). If we add homes headed by widows with children, the figure is considerably higher. And this says nothing of the million or more homes headed by fathers alone as a result of the same causes. Such statistics make it apparent that millions of parents and children are confronted with the stress of family disruption and the problems that accompany it.

A number of studies have shown the traumatic effects divorce can have on a child. Feelings of insecurity and rejection may be aggravated by conflicting loyalties and, sometimes, by the spoiling the child receives while staying with one or the other parent—maybe not the one he or she would prefer to be with. It would appear that divorce is much more traumatic for children whose homes were happy prior to the divorce than for those who came from unhappy homes.

It has been commonly assumed that the loss of a father is more traumatic for a son than for a daughter, but serious doubts have been raised about this assumption. For example, Hetherington (1973) found "the effects of father absence on daughters appear during adolescence and manifest themselves mainly as an inability to interact appropriately with males" (p. 52). In this context, one is also reminded of the bitterness of the daughter of a naval officer who stated, "I despise my father. He was never there. He was in the navy 120 years" (*Time,* 1967, p. 30).

The long-range effects of family disruption

Do we effectively develop and utilize the resources of our youth?

"The energy, idealism, and intelligence of youth are the prime resources of each nation; if these resources are to be widely spent, our youth must be involved in the mainstream of national life." This view, expressed by Eisenberg (1970, p. 1692) has been elaborated on by Bronfenbrenner (1974):

"Our children are not entrusted with any real responsibilities. Little that they do really matters. They are given duties rather than responsibilities; the ends and means have been determined by someone else and their job is to fulfill an assignment involving little judgment, decision making or risk. This practice is intended to protect children from burdens beyond their years, but there is reason to believe it has been carried too far in contemporary American society and has contributed to the alienation of young people and their alleged incapacity to deal constructively with personal and social problems. The evidence indicates that children acquire the capacity to cope with difficult situations when they have an opportunity to take on consequential responsibilities in relation to others and are held accountable for them." (p. 60)

In a similar vein, recent task force reports by both governmental and private agencies have suggested that young people be given the opportunity to participate more fully in our social institutions and to assume more responsibility for themselves and others.

----

on the child may vary greatly, even being favorable in many instances as contrasted to remaining in a home torn by marital conflict and dissension. Detrimental effects may be minimized if a substitute model for the missing parent is available, if the remaining family members are able to compensate for the missing parent and reorganize the family into an effective functioning group, or if the home is reconstituted by a successful remarriage that provides an adequate environment for child rearing. And if the remaining parent—usually the mother—is able to cope with her own emotional upset as well as the confusion, anxiety, or depression that may be aroused in the child, she may help to ease the transition through this crisis period.

In view of the very real stresses involved, however, it is not surprising that delinquency and other maladaptive behaviors are much higher among children and adolescents coming from disrupted homes than among those coming from intact ones, even when the education and social class of the parents is ruled out as a factor. The latter point is important, since the incidence of broken homes is proportionately much greater among families in the lower socioeconomic bracket.

The preceding categories are by no means discrete, and a given family may show a wide range of pathogenic behaviors. The point is that these family patterns have been labeled "pathogenic" because of the high frequency with which they are associated with problems in child development and later psychopathology. It may also be emphasized, however, that although healthy family environments are more likely to produce well-adjusted children than are unhealthy ones, this relationship is by no means inevitable. In fact, children coming from healthy family environments may show seriously maladaptive behavior, often leading to the question "Where did we go wrong?" on the part of parents and to unnecessary feelings of guilt.

In this context, it is relevant to note that pathogenic interpersonal relationships and interactions are by no means confined to the family, but may involve the peer group and other individuals outside the family. Particularly during adolescence, when young people are becoming progressively independent of parental controls, relationships outside the family are likely to be important influences on their further development.

Early psychic trauma

Most of us have had traumatic experiences that temporarily shattered our feelings of security, adequacy, and worth, and were important in influencing our later evaluations of ourselves and our environment.[4] The following illustrates such an incident.

---

[4]The terms *psychic trauma* and *traumatic* are used here to mean any aversive experience that inflicts serious psychological damage on the individual.

"I believe the most traumatic experience of my entire life happened one April evening when I was eleven. I was not too sure of how I had become a member of the family, although my parents had thought it wise to tell me that I was adopted. That much I knew, but what the term *adopted* meant was something else entirely. One evening after my step-brother and I had retired, he proceeded to explain it to me—with a vehemence I shall never forget. He made it clear that I wasn't a 'real' member of the family, that my parents didn't 'really' love me, and that I wasn't even wanted around the place. That was one night I vividly recall crying myself to sleep. That experience undoubtedly played a major role in making me feel insecure and inferior."

Such traumas are apt to leave psychological wounds that never completely heal. As a result, later stress that reactivates these early wounds is apt to be particularly difficult for the individual to handle and often explains why one person has difficulty with a problem that is not especially stressful to another. The following points are helpful in understanding this process:

a. Conditioned responses are readily established in situations that evoke strong emotions; such responses are often highly resistant to extinction. Thus one traumatic experience of being unable to swim and almost drowning in a deep lake may be sufficient to establish a fear of water that endures for years or a lifetime.

b. Conditioned emotional responses stemming from traumatic experiences may generalize to other situations. A child who has learned to fear water may also come to be fearful of riding in boats and other situations associated with even the remotest possibility of drowning.

c. Traumatic situations result in emotional conditioning rather than in responses learned through reasoning and problem solving. Consequently, exposure to similar situations tends to reactivate the emotional response instead of permitting a rational appraisal of the situation, which would provide more flexibility of response and be more likely to be adaptive.

The after-effects of early traumatic experiences depend heavily on the support and reassurance given the child by parents or other significant persons. This appears particularly important when the trauma involves an experience that arouses strong feelings of inadequacy and self-devaluation, such as being ridiculed by one's peers for stuttering or inability to learn to read.

Many traumatic experiences in childhood, though highly upsetting at the time, are probably of minor significance in their long-term consequences, and some children are less vulnerable than others and show more resilience and recoverability from any hurt or damage that may occur. However, a child exposed to repeated early trauma which keeps him off balance is likely to show a disruption in normal personality development. And even though subsequent experiences may have a corrective influence, the detrimental effects of such early traumas may never be completely obliterated.

Although we have emphasized the pathogenic effects of early psychic traumas on personality development and adjustment, such hurtful experiences at any age may adversely affect development and adjustment beyond that point. This is illustrated by the case of a young mother who had gone to visit a friend in the neighborhood and came back to find her home enveloped in flames and her two young children trapped inside. She was restrained from entering the burning structure by firemen who risked their own lives in a vain effort to save the children. A year later in therapy she made the following statement:

"I know I must put it in the past, that life must go on . . . that somehow I must think of the present and future. But I can't seem to forget. I shouldn't have left my children alone. . . . I can never really forgive myself. The memory of that awful night will haunt me as long as I live . . . and I can't bear the thought of having more children for fear something awful will happen to them too. . . . maybe I will do something irresponsible and crazy again."

In general, early traumas seem to have more far-reaching consequences than later ones, largely because critical evaluation, reflection, and self-defenses are not yet well-developed in children. During adolescence and adulthood, however, a traumatic experience may actually tend to immunize the individual to a similar later experience by making it a familiar phenomenon: its limits have been perceived, the individual has seen it in the perspective of other known experiences, and self-defenses have been developed.

Pathogenic interpersonal relationships

"Of all the endeavors that exert their influence on people's lives in our culture, the quest for intimate relationships must be the most . . . longed for, dreamed about, sung about, joked about, and cursed at. Few human experiences inspire the pangs, joys, ecstasies, fears, cheers, and tears that accompany the growth and development of intimacy. Such relationships are recognized as a major source of need fulfillment, stress, and challenge in our lives." (Coleman & Hammen, 1974, p. 259)

People differ markedly in their ability to give and receive love. Nevertheless, marital and other intimate relationships do represent a major source of need fulfillment in the lives of most of us. However, such relationships can also result in disillusionment, hurt, and trauma. In this section we will be concerned primarily with the role marital instability and other damaging interpersonal relationships play in maladaptive behavior.

Marital instability. For most of us the quest for an intimate relationship with another person takes the form of marriage, and the great majority of people in our society will marry at some time in their lives and attempt to establish a happy home life. In an extensive survey of Americans, including over 2000 personal interviews, more than 80 percent of those questioned selected a happy home life as their most desired goal (Eldrich, 1974).

Unfortunately, this goal seems to be an elusive one to achieve. The divorce rate in the United States is the highest in the world, with one in every three marriages ending in divorce. Over 700,000 marriages ended in divorce in 1974, and marital separations may also approach the same figure. Conservatively, this represents well over a million marital breakups each year. Heartache, bickering, feelings of wasted opportunity, of being tied down, and of marking time are very common. Thus it is not surprising that over half of all married partners say they would not pick the same mate if they had it to do over again. Where children are involved, marital dissatisfaction and instability are not only frustrating to the parents but also place the children under additional stress, often leading to what Satir (1967) has called "dysfunctional parenting."

In this context, it is relevant to note the changing role of marriage in contemporary life. Traditionally, authority was vested in the husband and the ties that bound marriage and family together were typically based on duty and economic necessity. Today marriage is likely to be viewed as a mutual undertaking for achieving an intimate and mutually need-fulfilling relationship with another person—a person with whom to share all aspects of one's life. However, to learn to share intimate experiences, to give and receive affection and emotional support, and to establish a secure "home base" in our changing and uncertain world is a difficult undertaking.

To add to the difficulty, modern urbanization has led to the decline of the extended family, with its relatively stable network of relationships and supports. In our mobile, urban society, it is difficult to establish and maintain close interpersonal relationships outside the nuclear family. As a consequence, increasing reliance for the satisfaction of emotional needs and personal fulfillment is being placed on the individual's immediate marital relationship. At the same time, the increasing demands on marriage have been accompanied by a growing acceptance of divorce as a viable choice in an unsatisfactory marital situation, as well as an acceptance of "trial marriage" and other forms of intimate relationships other than marriage. Thus there arises a modern dilemma in which marital stability has been reduced at the very time that the demands on marital relationships have increased.

Types of pathogenic relationships. In our review of the interpersonal model in Chapter 3, we noted that interpersonal relationships—particularly intimate ones—may be conducive either to need satisfaction and mental health or to personal distress and maladaptive behavior. Here we will briefly discuss three types of

pathogenic interpersonal relationships that have seriously detrimental effects on one or both partners: fraudulent interpersonal contracts, collusion, and discordant interpersonal patterns.

1. *Fraudulent interpersonal contracts.* This involves the terms of the relationship being violated by one person in such a way as to exploit the other. Such patterns may take a variety of forms, but Carson (1969) has delineated a common underlying sequence that may be summarized as follows:

(a) A offers B a type of relationship or "contract" in which B is interested because it seems to offer favorable possibilities for need satisfaction.

(b) B indicates acceptance of the terms of the contract and proceeds with activities appropriate to carrying out the terms agreed upon.

(c) A then assumes a stance that makes it seem justified to alter the terms of the contract.

(d) To maintain the relationship, B is forced to accept the new terms, thus enabling A to achieve the type of relationship he or she was presumably aiming for in the first place.

Such an approach is considered "fraudulent" because A's real goals were achieved by deceit and fraud—by "setting B up as a mark." B, however, has been "had" and is likely to resent it, and the new terms of the relationship are likely to prove frustrating and damaging to the relationship. If B feels strongly enough about the situation, he or she may decide to terminate it, in which case A is also the loser.

2. *Collusion.* In collusion a relationship is established and maintained only because the partners tacitly agree to follow certain maladaptive rules and norms of their own choosing, rather than socially established adaptive ones. In effect, the partners have entered into a conspiracy or collusion.

One person usually takes the initiative in outlining the rules and norms which both partners are then expected to follow. Typically this involves the joint agreement to deny or falsify certain aspects of reality. For example, a person who drinks excessively may agree to enter into an intimate relationship only if the excessive drinking is accepted as normal by the other person. The other person may not actually wish to accept these terms but may do so in order not to lose the relationship, perhaps anticipating rewards that will outweigh the costs or hoping that the other individual "will change."

The ensuing relationship is maladaptive, however, because the rewards do not in fact justify the costs. The excessive drinking of one partner is likely to interfere with his own adjustment as well as sexual, social, and other aspects of the couple's relationship. If hospitalization is eventually required, then tremendous stress may be placed on the other partner. In nonmarital relationships as well as marital ones, the results of such a contract are likely to be highly detrimental to the persons involved, and may lead to a termination of the relationship.

In some instances of collusion the terms are not initiated by one person. Two persons who share the same type of maladjustment may enter into such a contract. For example, two excessive drinkers may agree to accept their drinking as normal. Here the terms are mutually satisfactory to both partners, but over time their excessive drinking is likely to create serious problems for one or both of them and make a satisfactory relationship impossible.

3. *Discordant interpersonal patterns.* Serious and continued dissension, disagreements, and conflicts are detrimental to the quality and stability of the relationship as well as to the persons involved. Such discordant interactions may result when one or both partners do not play their agreed-upon or expected roles in the relationship. In other cases, one or both partners who are not gaining satisfaction from the relationship may express feelings of frustration and disillusionment in hostile ways such as nagging, belittling, and doing things purposely to annoy the other person. A common source of conflict and dissatisfaction stems from value differences, which may lead to serious disagreements about a variety of topics, including sexual behavior and how money is spent. Whatever the reasons for difficulties, seriously discordant relationships are likely to be frustrating, hurtful, and generally pathogenic in their effects.

As one might expect, immature and maladjusted persons are likely to find it especially difficult to establish and maintain a successful marital or other intimate relationship.

Severe stress

The various causes of abnormal behavior we have discussed—such as psychic trauma and marital difficulties—are also sources of severe stress. In addition, there are certain other common sources of stress in our society which appear directly relevant to understanding maladaptive behavior.

Devaluating frustrations. In contemporary life there are a number of frustrations that lead to self-devaluation and hence are particularly difficult to cope with. Among these are failure, losses, personal limitations and lack of resources, guilt, and loneliness.

1. *Failure.* The highly competitive setting in which we live almost inevitably leads to occasional failures. No team is likely to win all the time, nor can all succeed who aspire to become movie or television stars or to achieve high political office. For each person who succeeds, there is an inevitable crop of failures. Furthermore, some people seem to court failure by setting unrealistically high goals or by undertaking new ventures without adequate preparation.

Repeated failures or failure in an endeavor in which we are emotionally involved and want very much to succeed, such as marriage, can be especially devaluating and frustrating. Often it is important that failure experiences be "worked through," that we not only accept them but that we learn from them. In this context, it is interesting to note a report by Harmeling (1950) that the Eskimos at Cape Prince of Wales conducted a primitive form of psychodrama in their community igloo during the six-month winter. Accompanied by an orchestra of drums, they staged a pantomime of the failure experiences in their lives and laughed at their own mistakes thus objectively viewed.

2. *Losses.* Closely related to failure are the many losses that people inevitably experience—losses involving objects or resources they value or individuals with whom they strongly identify.

Among the most distressing material losses are those of money and status. In our society money gives its owner security, self-esteem, and the use of desired goods and services; thus an appreciable financial loss is apt to lead to severe self-recrimination and discouragement. Similarly, loss of social status—whether it stems from loss of economic position or some other cause—tends to devalue an individual in his own eyes as well as in the eyes of others.

Interpersonal losses are probably more stressful than material ones for most people. As we noted in Chapter 4, for example, Holmes and his associates (1970) found death of spouse, divorce, and marital separation to be the three most stressful events reported by adults in our society. Here it may be noted that the death rate for widowers is double that for married men, and that 75 percent of American women will one day be widowed (Caine, 1974; Harvey & Bahr, 1974).

3. *Personal limitations and lack of resources.* Being "on the low end of the totem pole" with regard to material advantages and possessions is a powerful source of frustration, one afflicting members of disadvantaged minorities in our society with special severity. Constantly being exposed to TV commercials and other advertising depicting desirable objects and experiences in our allegedly affluent society—while seeming to be "on the outside looking in"—can be highly frustrating for those whose aspirations and hopes seem to have been bypassed by society. But probably from time to time most of us make envious *status comparisons* in which we see others as more favorably endowed with personal and material resources than we are.

In addition, physical handicaps and other personal limitations that restrict one's activities—and possibly attractiveness to members of the opposite sex—can be highly stressful. Here again, dwelling on comparisons with others who seem more favorably endowed can unnecessarily increase frustration and self-devaluation.

4. *Guilt.* To understand feelings of guilt it is useful to note that (a) various value assumptions concerning right and wrong are learned and accepted; (b) these value assumptions are then applied to the appraisal of one's own behavior; and (c) it is learned, often by hard experience, that wrongdoing leads to punishment. Thus behaving in ways that one considers immoral leads to both self-devaluation and apprehension. Because of this orientation,

depressed persons commonly search back through past events, locating and exaggerating misdeeds that have presumably led to present difficulties.

Guilt is likely to be particularly stressful if it seems that nothing can be done to rectify one's misdeed. In fact, Gelven (1973) concluded that "Of all the forms of mental suffering, perhaps none is as pervasive or as intense as the ache of guilt" (p. 69). Since guilt is heavily infused with self-recrimination and anxiety, this conclusion seems to be well supported.

5. *Loneliness.* Probably most people experience painful feelings of isolation and loneliness at some time in their lives. As the novelist Thomas Wolfe (1929) has expressed it:

"Which one of us has known his brother? Which of us has looked into his father's heart? Which of us has not remained forever prison-pent? Which of us is not forever a stranger and alone?" (p. 3)

Being unloved and lonely has been called "the greatest poverty." Perhaps for more people than we ever realize, the world is a lonely place.

Here it is useful to make a distinction between pathological and existential loneliness, although it is difficult to draw a line between the two. The former involves the individual who is uncommitted, unconcerned, and unloving and who does not attempt to deal with loneliness through close interpersonal relationships or commitment to the human enterprise, while the latter involves the caring, committed, loving person whose loneliness is the result of conditions beyond his or her control.

A pervasive source of frustration that is related to all of the stresses we have mentioned—but is particularly pertinent to understanding loneliness—is the inability to find meaning in one's life. As Becker (1962) pointed out: "Let it be stressed emphatically that the most difficult realization for man is the possibility that *life has no meaning*" (p. 30). Without meaning life is wasted, futile, and empty. There is little reason to try to be concerned, or even to hope. Thus again we sense the great need for self-identity, for feelings of relatedness, and for values that give direction to life.

Value conflicts. As we have seen, values play a key role in determining our "choices." If our value assumptions are unclear or contradictory, or if we have little faith in them, we are likely to experience difficulties in making choices and directing behavior.

Here we shall briefly mention some core conflicts of modern life that frequently lead to such tension and inner turmoil that the individual's adjustive capacities are seriously impaired.

1. *Conformity vs. nonconformity.* Group pressures toward conformity inevitably develop as a group tries to maintain itself and achieve its goals, although the degree of conformity required varies greatly from one situation to another and from one group to another. For example, the conformity needed in a military group is considerably greater than that needed in a classroom. Even in the latter case, however, certain ground rules are established and members are under some pressure to conform to them.

Usually people are most likely to conform to the demands of groups in which they value membership and which have the greatest power to meet or to frustrate their needs. Thus it is often easier for teen-agers to repudiate adult norms than it is for them to go against peer group pressures. But adults too are likely to find it difficult to go against the expectations, demands, and pressures of peer groups that are important to them.

Thus a problem which often proves deeply disturbing is when to conform or not to conform to group expectations and pressures. Usually blind conformity or nonconformity is considered maladaptive because it represents an abdication of responsible self-direction and often results in behavior at odds with the individual's own values. A choice based on rational thought and decision appears most likely to serve the long-term interests of both the individual and the group.

2. *Caring vs. noninvolvement.* Because of the impersonality and anonymity of modern urban society, many people find it difficult to experience a sense of relatedness to others or of concern for the human enterprise. And since efforts on behalf of others can jeopardize one's own safety, the risks associated with "getting involved" may seem too great a price

Conformity to the group's norms can go to extremes, as illustrated by these motorcycle gang members.

to pay for helping "strangers." As Seaman (1966) has put it:

"Often it seems painful but realistic to conclude that, in the last analysis, you and your family are alone, and the only ones you can count on for help and support are yourselves. No one else cares." (p. 35)

The conflict between commitment and non-involvement is by no means confined to inter-actions with strangers or to participation in broader programs to right social injustices. Even in close interpersonal relationships, an individual may choose to remain somewhat aloof. All caring has hazards, since the one who invests affection is vulnerable to being hurt, and a painless outcome can never be guaranteed. Noninvolvement, on the other hand, exacts a price in lost satisfactions, feel-ings of estrangement and alienation, and a lack of meaning in one's existence.

3. *Avoiding vs. facing reality.* Perhaps the first requisite of maturity is the ability to see oneself and the surrounding world objectively and to make the best of realities. But this is no simple task. Reality is often unpleasant and anxiety-arousing, and may undermine an indi-vidual's efforts to feel good about himself and his world. For example, facing the realization that failure in an important venture resulted from one's own inadequacies would be self-devaluating. Hence a person may tend to avoid facing this reality by rationalizing, pro-jecting, or using other defense mechanisms.

Similarly, a proud parent may screen out the fact that his son is drinking too much, or is unduly preoccupied with drugs and neglecting his studies; or the parent may attempt to min-imize the undesirable behavior by saying that young people go through "phases" and that there is really no cause for concern.

While screening out unpleasant reality — whether it relates to oneself or the environ-ment — may help the individual feel adequate in facing life's problems, it may also keep him from making needed changes in his frame of reference and modes of adjustment.

4. *Fearfulness vs. positive action.* It has been said that anyone who lives in the latter half of the twentieth century and does not ex-perience a certain amount of fear and anxiety

is either stupid, insensitive, or atrophied. But many people, instead of taking constructive ac-tion to improve conditions, overreact to per-ceived dangers with disproportionate feelings of fear and inadequacy.

Although most people are familar with the increased tension and desire to flee that ac-company fear, few realize that fatigue, worry, indecision, and oversensitivity may also be disguised manifestations of fear. The perva-sive effects of fear are illustrated by the per-son who is afraid to go out in the dark alone after watching a terrifying murder mystery on television; if the person does go out anyway, he is prone to jump at the slightest sound. This increased sensitivity is characteristic of the many frightened, insecure persons who go through life overreacting to the slightest threat. Their fears rob them of courage and cripple their reasoning and other adjustive capacities.

Probably all of us experience some degree of fear in facing the problems of living. The brave person is not the one who experiences no fear, but the one who acts courageously despite fear. Not realizing this, many people expend their efforts trying to deny or conceal their fears, instead of learning to function effectively in spite of them.

5. *Integrity vs. self-advantage.* The term *integrity* essentially refers to being honest with oneself and others. At times it may appear that one's needs would best be served by ac-tions that are strongly in conflict with the person's ethical beliefs. An individual may be tempted, for example, to cheat on an examina-tion, to be devious in a business transaction, to lie in order to achieve some end, or simply to fail to stand up for values in which he believes. The temptation to engage in such behavior may be especially great when one sees others engage in it with seemingly successful results. In fact, a certain amount of deceit seems not only common but apparently acceptable in our society.

But most people find it guilt-arousing and self-devaluating to behave in ways that con-flict with what they believe to be right. In addi-tion, lack of self-integrity usually leads to a loss of respect from others and makes it vir-tually impossible to build satisfying interper-sonal relationships. As the biologist Herrick

(1956) so succinctly stated, "The wages of sin is death, if not of the person, certainly of his richest values and satisfactions" (p. 148).

6. *Sexual desires vs. restraints.* As a result of social prohibitions centering around sexual behavior, many people experience intense conflict in this area. Initially, sexual conflicts may be related to masturbation and may persist as a running battle between strong sexual desires and the belief that masturbation is a vile habit engaged in only by those who lack moral fiber and willpower. With the advent of adolescence and young adulthood, sexual conflicts are likely to arise over questions of premarital and extramarital relations.

Adding to young people's difficulty is the confusion and disagreement they see around them concerning what is acceptable and unacceptable in sexual behavior. In recent years our society has become more permissive with respect to norms governing sexual expression, but guidelines are far from clear and sexual values may differ markedly among different ethnic, socioeconomic, and religious groups as well as from one person to another. It's not surprising then that many young people experience intense conflict as they try to work out an acceptable code of sexual ethics to guide their behavior.

Pressures of modern living. Each person faces his own unique pattern of pressures, but in a general way most of us face the pressures of competing with others, meeting educational, occupational, and marital demands, and coping with the complexity and rapid pace of modern living.

1. Competition. In our highly competitive society, we compete for grades, athletic honors, jobs, marital partners, and almost everything

Every student can probably identify to an extent with the frustrations of class registration, just one of the many stressful demands education can make.

else we want, and in this competitive struggle we are encouraged to surpass others, to excel, to "get to the top." While we may give grudging credit for "a good try," it is success that gains the rewards. The winning football team attracts the crowds, the outstanding student gains the opportunity for admission to graduate school and advanced training. Consequently, many people feel compelled to drive themselves mercilessly toward high levels of achievement, subjecting themselves in the process to sustained and severe pressure.

Competitive pressures have been acclaimed as leading to greater productivity, to an increased sense of purpose, and to higher standards of excellence. Yet inappropriate or indiscriminate competition, particularly competition where one person can achieve or succeed only at the expense of others, may be especially harmful for the individual and divisive to the group. If competition leads to sustained "overloading," it may ultimately be harmful to winners and losers alike.

2. *Educational, occupational, and family demands.* Closely related to the pressures of competition are those of sustained effort stemming from educational, occupational, and family demands. The long hours of study, the tension of examinations, and the sustained concentration of effort over many years result in considerable stress for many students. Where a student is handicapped by inefficient study habits, inadequate financial resources, personal problems, or other difficulties, the continuing effort for grades and academic achievement may be highly stressful.

Occupational demands can also be highly stressful. Many jobs make severe demands in terms of responsibility, time, and performance, and Buck (1972) has reported a negative relationship between pressure on the job and the mental health of the worker. Regardless of the actual demands of the work situation, if the individual is not really interested or well suited to the work, occupational demands are likely to be a major source of stress.

Marriage and family make demands on both partners, demands that may be especially stressful if either partner is immature and poorly prepared for the responsibilities involved, if there are basic incompatibilities between the partners, or if financial or other problems make the external situation unfavorable. Particularly if a marriage is already making difficult adjustive demands, the arrival of children and problems of parenthood may markedly increase the pressures on both partners.

3. *Complexity and pace of modern living.* The mere complexity and pace of modern living tend to "overload" the human organism; the stress of living under such highly complicated and demanding conditions can play havoc on both biological and psychological levels. For example, we have mentioned the role of severe stress in the incidence of heart attacks and other "psychosomatic" disorders, as well as the general lowering of adaptive efficiency over time.

Many other frustrations, conflicts, and pressures could be mentioned in our discussion, including insufficient time to deal with the many adjustive demands that confront us and the necessity of making choices before adequate information is available. And ever lurking in the background are the possibility of thermonuclear war and the other problems of global scope that confront us in our contemporary world.

Sociocultural Factors

In addition to the biological and psychosocial factors that we have reviewed as conducive to abnormal behavior in our society, there are other conditions especially characteristic of our time and place in history that put stress, directly or indirectly, on most of us. Among these are the problems of war and violence, group prejudice and discrimination, economic and employment problems, and rapid social change and existential anxiety.

Since we shall extend our discussion of these problems in later chapters—particularly in Chapter 18, dealing with the maladaptive behavior of groups—we shall keep our present discussion brief.

War and violence

A history of the United States—or of the world in general—must of necessity devote a sizeable amount of space to a consideration of wars. Although wars have sometimes been necessary to achieve or maintain freedom and human rights, the conditions of warfare have placed great stress on large numbers of people. Privation, mutilation, death, grief, and social disorganization have been inevitable accompaniments of war.

Today we live in the shadow of the new and incredibly destructive instruments of modern warfare, which are becoming available to an increasing number of nations on our planet. Although most people try not to think about the possibility of humanity being consumed in a thermonuclear holocaust, the possibility does exist and adds its own distinctive note of fear to our lives.

While "small wars" and civil violence continue to smolder on our planet, we have also witnessed an ever-increasing rate of violent crime in our own society—an increase that makes many communities unsafe even in the daytime and adds its own grim note to the uncertainties of our times.

Supportive and destructive human environments

Each human environment has characteristics that affect the behavior of people in it in many subtle ways; this is especially important in dealing with sociocultural sources of stress. As Inself and Moos (1974) have described it:

"Like people, environments have unique personalities. Just as it is possible to characterize a person's 'personality,' environments can be similarly portrayed with a great deal of accuracy and detail. Some people are supportive; likewise, some environments are supportive. Some men feel the need to control others; similarly, some environments are extremely controlling. Order and structure are important to many people; correspondingly, many environments emphasize regularity, system, and order." (p. 179)

Such characteristics may reflect the prevailing attitudes and values of the individuals within them; in other instances, however, as in the case of mental clinics and hospitals, the characteristics of the environment may reflect the attitudes of administrative and other professional personnel in charge of the facility. In either case, an environment may be helpful and conducive to the physical and mental health of those within it, or it may be destructive and pathogenic.

Moos and his associates (1974) studied eight different treatment environments—psychiatric wards and correctional institutions—all supposedly trying to help people become better able to cope and play a constructive role in society. They found marked differences in treatment orientation and environmental climates, with resulting differences in patient or inmate responses. For example, some ward environments appeared to be supportive and constructive in their effects, while others appeared conducive to the patients' acting "crazy" and were considered pathogenic.

Studying the characteristics of a given treatment environment should prove helpful in determining whether it: (1) predisposes individuals to maladaptive behavior; (2) serves as a precipitating cause of maladaptive behavior; and/or (3) reinforces and maintains maladaptive behavior. This same approach can be used to assess the extent to which a given environment helps alleviate maladaptive behavior, or to plan human environments which are conducive to mental health.

In a broad sense, the study of human environments represents one application of the general systems approach, and it can be applied to family and other small group environments as well as to organizations and societies.

The term *anomie* refers to a state of societal disregulation or disorganization during which value conflicts tend to spread through the social system. There is little sense of community or group identification and a lack of widely shared norms to guide and control behavior. Often there tends to be a fragmentation of society into conflicting pressure groups.

One of the primary consequences of anomie are feelings of alienation on the part of large numbers of people. Such alienation is accompanied by confusion about who one is or what one should be, by a lack of needed values for distinguishing between the desirable and undesirable, by inability to establish authentic interpersonal relationships, and by feelings of being disconnected from the basic political and social processes of one's society.

The behavioral manifestations of alienation may vary widely, from cynicism and apathy at one extreme to brutal and senseless violence at the other. In some instances, individuals enter into highly damaging and pathogenic interpersonal relationships; others concentrate on getting "their share" with little or no concern for other people or the broader society; others join social groups or movements which often have high sounding ideals but are basically destructive and nihilistic; still others drift aimlessly or commit suicide.

In our complex, rapidly changing, and impersonal mass society, many people do seem alienated in varying degree from themselves, from others, and from society as a whole. In essence, they seem unable to find a truly authentic, meaningful, and fulfilling way of life.

Based on Bronfenbrenner (1974).

Group prejudice and discrimination

One of the most destructive forms of group prejudice is that of racial discrimination. While it is loudly decried in our society, it seems to be among our most ingrained cultural habits. All of society suffers as a result of this prejudice, but the victims lose most by it.

One index of the toll that such conditions take is Harlem's rate of admissions to mental hospitals—three times that of the rest of New York City—and its startlingly high rates for suicide, drug abuse, delinquency, crime, and other maladaptive behaviors. Racial discrimination, poverty, and social disorganization tend to debase and confuse human beings. Children reared in such a setting have the almost impossible task of trying to learn what is predictable and possible, of striving to develop healthy motives and values, and of attempting to achieve educational and other competencies essential for effective participation in our highly technological society. A report of the National Institute for Mental Health (1969) concluded that

". . . a child of parents at the bottom of the socioeconomic scale who comes into the world with the same basic intellect as a child of parents at the top is less likely, for lack of stimulation and opportunity, to develop it. Moreover, poverty often interferes with the development not only of intelligence but also of a healthy personality. There is evidence, too, of an association between poverty on the one hand and, on the other, ignorance and distrust of democratic ideals and institutions. Violence, too, breeds in an atmosphere of deprivation and despair." (p. 2)

Thus we see the beginning of the vicious circle of educational underachievement, menial jobs, broken homes, and the perpetuation of the culture of poverty.

The effects of group prejudice and discrimination are by no means limited to racial minorities in our society. In recent years, for example, we have witnessed the struggle for women's rights in educational, occupational, marital, and other areas where women have not had equal opportunity with men. Similarly, we could point to the discrimination against older people who are forced to adjust to arbitrary retirement, a marked reduction in income, and feelings of no longer being useful or even wanted.

Economic and employment problems

Inflation, unemployment, and job dissatisfaction are sources of stress for many people in our society. Inflation, for example, has imposed special hardships on people whose finances cannot keep pace with the economic spiral, such as those on fixed retirement incomes. Unemployment has placed a burden on a sizeable segment of our population, bringing with it both financial hardships and self-devaluation. In fact, unemployment can be as debilitating psychologically as it is financially (Nelson, 1974a). As an indication of the toll that unemployment exacts, periods of extensive unemployment are typically accompanied by increases in certain types of maladaptive behavior, such as depression, suicide, and crime (Brenner, 1973). Hardest hit by economic and employment problems are those at the bottom of the social ladder who are already handicapped by poorer education, poorer nutrition, more broken or unstable families, overcrowding, inadequate housing, and feelings of helplessness and of rejection by the larger society.

For many people who are employed, a major source of stress is job dissatisfaction. This point takes on particular significance in view of findings that job dissatisfaction is related to anxiety, tension, and a wide range of psychosomatic disorders; it has also been related to impaired marital and family relationships.

Whatever the possibilities for job satisfaction in an increasingly computerized and complicated society, the demand for it seems to be increasing (Gartner & Riessman, 1974). People are no longer content with only money as a return for their investment of time and energy; today there appears to be a widespread and growing demand for meaningful employment and for the integration of education, work, and increased leisure into a more fulfilling life pattern.

Prominent among the victims of racial prejudice and discrimination are the children, like these boys growing up in an urban ghetto.

Accelerating technological and social change

Accelerating change in our contemporary world has played havoc with established norms and values and with many people's assumptions about the meaning of human existence. With the advent of the space age, we are confronted with a new perspective of time and space and the problem of finding the meaning of human existence in a universe in which the earth may be no larger in relation to the whole than an atom is to the earth.

The rate and pervasiveness of change today are different from anything our ancestors ever experienced, and all aspects of our lives are affected—our education, our jobs, our family life, our leisure pursuits, our economic security, and our beliefs and values. Constantly trying to keep up with the new adjustments demanded by these changes is a source of considerable stress. In fact, Toffler (1970) proposed the term "future shock" to describe the profound confusion and emotional upset resulting from social change that has become too rapid.

As a result, many people in our society are groping about, bewildered and bitter, unable to find satisfying values to guide their lives. Despite their television sets, well-stocked refrigerators, and other signs of material affluence, the meaning of life seems to be escaping them. In essence, they are alienated from the broader society and suffering from *existential anxiety*—from doubt and concern about their ability to find a meaningful and fulfilling way of life.

Rapid change and pervasive anxiety are by

Their faces reflecting their feelings, these people wait in line at an unemployment office.

no means restricted to the United States. In the developing nations, as well as in the industrialized world, people are demanding the better way of life that they feel modern technology can bring them. Vast social changes seem to be the order of the day; unfortunately, these changes are accompanied by considerable turmoil and stress as old patterns and values give way to new ones.

In this chapter we have reviewed different models of causation in maladaptive behavior, and we noted our changing views of causal relationships. In the latter context, we defined the concepts of primary, predisposing, precipitating, and reinforcing causes; and we emphasized the concept of feedback and circularity in establishing the "vicious circles" that often characterize the clinical picture in abnormal behavior. We then reviewed some of the specific biological, psychosocial, and sociocultural factors that are commonly involved in the development of abnormal behavior in our society. Throughout we have emphasized the interaction of these factors in the total causal pattern.

We shall find this general perspective on causation most helpful as we turn now to an examination of specific patterns of abnormal behavior.

II
Patterns of Abnormal (Maladaptive) Behavior

6

Transient Situational Disorders

As we noted previously, any one of us may break down if the going gets tough enough. When conditions of overwhelming stress occur—as in terrifying accidents, imprisonment, physical mutilation, or military combat—temporary mental disorders may develop, even in previously stable personalities. The personality decompensation may be sudden, as in the case of an individual who has gone through a severe accident or fire; or it may be gradual, as in the case of a person who has been subjected to conditions in a prisoner-of-war camp or even to a very difficult situation in civilian life. Usually the individual shows good recoverability once the stress situation is over, although in some cases there is residual damage to the self-structure and an increased vulnerability to certain types of stress. In the case of individuals who are marginally adjusted to begin with, of course, the situational stress may precipitate more serious psychopathology.

Perhaps the special value of starting our discussion of the kinds of abnormal behavior with these transient personality disturbances, particularly with reactions to the acute stress of combat, lies in the perspective that they can give us on the development of the more typical maladaptive patterns that occur in less extreme situations. World War II, as well as the wars in Korea and Vietnam, furnished the social sciences with a laboratory in which the effects of severe environmental stresses on the personality integration of thousands of men could readily be evaluated. As Grinker (1969) has pointed out:

"The entire range of factors from the biological to the sociological were sharply etched in miniature and required only a magnified view for understanding. Likewise time was compressed so that in rapid succession we could view predisposition, precipitation, breakdown, and recovery." (p. 3)

Abhorrent as war is, it has provided a research setting that could perhaps never be duplicated in civilian life. As a result of this unique situation, plus the pressure of military necessity growing out of the large number of men who developed transient reactions to combat—particularly in World War II and the initial phases

Traumatic Reactions to Combat
Reactions to Civilian Catastrophes
Reactions to Chronic Situational Stress
Psychological Problems in Space Flights

of the Korean War—marked strides were made in the understanding and treatment of psychopathology.

These forward strides led, in turn, to a better understanding of mental disorders by the general public. For the first time, millions of people became aware of the potential effects of extreme stress on personality integration. They learned that such stress could seriously impair adaptive behavior or even incapacitate the individual; and they learned that this was not a disgrace—it could happen to anyone.

We shall begin our discussion with the psychological casualties of World War II and of the conflicts in Korea and Vietnam, particularly those cases involving army personnel subjected to combat; then we shall attempt to show the general implication of these findings for typical civilian mental disorders. Next we shall examine transient reactions to civilian catastrophes and to other situations of unusual and severe stress. Although we shall see similarities, we shall also see differences between combat and civilian stress reactions. Finally, we shall discuss some of the special stresses associated with the exploration of space.

Traumatic Reactions to Combat

During World War I traumatic reactions to combat conditions were called "shell shock," a term coined by a British pathologist, Col. Frederick Mott, who regarded such reactions as organic conditions produced by minute hemorrhages of the brain. It was gradually realized, however, that only a very small percentage of such cases represented physical injury from concussion of exploding shells or bombs. Most of these men were suffering instead from the general combat situation with its physical fatigue, ever-present threat of death or mutilation, and severe psychological shocks. During World War II, traumatic reactions to combat passed through a number of classifications, such as "operational fatigue" and "war neuroses," before finally being termed "combat fatigue" or "combat exhaustion" in the Korean War and the Vietnam conflict.

Even the latter terms were none too aptly chosen, since they implied that physical exhaustion played a more important role than was usually the case. However, they did serve to distinguish such disorders for purposes of treatment from neurotic, psychotic, and other disorders that happened to occur under war conditions but might well have occurred in civilian life—for example, among individuals showing a history of maladaptive behavior that was aggravated by the increased stress of military life. In the great majority of cases, men who became psychological casualties under combat conditions had adjusted satisfactorily to civilian life and to prior military experiences.

In World War II an estimated 10 percent of the men in combat developed combat exhaustion; however, the actual incidence is not known, since many received therapy at their battalion aid station and were returned to combat within a few hours. Records were kept mainly on men evacuated from the front lines who were considered the more seriously disturbed cases. Of the slightly over 10 million men accepted for military service during World War II, approximately 1,363,000 were given medical discharges, of which approximately 530,000 – 39 percent – were for neuropsychiatric disorders. In fact, what we now call combat exhaustion was the disability causing the single greatest loss of manpower during that war (Bloch, 1969). In the Korean War the incidence of combat exhaustion dropped from an initial high of over 6 percent to 3.7 percent; 27 percent of medical discharges were for psychiatric reasons (Bell, 1958). In the Vietnam War the figure dropped to less than 1.5 percent for combat exhaustion, with a negligible number of discharges for psychiatric disorders (Bourne, 1970; Allerton, 1970).

The marked decrease in combat exhaustion cases in the Vietnam War was apparently due to a number of factors, including (a) improved methods of selection and training, (b) confidence in military leadership, (c) the sporadic nature of the fighting, in which brief intensive encounters were followed by periods of relative calm and safety – as contrasted with weeks and months of prolonged combat that many soldiers went through in World War II and the Korean War – and (d) a policy of rotation after twelve months of service (thirteen months for Marines). Apparently it is easier for soldiers to tolerate combat stress for a known period of time, after which it becomes "somebody else's war."

Clinical picture

The specific symptoms in combat exhaustion have varied considerably, depending on the branch of the service, the severity and nature of the traumatic experience, and the personality makeup of the individual. Common symptoms among combat troops were dejection, weariness, hypersensitivity, sleep disturbances, and tremors. In air-corps personnel, after long combat flying, the more typical symptoms were anxiety, frequently with accompanying dejection and depression, phobias toward combat missions, irritability, tension, and startle reactions. In addition, where the stress was cumulative, symptoms often differed from those brought on by a sudden and particularly intense combat situation.

Despite such variations, however, there was surprising uniformity in the general clinical picture in both World War II and the Korean War. The first symptoms were a failure to maintain psychological integration, with increasing irritability, disturbances of sleep, and often recurrent nightmares.

"The irritability is manifested externally by snappishness, over-reaction to minor irritations, angry reactions to innocuous questions or incidents, flareups with profanity and even tears at relatively slight frustrations. The degree of these reactions may vary from angry looks or a few sharp words to acts of violence.

"Subjectively, the state of irritation is perceived by the soldier as an unpleasant 'hypersensitiveness' and he is made doubly uncomfortable by a concomitant awareness of his diminishing self-control. One patient put this very vividly by saying – 'The first thing that brought home to me the fact that I was slipping was this incident: A fellow next to me took some cellophane off a piece of hard candy and crumpled it up, and that crackling noise sounded like a forest fire. It made me so mad I wanted to hit him. Then I was ashamed of being so jumpy.'

"In association with this 'hypersensitiveness' to minor external stimuli, the 'startle reaction' becomes manifest (increasingly so as time goes on). This is a sudden leaping, jumping, cringing, jerking or other form of involuntary self-protective motor response to sudden, not necessarily very loud noises, and sometimes also to sudden movement or sudden light.

"The disturbances of sleep, which almost always accompany the symptom of increased irritability, consist mainly in the frustrating experience of not being able to fall asleep even upon those occasions when the military situation would permit. Soldiers have to snatch their rest when they can. . . . Opportunities for sleep become very precious and an inability to use them very distressing. Difficulties were experienced also in staying asleep because of sudden involuntary starting or leaping up, or because of terror dreams, battle dreams and nightmares of other kinds.

"This triad of increased 'sensitivity,' irritable reactions and sleep disturbances represents the incipient state of 'combat exhaustion.' It usually does not lead to referral [for treatment]. It may exist without much change for days, weeks or even months. Sooner or later, often upon the occasion of some incident of particularly traumatic significance to the soldier, the marginal and very unstable equilibrium is upset and the soldier becomes a casualty." (Bartemeier et al., 1946, pp. 374–75)

Breakdown of combat personnel who had been most resistant to personality decompensation

In studying the eventual breakdown of the army personnel who had been most resistant to personality decompensation, Sobel (1949) found that such individuals seemed to have been protected by five "defensive layers." These were surrendered progressively in the face of too-severe stress and threat. Distant ideals like "democracy" and "the four freedoms" went first. Loyalty to the group was the last to be given up.

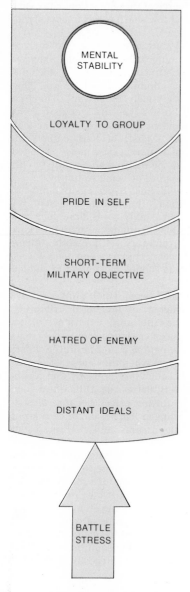

MENTAL STABILITY

LOYALTY TO GROUP

PRIDE IN SELF

SHORT-TERM MILITARY OBJECTIVE

HATRED OF ENEMY

DISTANT IDEALS

BATTLE STRESS

When the combat casualties reached the aid station or the clearing station, they presented a somewhat typical pattern of symptoms, differing only in the degree of personality decompensation.

"In the majority of cases they followed a stereotyped pattern: 'I just can't take it any more'; 'I can't stand those shells'; 'I just couldn't control myself.' They varied little from patient to patient. Whether it was the soldier who had experienced his baptism of fire or the older veteran who had lost his comrades, the superficial result was very similar. Typically he appeared as a dejected, dirty, weary man. His facial expression was one of depression, sometimes of tearfulness. Frequently his hands were trembling or jerking. Occasionally he would display varying degrees of confusion, perhaps to the extent of being mute or staring into space. Very occasionally he might present classically hysterical symptoms." (Menninger, 1948, p. 143)

In extreme cases where the soldier has undergone an unusually traumatic combat experience, the entire episode may be repressed so that he is amnesic for the entire battle experience.

The following diary covers a period of about six weeks of combat in the South Pacific area and illustrates the cumulative effect of combat stresses on an apparently stable personality.

"Aug. 7, 1942. Convoy arrived at Guadalcanal Bay at approximately 4 A.M. in the morning. Ships gave enemy a heavy shelling. At 9 A.M. we stormed the beach and formed an immediate beachhead, a very successful landing, marched all day in the hot sun, and at night took positions and rested. Enemy planes attacked convoy in bay but lost 39 out of 40 planes.

"Aug. 8, 1942. Continued march in the hot sun and in afternoon arrived at airport. Continued on through the Jap village and made camp for the night. During the night, Jap navy attacked convoy in battle that lasted until early morning. Enemy had terrific losses and we lost two ships. This night while on sentry duty, I mistook a horse for a Jap and killed it.

"Aug. 19, 1942. Enemy cruiser and destroyer came into bay and shelled the beach for about two hours. The cruiser left and the destroyer hung around for the entire morning. We all kept under shelter for the early afternoon a flying fortress flew over, spotting the ship and bombed it, setting it afire we all jumped and shouted with joy. That night trouble again was feared and we again slept in foxholes.

"Aug. 21, 1942. The long awaited landing by the enemy was made during the night 1500 troops in all and a few prisoners were taken and the rest were killed. Bodies were laying all over beach. In afternoon planes again bombed the Island. [Here the writing begins to be shaky, and less careful than previously.]

"Aug. 28, 1942. The company left this morning in higgins Boats to the end of the Island, landed and started through thick Jungle and hills. It was hot and we had to cut our way through. In afternoon we contacted the japs. our squad was in the assault squad so we moved up the beach to take positions the enemy trapped us with machine gun and rifle fire for about two hours. The lead was really flying. Two of our men were killed, two were hit by a hand greade and my corporal received a piece of shrampnel in back,—was wounded in arm, out of the squad of eight we have five causitry. We withdrew and were taken back to the Hospital.

"Sept. 12, 1942. Large jap squadron again bombed Island out of 35 planes sent over our air force knocked down 24. During the raid a large bomb was dropped just sevety yards from my fox hole.

"Sept. 13, 1942. At on o'clock three destroyers and one cruiser shelled us contumally all night The ships turned surch lights all up and down the beach, and stopped one my foxhole seveal time I'm feeling pritty nervese and scared, afraid I'll be a nervas reack be for long. slept in fox hole all night not much sleep. This morning at 9:00 we had a nother air raid, the raid consisted of mostly fighter planes. I believe we got several, this afternoon. we had a nother raid, and our planes went out to met them, met them someplace over Tulagi, new came in that the aircraft carrier wasp sent planes out to intersept the bombers. This eving all hell broke lose. Our marines contacted enemy to south of us and keep up constant fire all night through.

"Sept. 14, 1942. This morning firing still going on my company is scaduted to unload ships went half ways up to dock when enemyfire start on docks, were called back to our pososeion allon beach, company called out again to go after japs, hope were lucker than we were last time [part of this illegible.] Went up into hills at 4:00 P.M. found positions, at 7:00 en 8 sea planes fombed and strifed us, 151942 were strifed biy amfibious planes and bombed the concussion of one through me of balance and down a 52 foot hil. I was shaking likd a leaf. Lost my bayanut, and ran out of wathr. I nearves and very jumpy, hop I last out until morning. I hope sevearly machine s guns ore oping up on our left flank there going over our heads

"Sept. 16. this morning we going in to take up new possissons we march all moring and I am very week and nerves, we marched up a hill and ran in to the affaul place y and z company lost so many men I hardly new what I was doing then I'm going nuts.

"Sept. 17. don't remember much of this day.

"Sept. 18. Today I'm on a ship leaving this awful place, called Green Hell. I'm still nearves and shakey." (Stern, 1947, pp. 583–86)

In the Vietnam War, soldiers were seldom exposed to prolonged periods of shelling and bombardment; combat reactions were typically more sudden and acute as a result of some particular overwhelming combat experience. This is well illustrated in the following case.

"A 21-year-old rifleman was flown directly to the hospital from an area of fighting by a helicopter ambulance. No information accompanied him, he had no identifying tags on his uniform, and he was so completely covered with mud that a physical description of his features was not possible. His hands had been tied behind him for the flight, and he had a wild, wide-eyed look as he cowered in a corner of the emergency room, glancing furtively to all sides, cringing and startling at the least noise. He was mute, although once he forced out a whispered 'VC' and tried to mouth other words without success. He seemed terrified. Although people could approach him, he appeared oblivious to their presence. No manner of reassurance or direct order achieved either a verbal response or any other interaction from him.

"His hands were untied, after which he would hold an imaginary rifle in readiness whenever he heard a helicopter overhead or an unexpected noise. The corpsmen led him to the psychiatric ward, took him to a shower, and offered him a meal; he ate very little. He began to move a little more freely but still offered no information.

"He was then given 100 mg. of chlorpromazine (Thorazine) orally; this dose was repeated hourly until he fell asleep. He was kept asleep in this manner for approximately 40 hours. . . . Although dazed and subdued upon awakening, his response in the ward milieu was dramatic. This was aided by the presence of a friend from his platoon on an adjoining ward, who helped by filling in parts of the story that the patient could not recall. The patient was an infantryman whose symptoms had developed on a day when his platoon had been caught in an ambush and then was overrun by the enemy. He was one of three who survived after being pinned down by enemy fire for 12 hours. His friend told him that toward the end of that time he had developed a crazed expression and had tried to run from his hiding place. He was pulled back to safety and remained there until the helicopter arrived and flew him to the hospital.

These pictures, taken during the war in Southeast Asia, give some indication of the extreme stress to which soldiers are subjected during combat. Near right, a paratrooper guides a medical evacuation helicopter to a landing while others aid their wounded buddies. Below, a chaplain comforts a wounded soldier. Far right, the looks on the soldiers' faces convey their stress and tension. Below, a rare moment of relief, as two friends discover that each has survived and embrace in happiness; the radio corpsman looks on.

"Within 72 hours after his admission the patient was alert, oriented, responsive, and active—still a little tense but ready to return to duty. He was sent back to duty on his third hospital day and never seen again at our facility. It should be noted that he had no history of similar symptoms or emotional disorder." (Bloch, 1969, p. 42)

In the recorded cases of combat exhaustion among soldiers in all three wars, the common core was usually overwhelming anxiety. In World War II, however, an exception was noted in the case of troops from India to whom admission of fear was unacceptable. They rarely showed anxiety reactions, instead resorting occasionally to self-mutilation and other "honorable" ways of avoiding further combat (Williams, 1950).

It is interesting to note that wounded soldiers showed less anxiety or other combat exhaustion symptoms—except in cases of permanent mutilation. Apparently the wound, in providing an escape from the stressful combat situation, removed the source of the anxiety state. In fact, it was not unusual for a soldier to admit that he had prayed to be hit or to have something "honorable" happen to remove him from battle. When they were approaching full recovery and the necessity of returning to combat, injured soldiers sometimes showed prolongation of their symptoms or a delayed traumatic reaction of nervousness, insomnia, and other symptoms that were nonexistent when they were first hospitalized.

Similarly, some soldiers who had stood up exceptionally well under intensive combat experiences developed what might be called "delayed combat reactions" upon their return home—often in response to relatively minor stresses in the home situation that they had previously been capable of handling. Evidently there had been underlying damage to their adaptive capabilities, in some cases complicated by memories of killing enemy soldiers or civilians, tinged with feelings of guilt and anxiety (Karpe & Schnap, 1952; Polner, 1968; Van Putten & Emory, 1973).

Causal factors

In a combat situation, with the continual threat of injury or death and repeated narrow escapes, one's ordinary methods of coping are relatively useless. The adequacy and security feelings the individual has known in a relatively safe and dependable civilian world are completely undermined. As one combat medic expressed it:

"I was always afraid. In fact, I can't remember not being afraid. For one thing, a combat medic doesn't know what's happening. Especially at night, everybody screaming or moaning and calling, 'Medic, medic.' I always saw myself dying, my legs blown off, my brains spattered all about, shivering in shock, and talking madly. This is what I *saw* in reality." (Polner, 1968, p. 18)

However, we must not overlook the fact that even in World War II, about 90 percent of the soldiers subjected to combat did *not* become psychiatric casualties, although most of them evidenced severe fear reactions and other symptoms of ego disorganization that were not serious enough to be incapacitating. In addition, many soldiers tolerated almost unbelievable stress before they broke, while others became casualties under conditions of relatively slight combat stress.

Consequently, it appears that to understand traumatic reactions to combat, we need to examine other factors such as constitutional predisposition, personal maturity, loyalty to one's unit, and confidence in one's officers—as well as stress.

Biological factors. Do constitutional differences in sensitivity, vigor, and temperament affect one's resistance to the stress of combat? The probabilities are that they do, but there is a dearth of actual evidence.

Factors about which we have more information are the conditions of battle that tax the soldier's physical stamina. Grinker and Spiegel describe this vividly in a World War II study:

"Battle conditions are notoriously destructive to health. Frequently men must go for days without adequate sleep or rest. . . . The purely physiological effects of nearby blasts are also a factor. Many men are repeatedly subjected to minimal doses of blast. They are knocked over by the compression wave, or perhaps blown slightly off the ground, if they are lying prone. In some instances they are temporarily numbed or even stunned. . . . Lastly, the continued auditory irritation of constant explosions, bangs, snaps of machine guns, whines of artillery shells, rustle of mortars . . . wears down resistance." (1945, pp. 68–70)

Add other factors that have often occurred in combat situations—such as severe climatic conditions, malnutrition, and disease—to the strain of continual emotional mobilization, and the result is a general lowering of the individual's resistance to all stress.

Psychological and interpersonal factors. A number of psychological and interpersonal factors may contribute to the overall stress load experienced by a soldier and predispose him to break down under the increased burden of combat. Such factors include a reduction in personal freedom, frustrations of all sorts, and separation from home and loved ones. Letters from home that create worry or hurt add to the soldier's already difficult adjustive burden—particularly since he is far away and helpless to take any action. A soldier who has withstood months of combat may break when he finds that his wife has been unfaithful, or when she stops writing, or when she writes him a "Dear John" letter stating that she is leaving him for someone else.

Of particular importance is the toll of adjustive resources taken by prior combat experiences as well as anxiety, fear, and other factors directly related to the nature of combat.

1. *Fear and anxiety.* Although not all soldiers experience the same degree of threat and anxiety in combat situations, there is an emergency mobilization of emotional resources that is sustained as long as the crisis exists. With time, there are usually increasingly severe feelings of threat and anxiety as one sees his buddies killed or wounded and experiences narrow escapes himself.

The hypersensitivity shown in the startle reaction follows directly from this continued fear and anxiety. Consequently, the buzz of a fly or the striking of a match may produce marked overreactions. This hypersensitivity is, of course, intensified when the stimulus bears a direct association with some traumatic combat experience. A soldier who has been strafed by attacking planes may be terrified by the sight of approaching aircraft. As continued emotional mobilization and fatigue take their toll of adjustive resources, the common symptom of irritability makes its appearance and adds to the soldier's anxiety by making him aware of his diminishing self-control. In our normal lives, too, prolonged emotional stress and fatigue tend to keep our nerves "on edge" and to increase irritability.

Difficulties in falling asleep and other sleep disturbances are common accompaniments of fear and sustained emotional arousal, and in combat conditions, men often go for days without adequate sleep. However, the dynamic significance of the recurrent nightmares is not fully understood. How and why does the traumatic material become reactivated during sleep, when the soldier desperately needs quiet and rest? In some cases the repeated dreams are so terrifying that the soldier is even afraid to go to sleep. It may be, however, that the continual reliving of a traumatic battle experience in dreams gradually serves to discharge the anxiety associated with it and to desensitize the individual to the point where he can assimilate the experience.

In severe combat exhaustion cases, the stupor or amnesia is thought to result from temporary repression, enabling the individual to avoid consciousness of the traumatic experience until its emotional intensity has cooled down to the point where he can tolerate memory of it. Here the defensive function of repression is clearly demonstrated since the repressed material can be brought to consciousness in full detail under the influence of hypnosis or various drugs, such as sodium pentothal.

2. *Strangeness and unpredictability of the combat situation.* Strangeness and unpredictability can be a source of severe threat and stress. When the soldier knows what to expect and what to do, the chances are much better of coming through with a minimum of psychological disorganization. But even the best training cannot fully prepare a soldier for all the conditions of actual battle. The factor of unpredictability also partly explains the effectiveness of new "secret weapons" for which enemy soldiers are not prepared.

Conditions that necessitate immobilization in the face of acute danger also lower the soldier's stress tolerance. The case cited on page 189 — the soldier who was pinned down by enemy fire for twelve hours in an enemy ambush — shows the effects of immobilization on a person in extreme danger. Some activity or duty to perform, even though it does not lessen the danger, appears to provide an outlet for tension and thus to help a soldier keep his fear and anxiety within manageable limits.

3. *The necessity of killing.* Having to kill enemy soldiers and sometimes civilians can also be an important factor in combat reactions. Most of us have strong moral convictions against killing or injuring others, and for some soldiers it is psychologically almost impossible to engage in ruthless killing. In extreme cases, such soldiers may even be unable to defend themselves when attacked. In other instances, the soldiers engage in killing but later experience intense feelings of guilt, together with fear of retaliation and punishment.

A good fighter, a machine gunner, one day killed five of the enemy almost simultaneously. "His first reaction was elation — but suddenly he felt that it was wrong to enjoy this and thereupon developed anxiety with some depression, so severe that he was incapacitated." (Saul, 1945, p. 262)

Over time, such a soldier may become habituated to killing enemy soldiers and may even take pride in it — perhaps as a job well done for which he is reinforced by the praise of his buddies. In this context, Lifton (1972) has referred to "numbed warfare," in which the enemy is reduced to nonhuman status — to "Huns" or "Gooks" — so the soldier can feel that he is merely getting rid of animals or scum or devils. This attitude was epitomized by the statement of an American officer that the mass slaughter of civilians at My Lai was "no big deal."

On the other hand, the soldier may come to see further combat as the means by which he is inevitably to receive dreaded retaliation and punishment for his actions. Thus, anxiety arising out of combat experience may reflect not only a simple fear of death or mutilation but also emotional conflicts and guilt feelings generated by the experience of killing other human beings.

4. *Length of combat duty.* The longer a soldier is in combat, the more vulnerable — and more anxious — he is likely to feel. Although, as Tuohy (1967) found, most soldiers on their arrival in Vietnam had the notion of their invulnerability — that anyone but themselves was likely to get killed — they soon found that Vietnam was a dangerous place and that "war really is hell." This time of realization is when many soldiers show their first signs of anxiety. And after a soldier has been in combat and has seen many of his buddies killed and wounded as well as having had narrow escapes himself, he usually loses whatever feeling of invulnerability he may have had. Often the death of a buddy leads to a serious loss of emotional support as well as to feelings of guilt if the soldier cannot help feeling glad that it was his buddy and not himself who was killed. When a soldier has almost completed the number of missions or duration of duty necessary for rotation, he is particularly apt to feel that his "luck has run out" and that the next bullet coming his way will "have his name on it."

The effect of prolonged combat in lowering stress tolerance was exemplified in World War II by "the old sergeant syndrome," in which men of established bravery exhibited anxiety, depression, tremulousness, and impairment of self-confidence and judgment after prolonged combat experience — usually 150 to 350 days of combat (Bell, 1958). The progressive lowering of stress tolerance under prolonged combat is illustrated in the case on page 188.

5. *Personal characteristics.* Any personality characteristics that lower the individual's resistance to stress or to particular types of stress may be important in determining his reactions to combat. Personal immaturity — often stemming from parental overprotection — is commonly cited as making the soldier more vulnerable to combat stress.

Interestingly enough, a background of personal maladjustment does not always make an individual a "poor risk" for withstanding the stresses of combat. Some anxiety neurotics are so accustomed to anxiety that they can cope with it more or less automatically, whereas soldiers who are feeling severe anxiety for the first time may be terrified by the experience, lose their self-confidence, and go to pieces. It has also been observed that socio-paths, though frequently in trouble in the armed services during peacetime for disregarding rules and regulations, have often demonstrated good initiative and effective combat aggression against the enemy. However, the soldiers who function most effectively and are most apt to survive the rigors of combat usually come from backgrounds that fostered self-reliance, ability to function in a group, and ready adjustment to new situations (Bloch, 1969; Grinker, 1969; Lifton, 1972; Borus, 1974).

Sociocultural factors. In the preceding section our focus was on psychological and interpersonal factors related to combat stress. Here we are concerned with more general sociocultural factors that may play an important part in determining an individual's adjustment to combat. These include the clarity and acceptability of war goals, the identification of the soldier with his combat unit, *esprit de corps*, and the quality of leadership.

1. *Clarity and acceptability of war goals.* In general, the more concretely and realistically war goals can be integrated into the values of the individual in terms of "his stake" in the war and the worth and importance of what he is doing, the greater will be their supportive effect on him. The individual who is fighting only because he is forced to, or to "get the damned war over with," is not as effective and does not stand stress as well as the soldier who knows what he is fighting for and is convinced of its importance. Time and again men who have felt strongly about the rightness of their cause and its vital importance to themselves and their loved ones have shown incredible endurance, bravery, and personal sacrifice under combat conditions.

Of course, in the actual combat situation the soldier's concern about the political goals of the war is somewhat remote; he is fighting for survival. Perhaps this is the reason why distant ideals—such as "democracy"—were the first to go in the personality decompensation associated with prolonged combat (Forrest, 1970).

2. *Identification with combat unit.* It has been found particularly important to maintain good group identification in combat troops.

The soldier who is unable to identify himself with or take pride in his group lacks the feeling of "we-ness" that is a highly supportive factor in maintaining stress tolerance. Lacking this, he stands alone, psychologically isolated and less able to withstand combat stress. In fact, the stronger the sense of group identification, the less chance that the soldier will crack up in combat.

In cases of combat exhaustion, the soldier often returns to his unit with feelings of apprehension that his unit will not accept him or have confidence in him in the future (Tuohy, 1968). If the group does accept him, he is likely to make a satisfactory readjustment to further combat; if it does not, he is highly vulnerable to subsequent breakdown. In general, group identification and acceptance appear to be highly important in maintaining his appropriate role behavior.

3. *Esprit de corps.* Closely related to group identification is the matter of *esprit de corps*, the morale of the group as a whole. The spirit of the group seems to be contagious. When the group is generally optimistic and confident prior to battle, the individual is also apt to show good morale. If the unit has a reputation for efficiency in battle, the individual soldier is challenged to exhibit his maximum effort and efficiency.

On the other hand, when the unit is demoralized or has a history of defeats and a high loss of personnel, the individual is likely to succumb more easily to anxiety and panic. This is particularly true if low *esprit de corps* is associated with lack of confidence in leaders or in the importance of immediate combat objectives.

4. *Quality of leadership.* Confidence in military leaders is also of vital importance. When the soldier respects his leaders, has confidence in their judgment and ability, and can accept them as relatively strong father or brother figures, his morale and resistance to stress are bolstered. On the other hand, lack of confidence or actual dislike of leaders is highly detrimental to morale and to combat stress tolerance.

Several other supportive factors merit brief mention. The "buddy system," in which the individual is encouraged to develop a close personal relationship with another member of his unit, often provides needed emotional support. The pursuit of short-range military objectives appears, in general, to cause less stress than the pursuit of long-range ones, where there always seems to be another hill or town to take. Finally, hatred of the enemy appears to be a factor that tends to raise the combat soldier's stress tolerance.

In summary, it may be emphasized that the terrifying nature of the combat situation is usually only one of the causes of combat exhaustion. A complex of other factors may be involved, such as the morale of the group, the soldier's relationships with buddies, his confidence in the competence of leaders, his degree of physical fatigue, the adequacy of his training, his family situation and problems, and his own motivation and stress tolerance in general. And as we have seen, the duration of combat and the approach of rotation—when the war will become "somebody else's war"—are also important considerations.

Treatment and outcomes

In most cases the decompensation brought on by the acute stress of combat conditions was quickly reversed when the soldier was taken out of combat and given brief therapy—usually warm food, sedation to help him get some rest, and supportive psychotherapy.

In World War II, many men were able to return to combat after a night or two of such relief. Soldiers whose symptoms proved resistant to such treatment were evacuated to medical facilities behind the lines. It was found, however, that the farther the soldier was removed from the combat area, the less likely he was to be able to return to battle. Removal to an interior zone seemed to encourage the maintenance of symptoms and a reluctance to return to his unit. During the first combat engagements of American forces in North Africa, combat exhaustion cases were transported to base hospitals hundreds of miles behind the battle lines; under these conditions less than 10 percent of the soldiers were able to return to duty (Menninger, 1948). In contrast, approximately 60 percent of those treated immediately within fifteen to twenty miles of the front lines were sent back to

combat duty, and apparently the majority readjusted successfully (Ludwig & Ranson, 1947). Such statistics varied, however, ranging from a high of 80 to 90 percent returning to duty for soldiers from units with only a month or so of combat, down to 30 to 35 percent for "old" divisions.

Comparable statistics were obtained in the Korean War, with some 65 to 75 percent of the soldiers treated at the division level or forward being returned to combat duty, and less than 10 percent of those returned showing up as repeaters (Hausman & Rioch, 1967). Statistics for the Vietnam War are not entirely clear, but the percentage of soldiers responding favorably to treatment appears even higher (Bloch, 1969; Allerton, 1970).

The lessons learned in World War II were translated in the Korean and Vietnam wars into the principles of *immediacy, proximity,* and *expectancy.*

1. *Immediacy* refers to the early detection of signs of combat exhaustion, such as sleeplessness, tremulousness, and crying spells, and the removal of the soldier for immediate treatment.

In the Vietnam War, for example, officers were taught to watch for these symptoms in combat personnel. When a soldier manifested such symptoms he was taken to the nearest outpost, where a specially trained medic administered to him—usually urging him to review the traumatic events, reassuring him, providing him with a hot meal when possible, and recommending medication for ensuring a restful night. The soldier was then returned to duty the next morning.

2. *Proximity* refers to the treatment of the soldier as near to his combat unit and the battle zone as possible. As we have seen, mild cases were taken to the nearest outpost and given brief supportive therapy by specially trained medics. In the Vietnam War, soldiers who showed more severe combat reactions or whose symptoms did not respond to this brief supportive therapy were often evacuated by helicopter to the division base camp, where a similar but more intensive program of rest and supportive therapy was instituted. Usually after three days of such treatment the soldier felt "like his old self again" and could return to his unit. In exceptionally refractory

Archibald and Tuddenham (1965) made a follow-up study of 62 World War II combat exhaustion cases in an investigation of residual effects of combat exhaustion. Taking symptoms reported by members of this group and the same symptoms as reported by a control group of 20 World War II veterans who had not suffered combat exhaustion, the investigators compared the rate of incidence. The chart, on which a representative number of symptoms are listed, indicates the far greater percent of incidence among the veterans who had suffered combat exhaustion. The absence of the second (lighter) line for the last symptom means that it was not observed in the "healthy" group.

The more severe combat exhaustion cases revealed additional symptoms, including difficulties in work and family relationships, social isolation, and narrowing of interests. Alcoholism was a problem for about 20 percent of both the combat exhaustion and noncombat exhaustion cases.

Archibald and Tuddenham concluded that the residual symptoms in the combat exhaustion cases represented gross stress reactions, which are found among persons throughout the world who have been subjected to different kinds of severe stress. In many such instances, symptoms appear to clear up when the stress is over, only to reappear in chronic form later. Thus, intense and sustained stress apparently can lead to lasting symptoms unless the victims receive adequate treatment and follow-up care.

These same investigators obtained corresponding findings in a follow-up study of 15 Korean War combat exhaustion cases. Although both this group and the World War II combat exhaustion veterans in the study just cited were receiving assistance at a Veterans Administration outpatient psychiatric clinic, none was receiving disability compensation, to which a prolongation of symptoms might otherwise be attributed.

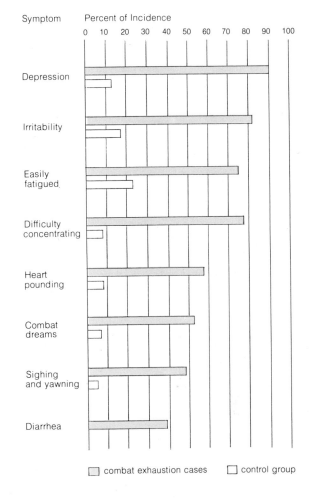

Chart adapted from Archibald and Tuddenham (1965), omitting statistics for noncombat psychiatric military cases.

Residual symptoms in combat veterans of the Vietnam War

Although long-range effects of combat on the veterans of the war in Southeast Asia are not yet available, DeFazio, Rustin, and Diamond (1975) have arrived at some preliminary findings. Based on a questionnaire checklist obtained from 207 veterans who had been separated from the armed forces for over 5 years, these findings show the percentage of veterans who had these symptoms:

Symptom	% Incidence
Frequent nightmares	68
Considers self a hothead	44
Many fears	35
Worries about employment	35
Difficulties with emotional closeness	35
Tires quickly	32

These symptoms were significantly more severe than those reported by noncombat veterans. Often the symptoms appeared to be exacerbated by stimuli associated with their combat experiences. For example, 2 combat veterans reported that each time the temperature in their apartments rose to about 75 to 80 degrees F, they experienced an increase in terrifying nightmares. These investigators concluded that prolonged exposure to stress situations that engender fear and anxiety result in disturbances in psychological functioning and outright symptom development.

---

cases, the soldier was sent to a hospital in the zone of the interior containing a psychiatric ward staffed by medical, psychological, and social work personnel.

3. *Expectancy* refers to (a) a "duty-expectant" attitude—the attitude that anxiety, fear, and tension are not conditions of sufficient severity to require permanent removal from battle and that every soldier, despite anxieties and traumatic experiences, is expected to perform combat duties; and (b) the removal, insofar as possible, of any gain to the soldier from maintaining these symptoms—for example, reassignment to noncombatant duty when not fully justified—such as apparently occurred in World War II.

Such an approach on the part of treatment personnel—who often were themselves in the forward area under enemy fire—reminded the soldier that he was a morally responsible person who could hold up as the going got tougher and perform his combat duties despite his fear and tension. The decision was up to him.

In essence, personal responsibility and a "doing role" were stressed rather than a "sick role," with a relinquishing of responsibility for one's recovery and behavior. The result was that most soldiers found themselves able to bear much more stress than they would have believed possible and that the number of combat exhaustion cases who were declared unfit for further combat duty was minimized.

In a minority of cases, the residual effects of combat exhaustion persist for a sustained period of time. In a follow-up study of ninety-two combat veterans of the Vietnam War, Polner (1968) cited a number of cases in which combat experiences continued to disturb the men after their return to civilian life. In most instances the difficulties appeared to center around killing and guilt feelings. For example, one veteran said, "I can't sleep, I'm a murderer." He continued:

"We were outside Bac Lieu, out on an eight man patrol along with 15 ARVNs.[1] Our orders were to move ahead and shoot at anything suspicious. My God, how I remember that damned day! It was hot and sticky. The mosquitoes were driving me crazy. And there was this boy, about 8 or 9. He had his hand behind his back, like he was hiding something. 'Grab him,' someone screamed, 'he's got something!' I made a move for him and his hand moved again. 'Shoot!' I fired. Again and again, until my M-2 was empty. When I looked he was there, all over the ground, cut in two with his guts all around. I vomited. I wasn't told. I wasn't trained for that. It was out-and-out murder. . . .

"Another time, in a village, I was serving as an adviser when a woman ran out of her hut with a rifle held high above her head. She wasn't shooting it, only carrying it high, moaning and crying. One of the ARVNs then began shouting, 'VC! VC!' I fired once, twice. She fell dead. You know I killed nine people as an adviser." (p. 12)

Many of the other veterans interviewed by Polner, however, felt that they had simply done their duty in a worthwhile cause.

In another study of Vietnam returnees, Strange and Brown (1970) compared combat

---

[1] South Vietnamese soldiers.

and noncombat veterans who were experiencing emotional difficulties. The combat group showed a higher incidence of depression and of conflicts in their close interpersonal relationships. They also showed a higher incidence of aggressive and suicidal threats but did not actually carry them out. In a later study of veterans of Vietnam who were making a satisfactory readjustment to civilian life, DeFazio, Rustin, and Diamond (1975) found that the combat veterans still reported certain symptoms twice as often as the noncombat veterans. Among these were recurrent nightmares, nervousness, difficulty in concentrating, easy fatigability, and difficulty "getting close to other people."

Studies by the VA's Department of Medicine and Surgery indicate that despite the low rate of combat exhaustion during active service, serious and prolonged readjustment problems were prevalent among the returning veterans (Scharr, 1974). Undoubtedly the readjustment problem for these veterans was aggravated by a society that wanted to forget about the Vietnam War—and in a sense the Vietnam veteran along with it. Of course, for soldiers who suffered physical mutilation and were totally or partially disabled, readjustment problems were markedly intensified.

Current military psychology and psychiatry

Current military psychology and psychiatry are concerned with many problems, including the screening of inductees, training and utilization of personnel, maintenance of morale and effectiveness, training for survival in the event of capture, and prevention and treatment of combat exhaustion. For the moment we are concerned with the last three tasks.[2]

---

[2]Some psychologists and psychiatrists are presented with an ethical dilemma in viewing their training in the health and healing professions as incompatible with treating a combat-exhaustion case so that he may live to kill again or be killed. The question arises as to whether they are justified in using their skills to "adjust" a mind to the brutalities of combat, particularly when that mind has been traumatized by or has rejected these brutalities. We shall consider the problems of war and violence in more detail in Chapter 18. It may suffice to point out here that the ultimate answer appears to lie in coping with the problem of war itself.

Maintenance of morale and effectiveness. There has been an increasing awareness that noneffective military behavior stems more often from difficulties in the environment—particularly in interpersonal relationships—than from individual psychopathology. As a consequence, there has been a gradual shifting of mental health personnel from their traditional roles and locations in military clinics and hospitals to the military community itself. The close working relationship between officers and mental health personnel which has resulted permits utilization of the "milieu"—the setting in which the soldier functions—for the treatment and prevention of ineffective behavior.

This new orientation has fostered three kinds or levels of assistance: (a) *primary prevention*, aimed at establishing conditions in the military environment that are likely to reduce the incidence of behavior problems and maladjustment; (b) *secondary prevention*, emphasizing the early recognition and prompt treatment of maladaptive behavior in the area of the soldier's unit; and (c) *tertiary prevention*, employing milieu therapy and intensive treatment for personnel with mental disorders requiring hospitalization, with the aim of heading off the development of chronic disabling conditions and returning the soldier to active duty as soon as possible.

In Chapter 21 we shall deal with the application of these principles to the prevention of psychopathology in civilian life.

Preparation for survival if captured. In the preparation of personnel for honorable survival as prisoners of war, the following points have been emphasized: (a) a clear understanding of what the soldier can expect as a prisoner and what is expected of him in the way of resisting collaboration; (b) a clear understanding of the futility and genuine hazards of collaboration, including the effects of ostracism by his own group; and (c) a strong identification with the military group and commitment to the civilian community for which he is fighting. It also appears that simulated capture and interrogation is a useful training procedure in preparing the soldier more realistically for what to expect and what to do in the event of capture.

Prevention and treatment of combat reactions in future wars. Since the stresses in any future war—and presumably the combat reactions—would differ from those of past wars, methods of treatment and prevention would have to be adapted accordingly. Where conditions were comparable with those of the past, however, treatment procedures would probably not differ greatly from those used in the Korean and Vietnam wars. It would, in any case, seem even more important than in the past to prepare the soldier to know what to expect and what to do; to foster strong identification with his unit and the broader military community; to emphasize his role as a self-reliant and morally responsible individual; and to foster understanding and commitment to his country and what it stands for and is trying to achieve.

In the event of a global atomic holocaust, the outcome would be catastrophic but somewhat unpredictable. Thus soldiers of the future must be prepared for eventualities which have never before been faced—at least not on the same scale—such as the probable death or wounding of hundreds of millions or perhaps billions of people during the first few hours of warfare. Also, with the dispersion of troops necessitated by nuclear warfare, any soldiers who survived would be subjected to many situations in which they would have to function alone in the face of tremendous stress. Such conditions would demand great adaptability, self-reliance, and moral responsibility on the part of any remaining civilian as well as military personnel if the human race were to survive and rebuild civilization. It has become apparent, however, as John F. Kennedy said, that "Mankind must put an end to war or war will put an end to mankind."

Reactions to Civilian Catastrophes

In civilian life, people exposed to plane crashes, automobile accidents, explosions, fires, earthquakes, tornadoes, sexual assault, or other terrifying experiences frequently show "shock" reactions—transient personality decompensation.

In an early study of reactions to civilian catastrophes, it was found that over half of the survivors of the disastrous Cocoanut Grove nightclub fire—which cost the lives of 492 people in Boston in 1942—required treatment for severe psychological shock (Adler, 1943). Similarly, when two commuter trains collided in Chicago in 1972, leaving 44 persons dead and over 300 injured, the tragedy also left scores of persons with feelings of fear, anxiety, and guilt (Uhlenhuth, 1973). More than 80 of them attended a voluntary "talk session" arranged by the psychiatric adult outpatient clinic of the University of Chicago.

Other events, such as the sudden loss of loved ones, social disgrace, imprisonment, and severe financial losses may also prove extremely traumatic. For our immediate purposes, however, we shall focus our discussion on reactions to terrifying experiences associated with civilian catastrophes. These will serve as models for understanding the general principles in other types of transient personality disorders in civilian life and will keep the discussion roughly parallel to that of combat exhaustion.

Clinical picture

Civilian "shock" cases may show a wide range of symptoms depending on the nature and severity of the terrifying experience, the degree of surprise, and the personality makeup of the individual. Among the victims of tornadoes, fires, and other civilian catastrophes, a "disaster syndrome" has been delineated that appears to characterize a sizeable number of people in the disaster area. This syndrome may be described in terms of both initial reactions to the traumatic experience and possible later post-traumatic complications.

Initial "disaster syndrome." This syndrome typically involves the three following stages:

1. *Shock stage*, in which the victim is stunned, dazed, and apathetic. Frequently he is unaware of the extent of his injuries, tends to wander about aimlessly until guided or directed by someone else, and is unable to make more than minimal efforts at aiding himself or others. In extreme cases the individual may be stuporous, disoriented, and amnesic for the traumatic event.

2. *Suggestible stage*, in which the individual tends to be passive, suggestible, and willing to take directions from rescue workers or others less affected than himself. Here the individual often expresses extreme concern over the welfare of others involved in the disaster and attempts to be of assistance; however, his behavior tends to be highly inefficient even in the performance of routine tasks.

3. *Recovery stage*, in which the individual may be tense and apprehensive and show generalized anxiety, but gradually regains his psychological equilibrium—often in the process showing a need to repetitively tell about the catastrophic event.

These three stages are well illustrated in the *Andrea Doria* disaster.

"On July 25, 1956, at 11:05 P.M., the Swedish liner *Stockholm* smashed into the starboard side of the Italian liner *Andrea Doria* a few miles off Nantucket Island, causing one of the worst disasters in maritime history. . . . During the phase of initial shock the survivors acted as if they had been sedated . . . as though nature provided a sedation mechanism which went into operation automatically." During the phase of suggestibility "the survivors presented themselves for the most part as an amorphous mass of people tending to act passively and compliantly. They displayed psychomotor retardation, flattening of affect, somnolence, and in some instances, amnesia for data of personal identification. They were nonchalant and easily suggestible." During the stage of recovery, after the initial shock had worn off and the survivors had received aid, "they showed . . . an apparently compulsive need to tell the story again and again, with identical detail and emphasis." (Friedman & Linn, 1957, p. 426)

In some cases the clinical picture may be complicated by intense feelings of grief and depression. Where the individual feels he has failed loved ones who perished in the disaster the picture may be further complicated by strong feelings of guilt. This pattern is well brought out in the following case of a husband who failed in his attempt to save his wife but saved himself.

A man aged thirty-five had received only minor burns from the Cocoanut Grove fire. By the end of the fifth day of hospitalization he was apparently well on the road to recovery and was informed that his wife had died in the fire. He seemed to accept the news quite well and appeared somewhat relieved of his worry about her fate. Shortly after, however, he developed severe feelings of guilt and depression. With intense morbid guilt feelings he reviewed incessantly the events of the fire. When he had tried to save his wife, he had fainted and was shoved out by the crowd. She was burned while he was saved. "I should have saved her or I should have died too." Again he appeared to be on the road to recovery when he skillfully distracted the attention of his special nurse and jumped through a closed window to a violent death. (Adapted from Lindemann, 1944, p. 146)

In some instances "the guilt of the survivors" seems to center around the view that they may have deserved to survive no more or perhaps even less than others. As one stewardess expressed it after the crash of a Miami-bound jet in the Everglades of Florida which took many lives, "I kept thinking, I'm alive. Thank God. But I wondered why I was spared. I felt, it's not fair . . ." (*Time*, Jan. 15, 1973, p. 53).

Post-traumatic "disaster syndrome." As in combat cases, some civilians who undergo such terrifying experiences reveal a somewhat typical post-traumatic pattern which may endure for weeks, months, or even years (Modlin, 1967; Warnes, 1973; Schanche, 1974). It includes the following symptoms: (a) anxiety, varying from mild apprehension to episodes of acute anxiety commonly associated with situations that recall the traumatic

The emotional aftermath of a devastating tornado

"Many saw it coming. At first it looked like a huge, mushroom-shaped black cloud with three narrow stems. Then the stems merged into one devastating funnel, six-tenths of a mile wide. Winds in the funnel reached 318 miles an hour, four times the force of a hurricane. . . . The tornado took only 22 minutes to cut a horrifying 16-mile path from the outskirts of Xenia, directly through the main intersection of town. . . . Almost half of the seven-square-mile town [was] destroyed in a tornado that may have been the largest ever observed on earth. . . . (Schanche, 1974, p. 18)

"The power of the storm was incredible. . . . Automobiles were wrapped like untidy Band-Aids around the shattered trees. . . . Of 2,757 homes damaged by the storm, 1,095 were totally destroyed. The three-story high school and both junior high schools were demolished. . . . Twenty-five people died quickly; seven others lingered a day or two in hospitals before they expired. About 2,500 were injured, some very seriously. . . ." (pp. 18–19)

The immediate reactions of "direct victims," who had lived through the full impact of the tornado, tended to follow the stages of the acute disaster syndrome—initial feelings of disbelief and numbness, followed by repetitive talking about the disaster experience, and gradual progress toward assimilation of the experience and adjustment to it. Where loved ones were lost, the pattern was, of course, much more complicated.

Prominent among the residual symptoms two months after the disaster were anxiety reactions relating to fear of another tornado and feelings of depression that had not yet fully cleared up. The most significant residual effects were found among the very young who appeared to develop a "school phobia," characterized by fear of leaving home and refusal to return to school. Often this pattern appeared to be exacerbated by parents who were afraid to let the children leave.

While the "direct survivors" of the disaster were most seriously affected, the "indirect survivors" who had not experienced the major impact of the tornado also evidenced emotional reactions, such as guilt for being spared, difficulty in sleeping, and uncharacteristic conflicts with their husbands or wives. As Schanche expressed it, "Such natural disasters seem invariably to suck an emotional storm in their wake that frequently cuts a wider swath than the disaster itself. In this psychological aftermath, the nonvictims often suffer as much, if not more, than the direct victims of the tragedy" (p. 19).

experience; (b) chronic tension and irritability, often accompanied by fatigability, insomnia, the inability to tolerate noise, and the complaint that "I just can't seem to relax"; (c) repetitive nightmares reproducing the traumatic incident directly or symbolically; (d) complaints of impaired concentration and memory; and (e) feelings of depression. In some cases there may be social withdrawal and avoidance of experiences that might increase excitation—commonly manifested in the avoidance of interpersonal involvement, loss of sexual interest, and an attitude of "peace and quiet at any price."

This post-traumatic syndrome may be complicated by a physical mutilation that necessitates changes in one's way of life; it may also be complicated by the psychological effects of disability compensation or damage suits, which tend to prolong post-traumatic symptoms (Keiser, 1968; Okura, 1975).

Causal factors

The causes behind civilian "shock" reactions seem to be similar to those involved in traumatic reactions to combat. Here too the world, which has seemed relatively secure and safe, suddenly becomes a terrifying place.

One survivor of the jet crash in the Everglades remembered reading a book one minute and the next "waking up in a puddle of water with one shoe, my jacket and glasses gone, and an engine lying not far from my head." (*Time*, Jan. 15, 1973, p. 53)

During the initial reaction to the catastrophe, symptoms of being stunned, dazed, and "numbed" appear to stem in part from psychological decompensation associated with the traumatic event; they also appear in part to be defense mechanisms protecting individuals from the full impact of the catastrophe until they are better prepared to assimilate the trauma into their life experience. The stage of suggestibility apparently results from the individual's temporary inability to deal with the situation alone, plus a tendency to regress to a passive-dependent position in which the direction and help of others is gratefully received.

During the stage of recovery, the recurrent nightmares and the typical need to tell about the disaster again and again with identical detail and emphasis appear to be mechanisms for reducing anxiety and desensitizing the individual to the traumatic experience. The tension, apprehensiveness, and hypersensitivity that often accompany the recovery stage appear to be residual effects of the shock reaction and to reflect the individual's realization that the world can become overwhelmingly dangerous and threatening. Feelings of guilt in civilian disasters typically center around a sense of having failed to protect loved ones who perished or were seriously injured; such feelings may be quite intense in situations where responsibility can be directly assigned.

Contrary to popular opinion, panic reactions are not common among people in the impact area of a disaster. *Panic*, defined as acute fear followed by flight behavior, tends to occur only under fairly specific conditions: (a) when a group of persons is directly threatened, for example, by fire, (b) when the situation is viewed as one in which escape is possible at the moment but maybe only for a few minutes or not for everyone, and (c) when the group is taken by surprise and has no prearranged plan for dealing with such a disaster (McDavid & Harari, 1968).

Under such conditions there may be a complete disorganization or demoralization of the group, with each individual striving to save himself; the emotional, panic-stricken behavior of others seems to be contagious, and a person may be overwhelmed by fear. Behavior may be extremely irrational and nonadaptive and can actually result in needless loss of life. For example, in the disastrous Iroquois Theater fire in Chicago in 1903, five hundred people were killed in less than eight minutes due to trampling and asphyxiation rather than burns. Similarly, in the catastrophic Cocoanut Grove fire no lives need have been lost had people exited in an orderly way. Instead the exits were jammed by a rush of panic-stricken people so that many were trampled and those behind them could not get out.

In broader perspective, however, the Disaster Center at Ohio State University, which has studied over 100 disasters, has concluded that most civilians function relatively well in natu-

Victims trapped on a balcony of a burning high-rise building in Sao Paulo, Brazil, attempt to escape the fire by jumping. Panic is not an unusual reaction in such terrifying situations.

ral catastrophes, and, in fact, many behave with heroism (Quarantelli & Dynes, 1972).

Both precipitating and predisposing conditions in civilian life are apt to differ considerably from those in combat situations, for in the former the individual is not typically far from home, extremely fatigued, or exposed to prolonged fear and conflict over physical danger. But here, too, predisposing factors may determine which survivors develop traumatic reactions and which do not, and why some recover much more rapidly than others. In general, the civilian is less prepared for coping with catastrophe than is the combat soldier, who knows that he can expect danger and has been specially trained to deal with it. Nevertheless, as we have seen, soldiers may evidence acute traumatic reactions to combat as well as prolonged post-traumatic reactions much like traumatic reactions to civilian disasters. And in both acute and long-term reactions, conditioned fear—the fear associated with the traumatic experience—appears to be a key causal factor. Thus prompt psychotherapy following the traumatic experience is considered important in preventing such conditioned fear from "building up" and becoming resistant to change.

Treatment and outcomes

Mild reassuring therapy and proper rest (induced by sedatives if necessary) usually lead to the rapid alleviation of symptoms in civilian shock reactions. It would also appear that repetitive talking about the experience and repetitive reliving of the experience in fantasy or nightmares may serve as built-in repair mechanisms in helping the individual adjust to the traumatic experience. As Horowitz has concluded from his own experimental findings and a review of available literature:

"A traumatic perceptual experience remains in some special form of memory storage until it is mastered. Before mastery, vivid sensory images of the experiences tend to intrude into consciousness and may evoke unpleasant emotions. Through such repetitions the images, ideas, and associated affects may be worked through progressively. Thereafter, the images lose their intensity and the tendency toward repetition of the experience loses its motive force." (1969, p. 552)

While the majority of civilian shock reactions clear up in a matter of days or weeks, a minority of cases, as we have seen, evidence a post-traumatic syndrome which may persist over a sustained period of time. Here the individual often remains sensitized to certain types of hazardous situations and simply does not regain his self-confidence in dealing with them. In a study by Leopold and Dillon (1963) of 34 seamen who survived an explosion and fire on board a gasoline tanker, it was found that 3½ to 4½ years after the disaster 12 of the survivors—who had succeeded in lowering a lifeboat and getting away from the inferno—had never returned to work, or had been forced to give it up, as a result of post-trau-

matic symptoms. Of those who continued to work at sea, all showed similar post-traumatic symptoms—tension, fearfulness, and anxiety aboard ship.

In general, the more stable and better integrated the personality and the more favorable the individual's life situation, the quicker will be his recovery from a civilian shock reaction.

It would also appear to be important to work through the traumatic experience if post-traumatic symptoms are to be avoided. For example, Leopold and Dillon (1963) concluded that with prompt psychotherapy after the disaster, the post-traumatic syndromes evidenced by the seamen could have been prevented.

This poignant award-winning photo shows South Vietnamese children fleeing in terror from a misdirected napalm attack.

Reactions to Chronic Situational Stress

In addition to the decompensation under acute stress seen in combat exhaustion and civilian shock reactions, transient disturbances may also occur when the individual continues for an extended time in a situation where he feels threatened, seriously dissatisfied, or inadequate. Regimentation may make army life intolerable for some; many people feel trapped and frustrated by unhappy marriages which they feel they must maintain because of children; and many other persons are deeply dissatisfied with their work but feel compelled to stick to it because of heavy financial responsibilities or lack of training for any other kind of job. Even living in a society from which the individual feels alienated may eventuate personality disturbances.

The symptoms of situational maladjustment may vary greatly depending on the individual and the severity of his life situation. In civilian life, however, chronic fatigue, lowered efficiency, and excessive drinking and drug usage are common; in extreme cases the individual may engage in destructive acting out behavior or even commit suicide. In the military, gambling, drinking, and going to prostitutes are common means of reducing feelings of boredom and frustration. Some soldiers develop a particularly embittered attitude and are resistant, irritable, fault-finding, and highly resentful about being "shoved around"; others, particularly those exposed to a highly restricted environment, such as assignment to an isolated outpost, may become apathetic or show a wide range of other symptoms.

Studies of persons confined to submarines for periods of sixty days—during which the vessels were continuously submerged—have shown that some 4 to 5 percent of the men

Cruelty, torture, and mass extermination cost the lives of some
ten million people in Nazi concentration camps—and left thousands of others emotionally and
physically scarred for life. The
two pictures were taken by American military photographers during the closing phases of World
War II.

developed psychological disturbances apparently stemming from the constant environmental stress (Satloff, 1967; Serxner, 1968). Common symptoms included anxiety, depression, insomnia, headaches, and other somatic concerns. Similarly, Popkin and his associates (1974) studied the behavior of a 22-man team—14 Navy men and 8 civilian scientists—in a South Pole station during the 6-month antarctic winter "night." They found that 12 of the 22 men showed a condition called "drifting," characterized by persistent apathy, inattention, and a general lowering or impairment of cognitive functioning.

In the discussion which follows, we shall focus on two extreme types of chronic situational stress—prisoner-of-war and concentration camp experiences. These will help highlight the nature of reactions to chronic situational stress and will keep our discussion roughly parallel with traumatic reactions to combat and to civilian catastrophes.

Reactions of prisoners of war

The symptoms of situational maladjustment under extreme conditions are well illustrated by prisoner-of-war experiences. One of the best descriptions is that of Commander Nardini, an eyewitness and participant, who described the effects of imprisonment and mistreatment on American soldiers following the fall of Bataan and Corregidor during the early part of World War II.

"Our national group experience accustoms us to protection of individual rights and recourse to justice. The members of this group found themselves suddenly deprived of name, rank, identity, justice, and any claim to being treated as human beings. Although physical disease and the shortages of food, water, and medicine were at their highest during this period, emotional shock and reactive depression . . . undoubtedly contributed much to the massive death rate during the first months of imprisonment.

"Conditions of imprisonment varied from time to time in different places and with different groups. In general there was shortage, wearisome sameness, and deficiency of food; much physical misery and disease; squalid living conditions; fear and despair; horrible monotony . . . inadequate clothing and cleansing facilities; temperature extremes; and physical abuse.

The trauma this Polish girl suffered during World War II shows in her eyes and in the picture she is drawing—a depiction of war.

". . . Hungry men were constantly reminded of their own nearness to death by observing the steady, relentless march to death of their comrades. . . . Men quibbled over portions of food, were suspicious of those who were in more favored positions than themselves, participated in unethical barter, took advantage of less clever or enterprising fellow prisoners, stole, rummaged in garbage, and even curried the favor of their detested captors. There was a great distortion of previous personality as manifested by increased irritability, unfriendliness, and sullen withdrawal. . . . Hungry, threatened men often found it difficult to expand the horizon of their thinking and feeling beyond the next bowl of rice. . . .

"Disease was abundant . . . fever, chills, malaise, pain, anorexia, abdominal cramps from recurrent malaria (acquired in combat), and dysentery plagued nearly all and killed thousands. . . . most men experienced bouts of apathy or depression. These ranged from slight to prolonged deep depressions where there was a loss of interest in living and lack of willingness or ability to marshal the powers of will necessary to combat disease. An ever-present sign of fatal withdrawal occurred 3 to 4 days before death when the man pulled his covers up over his head and lay passive, quiet, and refusing food.

". . . One of the most distressing features was the highly indefinite period of imprisonment. The future offered only visions of continued hunger, cold, disease, forced labor, and continued subservience in the face of shouting, slappings, and beatings. . . . Strong hostility naturally arose from the extreme frustration. . . . Little could be done with these hostile feelings. . . . It was not possible to demonstrate recognizable signs of hostility to the captors for obvious reasons. Therefore, where there were mixed groups of Allied prisoners, much hostility was turned from group to group and in other instances to individuals within the group. . . . In many cases hostile feelings were obviously turned inward and joined with appropriate feelings of frustration to produce serious waves of depression. . . . Self pity, in which some indulged, was highly dangerous to life. . . . (Nardini, 1952, pp. 241–44)

Similar reactions were observed among prisoners held by the North Koreans and Chinese Communists during the Korean War (Lifton, 1954; Segal, 1954; Strassman, Thaler, & Schein, 1956). Here, however, the picture was further complicated by "brainwashing" techniques, described in the chart on p. 210.

A common syndrome manifested by POW's during the Korean War was delineated by Farber, Harlow, and West (1956). They re-ferred to this syndrome as "DDD"—debility, dependency, and dread. *Debility* was induced by semistarvation, disease, and fatigue, and led to a sense of terrible weariness and weakness. *Dependency* was produced by a variety of techniques, including the use of solitary confinement, the removal of leaders and other accustomed sources of support, and occasional and unpredictable respites that reminded the prisoners that they were completely dependent on their captors for what happened to them. *Dread* was described as a stage of chronic fear that their captors attempted to induce—fear of death, of pain, of nonrepatriation, and of permanent deformity or disability due to neglect or inadequate medical treatment. The net effect of these conditions was a well-nigh intolerable state of mental and physical discomfort that rendered the men more amenable to brainwashing.

In the Vietnam War, soldiers were better prepared in terms of what to expect and what to do in the event of capture. Consequently they fared much better, in general, than did the POW's referred to above. However, occasional exceptions were noted. For example, Kushner (1973)—a medical doctor and fellow prisoner—reported that 2 of the 22 men in a Viet Cong POW camp, in which conditions were particularly bad, simply gave up and died.

Descriptions of prisoners in Nazi concentration camps, who were subjected to even more inhuman and sadistic conditions, emphasize similar symptomatology (Bettelheim, 1943, 1960; Chodoff, 1970; Eitinger, 1961, 1962, 1969; Frankl, 1963; Friedman, 1948; Hafner, 1968). Inmates of concentration camps also showed greater use of the defense mechanisms of denial and isolation of affect. The feeling that "This isn't really happening to me" was widespread. Chodoff (1970) has cited the case of a young prisoner "who would not see the corpses she was stepping over" and the even more poignant picture "of her fellow inmates who refused to believe that the smoke arising from the crematorium chimneys came from the burning corpses of their mothers" who had been selected—because of age—to be killed first. Isolation of affect apparently reached the degree of almost total emotional anaesthesia in the case Chodoff cited of a

Problems related to the individual's adjustment to close group interdependence, monotony of environment, and absence of accustomed sources of emotional gratification have been studied among groups of volunteers subjected to isolated antarctic living for 6 to 8 months at isolated U.S. bases. Scientists, officers, and enlisted personnel lived in groups of 12 to 40, with each man assigned a specific job and hence dependent on every other man. Technical competence, responsibility, and stability in job performance thus became key factors in determing group acceptance and status. Reactions such as those cited below are of special interest in terms of their possible relationship to reactions to the conditions of space travel.

Symptoms observed

Intellectual inertia	Lack of energy for intellectual pursuits, especially during winter. Earlier plans to catch up on reading or learn a foreign language rarely realized.
Impaired memory and concentration	Varied from absentmindedness and poor concentration to marked lowering of intellectual acuity and periods of amnesia. Most pronounced during winter months.
Insomnia	Varying degrees of sleeplessness, again mostly in winter. Individual felt tired but unable to relax.
Headaches	Frequent headaches, more common among officer-scientist group than among enlisted men. Appeared to be of psychogenic origin and possibly related to repression and control of hostility.
Hostility	Relatively little overt hostility expressed, probably because of the tremendous need for relatedness and group acceptance in these small, isolated groups. Social censure, in the form of the "silent treatment," inflicted on the occasional troublesome individual, resulted in "long-eye" syndrome — varying degrees of sleeplessness, crying, hallucinations, deterioration in personal hygiene, and a tendency to move aimlessly about or to lie in bed staring blankly into space until the man was again accepted by group.
Depression	Low-grade depression prevalent, particularly during winter months. Of 6 men who became psychiatric casualties, 3 diagnosed as cases of relatively severe neurotic depression.
Appetite	Appetite for food greatly increased, possibly because of absence of other gratifications. Weight gains of 20 to 30 pounds not unusual.

This program was initiated during the International Geophysical Year 1957–1958, and is still continuing on a reduced scale. Findings of a more recent study involving a 22-member team — 14 Navy personnel and 8 civilian scientists — who wintered over in a small station during the 6-month antarctic winter "night" tend to support and extend some of the results described in this chart (Popkin et al., 1974). Some of the findings of the latter study are summarized on page 207.

Brainwashing of American prisoners during the Korean War

In his novel *1984*, George Orwell (1949) described the process of "brainwashing," in which the environment around a person is controlled so completely that the effects are similar to those of removing the person's brain and literally washing it clean of all thoughts considered socially undesirable by those in control. Orwell's fictional concept became a frightening reality during the Korean conflict, when the Chinese Communists launched a systematic program to indoctrinate prisoners of war with Communist values and to achieve their collaboration.

During the early part of the war, the men captured by the North Koreans were subjected to a variety of cruelties, including forced "death marches," inadequate diet, exposure to freezing weather without adequate clothing or shelter, and vicious beatings for minor or alleged transgressions. Physical treatment improved somewhat after the Chinese Communists took charge of all POW's—but with the improvement came the emotional assault of brainwashing. The approach used by the Communists can be described in terms of three phases, which were in simultaneous and continuous operation: isolation, thought control, and political conditioning.

Phase	How carried out	Results
Isolation	Removal of leaders: officers transferred to a separate camp, and natural leaders, as they emerged, removed silently to "reactionary" camps. Informers rewarded to discourage personal ties and interaction. Home ties cut—pessimistic, complaining letters delivered while other mail withheld. In some instances a prisoner was subjected to complete isolation, increasing his need for companionship and making him more suggestible—"softening him up" for thought control.	Creation of a group of "isolates" with low morale and no *esprit de corps*. Social and emotional isolation robbed soldier of usual sources of strength and prevented him from validating his beliefs and values through discussion with others. Led to loss of strength to resist, increased suggestibility, and vulnerability to both threats and bribes.
Thought control	Prisoners forced to choose between "cooperation" and possible starvation, torture, and death. Ethical values, loyalty, religion, and self-identity placed in direct opposition to self-preservation and bodily needs: resistees subjected to threat, punishment, and marginal living conditions; cooperators rewarded with increased food, privileges in camp, and promises of early repatriation. Guilt feelings concerning prior behavior stimulated by mandatory "confessions" and self-criticism. Alternate harshness and friendliness by "inscrutable authority."	Fear, anxiety, guilt, confusion, and conflict about how to behave. "Playing it cool"—being inconspicuous, holding back strong feelings, being minimally communicative and noncommittal on everything, "cooperating" a little when necessary but avoiding major collaboration. Withdrawal of emotional involvement, marked apathy. Listlessness and apparent indifference.
Political conditioning	Daily "instruction" with repetitious teaching of communist catch phrases and principles. Appeals to be "open-minded" and to "just listen to our side of the story." Only anti-American books and newspapers available, stressing inequalities and injustices in U.S. Communists portrayed as "peace seekers," prisoner offered "opportunity to work for peace." Intensive pressure applied to those who seemed most susceptible; those already convinced used to indoctrinate others. Constant use of reward for cooperation and punishment for resistance.	Little actual conversion to communism but considerable confusion and doubt about America's role in war; poor morale and discipline; breakdown of group loyalty. Men turned against each other—"progressives" versus "reactionaries." Difficulty in relating to others even after release. Five percent later won commendation as resisters, 15 percent were judged to have complied unduly; the remaining 80 percent were relatively passive.

When prisoners were first released, they were apathetic, detached, dazed, without spontaneity, and at the same time tense and suspicious of their new surroundings. Large memory gaps were present, particularly for the period of their capture and for so-called death marches. They were ambivalent in their feelings about the Chinese Communists, showed strong guilt about all phases of their POW experience, and were not anxious to return home to the U.S. This "zombie reaction" wore off after three to five days and was followed by a period of greater spontaneity. However, they still appeared "suspended in time" — confused by their newly acquired status and incapable of making decisions concerning future courses of action. All the men felt alienated from others who had not shared their POW experience and were apprehensive about homecoming; they tended to band together in small, uneasy groups and maintained isolation from nonrepatriates.

On their return home, some got into difficulty over indiscriminate outbursts of misdirected, long-pent-up hostility. Expecting at last to be free of stress, some became disillusioned and discouraged in their efforts to adjust to economic and other changes and to communicate with others. Physical disabilities, chronic fatigue, and a confused self-picture complicated the adjustment problems of many. But although some drank too much or managed other escape measures, the majority of these men eventually made adequate adjustments. In a few cases their weathering of the prison experience seemed to have given them increased inner strength and greater capacity for achievement.

Material for this chart taken from Kinkead (1959); Lifton (1954); Schein, Schneier, and Barker (1961); Segal (1954); Strassman, Thaler, and Schein (1956); and West (1958). For information on the application of similar techniques to civilian populations — for example, in Russia and China — see Hinkle and Wolff (1956); Hunter (1954); Lifton (1961); and Watzlawick, Beavin, and Jackson (1967).

young female prisoner who stated "I had no feelings whatsoever" while being stripped naked and having all her hair shaved off in front of SS troopers (p. 83).

Concentration camp inmates also tended to form hopes of deliverance via miraculous events, possibly because their situation was even more hopeless than that of the POW's, and any hope would have had to be rather unrealistic.

Causal factors

Reactions to situational stress vary with the individual as well as with the nature and severity of the stress itself. Some people adjust fairly readily to chronic frustration and other disagreeable conditions, while others find it difficult to cope with them. With chronic stress, as with acute stress, the reaction of a particular individual depends on the pattern of biological, psychosocial, and sociocultural factors. In general, of course, the more severe and chronic the stress situation, the greater the degree of personality disturbance that is likely to be elicited. In fact, when situational stress is severe and long-lasting, there may be a marked lowering of adaptive resources accompanied by severe personality decompensation.

One common reaction to continued severe, inescapable stress is apathy. This pattern of defense — by partially depriving the situation of its power to hurt — apparently helps individuals to continue in the face of severe and sustained stress which, as far as they know, may continue indefinitely. Extreme apathy and loss of hope, however, can ultimately lead to death.

Another defense is to "play it cool," putting out the minimum essential effort and trying not to be emotionally involved. In a prisoner-of-war situation, this means being cautious, noncommittal, and minimally communicative, avoiding major collaboration while at the same time not getting "on the wrong side" of the captors.

The permanent POW's

Being in combat or captured by the enemy are not the only stress situations caused by war. One medic's experiences may present a different perspective on being a "prisoner of war."

Pete Rios (1973) was seriously wounded and left for dead in Vietnam. Saved by a buddy who was also seriously wounded, the soldiers, the only survivors of their combat unit, were finally removed from the battle site by helicopter.

"A week later we were flown to Travis AFB, Calif., and psychologically we were in pretty bad shape because we knew we were permanently disabled. . . ."

After one day at Travis, Rios was sent to Walter Reed Army Hospital in Washington, D.C., where he was given intensive physical therapy; at the end of his two-month stay, he could walk with leg braces and crutches. But then he was discharged from the Army and sent to a veteran's hospital, where he was told it was "impossible" for him to walk with such a "young [recent] injury." His actual achievement was discounted.

"I suppose the main thing I object to is always being categorized as 'a patient.' There is a nurse, a patient. There is a doctor, a patient. Never Pete Rios. You are in a wheelchair, so you are 'a spinal-cord injury' — not a person. You are 30 years old, and you've had more than your share of experiences, but you are treated as if you were a child. . . .

"Since you are 'a patient' and expected not to think, you should not ask questions about your own body. You don't need to know why your bowels won't work, why you can't have sexual relations, why you are spastic, why one foot is colder than another, why you have pain. . . .

"I have been disappointed to find that the public seems cognizant only of the fact that many Americans (about 47,000) were killed or missing in Vietnam and that the remaining hundreds of thousands who served there came home. Nobody seems to think of the fact that 153,000 were wounded or that 7,750 came back blind or with missing or useless legs. . . . If you want to see the aftermath of Vietnam, take a stroll through the second-floor spinal injuries section at Hines [Veterans Hospital]. . . .

"People not only don't give a damn today, but some of them are downright antagonistic toward you. . . ."

Rios tells the story of the time he was seated in a special section for wheelchairs at a restaurant—ahead of some patrons who had been waiting longer than he had. An older woman berated him for being disrespectful to his elders, and asked him how he had gotten hurt. When he told her he had been shot in Vietnam, she replied, "you certainly deserved it."

"Where do you suppose are the people and the flags," he wonders. *"They were greatly in evidence for the returning prisoners of war. . . .*

"Most severely disabled veterans, frankly, are not overly impressed that an American prisoner spent 22 years in China or eight years in Hanoi. We're glad, of course, that they came back.

"But now we are the only POWs.

"Guys who are blind or crippled are going to be POWs as long as they live.

"There is no time limit—not eight years, nor 22—on that kind of imprisonment."

Treatment and outcomes

Mild situational reactions usually clear up very rapidly when the individual is removed from the stressful situation. Yet such a simple therapeutic procedure is often impossible or undesirable. In such cases, counseling and psychotherapy may often be of assistance in modifying the stress situation or in helping the individual develop more effective coping techniques.

In the case of prisoners of war and concentration-camp survivors subjected to extreme and inhuman conditions, there is also often residual organic as well as psychological damage and a lowering of tolerance to stress of any kind.

Even when there is little evidence of residual physical pathology, survivors of prisoner-of-war camps commonly evidence impaired resistance to physical illness, low frustration tolerance, frequent dependence on alcohol and drugs, irritability, and other indications of emotional instability (Chambers, 1952; Goldsmith & Cretekos, 1969; Strange & Brown, 1970; Wilbur, 1973).

The residual damage to survivors of concentration camps is often more extensive and commonly includes anxiety, insomnia, headaches, irritability, depression, nightmares, impaired sexual potency, and "functional" diarrhea (Eitinger, 1964, 1969, 1973; Sigal, Silver, Rakoff, & Ellin, 1973; Warnes, 1973). "Functional" diarrhea means that this symptom occurs in any situation of stress, even ones of a relatively mild nature. Such symptoms are attributable not only to the psychological stresses of concentration-camp experiences but also to biological stresses, such as head injuries, prolonged malnutrition, and serious infectious diseases.

Another measure of the toll taken by the prolonged stress of being in a POW or concentration camp is the higher death rate after return to civilian life. Among returning POW's from the Pacific area after World War II, Wolff (1960) found that within the first six years, nine times as many died from tuberculosis as would have been expected in civilian life, four times as many from gastrointestinal disorders, over twice as many from cancer, heart disease, and suicide, and three times as many from accidents. Comparable figures have been reported for concentration-camp survivors by Eitinger (1973). And in analyzing the preceding statistics, it may be noted that we are dealing with select groups. For example, about half the American prisoners in Japanese POW camps died during their imprisonment; an even higher incidence of deaths occurred among inmates of Nazi concentration camps.

Nardini (1926b) has suggested the following qualities as being positive factors in both physical and psychological survival of POW experiences: a philosophical, fatalistic, yet nondefeatist attitude; intense application of life energies to the present; an ability to retain hope in the face of the greatest hardships; the ability to manage hostility and fight depression; personal maturity and ego strength; a strong sense of self-identity and self-respect; and the intangible but all-inclusive determination to live. Frankl (1963) has emphasized similar characteristics as fostering survival in concentration camps. Of course, in both POW and concentration camps, chance factors often played an important or even crucial role in the survival or death of the prisoner.

Here it may be noted that the "reentry problem" is often a difficult one for both POW's and concentration-camp survivors as they try to adjust to the sudden and major change in their world as well as to social changes that have taken place during their imprisonment. While most former prisoners do make a successful readjustment, some will spend the remainder of their lives "rattling the emotional chains" forged by the inhuman conditions of their imprisonment.

This picture of astronaut Edwin "Buzz" Aldrin walking on the lunar surface symbolizes some of the stress-inducing hazards of space flights, especially the danger in being isolated from Earth and the complete dependence on the lunar module and the space ship for a safe return.

Psychological Problems in Space Flights

With the landing of men on the moon and preparation for more extended space travel to other planets, the psychological problems of space flight have become of increasing importance. Present knowledge of psychological problems in extended space flight is based partly on our relatively limited experience and partly on inference. However, it would appear that these are key stresses: separation from earth; prolonged exposure to danger; difficulties in adjustment of the individual to the group, especially in a small space for a prolonged time; sameness of the environment; and the absence of many accustomed sources of emotional gratification. Some of these hazards, such as loneliness and a sense of ever-present danger, can be anticipated but not simulated.

Problems relating to the adjustment of the individual to the group, to monotony, and to absence of many accustomed sources of gratification were studied among a small group of scientists, officers, and enlisted personnel who voluntarily subjected themselves to isolated antarctic living for almost a year. Typical reactions to this experience are summarized in the chart on page 209. From an overall viewpoint, the Navy found that the most important single factor in successful adjustment in the antarctic was work efficiency, in the sense that the effective functioning of the small group depended on each individual's performing his assigned task efficiently. The next most important factor was the individual's adjustment to the small isolated group.

The more recent study by Popkin (1974) and his associates of a group of 22 men in a South Pole station during the 6-month antarctic winter "night" (referred to on p. 207) raises some important questions concerning the "novel behaviors" of personnel in extreme environments. It may be recalled that 12 of the 22 men manifested "drifting," a persistent condition involving both apathy and impaired cognitive functioning.

In space flights the smaller crews, more confined quarters, more alien environment, and greater danger can be expected to render problems of technical proficiency, adjustment to the group, and adaptability to diverse stresses even more crucially significant. Thus the problem of assembling a crew who can function effectively as a team during a prolonged space flight is a vitally important one. Here the questions raised by Haythorn and Altman (1967) still seem particularly relevant:

"So what kinds of people can get along together with the least amount of open friction in isolation? What kinds can accomplish most work when locked up together? What kinds simply sentence one another to mutual tedium?" (p. 19)

Such psychological problems, as well as physiological ones associated with the development of an artificial environment that can support effective human functioning during relatively long periods of time, have received a good deal of experimental attention. Included here are problems related to oxygen supply, radiation, weightlessness, isolation from earth, confinement, restrictions in the perceptual field, fatigue, and exposure to prolonged danger. Under conditions that simulate long space missions, some subjects have shown impairment in judgment; inaccurate perceptions, including distortions of space and time; peculiar changes in body image; sensations of an alien presence; and even delusions and hallucinations. Negative reactions of some subjects have required termination of the simulated missions. Of course, actual space missions have increased our understanding and capabilities of dealing with such problems.

Even mild thought disturbances, of course, might have serious consequences if they occurred during an actual space mission. We know from our studies of sensory deprivation that both variety and meaningfulness of sensory input (stimulation and information) are essential for preventing the disorganization of perception and thought.

A relatively new approach to the problem of effective human functioning in space is directed toward the modification of the human system itself. As White (1958–1959) has pointed out, a human being is "a sea-level,

low-speed, one-g, 12-hour animal." For greater adaptability in functioning under various extraterrestrial conditions, chemical and electrical techniques are being developed to modify some of the body's homeostatic controls—both on physiological and psychological levels. For example, it may be possible to use drugs or other techniques to have the pilot or other crew members sleep twenty-three hours out of the day. Of course, there would be procedures for waking them in the event of an emergency. It may also be that the amount of "earth environment" that crew members must take with them may be reduced by controlling their cardiovascular rate, body temperature, metabolic systems, and even thought processes.

In the human-machine system required for space flight, it becomes apparent that not only the life-support system, but also the limitations of the human organism, make up the baseline determining the efficiency of the total system. However, with our successful landing of men on the moon and their safe return to earth, it would appear likely that human beings can learn to cope with the greater physiological and psychological hazards of longer space flights—that as habitable space ships for longer missions are constructed, crews will be trained to manage them effectively.

In this chapter we discussed transient situational disorders which occur under conditions of unusual and excessive stress, such as military combat and civilian catastrophes. These disorders may involve a variety of symptoms, including intense anxiety, denial, repression, apathy, depression, and the lowering of ethical standards. In most cases the symptoms recede as the stress diminishes, especially if the individual is given brief supportive psychotherapy. However, in extreme cases, such as those involving the survivors of concentration camps, there may be residual psychological as well as physical damage.

While space exploration imposes somewhat different stresses, the problems of acute situational maladjustment and decompensation under excessive stress are still applicable. But with the successful landing of human beings on the moon, it would appear that we can learn to cope with the psychological and physiological stresses of longer space flights.

7

Neuroses

In our discussion of transient situational disorders we dealt primarily with stable personalities who had been subjected to excessive stress. In the neuroses we find faulty learning, often in early development, leading to persistent feelings of threat and anxiety in facing the everyday problems of living. Since the individual's ordinary methods of coping—including the "normal" use of ego-defense mechanisms—prove inadequate, the person tends to rely increasingly on one or more neurotic patterns.[1] These patterns share in common a search for relief from feelings of threat and anxiety. While they may alleviate such feelings, they exact a high price in self-defeating behavior.

The individual is said to exhibit neurotic behavior if he frequently misevaluates adjustive demands, becomes anxious in situations that most people would not regard as threatening, and tends to develop behavior patterns aimed at avoiding rather than coping with his problems. Curiously, he may realize his behavior is irrational and maladaptive—as in the case of a severe phobia for germs—but feel unable to alter it. Although neurotic behavior is maladaptive, it does not involve gross distortion of reality or marked personality disorganization, nor is it likely to result in violence to the individual or to others. Rather, neurotics are typically anxious, ineffective, unhappy, and often guilt-ridden individuals who do not ordinarily require hospitalization but nevertheless are in need of therapy. The incidence of neuroses is difficult to determine, but it has been estimated that there are at least 20 million individuals in the United States who might be classified as neurotic.

In this chapter we will begin by considering the basic nature of neurotic behavior; then we will examine specific neurotic patterns, such as anxiety and phobic reactions and describe the clinical picture, causal factors, and pertinent aspects of treatment for each one. Finally, we will deal with more general causal factors, methods of treatment, and outcomes in the neuroses.

The Basic Nature of Neuroses

Specific Neurotic Patterns

General Causal Factors, Treatment, and Outcomes

---

[1]The term *neurosis* was coined by the Englishman William Cullen in his *System of Nosology*, published in 1769, to refer to disordered sensations of the nervous system (Knoff, 1970).

The Basic Nature
of Neuroses

While the neuroses embrace a wide range of behaviors, the common core is a maladaptive life-style typified by anxiety and defense-oriented avoidant behavior. Basic to this neurotic life-style are (a) the *neurotic nucleus*—the faulty evaluation of reality and the tendency to avoid rather than cope with stress; and (b) the *neurotic paradox*—the tendency to maintain this life-style despite its self-defeating and maladaptive nature.

The neurotic nucleus

The neurotic nucleus is a circular process in which the individual feels basically inadequate, evaluates everyday problems as threatening, and attempts to deal with the resulting anxiety by avoidance and defense-oriented reactions. The end result is a self-defeating life-style which blocks personal growth and self-fulfillment. Usually the neurotic has trouble establishing and maintaining satisfying interpersonal relationships, feels vaguely guilty for trying to avoid rather than cope with reality, and is dissatisfied and unhappy with his way of life.

Three key facets of the neurotic nucleus merit brief mention:

1. *Feelings of inadequacy and anxiety.* The neurotic feels basically inadequate and insecure in a world which he perceives as dangerous and hostile. Consequently, he sees many everyday situations as threatening—situations which would not be so evaluated by most people. This "threat vulnerability" leads to a dread of competitive situations and a tendency to overreact to minor setbacks and failures. Even success may contribute to his underlying sense of inadequacy: a job promotion, for example, may raise fears that his "real lack of ability" will inevitably be exposed.

Threat in turn elicits anxiety, which is a key characteristic of the neuroses.

2. *Avoidance instead of coping.* Typically the neurotic develops a life-style characterized by defensive and avoidant behavior that enables him to escape from anxiety-arousing stress. For example, alleged physical ailments may provide an excuse for lack of competitive achievement, or irrational fears will enable him to avoid situations perceived as dangerous. However, his defenses are rarely adequate, and a considerable amount of anxiety usually remains. This anxiety may be augmented by the fact that the neurotic often realizes the irrationality of his own behavior.

3. *Self-defeating behavior and blocked personal growth.* In essence, the neurotic is enmeshed in a quagmire of "covering up," defending, escaping, and avoiding—a coping pattern that inevitably leads to rigid, egocentric, and self-defeating behavior. Since the neurotic often feels that he is fighting for his very life in a hostile and threatening world, his main energies are focused on clinging rigidly to the defenses he has been able to erect; it is not surprising that he has no time or energy for concern for others. This lack of flexibility and real concern for others, in turn, usually plays havoc with his personal relationships, thus adding to his difficulties. In short, the neurotic's life-style together with the complications it creates is not only self-defeating and maladaptive but tends to block his growth and fulfillment as a person.

Usually the neurotic vaguely senses that something is missing, that he is not fulfilling himself or leading a truly meaningful life. And this, in turn, leads to feelings of futility and unhappiness, to a "loss of joy in living."

The neurotic paradox

Human beings tend to be highly pragmatic in doing what works—in learning and modifying their behavior in accordance with adjustive demands. Yet the neurotic clings to his established coping pattern despite the fact that it is ineffective, self-defeating, and leads to dissatisfaction and unhappiness. The question then arises as to why this neurotic life-style is maintained. This puzzling situation is referred to as the *neurotic paradox*.

The neurotic paradox can be understood in terms of two basic patterns: (a) the immediate relief from anxiety that comes from the momentary avoidance of situations perceived as threatening; and (b) the continued and inappropriate perception of certain everyday situations as threatening. These patterns may operate in varying degrees and combinations, but their net effect is the tendency to maintain neurotic coping behavior despite its self-defeating nature.

Since the neurotic responds by avoidance to the earliest cues signifying the approach of the feared stress, he is able to protect himself from anxiety. But at the same time, he is prevented from testing the situation to see if what he fears is, in fact, realistic.

For example, let us take the case of a young man who is very much in love with a woman. They are engaged and have made wedding plans. However, she meets someone else to whom she is greatly attracted and abruptly breaks the engagement, terminating their relationship. He reacts with intense feelings of self-devaluation, anxiety, and depression, coupled with a considerable measure of hostility. Then his behavior follows a new pattern. Whenever a relationship with a woman begins to get serious, he experiences anxiety and breaks it off. In short, he has acquired a conditioned fear of close relationships with members of the opposite sex, and his anxiety and avoidance behavior do not permit him to try out the possibility that he might be more successful this time. Thus the fear and avoidance behavior are maintained because they are reinforced by the reduction of anxiety each time he breaks off a relationship that is starting to become serious.

The basic pattern we are dealing with in the neuroses thus involves conditioned fears which render the individual particularly vulnerable to stresses that most people can cope with effectively. This vulnerability, in turn, leads to a causal chain of *stress—anxiety—avoidance—reinforcement*. In this way, neurotic avoidance behavior tends to be both self-defeating and self-perpetuating.

Specific Neurotic Patterns

In this section we shall consider seven specific neurotic patterns:[2]

1. *Anxiety neurosis*—involves diffuse but often severe anxiety not referable to a particular situation or threat.

2. *Phobic neurosis*—involves various fears the individual realizes are irrational but from which he cannot free himself.

3. *Obsessive-compulsive neurosis*—involves thoughts and actions the individual recognizes as irrational but which still persist.

4. *Hysterical neurosis*—consists of two types: (a) *conversion type*, with symptoms of physical illness such as paralysis or loss of hearing without underlying physical pathology; and (b) *dissociative type*, including such reactions as amnesia and multiple personality.

5. *Hypochondriacal neurosis*—involves preoccupation with one's bodily functioning and various presumed diseases.

6. *Neurasthenic neurosis*—involves chronic fatigue, weakness, and lack of enthusiasm.

7. *Depressive neurosis*—involves abnormally prolonged dejection, associated with internal conflict, interpersonal loss, or environmental setback.

Our review of specific neurotic patterns will also deal with the question of whether there is an "existential neurosis"—involving feelings of meaninglessness with chronic alienation and apathy.

At this point, it may be noted that specific neurotic patterns may vary from time to time, and that aspects of different patterns may be combined in a given case.

---

[2]In addition to the seven categories listed, the APA classification also includes the category of *depersonalization neurosis,* which we shall not discuss because of the lack of information concerning depersonalization as a distinct neurotic pattern. However, we shall deal with the phenomenon of depersonalization in our later discussion of psychotic disorders.

Anxiety neurosis

Anxiety neurosis is the most common of the various neurotic patterns, constituting 30 to 40 percent of all neurotic disorders.[3] It is characterized by chronic anxiety and apprehensiveness, which may be punctuated by recurring episodes of acute anxiety. But since neither the anxious expectations nor the acute anxiety attacks appear to stem from any particular threat, the pervasive anxiety is said to be "free-floating." As Wolpe (1969) has emphasized, this indicates that the eliciting stimuli are obscure, complex, and quite pervasive.

In addition to free-floating anxiety, the predominant symptoms in anxiety neurosis typically include:

Inability to concentrate
Difficulty in making decisions
Extreme sensitivity
Discouragement
Sleep disturbances
Excessive sweating
Sustained muscle tension

It can be readily seen that these symptoms are directly related to the basic anxiety that is characteristic of this pattern. In other neurotic reactions the anxiety is ameliorated by the development of phobias, compulsions, and other defensive reactions. Aside from partial repression, the anxiety neurotic is largely without these supplementary defenses.

Clinical picture. The anxiety neurotic lives in a relatively constant state of tension, worry, and diffuse uneasiness. He is oversensitive in interpersonal relationships, and frequently feels inadequate and depressed. Usually he has difficulty concentrating and making decisions, dreading to make a mistake. His high level of tension is often reflected in strained postural movements, overreaction to sudden or unexpected stimuli, and continual nervous movements. Commonly, he complains of muscular tension, especially in the neck and upper shoulder region, chronic mild diarrhea, fre-

quent urination, and sleep disturbances that include insomnia and nightmares. He perspires profusely and his palms are often clammy; he may show cardiovascular changes, such as elevated blood pressure and increased pulse rate; and he may experience heart palpitations for no apparent reason.

No matter how well things seem to be going, anxiety neurotics are chronically apprehensive and anxious. Their vague fears and fantasies combined with their general sensitivity keep them continually upset, uneasy, and discouraged. Not only do they have difficulty making decisions, but after decisions have been made they worry excessively over possible errors and unforeseen circumstances that may lead to disaster. The lengths to which they go to find things to worry about is remarkable; as fast as one cause for worry is removed, they find another, until relatives and friends lose all patience with them.

Even after going to bed, the anxiety neurotic is not likely to find relief from his worries. Often he reviews each mistake, real or imagined, recent or remote. When he is not reviewing and regretting the events of the past, he is anticipating all the difficulties that are going to arise in the future. Then, after he has crossed and recrossed most of his past and future bridges and has managed to fall asleep, he frequently has anxiety dreams—dreams of being choked, falling off high places, being shot, or being chased by murderers, with the horrible sensation that his legs will move only in a slow-motion fashion and that his pursuers, try as he will to elude them, are gradually overtaking him.

The persistent raised level of anxiety may be punctuated from time to time by acute *anxiety attacks*—recurring periods of acute panic that last anywhere from a few seconds to an hour or more. These attacks usually come on suddenly, mount to high intensity, then subside. Symptoms vary from one person to another, but typically they include "palpitations, shortness of breath, profuse sweating, faintness and dizziness, coldness and pallor of the face and extremities, urge to micturate, gastric sensations and an ineffable feeling of imminent death" (Lader & Mathews, 1970, p. 377). The physiological symptoms together with the sensation of impending death or ca-

---

[3]Incidence statistics relative to the various neurotic patterns are rough estimates based on cases diagnosed in clinics and hospitals. Sources for these estimates include Eiduson (1968), Goodwin, Guze, and Robbins (1969), Marks (1970), Prusoff and Klerman (1974), and Templer and Lester (1974).

tastrophe make an anxiety attack a terrifying experience while it lasts.

Usually the attack subsides after a few minutes. If it continues, the individual may frantically implore someone around him to summon a doctor. After medical treatment has been administered, commonly in the form of reassurance and a sedative, he gradually quiets down. Such attacks vary in frequency from several times a day to once a month or even less often. They may occur during the day, or the person may awaken from a sound sleep with a strong feeling of apprehension which rapidly develops into an attack. Between attacks he may appear to be relatively unperturbed, but mild anxiety and tension usually persist.

Studies of large numbers of anxiety neurotics also reveal that many of them suffer from mild depression as well as chronic anxiety

(Prusoff & Klerman, 1974; Downing & Rickels, 1974). This finding is not unexpected in view of their generally gloomy outlook on the world. Nor is it surprising that excessive use of tranquilizing drugs, sleeping pills, and alcohol often complicates the clinical picture in anxiety neuroses.

Causal factors. Anxiety reactions reflect the individual's acute feelings of inadequacy in the face of inner and outer stresses perceived as threatening. Such reactions are considered normal when the stress situation is sufficiently severe to justify them. In our present highly unsettled world, many of us feel uneasy a good deal of the time and may even experience occasional mild anxiety attacks. Similarly, severe financial reverses, loss of employment, and other unusual stresses may activate rather severe but perfectly normal feelings

The psychological distress of the anxiety neurotic is typically accompanied by heightened muscular tension, emotional strain, and sleep disturbances. This picture vividly portrays the inner distress that is characteristic of the anxiety neurotic.

of anxiety. Thus it is not the anxiety per se but the type and degree of stress eliciting it that determines its normality or abnormality. In neurotic reactions the anxiety is considered pathological because it tends to be chronic and is elicited by stress situations that the average individual handles without too much difficulty.

1. *Conditioning.* As we have seen in our discussion of faulty development, a tense and anxious mother can transmit her anxiety to even a very young infant. If interactions with such a faulty parental model continue, the child may learn anxiety reactions similar to those of the parent. In his studies of the behavior disorders of children, Jenkins (1966, 1968, 1969) found that overanxious children tend to have neurotic mothers who are themselves anxious. As one neurotic young adult expressed the problem in the course of psychotherapy, "I guess there is more of my overanxious neurotic mother in me than I had realized."

Jenkins (1968, 1969) also pointed out that anxiety neurotics often come from families in which parents have high expectations for their child while at the same time rejecting his actual accomplishments as substandard. An individual reared in such a setting often appears to adopt perfectionistic parental standards for himself and to become self-critical and anxious if he fails or thinks he is in danger of failing to meet them.

After ten years of very successful practice, a 34-year-old dentist noted that his practice had declined slightly during the closing months of the year. Shortly after this he began to experience mild anxiety attacks and complained of continual worry, difficulty in sleeping, and a vague dread that he was "failing." As a result, he increased his hours of practice during the evenings from one to five nights and began driving himself beyond all reason in a desperate effort to "insure the success of his practice." Although his dental practice now increased beyond what it had been previously, he found himself still haunted by the vague fears and apprehensions of failure. These, in turn, became further augmented by frequent heart palpitations and pains that he erroneously diagnosed as at least an incapacitating if not a fatal heart ailment. At this point his anxiety became so great that he voluntarily came to a clinic for assistance.

In the course of assessment and treatment, the preceding case appeared typical of many ambitious, conscientious individuals who have habitually driven themselves toward well-defined material goals. When such individuals have a history of feeling inadequate and insecure, and of evaluating themselves in terms of high parental expectations, they tend to react to the slightest suggestion or threat of failure with apprehension and anxiety out of all proportion to the actual degree of threat. In the preceding case, such a threat precipitated a rather common form of anxiety reaction.

2. *Inability to handle "dangerous" impulses.* The neurotic is likely to experience intense anxiety in situations that elicit "dangerous" feelings—that is, feelings that would devalue his self-image or endanger his relationships with other people. The handling of hostility, for example, is usually especially difficult for the neurotic, who typically feels forced to take a compliant, subservient, self-suppressing attitude toward others as the price of security, love, and acceptance. This blocking of his own strivings to be a person, however, leads inevitably to strong feelings of aggression and hostility, yet it seems that these feelings must be controlled and denied at all costs to avoid possible rejection by others and to maintain an image of himself as a worthy person. Sometimes such repressed hostility reveals itself in indirect ways, such as in fantasies of killing or injuring other people, perhaps even someone he loves or feels dependent upon for acceptance and security.

An 18-year-old male student developed severe anxiety attacks just before he went out on dates. In therapy it was revealed that he came from a very insecure home in which he was very much attached to an anxious, frustrated, and insecure mother. Intellectually capable and a good student, he had entered college at 16. But during his two years on campus he had difficulty getting dates, especially with college women of his choice. The student he had been dating recently, for example, would not make any arrangements to go out until after 6:00 P.M. of the same day, after her chances for a more preferable date seemed remote. This had increased his already strong feelings of inferiority and insecurity and had led to the development of intense hostility toward the opposite sex, mostly on an unconscious level.

Fantasies of anticipated harm by anxiety neurotics

In a study of 32 anxiety neurotics, Beck, Laude, and Bohnert (1974) found unrealistic expectations and fantasies of harm associated with these patients' heightened levels of anxiety and with anxiety attacks. The degree of anxiety was related to the severity of anticipated harm and to its probability of happening as perceived by the patient.

These expectations and fantasies centered around both physical and psychological dangers — such as being involved in an accident, becoming sick, being violently attacked, humiliation, failure, and rejection by significant others. In this context, the following examples are instructive:

Patient	Fantasy of anticipated harm	Stimuli triggering anxiety
Physician Male, age 32	Fear of sudden death	Any gastrointestinal symptoms
Teacher Male, age 25	Fear of inability to function as a teacher and of ending up on skid row	Anticipation of giving lecture
Housewife Age 30	Fear of physical catastrophe happening to member of family	Sirens, news of deaths, fires, accidents, etc.
Student Male, age 26	Fear of psychological harm, school failure, rejection by everyone, illness	Schoolwork, confrontation with people, any physical symptom
Laborer Male, age 35	Continuous visual fantasies of accident, fear of imminent death	Any noises that might suggest danger (e.g., traffic noises)
Psychologist Male, age 40	Fear of heart attack, cerebral hemorrhage, fainting in public and subsequent disgrace	Physical sensations in chest or abdomen, back pains, hearing about heart attacks
Artist Female, age 35	Interpretation of subjective body sensations as heart attacks	Exertion, anticipation of exertion, reading or hearing about heart attacks
Student Male, age 18	Fear of appearing foolish and subsequent rejection by others	Contact with or anticipated contact with others

Often the fantasies and images reported by a given patient related to past personal experiences. For example, in the preceding cases the housewife had experienced the death of a close friend and the artist's mother had died of a heart attack. These investigators concluded that the expectations and fantasies of anxious patients "not only hold up mirrors to their psychopathology but provide entry points for treating it." (p. 325)

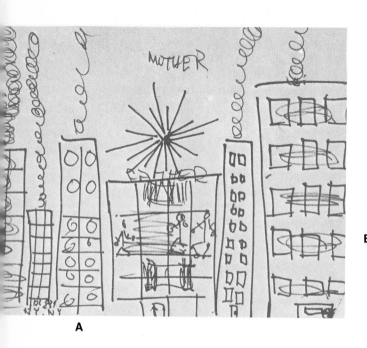

A

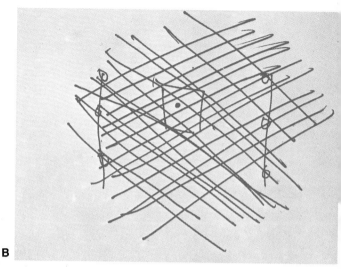

B

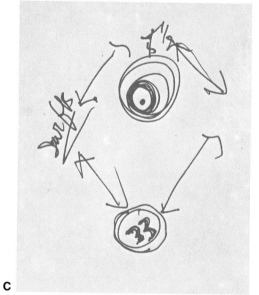

C

Drawing is often considered a primitive but effective method of communicating one's inner thoughts and feelings. Of course, the therapist must exercise caution to avoid misinterpretation. The four pictures shown here were drawn by a woman assessed as suffering from an acute anxiety neurosis. Although she was a successful businesswoman, having risen progressively through jobs of greater and greater responsibility, she felt herself incapable of achieving further advancement—that she had "reached the end of the line." Subsequently, she experienced feelings of frustration, inadequacy, and anxiety.

Sketch A was hurriedly drawn under great tension. The smoking buildings on the left represent New York City, the woman's place of employment, and buildings on the right, her desired place of employment. Separating the two is the middle structure, which contains the "aggressive, agitated figures of her male competitors in the business world."

In **Sketch B,** the woman appeared to represent herself in a cage by the boxed-in dot. She then partially blotted out the crude diagram "by rapidly placed crosshatching, as though to deny the admission that she found herself so trapped." **Sketch C** appears to represent "the merry-go-round on which she has been moving, from one firm to another, around and around, always seeking advancement, without finding any satisfying fulfillment." Finally, **Sketch D** indicates her anxiety over her present dilemma—"What road today? What road tomorrow?" (Adapted from Brown, 1957, pp. 171–74)

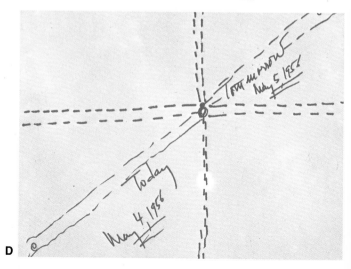

D

About two months before coming to the college clinic for assistance, he had experienced the anxiety-arousing fantasy of choking the young woman to death when they were alone together. As he put it, "When we are alone in the car, I can't get my mind off her nice white throat and what it would be like to choke her to death." At first he put these thoughts out of his mind, but they returned on subsequent nights with increasing persistency. Then, to complicate the matter, he experienced his first acute anxiety attack. It occurred in his car on the way over to pick up his date and lasted for only a few minutes, but the youth was panic-stricken and thought that he was going to die. After that he experienced several additional attacks under the same conditions.

The relationship of the repressed hostility to the persistent fantasies and anxiety attacks seemed clear in this case. Yet it was not at all apparent to the young man, who was at a complete loss to explain either his fantasies or anxiety attacks.

Similarly, repressed sexual desires may threaten to break through existing defenses and elicit intense anxiety. For example, a man may attempt to repress homosexual impulses that he considers highly immoral and completely incompatible with his self-concept. For a time the repression protects him, but repression is rarely—if ever—complete, and the individual is likely to experience periodic flare-ups of anxiety even though he may be unaware of the reason for them. In addition, some change in his life situation—perhaps a friendly relationship with an effeminate man—may intensify his homosexual impulses, posing a major threat to his repressive defenses and eliciting intense anxiety.

3. *Anxiety-arousing decisions.* We have noted that anxiety neurotics tend to have difficulty in making decisions. Under certain conditions—such as conflicts involving moral values or possible loss of security and status—there may be acute anxiety and paralyzing indecision.

A college sophomore, Mary ———, wanted very much to marry a young man she had met in school. However, he insisted on having premarital sex relations "to be sure that they would be sexually compatible." This was contrary to her ethical and religious training, yet she found herself strongly attracted to him physically as well as very much in love. As a consequence, the thought of giving in to his demands persisted, but she was unable to make up her mind. Eventually, she began to experience periodic anxiety attacks, had serious difficulty in concentrating on her studies, and suffered from insomnia, during which she would go over and over the conflict situation.

When Mary came to the college clinic for assistance it seemed apparent that two factors had contributed to the development of her anxiety attacks. The first factor was a devaluated self-concept; she viewed herself as unattractive and was apprehensive about her relations with males. This basic insecurity and sense of inadequacy appeared to pave the way for the second factor, which precipitated the anxiety attacks—namely, the conflict between her guilt-arousing desire for sexual relations, which she considered highly immoral, and her fear of losing the man she loved if she continued to refuse. The situation was also fraught with other anxiety-arousing uncertainties. Even if she did yield to his demands, she had to face the possibility that he was only trying to seduce her or that even if he were sincere, he might not find her sexually compatible. In addition, she had vague feelings of apprehension that she would somehow be punished if she indulged in such behavior, perhaps by becoming pregnant or causing him to lose his respect for her.

In cases where the neurotically insecure person has achieved some degree of real success and consequently of security, anxiety attacks may develop when his proposed behavior jeopardizes this security.

A successful business executive developed acute anxiety attacks about once every two or three months. His wife was eight years older than he, and he was no longer physically attracted to her. He had found himself increasingly interested in younger women and had begun to think how much more enjoyable it would be to have a younger, more companionable wife. During this period he met a woman with whom he was sure he had fallen in love. It was shortly thereafter that the anxiety attacks began to occur. They were preceded by a period of several days of increased tenseness and anxiety, but the attacks came on suddenly and were intense.

This man, too, was at a complete loss to explain his attacks. But the explanation was not difficult to find. He had had a poverty-stricken and insecure childhood and felt basically inferior, insecure, and threatened by a harsh world. These feelings had been intensified when he had failed college courses in his second year, even though the failure had resulted primarily from excessive outside work. He had been able to achieve some security, however, by marrying an older and very strong woman who had instilled considerable self-confidence and initiative in him. The relationship had proved very fruitful financially, and the man was living in a style which, as a youth, "I hadn't dared to imagine in my wildest dreams!" His persistent thoughts about divorcing his wife, on whom he felt dependent for his security and style of life, thus represented a severe threat to the moderately successful adjustment he had been able to achieve. The anxiety attacks followed.

Life often poses problems in which the pursuit of increased satisfactions involves giving up present hard-won security and taking new risks. For the neurotic, this is likely to prove a difficult and anxiety-arousing conflict situation.

4. *Reactivation of prior trauma.* A stressful situation that parallels some earlier trauma may elicit intense anxiety in an individual who is basically insecure. The following reactions are those of a man who sought treatment after being absent from his job for three days as a result of "sickness."

"I've just reached the point where I can't go on. Got no fight left. And not enough guts to end it here. Best damn job I ever had. Almost can see my way out of debt. And it's all going to hell, and I'm getting so I don't care about anything, except not going back to work. I can't kid myself, I just can't take it anymore. And I'll have to confess I have no faith left in anything including your profession. Or faith in myself. Maybe if I can tell someone how I feel, how balled up I am, I can see the light. I can't afford to take time off work. I can't afford to relax a couple of weeks on some warm beach, or forget my troubles with some floozy blonde. Hell, that's for the books on the best seller's lists. I've just got to go about acting like my normal stupid self and something's got to blow. It goes in waves. Sometimes, I'm alright and then I get anxiety feelings, and my heart pounds. I get to shaking all over, and think I'm going to die. God, it's awful!"

Interestingly enough, the primary cause of the intense anxiety reactions in this case was found to be associated with a new and rather critical supervisor at work. In response to criticisms from the supervisor that may have annoyed but did not completely disrupt the behavior of other employees, this man became anxious and depressed. His reaction was traced to his relationship with his father, who had died some five years before. From his earliest memory, the patient had idolized his father and had practically lived for the occa-

sional hard-won compliments he received from him. Conversely, when his father had criticized him, the patient had been so upset that he would go to his room completely distraught and cry for hours at a time. Now, as an adult, this dependent, insecure individual experienced these same feelings of distress when criticized by an exacting supervisor. Apparently the new supervisor had reactivated an old "weak spot" and thus precipitated the anxiety reaction.

Although we have emphasized the inadequacy, oversensitivity, and low stress tolerance of the anxiety neurotic, it may be pointed out that he often puts up a good battle in view of his faulty evaluations of himself and his environment. As Portnoy (1959) has pointed out: "To the picture of an anxious individual apprehensively coping with life in the face of inner and outer dangers must also be added the picture of a human being with courage, able to endure this much anxiety without the more massive defenses and character distortions which characterize the other psychiatric syndromes" (p. 320). This statement seems particularly relevant when we realize that repression—which is seldom adequate—represents the principal defense mechanism utilized by the anxiety neurotic. And as we have noted in our discussion of combat reactions, some anxiety neurotics function very effectively when confronted with an actual danger that both demands and permits definitive action.

Aspects of treatment. Anxiety neurotics often find some relief in mild tranquilizers, although such medication is not likely to modify their basic life-style. Psychotherapy is typically directed at helping the anxiety neurotic discriminate between real and imagined dangers, learn more effective methods of coping, and modify conditions in his life situation that are serving to maintain the maladaptive behavior. Anxiety neurotics usually respond well to treatment, although it appears that their chronic anxiety is seldom completely removed. But as we shall see in the general section on treatment, newer therapeutic innovations are providing a brighter picture concerning the outcome of treatment.

Phobic neurosis

A phobia is a persistent fear of some object or situation that presents no actual danger to the person or in which the danger is magnified out of all proportion to its actual seriousness. The following list of the common phobias and their objects will give some hint of the variety of situations and events around which phobias may be centered:

Acrophobia—high places
Agoraphobia—open places
Algophobia—pain
Astraphobia—storms, thunder, and lightning
Claustrophobia—closed places
Hematophobia—blood
Mysophobia—contamination or germs
Monophobia—being alone
Nyctophobia—darkness
Ocholophobia—crowds
Pathophobia—disease
Pyrophobia—fire
Syphilophobia—syphilis
Zoophobia—animals or some particular animal

Some of these phobias involve an exaggerated fear of things that most of us fear to some extent, such as darkness, fires, disease, and snakes. Others, such as phobias of open places or crowds, involve situations that do not elicit fear in most people.

Many people develop specific phobias which are not part of a neurotic pattern, as in the case of most snake phobias. In *phobic neurosis*, however, the phobia is a central feature in a neurotic life-style characterized by irrational fears and avoidance behaviors. About 10 percent of all neurotics seeking professional assistance suffer from phobic neurosis. This neurotic pattern occurs more commonly among adolescents and young adults than older people, and it is more common among females than males, possibly because strong fears have traditionally been more compatible with female roles than with male roles in our society.

Clinical picture. Most of us have minor irrational fears, but in phobic reactions such fears are intense and interfere with everyday activities. For example, a claustrophobic may go to great lengths to avoid entering a small room or passageway, even when it is essential for him to do so. Neurotics usually admit that

Specific snake phobias, which are usually not part of a neurotic pattern, are nonetheless relatively common. The subject shown here watched a model make a series of approaches to the snake; the subject then did the same, gradually learning to handle the snake until she overcame her phobic behavior and allowed the snake to crawl around on her.

they have no real cause to be afraid of the object or situation, but say they cannot help themselves. If they attempt to approach rather than avoid the phobic situation they are overcome with anxiety, which may vary from mild feelings of uneasiness and distress to a full-fledged anxiety attack.

Phobic neurotics usually show a wide range of other symptoms in addition to their phobias, such as tension headaches, back pains, stomach upsets, dizzy spells, and fear of "cracking up." At times of more acute panic, such individuals often complain of feelings of unreality, of strangeness, and of "not being themselves." In some instances, phobic neurotics also have serious difficulty in making decisions—a condition that Kaufman (1973) has somewhat facetiously called *decidophobia*.

The particular phobias that do develop are often influenced by cultural factors. For example, a phobia of flying would not likely have become common until we entered the age of commercial air travel. In some cases, phobic reactions may also be obsessive, as when a persistent obsessive fear of contamination dominates the neurotic's consciousness. Fears of this type will be dealt with in the next section under "obsessive-compulsive" neuroses.

Causal factors. Phobias may occur in a wide range of personality patterns and abnormal syndromes, reflecting the part that anxiety and avoidance play in many manifestations of abnormal behavior. In general, phobias have been thought of as attempts to cope with specific internal or external dangers by carefully avoiding situations likely to bring about whatever is feared. Thus phobias have been seen as simple defensive reactions in which the person feels he *must* give in to his fears in order to protect himself. This same view is applicable to phobic neurosis, although the focus has shifted from specific phobias to the more general role of phobias in an overall neurotic life-style of defensive and avoidant behaviors.

Three major causal patterns have been emphasized in the development of phobias: conditioning and avoidance learning, defense against threatening impulses, and the displacement of anxiety.

1. *Conditioning and avoidance learning.* As we saw in Watson's case of "little Albert"—who was conditioned to fear a white rat—a phobia may be the learned result of prior trauma in the feared situation. And this fear, as happened in the case of little Albert, may generalize to similar situations.

Phobias of this type are not difficult to understand because most of us probably have mild phobias based on previous learning. A person who has been attacked and bitten by a vicious dog may feel uneasy around dogs, even though some reconditioning experiences have intervened. A pervasive pattern of fear and avoidance behavior can be learned in much the same way. For example, if a child's fumbling attempts to master new skills are ridiculed by her parents, or if she is discouraged from becoming independent, she may never develop the confidence she needs to cope with new situations. In effect, she learns that avoidance is the "appropriate" response where risk or uncertainty is involved.

In addition, a phobia may generalize to a fear of situations only minimally related to the basic trauma.

An 18-year-old woman had been given strict "moral" training concerning the evils of sex, and she associated sexual relations with vivid ideas of sin, guilt, and hell. This basic orientation was reinforced when she was beaten and sexually attacked by a young man on her fifteenth birthday. Nevertheless, when the young man she was dating kissed her and "held her close," it aroused intense sexual desires—which were extremely guilt arousing and which led to a chain of avoidance behaviors. First she stopped seeing him in an effort to get rid of her immoral thoughts; then she stopped all dating; then she began to feel uncomfortable with any young man she knew; and finally she became fearful of any social situations where men might be present. At this point her life was largely dominated by her phobias, and she was so "completely miserable" that she requested professional help.

In the following case, the phobic reaction apparently served two protective functions but also led to complications.

A 22-year-old woman sought psychological assistance because of an intense fear of syphilis which made it impossible for her to have sexual relations with her husband. She explained that her husband was a wealthy and much older man to whom she had been married for about a year; she expressed concern that her phobia was interfering with her marital relationship.

In the course of therapy it was brought out that she considered her husband "a haven of refuge from the lousy world out there." However, she found sexual relations with him repulsive, "sort of like sleeping with your father." She was attracted to younger men and had engaged in a series of extramarital affairs. Although she was "discreet" in these matters, she was terrified that her husband would find out and leave her, taking away "the only real security I have ever had."

Prior to the onset of the phobia, she had had sexual relations with a stranger she met in a bar. He was slightly intoxicated and mentioned afterward that he had recently been treated for syphilis. She stated that at the time she didn't think anything about what he said: "I assumed his treatment had been completed." However, about 2 weeks later she inexplicably developed a morbid fear of syphilis which had continued unabated for over a month.

In this case, it seemed clear the patient's development of syphilophobia was related to the protection it afforded her from engaging in the extramarital affairs, in which she found little or no satisfaction, that endangered her marriage. At the same time, it relieved her of having to have intercourse with her husband, which she found repugnant. However, the phobia was not without its cost, for her husband seemed both puzzled and dissatisfied with the situation.

2. Defense against threatening impulses. A phobia may represent a defensive reaction that protects the individual from situations in which his repressed aggressive or sexual impulses might become dangerous. Thus a husband may develop a phobia of lakes, swimming pools, and other bodies of water because on previous occasions he had persistent ideas of drowning his wife; similarly, a young mother may develop a phobia of being alone with her unwanted baby because of recurring fantasies about strangling him.

3. Displacement of anxiety. A phobia may represent a displacement of anxiety from some external threat that elicited it to some other object or situation. This concept is strongly emphasized in the psychoanalytic model and stems largely from Freud's case history of little Hans, published in 1909. On the basis of this case and subsequent clinical experience, Freud concluded that phobias represent displaced anxiety associated with the Oedipus complex. Presumably a small boy desires to possess his mother sexually and is jealous and hostile toward his father. He therefore fears his father—and in particular dreads being castrated. The fear of the avenging father may then be displaced to some external and formerly innocuous object. In the case of 5-year-old Hans, the horse pulling the carriage in which he and his mother were riding fell down and was hurt. Hans had become very frightened, and according to Freud this dramatic situation led to the displacement of his fear of castration by his father to a fear of being bitten by horses. Freud concluded that phobias in adults develop only in people with disturbed sexual relationships.

Later investigators have disagreed with Freud's interpretation of little Hans' phobia, and have pointed out that many kinds of stress situations may lead to phobic reactions through the mechanism of displacement. For example, a basically insecure person who feels that she may be discharged from her job for inefficiency may develop an elevator phobia. Since she works in an office on the fortieth floor of a large building, this makes it impossible for her to get to work—which in turn protects her from the possible embarrassment and self-devaluation of being fired.

Regardless of how it begins, phobic behavior tends to be reinforced by the reduction in anxiety that occurs when the individual avoids the feared situation or stress. In addition, phobias may be maintained in part by secondary gains, such as increased attention, sympathy, and some control over the behavior of others. For example, a phobia of driving may enable a housewife to escape from responsibilities outside the home, such as shopping or transporting her children to and from school.

Aspects of treatment. Newer methods of behavior therapy have proven highly effective in the treatment of specific phobias as well as more extensive phobic neuroses; consequently, it is rarely necessary for the individual to continue to suffer the personal distress occasioned by phobic behaviors. Usually one of two basic strategies is followed in treatment.

Treatment of a patient with multiple phobias by a self-directing and self-reinforcing imagery technique

Frankel (1970) has reported on the treatment of a 26-year-old married woman who suffered from disabling fears of sexual relations, earthquakes, and enclosed places. The background of the case, the treatment procedure, and the outcome are summarized below.

Symptoms

1. The sexual fear. The woman reported that she had been able to have sexual relations with her husband only about 10 times in their 3 years of marriage. Her sexual phobia appeared to have a learned basis. She had been molested by an older male at age 5, had been raped by a gang of juvenile delinquents when she was 15, had been "pawed" by intoxicated male visitors of her divorced mother, and had had sexual relations with 3 men prior to her marriage — each of whom had professed love for her but stopped seeing her after the sexual contact. In an effort to "hold her husband" she had had sexual relations with him a few times, but she always had "a cold feeling, like I'm going to suffocate — like I can't breathe" during sexual relations. In the third month of marriage, the couple conceived a son, after whose birth they had sexual relations only twice.

2. The earthquake fear. The woman stated that several times a day her thoughts were occupied by an uncontrollable fear of being in an earthquake. Her sequence of thoughts was always the same. First she would imagine that the ground was shaking and the house rocking, and that she rushed to pick up the baby. She would next imagine herself standing in a doorway, with the house collapsing around her. At this point the anxiety would become "unbearable." The recurrent thoughts about being in an earthquake were especially prominent when she tried to go to sleep, with the result that she was physically tired, irritable, and anxious during the day. Although a physician had prescribed tranquilizers, she reported that they did not help. On several occasions, she had arisen during the night, picked up her son, and rushed to a doorway. Interestingly enough, she had never been in an earthquake, nor did she personally know anyone who had.

3. Fear of closed places. The woman reported that she had always been fearful of elevators, small rooms, and even being surrounded by people. However, she did not recall ever being locked up in a small enclosure, and did not know anyone who had. She would climb many flights of stairs rather than take an elevator. Just prior to seeking therapy, she had been caught up in a large crowd greeting a visiting dignitary. She reported feeling anxiety, panic, and fear of suffocation. She screamed and pushed people out of the way until she was able to flee.

Treatment

Since the woman's most disabling fear was that of earthquakes, it was decided to treat that fear first, then the fear of sexual relations, and finally the fear of enclosed places. The innovative treatment procedure was a variation of implosive therapy, in which the woman was instructed to proceed through sequences of thoughts and images of herself in the fear-producing situation.

"*The implosive technique raises the client's anxiety level and maintains it until it passes a peak and begins to decline. This reduction in anxiety is seen as the beginning of extinction of the fear response, but it also may be seen as providing the occasion for reinforcement for the toleration of a high degree of anxiety. That is, the ability to proceed through an imagery sequence which elicits high anxiety is itself reinforced first by success in sustaining anxiety and then by mastery implied by its reduction.*" (p. 497)

Thus, whenever the woman became "too upset to go on" — a point at which she had previously put the imagery "out of her mind" — she was encouraged to continue with the description of her imagery and her feelings toward it. For example, in the earthquake sequence where she imagined that the house was collapsing around her as she stood in the doorway with her son, she was asked such questions as "What's happening now?" "What's happening next?"

"*The content produced by the client involved the house collapsing on her, her son trapped under her as large beams fell on her, the earthquake finally ending, her being pinned under beams and being unable to move, screaming for help for several hours with no one coming to her aid, and finally being able to move a beam, stand up, walk away from the rubble, and breathe a sigh of relief at being alive and unharmed.*" (p. 498)

The imagery sequences lasted from 15 to 30 minutes, and the remainder of each 50-minute therapy session centered on the discussion of the vividness of the imagery sequences and the feelings they elicited. Since the woman could come in only once a week for therapy, she was instructed to proceed along the entire imagery sequence on her own whenever the fear of earthquakes entered her thoughts. She was instructed not to put the thoughts "out of her mind" under any circumstances. This treatment was continued until the fear of earthquakes no longer troubled her. A similar procedure was used in dealing with her sexual fear and her fear of enclosed places.

Outcome

The entire treatment procedure lasted five months, but the fear of earthquakes was reduced from the highest to the lowest rating (on a 10-point scale) in four sessions. The woman reported that she thought less and less about earthquakes and had no difficulty sleeping. Even though a mild earthquake did occur about six weeks after treatment began, she stated that she was "not bothered in the slightest by its occurrence." Six months after the treatment ended, she showed no recurrence of the fear or evidence of symptom substitution. An interesting finding, however, was that the reduction in the fear of earthquakes did not generalize to her other fears, which maintained their original intensity.

With respect to the sexual phobia, treatment enabled the woman to resume sexual relations with her husband. At first she did not enjoy the sex act; six months after treatment ended she felt increasing pleasure and confidence but was still unable to have an orgasm; and at the end of a year she reported that she was able to gain a great deal of pleasure in sex and to have an orgasm about once in every three or four sexual experiences. Her overall relationship with her husband improved also.

The fear of enclosed places decreased from a fairly high rating to zero after seven sessions. During the fifth session of treatment, the woman remembered that she had accidentally been trapped in an airtight cabinet at about age 6, and would have suffocated if her mother had not found her in time. Memory of the event came after she successfully rode down three floors in an elevator. Thus it would appear that behavior change can be followed by "insight."

In reporting this case, Frankel related the comparatively brief period required for the reduction and elimination of the woman's fears to the fact that none of the fears reappeared after the conclusion of treatment, and to the lack of symptom substitution. He also emphasized the point that the treatment was largely self-administered, a marked advantage over more typical therapy approaches.

The first—based on the assumption that phobias are symbolic representations of more basic anxieties—focuses on helping the patient understand his phobia and learn more effective techniques for coping with his anxiety and with the feared situation. However, this approach has not proven very effective. As Salzman has pointed out, "It has been known for some time that understanding, alone, is ineffectual in resolving the phobic state. It is a commonplace that, while the patient may have adequate insight into the origin, symbolism, and function of his phobia, he is still unable to risk the initial venture into the heretofore out-of-bounds area of living" (1968, pp. 464–65).

Consequently, the second major strategy, involving desensitization and other behavior-modification techniques, is being increasingly used to deal directly with the hierarchy of fears and avoidance behaviors. For example, the girl described on page 228, who had become fearful of any situation where men might be present, was first taught to relax while imagining herself in a social situation in which men were present. Next, she was encouraged to attend such a gathering, and found herself able to do so without experiencing the usual fear. Treatment then proceeded through each step of the fear hierarchy until she could behave normally in heterosexual relationships.

Other behavior-modification techniques that can be used in the treatment of phobias will be dealt with later. Here it may be pointed out that the successful treatment of phobias may lead to changes in the patient's entire lifestyle. This is well brought out in a case cited by Bandura, Blanchard, and Ritter (1969), in which the individual had been successfully treated for a fear of snakes.

"My success in gradually overcoming this fear of snakes has contributed to a greater feeling of confidence generally in my abilities to overcome any other problem which may arise. I have more faith in myself." (p. 197)

In essence, discovering that he can perform behaviors that he formerly avoided can help the individual gain confidence in himself and his ability to cope with stressful situations in general.

Obsessive-compulsive neurosis

In obsessive-compulsive neurosis the person feels compelled to think about something that he does not want to think about or to carry out some action against his will. As in the case of phobias, the individual usually realizes that his behavior is irrational but cannot seem to control it.

The incidence of obsessive-compulsive neuroses has been variously estimated to be from about 12 to 20 percent of the neurotic population. Age and sex differences have not been systematically studied.

Clinical picture. As Nemiah (1967) has pointed out, there is a wide range of obsessive-compulsive behaviors.

"The phenomena may be manifested psychically or behaviorally; they may be experienced as ideas or as impulses; they may refer to events anticipated in the future or actions already completed; they may express desires and wishes or protective measures against such desires; they may be simple, uncomplicated acts and ideas or elaborate, ritualized patterns of thinking and behavior. . . ." (p. 916)

Most of us have experienced minor obsessional thoughts, such as persistent thoughts about a coming trip or date, or a haunting melody that we cannot seem to get out of our mind. In the case of obsessive reactions, however, the thoughts are much more persistent, appear irrational to the individual, and interfere with his everyday behavior.

In neurotic reactions obsessive thoughts may center around a wide variety of topics, such as concern over bodily functions, committing immoral acts, attempting suicide, or even finding the solution to some seemingly unsolvable problem. Particularly common are obsessive thoughts of committing some immoral act. A wife may be obsessed with the idea of poisoning her husband, a daughter of pushing her mother down a flight of stairs.

Even though obsessive thoughts are not carried out in action, they remain a source of torment to the individual. This pattern is well illustrated in a classic case described by Kraines (1948) of a girl who

"complained of having 'terrible thoughts.' When she thought of her boy-friend she wished he were dead; when her mother went down the stairs, she 'wished she'd fall and break her neck'; when her sister spoke of going to the beach with her infant daughter, the patient 'hoped that they would both drown.' These thoughts 'make me hysterical. I love them; why should I wish such terrible things to happen? It drives me wild, makes me feel I'm crazy and don't belong to society; maybe it's best for me to end it all than to go on thinking such terrible things about those I love.' " (p. 183)

As in the case of obsessive thoughts, most of us show some compulsive behavior—stepping over cracks in sidewalks, walking around ladders instead of under them, or turning away when a black cat crosses our path—but without the degree of compulsiveness of the neurotic. Most of us also resort to minor obsessive-compulsive patterns under severe pressure or when trying to achieve goals that we consider of critical importance. Many historical figures have shown an "obsessive-compulsive" adherence to their goals despite discouragement and ridicule—Columbus persisted for 18 years in his efforts to secure financial backing for his expedition to "India," and Darwin assembled evidence for 22 years before he would present his ideas on evolution.

In neurotic-compulsive reactions, the person feels compelled to perform some act which seems strange and absurd to him and which he does not want to perform. Such compulsive acts may vary from relatively mild ritual-like behavior, such as making the sign of the cross periodically during the day, to more extreme behavior, such as washing one's hands as often as ten times each hour. The performance of the compulsive act usually brings a feeling of reduced tension and satisfaction (Carr, 1971, 1974; Hodgson & Rachman, 1972). On the other hand, if the person tries to resist the compulsion, he is overcome with anxiety.

An obsessive-compulsive neurosis is considered maladaptive because it represents irrational and exaggerated behavior in the face of stresses that are not unduly upsetting to most people, and because such patterns reduce the flexibility of behavior and the capability for self-direction. In general, such behavior takes place in the context of a personality characterized by feelings of inadequacy and insecurity, rigid conscience development, a tendency toward feelings of guilt, and high vulnerability to threat.

Causal factors. Either the obsessive thoughts or the compulsive actions may predominate in a given case, but both are parts of a total reaction pattern, and their causes are essentially the same. Several patterns have been delineated.[4]

1. *Substitutive thoughts and activities.* The obsessive-compulsive may defend himself from anxiety by persistently thinking of or doing something else each time threatening thoughts or impulses make their appearance. A man walking in a lonely place late at night might find the following thought continually persisting in his mind: "There is nothing to be afraid of—I am not afraid." In this way he attempts to allay his underlying fear. In essence, "safe" obsessive thoughts are substituted for more unpleasant or dangerous ones.

The same causal pattern may underlie compulsive preoccupation with some activity, such as working on a new invention, writing the "truly great" novel, or developing a system to beat the horses. The task may never be completed, but by working on it so hard the individual is kept too busy to deal with unpleasant problems and is too engrossed to think disturbing thoughts. In many cases the compulsive behavior may, of course, be directed toward a constructive task. It is judged neurotic because it is used as an escape from marital, sexual, interpersonal, or other problems with which the individual must cope if he is to achieve effective adjustment.

In some instances, substitutive thoughts may be more complicated, and may involve the defense mechanism of *reaction forma-*

---

[4]Obsessive thoughts and compulsive actions may, of course, occur as part of other clinical syndromes. Masserman (1961) has cited the case of a soldier who in an acute fatigue state kept throwing out his arms in a peculiar gesture. This gesture could not be explained until the patient recalled under narcosis that in the heat and excitement of a night battle, he had machine-gunned a friend, and had suffered a remorse so great that he had an overpowering desire to throw away his gun and run blindly from the unbearable horror of the situation. In our later discussion of psychotic disorders, we shall see how obsessive-compulsive reactions may be related to delusional and hallucinatory behavior.

Obsessions of infanticide

Obsessions of infanticide—referring to the murder of a newborn or preadolescent child—were a central clinical feature in 44 of 1317 consecutive patients at the University of Kansas Medical Center. Thirty-eight of these patients were women and 6 were men. Of the patients, 17 were diagnosed as schizophrenic—all of the male patients were so considered—and were characterized by bizarre and paranoid ideation; 11 were diagnosed as depressive even though they evidenced both depressive and obsessional ideation; and 7 were diagnosed as obsessive-compulsive neurotics.

Interestingly enough, in the latter group "the obsessional thoughts were typically experienced not so much as an impulse to harm the child but as an apprehension that such an impulse might occur and be uncontrollably acted upon" (p. 238). These patients then viewed the child as an object to be avoided if possible, for fear they would harm him. At the same time they expressed feelings of guilt and self-devaluation often reflected in statements such as "I'm not a good mother" (p. 238). Eventually the situation became so anxiety arousing that the patients sought hospitalization.

The following excerpt was written spontaneously by a 32-year-old mother and was considered typical of these obsessive-compulsive patients:

"When I found out I was pregnant I did not want the baby because of all my physical problems and my nervousness. I felt I wasn't equipped to handle another child just then, but I didn't and wouldn't do anything to harm the baby I was carrying. And I seemed in time to become adjusted to my pregnancy. The premature arrival of the baby upset me because I had lost three premature babies. When he had trouble the first few days of life, my fears for him were great. He was in the hospital three weeks. When it was time to go home, I became very tense and fearful of caring well for him. . . . He was home for six weeks and then became (severely) ill with bronchitis. (This) lasted nine days. During this illness my fears, my appetite loss, and the bad dreams all began. I felt I had failed in my care as a mother. Since bringing him home (the second time) I notice that I can't feel tender or relaxed or loving as I want to, and I do everything automatically." (p. 238)

This mother, like the other obsessive-compulsive patients, felt fearful of impending loss of control and the inadvertent acting out of her fantasies of infanticide.

In contrast to the neurotic group, the clinical picture in the psychotic group was dominated by actual impulses to harm the child which might well have been acted on.

Based on Button and Reivich (1972).

tion. Here the individual may think or act in ways directly contradictory to his dangerous thoughts or impulses. For example, a prisoner may repress dangerous thoughts about killing a hated guard and persistently think about "brotherly love."

Obsessive fantasies may also help satisfy repressed desires and provide a substitute for overt action.

A farmer developed obsessive thoughts of hitting his three-year-old son over the head with a hammer. The father was completely unable to explain his "horrible thoughts." He stated that he loved his son very much and thought he must be going insane to harbor such thoughts. In the treatment of this case it became apparent that the patient's wife had suffered great pain in childbirth and had since refused sexual relations with him for fear of again becoming pregnant. In addition, she lavished most of her attention on the son, and their previously happy marriage was now torn with quarreling and bickering.

The farmer's obsessive thoughts of violence toward his son had apparently developed out of a combination of repressed hostility toward the boy, who had replaced him in his wife's affection, and wishful thinking in the direction of a return to his previously happy marital state, once the son was out of the way. However, the man vigorously and sincerely denied this explanation when it was suggested to him. Because his fantasies were lacking in affect, they did not seem to represent his real feelings at all; and, at the same time, they permitted expression of his hostility without any attendant feelings of guilt. Of course, not all neurotics with obsessive thoughts of violence toward loved ones escape guilt feelings.

2. *Guilt and fear of punishment.* Obsessive-compulsive behavior often seems to stem from feelings of guilt and self-condemnation. Lady Macbeth's symbolic handwashing after her participation in the bloody murder of King Duncan is a well-known literary example of ritualistic behavior aimed at the cleansing of guilt for immoral behavior. In the following case, the development of obsessive-compulsive patterns seems to be associated with a belief that "unforgivable" behavior will inevitably be punished.

A 32-year-old high-school cooking teacher developed marked feelings of guilt and uneasiness, accompanied by obsessive fears of hurting others by touching them or by their handling something she had touched. She dreaded to have anyone eat anything she had prepared, and if students in her cooking class were absent, she was certain they had been poisoned by her cooking. In addition, she developed the obsessive notion that a rash at the base of her scalp was a manifestation of syphilis, which would gnaw at her brain and make a "drooling idiot" of her.

Accompanying the obsessive fears were compulsions consisting primarily of repeated hand-washings and frequent returns to some act already performed to reassure herself that the act had been done right, such as turning off the gas or water.

In treatment it became clear that the patient was a self-centered but highly sensitive and conscientious person. She had graduated from college with honors and considered herself highly intelligent. About three years before her present difficulties she had married a noncollege man of whom she had been very much ashamed because of his poor English, table manners, and other characteristics which she thought led to a very poor social showing. As a result, she had rejected him in her thinking and behavior and had treated him in what she now considered a very cruel manner. On one occasion she had also been unfaithful to him, which was directly opposed to her moral training.

Over a period of time, however, she came to realize that he was a very fine person and that other people thought highly of him despite his lack of social polish. In addition, she gradually came to the realization that she was very much in love with him. At this point she began to reproach herself for her cruel treatment of him. She felt that he was a truly wonderful husband, and that she was completely unworthy of him. She was sure her past cruelty and unfaithfulness could never be forgiven. "Heaven knows that every word he says is worth fifty words I say. If I were real honest and truthful I would tell my husband to leave me."

This woman's obsessive fear of contaminating other people and of having syphilis apparently grew out of a feeling that her past "sins" had caught up with her. They also served the function of protecting her from acting upon her occasionally returning desire for sexual relations with other men.

In some instances the individual may attempt to counteract forbidden desires or be cleansed of guilt by means of compulsive rituals. For example, a high-school senior's hostile fantasies toward her domineering mother were so acutely traumatic that she repressed them. However, this repression proved to be a precarious defense, and the dangerous hostility threatened to break through into consciousness. As a result, the patient developed a compulsive ritual of a defensive nature: at crucial moments she felt compelled to make the sign of the cross, repeating "God protect my dearly beloved mother." Yet she had not the vaguest idea why she had to perform this action. It seemed senseless and silly to her and was interfering with her classwork and social relationships.

3. *Assurance of order and predictability.* A rigid ordering of behavior can be temporarily adaptive in particularly difficult stress situations. The autobiographical accounts of Admiral Richard Byrd, who spent 6 solitary months in the antarctic, and of Dr. Alain Bombard, who sailed alone across the Atlantic for 65 days on a life raft (see page 99), show that the two men—dedicated scientists—reacted to their isolation and loneliness in almost identical ways.

"Both explorers found that while their lives were threatened daily by the hazards of their milieu, it was the constancy of their surroundings which seemed like a force which would destroy them. Both men felt that they could control themselves and their environment only by thoroughly organizing their days, assigning themselves to a strict routine of work, and spending no more than one hour at a time doing a task. In this way, each felt he proved to himself that he could control both himself and his environment. . . . Both men used the same mechanisms to fight off depression: controlling their thoughts, dwelling only on pleasant past associations and experiences and refusing to allow themselves to think about the anxiety-producing aspects of their situations." (Solomon et al., 1957)

Similarly, the neurotic, confronted with a world that seems highly dangerous, may attempt to maintain some semblance of order and control by becoming unduly meticulous and methodical. A rigid pattern of behavior helps to prevent anything from going wrong, and hence provides some security and predictability. But if the slightest detail gets out of order, the entire defensive structure is endangered and the individual feels threatened and anxious.

A case that illustrates this pattern is that of a patient who, prior to hospitalization, had had his life ordered in the most minute detail. He arose in the morning precisely at 6:50, took a shower, shaved, and dressed. His wife had breakfast ready precisely at 7:10 and followed a menu that he worked out months in advance. At exactly 7:45 he left for the office where he worked as an accountant. He came home precisely at 5:55, washed, then read the evening paper, and had dinner precisely at 6:30, again as per menu. His schedule was equally well worked out for evenings and weekends, with a movie on Tuesday, reading on Wednesday, rest on Monday and Thursday, and bridge on Friday. Saturday morning he played golf and Sunday morning and evening he attended church. Saturday evening usually involved having guests or visiting others. He was fastidious in his dress. Each shirt had to be clean and unwrinkled, his suit pressed every two days, and so on. His demands, of course, also included his wife, who was inclined to be easy-going and was upset when he "blew up" at the smallest variation from established routine.

By means of his carefully ordered existence the patient had managed to make a reasonably successful adjustment until he became involved in a business deal with a friend and lost a considerable sum of money. This proved too much for him and precipitated a severe anxiety reaction with considerable agitation and depression, necessitating hospitalization.

In this case the individual's primary means of defense against *external* threats was to try to impose rigid order, thus making the world safer and more predictable. In other instances such a compulsive following of a daily routine, particularly a socially desirable and ethical one, helps the individual establish automatic control over dangerous inner desires. He avoids situations that might stimulate such desires, as well as situations that might permit their expression.

In a general sense, this pattern seems similar to the repetitive and rigid rituals long used by primitive peoples as a means of warding off evil forces in an unpredictable world. If they are to be effective, such rituals must be faithfully observed and performed in rigidly prescribed ways.

Aspects of treatment. Therapy in obsessive-compulsive neuroses tends to follow three basic strategies: (a) helping the individual to discriminate between thought and action, to accept his "forbidden" desires as common to most people, and to integrate them into his self-structure; (b) helping the individual to discriminate between objective and imagined dangers and to respond selectively to each; and (c) blocking obsessive-compulsive rituals by consistently rewarding the person when he departs from or abandons the use of such neurotic behavior. All these strategies are aimed at eliminating neurotic defenses and helping the individual realize that catastrophe does not follow their removal.

Although changing a person's basic obsessive-compulsive life style is not always possible, therapy does ordinarily lead to a marked alleviation of symptoms and paves the way for long-range improvement. The following case represents the nature and outcome of treatment in one rather typical case.

A middle-aged married woman had the compulsion to shake every article of her own clothes and those of her children. The shaking ritual—which occupied over an hour of her time each morning—required that each piece of clothing be shaken three times in each of three different directions and at each of three different levels. In addition, most of the clothes had to be brushed inside and out; whenever anything was washed, it had to be washed three times. The woman also found it difficult to stop washing her hands once she had started and repeatedly felt a compulsion to rub her hands together in each of three different ways.

Interview assessment indicated that much of the woman's compulsive behavior was associated with vague fears of germs and disease. A treatment program was formulated that (a) helped her discriminate between stimuli that were objectively "dirty" and unhygienic and those that were not—thus eliminating unnecessary fears and helping her make realistic decisions about standards of cleanliness; (b) consistently reinforced her behavior when she abandoned her compulsive rituals; and (c) utilized verbal instructions by the therapist to prevent their repetition whenever possible.

Therapy began in February, and by November of the same year the woman's ritualistic behavior had been completely eliminated. She was able to make her own decisions about cleaning and washing and was more confident about her standards of cleanliness. (Adapted from Mather, 1970)

Hysterical neurosis: conversion type

The conversion type of hysterical neurosis involves a neurotic pattern in which symptoms of some physical illness appear without any underlying organic pathology. It is one of the most intriguing and baffling patterns in psychopathology, and we still have much to learn about it.

The term *hysteria* is derived from the Greek word meaning "uterus." It was thought by Hippocrates and other ancient Greeks that this disorder was restricted to women and that it was caused by sexual difficulties, particularly by the wandering of a frustrated uterus to various parts of the body because of sexual desires and a yearning for children. Thus the uterus might lodge in the throat and cause choking sensations, or in the spleen, resulting in temper tantrums. Hippocrates considered marriage the best remedy for the affliction.

The concept of the relationship of sexual difficulties to hysteria was later advanced in modified form by Freud. He used the term *conversion hysteria* to indicate that the symptoms were an expression of repressed and deviated sexual energy—that is, the psychosexual conflict is *converted* into a bodily disturbance. For example, a sexual conflict over masturbation might be solved by developing a paralyzed hand. This is not done consciously, of course, and the person is not aware of the origin or meaning of his symptom.

In contemporary psychopathology, hysterical reactions of this type are no longer interpreted in Freudian terms as the "conversion" of sexual conflicts or other psychological problems into physical symptoms. Rather, the physical symptoms are now usually seen as serving a defensive function, enabling the individual to escape or avoid a stressful situation. Despite this change in interpretation, however, the term *conversion reaction* has been retained.

In World War I conversion reactions were the most frequent type of psychiatric syndrome. For many soldiers this involved a highly threatening approach-avoidance conflict, in which military orders and doing one's duty were pitted against fear of being killed or maimed in the crude bayonet charges that

Conversion reactions in student naval aviators

Mucha and Reinhardt (1970) have reported on a study of 56 student aviators with conversion reactions who were assessed at the U.S. Naval Aerospace Medical Institute in Pensacola, Florida. In the group, representing 16 percent of a total population of 343 patients at the Institute, four types of conversion symptoms were found. These were, in order of frequency: visual symptoms, auditory symptoms, paralysis or paresthesias of extremities, and paresthesia of the tongue. The chart at lower right indicates the rates of incidence.

Generally, the 56 students came from middle-class, achievement-oriented families. The fathers of 80 percent of them were either high-school or college graduates, and were either professional men or white-collar workers. Interestingly enough, 89 percent of the students with conversion reactions had won letters in one or more sports in high school or college; all were college graduates and presently were flight students, officer candidates, or officers.

Commenting on the relatively high incidence of conversion reactions among the patients at the Institute, Mucha and Reinhardt emphasized three conditions which they considered of etiological significance:

1. Unacceptability of quitting. In the students' previous athletic training, physical illness had been an acceptable means of avoiding difficult situations, whereas quitting was not. Moreover, the present training environment tended to perpetuate this adaptation, since the military is also achievement-oriented, and does not tolerate quitting as a means of coping with stress situations.

2. Parental models. Seventy percent of the parents of these students had had significant illnesses affecting the organ system utilized in the students' conversion reactions; and a majority of the students had had multiple physical symptoms—often as a result of athletic injuries—prior to enlistment.

3. Sensitization to the use of somatic complaints. As a result of their previous experience, the students were sensitized to the use of somatic complaints as a face-saving means of coping with stressful situations.

"When faced with the real stress of the flight training program and with frequent life-or-death incidents, they resorted to this unconscious mechanism to relieve the stress and to avoid admitting failure. To admit failure would be totally unacceptable to the rigid demands of their superegos." (p. 494)

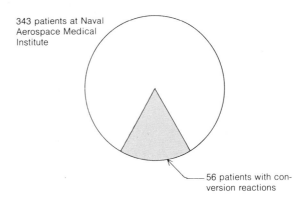

343 patients at Naval Aerospace Medical Institute

56 patients with conversion reactions

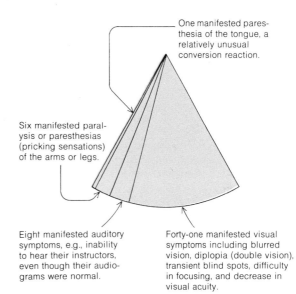

One manifested paresthesia of the tongue, a relatively unusual conversion reaction.

Six manifested paralysis or paresthesias (pricking sensations) of the arms or legs.

Eight manifested auditory symptoms, e.g., inability to hear their instructors, even though their audiograms were normal.

Forty-one manifested visual symptoms including blurred vision, diplopia (double vision), transient blind spots, difficulty in focusing, and decrease in visual acuity.

characterized this war. Here, conversion symptoms—such as being paralyzed in the legs or unable to straighten one's back—enabled the soldier to avoid the combat situation without being labeled a coward or being subjected to court-martial. Conversion reactions were also relatively common among combat personnel in World War II. These conversion reactions typically occurred in association with the highly stressful conditions of combat, and involved men who ordinarily would be considered stable.

Conversion reactions were once relatively common in both civilian and military life, but today they constitute only 5 percent of all neuroses treated. Interestingly enough, their decreasing incidence seems to be closely related to our growing sophistication about medical and psychological disorders: a hysterical disorder apparently loses its defensive function if it can be readily shown to lack an organic basis. The educational factor may help explain why the incidence of conversion reactions is highest among individuals with low socioeconomic status.

Clinical picture. In an age that no longer believes in such phenomena as being "struck" blind or suddenly afflicted with an unusual and dramatic paralysis with no obvious organic basis, conversion patterns increasingly simulate more exotic physical diseases that are harder to diagnose, such as mononucleosis or convulsive seizures. Conversion reactions are great imitators, however, and the range of symptoms is practically as diverse as it is for real physical ailments.

In describing the clinical picture in conversion hysteria, it is useful to think in terms of three categories of symptoms: sensory, motor, and visceral.

1. *Sensory symptoms.* Any of the senses may be involved in sensory conversion reactions. The most common forms of these reactions are:

Anesthesia—loss of sensitivity
Hypesthesia—partial loss of sensitivity
Hyperesthesia—excessive sensitivity
Analgesia—loss of sensitivity to pain
Paresthesia—exceptional sensations, such as tingling

Some idea of the range of sensory symptoms that may occur in conversion reactions can be gleaned from Ironside and Batchelor's (1945) study of hysterical visual symptoms among airmen in World War II. They found blurred vision, photophobia, double vision, night blindness, a combination of intermittent visual failure and amnesia, deficient stereopsis (the tendency to look past an object during attempts to focus on it), restriction in the visual field, intermittent loss of vision in one eye, color blindness, jumbling of print during attempts to read, and failing day vision. They also found that the symptoms of each airman were closely related to his performance duties. Night fliers, for example, were more subject to night blindness, while day fliers more often developed failing day vision. Results of a more recent study of student military aviators who developed conversion reactions are reported in the illustration on page 237.

The other senses may also be subject to a wide range of disorders, but anesthesias that formerly were common—such as loss of vision or hearing—have become increasingly rare. However, Parry-Jones and his colleagues (1970) have described a case of hysterical blindness, and the illustration on page 239 presents an interesting case of hysterical deafness. A puzzling and unsolved question in hysterical blindness and deafness is whether the individual actually cannot see or hear, or whether the sensory information is received but screened from consciousness (Theodor & Mandelcorn, 1973). In general, the evidence supports the latter hypothesis.

2. *Motor symptoms.* Hysterical motor disorders also cover a wide range of symptoms, but only the most common need be mentioned here.

Hysterical paralyses are usually confined to a single limb, such as an arm or a leg, and the loss of function is usually selective. For example, in "writer's cramp" the person cannot write but may be able to use the same muscles in shuffling a deck of cards or playing the piano. Tremors (muscular shaking or trembling) and tics (localized muscular twitches) are common. Occasionally there are contractures that usually involve the flexion of fingers and toes, or there is rigidity of the larger joints, such as the elbows and knees. Paralyses and contractures frequently lead to walking disturbances. A person with a rigid knee joint may be forced to throw his leg out in a sort of arc as he walks. Another walking disturbance worthy of mention is *astasia-abasia,* in which the individual can usually control his leg movements when sitting or lying down, but can hardly stand and has a very grotesque, disorganized walk, with his legs wobbling about in every direction.

The most common hysterical disturbances of speech are *aphonia,* in which the individual is able to talk only in a whisper, and *mutism,* in which he cannot speak at all. Interestingly enough, a person who can talk only in a whisper can usually cough in a normal manner. In true laryngeal paralysis both the cough and the voice are affected. Aphonia is relatively common in hysterical conversion reactions and usually occurs after some emotional shock, whereas mutism is relatively rare. Occasionally, conversion symptoms may involve convulsions, similar to those in epilepsy. However, the hysteric shows few of the usual characteristics of true epilepsy—he rarely, if ever, injures himself, his pupillary reflex to light remains unaffected, and he is not incontinent.

3. *Visceral symptoms.* Hysterical visceral symptoms also cover a wide range of disorders, including headache, "lump in the throat" and choking sensations, coughing spells, difficulty in breathing, cold and clammy extremities, belching, nausea, and so on. Occasionally there is persistent hiccoughing or sneezing.

Conversion reactions can simulate actual disease symptoms to an almost unbelievable degree. In a pseudo-attack of acute appendicitis, not only may the person evidence pain in the lower abdominal region and other typical symptoms of acute appendicitis, but his temperature may also shoot up far above normal. Cases of psychogenic malaria and tuberculosis have also been cited in the literature. In the latter, for example, the individual may show all the usual symptoms—coughing, loss of weight, recurrent fever, and night sweats—without actual organic disease. Even cases of pseudo-pregnancy have been cited, in which the menstrual cycle ceases, there is an enlargement of the abdominal area, and the individual experiences morning sickness.

The story of Anne: a case of hysterical deafness

Anne, a young woman of 19, became hysterically deaf, apparently as a result of family tensions. Her relations with her mother had been particularly strained, and the deafness was thought to be a type of avoidant behavior for screening out her mother's nagging voice. Anne showed no overt startle responses to sudden loud noises; however, she revealed covert responses to sound in the first of two trials to measure muscle contractions via an electromyogram (EMG). The first EMG trial revealed muscle contractions in Anne's neck when a loud sound was made, but the second trial 60 seconds later revealed no contractions. Some strong inhibitory neural changes must have come into operation in the brief time between the two trials, because complete inhibition of muscle contractions—covert ones, at least—is seemingly beyond the voluntary control of anyone suddenly exposed to loud noise.

Since Anne could read lips, the therapist combined conditioning with suggestion—telling Anne that she would soon be able to hear. The conditioning involved the removal of a negative reinforcer, which was an electric shock that closely followed the sounding of a tone for 150 trials. The first time the shock was withheld, the EMG picked up a burst of covert muscle contractions. These promising early results of treatment were given an unexpected boost when a near-accident caused Anne's hearing to be suddenly restored. Crossing a busy street, she was narrowly missed by a driver who honked his horn and shouted at her. The hearing that she instantly regained has subsequently remained intact.

Adapted from Malmo (1970).

Since the symptoms in conversion hysteria are capable of simulating almost every known disease, differential diagnosis can be a problem. However, in addition to specialized medical techniques, there are several criteria that are commonly used for distinguishing between hysterical and organic disturbances:

a) A certain *belle indifference,* in which the patient makes his complaints in a rather matter-of-fact way, with little of the anxiety and fear that would be expected in a person with a paralyzed arm or loss of sight. Mucha and Reinhardt (1970) reported that all of the 56 student fliers in their study (page 237) evidenced this pattern, seeming to be completely unconcerned about the long-range effects of their disabilities.

b) The frequent failure of the dysfunction to clearly conform to the symptoms of the particular disease or disorder. For example, there is no wasting away or atrophy of the paralyzed limb in hysterical paralyses, except in rare and long-standing cases.

c) The selective nature of the dysfunction. For example, in hysterical blindness the individual does not usually bump into people or objects. Paralyzed muscles can be used for some activities and not others; and hysterical contractures usually disappear during sleep.

d) The interesting fact that under hypnosis or narcosis the symptoms can usually be removed, shifted, or reinduced by the suggestion of the therapist. Similarly, if the individual is suddenly awakened from a sound sleep, he may be tricked into talking or using a "paralyzed" limb.

Of course, where conversion symptoms are superimposed on an actual organic disorder, the difficulty in making a diagnosis may be increased. However, it is usually fairly easy to distinguish between conversion hysteria and *malingering*. The malingerer is consciously perpetrating a fraud by faking the symptoms of a disease, and this fact is reflected in his demeanor. The hysteric is usually dramatic and apparently naive, whereas the malingerer is inclined to be defensive, evasive, and suspicious. When inconsistencies in his behavior are pointed out, the hysteric is usually unperturbed, whereas the malingerer immediately becomes even more defensive. Finally, the hysteric is concerned mainly with his symptoms and willingly discusses them, whereas the malingerer is apt to be reluctant to be examined and slow to talk about his symptoms, lest his pretense be discovered. Thus conversion hysteria and malingering are considered distinct patterns, although sometimes they overlap.

The phenomenon of *mass hysteria*, as typified by outbreaks of St. Vitus's dance and biting manias during the Middle Ages (see page 32), has become a rarity in modern times. However, an outbreak of mass hysteria that resulted in the temporary shutting down of a textile mill has been reported by Kerckhoff and Back (1969). The mass hysteria involved a "mysterious illness"—with symptoms of nausea and a body rash—presumably caused by an insect in a shipment of cloth that had arrived from England. The report quoted one victim:

" 'Some of those women were deathly sick. They were passing out, and they were taking them out of here like flies. I don't know what happened to me.' State and Federal health officials were called into the case; but the victims were reported to be suffering from 'nothing more than extreme anxiety.' " (p. 46)

Suggestibility clearly plays a major role in the development of mass hysteria, in which a conversion reaction in one individual rapidly spreads to others.

Causal factors. In the development of conversion patterns there is usually the following chain of events: (a) a desire to escape from some unpleasant situation; (b) a fleeting wish to be sick in order to avoid the situation (this wish, however, is suppressed as unfeasible or unworthy); and (c) under additional or continued stress, the appearance of the symptoms of some physical ailment. The individual sees no relation between his symptoms and the stress situation. The particular symptoms that occur are usually those of a previous illness or are copied from other sources such as illness symptoms observed among relatives or on television or read about in magazines. However, they may also be superimposed on an existing organic ailment, be associated with anticipated secondary gains, or be symbolically related to the conflict situation.

Unfortunately, the neurophysiological processes involved in the simulation of various disease symptoms, such as malarial fever, are not well understood. However, there is increasing research evidence of the remarkable extent to which an individual can control his own bodily functions. For example, recent studies with animals and humans have shown that blood pressure, heart rate, kidney function, and even the distribution of blood flow can be altered by selective reinforcement procedures, which we shall describe in Chapter 8. Although we have much to learn about the physiological mechanisms involved, it seems possible for bodily functioning to be markedly altered to meet the psychological needs of the individual.

1. *Personality and role factors.* What can be said about the personality of the individual who attempts to solve serious problems by getting sick? Here it may be recalled that most of us at some time or other have probably solved some problem or avoided something we did not want to do by pleading sickness. In fact, the common sayings "I don't feel like doing it" or "I don't feel up to it" show the prevalence of this type of reaction. The conversion hysteric, however, unconsciously commits himself to this pattern in the face of everyday life problems that most persons can deal with more effectively.

In relation to other neurotic types, the conversion hysteric tends to be highly suggestible and dramatic—a "histrionic personality": excitable but shallow in emotional responsiveness, particularly capable of ignoring, denying, and repressing what he does not want to perceive, prone to exaggeration, and demanding and manipulative in interpersonal relationships (Alarcon, 1973; Chadoff, 1974; O'Neill & Kempler, 1969; Slavney & McHugh, 1974; Steele, 1969; Verbeek, 1973). Female conversion hysterics have also been described as sexually seductive but often frigid in actual sexual relations.

The following excerpts from a therapy hour provide an excellent illustration of a hysterical personality.

"The patient, a 30-year-old married woman, sought therapy because of nervousness, depression, headache, and severe menstrual cramps. She entered the office with a despondent air which contrasted sharply with her colorful, almost flashy, dress. She wore a low-cut blouse and crossed her legs in a seductive manner as she sat down. The following interchange took place.

Pt: Well, you know what's bothering me. Why don't you talk today.
[The patient's attempt to control the interchange is immediately apparent.]
Th: Silent
Pt: I don't know why I come here. I have been coming to see you for six months now (actually four months) and I feel worse than ever. My head hurts so much (patient dramatically touches head) and I wonder more each day if life is worth living.
[This communication illustrates the patient's atten-

tion-seeking and histrionic behavior; there is also some obvious dishonesty.]
Th: Silent
Pt: I keep thinking that life isn't worth living. I'm worrying that I may kill myself.
Th: I have noticed that when I don't respond to you immediately you begin to complain more and feel sicker.
Pt: (Suddenly angry) You get me so mad. I come here for help and all you can do is interpret. You and your worship of Freud. I know all about the years you spent studying but I'm not impressed. Somebody like me is miserable and finds every minute of life pure hell and you attribute all kinds of unconscious motives to my suffering. You don't know how much courage it takes for me to just go on from hour to hour.
[The communication again illustrates the patient's controlling and attention-seeking behavior.]
Th: Somehow I can't feel your misery as that powerful or real. Can't we go beyond it and look at what's so unsatisfying in your life?
Pt: (Angrily exploding) I only wish you could feel what I'm feeling. (She reaches for an ash tray on the desk and postures as if she is going to throw it on the floor; then she changes her mind and shouts.) Damn you, nobody cares, nobody, nobody, nobody. (Sobs for several minutes while the therapist is silent, then slowly and dramatically) I guess you win, there's no beating you at your own game while I am so sick and helpless. I need you too much. (Suddenly she perks up and smiles coquettishly) Well, what do you want me to talk about today.
[Here she is again controlling, playing as if helplessly dependent, and demonstrating a reluctance to assume responsibility.]
Th: (Somewhat irritated) You know we've been over that before.
Pt: (Teasingly) Sure, I'm supposed to talk about my conflicts, bare my soul, search out my hidden oedipal wishes and my frustrations. (Suddenly more dramatic) But I know those things and so do you. You know how my mother treated me so cruelly, and how she paid more attention to my brothers, how my father ignored me, and what a bastard my husband is. You know what the problem is and what the answer is, I'll always be miserable and trapped with that no good impotent husband of mine. Why didn't I marry John? I had my choice and I goofed it. If only my parents had helped me I wouldn't have made such a miserable choice. Now I am trapped, trapped, trapped.
[In this communication the patient almost assumes responsibility for her choice, but then backslides and blames it on her parents.]
Th: Sounds like you and your husband have been fighting again.

Pt: (More seriously and sober) We had an awful fight after a party this weekend. Phil thought I was paying too much attention to one of our guests and . . . (Patient goes on to give a fairly nondramatic account of her flirtatiousness and ensuing verbal and physical battle with her husband.)" (Halleck, 1967, pp. 751–52)

In describing the "sick role" enactment of the conversion hysteric, it is useful to note that (a) the role is useful only in a culture that provides sympathy and support for sick persons and enables them to avoid normal responsibilities; (b) the role is enacted or modeled on the basis of information the individual has concerning the physical ailment he is simulating; (c) the role tends to be self-perpetuating, since it is reinforced by anxiety reduction and other gains—in essence, it works. Here it may be emphasized again that the conversion hysteric is not consciously aware of playing a sick role, for if he were, the psychological benefit to him would be lost. This need not be considered a mysterious phenomenon, since the literature on learning includes many instances in which behavior is altered by reinforcement without the person's awareness of the relationship between his changed behavior and the reinforcing conditions (Bandura, 1969).

2. *Avoidance of or defense against threat.* Typically a conversion pattern enables the individual to avoid or defend himself against a threatening stress situation. This avoidance pattern seemed clear in the case of a youth who fainted on his way to the altar on two separate occasions, each time planning to wed the same girl. In another instance, a divorcee lost her sense of smell when she noticed a sweet and pungent odor that she suspected to be "pot" in the room of her adolescent son—on whom she was strongly dependent for affection and meaning in her life. In an early report, Halpern (1944) cited 15 cases of hysterical amblyopia—markedly diminished visual acuity—in the armed forces, which developed at a port of embarkation and cleared up when the soldiers were removed from the conflict situation by hospitalization. These reactions have sometimes been called "gangplank fever."

The following case of astasia-abasia (see page 239) has been described by Hammer

(1967). The case involves an athletically inclined youth who did well in preparatory school and was admitted to the United States Military Academy at West Point.

Early in cadet training, when new cadets are under considerable pressure, he suffered a shoulder separation while playing football. Surgery was performed, he responded well, and after a thorough physical examination was returned to duty. Back on duty, however, his activities were significantly changed. Losing the privileges accorded a member of the football squad, he became just another "plebe." This change in his status was considered significant, for within two weeks he returned to the hospital with acute vertigo and temporary loss of consciousness. A physical examination at the time he reentered the hospital showed nothing significant.

Shortly after hospitalization, the student developed a markedly ataxic gait and had difficulty standing erect; however, when he was in a sitting or reclining position his coordination and tonus remained normal. With the continuation of hospitalization, the cadet's symptoms gradually intensified. On rare occasions when he showed some improvement, a return to duty was suggested. This was promptly followed by a recurrence in intensity of symptoms.

Psychological and psychiatric evaluation revealed ambivalent feelings about his remaining at West Point, and a concomitant increase in overt dependency needs. The psychologist's conclusions follow:

"This cadet shows an emotionally unstable, impulse-ridden, hysteroid, neurotic character makeup, manifested by difficulty in accepting authority, low tolerance for frustration of his egocentric compensatory need to prove his manliness, and inadequacy in interpersonal relations generally. He appears to be acting out conversion symptoms which are persistent largely because of secondary gains in defying authority and avoiding having to come to grips with his problem in adjusting to the normal demands of the United States Military Academy."

Following 60 days of hospitalization the cadet was separated from the Corps of Cadets. He returned home and accepted work as a bank clerk. A 6-month follow-up study revealed that his symptoms cleared up within a week after he returned home, that he had no further educational plans, and that he had remained symptom-free during the intervening period. (Adapted from Hammer, 1967, pp. 672–73)

Conversion reactions may also represent defenses against dangerous desires and impulses. Abse (1959) has cited the case of a middle-aged male patient who suffered total paralysis of his legs after his wife left him for another man. During the course of treatment it became apparent that he had a strong wish to pursue his wife and kill her and her lover. Although the wish had been repressed, it was quite intense, and the paralysis apparently represented a massive defense against the possibility that this vengeful wish might be carried out.

Sometimes, conversion reactions seem to stem from feelings of guilt and the necessity for self-punishment. In one case, for example, a female patient developed a marked tremor and partial paralysis of the right arm and hand after she had physically attacked her father. During this incident she had clutched at and torn open his shirt with her right hand, and apparently the subsequent paralysis represented a sort of symbolic punishment of the "guilty party," while preventing a recurrence of her hostile and forbidden behavior.

3. *Secondary gains stemming from actual illness or injury.* In some instances conversion symptoms develop following physical illness or an accident in which the individual may or may not have been injured. If pneumonia temporarily enables a patient to avoid unpleasant occupational responsibilities—as well as receive the sympathy and attention of others—he may unconsciously prolong his invalidism. An injury may lead to the same pattern.

Not uncommonly, conversion symptoms develop following some accident or injury as a result of which the individual hopes to receive monetary compensation. These reactions usually occur after accidents in which the individual might have been seriously injured but is actually only shaken up or slightly injured. Later, in discussions with family or friends, it may be agreed that he would have had a strong legal case if he had been injured. Is he sure he is all right? Could he possibly have injured his back? Perhaps there *is* something wrong with it. With the aid of a sympathetic lawyer, he may proceed to file suit for compensation for his alleged injuries.

Here it is especially hard to distinguish between the malingerer's deliberate simulation of injury and the unconscious deception of a hysteric (Lewis, 1974). Apparently in many hysterical cases there is a combination of the two, in which conscious acting is superimposed on unconscious acting or role playing. In these cases the patient shows an amazingly rapid recovery once he has been properly compensated for his "injuries." In this general context, Liebson (1969) reported an interesting case in which a machinist's helper experienced pain and weakness in both legs.

About five years after the initial occurrence of his symptoms, this man had to stop work and was put on welfare payments. Although no organic pathology could be found, he finally required hospitalization.

A variety of treatments were tried, including a substantial number of drugs, all without success. At this time, behavior therapy—focusing on the reinforcement contingencies of his symptoms—was begun. Although the causal factors were not clear, it was felt that the symptoms might have been induced and maintained because of their reinforcing consequences—that is, the avoidance of a job he disliked and the receipt of welfare payments. The treatment program was worked out in collaboration with the patient, and focused on the target behaviors of walking and doing a day's work. A job was found for him, and to add to his $235 monthly welfare payments, he could earn $3.00 per day working, with a bonus of $1.00 for getting there on time and a second bonus of $1.00 if his work was approved by his instructor.

The patient progressed at his own rate, beginning with a two-day-per-week schedule, and despite occasional mild setbacks, was able to work a five-day week by the seventh month. Four months later he accepted a full-time job similar to his old one, and no longer required welfare aid. A follow-up study six months later showed that the man was still on the job, although he occasionally experienced symptoms similar to his initial ones. (Adapted from Liebson, 1969, pp. 217–18)

Whatever specific causative factors may be involved, however, the basic dynamic pattern in conversion hysteria seems to be the avoidance or reduction of anxiety-arousing stress by getting sick—thus converting an intolerable emotional problem into a face-saving physical one. The initial learning of the reaction and its maintenance are reinforced, both by anxiety reduction and by the interpersonal gains—in terms of sympathy and support—that result from being sick.

Aspects of treatment. Conversion symptoms can usually be removed by means of hypnosis or drug interviews, thus paving the way for a more extensive therapy program aimed at alleviating the conditions that appear to have influenced the development and maintenance of the symptoms. While more extensive treatment may be necessary to modify the basic life-style of the hysterical personality, the preceding measures are usually effective in helping the person through an immediate crisis and avoiding a chronic pattern of dealing with a given problem by "sickness." This is particularly true where the stress situation can be alleviated to some extent.

Hysterical neurosis: dissociative type

Like conversion hysteria, the dissociative type of hysteria is a way of avoiding stress while gratifying needs—in a manner permitting the person to deny personal responsibility for his unacceptable behavior. Dissociative patterns include amnesia, fugue states, and multiple personality.[5] These patterns are relatively rare, constituting less than 2 percent of all neuroses.

Amnesia and fugue. Amnesia is partial or total inability to recall or identify past experience. It may occur in neuroses, psychoses, or brain pathology, including delirium, brain injury, and diseases of the nervous system. Where the amnesia is caused by brain pathology, it generally involves an actual failure of retention. That is, either the information is not registered and does not enter memory storage, or it is not retained in storage—it is truly lost.

Psychogenic amnesia, on the other hand, is usually limited to a failure to recall. The "forgotten" material is still there beneath the level of consciousness, as becomes apparent under hypnosis, narcosis interviews, and in cases where the amnesia spontaneously clears up. As we have noted, amnesia is fairly com-

mon in reactions to intolerably traumatic experiences, such as those occurring under combat conditions of warfare and the "shock" conditions of civilian life. In hysterical amnesia, however, the reaction occurs in the face of life stresses with which most people deal more effectively.

1. *Clinical picture.* In the typical neurotic amnesic reaction, the individual cannot remember his name, does not know how old he is or where he resides, and does not recognize parents, relatives, or friends; yet his basic habit patterns—such as his ability to read, talk, and so on—remain intact, and he seems quite normal aside from the amnesia.

In this amnesic state the individual may retreat still farther from his problems by going away in what is called a "fugue state." A fugue reaction is a defense by actual flight—the individual wanders away from home, and then days, weeks, or sometimes even years later suddenly finds himself in a strange place, not knowing how he got there and with complete amnesia for the period of the fugue. His activities during the fugue may vary from merely going on a round of motion pictures to traveling across the country, entering a new occupation, and starting a new way of life.

2. *Causal factors.* The pattern in psychogenic amnesia is essentially the same as in conversion reactions, except that instead of avoiding some unpleasant situation by getting sick the person does it by avoiding thoughts about it. This avoidance of areas of thought may represent a pattern of avoidance learning without awareness, or it may involve more conscious suppression. In patterns involving suppression, the individual apparently tells himself that he will not remember some traumatic event or situation; subsequently he tries to believe and behave as though he were amnesic for that time. For example, in a study of 98 amnesia cases, primarily among military personnel, Kiersch (1962) found 41 to be of this "feigned" type.

In actual psychogenic amnesia we typically find an egocentric, immature, highly suggestible personality faced with an acutely unpleasant situation from which he sees no escape. There is often a conscious impulse to "forget" and run away from it all, but this solution is

---

[5]Somnambulism, or sleepwalking, could be included here, but we shall deal with this dissociative pattern in our discussion of the behavior disorders of childhood (Chapter 15).

too cowardly to be accepted. Eventually, however, the stress situation becomes so intolerable that large segments of the personality and the stress situation itself are repressed, while more congenial patterns carry on in an amnesic or fugue reaction. As O'Neill and Kempler (1969) have pointed out, this process of amnesia is highly selective and involves only material that is basically intolerable or threatening to the self.

During such dissociative reactions the individual appears normal and is able to engage in complex activities, that are often of a wish-fulfilling or compensatory nature. This is well illustrated in an interesting case described by Masserman (1961).

"Bernice L., a forty-two-year-old housewife, was brought to the Clinics by her family, who stated that the patient had disappeared from her home four years previously, and had recently been identified and returned from R———, a small town over a thousand miles away. On rejoining her parents, husband and children she had at first appeared highly perturbed, anxious, and indecisive. Soon, however, she had begun to insist that she really had never seen them before, that her name was not Bernice L—but Rose P—and that it was all a case of mistaken identity; further, she threatened that if she were not returned to her home in R——— immediately, she would sue the hospital for conspiracy and illegal detainment. Under treatment, however, the patient slowly formed an adequate working rapport with the psychiatrist, consented to various ancillary anamnestic procedures such as amytal interviews and hypnosis, and eventually dissipated her amnesias sufficiently to furnish the following history:

"The patient was raised by fanatically religious parents, who despite their evangelical church work and moralistic pretenses, accused each other of infidelity so frequently that the patient often questioned her own legitimacy. However, instead of divorcing each other, the parents had merely vented their mutual hostility upon the patient in a tyrannically prohibitive upbringing. In the troubled loneliness of her early years the patient became deeply attached to her older sister, and together they found some security and comfort; unfortunately, this sister died when the patient was seventeen and left her depressed and unconsolable for over a year. After this, at her parents' edict, the patient entered the University of A——— and studied assiduously to prepare herself for missionary work. However, during her second semester at the University, she was assigned to room with an attractive, warm-hearted and gifted girl, Rose P—, who gradually guided the patient to new interests, introduced her to various friendships, and encouraged her to develop her neglected talent as a pianist. The patient became as devoted to her companion as she had formerly been to her sister, and was for a time relatively happy. In her Junior year, however, Rose P— became engaged to a young dentist, and the couple would frequently take the patient with them on trips when a chaperone was necessary. Unfortunately, the patient, too, fell 'madly in love' with her friend's fiancé, and spent days of doubt and remorse over her incompatible loves and jealousies. The young man, however, paid little attention to his fiancée's shy, awkward and emotionally intense friend, married Rose P— and took her to live with him in Canada. The patient reacted with a severe depression, the cause of which she refused to explain to her family, but at their insistence, she returned to the University, took her degree, and entered a final preparatory school for foreign missionaries.

"On completion of her work she entered into a loveless marriage with a man designated by her parents and spent six unhappy years in missionary outposts in Burma and China. The couple, with their two children, then returned to the United States and settled in the parsonage of a small midwest town. Her life as a minister's wife, however, gradually became less and less bearable as her husband became increasingly preoccupied with the affairs of his church, and as the many prohibitions of the village (e.g., against movies, recreations, liberal opinions and even against secular music) began to stifle her with greater weight from year to year. During this time the patient became increasingly prone to quiet, hazy reminiscences about the only relatively happy period she had known—her first two years in college with her friend, Rose P——and these years, in her day-dreaming, gradually came to represent all possible contentment. Finally, when the patient was thirty-seven, the culmination of her disappointments came with the sickness and death of her younger and favorite child. The next day the patient disappeared from home without explanation or trace, and her whereabouts, despite frantic search, remained unknown to her family for the next four years.

"Under treatment in the Clinics, the patient recollected that, after a dimly remembered journey by a devious route, she finally reached A———, the college town of her youth. However, she had lost all conscious knowledge of her true identity and previous life, except that she thought her name was Rose P—. Under this name she had begun to earn a living playing and teaching the piano, and was so rapidly successful that within two years she was the assistant director of a conservatory of music. Intuitively, she chose friends who would not be curious about her past, which to her remained a mysterious blank, and thereby eventually established a new social identity which soon removed the need for introspections and ruminations. Thus the patient lived for four years as though she were another person until the almost inevitable happened. She was finally identified by a girlhood acquaintance who had known both her and the true Rose P— in their college years. The patient at first sincerely and vigorously denied this identification, resisted her removal to Chicago, where her husband was now assigned, and failed to recognize either him or her family until her treatment in the Clinics penetrated her amnesia. Fortunately, her husband proved unexpectedly understanding and cooperative, and the patient eventually readjusted to a fuller and more acceptable life under happily changed circumstances." (pp. 35–37)

In his analysis of this case, Masserman pointed out that the patient's behavior enabled her to flee from an intolerable mode of living as Mrs. Bernice L—, the unhappy wife, and to substitute an intensely desired way of living, personified by Rose P—, the loved and successful artist. Her "new personality" was in no sense completely novel, but represented an unconscious selection and integration of certain patterns of the old.

It is interesting to note that a person rarely engages in activities that would have been morally incompatible with his pre-fugue personality. Thus, in her identity as Rose P—, the patient neither married again nor engaged in any direct sexual activity, since "bigamy or unfaithfulness, conscious or not, would have been untenable."

Multiple personality. Dual and multiple personalities have received a great deal of attention and publicity in fiction, television, and motion pictures. Actually, however, they are rare in clinical practice. Only slightly more than a hundred cases can be found in psychological and psychiatric records.

1. *Clinical picture.* Multiple personality is a dissociative reaction to stress in which the patient manifests two or more complete systems of personality. Each system has distinct, well-developed emotional and thought processes and represents a unique and relatively stable personality. The individual may change from one personality to another at periods varying from a few minutes to several years. The personalities are usually dramatically different; one may be gay, carefree, and fun-loving, and another quiet, studious, and serious.

Various types of relationships may exist between the different personalities. Usually the individual alternates from one personality to the other, and cannot remember in one what happened in the other. Occasionally, however, while one personality is dominant and functions consciously, the other continues to function subconsciously and is referred to as a *co-conscious* personality. In these cases the co-conscious personality is usually intimately aware of the thoughts of the conscious personality and of things going on in the world, but indicates its awareness through automatic writing (in which the individual writes a message without full awareness or conscious control) or in some other roundabout way. The conscious personality, however, usually knows nothing of the co-conscious personality.

Relationships may become highly complicated when there are more than two personalities, as in the case described on page 247. Some of the personalities may be mutually amnesic while others are only one-way amnesic.

2. *Causal factors.* In a sense, we are all multiple personalities, in that we have many conflicting and warring tendencies and frequently do things that surprise both ourselves and others. This is illustrated by many common sayings, such as "I don't know why I did it" or "I didn't think he had it in him." It is also illustrated by the changed behavior many persons indulge in at conventions when they are away from their families and associates and "cut loose." In pathological cases, there is evidently such a deep-seated conflict between contradictory impulses and beliefs that a resolution is achieved through separating the conflicting parts from each other and elaborating each into more-or-less autonomous personality systems. In this way the individual is able to carry out incompatible systems of behavior without the stress, conflict, and guilt that would otherwise occur. As Murphy (1947) has pointed out, "the main dynamics in most cases of double and multiple personality

The four faces of Eve

A dramatic example of multiple personality was the widely publicized case of Eve White, a 25-year-old woman who sought therapy because of "severe and blinding headaches" often followed by "blackouts." Eve had been having serious marital conflicts and was separated (and subsequently divorced) from her husband. For financial reasons, her 4-year-old daughter lived with grandparents some 100 miles away from where Eve worked. Concern about the happiness of her daughter and fear of becoming a stranger to her added to Eve's stresses.

In therapy, Eve gave the appearance of a demure, retiring, and gently conventional person trying somewhat stoically to cope with severe personal frustrations. Then one day, during an early therapy session she appeared to be seized by a sudden pain and put both hands to her head. "After a tense moment of silence, her hands dropped. There was a quick, reckless smile and, in a bright voice that sparkled, she said, 'Hi there, Doc!' . . . there was in the newcomer a childishly daredevil air, an erotically mischievous glance, a face marvelously free from the habitual signs of care, seriousness, and underlying distress, so long familiar in her predecessor. This new and apparently carefree girl spoke casually of Eve White and her problems, always using *she* or *her* in every reference, always respecting the strict bounds of a separate identity. When asked her own name she immediately replied, 'Oh, I'm Eve Black' " (Thigpen & Cleckley, 1957, p. 137).

The traits of the two personalities, as they continued to present themselves in ensuing therapy hours, may be summarized as follows:

	Eve White	Eve Black
Appearance	Face: quiet sweetness, sadness Movements: careful, dignified Voice: gently modulated Dress: neat, conservative, inconspicuous No allergy to nylon	Face: pixielike, mischievous, seductive Movements: suggested lightheartedness Voice: coarse, mirthful, teasing Dress: a little provocative, expensive Skin reacted to nylon by breaking out
Personality	Industrious worker and good housekeeper, literary tastes, not spontaneous, not deceitful, devoted to child, passive strength of character, admired by others	Attractive, likable, heedless, unthinking, quick, vivid, a rowdy wit, ready for any adventure, enjoyed teasing Eve White
Role	Role involved unspoken pathos; one felt she was doomed to be overcome.	Seemed strangely secure from stresses of everyday life and from grief

After about 8 months of therapy, a third personality, Jane, appeared. Jane was more mature and capable than the retiring Eve White and had a much more vivid personality. Unlike Eve Black, Jane had positive attitudes both toward herself and toward cultural values. She remained conscious when either of the two Eves was in control, but for a long time had no memory of her past.

At last, after recalling and working through a highly traumatic experience—in which she had been forced by her mother to kiss her dead grandmother—a somewhat new personality emerged who was like Jane but more complete. This personality appeared to represent a resolution of the separate entities of Eve White and Eve Black and decided to call herself Evelyn (Eve's full legal name). Evelyn remarried and at last report had managed to establish a stable marriage and family life (Lancaster & Poling, 1958; Thigpen & Cleckley, 1954, 1957).

seems to be an exaggeration of a conflict situation which is present in nearly all of us, namely, a conflict between a conforming and a guilty non-conforming trend" (p. 443).

This dynamic pattern is well brought out in Lipton's comprehensive and excellent analysis of the case of Sara and Maud K., excerpts of which are given below.

". . . in general demeanor, Maud was quite different from Sara. She walked with a swinging, bouncing gait contrasted to Sara's sedate one. While Sara was depressed, Maud was ebullient and happy.

". . . in so far as she could Maud dressed differently from Sara. Sara had two pairs of slippers. One was a worn pair of plain gray mules; the other, gaudy, striped, high-heeled, open-toed sandals. Sara always wore the mules. Maud would throw them aside in disgust and don the sandals. Sara used no make-up. Maud used a lot of rouge and lipstick, painted her fingernails and toenails deep red, and put a red ribbon in her hair. She liked red and was quickly attracted by anything of that color. Sara's favorite color was blue.

"Sara was a mature, intelligent individual. Her mental age was 19.2 years, I.Q., 128. A psychometric done on Maud showed a mental age of 6.6, I.Q., 43. Sara's vocabulary was larger than Maud's, and she took an intelligent interest in words new to her. When Maud heard a new word, she would laugh and mispronounce it, or say, 'That was a twenty-five cent one.' In sharp contrast to Sara, Maud's grammar was atrocious. A typical statement was, 'I didn't do nuttin'.' Sara's handwriting was more mature than Maud's.

"Sara did not smoke and was very awkward when she attempted it. Maud had a compulsion to smoke. At times she insisted she 'had to' and would become agitated and even violent if cigarettes were denied her. She would smoke chain fashion as many cigarettes as were permitted but two would satisfy her for a while. . . .

"Maud had no conscience, no sense of right and wrong. She saw no reason for not always doing as she pleased. She felt no guilt over her incestuous and promiscuous sexual relationships. Sara on the other hand had marked guilt feelings over her previous immoral sexual behavior.

"It seemed that Sara changed to Maud at the point when Sara's feeling of guilt was greatest." (1943, pp. 41–44)

Judging from the previous history of this patient, it would appear that the development of a dissociated personality in the form of Maud had, among other things, enabled Sara to gratify her sexual desires by engaging in promiscuous sexual relations without conscious knowledge and hence without guilt feelings. Apparently Sara reverted to Maud when her guilt feelings over her own previous promiscuous sexual behavior became too intense and self-devaluating.

Further light is cast on Sara's background by the report of two of her previous high-school friends that "she was 'boy crazy' and was always chasing after some boy, often being rude to her girl friends, that she dyed her hair red, and that she smoked and used Listerine to deceive her mother about smoking. Sara denied all this but Maud readily recalled it" (Lipton, 1943, p. 47). It is interesting to note that this patient later became psychotic, apparently as a result of the failure of the dissociative reaction to solve her inner conflicts satisfactorily.

Because multiple personalities can be induced experimentally, the question has been raised as to whether such cases are only artificial creations produced inadvertently by suggestions of the therapist. Although this seems unlikely, some of the cases reported in the literature probably do fall in this category.

Aspects of treatment. Treatment for dissociative hysteria is essentially the same as for the conversion type. Usually the immediate amnesia can be readily cleared up by means of hypnosis or narcosis interviews, and in some cases, as we have noted, the individual's amnesia clears up spontaneously. The latter appears especially likely in fugue reactions in which the individual finds himself in an even worse situation than the one from which he was trying to escape. Where the conflict and subsequent dissociative reaction stem from some special stress rather than a chronic life situation, and the situation changes or the stress can be alleviated, amelioration of symptoms via hypnosis or other treatment procedures is likely to be followed by a more adequate life adjustment. Also of key importance in treatment is helping the patient learn more effective methods of coping, which make his neurotic avoidant behavior unrewarding and unnecessary.

Hypochondriacal neurosis

In hypochondriacal neurosis the individual is preoccupied with his state of health and with various presumed disorders or diseases of bodily organs. Although some hypochondriacal symptoms occur in many neurotic patterns—as well as in other forms of psychopathology—hypochondriacal neurosis is relatively rare, occurring in about 5 percent of the neurotic population. This pattern appears to be particularly common during later adulthood, and is found more frequently among women than men (Kenyon, 1966; Bianchi, 1973).

Clinical picture. Hypochondriacs are characterized by their multiplicity of complaints about physical illness—complaints that are usually not restricted to any logical symptom pattern. Thus, they may complain of uncomfortable and peculiar sensations in the general area of the stomach, the chest, the head, the genitals, or anywhere else in the body.

Usually they have trouble giving a precise description of their symptoms. They may begin by mentioning pain in the stomach, which on further questioning is not a pain but a gnawing sensation, or perhaps a feeling of heat. Their general mental orientation keeps them constantly on the alert for new illness manifestations. They are often avid readers of popular magazines on medical topics, and are apt to feel certain they are suffering from every new disease they read or hear about. Tuberculosis, cancer, tumors, and numerous other disease conditions are readily diagnosed by hypochondriacs. Their morbid preoccupation with bodily processes, coupled with their ignorance of medical pathology, often leads to some interesting diagnoses. One patient diagnosed his condition as "ptosis of the transvex colon," and added, "If I am just half as bad off as I think, I am a dead pigeon."

This attitude appears to be typical: hypochondriacs are sure they are seriously ill and cannot recover. Yet—and this is revealing—despite their exaggerated concern over their health, they do not usually show the fear or anxiety that might be expected of those suffering from such horrible ills. The fact is that they are usually in good physical condition. But it does not follow that the hypochondriac is malingering; he is sincere in his conviction that his symptoms represent real illness. Indeed, in some cases a hypochondriacal reaction may be superimposed on actual organic pathology, which is then magnified out of all proportion and becomes the focal concern of the person's life.

A classic illustration of the shifting symptoms and complaints in a very severe hypochondriacal neurosis is presented in the following letter that a hospitalized patient wrote to her anxious relatives.

"Dear Mother and Husband:

"I have suffered terrible today with drawing in throat. My nerves are terrible. My head feels queer. But my stomach hasn't cramped quite so hard. I've been on the verge of a nervous chill all day, but I have been fighting it hard. It's night and bedtime, but, Oh, how I hate to go to bed. Nobody knows or realizes how badly I feel because I fight to stay up and outdoors if possible.

"I haven't had my cot up for two days, they don't want me to use it.

"These long afternoons and nights are awful. There are plenty of patients well enough to visit with but I'm in too much pain.

"The nurses ignore any complaining. They just laugh or scold.

"Eating has been awful hard. They expect me to eat like a harvest hand. Every bite of solid food is agony to get down, for my throat aches so and feels so closed up. . . .

"With supper so early, and evening so long, I am so nervous I can't sleep until so late. I haven't slept well since I've been here. My heart pains as much as when I was at home. More so at night. I put hot water bottle on it. I don't know if I should or not. I've been wanting to ask some Dr.

"I had headache so badly in the back of my head last night and put hot water bottle there. My nurse said not to.

"They don't give much medicine here. Mostly Christian Science it seems! Well I must close or I never will get to sleep. My nurse gets off at 8:15 so she makes me go to bed by then.

"My eyes are bothering me more.

"Come up as soon as you can. My nose runs terrible every time I eat.

"The trains and ducks and water pipes are noisy at night.

ANNIE"
(Menninger, 1945, pp. 139–40)

Hypochondriacs often show a morbid preoccupation with digestive and excretory functions. Some keep charts of their bowel movements, and most are able to give detailed information concerning diet, constipation, and related matters. Many of them also keep up with "the latest" in medical treatment, by reading newspapers or popular magazines, and are prone to the indiscriminate use of a wide range of medications. However, they do not show the losses or distortions of sensory, motor, and visceral functioning of conversion hysterics; nor do their complaints have the bizarre delusional quality—such as "insides rotting away" or "lungs drying up"—more typical of somatic complaints by psychotics.

Causal factors. Most of us are interested in our bodily functioning and state of health. In fact, health ranks high on the list of subjects that are of general interest. The hypochondriac, however, shows a morbid exaggeration of this common interest and concern—an exaggeration that sometimes seems to function like a phobia of illness and dying, but more commonly enables him to avoid certain difficult life stresses and achieve various interpersonal gains.

1. *Overemphasis on body functions in early life.* A variety of early experiences may predispose an individual to the later development of hypochondriacal reactions. Among the most important of these are exposure to faulty parental models and being the object of parental overconcern. The child may learn to be oversensitive to and concerned with his bodily processes from the model presented by a parent who is inclined to be hypochondriacal. Similarly, when the parent is continually commenting on and worrying about the child's every sneeze, cough, digestive upset, or other possible illness manifestation, the child, in turn, may learn to attach undue significance to such manifestations in himself. A third important predisposing factor is an actual early illness or injury—which focuses the attention of parents and the child himself on his condition and may lead to a highly gratifying position in the family, in terms of attention and care.

2. *A disappointing life situation as a precipitating factor.* A predisposed individual is especially likely to experience hypochondriacal reactions during his forties or fifties, for he is forced to the realization that his life is more

than half over and that his life pattern is fairly well determined—for better or worse. When his evaluation of his life situation is unfavorable—that is, when he feels he has failed to achieve his hopes and dreams, and perhaps finds his occupational and marital situation far from satisfactory—the stage is set for a hypochondriacal or other maladaptive reaction.

3. *Maintenance of the hypochondriacal pattern by reinforcement.* As in the case of conversion hysteria, the hypochondriacal pattern enables the individual to avoid the demands and stresses of an unpleasant life situation while at the same time gaining sympathy and support from significant others, plus some measure of control over their behavior. We obviously cannot hold a "sick" person responsible for the same level of achievement we expect of well persons. Thus the hypochondriac's feelings of adequacy and worth are protected in his own eyes as well as in the eyes of others, and he need no longer strive toward difficult or unattainable achievements or accept other unpleasant responsibilities. In a general way, the anxiety aroused by his stressful life situation—often including the failure to achieve important goals—is displaced to a concern and preoccupation with his body and its functioning.

In addition, the increased attention that the hypochondriacal individual devotes to himself and receives from others may endow him and his body with increased significance. Most of us feel fairly important when we have the undivided attention of physicians and the sympathetic interest of our family and friends. And by maneuvering his symptoms with a measure of finesse, the hypochondriac can often control the behavior of those around him. For example, when some activity is planned in which he does not wish to participate, an unexpected intensification of his pain or other symptoms may force others to give up their plans and accede to his wishes. In one case a mother very effectively kept either her husband or son at home and attentive to her every need by her physical complaints, often including statements that she could feel a heart attack coming on. Usually she was not believed, but when she was left alone the family members paid a high price on their return.

The recitation of what she had "gone through" in their absence, accompanied by the theme of "Look what you did to me," exacted its toll—and prevented her from being ignored very long or often.

In cases where the hypochondriacal pattern is superimposed on actual organic pathology—as in the case of a chronic disease or lasting injury—the causal factors are essentially the same as described above. The hypochondriac utilizes actual physical disability as a defense against feelings of failure and as an escape from future striving. But where he evaluates his injury or illness as so severe that it puts him "out of the running," his evaluation automatically prevents him from developing the healthy attitudes and coping patterns that could overcome or alleviate the consequences of his handicap. Thus whatever short-range gains an individual may obtain with hypochondriacal patterns, he will find that they tend to exacerbate rather than resolve his problems. Like other avoidant neurotic behaviors, they are self-defeating in the long run.

Aspects of treatment. These individuals are usually very resistant to treatment, since a hypochondriac must believe in his symptoms if he is to avoid the difficult stresses in his life situation. Such patients, therefore, are apt to discontinue therapy when told there is nothing organically wrong with them, but as long as a therapist is willing to listen to their long list of complaints, they are usually willing to continue in "treatment." It can be hoped that behavior-modification techniques and other new therapeutic approaches will be able to provide effective means for helping such individuals.

Neurasthenic neurosis

The neurasthenic pattern is characterized by chronic mental and physical fatigue and by various aches and pains. There is disagreement on estimates of incidence, but usually the figure is put at approximately 10 percent of all neuroses. In milder form, neurasthenic neuroses seem to be relatively common among young adults, particularly frustrated housewives.

Clinical picture. The neurasthenic's principal complaint is tiredness. Mental concentration is difficult and fatiguing; the person is easily distracted and accomplishes little. He lacks the vigor required to carry activities through to completion. Even minor tasks seem to require herculean effort. He usually spends a good deal of time sleeping in an attempt to counteract fatigue, yet regardless of the amount of sleep he gets, he awakens unrefreshed.

Typically, he sleeps poorly and feels "just rotten" when he drags himself out of bed in the morning. On the rare occasions when he does feel refreshed, he is completely upset by minor emotional setbacks, such as some criticism of his behavior, and his fatigue and listlessness return. Even when things seem to be going relatively well, the fatigue tends to get worse as the day wears on, although by evening he may feel somewhat better and may go to a movie or a party without experiencing anything like his usual exhaustion. In fact, one of the most significant things about the neurasthenic's fatigue is its selective nature. He often shows relatively good energy and endurance in playing tennis, golf, or bridge or in doing anything else that really interests him. In the face of family, occupational, and other routine activities, however, he is usually a monument of listlessness, lack of enthusiasm, and general tiredness.

The incidence of neurasthenic reactions seems highest among married women whose husbands have become neglectful and who feel that they are trapped in the role of "housewife," cheated of the satisfactions that other people seem to enjoy. Those who develop such reactions typically have a childhood history of delicate health and parental overprotection. As adults, they have become almost totally dependent on (if also highly resentful of) their husbands. Now their life situation seems hopeless to them, and they react with discouragement, listlessness, and preoccupation with various somatic complaints. The following excerpts are taken from an interview with a middle-aged married woman who felt, and with good reason, that her husband was no longer interested in her.

The woman's husband often failed to come home for several days at a time, and when he was home,

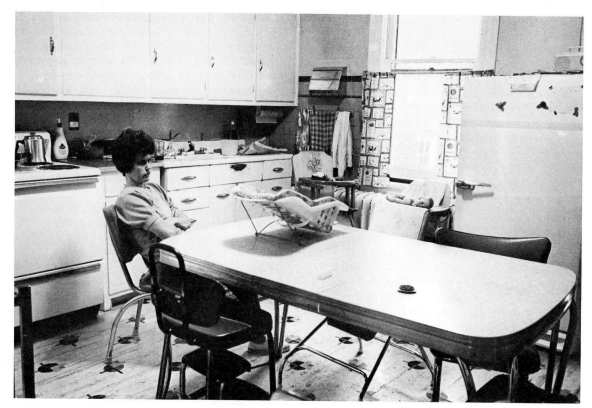

Neurasthenic neurosis is often seen in young housewives who may have frustrated ambitions or feel too heavily burdened with the demands of keeping house and rearing children.

he showed little evidence of interest or affection. Although the patient had completed high school, she had no occupational skills and felt completely dependent on her husband for support and protection. She was self-pitying in her attitude, prone to relating her symptoms almost endlessly, and very demanding in her attitude toward the therapist.

Pt.: I used to talk rather fluently, but now I'm more nervous than I've ever been and my tongue seems to catch on my teeth so that I don't speak plainly. Everything seems such an effort . . . like I had an anchor tied to me or something. I no longer care to play cards or even talk to people any more. . . . Even the simplest things are too much for me.

Dr.: Even the simplest things . . .

Pt.: Ah, hm, I mean, the phone is there and I'm lonesome and yet I don't even phone. . . . I don't even talk to my neighbors much any more even though I know that I should be with people and I like people, but I've gotten so that . . . (long pause) . . . that . . . (sigh) . . . I feel too bad to even talk or do anything (voice breaks and tears).

I've tried so many things to get well, but it's just awful . . . I mean . . . sometimes I can just barely live . . . I mean just listen to the radio or read, or eat . . . I mean just like being in a daze or something . . . I don't know . . . I just feel so horribly tired and sick.

Two months ago I felt better than I had been. I mean I was able . . . well I went to several shows and I actually even went to a dance. Often I would begin to get tired, and I was very frightened that I would break down, but I would go on . . . I mean like some people would go to a battle or to a battle-front (proud tone of voice). But . . . now . . . well I am just so tired and run-down that I can't even go to a show . . . if I do go . . . I have to leave in the middle because I am not strong enough . . . I mean I don't have enough strength to sit through it.

Dr.: Two months ago you felt better?

Pt.: Well, yes . . . you see my husband's brother

came to visit us . . . and he would talk to me and he had such a way of diverting me and he was very interesting, and you'd be amazed, within a few minutes or a few hours I'd be just different . . . and he took me to several shows and to the dance. I felt so much better and I had a really good time. So I can see it isn't sleeping or eating. I mean . . . I need someone who'd give me something different to think about . . . someone who'd show you some affection . . . enough interest in you so that you would improve. But my husband . . . well I just can't understand how he can treat a woman who is ill . . . and trying her best . . . well (tears) . . . I have just sort of withdrawn . . . he has really made me sick . . .

Causal factors. Historical attempts to explain the causal factors of neurasthenic reactions centered around the concept of "nerve weakness," which is the literal meaning of the older term *neurasthenia*. Beard (1905), an early American psychiatrist who first applied the term to the fatigue syndrome, attributed the condition to prolonged conflict and overwork, which presumably depleted the nerve cells of essential biochemical elements.[6] This conception later gave rise to the Weir Mitchell method of treatment for "nervous exhaustion," which involved a long period of complete rest and relaxation for the patient. Neurasthenic patients, however, rarely reveal a history of overwork, nor is rest what they most need.

Today neurasthenia is looked on primarily as a psychological rather than a physical fatigue reaction. It is not overwork but prolonged frustration, discouragement, and hopelessness that reduce motivation and lead to the characteristic listlessness and fatigue. In addition, there are likely to be sustained emotional conflicts centering around hostility toward one's mate and guilt over the abandonment of cherished goals.

We all feel tired and listless when we are discouraged and forced to do something that does not interest us. Those of us who have worked at jobs that were boring and frustrating can readily understand how feelings of

listlessness and tiredness can arise in such situations. In the neurasthenic these feelings are elaborated into a chronic fatigue reaction similar to the fatigue reaction commonly found in acute situational maladjustment. Of course, the chronic anxiety, disturbed sleep, and overreactivity of the neurasthenic may eventually lead to a very real depletion of bodily reserves. Although such somatic conditions may complicate the clinical picture and require treatment in their own right, they are results of the neurasthenic reaction—not the basic cause.

As in other neurotic reactions, neurasthenic symptoms may have important secondary gains. They tend to force others to show sympathy and concern, and may even be used aggressively to control the behavior of others. For example, a wife's obvious difficulties and complaints may prevent her husband from obtaining a contemplated divorce, may force additional attention and time from him, such as any sick person would merit, and may largely control the family's social life. Much of the psychological benefit derived from these patterns is due to the neurasthenic's sincerity—he uses his symptoms without awareness of their actual function.

The neurasthenic often gets credit for putting up a noble battle against heavy odds. In general, however, such individuals eventually wear out the patience of their family and friends. Their listlessness, morbid outlook, self-centered attitudes, and continual complaining are not conducive to the maintenance of happy social relationships. Poorly repressed hostility toward their mate or other loved ones—whom they hold accountable for their difficulties—may further damage their personal relationships.

In understanding the causal factors of neurasthenic patterns, it is important to note that feeling fatigued and unable to cope with the world are common in our high-pressure society, but the normal individual carries on and makes a fairly satisfactory adjustment. The neurasthenic, by contrast, is typically a person who lacks self-confidence, is overdependent on others, and feels completely inadequate in the face of a situation he perceives as frustrating and hopeless. His symptoms enable him to escape the necessity of dealing with his

[6]At one time certain cases of neurasthenia were thought to be the outcome of unsolved sexual problems. Masturbation, for example, was presumed to result in depletion of bodily energy and chronic fatigue. Where sexual practices do constitute a problem, they are now considered to be merely the focal point of a much more general maladjustment.

problems, for he is just too tired and sick. However, they exact a heavy toll in the restriction of his life activities, in blocked self-fulfillment, and in reduced satisfactions in living.

Aspects of treatment. Neurasthenic reactions are frequently very resistant to treatment. Often it is difficult or impossible to ameliorate the neurasthenic's life situation, and it is difficult for him to accept the fact that his problems are psychological and not somatic. In fact, he may actually feel relieved if medical examination reveals some organic pathology. For since he does not understand why he feels tired all the time, he is continually searching for bodily ailments that might account for his fatigue.

Although they may alleviate some of the underlying anxiety, tranquilizing drugs have not proven very helpful in the treatment of neurasthenia. In general, treatment to date has centered around helping the neurasthenic gain some understanding of his problems, learn more effective coping techniques, and achieve enough self-confidence and courage to stop feeling sorry for himself and get back into the "battle of life."

Depressive neurosis

In neurotic depressive reactions the individual reacts to some distressing situation with more than the usual amount of sadness and dejection and often fails to return to normal after a reasonable period of time. Although such reactions may last for weeks or even months, they do eventually clear up. In some cases a mildly depressed mood remains after more severe symptoms have abated. Neurotic depressive reactions appear to have increased during recent years and are now estimated to constitute some 30 percent or more of neurotic disorders. The incidence appears to be higher in females than males.

Clinical picture. The general appearance of the individual is one of dejection, discouragement, and sadness. Typically there is a high level of anxiety and apprehensiveness, together with diminished activity, lowered self-confidence, constricted interests, and a general

loss of initiative. The person usually complains of difficulty in concentrating, although his actual thought processes are not slowed up. Often he has difficulty in going to sleep, and during the night he may awaken and be unable to go back to sleep. In many cases he has somatic complaints and experiences feelings of tension, restlessness, and hostility. Most persons suffering from depressive neurosis can describe the traumatic situation that led to their depression, although they may not be able to explain their overreaction to it.

The following is typical of a conversation with a neurotic depressive and illustrates the characteristic feeling tone.

Pt: Well, you see, doctor, I just don't concentrate good, I mean, I can't play cards or even care to talk on the phone, I just feel so upset and miserable, it's just sorta as if I don't care any more about anything.
Dr.: You feel that your condition is primarily due to your divorce proceedings?
Pt.: Well, doctor, the thing that upset me so, we had accumulated a little bit through my efforts—bonds and money—and he (sigh) wanted one half of it. He said he was going to San Francisco and get a job and send me enough money for my support. So (sigh) I gave him a bond, and he went and turned around and went to an attorney and sued me for a divorce. Well, somehow, I had withstood all the humiliation of his drinking and not coming home at night and not knowing where he was, but *he* turned and divorced me and this is something that I just can't take. I mean, he has broken my health and broken everything, and I've been nothing but good to him. I just can't take it, doctor. There are just certain things that people—I don't know—just can't accept. I just can't accept that he would turn on me that way.

The clinical picture in neurotic depression is often similar to that in neurasthenia. However, the neurotic depressive usually shows greater depression as well as lowered levels of activity and initiative. In very severe cases the person may be unable to work and may sit alone hopelessly staring into space, able to see only the dark side of life. In such cases he is likely to need hospitalization for treatment and safeguard against possible suicide.

Causal factors. Most of us have probably felt depressed at one time or another as a result of a disappointment in love, an accident, a hurtful failure, or the death of a loved one. Neurotic depressive reactions, however, occur in a personality predisposed to overreact to such stresses and lacking the resiliency most people show.

The neurotic depressive usually reveals low stress tolerance, together with rigid conscience development and a proneness to guilt feelings. Typically the stress situation seems to center around the individual's "Achilles' heel"—that is, some stress situation that reactivates earlier conflict or trauma, like the death of one's husband may reactivate insecurities and conflicts associated with the death of one's father many years before. Thus it is not surprising that feelings of anxiety often complicate the clinical picture in neurotic depressive reactions (Prusoff & Klerman, 1974; Downing & Rickels, 1974). Interestingly enough, while most persons manifest such "pathological mourning" immediately after the death of a loved one, a sizeable number manifest the symptoms on anniversaries of the death (Volkan, 1973).

Often in depressive neurosis the picture is complicated by hostility toward the loved one. This hostility is typically repressed because of its dangerous and unethical implications, but it may manifest itself in hostile, guilt-arousing fantasies. Should the loved one die, the person's grief is augmented by his intense guilt, as if his hostile fantasies had somehow brought about the tragedy. Where the individual was indeed partially responsible for the loved one's death, as in an automobile accident in which he was driving, his feelings of guilt and self-condemnation may be extremely severe.

Like other types of neurotics, neurotic depressives sometimes use their symptoms to force support and sympathy from others. One woman telephoned her therapist and told him that she was going to commit suicide. Special precautions were taken, although the woman made no serious suicide attempt. In a later therapeutic session the therapist asked her why she had called him and threatened suicide. The woman explained that she thought the therapist was not taking her symptoms and hopeless situation seriously enough and was not showing proper sympathy and appreciation for her desperate plight. By her threat

of suicide she hoped to make him realize that he "just had to do something for her immediately."

Aspects of treatment. Electroshock therapy may be used for clearing up the depression in more severe cases of depressive neurosis, although newer drug therapies have made this more drastic procedure largely unnecessary. Usually antidepressant drugs, supportive measures, and short-term psychotherapy are effective in alleviating the depression and helping the patient achieve better personal adjustment.

Symptoms of types of neuroses

Anxiety
"Free floating" anxiety, usually punctuated by acute attacks.

Phobic
Irrational fears which lead to anxiety if not heeded; may lead to a pervasive pattern of avoidance behavior.

Obsessive-compulsive
Repetitive thoughts and impulses which the individual realizes are irrational, but which persist nonetheless.

Hysterical (conversion type)
Simulation of actual organic illness, such as paralysis or loss of vision, without organic pathology.

Hysterical (dissociative type)
Dissociation of certain aspects of consciousness or identity from self-structure; symptom pattern may take the form of amnesia, fugue, or multiple personality.

Hypochondriacal
Preoccupation with bodily processes and presumed disease.

Neurasthenic
Chronic fatigue, weakness, lack of enthusiasm.

Depressive
Abnormally prolonged dejection associated with life stress.

"Existential"
Feelings of meaninglessness, alienation, and apathy, with little sense of purpose or control over one's life.

The basic clinical picture in all of these neurotic reactions involve coping with perceived stress situations by means of avoidant behavior.

Is there an existential neurosis?

As we have seen, existentialists are very much concerned about the human situation; they point to the breakdown of traditional values, the depersonalization of human beings in a mass society, and the loss of meaning in human existence. The tasks of shaping one's own identity, finding satisfying values, and living a constructive and meaningful life are seemingly more difficult today than ever before.

Maddi (1967) has suggested the term "existential neurosis" to refer to the individual's inability to succeed in this quest. He has described it basically as follows:

The personal identity out of which this neurosis originates involves a definition of self as simply an embodiment of biological needs and a player of social roles. Such a self-identity is highly vulnerable to various stresses, such as rapid social change and new role expectations, interpersonal relations that victimize a poorly differentiated and confused individual, and acute awareness of the superficiality of one's existence. The resulting symptom pattern is characterized by chronic alienation, aimlessness, and meaninglessness. (Adapted from pp. 311–25)

Many students of psychopathology would not consider the syndrome described by Maddi to be a distinct pattern of neurosis. Most would readily agree, however, that feelings of purposelessness and alienation are severely disturbing to the individual and often play a key role in the development of neurotic behavior.

In fact, many people in our society, after "taking stock," are confronted with the sickening realization that their busy and seemingly important lives have really not proven meaningful or fulfilling. In fact, Adams (1972) has commented on "middle-class alienation" and neuroses in contemporary mass society. Thus the question of whether there is an existential neurosis seems a meaningful one, and a question likely to be answered in the affirmative by many psychologists and psychiatrists.

General Causal Factors, Treatment, and Outcomes

In our preceding discussion we have focused on the basic nature of neurotic behavior, various specific neurotic patterns, and some aspects of treatment. Now let us take a more detailed look at general causal factors, treatment strategies, and outcomes in the neuroses.

Development and maintenance of neuroses

In the development and maintenance of neurotic behavior, as in other psychopathology, it is relevant to consider the role of biological, psychological, and sociocultural factors.

Biological factors. The precise role of genetic and constitutional factors in the neuroses has not been delineated. Ample evidence from army records and civilian studies indicates that the incidence of neurotic patterns is much higher in the family histories of neurotics than in the general population, but the extent to which such findings reflect the effect of heredity is not known.

In a study of concordance rates of neuroses in identical and fraternal twins in the military, Pollin et al. (1969) found that among identical twins the rate was only 1½ times as high as it was among fraternal twins. Since the environmental background of identical twins is likely to be more similar than that of fraternal twins, these investigators concluded that heredity plays a minimal role in the development of neuroses. After an evaluation of available evidence, Cohen (1974) came to a similar conclusion: "the concept of a genetically based disease or defect can not provide a satisfactory explanation for the diversity and variability of most neurotic phenomena" (p. 473).

Sex, age, glandular functioning, and other physiological factors have also been investigated without illuminating the causal picture. It is known, of course, that stress tolerance is lowered by the loss of sleep, poor appetite, and increased irritability associated with prolonged emotional tension seen in some neurotic patterns—but such conditions are by no means exclusive to the neuroses. A more promising possibility centers around constitutional differences in ease of conditioning. For example, extreme sensitivity and autonomic lability may predispose the individual to a "surplus" of conditioned fears and hence to avoidance behavior. But as yet the evidence is inconclusive; a great deal more research is needed to clarify the role of constitutional and other biological factors in the development of neuroses.

Psychological and interpersonal factors. The causal factors in maladaptive behavior that we reviewed in Chapter 5 are directly applicable to the neuroses. Particularly relevant here are early psychic trauma, pathogenic parent-child and family patterns, and disturbed interpersonal relationships.

Also of particular relevance are the "viewpoints of causation" which we reviewed. Here it is useful to comment on three of these causal factors as they relate to neurotic behavior.

1. *Anxiety-defense.* Traditionally, the neuroses have been explained within the framework of anxiety-defense as set down by Freud and elaborated by later investigators. According to this view, threats stemming from internal or external sources elicit intense anxiety; this anxiety, in turn, leads to the exaggerated use of various ego-defense mechanisms and to maladaptive behavior. Today anxiety-defense is far less widely used to explain neurotic behavior, but we have seen that it does appear directly applicable to a sizeable number of cases.

2. *Faulty learning.* The failure of neurotics to learn needed competencies and coping behaviors, and/or their learning of maladaptive ones, can be seen as stemming from faulty learning. Lacking such competencies, the individual is likely to feel basically inadequate and insecure in a highly competitive and hostile world. Such an orientation, of course, is ideally suited to the development of a defensive and avoidant life-style; since this life-style does lead to some alleviation of anxiety, it tends to be reinforced and maintained. Faulty learning as a causal factor has become the most widely used explanation of the development and maintenance of neurotic behaviors.

3. *Blocked personal growth.* We have noted the emphasis placed by the humanistic and existential psychologists on values, meaning, personal growth, and self-fulfillment; we have also seen how stressful one's life situation can become when it is devoid of meaning and hope, as depicted by reports of former inmates of concentration and POW camps. In civilian life, lack of meaning and blocked personal growth often appear to stem from a lack of needed competencies and resources. As a result, the individual's main efforts are devoted to maintenance and simply trying to meet his basic needs, rather than to personal growth. The ultimate result of such a life-style are feelings of anxiety and futility, feelings which underlie many neurotic reactions.

It is apparent that the preceding views of causation—as well as the interpersonal and stress-decompensation factors—are interrelated and may apply in varying degrees to a given case. As Bandura (1969) has pointed out, the causal factor attributed to a particular neurotic case usually depends heavily on the orientation of the therapist. Psychoanalysts are likely to unearth anxiety-arousing desires and exaggerated ego-defense mechanisms; behaviorists to point out learned maladaptive patterns and their maintenance through reinforcement; and humanistic and existential psychologists to discover blocked personal growth and existential anxiety. Nevertheless, all of these factors are useful in understanding the development of neurotic behaviors.

Sociocultural factors. Reliable data on the incidence of neurotic disorders in other societies is meager. Kidson and Jones (1968) failed to find classical neurotic patterns among the aborigines of the Australian western desert, but noted that as these groups were increasingly exposed to contemporary civilization, hypo-

The induction of "experimental neuroses" in animals

An unusual series of experiments on "neurotic" behavior in animals has been carried out by Dr. Jules Masserman. Although we do not know how far the findings of such studies can be applied on the human level, there clearly are many parallels between human reactions to conflict and those observed in Masserman's animal subjects. Masserman's studies were carried out with both cats and monkeys.

The first step in Dr. Masserman's procedure was to condition the animals to respond to a food signal—a light, a bell, or an odor—by pressing a treadle which was connected to a switch. A proper response opened the plastic lid of a food box in which the animal found the reward (A). When this behavior had been learned, conflict was introduced by associating a noxious stimulus with the feeding situation. Cats were subjected to a brief electric shock or had a strong puff of air directed at their heads when they tried to obtain the food. Monkeys were commonly exposed to a toy snake, which was presented in the food box or through the wall of the apparatus. These stimuli all produced strong avoidance reactions when initially presented. After a few experiences with the noxious stimulus the basic conflict was well established: the animal faced the choice of resisting his fear in order to satisfy his hunger or withdrawing and remaining hungry in order to avoid the fear.

Under these conditions many apparently neurotic reactions were observed. Cats displayed typical symptoms of anxiety: they crouched and trembled; their hair stood on end and their pupils dilated; their breathing was rapid, shallow, and irregular; their pulses were rapid; their blood pressure was markedly increased. They showed severe startle reactions and phobic aversions to sudden lights or sounds, to constricted spaces or to restraint, and to any sensory stimulation in the modality associated with the traumatic experience. Some refused to take any food even when it was presented outside the food box on the floor of the cage. Animals that had willingly entered the cage and had resisted removal during the initial learning period became eager to escape after conflict had been established. Often they would crouch near the sliding glass door of the experimental cage, waiting to be removed (B, C).

Monkeys, in addition to anxiety and phobic reactions like those shown by the cats, displayed even more profound disturbances. Somatic and motor dysfunctions included diarrhea and gastrointestinal disorders resulting in rickets and severe neuromuscular weakness. In contrast to their previous behavior, some monkeys after experimental treatment spent long periods in stereotyped, repetitive activity, such as "pacing" back and forth in the experimental cage (D). Sometimes this behavior alternated with states of tense, apprehensive immobility (E). Some animals would stare fixedly for hours if left undisturbed (F). Often these monkeys would sleep or lie immobile in their home cages until mid-afternoon. Homosexual and autoerotic activity increased markedly, even in the presence of receptive females. One monkey attempted coitus only once in six months. "Neurotic" animals also lost their former positions of dominance in relation to other animals and were frequently attacked by other members of the colony.

A

B

C

D

E

F

chondriacal concerns and other somatic complaints occurred. In general, however, it would appear that hysterical neurosis is common among the people of most underdeveloped countries, while anxiety, obsessive-compulsive, and existential neuroses are more common in technologically advanced societies. The most common type of neurotic disorder in the Soviet Union appears to be neurasthenia, although the reasons for this are unclear.

In our own society, neurotic disorders are found among all segments of the population. There appear to be significant differences, however, in the incidence and types of neurotic patterns manifested by particular subgroups. In general, neurotic individuals from the lower educational and socioeconomic levels appear to show a higher than average incidence not only of conversion hysteria but also of aches, pains, and other somatic symptoms. Middle- and upper-class neurotics, on the other hand, seem especially prone to anxiety and obsessive-compulsive neuroses—with such subjective symptoms as "unhappiness" and a general feeling of dissatisfaction with life.

Although there has been little systematic research on the effects of specific sociocultural variables in the development of neuroses, it seems clear that the individual's social milieu influences the likelihood of his becoming neurotic as well as the pattern of neurosis he is most likely to develop. Thus, as social conditions continue to change in our own society and elsewhere, we can expect that there will be corresponding changes in both the incidence and prevailing types of neurotic behavior.

Treatment and outcomes

The treatment of neuroses may involve a wide range of goals and procedures. Treatment may be aimed at alleviating distressing symptoms, changing the individual's basic defensive and avoidant life-style, or both; it may include drug therapy, psychotherapy, or sociotherapy, or some combination of these approaches. As we have noted, anxiety, phobic, conversion, and depressive reactions usually respond more readily to treatment than do other neurotic patterns, but, in general, the

outlook for the neuroses is highly favorable.

For present purposes, we shall keep our discussion brief and focused on the aspects of treatment that are particularly relevant to the neuroses.

Drug therapy and other biological approaches. Depending on the neurotic pattern involved, tranquilizing and antidepressant drugs may prove helpful in the treatment of neurotic reactions by reducing anxiety, clearing up depressive symptoms, and stabilizing emotional reactivity. Available statistics indicate that some 70 percent or more of neurotic patients show some alleviation of symptoms following drug therapy, and most of them are able to function more effectively (Covi et al., 1974; Engelhardt, 1974; Kline, 1967; Prusoff & Klerman, 1974).

But these drugs can have undesirable effects—such as drowsiness—and in some cases the patient develops an increasing tolerance for and dependence on the drug. In addition, many persons expect too much of drug medication, and the masking of their symptoms may prevent them from seeking needed psychotherapy.

Other biological treatment procedures have been used for the neuroses with mixed results. Electrosleep—a relaxed state of sleep induced by means of the transcranial application of low-intensity electric current—has led to both promising and disappointing results with anxiety neurotics (Rosenthal & Wulfsohn, 1970; Hearst et al., 1974). Similarly, biofeedback-induced muscle relaxation has produced mixed findings with respect to the treatment of chronic anxiety (Raskin, Johnson, & Rondestvedt, 1973; Blanchard & Young, 1974). Acupuncture is being tested for possible use with anxiety and other neuroses, and megavitamin or orthomolecular therapy has both its avid proponents and its strong opponents, although the latter seem to predominate (Graber, 1973; Trotter, 1973). A good deal of further research is needed before the potential effectiveness of the preceding biological methods of treatment can be ascertained.

An interesting method of treatment that progresses from biological measures to psychotherapy is Morita therapy, which has produced favorable results in the treatment of anxiety neuroses, neurasthenia, and obsessional fears (Gibson, 1974; Kora & Ohara, 1973). Initially the patient is subjected to absolute bed rest for a period of four to seven days with no reading, writing, visitors, or other such external stimuli permitted. By the end of this period, the patient usually finds positive reinforcement in responding to external stimuli—undergoing a graded series of tasks beginning with light work and proceeding through heavy manual labor to a focus on interpersonal relationships and the reestablishment of purposive, goal-directed behavior designed to eliminate his neurotic life-style and reorient his life pattern.

Psychotherapy. Both individual and group psychotherapy have been utilized in the treatment of neuroses. The various specific approaches may be divided into two general categories: cognitive therapy and behavior therapy.

1. *Cognitive therapies.* Therapeutic approaches like psychoanalysis, existential therapy, Gestalt therapy, and encounter groups are classified broadly as cognitive therapy, since they are oriented toward helping the individual achieve greater knowledge and understanding of himself and his problems. The various types of therapy included in this general category differ somewhat in their specific goals and procedures—each reflecting the particular psychosocial model or models on which it is based—but all stress the need for self-understanding, a realistic frame of reference, and a satisfying pattern of values, as well as the development of more effective techniques for coping with adjustive demands.

Patients with cynophobia, or fear of dogs, watch a series of slides of dogs, beginning with small, cuddly ones and progressing to lunging, hostile ones, like the snarling German shepherd shown here. Eventually the phobia sufferers should be able to overcome their fear and touch live animals.

Mary, who was 27, had recently separated from her 29-year-old husband, Bill. Since Mary had tried to be the perfect wife, it came as quite a shock to her when Bill, after one year of marriage, told her he was no longer in love with her. Feeling responsible for the difficulties in her marriage, and anxious about her ability to establish meaningful marital or other interpersonal relationships, Mary joined an encounter group which met one evening a week for 2½ hours. The group was cofacilitated by two nonprofessional leaders who were being trained by and working under the local Growth Center, the group's sponsor. The male facilitator was a 27-year-old high-school teacher and the female facilitator was a 35-year-old housewife with three children. The group consisted of 4 male and 5 female participants ranging in age from 19 to 40.

At first during the meetings, Mary remained relatively quiet and listened politely as others spoke. She made only positive comments when she did speak—avoiding saying anything negative to anyone.

During the fourth meeting, one of the members—Sid, aged 38—confronted Mary about her uniform politeness and seeming superficiality, an exchange in which the facilitator also took part:

Sid: Mary, I would like to get to know you better, but your polite sweet manner puts me off. Frankly, your sweetness makes me a little angry with you.

Fcltr.: In your anger, Sid, what do you need to say to Mary?

Sid: (in a loud and moderately angry voice) Damn it, Mary, come out from behind that phony sweet façade of yours! Stop putting me off!

Mary: (with a polite smile and pleasant tone) Gee, I'm sorry, I really don't want to put you off.

Fcltr.: Mary, become aware of your smile and tone of voice.

Mary: (again smiling) I guess I was smiling (followed by a childish chuckle).

Sid: Mary, you're impossible! (said in a tone implying that he did not think Mary capable of being aware of her pattern of behavior).

Mary: (in a more somber tone) I really don't understand, Sid, why you are angry at me. I'm trying to . . . (long pause followed by an embarrassed look).

Fcltr.: Would you be willing to look at Sid and express your embarrassment to him?

Mary: Yes (then looking at Sid). I stopped my sentence because I was going to say . . . "I'm trying to be polite so that you'll like me."

Sid: Mary, that's the trouble. I don't like your politeness—it seems phony to me. I'd feel closer to you if I knew what you *really* were thinking and feeling.

Mary: You know it's true that I don't really feel all the nice things I say—but to imagine not being polite and sweet . . . just really scares me.

Fcltr.: What is your fear?

Mary: I'm afraid nobody will like me.

Sid: I'm liking you right now.

Mary: You know when you said you like me, it made me feel anxious and confused. (She looks to facilitator.) I'm at a loss to figure out what's going on with me. Why do I feel confused?

Fcltr.: Mary, right now the "why" of your confusion is secondary to the fact that you *are* feeling confused *right now*. Try to get the feel of your confusion. In other words, become aware of your sensations and let them emerge on their own.

Mary: (mildly distressed) I feel overcome by a growing sense of emptiness which I feel in my stomach.

Fcltr.: Let your emptiness have its say. You're at the point at which you don't get support from others and you can't quite get it from yourself.

Mary: (mildly fearful) I feel awful. I feel like nothingness—I feel so empty.

Fcltr.: (noting Mary's eyes becoming moist) What do your tears have to say to us, Mary?

Mary: (breaking into deep sobs) I feel unloved and unappreciated for what I am; I so much need everyone's approval. I really don't like myself. (Mary continues crying for several minutes, then adds as she looks down at the floor) Now I feel silly; everyone must think I'm a jerk!

Fcltr.: Mary, you will get yourself into trouble by imagining what people are thinking. Right now, look at each person in the group and tell us what you see.
(As Mary looks around the group, she sees the members looking at her sympathetically; several have been moved to tears by her outpouring of feeling.)

Mary: (responding to the warmth and support she sees around her) I feel so happy, so free right now. I want to express my warm feelings to all of you. (She goes around the group making contact by touching, holding, or talking to each member.)

As the group sessions continued, Mary became able to drop her "polite good-girl" role, to begin to understand and trust herself, and to improve her competence and authenticity in relating to others.

Case material supplied by Bryant Crouse, Psychology Clinic, The University of California at Los Angeles, 1971.

These objectives seem deceptively easy to achieve; actually there are a number of common stumbling blocks. First is the problem of creating a therapeutic situation in which the patient feels safe enough to lower his defenses and explore his innermost feelings, thoughts, and assumptions. Second is the problem of providing him with needed opportunities for learning new ways of perceiving himself and his world, and new ways of coping. Involved here is a process of exploration and reeducation, in which he gradually comes to realize that his previous assumptions and values are neither as necessary nor as desirable as he had assumed—that there are other alternatives open to him that would yield greater satisfaction and fulfillment. Third is the problem of helping the individual transfer what he has learned from the therapy situation to real life; for while the patient may have achieved adequate understanding of the nature and causes of his self-defeating behavior and learned that more effective coping techniques are available, he may still be "unable to risk the initial venture into the heretofore out-of-bounds area of living" (Salzman, 1968, p. 465). And fourth is the problem of dealing with conditions in the patient's life situation that may be maintaining his neurotic life-style. For example, a domineering and egocentric husband who will not participate in the therapy program may tend to block his wife's efforts toward self-direction and make it more difficult for her to give up her insecure, neurotic behavior; or he may even manage to sabotage the entire treatment program.

2. *Behavior therapy.* As we have seen, behavior therapy focuses on (a) the removal of specific symptoms or maladaptive behaviors; (b) the development of needed competencies and adaptive behaviors; and (c) the modification of environmental conditions that may be reinforcing and maintaining the maladaptive behaviors. In this last context, Bandura (1969) has stated, "A treatment that fails to alter the major controlling conditions of the deviant behavior will most certainly prove ineffective" (p. 50). Although behavior modification does not emphasize self-understanding, changes in values, or personal growth, it often leads in that direction.

Many procedures may be utilized in behavior therapy. Perhaps the simplest and most commonly used in the treatment of neuroses is systematic desensitization. Here the person is placed—symbolically or actually—in situations that are increasingly closer to the situation he finds most threatening, and an attempt is made to associate the fear-producing stimuli or situations with emotional states that are antagonistic to anxiety. The prototype of this model was the classic experiment by Mary Cover Jones (1924) in treating three-year-old Peter's phobia of furry objects. As we discussed in Chapter 3, she introduced a white rabbit in a cage at the end of the room while Peter was eating and brought the rabbit a little closer each day until Peter's phobia was extinguished.

In an early study utilizing systematic desensitization, Wolpe (1958) reported the apparent recovery of 188 out of 210 neurotic cases, in an average of 35 sessions. Although a wide range of neurotic reactions were represented, the majority of these cases (135) were labeled as anxiety reactions. In more recent reports, the results of desensitization and other forms of behavior therapy have continued to be very positive (Paul, 1968; Razani, 1974; Bandura, 1973; Rachman, Marks, & Hodgson, 1973). In fact, after a review of 20 studies that utilized control groups for purposes of comparison, Paul concluded: "The findings were overwhelmingly positive, and for the first time in the history of psychological treatments, a specific therapeutic package reliably produced measurable benefits for clients across a broad range of distressing problems in which anxiety was of fundamental importance" (p. 159).

In our discussion of specific types of neuroses, we have seen how maladaptive behaviors—such as conversion symptoms—may be extinguished by removing reinforcements that maintain the behavior while simultaneously providing reinforcements that enhance the learning of more responsible and effective coping patterns. Other maladaptive behaviors—such as obsessive thoughts and compulsions—can often be removed by mild aversive conditioning (Bandura, 1969, 1973; Stern, Lipsedge, & Marks, 1973). The illustration on page 230 describes the treatment of a phobic neurosis with a self-directed and self-reinforcing imagery technique. We shall have occasion to refer to these and other behavior modification techniques in subsequent chapters.

Although behavior therapy is usually directed at changing specific "target behaviors"—such as removing phobias—it often seems to have more far-reaching positive results. As we noted in the statement of the patient on page 231, in overcoming her snake phobia she gained confidence in her ability to overcome other problems. Ultimately such a patient learns that coping effectively with adjustive demands is more rewarding than trying to avoid them. Thus while cognitive therapies usually focus more on modifying the basic neurotic life-style of the patient and behavior therapy focuses more on the removal of specific target symptoms, the outcomes of these two forms of therapy are often comparable. In fact, behavior modification techniques are being increasingly used in the cognitive therapies and vice versa. In this context, London (1972) has pointed to a deemphasis on ideology in both behavior therapy and cognitive therapy, and a tendency to use the methods "that work" for the particular patient.

Here it may be pointed out that psychotherapy often requires a great deal of courage and persistence on the part of the patient as he musters the courage to face his problems realistically and give up the defensive and avoidant life-style that has helped alleviate feelings of inadequacy and anxiety. In some cases, however, the neurotic may present himself in such a way as to put the whole responsibility for his well-being and happiness on the therapist. As Weiss and English (1943) so succinctly described it:

"There's my story, doctor (after taking plenty of time to tell it in detail). Now you pat me . . . and take my pains away . . . and give me inspiration and happiness and tell me how to be successful, and while you are about it, get my mother-in-law out of the house and I'll pay you when I get a job." (Weiss & English, 1943, p. 119)

Despite the difficulties involved, however, powerful forces are aligned on the side of psychotherapy. For one thing, the person who seeks help is usually experiencing considerable inner distress, so that he is motivated to change his behavior. And when helped to understand his problems, to discriminate more effective ways of coping with them, and to open paths for achieving personal growth and fulfillment, he usually will find the courage "to see it through." However, the outcome may vary considerably with regard to the degree of change that is brought about in his basic neurotic life-style.

Sociotherapy. Here the focus is on the modification of circumstances in the individual's life situation that tend to perpetuate his neurosis. Often there are pathogenic family interactions that keep the neurotic patient in a continually "sick situation." As the psychiatrist in T. S. Eliot's *The Cocktail Party* says:

"Indeed it is often the case that my patients
Are only pieces of a total situation
Which I have to explore. The single patient
Who is by himself is rather the exception."

Scientific studies have yielded similar findings (Melville, 1973; Hurvitz, 1974; Cookerly, 1973). As Melville (1973) has expressed it, "In a family there is no such thing as one person in trouble" (p. 17). As a consequence of such findings, increasing emphasis has been placed on treating the family system rather than focusing primarily on the individual neurotic. In broad perspective, both psychotherapy and sociotherapy are concerned with the alleviation of culture-induced stresses that foster the production of neuroses and other psychopathology.

With appropriate therapy—usually involving the integration of biological, psychosocial, and sociological measures—the outlook for the neuroses is good. In this context, the differences in the use of such terms as *recovered* and *markedly improved* are important in evaluating reports of treatment outcomes. In addition, it is important to differentiate between *short-term* and *long-term* results. But even though the results of therapy are often difficult to assess, it would appear that the great majority of neurotics—90 percent or more—can benefit substantially from appropriate kinds of help. In many cases, the use of periodic "booster treatments" can probably improve long-range results.

In concluding our discussion of the neuroses, several additional points may be mentioned. Fear of committing suicide is a common neurotic symptom, but the actual incidence of suicide among neurotics does not appear to be higher than for the general population. Nor does the life span of neurotics appear adversely affected by their chronic tension and somatic disturbances, although there are few conclusive statistics on this point. The question has also been raised as to whether neurotics are likely to become psychotic, and the answer seems to be a definitive *no*. However, in a minority of cases—5 percent or less—excessive life stress may lead to severe personality decompensation and psychotic patterns.

Finally, the question has been raised as to how a neurosis affects creativity and productiveness. Many authors have declared neurotics to be "pleasantly different" and more likely than the "normal" person to be innovative and productive. In general, however, the evidence indicates that the neurotic's reliance on defensive strategies reduces his potential for positive accomplishment as well as his enjoyment of life.

In the beginning of this chapter we focused on the basic nature of neuroses—characteristics that seem common to various patterns of neurotic behavior. We noted that these characteristics may be described in terms of the *neurotic nucleus* and the *neurotic paradox*. The neurotic nucleus involves (a) pervasive anxiety resulting from basic feelings of inadequacy and the evaluation of everyday problems as threatening; (b) the tendency to avoid such problems by means of various defensive maneuvers rather than to cope with them; and (c) self-defeating and maladaptive behavior which blocks personal growth and leads to feelings of futility and unhappiness. Why does the neurotic cling to such self-defeating patterns of behavior? This is the neurotic paradox, which can be explained in terms of (a) the relief from anxiety which results from defensive and avoidance maneuvers; and (b) avoidance at the earliest cues signifying the approach of the feared stress, thus preventing the neurotic from testing the situation to see if his fears are realistic. The net result is the tendency to cling rigidly to the defensive and avoidant life-style which characterizes the neuroses.

We then discussed the clinical pictures, causal factors, and treatment and outcomes characteristic of specific neurotic patterns, including anxiety neurosis, phobic neurosis, obsessive-compulsive neurosis, hysterical neurosis, hypochondriacal neurosis, neurasthenic neurosis, and depressive neurosis. We also examined the concept of an "existential neurosis"—a maladaptive pattern characterized by chronic meaningless, alienation, and apathy.

To round out our discussion, we surveyed the general role of biological, psychological and interpersonal, and sociocultural factors in the development of neurotic behavior; we noted that the anxiety-defense, faulty learning, blocked personal growth, and other causal factors were directly applicable to the neuroses. Finally, we noted some contemporary approaches to treatment and the results they have achieved.

8

Psychosomatic Disorders

Traditionally, the medical profession has been concerned with physical illness and has concentrated research efforts on understanding and controlling the organic factors in disease. In psychopathology, on the other hand, interest has centered primarily on uncovering the psychological and emotional factors that lead to the development of mental disorders. Today we realize that both of these approaches are limited; although an illness may be primarily physical or psychological, it is always a disorder of the whole person—not just of the lungs or psyche. Fatigue or a bad cold may lower our tolerance for psychological stress; an emotional upset may lower our resistance to physical disease. In short, the individual is a psychobiological unit in continual interaction with the environment.

Recognition of the importance of sociocultural influences is an important part of this interactional view, for the environment affects the types and incidence of disorders found in different groups. The ailments to which people are most vulnerable—whether physical, psychological, or both—are determined in no small part by when and where they live. Likewise, on a more specific level, the life situation of an individual has much to do with the onset of a disorder, its form and duration, and whether or not he recovers. If the individual's family supports him and cooperates in his treatment program, and if he is eager to resume his usual activities, recovery is more probable and apt to be more rapid than if he faces a return to an unpleasant marriage or a frustrating job.

The interdisciplinary approach to all disorders—which fits relevant biological, psychosocial, and sociocultural data into a coherent picture—is also referred to as the *psychosomatic approach*. It is now reflected in medical and psychological thinking, with respect to the treatment not only of physical illnesses brought on by emotional tension, but also of those cases where no causes other than physical ones are obvious. We might, for example, ask whether emotional factors have lowered the resistance of a tuberculosis patient and hence contributed to the onset of the disease. We might also ask how the individual will react to changes in his life situation brought

Clinical Picture

General Causes of Psychosomatic Disorders

Treatment and Outcomes

about by the disease. Will he fail to cooperate in treatment and welcome death as a solution to his problems, or will he fight the disease with a determination to get well? Some patients apparently give up when medically the chances seem good that they will recover. Others with more serious organic pathology recover, or survive for long periods of time. In fact, a pioneer in the field of psychosomatic medicine, Flanders Dunbar (1943), concluded that it is often "more important to know what kind of patient has the disease than what kind of disease the patient has" (p. 23).

Since this is not a book about medicine, we shall not go deeply into the role of emotional factors in primarily physical diseases, such as tuberculosis, pneumonia, and cancer. Rather we shall focus on disorders such as peptic ulcers, tension headaches, and high blood pressure, in which the physical symptoms are usually brought on in large part by sustained emotional tension. In these disorders there is a tendency for a single organ system to be involved, such as the respiratory or gastrointestinal system. Where tissue damage occurs, it may be relatively mild, or, in some instances—as in hemorrhaging ulcers—it may actually threaten the person's life.

Clinical Picture

In contrast to the neuroses, the psychosomatic disorders involve a clinical picture dominated by maladaptive changes in bodily systems rather than overt maladaptive behavior. The incidence of psychosomatic disorders is indicated by the estimate that at least half of those who seek medical aid suffer from physical illnesses directly related to emotional stress.

In the present section we shall note the various categories of disorders included in this very broad classification and then briefly describe several specific reaction patterns.

Classification of psychosomatic disorders

Psychosomatic disorders are classified according to the organ system affected, and it seems that no part of the body is immune.[1] In the APA classification, ten categories of these disorders are listed, each one preceded by the word *psychophysiologic* to emphasize that we are talking about disorders caused and maintained primarily by psychological and emotional factors rather than organic ones. The ten groups and some of the specific disorders in each are:

1. *Psychophysiologic skin disorders*—neurodermatosis, atopic dermatitis, eczema, and some cases of acne and hives.

2. *Psychophysiologic musculoskeletal disorders*—backaches, muscle cramps, tension headaches, and some cases of arthritis.

3. *Psychophysiologic respiratory disorders*

[1]The APA uses the term *psychophysiologic* when referring to specific disorders—reserving *psychosomatic* for the general approach to medicine in which physical, psychosocial, and sociocultural factors are taken into consideration. In some countries *corticovisceral* is preferred over either *psychophysiologic* or *psychosomatic*, but we shall use these terms as roughly synonymous.

Advocates of the psychosomatic approach to medicine maintain—as Galen and others did many centuries ago—that it is unrealistic to compartmentalize "mind," "body," and "environment" when assessing and treating maladaptive patterns, whether such patterns are primarily physical or psychological in nature. This view is supported by the striking correlations which a number of investigators have found between the incidence of physical illness and emotional disturbances.

In their pioneering study of illness in relatively healthy populations, for example, Hinkle and Wolff (1957) found that persons who had the greatest number of physical illnesses, regardless of kind, were also the ones who experienced the greatest number of disturbances in mood, thought, and behavior. Similarly, in a study of almost 400 subjects in a 10-year period, Rahe and Holmes (1966) found that major health changes were evidenced by 70 percent of those who experienced severe life crises, while the figure was only 37 percent for those who experienced moderate crises. In fact, Matarazzo, Matarazzo, and Saslow (1961) concluded that the incidence of physical illness in a population is a good predictor of mental disturbances, and vice versa.

The correlation between physical and emotional disturbances is well brought out in the reports of Jacobs et al. (1970, 1971) of their initial and follow-up evaluations of 179 college students in the Boston area—106 of whom sought medical help for respiratory infections. The ill subjects were significantly more likely than the "normals" to perceive the year preceding their illness as one characterized by failure and disappointment; and the more severely ill they were, the more frequent and intense were their reports of unpleasant and stressful events and emotions. A follow-up study revealed recurrences of illness and repetition of treatment-seeking behavior, while the healthy controls tended to stay healthy. Finding that the chief point of difference between the ill and healthy subjects was the style and intensity of the formers' maladaptive coping behavior, the investigators concluded that a direct association could be made between maladaptive coping styles and physical illness, as well as psychiatric complaints.

An explanation for such concurrences in physical and emotional disturbances may be found in Schwab's (1970) observation that there is often a vicious circle in which emotional disturbances adversely affect the body's functioning and lower its resistance to disease; and disease, in turn, tends to elicit and exacerbate feelings of anxiety, depression, and, often, hopelessness. Thus, Schwab did not find reports of both physical and mental distress by emotionally disturbed persons surprising—noting that "The concurrence of mental and physical symptomatology should be regarded as natural when we view man as a biosocial organism whose nervous system functions as the central integrating medium" (p. 594). As we noted in Chapter 4, it would appear that each highly stressful experience leaves a person with an "indelible scar" to the extent that it uses up bodily reserves that cannot be entirely replaced and contributes to the process we call "aging."

—bronchial asthma, hyperventilation syndromes, hiccoughs, and recurring bronchitis.

4. *Psychophysiologic cardiovascular disorders*—hypertension, paroxysmal tachycardia, vascular spasms, heart attacks, and migraine headaches.

5. *Psychophysiological hemic and lymphatic disorders*—disturbances in the blood and lymphatic systems.

6. *Psychophysiologic gastrointestinal disorders*—peptic ulcers, chronic gastritis, and mucous colitis.

7. *Psychophysiologic genitourinary disorders*—disturbances in menstruation and urination.

8. *Psychophysiologic endocrine disorders*—hyperthyroidism, obesity, and other endocrine disorders in which emotional factors play a causative role

9. *Psychophysiologic disorders of organs of special sense*—chronic conjunctivitis. (Conversion reactions are excluded.)

10. *Psychophysiologic disorders of other types*—disturbances in the nervous system in which emotional factors play a significant role, such as multiple sclerosis.

From the foregoing, it is apparent that psychosomatic disorders cover a wide range of disturbances in which life stress plays a causal role; even heart attacks and a number of other disorders formerly assumed to be strictly physical in origin have recently been added to the category of psychosomatic disorders. It should be emphasized, however, that a given case of tension headache, ulcers, or high blood pressure should not be diagnosed as psychosomatic until a thorough medical examination has ruled out organic factors as the primary cause.

Some specific reaction patterns

The clinical picture in psychosomatic disorders tends to be *phasic:* typically there is an upsurgence of symptoms followed by their waning or disappearance. The sequence of their appearance and disappearance appears to be directly related to the amount of stress in the individual's life situation. For example, a hard-pressed and insecure business executive may find his ulcers quiescent during a three-week vacation. However, there are many exceptions to this general trend. It is also of interest to note that there are often marked differences between the sexes in the incidence of specific disorders; for example, ulcers are much more common among men than women, while the reverse is true of rheumatoid arthritis.

Here we shall briefly review five of the most common types of psychosomatic reactions—peptic ulcers, migraine and tension headaches, asthma, high blood pressure, and heart attacks.[2]

Peptic ulcers. Peptic ulcers first came into prominence in our Western culture during the early part of the nineteenth century. In the be-

[2]Emotional stress usually plays a key causal role in the development of these reactions; hence they are listed as psychophysiologic or psychosomatic disorders. However, in a sizeable number of cases there may be little or no direct emotional involvement, as in migraine headaches resulting directly from dietary factors or heart attacks stemming directly from genetic defects or other biological conditions. In such cases the reactions would not be labeled psychosomatic.

These references were used in estimating the incidence and related statistics concerning these psychosomatic disorders: Cailliet (1968), Edwards (1973), Miller (1974), Murata (1973), Necheles (1970), Schwab et al. (1970), and *U.S. News & World Report* (October 8, 1973, p. 52).

ginning they were observed primarily in young women, but in the second half of the nineteenth century there was a shift, and today the incidence of ulcers is some 2 or 3 times higher among men than women. Contemporary civilization apparently is conducive to the chronic emotional reactions that lead to peptic ulcers, and it is estimated that about 1 in every 10 Americans now living will at some time develop a peptic ulcer.

The ulcer itself results from an excessive flow of the stomach's acid-containing digestive juices, which eat away the lining of the stomach or duodenum, leaving a craterlike wound. Although dietary factors, disease, and other organic conditions may lead to ulcers, it is now recognized that worry, repressed anger, resentment, anxiety, and other negative emotional states may stimulate the flow of stomach acids beyond what is needed for digestion.

In a historic study, Wolf and Wolff (1947) observed a subject, Tom, who as a consequence of an operation literally had a window over his stomach. When Tom was subjected to interview experiences designed to elicit strong resentment, hostility, and anxiety, there was a marked increase in acid production, engorgement of the stomach with blood, and rhythmic contractions—in essence, digestive functions occurred as if his stomach were full of food. A number of more recent studies have shown comparable findings. Most people, of course, get over emotional upsets and return to normal bodily functioning. But if the emotional tension is sustained long enough—if anger and resentment, for example, are repressed or denied adequate expression—the excess digestive acids may eat into the gastric lining and cause ulceration.

Migraine and tension headaches. Although headaches can result from a wide range of organic conditions, the vast majority of them—about 9 out of 10—seem to be related to emotional tension. An estimated 20 million or more Americans suffer from such recurrent tension and migraine headaches with the incidence apparently being higher among women than men. Research in this area has focused primarily on migraine, an intensely painful headache that recurs periodically. Although typically involving only one side of the head, migraine is sometimes more generalized; it may also shift from side to side. In addition to these "ordinary" types of migraine headache, there is the sharp, stabbing "cluster" type that occurs in multiple episodes, often following a period of REM sleep (the initial period of sleep characterized by rapid eye movements and dreaming).

Migraine was extensively described by Galen and other medical writers of antiquity, but the cause of the pain remained a mystery until recently, when interest was focused on the pain-sensitive arteries of the head. By dilating these arteries with an injection of histamine, researchers found it possible to reproduce the pain of migraine. Turning to actual cases of migraine, they discovered that the onset of the headaches was accompanied by progressive dilation of these cranial arteries. In addition, persons with unilateral headaches showed dilation of the cranial artery only on the side where the pain occurred. As the attack subsided, either spontaneously or following the administration of drugs, the pain diminished and the arteries returned to their normal size.

It has also been shown that a variety of experimentally induced stresses—frustrations, excessive performance demands, and threatening interviews—cause vascular dilation among migraine sufferers but not among other persons. The graph on page 272 traces the course of a headache induced during a discussion that evoked feelings of hostility in the subject—a migraine sufferer.

The vast majority of headaches are so-called "simple" tension headaches. These, too, involve stress and vascular changes, but the changes are different from those in migraine headaches. As a consequence of emotional stress, muscles surrounding the skull contract; these contractions, in turn, result in vascular constrictions, which the person commonly experiences as "a band of pain that seems to circle my head."

Both tension and migraine headaches usually make their appearance during adolescence and reoccur periodically during periods of stress, often being so painful as to be temporarily incapacitating unless they are alleviated or stopped by some form of treatment. Of the two types, however, migraine headaches are usually more painful and difficult to

The development of peptic ulcers

In some individuals the lining of the stomach or the duodenum may be eaten away by acid-containing digestive juices, leaving a peptic ulcer. Nervous tension and general emotional stress are recognized as key factors in the excessive production of digestive juices; thus, the drawing below depicts the nerves, as well as the organs, primarily involved in the development of peptic ulcers.

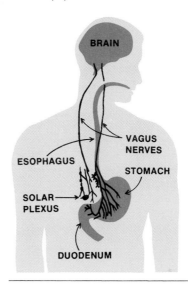

treat than simple tension headaches, in which the pain can often be relieved with simple analgesics.

Asthma. Like migraine, asthmatic attacks have been described by medical writers since ancient times. The actual attack occurs when airways become restricted, making breathing difficult. Many asthmatics begin to wheeze in the presence of household dust, tobacco smoke, cold air, and other conditions that do not bother other people so much. Attacks may be mild or severe and may continue for hours or even days. In severe cases the individual may become extremely distressed, fight for air, and suffer convulsive coughing. Between attacks, he is relatively symptom-free. The actual incidence of asthma is unknown, but it is considered the leading chronic illness among persons under 17 years of age.

Migraine headaches

The side-view drawing of the head at left below shows the location of pain-sensitive cranial arteries, with the dotted lines marking the areas where the headache is felt as various parts of the arteries dilate.

The graph traces the course of a headache induced during a discussion which evoked feelings of hostility in a subject. Both the changes in the amplitude of the artery pulsations and the corresponding increase and diminution in the intensity of the pain are shown. The headache was completely relieved by means of an injection which the subject believed would end the suffering but which actually could have had no physical effect.

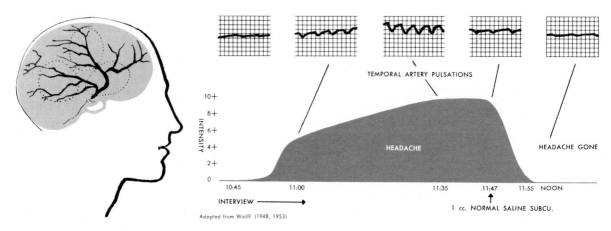

TEMPORAL ARTERY PULSATIONS

HEADACHE

HEADACHE GONE

INTENSITY

10+
8+
6+
4+
2+
0

10:45   11:00   11:35   11:47   11:55 NOON

INTERVIEW ⟶

1 cc. NORMAL SALINE SUBCU.

Adapted from Wolff (1948, 1953)

Head redrawn from H. G. Wolff's *Headache and other head pain,* revised by Donald J. Dalessio. Copyright © 1948, 1963, 1972 by Oxford University Press, Inc. Reprinted by permission.

There appear to be several types of asthma, each with its own causes and triggering stimuli. Probably the most common is allergic asthma, initiated by something in the environment to which the individual has become sensitized, such as ragweed pollen (Ellis, 1970). Although the precise way in which sensitization occurs is not known, once it takes place the individual will develop symptoms in the presence of the allergen.

Other cases of asthma are associated with infectious conditions, and in still other cases asthma appears to be "intrinsic"—that is, there is no apparent sensitization to any given allergen, nor is any infectious condition present. This last form of asthma may be triggered by emotional stimuli and may occur in infancy as well as later life.

Knapp (1969) has cited the case of a young married woman who suffered from severe episodes of asthma. Medical examination revealed no selective sensitivity to particular allergens; rather, the asthma attacks appeared to be directly related to her difficulty in handling hostility aroused by interpersonal relationships. The following excerpts are illustrative of the clinical picture.

"I just feel rotten and I can't breathe and I just have to keep using the spray, and if I cough my lungs out it'll go away. . . . When I'm mad or something's bothering me it can happen. If I'm mad, inside mad, this can go off. Now whether it's because there's anxieties or nerves or worries I don't know, but if I get mad and I'm holding it in, and I'm thinking about something, it can happen." (pp. 141–42)

Hypertension. Of the various organ systems, the heart probably is the most sensitive to emotional stress. During states of calm, the beat of the heart is regular, pulse is even, blood pressure is relatively low, and the visceral organs are well supplied with blood. With emotion-arousing stress, however, the vessels of the visceral organs are constricted, and blood is directed in greater quantity to the muscles of the trunk and limbs—changes that help put the body on an emergency footing for maximum physical exertion. The tightening or restricting of the tiny vessels to visceral organs forces the heart to work harder. As it beats faster and with greater force, the pulse quickens and blood pressure mounts. Usually, when the stress or crisis passes, the body resumes normal functioning and the blood pressure returns to normal. But under chronic emotional strain, high blood pressure may become chronic.

Over 23 million persons in the United States suffer from chronically high blood pressure, or *hypertension*. It is the primary cause of about 60,000 deaths each year, and a major underlying factor in another million or more deaths a year from strokes and cardiovascular disease. Hypertension is also a risk factor in kidney failure, blindness, and a number of other physical ailments. For reasons that are not entirely clear but apparently relate in part to diet, the incidence of hypertension is about twice as high among blacks as among whites (Edwards, 1973; Mays, 1974). In fact, for every black person who dies from sickle-cell anemia, an estimated one hundred die from hypertension.

Unlike the other psychosomatic disorders we have dealt with, there are usually no symptoms to signal high blood pressure. The individual experiences no personal distress. In severe cases, some persons complain of headaches, tiredness, insomnia, or occasional dizzy spells—symptoms often easy to ignore—but most persons suffering from hypertension receive no warning symptoms. In fact, Nelson (1973) reported on one survey encompassing three middle-class neighborhoods in Los Angeles which revealed that a third of the adults tested had high blood pressure; only half of them were aware of it. As Mays (1974) has described the situation:

"In most instances . . . the disease comes as silently as a serpent stalking its prey. Someone with high blood pressure may be unaware of his affliction for

The problem of eczema

Eczema is a superficial inflammation of the skin characterized by redness, itching, pimples, and the formation of crusts. Since the skin is well supplied with blood vessels, it is a highly sensitive indicator of emotional states. For example, when an individual feels embarrassed or angry, his skin tends to flush; when he is severely frightened, the blood tends to be drawn away from the small capillaries of the skin and his face may blanch or turn pale.

Often people who are under severe stress and emotionally upset develop a rash or other psychosomatic skin reaction. In a study of 82 cases of eczema referred to the Skin Department of the Middlesex Hospital in England, as contrasted with 123 dental patients used as controls, D. G. Brown (1972) reported that the eczema patients tended to describe themselves as "bottling up" their emotional problems and reported to a significant degree more often "feeling frustrated and unable to do anything about it," and more often "getting really angry" (p. 323). Brown also pointed to a significantly higher incidence of separation experiences—such as marital separation and divorce—to which the eczema patients had apparently been sensitized by separation experiences, other than bereavement, in childhood.

Eczema reactions associated with emotional stress (such reactions may stem primarily from physical causes) typically clear up when the stress situation is alleviated. However, there may be residual scars, particularly if the skin itches and is continually scratched, which may have a detrimental effect on the individual's self-concept and interpersonal relationships. Thus as Shelley and Edson (1973) have pointed out, eczema and other skin disorders may not take a person's life, but they "could take the enjoyment out of it" (p. 26).

many years and then, out of the blue, develop blindness or be stricken by a stroke, cardiac arrest or kidney failure." (p. 7)

Since there is no such thing as "benign hypertension," high blood pressure is considered an insidious and dangerous disorder. Ironically, high blood pressure is both simple and painless to detect by means of a medical examination.

In many cases a physical cause of hypertension can be identified. For example, it may be attributable to certain diseases of the kidney, to a narrowing of the aorta or one of its arteries, to the excessive use of certain drugs, or to dietary factors. But a number of investigators, following the lead of Wolff (1953), have shown that chronic hypertension may be triggered by emotional stress. For example, a highly stressful job markedly increases the risk of high blood pressure (Edwards, 1973), and the stresses of ghetto life—as well as dietary factors—have been identified as playing a key role in hypertension among black people (Mays, 1974).

As the following case illustrates, hypertensive reactions may appear even in young people.

Mark ———, a senior in law school, evidenced episodes of extreme hypertension whenever he was subjected to stress. He became aware of these episodes when he failed to pass his physical examination of induction into the armed forces because of exceptionally high blood pressure. In a later check at a medical clinic, under nonstressful conditions, his blood pressure was normal; however, under simulated stress conditions, his blood pressure showed extreme elevation, and it happened again when he returned for another physical examination at the induction center.

Although most people show alterations in blood pressure under stress, it would appear that under severe and sustained stress, persons like Mark run a high risk of developing chronic hypertension.

Heart attacks. Heart attacks are often referred to as "the twentieth-century epidemic." More people in the United States die from heart attacks than from any other cause, to say nothing of the many additional thousands who survive but suffer crippling effects.[3] Although there are various types and causes of heart attacks, the common denominator is hypertension—itself a leading psychosomatic disorder.

In a study of sudden cardiac death, Rahe and Lind (1971) gathered life-change data on 39 subjects over the last three years of their lives prior to their sudden cardiac deaths. (The chart showing life-change units is on p. 117). Both for those with prior histories of coronary heart disease and for those without, there was a threefold increase in the number and intensity of life-change units during the final six months of their lives as compared to the rest of the three years prior to death. Similarly, in a study of 50 patients, aged 40 to 60, admitted consecutively to a hospital following their first heart attack—as contrasted with 50 healthy controls—Thiel, Parker, and Bruce (1973) found significant differences between the two groups with respect to the incidence of divorce, loneliness, excessive working hours, sleep disturbances, nervousness, anxiety, and depression. While leaving room for exceptions resulting primarily from biological factors, these investigators, as well as Rahe and Lind, concluded that their findings point to a direct relationship between life stress and heart attacks.

Finally, in a study of 229 men from three different countries (Finland, Sweden, and the United States) who had recently survived a myocardial infarction—one type of heart attack—it was found that common background factors included heavy work responsibility, time urgency coupled with hostility when slowed by others, and dissatisfaction with the achievement of life goals (Romo, Siltanen, Theorell, & Rahe, 1974). Again it would appear that severe stress and heart attacks tend to be causally related.

We could describe a number of other psychosomatic disorders—including acute backache, which is typically the result of life stress rather than physical injury and affects over 8 million Americans. Hopefully, however, the preceding discussion will suffice to provide a typical picture of these disorders.

---

[3]Although "heart attack" implies a sudden episode rather than a continuing condition, it is a "wastebasket" term that includes a variety of heart disorders, such as cardiac arrest, coronary insufficiency, coronary thrombosis, myocardial infarction, and angina pectoris. The broader terms *cardiovascular disorders* and *coronary heart disease* are used as roughly synonymous with *heart attack.*

General Causes of Psychosomatic Disorders

In this section we shall be concerned both with the general causes of psychosomatic disorders and with the problem of organ specificity—of why, under stress, one individual develops bronchial spasms, another hypertension, and still another migraine headaches.

Much remains to be learned about the interacting roles of biological, psychosocial, and sociocultural variables in predisposing an individual to psychosomatic disorders as well as in precipitating and maintaining them. However, the theme that underlies all of these disorders is *life stress*. In essence, chronic emotional tension elicited by life stress perceived as threatening can cause profound changes in the physiological functioning of the human body; these changes, in turn, can play an important causal role in the various disorders we refer to as *psychosomatic*.

In general, the development of psychosomatic disorders appears to involve the following sequence of events: (a) the arousal of negative emotions in response to stress situations—the degree of arousal depending not only on the nature of the stress situation, but also on the individual's perception of the situation and his stress tolerance; (b) the failure of these emotions to be dealt with adequately—either through appropriate expression or through a changed frame of reference or improved competence—with the result that the emotional arousal continues on a chronic basis; and (c) response stereotypy—the damaging effects of chronic arousal becoming concentrated in a specific organ system. In the discussion that follows, we shall be concerned with the possible significance of particular biological, psychosocial, and sociocultural variables in contributing to this chain of events.

Biological factors

A number of biological factors have been implicated in psychosomatic disorders, directly or indirectly. These include genetic factors, differences in autonomic reactivity, somatic weakness, and alterations in corticovisceral control mechanisms.

Genetic factors. Research by Gregory and Rosen (1965) has demonstrated that the brothers of ulcer patients are about twice as likely to have ulcers as comparable members of the general population. Increased frequencies of asthma, hypertension, migraine, and other reactions have also been reported for close relatives, and these frequencies are specific to given reactions—that is, the relatives of bronchial asthma cases show an increased frequency of bronchial asthma but not of other psychosomatic disorders.

It used to be considered unlikely that such increased frequencies could be due to parental example and learning, since the autonomic nervous system was presumably much less vulnerable to conditioning and learning than the cerebrospinal system. More recent studies of learning in the autonomic system, however, indicate that increased incidence of specific psychosomatic conditions in given families could result from common experience and learning. Further research evidence is needed, but genetic factors should not be ruled out—particularly in such disorders as bronchial asthma, where allergens often play a key role.

Here it is of interest to note the findings of Liljefors and Rahe (1970) who studied the role of life stress in coronary heart disease among twins. The subjects consisted of 32 pairs of identical male twins, between 42 and 67 years of age, in which only one twin in each pair suffered from coronary heart disease while the other did not. These investigators found that twins suffering heart disease were more work oriented, took less leisure time, had more home problems, and, in general, experienced greater dissatisfactions in their lives.

Differences in autonomic reactivity. In our earlier discussion of personality development in Chapter 4, we noted that individuals vary significantly in "primary reaction tendencies."

Biological clocks

The 24-hour rhythmic fluctuations observable in the activity and metabolic processes of plants and animals—indeed, all living creatures on earth—are referred to as *circadian* cycles, from the Latin words meaning "about a day." Thus, normal functioning for each system or individual appears to follow a biological clock; and an upset in this cycle, caused by changes in schedule or other factors, may cause malfunctioning in the form of somatic or psychosomatic complaints.

Thousands of experiments with lower animals have established the relationship between biological clocks and normal functioning. And humans—although found to be somewhat more adaptable to environmental changes than lower animals—have revealed similar cyclic fluctuations in activity and sleep, body temperature, chemical constituents of the blood, and so on. Interestingly enough, these cycles have remained essentially the same even for human subjects who have lived in caves, cut off from all means of knowing whether it was day or night for periods as long as several months.

In studies of disturbances in circadian cycles in humans—e.g., a sudden reversal of sleep schedules from night to daytime—subjects have demonstrated various degrees of adaptability. And in experiments that simulated manned space flights, some subjects reacted well to unusual schedules of work and rest—e.g., working for 4 hours, then resting for 4 hours—while others were unable to adapt to them.

A report prepared for the National Institute of Mental Health by Weitzman and Luce (1970) has noted the potential adverse effects of technological change—including abrupt time changes associated with jet travel—on "the invisible circadian cycle that may govern our susceptibility to disease or shock, our emotions, our performance, our alertness or stupefaction" (p. 279).

Even very young infants reveal marked differences in their sensitivity to aversive stimuli; some infants react to such stress by developing a fever, others by digestive upset, and still others by disturbances in sleeping. Such differences in reactivity continue into adult life, and presumably help to account for individual differences in susceptibility to psychosomatic disorders as well as for the type of disorder a given individual is most likely to develop.

In connection with the latter point, Wolff (1950) suggested that people can be classified as "stomach reactors," "pulse reactors," "nose reactors," and so on, depending on what kinds of physical changes that stress characteristically triggers in them. For example, a person who characteristically reacts to stressful situations with a rise in blood pressure will be particularly vulnerable to hypertension, whereas one who reacts with increased secretions of stomach acids will be more likely to develop peptic ulcers.

Somatic weakness. The organ affected may be one that is especially vulnerable. Factors as diverse as heredity, illness, or prior trauma may produce somatic weakness in a particular organ system, making it more vulnerable to stress than others. The person who has inherited or developed a "weak" stomach presumably will be prone to gastrointestinal upsets during anger or anxiety. The person who has had a respiratory infection may have especially vulnerable lungs or nasal passages, and emotional stress may bring on attacks of bronchitis or asthma. Such respiratory infections have in fact been found in the prior histories of most asthmatic patients (Rees, 1964; Bulatov, 1963).

Presumably, the weakest link in the chain of visceral organs will be the organ affected. However, caution must be exercised to avoid *ex post facto* reasoning, since it would not be safe to conclude when a particular organ system is affected that it must have been weak to begin with. Also, as we shall see, conditioning may play a key role in determining which organ system is involved.

Inadequate corticovisceral control mechanisms. Other biological explanations have focused on the role of cortical control mechanisms in regulating autonomic functioning. Presumably corticovisceral control mechanisms may fail in their homeostatic functions, so that the individual's emotional response is exaggerated in intensity and he does not regain physiological equilibrium within normal time limits (Halberstam, 1972; Lebedev, 1967).

A combination of response stereotypy and faulty visceral control mechanisms appears to predispose the individual to psychosomatic disorders in the face of continued stress. On the other hand, efficient corticovisceral control mechanisms can prevent psychosomatic reactions even in the face of response stereotypy and severe, sustained stress:

"If a person with marked response stereotypy is continually exposed to stressful situations, he may nevertheless avoid having psychosomatic symptoms if his autonomic feedback and control mechanisms operate efficiently. The individual's own autonomic balance (homeostasis) may be kept within the limits of normal functioning by the reflex mechanisms . . . which prevent either responses or rebounds from being of such magnitude that tissue damage occurs." (Sternbach, 1971, p. 141)

In assessing the role of biological factors in psychosomatic disorders, most investigators would take into consideration each of the factors we have described. Perhaps the greatest emphasis at present would be placed on the characteristic autonomic activity of given individuals, the vulnerability of affected organ systems, and possible alterations in cortical control mechanisms that normally regulate autonomic functioning.

Psychosocial factors

The role of psychosocial factors in psychosomatic disorders is still not altogether clear. Factors that have been emphasized include personality characteristics, including failure to learn adequate coping patterns, kinds of stress, interpersonal relationships, and learning in the autonomic nervous system.

Personality characteristics and inadequate coping patterns. The work of Flanders Dunbar (1943, 1954) and a number of other early investigators raised the hope of identifying specific personality factors associated with particular psychosomatic disorders, for example, rigidity, high sensitivity to threat, and proneness to chronic underlying hostility among those who suffer from hypertension. If it were possible to delineate ulcer types, hypertensive characters, accident-prone personalities, and so on, such findings would, of course, be of great value in understanding, assessing, and treating psychosomatic disorders—and perhaps even in preventing them.

More recent research evidence, however, suggests that such an approach is oversimplified. For example, although Kidson (1973) found hypertensive patients to be significantly more insecure, anxious, sensitive, and angry than a nonhypertensive control group, a sizeable number of control-group members also showed these characteristics. Similarly, Jenkins (1974) identified what he called "Type A" people—those who strive diligently to achieve, are time-conscious, tense, unable to relax, and active. In this study, 2700 men who had not had heart attacks were given computer-scored test questionnaires and their lives followed over a four-year period. The men who scored high on Type A behavior had twice as many heart attacks during this follow-up period as those who scored low. But the majority of high scorers did not have heart attacks, and some of the low scorers did.

So even though personality makeup seems to play an important role, we still do not know why some individuals with similar personality characteristics do *not* develop psychosomatic disorders; nor can we account adequately for the wide range of personality makeup among individuals suffering from heart attacks and other psychosomatic disorders. In addition, in cases where people already suffering from a chronically painful and disabling disease like rheumatoid arthritis are studied, the personality similarities found may be the result rather than the cause of the disorder (Robinson, Kirk, Frye, & Robertson, 1972). This point seems particularly important, since Crown and Crown (1973) failed to find a definitive personality type in *early* rheumatoid arthritis.

A related approach has focused on the possible relationship between an individual's attitudes toward stressful situations and the coping pattern he develops. Graham (1962) found

Many cases have been reported of terminally ill patients who managed to stay alive until an important event took place, such as a birthday, a wedding anniversary, or the birth of a grandchild. Of the first four presidents of the U.S. to die, three died on the Fourth of July. Sigmund Freud and Carl Sandburg have been cited as examples of persons where specific dates became "emotionally invested deadlines" for living.

Even among people in good health, the setting of such "target dates" for death is relatively common. The prospect of life without the companionship of one's mate has caused many happily married older people to say that they want to die when their mates do, and in many instances they do die shortly after the death of their spouses. Similarly, many middle-aged persons, when asked, will state that they want to live until New Year's Day of the year 2000, to see the dawning of the twenty-first century.

A number of cases have also been recorded of persons in good health who actually died on the target dates for death that they set for themselves. Harry Oliver, a two-time Oscar-winning art director in the film industry, died on the Fourth of July at the age of 85 — as he predicted he would. One of the most interesting cases with respect to target dates for death is that of Mark Twain (shown at left). He was born on November 30, 1835, when Halley's comet made its spectacular appearance in the sky, and he died — as he had predicted — on April 21, 1910, when Halley's comet returned. Death was attributed to angina pectoris, but the question still remains as to the underlying cause. Was it the excitement surrounding the fiery comet's return, or the conviction that the incontrovertible date for death had arrived?

Based on Fischer and Dlin (1972), Rawitch (1973), and Weisman (1972).

the following attitude and coping patterns to be fairly typical:

Ulcers—feels deprived of what is due him, and wants to get what is owed or promised and to get even.

Migraine—feels something has to be achieved, drives self to reach a goal, and then feels let down.

Asthma—feels unloved, rejected, left out in the cold, and wants to shut the person or situation out.

Eczema—feels he is being frustrated, but is helpless to do anything about it except take it out on himself.

Hypertension—feels endangered, threatened with harm, has to be ready for anything, to be on guard.

Although the work of Graham has evoked a great deal of interest and considerable acceptance, there is still a lack of definitive follow-up studies to support his findings.

Araujo, van Arsdel, Holmes, and Dudley (1973), studying a sizeable number of asthmatic patients, found a lack of essential competencies and psychosocial assets, resulting in limited coping ability. Undoubtedly many psychosomatic disorders are largely the result of faulty learning—failure to learn needed competencies and the learning of maladaptive behavior instead.

Many individuals suffering from psychosomatic disorders also appear unable to express their emotions adequately by verbal means, nor have they learned to use various ego-defense mechanisms—such as rationalization, fantasy, and intellectualization—to alleviate their emotional tension. As a consequence, they rely primarily on repression, which does screen their feelings from conscious awareness. However, the physiological components of the emotion continue and finally lead to structural damage.

When individuals are subjected experimentally to frustrating experiences and then given an opportunity to express physical or verbal aggression against the frustrator, there is a rapid return to normal blood pressure and heart rate. Those who are permitted only fantasy aggression or no aggression at all, however, return much more slowly to normal physiological functioning (Hokanson & Burgess, 1962). Thus in addition to the individual's ability to cope with the stress itself, it seems necessary to consider his ability to deal adequately with the emotional tensions elicited by the stress.

In general, it would appear that the possible role of attitudes, coping patterns, and other personality factors merits further exploration. At present, however, it seems likely that these factors are part of the total causal pattern rather than being of primary causal significance.

Kinds of stress. Approaching the problem from the standpoint of stress rather than personality factors, Alexander (1950) hypothesized that each type of psychosomatic disorder could be associated with a particular kind of stress. He concluded that peptic ulcers, for example, are typically associated with frustration of the needs for love and protection. Presumably, the frustration of these needs would give rise to such emotions as anxiety and anger, and these emotions, in turn, would trigger excessive secretions of stomach acid—leading eventually to peptic ulcers. Subsequent research, however, has failed to demonstrate a consistent relationship between particular disorders and particular types of stress. Rather it would appear that a wide range of stress situations can lead to a given type of disorder—and, conversely, that a wide range of disorders can

result from a given type of stress. In a sample of 192 men between the ages of 30 and 60, Payne (1975) found that long-standing physical and psychological health problems were related to higher life-change values.

Often it appears that severe stress, regardless of the kind, serves to pave the way for, precipitate, or aggravate a physical disorder in a person already predisposed to the disorder (G. W. Brown, 1972). The individual who is allergic to a particular protein may have his resistance further lowered by emotional tension; similarly, where an invading virus has already entered the body—as is thought to be the case in multiple sclerosis—emotional stress may interfere with the body's normal defensive forces or immunological system. In like manner, stress may tend to aggravate and maintain certain specific disorders, such as rheumatoid arthritis (Astor, 1973; Robinson, et al., 1972). As another pioneer in psychosomatic disorders, Day (1951), once pointed out, "To develop chronic active pulmonary tuberculosis a person needs some bacilli, some moderately inflammable lungs . . . and some internal or external factor which lowers the resistance to the disease." He noted further that unhappiness was among the stress factors that could lower resistance.

Here we can see the potential role of stress in the development of physical disorders, including those labeled "psychosomatic" as well as many that are not.

Interpersonal relationships. In our previous discussion, we have repeatedly noted the destructive effects that stressful interpersonal patterns—including marital unhappiness, divorce, and bereavement—may have on personality adjustment. Such patterns may also influence physiological functioning. For example, in a study of widowers, Parkes, Benjamin, and Fitzgerald (1969) reported that during the six-month period following the death of their wives, the widowers' death rate was 40 percent above the expected rate. In fact, the incidence of cardiac deaths among them was so high that the investigators referred to these findings as "the broken-heart syndrome."

Other studies have focused on the role of pathogenic family patterns. For example, studies of asthmatic patients have found that

Ulcers in "executive monkeys": an unsolved riddle?

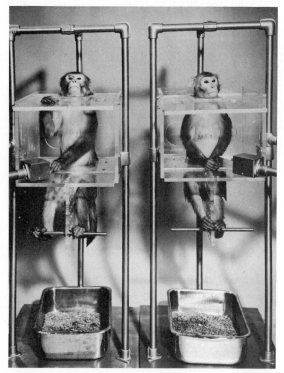

In a well-known series of experiments at Walter Reed Army Hospital, Brady and his associates (1958, 1970) produced ulcers in "executive monkeys." The "executive monkey" (at left) learned to press a lever at least once every 20 seconds to prevent electric shocks to himself and a control monkey. The control monkey (at right) had no responsibility in avoiding the shock, since his lever was actually useless, so he soon lost interest in lever pressing. Only the executive monkey in each pair developed ulcers.

Though these experiments are of interest regarding the ulcer-inducing effect of stress, several questions remain unanswered:

1. **The question of scheduling.** The only schedule that was found to produce ulcers was one involving 6 hours of rest followed by 6 hours of lever pressing. A schedule of 30-minutes-off followed by 30-minutes-on, for example, did not produce ulcers. Why did other schedules fail while the 6-hour schedule could produce ulcers "to order"?

2. **The question of symptoms.** A second question focuses around why the executive monkeys developed ulcers rather than other symptoms, such as hypertension, depression, headaches, or even an "experimental neurosis"?

3. **The question of causal factors.** Since the 30-minute-on and 30-minute-off schedule was more strenuous, it apparently was not the severity of stress that resulted in the ulcers. Could it have been the type of stress, the way the monkey perceived the stress situation, or possibly a disturbance in biorhythms?

4. **The question of selection.** Rather than selecting the monkeys for the experiment randomly, the experimenters chose monkeys who had demonstrated the most initiative in pressing levers to be the "executives" and the more passive monkeys as controls. It has since been found that more "emotional" monkeys respond more quickly to shock, thus suggesting that these monkeys might already have had a tendency toward being more susceptible to stress.

While the results of these studies have frequently been cited as having direct relevance for the development of ulcers in human beings, these unresolved questions leave their implications an unsolved riddle.

the mothers of such patients have in many cases felt ambivalent toward their children and tended to reject them, while at the same time being overprotective and unduly restrictive of the children's activities (Lipton, Steinschneider, & Richmond, 1966; Olds, 1970). Since individuals coming out of such family backgrounds tend to be overdependent and insecure, it would hardly be surprising if they should react with chronic emotional mobilization to problems that do not seem threatening to most people. At the same time, we may wonder why some of these individuals develop psychosomatic disorders rather than another form of psychopathology—and indeed, why others achieve adequate adjustment. We again appear to be faced with an interaction of factors in which parent-child, family, and other interpersonal patterns may play roles of varying importance, depending on the case.

Learning in the autonomic nervous system. While Pavlov and other investigators demonstrated that autonomic responses can be conditioned—as in the case of salivation—it has long been assumed that we could not learn to control such responses voluntarily. More recent evidence indicates that this assumption is not valid. Not only can autonomic reactivity be conditioned involuntarily via the classical Pavlovian model, but operant learning in the autonomic nervous system can also take place. For example, Turnbull (1962) demonstrated that by reinforcing certain breathing behavior an experimenter can induce respiratory patterns that are progressively closer approximations of asthmatic breathing.

Thus the hypothesis developed that psychosomatic disorders may arise through accidental conditioning and reinforcement of such patterns. "A child who is repeatedly allowed to stay home from school when he has an upset stomach may be learning the visceral responses of chronic indigestion" (Lang, 1970, p. 86). Similarly, an infant may get little or no attention from crying, but the gasping or wheezing reactions that often follow crying spells may obtain immediate attention and concern for him. If this pattern is repeated, the infant might learn an asthmalike response as a means of obtaining parental attention and

alleviating distress. By virtue of its anxiety-reducing quality, it would continually be reinforced, and hence tend to persist and generalize to any stressful situation.

Regardless of how a psychosomatic response may have developed, it may be elicited by suggestion and maintained by secondary gains. The role of suggestion was demonstrated by a study in which 19 of 40 volunteer asthmatic subjects developed asthma symptoms after breathing the mist of a salt solution that they were told contained allergens, such as dust or pollen. In fact, 12 of the subjects had full-fledged asthma attacks. When the subjects then took what they thought was a drug to combat asthma (actually the same salt mist), their symptoms disappeared immediately (Bleeker, 1968). Why the other 21 subjects remained unaffected is not clear, but in 19 of the 40 subjects we see the effect of suggestion on an autonomically mediated response.

It would also seem possible for some psychosomatic reactions to be elicited and maintained by secondary gains. Thus a little boy with asthma who does not like to be left at home with a baby-sitter may develop an acute attack when his parents are planning to go to some social event; a wife who feels neglected by her husband may find her symptoms provide a convenient means of obtaining sympathy and attention as well as some measure of control over his activities.

In short, it would appear that some psychosomatic disorders may be acquired and maintained in much the same way as other behavior patterns.

Sociocultural factors

The incidence of specific disorders, both physical and mental, varies in different societies, in different strata of the same society, and over time, as we have seen. In general, psychosomatic disorders, including ulcers, hypertension, rheumatoid arthritis, tension headaches, and asthma, occur among all major groups—from Africans to Australians, from Japanese to Russians, and from Americans to Chinese.

On the other hand, such disorders appear to be extremely rare among primitive societies

Although attributing death to voodoo spells may appear naive, Cannon (1942) — in what is probably the only comprehensive study of the scientific literature on the subject — has cited a good deal of evidence to substantiate its occurrence. Included among Cannon's sources were competent scientific observers who had lived among the natives of Africa, Australia, New Zealand, and South America, as well as nearby Haiti. One such observer was Leonard (1906), whom Cannon quoted as follows:

"I have seen more than one hardened old Haussa soldier dying steadily and by inches because he believed himself to be bewitched; no nourishment or medicine that were given to him had the slightest effect either to check the mischief or to improve his condition in any way, and nothing was able to divert him from a fate he considered inevitable." (Leonard, p. 257)

Another statement, from *The Australian Aboriginal* by Basedow (1927), concerns the effect of "bone pointing" on its victim:

"The man who discovers that he is being boned by an enemy is, indeed, a pitiable sight. He stands aghast, with his eyes staring at the treacherous pointer, and with his hands lifted as though to ward off the lethal medium, which he imagines is pouring into his body. His cheeks blanch and his eyes become glassy and the expression of his face becomes horribly distorted. . . . He attempts to shriek but usually the sound chokes in his throat, and all that one might see is froth at his mouth. His body begins to tremble and the muscles twitch involuntarily. He sways backwards and falls to the ground, and after a short time appears to be in a swoon; but soon after he writhes as if in mortal agony, and, covering his face with his hands, begins to moan. After a while he becomes very composed and crawls to his wurley. From this time onwards he sickens and frets, refusing to eat and keeping aloof from the daily affairs of the tribe. Unless help is forthcoming in the shape of a counter-charm administered by the hands of the Nangarri, or medicine-man, his death is only a matter of a comparatively short time." (pp. 178–79)

Cannon's study of such sources led him to answer in the affirmative the question of whether those who had reported voodoo deaths exercised good critical judgment, and in the negative to that of whether the deaths might have been due to natural causes or poisoning rather than to black magic. He cited the example of Dr. P. S. Clarke, who reported having attended a native in North Queensland to whom an evil spell proved fatal in a few days, even though routine hospital tests preceding death and a postmortem examination disclosed no pathological physical causes. In further support of his conclusions Cannon received a letter from Dr. J. B. Cleland, author of an article on voodoo death in the *Journal of Tropical Medicine and Hygiene* (1928), who "entirely ruled out" the possibility that the deadly effects of bone pointing among Australian natives might be caused by poisoning.

Then how can we account for the effectiveness of voodoo death spells? Cannon emphasized three interrelated factors:

1. Debilitating consequences of intense fear. Studies of humans — and other animals — have shown that intense fear, continued over time, may have serious and even fatal consequences. The deaths of soldiers within 3 to 4 days of suffering severe emotional shock and "malignant anxiety," and the results of postmortem findings in such cases have seemed, according to Cannon, to "fit well with fatal conditions reported from primitive tribes" (p. 180). In many cases, of course, physiological disturbances induced by fear are exacerbated by the victim's refusal of food and liquids.

2. Deep-seated nature of tribal superstitions. The firm belief of primitive peoples in the calamitous effects of voodoo spells explains the very real terror the spells have inspired. Cannon noted that the victim of bone pointing succumbs to dread, as described above, because ". . . death is sure to intervene. This is a belief so firmly held by all members of the tribe that the individual not only has that conviction himself but is obsessed by the knowledge that all his fellows likewise hold it" (p. 176).

3. Abandonment of victim. As Cannon noted, in some groups the member marked for death "becomes a pariah, wholly deprived of the confidence and social support of the tribe" (p. 176). All people who stand in any kinship to him withdraw their sustaining support; in addition the group appoints a ceremonial leader, a person of very near kin, who conducts the fateful ritual of mourning. Thus effectively cut off from the ordinary world and placed in the world of the dead, the victim—highly suggestible and fearful—responds to group expectations and "assists in committing a kind of suicide" (p. 174).

Although there is a dearth of more recent systematic data on the effects of voodoo sorcery, Watson (1973) has reported findings which strongly support Cannon's data and conclusions. While serving in an African jungle hospital in central Zaire, Watson reported that he witnessed an average of one "death by cursing" every three months. As in the cases described by Cannon, the victims typically became comatose and died, some gradually and others on the same day they were admitted to the hospital. Although it is not known how such death curses work, we saw in Chapter 6 that feelings of hopelessness and despair have been considered to be key factors in the death of prisoners in concentration and prisoner-of-war camps, and we noted the adverse effects (in the "long-eye" syndrome) of the "silent treatment" to which a group wintering over in the antarctic occasionally subjected a difficult member.

like the aborigines of the Australian Western Desert (Kidson & Jones, 1968) and among the Navajo Indians of Arizona and certain primitive groups in South America (Stein, 1970). As these "primitive" societies are exposed to social change, however, gastrointestinal, cardiovascular, and other psychosomatic disorders begin to make their appearance. There is evidence of change in the nature and incidence of psychosomatic disorders in Japan paralleling the tremendous social changes that have taken place there since World War II (Ikemi et al., 1974). For example, the incidence of bronchial asthma and irritable colon have shown a marked increase among the young, while hypertension and heart attacks have increased markedly among adults.

In our own society, a number of early studies found a disproportionately high incidence of psychosomatic disorders at the two extremes of the socioeconomic scale (Faris & Dunham, 1939; Pasamanick, 1962; Rennie & Srole, 1956). For example, arthritis was most commonly found on lower socioeconomic levels, while ulcers and cardiac problems were believed most common among executives. More recently, however, reports have cast doubts on these early findings. After an extensive review of the literature, Senay and Redlich (1968) found that psychosomatic disorders—including peptic ulcers, rheumatoid arthritis, asthma, and hypertension—were no respectors of social class or other major sociocultural variables. Similarly, Kahn (1969) found that only a small number of executives develop peptic ulcers; in fact, blue-collar workers who are dissatisfied with their jobs are more likely to develop ulcers than successful business executives who are moving up on the occupational ladder. And while black people in our society show a higher incidence of hypertension than whites, this finding is confounded by the dietary habits among many black citizens, including the excessive use of salt (Mays, 1974).

This statement is not meant to minimize the importance of ghetto life stresses, but stress is also common in other communities as well. For example, we noted that one survey found a third of the adults in three middle-class neighborhoods in Los Angeles to be suffering from hypertension. Although differences in stress level probably contribute to the differential incidence of hypertension among blacks and whites, they apparently do not provide the entire explanation.

In general, it would appear that any sociocultural conditions that markedly increase the stressfulness of living tend to play havoc with the human organism and lead to an increase in psychosomatic disorders as well as other physical and mental problems.

From our discussion so far, we can conclude:

1. Attempts to delineate specific personality profiles associated with given disorders have met with very limited success. A wide range of personality types may, in fact, be associated with peptic ulcers, hypertension, and other psychosomatic disorders. The same conclusion holds for family patterns. However, it would appear that faulty learning—resulting in an inability to cope effectively with the stresses of life—is an important factor in the causal pattern.

2. While efforts to relate specific stresses to specific psychosomatic disorders have not been successful, stress is a key underlying theme in these disorders. Stress may serve as a predisposing, precipitating, or reinforcing factor in the causal pattern, or it may merely serve to aggravate a condition, such as rheumatoid arthritis, which would have occurred anyway. Often the stress appears to speed up the onset rate, increase the severity of the disorder, and/or interfere with the body's immunological defenses and other homeostatic functions.

3. Constitutional predisposition—whether as a result of genetic, disease, or other biological factors—appears to play an important role in the development of psychosomatic disorders and in the involvement of specific organ systems. Predisposition may include autonomic reactivity, somatic weakness, and inadequate corticovisceral control mechanisms.

4. Many psychosomatic disorders may be acquired via learning processes in the autonomic nervous system, which are not essentially different from other types of learning through reinforcement.

5. General sociocultural patterns, such as severe stresses associated with rapid social change, are directly related to the nature and incidence of psychosomatic disorders.

Treatment and Outcomes

Some psychosomatic disorders that endure over prolonged periods of time—such as hypertension and coronary heart disease—result in organic changes that tend to be irreversible. Thus the removal of given stresses or the development of more effective coping techniques may be insufficient from the standpoint of treatment.

Once the psychosomatic disorder has developed, it therefore becomes of crucial importance to assess the nature and severity of the organic pathology involved as well as the roles of psychosocial and organic factors in the total causal pattern. In hypertension, for example, the role of dietary factors may far outweigh that of current psychosocial conditions in causation. Dietary patterns, however, reflect cultural patterns and attitudes that also may have to be reckoned with. Thus a thorough assessment involving the roles of biological, psychosocial, and sociocultural factors seems to be an essential starting point for formulating an effective treatment program.

Except for psychosomatic disorders involving serious organic pathology, treatment is similar to that of the neuroses; the outcomes of treatment are likewise usually favorable. It is not necessary to go into detail concerning specific methods of treatment and outcomes for each type of psychosomatic disorder; however, it is useful to briefly summarize the general treatment measures that are used.

Biological measures

Aside from immediate and long-range medical measures, such as emergency treatment for bleeding ulcers or long-range treatment for coronary heart disease, biological treatment typically focuses on the use of mild tranquilizers aimed at reducing emotional tension. Such drugs, of course, do not deal with the stress situation or the coping reactions in-

Obesity—etiology and treatment procedures

Obesity, the condition characterized by an "excess accumulation of body fat," is a major health problem in our society. Obese persons number in the millions, and obesity is associated with high blood pressure, coronary heart disease, and other physical disorders.

Etiological factors in obesity are diverse, with psychosocial and sociocultural—rather than physiological—influences being the most commonly involved. However, a sizeable number of persons reveal endocrine and metabolic anomalies that may account for the continuance of obesity from infancy through old age (Mayer, 1973). In many cases the key determinants appear to be familial and cultural associations or norms, as well as psychological factors. Thus, in some families the customary diet may lead to obesity in its members; and in some cultural groups obesity is regarded as a sign of social influence and power. And, of course, learned responses typically play a major role; some persons have apparently learned in childhood to overeat as a means of alleviating emotional distress, and this pattern may continue into adulthood. The consequences of such overeating following a traumatic experience has been labeled as "reactive obesity."

In general, it would appear that the eating behavior of obese persons is not triggered by the same internal stimuli as that of persons of normal weight. For example, while hunger and its satisfaction dictate the eating patterns of persons of normal weight, obese persons seem to be much more at the mercy of environmental cues. Regardless of how recently or amply they have eaten, they may be prompted to eat again simply by the sight or smell of food. Thus Stuart (1971) has emphasized the importance of environmental controls in treating obesity, utilizing: (1) cue elimination—e.g., restricting all eating activity to one place; (2) cue suppression—e.g., preparing and serving only small quantities of food; and (3) cue strengthening—e.g., keeping weight charts and displaying pictures of desired clothing, appearance, and activities. Preliminary results of this behavioristic approach have been described as highly positive. In this context, it is interesting to note that a group of overweight persons who had failed to maintain their weight loss over a 1-year period following treatment—as contrasted with a group who were successful in maintaining their weight loss—showed that "the regainers ate high-caloric snacks in a greater variety of situations unrelated to internal cues of hunger" (Leon & Chamberlain, 1973, p. 108).

While immediate success has been reported with a variety of psychological methods—including group therapy, behavior therapy, and a combination of the two—long-range follow-up studies are required to assess the effectiveness of given treatment approaches and programs. A useful review of behavioral approaches to weight control may be found in Abrahamson (1973).

Medical measures have usually focused on the use of appetite-dulling drugs to reduce the individual's food intake and are usually only temporarily effective; the lost weight is regained unless a change in eating behavior takes place. Surgical procedures to reduce food intake and/or absorption are undergoing experimental evaluation.

Based on Abramson (1973), Crisp (1970). Hall et al. (1975), Horan et al. (1975), Leon and Chamberlain (1973), Mason and Ito (1969), Mayer (1973), Penick et al. (1971), Rau and Green (1975), Schachter (1971), and Stuart (1971).

---

volved. But by alleviating emotional tension and distressing symptoms, they may provide the individual with a "breathing spell," during which he can regroup his coping resources.

Other drugs, such as those used to control high blood pressure, are prescribed on a more specific basis. Dietary measures may be indicated in certain psychosomatic reactions, including peptic ulcers, migraine headaches, and hypertension. Acupuncture as a method of treatment is still undergoing intensive research, although it does appear useful in alleviating backache, tension and migraine headaches, and the pain of rheumatoid arthritis (Suback-Sharpe, 1973; Gwynne, 1974; Bresler, 1975). Electrosleep—cerebral electrotherapy—has produced mixed results in the treatment of psychosomatic disorders as it has in the neuroses. Preliminary findings appear promising in the use of this method for insomnia, but more research is needed (Hearst, Cloninger, Crews, & Cadoret, 1974; Miller, 1974; Rosenthal, 1972).

Morita therapy, which progresses from biological to psychological measures and was described on page 260, has been reported as being effective with a number of psychophysiologic as well as neurotic disorders (Murase & Johnson, 1974).

Psychosocial measures

Although family therapy has shown promising results in the treatment of children with bronchial asthma and other psychosomatic disorders, cognitive psychotherapies—aimed at helping the individual understand his problems and achieve more effective coping techniques—have been relatively ineffective. The most promising psychological measures appear to lie in the direction of behavior therapy and biofeedback.

Behavior therapy. Behavior modification techniques are based on the assumption that since autonomic responses can be learned, they can also be unlearned via extinction and differential reinforcement. In one case, the patient, June Clark, was a 17-year-old girl who had been sneezing every few seconds of her waking day for a period of 5 months. Medical experts had been unable to help her, and Kushner, a psychologist, volunteered to attempt treatment by behavior therapy.

"Dr. Kushner used a relatively simple, low power electric-shock device, activated by sound—the sound of June's sneezes. Electrodes were attached to her forearm for 30 minutes, and every time she sneezed she got a mild electric shock. After a ten-minute break, the electrodes were put on the other arm. In little more than four hours, June's sneezes, which had been reverberating every 40 seconds, stopped. Since then, she has had only a few ordinary sneezes, none of the dry, racking kind that had been draining her strength for so long. 'We hope the absence of sneezes will last,' said Dr. Kushner cautiously. 'So do I,' snapped June. 'I never want to see that machine again.' "(*Time*, 1966, p. 72)

In a follow-up report, Kushner (1968) stated that once the patient had stopped sneezing a program of maintenance therapy was instituted, and at the end of 16 months the intractable sneezing had not recurred.

Wolpe (1969) has reported a strategy involving deconditioning of the anxiety reaction to particular stresses; he has had success with peptic ulcers, asthma, migraine, neurodermatitis, and many other psychosomatic disorders. To illustrate, he cited the case of an extremely capable and active 49-year-old woman who suffered from asthma. Her disorder began after the birth of her fourth child. Attacks were brought on by her annoyance with her husband—particularly with respect to family finances—and by seeing anything connected with death or physical disability. Wolpe encouraged her to express her feelings to her husband, and he readily changed. Then Wolpe used routine desensitization procedures to extinguish the woman's fears concerning physical disability and death. Improvement was rapid, and even after 9 years the woman was reported to have maintained her gains.

A number of behavior therapists have relied heavily on suggestion and training in relaxation to treat various psychosomatic disorders. For example, Philipp, Wilde, and Day (1972), utilizing this approach, reported the alleviation of symptoms in asthma, and Tasto and Hinkle (1973) reported success in the treatment of tension headaches. Similarly, investigators in the Veterans Administration reported the successful treatment of hypertension with a combination of hypnosis and relaxation training (*Science News*, Oct. 6, 1973, p. 217); Shoemaker and Tasto (1975) have also reported promising results using relaxation training in the treatment of high blood pressure.

Finally, we may note an interesting study by Kahn, Staerk, and Bonk (1973) who treated twenty asthmatic children by means of counterconditioning. Utilizing biofeedback, which is described in the next section, these investigators trained the children to substitute bronchodilation for bronchoconstriction when faced by stimuli that had previously elicited asthmatic attacks. During a 1-year follow-up period, these children showed a significant reduction in the frequency and severity of asthmatic attacks. Lukeman (1975), too, cited several cases of successful treatment of childhood asthma using conditioning methods, but she also pointed to the need to deal with emotional problems resulting from the asthma.

Biofeedback. In bowling or serving a tennis ball, we receive immediate feedback and can correct our behavior accordingly, but such

A case of anorexia nervosa

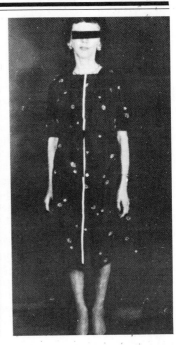

The woman in these pictures was diagnosed as suffering from anorexia nervosa, a disorder characterized by severe loss of appetite and weight due to emotional factors. At the age of 18 (above, left), she weighted 120 pounds, but over a period of years her weight dropped to 47 pounds (center). The photo at right, in which she weighed 88 pounds, was taken after she had undergone behavior therapy.

Treatment of anorexia nervosa is often difficult, and about 10 percent of anorexic patients literally starve themselves to death. The disorder—much more common among females than males—can occur from childhood to adulthood but is seen most frequently among adolescents. The reasons behind the refusal of food hold the key to the etiological puzzle in these cases. As noted above, emotional factors are typically involved, and this view is not negated by the fact that there is often a prior nutritional disorder, for both disorders may result from similar underlying causes. Often obesity precedes anorexia nervosa. Here, the individual reverses previous eating habits, going from one extreme to another, perhaps in reaction to teasing about being "fat." In anorexic children refusal to eat may be associated with unbearable hurt or a desire to get even with parents for perceived mistreatment. Factors implicated among other age groups include depression and sexual conflicts. The latter appear to lead to an association between eating, sex, and fear of impregnation.

In the treatment of anorexia nervosa, medical procedures typically are required in combination with psychotherapeutic procedures. Liquid feeding—intravenously or by tube—may be indicated for persons whom the disorder has rendered too weak to eat; and with children, forced feeding is sometimes resorted to. Other procedures commonly utilized include chemotherapy, individual psychotherapy, and behavior therapy, with the latter appearing to offer the most promise.

In the case of the woman pictured here, Bachrach, Erwin, and Mohr (1965) utilized a program of environmental control designed to reinforce and shape eating behavior, while denying her pleasures when she did not eat. The program proved effective, and a follow-up report revealed that the woman was working as a nurse at the university hospital where she had undergone treatment.

Based on Bachrach, Erwin, and Mohr (1965), Crisp (1970), Halmi, Powers, and Cunningham (1975), Liebman, Minuchin, and Baker (1974), See (1975), Szyrynski (1973), and Warren (1968).

Use of biofeedback in the treatment of asthma

Asthmatics suffer because they are overly sensitive to environmental agents like dust, fumes, and various plants. However, their attacks often appear to be complicated by emotional reactions to such stimuli. For example, an asthma patient whose attacks are provoked by roses may not wheeze when he first enters a room full of roses; rather he may react with a feeling like "oh, damn," for finding himself in that situation. This, in turn, elicits an emotional reaction followed by wheezing. Fried (1974) has reported on a program at the National Jewish Hospital utilizing biofeedback in the treatment of asthma patients:

"An asthmatic enrolled in the hospital's biofeedback program is placed in a large, comfortable, soundproof room. Electrodes are connected to his forehead, where they can detect electrical activity in the muscles just above the eyebrow. A companion instrument transforms the signals into loud clicks. If the patient is relaxed, little electricity courses through them, and the patient hears only a slow, lethargic series of clicks. If the patient is tense, the forehead muscles knot up, electrical activity intensifies, and, like a Geiger counter aimed at a deep, rich lode of uranium, the machine bursts forth with fast, frantic clicking.

"Once the patient has been connected and has been given time to adjust to the surroundings, the training process begins. Pictures of flowers, trees, fields of grass, dust—whatever threatens an attack of asthma in the patient—are flashed onto a screen. As the patient reacts instinctively to the scene, the biofeedback equipment, reflecting mounting anxiety, goes into action, clicking at an increasing speed.

"When the patient hears the mounting crescendo, he knows that he is laying the groundwork for an intensified asthma attack. Over the course of several sessions in the training room, the patient learns to keep the clicks coming at a slow rate by keeping tension down. (Just how the patient does this, he cannot explain, any more than he can explain exactly how he learns to ride a bicycle.)" (p. 19)

While this treatment procedure does not "cure" the patient's asthma, it does serve as a valuable adjunct to treatment by reducing the number and/or severity of attacks, and helping the patient feel that he has more control over the situation.

feedback is usually not available with respect to autonomic functions, such as heart rate and brain waves. The new biofeedback devices are designed to provide such feedback: they monitor these functions and convert the information into signals like lights or sounds that the individual can readily perceive.

In an early study involving the control of heart rate, for example, Lang et al. (1967) provided subjects with equipment that measured heart rate. The subjects received visual feedback on the dial and were instructed to maintain their heart rates within prescribed limits. With learning, subjects became able to do so. In such studies, the subject may not be aware of how he learns to lower or raise his heart rate or blood pressure, but mental set and exposure to feedback information enable him to achieve the desired result.

More recent studies have dealt with control of a wide range of psychosomatic and other disorders, including hypertension, headache, backache, muscular spasms, teeth grinding, epilepsy, sexual impotency, irregular heartbeat, and asthma. However, the actual magnitude and duration of results is a matter of some controversy. For example, Davis, Saunders, Creer, and Chai (1973) used relaxation training facilitated by biofeedback training in the treatment of bronchial asthma in children. Asthma symptoms were reduced in nonsevere cases but not in cases considered as severe. On the other hand, Murata (1973), Blanchard and Young (1974), and Budzynski (1974) have pointed to the success of biofeedback in treating migraine and tension headaches. In fact, Budzynski reported that 81 percent of his patients with migraine headaches were helped to a significant extent by biofeedback training.

Results with respect to the self-control of cardiac functioning are not definitive at this time. In a review of available research findings, Blanchard and Young (1973) found that four cardiac functions were indeed subject to self-control—heart rate level, heart rate variability, cardiac arrhythmias, and blood pressure. But the changes, while statistically significant, were not sufficiently great to be of help therapeutically.[4]

[1]A useful review of the potentialities of biofeedback in the control of autonomic functions may be found in Brown (1974) and Miller (1969, 1975).

As more sophisticated biofeedback devices and procedures are developed, it may become possible for the individual to control many autonomic functions—including heart rate, blood pressure, stomach acid secretion—and thus prevent or cope with many psychosomatic disorders on his own. The overall effectiveness of autonomic learning as therapy may depend, however, on concomitant efforts to change the individual's attitudes and coping techniques in dealing with particular stresses as well as alleviating unusual stresses in his life situation so that he has a better opportunity to make an effective adjustment.

Sociocultural measures

Treatment measures here are concerned with modifying conditions in the community and broader society that place severe and sustained stress on large numbers of people. Sociocultural measures are also concerned with changing cultural patterns that make people more vulnerable to certain types of psychosomatic disorders, including hypertension and heart attacks.

As we learn more about the role of biological, psychosocial, and sociocultural factors in the etiology of psychosomatic disorders, it becomes increasingly possible to delineate "high-risk" individuals and groups—such as the heart attack prone "Type A" personalities identified by Jenkins (p. 277). This, in turn, enables treatment efforts to focus on early intervention and prevention.

In this context, broadly based educational, counseling, and related programs seem eminently worthwhile in fostering changes in the life-styles of individuals and families—as well as in pathological social conditions—which will help to minimize the development of psychosomatic disorders.

In this chapter we have noted the high incidence of tension headaches, high blood pressure, and other psychosomatic disorders in our society. In discussing the development of these disorders, we noted that they typically seem to involve (a) the arousal of emotional tensions in response to stress situations; (b) the failure of such tensions to be adequately discharged, with the result that emotional arousal becomes chronic; and (c) the channeling of undischarged tensions to a particular organ system, which sustains physiological damage.

As yet we do not have adequate answers to the question of why some people develop psychosomatic disorders under sustained stress and others do not, or why some persons develop peptic ulcers and others hypertension. But in the course of our discussion we did see the extent to which the organism reacts to stress as a psychobiological unit—that although a disorder may be primarily physical or psychological in nature, it is always a disorder of the whole person. We observed that learning may occur in the autonomic nervous system to a much greater extent than had previously been supposed, and that learning principles can be applied to treatment of psychosomatic disorders. Since faulty autonomic responses may be learned, they also may be unlearned. This unlearning involves the utilization of feedback, reinforcement, and other learning principles to regulate the functioning of various organ systems. The development of more effective coping methods and the alleviation of severe stress in the individual's life situation also appear to be key objectives in a comprehensive treatment program.

9

Schizophrenia and Paranoia

As we go from the neuroses and psychosomatic disorders to schizophrenia and other psychoses, we encounter a new realm of symptoms that typically includes delusions, hallucinations, and various kinds of bizarre behavior. Here we are dealing with individuals who are either temporarily or chronically unable to cope with their problems and evidence severe psychological decompensation. Typically, they require professional help and supervision, often involving hospitalization. Thus, in general, the psychoses are more serious and disabling — at least psychologically — than the neuroses or the psychosomatic disorders. It may be emphasized, however, that there is not always a sharp dividing line between them, particularly between neuroses and psychoses. Occasionally, for example, a neurotic disorder may blend almost imperceptibly into a psychosis if stress and personality decompensation become increasingly severe.

As distinguished from psychoses associated with *organic* brain syndromes, the disorders classified as *functional* psychoses are considered to be primarily psychological in origin. However, genetic and other biological factors often appear to play a significant role in the overall causal pattern. These disorders can be divided into three major categories: (a) schizophrenia, (b) paranoid disorders, consisting of paranoia and paranoid states, and (c) affective disorders, including manic-depressive reactions and involutional melancholia. Psychotic patterns may also be associated with senile brain deterioration and other brain pathology.

Schizophrenia and paranoia are considered to be *thought* disorders, while the affective psychoses are dominated by *mood* disturbances. Paranoid disorders are distinguished from schizophrenia primarily by the narrower limitations of their distortion of reality and by the absense of other psychotic symptoms. We shall deal with schizophrenia and paranoid disorders in this chapter, with the affective disorders in Chapter 10, and with psychoses associated with known brain pathology in Chapter 13. Our discussion of schizophrenia will be detailed, since it is the most common of the functional psychoses and has long served as the "proving ground" in efforts to understand why and how these psychoses develop.

Schizophrenia
Paranoia

Schizophrenia

Schizophrenia is the descriptive term for a group of psychotic disorders characterized by gross distortions of reality; withdrawal from social interaction, and the disorganization and fragmentation of perception, thought, and emotion. While the clinical picture may differ in schizophrenic reactions, the disorganization of experience that typifies acute schizophrenic episodes is well illustrated in the following description:

"Suspicious and frightened, the victim fears he can trust neither his own senses, nor the motives of other people . . . his skin prickles, his head seems to hum, and 'voices' annoy him. Unpleasant odors choke him, his food may have no taste. Bright and colorful visions ranging from brilliant butterflies to dismembered bodies pass before his eyes. Ice clinking in a nearby pitcher seems to be a diabolic device bent on his destruction.

"When someone talks to him, he hears only disconnected words. These words may touch off an old memory or a strange dream. His attention wanders from his inner thoughts to the grotesque way the speaker's mouth moves, or the loud scrape his chair makes against the floor. He cannot understand what the person is trying to tell him, nor why.

"When he tries to speak, his own words sound foreign to him. Broken phrases tumble out over and over again, and somewhat fail to express how frightened and worried he is." (Yolles, 1967, p. 42)

Schizophrenic disorders were at one time attributed to a type of "mental deterioration" beginning in childhood. In 1860 the Belgian psychiatrist Morel described the case of a 13-year-old boy who had formerly been the most brilliant pupil in his school, but who, over a period of time, lost interest in his studies, became increasingly withdrawn, seclusive, and taciturn, and appeared to have fogotten everything he had learned. He talked frequently of killing his father, and evidenced a kind of inactivity that bordered on stupidity. Morel thought the boy's intellectual, moral, and physical functions had deteriorated as a result of hereditary causes and hence were irrecov-

erable. He used the term *démence précoce* (mental deterioration at an early age) to describe the condition.

The Latin form of this term—*dementia praecox*—was subsequently adopted by the German psychiatrist Kraepelin to refer to a group of rather dissimilar conditions that all seemed to have the feature of mental deterioration beginning early in life. Actually, however, the term was rather misleading, since schizophrenia usually becomes apparent not during childhood but during adulthood, and there is no conclusive evidence of permanent mental deterioration.

It remained for a Swiss psychiatrist, Bleuler, to introduce in 1911 a more acceptable descriptive term for this disorder. He used *schizophrenia* (splitting of the personality) because he thought the disorder was characterized primarily by disorganization of thought processes, a lack of coherence between thought and emotion, and an inward orientation away from reality.

Schizophrenia occurs in all societies, from the aborigines of the Australian western desert and the remote interior jungles of Malaysia to the most technologically advanced societies. Apparently mental disorders are not simply the result of the jungle being made of concrete.

In the United States the estimated incidence of schizophrenia is about 1 percent of the population, a figure that has been quite stable over time. About one-fourth of the patients admitted each year to mental hospitals and clinics are diagnosed as schizophrenics, and since schizophrenics often require prolonged or repeated hospitalization, they usually constitute about half the patient population.

Although schizophrenic disorders sometimes occur during childhood or old age, about three-fourths of all first admissions are between the ages of 15 and 45, with a median age of just over 30. The incidence rate is about the same for males and females. Because of its complexity, its high rate of incidence, especially during the most productive years of life, and its tendency to recur and/or become chronic, schizophrenia is considered one of the most serious of all psychotic disorders as well as one of the most baffling.

Clinical picture in schizophrenia

Often schizophrenia develops slowly and insidiously. Thus, the early clinical picture may be dominated by seclusiveness, gradual lack of interest in the surrounding world, excessive daydreaming, blunting of affect, and mildly inappropriate responses. This pattern is referred to as *process schizophrenia,* and the outcome is considered generally unfavorable—partly because the need for treatment usually is not recognized until the behavior pattern has become firmly entrenched. In the majority of cases, however, schizophrenia has a sudden onset, typically marked by intense emotional turmoil and a nightmarish sense of confusion. This pattern, which usually appears to be related to specific precipitating stresses, is referred to as *reactive schizophrenia.* Here the symptoms usually clear up in a matter of weeks, though in some cases an acute episode is the prelude to a more chronic pattern.

In both process and reactive schizophrenia, specific symptoms are legion and vary greatly from one individual to another, as well as with time. The basic experience in schizophrenia, however, seems to be one of disorganization in perception, thought, and emotion. Five categories of symptoms are commonly involved.

Breakdown of perceptual filtering. The normal individual—by means of complex processes of "filtering"—can selectively attend to and cope with the great mass of incoming sensory information to which he is exposed. Thus he perceives his world in an orderly and meaningful way. The schizophrenic, by contrast, is apparently unable to screen out distractions or to discriminate between relevant and irrelevant input. He is highly sensitive to stimuli of all kinds—from both internal and external sources—and is unable to integrate his perceptions into a meaningful pattern.

This point is well illustrated by excerpts from statements made by schizophrenics during the early phases of their breakdowns.

"I feel like I'm too alert . . . everything seems to come pouring in at once . . . I can't seem to keep anything out . . ."

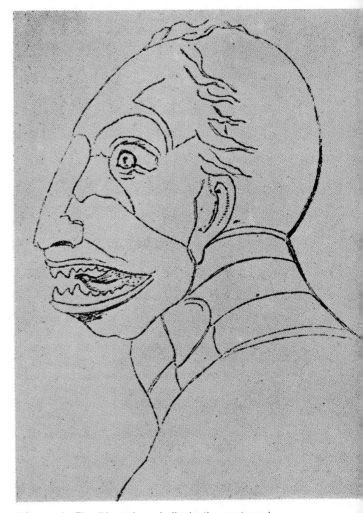

"Ghost of a Flea," based on a hallucination portrayed by William Blake. According to Blake, this flea was in the room and told him that fleas contained the damned souls of bloodthirsty men. Blake, in both his poetry and his etchings, gave many evidences of schizophrenic ideation (Born, 1946).

"My nerves seem supersensitive . . . objects seem brighter . . . noises are louder . . . my feelings are so intense. . . . things seem so vivid and they come at me like a flood from a broken dam."

"It seems like nothing ever stops. Thoughts just keep coming in and racing round in my head . . . and getting broken up . . . sort of into pieces of thoughts and images . . . like tearing up a picture. And everything is out of control . . . I can't seem to stop it."

In these excerpts, we see not only the breakdown of filtering but increased intensity of stimulation and fragmentation of experience.

Disorganization of thought and emotion. Accompanying the breakdown of filtering is a disorganization of thought processes. This includes difficulty in concentrating, impaired ability to sort relevant from irrelevant stimuli and to maintain order in the association of thoughts, and a marked reduction in problem-solving and decision-making ability. As one patient expressed it, "I start out thinking about one problem, but I seem to wander off in the wrong direction and end up thinking about something else without ever knowing how I really got there."

In other instances the patient experiences a sense of being "locked in" on particular themes over which he has no control:

"My mind seems to have a will and direction of its own. It seems to take over my thoughts . . . without telling me what it's up to. Like, you know, this one idea . . . well it keeps going around in my mind . . . and I don't want to think about it . . . but I can't seem to stop. It's . . . well . . . as if . . . my mind were running me."

Since our emotions are strongly influenced by cognitive processes, it is not surprising that the disorganization of thought is accompanied by distortions in affective responses.

"Half the time I am talking about one thing and thinking about half a dozen other things at the same time. It must look queer to people when I laugh about something that has got nothing to do with what I am talking about, but they don't know what's going on inside and how much of it is running round in my head. You see I might be talking about something quite serious to you and other

things come into my head at the same time that are funny and this makes me laugh. If I could only concentrate on the one thing at the one time I wouldn't look half so silly." (McGhie & Chapman, 1961, pp. 109–10)

Often, however, the patient has less insight than this, and his feelings seem as confused and out of control as his thoughts.

Anxiety and panic. Loss of control over one's thoughts and feelings—as when the individual can't filter incoming stimuli and attend selectively, when he is plagued by racing thoughts or "locked in" on a particular theme, and when his thoughts don't line up with his feelings—appears to be an important factor in the intense anxiety and panic that characterize the acute schizophrenic reaction.

Not only does the disorganization of thought and emotion involve the environment, it involves the self-structure as well. The self, which normally functions as the integrating core of the personality, becomes diffused, fragmented, and chaotic. The individual may experience varying degrees of confusion concerning who and what he is, accompanied by some measure of depersonalization. Thus it is not uncommon to hear a patient ask such questions as "Who am I?" "What is happening to me?" "What is the meaning of it all?" Referring to this aspect of her schizophrenic breakdown, one patient recalled:

"Everything seemed different and strange. It was like I had entered an alien world where nothing was the same as I had known it. I no longer knew who I was, or even where the environment left off and I began. I didn't even seem to exist anymore as a distinct person—just parts of me 'floating around' here and there in space."

The loss of control over one's thoughts and feelings, combined with fragmentation of the self and a sense of depersonalization, adds up to acute panic. As one patient expressed it, "It's like no other experience on earth. It's just sheer terror."

Delusions and hallucinations. For many schizophrenics, the inner turmoil and anxiety are accompanied by *delusions*—beliefs maintained despite their logical absurdity or objec-

Comparison of neuroses and functional psychoses

	Neuroses	Functional psychoses
General behavior	Maladaptive avoidance behavior, with mild to moderate impairment of personal and social functioning.	Severe personality decompensation; marked impairment of contact with reality; severe impairment of personal and social functioning.
Nature of symptoms	Wide range of psychological and somatic symptoms, but no hallucinations or other extreme deviations in thought, affect, or action.	Wide range of symptoms, with extreme deviations in thought, affect, and action—e.g., delusions, hallucinations, emotional blunting, bizarre behavior.
Orientation to the environment	Slight, if any, impairment of orientation to environment with respect to time, place, and person.	Frequent loss of orientation to environment with respect to time, place, and person.
Insight (self-understanding)	Frequently some understanding of own maladaptive behavior, but with a seeming inability to change it on one's own.	Markedly impaired understanding of current symptoms and behavior.
Physically destructive behavior	Behavior rarely dangerous or physically injurious to anyone.	In some cases behavior may be dangerous to self or others.
Causal factors	Emphasis on failure to acquire needed competencies, and/or on learned maladaptive behaviors.	Emphasis on maladaptive learning, decompensation under excessive stress, and possible biochemical irregularities.

tive evidence showing they lack any foundation in reality. Thus a patient may develop a delusion of influence, being convinced that his "enemies" are using a complicated electronic device to transmit high-frequency sound waves that interfere with his thought processes or "pour filth" into his mind. The most common types of delusions are summarized on page 296. Such delusions may vary greatly in the degree to which they are organized into a systematic or coherent explanation of the experiences that the schizophrenic is undergoing.

The schizophrenic may also evidence *hallucinations*—the perception of objects and events without any appropriate stimuli. Thus he may hear voices telling him what to do or commenting on or criticizing his actions. In some instances the voices are ascribed to relatives or friends, in others to "enemies" who are interfering with or persecuting him, and in still other cases the messages are received

"from God" or from some organization and tell him of great powers that have been conferred on him or of his mission to save humanity. Occasionally the individual insists that he has not the vaguest idea of the identity of the person or persons talking to him. Often he has difficulty localizing the source of the voices—they may come from a light fixture, from a television set that is not turned on, or even from an imaginary telephone receiver that he holds to his ear. Sometimes the voices seem to come from all directions. Although auditory hallucinations are the most common, visual and other sensory modalities may also be involved. Thus the schizophrenic may see angels in heaven, or smell noxious gas that has been injected into his room, or taste poison in his food. As in the case of delusions, his evaluations of stimuli are distorted by the disorganization and fragmentation of thought and experience. And, of course, delusions and hallucinations may occur at the same time.

Delusions and hallucinations in the psychoses

Delusions and hallucinations of various kinds are among the most characteristic symptoms of psychotic disorders. *Delusions* are irrational beliefs that the individual defends vigorously, despite their logical absurdity and despite objective evidence showing them to be untrue. Some of the most common types of delusions are listed below. *Hallucinations* are perceptions of various kinds of strange objects and events without any appropriate "external" sensory stimuli. As the examples indicate, hallucinations may involve any of the senses.

Delusions

Delusions of reference	Delusional beliefs of an individual that other people are talking about him, referring to him, portraying his life on television, or otherwise making references to him in their activities.
Delusions of influence	Delusional beliefs of an individual that "enemies" are influencing him in various ways, as with complicated electronic gadgets which send out waves that interfere with his thoughts or "pour filth" into his mind.
Delusions of persecution	Delusional beliefs of an individual that he is being deliberately interfered with, discriminated against, plotted against, threatened, or otherwise mistreated.
Delusions of sin and guilt	Delusional beliefs of an individual that he has committed some unforgivable sin that has brought calamity to others, and that he is evil and worthless.
Hypochondriacal delusions	Delusional beliefs relating to having various horrible disease conditions, such as "rotting," being "eaten away," or having one's brain turn to dust.
Delusions of grandeur	Delusional beliefs in which an individual views himself as some great and remarkable person, such as a great economist or inventor, a religious savior, a historical figure, or even God.
Nihilistic delusions	Delusional beliefs associated with the conviction that nothing exists. The individual may insist that he is living in a "shadow world" or that he died several years before and that only his spirit, in a sort of vaporous form, remains.

Hallucinations

Auditory hallucinations	Hallucinations involving the sense of hearing: the individual may hear voices telling him what to do, commenting on or criticizing his actions, or warning him that he will be punished unless he repents.
Visual hallucinations	Hallucinations involving the sense of sight: the individual may see angels in heaven, the pitfires of hell, or just clouds and open space when he is in an enclosed room.
Olfactory hallucinations	Hallucinations involving the sense of smell: the individual may smell poison gas that he believes has been injected into his room by his enemies.
Gustatory hallucinations	Hallucinations involving the sense of taste: the individual may taste poison that he believes to have been put into his food or coffee.
Tactual hallucinations	Hallucinations involving the sense of touch: the individual may feel cockroaches crawling over him or small bugs crawling around under his skin.

Delusions of reference, influence, persecution, and sin and guilt are the most common in the functional psychoses. However, delusions of grandeur, hypochondriacal delusions, and nihilistic delusions are also common. Interestingly enough, delusions of persecution usually develop before those of grandeur. Of the hallucinations, auditory and visual ones are the most common, but olfactory and gustatory hallucinations are not infrequent, especially in association with delusions of persecution. Delusions and hallucinations may result from a variety of biological and psychological conditions. Among these are extreme fatigue, drugs, delirium accompanying fever, brain pathology, sensory deprivation, and exaggeration of ego-defense mechanisms.

Withdrawal from reality. In acute schizophrenic episodes, the individual tends to withdraw temporarily from interaction with others and to become preoccupied with his own inner world of experiencing. In chronic cases, the withdrawal tends to be more enduring; in essence, the individual withdraws from the external world—which he finds highly aversive—into his own private world.

Typically this withdrawal is accompanied by a loss of interest in people and events in the "real" world. For example, a patient may be completely indifferent when informed that her daughter or son has terminal cancer. The degree of such "emotional blunting" varies markedly from one patient to another, but in chronic schizophrenics it is usually pronounced. Efforts to lead or force the patient back into the world of reality are likely to arouse negativistic and hostile behavior. Often, however, even where the patient evidences emotional blunting there is still a residual of acute anxiety underneath his seeming indifference. Thus many patients—in their own way and at their own pace—do attempt to reestablish contact with reality. An extreme example is depicted in Hannah Green's autobiographical novel *I Never Promised You a Rose Garden* (1964), which describes how a young girl—hospitalized for schizophrenia while in her teens—burned herself repeatedly with cigarette butts to relieve intolerable inner pressures and to "prove to herself finally whether or not she was truly made of human substance."

As the preceding example illustrates, the clinical picture in schizophrenia may include bizarre behavior. A patient may exhibit peculiarities of movement, gesture, and expression; act out inappropriate sexual and other fantasies; or simply sit apathetically staring into space. We shall elaborate on these and other behavior anomalies in describing the various types of schizophrenia.

With regard to the clinical picture in schizophrenia, it is relevant to note that (a) not all symptoms occur in a particular case; (b) the symptom picture may differ markedly from one patient to another; (c) the symptom picture may be influenced by the individual's being labeled as a schizophrenic and given a "sick" role; and (d) the symptom picture may vary markedly with time, both episodically and over long-range periods. Most schizophrenics "fade in and out of reality" as a function of their own inner state and the environmental stimuli present. Thus the patient may be in "good contact" one day and evidence delusions and hallucinations the next; or an acute schizophrenic reaction may clear up fairly rapidly or progress to a chronic condition.

Types of schizophrenia

The American Psychiatric Association classification of mental disorders lists ten subtypes of schizophrenia, which are summarized on page 308. We shall consider five of these subtypes in our present discussion: acute, paranoid, catatonic, hebephrenic, and simple. Of these, the acute and paranoid types are the most common.

Acute type. Since most types of schizophrenia are subject to acute episodes, the classification of *acute schizophrenia* as a distinct type may seem somewhat arbitrary.[1] However, this reaction has several distinguishing characteristics. It comes on suddenly, often in a person whose behavior has previously been relatively normal; it is undifferentiated, involving a wide range of symptoms associated with personality disorganization; and the schizophrenic symptoms tend to clear up as the episode abates. Paranoid, catatonic, and other types of schizophrenia, by contrast, have distinct symptom patterns that may be intensified during acute episodes but tend to persist during the course of the disorder.

The case of David F. illustrates the onset of an acute schizophrenic episode (Bowers, 1965). David felt great apprehension about his future as he approached the end of his undergraduate days. He also felt inadequate in his relationship with his girlfriend, Laura—a relationship characterized by emotionally charged separations and reconciliations, as well as by sexual experimentation, in which David frequently doubted his sexual adequacy. When Laura dated another boy and refused to tell

---

[1]The acute type of schizophrenia is also referred to as the *undifferentiated* type.

Diagnostic signs or symptoms of schizophrenia

In an International Pilot Study of Schizophrenia, sponsored by the World Health Organization, investigators from nine countries collected behavioral data on a large number of schizophrenic patients. On the basis of this data, 12 signs or symptoms were delineated which are used for the identification of schizophrenia in many countries throughout the world. Presence of these signs, together with absence of signs followed by (−), favors a diagnosis of schizophrenia. Following the sign or symptom is the diagnostic observation of the sign or examples of questions to elicit the symptom if it is present.

Restricted affect: Blank, expressionless face. Very little or no emotion shown when delusion or normal material is discussed which would usually bring out emotion.

Poor insight: Overall rating of insight.

Thoughts aloud: Do you feel your thoughts are being broadcast, transmitted, so that everyone knows what you are thinking? Do you ever seem to hear your thoughts spoken aloud? (Almost as if someone standing nearby could hear them?)

Waking early (−): Have you been waking earlier in the morning and remaining awake? (Rate positive if 1 to 3 hours earlier than usual.)

Poor rapport: Did the interviewer find it possible to establish good rapport with patient during interview? Other difficulties in rapport.

Depressed facies (−): Facial expression sad, depressed.

Elation (−): Elated, joyous mood.

Widespread delusions: How widespread are patient's delusions? How many areas in patient's life are interpreted delusionally?

Incoherent speech: Free and spontaneous flow of incoherent speech.

Unreliable information: Was the information obtained in this interview credible or not?

Bizarre delusions: Are the delusions comprehensible?

Nihilistic delusions: Do you feel that some part of your body is missing, for example, head, brain, or arms? Do you ever have the feeling that you do not exist at all, that you are dead, dissolved?

Based on Carpenter, Strauss, and Bartko (1973).

David the details, David thought the date had involved intercourse, and he wrote a vindictive poem in which he called Laura a whore. After mailing the poem he felt guilty, and he was quite disturbed to find that his best friend sided with Laura. David began to stay in his room more, attending only a few classes.

The following excerpts from David's diary were written during the month preceding his hospitalization.

". . . and there's old Hawthorne's bosom serpent for you eating away hissing all night I lie there and I lie there and think and think and think all the time trying not to think I think anyway or reminisce rather (delightful pastime) until pow I feel like the top of my head blows off and I smash my fist into something and begin all over again like a one cycle engine." (p. 348)

"Tuesday, March 10, 10 P.M. I can't cope, I can't come to grips . . . it's Hawthorne's disease blazing away, red guilt or little stringy black warts (they're growing with a virulence I swear I never noticed before) . . . music helps a bit and I've conducted the Eroica all over the room three times already today, waving my arms and occasionally hitting things . . . all very dramatic . . . to think I worried myself about sleeping too much last fall! I've given the jargon a once over; it stems from incest drives, castration fears, masturbation complexes, homosexual doubts, oedipal fixations bullshit bullshit it was around before the jargon and its got me . . . already at table I've been making curious unconscious slips as if the synapses suddenly rot away and I come disconnected its all right its all right I'm going to be a lawyer and make lots of money and grow up to be as weak as my father as torn as my mother look ahead!!" (p. 349)

"Midnight Tuesday. . . . Boy, that Nathan and Laura business really pulled the cork I'm bad or mad or just dull? Down on my knees before the crescent moon I got my pants dirty. This is undoubtedly one of the most prolix records of a scarringover process (I'm sealing like one of those puncture proof tires, but in slow motion) I should be back to my habitual state of callousness in a couple of days with no apparent damage, maybe I can even go on staving off like this ("a poem is a momentary stay against confusion" Frost . . . this is quite a poem) till I die." (p. 351)

"Thursday, March 12, 11 A.M. I'm out! I'm through . . . boomed out of the tunnel sometime last night and it's raining stars. . . . whooey . . . its nice out there's time for everything. . . . I can do it I did it and if it happens again I'll do it again twice as hard I got a dexamyl high going and I'm not on dexamyl and I've been up for forty eight or more hours and I'm giddygiddygiddy and I took a test this morning and it was on Voltaire and I kicked him a couple of good ones for being down on Pascal that poor bastard with his shrivelled body and bottomless abysess they're not bottomless!! You get down far enough and it gets thick enough and black enough and then you claw claw claw your way out and pretty soon you're on top again. And I licked it by myself, all alone. No pandering psychiatrists or priests or friends by myself. Now, I must admit I'm a little leery; I dashed back to the typewriter to give it form to write it down and sew it in my vest like Pascal so if the Thing hits me again I'll have this in my vest and I'll kick it in the teeth again but Pascal saw God and yet still it hit him again . . . will it hit me again? Who cares . . . I just sat in on one of those weddings of the soul and I tooted tooted . . . I don't care I can use it I can run on it it will be my psychic gasoline now I don't have to sleep sleep all the time to get away with it . . . but if I lose my typewriter?" (p. 351)

"Saturday, March 14, 11 A.M. . . . Falling asleep last night a thousand million thoughts bubbled then the number the age 18 what happened when I was 18? (my stomach hurts . . . it really physically does . . . that blue bear has all kinds of tricks . . . I'm going out for coffee) Well I DO have to go out to get some money but I MUST be merciless with the blue bear. He has no quarter for me. . . . and not scare myself with eery consequences . . . the newspaper odds are AGAINST automobile deaths, that was the resistance mechanism trying to stop me again I'm hot on your tail blue bear that doesn't mean anything what does that mean it means that I'm feeling the denied homosexual instincts, feeling the woman in me and getting over her that's it that's what Faulkner's bear was a woman I have the quotes up on my wall I wrote them down a week ago. . . . woman is a bear you must kill the bear to be a man no that isn't what I've got on my wall the quotes go 'Anyone could be upset by his first lion.'" (p. 356)

David was hospitalized four days after writing this. His experiences illustrate well the massive breakdown of filtering, the panic at loss of control, and the desperate attempts to understand what is going on that are typical in acute schizophrenia.

The individual does not remain in a state of acute schizophrenia over a sustained period of time. Usually the patient "works through" his problems and recovers in a few weeks or months. However, recurrent episodes are common in the acute type of schizophrenia; in

In some schizophrenic episodes the individual experiences extreme excitement and may engage in impulsive acts which harm himself or others. Formerly such patients were often placed in straitjackets, but improved methods of treatment have made such crude procedures unnecessary.

some instances, the clinical picture changes to a more chronic type of schizophrenic reaction.

Paranoid type. Formerly about one-half of all schizophrenic first admissions to mental hospitals and clinics were of the paranoid type. In recent years, however, the incidence of the paranoid type has shown a substantial decrease, while the acute type has shown a marked increase.

Frequently paranoid type patients show a history of growing suspiciousness and of severe difficulties in interpersonal relationships. The eventual symptom picture is dominated by absurd, illogical, and changeable delusions. Persecutory delusions are the most frequent, and may involve a wide range of ideas and all sorts of plots. The individual may become highly suspicious of his relatives or associates and may complain of being watched, followed, poisoned, talked about, or influenced by electrical devices rigged up by his enemies.

All the attention he receives may lead him to believe that he must possess remarkable qualities or be some great person. Why else would his enemies persecute him? Consequently, he may develop delusions of grandeur and believe that he is the world's greatest economist or philosopher, or some prominent person of the past such as Napoleon. These delusions are frequently accompanied by vivid auditory, visual, and other hallucinations. The patient may hear singing, or God speaking, or the voices of his enemies, or he may see angels or feel electric rays piercing his body at various points.

The individual's behavior becomes centered around these delusions and hallucinations, resulting in loss of critical judgment and in erratic, unpredictable behavior. In response to a command from a "voice" he hears, he may break furniture or commit other violent acts. Occasionally a paranoid schizophrenic can be dangerous, as when he attacks someone he is sure is persecuting him. In general, there is less extreme withdrawal from the outside world than with most other types of schizophrenia. The illogical, delusional picture, together with continued attention to external data that are misinterpreted, is brought out in the following conversation between a doctor and a chronic paranoid schizophrenic.

Dr.: What's your name?
Pt.: Who are you?
Dr.: I'm a doctor. Who are you?
Pt.: I can't tell you who I am.
Dr.: Why can't you tell me?
Pt.: You wouldn't believe me.
Dr.: What are you doing here?
Pt.: Well, I've been sent here to thwart the Russians. I'm the only one in the world who knows how to deal with them. They got their spies all around here though to get me, but I'm smarter than any of them.
Dr.: What are you going to do to thwart the Russians?
Pt.: I'm organizing.
Dr.: Whom are you going to organize?
Pt.: Everybody. I'm the only man in the world who can do that, but they're trying to get me. But I'm going to use my atomic bomb media to blow them up.
Dr.: You must be a terribly important person then.
Pt.: Well, of course.
Dr.: What do you call yourself?
Pt.: You used to know me as Franklin D. Roosevelt.
Dr.: Isn't he dead?
Pt.: Sure he's dead, but I'm alive.
Dr.: But you're Franklin D. Roosevelt?
Pt.: His spirit. He, God, and I figured this out. And now I'm going to make a race of healthy people. My agents are lining them up. Say, who are you?
Dr.: I'm a doctor here.
Pt.: You don't look like a doctor. You look like a Russian to me.
Dr.: How can you tell a Russian from one of your agents?
Pt.: I read eyes. I get all my signs from eyes. I look into your eyes and get all my signs from them.
Dr.: Do you sometimes hear voices telling you someone is a Russian?
Pt.: No, I just look into eyes. I got a mirror here to look into my own eyes. I know everything that's going on. I can tell by the color, by the way it's shaped.
Dr.: Did you have any trouble with people before you came here?
Pt.: Well, only the Russians. They were trying to surround me in my neighborhood. One day they tried to drop a bomb on me from the fire escape.
Dr.: How could you tell it was a bomb?
Pt.: I just knew.

Although there is considerable disorganization in paranoid schizophrenia, it is not so extreme as to cause the person to give up attempts to understand and deal with his condition through delusional interaction with the

THE TRIAL: Schizophrenia in literature

Some students of psychopathology have suggested that "madness" of the schizophrenic may be largely a reflection of the "madness" of society itself. An interesting perspective on this issue is provided by Franz Kafka's novel *The Trial*. The bizarre experiences of its central character—known simply as "Joseph K."—have been interpreted by some readers as a symbolic indictment of social injustice and, by others, as an almost clinical depiction of a paranoid schizophrenic. The following synopsis (Grant, 1956) reflects the latter view. The novel's ending, however, suggests that Joseph K. may have been the victim of something more than his own delusions.

"[The Trial] *begins with the arrest, for no reason he is aware of, of its central figure:* 'Someone must have been telling lies about Joseph K. . . .' *The charge against him is undefined; he is simply informed that he is under arrest, but he is not detained. Called to an interrogation chamber, before an audience, he takes an aggressive attitude and makes accusations of unfair treatment; back of his arrest, he thinks, a* 'great organization' *is at work, by which the innocent are accused of guilt. K. observes the magistrate making a* 'secret sign' *to someone in the audience; he sees* 'artifices'; *he notes certain badges among the onlookers and concludes that they are in league with the magistrate and are there to spy upon him. He observes peculiar movements in the assembly, the people on the right side of the room behaving differently from those on the left. Strange and seemingly irrelevant incidents occur from time to time in the course of the narrative; e.g., K. is distracted, during his speech in the interrogation chamber, by an assault, apparently sexual, by a male spectator upon a* 'washerwoman,' *who turns out later to be connected with the court through her husband, and who promises him aid in his case. Other people, also, who would assumedly be unrelated to the action, are disclosed to have such* 'connections,' *including even some urchin-like girls at play in a tenement. In the same vein K. finds that various people whom he would have supposed were outsiders are familiar with his case; the news has travelled surprisingly. The concept of peculiar* 'signs' *appears again: there is a superstition that one may read, from the expression of a defendant's mouth, the outcome of his case; from the* 'line' *of his own lips, K. is told, people have judged that he will very soon be declared guilty; again, a man to whom he had spoken was shocked to read his own condemnation on K.'s mouth.*

"*Much of the novel is devoted to sustained preoccupation . . . with the details of litigation. . . . An important feature, in this context, is the [implication] that the guilt is subjective, and that the culprit's doom is inescapable. K. himself asserts that the trial is a trial* 'only . . . if I recognize it as such.' *Following his first visit, he returns to the court without being ordered to do so. Though under arrest he is permitted to go about his usual business as a bank executive. There is no indication of force, or mention of physical punishment, imprisonment, etc. The case is a criminal one, but it* 'is not a case before an ordinary court.' *K. feels that he could formulate, himself, all the questions for his own cross-examination; in planning a written defense he considers giving an account of his life, with a moral appraisal of each important action. . . .*

"*It is equally clear that the final judgment will not be determined by the merits of the case. The court is arbitrary, capricious, and irritable. K. is advised that the* 'first plea' *of his case might determine everything, but also that it might be mislaid or even lost altogether. The defense will be difficult because the charge is unknown to the defense counsel as well as to the accused, though later it might be* 'guessed at.' *The right of defense itself, in fact, is merely tolerated, rather than legally recognized. The bringing of a charge is, in fact, equivalent to conviction of guilt, in the eyes of the court; one might as well plead innocence, K. is told, before a row of judges painted on canvas. Actual acquittal is almost unknown; there is* 'ostensible' *acquittal, but this may be followed by a second arrest, a second acquittal by a third arrest and so on.*

"*The unorthodox procedures of the court continue, through a rather eerie tableau in an empty cathedral to a sinister climax; the novel ends when 2 callers walk K., unenlightened yet not unwilling, to a suburban quarry, and there thrust a knife into his heart.*

"*The Trial is notable for the unaccountable actions of its characters, and for bizarre unrealities presented with matter-of-fact and circumstantial realism. More important, the impression is strong that the interest, the motivation for a novel so obsessed with such a theme must be intimately related to something uniquely personal in its author. . . .*" (Grant, 1956, pp. 143–44)

An assassin diagnosed as a chronic paranoid schizophrenic

Sirhan B. Sirhan, the convicted assassin of Senator Robert F. Kennedy, was diagnosed as a chronic paranoid schizophrenic by expert witnesses—psychologists and psychiatrists—appointed by the court.

Although proud of his deed and believing himself to have been a great patriot who acted on behalf of the Arab people (Kennedy had proposed a short time previously that the United States send 50 military aircraft to Israel), Sirhan seemed to have no recollection of the actual assassination. Diamond (1969), who examined Sirhan, suspected that the amnesia covered a psychotic break. He hypnotized Sirhan and was able to observe an entirely different individual, one who vividly remembered killing Kennedy and who was intensely emotional when asked any question about the Arab-Israeli conflict. For example, when asked about a terrifying experience of his boyhood, the bombing of Jerusalem by the Israelis in 1948, Sirhan "suddenly crumpled in agony like a child, sobbing and shivering in terror. The tears poured down his face" (p. 54).

According to Diamond, Sirhan planned the killing under self-hypnosis and lacked conscious awareness of it (see facing page). An example of a "truly split" personality, whose arrogance and "cool front" provided a "simulation of sanity," Sirhan apparently preferred to think of himself as a sane patriot and be convicted of the assassination—rather than face his psychotic behavior and the possibility of being declared criminally insane.

Pages from Sirhan's "trance" notebooks were introduced in evidence at his trial for Robert F. Kennedy's murder. Commenting on them, Diamond (1969) said: "Sirhan's trances obviously took his mind into a voodoo world. He thought he saw Kennedy's face come before him in the mirror, blotting out his own image, and he began to write kill-Kennedy orders to himself . . . 'RFK must die,' he wrote, 'Robert F. Kennedy must be assassinated before June 5, 1968.' . . . Actually his self-hypnosis worked better than he knew. Without real knowledge or awareness of what was happening in the trances, he rigorously programmed himself for the assassination exactly the way a computer is programmed by magnetic tape. In his unconscious mind there existed a plan for the fulfillment of his sick, paranoid hatred of Kennedy and all who might want to help the Jews. In his conscious mind there was no awareness of such a plan or that he, Sirhan, was to be the instrument of assassination" (p. 50). While interesting and persuasive, it may be pointed out that other clinical psychologists or psychiatrists might place a different interpretation on these comments from Sirhan's notebook.

---

world. A case cited by Enders and Flinn (1962)—which represents a typical paranoid schizophrenic reaction—will help fill in the symptom picture for this reaction type. It is a particularly interesting case, since it involves an officer in the Air Force, whose rigorous selection and training procedures screen out individuals with conspicuous emotional difficulties. In addition, the patient had had an excellent service record as a pilot and had tolerated severe combat stress.

"The case to be reported occurred in a 41-year-old command pilot with 7,500 hours, who had flown 135 combat missions . . . in World War II and Korea. At the time of his illness, he was a chief pilot in a command headquarters. He was an excellent pilot . . . and had consistently received superior ratings because of his conscientious and dependable performance. The overt onset of his illness was related to a period of TDY [temporary tour of duty] at a conference where flight procedures on a new type aircraft were being drafted. However, in retrospect, it was learned that for several weeks he had been preoccu-

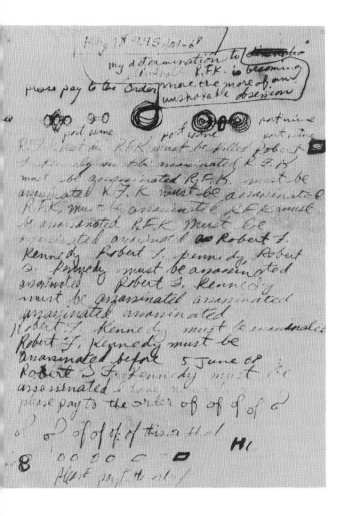

his associates were trying to 'teach' him something, and puzzled them several times when he confronted them with a demand that they tell him openly whatever they wanted him to learn. They became further concerned when he became increasingly upset, tearful and incoherent, and when he did not improve after several days of 'rest' at his brother's home, he was admitted to the hospital.

"On admission, he was suspicious of those about him, wondering whether they were dope-peddlers or communists, and he refused to talk to people who could not assure him they were cleared for top secret. He believed that he was accused of taking dope, that there were concealed microphones about the ward, and he had hallucinations consisting of voices which accused him of being 'queer.' He was often apprehensive and tearful, but this alternated with periods when he was inappropriately jovial. He was oriented in all spheres, and physical and neurological exams were entirely normal.

"A review of the patient's past history revealed no other evidence of emotional disturbance. He was the second of four children of a strict, moralistic, financially successful farm family. He did well in school and one year of college, but always felt inadequate in comparison with his peers. He entered the Air Corps and flew 32B-17 missions in World War II, was separated, then recalled in 1950 and flew 103 combat missions in Korea. He had been married for 18 years and had five children. He used alcohol only rarely, and there was no evidence that toxic or exogenous factors could have been implicated in his psychosis.

"The patient received psychotherapy and began to improve within a few days after admission. For this reason, no drug or other somatic treatment was instituted. He continued to improve over the course of the next several weeks and seemed greatly relieved after telling of an isolated extramarital adventure during the TDY. He gradually gained insight into the unreality of his experiences and was discharged from the hospital after one month."

[Following his discharge from the hospital, the officer was assigned to duties associated with supply and ground training, which he handled without difficulty. Despite his apparent recovery, however, some residuals of his previous thought disturbance remained in the background.]

". . . He wondered at times whether he had not been partly right about the events on TDY, and whether his fellow conferees had not been playing a practical joke on him. He had recently considered going to his Wing Commanding Officer to ask whether the experiences had been part of some kind of 'test' of his mental stability, but had decided against this because it might create an unfavorable impression if he were being tested. He had decided that

pied and upset, had sensed that he could read other people's minds by radio waves, and suspected those with whom he worked of being 'queer.'

"While at the conference, he developed ideas of reference, believing that certain comments which his companions made, or which he heard over the radio, had hidden meanings and were directed toward him. For example, when the conferees spoke of 'take-off,' he did not know whether they were referring to an airplane or a woman, and suspected they were suggesting he should have an illicit sexual relationship. He developed the delusional idea that whatever had happened, it was best forgotten, and through the use of this suppressive mechanism had continued to function effectively. Because of his clear-cut history of a psychotic disorder without an underlying organic basis, as well as the evidence of a continuing minimal thinking disorder, return to flying status was not considered to be consistent with flying safety." (pp. 730–31)

In commenting on this case, Enders and Flinn emphasized the patient's lifelong rigid, moralistic code, which made him unable to tolerate an impulse toward promiscuous behavior. As a result, he projected this unethical impulse to outside agencies; he now misconstrued comments heard on the radio or made by his companions as suggesting illicit activities.

Catatonic type. Catatonic reactions often make their appearance with dramatic suddenness, but usually the patient has shown a background of eccentric behavior, often accompanied by some degree of withdrawal from reality.

The APA classification distinguishes between *excited* and *withdrawn* catatonic schizophrenia, the first marked by "excessive and sometimes violent motor activity," the other by "generalized inhibition manifested by stupor, mutism, negativism, or waxy flexibility" (pp. 33–34). Many catatonics alternate between periods of extreme withdrawal and extreme excitement, but in most cases one reaction or the other is predominant. In a study of 250 patients labeled as catatonic schizophrenics, Morrison (1973) found that 110 were predominantly withdrawn, 67 predominantly excited, and 73 were considered "mixed." No significant differences were found between these groups with regard to age, sex, or education.

In the withdrawal reaction there is a loss of all animation and a tendency to remain motionless in a rigid, stereotyped position—mute and staring into space. The same position may be maintained for hours or even days, and the hands and feet may become blue and swollen because of the immobility. A patient may feel that he has to hold his hand out flat because the forces of "good" and "evil" are waging a "war of the worlds" on his hand; and if he moves it he may tilt the precarious balance in favor of the forces of evil. Surprisingly, despite his apparent lack of attention to his environment while in this condition, he may later relate in detail events that were going on around him.

Some of these patients are highly suggestible and will automatically obey commands or imitate the actions of others (*echopraxia*) or repeat phrases in a stereotyped way (*echolalia*). If the patient's arm is raised to an awkward and uncomfortable position, he may maintain it in this attitude for minutes or even hours. Ordinarily, however, a patient in a catatonic stupor is extremely negativistic. He is apt to resist stubbornly any effort to change his position and may become mute, resist all attempts to feed him, and refuse to comply with even the slightest request. He pays no attention to bowel or bladder control and saliva may drool from his mouth. The patient's facial expression typically becomes vacant, and his skin appears waxy. Threats and painful stimuli have no effect, and he has to be dressed and washed and have his eliminative processes taken care of.

Suddenly and without warning, the catatonic patient may pass from a state of extreme withdrawal to one of great excitement, during which he seems to be under great "pressure of activity." He may talk or shout excitedly and incoherently, pace rapidly back and forth, openly indulge in sexual activities such as masturbation, mutilate himself or attempt suicide, or impulsively attack and attempt to kill other persons. The suddenness and the extreme frenzy of these attacks make such patients very dangerous to both themselves and others. The excitement may last a few hours, days, or even weeks.

The following case illustrates some of the symptoms typical of catatonic reactions.

On admission, the patient, a 35-year-old male, appeared apathetic and withdrawn. He would answer questions only after they had been repeated several times and then his speech was so indistinct that it was difficult to understand what he said. After a period of 3 weeks on the ward, his behavior underwent a rather dramatic shift and he became mildly excited, heard the voice of God talking to him, and spent a good deal of time on his knees praying aloud. He occasionally turned to other patients and beseeched them to "get religion" before the devil

Art by emotionally disturbed patients

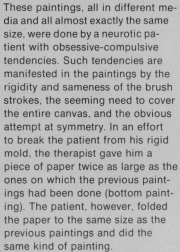

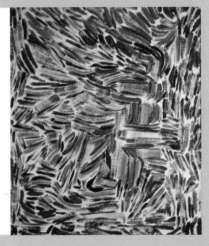

These paintings, all in different media and all almost exactly the same size, were done by a neurotic patient with obsessive-compulsive tendencies. Such tendencies are manifested in the paintings by the rigidity and sameness of the brush strokes, the seeming need to cover the entire canvas, and the obvious attempt at symmetry. In an effort to break the patient from his rigid mold, the therapist gave him a piece of paper twice as large as the ones on which the previous paintings had been done (bottom painting). The patient, however, folded the paper to the same size as the previous paintings and did the same kind of painting.

In these paintings of cats (above and on opposite page) by the English artist Louis Wain (1860–1939), there is a transition from realistic and recognizable portraits to representations that become more stylized and ornamental—so bizarre and abstract that they bear little resemblance to their subjects.

Wain was a well-known popular artist who drew pictures of cats in human situations, such as the one shown at left done in 1922. In the mid-1920s he suffered a schizophrenic breakdown and from then on was confined to mental institutions for most of his life. He continued to paint, however, and stuck with his chosen subject even during various schizophrenic episodes. Wain's art is remarkable for the clues it provides to his changing mental state and the distortions of perception characteristic of schizophrenia.

A male patient diagnosed as suffering from undifferentiated schizophrenia did hundreds of paintings over a period of about nine years; in these, the tops of the heads of males were always missing, but females were complete. In an attempt to maneuver the patient into a position to complete a man's head, the therapist drew the outine of a suit of clothes on a canvas (right), low enough so that a head would logically fit in the picture, and urged the patient to finish the drawing. However, the patient only finished the suit.

Another manifestation of this patient's disorder was his inability to communicate verbally: he spoke only in a "word salad." However, when asked about his life, he would often draw a "comic strip" that told a story, such as the one on the opposite page.

These three paintings are part of a series of approximately 20 paintings done over a six-month period by a patient diagnosed as an anxiety neurotic. The first painting indicates great hostility toward women, evidenced by the beetle on the forehead, pointed ears, and bald head. At this stage also the patient, while showing some obvious art ability, had difficulty finishing the painting, especially the background and edges.

The second painting was done after about three months in therapy. The fragmentation of the image was interpreted as indicating the patient's feelings of ambivalence and confusion at this stage.

The same woman is shown in the third painting at right, but she now has hair, the scarab is gone from her forehead, the pointed ears are modified, and her facial expression is less hostile. The patient, while not completely relieved of his hostility and paranoia toward women, was considered to have reached a point where he could express his feelings in a socially acceptable manner.

Both the pen-and-ink drawing (above) and the painting shown (left) were done by the same artist, a young male patient diagnosed as schizophrenic, paranoid type. Although at first glance the two works seem completely different, there are similarities that indicate the patient's symptoms, though they are shown in a more ''conventional'' manner in the drawing. The concentration on the self as subject matter is typical of schizophrenia; the paranoid delusional tendencies are shown by the watchful eyes and the grasping hands, which become like claws and tentacles in the painting. Both pieces of art are filled with symbols meaningful to the patient; the drawing, done during a time when the patient was in a very religious phase, has obvious Christ-like overtones, while the symbols of the painting are more obscure.

A

C

D

B

A patient diagnosed as schizophrenic, paranoid type, was unable to respond at all when asked by the therapist to do an original drawing; therefore, with the therapist's aid, a picture (A) was selected from a magazine for the patient to copy. One of his first attempts was picture B, a pencil drawing on manila paper. The great visual distortion, as well as the inability to use colors or perspective and to distinguish or reproduce letters of the alphabet, is a common manifestation of schizophrenia. The evident visual distortion was also a diagnostic aid for the psychologist, who was able to learn from it that the patient, who was extremely fearful, saw everything in this distorted way, partially causing his fear. In picture C the patient has shown obvious improvement, although it was not until about a year after therapy began that he was able to execute a painting with the realism of picture D.

got them. During this period the following conversation occurred with the ward physician:

Dr.: How are you today, Mr. ———?

Pt.: I am fighting, doctor—fighting sin and evil.

Dr.: Sin and evil?

Pt.: Yes, sin and evil. You know what sin and evil are, and you should be down here praying with me for your salvation. . . . God knows the answers. He has imparted some of his knowledge to Churchill. He knows but others are confused. He is the true hero of the British Empire. The Bible states that "By a man's actions ye shall judge him," and he is a man of action.

Dr.: Do you feel that you have found any answers?

Pt.: I am fighting, doctor. The devil tries to confuse you, but I am fighting. Why do people die, doctor? Why did my mother have to die? That's the crucial point, how can you beat sin and evil, how can you keep from moral and physical decay? God has all the answers!

On one occasion the patient impulsively attacked another patient on the ward who had asked him if he was trying to polish the ward floor with his knees. Afterwards, he stated that it was the devil who directed the attack.

The catatonic's immobility is apparently a way of coping with his reduced filtering ability and increased vulnerability to stimulation: it seems to give him a feeling of some control over external sources of stimulation though not necessarily over inner ones. Freeman has cited the explanation advanced by one patient: "I did not want to move, because if I did everything changed around me and upset me horribly so I remained still to hold onto a sense of permanence" (1960, p. 932).

Hebephrenic type. Hebephrenic reactions usually occur at an earlier age and represent a more severe disintegration of the personality than the other types of schizophrenia. Typically the individual has a history of oddness, over-scrupulousness about trivial things, and preoccupation with religious and philosophical issues. He frequently broods over the dire results of masturbation and minor infractions of social conventions. While his schoolmates are enjoying normal play and social activities, he is gradually becoming more seclusive and more preoccupied with his fantasies.

As the disorder progresses, the individual becomes emotionally indifferent and infantile in his reactions. A silly smile and inappro-

The creator of this macabre drawing of a "tree man," who holds a bleeding human head, was a hebephrenic girl who described her creation as a "comical print." Preoccupation with bizarre fantasies is characteristic of hebephrenic schizophrenics.

priate, shallow laughter after little or no provocation are common symptoms. If asked the reason for his laughter, the patient may state that he does not know, or he may volunteer some wholly irrelevant and unsatisfactory explanation. Speech becomes incoherent, and there may be considerable baby talk, childish giggling, a repetitious use of similar sounding words, and a derailing of thought along the lines of associated meanings that may give a punlike quality to speech. In some instances speech becomes completely incoherent.

Hallucinations, particularly auditory ones, are common. The "voices" may accuse the patient of immoral practices, "pour filth" into his mind, and call him vile names. Delusions are usually of a sexual, religious, hypochondriacal, or persecutory nature and are changeable and fantastic. For example, the patient may insist not only that he is being followed by enemies but that he has already been killed a number of times. In occasional cases, the patient becomes hostile and aggressive. Peculiar mannerisms and other bizarre forms of behavior appear. These may take the form of word salad (meaningless, stereotyped repetition of words or sentences), facial grimaces, talking and gesturing to himself, sudden inexplicable laughter and weeping, and in some cases an abnormal interest in urine and feces, which the patient may smear on walls and even on his person. Obscene behavior and absence of any modesty or sense of shame are characteristic. Although outbursts of anger and temper tantrums may occur in connection with his fantasy life, the patient is indifferent to real-life situations, no matter how horrifying or gruesome they may be.

The clinical picture in hebephrenic schizophrenia is well illustrated in the following interview:

The patient was a divorcée, 32 years of age, who had come to the hospital with bizarre delusions, hallucinations, and severe personality disintegration and with a record of alcoholism, promiscuity, and possible incestuous relations with a brother. The following conversation shows typical hebephrenic responses to questioning.

    Dr.: How do you feel today?
    Pt.: Fine.
    Dr.: When did you come here?
    Pt.: 1416, you remember, doctor (silly giggle).

    Dr.: Do you know why you are here?
    Pt.: Well, in 1951 I changed into two men. President Truman was judge at my trial. I was convicted and hung (silly giggle). My brother and I were given back our normal bodies 5 years ago. I am a policewoman. I keep a dictaphone concealed on my person.
    Dr.: Can you tell me the name of this place?
    Pt.: I have not been a drinker for 16 years. I am taking a mental rest after a "carter" assignment or "quill." You know, a "penwrap." I had contracts with Warner Brothers Studios and Eugene broke phonograph records but Mike protested. I have been with the police department for 35 years. I am made of flesh and blood—see, doctor (pulling up her dress).
    Dr.: Are you married?
    Pt.: No. I am not attracted to men (silly giggle). I have a companionship arrangement with my brother. I am a "looner" . . . a bachelor.

Simple type. Simple schizophrenia is characterized by a slow and progressive onset. Beginning fairly early in life, often during adolescence, there is a gradual reduction in external interests and attachments. The individual no longer cares whether he passes or fails in school, he withdraws from social relationships, and he no longer is concerned about his family or friends. Conversation becomes increasingly scanty and trivial, personal hygiene and appearance are neglected, interest in the opposite sex declines, and the individual has increasing difficulty concentrating on anything other than his own inner world of thoughts and fantasies. He makes no effort to work or assume responsibility, and seems content to lead a simple, indifferent, parasitic existence. Although such persons may show episodes of irritability and overt aggression, there is not the dramatic psychotic flare-up that we saw in the acute schizophrenic reaction. Rather, there is a progressive and insidious depletion of thought, affect, and behavior.

Lecturing, pleading, and encouragement by well-meaning family members are of no avail and often lead to obstinate, negativistic, and evasive behavior. But despite the individual's intellectual and emotional withdrawal, his mental functions may not be markedly impaired or disintegrated.

The following interview with a male patient who was diagnosed as a schizophrenic, simple type, illustrates the apathy and indifference typical of such patients.

Dr.: Do you know who I am?

Pt.: A doctor, I suppose.

Dr.: How do you feel?

Pt.: Oh—OK, I guess.

Dr.: Do you know where you are?

Pt.: It's a hospital.

Dr.: Why are you here?

Pt.: I don't know. . . . I don't think I should be here. I'm all right.

Dr.: Where would you rather be?

Pt.: I don't care, just out. . . . I don't know. Maybe with some fellows or something. I don't care. There were some guys I used to know.

Dr.: What did you do with those fellows?

Pt.: I don't know—just go around.

Dr.: How do you like it here?

Pt.: I don't know, I don't care. It's all right, I guess. I liked the boys though. I used to know them.

Dr.: And you used to like them?

Pt.: Yes—they were all right, I guess.

Dr.: Who is "they"?

Pt.: Some men. I don't know them by name.

Dr.: Can you think of any reason why you should be here?

Pt.: No, I'm all right. I feel all right. I'd like to be with the fellows I used to know.

Dr.: Are there any fellows here you like?

Pt.: I don't know. They're all right, I guess.

Dr.: Do you think the men who brought you here had it in for you?

Pt.: No. They were nice to me. They were all right. They didn't have it in for me or hate me or anything.

Dr.: Do you ever hear strange noises?

Pt.: No, I never do that. I'm not crazy.

This patient was hospitalized on the complaint of his sister-in-law, who stated that he had tried to force her at the point of a gun to have sexual relations with him. On admission to the hospital the patient appeared rather indifferent about the whole matter and explained that it must have been some "temporary impulse."

Although 30 years of age, the patient had been living with his parents and was completely dependent on them. His educational background was good. He made an A average in high school, but during his first year of college he lost interest in his studies and refused to attend classes despite his parents' pleadings. His parents then did their best to help him achieve some vocational adjustment, but the patient seemed indifferent to their efforts and hopes for him. After leaving college he did take several part-time jobs, including one in a grocery store, which he lost soon after because of his listless attitude and indifference to his duties. Thereafter he would neither look for nor accept work and was quite content to remain dependent on his parents. Although rather handsome, he had never gone out with girls. When questioned on this subject he stated that "I'm not interested in girls. All they ever do is get you in trouble."

Many simple schizophrenics are able to get by in the outside world. They may be cared for by their families, particularly during adolescence and early adulthood; or they may be able to support themselves through simple clerical or manual work. They usually make little or no progress in their jobs, resist efforts to change or complicate their routines, and impress others as being rather odd or stupid—curiously inaccessible, isolated, colorless, and uninteresting.

Careful study of patients who are hospitalized often reveals that episodes involving delusions, hallucinations, and bizarre behavior—such as the attempted rape by the patient described in the preceding case history—are not uncommon. However, psychological disorganization is typically less severe than in other types of schizophrenia, and some superficial contact with reality is usually maintained.

As we noted, the acute type of schizophrenia has become the most common, although the paranoid type still occurs frequently in chronic mental hospital populations. The other three types of so-called hard-core schizophrenia—catatonic, hebephrenic, and simple—are becoming relatively rare (Straker, 1974; Kuriansky, Deming, & Gurland, 1974). It may also be pointed out that these various subtypes are part of a more generalized clinical picture of schizophrenia, and it is not always possible or relevant to distinguish between them.

Summary of types of schizophrenia

Acute type — Characterized by a sudden onset of undifferentiated schizophrenic symptoms, often involving perplexity, confusion, emotional turmoil, delusions of reference, excitement, dreamlike dissociation, depression, and fear. The individual seems to undergo a massive breakdown of filtering processes, with the result that experience becomes fragmented and disorganized, taking on the qualities of a nightmare.

Paranoid type — A symptom picture dominated by absurd, illogical, and changeable delusions, frequently accompanied by vivid hallucinations, with a resulting impairment of critical judgment and erratic, unpredictable, and occasionally dangerous behavior. In chronic cases, there is usually less disorganization of behavior than in other types of schizophrenia, and less extreme withdrawal from social interaction.

Catatonic type — Often characterized by alternating periods of extreme withdrawal and extreme excitement, although in some cases one or the other reaction predominates. In the withdrawal reaction there is a sudden loss of all animation and a tendency to remain motionless for hours or even days, in a stereotyped position. The clinical picture may undergo an abrupt change, with excitement coming on suddenly, wherein the individual may talk or shout incoherently, pace rapidly, and engage in uninhibited, impulsive, and frenzied behavior. In this state, the individual may be dangerous.

Hebephrenic type — Usually occurs at an earlier age than most other types of schizophrenia, and represents a more severe disintegration of the personality. Emotional distortion and blunting typically are manifested in inappropriate laughter and silliness, peculiar mannerisms, and bizarre, often obscene, behavior.

Simple type — An insidious depletion of thought, affect, and behavior, beginning early in life and gradually progressing until the individual impresses others as being curiously inaccessible, isolated, colorless, and uninteresting. Because psychological disorganization is typically less severe than in other types of schizophrenia and some superficial contact with reality is usually maintained, hospitalization is less frequent.

Schizo-affective type — Characterized by a mixture of general schizophrenic symptoms, in conjunction with more pronounced obvious depression or elation — not typical of the usual surface pattern of "flattened affect."

Latent type — Characterized by various symptoms of schizophrenia but lacking a history of a full-blown schizophrenic episode.

Chronic undifferentiated type — Although manifesting definite schizophrenic symptoms in thought, affect, and behavior, not readily classifiable under one of the other types.

Residual type — Mild indications of schizophrenia shown by individuals in remission following a schizophrenic episode.

Childhood type — Preoccupation with fantasy, and markedly atypical and withdrawn behavior prior to puberty.

Biological factors in schizophrenia

Despite extensive research on schizophrenia, the etiology of this disorder is still unclear. Responsibility for its development has been attributed primarily to (a) biological factors, including heredity and various biochemical and neurophysiological processes; (b) psychological and interpersonal factors, including faulty learning, pathogenic interpersonal and family patterns, and decompensation under excessive stress; and (c) sociocultural factors, focusing on the role of pathological social conditions in determining the types and incidence of schizophrenic reactions. These three sets of factors are not mutually exclusive, of course, and may occur in varying combinations or causal patterns.

Heredity. In view of the disproportionate incidence of schizophrenia in the family backgrounds of schizophrenic patients, a number of investigators have concluded that genetic factors must play an important causal role. Evidence remains "circumstantial," however, based on demonstrations of high rates of schizophrenia—known as *concordance rates*—among close relatives of schizophrenics.

1. *Twin studies.* These studies are designed to find out whether the concordance rate is greater for *identical* (monozygotic) twins, who develop from a single fertilized egg and share the same genetic inheritance, than it is for *fraternal* twins, whose genetic inheritance is comparable to that of siblings.

While the incidence of schizophrenia among twins is no greater than for the general population, we noted in Chapter 5 that Kallmann (1953, 1958) found a much higher concordance rate among identical than fraternal twins—86.2 percent as contrasted with 14.5 percent, respectively. In a number of other early studies, concordance rates varied markedly, but typically ranged from about 60 to 75 percent for identical and 10 to 15 percent for fraternal twins. These findings contrast with an incidence figure for the general population of approximately 1 percent.

More recent studies using refinements in methodology have reported substantially lower concordance rates for twins. In a major study in Norway, Kringlen (1967) found a 38 percent concordance rate for identical twins as contrasted with 10 percent for fraternal twins; Cohen, Allen, Pollin, and Hruber (1972), studying a large sample of twin pairs who were veterans of the American armed forces, found a concordance rate of 23.5 percent for identical and 5.3 percent for fraternal twins.[2] Similarly, Gottesman and Shields (1972) found a concordance rate of 42 percent for identical and 9 percent for fraternal twins. They also found that the concordance was much higher for twins with severe schizophrenic disorders than for those with mild schizophrenic symptoms. In severe cases, when one identical twin became schizophrenic, it was usually just a question of time before the other did also.

Despite the differences in exact figures for concordance rates, these studies leave little doubt that the schizophrenia rate for identical twins is over 30 times greater than one would expect in the general population. Thus it is not surprising that all the preceding investigators emphasized the important role of genetic factors in the etiology of schizophrenia. Yet it should also be emphasized that the *discordance* rate for schizophrenia in identical twins is greater than the *concordance* rate; that is, there are far more identical twins who are discordant for schizophrenia than there are who are concordant. If schizophrenia were solely the result of genetic factors, the concordance rate for identical twins would approximate 100 percent.

2. *Children reared apart from their schizophrenic mothers.* Several studies have attempted to eliminate the possible influence of being raised by schizophrenic parents as a causal factor of schizophrenia. In a follow-up study of 47 persons who had been born to schizophrenic mothers in a state mental hospital and placed with relatives or in foster homes shortly after birth, Heston (1966) found that 16.6 percent of these subjects were later diagnosed as schizophrenic. In contrast, none of the 50 control subjects selected from

---

[2]The lower concordance rates in the Cohen et al. (1972) study may be partially explained by the fact that the veteran sample was not representative of the general twin population, since it consisted entirely of men who had been considered fit for military service.

Schizophrenia and drug-induced "model psychoses"

The similarities between the symptoms of schizophrenia and those produced by certain psychoactive drugs, particularly LSD, mescaline, and psilocybin, led many investigators to speculate that their biochemical basis may be similar. But schizophrenia and "model psychoses" produced by the preceding drugs differ significantly, not only in many particular respects, but, most importantly, in overall pattern.

	Schizophrenic reactions	Drug-induced "model psychoses"
Mood	Daydreaming and extreme withdrawal from personal contacts, ranging from sullen reluctance to talk to actual muteness.	Dreaming, introspective state, but preference for discussing visions and ruminations with someone.
Communication	Speech vague, ambiguous, difficult to follow; no concern about inability to communicate; past tense common.	Speech rambling or incoherent but usually related to reality; subjects try to communicate thoughts; present tense used.
Irrationality	Great preoccupation with bodily functions; illnesses attributed to unreasonable causes (the devil, "enemies").	Great interest in the vast array of new sensations being experienced; symptoms attributed to reasonable causes.
Hallucinations	Frequent, very "real" hallucinations, usually auditory and extremely threatening.	Hallucinations predominantly visual; rare auditory hallucinations not so personal or threatening; subjects attempt to explain them rationally.
Delusions	Delusions common, usually of reference, persecution, and grandeur.	Delusions rare; occurrence probably due to individual personality conflicts.
Mannerisms	Bizarre mannerisms, postures, and even waxy flexibility manifested by certain patients.	Strange and bizarre repetitive mannerisms rare.

These findings proved disappointing and led to reduced interest in drug-induced model psychoses. However, more recent and sophisticated research—particularly focusing on the effects of the amphetamines on "neurotransmitters," such as dopamine, which can facilitate or disrupt information processing in the central nervous system—has revived interest in the study of drug-induced psychoses. For example, Ellinwood, Sudilovsky, and Nelson (1973) noted a distinctive symptom pattern among patients being treated in a clinic setting for chronic abuse of amphetamines in amounts ranging from 150 to 2000 mg per day. This pattern was characterized by "delusions of persecution, ideas of reference, visual and auditory hallucinations, changes in body image, hyperactivity, agitation, and panic" (p. 1088).

Because of permanent damage to the nervous system resulting from the chronic abuse of amphetamines, this drug cannot ethically be used on human volunteers. Preliminary findings on laboratory animals, including primates, however, have produced results comparable to those reported by Ellinwood and his associates for human patients. These results have led to intensified research on drug-induced model psychoses, and on the application of such findings to understanding possible imbalances in dopamine and other neurotransmitters in schizophrenia.

among residents of the same foster homes—and whose mothers were not schizophrenic—later became schizophrenic. In addition to the greater probability of being labeled schizophrenic, the offspring of schizophrenic mothers were more likely to be diagnosed as mentally retarded, neurotic, and sociopathic. They also had been involved more frequently in criminal activities, and had spent more time in penal institutions. Thus Heston concluded that children born to schizophrenic mothers, even when reared without contact with them, were more likely not only to become schizophrenic but also to suffer a wide spectrum of other disorders.

Other studies of children having schizophrenic mothers and/or fathers but adopted at an early age and reared by presumably normal parents have found from 20 to 31.6 percent developing disorders in the "schizophrenic spectrum" (Rosenthal, 1970; Rosenthal et al., 1971; Wender, 1972; Wender, Rosenthal, & Kety, 1974).

3. *Family studies.* Another line of research has studied the incidence of schizophrenia among children reared by their schizophrenic parents. A review of the literature led Heston (1970) to report that about 45 percent of the children who have one schizophrenic parent would later become schizoid (borderline) or actually schizophrenic. The corresponding statistic for children with two schizophrenic parents approached 66 percent.

In a similar review, Rieder (1973) found a wide spectrum of psychopathology reported among the adult offspring of schizophrenics, ranging from schizophrenia to sociopathic disorders. The offspring of schizophrenic parents also showed a high incidence of psychological maladjustment as children—estimated at 20 percent—with two types being prominent, a withdrawn schizoid type and a hyperactive, asocial, delinquent type. Thus Rieder, too, concluded that the offspring of schizophrenics differ from the offspring of controls with nonschizophrenic parents.

Available research studies do indicate that genetic factors play an important role in the etiology of schizophrenia. But assuming that there is an inherited predisposition to schizophrenia, it would not appear to be an "all-or-nothing" factor but rather one of degree. Thus

---

"High-risk" children for schizophrenia

Research findings are making it increasingly possible to identify children who are "high risks" for the later development of schizophrenia, and to observe them over time to see if they do in fact develop schizophrenia.

Four groups of children are regarded as high risk: (a) children with schizophrenic mothers; (b) children with a history of serious prenatal or birth difficulties; (c) children who show unsocialized behavior, including extreme aggressiveness; and (d) children in highly aversive sociocultural environments.

As Rolf and Harig (1974) have pointed out, such studies have disadvantages as well as possible advantages. Studies of high-risk children must be carried out over a period of many years and are expensive; in addition, there is always the possibility that the factors being assessed will not prove to be of causal significance in schizophrenia. On the other hand, well-controlled studies can yield useful information about specific factors, and where such factors are of predictive value can pave the way for early therapeutic intervention and prevention.

---

a mild degree of predisposition presumably would lead to schizophrenia only in persons subjected to severe stress. On the other hand, a high degree of predisposition would increase the probability of becoming schizophrenic, since stress factors would be less important. Despite the forcefulness of this viewpoint, however, further research in this area is needed. This is not intended to minimize the importance of genetic factors in schizophrenia, but merely to emphasize that their specific role is at present unknown.

Biochemical factors. Research into the possibility of biochemical abnormalities in schizophrenic patients was given impetus when it was shown that the presence of some chemical agents in the bloodstream, even in minute amounts, can produce profound mental changes. Lysergic acid (LSD) and mescaline, for example, can lead to a temporary disorganization of thought processes and a variety of psychotic-like symptoms that have been referred to as "model psychoses." Such findings

After intensive study of schizophrenics and their offspring over time, Bleuler (1974) came to the following
conclusions:

*"One of the most lasting impressions brought home to
me by the family studies of our subjects is the fact that
even normal offspring who are successful in life can
never fully free themselves from the pressures imposed
by memories of their schizophrenic parents and their
childhood. Once one knows them intimately, it is not
rare to hear, as from the depths of their hearts, a long-
drawn sigh, and something like: 'When you've gone
through that . . . you can never really be happy, you can
never laugh as others do. You always have to be
ashamed of yourself and take care not to break down
yourself.' Children of schizophrenics commonly feel
that they are incompetent as partners in love or marriage, and could in no way assume the awesome responsibility of putting children of their own into the
world. Many eventually overcome such inhibitions. But
others never do; they plunge into their jobs and reject a
normal family life."* (p. 106)

Bleuler goes on to point out that many schizophrenics
can be good parents, and that their children do not
experience an unfavorable environment. In addition,
such children may learn to distinguish between what is
strange and "sick" and what is good and lovable in
their parent. On the other hand, as we have seen, subtle
emotional scars may remain.

encouraged investigators to look for an *endogenous hallucinogen*—a chemical arising within the body under stressful conditions—that
might account for the hallucinations and disorganization of thought and affect in schizophrenia and other psychotic disorders.

Perhaps the most exciting early finding was
that made by Heath and his associates at the
Tulane Medical School (1957, 1958). Using
two volunteers—convicts from the Louisiana
State Prison—these investigators were able to
produce manifestations of schizophrenia by
injecting *taraxein,* a substance obtained from
the blood of schizophrenic patients. One subject developed a brief catatonic type of reaction, the other a paranoid type.

In a series of follow-up studies, taraxein
was administered to additional nonpsychotic
volunteers, all of whom developed schizophrenic-like symptoms. The characteristic reaction
was mental blocking with disorganization and
fragmentation of thought processes. Other
common symptoms included delusions of reference, persecution, and grandeur; auditory
hallucinations; and subjective complaints of
depersonalization. The onset of the symptoms
was gradual, reaching a peak between 15 and
40 minutes following the injection and then
subsiding. In an additional experiment, rapid
blood transfusions were made from schizophrenic to normal subjects; the latter developed mild schizophrenic-like symptoms that
cleared up within an hour. On the basis of
these findings, it was concluded that there is a
metabolic defect in schizophrenia, perhaps
inherited, that is activated by severe stress.

Further studies by Heath and his associates
(1967, 1970) produced similar findings, leading
them to conclude that schizophrenia is a disease in which the body manufactures antibodies that act against its own brain cells. Presumably when the guilty antibody, taraxein,
reaches the brain, it disrupts the passage of
information from one cell to another and
hence the processing of information. Unfortunately—as in so many biochemical studies—
the findings of Heath and his associates have
not been generally supported by other investigators, at least in the United States. However,
Dearing (1969) has cited Russian research
supporting Heath's views of autoimmunolog-
ical antibodies produced by the human brain
under stress.

A number of other research reports have
provided promising leads to the possible role
of biochemical alterations in schizophrenia.
On the basis of his studies, Himwich (1970)
concluded that schizophrenics are "biologically different" and consequently convert certain
chemicals in their bodies into *psychotogenic*
(psychosis-producing) agents when they are
placed under stress. Strong support for this
conclusion has been provided by the findings
of Mandell, Segal, Kuczenski, and Knapp
(1972), who found an enzyme in the human
brain that can convert normal neural trans-
mitter chemicals, such as serotonin, into hal-
lucinogen-like compounds.

Once it was shown that the human brain
has the potential for making its own hallucino-

gens, it seemed only another step to demonstrate a simple chemical basis for psychosis. However, it soon became apparent that the regulatory processes of the brain are well designed to deal with such imbalances. In addition, no evidence was found that schizophrenics show a higher level of such hallucinogenic chemicals than non-psychotics. Finally, where such chemical imbalances do occur, they could result from rather than be the cause of schizophrenic disorders. Thus the probability of a single psychotic agent accounting for schizophrenia seems remote. This conclusion does not exclude the likelihood, however, that biochemical factors may play an important role in the total causal pattern.

Neurophysiological factors. A good deal of research has focused on the role of neurophysiological disturbances in schizophrenia. These disturbances are thought to include an imbalance in excitatory and inhibitory processes and inappropriate arousal to stress.

1. *Excitatory and inhibitory processes.* This line of investigation goes back to the early work of Pavlov (1941), who suggested that schizophrenics have abnormally excitable nervous systems. A key concept here is that, under intense stimulation, a process of protective ("transmarginal") inhibition occurs, which reduces the person's general level of excitability and reactivity. If the intense stimulation is sustained, however, there is a change in the process of protective inhibition, so that the normal relationship between strength of stimulation and excitation is reversed. Strong stimulation still results in inhibition, but weak stimuli are now capable of producing the cortical excitation that formerly were produced only by strong stimuli. Consequently, the individual may have difficulty distinguishing relevant from irrelevant stimuli, and may confuse vague memories, fears, and fantasies with present reality. No longer able to distinguish clearly between fact and fantasy, he falls prey to delusions and hallucinations.

2. *Arousal and disorganization.* Closely related to the concept of disturbances in excitatory and inhibitory processes is the view that schizophrenia may result in part from

---

The "reproductive fitness" of schizophrenics

A puzzling problem in the genetics of schizophrenia is the general estimate that the "reproductive fitness" of schizophrenics is not greater than 70 percent, mainly because of the diminished heterosexual aggressiveness and low marriage rate of schizophrenic males.

The seeming constancy in the incidence of schizophrenia, despite the lower-than-normal rate of reproduction among schizophrenics, may indicate that (1) the pool of pathological genes is being continually augmented by mutations; (2) many cases of schizophrenia do not involve a genetic predisposition; or (3) there is a higher than average rate of fetal or neonatal deaths among the offspring of schizophrenics.

With reference to the latter point, it is interesting to note that Sobel (1961) found a two-fold increase in the fetal or neonatal deaths among the offspring of schizophrenic mothers compared to mothers in the general population. Using a carefully matched control group of non-schizophrenic mothers, Rieder, Rosenthal, Wender, and Blumenthal (1975) also found a two-fold increase. They attributed this to one or more of the following: adverse genetic factors, an adverse intrauterine environment, or medical toxicity. While major tranquilizers are prescribed for many schizophrenic mothers, they could find no definitive evidence—based on a review of available research findings—of medical toxicity being a significant factor.

---

irregularities in the functioning of the autonomic nervous system, which predispose the individual to "overarousal" or "underarousal" in the face of stress.

This view is supported by research findings showing that in situations representing relatively mild stress for normal subjects, arousal tends to be abnormally high in schizophrenics; in response to more severe stress, however, the reactivity of schizophrenics is often lower than that of normal subjects (Broen, 1968; Gruzelier, Lykken, & Venables, 1972). After a review of the literature and a study of 28 schizophrenic and 14 control subjects, Fenz and Velner (1970) summarized the situation in this way:

". . . schizophrenics fall anywhere along the continuum of arousal, although in most cases toward the high or low end of this continuum. In addition, some schizophrenics show marked and sudden shifts in autonomic activity, now being 'overaroused' and now 'underaroused.' A common and basic deficit in all schizophrenics, nevertheless, lies in their inability to modulate effectively or change their level of autonomic responsiveness to correspond to variations in internal and external stimulation." (p. 27)

And once arousal has occurred, it would appear that schizophrenics are often slower than normal persons in returning to a state of physiological equilibrium.

In summary, the research data do indicate that various biochemical and neurophysiological processes are altered in schizophrenia. But the weeks and months of acute turmoil that ordinarily precede hospitalization are likely to affect nutrition, sleep, activity patterns, and the entire metabolic functioning of the individual. Hence cause and effect are difficult to determine. In addition, few of these changes are specific to schizophrenia. Here it would appear useful to note the conclusion of Horwitt (1956) concerning claims of biological anomalies in schizophrenia:

"Year after year, papers appear which purport to distinguish between the state of schizophrenia and that of normalcy. The sum total of the differences reported would make the schizophrenic patient a sorry physical specimen indeed: his liver, brain, kidney, and circulatory functions are impaired; he is deficient in practically every vitamin; his hormones are out of balance, and his enzymes are askew. Fortunately many of these claims of metabolic abnormality are forgotten in time . . . but it seems that each new generation . . . has to be indoctrinated— or disillusioned—without benefit of the experiences of its predecessors." (p. 429)

Over two decades later, it still seems wise to exercise caution in assessing the findings and claims of investigators concerning the role of biological factors in schizophrenia. Whether they are primary causes of schizophrenia, secondary effects of schizophrenia, or interactive factors in the total causal pattern remains to be clarified.

Psychological and interpersonal factors

Laing (1967) has observed:

"The experience and behavior that are labelled schizophrenic are a special sort of strategy that a person invents in order to live in an unlivable world. He cannot make a move . . . without being beset by contradictory pressures both internally, from himself, and externally, from those around him. He is in a position of checkmate." (p. 56)

This viewpoint contrasts sharply with that in which schizophrenia is held to be a biological condition caused by brain pathology. Here the schizophrenic is seen as an individual who escapes from an unbearable world and seemingly unsolvable conflicts by altering his inner representation of reality. Although biological factors may complicate the clinical picture, the origins of the disorder are held to be psychosocial.

In this section we shall deal with the psychological and interpersonal patterns that appear particularly relevant to the development of schizophrenia: (a) early psychic trauma and increased vulnerability; (b) pathogenic parent-child and family interactions; (c) faulty learning and exaggerated defenses; (d) destructive social roles and interpersonal patterns; and (e) excessive stress and decompensation.

Early psychic trauma and increased vulnerability. A number of investigators have placed strong emphasis on the early traumatic experiences of children who later become schizophrenic.

In a pioneering study of the psychoses of children and adolescents, Yerbury and Newell emphasized the total lack of security in human relationships, the severely disturbed home life, and the brutal treatment that many of these children had experienced. Of 56 psychotic cases,

"Ten of them had been shocked by the deaths of parents. . . . Four were so disoriented upon learning of their adoption that they could not reconcile themselves to the true situation. Four children had lived with mentally ill mothers who were finally hospitalized. Sex traumas were reported in 14 cases of children who were overwhelmed with guilt and

Schizophrenic writings

The personality decompensation in psychotic reactions is frequently manifested in the content and form of patients' letters and other spontaneous writings. These examples clearly reveal the "loosening" and deviations of thought, the distortion of affect, and the lowered contact with reality so common among schizophrenics.

The postcard is a reproduction of a card sent by a paranoid schizophrenic.

To: The football department and its members present and future
The University of New Mexico, Albuquerque, N. M.

I depend on correct, honest supplementation of this card by telepathy as a thing which will make clear the meaning of this card. There exists a Playing of The Great Things, the correct, the constructive, world or universe politics, out-in-the-open telepathy, etc. According to the Great Things this playing is the most feasible thing of all; but it is held from newspaper advertising and correct, honest public world recognition, its next step, by telepathic forces (it seems), physical dangers, and lack of money. Over 10,000 cards and letters on this subject have been sent to prominent groups and persons all over the world. Correct, honest contact with the honest, out-in-the-open world. This line of thought, talk, etc. rule. The plain and frank. Strangers. The Great Things and opposites idea. References: In the telepathic world the correct playings. Please save this card for a history record since it is rare and important for history.

The handwritten excerpts are from a letter written by an 18-year-old girl, also diagnosed as a paranoid schizophrenic. As is apparent from the first and last parts of the letter, shown here, the handwriting is of two quite different types, suggestive of the writer's emotional conflict and personality disorganization. Lewinson (1940) included this letter in her study of handwriting characteristics of different types of psychotics. Among psychotics generally, she found that handwriting typically showed abnormal rhythmic disturbances, with rigidity or extreme irregularity in height, breadth, or depth.

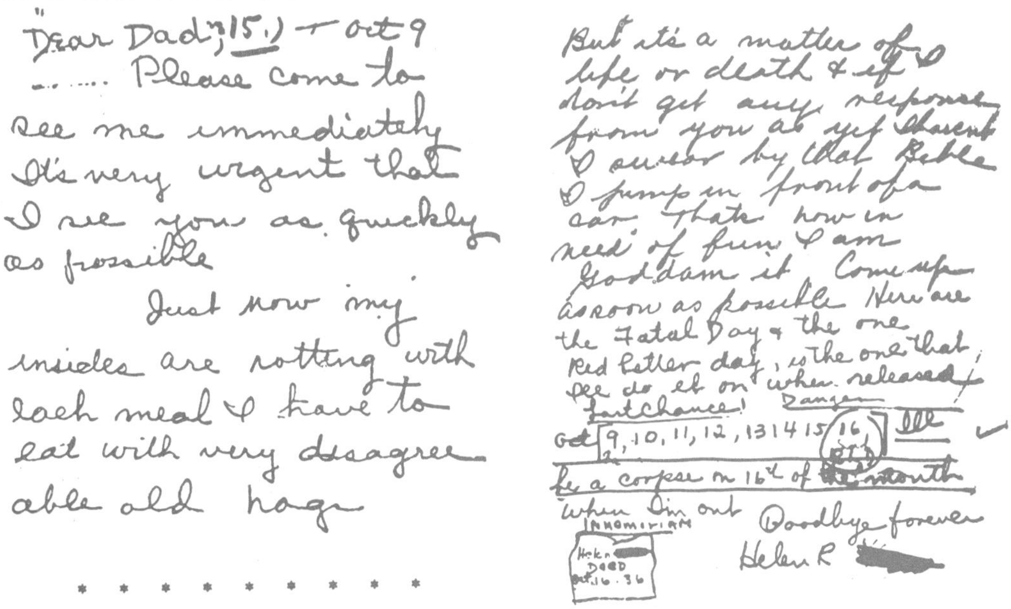

"Dear Dad, (15.) — Oct 9 ...... Please come to see me immediately It's very urgent that I see you as quickly as possible

Just now my insides are rotting with each meal & I have to eat with very disagreeable old hags

* * * * * * * *

But it's a matter of life or death & if I don't get any response from you at yet I haven't I swear by that Bible I jump in front of a car. I'm that now in need of fun & I am God damn it Come up as soon as possible Here are the Fatal Day & the one Red Letter day, is the one that, see do it on when released, Last Chance! Danger

Oct 9, 10, 11, 12, 13 14 15/16, be a corpse on 16th of this month when I'm out Goodbye forever Helen R fear. . . . Three children were horrified by incest in the home, and three girls had become pregnant. . . . Six children had been tormented, beaten, tied, and confined by their companions so that they were terrified in the company of children, and felt safe only with adults." (1943, p. 605)

Similarly, Bettelheim (1955) cited the poignant case of a boy who was rejected by his mother and placed in an orphanage. Here he never learned the names of any of the other boys but referred to them as "big guys" and "little guys"; he lived in a terrifying world of shadowy figures who had the power to beat him up and hurt him without reason.

Karl Menninger has provided a vivid picture of the defenses—and special vulnerabilities—of adolescents and young adults who have suffered deep hurts and have come to view the world as a dangerous and hostile place:

"Children injured in this way are apt to develop certain defenses. They cover up, as the slang expression puts it. They deny the injury which they have experienced or the pain which they are suffering. They erect a façade or front, 'All's well with me,' they seem to say. 'I am one of the fellows; I am just like everybody else. I am a normal person.' And indeed they act like normal persons, as much as they can. They go to the same schools, they complete the same work, they seek the same goals, they do the same things that all the rest of us do. Often they are noticeable only for a certain reticence, shyness, perhaps slight eccentricity. Just as often, they are not conspicuous at all. . . .

"What is underneath that front? One might say that the same sort of thing goes on in the emotional life that goes on when an abscess slowly develops beneath the surface of the body . . . concealed from the outsider. There is intense conflict and tension and anxiety and strong feelings of bitterness, resentment and hate toward those very people with whom the external relationships may be so perfectly normal. 'I hate them! They don't treat me right. They will never love me and I will never love them. I hate them and I could kill them all! But I must not let them know all this. I must cover it up, because they might read my thoughts and then they wouldn't like me and wouldn't be nice to me.'

"All this is covered up as long as possible. . . . For the chief problem in the person who is going to develop what we call schizophrenia is, 'How can I control the bitterness and hatred I feel because of the unendurable sorrow and disappointment that life has brought to me?' . . .

". . . the regimen under which they live has much to do with their successful adaptation. Given certain new stresses, the façade may break down and the underlying bitterness and conflict may break through. . . ." (1948, pp. 101–4)

Schizophrenic withdrawal from a dangerous world is not the only pattern that may emerge from early psychic trauma. In some instances the outcome seems to be a "stormy" personality. Here, instead of withdrawing, the individual tries aggressively to relate to people. He is highly vulnerable to hurt, however, and his existence is usually an anxious one. Often his life is a series of crises, precipitated by minor setbacks and hurts that he magnifies out of all proportion (Arieti, 1974). In other instances, the individual manifests a pattern of somewhat disorganized paranoid ideation often coupled with rebellious behavior involving pathological lying, episodes of unbridled aggression, and various types of delinquent behavior.

Although most children who undergo early psychic trauma show residual effects in later life, most do not become schizophrenics. Conversely, not all schizophrenics have undergone such traumatic childhood experiences. Thus early psychic trauma appears to be only one among many interactional factors that may contribute to schizophrenia.

Pathogenic parent-child and family interactions. Studies of interactions in schizophrenic families have focused on such factors as (a) "schizophrenogenic" parents; (b) destructive marital interactions; (c) pseudo-mutuality and role inflexibility; (d) faulty communication; and (e) the undermining of personal authenticity. Here it may be noted that the focus of research has shifted from parent-child to total family interactions.[3]

1. *"Schizophrenogenic" mothers and fathers.* Many studies have been made of the parents of schizophrenics—particularly the mothers of male patients. Typically, these mothers have been characterized as rejecting, dominating, cold, overprotective, and impervi-

---

[3]A comprehensive review of family interaction in disturbed and normal families may be found in Jacob (1975).

ous to the feelings and needs of others. While verbally such a mother may seem accepting, basically she rejects the child. At the same time, she depends on him rather than the father for her emotional satisfactions and feelings of completeness as a woman. Perhaps for this reason she tends to dominate, possessively overprotect, and smother the child—keeping him dependent on her. Often combined with this behavior are rigid, moralistic attitudes toward sex that make her react with horror to any evidence of sexual impulses on the child's part. In many instances the mother is overtly seductive in physical contacts with her son, thus augmenting his sexual conflicts. In general, the mother-son relationship in schizophrenia appears to foster immaturity and anxiety in the youth—depriving him of a clear-cut sense of his own identity, distorting his views of himself and his world, and causing him to suffer from pervasive feelings of inadequacy and helplessness.

Although the "schizophrenogenic" mother has long been a favorite target of investigators, the fathers have not come through unscathed—especially in regard to schizophrenic daughters. Available studies have typically revealed a somewhat inadequate, indifferent, or passive father who appears detached and humorless—a man who rivals the mother in his insensitivity to others' feelings and needs. Often, too, he appears to be rejecting toward his son and seductive toward his daughter. At the same time, he is often highly contemptuous and derogatory toward his wife, thus making it clear that his daughter is more important to him. This treatment of the wife tends to force her into competition with her daughter, and it devaluates her as a model for her daughter's development as a woman. In fact, the daughter may come to despise herself for any resemblance to her mother. Against this background, the daughter often moves into adolescence feeling an incestuous attachment to her father, which creates severe inner conflict and may eventually prove terrifying to her.

As might be expected, studies have shown a high incidence of emotional disturbance on the part of both mothers and fathers of schizophrenics. Kaufman et al. (1960) reported that both the mothers and fathers of 80 schizo-

Regression to "primary" thought processes in schizophrenia

Some investigators, particularly those adhering to the psychoanalytic model, have emphasized regression to more primitive levels of thinking as a primary feature of schizophrenia. In essence, more highly differentiated and reality oriented "secondary" thought processes, which follow the rules of logic and take external reality into consideration, are replaced by "primary" thought processes, which involve illogical ideas, fantasy, and magical thinking. Presumably, such primary thought processes characterize the thinking of children. The child lives in a world that is partly fantasy and partly real, and develops all manner of fantastic notions about things and events around him. He talks to imaginary playmates, personifies inanimate objects, and attributes various powers to these figments of his imagination. Not uncommonly, he feels that he is the center of the world and develops ideas of his omnipotence.

The regressed schizophrenic does not, however, perceive, think, and feel in ways precisely like those of a child. For example, the child, unlike the schizophrenic, can usually distinguish between his fantasies and the world of reality, and most children, despite their fantasies, imperfect logic, and lack of perspective, are clearly not schizophrenic. Thus, it would appear that regression in schizophrenia does not represent a return to childhood, but rather a defensive pattern that enables the individual to assume a position of dependency and hence avoid problems and responsibilities that he perceives as overwhelming.

phrenic children and adolescents studied were emotionally disturbed: the mothers almost uniformly used psychotic-like defense patterns, and the fathers used seriously maladaptive coping patterns. Later studies, such as that of Tsuang, Fowler, Cadoret, and Monnelly (1974), have generally supported earlier findings.

2. *Destructive marital interactions.* Of particular interest here is the work of Lidz and his associates, which has continued over some two decades. In an initial study of 14 families with schizophrenic offspring, Lidz et al. (1957, 1958) failed to find a single family that was reasonably well integrated. Eight of the 14 couples lived in a state of severe chron-

Folie à deux

A relatively neglected phenomenon in the functional psychoses is that of *folie à deux* — a form of psychological "contagion" in which one person copies and incorporates into his own personality structure the delusions and other psychotic patterns of another person. Familial relationships between individuals in 103 cases studied by Gralnick (1942) fell within one of the following four categories:

sister ⇌ sister	40 cases
husband ⇌ wife	28 cases
mother ⇌ child	24 cases
brother ⇌ brother	11 cases

Among the explanatory factors — all environmental — emphasized by Gralnick were the following: (1) length of association, (2) dominance-submission, (3) type of familial relationship, and (4) pre-psychotic personality. The high incidence in the husband-wife category is particularly striking since common heredity would play no part as an etiological factor in these cases.

In a more recent study, Soni and Rockley (1974) have reported on 8 cases of *folie à deux* seen at a European hospital. Their findings support those of Gralnick and emphasize the role of pathological pre-psychotic characteristics, such as increased suggestibility and submissive roles, as well as the type of relationship, in explaining why these patients acquired the delusions of their partners.

ic discord in which the continuation of the marriage was constantly threatened — a condition the investigators called *marital schism*. A particularly malignant feature was the chronic undermining of the worth of one marital partner by the other, which made it clear to the children that the parents did not respect or value each other. Each parent expressed fear that the child would resemble the other parent, and a child's resemblance to one parent was a source of concern and rejection by the other parent. The other 6 couples in this study had achieved a state of equilibrium in which the continuation of the marriage was not constantly threatened but in which the relationship was maintained at the expense of a basic distortion in family relationships, as when, for example, family members entered into a "collusion" in which the maladaptive behavior of one or more family members was accepted as normal. This pattern was referred to as *marital skew*.

On the basis of the preceding as well as additional studies of families with a schizophrenic offspring (Fleck, 1960; Lidz et al., 1963; Lidz, 1969, 1973), investigators emphasized these findings: (a) male schizophrenics usually came from skewed families with passive, ineffectual fathers and disturbed, engulfing mothers; (b) in over half the families, at least one parent was seriously disturbed emotionally; and (c) there was a great deal of reality distortion in these families. The net effect on the child was to "provide training in irrationality" and maladaptive behavior.

The extent to which irrational family patterns may go is well illustrated in a report by Anthony (1968). In this family

". . . a father with paranoid schizophrenia turned his home into a beleaguered fortress in which the family mounted watches against the enemy, and weapon training was rigorously enforced. A great deal of secrecy prevailed, and no one was allowed to come and go without an examination of credentials. A child who went out shopping was closely interrogated on his return. One of the children complained bitterly that he even had to report before going to the bathroom." (p. 307)

Such a family setting would certainly provide a distorted view of a child's world and more than adequate training in irrationality — conditions that Anthony referred to as "developmental precursors of adult schizophrenia."

3. *Pseudo-mutuality and role inflexibility.* Wynne et al. (1958) found that schizophrenic family relationships often had the appearance of being mutual, understanding, and open, but in fact were not—a condition they termed *pseudo-mutuality.* These investigators also found considerable rigidity in the family role structure, which tended to depersonalize the child and block his growth toward maturity and self-direction.

Similarly, Bowen (1959, 1960), studying the backgrounds of 12 schizophrenics, noted the "striking emotional distance" between the parents in all the studies. He referred to the emotional barrier as having the characteristics of an "emotional divorce." Although the parents in such families often maintained a façade of love—for example, making a big drama out of giving each other presents at Christmas—there was an underlying withdrawal accompanied by severe disappointment and often hostility. The patient's function had often been that of an unsuccessful mediator between the parents. In the case of the male patients, however, the most common pattern was an intense association between mother and son that excluded the father. Bowen also noted that, as the years passed, the son was threatened by signs of the mother's aging or by other characteristics that might prevent her from being the strong person upon whom he was dependent, while the mother was threatened by any signs of personality growth that might prevent the son from remaining "her baby."

Pseudo-mutuality seems related to a variety of role distortions in schizophrenic families. Stabenau et al. (1965) found that such families were characterized by the assignment of inflexible and simplified roles to each member. Brodey has expressed this as an analogy, using a model based on the theater:

"The family drama is unlike the modern theatre. It is more like the morality play of medieval times. Actors take allegorical role positions that are stereotyped and confined—one is Good; another, Evil; a third, Temptation." (1959, p. 382)

In general, it would appear that the rigid and inflexible roles played by the family members permit a façade of continuing relatedness with each other and with the world, and make the business of living seemingly understandable and controllable. But basically the role provided for the child is destructive to his personal growth.

4. *Faulty communication.* Bateson (1959, 1960) was one of the first investigators to emphasize the conflicting and confusing nature of communications among members of schizophrenic families. As we noted in Chapter 5, he used the term *double-bind* to describe the effect of one such pattern. Here the parent presents to the child ideas, feelings, and demands that are mutually incompatible. For example, the mother may be verbally loving and accepting but emotionally anxious and rejecting; or she may complain about the child's lack of affection but freeze up or punish him when he approaches her affectionately. The mother subtly but effectively prohibits comment on such paradoxes, and the father is too weak and ineffectual to intervene. In essence, a child is continually placed in situations where he cannot win. He becomes increasingly anxious; presumably, such disorganized and contradictory communications in the family come to be reflected in his own thinking.

Singer and Wynne (1963, 1965a, 1965b) have linked the thought disorders in schizophrenia to two styles of thinking and communication in the family—*amorphous* and *fragmented.* The amorphous pattern is characterized by failure in differentiation; here, attention toward feelings, objects, or persons is loosely organized, vague, and drifting. Fragmented thinking involves greater differentiation but lowered integration, with erratic and disruptive shifts in communication. Feinsilver (1970) found supporting evidence for such amorphous and fragmented thinking in the impaired ability of members of schizophrenic families to describe essential attributes of common household objects to each other. And Bannister (1971) has found that schizophrenic thinking tends to be even more "loose" and disordered when the individual is dealing with persons and interpersonal relationships than when he is dealing with objects.

5. *Undermining personal authenticity.* The philosopher Martin Buber (1957) pointed

out that a confirmation of each person's authenticity is essential to normal interpersonal relationships.

"In human society at all its levels, persons confirm one another in a practical way, to some extent or other, in their personal qualities and capacities, and a society may be termed human in the measure to which its members confirm one another. . . ." (p. 101)

Such confirmation apparently is often denied the person who later becomes schizophrenic. Several investigators have noted that the members of schizophrenic families, when they interact, often behave in ways that are inconsistent with what they themselves say. Often, too, the members of schizophrenic families consistently disqualify one or more member's statements and actions. In one family, for example, the father strongly approved of whatever the younger son did while he was equally disapproving of the behavior of the older son. Thus the brothers might make similar statements about some matter, and the father would agree with one and find some basis for disqualifying or discrediting the statement of the other. Similarly, at Christmas time, the younger son's present to his father was praised and appreciated, while that of the older son was criticized and found disappointing by the father. The mother and younger sister went along with this differential treatment. Later, at the age of 27, the older son was hospitalized and diagnosed as a paranoid schizophrenic.

Such contradictory and disconfirming communications subtly and persistently mutilate the self-concepts of one or more family members, usually that of a particular child, as in the preceding example. This pattern has been well described by Laing and Esterson (1964):

"The characteristic family pattern that has emerged from the study of families of schizophrenics does not so much involve a child who is subject to outright neglect or even to obvious trauma, but a child whose authenticity has been subject to subtle, but persistent, mutilation, often quite unwittingly. . . . (p. 91)

The ultimate of this mutilation process, as we noted in Chapter 3, occurs when

". . . no matter how [a person] feels or how he acts, no matter what meaning he gives his situation, his feelings are denuded of validity, his acts are stripped of their motives, intentions, and consequences, the situation is robbed of its meaning for him, so that he is totally mystified and alienated." (Laing & Esterson, 1964, pp. 135–36)

In the general context of faulty parent-child and family interactions, we may note that Lidz (1968, 1973) has characterized the parents of schizophrenics as "deficient tutors": they create a family milieu inappropriate for training a child in the cognitive abilities essential for categorizing experience, thinking coherently, and communicating meaningfully. Coupled with feelings of inadequacy and other damage to the child's emerging self-concept, this may help explain the later cognitive distortions, communication failures, difficulties in interpersonal relationships, and identity confusion that commonly occur in schizophrenia.

Yet most of the children from families with pathogenic characteristics do not become schizophrenic; thus, few investigators would maintain that all cases of schizophrenia develop from pathogenic family interactions. In assessing the relative contribution of genetic and family factors in schizophrenia, Eisenberg (1968) has hypothesized that (a) some family environments are so healthy and growth-producing that schizophrenia would rarely occur except in the presence of a marked genetic predisposition; (b) some family environments are so traumatic in their effects on the offspring that schizophrenia may occur with a minimal genetic loading or possibly even in the absence of any genetic predisposition; and (c) in average families the occurrence of schizophrenic episodes is usually caused by a combination of stress factors and genetic predisposition.

Faulty learning and coping. Faulty learning appears to play a key role in schizophrenia, as it does in most other forms of maladaptive behavior.

Early traumatic experiences—both within the family setting and in the outer world—may leave conditioned fears and vulnerabilities which lead to the perception of one's environment as a dangerous and hostile place.

Perhaps of even greater importance is faulty learning on a cognitive level resulting from the observation and imitation of pathological parental models, as well as from attempts to meet inappropriate expectations and demands.

1. *Deficient self-structure.* Such faulty learning is typically reflected in (a) grossly inaccurate assumptions concerning reality, possibility, and value; (b) a confused sense of self-identity coupled with basic feelings of inadequacy, insecurity, and self-devaluation; (c) personal immaturity often reflected in over-dependence on others and overemphasis on being a "good boy" or a "good girl"; and (d) a lack of needed competencies coupled with ineffective coping patterns. These characteristics appear capable of paving the way for schizophrenic and other seriously maladaptive behaviors.

Two areas in which the results of such faulty learning often seem apparent are in dealing with inner impulses and in establishing satisfying interpersonal relationships. In the sexual sphere, the schizophrenic's problems are often complicated by rigidly moralistic attitudes toward sexual behavior. At the same time, the individual usually has had few, if any, meaningful sexual relationships. As a consequence, his sexual fantasies—like those of the early adolescent—may be somewhat chaotic and encompass a wide range of sexual objects and behaviors. Such fantasies often lead to severe inner conflicts and to self-devaluation. Similarly, the hostility he may feel toward people important to him, as a result of the hurt and frustration they cause him, is apt to be particularly difficult for such a "good" individual to handle; he tends to view such hostility as both immoral and dangerous and does not know how to express it in socially acceptable ways. At the same time, he may be completely upset if he is the object of hostility from those on whom he feels dependent.

Lack of competencies in dealing with sexual and hostile fantasies and impulses combined with a general deficiency in social skills usually leads to disappointment, hurt, and devaluation in intimate interpersonal relationships. As we shall see, the stresses which commonly precipitate schizophrenic episodes typically center around difficulties in such relationships. Fortunately or unfortunately, the individual's inability to establish and maintain satisfying interpersonal relationships does not void his needs for acceptance, approval, and love; rather it reduces his chances for meeting these needs.

2. *Exaggerated use of ego-defense mechanisms.* Feeling inadequate and devaluated and lacking an adequate frame of reference and needed competencies, it is not surprising that the individual tends to rely excessively on ego-defense mechanisms rather than on task-oriented coping patterns.

Emotional insulation protects the individual from the hurt of disappointment and frustration. Regression enables him to lower his level of aspiration and accept a position of dependence. Projection helps him maintain feelings of adequacy and worth by placing the blame for his failures on others and attributing his own unacceptable desires to them. Wish-fulfilling fantasies give him some measure of compensation for feelings of frustration and self-devaluation.

The exaggerated use of such defense mechanisms as projection and fantasy appears particularly likely to lead to delusions and hallucinations, which not only represent the breakdown of organized perception and thought processes, but also—as part of the schizophrenic reorganization of reality—may have marked defensive value. Delusions of influence and persecution enable the individual to project the blame for his own inadmissible thoughts and behaviors; hallucinations—such as voices that "pour filth into his mind" or keep him informed of what his "enemies" are up to—may serve a comparable defensive purpose. Delusions of grandeur and omnipotence may grow out of simple wishful thinking and enable him to counteract feelings of inferiority and inadequacy, and hallucinations, such as conversations in which the individual hears the voice of God confer great power upon him and assign him the mission of saving the world, may likewise have comparable defensive value.

In acute schizophrenic episodes the initial picture is somewhat different, as we have seen, and is dominated by the massive breakdown of filtering, the individual's panic at the

A series of photographs shows the noticeable improvement this schizophrenic patient made after only a few days of treatment. When first admitted to the hospital, the patient had been agitated and crying, then became withdrawn, convinced everyone around her was hostile. In her first interview with the doctor, she answered a few questions, but then hid her face with her hand and only shrugged her shoulders in answer to further questions. But after only three days of hospitalization, the patient is able to talk openly to her doctor. Her treatment involved an intensive program of specially prescribed therapies, including drugs (chlorpromazine) and psychotherapy. This patient was released after almost seven weeks of treatment; follow-up treatment included periodic visits to a community health clinic, continuing medication, and the understanding of her husband and family. (Based on Wilson, 1964.)

All photos: Alfred Eisenstaedt, Time-Life Books.

Often the schizophrenic is deeply confused about who he is, what sort of world he lives in, and what an appropriate life pattern is for him. It is common to hear schizophrenics ask such questions as "Who am I?" "What is the meaning of it all?" and "Is there any future?" Typically he feels alone and overwhelmed by a complex and hostile world he does not understand — a world that seems to provide his existence with no sense of meaning.

The following excerpts from Curry's description of a 29-year-old female schizophrenic illustrate this picture:

"The world of this woman was a wasteland, a battlefield where the wreckage of interpersonal wars pressed her into isolation and suffocation. 'It is as if I'm a girl alone in an attic, with no air to breathe.' . . . [there] was only threat in her world — each human was at war with each other human. She could not get beyond this. Even in her intimate relations with men, there had been nothing: a fearfulness devoid of love and care.

"The structure of her existence was threat — impending attack, destruction. There was no orientation toward the future. . . . Each moment was but each moment, and like the first, long ago, filled with only emptiness. . . . In her distorted world there was only past, because she had had it; no future, because she could not make it. . . . What we called 'her psychosis' was her particular being-in-the-world, in all its pain and unauthenticity: a flight from true existence, a corruption of care. Gradually, she seemed to no longer need this world, having transcended it to, what she termed, 'beauty with eyes open.'" (1962, pp. 129–30, 133–35)

---

loss of control over his thoughts and feelings, and his desperate attempts to understand his terrifying experience. As yet he has not developed defenses to cope with his situation, but he cannot continue indefinitely in this state of panic and confusion. His acute schizophrenic episode either clears up eventually, or various extreme defenses, such as the ones mentioned above, are likely to develop.

Here it may be emphasized that the schizophrenic's reactions appear to represent a total defensive strategy rather than a conglomeration of individual defenses. In essence, the schizophrenic withdraws from the real world and evolves a defensive strategy that enables him to distort and "reshape" aversive experiences so that he can assimilate them without further self-devaluation. Even though this new defensive system may be illogical and far from satisfactory, it relieves much of his inner tension and anxiety and protects him from complete psychological disintegration.

Social role problems. Social role behavior has been tied into the development and course of schizophrenic reactions in several different ways. A factor emphasized by Cameron and Margaret (1949, 1951) in their intensive studies of schizophrenic patients was the schizophrenic's failure to learn appropriate role-taking behavior. Thus, inflexible in his own role behavior and uncomprehending of the role behavior of others, he does not know how to interact appropriately with them.

As we noted in Chapter 3, Laing (1967, 1969, 1971) has carried this view of role behavior a step further, to the schizophrenic's creation of his own social role to protect himself from destructive social expectations and demands. Describing the so-called normal world as a place where all of us are "bemused and crazed creatures, strangers to our true selves, to one another, and to the spiritual and material world" (1967, p. 56), Laing explains that a split arises between an individual's false outer self and his true inner self. When the split reaches a point where it can no longer be tolerated, the result is a psychotic breakdown which usually takes the form of schizophrenia. In this view the "madness" labeled schizophrenia represents the individual's attempts to achieve integration between the inner and outer world and to recover his wholeness as a human being.

In essence, according to Laing, the individual dons the "mask of insanity" as a social role and a barricade. Behind this "false self" and often turbulent façade, however, the real person — the "true inner self" — remains. In this hidden inner world, despite his outward role of madness, the schizophrenic's hopes and aspirations may remain very much intact. Thus Laing thinks treatment should focus less on removing "symptoms" than on finding a path to this remote and often inaccessible sanctuary and assisting the individual to regain his wholeness as a person.

Finally, it may be noted that whether or not the individual finds expected social role behavior destructive to his inner self, his inadequate role behavior leads to repetitive failures, to self-devaluation, and to a tendency to resort to defensive rather than task-oriented behavior. Eventually this vicious circle may lead to an ever widening breach between the individual and others, to the breakdown of his defensive barricade and the loss of control over his thoughts and feelings, and to the terrifying realization that he is "losing his mind"—followed by hospitalization and the "sick role" behavior associated with being labeled a schizophrenic.

Excessive stress and decompensation. Brown (1972) found a marked increase in the severity of life stress during the 10-week period prior to an actual schizophrenic breakdown. The life stress typically centered around difficulties in intimate personal relationships. Focusing on the type of stress, Forgus and DeWolfe (1974) found that schizophrenic patients seemed to have been defeated by their whole life situation as well as by difficulties in close personal relationships.

As we noted, the course of decompensation in reactive schizophrenia tends to be sudden, while that in process schizophrenia tends to be gradual. The actual degree of decompensation may vary markedly, depending on the severity of stress and the makeup of the individual. And the course of recovery or recompensation may also be relatively rapid or slow. Similarly, the degree of recovery may be complete, leading to a better integrated person; it may be partial but sufficient for the individual to cope with his life situation; or his defenses may be stabilized on a psychotic level eventuating in chronic schizophrenia.

General sociocultural factors

While disorders of thought and emotion are common to schizophrenia the world over, cultural factors may influence both the type and symptom content of schizophrenic disorders that occur in given societies. Carothers (1953, 1959) found the hebephrenic type of schizophrenia to be most common among African tribal groups in remote areas. He attributed this finding to a lack of well-developed ego-defense mechanisms among the members of these groups, thus making a complete disorganization of personality more likely when schizophrenia does occur. Similarly, Field (1960) described the initial schizophrenic breakdown among natives in rural Ghana as typically involving a state of panic. Here it was observed that when the individual was brought quickly to a shrine for treatment, he usually calmed down and in a few days appeared recovered. But when there was considerable delay before he reached the shrine, he presented a classic hebephrenic picture. In a more recent study of schizophrenia among the aborigines of West Malaysia, Kinzie and Bolton (1973) found the acute type to be by far the most common subtype; they also noted that symptom content often "had an obvious cultural overlay, for example, seeing a 'river ghost' or 'men-like spirits' or talking to one's 'soul'" (p. 773).

However, the clinical picture seems to be changing as rural Africans and other so-called "primitive" peoples are increasingly exposed to modern technology and social change (Copeland, 1968; Kinzie & Bolton, 1973; Torrey, 1973).

Focusing on sociocultural factors within our own society, Murphy (1968) has summarized the picture as follows:

"There is a truly remarkable volume of research literature demonstrating an especially high rate of schizophrenia . . . in the lowest social class or classes . . . of moderately large to large cities throughout much of the Western world. It is not altogether clear what is the direction of causality in this relationship—whether the conditions of life of the lowest social classes are conducive to the development of schizophrenia, or schizophrenia leads to a decline in social class position—but present evidence would make it seem probable that some substantial part of the phenomenon results from lower class conditions of life being conducive to schizophrenia." (p. 152)

Levy and Rowitz (1972) also found both a higher incidence of schizophrenia and a greater likelihood of relapse on lower socioeconomic levels, especially in areas of large cities that are undergoing rapid and drastic social change. Apparently the social disorganization, rapid changes, insecurity, poverty, and harshness characteristic of urban slums intensify personal problems and tend to increase the likelihood of schizophrenic and other psychopathology.

Here it may also be emphasized that alleged ethnic differences in the incidence and clinical pictures of schizophrenia—for example, between blacks, Chicanos, and Anglo-Americans—disappear when social class, education, and related socioeconomic conditions are equated.

In concluding our review of causal factors in schizophrenia, it may be pointed out that research on the causation of human behavior is, as Shakow (1969) has expressed it, "fiendishly complex," even with normal subjects.

"Research with disturbed human beings is even more so, particularly with those with whom it is difficult to communicate, among them schizophrenics. The marked range of schizophrenia, the marked variance within the range and within the individual, the variety of shapes that the psychosis takes, and both the excessive and compensatory behaviors that characterize it, all reflect this special complexity. Recent years have seen the complication further enhanced by the use of a great variety of therapeutic devices, such as drugs, that alter both the physiological and psychological nature of the organism. Research with schizophrenics, therefore, calls for awareness not only of the factors creating variance in normal human beings, but also of the many additional sources of variance this form of psychosis introduces." (Shakow, 1969, p. 618)

Or as Bannister (1971) has pointed out, "We will eventually have to develop a theory of what makes all people march before we can say very much about why some people march to a different drummer" (p. 84).

In general, however, it appears that there is no one clinical entity or causal sequence in schizophrenia. Rather we seem to be dealing with several types of maladaptive behavior— often referred to as "the schizophrenias"— resulting from an interaction of biological, psychosocial, and sociocultural factors; the role of these factors undoubtedly varies according to the given case and clinical picture.

Often the interaction appears to involve a vicious spiral, in which life stresses trigger metabolic changes that impair brain functioning. The latter, in turn, appears to intensify anxiety and panic as the individual realizes he is losing control. And so the spiral continues until more permanent defensive patterns are established, treatment is undertaken, or the disorder "has run its course."

Treatment and outcomes

Until recent times, the prognosis for schizophrenia was generally unfavorable. Under the routine custodial treatment in large mental hospital settings, the rate of discharge approximated only 30 percent.

Sommer and Osmond (1962) used the term "schizophrenic no-society" to refer to such chronic mental hospital wards. "Long-stay wards are inhabited by ghostly figures who, like the crew of the *Flying Dutchman,* are able to walk through one another without leaving a trace" (p. 244). These investigators noted that in 1883 Sir Francis Galton made a similar observation.

"There is yet a third peculiarity of the insane which is almost universal, that of gloomy segregation. Passengers nearing London by the Great Western Railway must have frequently remarked upon the unusual appearance of the crowd of lunatics who take their exercise in the large green enclosures in front of the Hanwell Asylum. They almost all, without exception, walk apart in moody isolation, each in his own way, buried in his own thoughts." (1883, p. 67)

For most schizophrenics, the outlook today is not nearly so dark. Improvement in this situation came with dramatic suddenness when the phenothiazines—major tranquilizing drugs—were introduced in the 1950s. Chemotherapy, together with other modern treatment methods, permits the majority of cases to be treated in outpatient clinics; a schizophrenic who enters a mental hospital or clinic as an inpatient for the first time has an 80- to 90-percent chance of being discharged within a matter of weeks or, at most, months. However, the rate of readmission is still extremely high, with 45 percent of all discharged patients being readmitted during the first year after release. Overall, about one third of schizophrenic patients recover; another third show partial recovery; and a final third remain largely or totally disabled. This ratio appears less favorable for children and adolescents than for adults (Bender, 1973; Gross & Huber, 1973; Morrison, 1974; Roff, 1974).

Different handling of acute and chronic cases. At the present time community-oriented treatment facilities appear to be conducting two parallel programs. The *first* concerns the newly admitted acutely disturbed schizophrenic patient whose family and community ties are still relatively intact. Most of these patients respond rapidly to treatment and can be discharged within 20 to 60 days provided they will receive adequate aftercare. The *second* program is devoted to more severe and chronic cases, whose family and community ties have been disrupted and whose post-hospitalization careers—if they recover sufficiently to leave the hospital setting—usually continue with the aid of aftercare in sheltered environments, such as halfway houses.

Chemotherapy. Modern drugs—tranquilizers and energizers—have proven of great benefit in the treatment of schizophrenic patients. Commonly used drugs are (a) major tranquilizers such as chlorpromazine and haldol, which are used to control excitement, agitation, and thought disorders; (b) antidepressants, which are used to increase alertness and interest and to elevate mood; and (c) antianxiety drugs—minor tranquilizers—which are used to decrease apprehension and tension and to promote sleep. These drugs are frequently used in combination with each other. In the overall treatment and follow-up program, major tranquilizers may be used for periods of months or even years, while the antidepressant and antianxiety drugs are usually used only for a short period of time and then intermittently during periods of special stress. In one major NIMH study, for example, Hogarty & Goldberg (1973) found that the continued use of chlorpromazine was highly effective in preventing relapse during the first year after discharge from the hospital. Similarly, Hogarty et al. (1974) reported

---

Is there a schizophrenic residual?

While many schizophrenic patients—particularly of the acute type—show a full recovery, a minority appear to evidence a "schizophrenic residual." This means that some degree of schizophrenic ideation may remain and render the individual susceptible to another schizophrenic episode under severe stress. For example, Strauss (1969) reported on a study of a woman who had been severely delusional during a schizophrenic episode. When first interviewed by a therapist after her breakdown, she had stood at attention, feeling that the devil willed her to do so; she had also thought that the devil was trying to get her to do "bad things." A follow-up study made a year after recovery showed that the woman no longer felt that the devil was trying to influence her. However, in response to one card of the Rorschach inkblot test, "she was startled to see the face of a malevolent devil commanding someone to do something." Strauss concluded that although the subject had apparently gone from schizophrenic to normal in terms of becoming free of delusions, a residual of her delusional ideas was still with her.

Similarly, in a study of recovery from delusions in schizophrenia, Sacks, Carpenter, and Strauss (1974) outlined three stages: the *delusional* stage, the *double-awareness* phase in which the patient begins to doubt his delusions, and the *nondelusional* phase indicating recovery. However, these investigators raised the question of whether these prior delusions "will provide focal points for the recurrence of delusions under future conditions of stress for the patient" (p. 120). In view of the relatively high recurrence of schizophrenic episodes, the question of a possible schizophrenic residual—and if it does exist, how to deal with it—appears to merit further study.

---

that during a two-year period following hospital discharge, 80 percent of schizophrenic patients treated with placebos had relapsed as contrasted with 48 percent on drug therapy.

Acute schizophrenic patients usually respond readily to drug treatment, showing a rapid alleviation of symptoms. The more severe and chronic patient responds more slowly, but his delusions and hallucinations are gradually eliminated or reduced to a point where he is no longer upset by them. For example, in paranoid schizophrenic reactions, the patient loses interest in his persecutors and begins

Conditions associated with favorable outcomes in the treatment of schizophrenia

1. Reactive rather than process schizophrenia, in which the time from onset of full-blown symptoms is 6 months or less.
2. Clear-cut precipitating stresses.
3. Adequate heterosexual adjustment prior to schizophrenic episode.
4. Good social and work adjustment prior to schizophrenic episode.
5. Minimal incidence of schizophrenia and other pathological conditions in family background.
6. Involvement of depression or other schizo-affective pattern.
7. Favorable life situation to return to and adequate aftercare in the community.

In general, the opposite of the preceding conditions — including poor premorbid adjustment, slow onset, and relatives with schizophrenia — are indicative of an unfavorable prognosis.

Here it may be noted that in a 5-year follow-up study of 61 schizophrenics in the U.S., Hawk, Carpenter, and Strauss (1975) failed to find any differences in long-range outcomes between acute and other subtypes of schizophrenia. (Data could be obtained on only 61 out of the original sample of 131 cases.) While this sample is too small to be definitive, this study is part of an International Pilot Study of Schizophrenia (IPSS) designed to include transcultural data on over 1200 patients in 9 countries — Colombia, Czechoslovakia, Denmark, India, Nigeria, Taiwan, U.S.S.R., the United Kingdom, and the United States.

Based on Caffey, Galbrecht, and Klett (1971), Fenz and Velner (1970), Hawk, Carpenter, and Strauss (1975), Morrison (1974), Roff (1974), Stephens, Astrup, and Mangrum (1966), Turner, Dopkeen, and Labreche (1970), Yarden (1974), and Yolles (1967).

---

to take more interest in his environment. "Voices" that have been a source of torment to him may still be heard but do not bother him anymore. Grinspoon et al. (1968, p. 1651) described one patient who "still heard voices while receiving thordiazine, but he no longer shouted at them or did cartwheels in response to their commands." And, as we have noted, chemotherapy enables the majority of schizophrenics to be treated in outpatient clinics and thus remain in their family and community settings.

Ideally, of course, treatment programs in schizophrenia involve much more than chemotherapy, for an individual whose symptoms have been alleviated by drugs may still remain schizophrenic in his basic ideation and feelings. In addition, several investigators have reported that drug therapy actually appears detrimental for certain patients — particularly those who have evidenced a relatively good adjustment prior to an acute onset of symptoms — possibly making it less likely that such patients will work through and resolve their problems and achieve better personality integration (Arieti, 1974; Goldstein et al., 1969; Goldstein, Rodnick, & Judd, 1971). Whatever its limitations, however, modern chemotherapy — as part of a total treatment program — has clearly improved the immediate and long-range outlook for most schizophrenics.

Psychosocial approaches to treatment. Various forms of psychotherapy have been used in an attempt to help schizophrenic patients reestablish bonds of human relatedness, eliminate specific psychotic symptoms, correct distorted attitudes, and develop needed interpersonal and other competencies for coping with the stresses of life.

In general, psychoanalysis and other forms of individual psychotherapy have not proven effective with schizophrenics. In fact, Bandura (1969) concluded from available evidence that schizophrenia can be treated more effectively in a group or social systems context than on an individual level. Group psychotherapy appears to be particularly helpful in providing the patient with a safe environment in which to test reality and develop increased understanding and competence in interpersonal and other life areas. At present, the vast majority of schizophrenic patients receiving psychological help are involved in some form of group therapy, including both hospitalized patients and those in aftercare programs. Interestingly, group psychotherapy appears to be a key component in the treatment of schizophrenia in China but not in Russia (Allen, 1973; Kety, 1974; Ratnavale, 1973).

In hospital or clinic settings for inpatients, two rather comprehensive therapeutic procedures have been used with promising results. The first is *milieu therapy,* in which the

This picture contrasts strongly with the ones on pp. 322–23; for mental patients, the picture is considerably brighter today than it was in 1947 when this scene in a mental hospital ward occurred. The attitude then was one of custody, rather than understanding and treatment.

entire facility is regarded as a therapeutic community, and the emphasis is on developing a meaningful and constructive environment in which the patients participate in the regulation of their own activities. Self-reliance and the formation of socially acceptable interpersonal relationships are encouraged, and a climate is provided that permits reality testing and fosters personal growth. A second approach has been to place entire wards on "token economy" programs, where individual responsibility and appropriate social interaction are rewarded by tokens that the patients can exchange for cold drinks and other things they want. In both of these treatment programs, patients have shown a marked improvement in initiative, responsibility, and appropriate social interaction (Ayllon & Azrin, 1965; Carlson, Hersen, & Eisler, 1972; Crowley, 1975; Paul, 1969; Schwartz & Bellack, 1975; Winkler, 1970, 1973).

Sociotherapy—directed toward working out family crises, alleviating pathogenic family conditions, and helping the patient make an adequate adjustment in the community—is receiving increasing emphasis as a crucial part of the overall treatment program. As we have noted, this approach may involve therapy for the entire family unit.

Community treatment and aftercare. As a consequence of more effective methods of treatment, an increasing number of schizophrenics are being treated in community clinics; also, an increasing number of hospitalized patients are being discharged—both recently admitted patients who had been acutely disturbed and many chronic cases as well. Thus, increased attention is being given to outpatient clinics and other supportive facilities in the community, and to sociotherapy with patients' families. In essence, the emphasis is now on community treatment, or—where hospitalization is required—on short-term hospitalization with long-term aftercare in the community. It is of interest to note that in Russia, extensive community programs—participated in by labor unions, housing councils, and other agencies—attempt to make the entire community a therapeutic milieu for the schizophrenic, helping him feel "you are not alone in the world" (Ziferstein, 1968).

A study by Caffey, Galbrecht, and Klett (1971) suggests that intensive hospital treatment for about 21 days followed by a comprehensive aftercare program may be more effective in most cases than longer hospitalization and may markedly reduce readmission rates. Further evidence in support of this view has been provided by Driemen and Minard (1971), who demonstrated that "preleave planning" and intensive aftercare in the community—for example, family therapy and assistance with financial and vocational plans as well as drug medication when necessary—reduced the usual readmittance rate of 40 to 70 percent to slightly less than 10 percent at Metropolitan State Hospital in California. These statistics call to mind Miller's (1966) conclusion that what is needed to keep most schizophrenics from returning to the hospital are the very things that most of us take for granted in our own lives, including an adequate livelihood, the love and support of family and friends, and feelings of competence and self-respect.

A great deal of research is being devoted to schizophrenia, and as we learn more about the role of biological, psychosocial, and sociocultural factors in the development of this mental disorder, it should be possible to understand, effectively treat, and ultimately prevent this pervasive human affliction.

Paranoia

The term *paranoia* has been in use a long time. The ancient Greeks and Romans used it to refer more or less indiscriminately to any mental disorder. Our present, more limited use of the term stems from the work of Kraepelin, who reserved it for cases showing delusions and impaired contact with reality but without the severe personality disorganization characteristic of schizophrenia.[4]

Currently two types of paranoid psychoses are included under the general heading of paranoid disorders:

a) *Paranoia*, with a delusional system that develops slowly, becomes intricate, logical, and systemized and centers around delusions of persecution and/or grandeur. Aside from the delusions, the patient's personality remains relatively intact, with no evidence of serious disorganization and no hallucinations (unlike the symptoms in paranoid schizophrenia, discussed on pp. 300–304).

b) *Paranoid state*, with transient and changeable paranoid delusions lacking the logical and systematic features of paranoia, yet not showing the bizarre fragmentation and deterioration often found in paranoid schizophrenia. Usually the condition is related to some evident stress and is a transient phenomenon. Paranoid states often color the clinical picture in other types of psychopathological reactions.[5]

Our primary focus in this section is on paranoia proper. Paranoia is rare in clinic and mental hospital populations, but this provides a somewhat misleading picture of its actual occurrence. Many exploited inventors, persecuted teachers and business executives, fanat-

---

[4]There is a marked dearth of recent research on paranoia, and in this section we have been forced to draw on a number of earlier but seemingly definitive studies.
[5]A comprehensive review of paranoid states may be found in Tanna (1974).

ical reformers, morbidly jealous spouses, and self-styled prophets fall in this category. Unless they become a serious nuisance, these individuals are usually able to maintain themselves in the community. In some instances, however, they are potentially dangerous.

Clinical picture in paranoia

In paranoia the individual feels that he is being singled out and taken advantage of, mistreated, plotted against, stolen from, spied upon, ignored, or otherwise mistreated by his "enemies." His delusional system usually centers around one major theme, such as financial matters, a job, an invention, an unfaithful spouse, or other life affairs.[6] A person who is failing on the job may insist that his fellow workers and superiors have it in for him because they are jealous of his great ability and efficiency. As a result, he may quit his job and go to work elsewhere, only to find friction developing again and his new job in jeopardy. Now he may become convinced that the first company he worked for has written to his present employer and has turned everyone here against him, so that he has not been given a fair chance. With time, more and more of the environment is integrated into his delusional system as each additional experience is misconstrued and interpreted in the light of his delusional ideas.

Although the evidence the paranoiac advances to justify his claims may be extremely tenuous and inconclusive, he is unwilling to accept any other possible explanation and is impervious to reason. He may be convinced of his spouse's unfaithfulness because on two separate occasions when he answered the phone the party at the other end hung up. Argument and logic are futile. In fact, any questioning of the paranoiac's delusions usually only convinces him that his interrogator has sold out to his enemies.

---

[6]At one time it was customary to distinguish several types of paranoid reactions in accordance with the delusional ideas manifested—whether persecutory, grandiose, erotic, jealous, or litigious. But a classification in terms of delusional content has been found not to be very helpful.

Milner cited the case of a paranoiac, aged 33, who murdered his wife by battering her head with a hammer. Prior to the murder, he had become convinced that his wife was suffering from some strange disease and that she had purposely infected him because she wished him to die. He believed that this disease was due to a "cancer-consumption" germ. He attributed his conclusion in part to his wife's alleged sexual perversion and also gave the following reasons for his belief:

"1. His wife had insured him for a small sum immediately after marriage.

"2. A young man who had been friendly with his wife before their marriage died suddenly.

"3. A child who had lived in the same house as his wife's parents suffered from fits. (He also believed that his wife's parents were suffering from the same disease.)

"4. For several months before the crime his food had had a queer taste, and for a few weeks before the crime he had suffered from a pain in the chest and an unpleasant taste in the mouth." (1949, p. 130)

Although ideas of persecution predominate in paranoid reactions, many paranoiacs develop delusions of grandeur in which they endow themselves with superior or unique ability. Such "exalted" ideas usually center around Messianic missions, political or social reforms, or remarkable inventions. Religious paranoiacs may consider themselves appointed by God to save the world and may spend most of their time "preaching" and "crusading." Threats of fire and brimstone, burning in hell, and similar persuasive devices are liberally employed. Many paranoiacs become attached to extremist political movements and are tireless and fanatical crusaders, although they often do their cause more harm than good by their self-righteousness and their condemnation of others.

Some paranoiacs develop remarkable inventions that they have endless trouble in patenting or selling. Gradually they become convinced that there is a plot afoot to steal their invention, or that enemies of the United States are working against them to prevent the country from receiving the benefits of their remarkable talents. Hoffman cited the case of an individual who went to Washington to get presidential assistance in obtaining a patent for a flamethrower that, he claimed, could destroy all the enemies of the United States. He would patiently explain who he was. "There's God who is Number 1, and Jesus Christ who is Number 2, and me, I am Number 3" (1943, p. 574).

Aside from his delusional system, the paranoiac may appear perfectly normal in his conversation, emotionality, and conduct. Hallucinations and the other obvious signs of psychopathology are rarely found. This normal appearance, together with the logical and coherent way in which he presents his delusional ideas, may make him most convincing.

In one case an engineer developed detailed plans for eliminating the fog in San Francisco and other large cities by means of a system of reflectors which would heat the air by solar radiation and cause the fog to lift. The company for whom he worked examined the plans and found them unsound. This upset him greatly and he resigned his position, stating that the other engineers in the company were not qualified to pass judgment on any really complex and advanced engineering projects like his. Instead of attempting to obtain other employment, he then devoted full time trying to find some other engineering firm who would have the vision and technical proficiency to see the great potentialities of his idea. He would present his plans convincingly but become highly suspicious and hostile when questions concerning their feasibility were raised. Eventually, he became convinced that there was a conspiracy among a large number of engineering firms to steal his plans and use them for their own profit. He reported his suspicions to the police, threatening to do something about the situation himself unless they took action. As a consequence of his threats, he was hospitalized for psychiatric observation and diagnosed as a paranoiac.

The delusional system is apt to be particularly convincing if one accepts the basic premise or premises upon which it is based. For example, where the delusional system develops around some actual injustice, it is difficult to distinguish between fact and fancy. As a result, the individual may convince his family, friends, and well-meaning public officials of the truth of his claims. However, his inability to see the facts in any other light, his typical lack of evidence for his far-reaching conclusions, and his hostile, suspicious, and uncommunicative attitude when his delusional ideas are questioned usually give him away.

The following case history is a rather classical description of a mild paranoid reaction; it reveals the development of a logically patterned delusional system and the pertinent selection of environmental evidence in an attempt to involve more and more individuals in the supposed conspiracy. Despite this paranoiac's delusional system, however, she was not severely out of touch with reality; there are many nonhospitalized cases in the community who reveal similar symptomatology to a more serious degree.

The patient was an attractive 31-year-old nurse who was commissioned a second lieutenant in the Army Nurse Corps shortly after the beginning of World War II. From the start she found it difficult to adjust to fellow nurses and to enlisted men under her supervision, the difficulty apparently arising from her overzealousness in carrying out ward regulations in the minutest detail. In any event, "No one could get along with her." After some 2 years of service, she was transferred to the European Theater of Operations.

". . . Initially she made an excellent impression, but soon showed herself to be a perfectionist, a hypercritical and domineering personality who insisted on the immediate, precise, exact and detailed execution of orders. Within a 14-week period she was transferred on three separate occasions from post to post, and at each new post her manner and her attitude, despite her precise and meticulous efficiency, constituted a virtual demand that nurses, wardmen, patients, and medical officers conform to her exceedingly rigid ideas about the management of ward and even departmental routines. . . .

"During the course of her last assignment, she received every possible help. She requested additional responsibility and was, therefore, assigned, as charge nurse, to the E.E.N.T. Clinic. Within a week she lodged a complaint with the commanding officer of the hospital, accusing the enlisted men of conspiring against her, the nurses of lying about her, and the officer in charge of lack of co-operation. She was, therefore, transferred to one of the wards, where she expected wardmen, nurses and patients to execute her orders on the instant, in minute and exact detail, and where she violently berated them because of their inability to do so. A week later, the responsible medical officer requested that she be relieved from duty there. Instead, she discussed the problem with the chief nurse and promised to correct her attitude. Within four days, the patients as a group requested her removal. Two weeks later, the ward officer repeated his request. She was, therefore, given a five-day leave, and during her absence all ward personnel were contacted in an attempt to help her adjust when she returned to duty.

"During this period she became convinced that she was being persecuted. She grew tense and despondent, kept rigidly to herself, was unable to sleep in a room with a ticking clock, and frequently burst into tears. As she herself said, 'Some of the nurses deliberately went out of their way to annoy and criticize me. They wanted to make me trouble. That's why I was so upset.' On three separate occasions, she requested the appointment of a Board of Officers to investigate these alleged discriminatory acts. Finally she demanded that a Board of Officers be convened to determine her efficiency as a nurse. Instead, she was ordered to report to our hospital for psychiatric observation.

"On admission, few details of her military history were known. She seemed alert and co-operative, was well oriented in all three spheres, and was thought to be in complete contact. Extreme care, however, was necessary when addressing her. Even fellow patients would warn newcomers to the ward. 'Be careful what you say when she's around. She won't mean it, but she'll twist your statements without changing your words, and give them some meaning you never intended.' In addition, she was bitter about the unfair treatment she had received in the Army, wished to reform the Medical Department and the Army Nursing Corps, and indignantly repudiated the existence of any condition that could justify placing her under NP [neuropsychiatric] observation. . . .

"The diagnosis of 'paranoia, true type' was made, and she was returned to the United States, one month after admission to the hospital, a rigid and overzealous individual whose inelasticity had antagonized her associates and aroused severe emotional strain within herself, firmly convinced that she was being persecuted because of the necessary and badly needed work which she had much too efficiently performed. And by one of those fortuitous circumstances that nevertheless occur so frequently, she was received in the States as a patient in the very hospital to whose psychiatric section she had previously, for so brief a period of time, been assigned as ward nurse." (Rosen & Kiene, 1946, pp. 330–33)

Paranoiacs are not always as dangerous as we have been led to believe by popular fiction and drama, but there is always the chance that they will decide to take matters into their own hands and deal with their enemies in the only way that seems effective. In one instance, a school principal who was a paranoiac became convinced that the school board was discriminating against him and shot and killed most of the members of the board. In

---

Sequence of events in paranoid mode of thinking

A number of investigators have concluded that the most useful perspective from which to view paranoia is in terms of a *mode of thinking*. The sequence of events which appears to characterize this mode of thinking may be summarized as follows:

1. Suspiciousness — the individual mistrusts the motives of others, fears he will be taken advantage of, is constantly on the alert.

2. Protective thinking — selectively perceives the actions of others to confirm suspicions, now blames others for own failures.

3. Hostility — responds to alleged injustices and mistreatment with anger and hostility, becomes increasingly suspicious.

4. Paranoid illumination — the moment when everything "falls into place"; the individual finally understands the strange feelings and events he is experiencing.

5. Delusions — of influence and persecution that may be based on "some grain of truth," presented in a very logical and convincing way; often later development of delusions of grandeur.

Over time additional life areas, people, and events may be incorporated into the delusional system, so that the individual builds a "pseudo community" whose purpose is to carry out some action against him. He may come to feel that all the attention he is receiving from others is indicative of his unique abilities and importance, thus paving the way for delusions of grandeur.

Based in part on Swanson, Bohnert, and Smith (1970).

another case a paranoiac shot and killed a group of 7 persons who he thought were following him. The number of husbands and wives who have been killed or injured by suspicious paranoid mates is undoubtedly large. As Swanson, Bohnert, and Smith (1970) have pointed out, such murderous violence is commonly associated with jealousy and the loss of self-esteem; the paranoiac feels that he has been deceived, taken advantage of, and humiliated. Paranoiacs may also get involved in violent and destructive subversive activities as well as political assassinations.

Causal factors in paranoia

Most of us on various occasions may wonder if we are not "jinxed," when it seems as if everything we do goes wrong and the cards seem to be "stacked against us." If we are generally somewhat suspicious and disposed to blame others for our difficulties, we may feel that most people are selfish and ruthless and that honest people, no matter what their ability, do not have a fair chance. As a result, we may feel abused and become somewhat bitter and cynical. Many people go through life feeling underrated and frustrated and brooding over fancied and real injustices.

In paranoia, the picture is similar but considerably more extreme. Such reactions usually occur in sensitive, rigid, and suspicious persons who in severe stress situations begin to selectively perceive certain aspects of reality in a distorted way—usually concluding that others are deliberately interfering with or mistreating them. In some instances, these delusions have some grounding in fact but become grossly exaggerated. Neither genetic nor biochemical alterations have been found to play a role in the causes of paranoia. Available evidence indicates that psychosocial factors are of primary importance.

Faulty learning and development. As children, most paranoiacs seem to have been aloof, suspicious, seclusive, stubborn, and resentful of punishment. When crossed, they become sullen and morose. Rarely do they show a his-

tory of normal play with other children or good socialization in terms of warm, affectionate relationships (Sarvis, 1962; Schwartz, 1963; Swanson, Bohnert, & Smith, 1970).

Often the family background appears to have been authoritarian and excessively dominating, suppressive, and critical. Such a family has often been permeated with an air of superiority that was a cover-up for an underlying lack of self-acceptance and feelings of inferiority, creating for the child, in turn, the necessity of proving that he is superior. Inevitably his family background colors his feelings about people in general and his way of reacting to them. His inadequate socialization keeps him from understanding the motives and point of view of others and leads him to suspicious misinterpretation of their unintentional slights. Also he tends to enter into social relationships with a hostile, dominating attitude that drives others away. His inevitable social failures then further undermine his self-esteem and lead to deeper social isolation and mistrust of others.

In later personality development these early trends merge into a picture of self-important, rigid, arrogant individuals who long to dominate others and readily maintain their unrealistic self-picture by projecting the blame for difficulties onto others and seeing in others the weaknesses they cannot acknowledge in themselves. They are highly suspicious of the motives of other people and quick to sense insult or mistreatment. Such individuals lack a sense of humor—which is not surprising, since the paranoid is suspicious of others and views life as a deadly serious struggle—and are incapable of seeing things from any viewpoint but their own. Typically, they categorize people and ideas into "good" and "bad" and have difficulty in conceiving of something as having both good and bad qualities or in shades of gray. Their goals and expectations are unrealistically high, and they refuse to make concessions in meeting life's problems by accepting more realistic goals. They expect to be praised and appreciated for even minor achievements, and when such praise is not forthcoming, they sulk and withdraw from normal contacts. Although such individuals may have broad interests and appear normal in general behavior, they usually are unable to relate closely to other persons; they appear inaccessible, are overly aggressive, and maintain a somewhat superior air.

Failure and inferiority. The history of the paranoiac is replete with failures in critical life situations—social, occupational, and marital—stemming from his rigidity, his unrealistic goals, and his inability to get along with other people. Such failures jeopardize his picture of himself as being adequate, significant, and important and expose his easily wounded pride to what he interprets as the rejection, scorn, and ridicule of others.

His failure is made more difficult to cope with by his inability to understand the causes for it. Why should his efforts to improve the efficiency of his company—which people approve in principle—lead to such negative reactions from others? Why should people dislike him when he strives so hard to do the best possible job down to the very last detail? Unable to see himself or the situation objectively, he simply cannot understand how he tends to alienate others and why they rebuff and reject him.

Although the paranoiac's feelings of inferiority are masked behind his air of superiority and self-importance, they are manifested in many aspects of his behavior. Clues in profusion are found in their pathetic craving for praise and recognition, their hypersensitivity to criticism, their exact and formal adherence to socially approved behavior, and their conscientious and overzealous performance of the most minute occupational tasks.

In essence, then, the paranoid individual is confronted with failure experiences that in effect say, "People don't like you," "Something is wrong with you," "You are inferior." But he is incapable of dealing with the stress situation in a task-oriented way. Instead, he tends to intensify his existing defenses, becoming more rigid, opinionated, and prone to blame others. This defensive pattern helps protect him from facing unbearable feelings of inferiority and worthlessness.

Elaboration of defenses and the "pseudo-community." A rigid, self-important, humorless, and suspicious individual such as we have described becomes understandably unpopular with other people. He is, in effect, an aversive stimulus. Thus as Lemert (1962) has noted, many times the paranoiac not only misconstrues the world "as if others were against him" but is, in fact, a target of actual discrimination and mistreatment. Ever alert to injustices, both imagined and real, the paranoid individual has little trouble finding "proof" that he is being persecuted.

In this context, Grunebaum and Perlman (1973) have pointed to the naivete of the preparanoid in assessing the interpersonal world—in terms of whom he can trust and whom he can't—as a fertile source of hurtful interactions. As they express it, "The ability to trust others realistically requires that the individual be able to tolerate minor and major violations of trust that are part of normal human relationships" (p. 32). But the preparanoid individual is unprepared for the "facts of life"; he tends to both trust and mistrust inappropriately and to overreact when others actually do or are perceived as letting him down.

Paranoid reactions usually develop gradually, as mounting failures and seeming betrayals force the individual to an elaboration of his defensive structure. To avoid self-devaluation, he searches for "logical" reasons for his lack of success. Why was he denied a much deserved promotion? Why was it given to someone less experienced and obviously far less qualified than he? He becomes more vigilant, begins to scrutinize his environment, searches for hidden meanings, and asks leading questions. He ponders like a detective over the "clues" he picks up, trying to fit them into some sort of meaningful picture.

Gradually the picture begins to crystallize—a process commonly referred to as "paranoid illumination." It becomes apparent that he is being singled out for some obscure reason, that other people are working against him, that he is being interfered with. In essence, he protects himself against the intolerable assumption "There is something wrong with me" with the projective defense "They are doing something to me." Now he has failed not because of any inferiority or lack on his part but because others are working against him. He is on the side of good and the progress of humankind while "they" are allied with the forces of evil. With this as his fundamental defensive premise, he proceeds to distort and falsify the facts to fit it and gradually develops a logic-tight, fixed, delusional system.

Cameron (1959) has referred to this process as the building up of a paranoid "pseudo-community" in which the individual organizes the people around him (both real and imaginary) into a structured group whose purpose is to carry out some action against him. Now the most trivial events may take on an ominous meaning. If a new employee is hired by his company, the person was obviously sent by the organization to spy on him. If an employee under his supervision makes a mistake, it is done to discredit his competence as a supervisor. Even the most casual conversation of others may have a hidden and sinister meaning. This pseudo-community is not all-inclusive, however, but remains limited in scope to those stress areas—such as occupational failure—that present the greatest threat to his feelings of adequacy and worth. In other life areas not directly involved with his paranoid system, he may be quite rational and may function adequately. Over a period of time, of course, additional life areas and experiences may be incorporated into his delusional system.

In many cases the attention the individual thinks he is receiving leads him to believe that he is a person of great importance, for why else would his enemies go to all this trouble? In one case, it was pointed out to a hospitalized patient that if his enemies were persecuting him in the way he insisted they were, it would be costing them about $10,000 per day, which was obviously a ridiculous figure. The patient drew himself up proudly and replied, "Why shouldn't they? After all, I am the world's greatest atomic scientist." As might be expected, the particular content of the grandiose ideas that develop is closely related to the individual's education, vocation, and special interests. A paranoid person with strong religious convictions may develop the notion that he is a great religious savior, whereas the individual interested in science is more likely to envision himself as a great inventor.

The role of perceptual selectivity in the development of these delusional systems should be emphasized. Once the individual begins to suspect that others are working against him,

he carefully notes the slightest signs pointing in the direction of his suspicions and ignores all evidence to the contrary. As Swanson, Bohnert, and Smith (1970) have pointed out:

"Suspicious thinking is remarkably rigid thinking. The suspicious person has something on his mind constantly. He looks at the world with a definite expectation. Suspiciousness requires intense attention. The paranoid reads more between the lines than he sees in the lines themselves, thus overlooking the obvious." (p. 14)

With this frame of reference, it is quite easy, in our highly competitive, somewhat ruthless world, to find ample evidence that others are working against us. And the individual's very attitude leads him into a vicious circle, for his suspiciousness, distrust, and criticism of others drive his friends and well-wishers away and keep him in continual friction with other people, generating new incidents for him to grasp hold of and magnify. Often people do in fact have to conspire behind his back in order to keep peace and cope with his eccentricities.

One additional factor often mentioned in connection with the development of paranoia is that of sexual maladjustment. Like schizophrenic patients, most paranoids do reveal sexual difficulties, not infrequently centering around homosexual conflicts. The factor of homosexuality was, in fact, strongly emphasized by Freud, who concluded that paranoia represents the individual's attempt to deal with homosexual tendencies that the ego is not prepared to acknowledge. Most contemporary investigators, however, believe that the critical factors in paranoia are the individual's serious difficulties in interpersonal relationships and overwhelming feelings of inadequacy and inferiority. While underlying sexual conflicts, both heterosexual and homosexual, may be involved in the clinical picture, they do not appear to be of primary significance.

Treatment and outcomes

In the early stages of paranoia, treatment with individual and/or group psychotherapy may prove effective, particularly if an individual voluntarily seeks professional assistance. Here, behavior therapy appears to show particular promise; for example, the paranoid ideation may be altered by a combination of aversive conditioning, removal of factors in the person's life situation that are reinforcing the maladaptive behavior, and development of more effective coping patterns.

Once the delusional system is well established, however, treatment is extremely difficult. It is usually impossible to communicate with the paranoiac in a rational way concerning his problems. In addition, such persons are not prone to seek treatment, but are more likely to be seeking justice for all the wrongs done to them. Unfortunately, hospitalization of paranoiacs is usually of little avail. To the paranoiac, it often seems more a form of punishment than of treatment. He is apt to regard himself as superior to other patients and will often complain that his family and the hospital staff have had him "put away" for no valid reason; thus he refuses to cooperate or participate in treatment.

Eventually, however, he may realize that his failure to curb his actions and ideas will result in prolonged hospitalization. As a result, he may make a pretext of renouncing his delusions, admitting that he did hold such ideas but claiming that he now realizes they are absurd and has given them up. After his release, he is often more reserved in expressing his ideas and in annoying other people, but he is far from recovered. Thus the prognosis for paranoia has traditionally been unfavorable.

In beginning our consideration of the psychoses with schizophrenia and paranoia, we have dealt with clinical manifestations considerably different from those found in the neuroses or psychosomatic illnesses. Thus in schizophrenia we noted severely impaired contact with reality and marked personality disorganization—involving disturbances in thought, affect, and behavior. We examined the major types of schizophrenia—acute, paranoid, catatonic, hebephrenic, and simple—and attempted to identify certain differences in the clinical picture of each type. We then dealt with various causal factors, noting that we still do not understand the development of schizophrenia. However, we examined evidence pointing to the significant role of genetic factors in schizophrenia; we also noted the possible role of neurophysiological and biochemical alterations in the impairment of normal brain functioning in schizophrenia, including the breakdown of filtering mechanisms. The precise nature of these alterations remains to be ascertained, as well as whether they precede or result from the mental disorder. We also considered the potential significance of various psychosocial factors, regarded by many investigators to be of primary importance in the etiology of schizophrenia. Finally, we noted how innovations in chemotherapy, psychosocial therapy, and aftercare programs have resulted in an increasingly favorable outlook for the schizophrenic patient.

In the latter part of the chapter we examined paranoia, characterized by the development of a highly systematized delusional system. Here, the evidence indicates that psychosocial factors are of primary importance, neither genetic nor biochemical alterations having been emphasized as causal factors in paranoia. Paranoid disorders involve less personality disorganization than most other types of psychosis, but they are highly resistant to presently available methods of treatment.

10

Major Affective Disorders

The term *affect* is roughly equivalent to *emotion,* and in the affective disorders extreme and inappropriate emotional responses, especially extreme elation or depression, dominate the clinical picture. By contrast, the disorders discussed in the preceding chapter primarily involve thought disturbances accompanied by emotional distortion.

Affective psychoses are not new in the history of humankind. Descriptions of affective disorders are found among the early writings of the Egyptians, Greeks, Hebrews, and Chinese; similar descriptions are found in the literary works of Shakespeare, Dostoevsky, Poe, and Hemingway. As we noted in Chapter 1, Saul, King of Israel in the eleventh century B.C., suffered from manic-depressive episodes, and King George III of England was subject to periods of manic overactivity. The list of historical figures who suffered from recurrent depression is a long and celebrated one, including Moses, Rousseau, Dostoevsky, Lincoln, Tchaikovsky, and Freud. Here it is apparent that we are again dealing with mental disorders that appear to be common to the human race, both cross-culturally and historically.

For our purposes, we shall focus on two subgroups of affective disorders: (a) *manic-depressive psychoses,* characterized by episodes of extreme elation and overactivity or extreme depression and underactivity or an alternation between the two; and (b) *involutional melancholia,* characterized by depression and agitation. In our own society, as we shall see, the incidence of these psychotic patterns has undergone considerable change in recent years.

In the final section of this chapter we shall briefly discuss the broader problem of depression in our society. We shall note its increasing incidence, the myriad forms that depressive patterns may take—particularly nonpsychotic ones in which the depression may not be obvious and is, in fact, often "disguised"—and the implications of these depressive patterns for adjustment. We shall also comment on the relevance of depressive episodes to the problem of suicide, to which we devote an entire chapter in Part Three.

Manic-Depressive Psychoses
Involutional Melancholia
Broader Aspects of Depression

Manic-Depressive Psychoses

The great Greek physician Hippocrates classified all mental disorders into three broad categories—mania, melancholia, and phrenitis. His descriptions of mania and melancholia, based on the clinical records of his patients, are strikingly similar to modern clinical symptomatology.

The sixth-century physician Alexander Trallianus was perhaps the first to recognize recurrent cycles of mania and melancholia in the same person, thus anticipating by several hundred years Bonet's (1684) "folie maniaco-mélancolique" and Falret's (1854) "folie circulaire." It remained for Kraepelin, however, in 1899, to introduce the term *manic-depressive psychosis* and to clarify the clinical picture. Kraepelin described the disorder as a series of attacks of elation and depression, with periods of relative normality in between and a generally favorable prognosis.

Actually, some individuals show only manic reactions and others only depressive reactions. Others, however, alternate between these two. Consequently, three major types of manic-depressive psychoses are commonly distinguished: (a) manic type, (b) depressed type, and (c) circular reactions.[1]

Clinic and hospital statistics indicate that the manic and circular types have decreased in incidence, while the depressive type has increased in recent years. In fact, it has been estimated that some 8 to 10 persons in 100—about 25 million Americans—will evidence a severe depressive episode at some time in their lives (Brown, 1974; Schanche, 1974). A large percentage of these will be labeled manic-depressive psychotics, depressive type. The great majority of cases occur between the ages of 25 and 65, although such reactions

---

[1]Recurrent manic or depressive reactions only are also referred to as *unipolar* disorders; circular reactions, involving alternating manic and depressive episodes, are sometimes referred to as *bipolar* disorders.

may occur from early childhood to old age. Poznanski and Zrull (1970) have described depressive reactions among children ranging from 3 to 12 years of age, and cases have been observed even after age 85. The incidence is higher among females than males, with a ratio of about 3 to 2.

Clinical picture

The clinical picture in manic-depressive reactions is colored by the predominant emotional mood of the patient, which may be one of elation or depression. Against this affective background, the patient may evidence a variety of psychological and behavioral symptoms, including delusions, hallucinations, and overtly aggressive or suicidal actions, that are roughly appropriate to the prevailing mood.

In manic reactions there are feelings of optimism and elation, accompanied by a speeding up of thought processes and activities and a decreased need for sleep. The individual is loud and boisterous, appears to have unbounded energy and enthusiasm, and is involved in all sorts of activities. He shows impaired ability to concentrate, is easily distracted, and changes rapidly from one trend of thought and activity to another. Judgment is impaired, sexual and other behavioral restraints are lowered, and the individual tends to be extremely impatient with any attempts to restrain his activities. Extravagant plans and delusions of grandeur are common: the person may envision himself as the ruler of the world, the most remarkable scientist who ever lived, or a great prophet who can solve the problems of all humankind.

In depressive reactions the individual experiences a feeling of profound sadness and loneliness, and the whole world becomes joyless and gray. Nothing seems worthwhile any more; emptiness prevails, and only bad things are expected. Thought processes and behavior are slowed down. The individual speaks slowly in a monotonous voice. He limits himself to brief answers to questions. He rarely poses questions; he avoids people and has a listless facial expression and a stooping posture. Self-accusatory and hypochondriacal delusions are common. The individual may accuse himself of having committed various crimes, participated in immoral sexual acts, been selfish and callous with loved ones. He feels guilty of "unpardonable sins" and regards himself as basically worthless and not fit to live. He may be convinced that he has an incurable disease, that his internal organs have disappeared or are rotting away, or that his body is undergoing peculiar changes. In older depressed persons, the delusional content often centers around ideas of poverty, of suffering from some terrible disease, and of being abandoned and doomed to die in loneliness and despair.

About 75 percent of depressed cases have suicidal thoughts and some 10 to 15 percent attempt suicide. Ianzito, Cadoret, and Pugh (1974) also found that about 10 percent of their sample of 89 depressed patients had homicidal thoughts. Occasionally, depressed patients commit infanticide or homicide—usually involving loved ones—and then take their own lives. Manic patients may become hostile if interfered with and threaten or assault others, but they rarely kill anyone.

Manic-depressive reactions tend to be episodic and relatively brief. Even in those cases where no formal treatment is received, manic reactions usually run their course in about three months and depressive reactions in about nine months. There are wide variations, however, with some psychotic episodes lasting only a few days and others as long as a year or more. At the conclusion of a manic or depressive episode, the individual usually returns to apparent normality. While some patients manifest recurrent episodes of manic, depressive, or circular reactions, Helzer and Winokur (1974) concluded from a review of available research findings that "the average number of episodes in all affective patients is probably two or less . . ." (p. 77). Patients who manifest only depression tend to have fewer episodes than those manifesting manic or circular reactions.

Manic types. Manic reactions are characterized by varying degrees of elation and psychomotor overactivity. Three degrees are commonly delineated, denoting the progression of behavior from mild to extreme degrees of manic excitement. Though these reactions differ in degree rather than kind, they merit separate consideration.

1. *Hypomania.* This is the mildest form of manic reaction and is characterized by moderate elation, flightiness, and overactivity. The individual feels "simply great," has unbounded confidence in his ability and knowledge, and will unhesitatingly express his opinion on any and all subjects. His thinking is speeded up and he may become particularly witty and entertaining. He seems tireless and gets practically no sleep, stating that he feels so well that he does not need any. During the day he engages in ceaseless activity, talking, visiting, keeping luncheon and other engagements, telephoning, writing, and working on various sure-fire schemes. Numerous appointments are made, postponed, and canceled. The mails frequently seem too slow to these persons, and they are fond of sending telegrams and special-delivery letters and making long-distance telephone calls.

The overall picture frequently appears at first to be one of an aggressive, brilliant, sociable individual who has many commendable enthusiasms and wonderful plans for the future. Initially he may seem an exciting person to be with, but he soon reveals his self-centeredness, becomes domineering, monopolizes the conversation, and shows difficulty in sticking to the subject. He is intolerant of criticism and may unsparingly denounce as a stupid fool anyone who dares to disagree with him or interfere with his plans. The details of his plans are seldom worked out; very few of them are ever put into action, and these few are not completed. However, the individual easily rationalizes his activities and concedes no mistakes. He spends money recklessly and in a short period of time may dissipate his entire savings. Moral restraint gives way, and he may engage in numerous promiscuous sexual acts and in alcoholic excesses.

Although these persons rarely show marked delusions or hallucinations, they do show very poor judgment and usually lack insight into their condition. Any suggestion that they seek professional assistance is met with angry abuse. They are ready with a rebuttal to all charges made against them and may threaten legal action against anyone who dares to interfere with them.

The following conversation with a hypomanic patient reveals the elated mood and pressure toward activity typical of this reaction pattern. The patient was a woman of 46.

Dr.: Hello, how are you today?

Pt.: Fine, fine, and how are you, Doc? You're looking pretty good. I never felt better in my life. Could I go for a schnapps now? Say, you're new around here, I never saw you before—and not bad! How's about you and me stepping out tonight if I can get that sour old battleship of a nurse to give me back my dress. It's low cut and it'll wow 'em. Even in this old rag, all the doctors give me the eye. You know I'm a model. Yep, I was No. 1—used to dazzle them in New York, London and Paris. Hollywood has been angling with me for a contract.

Dr.: Is that what you did before you came here?

Pt.: I was a society queen . . . entertainer of kings and presidents. I've got five grown sons and I wore out three husbands getting them . . . about ready for a couple of more now. There's no woman like me, smart, brainy, beautiful and sexy. You can see I don't believe in playing myself down. If you are good and know you're good you have to speak out, and I know what I've got.

Dr.: Why are you in this hospital?

Pt.: That's just the trouble. My husbands never could understand me. I was too far above them. I need someone like me with savoir faire you know, somebody that can get around, intelligent, lots on the ball. Say, where can I get a schnapps around here—always like one before dinner. Someday I'll cook you a meal. I've got special recipes like you never ate before . . . sauces, wines, desserts. Boy, it's making me hungry. Say, have you got anything for me to do around here? I've been showing these slowpokes how to make up beds but I want something more in line with my talents.

Dr.: What would you like to do?

Pt.: Well, I'm thinking of organizing a show, singing, dancing, jokes. I can do it all myself but I want to know what you think about it. I'll bet there's some schnapps in the kitchen. I'll look around later. You know what we need here . . . a dance at night. I could play the piano, and teach them the latest steps. Wherever I go I'm the life of the party.

2. *Acute mania.* The symptoms in acute mania are similar to those in hypomania but are more pronounced. This condition may develop out of a hypomanic reaction or may develop suddenly with little or no warning except for a short period of insomnia, irritability, and restlessness. Elation and pressure of activity become more pronounced, and the individual may laugh boisterously and talk at the top of his voice. He becomes increasingly boastful, dictatorial, and overbearing, and may order everyone around as if he were a super-dictator.

Irritability is easily provoked, and the individual's mood may change rapidly from gaiety to anger. Both before and during hospitalization, violent behavior is common, and the individual may break up furniture, deface the walls, and assault nurses and other patients. He is continually on the go, walking back and forth, gesturing to himself, singing, and banging on the walls and door, demanding release. Even persons who have had the most rigid moral backgrounds will show a complete abandonment of moral restraint and may be obscene in their talk, expose themselves, and make sexual advances to those around them.

There is a wild flight of ideas, frequently leading to incoherent speech. The alternation in ideas may be so rapid that at one moment the person engages in erotic activities and the next delivers a profound religious dissertation. There may be some confusion and disorientation for time, place, and person, with a tendency to misidentify those about him.

Transient delusions and hallucinations may occur, in which the person may have grandiose ideas of his wealth and abilities or in which he may hear voices and carry on conversations with persons whom he imagines to be present. Occasionally there may be short periods of relative calmness in which the individual shows some insight into his noisy behavior and may even apologize for it. In general, however, insight and judgment are severely impaired, and periods of insight are shortly followed by a resumption of manic activity.

The following brief description of an acute manic patient, though made over 30 years ago and involving a relatively extreme case, still serves to illustrate various typical symptoms as well today as it did then.

"On admission she slapped the nurse, addressed the house physician as God, made the sign of the cross, and laughed loudly when she was asked to don the hospital garb. This she promptly tore into shreds. She remained nude for several hours before she was restrained in bed. She sang at the top of her voice, screamed through the window, and leered at the patients promenading in the recreation yard. She

Comparison of clinical pictures in manic and depressive patterns

	Manic pattern	Depressive pattern
Emotional symptoms	Euphoric, elated mood Sociability Extreme impatience with restraint or criticism	Gloomy outlook, loss of hope Social withdrawal Marked irritability
Cognitive symptoms	Short attention span; racing of thoughts; flight of ideas Orientation toward action; impulsiveness; overtalkativeness Positive self-image; tendency to blame others Grandiose delusions	Slowing of thought processes Obsessional worrying; exaggeration of problems; indecisiveness Negative self-image; tendency to blame self Delusions of sin, guilt, disease, poverty
Motor symptoms	Hyperactivity Indefatigability Decreased need for sleep Variable appetite Increased sex drive	Decreased motor activity Fatigue Insomnia Loss of appetite Decreased sex drive

Such clear-cut differences cannot, of course, be drawn in the case of certain symptom patterns. For example, in involutional melancholia and "mixed" depressive reactions, the clinical picture may be complicated by agitation and overactivity.

Based in part on Akiskal and McKinney (1975). American Psychiatric Association (1968). Becker (1974), and Reich, Clayton, and Winokur (1969).

was very untidy and incontinent, smearing her excreta about the floor and walls. Frequently she would utter the words, 'God, Thou Holy One,' cross herself, laugh, and then give vent to vile expletives while she carried out suggestive movements of the body. She yelled for water, and, when this was proffered, she threw the tin cup across the room." (Karnosh & Zucker, 1945, p. 78)

3. *Delirious mania.* In the most severe type of manic reaction the individual is confused, wildly excited, and violent. The condition may develop out of hypomania or acute mania but often appears suddenly with few warning signs. The individual becomes incoherent and disoriented and may experience vivid auditory and visual hallucinations. It is impossible to converse with him or hold his attention. He shows the most extreme psychomotor overactivity, is violent and destructive, and spends his days and nights in restless pacing, singing, screaming, gesticulating, and incoherent shouting. His eyes may show a peculiar glare

and his features may be contorted beyond recognition. One moment he may refuse food and the next devour everything he can get hold of. His behavior is obscene and entirely shameless, and personal habits completely deteriorate. He may smear his excreta on his person or about the walls. He is dangerous to those about him and may seriously injure himself. In short, he fulfills the popular notion of a raving maniac.

This condition places a tremendous burden on all bodily functions, and the patient loses weight rapidly and may become utterly exhausted. As might be expected, vulnerability to heart attacks and strokes is increased and resistance to disease is lowered, particularly among older patients.

The following scene, which took place in the courtyard of a state mental hospital before the advent of newer treatment procedures, illustrates the extreme excitement that may occur during a severe manic reaction.

This picture and the one on the opposite page reveal the deep distress that is felt by depressed individuals. The look on the woman's face and the way the man is standing communicate in different ways their feelings of depression and despair, signs that personal resources are proving inadequate for dealing with their problems.

A manic patient had climbed upon the small platform in the middle of the yard and was delivering an impassioned lecture to a number of patients sitting on benches surrounding the platform. Most of the audience were depressed patients who were hallucinating and muttering to themselves and not paying a bit of attention to the speaker. However, the speaker had an "assistant" in the form of a hypomanic patient who would move rapidly around the circle of benches shaking the occupants and exhorting them to pay attention. If anyone started to leave, the assistant would plump him back in his seat in no uncertain terms. In the background were a number of apparently schizophrenic patients who were pacing a given number of steps back and forth, and beyond was a high wire fencing surrounding the yard.

The speaker herself was in a state of delirious mania. She had torn her clothing to shreds and was singing and shouting at the top of her voice. So rapidly did her thoughts move from one topic to another that her "speech" was almost a complete word hash, although occasional sentences such as "You goddam bitches" and "God loves everybody, do you hear?" could be made out. These points were illustrated by wild gestures, screaming, and outbursts of song. In the delivery of her talk, she moved restlessly back and forth on the platform, occasionally falling off the platform in her wild excitement. Her ankles and legs were bleeding from rubbing the edge of the platform during these falls, but she was completely oblivious of her injuries.

Fortunately, the degree of excitement in manic reactions can now be markedly reduced by means of various drugs, and scenes such as this need no longer occur.

Depressed types. The symptom picture in depressive reactions is in many ways the reverse of that in manic reactions. Here, too, there are differences in degree.[2]

1. *Simple depression.* The outstanding symptoms in simple depression are a loss of enthusiasm and a general slowing down of mental and physical activity. The individual feels dejected and discouraged. Work and other activities require tremendous effort and somehow do not seem worth bothering with anyway.

---

[2]There is also a category called *psychotic depressive reactions* in the APA classification, but the clinical picture is not significantly different from that in the depressive type of manic-depressive reactions described in this chapter. Consequently, we shall not discuss the other category separately.

Feelings of unworthiness, failure, sinfulness, and guilt dominate his sluggish thought processes. His loss of interest in things about him extends to eating and is usually reflected in loss of weight and digestive difficulties, such as constipation. Conversation is carried on in a monotone, and questions are answered with a meager supply of words. In general, the individual prefers just to sit alone, contemplating his sins and seeing no hope for the future. As we have noted, suicidal preoccupation is common and actual suicide attempts may be made.

Despite the mental and motor retardation, however, the person shows no real clouding of consciousness or actual disorientation. His memory remains unimpaired, and he is able to answer questions fairly satisfactorily if allowed sufficient time. Many of these individuals have some insight into their condition and understand that they need treatment, although they may not admit that they are depressed but rather emphasize various bodily ailments such as headaches, fatigue, loss of appetite, constipation, and poor sleep. In fact, mild depressive cases are sometimes diagnosed as neurasthenia. Unlike neurasthenic patients, however, the person usually insists that his ailments and other difficulties are punishment for various mistakes and sins committed in the past. The following is an excerpt from a conversation between a therapist and a young woman 25 years old who had been classified as a mild depressive.

Th.: Good morning, how are you today?

Pt.: (Pause) Well, o.k. I guess, doctor. . . . I don't know, I just feel sort of discouraged.

Th.: Is there anything in particular that worries you?

Pt.: I don't know, doctor . . . everything seems to be futile . . . nothing seems worth while any more. It seems as if all that was beautiful has lost its beauty. I guess I expected more than life has given. It just doesn't seem worth while going on. I can't seem to make up my mind about anything. I guess I have what you would call the "blues."

Th.: Can you tell me more about your feelings?

Pt.: Well . . . my family expected great things of me. I am supposed to be the outstanding member of the family . . . they think because I went through college everything should begin to pop and there's nothing to pop. I . . . really don't expect anything from anyone. Those whom I have trusted proved themselves less than friends should be.

Th.: Oh?

Pt.: Yes, I once had a very good girl friend with whom I spent a good deal of time. She was very important to me . . . I thought she was my friend but now she treats me like a casual acquaintance (tears).

Th.: Can you think of any reason for this?

Pt.: Yes, it's all my fault. I can't blame them—anybody that is . . . I am not worthy of them. I have sinned against nature. I am worthless . . . nobody can love me. I don't deserve friends or success. . . .

Th.: You sinned against nature?

Pt.: Well . . . I am just no good. I am a failure. I was envious of other people. I didn't want them to have more than I had and when something bad happened to them I was glad. Now I am being repaid for my sins. All my flaws stand out and I am repugnant to everyone. (Sighs) I am a miserable failure. . . . There is no hope for me.

2. *Acute depression.* In acute depressive reactions the mental and physical retardation is increased. The individual becomes increasingly inactive, tends to isolate himself from others, does not speak of his own accord, and is extremely slow in his responses. Feelings of guilt and worthlessness becomes more pronounced and the individual becomes increasingly self-accusatory. He may hold himself responsible for plagues, floods, or economic depressions, and may insist that he has committed all sorts of horrible sins that will bring disaster on everyone. Delusions may take a hypochondriacal turn, and in keeping with his morbid mood, the individual may believe that his brain is being eaten away, that his "insides are slowly petrifying," or that his bowels are completely stopped up. One hospitalized patient maintained that he had not had a bowel movement for over a month. The patient may refuse to eat because he has no stomach and is only a "living shell." He usually blames these ailments on early sex practices or other sins that have undermined his health and for which he is now being punished.

The individual experiencing acute depression sees absolutely no hope that things will ever improve. Feelings of unreality and mild hallucinations occasionally occur, particularly in connection with ideas of sin, guilt, and disease. There is a considerable danger of suicide, since death generally seems the only way out. The reactions of this 47-year-old patient are fairly typical:

Th.: Good morning, Mr. H., how are you today?
Pt.: (Long pause—looks up and then head drops back down and stares at floor.)
Th.: I said good morning, Mr. H. Wouldn't you like to tell me how you feel today?
Pt.: (Pause—looks up again) . . . I feel . . . terrible . . . simply terrible.
Th.: What seems to be your trouble?
Pt.: . . . There's just no way out of it . . . nothing but blind alleys . . . I have no appetite . . . nothing matters anymore . . . it's hopeless . . . everything is hopeless.
Th.: Can you tell me how your trouble started?
Pt.: I don't know . . . it seems like I have a lead weight in my stomach . . . I feel different . . . I am not like other people . . . my health is ruined . . . I wish I were dead.
Th.: Your health is ruined?
Pt.: . . . Yes, my brain is being eaten away. I shouldn't have done it . . . If I had any willpower I would kill myself . . . I don't deserve to live . . . I have ruined everything . . . and it's all my fault.
Th.: It's all your fault?
Pt.: Yes . . . I have been unfaithful to my wife and now I am being punished . . . my health is ruined . . . there's no use going on . . . (sigh) . . . I have ruined everything . . . my family . . . and now myself . . . I bring misfortune to everyone . . . I am a moral leper . . . a serpent in the Garden of Eden . . . why don't I die . . . why don't you give me a pill and end it all before I bring catastrophe on everyone. . . . No one can help me. . . . It's hopeless . . . I know that . . . it's hopeless.

3. *Depressive stupor.* In the most severe degree of psychomotor retardation and depression, the individual becomes almost completely unresponsive and inactive. He is usually bedridden and utterly indifferent to all that goes on around him. He refuses to speak or eat and has to be tube-fed and have his eliminative processes taken care of. Confusion concerning time, place, and person is marked and there are vivid hallucinations and delusions, particularly involving grotesque fantasies about sin, death, and rebirth. The following brief description illustrates this severe depressive reaction.

The patient lay in bed, immobile, with a dull, depressed expression on his face. His eyes were sunken and downcast. Even when spoken to, he would not raise his eyes to look at the speaker. Usually he did not respond at all to questions, but sometimes, after apparently great effort, he would mumble something about the "Scourge of God." He appeared somewhat emaciated, his breath was foul, and he had to be given enemas to maintain elimination. Occasionally, with great effort, he made the sign of the cross with his right hand. The overall picture was one of extreme vegetativelike immobility and depression.

With the newer treatment methods today, most depressive reactions can be rapidly ameliorated, and few hospitalized patients remain severely depressed for an extended period of time.

Circular type. The circular type of manic-depressive psychosis is distinguished by at least one episode of both mania and depression, and helps us understand why manic and depressed types are combined into a single category in the APA classification. Although manic-depressive reactions have been considered historically as circular reactions, only some 15 to 25 percent of manic-depressives actually show an alternation between manic and depressive episodes.

Jenner et al. (1967) have cited an unusual case of a manic-depressive patient whose manic phase lasted 24 hours and was then followed by a depressive phase of equal length. This cycle had persisted for 11 years. Similarly, Bunney, Murphy, Goodwin, and Borge (1972) refer to the case of a female patient who switched between mania and depression every 48 hours over a period of two years. Such cases are atypical, however. There is likely to be a 1- to 10-day period of relative normality between the end of depression and the start of mania. The switch the other way, from mania to depression, usually happens suddenly, with little or no warning, but in some cases there is an extensive period of normality in between. Thus an inpatient may recover from a manic episode and leave the hospital or clinic setting only to be readmitted several months or years later with a severe depression.

In a substantial number of cases, the clinical picture in manic-depressive psychoses is further complicated by the excessive use of alcohol (Reich, Davies, & Himmelhoch, 1974). In other cases the clinical picture may show a distinct schizophrenic coloring and is referred

The "switch" from depression to mania

Clinical study of patients in a metabolic research ward at the National Institute of Mental Health, Bethesda, Maryland, led a team of investigators to suspect that a biological switch mechanism may be a factor in sudden cyclic shifts from depression to mania. As an example of how the switch occurs, they described the case of a female patient. Twelve days prior to the onset of a manic episode, the woman was deeply depressed. For the next seven days she stayed in bed in her room, avoiding contact with the nurses and staff. She appeared sad and deep in thought. Then the "countdown" to switch day proceeded as follows:

'Switch day' minus 5   Patient remains alone, depressed but beginning to come out of it. She says to a nurse: 'I guess I'm in one of my low periods.'

'Switch day' minus 4   Patient still appears depressed and still secludes herself in her room, but there are times when she actually seems pleasant and not brooding.

'Switch day' minus 3   In the morning, the nurses find that the patient 'appears to be functioning on a good level' and not depressed. Her behavior is rated as normal. She says how good it would be to go home on a pass the next day and expresses concern about a new female patient.

'Switch day' minus 2   Patient is normal and spends the day out on a pass with her mother.

'Switch day' minus 1   Patient is still normal and returns from pass 'in excellent spirits.' She recounts many of the events at home: 'I washed my windows, gave my dog a bath, took care of other odds and ends and got my hair cut and styled.'

'Switch day'   Patient was up entire night. Sudden onset of mania was noted around midnight. After midnight she became loud, threatening and seductive, and provoked fights. She was very angry, sarcastic, euphoric at times, talking continuously. By afternoon, she was shouting, had dressed gaudily and had put on bizarre makeup.

"For the next 25 days she continued to be manic, very loud, threatening, shouting continuously, bizarre in dress, obnoxious, provocative, and extremely angry, with moods frequently vacillating from tears to forced laughter. By 'switch day' plus 26, she began to come down slowly. The cycle was starting again." (Bunney, Paul, & Cramer, 1971, pp. 1–2)

On the assumption that "Something must be happening in the body as well as the mind" of such patients, these NIMH investigators studied biochemical changes in 6 manic-depressive patients, who, with one exception, were not on medication. It was found that there was a brief but marked elevation in a biogenic amine (adenosine 3', 5'-monophosphate) in the urine of the depressed patients on the day of the switch. Patients with the most rapid onset of mania also showed the most marked elevation in this biogenic amine on the switch day. Although these investigators considered the biological alteration as a possible switch mechanism, it was their impression that identifiable environmental stresses also played a part. However, they were unable to identify such stresses in the change out of mania. This impression was supported in an additional study of patients switching from mania into depression as well as from depression to mania (Bunney, Murphy, Goodwin, & Borge, 1972).

to as schizo-affective psychosis. The latter pattern has led some investigators to speculate that schizophrenia and manic-depressive psychoses are not separate mental disorders, but rather are extremes of a continuum characterized by a shattering of thought processes at one end and relatively pure mood disturbances at the other, with gradations in between.

Causal factors in manic-depressive disorders

In considering the development of manic-depressive disorders, we shall again find it useful to examine the possible roles of biological, psychological and interpersonal, and sociocultural factors.[3]

Biological factors. A biological basis for manic and depressive reactions is suggested by the fact that once the reaction is underway, it becomes relatively "autonomous" until it runs its course or is interrupted by drugs or other medication. Attempts to establish a biological basis for manic-depressive disorders have run the familiar gamut from genetic and constitutional factors through neurophysiological and biochemical alterations, as well as implicating various related considerations, such as sleep disturbances.

1. *Hereditary predisposition.* As with schizophrenics, the incidence of manic-depressive disorders is considerably higher among the relatives of manic-depressives than in the population at large. In an early study, Slater (1944) found that approximately 15 percent of the brothers, sisters, parents, and children of manic-depressives were also manic-depressives, as compared with an expectancy of about 0.5 percent for the general population. Kallmann (1958) found the concordance rate for manic-depressive disorders to be much higher for identical than for fraternal twins; he also noted that when both twins became psychotic, they developed the same type of manic-depressive reaction. For

example, if one twin became depressed, the other would also become depressed rather than develop a manic or circular reaction.

More recent studies have supported these earlier findings in terms of incidence and concordance rates (Abrams & Taylor, 1974; Allen, Cohen, Pollin, & Greenspan, 1974; Helzer & Winokur, 1974; Ossofsky, 1974; Reich, Clayton, & Winokur, 1969). It has also been found that mothers with a history of such disorders were much more likely than similarly affected fathers to have offspring who later developed manic-depressive disorders.

As in schizophrenia, the evidence for some kind of hereditary predisposition to manic-depressive disorders is persuasive but not clear-cut because the factors of early environment and learning have been left uncontrolled. For example, the finding of a much higher incidence of mother-offspring concordance than of father-offspring concordance in these disorders could be interpreted as evidence of a sex-linked genetic factor, but it could also result from early environment and learning if the child is more influenced by his mother than his father during his early years. In short, the precise role of heredity is far from clear, although it seems realistic to consider it an important interactional factor in the total picture.

2. *Neurophysiological factors.* Following the early lead of Pavlov, a great deal of interest has been expressed in the possibility that imbalances in excitatory and inhibitory processes may predispose some people toward extreme mood swings. It is suggested that manic reactions may result from excessive excitation and weakened inhibition, and depressive reactions from excessive inhibition.

To support this viewpoint, several investigators have pointed out that in monkeys—highly excitable and unequilibrated animals—the processes of excitation do in fact predominate over the processes of inhibition. In many other species, including humans, there is a greater equilibrium of excitatory and inhibitory processes, but within any species there are wide individual differences, probably stemming from both genetic and environmental influences. Presumably such neurophysiological differences could predispose some individuals to manic-depressive disorders under stress.

---

[3]An overview of recent research in depression and the delineation of 10 causal models may be found in Akiskal and McKinney (1975).

Stress factors preceding severe depression

In an intensive study of 40 depressed patients, Leff, Roatch, and Bunney (1970) found that each patient had been subjected to multiple stressful events prior to early symptoms and to a clustering of such events during the month preceding the actual breakdown in functioning. The chart shows ten types of stress most frequently involved.

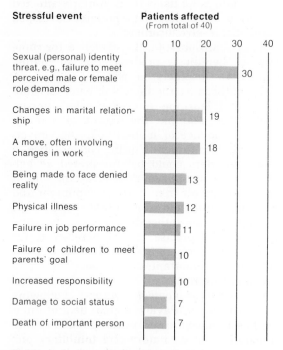

Stressful event **Patients affected**
(From total of 40)

Sexual (personal) identity threat, e.g., failure to meet perceived male or female role demands	30
Changes in marital relationship	19
A move, often involving changes in work	18
Being made to face denied reality	13
Physical illness	12
Failure in job performance	11
Failure of children to meet parents' goal	10
Increased responsibility	10
Damage to social status	7
Death of important person	7

Strikingly similar to the findings of Leff and her associates are those of Paykel et al. (1969). In that study, which involved 185 depressed patients, it was found that comparable stressful events preceded the onset of the depressive breakdown. In order of significance, these events were categorized as (a) marital difficulties, (b) work moves or changes in work conditions, (c) serious personal illness, and (d) death or serious illness of an immediate family member. More recent reports have supported these findings (Brown, 1972; Brown, 1974; Schanche, 1974).

In considering the possible role of neurophysiological factors in manic and depressive reactions, it is relevant to note Engel's (1962) conclusion that the central nervous system is apparently "organized to mediate two opposite patterns of response to a mounting need." The first is an active, goal-oriented pattern directed toward achieving the gratification of needs from external sources; the second, in contrast, is a defensive pattern aimed at reducing activity, heightening the barrier against stimulation, and conserving the energy and resources of the organism. Manic reactions appear to be an exaggerated form of the first response pattern, while depression appears to be an extreme form of the second.

But though the psychomotor retardation of the depressive and the psychomotor overactivity of the manic do suggest polar opposites in neural functioning, as well as behavior, this view appears to be oversimplified as an explanation of manic-depressive disorders. In any event, a great deal more research is needed before we can arrive at any definitive conclusions concerning the role of neurophysiological factors in manic-depressive disorders.

3. *Biochemical factors.* Kraepelin considered manic-depressive psychoses to be toxic, and a good deal of research effort has been directed toward finding possible metabolic alterations and brain pathology in individuals with these disorders. Particularly prominent during the last decade has been the "catecholamine hypothesis," in which both mania and depression are viewed as being related to the level of catecholamines (various biogenic amines) in the blood.

As we noted in Chapter 9, biogenic amines serve as neural transmitters or modulators, and treatment agents like electroshock, antidepressant drugs, and lithium carbonate influence the metabolism of these biogenic amines. Since these changes are in a corrective direction for manic-depressive patients, it is inferred that biochemical pathology must exist in these disorders.

Available studies have found evidence of altered brain chemistry in both manic and depressive reactions, as well as in rapidly alternating manic-depressive patterns (Akiskal & McKinney, 1975; Becker, 1974; Goodwin & Bunney, 1973). In addition to adrenal pitu-

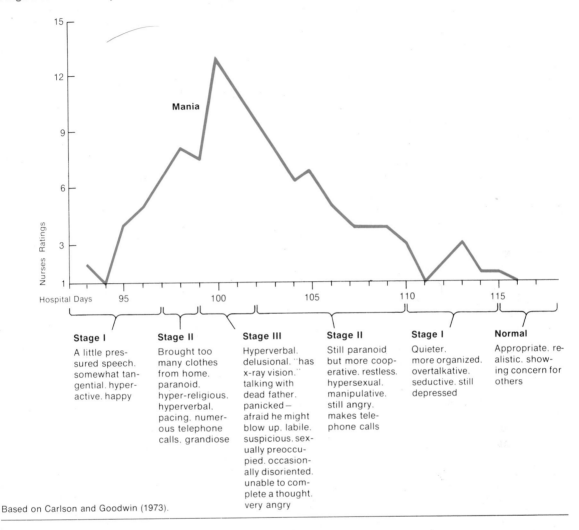

Stage I

A little pressured speech. somewhat tangential. hyperactive. happy

Stage II

Brought too many clothes from home. paranoid. hyper-religious. hyperverbal. pacing. numerous telephone calls. grandiose

Stage III

Hyperverbal. delusional. "has x-ray vision." talking with dead father. panicked—afraid he might blow up. labile. suspicious. sexually preoccupied. occasionally disoriented. unable to complete a thought. very angry

Stage II

Still paranoid but more cooperative. restless. hypersexual. manipulative. still angry. makes telephone calls

Stage I

Quieter. more organized. overtalkative. seductive. still depressed

Normal

Appropriate. realistic. showing concern for others

Based on Carlson and Goodwin (1973).

itary changes, the evidence suggests that catecholamine function may be decreased in depression and increased in mania. The question may be raised, however, as to which changes—such as those in adrenal pituitary functioning—are part of a general adaptation syndrome to stress, and which are specific to manic-depressive disorders. And again it may be noted that various mental disorders—including manic-depressive psychoses—may lead to alterations in brain biochemistry rather than the other way around.

In assessing the role of neurophysiological and biochemical factors in manic-depressive disorders, it is relevant—as in schizophrenia—to note the prolonged disturbances in metabolic processes that typically precede and accompany these disorders. Of particular importance are disturbances in sleep patterns. The psychomotor overactivity of the manic makes normal sleep all but impossible, and in acute mania, the individual may average less than an hour's sleep a night. Similarly, sleep disturbances involving less total sleep, less REM sleep, and less Stage 4 or deep sleep are characteristic of depressive reactions. Such sleep disturbances may, in turn, affect neurophysiological and biochemical processes, and hence play a contributing role in the total causal pattern. It may also be emphasized that without treatment both manic and depressive psychoses tend to run their course and clear up in a matter of months—again indicating a possible involvement of biochemical and/or neurophysiological alterations in these disorders.

In general, then, the available evidence suggests that (a) genetic and constitutional factors may predispose a person to manic-depressive reactions; (b) neurophysiological and biochemical factors appear to play an important interactional role in these disorders, but as yet their exact role remains to be clarified; and (c) sleep disturbances appear to be a by-product of these disorders and possibly also an interacting factor in the total pattern. These biological factors may act singly or in combination in influencing the onset, nature, and course of manic-depressive disorders.

Psychological and interpersonal factors. Following the early lead of Meyer (1948), many investigators view manic-depressive reactions as attempts, however ineffective, to cope with threatening stress situations.

In examining this general viewpoint, three basic questions arise: (a) Are there predisposing psychological factors, in addition to biological factors, which lead to manic-depressive reactions under stress? (b) How can we explain manic-depressive reactions as coping patterns? and (c) Once such patterns do come into operation, what accounts for their tendency to be maintained until they have "run their course"?

In the discussion that follows we shall attempt to deal with these specific questions as well as the more general role of psychological and interpersonal factors in the development of manic-depressive disorders.

1. *Predisposing family and personality factors.* It might be expected that exaggerated mood swings in the child would be fostered by observations of similar emotional patterns in the parents, and would then persist as learned maladaptive response patterns. The high inci-

dence of affective disorders in the families of manic-depressive patients would provide greater than average opportunities for such learning. In their study of 14 depressed children, for example, Poznanski and Zrull (1970) reported that 5 of the parents were depressed at the time of the child's referral; one father had committed suicide, apparently during an episode of depression. These investigators concluded:

" . . . in those cases where parental depression was known, one source of the child's depression could be based on identification with the parent, particularly the parent's affective reaction to stress and difficulties within his own life." (p. 14)

Attempts to delineate a typical premorbid personality pattern for adults who later suffer manic-depressive episodes have met with limited success. In general, however, manic patients—whatever their childhood backgrounds may have been—are described as ambitious, outgoing, energetic, sociable, and often highly successful, both prior to their psychotic breakdown and after remission. As contrasted with controls, they tend to place a higher conscious value on achievement, are very conventional in their beliefs, and are deeply concerned about what others think of them. Depressives share these characteristics, but they appear to be more obsessive, anxious, and self-deprecatory. They also show an unusually rigid conscience development, which prevents the overt expression of hostile feelings and makes them particularly prone to feelings of guilt and self-blame when things go wrong.[4]

On the other hand, manic-depressives are a heterogeneous group who differ greatly in personality makeup, and there are many persons who show these typical personality traits but do not suffer manic-depressive episodes.

2. *Severe stress.* Most investigators who have studied manic-depressive reactions have been impressed with the high incidence of

---

[4]The description of characteristics that are commonly ascribed to the personality makeup of manic-depressives is based on the following references: Akiskal and McKinney (1975), Bagley (1973), Beck (1971), Becker and Altrocchi (1968), Chodoff (1972), Ferster (1973), Grinker (1969), Lewinsohn and Graf (1973), Libet and Lewinsohn (1973), Peto (1972), and Schanche (1974).

aversive life events that apparently served as precipitating factors. In an early study, Rennie and Fowler (1942) found a disturbing life situation directly related to the onset of the disorder in about 80 percent of their manic-depressive patients. Only 20 percent of the disorders seemed to have arisen "out of the blue," and these cases may have been precipitated by life situations disturbing to the patient but not apparent to an objective observer.

Following this early lead, Arieti (1959) concluded that typical precipitating stresses in severe depressive reactions fall into three general categories: (a) death of a loved one; (b) failure in an important interpersonal relationship, usually with one's spouse; and (c) a severe setback or disappointment in the work or other goals to which an individual has been devoted. All of these precipitating conditions involve the loss of something that has been of great value to the individual.

A number of later studies have also emphasized the role of stress, finding a "general excess" of aversive life events prior to the onset of manic-depressive episodes (Paykel et al., 1969; Brown, 1972; Briscoe et al., 1973). These events typically fitted into the categories delineated by Arieti (1959), but also included such events as serious accidents and personal illness.

An interesting example of the possible role of aversive life events is that of a patient described by Hartmann (1968) who, between the ages of 44 and 59, had six severe manic episodes, all of which required hospitalization, and a number of depressive episodes, two of which required hospitalization. Typically, this patient tended to be hypomanic in his general functioning, but during the early autumn he usually ran for a political office himself or took an active role in someone else's campaign. In the process, he would become increasingly manic; when the ventures led to defeat—which they almost invariably did—he would become depressed in November or December, after the elections were over.

Although affective disorders may be precipitated by aversive life events, such disorders cannot be explained in terms of external events alone—many people suffer the death of a loved one, go through a divorce, or lose their job without becoming psychotically depressed.

The relation of cognition to affect in manic-depressive disorders

In attempting to understand manic-depressive reactions, it is helpful to remember that we all experience moods. We may feel particularly elated and self-confident at one time and vaguely anxious and depressed at another. In a pioneering study of euphoric and depressed moods in normal subjects, Johnson (1937) found striking differences in an individual's whole manner and approach to problems, depending on whether he was in a euphoric mood or a depressed one. In euphoric moods, subjects made more spontaneous and unnecessary conversation and reached decisions much more easily. In addition, they made more expansive movements in such psychomotor functions as writing. Depression, on the other hand, resulted in a very definite regression to childhood events in thought and memory, increased difficulty in making decisions, more cramped and smaller script and figures, and a judgment of distances as being greater than they actually were.

Findings like these in normal subjects help us understand the effects of more exaggerated mood swings in manic-depressive reactions. Whereas our cognitive processes ordinarily maintain adequate control over our perceptions and reactions to stress situations, it appears that in manic-depressive reactions, affective processes take over and largely determine an individual's appraisal of events and experiences. It is possible, of course, that changes in cognition—as when one begins to perceive his life situation as hopeless—may precede and pave the way for the affective reaction, or the relationship between cognition and affect may involve a vicious circle, in which the one augments the other.

Unfortunately there is little research evidence on the relationship between cognition and affect in manic-depressive disorders. Whatever the relationship, however, it is the exaggeration of affect which eventually dominates the clinical picture.

Based in part on Briscoe and Smith (1973) and Ferster (1973).

Rather, the key element may not be the stressful event itself but the individual's appraisal of the event in relation to himself; for example, he may experience feelings of helplessness and a catastrophic loss of self-esteem.

Thus, while severe stress appears to play a key causal role in manic-depressive disorders, the problem remains of accounting for differences in the way people react to such stressful life events, for, as we have seen, severe stress also appears to play an important causal role in schizophrenia and other mental disorders.

3. *Feelings of helplessness and loss of hope.* Feelings of helplessness and hopelessness as a reaction to aversive life events have been emphasized as basic to depressive reactions by investigators of differing theoretical orientations. Bibring (1953), a psychoanalyst, held that the basic mechanism of depression is "the ego's shocking awareness of its helplessness in regard to its aspirations . . . such that the depressed person . . . has lost his incentives and gives up, not the goals, but pursuing them, since this proves to be useless" (p. 39). In later studies, other investigators have referred to "learned helplessness" in severe depression; presumably the individual, perceiving no way of coping with the stress, eventually stops fighting and gives up (Hiroto & Seligman, 1975; Seligman, 1973; Weiss, 1974). As one recovered patient expressed her feelings, in retrospect, "I tried to cope with my situation, but nothing I did made a difference. I finally lost hope and just gave up."

Feelings of helplessness and hopelessness and their behavioral consequences have been dealt with from a behavioristic viewpoint by several investigators. Lazarus (1968) has concluded that ". . . depression may be regarded as a function of inadequate or insufficient reinforcers . . . some significant reinforcer has been withdrawn" (pp. 84–85). Similarly, Lewinsohn (1974) has concluded that feelings of depression—along with other symptoms of this clinical picture—can be elicited when the individual's behavior no longer results in accustomed reinforcement or gratification. The failure to receive positive reinforcement, in turn, leads to a reduction in effort and activity, thus resulting in even less chance of coping with aversive conditions and achieving need gratification. In essence, the individual is caught in a vicious circle of learned helplessness and hopelessness.

While the behavioristic interpretation seems helpful in understanding depressive reactions, it seems less applicable to manic reactions. However, one might speculate that the latter represents an attempt to obtain needed reinforcers via an indiscriminate increase in activity level. As in the case of depressive reactions, however, such reinforcers are not forthcoming. Here the conclusion of Ferster (1973) seems directly applicable: "It seems likely . . . that any factor which causes a temporary or long term reduction in positively reinforced ways of acting . . . will also produce bizarre or irrational behavior as a by-product" (p. 859). But still to be adequately accounted for in this explanation are the feelings of euphoria that characterize manic reactions.

4. *Extreme defenses.* Manic and depressive reactions may be viewed as two different but related defense-oriented strategies for dealing with severe stress.

In the case of mania, the individual tries to escape his difficulties by a "flight into reality." In less severe form, this type of reaction to stress is shown by the person who goes on a round of parties to try to forget a broken love affair, or tries to escape from a threatening life situation by restless activity in which he occupies every moment with work, athletics, sexual affairs, and countless other crowded activities—all performed with professed gusto but with little true enjoyment.

In actual manic reactions, the preceding pattern is exaggerated. With a tremendous expenditure of energy, the manic tries to deny his feelings of helplessness and hopelessness and to play a role of competence. Once this mode of coping with difficulties is adopted, it is maintained until it has spent itself in emotional exhaustion, for the only other alternative is an admission of defeat and inevitable depression. This is well brought out in the following case of a hypomanic patient.

"He neglected his meals and rest hours, and was highly irregular, impulsive, and distractible in his adaptations to ward routine. Without apparent intent to be annoying or disturbing he sang, whistled, told pointless off-color stories, visited indiscriminately, and flirted crudely with the nurses and female patients. Superficially he appeared to be in high spirits, and yet one day when he was being gently chided over some particularly irresponsible act he suddenly slumped in a chair, covered his face with his hands, began sobbing, and cried, 'For Pete's sake, doc, let me be. Can't you see that I've just got to act happy?'" (Masserman, 1961, pp. 66–67)

Unfortunately, as manic reactions proceed, any defensive value they may have had is negated, for the individual's thought processes are speeded up to a point where he can no longer "process" incoming information with any degree of efficiency. In a manner of speaking, "the programmer loses control of the computer," resulting in severe personality decompensation.

In the case of depression, the person apparently gains some relief from his intolerable stress situation by admitting defeat and giving up the fight. Also, the slowing down of thought processes may serve to decrease his suffering by reducing the sheer quantity of painful thoughts. However, his feelings of relief are gained at the expense of his sense of adequacy and self-esteem, and thus are accompanied by marked guilt and self-accusation. Like the soldier who panics and flees from combat, he may feel relieved to be out of an intolerable situation but also feel guilty and devaluated.

Since the depressive tends to blame himself for his difficulties, he often goes over his past with a microscope, picking out any possible sins of omission or commission and exaggerating their importance in relation to his present difficulties. He may even accuse himself of selfishness, unfaithfulness, or hostile acts that did not occur. These self-accusations seem to be attempts to explain and find some meaning in his predicament and at the same time achieve some measure of expiation and atonement.

The traditional Freudian view of depression has emphasized its association with bereavement. Apparently normal grief and depression may be intensified to a pathological degree if the individual feels guilty about having had strong feelings of hostility toward the deceased and/or some responsibility for the loved one's death. Here the turning inward of hostility, coupled with self-recrimination, apparently helps the individual work through his severe guilt and depression. This pattern is illustrated in the following case.

The patient, a 24-year-old woman, had eloped two years previously with a young man of whom her parents disapproved. Following the elopement the parents disowned her and refused to have anything to do with her. The patient and her husband then traveled to California, where he obtained employment as a shipping clerk in a wholesale company.

The daughter and her parents did not correspond, although the daughter had severe guilt feelings about letting her parents down—they had had great ambitions for her in college and had looked forward to her future marriage to a wealthy youth whose parents were old friends. During her first year in California she became pregnant and just before the baby was to arrive wired her parents of the forthcoming event. Unfortunately, the baby died during birth and the handsome presents her parents sent for the baby only served to intensify her disappointment. However, the event served to reestablish relations, and the parents made immediate arrangements to drive to California to visit the patient and her husband. But on the way they were involved in a tragic automobile accident. The father was killed outright and the mother died on the way to the hospital.

Upon the receipt of this news, the patient became extremely depressed and attempted suicide by taking an overdose of sleeping tablets. Emergency medical attention saved her life but she remained depressed and was extremely anxious and tense, unable to sit still or concentrate on any topic except her parents' death. She blamed herself for it and paced the floor in great agitation, muttering to herself and bewailing her guilt. During this period the following conversation took place.

Dr.: You feel that you are to blame for your parents' death?

Pt.: Yes, oh why didn't I obey them. Now they are dead . . . I have killed them. They were wonderful to me and I have repaid them by disobedience and murder. I deserve to die too. Oh God! I have killed my baby and now my parents! I don't deserve to live. . . . I am no good, evil. I will be punished too . . . Oh God what have I done!

It was thought in this case that the patient had felt considerable hostility toward her parents following their rejection of her, as well as guilt for disobeying them. She had never been able to express this hostility even to her husband. Apparently it added considerably to her guilt feelings and played an important part in the severe self-recrimination and depression which followed their death. With antidepressant medication and brief psychotherapy, she showed a rapid and apparently full recovery.

It may be that the remission of depressive reactions even without treatment occurs because the effort at expiation and atonement has been successful. In such cases, there may be a gradual working through of the individual's feelings of unworthiness and guilt, in which he pays the price for his failures by self-punishment and is thereby cleansed and ready for another go at life.

In circular reactions, the shift from mania to depression may tend to occur when the defensive function of the manic reaction breaks down. Similarly, the shift from depression to mania may tend to occur when the individual feels so devaluated and guilt-ridden by his inactivity and inability to cope that he feels compelled to attempt some countermeasure, however desperate.

While the view of manic-depressive reactions as extreme defenses seems plausible, there is still the possible role of biological and other factors to be reckoned with for a full understanding of the clinical picture in these psychotic disorders.

5. *Social roles and communications.* Two other factors merit consideration in understanding manic-depressive reactions—namely, social roles and communications.

Curiously enough, the manic tends to play a social role well suited to alienating himself from others, while the depressive tends to elicit their sympathy and support. In their discussion of "playing the manic game," Janowsky, Leff, and Epstein (1970) have observed:

"The acutely manic patient is often able to alienate himself from family, friends, and therapists alike. This knack is based on the facile use of maneuvers which place individuals relating to the manic in positions of embarrassment, decreased self-esteem, and anxious self-doubt. Those dealing with the manic frequently find themselves on the defensive, attempting to justify their actions and motivations. Commonly, they feel 'outsmarted' and 'outmaneuvered.' " (p. 253)

The manic apparently feels it threatening and unacceptable to rely on others or wish to be

taken care of. Instead, as a way of maintaining his self-esteem and feelings of adequacy and strength, he establishes a social role and position in which he is able to control and manipulate the people on whom he must rely (Janowsky, El-Yousef, & Davis, 1974).

On the other hand, the depressive tends to adopt a role that places others in the position of supporting and caring for him (Janowsky et al., 1970; Ferster, 1973). The frequent reinforcement of this "depressed role" in our society has been noted by Ullmann and Krasner (1969):

"Because most people respond with kindness to the cues called depressed behavior, there may well be immediate reinforcement for emitting such behavior. . . . If depressed role enactments continue, most other people will become less responsive. The effect over time is toward placing the person on an intermittent reinforcement schedule resistant to extinction." (p. 423)

The depressive generally does obtain some secondary gains from his symptoms via sympathy and support from others, and he may tend to play the depressive role in accordance with his own feelings and perceptions and the apparent expectations of others. However, depressive reactions are not as resistant to extinction as Ullmann and Krasner suggest: they tend to run their course with or without secondary gains. Thus it seems unlikely that they can be explained entirely in terms of a simple learned role.

Other investigators have seen depressive reactions as an attempt to communicate a particular message. As Hill (1968) has expressed it:

"Symptoms, then, whether they be verbal expressions, deviant behavior, or simple motor postures or movements, are forms of communication. They are postures in the sense that they communicate the internal need state of the patient, his distress, his fear and anger, his remorse, his humble view of himself, his demands, and his dependency." (p. 456)

Particularly in interpersonal relations with significant others, depressive reactions can often be seen as attempts of the individual to communicate his feelings of discouragement and despair—to say, in effect, "I have needs that you are failing to meet." Hopefully, this communication will elicit a helpful response from the other person, but often it goes unheeded. Thus in failing marriages, which are commonly associated with depressive reactions, we may see the curious spectacle of one partner trying to communicate his unmet expectations, distress, and dependency—and then becoming increasingly depressed and disturbed when the other partner fails to make the hoped-for response. In a study of combat returnees from Vietnam, Goldsmith and Cretekos (1969) found that whereas anxiety had been the most common reaction during combat, depression was the most common reaction to the interpersonal problems and conflicts they experienced on coming home. Here again we may speculate that the depression was at least partly a form of communication—a pleading that others meet their special needs.

General sociocultural factors. The incidence of manic-depressive reactions seems to vary considerably among different societies: in some, manic reactions are more frequent, while in others, depressive reactions are more common.

In early studies, Carothers (1947, 1951, 1959) found manic reactions fairly common among African natives, but depressive reactions relatively rare—the exact opposite of their incidence in the United States. He attributed the low incidence of depressive reactions to the fact that in traditional African cultures the individual has not usually been held personally responsible for his failures and misfortunes. The culture of the Kenya Africans may be taken as fairly typical in this respect:

Their behavior in all its major aspects is group-determined. Even religion is a matter of offerings and invocations in a group; it is not practiced individually and does not demand any particular attitude on the part of the individual. Similarly, grief over the death of a loved one is not borne in isolation, but appropriate rites are performed amid great public grieving. In these rites, the widowed person expresses his grief dramatically in ways prescribed by custom, and then resumes the tenor of his life as if no bereavement had occurred. Psychologically speaking, Kenyans receive security because they are part

---

Frequency of various symptoms in 52 manic patients

Taylor and Abrams (1973) reported the following symptoms in 23 male and 29 female manic patients. These investigators noted that while these patients evidenced the classical symptoms of mania, they also evidenced many symptoms characteristic of schizophrenia. As a consequence, they concluded that this may help explain the confusion in diagnosis which often occurs between these two disorders, particularly between manic reactions and acute schizophrenic episodes. In fact, some clinicians prefer to use the label *schizo-affective* psychosis when the patient evidences a pronounced combination of symptoms characteristic of both affective and schizophrenic disorders.

Symptom	Percent patients affected
Mood disorder	100
Irritable	80.8
Expansive	65.5
Euphoric	30.8
Labile, with depression	28.8
Hyperactivity	100
Rapid/pressured speech	100
Flight-of-ideas	76.9
Grandiose delusions	59.6
Assaultive/threatening behavior	48.1
Incomplete auditory hallucinations	48.1
Persecutory delusions	42.3
Confusion	32.7
Singing/dancing	32.7
Head decoration	32.7
Autochthonous ideas	26.9
Visual hallucinations	26.9
Nudity/sexual exposure	23.1
Fecal incontinence/smearing	19.2
Olfactory hallucinations	15.4
Catatonia (posturing, catalepsy, mannerisms, stereotypies, automatic cooperation)	13.5

Playing the manic game

Janowsky and his associates (1970, 1974), noting the extent to which the manic patient intentionally induces discomfort in those around him, pointed to the following techniques that are used in "playing the manic game."

1. Manipulating the self-esteem of others—either lowering or raising it—as a means of exerting leverage over them.

2. Discovering areas of sensitivity and vulnerability in others for purposes of exploitation.

3. Projecting responsibility in such a way that other people become responsible for the manic's own actions.

4. Progressively testing limits—avoiding the limits imposed on him by challenging them or finding loopholes in them.

5. Creating interpersonal distance between himself and others by deliberately evoking the anger of and alienating staff members.

Although the reasons for the use of these techniques are not clear, these investigators suggest that the manic's feeling of being threatened by and unable to rely on others may be a contributing factor. In any event, these interpersonal maneuvers appeared typical of the clinical picture in mania and disappeared when the manic episode remitted.

---

of a larger organism and are not confronted with the problems of individual self-sufficiency, choice, and responsibility that play such a large part in our culture. They do not set themselves unrealistic goals, and they have no need to repress or feel guilty about "dangerous" desires. Their culture actively discourages individual achievement of success, does not consider sexual behavior as evil, and is tolerant of occasional outbursts of aggressive hostility.

In addition, Kenyans feel a great humbleness toward their natural environment, which is often harsh in the extreme. They always expect the worst, and hence can accept misfortunes with equanimity. Here too, responsibility and blame are automatically placed on forces outside themselves. Although they attempt to counteract misfortune and assure success in their ventures by performing appropriate rituals, the outcome is in the hands of the gods. They are not personally responsible and hence do not ordinarily experience self-devaluation or the need for ego-defensive measures. When excessive stress and decompensation do occur, there tends to be a complete disorganization of personality—as in the hebephrenic type of schizophrenia, which is the

Needless to say, Africa today is changing rapidly, and the preceding patterns may no longer prevail. However, Carothers' description is of great value in helping us understand the role of sociocultural factors in depressive reactions and other types of mental disorders.

Even where depressive reactions are relatively common among so-called primitive peoples, they seem less closely associated with feelings of guilt and self-recrimination than in the developed countries (Kidson & Jones, 1968; Lorr & Klett, 1969; Zung, 1969). In fact, among several groups of Australian aborigines, Kidson and Jones (1968) found not only an absence of guilt and self-recrimination in depressive reactions but also no incidence of attempted or actual suicide. In connection with the latter finding, they stated:

"The absence of suicide can perhaps be explained as a consequence of strong fears of death and also because of the tendency to act out and project hostile impulses." (p. 415)

In our own society, the role of sociocultural factors in manic-depressive disorders remains unclear, but it would appear that conditions which increase life stress lead to a higher incidence of these as well as other disorders. For example, Jaco (1960) found that while manic-depressive disorders were distributed more evenly in the population than schizophrenia, they were significantly higher among the divorced than among the married and about 3 times higher in urban than in rural areas. Here it is of interest to note that Sethi, Nathawat, and Gapta (1973) reported that in India the incidence of depression was also much higher in urban as compared with rural areas in the ratio of about 4 to 1. These investigators concluded that modern technology along with rapidly changing social values and the increasing pace and complexity of modern civilization were contributing factors in urban areas, whereas the more intimate social contacts in small communities were probable deterrents of depression in their rural sample.

The investigators we have cited do not minimize the influence of biological, psychological, and interpersonal factors on the incidence rates and clinical picture of manic-depressive reactions, but their findings indicate that sociocultural factors, too, are important in the overall pattern.

Treatment and outcomes

Antidepressant, tranquilizing, and anti-anxiety drugs are all used with manic-depressive patients. Lithium salts, available for more than a century, were first tried for the treatment of affective disorders in the 1940s by Cade of Australia but were found to have adverse side effects. Thanks to a series of refinements since then, however, lithium therapy has become highly effective in the treatment of manic reactions and, more recently, in the treatment of depressive reactions as well (Brown, 1974; Johnson, 1974; Schou, 1974). In addition, lithium therapy can be used to prevent the recurrence of manic-depressive reactions. With depressive patients, antidepressant drugs such as imipramine or amitriptyline have also proven effective, both in treatment and the prevention of relapse (Prien, Klett, & Caffey, 1973; Raskin, 1974).

Since an estimated 60 percent or more of depressed patients are also anxious, tranquilizing and anti-anxiety drugs are commonly used in combination with antidepressants (Cole, 1974; Raskin, 1974). Here it is useful to note the reminder of Lehmann (1968) that

"Depression and anxiety are two symptoms which very often co-exist in the same patient. They are nevertheless different symptoms and they may vary independently in their intensity. Of the two symptoms, anxiety is by far the more conspicuous and depression the more dangerous." (p. 18)

Unfortunately, antidepressant drugs usually require a few days before their effects are manifested. Thus electroconvulsive therapy (ECT) is often used with patients who present an immediate and serious suicidal risk (Brown, 1974; Hurwitz, 1974). ECT is now considered both safe and effective; there is a complete remission of symptoms after about 4 to 6 convulsive treatments in over 90 percent of depressive patients. In such cases, maintenance dosages of antidepressant and anti-anxiety drugs ordinarily are used to maintain the treatment gains achieved by ECT until the depression has run its course.

Treatment is not ordinarily confined to drugs or ECT, but usually is combined with individual and/or group therapy directed at helping the patient develop a more stable long-range adjustment. The need for such therapy is indicated by the findings of Hauri (1974) and of Hauri, Chernik, Hawkins, and Mendels (1974), who studied the sleeping patterns of former depressed patients. While these patients were overtly recovered, they tended to evidence a "depressive life style" in their dreams; they also showed significantly more sleep disturbances than a matched "normal" control group, including delayed onset of sleep, more REM sleep, and greater night-by-night variability in sleep patterns.

A number of innovative techniques of psychotherapy have been developed in recent years, particularly for the treatment of depression. The following case of a 37-year-old homemaker who had been depressed since the recent death of her mother will serve as an example of an innovative method of behavior therapy. The treatment program was directed toward reinforcing behavior incompatible with depression and relieving feelings of helplessness and hopelessness. The therapist began the program by observing the patient in her home.

"The therapist recorded each instance of 'depressive-like' behavior, such as crying, complaining about somatic symptoms, pacing, and withdrawal. He also noted the consequences of these behaviors. Initially, she had a high rate of depressive behaviors and it was noted that members of her family frequently responded to them with sympathy, concern, and helpfulness. During this time, her rate of adaptive actions as a housewife and mother were very low, but she did make occasional efforts to cook, clean house, and attend to the children's needs. . . .

"The therapist, in family sessions, instructed her husband and children to pay instant and frequent attention to her coping behavior and to gradually ignore her depressed behavior. They were taught to acknowledge her positive actions with interest, encouragement, and approval. Overall, they were not to decrease the amount of attention focused on the patient but rather switch the contingencies of their attention from 'sick woman' to 'housewife and mother.' Within one week, her depressed behavior

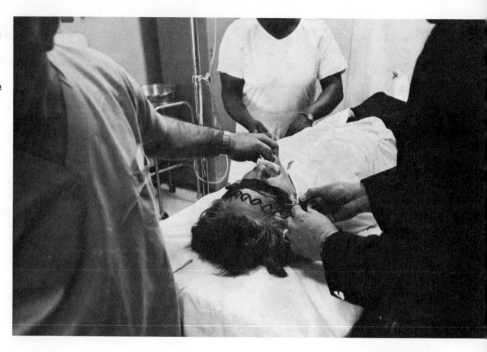

Electroconvulsive therapy is used for the rapid alleviation of symptoms in severely depressed patients who may represent a serious suicidal risk. Here a patient at a state mental hospital is being prepared for ECT.

decreased sharply and her 'healthy' behavior increased.

"A clinical experiment was then performed to prove the causal link between her behavior and the responses generated in her family. After the 14th day, the therapist instructed the family members to return to providing the patient with attention and solicitude for her complaints. Within three days, she was once again showing a high level of depressive behavior, albeit not as high as initially. When the focus of the family's attentiveness was finally moved back to her coping skills and away from her miserableness, she quickly improved. One year after termination, she was continuing to function well without depressive symptoms." (Liberman & Raskin, 1971, p. 521)

In the overall treatment program, it is important to deal also with unusual stresses in the patient's life, since an unfavorable situation may lead to a recurrence of the reaction as well as necessitating longer treatment.

Proper nursing care is important during acute depression because depressed patients are frequently very ingenious in their efforts to put an end to their suffering. Despite the patient's seemingly earnest assurance that he will do nothing to harm himself, he may cut his wrists with a small fragment of glass or set fire to his clothing with a cleverly concealed match. Because of the likelihood of suicide attempts, it is considered hazardous for family members to try to care for depressed patients in the home.

Even without formal therapy, as we have noted, the great majority of manic-depressives recover within less than a year. And with modern methods of treatment, the general outlook has become increasingly favorable, so that most hospitalized patients can now be discharged within 60 days. While relapses may occur in some instances, these can usually be prevented by maintenance therapy.

The mortality rate for depressive patients appears to be about twice as high as that for the general population, however, because of the higher incidence of suicide (Bratfos & Haug, 1968; Schanche, 1974). Thus while the development of effective drugs and other new approaches to therapy have brought greatly improved outcomes for manic-depressive psychoses, the need clearly remains for still more effective treatment methods, both immediate and long term. Also, there appears to be a strong need for additional "high-risk" studies of depression, and the application of relevant findings to early intervention and prevention.

How one patient felt before hospitalization for depression

It was a cold, rainy, gray Saturday afternoon but the gloom of the day could not possibly mirror the despondency which filled my whole being. There I sat, a 53-year-old man, happily married, professionally successful, financially affluent, crying like a lost child as I clenched and unclenched my fists. The psychiatrist, whom I had met only 10 minutes earlier, had just said, bluntly and finally, "I could prescribe more medicine for you, but I don't think that would help you get better. You need to get in another environment for a few days. There is a bed available this afternoon in the hospital I recommend."

Here was the verdict I had been secretly dreading for months: hospitalization. Willpower, vacations, tranquilizers, antidepressants, sporadic therapy—none had been able to stop my descent into uncontrollable depression. I had begun to dread what loomed ever larger as the only alternatives—a complete breakdown and hospitalization, or suicide.

In spite of years of study of social psychology, all my professional sophistication vanished now. "Insane" was only the worst of the frightening words that flashed through my disordered mind. "Institutionalized," "psychiatric ward," "mentally ill," "deviant," are only a few of the others that I can remember. Not only did I know that, in terms of what we sociologists call "labeling theory," my friends would hereafter perceive me differently; I was already experiencing the pain of a new self-definition. Just the day before I had gotten my driver's license renewed. One of the questions on the application had been, "Have you ever been hospitalized for mental illness?" Never again would I be able to answer "No" to this question. The realization was devastating.

Quoted from Killian and Bloomberg (1975).

At last, in anguish and desperation, I forced the words from my dry, constricted throat—"Yes, God damn it, I'll go!" Within a few minutes my wife was driving me to a hospital in a nearby town where I would become a patient in a "therapeutic community"—what I thought then was a euphemism for the psychiatric ward. I would have to learn for myself that the term was more than a sugar-coated label. Now, on the way to the hospital, I was still reacting to visions of the "snake pit." I cried out to my wife, "Oh, my God, they'll give me shock treatment." I could visualize myself in a straitjacket, or immersed in a tub of water for hydrotherapy. At the same time, I worried about the cost of the treatment, how many days of sick leave I had accumulated at my university, what would be done about my class and my administrative responsibilities, how my poor wife would get along in a lonely house—every concern that had ever crossed my mind now raced through it in a parade of problems about which I could do absolutely nothing.

I remember my admission to the hospital only in fragments. My recollection leaps in one bound from the hospital parking lot to the scene at the side of the bed which was to be mine for—I did not know how long. Weeping again, I kissed my wife goodbye and heard the appalling words, "No visitors for 72 hours," and then I was alone among strangers. I didn't care: I wanted to be alone, to lapse into the bliss of unconsciousness. But immediately the therapeutic community began to break through my shell. "Have you eaten supper, Lewis?" "We all use first names here—patients and staff; I'm Helen, I'm a nurse." "We ordered the house supper for you in case you hadn't eaten." "You'll be in this room by yourself tonight—your roommate is home on LOA [leave of absence] and will be back tomorrow." (pp. 42–43).

Involutional Melancholia

Involutional melancholia is differentiated from other depressive reactions by the initial appearance of the disorder during the climacteric (change of life), and by its tendency to run a long course unless treatment is undertaken. The involutional period is generally considered to occur in women of 45 to 60 and in men of 50 to 65. Involutional melancholia has shown a marked decline in recent years and constitutes some 2 percent or less of first admissions to mental hospitals and clinics (Hare, 1974). This reaction pattern occurs about 3 times more often among women than men.

Much of what we have already said about depression applies to involutional melancholia as well, and in recent years there has been very little research concerned with involutional reactions as distinct from other depressive psychoses. Thus we shall limit our present discussion to a brief description of the clinical picture and a consideration of those causal factors that appear to be particularly relevant.

Clinical picture

The onset of this disorder is gradual, with a slow buildup of pessimism, irritability, restlessness, and insomnia. Often there is excessive worry about minor matters, with unprovoked spells of weeping. The individual is worried about the past and sees little or no hope for the future. As the more acute symptoms make their appearance, he becomes increasingly depressed, anxious, and agitated, and develops marked feelings of guilt. Somatic complaints and hypochondriacal delusions are frequently present. The individual may insist that his bowels are stopped up and will never move again, that his stomach is rotting, that his body is all withered and dried up, that his brain has been eaten away, or that he has cancer or some other terrible disease. Feelings of unreality and nihilistic delusions are also common; the individual may feel that he is living in a shadow world, that his spouse and children are dead, and that nothing really exists.

The following case of a woman of 47 illustrates the feelings and thought content typical in involutional depressions.

> **Th.:** Hello—how do you feel today?
> **Pt.:** Oh (moaning), why don't you just let me die! It would be better for everybody.
> **Th.:** What is the matter?
> **Pt.:** Misery and death follow me around; everyone who gets close to me suffers. My mother and father, my children, and my husband suffered by my hand and died by my hand. (Gets up and paces back and forth.)
> **Th.:** Isn't the girl that visits you your daughter?
> **Pt.:** She says she is my daughter, but my children are all dead—and it is my fault. I should die a horrible death. God knows this and wants me to die. Why did I do it, there's nothing left for me but death. Nothing can be done for me—it's unforgivable; you should kill me. (Runs hands nervously through hair.)
> **Th.:** What did you do?
> **Pt.:** I let them die and now I should die. I am only dirt, there is only dirt left in me. There is no reason for me to eat because I am only dirt—filthy, smelly dirt. I treated everyone like dirt and now I am dirt—the worst sort and everyone knows it.
> **Th.:** Don't the people treat you well here?
> **Pt.:** They don't try to hurt me—but they will suffer like all the rest if they try to help me. They wouldn't try anyway—because they can see I am dirt turning to dirt. I am worthless and I can't do anything about it; no one can be my friend. They try to feed me. Can't they see that they can't feed dirt—earth into earth, that's the only place for me, and maybe I can atone for the evil I have caused.

Feelings of anxiety and depression in involutional reactions are usually accompanied by an increase in motor activity, which may range from mere restlessness to extreme agitation in which the individual paces the floor weeping, wringing his hands, pulling his hair, biting his lips, and bemoaning his fate. Despite the dramatic symptoms, however, the actual depressive affect is generally thought to be shallow as compared to that in other depressive reactions. Thought processes are not retarded, orientation is usually fairly good, and the individual may realize that he needs treatment. However, the danger of suicide is great even among individuals who show considerable insight into their condition and voluntarily seek help. It has been estimated that prior to the advent of modern treatment procedures some 25 percent of persons with involutional depression died by their own hands (English & Finch, 1954). This statistic seems pertinent since many cases of involutional depression do not receive professional assistance.

In some cases of involutional melancholia, the underlying depression is overlaid with delusions of persecution and other paranoid ideation. Since involutional psychotics with paranoid delusions can be dangerous, hospitalization is ordinarily considered desirable as a safeguard for other people as well as for themselves.

Causal factors

In general, involutional psychotic reactions have been distinguished from manic-depressive reactions by the following characteristics: (a) a lack of previous episodes of depression prior to the involutional period; (b) a rigid, obsessive, pre-psychotic personality as contrasted with one more subject to mood swings; (c) a gradual rather than abrupt onset of the disorder; (d) symptoms of agitation rather than of retardation; and (e) an absence of manic symptoms. In addition, involutional melancholia tends to run a longer course, with fewer spontaneous recoveries. With modern methods of treatment, however, involutional reactions are usually cleared up before they progress to a chronic pattern.

Biological factors. Many women during the beginning of the involutional period experience various disturbances referred to as the *menopause syndrome*. The symptoms consist primarily of hot flashes, headaches, periods of dizziness, excessive sweating, nervous irritability, insomnia, and difficulty in concentrating. There may be mild depression and the clinical picture may resemble a mild neurosis, but the disturbance is transitory. It is apparently due to a decrease in ovarian hormone production, and treatment with estrogen is helpful both physiologically and psychologically.

Although the menopause syndrome and involutional psychosis occasionally occur at the same time and the symptoms may be intermixed, the two conditions are distinct: involutional reactions are much more serious and do not respond to estrogen treatment. In general, studies of involutional melancholia have stressed the importance of psychological and interpersonal factors rather than endocrine imbalances or other organic pathology.[5] In fact, Winokur (1973) failed to find a greater risk of depression among women during the menopause than during other periods of adult life.

Psychological and interpersonal factors. The primary emphasis in the study of involutional melancholia has been on the reactions of a psychologically predisposed individual to the severe stresses typical of this life period. Although patterns of family interaction have not been investigated, the pre-psychotic personality of involutional patients has been fairly well delineated.

In an early study comparing manic-depressives, involutional melancholics, and normals, Titley (1936) found a distinctive pre-psychotic personality profile for the involutional patients, marked by overmeticulousness, overconscientiousness, rigid adherence to a high ethical code, anxiety, stubbornness, a narrow range of interests, and poor sexual adjustment. Other investigators have pointed to such traits as perfectionism, overconformity, insecurity, compulsiveness, and rigidity in everyday living habits (Gregory, 1961; Rosenthal, 1968). Where paranoid ideation is involved in involutional reactions, the pre-psychotic personality profile usually includes a tendency to be overly suspicious of other people's motives.

Individuals who are psychologically handicapped in these ways are especially vulnerable to the stresses that inevitably accompany the involutional period of life. In a study of 379 involutional patients, Tait and Burns

---

[5]In Chapter 13 we shall discuss some other psychoses associated with later life in which organic pathology does play a primary causative role.

More women than men are likely to suffer from involutional melancholia; the onset may be gradual, with the individual worrying about the past and seeing no hope in the future. Typically, such individuals consider themselves total failures, feel intensely guilty, and engage in self-recrimination.

(1951) found that the main precipitating factor was concern about the decline of the self. Almost without warning, many people become aware of getting "old." They lack their old strength and tire more easily; sexual desire tends to be lessened; and physical attractiveness is on the wane. Often they have to adjust to new stresses, which may range from seemingly minor concerns such as false teeth to major ones like chronic ailments. During the latter part of the involutional period, many people have to cope with the death of loved ones. Caine (1974) has pointed out, for example, that 75 percent of American women will one day be widowed; for a sizeable number of women this stress comes during the involutional period. Of crucial importance to many people is the realization that "time is running out"; and that it is increasingly difficult, if not impossible, to make major changes in their life pattern.

Each individual reacts to these stresses in his own way, depending on his general personality organization and on the degree of success and independence he has achieved, his family attachments, and so on. Some people accept the inevitable with philosophical calm, perhaps tinged with a little sadness, and grow old gracefully; others begin the downward path as they climbed up, without much thought or awareness. Others, however, find this a most trying and difficult period, especially if the general disappointment and frustration are accompanied by other stressful conditions, such as financial losses or the death of a loved one. The following poem by an involutional patient clearly conveys her feelings of hopelessness and despair:

"My kin all dead, my childless home a hall
Of spells and spectres deforming the windowed sun,
Friends few and far, and passing one by one,
My body yoked here like an ox in stall
By long disease. . . ."

The developmental pattern involved in invo-lutional melancholia seems readily under-standable and might almost be predicted. In response to the very real stresses at this time of life, lonely, overconscientious, perfectionis-tic individuals easily become worried, anx-ious, and depressed. As past failures and dis-appointments loom large and as the future holds potentially less and less, the increased self-centering of interests and hypochondria-cal concern provide a measure of substitute satisfaction. Then, as the involutional reac-tion becomes exaggerated, these hypochon-driacal factors may develop into definite delu-sions.

Ideas of unreality probably develop out of this same self-centering of interests and the accompanying loss of interest in others and in the environment. It has been pointed out that, to a large extent, things feel real to us in pro-portion to the amount of interest we take in them; if we gradually become preoccupied with our own thoughts and difficulties, the external world can be expected to become progressively less real and to take on a some-what shadowy aspect.

Delusions of sin grow naturally out of feel-ings of failure and self-recrimination. The in-dividual begins to feel that the failure must have been deserved (for it is common in our culture to assume that a really good and de-serving person who works hard is bound to be a success). It is then only another step to magni-fy the most trivial mistakes to cardinal and un-pardonable sins and to distort them as a means of explaining their present predicament.

Like other depressives, involutional patients may even derive some satisfaction out of their exaggerated self-accusations. Statements such as "I am the greatest sinner that ever lived and the whole world knows it" may not only express feelings of extreme guilt and unworthiness, but at the same time help to build feelings of esteem and importance as a unique person. Also, the excessive self-recrimination probably ensures some measure

Some unanswered questions concerning the affective psychoses

Research into the affective psychoses has yet to provide answers to the following questions:

1. Why are most affective disorders—particularly manic-depressive reactions—of relatively brief duration?

2. Why do affective disorders tend to recur?

3. Why are affective disorders relatively "autonomous," tending to run their course even without treatment?

4. Why, in severe depression, does the individual se-lect from a lifetime of experience the most painful thoughts and memories?

5. What precise role is played in the affective psychoses by neurophysiological, biochemical, and psychosocial processes?

In psychology, as in the other sciences, research pro-vides answers to some questions while leaving others unanswered; and sometimes the answers themselves give rise to other, more difficult, questions. As Lipton (1970) has said, ". . . sound research is characterized not only by the questions it answers but also by the many others it generates." (p. 357)

of expiation and atonement. However, the fail-ure of these defensive measures and the con-tinued feelings of hopelessness and depres-sion are reflected in the tendency of these reactions to become chronic if treatment is not undertaken.

In the minority of cases where these individ-uals do evidence paranoid ideation, it would appear that the patient reacts to his disap-pointments and feelings of failure by project-ing the blame for his difficulties onto others instead of blaming himself. Again this pattern might be predicted in the context of a rigid and suspicious person who becomes increas-ingly concerned with his seemingly hopeless life situation and increasingly isolated from meaningful interaction with others.

General sociocultural factors. Differences in the incidence of involutional reactions have been reported for different societies. Some years ago, Henderson and Gillespie (1950) referred to the high incidence of involutional reactions in the rural areas of Scotland. Carothers (1947), on the other hand, found that involutional reactions constituted only 1.4 percent of total admissions among Kenya Africans, as contrasted with some 4 to 5 percent in the United States at that time. He also found no guilt in the Kenyan reactions, as we might have anticipated, since behavior is primarily the responsibility of the group rather than of the individual. In general, however, it would appear that the symptoms of involutional melancholia are much the same in all societies. As Field (1960) has described it, such persons are typically "unshakenly convinced of their own worthlessness and wickedness and irrationally accuse themselves of having committed every unforgivable sin" (p. 36).

Field has also described the way in which social customs and expectations may foster the development of involutional reactions and then shape the form they take. He noted that in rural Ghana women experiencing involutional depression travel to Ashanti religious shrines and there accuse themselves of vile witchcraft. To explain this phenomenon, Field pointed out that the Ashanti woman raises a large family with extreme care, is an excellent housekeeper, and is an efficient business manager. In short, she has a role to play which provides ample meaning in her life. But when she grows old and the children have left the family, the husband often takes on a younger bride on whom he lavishes his possessions and affection. Here the wife's life style, which has had integrity and meaning, is suddenly undermined. Interestingly enough, however, the culture provides a ready rationalization that provides some continuity and meaning for her existence. The woman can simply acknowledge that all along she has really been a witch, and that she therefore deserves the evil that has befallen her. Thus society provides a transitional role which is intropunitive but which explains the sudden change in her life situation and paves the way for her new role as a discarded wife—which she will assume after her cure as a "witch" at the shrine.

In our own highly competitive and age-conscious society, in which many middle-aged and older people are alienated from close family and broader societal ties, we would expect to find a substantial incidence of depression during the involutional and later life periods. And statistics bear out this expectation, not only with respect to the incidence of depression but also of suicide.

Treatment and outcomes

Prior to the advent of modern treatment approaches, the course of involutional melancholia was a long one, estimated at one to four years for those patients who recovered spontaneously—some 30 to 60 percent (Rosenthal, 1968). The other 40 or more percent became chronic hospital cases. With the use of ECT, the duration of the disorder has been shortened to three to six weeks in many cases; the great majority of patients respond to broadly based treatment programs that include the use of antidepressant drugs, psychotherapy, and sociotherapy.

The importance of psychotherapy and sociotherapy seems particularly important in involutional melancholia. As we have seen, the manic-depressive is apparently only temporarily defeated; once he has worked through his feelings of loss, hopelessness, and self-devaluation, he can return to the struggle of life. On the other hand, the depressed involutional patient, more rigid and perfectionistic, older and probably actually facing a more hopeless future, has little incentive to recover and reenter the fight to build a meaningful and fulfilling life in the time remaining. Thus, additional and long-range supportive measures are needed for an adequate readjustment. As in other depressive patterns, the delineation of high-risk groups and individuals combined with early intervention—and where possible, prevention—appear definitely indicated.

Broader Aspects of Depression

In Chapter 7 we dealt with neurotic depressive reactions, and in this chapter we dealt with severe depression of a psychotic type. However, these cases represent only a small and visible "tip of the iceberg" of depression in our society. There are literally hundreds of thousands of Americans—an estimated 1 person in 7—who each day evidence "mild" depression. Such depression usually occurs in response to very real life stress, and, while considered mild, it can be partially or even totally disabling.

The clinical picture in mild depression includes many of the same symptoms as the early stages of psychotic depressive episodes, especially loss of appetite, sleep disturbances, markedly lowered sex drive, difficulty in concentrating and making decisions, and lowered productivity. The individual derives little or no enjoyment from life, even from being with loved ones or engaging in leisure-time activities he formerly entered into with enthusiasm. Instead, he focuses on the negative or aversive aspects of his life situation, and has a devaluated self-image. In essence, he has a "lousy view of himself and his world."

The complexity and rate of technological and social change in our society, economic problems and uncertainties, and the unhappiness and instability of many marriages and other intimate personal relationships are among the many stresses which apparently take their toll in episodes of depression as well as in other physical and mental disorders. Often a vicious circle is established in which the individual's marital or other problems lead to the depression and are, in turn, intensified by it (Briscoe & Smith, 1973).

We can also point to the high incidence of depression among older people, particularly those faced with difficult or aversive life situations—but depression is by no means confined to this age group. Episodes of depression are affecting an increasing number of people of all ages, including teen-agers. In fact, among teen-agers the suicide rate—the ultimate expression of the aversiveness of one's life experience—has shown a significant increase in recent years. In Chapter 17, we shall deal in more depth with the role of stress and depression in suicide. Here we will simply reemphasize that the problem of depression in contemporary society is of tremendous scope, and may directly or indirectly affect our lives in many ways.

In this chapter we have dealt with the affective disorders, which involve severe mood disturbances in the direction of elation or depression, and associated thought disturbances. In manic reactions we observed psychomotor overactivity accompanied by feelings of elation and a seeming "flight into reality" as a means of coping with excessive stress. In depressive reactions we observed psychomotor retardation accompanied by severe feelings of dejection and often of guilt and self-recrimination. Such depressive reactions appear to provide some relief from overwhelming stress through the admission of defeat and giving up, but take their toll in a catastrophic loss of self-esteem. In involutional melancholia we observed a clinical picture of agitated depression—with a similar but even greater loss of hope in an aversive life situation.

While emphasizing the importance of psychosocial factors in the etiology of affective disorders, we have also noted the growing body of research, indicating that neurophysiological and biochemical factors are often significantly involved.

Finally, we noted the broader problem of depression in our society, emphasizing the importance of severe but nonpsychotic episodes in the lives of millions of Americans.

11

Sociopathic Disorders, Delinquency, and Crime

In this chapter we shall be dealing primarily with patterns of personality and behavior that have been classified by the American Psychiatric Association as "Personality Disorders and Certain Other Non-Psychotic Mental Disorders." This category of disorders is a broad one which includes *antisocial personality* and several other maladaptive behavior patterns such as alcoholism, drug dependence, and certain sexual deviations. For the moment, we shall focus on the antisocial personality pattern, the compulsive gambler, and the related problems of delinquency and crime. In later chapters we shall deal with alcoholism and other maladaptive behavior patterns included in the category of "Personality Disorders."

Pathological personality disturbances, unlike many neurotic, psychosomatic, and psychotic disorders, typically do not stem from defenses against anxiety or from personality decompensation. Rather they represent immature and distorted personality development, resulting in individuals who meet their needs in unethical ways at the expense of others. Their behavior tends to be irresponsible, impulsive, and selfish; they "act out" their desires and feelings with little or no sense of guilt or personal distress.[1] Often these patterns of personality and behavior are recognizable by adolescence and continue into adult life.

Compulsive gambling, though not yet well understood, appears to merit consideration as a personality-pattern disturbance. As we shall see, it involves many traits that are also characteristic of the antisocial personality.

Although delinquent and criminal behaviors do not constitute distinct patterns of personality disturbance, they may be closely allied not only with the antisocial personality pattern but also with other types of psychopathology. In considering the topics of delinquency and crime, we shall concern ourselves not only with the varied nature and causes of such behavior, but also with programs of treatment and prevention.

Antisocial (Psychopathic) Personality

Compulsive Gambling

Delinquent Behavior

Criminal Behavior

[1]Sometimes behavior patterns similar to those in the personality disorders are determined primarily by the residual effects of head injuries or other brain pathology. Such cases will be considered in our discussion of brain disorders (Chapter 13).

Antisocial (Psychopathic) Personality

In current usage the terms *antisocial* and *psychopathic* personality are used interchangeably to refer to personality characteristics and behavior patterns that lead to serious difficulties in interpersonal relationships and usually bring the individual into repeated conflict with society.[2] Antisocial personalities are not classifiable as mentally retarded, neurotic, or psychotic. Their outstanding characteristics are a marked lack of ethical or moral development and an inability to follow approved models of behavior. Basically, they are unsocialized and incapable of significant loyalty to other persons, groups, or social values.

The category called antisocial personality includes a mixed group of individuals: unprincipled businessmen, shyster lawyers, quack doctors, high-pressure evangelists, crooked politicians, imposters, drug pushers, a sizeable number of prostitutes, and assorted delinquents and criminals. Few of these individuals find their way into community clinics or mental hospitals. A much larger number are confined in penal institutions, but, as the APA manual points out, a history of repeated legal or social offenses is not sufficient justification for labeling an individual a psychopath. In point of fact, the great majority of psychopaths manage to stay out of corrective institutions, although they tend to be in constant conflict with authority.

The incidence of psychopathic personality is difficult to estimate. In the United States, however, incidence figures are thought to exceed five million. This behavior pattern is considered to be much more common among males than females and more common among younger than older people.

---

[2]The term *sociopath* is also commonly used in this context.

Clinical Picture

Typically intelligent, spontaneous, and very likeable on first acquaintance, antisocial personalities are deceitful and manipulative, callously using others to achieve their own ends. Often they seem to live in a series of present moments, without consideration for the past or future. The following example is illustrative.

Two 18-year-old youths went to visit a teen-ager at her home. Finding no one there, they broke into the house, damaged a number of valuable paintings and other furnishings, and stole a quantity of liquor and a television set. They sold the TV to a mutual friend for a small sum of money. Upon their apprehension by the police, they at first denied the entire venture and then later insisted that it was all a "practical joke." They did not consider their behavior particularly inappropriate, nor did they think any sort of restitution for damage was called for.

In other cases psychopaths are capable of assuming responsibility and pursuing long-range goals, but they do so in unethical ways with a complete lack of consideration for the rights and well-being of others. In describing the "Case of Dan," a wealthy actor and disc jockey, McNeil (1967) pointed to Dan's lifestyle of abusing other people for his own amusement and profit. Dan had

"an unbelievable set of deceptive ways to deal with the opposition. Character assassination, rumor mongering, modest blackmail, seduction, and barefaced lying were the least of his talents. He was a jackal in the entertainment jungle, a jackal who feasted on the bodies of those he had slaughtered professionally." (p. 86)

Also included in the general category of antisocial personality are "hostile psychopaths" who are prone to acting out their impulses in remorseless and often senseless violence.

To fill-in the clinical picture, let us begin by summarizing characteristics which antisocial personalities tend to share in common; then we shall describe three quite different cases which serve to show the wide range of behavior patterns that may be involved.

Common characteristics. While all the following characteristics are not usually found in a particular case, they are typical of psychopaths in general.

1. *Inadequate conscience development and lack of anxiety or guilt.* The antisocial personality is unable to understand and accept ethical values except on a verbal level. Because of the marked discrepancy between his level of intelligence and his conscience development, he has been referred to as a "moral moron." His glib verbalizations and claims of adherence to high standards of morality are usually false and deceptive. He tends to "act out" tensions and problems rather than to worry them out. Often hostile and aggressive, he has little or no sense of guilt. His lack of anxiety and guilt, combined with his apparent sincerity and candor, may enable him to avoid suspicion and detection for stealing and other illegal activities. He often shows contempt for those he is able to take advantage of — the "marks."

2. *Irresponsible and impulsive behavior; low frustration tolerance.* The antisocial personality generally has a callous disregard for the rights, needs, and well-being of others. He is typically a chronic liar, and has learned to take rather than earn what he wants. Prone to thrill seeking and deviant and unconventional behavior, he often breaks the law impulsively and without regard for the consequences. He seldom foregoes immediate pleasure for future gains and long-range goals. He lives in the present, without realistically considering the past or future. External reality is used for immediate personal gratification. Unable to endure routine or to shoulder responsibility, he frequently changes jobs.

3. *Ability to put up "a good front" to impress and exploit others, and to project the blame for his own socially disapproved behavior.* Often the psychopath is charming and likeable, with a disarming manner that easily wins friends. Typically, he has a good sense of humor and an optimistic outlook. If detected in lies he will often seem sincerely sorry and promise to make amends but not really mean it. He seems to have good insight into the needs and weaknesses of other people and is very adept at exploiting them. For example, psychopaths are prone to engaging in unethical sales schemes in which their charm and the confidence they inspire in others is used to make "easy money." He readily finds excuses and rationalizations for his antisocial conduct, typically projecting the blame onto someone else. Thus he is often able to convince other people — as well as himself — that he is free of fault.

4. *Rejection of authority and inability to profit from experience.* The psychopath behaves as if social regulations do not apply to him — he does not play by the rules of the game. His rejection of constituted authority may show itself in impulsive, hostile, criminal acts. Frequently he has a history of difficulties with educational and law-enforcement authorities. Although he often drifts into criminal activities, he is not typically a calculating professional criminal. Despite the difficulties he gets into and the punishment he may receive, he goes on behaving as if he were immune from the consequences of his actions.

5. *Inability to maintain good interpersonal relationships.* Although initially able to win the liking and friendship of other people, the psychopathic personality is seldom able to keep close friends. Irresponsible and egocentric, he is usually cynical, unsympathetic, ungrateful, and remorseless in his dealings. He seemingly cannot understand love in others or give it in return. As Horton, Louy, and Coppolillo (1974) have expressed it, the psychopath "continues to move through the world wrapped in his separateness as though in an insulator, touched rarely and never moved by his fellow man" (p. 622).

The psychopath not only poses a menace to acquaintances but may also set up family and friends as "marks" and create a great deal of unhappiness for them. Manipulative and exploitive in his sexual relationships, he is irresponsible and unfaithful as a mate. Though he often promises to change, he rarely does so for any length of time; seemingly he is incorrigible.

Many of the preceding characteristics may be found in varying degrees in neurotics, in those dependent on drugs, and in those showing other maladaptive behavior patterns. In the case of the antisocial or psychopathic personality, however, these characteristics are extremely pronounced and occur apart from other "symptoms" of psychopathology. Whereas most neurotics, for example, are beset by

worry and anxiety and have a tendency to avoid difficult situations, the antisocial personality acts out his impulses fearlessly, with little or no thought for the consequences.

Patterns of behavior. The following cases are useful in illustrating the range and variability of behavior that may be found among individuals labeled as psychopathic personalities.

"Donald S., 30 years old, has just completed a three-year prison term for fraud, bigamy, false pretenses, and escaping lawful custody. The circumstances leading up to these offenses are interesting and consistent with his past behavior. With less than a month left to serve on an earlier 18-month term for fraud, he faked illness and escaped from the prison hospital. During the ten months of freedom that followed he engaged in a variety of illegal enterprises; the activity that resulted in his recapture was typical of his method of operation. By passing himself off as the "field executive" of an international philanthropic foundation, he was able to enlist the aid of several religious organizations in a fund-raising campaign. The campaign moved slowly at first, and in an attempt to speed things up, he arranged an interview with the local TV station. His performance during the interview was so impressive that funds started to pour in. However, unfortunately for Donald, the interview was also carried on a national news network. He was recognized and quickly arrested. During the ensuing trial it became evident that he experienced no sense of wrongdoing for his activities. He maintained, for example, that his passionate plea for funds "primed the pump"—that is, induced people to give to other charities as well as to

the one he professed to represent. At the same time, he stated that most donations to charity are made by those who feel guilty about something and who therefore deserve to be bilked. This ability to rationalize his behavior and his lack of self-criticism were also evident in his attempts to solicit aid from the very people he had misled. Perhaps it is a tribute to his persuasiveness that a number of individuals actually did come to his support. During his three-year prison term, Donald spent much time searching for legal loopholes and writing to outside authorities, including local lawyers, the Prime Minister of Canada, and a Canadian representative to the United Nations. In each case he verbally attacked them for representing the authority and injustice responsible for his predicament. At the same time he requested them to intercede on his behalf and in the name of the justice they professed to represent. . . .

"By all accounts Donald was considered a willful and difficult child. When his desire for candy or toys was frustrated he would begin with a show of affection, and if this failed he would throw a temper tantrum; the latter was seldom necessary because his angelic appearance and artful ways usually got him what he wanted. Similar tactics were used to avoid punishment for his numerous misdeeds. At first he would attempt to cover up with an elaborate facade of lies, often shifting the blame to his brothers. If this did not work, he would give a convincing display of remorse and contrition. When punishment was unavoidable he would become sullenly defiant, regarding it as an unjustifiable tax on his pleasures.

"Although he was obviously very intelligent, his school years were academically undistinguished. He was restless, easily bored, and frequently truant. His

As part of an experiment to study vandalism, an "abandoned" automobile was left on a New York City street and photographers hidden to record the action. Although it was expected that most of the vandals would be teen-agers and children, that prediction was not confirmed; the picture on the left shows the first vandals, a white middle-class family who stripped the car of its most valuable components; second, an adult male takes the best tires. Finally, after the car had been completely stripped, the destruction began: passers-by stopped to look, then broke windows and bashed in the metal until only a useless hulk remained. (Based on Zimbardo, 1973.)

behavior in the presence of the teacher or some other authority was usually quite good, but when he was on his own he generally got himself or others into trouble. Although he was often suspected of being the culprit, he was adept at talking his way out of difficulty. . . .

"His sexual experiences were frequent, casual, and callous. When he was 22 he married a 41-year-old woman whom he had met in a bar. Several other marriages followed, all bigamous. In each case the pattern was the same: he would marry someone on impulse, let her support him for several months, and then leave. One marriage was particularly interesting. After being charged with fraud Donald was sent to a psychiatric institution for a period of observation. While there he came to the attention of a female member of the professional staff. His charm, physical attractiveness, and convincing promises to reform led her to intervene on his behalf. He was given a suspended sentence and they were married a week later. At first things went reasonably well, but when she refused to pay some of his gambling debts he forged her name to a check and left. He was soon caught and given an 18-month prison term. As mentioned earlier, he escaped with less than a month left to serve.

"It is interesting to note that Donald sees nothing particularly wrong with his behavior, nor does he express remorse or guilt for using others and causing them grief. Although his behavior is self-defeating in the long run, he considers it to be practical and possessed of good sense. Periodic punishments do nothing to decrease his egotism and confidence in his own abilities, nor do they offset the often considerable short-term gains of which he is capable." (Hare, 1970, pp. 1–4)

The most dangerous psychopaths from the standpoint of society as a whole are those who are not only intelligent and completely unscrupulous but also show sufficient self-control and purposefulness of behavior to achieve high political office. This point is well illustrated by the case of Nazi Field Marshal Goering.

"Goering had a better family background than most of his Nazi associates. His father had been Governor of German Southwest Africa and Resident Minister at Haiti. Hermann attended several boarding schools but he was bored and restless till he got to the Military Academy, where he settled down to his studies. He entered the army as an infantryman but he took flying lessons surreptitiously and got himself transferred to the Air Force against the wishes of his superior officers. He was a courageous and impetuous flyer and after the death of Richthofen he took charge of The Flying Circus.

"At the close of the First World War Goering went to Sweden where he worked as a mechanic and as a civil aviator. He married a wealthy woman and was able to return to Germany and enroll at the University of Munich. In Munich he met Hitler and joined the Nazi movement. . . .

"Goering's manner of living is described as 'Byzantine splendor' and as 'piratical splendor.' He built a pretentious country home near Berlin and furnished it magnificently with tapestries and paintings and antiques. He had a private zoo. He required his servants to address his wife as Hohe Frau, thus giving her the distinction of nobility. He felt that the Germans liked his display of luxury—that it gave food for their imagination and gave the people something to think about. Goering was given to

In addition to the antisocial personality, the APA Diagnostic Manual lists a number of other personality trait disturbances—disorders that are relatively heterogeneous and appear to have little in common except that each involves personality traits or patterns that lead to maladaptive behavior.

Paranoid personality	This pattern is characterized by suspiciousness, hypersensitivity, rigidity, envy, and excessive self-importance, plus a tendency to blame others for one's own mistakes and failures and to ascribe evil motives to others.
Cyclothymic (affective) personality	This pattern is a milder version of manic-depressive reactions, and is characterized by recurring and alternating periods of elation and depression. The periods of elation may involve enthusiasm, ambition, optimism, high energy, and warmth, while the periods of depression tend to be marked by worry, low energy, pessimism, and a sense of futility. Usually the mood variations are not readily attributable to stressful situations.
Schizoid personality	In this behavior pattern, the individual manifests seclusiveness, shyness, oversensitivity, avoidance of competitive or close interpersonal relationships, and often, ego-centricity. Autistic thinking and daydreaming are common, although the individual does not lose the capacity to recognize reality. The schizoid personality has difficulty expressing ordinary aggressive feelings or hostility, and tends to react to disturbing stress situations with apparent detachment.
Explosive personality	This behavior pattern is characterized by gross verbal or physical aggressiveness and outbursts of rage. Such outbursts are strikingly different from the individual's usual behavior, and he may be quite regretful and repentant about them. The individual is generally considered excitable and overresponsive to environmental stresses. The intensity of the outbursts and the individual's seeming inability to control them are the distinguishing characteristics of this pattern.
Obsessive-compulsive personality	In this behavior pattern the individual manifests excessive concern with conformity and rigid adherence to standards of conscience. Such an individual tends to be over-inhibited, overconscientious, overdutiful, rigid, and to have difficulty relaxing. This disorder is a milder version of obsessive-compulsive neurosis, to which it may actually lead.
Hysterical personality	This type of personality is characterized by immaturity, excitability, emotional instability, and self-dramatization. Whether or not the individual is aware of his motives, such self-dramatization is attention-seeking and often seductive. Such persons, who have also been referred to as histrionic personalities, are usually self-centered, vain, and quite concerned about the approval of others.
Asthenic personality	In this type of personality pattern, the individual manifests a mild version of neurasthenia, with low energy level, easy fatigability, lack of enthusiasm, oversensitivity to physical and emotional strain, and a marked incapacity to enjoy life. Typically he is very self-pitying and tends to place the main responsibility for his difficulties and for helping him out of them upon others.
Passive-aggressive personality	This pattern is characterized by both passivity and aggression. The latter is typically expressed nonviolently—e.g., by procrastination, obstructionism, pouting, intentional inefficiency, or stubbornness. Often the individual's behavior reflects a hostility that he does not dare express openly, and his behavior commonly stems from a frustrating interpersonal or institutional relationship on which he is overdependent.

Inadequate personality	This behavior pattern is characterized by ineffectual responses to stress—particularly to emotional, intellectual, social, and physical demands. While the individual does not appear to be mentally retarded or physically deficient, he does manifest ineptness, poor judgment, social instability, poor adaptability, and a lack of physical and emotional stamina.
Other personality disorders	This category includes such patterns as immature personality and passive-dependent personality.

In general, it is risky to use the above categories in labeling a given individual, since few persons appear to fit into a given category very adequately. Small et al. (1970) did find a number of common characteristics in a study of passive-aggressive personalities, but these were hospitalized cases and not necessarily representative, since personality trait disturbances usually are not incapacitating. Of course, persons with these disturbances may be more vulnerable to life stresses than normal persons.

exhibitionism and he had a passion for uniforms, gold braid, medals, and decorations. . . . Goering would strut and swagger in private and public. In political rallies he made himself a flamboyant master of pomp and pageantry. He was an exhibitionist in the psychopathic pattern.

"Goering was coarse and gross. He was a Gargantuan eater and drinker. He was ribald in jest. He laughed uproariously when his pet lion urinated on a lady's dress. He once horrified his men and women guests at his country estate by having a bull and a cow mate before them. Personally he enjoyed the spectacle and declared that it was an old Teutonic custom.

"'Our Hermann' was popular with the masses and they smiled goodnaturedly at his antics and self-display. He demanded that they make sacrifices in order to win victory and exhorted them to choose guns instead of butter. He patted his fat belly and said that he had lost forty pounds in the service of his country. The Germans appreciated his sense of humor. . . .

"Goering was unscrupulous in his exercise of authority. He was said to be courageous, hard, challenging and authoritative in the Prussian manner. He was described as an affable, hearty butcher. . . . When he was made Chief of the Prussian Police he told his men to shoot first and inquire afterward. 'If you make a mistake, don't talk about it.' 'The faults which my officials commit are my faults; the bullets which they fire are my bullets.' Goering regarded his bullets as an effective form of propaganda. He introduced the concentration camp and

declared that it was not his duty to exercise justice, but to annihilate and exterminate. He reintroduced decapitation as an honest old German punishment. Goering is given credit for plotting the Reichstag Fire and for the planning and direction of the Blood Purge. Goering admitted that he had no conscience; his conscience was Adolf Hitler.

"Like many a psychopath Goering had a tender side. He was fond of animals, including his lion cubs. He declared that 'He who torments an animal hurts the feelings of the whole German people.' . . .

"Goering was often considered the most normal and the most conservative of the Nazi leaders. Like most psychopaths he would appear normal in his social relationships and he might seem genial and kindly with his humor and laughter. His pattern of behavior, however, identifies him as a constitutional psychopath and he presents a fair example of this personality disorder." (Bluemel, 1948, pp. 78–82)

Found guilty as a war criminal at the Nuremberg trials following World War II, Goering was sentenced to death on the gallows. However, he managed to evade his punishment by obtaining a capsule of cyanide—an extremely fast-acting poison—and taking his own life.

One of the most interesting types of persons found in the category of antisocial personality is the impostor, whose abilities are often outstanding and might seemingly have been channeled in socially approved ways. This is well brought out in the following unusual case.

One of the boldest impostors of recent times was Ferdinand Waldo Demara, Jr. As an adolescent, he ran away from a rather tragic family situation and after unsuccessful attempts first to become a Trappist monk and then to teach school, he joined the army. Soon thereafter he went AWOL, joined the navy, and was assigned to duty on a destroyer during World War II. Here, by a ruse, he got hold of some navy stationery with which he managed to obtain the transcript of college grades of an officer who was on leave. He then "doctored" this transcript by substituting his own name and adding some courses; when photostated, it looked so impressive that he used it to apply for a commission. While waiting for his commission to come through, he amused himself by obtaining other records, including the full credentials of a Dr. French, who had received a Ph.D. degree in psychology from Harvard. Informed during a visit to Norfolk that he could expect his commission as soon as a routine security check was completed, he realized that such a check would surely expose him. Under cover of darkness, he left his navy clothes on the end of a pier with a note that "this was the only way out."

Now that Demara was "dead"—drowned in the oily waters off Norfolk—he became Dr. French. He obtained an appointment as Dean of Philosophy in a small Canadian college and taught courses in general, industrial, and abnormal psychology. Eventually, however, he had a disagreement with his superior and reluctantly left.

During this period he had become friends with a physician by the name of Joseph Cyr and had learned a considerable amount about the practice of medicine from him during the cold winter months when neither man had much to occupy his time. Interested in the possibility of getting a license to practice in the States, the trusting doctor had given Demara a complete packet including his baptism and confirmation certificates, school records, and his license to practice medicine in Canada.

Using these credentials, without Dr. Cyr's knowledge, Demara now obtained a commission for himself as lieutenant in the Royal Canadian Navy. His first assignment was to take sick call each morning at the base. To help solve his problem of lack of knowledge in the field, he went to his superior officer and stated that he had been asked to work up a rule-of-thumb guide for people in lumber camps, most of whom did not have physicians readily available. His senior officer, delighted with the project, prepared a manual covering the most serious medical situations, which served as a basic guide for amateur diagnosticians. Demara then used this manual faithfully as his own. He also studied medical books and evidently picked up considerable additional knowledge.

Assigned to duty on the aircraft carrier HMCS *Magnificent*, Demara was criticized by his senior medical officer for his lack of training in medicine and surgery, especially for his deficiency in diagnosing medical problems. Learning of the report, Demara took characteristic bold action. He commandeered several seamen's compartments in the lower area of the ship, posted them with quarantine signs, and sent there for observation the patients whom he was having trouble diagnosing—in the meantime giving them penicillin. The chief medical officer knew nothing of this plan—Demara had confided only in a bosun's mate—and the reports of Demara's performance, based only on cases that Demara reviewed with his superior officer, became more favorable.

Perhaps the climax of Demara's incredible career came during the Korean War when—still as Lieutenant Cyr—he was assigned as the ship's doctor to the Canadian destroyer *Cayuga*. As the *Cayuga* proceeded to the combat zone, Demara studied medical books and hoped that his skill would never be put to the test. But fate decreed otherwise. One afternoon the destroyer spotted a small Korean junk littered with wounded men who had been caught in an ambush. "Dr. Cyr" was summoned and knew that there was no escape for him.

"Nineteen suffering men were lifted tenderly from the junk. Three were so gravely wounded that only emergency surgery could save them. Demara had read books on surgery, but had never seen an operation performed.

"The self-taught 'M.D.' cleaned and sutured the 16 less seriously wounded men, while gathering his courage for the great ordeal. Then he commandeered the captain's cabin as an emergency operating room. Working hour after hour with slow, unskilled hands, but drawing on all the resources of his great memory and natural genius, Demara performed miracles, while the ship's officers and dozens of enlisted men helped and watched.

"From one wounded man he removed a bullet that had lodged near the heart; from the second, a piece of shrapnel in the groin. For the third man, Demara collapsed a lung which had been perforated by a bullet.

"The operations began at midnight. When the pseudo surgeon looked up after the last operation, the light of dawn was shining through the portholes. Drenched in his own sweat, with the cheers of officers and crew ringing in his ears, he took a long drink of the ship's rum, went to his cabin, and collapsed in a stupor of sleep."

When his ship was sent to Japan for refitting, an eager young press officer seized on "Dr. Cyr's" exploits and wrote them up in full. His story was released to the civilian press, and the "miracle doctor" became world famous. This publicity proved to be Demara's temporary undoing, for it led to queries from the real Dr. Joseph Cyr as to whether the physician mentioned in the press releases was a relative, and when Dr. Cyr saw the newspaper picture, he was shocked to find it was that of an old friend.

Dropped from the Canadian navy without fanfare—largely because he had managed to get a license to practice medicine in England and was now a licensed physician—Demara went through a difficult period. Wherever he went, he was soon recognized, and he lost job after job. He managed to work for a year at a state school for retarded children and did so well that he received a promotional transfer to a state hospital for the criminally insane. Here he found that the patients seemed to like him and that he was able to communicate with them. The experience began to bother him and he started to drink heavily and eventually resigned.

One morning after a prolonged drinking bout, he woke up in a southern city and realized his drinking was getting out of hand. He joined the local chapter of Alcoholics Anonymous as Ben W. Jones, whose credentials he had acquired along the way. With the help of sympathetic friends in Alcoholics Anonymous and a few fraudulent references obtained by ingenious methods, he was hired as a guard in a state penitentiary. Here he did a remarkable job, instituting a number of badly needed reforms in the maximum security block. Again he found himself able to communicate with the men, and he was promoted to assistant warden of maximum security. Ironically, one of his reform measures was to ask the townspeople to contribute old magazines, and before long one of the prisoners read the issue of *Life* that contained his picture and case history and recognized the new assistant warden.

Trying to get away lest he wind up as a prisoner in the same penitentiary, Demara was jailed in a nearby state and given considerable publicity but eventually released. Some time later he telephoned Dr. Crichton, from whose report most of this material has been adapted, to say "I'm on the biggest caper of them all. Oh, I wish I could tell you." (Summarized from Crichton, 1959; quoted passages from Smith, 1968.)

By way of a postscript, it may be mentioned that in early 1970 there was a newspaper report of Demara functioning successfully as a minister in a small northwestern community, this time with the congregation's full knowledge of his past. As we shall see, many persons labeled as "antisocial personalities" do eventually settle down to responsible positions in the community.

Causal factors

The personality characteristics and behavior patterns that we now label "antisocial" or "psychopathic" have been part of the human scene since ancient times, and are found in primitive as well as highly developed societies. However, the causal factors in such antisocial reactions are still not fully understood, though it would appear that these factors differ from case to case as well as from one socioeconomic level to another.

Contemporary research in this area has variously stressed constitutional deficiencies, the early learning of antisocial behavior as a coping style, and the influence of particular family and community patterns.

Constitutional factors. Because the psychopath's impulsiveness, acting out, and intolerance of discipline tend to appear early in life, several investigators have focused on the role of constitutional deficiencies as causative factors in antisocial personality disturbances.

1. *Malfunction of inhibitory mechanisms in the central nervous system.* In a review and interpretation of studies indicating a relatively high incidence of EEG abnormalities among psychopaths, particularly involving slow-wave activity in the temporal lobe of the brain, Hare (1970) concluded that such abnormalities reflect the malfunction of inhibitory mechanisms in the central nervous system, and that "this malfunction makes it difficult to learn to inhibit behavior that is likely to lead to punishment" (pp. 33–34).

It may be emphasized, however, that most psychopaths do not show abnormal EEGs, and when they do, there is no conclusive evidence that the EEG patterns are directly related to the development of antisocial personalities. In addition, many individuals who show similar EEG patterns are not psychopathic. So when brain anomalies do occur in antisocial personalities, they are probably interactive factors rather than primary determinants of the maladaptive behavior.

2. *Deficient emotional arousal.* A good deal of research evidence indicates that psychopaths are deficient in emotional arousal; this presumably renders them less prone to fear and anxiety in stressful situations and less prone to normal conscience development and socialization.

In an early study, for example, Lykken (1957) concluded that psychopaths have fewer inhibitions about committing antisocial acts because they suffer little anxiety. Similarly, Eysenck (1960) concluded that psychopaths are less sensitive to noxious stimuli and have a slower rate of conditioning than normal individuals. As a result, psychopaths presumably fail to acquire many of the conditioned reactions essential to normal avoidance behavior, conscience development, and socialization. Support for this viewpoint is found in the more recent findings of Chesno and Kilmann (1975) who concluded that psychopaths, as contrasted with normals, "were relatively unsuccessful in acquiring active avoidance responses" (p. 150).

Hare (1970) and other later investigators have reported comparable findings with respect to the psychopath's lack of normal fear and anxiety reactions and failure to learn readily from punishment. However, the latter point merits qualification. Schmauk (1970) found that psychopaths were less adept than nonpsychopaths in learning to avoid physical and social punishments, but they were more adept than normals in learning to avoid the loss of money — a type of punishment that was apparently *meaningful* to them. These findings are more understandable when it is added that the psychopaths in this experiment were inmates of a penal institution where punishments were relatively mild for most forms of misbehavior, whereas money was both hard to come by and very valuable for obtaining niceties beyond the grim prison fare. While psychopaths do not experience the aversive consequences of misbehavior as negatively as do most people, when punishment is related to their values and important to them, apparently they can learn avoidance behavior quite readily.

In addition, it may be noted that while the psychopath's lack of normal emotional arousal may be based on constitutional deficiencies, it may also be based partially on learning. Often in the past they have managed to avoid the full consequences of their antisocial behavior by such devices as lies and plausible excuses, dramatic shows of remorse, and empty but convincing promises of "good" behavior in the future. But regardless of its origin, psychopaths show a general lack of fear and anxiety in situations that would be stressful and anxiety-arousing to most people.

3. *Stimulation seeking.* In his study of criminal psychopaths, Hare (1968) reported that these individuals operate at a low level of arousal and are deficient in autonomic variability. He considered these findings — together with the psychopath's lack of normal conditioning to noxious and painful stimuli — indicative of a "relative immunity" to stimulation that is likely to make the psychopath seek stimulation and thrills as ends in themselves. In a study comparing psychopaths and normals, Fenz (1971) similarly found that psychopaths seem to have an insatiable need for stimulation.

Such findings support the earlier view of Quay (1965), who concluded that psychopathic behavior is an extreme form of stimulation-seeking behavior:

"The psychopath is almost universally characterized as highly impulsive, relatively refractory to the effects of experience in modifying his socially troublesome behavior, and lacking in the ability to delay gratification. His penchant for creating excitement for the moment without regard for later consequences seems almost unlimited. He is unable to tolerate routine and boredom. While he may engage in antisocial, even vicious, behavior, his outbursts frequently appear to be motivated by little more than a need for thrills and excitement. . . . It is the impulsivity and the lack of even minimal tolerance for sameness which appear to be the primary and distinctive features of the disorder." (p. 180)

What such extreme stimulation-seeking might mean in the total context of a personality characterized as impulsive, lacking in judgment, deficient in inner reality and moral controls, and seemingly unable to learn from punishment and experience can only be surmised. Though further investigation is needed, it seems plausible that stimulation-seeking "unchecked by conditioned fear response is a two-edged sword for antisocial behavior" (Borkovec, 1970, p. 222).

Family relationships. Perhaps the most popular generalization about the development of the antisocial personality is the assumption of some form of early disturbances in family relationships.

1. *Early parental loss and emotional deprivation.* A number of earlier studies reported that an unusually high number of psychopaths had experienced the trauma of losing a parent at an early age—usually through the separation or divorce of their parents. For example, Greer (1964) found that 60 percent of a sample of psychopaths had lost a parent during childhood, as contrasted with 28 percent for a control group of neurotics and 27 percent for a control group of normal subjects.

Since many normal people have experienced the loss of a parent at an early age, it would seem to require considerably more than parental loss to produce a psychopath. In reviewing the available evidence, Hare (1970) suggested that the factor of key significance was not the parental loss per se, but rather the emotional disturbances in the family relationships created before the departure of a parent.

This point is supported by the findings of Wolkind (1974) who found a high incidence of "affectionless psychopathy" in a group of 92 institutionalized children. In many of these cases the antisocial disorder seemed to have been caused by pathogenic family situations prior to the children's being placed in an institution.

2. *Parental rejection and inconsistency.* A number of studies have attempted to relate parental rejection and inconsistent discipline to inadequate socialization and antisocial personality. After an extensive review of the available literature, McCord and McCord (1964) concluded that severe parental rejection and lack of parental affection were the primary causes of psychopathic personality.

Another aspect of this picture has been pointed out by Buss (1966), who concluded that two types of parental behavior foster psychopathy. In the first, parents are cold and distant toward the child and allow no warm or close relationship to develop. If the child imitates the parental model, he will become cold and distant in his own later relationships; although he learns the formal attributes and amenities of social situations, he does not develop empathy for others or become emotionally involved with them. The second type of parental behavior involves inconsistency, in which parents are capricious in supplying affection, rewards, and punishments. Usually they are inconsistent in their own role enactments as well, so that the child lacks a stable model to imitate and fails to develop a clear-cut sense of self-identity. Often the parents reward not only "superficial conformity" but "underhanded nonconformity"—that is, nonconformity that goes undetected by outsiders. Thus, they reinforce behaviors that lead to psychopathic behavior. Similarly, when the parents are both arbitrary and inconsistent in punishing the child, avoiding punishment becomes more important to him than receiving rewards. Instead of learning right from wrong, the child learns how to avoid blame and punishment by lying or other manipulative means.

In Chapter 5 we noted that among the damaging effects of parental rejection and inconsistent discipline are slow conscience development and aggression on the part of the child. We also noted that children subjected to inconsistent reward and punishment for aggressive behavior were more resistant to the extinction of such behavior than were children who experienced more consistent discipline. In addition, Campagna and Harter (1975) concluded from their findings that later antisocial personality is related to an arrest in moral development on the part of the child. However, it seems desirable to exercise caution in using parental rejection and inconsistency as basic explanations of psychopathic personalities. These same conditions have been implicated in a wide range of later maladaptive behaviors, and many children coming from such family backgrounds do not become psychopaths or evidence other serious psychopathology.

3. *Faulty parental models and family interactions.* In an early study of 40 male psychopathic personalities, Heaver (1943) emphasized the influence exerted by faulty parental models—typically a mother who overindulges her son and a father who is highly successful, driving, critical, and distant.

Greenacre (1945) added a number of details that have been supported by later studies of psychopaths from middle-class families. The father is a successful and respected member of the community and is distant and fear-inspiring to his son. The mother, on the other hand, is indulgent, pleasure-loving, frivolous, and often tacitly contemptuous of her husband's importance. When such families are heavily dependent on the approval and admiration of their communities—as in the case of some clergymen and politicians—it is crucial that they maintain the illusion of a happy family by concealing and denying any evidence of bickering or scandal. Thus the children learn that appearances are more important than reality, and they, too, become part of the show-window display, where a premium is put on charm and impressing others, rather than on competence and integrity. This need to please and to win social approval for their parents' sake seems to bring out a precocious but superficial charm in some of these children, together with great adroitness in handling people for purely selfish ends.

The son in such a family cannot hope to emulate his successful and awe-inspiring father, but, aware of the extension to himself of the high evaluation that is placed on his father, he develops a feeling of importance and of being exempt from the consequences of his actions. Frequently the prominence of the father does, in fact, protect the child from the ordinary consequences of antisocial behavior. If we add one additional factor—the contradictory influence of a father who tells his son of the necessity for responsibility, honesty, and respect for others, but who himself is deceitful and manipulative—we appear to have a family background capable of producing a middle-class psychopath.

Supporting this explanation is Hare's (1970) finding of a high incidence of psychopathic personalities—particularly fathers—in the families of children who later manifest such behavior themselves. In this context, Hare concluded that "at least part of a psychopath's behavior results from modeling another individual's psychopathic behavior" (p. 107).

The life-style of the psychopath seems especially resistant to change, since it is intermittently reinforced by short-term gains and by the avoidance of punishment or other noxious situations. With relative freedom from anxiety, guilt, and remorse, there is little motivation to change.

Sociocultural factors. Although we have emphasized the part played by constitutional and family factors in the formation of psychopathic personalities, it would appear that social conditions such as those found in our urban ghettos also produce their share of psychopaths. An environment characterized by the breakdown of social norms and regulations, disorganization, undesirable peer models, and a climate of alienation from and hostility toward the broader society appears to produce a type of psychopathic personality. This personality is manifested by inadequate conscience development, lack of concern for others, and destructive antisocial behavior. On a family level, the picture is often aggravated by broken homes, parental rejection, and inconsistent discipline, leading to distrust, a confused sense of personal identity, self-devaluation, and feelings of hurt and hostility. The end result may be overt aggressive behavior, directed especially at the representatives of "conventional" society.

In one high school in a disadvantaged area, two black youths held a white teacher while a third poured gasoline over him and set him on fire. Fortunately, another teacher came to the rescue and was able to extinguish the flames before the teacher was seriously burned. The youths were apprehended and detained in a juvenile facility, since they were under 18 years of age. Interviewed by a social worker, they showed no remorse for their act, did not consider it wrong, and were disappointed that they had not succeeded in killing the teacher. The youths were not in any of his classes, nor did they know him personally. The apparent leader of the group stated that "Next time we'll do it right, so there won't be nobody left around to identify us."

Melges and Bowlby (1969) have pointed out that such hostile psychopaths believe other people cannot be counted on and see their own future as out of their control. In essence, they feel helpless and hopeless—as well as resentful and hostile—in relation to their aversive life situations. Seeing no possible way they can "make it," they lash out to make others suffer too.

In summary, antisocial personalities are a mixed group of individuals who nevertheless have certain characteristics in common. Although the causal factors are not clear and may differ from case to case, varying combinations of constitutional, psychosocial, and sociocultural factors appear to be involved.

Treatment and outcomes

Since individuals with antisocial personalities do not exhibit obvious psychopathology and can function effectively in most respects, they seldom come to the attention of mental hospitals or clinics. Those who run afoul of the law may participate in rehabilitation programs in penal institutions, but thus far these programs have not proven generally effective. Even if more and better therapeutic facilities were available, effective treatment would still be a challenging task.

Some early case reports pointed to favorable results with intensive psychotherapy, but, in general, traditional psychotherapeutic approaches have not proven effective. Nor have various biological measures, including electroshock therapy, the use of drugs, and psychosurgery, fared any better.

More recently, behavior therapists have dealt successfully with specific antisocial behaviors, and modern behavior therapy techniques appear to offer promise of more effective treatment. However, behavior therapy is also somewhat at a disadvantage since we are dealing with a total life-style rather than with a specific maladaptive behavior like a phobia, that can be targeted for treatment. And as we have noted, intermittent reinforcement by short-term gains and avoidance of punishment combined with a lack of anxiety and guilt do not motivate the psychopath to change his way of life.

On the basis of an extensive review of research findings, Bandura (1969, 1973) has suggested three steps that can be used to modify antisocial behavior through the application of learning principles: (a) the withdrawal of reinforcements for disapproved antisocial behavior, and, where appropriate, the use of punishment for such behavior; (b) the modeling of desired behavior by "change agents"—the therapist and/or other behavioral models—and the use of a graded system of rewards or reinforcers for imitating such behavior; and (c) the reduction of material incentives and rewards as the individual's behavior is increasingly brought under the control of self-administered, symbolic rewards. Essentially, the objective is to effect the gradual transfer of evaluative and reinforcement functions to the antisocial individual himself by helping him develop inner controls that minimize the need for external ones. An important facet of this approach is providing situations in which the psychopath's improved behavior becomes a model for other individuals in treatment; he thus functions as a "change agent" or therapist in helping others, while also furthering the long-range modification of his own behavior.

Fortunately, many psychopathic personalities improve after the age of 40 even without treatment, possibly because of weaker biological drives, better insight into their self-defeating behavior, and the cumulative effect of social conditioning. Such individuals are often referred to as "burned-out" psychopaths. However, psychopaths create a great deal of havoc before they reach 40 — as well as afterward if they do not change. In view of the distress and unhappiness they inflict on others and the social damage they cause, it seems desirable — and more economical in the long run — to put increased effort into the development of effective treatment programs.

Compulsive Gambling

Gambling is usually defined as wagering on games or events in which chance largely determines the outcome. In modern societies money is typically the item of exchange; in other societies, seashell currency, beads, jewelry, and food are often used. The ancient Chinese frequently wagered hairs of their head — and sometimes even fingers, toes, and limbs — on games of chance (Cohen & Hansel, 1956). Occasionally the Mojave Indians wagered their wives (Devereaux, 1950). But regardless of the item of exchange, gambling seems to be an enduring human proclivity. Judging from written history and the studies of anthropologists, gambling has occurred and continues to occur almost universally and among all social strata.

Clinical picture

Gambling in our society takes many forms, from the casino gambling of Las Vegas, to betting on horse races (legally or otherwise), to numbers games, lotteries, dice, bingo, and cards. The exact sums that change hands in legal and illegal gambling are unknown, but it has been estimated that habitual gamblers in the United States lose more than 20 billion dollars each year.[3]

If one were to define gambling in its broadest sense, even playing the stock market might be considered a game of chance. Sherrod (1968) has humorously pointed to the need for a clearer definition of terms:

"If you bet on a horse, that's gambling. If you bet you can make three spades, that's entertainment. If you bet cotton will go up three points, that's business. See the difference?" (p. 619)

[3]Statistics in this section are based on Solomon (1972), Strine (1971), and Livingston (1974).

In any event, gambling appears to be one of our major national pastimes, with some 50 percent of the population gambling at one time or other on anything from horse races to Saturday-night poker games. Usually, such gambling is a harmless form of social entertainment; the individual places a bet and waits for the result. Win or lose, that is that. But while most people can take it or leave it, an estimated 6 to 10 million Americans get "hooked" on gambling.

These compulsive gamblers[4] are habitual losers who are practically always out of luck, usually in debt, and sometimes in jail. Despite their difficulties, however, they tend to be of average intelligence or above, and many have completed one or more years of college. They are usually married and often have responsible managerial or professional positions that provide a reasonably good income. It is generally assumed that far more men than women are compulsive gamblers, but there are no reliable data concerning the actual sex ratio.

Causal factors

One of the first attempts to explain the role of psychological factors in compulsive gambling was made by Sigmund Freud. Using the compulsive gambling of Dostoevsky as an example, Freud concluded that compulsive gamblers were guilt-ridden masochists who wanted to be punished. Freud emphasized Dostoevsky's hatred of his father and subsequent guilt feelings after his father was murdered when Dostoevsky was 18 years old.

Although a few psychologists and psychiatrists have dealt with the topic of compulsive gambling, very little systematic research has been done in this area. As a result, the causal factors in compulsive gambling are not yet well understood. It seems to be a learned pattern that is highly resistant to extinction. Often the person who becomes a compulsive gambler wins a substantial sum of money the first time he gambles; chance alone would dictate that a certain percentage of individuals would have "beginner's luck." Bolen and Boyd (1968) consider it likely that the reinforcement an individual receives during this introductory phase is a significant factor in his later pathological gambling. And since anyone is likely to win from time to time, the principles of intermittent reinforcement could explain the addict's continued gambling despite excessive losses. Bolen and Boyd were struck particularly by the similarity between female slot-machine players and Skinner's laboratory pigeons; the latter, which had been placed on a variable reinforcement schedule, "repetitively and incessantly pecked to the point of exhaustion and eventual demise while awaiting the uncertain appearance of their jackpot of bird seed" (1968, p. 629).

Despite his awareness that the odds are against him, and despite the fact that he never, or rarely, repeats his early success, the compulsive gambler continues to gamble avidly. To "stake" his gambling he often dissipates his savings, neglects his family, defaults on bills, and borrows money from friends and loan companies. Eventually he may resort to writing bad checks, embezzlement, or other illegal means of obtaining money, feeling sure that his luck will change and that he will be able to repay what he has taken.

On a superficial level, the compulsive gambler tends to be quite personable and is often socially facile and responsive. His personal relationships, however, are usually manipulatory and shallow. In addition, his gambling activities tend to alienate him from family and friends. Whereas others view his gambling as unethical and disruptive, he is likely to see himself as a man taking "calculated risks" to build a lucrative business. Often he feels alone and resentful that others do not understand his activities.

In a pioneering and well-controlled study of former compulsive gamblers, Rosten (1961) found that as a group they tended to be rebellious, unconventional individuals who did not seem to fully understand the ethical norms of society. Half of the group described themselves as "hating regulations." Of 30 men studied, 12 had served time in jail for embezzlement and other crimes directly connected with their gambling.

---

[4]Although these individuals have traditionally been called compulsive gamblers, they are closer to psychopathic personalities than to obsessive-compulsives. Thus it has been suggested that the label be changed to pathological gamblers.

One reason for compulsive gambling may be found in the intermittent reinforcement of winning—exemplified here by the occasional payments the slot machine metes out to this woman, so intent on her playing. As we have noted, a given response, whether maladaptive or adaptive, tends to be maintained through such a pattern of reinforcement.

Rosten also found that the men were unrealistic in their thinking and prone to seek highly stimulating situations. In the gambler's own words, he "loves excitement" and "needs action." Although these men admitted that they had known objectively the all-but-impossible odds they faced while gambling, they had felt that these odds did not apply to them. Often they had the unshakable feeling that "tonight is my night"; typically they had also followed the so-called Monte Carlo fallacy—that after so many losses, their turn was coming up and they would hit it big. Many of the men discussed the extent to which they had "fooled" themselves by elaborate rationalizations. For example, one gambler described his previous rationalizations as covering all contingencies: "When I was ahead, I could gamble because I was playing with others' money. When I was behind, I had to get even. When I was even, I hadn't lost any money" (Rosten, 1961, p. 67).

It is of interest to note that within a few months after the study, 13 of Rosten's 30 subjects either had returned to heavy gambling, had started to drink excessively, or had not been heard from and were presumed to be gambling again.

Later studies of compulsive gamblers are sparse, but the few that are available strongly support the earlier findings of Rosten, typically describing compulsive gamblers as immature, rebellious, thrill-seeking, superstitious, and basically psychopathic (Bolen & Boyd, 1968; Solomon, 1972; Caldwell, Bolen, & Boyd, 1972; Livingston, 1974).

The most comprehensive study is that of Livingston, who observed, interviewed, and tested a group of 55 admitted compulsive gamblers who had joined Gamblers Anonymous to try to stop gambling. These individuals were all male and mostly working class. Livingston found that these men often referred to their "past immaturity" in explaining their habitual gambling. They also described themselves as having a "big ego" and acknowledged a strong need for recognition and adulation from others. Livingston noted that "money seems to be the key to such adulation, since they equate it with smartness, shrewdness, and success" (1974, pp. 51–52).

The gamblers in this sample were extremely impatient and seemingly incapable of sustained effort toward achievement in one area—other than gambling.

Although these men had usually been able to cover up their losses early in their gambling careers, the course was downhill, leading to financial, marital, job, and often legal problems. Eventually the gambler's life situation became so bad that it seemed the only way out of his difficulties was the way he got in—by gambling.

It is of interest to note that these findings, based largely on working-class subjects, are not markedly different from those of Rosten. However, the influence of social class standing on compulsive gambling remains to be explored. And since the subjects of both investigations were all men, we can only speculate as to how their findings would generalize to women gamblers.

Treatment and outcomes

Treatment of compulsive gamblers is still a relatively unexplored area. However, Boyd and Bolen (1970) have reported on a study in which compulsive gamblers and their spouses were treated together through group psychotherapy—an approach based on the finding that the compulsive gambler's marital relationship is generally chaotic and turbulent, with the spouse frequently showing seriously maladaptive behavior patterns. Of the eight gamblers treated, there was a complete cessation of gambling in three and a near cessation in the other five. The extent to which changes in the gamblers' marital relationships influenced the outcome of treatment can only be surmised—six of eight couples showed a significant improvement. Other treatment approaches, including aversion therapy, have been tried with individual cases, but further studies are needed before we can evaluate the potential effectiveness of psychotherapy in the treatment of compulsive gambling.

Some compulsive gamblers who want to change find help in doing so through membership in Gamblers Anonymous. This organization was founded in 1957 in Los Angeles by two compulsive gamblers who found that they could help each other control their gambling by talking about their experiences. Since then,

---

John ———: A case of compulsive gambling

John ——— was a 40-year-old rather handsome man with slightly greying hair who managed an automobile dealership for his father. For the previous two years, he had increasingly neglected his job and was deep in debt as a result of his gambling activities. He had gambled heavily since he was about 27 years old. His gambling had occasioned frequent quarrels in his first marriage and finally a divorce. He married his second wife without telling her of his problem, but it eventually came to light and created such difficulty that she took their two children and returned to her parents' home in another state.

John joined an encounter group in the stated hope that he might receive some assistance with his problems. In the course of the early group sessions, he proved to be an intelligent, well-educated man who seemed to have a good understanding of his gambling problem and its self-defeating nature. He stated that he had started gambling after winning some money at the horse races. This experience convinced him that he could supplement his income by gambling judiciously. However, his subsequent gambling—which frequently involved all-night poker games, trips to Las Vegas, and betting on the races—almost always resulted in heavy losses.

In the group, John talked about his compulsive gambling freely and coherently—candidly admitting that he enjoyed the stimulation and excitement of gambling more than sexual relations with his wife. He was actually rather glad his family had left since it relieved him of certain responsibilities toward them as well as feelings of guilt for neglecting them. He readily acknowledged that his feelings and behavior were inappropriate and self-defeating, but stated that he was "sick" and that he desperately needed help.

It soon became apparent that while John was willing to talk about his problem, he was not prepared to take constructive steps in dealing with it. He wanted the group to accept him in the "sick role" of being a "compulsive gambler" who could not be expected to "cure" himself. At the group's suggestion he did attend a couple of meetings of Gamblers Anonymous but found them "irrelevant." It was also suggested that he try aversive therapy, but he felt this would not help him.

While attending the group sessions, John apparently continued his gambling activities and continued to lose. After attending the eighth encounter group session, he did not return. Through inquiry by one of the members, it was learned that he had been arrested for embezzling funds from his father's business, but that his father had somehow managed to have the charges dropped. John reportedly then left for another state and his subsequent history is unknown.

Compulsive Gambling   **385**

groups have been formed in most of the major cities in the United States. The groups are modeled after Alcoholics Anonymous, and the only requirement for membership is an expressed desire to stop gambling. In group discussions, members share experiences and try to gain insight into the irrationality of their gambling and to realize its inevitable consequences. They consider it their obligation to help each other when a member feels he cannot control himself or has had a relapse. Gamblers Anonymous has no policy for influencing legislation to control gambling but emphasizes the view that each person who gambles is personally responsible for his own actions.

Unfortunately, only a small fraction of compulsive gamblers find their way into Gamblers Anonymous; of those who do, only about 1 in 10 manages to overcome the addiction to gambling (Strine, 1971).

Delinquent Behavior

In this section and the next, we will be considering patterns in which delinquent or criminal behavior is the central feature. While the APA classification has no specific category for such patterns, they may be generally placed in the group of sociopathic disorders.

Delinquency refers to behavior by youths under 18 years of age which is not acceptable to society and is generally regarded as calling for some kind of admonishment, punishment, or corrective action.[5] Thus, delinquent behavior may range from truancy, "incorrigibility," and the use of illegal drugs to homicide and other serious criminal offenses.

The actual incidence of juvenile delinquency is difficult to determine, since many delinquent acts are not reported. In addition, the states differ somewhat in their definitions of delinquent behavior—particularly regarding minor offenses—so that what is considered delinquent behavior in Texas may not be so considered in California or New York. Of the approximately two million young people who go through the juvenile courts each year in the United States, about half have done nothing that would be considered a crime in the case of an adult. However, many of this group are returned to the courts at a later time for having committed serious offenses. Delinquency has become a cause for national concern not only in our own society but in most modern countries throughout the world.

Incidence

Between 1968 and 1975, arrests of persons under 18 years of age for serious crimes in-

---

[5]It may be noted here that children under 8 are not considered delinquents, because it is assumed that they are too immature to understand the significance and consequences of their actions.

creased more than 100 percent—some four times faster than the increase in population for this age group.[6] In 1974, juveniles accounted for over 1 out of 3 arrests for robbery, 1 out of 5 arrests for rape, and 1 out of 10 arrests for murder. Although the great majority of "juvenile crime" was committed by males, the rate of increase has risen sharply for females. In 1974 about 1 teen-ager out of every 15 in the nation was arrested, and almost half of all serious crimes in the United States were committed by juveniles.

Well over half of the juveniles who are arrested each year have prior police records. Female delinquents are commonly apprehended for drug usage, sexual offenses, running away from home, and "incorrigibility," but crimes against property, such as stealing, have markedly increased among them. Male delinquents are commonly arrested for drug usage and crimes against property; to a lesser extent, they are arrested for armed robbery, aggravated assault, and other crimes against the person. However, crimes of violence by juveniles are increasing in our large metropolitan centers, contributing materially to the fact that in many areas the streets are considered unsafe after dark. If current trends continue, the chances are estimated to be about 1 in 3 of a juvenile acquiring a police record by the time he is 18 (Polk, 1974).

In general, it has been assumed that both the incidence and severity of delinquent behavior is disproportionately high for slum and lower-class youth. This view has been supported by findings of the President's Commission on Law Enforcement and Administration of Justice (1967) as well as by later reports of law enforcement officials (Ostrow, 1974). Other investigators, however, have found no evidence that delinquency is predominately a lower-class phenomenon. In a study of 433 teen-agers who had committed almost 2500 delinquent acts, Haney and Gold (1973) found "no strong relationship between social status and delinquent behavior" (p. 52). It may also be noted that the delinquency rate for socially disadvantaged youth appears about equal for whites and nonwhites.

---

[6]Statistics in this and the following section on Criminal Behavior are based mainly on Uniform Crime Reports (1975).

Causal factors

Various conditions, singly and in combination, may be involved in the development of delinquent behavior. In general, however, there appear to be three key variables: (a) personality characteristics, (b) family patterns and interactions, and (c) delinquent gangs and subcultures. We shall also see that certain delinquent acts may be triggered by unusual stresses.

Personal pathology. A number of investigators have attempted to "type" delinquents in terms of pervasive patterns of personal pathology.

1. *Brain damage and mental retardation.* In a distinct minority of cases of delinquency—an estimated 1 percent or less—brain pathology results in lowered inhibitory controls and a tendency toward episodes of violent behavior (Caputo & Mandell, 1970; Kiester, 1974). These youths are often hyperactive, impulsive, emotionally unstable, and unable to inhibit themselves when strongly stimulated. Fortunately their inner controls appear to improve during later adolescence and young adulthood.

In some 5 percent of delinquents, low intelligence appears to be of causal significance. Here the individual may be unable to foresee the probable consequences of his actions or understand their significance. This is particularly true of mentally retarded, sexually delinquent girls, but it also applies to delinquent male retardates who typically commit impulsive offenses, such as petty thievery and minor acts of aggression, often against the person. Frequently delinquent retardates fall prey to brighter psychopaths or delinquent gangs that dominate and exploit them.

2. *Neuroses and psychoses.* An estimated 3 to 5 percent of delinquent behavior appears to be directly associated with neurotic disorders, and about the same percentage with psychotic disorders. In the former, the delinquent act may take the form of a compulsion, such as "peeping" or stealing things that are not needed. Such compulsions often seem related to deviant sexual gratification in overinhibited adolescents who have been indoctrinated in the belief that masturbation and other overt forms of sexual release are terribly evil and sinful. Often such individuals fight their inner

impulses before committing the delinquent act, and then feel guilty afterward. Disturbances of this sort have shown a marked decline in recent years, possibly because parents are no longer so prone to induce overinhibition in sexual behavior.

In delinquent acts associated with psychotic behavior there is often a pattern of prolonged emotional hurt and turmoil, culminating after long frustration in an outburst of violent behavior (Bandura, 1973). In both neurotic and psychotic delinquents, the delinquent act is a by-product of severe personality maladjustment rather than a reflection of consistent antisocial orientation.

3. *Psychopathic personality.* A sizeable number of habitual delinquents appear to share the traits typical of the antisocial or psychopathic personality—they are impulsive, defiant, resentful, devoid of feelings of remorse or guilt, incapable of establishing and maintaining close interpersonal ties, and unable to profit from experience. Because they lack needed reality and ethical controls, they often engage in seemingly "senseless" acts that are not planned but occur on the "spur of the moment." They may steal a small sum of money they don't need, or they may steal a car, drive it a few blocks, and abandon it. In some instances they engage in impulsive acts of violence—against either property or persons—which are not committed for personal gain but rather reflect underlying resentment and hostility toward their world. In essence, these individuals are "unsocialized delinquents."

The following case provides an extreme example of a juvenile psychopath.

At the age of 12, Benny hurled a brick from the roof of an apartment building, striking another boy on the head and killing him. Benny first told the police that "it was all an accident," the brick having slipped out of his hand. He later stated that a friend had hurled the brick and that he had tried to stop him. He absolutely refused to discuss the episode again.

Benny was a cherubic-looking boy who was superficially cheerful and seemed to relate easily to other people. Yet he had thrown puppies and kittens from the roof of the apartment building where he lived; had engaged in stealing, truancy, and glue-sniffing, and had frequently gotten into terrific fights with other boys, alternately experiencing savage beatings and bloody triumphs. He kept a flock of pigeons on the roof, and his concern for the birds appeared to be touching. However, when a pigeon was injured "in a bad fight," he would dispose of it by throwing it down the incinerator alive.

Over a period of time Benny had been sent to various juvenile correctional facilities. At each institution, the same behavior pattern was noted. Benny would be warm and charming for a time, but just when it appeared that he was responding to the treatment program, he would engage in defiant behavior culminating in escape. He escaped from various institutions more than twenty times and boasted that "the place hasn't been built that can hold me." His eventual course was a tragic one, ending in death when he escaped from a maximum security installation and slammed a stolen bicycle into a parked car, suffering a fatal cerebral injury. (Adapted from Greenberg & Blank, 1970).

Although research has focused primarily on male delinquents, several investigators have also emphasized the high incidence of psychopathic personalities among females in state correctional institutions (Cloninger & Guze, 1970; Fine & Fishman, 1968; Konopka, 1964, 1967). In a study of 115 girls in a state correctional institution in Kentucky, Fine and Fishman (1968) emphasized a personality picture characterized by rebelliousness, impulsiveness, inadequacy, instability, and immaturity—characteristics commonly found in the psychopathic personality.

Here it is interesting to note that Ganzer and Sarason (1973) found that both male and female delinquents with multiple arrests were more frequently assigned the label of sociopathic personality than were nonrecidivists (those arrested only once). It was also noted that "Females more frequently came from personally and socially disorganized families than did males" (p. 1).

4. *Drug abuse.* A sizeable number of delinquent acts—particularly theft, prostitution, and assault—are directly associated with drug problems. Most youths who are addicted to hard drugs, such as heroin, are forced to steal in an attempt to maintain their habit, which can be highly expensive. In the case of female addicts, theft may be combined with or replaced by prostitution as a means of obtaining money. The two most common drugs associated with physical assault are secobarbital and alcohol, although the amphetamines may also be involved in impulsive antisocial acts, including crimes against the person.

We shall deal more extensively with the relation of drug problems to delinquent and criminal behavior in the next chapter.

Pathogenic family patterns. Of the various pathogenic family patterns that have been emphasized in the research on juvenile delinquency, the following appear to be the most important.

1. *Broken homes.* A number of investigators have pointed to the high incidence of broken homes and multiple parental figures in the background of delinquent youths. In general, delinquency appears to be much more common among youths coming from homes broken by parental separation or divorce than from homes broken by the death of a parent.

As we have seen, however, the effects of broken homes vary greatly. Even when the disruption is due to parental separation or divorce, the effects on the child may be more favorable than when he is raised in a home torn by parental conflict and dissension.

2. *Parental rejection and faulty discipline.*

Here we are not referring to broken homes but to homes in which one or both parents reject the child. When the father is the rejecting parent, it is difficult for a boy to identify with him and to use him as a model for his own development. In an early study of 26 aggressively delinquent boys, Bandura and Walters (1963) delineated a pattern in which father rejection was combined with inconsistent handling of the boy by both parents. To complicate the pathogenic picture, the father typically used physically punitive methods of discipline, thus augmenting the hostility the boy already felt toward him as well as modeling aggressive behavior. The end result of such a pattern was found to be a hostile, defiant, inadequately socialized youth who lacked normal inner controls and tended to act out his aggressive impulses in antisocial behavior.

Similarly, Shainberg (1967), in a study of 1500 young "military delinquents" (primarily servicemen who had been A.W.O.L.), reported that 90 percent of them had had severe difficulties with their fathers, whom they perceived as vague, lacking in warmth, and difficult to communicate with. The relationships were so full of conflict that the sons had given up trying to maintain them, while the fathers, unable to communicate with or discipline their sons, had abandoned their roles in child rearing altogether. On the other hand, the sons frequently reported having had good relationships with their mothers. In this context, it is interesting to note the findings of Bacon, Child, and Berry (1963) who studied the incidence of crime in 48 nonliterate societies. They found a much higher incidence of theft and personal crime in societies where the family typically restricted opportunities for the young boy to identify with his father.

The detrimental effects of parental rejection and inconsistent discipline are by no means attributable only to the father. As we have seen, such behavior by either parent is associated with aggression, lying, stealing, running away from home, and a wide range of other difficulties (Langner et al., 1974; Lefkowitz, Huesmann, Walder, & Eron, 1973; Pemberton & Benady, 1973). Often, too, inconsistent discipline may involve more complex family interactions, as when a mother imposes severe restrictions on a youth's behavior and then leaves

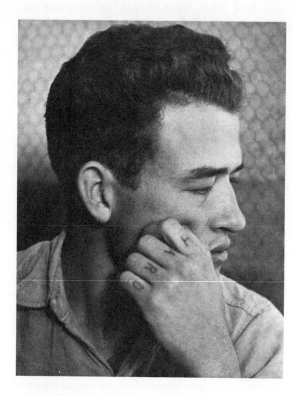

Exploding into the headlines in the early 1950s was the story of Billy Cook, hard-luck killer from Joplin, Missouri, whose days were ended in the gas chamber at San Quentin. He was captured by a Mexican posse in Lower California after a murderous rampage which extended across several states from Missouri to California. Cook's life motto was "Hard Luck," which he had tattooed on the knuckles of his left hand.

"Hard luck" was an appropriate motto for the youth; his mother died when he was 5 years old, and his father thereupon abandoned him, with his brothers and sisters, in a mine cave. In addition, he was handicapped with a deformed right eyelid. Nobody wanted Billy when he was offered for adoption, resentful and squint-eyed, and it was only a matter of time until his tantrums became too much for county-appointed guardians to control. Billy quit school at the age of 12, and when brought before the court he was sent to the reformatory at his own request. From then on, almost all of his life was spent behind bars, first in the reformatory and then in the state penitentiary, to which he was "graduated" at 18.

Released from prison, Cook looked up his father and announced his intention to "live by the gun and roam." He got a job washing dishes, bought a gun, and was on his way—stealing his first car from a Texas mechanic with whom he hitched a ride. Robbed and locked in the trunk, the mechanic escaped to freedom by prying open the lid, but the next kidnap victims—an Illinois farmer, his wife, and three small children who picked Cook up near Oklahoma City when the first stolen car broke down—were not so lucky. Not daring to set them free, Cook forced them to drive back and forth through four states while he decided what to do with them. It was a three-day nightmare which included a foiled escape attempt; it finally ended in Joplin where Cook shot them and threw their bodies down a mine shaft.

A horrible pattern of kidnapping and murder had been set in motion, and as the hunted Cook desperately attempted to elude the law, he hitched three more rides and took the cars' occupants as captives. He spared the life of one kidnap victim, a Blythe, California, deputy officer whom he left tied up in the desert; but he shot and killed a Seattle businessman—the crime for which he eventually received the death penalty. The big interstate manhunt that was on for Cook spread into Mexico when he was reported seen there with two companions—California prospectors who picked him up below the border and were his prisoners for eight days. When Cook was apprehended, less than a month had gone by since he had hitched the ride with the Texas mechanic. But though the time was brief, the toll was high: 9 people kidnapped, 6 killed.

As if in explanation of his deeds, Billy Cook said when arrested, "I hate everybody's guts, and everybody hates mine."

Both before and after the Billy Cook case, a number of gruesome homicide cases have been reported. Among these are Jack the Ripper, the Boston Strangler, Richard Speck, the Manson family, and the "horror story" of the brutal murder of 27 teen-age boys in Texas. In the case of Billy Cook, however, there seems to be an almost classic portrayal of the extent to which extreme parental and societal rejection, undesirable peer group models, and a life spent mainly as an inmate of penal institutions combined to produce a psychopathic killer.

Based on *Life* (1951) and *Time* (1951, 1952).

"policing" to a timid or uncaring father who fails to follow through. In a study of middle-class families with a delinquent offspring, for example, Singer (1974) found that the result of such a family pattern was a buildup of resentment and tension on the part of the adolescent toward the mother followed by acting out in antisocial behavior.

3. *Sociopathic parental models.* Several investigators have found a high incidence of sociopathic traits in the parents of delinquents—particularly but not exclusively in the father (Glueck & Glueck, 1969; Ulmar, 1971; Bandura, 1973). These included alcoholism, brutality, antisocial attitudes, failure to provide, frequent unnecessary absences from home, and other characteristics that made the father an inadequate and unacceptable model. Elkind (1967), for example, cited the case of a "father who encouraged his 17-year-old son to drink, frequent prostitutes, and generally 'raise hell.' This particular father was awakened late one night by the police who had caught his son in a raid on a so-called 'massage' parlor. The father's reaction was, 'Why aren't you guys out catching crooks?' This same father would boast to his co-workers that his son was 'all boy' and a 'chip off the old block' " (p. 313).

Sociopathic fathers—and mothers—may contribute in various ways to delinquent behavior of girls as well. Covert encouragement of sexual promiscuity is fairly common, and in some instances there is actual incest with the daughter. In a study of 30 delinquent girls, Scharfman and Clark (1967) found evidence of serious psychopathology in one or both parents of 22 of the girls, including 3 cases of incest and many other types of early sexual experience. These investigators also reported a high incidence of broken homes (only 11 of the 30 girls lived with both parents) and harsh, irrational, and inconsistent discipline:

"Any form of consistent discipline or rational setting of limits was unknown to the girls in their homes. Rather, there was an almost regular pattern of indifference to the activities or whereabouts of these girls, often with the mother overtly or indirectly suggesting delinquent behavior by her own actions. This would alternate with unpredictable, irrational, and violent punishment." (p. 443)

Scharfman and Clark concluded that the key factors in the girls' delinquent behavior were: (a) broken homes, combined with emotional deprivation; (b) irrational, harsh, and inconsistent parental discipline; and (c) patterns of early sexual and aggressive behavior modeled by psychopathic parents. Here we can readily see the interaction of pathogenic family conditions in the etiology of delinquent behavior.

In evaluating the role of pathogenic family patterns in delinquency, it may be emphasized that a given pattern is only one of many interacting factors. For example, the term "broken home" is a catchall term to describe the absence of one or both parents because of a variety of conditions, including desertion, separation, death, or imprisonment. A home may be "broken" at different times, under varying circumstances, and have differing influences, depending on the individual involved and his total life situation. Consequently the effects of a given family pattern can only be assessed adequately in relation to the total situation.

Undesirable peer relationships. While not typically a gang experience, delinquency does tend to be a shared experience for both males and females. In their study of delinquents in the Flint, Michigan, area, Haney and Gold (1973) found that about two-thirds of delinquent acts were committed in association with one or two other persons, and most of the remainder involved three or four other persons. Usually the offender and companion or companions were of the same sex. Interestingly enough, girls were more likely than boys to have a constant friend or companion in delinquency. Unfortunately, there is little research data on the effects of associating with delinquent friends or companions, and such effects probably vary, depending on the individual.

General sociocultural factors. Here, we are concerned with broad social conditions that tend to produce delinquency. Interrelated factors that appear to be of key importance include alienation and rebellion, social rejection, and the psychological support afforded by membership in a delinquent gang.

1. *Alienation and rebellion.* Feelings of alienation and rebellion are common to many teen-agers today from all socioeconomic levels. For example, we find middle-class youth who are uncommitted to the values of their parents or the "establishment" but at the same time are confused about their own values and sense of identity. Often they view the adult world as a hostile and phony place, inhabited by people who work at useless jobs that they pompously assume are meaningful and who try to "sell" the younger generation on a fraudulent and inevitably unfulfilling way of life. Outwardly the youths may passively submit to their elders' demands, or they may openly disobey parental and other adult authority and create no end of problems for themselves and their families. In either event, alienation from family and the broader society exposes the youth to becoming a "captive of his peers"—to whom he may turn for guidance and approval. Thus he is likely to identify with and join peer groups that engage in the use of illegal drugs or other behavior considered delinquent. In some instances these alienated youths may rebel, leave home, and drift into groups in which delinquent behavior is the way of life, as in the case of runaway teen-age girls who become affiliated with organized prostitution. The alienated and rebellious behavior of socially disadvantaged youth may lead to the same pattern, although its onset is much more likely to be directly associated with poverty, deprivation, and discrimination.

2. *The "social rejects."* A new population element is making itself increasingly felt in our society. This consists of young people who lack the motivation or ability to do well in school and "drop out" as soon as they can. With increasing automation and the demand for occupational skills—whether in the trades or in managerial or professional fields—there are few jobs for which they can qualify. Augmenting this population are students who graduate from high school but whose training does not qualify them for available occupational opportunities.

Whether they come from upper-, middle-, or lower-class homes, and whether they drop out or continue through high school, they have one crucial problem in common—they discover they are not needed in our society. They are victims of "social progress"—"social rejects."

While some are able to obtain additional training in specific job areas, others appear unable to find or hold jobs, and still others drift aimlessly from one unsatisfactory job to another.

In a study of 177 institutionalized teen-age male delinquents, McCandless, Parsons, and Roberts (1972) found an average of 5 years' academic retardation, with reading at less than the fourth-grade level. With that academic handicap, such teen-agers are at a serious disadvantage in the job market; many may engage in delinquent behavior partly as a result of underlying feelings of frustration, confusion, and hopelessness. In this context, it is interesting to note that Odell (1974) found a program that combined educational development and job placement—facilitating entry into the "opportunity structure"—more effective than traditional case-work methods in preventing juvenile recidivism.

3. *Delinquent gang cultures.* Here we are dealing not so much with personal psychopathology per se as with organized group pathology, involving rebellion against the norms of society. As Jenkins (1969) has expressed it:

"The socialized delinquent represents not a failure of socialization but a limitation of loyalty to a more or less predatory peer group. The basic capacity for social relations has been achieved. What is lacking is an effective integration with the larger society as a contributing member." (p. 73)

While the problem of delinquent gangs is most prevalent in lower socioeconomic areas, it is by no means restricted to them, nor does it occur only in particular racial, ethnic, or social groups. While there are many reasons for joining delinquent gangs—including fear of personal injury by gang members if one does not join—most members of delinquent gangs appear to feel inadequate in and rejected by the larger society. Gang membership gives them a sense of belonging and a means of gaining some measure of status and approval. It may also represent a means of committing robberies and other illegal acts for financial gain—acts that the individual could not successfully perform alone (Feldman & Weisfeld, 1973).

Juvenile and other law enforcement authorities in major U.S. cities have expressed concern about the increasing number and violence of delinquent juvenile gangs. In Los Angeles, for example, there are an estimated 200 such gangs, of which some 40 or more are considered well organized and dangerous (Hazlett, 1974). Police estimate that there are over 800 hard-core leaders, each with a record of 10 or more arrests. The typical gang activist is between 14 and 22 years of age, but a sizeable and increasing number are under 14 years of age. The better organized and more violent gangs have turned from knives and zip guns to more lethal weapons, including sawed-off shotguns and automatic rifles; their activities range from "warfare" with rival gangs to purse snatching, robbery, assault, and homicide. As one Los Angeles police captain expressed it to Hazlett (1974):

"We're caught up in an epidemic of violence, murder has no meaning, killing has become a game, a way of life. . . .
"The whole attitude has changed. The kids aren't afraid anymore – the public is!" (p. 1)

Nor are delinquent gangs confined to males. Female gangs have developed in recent years and provide much the same function for confused, resentful, and defiant girls as male gangs do for boys. In these gangs the girls create their "own world" for purposes of belonging, protection, and defiance. In the gang they find acceptance, rules, loyalty, authority, discipline, and many of the other components that they cannot find or accept in the adult world. Many of these female gangs are affiliated with male gangs, while maintaining their own separate organizations. Statistics indicate that girls are involved in about 15 to 30 percent of all delinquent gang activities that come to the attention of police.

It should be emphasized that the majority of delinquents do not belong to delinquent gangs, nor do the majority of juvenile gangs fall in the delinquent category. Many are organized for recreational and other constructive purposes. And not all delinquent gangs are highly organized, cohesive groups. Observing several hundred black and Mexican-American gangs, both male and female, Klein (1968) found low cohesiveness, shifting roles, and little relation to adult criminal groups. More recently, however, there appears to be an increase in both the organization and cohesiveness of delinquent gangs as well as in the violent nature of their activities. Ironically, the areas in which delinquent gangs appear to be best organized and to operate most widely are generally provided with first-rate public recreation facilities, which such gangs typically use as convenient meeting places.

Unusual stresses and other factors. We have noted that many delinquent acts are based on momentary impulses or are part of the regular activities of a delinquent gang. Delinquent behavior may also be precipitated by some relatively minor event, as when a riot is triggered by a fight between two youths. And, of course, it may sometimes be inadvertent, resulting from innocent pranks that backfire.

In some instances, traumatic experiences in the life of a boy or girl appear to act as precipitating events (Coleman, 1973). In an early study of 500 delinquent boys, Clarke (1961) found that in about a third of the cases it was possible to isolate highly stressful events that preceded the delinquency, such as death of parents, disruption of family life, or discovery that they had been adopted. These events had proved highly disorganizing and often had led to poor school performance, truancy, brooding, and – eventually – delinquent behavior. Burks and Harrison (1962) also emphasized the importance of stresses that undermine a youth's feelings of adequacy and worth as precipitating factors in some cases of aggressive antisocial behavior. In an analysis of 4 case histories – involving arson, murder, and breaking and entering – Finkelstein (1968) found an "accumulation of emotional tensions [leading] at times to temporary disintegration, or at least to a state in which the person in full awareness of what he is doing loses his ego control" (p. 310).

We shall deal with the more general causes of destructive violence in America in Chapter 18. Suffice it to point out here that Bandura (1973), Patterson (1974), and other investigators have concluded that, with rare exceptions involving unusual brain damage, children are not born violent but learn to be that way.

Dealing with delinquency

If they have adequate facilities and personnel, juvenile institutions and training schools can be of great help to youths who need to be removed from aversive environments and given a chance to learn about themselves and their world, to further their education and develop needed skills, and to find purpose and meaning in their lives. In such settings the youths may have the opportunity to receive psychological counseling, group therapy, and guided group interaction. Here it is of key importance that peer-group pressures are channeled in the direction of resocialization, rather than toward repetitive delinquent behavior. Behavior-therapy techniques—based on the assumption that delinquent behavior is learned, maintained, and changed according to the same principles as other learned behavior—have shown marked promise in the rehabilitation of juvenile offenders who require institutionalization.[7] Counseling with parents and related sociotherapeutic measures are generally of vital importance in the total rehabilitation program.

Probation is widely used with juvenile offenders, and may be granted either in lieu of or after a period of institutionalization. In keeping with the trend toward helping troubled persons in their own environments, the California Youth Authority conducted The Community Treatment Project, a 5-year experiment in which delinquents—other than those involved in such crimes as murder, rape, or arson—were granted immediate probation and supervised and assisted in their own communities. The 270 youths treated in this project showed a rehabilitation success rate of 72 percent during a 15-month follow-up period. In contrast, a comparable group of 357 delinquents who underwent institutional treatment and then were released on probation showed a rehabilitation success rate of only 48 percent (Blake, 1967). Since 90 percent of the girls and 73 percent of the boys committed to the California Youth Authority by juvenile courts were found eligible for community treatment, it would appear that most delin-

Placing juvenile offenders behind bars in dehumanizing penal institutions appears to be not only ineffective but often accomplishes the opposite of what is intended by turning the youth into a hardened criminal.

[7]A review of studies dealing with the application of behavior therapy to juvenile delinquency may be found in Davidson and Seidman (1974).

quents can be guided into constructive behavior without being removed from their family or community. It may be noted, however, that a key factor in the success of this pioneering research project was a marked reduction in the case load of supervising probation officers. Here it may be emphasized that the recidivism rate—the most commonly used measure for assessing rehabilitation programs—depends heavily on the type of offenders being dealt with as well as the particular facility (Roberts, Erikson, Riddle, & Bacon, 1974). While specific figures are not available, the recidivism rate for delinquents sent to training schools has been estimated to be as high as 80 percent (*Time*, June 30, 1975).

Institutionalization seems particularly questionable in the case of "juvenile status offenders," youths whose offenses have involved acts that would not be considered criminal if committed by an adult, such as running away from home or engaging in sexual relations. In such instances, institutionalization may aggravate behavioral problems rather than correct them. For example, mixing juvenile status offenders and "real" delinquents in detention facilities may provide learning experiences for nondelinquents on how to become delinquents. On the other hand, failure to institutionalize delinquents who have committed serious offenses such as robbery, assault, and murder, may be a disservice to both the delinquents and the public. In essence, it seems essential to correct the "bizarre lumping" of major felonies, minor misdemeanors, and trivial violation of social norms under the general label of "juvenile delinquency." This would enable many delinquencies to be dealt with by educational and social-work agencies rather than the justice system and would make it possible for treatment programs to better meet the needs of individual delinquents.

One key task in dealing with troubled youth is that of opening lines of communication with them. The behavior of even some of the most "hard-core" delinquent gangs has shown marked improvement when social workers or police officers have managed to win their confidence and respect. Often such personnel can help channel the youths' activities into automobile or motorcycle rallies and other programs that provide both recreational and learning opportunities. Too often, however, as in the case of institutional and probation programs, lack of trained personnel and other resources prevent such programs.

Fortunately, there is growing concern about the inadequacies of our correctional system for juveniles, and recently the federal government established the Office of Juvenile Justice and Delinquency Prevention to foster these and related goals. The big need, of course, is not only for more effective rehabilitation programs, but also for long-range programs aimed at the prevention of delinquency. This would mean alleviation of slum conditions, provision of adequate educational and recreational opportunities for disadvantaged youth, education of parents, and delineation of a more meaningful societal role for adolescents—tasks for the whole society.

Criminal Behavior

In our society, criminal behavior is classified for the most part as falling into one of two major categories: felonies or misdemeanors. Felonies are serious crimes such as murder and robbery for which there are severe legal penalities. Misdemeanors, as the name implies, are minor offenses such as disorderly conduct and vagrancy. The particular behaviors classified as misdemeanors often vary considerably from state to state—illustrating once again the importance of social definitions in the labeling of behavior as "abnormal."

Although criminal behavior sometimes has its roots in juvenile delinquency, most juvenile delinquents do not become criminals as adults, and many criminals have no prior history of juvenile delinquency. The range of offenses, motivations, and causal factors are much the same, however. In the following discussion we shall attempt to highlight both the likenesses and the differences between these two categories of sociopathic behavior.

Incidence

Official figures compiled by the Federal Bureau of Investigation indicate that the crime rate is higher in the United States than in most other countries, and that the rate is continuing to rise. In 1974 the FBI reported the commission of over 10 million crimes of the type classified as serious: homicide, forcible rape, robbery, aggravated assault, burglary, larceny, and auto theft.[8] In actual fact, the problem is even more serious since it has been estimated that from one-third to one-half of all serious crimes are not reported to the police (Uniform Crime Reports, 1975; Law Enforcement Assistance Administration, 1974a).

Some investigators have pointed out that

[8] Based on reports of some 11,000 state and local law enforcement agencies to the FBI.

the figure for serious crime is not as ominous as it seems, since it includes over a million auto thefts, which many people feel should not be included in this classification. But there would appear to be little room for complacency when it is realized that *violent* crimes—the first four types listed above—increased 11 times faster in the 1960s than population size, and that during the first half of the 1970s they rose over 15 times as fast as population size. As shown by the FBI "crime clocks" in the illustration on p. 398, violent crimes in 1974 occurred at the rate of one every 30 seconds, while the overall rate for serious crimes was 19 per minute.

Among lower-income groups, blacks are almost twice as likely as whites to be victims of crimes of violence, but they are only slightly more likely than whites to be victims of crimes against property. Middle- and upper-income groups, whether black or white, are about equally exposed to crime, but crimes against property are much more common than crimes against the person. By and large, whites tend to victimize whites and blacks to victimize blacks. Criminals most often strike in the vicinity in which they live, and often they know their victims personally.

Crime rates vary considerably from one region of the country to another, from city to city, and from metropolitan to suburban and rural areas. They are much higher in the West than in the Northwest or South, higher in New York City and Los Angeles than in Philadelphia, and much higher in metropolitan centers than in smaller cities and rural areas. However, the crime rate is increasing more rapidly in the latter than in metropolitan centers.

More than 10 million Americans come into contact with some agency of criminal justice each year for having committed, or for suspicion of having committed, a serious crime. Approximately 80 percent of both juvenile and adult offenders are male; the great majority of violent crimes are committed by males. However, American females are committing an increasing number of murders, armed robberies, assaults, and other serious crimes, and their rate is increasing faster than that for males. Almost half of all serious crimes are committed by persons under 18 years of age, and about 75 percent by persons under 25. As a consequence of apprehension and conviction for such crimes, over 500,000 individuals, including over 80,000 women, are in federal, state, and local prisons. In addition, more than a million others, both male and female, are on probation.

The cost of crime in the United States each year is estimated at over $85 billion, an incredible and wasteful financial toll; and this says nothing of the toll in human resources and human suffering.

Causal factors

In our discussion of delinquency, we noted the importance of pervasive personal pathology, of pathogenic family and peer patterns, of general sociocultural factors that foster antisocial behavior, and of severe stress. These factors have also been examined in relation to adult criminal behavior, as have some additional factors, including chromosomal aberrations, crime as a profession, and organized crime.

Chromosomes and crime. A number of early investigators attributed criminal behavior to heredity. Prominent among these investigators were Lombroso and his followers, who became known as the "Italian School of Criminology" (Lombroso-Ferrero, 1911). According to Lombroso, the criminal was a "born type" with "stigmatizing" features—such as a low forehead, an unusually shaped head and jaw, eyebrows growing together above the bridge of the nose, and protruding ears—that clearly distinguished him from normal people. These stigmata were considered to be a throwback to "savage man" and were believed to predispose the individual to criminal behavior.

Although Lombroso's view has long since been discarded, a number of recent investigators have dealt with the possibility that an extra Y chromosome—a genetic anomaly that may occur in males—is associated with criminal behavior. Although there are many exceptions, men of the XYY chromosomal type are characterized by unusual height, borderline intelligence, and a tendency to show excessive episodes of aggressive behavior.

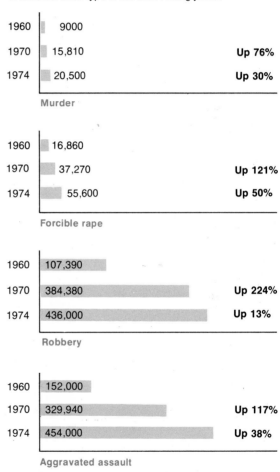

Increase of violent crimes in the 1960s and 1970s

During the 1960s, the incidence of violent crimes in the United States increased 10 times faster than the general population; this increase continues into the 1970s. The following chart, based on figures released by the FBI, shows the approximate incidence of various types of crimes for 1960, 1970, and 1974, and the respective increase for each type in the intervening years.

1960	9000	
1970	15,810	Up 76%
1974	20,500	Up 30%

Murder

1960	16,860	
1970	37,270	Up 121%
1974	55,600	Up 50%

Forcible rape

1960	107,390	
1970	384,380	Up 224%
1974	436,000	Up 13%

Robbery

1960	152,000	
1970	329,940	Up 117%
1974	454,000	Up 38%

Aggravated assault

Serious crimes in the United States — which include all the offenses represented by the seven "crime clocks" shown — occurred at the rate of 19 per minute in 1974, up from 11 per minute in 1970. For offenses in the subcategory of violent crimes — murder, forcible rape, robbery, and assault to kill — the rate of occurrence was over one every 33 seconds, as compared with one every 43 seconds in 1970. Since an estimated one-third or more of all violent crimes are not reported, the actual incidence is probably much higher than the figures used here, all of which are based on Uniform Crime Reports (1975). Specific figures on the increase in violent crimes in the 1970s are provided in the illustration on p. 397.

During the mid-1970s only about 20 percent of the serious crimes were "cleared" by arrests, and only about 5 percent were "solved" by convictions as charged: the highest clearance rate is for murder, with arrests made in over 75 percent of all cases, followed by aggravated assault (60 percent), forcible rape (50 percent), robbery (25 percent), larceny (20 percent), and auto theft (15 percent). Rates for conviction as charged, however, are considerably lower than the arrest rates for these serious crimes, and, in addition, a steadily decreasing number of those convicted are sent to prison. Thus it would appear that a high percentage of criminals beat the risk and find crime profitable.

Based on Uniform Crime Reports, 1971.

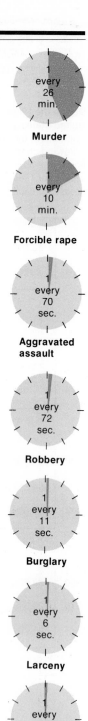

Murder
1 every 26 min.

Forcible rape
1 every 10 min.

Aggravated assault
1 every 70 sec.

Robbery
1 every 72 sec.

Burglary
1 every 11 sec.

Larceny
1 every 6 sec.

Auto theft
1 every 33 sec.

The pioneering study in this area was that of Jacobs and her colleagues (1965) who published their findings on 197 mentally abnormal inmates of a special security institution in Scotland. All were considered to have violent and dangerous criminal tendencies. Seven — 3.5 percent — were of the XYY chromosomal type.

In an intensive review of later research findings, Jarvik, Klodin, and Matsuyama (1973) reported that the total frequency of XYY males in the criminal population approximated 2 percent. This frequency is about 15 times that found for the male population in general.

Presumably the extra Y chromosome stimulates excessive production of testosterone, the male hormone that has been linked by some investigators to aggression. However, this hypothesis is not as simple as it first seems. For one thing, not all XYY males are aggressive. In addition, their crimes are more often against property than persons. To resolve this seeming paradox, Ginsburg (1974) has advanced evidence to show that the aggressiveness of an XYY male depends on whether the extra chromosome is inherited from an aggressive father or a mild one; he has also suggested that when aggression does occur it may reflect defects in brain structure and functioning stemming from this genetic anomaly rather than excessive testosterone.

Until more definitive research evidence becomes available, the conclusion of Jarvik et al. (1973) seems to be a sound one:

"Although the majority of violent crimes are committed by chromosomally normal persons, the increased frequency of XYY individuals among perpetrators of such crimes suggests that an extra Y chromosome predisposes to aggressive behavior." (p. 680)

These investigators then go on to emphasize the importance of the environment — for example, whether it fosters violent or nonviolent behavior — in determining whether or not individuals with this genetic condition will show aggressive behavior. This chromosome complement appears to play a much less significant role in delinquency than in adult crime.

Other biological factors. Tendencies toward violent behavior have been related to several other biological variables, including brain

Electro Encephalo grams.

damage, mental retardation, psychomotor epilepsy, and degenerative brain changes associated with old age. An estimated 10 to 20 million Americans have some form of minor brain damage, and a number of investigators are exploring the possibility of a link between such conditions and antisocial behavior, particularly in conjunction with other factors such as severe stress or the use of alcohol or other drugs (Kiester, 1974).

Although a disproportionately high incidence of abnormal EEG's have been reported for both male and female prisoners, there is no conclusive evidence of the relation of brain lesions to serious crime except in a distinct minority of cases (Small, 1966; Climent et al., 1973). Interestingly enough, Small found that felons with abnormal EEG's were less likely to have engaged in "skilled" criminal behavior but were usually guilty of repeated theft; those with no demonstrable evidence of central nervous system lesions accounted for the most serious crimes, such as assault, murder, and forcible rape.

Personal, family, and social pathology. Among criminals who show no biological pathology related to their antisocial behavior, personal pathology is common. In an early study, Arief and Bowie (1947) used 18 diagnostic categories to describe shoplifters for evaluation by the Chicago Municipal Court. In a study of 300 bad-check writers, MacDonald (1959) found not only a high incidence of psychopathic personalities and chronic alcoholics, but also a lesser number of schizophrenics, manics, seniles, and mentally retarded individuals. In general, the most common forms of psychopathology associated with serious crimes appear to be antisocial personality, alcoholism, and drug dependence; however, there is also a disproportionately high number of borderline and actual psychotics (Guze, Goodwin, & Crane, 1969; Sutker & Moan, 1973). Severe life stress, particularly in conjunction with personal pathology, also appears to be an important factor in triggering impulsive acts of violence and other antisocial behavior.

Many criminals who show pervasive personal pathology come from homes torn by conflict and dissension, often resulting in parental separation or divorce; frequently found in their family backgrounds also are parental rejection and inconsistent and severe punishment. These characteristics appear to be particularly common in—but not exclusive to—prison inmates who have committed crimes of violence (Climent et al., 1973; Sutker & Moan, 1973). Again, however, it is risky to draw causal inferences, since many persons coming from similar backgrounds do not evidence personal pathology or engage in criminal behavior.

Often personal pathology appears to stem primarily from social pathology, as evidenced by the unusually high incidence of both juvenile and adult offenses in the slums of our large cities. These areas are characterized by severe social disorganization that, in some ways, reverses the usual forms of socialization and social regulations. The values of the larger society are often held in low repute or discarded, and there are widespread feelings of helplessness and hopelessness combined with hostility toward established authority. Under such conditions, aggressive and antisocial behavior may become the norm for an entire subgroup.

Crime as a profession. The term *dyssocial personality* is used to refer to individuals who are not psychopathic personalities but who follow a predatory criminal life-style—people such as drug pushers, hired killers, burglars, and forgers. Such individuals are economically motivated, usually nonviolent, often highly skilled. Typically they come from subcultures in which they were exposed early to deviant codes of behavior and criminal models.

The concept of *differential association*, first developed by Sutherland in the late 1930s, has provided a framework for understanding the importance of subcultural influences in the "training" of the professional criminal (Sutherland & Cressey, 1966). As Sutherland noted, the basic process of socialization is much the same for everyone: the individual comes to accept as his own the values and behavioral standards emphasized by those with whom he associates on a repeated and intimate basis—most notably, his parents and peers. But in the case of a young person growing up in a subculture where antisocial behavior is the norm, the values and standards in-

Facts about homicide

Homicides are classified, in terms of intent, into: (1) first degree murder, characterized by premeditation and planning, or committed during a felony, such as rape or robbery; (2) second degree murder, in which there is no premeditation or planning, e.g., as when the homicide is committed "in the heat of passion"; and (3) manslaughter, committed without malice aforethought, as when a driver accidentally kills a pedestrian in a crosswalk. Relevant to these three categories are the following data concerning homicide in the United States.

Incidence	For reasons that are unclear, the homicide rate started to rise sharply in 1963 and has continued to rise since. As shown in the chart on p. 397, the incidence of homicide increased 240 percent from 1963 to 1975. In 1974, 20,500 homicides were committed in the United States. For each actual murder, it may be noted that many attempts are unsuccessful and the victim lives (80 percent of gunshot victims and 90 percent of stab victims). Thus, homicidal acts are far more common in our society than the statistics on homicide would indicate.
Who kills whom?	Ten percent of all homicides are committed by youths under 18 years of age, and 45 percent are committed by persons under 25. Males outnumber females as victims at a ratio of 4 to 1, and as offenders in a ratio of 5 to 1. More murder victims are individuals in the 20- to 29-year age bracket than in any other 10-year age span. In the great majority of murders, the victims are of the same race. Blacks are disproportionately represented as both victims and offenders. Apprehending the offender is often relatively easy, since in most cases offender and victim are relatives, friends, or close acquaintances. In one-fourth of all murders, offender and victim are members of the same family; about half of these family killings involve spouse killing spouse. Another 7 percent or so involve "lover's quarrels." Homicides associated with felonies—usually armed robbery involving strangers—make up about 30 percent of all homicide cases.
Methods or weapons used	By far the greatest number of homicides result from shooting (67 percent), followed by cutting or stabbing (19 percent), use of other impersonal weapons such as clubs or poisons (7 percent), and use of personal weapons, such as hands (9 percent). The high incidence of murders committed by firearms is not surprising in view of the widespread possession of guns by civilians in the U.S., exceeding that in any other country.
Motives	As we have noted in listing the three categories of homicide, motives may be diverse, or the homicide may even be accidental. However, aside from murders committed for calculated monetary gains by individuals or professional killers associated with organized crime, homicide is typically considered a "crime of passion." It often results from quarrels combined with a lowering of inner reality and ethical restraints; for example, intoxicants complicate the motivational picture in about half of all homicide cases. In some instances the victim—for whatever reason—seems to invite being killed, as by striking the first blow; and, as we have seen, homicide may be associated with such mental disorders as schizophrenia and paranoia.
Psychosocial factors	Although diverse personality types may commit homicide, offenders tend to come from homes or neighborhoods in which violence is an aspect of daily life. Often they have a history of violent tendencies and behavior. In ghetto slums among socially disadvantaged blacks, homicide rates are disproportionately high. Homicide rates also show marked cross-cultural differences—with Iceland and Colombia, South America, representing extremes in rates of incidence among the major countries. Iceland's rate is zero, while that for Colombia is 5 times that of the United States.
	In general, it would appear that an increase in homicidal acts tends to accompany technological and social change.
	Statistics are approximate, based on 1974 and available 1975 data (Uniform Crime Reports, 1975).

ternalized – and the skills learned – are likely to be quite different from those emphasized in conventional society. Thus, the individual who becomes a professional criminal usually acquires his training in much the same way that legitimate professionals do, responding to the learning opportunities, values, and reinforcements that his environment has provided. Unlike the antisocial or psychopathic personality, he is socialized – but in a deviant way.

Typically, the professional criminal specializes in a particular type of crime, such as forgery or burglary, and develops a particular style of operation. His goal is to make money in the quickest and safest way possible. In general, he attempts to avoid violence, since it would greatly increase the risk of detection and imprisonment. His crimes are usually well planned and may even be rehearsed.

By and large, professional criminals do not appear to show significant personality deviations, aside from their adherence to the values and codes of their own group. But Stojanovich (1969) has sounded a note of caution. While many professional criminals he studied did manifest so-called dyssocial characteristics – such as predatoriness, good control of inner impulses, and ability to profit from experience – others showed characteristics more typically associated with the psychopathic personality. Apparently we are dealing with a continuum that has antisocial personality at one end, dyssocial personality at the other end, and a combination of antisocial and dyssocial personalities in between.

Of course, even typical dyssocial professional criminals are not immune to mental disorders, and the stressful life situation they typically live under often leads to some degree of personality decompensation, which may reach neurotic or psychotic levels. In general, however, their background or training and their emotional insulation protect them from stress and personality decompensation, even during imprisonment. Possible arrest and imprisonment are hazards of their profession: should he be imprisoned, the criminal tries to adapt to prison life and do "easy time."

Organized crime. It is difficult to assess or discuss the nature and incidence of organized crime, since it has not been defined legally in the same sense as individual criminal *acts* like forcible rape and homicide. In addition, organized crime actively maintains a low level of social visibility. In general, however, the "organized criminal" is an individual who commits criminal acts while occupying a position in an organization specifically set up for perpetrating specific criminal activites.

The largest criminal organization in the United States, by all accounts, is La Cosa Nostra, also known as "the Mafia," "the Syndicate," and "the Mob." The gross annual income of Cosa Nostra has been variously estimated at between $40 and $50 billion. In 1969 the Attorney General reported a figure of not less than $50 billion – more than the total national revenue of all but a few of the world's major countries (Alsop, 1969) – and there is little reason to believe that the amount has decreased since then. About 70 percent of the mob's illegal income is estimated to be derived from gambling, and most of the remainder from narcotics, hijacked goods, and interest from loan sharking (*U.S. News & World Report*, Dec. 16, 1974).

Of course, as our society changes, the patterns of organized crime also change; and activities that the syndicate once found economically rewarding – such as prostitution – may now be deemphasized in favor of more lucrative pursuits, such as gambling. In recent years, Cosa Nostra money has been invested in various legitimate businesses, thus implementing its income. In his authoritative book *Theft of a Nation*, Cressey (1969) estimated Cosa Nostra's minimum contribution to our political campaigns at about 15 percent of their total cost. Operating in most, if not all, of the big cities and many smaller ones, the syndicate represents a powerful and pervasive force.

In their fight against organized crime, law-enforcement agencies must obtain evidence and seek convictions; however, since violence and intimidation are such an integral part of organized crime, evidence is extremely difficult to obtain. As J. Edgar Hoover (1968) described it, violence

". . . is a coldly calculated tactic to maintain the group's dominance over its own members and over

What a professor learned when he became a "cop"

Dr. George L. Kirkham (1974), an assistant professor in the department of criminology at Florida State University, decided to study law enforcement at first hand. After taking a leave of absence, he attended a police academy and became a patrolman in the Jacksonville-Duval County police force.

In reporting on his 6 months of duty as a patrolman, Dr. Kirkham found that the stereotyped image of a police officer as a brutal, racist, discourteous, or crooked cop that is so common among much of the general public failed to take into consideration "the image of thousands of dedicated men and women struggling against almost impossible odds to preserve our society and everything in it which we cherish" (p. 70).

As a patrolman he found that there was a world of difference between encountering individuals in correctional settings and encountering them face to face in the real world as a police officer does. For the first time, he began to see the offender as a menace to the security of society as well as his own personal safety, not as a harmless figure sitting across a prison desk, the "victim" of society to be treated with compassion and leniency. As with other police officers, fear ceased to be an impersonal thing and became a regular experience. "I could taste it as a dryness in my mouth as we raced with blue lights and siren toward the site of a "Signal Zero (armed and dangerous) call" (p. 71).

One incident in particular taught him the meaning of fear. It started on a routine patrol in an unsavory part of town, when Kirkham and his partner politely asked a man who was double-parked to either park or drive on. The man, however, began to curse them and shout that the police couldn't make him go anywhere, attracting the attention of an angry crowd who became convinced that the police were harassing the man.

"As a criminology professor . . . I would have urged that the police officer who was now myself simply leave the car double-parked and move on rather than risk an incident.

"As a police officer, however, I had come to realize that

an officer can never back down from his responsibility to enforce the law. . . ."

In the meantime, the crowd grew more unruly, and eventually began to converge on the policemen.

"Suddenly, I was no longer an 'ivory-tower' scholar watching typical police 'overreaction' to a street incident—but I was part of it and fighting to remain alive and uninjured. I remember the sickening sensation of cold terror which filled my insides as I struggled to reach our car radio. I simultaneously put out a distress call and pressed the hidden electric release button on our shotgun rack as my partner sought to maintain his grip on the prisoner and hold the crowd at bay with his revolver.

"How readily as a criminology professor I would have condemned the officer who was now myself, trembling with fear and anxiety and menacing an 'unarmed' assembly with an 'offensive' weapon. . . . As someone who had always been greatly concerned about the rights of offenders, I now began to consider for the first time the rights of police officers. As a police officer, I felt that my efforts to protect society and maintain my personal safety were menaced by many of the very court decisions and lenient parole-board actions I had always been eager to defend" (p. 71)

Professor Kirkham came away from his experience as a patrolman with an entirely new perspective on crime, criminals, and policemen: "I wish that they [psychologists, psychiatrists, prison counselors and parole officers], and every judge and juror in our country, could see the ravages of crime as the cop on the beat must: innocent people cut, shot, beaten, raped, robbed and murdered. . . .

"For all the human misery and suffering which police officers must witness in their work, I found myself amazed at the incredible humanity and compassion which seems to characterize most of them. My own stereotypes of the brutal, sadistic cop were time and again shattered by the sight of humanitarian kindness on the part of the thin blue line. . . ." (p. 72)

the members of the society in which it operates rather than terror for terror's sake.

"The peculiar evil of this type of 'corporate' violence is not the individual sadism and brutality of the 'enforcers' and 'strong-arm men,' but the monopolistic position it enables racket leaders to gain and hold in their legitimate, as well as their illicit, activities.

"Force and threats of force are employed to eliminate rivals, collect on gambling and loan-sharking debts, frighten potential witnesses, enforce internal discipline, and gain possession of various business chattels. In the greater Chicago area alone, there have been more than 1,000 gangland slayings since 1919, only 17 of which have been solved; in the greater Boston area there have been more than 50 during the past four years, only 11 of which have been solved." (p. 62)

Since organized crime is a major threat to a democratic society based on justice, law, and order, our country is striving to find more effective methods of dealing with it.

Changes in criminal types. During the early 1960s a number of investigators noted the growing prevalence of individuals who committed criminal acts primarily for ego-satisfactions and "kicks." A thrill is derived from performing some taboo act—usually a senseless act of violence—which serves to intensify the present moment, clearly differentiating it from the routine of daily life. Whereas most "old" types of criminals carefully calculate their acts, usually with an eye on material gain with minimum risk, this new criminal type commits violent acts on impulse, simply because it "makes me feel good." As one youth told Yablonsky (1962) after a gang killing:

"If I would of got the knife, I would have stabbed him. That would of gave me more of a build-up. People would have respected me for what I've done and things like that. They would say, 'There goes a cold killer.'"

Typically, the illegal acts of such criminals are spontaneous and unpremeditated; in most cases there is no evidence that he has even had prior contact with his victim. Even when he does participate in planned criminal acts, he is still interested primarily in kicks. Unlike most other criminals, he seeks no gain other than the pleasure to be derived from the criminal act itself.

More recently still, another new type of criminal has emerged, who now constitutes a large segment of today's prison population. As Alexander (1974) has described them:

"They are mostly losers, mostly poor and black. Their chief crime, in Huey Newton's memorable phrase, is being 'illegitimate capitalists,' unemployables whose only hope of enjoying the good things of life is in ripping off the system." (p. 35)

The poor, the powerless, and the undereducated are much more likely to be caught, prosecuted, punished, or even held in jails for months before they are tried. And if found guilty, their sentence is likely to be more severe.

While the affluent have probably always fared somewhat better, there is evidence of a widening "class gap" in the organization and administration of our legal system. As Doleschal and Klapmuts (1974) have pointed out, the rich, powerful, and intelligent members of our society are rarely caught, prosecuted, or punished. This gap increases the resentment of those at the bottom and heightens their feelings of not being part of the broader society and their feelings of justification in simply taking what they want.

Admittedly the causes of violence and other forms of crime in the United States are both complex and varied. But as a United States Attorney General has pointed out,

"Much crime develops from poverty and deprivation. Most victims of crime are the poor themselves. There will be no marked crime reduction until we understand that—but more importantly, until we act upon it." (Saxbe, 1974, p. 12)

Approaches to dealing with criminals

"Man has never been able to develop a completely rational and satisfactory set of alternatives for dealing with convicted violators of the criminal law. The more primitive forms of criminal sanctions were based primarily on ideas of revenge and retribution. Execution, physical torture, and public degradation were the most common methods in use until near the close of the eighteenth century. Imprisonment as the principal method did not come into general use until the beginning of the nineteenth century.

Concepts of retributive punishment have persisted, but superimposed upon them were other purposes, such as deterrence, public protection, and rehabilitation. The trend in Western civilization for the past 150 years has been steadily in the direction of more and more commitment to rehabilitation and resocialization of offenders. Implementation of these ideas has been extremely slow and hampered by lack of financial support and the excessive fragmentation of the public agencies responsible. The movement is now away from the excessive use of imprisonment and more and more toward the development of community-based programs making use of the social sciences. The correctional field is on the threshold of revolutionary changes which will take place gradually, tested by scientific methods." (McGee, 1969, p. 1)

As is apparent from the preceding excerpt, the trends in dealing with criminal behavior have in many ways paralleled those used for psychopathology in general. It is obvious that similar treatment procedures apply throughout, such as early detection and correction of unhealthy personality trends, correction of undesirable social conditions, and provision of adequate treatment personnel and facilities. But since crime represents a vast range of individuals and behaviors, it is also apparent that no simple formula or single generalization can either explain it or suggest an easy solution to it. Because its complex social, economic, and psychological bases are not fully understood, its eradication must be considered a long-range, rather than an immediately achievable, goal.

For present purposes let us briefly examine three aspects of the treatment of criminal offenders: (a) the traditional reliance on punishment, (b) rehabilitation, and (c) some correctional trends and prospects.

Traditional reliance on punishment. In 1843, Jeremy Bentham concluded that if punishment were certain, swift, and severe, many a person would avoid criminal behavior. The view is still widely held that punishment—usually involving imprisonment—is the most effective way of making offenders realize the error of their ways and curing them of their criminal tendencies. Such punishment has actually been thought to serve three purposes: (a) revenge by society—"giving the criminal his due"; (b) protection of society; and (c) deterrence from future crimes—both for the offenders who are punished and for others, through example.

1. *Revenge.* This approach is based on the premise that the guilty, who have brought distress to others, ought to suffer themselves. As Henley (1971) has noted, "Many crime victims carry unseen and long-lasting psychological scars" (p. 39). He might have added that many also carry physical injuries that impair their health and earning ability. And in the tens of thousands of cases where victims are killed, great suffering and hardship may result for their loved ones.

Another basis for this approach is the view that if society does not establish legal procedures for punishing criminal offenders, individuals or groups will take the law into their own hands. Even with established laws, the early history of our society reveals numerous incidents of lynchings and illegal hangings.

2. *Protection of society.* The protection of society by the imprisonment of the offender is assured while he is serving his term, but not thereafter. Without rehabilitation, imprisonment may simply serve to expose the offender to prison codes of behavior, to reinforce his criminal values, to permit his learning of new criminal skills or refining old ones, and to augment his degradation and feeling of separateness from society.

In extreme cases, for example, young offenders are subjected to sexual assault by tougher convicts and may be sent back to society filled with confusion, shame, and hatred. In other cases, prisoners are the victims of stabbings and other forms of physical assault that result in serious injuries and even death. Thus the criminal offender himself does not appear to be well protected while serving his term, and from such an environment he may return to society more hardened and criminally inclined than before. It is a strange paradox that our prisons have been referred to as "universities of crime" and often seem to accomplish the opposite of what they were designed for—to reduce and not increase serious crimes.

3. *Deterrence.* Efforts at deterrence are based on the premise that punishment for criminal acts will both deter the individual offender in the future and keep others from committing similar acts. The failure of our present system to do this is shown by the rapidly rising crime rates and by the fact that the rate or recidivism among past prisoners is over 66 percent nationwide and as high as 90 percent in some areas of the country, including New York City (Murphy, 1970; Goldfarb, 1974).

Several factors limit the deterrent effect of punishment—among them the lack of guilt feelings in those who are punished and the uncertainty and delay that often surround the punishment. Many young black prisoners see themselves as victims of a "racist society" rather than as perpetrators of antisocial acts. Similarly, many imprisoned offenders see their problem as one of getting caught—as "bad luck" rather than "bad character." In addition, the long delay that commonly separates sentencing from the offense lessens the impact of punishment as a deterrent force. During the last decade spiraling caseloads have strained our judicial system to the point where there are often delays of several months or longer between arrest and trial. In addition, large numbers of offenders manage to avoid imprisonment for their crimes.

Logically, it might seem that the more severe the punishment, the greater its deterrent effect, but for certain crimes at least—including homicide and rape—this has not been the case (Schwartz, 1968; Melville, 1973). For example, states that have used the death penalty have had homicide rates as high or higher than those that have not. For other types of crimes, the deterrent effect of increasingly severe punishment may be different, but no conclusive evidence is presently available. In addition, severe penalties may lead to the take-over of some criminal activities—such as drug peddling—by organized crime if the profits are considered worth the risk.

In 1970 drastic new anticrime measures were passed by Congress, aimed both at the apprehension of criminals and the stiffening of legal penalties. And in the 1970s, we have witnessed efforts to speed up "justice"—to shorten the time between the apprehension and the sentencing of the offender. The long-range effectiveness of these measures remains to be ascertained.

Human rights vs. "treatment" for offenders who commit violent criminal acts

During the eighteenth and nineteenth centuries the criminal offender was viewed as having "free will" and being "morally depraved." Because the criminal was viewed as a serious menace to society, the primary method of crime control centered around detection and long periods of imprisonment. During the latter part of the nineteenth century and the first half of the twentieth, the preceding view changed to one emphasizing "treatment" and "rehabilitation" of the offender, based largely on the assumption that his behavior was the result of underlying maladjustment. The individual was "sick" and needed treatment.

In the latter half of this century, a new view of criminology has emerged which views our society, rather than the criminal offender, as "sick." In essence, the offender is the end product of the failures of the "establishment." From this viewpoint, more drastic methods of "treatment"—such as long prison sentences and the use of powerful behavior modification techniques—are considered both misdirected and a violation of the offender's rights as a person, for the emphasis is on forcing the offender to adjust to a sick society, rather than on changing pathological social conditions which presumably resulted in the criminal behavior.

In the light of available evidence, it would seem more realistic to adopt an interactional view which focuses on needed changes in both society and in criminal offenders. Until the former can be achieved, however, the immediate problem of what to do with offenders who commit violent criminal acts such as homicide, assault, robbery, and rape is a difficult one to resolve.

It would appear, however, that society has three general options for dealing with this problem:
1. *Release of the offender*—including probationary release, but with the full knowledge that his past history indicates the likelihood of his repeating acts of violence.
2. *Drastic punishment*—including capital punishment or long imprisonment for offenders, either for the first offense or for repeated offenses.
3. *Drastic treatment*—including the use of powerful behavior modification techniques which are likely to prevent the recurrence of violent criminal offenses.

At the present time, there is obviously a good deal of controversy and confusion concerning the rights of society, the rights of offenders, and the most appropriate and effective solution to the problem of violent crime. In the meantime, crimes of violence in our society continue their alarming rise.

Based on Doleschal & Klapmuts (1974) and LEAA (1974b).

No prison is a "country club," but some prisons are better than others, as a comparison of these two pictures shows. A recreation room where prisoners can play games normally, no matter how barren, is certainly less dehumanizing than being forced to play cards through the bars of the cell door.

Rehabilitation. Less than 4 percent of the persons working in penal institutions are treatment staff – the rest are guards, administrators, and other personnel. Less than 13 percent of state and local correctional personnel handle probations and parolees, although the latter constitute more than two-thirds of the nation's criminal offender population. In view of these figures, both treatment facilities in penal institutions and supervision facilities for parolees appear to be sadly inadequate, which helps explain the high recidivism rate.

Aside from the dehumanizing treatment to which most prisoners are subjected, nonviolent offenders, and sometimes even juvenile offenders who have committed minor offenses, are confined with hardened and inveterate offenders, many of whom have committed repeated crimes of violence. The result is that the nonviolent offender who has committed a less serious crime often emerges from prison more brutalized and less fit for society than when he entered.

Imprisonment of some offenders may be necessary and may even have positive value providing it includes opportunities for rehabilitation – for atonement, reeducation, and resocialization, including the development of a sense of purpose and responsibility to society. Imprisonment without such redeeming characteristics is neither a major deterrent to criminal behavior nor a helpful form of treatment. In fact, Menninger (1968) has referred to imprisonment as "the crime of punishment" and has concluded that vengeful punishment only aggravates crime. In addition, "The most hardened wardens agree that 80 to 90 percent of prisoners could be released without constituting any menace to society" (Alexander, 1974, p. 35). The problem is that not even the most experienced criminologists can positively identify the 10 percent who will again commit crimes of violence.

In line with the concept of rehabilitation rather than punishment of criminal offenders, a number of approaches have been introduced during recent years:

1. *Indeterminate sentences and paroles.* In view of the deplorable conditions existing in penal institutions, the courts became increasingly reluctant to send offenders to prison unless it was considered absolutely necessary; thus the indeterminate sentence came into wide use. It was intended to (a) enable qualified rehabilitation personnel – within broad limits – to determine when an offender should be released; (b) introduce flexibility into the widely disparate ideas of different judges about the appropriate sentences for convicted offenders; and (c) facilitate return to the community of prisoners who meet qualifications for parole.

Unfortunately, the indeterminate sentence also makes a prisoner's fate more subject to the whim of those who have power over him, particularly when it is capriciously applied. In fact, it may give the prisoner less control over what happens to him, since he can no longer be sure that after X months or years he will be freed on parole. Putting in time is no longer enough. He must conform in ways that may seem alien or impossible or even wrong to him. Many inmates would prefer a clear penalty to an indeterminate sentence in which they have to please the authorities in order to get out. In addition, this whole structure is based on the questionable assumption that law enforcement personnel can predict the behavior of paroled offenders.

As a consequence of such considerations, the indeterminate sentence has been subjected to severe criticism and is being used less than it formerly was.

2. *Plea bargaining.* Delays and heavy workloads in the courts have resulted in an informal system of pretrial bargaining and settlement known as *plea bargaining*. A suspect may be induced to admit part or all of the crime charged in return for a specified punishment rather than await trial with the possibility of either acquittal or a more serious punishment. In some cities 80 percent or more of felony cases have been disposed of by plea bargaining, providing cheaper and swifter "justice" and punishment, more flexible and better fitted to the needs of the individual (Howard, 1974). However, plea bargaining has several dangers, one of which is presumption of guilt without trial. Even an innocent suspect may confess in order to have the matter settled promptly. But despite its limitations, plea bargaining has effected major changes in our judiciary system. How permanent these changes will be remains to be seen.

Patuxent: "Therapeutic" prison

A unique correctional institution named Patuxent was established in Jessup, Maryland, in January 1955 to demonstrate decades of progress in correctional psychology and to serve as a model facility for treatment of criminal offenders. Designed for some 400 to 500 offenders and staffed by a large number of mental health personnel, it is also run as a maximum security institution with the usual complement of guards and related personnel. Despite the well-intentioned plans, by 1975 it had become a focus of controversy. Some of the following data reported by Trotter (1975) may help reveal the complexity of the situation at that time.

1. Requirements for admission. An offender "must have been convicted and sentenced for a felony, a misdemeanor punishable by imprisonment in the state penitentiary, a crime of violence or one of a number of specified sex crimes" (p. 1). In addition, though considered legally sane, the offender must have evidenced persistent, aggravated criminal or antisocial behavior.

2. Length of sentence. "All commitments to Patuxent are for an indeterminate period of time (meaning everyone is potentially there for life). In keeping with the therapeutic intent of the institution, all inmates are there to be treated and no one released until considered cured" (p. 1). The concept of making release contingent on rehabilitation is considered essential for motivating the inmate to take part in treatment programs and "to cure his condition." While participation in treatment is voluntary, all inmates are expected to participate in order to achieve changes in themselves and in their behavior in order to be released.

3. Treatment procedures. The basic treatment program is based on "psychological learning principles" utilizing the "graded-tier system." The new patient or inmate starts on the bottom level and earns more privileges as he works his way up through the four levels. Treatment procedures also include the use of punishment in the form of "segregation cells" — called "the hole" by the inmates — as "negative reinforcers. . . ." (p. 4). Since there are not enough therapists to treat 400 men individually, treatment is based heavily on group therapy. Finally, the entire institutional setting was designed to represent a "therapeutic milieu," despite the maximum security nature of the correctional institution.

4. Outcomes of treatment and reasons for controversy. The following points seem particularly relevant here:

a) During the first 18 years of Patuxent's existence, only 135 men were released as "cured"; another 337 men were released by the courts against the advice of the Patuxent staff. The recidivism rate calculated for both groups was only 7 percent, an exceptionally low figure. However, critics have questioned the methodology on which the recidivism figure is based and have suggested that if inmates are kept locked up more or less indefinitely, it is easy to have a low recidivism rate.

b) Patuxent has been accused of overusing negative reinforcement procedures, such as keeping men in "segregation cells" for long periods of time, and has been ordered by the court to limit the stay there to 15 days to avoid "cruel and unusual punishment." It has also been criticized by an investigating committee for guard brutality, use of a "goon squad," inadequate training of the custodial staff, and lack of communication between custodial and professional staff.

c) "Shamming." The nature of the treatment program has been accused of encouraging inmates to put up false fronts in therapy groups to impress the staff with their self-understanding and progress in self-control. Apparently the staff feels that shamming is irrelevant, for it can be interpreted as indicating that the individual has developed necessary inner controls.

d) *Abuse of the indeterminate sentence.* Since release from Patuxent depends on the approval of a small committee of staff and outside professional personnel, the inmate can be confined for long periods unless his behavior meets with their approval. In one case, for example, a Baltimore pipefitter was sentenced to two years on a relatively minor assault charge, but was confined for ten years because of attempting to gain his release on legal grounds and refusing to participate in group therapy.

e) *Enforced "treatment."* Another element of the controversy centers around the concept of enforced treatment. Unless the men cooperate — regardless of their own inclinations or values — they simply remain confined, even though they might or might not be dangerous to society. The pipefitter cited earlier maintained that his legal battle and refusal to engage in group therapy was interpreted by the staff as hostility, and he was therefore labeled as a danger to society. "Whether or not his position was justified, it raises the issue that "to assert one's rights or one's dignity against an institution that is by definition benign, is automatically to be branded recalcitrant, or simply sick" (p. 12).

Trotter concluded that "Therapy in a setting where the patient has no alternative tends to magnify the imperfections of a discipline that is still more art than science, and leads many mental health professionals to recommend extreme caution lest they inadvertently become more jailer than healer" (p. 12).

3. *Other innovative approaches to treatment.* A number of other innovative approaches to dealing with criminal offenders have also been suggested, and some have been tried out on a limited basis. Among these have been study and work furloughs, sexual integration of prisons, conjugal visits, and integration of family and institutional treatment programs.

Although imprisonment means different things to different people, it tends in general to be degrading, as well as to create serious sexual problems that may lead to homosexual behavior—particularly since about 50 percent of the prisoners are under 25 years of age. And where the prisoner is married and has a family, his imprisonment places a tremendous burden on his spouse and children. To help counteract this problem, prisons in Mexico, Sweden, India, and a number of other countries allow conjugal visits. In the United States the first prison to allow conjugal visits was the Mississippi State Penitentiary. This practice, including overnight visits by women friends of unmarried male prisoners, seems to be gaining support in the United States.

Other innovative approaches to rehabilitation range from transcendental meditation, through behavior therapy techniques, to the use of drugs and other medical measures for prisoners who have brain abnormalities that apparently make them prone to anger and impulsive violence. However, the "treatment" of offenders by medical and psychological procedures has become a matter of considerable controversy.

At the present time, there is a strong trend away from the goal of rehabilitation for those offenders who require imprisonment and toward punishment and deterrence. While some people feel that the ideal of rehabilitation has not been given a fair chance, the high rate of recidivism has led most to conclude that rehabilitation simply doesn't work. As Schwartz (1975) has expressed it, " 'Rehabilitation' in prison is at best a myth and at worst a fraud" (p. 5).

Some correctional trends and prospects. While serious efforts are being made to improve law-enforcement and correctional procedures, there is a good deal of disagreement among

Prison inmates march with drill-like precision. In the prison environment a convict loses his individuality and becomes a number. Subject to rigid regimentation, deprived of his civil rights, and exposed to highly undesirable models, it is not surprising when he returns to the community unrehabilitated—traumatized by prison experiences and bearing the additional burden of the label "ex-con." Because of the high rate of recidivism, many jails and prisons have been referred to by investigating committees as "crime hatcheries," or breeding grounds of bitter social outcasts.

1817 Inauguration in New York State of the first parole system in the U.S.

1841 Adoption by the city of Boston, Massachusetts, of probation procedures—the first in the U.S.

1855 Opening of an institution for the criminally insane—the first in the U.S.—adjacent to Auburn State Prison, New York

1899 Establishment at Chicago, Illinois, of the first juvenile court in the U.S.

1915 Formal report by Paul E. Bowers, psychiatrist at Indiana State Prison, of comprehensive studies on the relationship between crime and mental illness

1922 Establishment of the Division for the Prevention of Delinquency by the National Committee for Mental Hygiene

1930 Congressional passage of law reorganizing federal prisons and providing for medical services to prisoners

1940 First publication of the *Journal of Criminal Psychopathology*

1948 Utilization in the New Jersey prison system of group therapy techniques

1952 Inauguration by the State of Wisconsin of the first program in the U.S. for adequate treatment of sex offenders

1956 The rendering, by the U.S. Court of Appeals for the District of Columbia, of the Durham decision, in which the provision is made that a defendant is not criminally responsible if his criminal act was the product of mental disease or mental defect

1958 Congressional passage of Public Law 752, providing for psychiatric examination of convicted federal offenders before imposition of sentence

1965 Congressional passage of the Prisoner Rehabilitation Act, authorizing the daytime release of selected inmates for education or work in nearby communities

1965 The rendering, by the U.S. Supreme Court, of the Miranda decision, which requires that a person accused of a crime be informed of his right to counsel before he is questioned

1970 Congressional passage of "preventive detention" and other new anticrime legislation

1972 Supreme Court decision holding that the death penalty as imposed under some state laws violates the Eighth Amendment of the Constitution, which bans "cruel and unusual punishment." However, the precise meaning of the decision remains unclear, and further action is expected

1974 Congressional passage of the Juvenile Justice and Delinquency Prevention Act, providing for an office to foster research into treatment and prevention, develop training programs for professionals and paraprofessionals, and serve as a national clearing house for information

1975 Decision of the Supreme Court to extend to juveniles the guarantee against double jeopardy (being tried twice for the same crime)

In addition to the events listed, there has been a trend during the 1960s and 1970s toward the use of clinical psychologists and psychiatrists as "expert witnessess" in selected criminal cases. Such testimony is directed toward providing a jury with information concerning a defendant's mental status and assisting the jury in drawing inferences from certain types of psychological data. For a discussion of the role of psychologists and psychiatrists as expert witnesses, the reader is referred to the Group for the Advancement of Psychiatry (1974). Silber (1974), and Silverman (1969).

governmental agencies, law-enforcement officials, and criminologists and other social scientists concerning the most effective measures to take. There appears, however, to be increasing agreement on the following points:[9]

1. At the present time, there are no methods of rehabilitation that are both predictably effective and socially acceptable. Therefore, some people must be imprisoned to protect society.

2. Such criminal offenders should be given a flat maximum sentence to "fit the crime," but with time off for good behavior—for example, for each day the individual abides by prison rules.

3. Rehabilitation programs should be available in prison for those who want them, but participation in such programs should not be made a condition of parole, at least until they have been proven effective.

4. Giant human warehouses such as Attica and San Quentin should be phased out and replaced with smaller, more flexible, and less dehumanizing prisons. Prison facilities such as libraries should be improved.

5. Treatment of all prisoners should be equal, regardless of sex, race, or social class. Standards for correctional personnel should be established and maintained, and facilities for helping paroled prisoners make the transition to society should be available.

Implicit in the above measures is the realization that prison is not presently a good place to send people for rehabilitation. As Guthrie (1975) quoted one former state prison official as saying, "If you had a friend who was having some adjustment problems unrelated to crime, you wouldn't think of sending him to San Quentin for a couple of months to get rehabilitated" (p. 5). With this in mind, probation or early parole would be used for offenders who have not committed violent or serious crimes, and a concentrated effort would be made to integrate institutional, family, and community facilities into a broadly based correctional program.

Ultimately, of course, any effective approach to crime must elicit the citizen and community involvement essential for dealing with the root causes of crime, insofar as we

understand them, as well as injustices in our legal system.

In this chapter we have dealt with sociopathic personality disorders, including antisocial personality and compulsive gambling, and with delinquency and crime. We noted that sociopathic disorders are usually recognizable in childhood or adolescence and tend to continue into adult life, and that they stem primarily from faulty learning, rather than anxiety or other factors associated with excessive stress.

Initially focusing on the antisocial personality, we noted the various traits that tend to characterize this disorder, and the role of such traits in faulty interpersonal relationships and self-defeating behavior. We then discussed the closely related problem of compulsive gambling.

In the latter part of the chapter we dealt with delinquency and crime, noting the increasing incidence and social dangers of both, as well as the complex causal patterns that may be involved. We have seen that although these patterns are considered separately, a certain amount of overlapping characterizes the range of offenses, motivations, causal factors, and treatment procedures. Finally, we have seen the inadequacy of present methods of dealing with crime, and we noted some of the innovative approaches and new trends for coping with this major social problem.

---

[9]Based in part on Holden (1975) and Schwartz (1975).

12

Alcoholism and Drug Abuse

During the last decade we have seen a marked increase in the use of psychoactive, or mind-altering, drugs in our society. Concurrent with their rising use has come their misuse—with which we are primarily concerned in the present chapter.

The misuse of drugs may take the form of dependence or abuse. In traditional usage, *dependence* signified psychological reliance on a particular drug, while *addiction* was reserved for physiological dependence, as indicated by withdrawal symptoms if the drug were to be discontinued. Recently, however, *drug dependence* has come to denote both psychological and physiological dependence. The term *drug abuse* is used to indicate the excessive consumption of a drug, regardless of whether an individual is truly dependent on it. Of course, drug abuse often leads to drug dependence.

The most commonly used problem drugs are alcohol, barbiturates, amphetamines, heroin, and marijuana. Some of these drugs, such as alcohol, can be purchased legally by adults; others, such as the barbiturates, can be used legally under medical supervision; still others, such as heroin, are illegal. Currently, drug legislation—particularly in relation to marijuana—is a controversial matter.

The increasing problem of alcoholism[1] and drug abuse and dependence in our society has caused both public and scientific attention to be focused on it. In the past, abuse and dependence—particularly in relation to alcohol and heroin—were considered to be manifestations of "moral weakness." But exhortation and other treatment approaches based on this concept—such as imprisonment—proved singularly ineffective. Thus, until recently, little progress was made toward the identification of causal factors or the development of effective methods of treatment. Although our present knowledge concerning alcohol and drug abuse and dependence is far from complete, investigating them as maladaptive patterns of adjustment to life's demands rather than as moral deficiencies is leading to rapid progress in both understanding and treatment.

Alcohol Abuse and Alcoholism
Drug Abuse and Drug Dependence

---

[1]The term *alcoholism* is gradually being replaced by *the alcoholisms*, since many types or patterns and causal factors appear to be involved.

Alcohol Abuse and Alcoholism

As we noted in Chapter 1, Cambyses, King of Persia in the sixth century B.C., had the dubious distinction of being one of the first alcoholics on record. People of many other early cultures, including the Egyptian, Greek, and Roman, made extensive and often excessive use of alcohol, principally wine. The oldest surviving winemaking formulas were recorded by Marcus Cato in Italy almost a century and a half before the birth of Christ. About A.D. 800 the process of distillation was developed by an Arabian alchemist, thus making possible an increase in both the range and potency of alcoholic beverages. However, both before and since that time, many notable historical figures have had their difficulties with alcohol.

Incidence and effects of alcoholism

Despite the publicity given during the 1960s to a few drugs—notably LSD, heroin, and marijuana—alcohol has long been and continues to be the most widely used and popular of the "mind-bending" drugs. And with the recent deemphasis on marijuana and the decreased use of heroin, alcohol has regained its rightful place as the Number One problem drug in our society.

The potentially detrimental effects of alcoholism—for the individual, his loved ones, and society—are legion. In relation to alcohol, Bengelsdorf (1970a) has pointed out that:

". . . its abuse has killed more people, sent more victims to hospitals, generated more police arrests, broken up more marriages and homes, and cost industry more money than has the abuse of heroin, amphetamines, barbiturates and marijuana combined." (p. 7)

Similarly, the National Institute on Alcohol Abuse and Alcoholism, as well as other national agencies, has concurred that alcoholism is by far the most devastating drug problem in the United States today.

The technical name of the drug in alcoholic beverages is *ethanol,* or *ethyl alcohol;* popularly, it is known simply as alcohol. There are more than 100 million users of alcohol in the United States, the preponderance of their drinking being social, moderate, and generally approved. Most users rarely, if ever, cause trouble to themselves or others. In fact, a task force of the U.S. Department of Health, Education, and Welfare (1974) concluded that "moderate consumption of alcohol is generally not harmful" (p. xi).

Unfortunately, however, an estimated 12 to 15 million Americans experience episodes of abusive use of alcohol and are labeled *alcoholics:* individuals whose drinking seriously impairs their life adjustment in terms of health, personal relationships, and/or occupational functioning. Such episodes of alcohol abuse may range from infrequent to frequent and may be manifestations of early, intermediate, or later phases of alcoholism. In addition to the serious problems they create for themselves, these excessive drinkers pose serious difficulties for, on the average, some 4 to 6 other persons, including mates, children, friends, employers, and even total strangers, as in cases where they are involved in automobile accidents while under the influence of alcohol.

Alcoholism is on the rise in the United States: there are some 200,000 or more new cases each year, and an increasing proportion of these cases are teen-agers. In fact, alcoholism has been called the "teen-age tragedy of the Seventies." Alcohol has been associated with over half the deaths and major injuries suffered in automobile accidents each year, and with about 50 percent of all murders, 40 percent of all assaults, 35 percent or more of all rapes, and 30 percent of all suicides. About one out of every three arrests in the United States results from the abuse of alcohol. The financial drain imposed on the economy by alcoholism is estimated to be over 25 billion dollars a year, in large part comprised of losses to industry from absenteeism, lowered work effi-

Many young people think it's smart and sophisticated to "fool around" with alcohol, but the effects of the type of "fooling around" these boys are doing can be tragic, either immediately, as in automobile accidents, or much later, if it leads to alcoholism.

ciency, and accidents, as well as the costs involved in the treatment of alcoholics. The life span of the average alcoholic is about 12 years shorter than that of the average nonalcoholic, and alcohol now ranks as the third major cause of death in the United States, behind coronary heart disease and cancer.[2]

Alcoholism in the United States cuts across all educational, occupational, and socioeconomic boundaries. It is considered a serious problem in industry, in the professions, and in the military; it is found among such seemingly unlikely candidates as airline pilots, surgeons, and law enforcement officers. The once popular image of an alcoholic as an unkempt

resident of Skid Row is inaccurate. In fact, the latter group constitutes less than 5 percent of all alcoholics; it is even estimated that half or more of the people on Skid Row – such as the Bowery in New York – are either moderate drinkers or nondrinkers. Alcoholism may develop during any life period from early childhood through old age. However, the great majority of alcoholics are men and women who are married and living with their families, still hold jobs – often important ones – and are accepted members of their communities. And although alcoholism has traditionally been considered to be more prevalent among males than females, this distinction seems to be disappearing in our society. Since many women do not work outside the home, it is often easier for them to conceal their alcoholism (Gunther, 1975). Thus the commonly

---

[2]The statistics in this section are based on Levitt (1974), U.S. Dept. of Health, Education, and Welfare (1974), *U.S. News & World Report* (April 14, 1975), and National Institute on Alcohol Abuse and Alcoholism (1974/1975).

Alcohol levels in the blood after drinks taken on an empty stomach by a 150-pound person

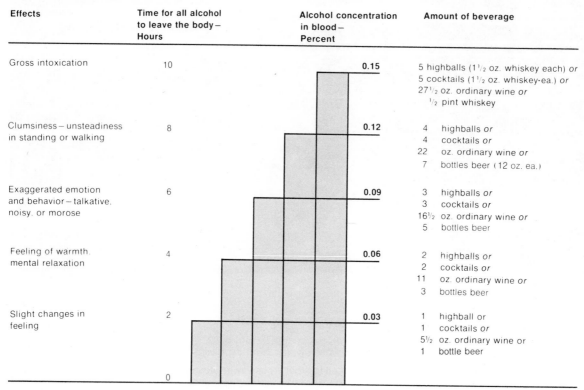

Effects	Time for all alcohol to leave the body— Hours	Alcohol concentration in blood— Percent	Amount of beverage
Gross intoxication	10	0.15	5 highballs (1½ oz. whiskey each) or 5 cocktails (1½ oz. whiskey·ea.) or 27½ oz. ordinary wine or ½ pint whiskey
Clumsiness—unsteadiness in standing or walking	8	0.12	4 highballs or 4 cocktails or 22 oz. ordinary wine or 7 bottles beer (12 oz. ea.)
Exaggerated emotion and behavior—talkative. noisy. or morose	6	0.09	3 highballs or 3 cocktails or 16½ oz. ordinary wine or 5 bottles beer
Feeling of warmth. mental relaxation	4	0.06	2 highballs or 2 cocktails or 11 oz. ordinary wine or 3 bottles beer
Slight changes in feeling	2	0.03	1 highball or 1 cocktails or 5½ oz. ordinary wine or 1 bottle beer
	0		

Calories

5½ oz. wine	115
12 oz. beer	170
1½ oz. whiskey	120

used incidence figure of 4 males to 1 female is considered invalid.

Our present discussion will center on the problem of alcoholism in the United States. This problem, however, is by no means limited to any particular country or racial or ethnic group but is found all over the world. In fact, there has been a recent upsurge of alcoholism in a number of industrialized nations, including the Soviet Union.

Clinical picture

The Roman poet Horace, in the first century B.C., wrote lyrically about the psychological effects of wine:

"It discloses secrets; ratifies and confirms our hopes; thrusts the coward forth to battle; eases the anxious mind of its burthen; instructs in arts. Whom has not a cheerful glass made eloquent! Whom not quite free and easy from pinching poverty!"

Unfortunately, the effects of alcohol are not always so benign or beneficial. According to the Japanese proverb, "First the man takes a drink, then the drink takes a drink, and then the drink takes the man."

General effects of alcoholic intoxication. Alcohol is a depressant which attacks and numbs the higher brain centers, impairing judgment and other rational processes and lowering self-control. As behavioral restraints decline, more primitive emotional responses appear, and the drinker may indulge in the satisfaction of impulses he ordinarily holds in check. In fact, alcohol has been called a "catalyst" for violence, including homicide, assault, and rape.

Some degree of motor incoordination soon becomes apparent, and the drinker's sense of discrimination and perception of cold, pain, and other discomforts are dulled. Typically he experiences a sense of warmth, expansiveness, and well-being. In such a mood, unpleasant realities are screened out and the drinker's feelings of self-esteem and adequacy rise. Casual acquaintances become the best and most understanding of friends, and the drinker enters a generally pleasant world of unreality in which worries are temporarily left behind.

When the alcohol content of the bloodstream reaches 0.1 percent, the individual is considered to be intoxicated. Muscular coordination, speech, and vision are impaired, and thought processes are confused. When the blood alcohol reaches approximately 0.5 percent, the entire neural balance is upset and the individual "passes out." Here unconsciousness apparently acts as a safety device, since concentrations above 0.55 percent are usually lethal.

In general, it is the amount of alcohol actually concentrated in the bodily fluids, not the amount consumed, that determines intoxication. However, the effects of alcohol vary with the individual—his personality, his physical condition, the amount of food in his stomach, and the duration of his drinking. In addition, the user of alcohol gradually may build up a tolerance for the drug so that ever-increasing amounts may be needed to produce the desired effects. The attitude of the drinker is important, too: although actual motor and intellectual abilities decline in direct ratio to the blood concentration of alcohol, many persons who consciously try to do so can maintain adequate control over their behavior, showing few outwards signs of being intoxicated, even after drinking relatively large amounts of alcohol.

Exactly how alcohol works on the brain is not yet fully understood, but several physiological effects are common. One is a tendency toward increased sexual stimulation but, simultaneously, lowered sexual performance.

As Shakespeare wrote in *Macbeth*, alcohol "provokes and unprovokes. It provokes the desire, but it takes away the performance." Another phenomenon which occurs in an appreciable number of cases is the "blackout"—a lapse of memory after moderate drinking in which there typically have been no signs of obvious intoxication. Here the drinker may carry on a rational conversation and engage in other relatively complex activities but have no trace of recall the next day. Blackouts may also occur in association with heavy drinking, but in such instances the individual usually acts as if he is intoxicated. A third curious phenomenon associated with alcoholic intoxication is the "hangover," which many drinkers experience at one time or another. As yet, no one has come up with a satisfactory explanation or remedy for the symptoms of headache, nausea, and fatigue which are characteristic of hangovers.

Alcohol dependence and deterioration. Although many investigators have maintained that even in very small amounts alcohol is a dangerous systemic poison, newer studies indicate that in moderate amounts—up to about three shots of whiskey, half a bottle of wine, or four glasses of beer per day—alcohol is not harmful to most people and may actually be beneficial (U.S. Dept. of Health, Education, and Welfare, 1974).

For individuals who drink immoderately, however, the picture is highly unfavorable. For one thing, the alcohol that is taken in must be assimilated by the body, except for about 5 to 10 percent which is eliminated through breath, urine, and perspiration. The work of assimilation is done by the liver, but when large amounts of alcohol are ingested, the liver may be seriously overworked and eventually suffer irreversible damage. In fact, over time the excessive drinker has a 1-in-10 chance of developing cirrhosis of the liver, a pathological condition in which liver cells are irreparably damaged and replaced by fibrous scar tissue.

For another thing, alcohol is a high-calorie drug; drinking a pint of whiskey—enough to make about 8 to 10 ordinary cocktails—provides about 1200 calories, which is approximately half the ordinary caloric requirement for a day and thus reduces the drinker's appetite for other food. But since alcohol has no nutritional value, the excessive drinker often suffers from malnutrition; furthermore, since heavy drinking impairs the body's ability to utilize nutrients, the deficiency cannot be made up by popping vitamins. The excessive intake of alcohol also impairs the activity of the white blood cells in fighting disease and is associated with a greatly increased risk of cancer (U.S. Dept. of Health, Education, and Welfare, 1974). And in addition to his other problems, the alcoholic usually suffers from chronic fatigue, oversensitivity, and depression.

Initially alcohol may provide a seemingly useful crutch for dealing with the stresses of life, especially during periods of acute stress, by helping screen out intolerable reality and enhancing the drinker's feelings of adequacy and worth. Eventually, however, the excessive use of alcohol becomes counterproductive, resulting in lowered feelings of adequacy and worth, impaired reasoning and judgment, and gradual personality deterioration. The individ-

ual's behavior typically becomes coarse and inappropriate, he assumes increasingly less responsibility, loses pride in his personal appearance, neglects his family, and becomes generally touchy and irritable about his drinking. As his judgment becomes impaired, the excessive drinker may find himself unable to maintain employment and generally unqualified to cope with any new demands that are made upon him. By this time, he is likely to have seriously weakened his general health as well as to be suffering from brain damage; his general life situation is likely to reflect— for example, in loss of employment and/or a marital breakup—his personal disorganization and deterioration.

Psychoses associated with alcoholism. Several psychotic reactions commonly develop in individuals who have been drinking excessively over long periods of time, or who—for various reasons, such as brain lesions—have a reduced tolerance for alcohol. Such acute reactions usually last only a short time and generally consist of confusion, excitement, and delirium. There are four commonly recognized subtypes.

1. *Pathological intoxication* is an acute reaction that occurs in persons whose tolerance to alcohol is chronically very low (such as epileptics or those of an unstable personality makeup) or in normal persons whose tolerance to alcohol is temporarily lessened by exhaustion, emotional stress, or other conditions. Following the consumption of even moderate amounts of alcohol, these individuals may suddenly become disoriented, and may evidence a homicidal rage—sometimes committing violent crimes. This confused, disoriented state is usually followed by a period of deep sleep, with complete amnesia occurring afterward. The following case history illustrates this pattern.

The patient was hospitalized following an altercation in a bar in which he attacked and injured a woman and her escort. On admission to the hospital he seemed very friendly and cooperative—in fact, almost servile in his desire to please those in authority. His personal history revealed that he had been involved in five such incidents during the previous two years. His family background was torn with bickering and dissension. Both parents were stern disciplinarians and severely punished him for the most minor disapproved behavior. He was taught to feel that sex was very evil.

In his previous altercations he had been arrested twice for disturbing the peace. In each case these incidents took place in bars where, after a few drinks, he would become aggressive, loud, and abusive, daring any and all to do anything about it. His latest escapade and arrest involved an attack on a woman; this had apparently been provoked by her kissing her escort and making what the patient interpreted as sexual overtures in public. He approached the woman in a threatening manner, slapped her, knocked her escort out when he attempted to intervene, and then hit her several times with his fists before he was forcibly restrained by other customers. He was amnesic for the entire episode, apparently "coming to" on his way to the hospital.

It was felt in this case that the woman's behavior aroused unacceptable and therefore threatening sexual desires in the patient, against which he defended himself by becoming hostile and attacking her. The alcohol apparently served to lower his normal behavioral restraints, permitting his hostility to be expressed in overt antisocial behavior.

2. *Delirium tremens* is probably the best known of the various alcoholic psychotic reactions. A fairly common occurrence among those who drink excessively for a long time, this reaction may follow a prolonged alcoholic debauch, appear during a period of abstinence, be associated with a head injury or infection, or occur upon the withdrawal of alcohol after prolonged drinking.

The delirium usually is preceded by a period of restlessness and insomnia during which the person may feel generally uneasy and apprehensive. Slight noises or sudden moving objects may cause considerable excitement and agitation. The full-blown symptoms include (a) disorientation for time and place in which, for example, a person may mistake the hospital for a church or jail, friends are no longer recognized, and hospital attendants may be identified as old acquaintances; (b) vivid hallucinations, particularly of small, fast-moving animals like snakes, rats, and roaches, which are clearly localized in space; (c) acute fear, in which these animals may change in form, size, or color in terrifying ways; (d) extreme suggestibility, in which a person can be made to see almost any form of animal if its presence

is merely suggested to him or if he is asked what he sees on the wall; (e) marked coarse tremors of the hands, tongue, and lips—as indicated by the name of this disorder; and (f) other symptoms, including perspiration, fever, a rapid and weak heartbeat, a coated tongue, and a foul breath.

The hallucinatory animals the person sees may cause him to cower, terrified, in a corner, or to stand up in his bed and desperately fight them off. This acute fear may be combined with a generalized state of terror in which he feels that something horrible is going to happen to him. As a result, he may even attempt suicide.

The delirium typically lasts from three to six days and is generally followed by a deep sleep. When the person awakens, he has few symptoms—aside from possible slight remorse—but frequently he will have been rather badly scared, and may not resume drinking for several weeks or months. Usually, however, there is eventual resumption, followed by a return to the hospital with a new attack. The death rate from delirium tremens as a result of convulsions, heart failure, and other complications has approximated 10 percent (Tavel, 1962). With such newer drugs as chlordiazepoxide, however, the current death rate during delirium tremens and acute alcoholic withdrawal has been markedly reduced.

The following is a brief description of a 43-year-old male delirium tremens patient.

The subject was brought forcibly to the psychiatric ward of a general hospital when he fired his shotgun at 3:30 A.M. while "trying to repel an invasion of cockroaches." On admission he was confused and disoriented and had terrifying hallucinations involving "millions and millions" of invading cockroaches. He leaped from his bed and cowered in terror against the wall, screaming for help and kicking and hitting frantically at his imaginary assailants. When an attendant came to his aid, he screamed for him to get back out of danger or he would be killed too. Before the attendant could reach him he dived headlong on his head, apparently trying to kill himself.

The subject's delirium lasted for a period of 3½ days, after which he returned to a state of apparent normality, apologized profusely for the trouble he had caused everyone, stated he would never touch another drop, and was discharged. However, on his way home he stopped at a bar, had too much to drink, and on emerging from the bar collapsed on the street. This time he sobered up in jail, again apologized for the trouble he had caused, was extremely remorseful, and was released with a small fine. His subsequent career is unknown.

3. In *acute alcoholic hallucinosis*, the main symptoms are auditory hallucinations. At first the individual usually hears a voice making certain simple statements. With time, however, the hallucinations usually extend to the voices of several people, all of them critical and reproachful. The individual's innermost private weaknesses, particularly sexual ones, are itemized and discussed, and various horrible punishments are then proposed for him. He may hear the clanking of chains, the sharpening of knives, the sound of pistol shots, or footsteps approaching in a threatening manner. Terror-stricken, he may scream for help or attempt suicide.

This condition may continue for several days or even weeks, during which time the person is depressed but fairly well oriented and coherent, apart from his hallucinations. After recovery, he usually shows considerable remorse as well as some insight into his previous behavior.

Investigators are less inclined than formerly to attribute this psychotic reaction solely to the effects of alcohol. Generally, it seems to be related to a broad pattern of maladaptive behavior, as in the following case.

The subject was hospitalized after a suicide attempt in which he slashed his wrists. He had been hospitalized once before after a similar incident in which he tried to hang himself with a bath towel. He was unmarried and lived alone.

The patient had been drinking excessively for a three-year period. He was not in the least particular about what he drank as long as it contained alcohol. For several days prior to his last suicide attempt he had heard voices that accused him of all manner of "filthy sex acts." He was particularly outraged when they accused him of having committed homosexual acts with his mouth and of having had relations with animals. He complained of a terrible taste in his mouth and imagined that his food had been poisoned as a means of punishing him for his sins. He was generally fearful and apprehensive and slept poorly.

After a stay of two weeks in the hospital, the patient made a good recovery and was discharged. At this time he seemed to have some insight into his difficulties, stating that he felt that his sexual problems had something to do with his suicide attempt.

The psychotic symptoms of the individual were apparently triggered by alcohol, but it seems probable that they could have been similarly brought on by other drugs, illness, exhaustion, or other types of stress.

4. *Korsakoff's psychosis* was first described by the Russian psychiatrist Korsakoff in 1887. The outstanding symptom is a memory defect (particularly with regard to recent events) which is concealed by falsification. An individual may be unable to recognize pictures, faces, rooms, and other objects as identical with those just seen, although they may appear to him as similar. Such persons increasingly tend to fill in gaps with reminiscences and fanciful tales that lead to unconnected and distorted associations. These individuals may appear to be delirious, hallucinated, and disoriented for time and place, but ordinarily their confusion and disordered conduct are closely related to their attempts to fill in memory gaps. The memory disturbance itself seems related to an inability to form new associations. Such a reaction usually occurs in older alcoholics, after many years of excessive drinking.

The symptoms of this psychosis are now considered to be due to vitamin B deficiency and other dietary inadequacies. A diet rich in vitamins and minerals generally restores the patient to more normal physical and mental health. However, some personality deterioration usually remains in the form of memory impairment, blunting of intellectual capacity, and lowering of moral and ethical standards.

Stages in alcohol dependence

Without suitable intervention, excessive drinking tends to progress insidiously from early- to middle- and late-stage alcoholism. In an extensive study of over 2000 alcoholics, Jellinek (1952, 1971) found the following stages which are common in the development of alcohol dependence.

1. *The prealcoholic symptomatic phase.* The candidate for alcoholism starts out drinking in conventional social situations but soon experiences a rewarding relief from tension—a feeling that is strongly marked in his case, either because his tensions are greater than others' or because he has not learned to handle them effectively. Initially, he may seek this relief of tension only occasionally. Gradually, however, his tolerance for tension decreases to such an extent that he resorts to alcohol almost daily. This transition from occasional to frequent drinking may take several months or as long as two years.

2. *The prodromal phase.* This phase is marked by the sudden onset of blackouts; the drinker may show few, if any, signs of intoxication and may be able to carry on a reasonable conversation or go through quite elaborate activities, but will have no memory of these events the next day. Occasionally average drinkers experience such amnesic episodes when they drink excessively during a state of emotional or physical exhaustion, but this is very rare. Consequently, Jellinek considered this amnesia without loss of consciousness and sometimes even without intake of extremely large amounts of alcohol to be an indication of a heightened susceptibility to alcohol.

Certain correlated behaviors now make their appearance, among which are (a) surreptitious drinking, in which the drinker seeks occasions for having a few drinks, unknown to others, for fear that they will misjudge him; (b) preoccupation with alcohol, which often takes the form of worrying about whether there will be enough to drink at a social gathering to which he is going—and perhaps having several drinks ahead of time in anticipation of a possible shortage; (c) avid drinking, in which the drinker gulps the first one or two drinks; (d) guilt feelings about drinking behavior, which he begins to realize is out of the ordinary; and (e) avoidance of references to alcohol in his conversation.

3. *The crucial phase.* This stage is characterized by the loss of control over drinking, which means that any consumption of alcohol seems to trigger a chain reaction that continues until the individual is either too intoxicated or too sick to drink any more. But although he has lost the ability to regulate his drinking once he has begun, he still can control whether he will drink on any given occasion. This is

evidenced by periods of abstinence or "going on the wagon" following recovery from severe intoxication.

Almost simultaneously with this loss of control, the alcoholic begins to rationalize his drinking behavior and produces the familiar alcoholic alibis. He devises explanations to convince himself that he did not lose control—that he had good reason for getting intoxicated. These justifications also serve to counter the social pressures that arise as the drinker's behavior becomes more conspicuous.

In spite of his rationalizations, there is a marked lowering of the drinker's self-esteem,

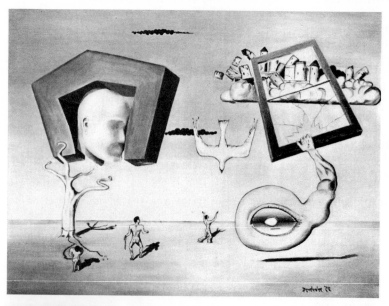

These paintings were done by W———, a 40-year-old male with a history of alcoholism, repeated loss of employment, and hospitalization for treatment. His interest in painting, which gradually became the key aspect of his treatment program at an alcoholism treatment center, also led to a new way of life following his discharge. In the painting at top, W——— depicted alcoholism as a magnetlike vise that drew and crushed his consciousness. He symbolized his feelings in sober periods between drinking sprees as the chained tree, and the nebulous higher power to which he looked for help as a descending dove. The egg and the eye, a motif W——— used in earlier work to depict his unrealistic view of alcohol, are merged into a straining muscular arm reaching back to the more placid past and unattainable dream castles—futile quests with which W——— associated his past abuses of alcohol.

In the second painting, the overriding concept is of constructive action. Contrasting with segments at left and right—a world "blown to hell," an aimless passing through one span of sobriety to the barrenness beyond, and the dismal choice offered by the portals to an abyss or barren sobriety—is the cross symbolizing hope. Through this hope W——— sees the landscape representing goal or purpose. The crosslike shape of the hope segment, while not signifying formal religious affiliation, is indicative of W———'s view of the suprahuman nature of one of the forms of help available to him.

and he may now attempt to compensate for this trend with extravagant expenditures and other grandiose behaviors and by projecting the blame for his difficulties onto others. But these defenses do not work well and he remains remorseful, which further increases his tension and provides added reason for drinking. This remorse, however, together with social pressures, may also lead to periods of total abstinence. As tensions persist, it may even occur to the drinker that his troubles arise not from the drinking *per se,* but rather from the type of beverage he drinks. So now he may attempt to control his problem by changing his pattern — consuming different beverages, setting up rules about drinking only after a certain hour of the day, and so on.

During this phase the alcoholic usually begins drinking in the afternoon and is intoxicated during the evening. The aftereffects of the evening's drunkenness may cause some loss of time from his job, but he still struggles to maintain his employment and social standing, even though he has now begun a pattern of progressive withdrawal from his environment.

The entire struggle subjects the drinker to severe stress. He begins to drop friends and quit jobs. In some cases, of course, he is abandoned by associates and dismissed by employers, but usually he takes the initiative as an anticipatory defense. This process leads to increased isolation and to further centering of his behavior around alcohol. He now becomes concerned with how his activities may interfere with his drinking rather than with how his drinking may affect his activities.

About this time, too, the alcoholic takes steps to protect his supply by laying in a large stock of alcoholic beverages which he hides in the most unlikely places. Similarly, his neglect of proper nutrition begins to aggravate the effects of heavy drinking, and the first hospitalization for some alcoholic complaint may occur. Improper nutrition and other complications also induce a marked decrease in sexual drive, a factor which increases the hostility of the alcoholic toward his spouse and gives rise to the well-known "alcoholic jealousy syndrome," in which the drinker blames his loss of sexual drive on his mate's alleged extramarital affairs.

By now, the alcoholic has begun to feel that he cannot start the day without a drink to steady himself. This is the beginning of "morning drinking" and foreshadows the start of the chronic phase.

4. *The chronic phase.* As alcohol becomes increasingly dominant in the drinker's life, he may find himself intoxicated during the daytime on a weekday and may continue in this state for several days until he is entirely incapacitated.

These drawn-out drinking bouts are usually associated with a marked impairment of thinking and with ethical deterioration — processes which, however, are reversible. The alcoholic no longer is selective about the persons he drinks with, and if his normal sources of liquor are not available he will drink almost anything, even hair tonic or rubbing alcohol. At this time, true alcoholic psychoses, such as delirium tremens, may occur.

Also commonly noted at this time is a loss of tolerance for alcohol: half the amount previously required may be sufficient to produce an alcoholic stupor. Indefinable fears and tremors become persistent, and are especially pronounced as soon as the alcohol disappears from his system. Consequently the alcoholic "controls" the symptoms by continuous drinking.

In this chronic phase the alcoholic's rationalizations begin to fail as they are mercilessly tested against reality. And in many alcoholics — approximately 60 percent — vague religious desires begin to develop. As the rationalization system finally gives way, the alcoholic may admit defeat and become amenable to treatment. However, unless he seeks and receives outside help, his obsessive drinking continues. He is unable to help himself.

Here it should be emphasized that although the stages outlined by Jellinek appear to characterize the course followed by many alcoholics, others do not fit this typical pattern. For example, there are so-called spree drinkers who remain sober and handle responsible positions for long periods of time, but then in the face of some stressful situation will lose control completely — usually winding up in a hospital or jail. It has also been shown that not all alcoholics have blackouts, and that often such experiences occur in later, rather than earlier, stages of alcoholism. And in some instances, individuals appear to skip even the social drinker phase, becoming what has been referred to as "instant alcoholics." Finally, a new trend has become apparent in our society, involving "multiple addictions," in which dependence on alcohol is complicated by the concurrent use of barbiturates, amphetamines, and/or other psychoactive drugs. This is apparently particularly common among young alcoholics and, of course, may markedly change the nature and course of the clinical picture.

Causes of alcoholism

In trying to identify the causes of alcoholism, some researchers have stressed the role of genetic and biochemical factors; others have viewed alcoholism as a maladaptive pattern of adjustment to the stresses of life; still others have emphasized sociocultural factors, such as the availability of alcohol and social approval or disapproval of excessive drinking. As with most other forms of maladaptive behavior, it would appear that alcoholism has multiple causes; its development can best be viewed in terms of the interaction of biological, psychosocial, and sociocultural factors.

Biological factors. After an inordinate intake of alcohol, an individual who is not an alcoholic may develop a severe hangover; however, the nonalcoholic can usually control this toxic reaction merely by abstaining from subsequent overindulgence in the drug. But if the chronic alcoholic tries to stop, he experiences withdrawal symptoms, which indicate that cell metabolism has adapted itself to the presence of alcohol in the bloodstream. These symptoms may be relatively mild, involving a craving for alcohol, tremors, perspiration, and weakness, or more severe, such as nausea, vomiting, fever, tachycardia, convulsions, and hallucinations.

In terms of learning principles, each drink now serves to reinforce alcohol-seeking behavior because it reduces the craving. As Bandura (1969) has expressed it, "After the person thus becomes physically dependent on alcohol, he is compelled to consume large quantities of liquor both to alleviate distressing physical reactions and to avoid their recurrence" (p. 533). In essence, a recurrent cycle of alcohol-induced need-arousal and need-reduction is established.

A question that has been raised is whether certain individuals have a physiological predisposition to alcoholism—perhaps an unusual craving for alcohol once it has been experienced, and hence a greater-than-average tendency toward loss of control. Presumably such a craving could result from some genetic vulnerability, such as a lack of one or more of the enzymes needed for the breakdown of alcohol in body metabolism.

Research studies over the past three decades have shown that alcoholism does tend to run in families. In a study of 259 hospitalized alcoholics, for example, Winokur et al. (1970) found that slightly over 40 percent had a parent—usually the father—who was an alcoholic. Whether this familial incidence results from shared genes or a shared alcoholic environment is a matter of some controversy. In an early study, Roe, Burks, and Mittelmann (1945) followed the case histories of 36 children who had been taken from severely alcoholic parents and placed in foster homes. The likelihood of their becoming alcoholic was no greater than that of a control group of 25 children of nonalcoholic parents. In a review of a number of available studies, Rose and Burks (1968) reported comparable results, thus casting doubt on the genetic hypothesis.

More recent studies, however, have strongly supported the genetic viewpoint. For example, Goodwin et al. (1973) found that children of alcoholic biologic parents who had been adopted by nonalcoholic foster parents still had nearly double the number of alcohol problems by their late twenties as did a control group of adopted children whose biologic parents did not have a history of alcoholism. In another study, Goodwin and his colleagues (1974) compared the sons of alcoholic biologic parents adopted in infancy by nonalcoholic parents with those raised by their alcoholic parents. Both the adopted and nonadopted sons later evidenced high rates of alcoholism—25 percent and 17 percent respectively—and these investigators concluded that it was being born to an alcoholic biologic parent rather than being raised by one that increased the risk of the son becoming an alcoholic.

On the other hand, the great majority of children having alcoholic biologic parents do not themselves become alcoholics—whether or not they are raised by their real parents. Thus as yet we do not know the precise role of genetic factors in the etiology of alcoholism; however, available evidence suggests their importance as predisposing causes. Of course, a possible constitutional predisposition to alcoholism could be acquired as well as inherited. But it is not known if there are acquired conditions, such as endocrine or enzyme imbalances, that increase an individual's vulnerability to alcoholism.

Psychological and interpersonal factors. Not only does the alcoholic become physiologically dependent on alcohol; he develops a powerful psychological dependency as well. Since excessive drinking impairs the total life adjustment of an individual, the question arises as to why the individual becomes psychologically reliant upon it. A number of psychological and interpersonal factors have been advanced as possible answers.

1. *Psychological vulnerability.* The query as to why some individuals lose control over their drinking is often posed in terms of psychological vulnerability; in other words, is there an "alcoholic personality"—a type of character organization that predisposes a given individual to the use of alcohol rather than to some other defensive pattern of coping with stress?

In efforts to answer this question, investigators have reported that alcoholics, in terms of pre-alcoholic personality, tend to be emotionally immature, to expect a great deal of the world, to require an inordinate amount of praise and appreciation, to react to failure with marked feelings of hurt and inferiority, to have low frustration tolerance, and to feel inadequate and unsure of their ability to play expected male or female roles. With respect to the latter characteristic, for example, Winokur et al. (1970), Pratt (1972), and McClelland et al. (1972) have viewed heavy drinking by some young men as an attempt to prove their masculinity and achieve feelings of adequacy and competency. Similarly, Wilsnack (1973a,

---

The psychology of development, reversal, and remission in alcoholism

1. **Escape into alcohol** to avoid, minimize, and seek temporary relief from aversive life conditions, including failure, anxiety, loneliness, and other stresses.

2. **Vague sensing that this escape route is not working,** that alcohol is destroying any possibility of the individual's attaining what he really wants.

3. **Search for an escape from alcohol,** disguised cries for help in coping with his "failure type" drinking, some of which may be heard by others.

4. **Awareness of alternatives to "failure type" drinking,** arousal of hope and tentative trying out of alternative to drinking, with occasional regressions.

5. **Establishment of a nonalcoholic life-style,** as the aversive consequences of alcohol abuse are avoided and the individual learns to share the values and rewards of a life freed from alcoholism.

Adapted from Erdmann (1975).

1973b) concluded that the potential female alcoholic places strong value on the traditional female role, while at the same time her sense of adequacy as a female is highly fragile.

"She may manage to cope with her fragile sense of feminine adequacy for a number of years, but when some new threat severely exacerbates her self-doubts she turns to alcohol in an attempt to gain artificial feelings of womanliness. Her excessive drinking may then begin a vicious circle that culminates in the alcoholic's characteristic loss of control over her drinking." (1973a, p. 96)

Antisocial personality and depression are two clinical syndromes that have also been commonly associated with later excessive drinking (Jones, 1968, 1971; Seixas & Cadoret, 1974; Woodruff et al., 1973).

While such findings provide promising leads, it is difficult to assess the role of specific personality characteristics in the development of alcoholism. Certainly there are many persons with similar personality characteristics who do not become alcoholics, and others with dissimilar ones who do. The only characteristic that appears common to the backgrounds of most problem drinkers is personal maladjustment, yet most maladjusted people do not become alcoholics. And since the personality of alcoholics may be a result rather than a cause of their dependence—for example, a depressed person may turn to the excessive use of alcohol, or the excessive use of alcohol may lead to depression, or both—it is apparent that longitudinal studies are needed to delineate those characteristics that may predispose an individual to lose control over his drinking.

Although the concept of a pre-alcoholic personality remains indefinite, alcoholics do tend to show a distinct cluster of personality traits once their drinking pattern has been established. Included here are low stress tolerance, a negative self-image, and feelings of inadequacy, isolation, and depression. By the time the alcoholic comes to the attention of a clinic or hospital, he also tends to manifest a number of other characteristics, including the exaggerated use of ego-defense mechanisms—particularly denial, rationalization, and projection—a lack of responsibility, impaired impulse control, and a decided tendency toward deceitfulness. In this context, Wikler (1973) has pointed out that during the later stages of alcoholism, there tends to be a "curious twist in the alcoholic's thinking" (p. 10). For example, instead of blaming herself for drinking excessively and letting the dinner burn, a housewife may excuse herself and project the blame onto her husband, who is now perceived as a "nag." And as the alcoholic's life situation continues to deteriorate and stress increases, there is a tendency to rely increasingly on such ego-defense mechanisms.

2. *Stress, tension reduction, and reinforcement.* A number of investigators have pointed out that the typical alcoholic is discontented with his life situation and is unable or unwilling to tolerate tension and stress (AMA Committee on Alcoholism and Drug Dependency, 1969). In fact, Schaefer (1971) has concluded that alcoholism is a conditioned response to anxiety. The individual presumably finds in alcohol a means of relieving anxiety, resentment, depression, or other unpleasant feelings resulting from stressful aspects of his life situation. Each time he drinks and experiences relief of tension, his drinking pattern is reinforced; eventually it becomes his habitual way of coping with stress.

Some investigators hold that anyone—regardless of his life situation—who finds alcohol to be tension-reducing is in danger of becoming an alcoholic. However, if this were true, we would expect alcoholism to be far more common than it is, since alcohol tends to reduce tensions for most persons who use it. In addition, this model does not explain why some excessive drinkers are able to maintain control over their drinking and to function in society, while others are not.

At the opposite end of the spectrum are investigators who reject the view that alcoholism is simply a learned maladaptive response which is reinforced and maintained by tension reduction. They point out that the devastating long-range consequences of excessive drinking far outweigh its temporary relief value. However, as Bandura (1969) has pointed out,

"This argument overlooks the fact that behavior is more powerfully controlled by its immediate, rather than delayed, consequences, and it is precisely for this reason that persons may persistently engage in immediately reinforcing, but potentially self-destructive behavior. . . ." (p. 530)

It seems "the alcoholic drinks not to feel bad," even though he knows he will feel worse later.

For many people—both men and women—it is the severity of stress in their life situations that appears to lead to excessive drinking in an attempt to screen out unbearable reality, to relieve feelings of depression, or to simply cope.

3. *Marital and other intimate relationships.* As we have noted, alcoholism tends to run in families. But while genetic factors may be an influence, it is clear that an alcoholic parent also constitutes a highly undesirable model for the child. Thus an alcoholic's child may have special problems in learning who he is, what is expected of him, and what to esteem in others. Further, his range of coping techniques is likely to be more limited than that of the average child.

Of course, in some cases a child may learn to perceive the parent as a negative model—as someone *not* to emulate or model his behavior after. Here it would appear that an alcoholic parent creates so many problems for the family that the child comes to see the alcoholic behavior as highly aversive. This learning process is well illustrated in the case of a 26-year-old Miami divorcée.

"After attending a Dade County alcohol rehabilitation center for the past three months, Barbara is sober and plans to remain that way. She fears, however, that her drinking may have permanently hurt her children. 'They remember my wine-drinking days when I'd throw up in their wastebasket. Now if they see me drinking a Coke, my older girl will come over and taste it and then reassure the younger one: "It's O.K." ' " (*Time*, April 22, 1974, p. 81)

Excessive drinking often begins during crisis periods in marital or other intimate personal relationships, particularly crises which lead to hurt and self-devaluation. For example, in a study of 100 middle- and upper-class women who were receiving help at an alcoholism treatment center, Curlee (1969) found that the trauma which appeared to trigger the alcoholism was related to a change or challenge in the subject's role as wife or mother, such as divorce, menopause, or children leaving home (the so-called empty-nest syndrome). Many women appear to begin their immoderate drinking during their late thirties and early forties when such life situation changes are common.

After a review of available literature, Siegler, Osmond, and Newell (1968) described a more general pattern of family interaction in alcoholism:

"Alcoholism, like drug addiction and schizophrenia, is best seen as a form of family interaction in which one person is assigned the role of the 'alcoholic' while others play the complementary roles, such as the martyred wife, the neglected children, the disgraced parents, and so forth. As this deadly game is played by mutual consent, any attempt to remove the key actor, the alcoholic, is bound to create difficulties for the other family members, who will attempt to restore their former game. As the game is of far greater interest to the family than to the therapist, the family is almost bound to win. The family may succeed in including the therapist as another role in the game." (p. 579)

Since in this conceptualization alcoholism represents a long drawn-out family game

which is circular and self-reinforcing, it appears relatively useless to ask how it all began.

In this context Al-Anon (1971) has pointed out that a husband who lives with an alcoholic wife is often unaware of the fact that, gradually and inevitably, many of the decisions he makes every day are based on the expectation that his wife will be drinking. In a case such as this, the husband is becoming "drinking-wife-oriented." These expectations, in turn, may make the behavior more likely. Eventually the entire marriage may be dominated by and center around the drinking of the alcoholic spouse. And in some instances, the husband or wife may also begin to drink excessively, possibly through the reinforcement of such behavior by the drinking mate, or to blank out the disillusionment, frustration, and resentment that are often elicited by an alcoholic spouse. Of course, such relationships are not restricted to marital partners but may also occur in those involved in love affairs or close friendships.

Excessive use of alcohol is the third most frequent cause of divorce in the United States, and persons who abuse alcohol are about 7 times more likely to be divorced or separated than nonabusers (Levitt, 1974). The deterioration in the alcoholic's intimate interpersonal relationships further augments the stress and disorganization in his life situation.

General sociocultural factors. In a general sense, our culture has become dependent on alcohol as a social lubricant and a means of reducing tension—it is the "drug of choice." Thus numerous investigators have pointed to the role of sociocultural as well as physiological and psychological factors in the high rate of alcohol abuse and alcoholism among Americans.

Here it is of interest to note the conclusions of Pliner and Cappell (1974) concerning the reinforcing effects of social drinking in our society, in which liquor has come to play an almost ritualistic role in promoting gaiety and pleasant social interaction.

"According to the present results, if it is the case that much of the early drinking experience of . . . individuals takes place in such convivial social settings, drinking will be likely to become associated with positive affective experiences. This reinforcing consequence may in turn make drinking more probable in the future. Thus, to the extent that a social context can enhance the attraction of alcohol, for some individuals it may play a crucial role in the etiology of pathological patterns of alcohol consumption." (p. 425)

The use of alcohol may also be related to the level of stress in a given culture. In a pioneering study of 56 primitive societies, Horton (1943) found that the greater the insecurity level of the culture, the greater the amount of alcohol consumption—due allowance having been made for the availability and acceptability of alcohol. Carrying matters a step further, Bales (1946) outlined three cultural factors that appear to play a part in determining the incidence of alcoholism in a given society: (a) the degree of stress and inner tension produced by the culture; (b) the attitudes toward drinking fostered by the culture; and (c) the degree to which the culture provides substitute means of satisfaction and other ways of coping with tension and anxiety. Today it would seem appropriate to include the effects of rapid social change as well as social disintegration. For example, the U.S. Public Health Service's Alaska Native Medical Center has reported excessive drinking to be a major problem among Eskimos in many places in rural Alaska (*Time*, April 22, 1974). This problem is attributed primarily to rapid change in traditional values and way of life, in some cases approaching social disintegration. It is also relevant to note that alcoholism is a major problem in two of the world's superpowers—the United States and the Soviet Union.

Finally, the effect of cultural attitudes toward drinking is well illustrated by Moslems and Mormons, whose religious values prohibit the use of alcohol, and by the Jews, who have traditionally limited its use largely to religious rituals. The incidence of alcoholism among these groups is minimal. On the other hand, the incidence of alcoholism is proportionately higher among the French and Irish, where cultural approbation is greater—in fact, the French appear to have the highest rate of alcoholism in the world, approximating 10 to 12 percent of the population. Thus it appears that religious sanctions and social custom, as well as the degree of socially induced stress, can determine whether alcohol is one of the modes of coping commonly used in any given group or society.

But while there are many reasons why people drink—as well as many conditions that predispose them to and reinforce drinking behavior—the factors that result in a person's becoming an alcoholic are still unknown.

Treatment and outcomes

A multidisciplinary approach to treatment of alcoholism appears to be most effective because alcoholism is a highly complex disorder, requiring flexibility and individualization of treatment procedures. Also, the needs of the alcoholic change as treatment progresses.

Formerly it was considered essential that treatment of an alcoholic take place in an institutional setting, which removed the individual from an aversive life situation and asserted more control over his behavior—particularly his drinking. However, an increasing number of alcoholics are now being treated in community clinics, especially those alcoholics who do not require hospitalization for withdrawal treatment. Halfway houses are being used increasingly to bridge the gap between institutionalization and return to the community and to add to the flexibility of treatment programs.

The key objective of a treatment program is the recovery of the alcoholic: his physical rehabilitation, his control over the craving for liquor, his abstinence from drinking, and his subsequent realization that he can cope with the problems of living and lead a much more rewarding life without alcohol.

Biological measures. Included here are a variety of treatment measures ranging from detoxification procedures to aversion therapy and brain surgery.

1. *Medical measures in detoxification.* In acute intoxication, the initial focus is on detoxification, or elimination of the harmful alcoholic substances from the individual's body; on treatment of withdrawal symptoms; and on a medical regimen for physical rehabilitation. These can best be handled in a hospital or clinic setting, where drugs, such as chlordiazepoxide, have largely revolutionalized the treatment of withdrawal symptoms. Such drugs function to overcome motor excitement, nausea and vomiting, prevent delirium tremens and convulsions, and help alleviate the tension and anxiety associated with withdrawal.

Detoxification is usually followed by psychosocial measures, including family counseling, and the use of resources in the community relating to employment and other aspects of the alcoholic's social readjustment.

It should be noted that although mild tranquilizing drugs are often used in helping the alcoholic sleep and alleviating anxiety during acute reactions, their effectiveness in long-range reduction of the need for alcohol has not been demonstrated. In fact, the alcoholic usually has to abstain from tranquilizers as well as from alcohol, since he tends to misuse the one as well as the other. And under the influence of tranquilizers he may even return to the use of alcohol.

2. *Aversion therapy.* A treatment approach that has received considerable research attention is aversion therapy. The Romans employed this technique by placing a live eel in a cup of wine; forced to drink this unsavory cocktail, the alcoholic presumably would feel disgusted and from then on be repelled by wine.

Today there are a variety of pharmacological and other deterrent measures that can be

---

Problem drinkers on the job

The abuse of alcohol is a major cause of substandard job performance, resulting in absenteeism, poor or defective work output, accidents, and faulty judgment and decisions. It has been estimated that problem drinkers cost business and industry well over 10 billion dollars per year. The cost in the state of Illinois alone approximates 1 billion dollars and the problem in this state is probably not essentially different from that in California, Florida, New York, and many others.*

As a result, increased emphasis has been placed on occupational programs for the early detection and treatment of problem drinkers. The U.S. Dept. of Health, Education, and Welfare (1974) has formulated the following guidelines that are considered essential to the success of such programs:

1. **A written policy** specifying the procedures for early identification, such as frequent absenteeism without justification, and for assurance that employees who seek assistance will not be penalized.

2. **Specific channels for referral,** possibly including referral to a company counselor or rehabilitation program or to appropriate facilities in the community. This requires a program coordinator and close cooperation between industry, government, and public organizations.

3. **Training of managerial and supervisory personnel,** including a basic orientation to the alcohol problem and their roles and responsibilities in implementing the program.

4. **Education of the entire work force** in order to clarify overall company policy, procedures, and the provision that help-without-penalty for problem drinking can be obtained by employees with a drinking problem.

5. **Cooperation between management and labor unions** as well as other employee organizations to ensure needed support for the program, its implementation, and its continuity.

The main thrust of such programs is to detect and correct problem drinking before it progresses to a later stage of alcoholism and is far more difficult and expensive to treat. It has been estimated that the effective implementation of such programs could help over three-fourths of employees with drinking problems overcome them, with tremendous long-range savings to industry, labor unions, and to the employees and their families.

*As described in the Illinois State Plan for the Prevention, Treatment and Control of Alcohol Abuse and Alcoholism, this state instituted in 1974–75 one of the most comprehensive and advanced programs for coping with the problem of alcoholism of any state in the U.S. (Levitt, 1974)

---

employed after detoxification has been accomplished. One approach utilizes the intramuscular injection of emetine hydrochloride, an emetic. Prior to the nausea that results from the injection, the patient is given alcohol, so that the sight, smell, and taste of the beverage become associated with severe retching and vomiting. With repetition, this classical conditioning procedure acts as a strong deterrent to further drinking—probably in part because it adds an immediate and unpleasant physiological consequence to the more general socially aversive consequences of excessive drinking.

Disulpherim (Antabuse), a drug that creates extremely uncomfortable effects when followed by alcohol, may also be administered to prevent an immediate return to drinking. However, such deterrent therapy is seldom advocated as the sole approach, since pharmacological methods alone have not proven effective in treating alcoholism. For example, an alcoholic may simply discontinue the use of Antabuse when he is released from the hospital or clinic, and return to his former drinking patterns. In fact, the primary value of drugs of this type appears to lie in their interruption of the alcoholic cycle for a period of time, during which therapy may be undertaken.

Among other aversive methods has been the use of electroshock, which presumably enables the therapist to maintain more exact control of the aversive stimulus, reduces possible negative side effects and medical complications, and can even be administered by means of a portable apparatus that can be used by the patient for self-reinforcement. Utilizing a procedure which paired electroshock with stimuli associated with drinking, Claeson and Malm (1973) reported successful results—no relapses after 12 months—in 24 percent of a patient group that consisted mostly of advanced-stage alcoholics.

However, in an extensive comparison of available studies on chemical and electroaversive therapy with alcoholics, Davidson (1974) concluded that despite a number of positive results reported in the literature, there were insufficient data to assess the long-range effectiveness of aversion therapy on alcoholism.[3]

---

[3] A review of behavior-therapy approaches to alcoholism can be found in Bassin (1975) and Callner (1975).

3. *Brain surgery.* In a report from Göttingen University in Germany, Fritz Roeder and his associates (1974) stated that

"Our research has revealed that dependence on drugs or alcohol assumes the proportions of a natural urge after a certain period and, like the sexual drive or the urge to eat, is controlled by a certain brain center. Neutralizing this center, which is no more than 50 cubic millimeters in volume, will cure the patient for all time." (p. 106)

No undesirable side effects were reported by these investigators after 22 operations, but such a drastic procedure as brain surgery in the treatment of alcoholism is a highly controversial matter. At this time it would appear to be a treatment of last resort, justified only in the case of patients in the most advanced stages of alcoholism where all other treatment measures have proven ineffective.

In general, biological measures alone have not proven adequate in the treatment of alcoholism, although medical measures focusing on detoxification and general health problems are often of crucial importance in the total treatment program. And aversion therapy does appear to merit further research both as the focus of treatment and as an adjunct to a broader treatment program.

Psychosocial measures. Although individual psychotherapy is sometimes effective, the focus of psychosocial measures in the treatment of alcoholism more often involves group therapy, sociotherapy, and the approach of Alcoholics Anonymous.

1. *Group therapy.* Usually the first and most important step in group therapy is to get the alcoholic to concede that he has a drinking problem and that there are resources available for helping him deal with it. In the rugged give-and-take of group therapy, the alcoholic is usually forced to face his problem and to recognize its possible disastrous consequences. Often, but by no means always, this recognition paves the way for learning more effective methods of coping and other positive steps toward dealing with his drinking problem.

In some instances the spouse of an alcoholic and even his children may be invited to join in

An actor's challenging off-screen role

The veteran actor has had an outstanding record of success in motion pictures, and his credits include starring roles in two top-rated television series; yet the most challenging role of his life has been as protagonist in an intensely personal drama. This story pits him—in a battle waged over many years—against feelings of inferiority and fear. When an increasing reliance on alcohol threatened to prove his undoing, a showdown inevitably occurred.

As he looks back on the unfolding of this drama, the actor reports that during most of his 40-year career he was apprehensive and fearful of failing (Haber, 1971, p. 13). No matter how well he was doing, he felt unworthy of the success he achieved, and worried time after time that his contract would be canceled and that he was "washed up."

Fear and apprehension had their physical symptoms—tension and painful headaches. Turning to alcohol to ease his difficulties, the actor found that drinking itself became a major problem. He now feels that if he had not mastered it, alcoholism would have ruined his career and his health. A warning of this came in 1966 when, touring the country in a play, he suffered a physical collapse (Haber, 1971, p. 13).

The actor spent some 4 years fighting—and finally winning—the battle against alcoholism. He attributes his victory largely to the understanding and emotional support of his wife and to Alcoholics Anonymous (Ellison, 1971, p. 27). However, it is the individual's motivation to change his behavior which is crucially important.

" 'If you suffer enough, you will either jump out the window or do something about it,' " the actor said. " 'In principle, it's the same as a toothache. You can either sit there and suffer or you can go to a dentist.' " (Haber, 1971, p. 13)

Although the actor would probably be the last person to claim that he has completely conquered his feelings of fear and tension, he is no longer so troubled by personal problems or the demands of his profession as to rely on the self-defeating crutch of alcohol.

A young teacher's continuing battle

Mary————— is an intelligent, attractive, elementary-school teacher who is married to a writer some 10 years her senior. At age 29 she had been teaching for 7 years, and as a result of her high degree of competence had been given increasingly difficult classes. Mary stated that after a difficult day at school she had many unresolved problems that she needed to discuss with someone but seldom could do so with her husband, who was under sustained pressure himself and away on assignments a good deal of the time.

Thus, with her husband either away or too busy to talk, Mary turned to alcohol:

"I started having two or three cocktails every evening to 'settle my nerves.' And as the pressure seemed to build up about 3 years ago, I found myself drinking heavily every night to blot out the events of the day. I seemed to have this insatiable craving for alcohol, and I could hardly wait to get home after school to get a drink. And on weekends, I was drunk from Friday evening through Sunday. On Monday mornings, my hangovers were something awful, and I started calling in sick. I knew my drinking was interfering with my work, but I couldn't seem to cope with either. Frankly, I became just plain desperate."

The principal of Mary's school became aware of the problem and suggested that she take a sick leave and obtain medical assistance. Examination revealed serious liver damage, and the physician informed Mary that if she continued to drink she would kill herself. He prescribed Antabuse to help her stop drinking. Although she had the prescription filled, Mary did not take the drug right away: "I was so terrified by what the doctor told me that I just had to have a drink to calm me down. Then I was going to try the Antabuse, I really was." That drink led to 3 days of intoxication; finally, going into convulsions, Mary was hospitalized.

When she improved sufficiently to leave the hospital, Mary volunteered to join a local chapter of Alcoholics Anonymous and to continue seeing a therapist. Her crucial battle with alcoholism was just beginning.

group therapy meetings. In other situations, family treatment is itself the central focus of therapeutic effort. In the latter case, the alcoholic individual is seen as a member of a disturbed family in which he and the other members each have a responsibility for cooperating in treatment. Since family members frequently have been the persons most victimized by the alcoholic's addiction, they often tend to be judgmental and punitive, and the alcoholic, who has already passed harsh judgment on himself, tolerates this further source of devaluation very poorly. In other instances, members of a family may unwittingly encourage an alcoholic to remain addicted, as, for example, when a wife with a need to dominate her husband finds that a continually drunken and remorseful spouse best meets her need.

2. *Sociotherapy.* As with other serious maladaptive behaviors, the total treatment program in alcoholism usually requires measures to alleviate the patient's aversive life situation. Often as a result of his drinking he has become estranged from family and friends, and his job has been lost or jeopardized. Typically the reaction of those around him is not likely to be as understanding or supportive as it would have been had he had a physical illness of comparable magnitude. Simply helping him learn more effective coping techniques may not be enough if his social environment remains hostile and threatening. For alcoholics who have been hospitalized, halfway houses—designed to assist the alcoholic in his return to family and community—are often an important adjunct to the total treatment program.

Relapses and continued deterioration are generally associated with a lack of close relationships with family or friends, or with living in a high-risk environment. In a study of black male alcoholics, for example, King et al. (1969) have pointed to the ghetto cycle of broken homes, delinquency, underemployment, alcoholism, and, once again, broken homes. In general, it would appear unlikely that an alcoholic will remain abstinent after treatment unless the negative psychosocial reinforcements that operated in the past are dealt with.

As a consequence, the concept of a "community reinforcement approach" has de-veloped which focuses on helping problem drinkers achieve more satisfactory adjustments in key areas of their lives, such as marriage, work, and social relations. Unfortunately, it is not always possible to make needed changes in the individual's aversive life situation. But this approach seems to offer a promising conceptual basis for the direction of future treatment programs.

3. *Alcoholics Anonymous.* A practical approach to the problem of alcoholism which has met with considerable success is that of *Alcoholics Anonymous* (AA). This organization was started in 1935 by two individuals, Dr. Bob and Bill W. in Akron, Ohio. Bill W. recovered from alcoholism through a "fundamental spiritual change," and immediately sought out Dr. Bob, who, with Bill's assistance, achieved recovery. Both in turn began to help other alcoholics. Since that time AA has grown to over 10,000 groups with over a million members. In addition, AA groups have been established in many other countries of the world.

Alcoholics Anonymous operates primarily as a psychotherapeutic program in which both person-to-person and group relationships are emphasized. AA accepts both teen-agers and adults with drinking problems, has no dues or fees, does not keep records or case histories, does not participate in political causes, and is not affiliated with any religious sect, although spiritual development is a key aspect of its treatment approach. To ensure the anonymity of the alcoholic, only first names are used. Meetings are devoted partly to social activities, but consist mainly of discussions of the participants' problems with alcohol, often with testimonials from these who have recovered from alcoholism. Here, recovered members usually contrast their lives before they broke their alcohol dependence with the lives they now live without alcohol.[4]

An important strength of AA is that it lifts the burden of personal responsibility from the shoulders of the alcoholic by helping him realize that alcoholism, like many other problems,

---

[4]The term *alcoholic* is used by AA and its affiliates to refer either to individuals who currently are drinking excessively or to persons who have recovered from such a problem but must continue to abstain from alcohol consumption in the future.

is bigger than he. Henceforth, he can see himself not as weak-willed or lacking in moral strength, but rather simply as having an affliction—he cannot drink—just as other people may not be able to tolerate certain types of medication. By mutual help and reassurance through participation in a group composed of others who have shared similar experiences, many an alcoholic acquires insight into his problems, a new sense of purpose, greater ego strength, and more effective coping techniques. And, of course, continued participation in the group helps prevent the crisis of a relapse. For persons in hospitals and halfway houses, there are usually AA groups available in which the individual may participate.

An affiliated movement, Al-Anon Family Groups, has been established for the relatives of alcoholics. By meeting together and sharing their common problems and experiences, the wives or husbands of alcoholics are helped to better understand the nature of alcoholism, the effects of the spouses' drinking upon them personally, and the best techniques for helping their alcoholic mates, as well as themselves. They learn to understand, for example, the necessity of their alcoholic spouses' attendance at AA meetings several nights a week on a sustained basis if relapses are to be prevented. They are also helped to see their mates in a less "drinking-wife-" or "drinking-husband-oriented" perspective, and they are provided with suggestions for reasonable courses of action. Finally, they are relieved from guilt feelings over being the causes of their spouses' drinking, for they come to realize that many factors may contribute. In addition, it is made clear that the initial choice of using alcohol as a coping mechanism lies with the individual.

An outgrowth of the Al-Anon movement has been the Ala-teen movement, designed to help teen-agers understand the drinking problems of their parents and find support in a group setting.

Results of treatment. Statistics on the long-range outcome of treatment for alcoholism vary considerably, depending both on the population studied and the treatment facilities and procedures employed. They range from a very low rate of success for hardcore, Skid

---

Alcoholics treated by "individualized behavior therapy"

Sobell and Sobell (1973) have described the range of procedures utilized in what they term "individualized behavior therapy" for alcoholics. This treatment used both individual and group procedures but attempted to tailor the treatment to meet the needs of each particular patient.

"Procedures included subjects being videotaped while intoxicated under experimental conditions, providing subjects when sober with videotape self-confrontation of their own drunken behaviors, shaping of appropriate controlled drinking or non-drinking behaviors respective to treatment goal, the availability of alcoholic beverages throughout treatment, and behavior change training sessions. 'Behavior change training sessions' is a summary phrase to describe sessions which concentrated upon determining setting events for each subject's drinking, training the subject to generate a series of possible alternative responses to those situations, to evaluate each of the delineated alternatives for potential short- and long-term consequences, and then to exercise the response which could be expected to incur the fewest self-destructive long-term consequences. Behavior change training sessions consisted of discussion, role playing, assertiveness training, role reversal or other appropriate behavioral techniques, respective to the topics under consideration during a given session." (p. 601)

The subjects consisted of 70 male alcoholics in a state mental hospital who were treated for a period of one year. The subjects were initially divided into two groups in terms of treatment goals, either controlled drinking or complete abstinence, whichever was considered most appropriate for the given subject. Then the subjects from each group were assigned at random to either the experimental group, which participated in the program described above, or a control group, which received routine hospital treatment. The subjects were then followed up during a six-month post-discharge period; it was found that "experimental subjects functioned significantly better than control subjects, regardless of treatment goal" (p. 601).

A critical review of research studies dealing with the results of behavior therapy for drug abuse—including counterconditioning, aversion therapy, and positive reinforcement—may be found in Callner (1975).

Row alcoholics to recoveries of 70 to 90 percent where modern treatment and aftercare procedures are utilized. The outcome is most likely to be favorable when the drinking problem is discovered early, the individual realizes that he needs help with his drinking, and adequate treatment facilities are available.

Over the past few years, great progress has been made in the treatment of alcoholism by the introduction of employee programs in both government and industry. Such programs have proven highly effective in detecting drinking problems early, in referring drinkers for treatment, and in ensuring the effectiveness of aftercare procedures. When it is realized that an estimated 5 percent of the nation's work force are alcoholics and an additional 5 percent are considered alcohol abusers, it is apparent that such programs can make a major impact in coping with the alcohol problem in our society (Levitt, 1974).

Unfortunately, many alcoholics refuse to admit they have an alcohol problem and seek assistance before they "hit bottom"—which in many cases is the grave. Nor is there a miracle "cure" for those who do seek treatment. Nevertheless, it would appear that for the great majority of alcoholics there is a treatment program that can be tailored to the individual's needs and provide him with a good chance for recovery.

New hope for alcoholics. During the 1970s we have witnessed increasing national momentum for efforts to combat alcoholism. One of the most significant early advances was the passage of congressional legislation in 1970 providing for the establishment of The National Institute on Alcohol Abuse and Alcoholism. Some 1000 or more federally supported community alcoholism centers throughout the nation were projected by the Institute during its first 10 years (Chafetz, 1971). Although this goal is still far from achievement, it has led to substantial federal funding for rehabilitation centers and halfway houses that would probably never have been established without federal assistance. The objectives of the Institute include improved health insurance for alcoholism, fostering research aimed at improving programs for the treatment and prevention of alcoholism, and the establishment of the best possible treatment services for alcoholics on a community level.

Following the gradual change of attitude toward alcoholism in the United States, many states have enacted laws removing drunkenness—but not drunk driving—from the criminal statutes. Consequently many problem drinkers are not hauled off to jail to dry out in a "drunk tank" but are taken to a hospital or Local Alcoholism Reception Center (LARC). Here the individual is detoxified, if it is medically indicated, and then transferred to another facility for further treatment. This approach makes it possible to reach many problem drinkers early and to assist them with conditions in their life situations, such as job and marital difficulties, which may be significant factors in their alcohol abuse or alcoholism.

Pending possible breakthroughs in research leading to biochemical methods of prevention, programs designed to cope with the problem of alcohol abuse and alcoholism must rely heavily on educational measures concerning the use of alcohol and its dangers. The long-range objective of such programs is not to prevent the use of alcohol but to help people learn to drink in moderation and under appropriate social conditions.

Drug Abuse and Drug Dependence

The earliest records contain not only references to human familiarity with alcoholic beverages but to a variety of other psychoactive drugs—drugs that affect mental processes. Hallucinogenic drugs were made from a variety of mushrooms by paleolithic peoples in Siberia and the Far East to induce cheer, intoxication, and courage during tribal clashes. The substances used apparently had many of the effects of modern hallucinogenic drugs, such as LSD (Brekhman & Sam, 1967). Various narcotic drugs, such as hyoscyamus and hemlock, are also known to have been used in ancient times.

Aside from alcohol, the psychoactive drugs most commonly associated with abuse and dependence in our society appear to be (a) narcotics, such as opium and its derivatives; (b) sedatives, such as barbiturates; (c) stimulants, such as amphetamines; (d) mild tranquilizers, such as meprobamates; and (e) hallucinogens, such as marijuana. Caffeine and nicotine are also drugs of dependence, but they are not included in the APA classification, and we shall not deal with them in our present discussion.

Drug abuse and dependence may occur at any age, but seem to be most common during adolescence and young adulthood. Clinical pictures vary markedly, depending on the type, amount, and duration of drug usage, the physiological and psychological makeup of the individual, and, in some instances, the social setting in which the drug experience occurs. Thus it appears most useful to deal separately with some of the drugs more commonly associated with abuse and dependence.[5] For historical reasons, we shall first deal with opium and its derivatives.

Opium and its derivatives

People have used opium and its derivatives for over 5000 years. Galen (A.D. 130–201) considered theriaca, whose principal ingredient was opium, to be a veritable panacea:

"It resists poison and venomous bites, cures inveterate headache, vertigo, deafness, epilepsy, apoplexy, dimness of sight, loss of voice, asthma, coughs of all kinds, spitting of blood, tightness of breath, colic, the iliac poisons, jaundice, hardness of the spleen, stone, urinary complaints, fevers, dropsies, leprosies, the trouble to which women are subject, melancholy and all pestilences."

Even today, opium derivatives are still used for some of the conditions Galen mentioned.

Opium is a mixture of about eighteen nitrogen-containing agents known as *alkaloids*. In 1805 it was found that the alkaloid present in the largest amount (10 to 15 percent) was a bitter-tasting powder that proved to be a powerful sedative and pain reliever; it was thus named *morphine* (after Morpheus, god of sleep in Greek mythology). After introduction of the hypodermic needle in America about 1856, morphine was widely administered to soldiers during the Civil War, not only to those wounded in battle but also to those suffering from dysentery. As a consequence, large numbers of Civil War veterans returned to civilian life addicted to the drug, a condition euphemistically referred to as "Soldier's Illness."

Scientists concerned with the addictive properties of morphine hypothesized that one part of the morphine molecule might be responsible for its analgesic properties[6] and another for its addictiveness. Thus, at about the turn

---

[5]It may be noted that the most common function of all drugs—even those which are medically prescribed—is their alteration of cell metabolism. Typically, this change in cellular action is a temporary one designed to help combat the patient's problem. Nevertheless, the changes that drugs bring about in "target cells" are in a direction *away from normal functioning*. Thus, medication does not result in cells performing "better than ever." Of course, some drugs—such as hormones—do replace or supplement substances which are normally present in the body, and in this sense, they may improve the normal functioning of various organs and cells; but in general, drugs tend to block some important functions of cells. Hence, the general rule of thumb is the fewer drugs the better.

[6]An analgesic is a drug that alleviates pain without inducing unconsciousness.

of the century it was discovered that if morphine were treated by an inexpensive and readily available chemical called *acetic anhydride,* it could be converted into another powerful analgesic called *heroin.* Heroin was hailed with enthusiasm by its discoverer, Heinrich Dreser[7] (Boehm, 1968). Leading scientists of his time agreed with Dresser on the merits of heroin, and the drug came to be widely prescribed in place of morphine for pain relief and related medicinal purposes. However, heroin turned out to be a cruel disappointment, for it proved to be an even more dangerous drug than morphine, acting more rapidly and more intensely and being equally if not more addictive. Eventually heroin was removed from use in medical practice.

As it became apparent that opium and its derivatives—including codeine, which is used in some cough syrups—were perilously addictive, the United States Congress enacted the Harrison Act in 1914. Under this and later acts, the unauthorized sale and dispensation of narcotic drugs became a federal offense; physicians and pharmacists were held accountable for each dose they dispensed. Thus, overnight, the role of a narcotic user changed from that of addict—which was considered a vice, but tolerated—to that of criminal. And now, unable to obtain narcotic drugs through legal sources, many turned to illegal ones, and eventually to other criminal acts as a means of maintaining their suddenly expensive drug supply. The number of addicts declined, however, and remained at about 40,000 for several decades.

During the 1960s there was a rapid increase in the use of heroin—the peak year being 1969 when there were an estimated 150,000 or more addicts in New York City alone, and some 300,000 in the country as a whole—and public attention was focused on the "heroin epidemic" (Bazell, 1973; Greene & Dupont, 1974). Largely as a result of strict control by federal and local authorities, programs of public education, and more effective methods of detection and treatment, heroin addiction has markedly decreased during the 1970s. Beginning about 1974, however, there appears

to have been a tendency for heroin usage to spread from large cities to rural communities (DuPont, 1975; Wilson, 1975).

Effects of morphine and heroin. Morphine and heroin are commonly introduced into the body by smoking, "snorting" (inhaling the bitter powder), eating, "skin popping," and "mainlining," the last two being methods of introducing the drug via hypodermic injection. *Skin popping* refers to injecting the liquified drug just beneath the skin, and *mainlining* to injecting the drug into the bloodstream. In the United States, the young addict usually progresses from snorting to mainlining.

Among the immediate effects of heroin is a euphoric spasm of 60 seconds or so, which many addicts compare to a sexual orgasm. This is followed by a "high," during which the addict typically is in a lethargic, withdrawn state in which bodily needs, including those for food and sex, are markedly diminished; pleasant feelings of relaxation, euphoria, and reverie tend to dominate. These effects last from 4 to 6 hours and are followed—in addicts—by a negative phase which produces a desire for more of the drug.

The use of opium derivatives over a period of time usually results in a physiological craving for the drug. The time required to establish the drug habit varies, but it has been estimated that continual usage over a period of 30 days or longer is sufficient. The user will then find that he has become physiologically dependent upon the drug, in the sense that he will feel physically ill when he does not take it. In addition, the user of opium derivatives gradually builds up a tolerance to the drug so that ever larger amounts are needed for the desired effects.

When persons addicted to opiates do not get a dose of the drug within approximately 8 hours, they start to experience *withdrawal symptoms.* The character and severity of the reaction depends on many factors, including the amount of the narcotic habitually used, the intervals between doses, the duration of the addiction, and especially the addict's health and personality.

Contrary to popular opinion, withdrawal from heroin is not always dangerous or even very painful. Many addicted persons are able

---

[7]Dreser shortly thereafter introduced aspirin—an effective but nonaddictive analgesic for relief of minor pains.

to withdraw without assistance. However, in some instances withdrawal is both an agonizing and perilous experience.

Initial symptoms usually include a running nose, tearing eyes, perspiration, restlessness, increased respiration rate, and an intensified desire for the drug. As time passes, the symptoms become more severe, usually reaching a peak in about 40 hours. Typically there may be chilliness alternating with vasomotor disturbances of flushing and excessive sweating (this may result in marked pilomotor activity so that the skin of the addict comes to resemble that of a plucked turkey—a condition commonly described as "goose flesh"), vomiting, diarrhea, abdominal cramps, pains in the back and extremities, severe headache, marked tremors, and insomnia in varying degrees. Beset by these discomforts, the individual refuses food and water, and this, coupled with the vomiting, sweating, and diarrhea, results in dehydration and weight losses of as much as 5 to 15 pounds in a day. Occasionally there may be delirium, hallucinations, and manic activity. Cardiovascular collapse may also occur, and may result in death. If morphine is administered at any point along the way, the subjective distress of the addict ends, and physiological equanimity is restored in about 5 to 30 minutes.

Usually the withdrawal symptoms will be definitely on the decline by the third or fourth day, and by the seventh or eighth day will have disappeared. As his symptoms subside, the individual resumes normal eating and drinking, and rapidly regains his lost weight. An additional hazard now exists in that after withdrawal symptoms have ceased, the individual's former tolerance for the drug also will have disappeared, and death may now result from his taking the former large dosage of the drug.

In rare cases an individual will have enough self-control to use opiates without allowing them to interfere with his work and ruin his life, but the danger in the use of such drugs—especially heroin—is very great. Tolerance may be built up so rapidly that larger and more expensive amounts of the drug are soon required, and withdrawal treatments are likely to do little to end the problem. Most addicted individuals—even after withdrawal—find it

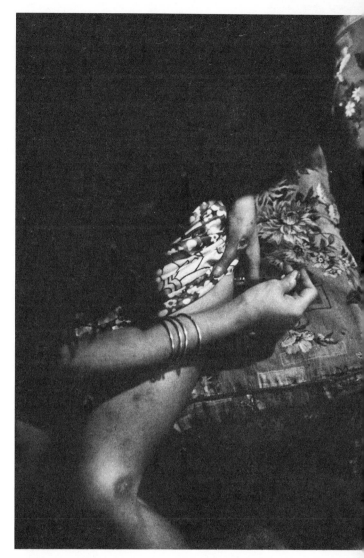

Unable to find any more functioning surface veins into which she can inject heroin, a 26-year-old addict (who later died of an overdose) shoots the drug directly into skin tissue. The abscesses were caused by impure drugs and dirty needles.

extremely difficult to break their dependency. Biochemical alterations appear to be at least partly responsible for the individual's continued craving for the narcotic drug even after completion of the withdrawal treatment.

Typically, the life of a narcotic addict becomes increasingly centered around obtaining and using drugs, so the addiction usually leads to socially maladaptive behavior as the individual is eventually forced to lie, steal, and associate with undesirable companions in order to maintain his supply of the drug. Contrary to the common picture of a "dope fiend," however, most narcotic addicts are not major criminals. Those who have police records usually confine themselves to petty offenses, and very few commit crimes of violence. Female addicts, for example, commonly turn to prostitution as a means of financing their addiction.

Along with the lowering of ethical and moral restraints, addiction has adverse physical effects on the well-being of the individual. Lack of an adequate diet may lead to ill health and increased susceptibility to a variety of physical ailments. The use of unsterile equipment may also lead to a variety of ailments, including liver damage from hepatitis. In addition, the use of such a potent drug as heroin without medical supervision and government controls to assure its strength and purity can result in perilous overdosage. If the heroin user injects too much, his respiration is slowed, which can cause coma and death. In 1969 in New York City—a peak year for heroin addiction in the United States—there were more than 900 deaths associated with heroin usage, 224 of which were of teen-agers who died from overdoses or heroin-related infections (Abelson, 1970).

Usually, however, addiction to opiates leads to a more gradual deterioration of well-being. The ill health and general personality deterioration often found in opium addiction do not result directly from the pharmacological effects of the drug, but are generally the product of the sacrifice of money, proper diet, social position, and self-respect, as the addict becomes more desperate in his efforts to procure his required daily dosage. On the other hand, narcotic addicts with financial means to maintain both a balanced diet and an ade-

quate supply of the drug without resorting to criminal behavior may maintain their drug dependence over many years without any appreciable symptoms of either physical or mental disorders.

The following case history gives a brief view of a teen-age addict arrested by the Los Angeles police.

"The boy was seventeen years of age. He had a pleasant way of talking, punctuating his remarks with an occasional smile. His excellent grammar and quiet manners indicated a good home and background. . . .

"Is this a 'dope fiend'? This is an inaccurate . . . term, but by all common standards and definitions the answer would be yes. Gene R____, the boy in custody, is a confirmed heroin addict, a 'mainliner' injecting heroin directly into the main blood vessels of his arm. His body requires five 'pops' every day, costing him from $20 to $25 every twenty-four hours. He has managed to earn this amount by 'introducing' other teen-agers into the mysteries of . . . heroin. The police report five separate cases where Gene R____ has inflicted the dope habit upon 'girl friends,' all minors. Investigation indicates that four of these girls now pay for his, and their own, drug supply by means of prostitution." (Los Angeles Police Department, 1952, pp. 3–4)

This case, reported over two decades ago, is of particular interest, since it would still appear typical of the narcotic scene among middle-class teen-agers who become addicted to heroin today—except that the daily cost of maintaining the habit has greatly increased.

Causal factors in narcotic addiction. There is no single causal pattern that fits all narcotic addiction. In addition to the physiological and psychological dependence that itself becomes a driving factor, life stress, personal maladjustment, and sociocultural conditions enter into the total causal picture.

Admittedly, the following categorization of causal factors is somewhat artificial, but it does provide a convenient means of ordering our discussion.

1. *Neural bases for physiological addiction.* Research teams have isolated and studied receptor sites for narcotic drugs in the brain (Pert & Snyder, 1973; Goldstein, et al., 1974). Such receptor sites are specific nerve cells into which given psychoactive drugs fit like

keys into the proper lock. This interaction of drug and brain cell apparently results in the action of the drug and in the case of narcotic drugs leads to addiction. Preliminary findings indicate that there are two or more receptor sites mediating the effects of these drugs; apparently one site mediates the pleasurable euphoria, while another mediates the pain-killing action.

Although these research findings were made on the brains of mice, researchers believe that similar receptor sites are involved in human addiction. Hopefully, by studying the changes in receptor sites resulting from the use of addictive drugs, it will be possible to understand what actually happens in addiction as well as to provide a basis for the development of treatment procedures. For example, it might be possible to correct the changes produced by narcotic drugs in receptor sites, or a less harmful drug that has a greater affinity for the opiate receptor site could possibly be used as an antagonist to heroin.

2. *Addiction associated with the relief of pain and with professional persons who have access to narcotic drugs.* Many patients are given narcotic drugs, such as morphine, to relieve pain during illness or following surgery or serious injury. The vast majority of such patients never develop an addiction, and when their medication is discontinued, they do not again resort to the use of morphine. Those narcotic addicts who blame their addiction on the fact that they used drugs during an illness usually show personality deficiencies which predisposed them to the use of drugs—such as immaturity, low frustration tolerance, and the ability to distort and evade reality by way of a flight into drug-induced fantasy.

Occasionally, professional people entrusted with the handling of narcotics, such as doctors and nurses, become addicted to these drugs. They may be tempted by curiosity, but more commonly their drug use appears to represent an attempt to ward off anxiety or depression induced by some environmental stress, such as divorce. These persons get little or no emotional satisfaction from the drug; they are not psychologically dependent on its use as a long-range means of escaping unpleasant reality. When their traumatic life situation has improved and their physiological

---

Tolerance in drug usage

Tolerance to a drug develops in an individual when the same dosage produces decreased effects after repeated use. The degree of tolerance and the rate at which it is acquired depend on the specific drug, the person using it, and the frequency and magnitude of its use. Dosages of drugs that produce tolerance—e.g., alcohol, barbiturates, and heroin—tend to be increased by persons using them as their tolerance to a particular drug increases.

The mechanisms by which physiological tolerance is acquired are not fully understood. There is some evidence that the central nervous system develops some degree of tolerance for various drugs; but, in addition, learning may play an important role in changing an individual's attitude toward a drug and his response to it after repeated use. Thus with some drugs, such as marijuana, the individual may learn to control some effects and maintain relatively normal functioning.

Two aspects of drug tolerance that merit brief mention are "cross-tolerance" and "reverse tolerance." "Cross-tolerance" may occur when the individual who develops tolerance to one drug also shows tolerance to drugs whose effects are similar. A heavy drinker, for example, may not only show tolerance to alcohol but also to barbiturates, tranquilizers, and anesthetics. "Reverse tolerance" may occur in the use of some drugs, such as the psychedelics; here, with experience, the desired effects may be achieved through the use of smaller doses. Both physiological and psychological (learning) factors appear to play a significant part in this process.

Based on Commission of Inquiry into the Non-Medical Use of Drugs (1970).

---

dependence on the drug is broken, they usually feel no strong desire to return to its use. Fortunately, the addiction of professional persons has become far less common since the advent of tranquilizing and antidepressant drugs.

3. *Addiction associated with psychopathology.* During the 1960s, studies placed strong emphasis on the high incidence of psychopathic personalities among heroin addicts. In a comparison between a group of 45 young institutionalized male addicts and a control group of nonaddicts, Gilbert and Lombard (1967) found that distinguishing features were "the addict's psychopathic traits, his depression, tension, insecurity, and feelings of inadequacy, and his difficulty in forming warm and lasting interpersonal relationships" (p. 536). Similarly, in a study of 112 drug abusers admitted to Bellevue Psychiatric Hospital in New York, Hekimian and Gershon (1968) found that heroin users were usually psychopaths.

Although very little research has been done on female narcotics users, Chinlund (1969) reported a sociopathic personality pattern as being characteristic of female addicts studied over a period of seven years in New York City. He concluded that a female addict has three key goals: (a) a conscious wish to lose control of her drug usage so that she can blame her failures on the drug; (b) a desire to obliterate all sense of time—to blot out what is happening in her frustrating life situation; and (c) a need to deny cause-and-effect relationships in her life—for example, the relationship between sexual intercourse and pregnancy.

While the thrill-seeking and uninhibited behavior characteristic of psychopathic personalities appears to render them particularly vulnerable to drug dependence, including heroin addiction, the picture of the typical addict seems to have changed during the 1970s. In an extensive study, Berzins et al. (1974) assessed the personality makeup of 1500 hospitalized opiate addicts, 750 males and 750 females. They found that the majority of addicts—60 percent—showed a variety of emotional disturbances and related characteristics that did not fit any major personality profiles. The remaining 40 percent of the subjects, however, could be classified into two groups:

"Type I subjects were characterized by high levels of subjective distress, nonconformity, and confused thinking; they attributed a wide range of psychopathology to themselves and also deprecated themselves *as addicts.* In contrast . . . Type II subjects appeared self-satisfied both as persons and as addicts." (p. 72)

In fact, it was concluded that had Type II subjects not been hospitalized for opiate addiction, they might have been regarded as above average in personal-social competence.

On the basis of their findings, Berzins and his associates speculated that "Type I subjects may employ drugs to control or attenuate feelings of anxiety, depression, distress, and so on, while Type II subjects may use them to enhance hedonistic pursuits or, possibly, to reduce feelings of hostility and resentment" (p. 72). Type I subjects constituted 33 percent of the total addict population and were considered more amenable to treatment than Type II subjects who constituted only 7 percent of the total addict population. Although Type II subjects were not labeled as psychopaths, they did evidence many characteristics of this personality disorder.

In general, it would appear that narcotic dependence tends to develop in association with antisocial personality and other psychopathology. As in the case of alcoholism, however, it seems essential to exercise caution in distinguishing between personality traits before and after addiction, for the high incidence of psychopathology among narcotic addicts may result in part from the long-term effects of addiction rather than precede it.

4. *Addiction associated with sociocultural factors.* The influence of sociocultural factors in drug dependence, including alcohol and opium addiction, is well depicted in the experience of the Meo, a tribal people who inhabit the mountains of several countries in Southeast Asia (Westermeyer, 1971). Although alcohol is used, it is employed with rigid restraints, and alcoholism does not occur. On the other hand, opium is a major cash crop and is widely used among the Meo, and opium addiction does occur. Westermeyer (1974) also reported the widespread use of opium in Laos. He noted that "Most Western observers have depicted the Oriental opium den as an unsavory place that leads only to ruin" (p. 237), but found, however, that in Laos the opium den tended to play about the same role as the neighborhood tavern in Western countries.

In our own society there are no opium dens, but there are so-called narcotic subcultures, in which it is easier for an addict to obtain drugs and to protect himself against the sanctions of society. Apparently the majority of narcotic addicts do participate in the drug culture. The decision to join this culture has important implications for the future life of an addict, for from that point on he will center his activities around his role of drug user. In short, his addiction becomes his way of life.

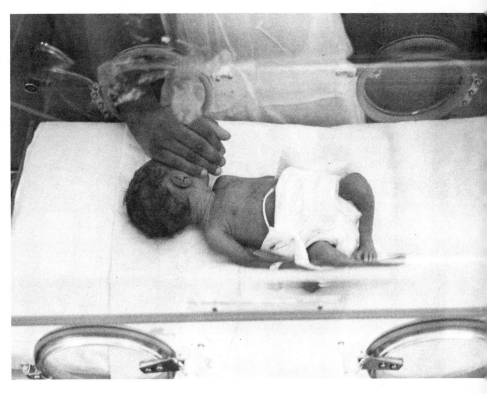

Infants such as this one, whose mothers are dependent on narcotic drugs such as opium, morphine, heroin, or methadone, may be born addicted themselves and show serious withdrawal symptoms from birth to about 4 days. If the problem is not detected and treated, the infant may die of a convulsion or of dehydration. There have been no follow-up studies to determine how prenatal exposure to narcotics may influence later development and behavior.

With time, most young addicts who join the drug culture become increasingly withdrawn, indifferent to their friends (except those in the drug group), and apathetic about sexual activity. They are likely to abandon scholastic and athletic endeavors, and to show a marked reduction in competitive and achievement strivings. Most of these addicts appear to lack good sex-role identification, and to experience feelings of inadequacy when confronted with the demands of adulthood. While feeling progressively isolated from the broader culture, they experience a bolstering of their feelings of group belongingness by continued association with the addict milieu; at the same time, they come to view drugs both as a means of revolt against constituted authority and conventional values and as a device for alleviating personal anxieties and tensions.

But even as a member of this subculture, an addict finds his drug habit costly, and he almost inevitably is forced into various types of criminal activity to finance it. In the late 1960s, it was estimated that heroin users alone cost New York City over 3.5 billion dollars per year, largely from such crimes as theft, burglary, and shoplifting (Hekimian & Gershon, 1968). However, for reasons which are not entirely clear, there appears to have been a decrease in crimes committed by heroin addicts. And although heroin is still widely used in the ghetto areas of large cities—and appears to be spreading to some smaller communities—the most popular drug now is alcohol.

Treatment and outcomes. Treatment for heroin addiction is initially similar to that for alcoholism, in that it involves building up the addict both physically and psychologically and helping him through the withdrawal period. Often the discomfort of the latter is greatly feared by the addict; however, withdrawal in a hospital setting is not abrupt, but usually involves the administration of a synthetic drug that eases the distress.

After withdrawal has been completed, treatment focuses on helping the former addict

Drug Abuse and Drug Dependence   **441**

make an adequate adjustment to his community and abstain from the further use of narcotics. Traditionally, however, the prognosis has been unfavorable. Despite the use of counseling, group therapy, and other rehabilitative measures, only about 15 percent of persons formerly discharged from U.S. Public Health Service Hospitals did not become readdicted, and comparable findings were reported for other treatment facilities. These findings led to the realization that withdrawal does not remove the craving for heroin and that a key target in treatment must be the alleviation of this craving.

An approach to dealing with the problem of physiological craving for heroin was pioneered by a research team at the Rockefeller University in New York. Their approach involved the use of methadone in conjunction with a rehabilitation program (counseling, group therapy, and other procedures) directed toward the "total resocialization" of the addict (Dole & Nyswander, 1967; Dole, Nyswander, & Warner, 1968). Methadone hydrochloride is a synthetic narcotic which is related to heroin and is equally addictive physiologically. Its usefulness in treatment lies in the fact that it satisfies the addict's craving for heroin without producing serious psychological impairment. For example, of 863 volunteer addicts—all of whom were between the ages of 20 and 50, had injected heroin for at least four years, and had failed in other treatment programs—750 stopped using heroin. Although they were now methadone addicts, they were nonetheless productive and responsible members of their communities. The results of a four-year trial showed that nine out of ten former heroin addicts abstained from the further use of heroin—a figure that contrasts sharply with the poor record of success achieved by most earlier treatment programs.

In evaluating the preceding study, it may be pointed out that the average age of addicts in the program was older than that of the addict population in general, and participants were perhaps more strongly motivated to undertake treatment than are younger heroin addicts. In a second study of criminal addicts, however, Dole and Robinson (1969) randomly selected 12 who were prison inmates to receive the methadone treatment, as well as a control group of 16 convict-addicts. All had been addicts for at least five years, had had five or more jail sentences, and had volunteered for treatment. The results were impressive: none of the 12 addicts who were treated with methadone became readdicted to heroin, and 9 had no criminal convictions during a 50-week follow-up period. Of the 16 controls, by contrast, all but one became readdicted after release from jail, and 15 were also convicted of crimes committed during the same follow-up period. These investigators concluded that at least 50 percent of all criminal addicts could be rehabilitated permanently by the methadone program of treatment. Similarly, in a five-year study of a methadone maintenance program involving over 2000 narcotic addicts, Gearing (1970) reported that previous antisocial behavior, as measured by arrests and related criteria, was eliminated or markedly reduced, and that there was a corresponding increase in employment and social adjustment.

As a result of such impressive preliminary findings, the federal government in 1972 agreed to a licensing program for physicians and clinics utilizing methadone in the treatment of narcotic addicts. But as methadone treatment became more widely employed, it became apparent that methadone alone does not appear sufficient to rehabilitate narcotic addicts. Although some former addicts do make good adjustments with little ancillary treatment, most require vocational training and other supportive measures if the overall treatment program is to prove effective. It would also appear essential that methadone treatment be monitored very carefully, since there are a limited but rising number of reports of liver damage and other undesirable side effects following the long-term use of methadone (Thornton & Thornton, 1974). In addition, it is important to prevent the illicit use of methadone, since there are serious dangers—including overdosage—when it is not used in a well-organized heroin treatment program (Greene, Brown, & DuPont, 1975).

There is also the ethical problem of weaning the addict from heroin only to addict him to another narcotic drug that may be required for life. A response might be that addicts on methadone can function normally and hold jobs—not possible for most heroin addicts. In addition, methadone is available legally, and its quality is controlled by government standards. Nor is it necessary to increase the dosage over time. In fact some patients can eventually be taken off methadone without danger of relapse to heroin addiction. Many heroin addicts can also be treated without undergoing initial hospitalization, and during treatment are able to hold jobs and function in their family and community settings.[8]

In addition to methadone, other drugs not considered narcotics are being tested as possible "antagonists" for overcoming a craving for heroin. These drugs are still in the experimental stage, but some appear capable of suppressing the craving for a much longer period of time than does methadone. In any event, we appear to be achieving a major breakthrough in the treatment of narcotic addiction through the methadone-maintenance approach.

The barbiturates

In the 1850s, new chemical compounds known as *bromides* were introduced. They immediately became popular as sedatives and were taken by millions of people. But with use came abuse; and the excessive consumption of bromides resulted in toxic psychoses—involving delusions, hallucinations, and a variety of neurological disturbances—which for a time became a leading cause of admissions to mental hospitals (Jarvik, 1967). Misuse of bromides waned in the 1930s, however, when more powerful sedatives, called *barbiturates,* were introduced.

While the barbiturates have their legitimate medical uses, they are extremely dangerous drugs commonly associated with both physiological and psychological dependence as well as with lethal overdoses (American Psychiatric Association, 1974).

The result of an 18-month survey by a subcommittee of the United States Senate, released in 1972, indicated that as many as 1

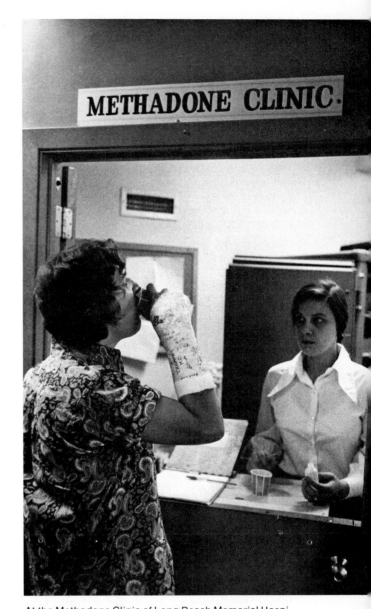

At the Methadone Clinic of Long Beach Memorial Hospital in New York, a patient drinks his methadone medication under the supervision of a nurse. Each patient enrolled at the clinic—which has a complete drug therapy program—has his own bottle with his name on it. After the patient has had his dosage the bottle is refilled by the nurse and stored in a safe until the next visit.

[8]The legalization of narcotics for addicts in England, under medical supervision, is a policy which has resulted in a marked reduction in known cases of addiction. The question of whether such a program is feasible or desirable in the United States has not been resolved.

Drug Abuse and Drug Dependence   **443**

Judi A. was a young attractive girl from a middle-class family who apparently was seeking something that eluded her. She died of an overdose of barbiturates. The newspaper account of her death began with a statement from the autopsy report:

"The unembalmed body for examination is that of a well-developed, well-nourished Caucasian female measuring 173 cm. (68 inches), weighing 100-110 pounds, with dark blonde hair, blue eyes, and consistent in appearance with the stated age of . . . .

"Judi A. had lived only 17 years, 5 months and 27 days before her nude body was found on a grimy bed which had been made up on the floor of a rundown apartment in Newport Beach [California].

"The inside of her mouth and her tongue were a bright red. The fingers of both hands were stained with the same color . . . A small pill was found on the bed near the body, another was discovered on the floor.

"Judi's death was classified as an accident because there was no evidence that she intended to take her own life. Actually it was about as accidental as if she'd killed herself while playing Russian roulette.

"Judi didn't intentionally take too many reds. She was familiar with them, had taken them before, knew what to expect. She'd even had an earlier scare from a nonfatal overdose.

"But her mind, clouded by the first few pills, lost count and she ingested a lethal number. She was dying before she swallowed the last pill. . . ." (Hazlett, 1971, p. 1)

A complete investigation was ordered, in which it came to light that Judi took drugs when she was unhappy at home, apparently often feeling unloved and unwanted. Following the breakup of her parents' marriage, she lived with her grandparents—neither of whom seemed to have been aware of her drug problem and hence had not attempted to help her with it.

Judi escalated the odds against herself by combining barbiturates with alcohol. Her friends said she was not particularly different from the other girls they knew, most of whom also took pills in combination with beer or wine. In Judi's case, however, the combination was lethal. She never found the something that eluded her, but she did find death.

million Americans were addicted to barbiturate drugs, most of them between 30 and 50 years old (Bayh, 1972). And it would appear that the number of addicted persons has not appreciably decreased since that time. Literally billions of barbiturate pills, including pills with fixed combinations of barbiturates and amphetamines, are manufactured each year in the United States.

Effects of barbiturates. The barbiturates are the primary sedative drugs used by physicians to calm patients and/or induce sleep. They act as depressants—somewhat like alcohol—to slow down the action of the central nervous system. Shortly after taking the drug, the individual experiences a feeling of relaxation in which tensions seem to disappear, followed by a physical and intellectual lassitude and a tendency toward drowsiness and sleep—the intensity of such feelings depending on the type and amount of the barbiturate taken. Strong doses produce sleep almost immediately; excessive doses are lethal because they result in paralysis of the respiratory centers of the brain.

Excessive use of barbiturates leads to increased tolerance as well as to physiological and psychological dependence. The barbiturates most often involved in such abuse are the short-acting ones such as seconal ("red devils") and tuinal ("rainbows"): long-acting barbiturates, such as phenobarbital, are not so subject to abuse because of their failure to produce quick results.

In addition, excessive use of barbiturates leads to a variety of undesirable side effects, including sluggishness, slow speech, impaired comprehension and memory, lability of affect, motor incoordination, and depression. Problem solving and decision making require great effort, and the individual usually is aware that his thinking is "fuzzy." Prolonged excessive use of this class of drugs leads to brain damage and personality deterioration. And, whereas building tolerance to the opiates raises the amount that is lethal, this is not true for the barbiturates, which means that death can easily occur through an overdose, whether intentional or accidental. Indeed, barbiturates are associated with more suicides than any other drug.

Causal factors in abuse and dependence. Though many young people experiment with barbiturates, or "downers," most do not become dependent. In fact, the individuals who do become dependent on barbiturates tend to be middle-aged and older persons who often rely on them as "sleeping pills" and who do not commonly rely on other classes of drugs with the possible exception of alcohol and the minor tranquilizers. Often these persons are referred to as "silent abusers" since they take the drugs in the privacy of their homes and ordinarily do not become public nuisances. Dependence occurs as a result of the gradual building of tolerance and the concomitant tendency to take an increased dosage to get the required effect. Physiological dependence does not occur in persons who have maintained the normal dosage range. As with alcoholism, barbiturate dependence seems to occur in the emotionally maladjusted person who seeks relief from feelings of anxiety, tension, inadequacy, and the stresses of life.

An exception to the above picture has occurred in recent years with the introduction of "new, improved" diet pills. Previous diet pills had usually been amphetamines alone, but the new pills are fixed-ratio combinations of amphetamines and barbiturates—the latter being added to reduce the "jitteriness" often caused by the amphetamines alone. Unfortunately, both of these drugs are highly addictive, either separately or in combination, and since the addition of barbiturates may make the amphetamines more tolerable, the "addiction prone" person may rapidly increase his pill intake, thus increasing the possibility of addiction to both drugs (Kunnes, 1973).

In addition to being used with amphetamines, barbiturates are also commonly used with alcohol. Some teen-agers claim they can achieve a "far out" effect—a kind of controlled hypersensitivity—by combining barbiturates, amphetamines, and alcohol. However, one possible "far out" effect of combining barbiturates and alcohol is death, since each drug *potentiates* (increases the action of) the other.

Treatment and outcomes. As with many other drugs, it is often essential in treatment to distinguish between barbiturate intoxication,

---

The use and abuse of minor tranquilizers

Minor tranquilizing drugs, such as Librium, Miltown, and Valium, are widely used in our society for reducing anxiety and tension, particularly in relation to specific life stresses. However, minor tranquilizers are potentially dangerous because of possible side effects, because of ill-advised practices associated with their use, and because physiological and psychological dependence may result from their continued use.*

Drowsiness and motor impairment are common side effects of the minor tranquilizers. Thus it is illegal in many states to drive while under the influence of tranquilizers; such drugs can also be dangerous to people in occupations that require continual alertness and a high level of motor coordination. In fact, it would appear that far more accidents, both on and off the job, are associated with the misuse of legal drugs than with the use of illegal ones. There is also evidence that the meprobamates have been implicated in an increasing number of suicide attempts. And, of course, mixing mild tranquilizers with other psychoactive drugs may have potentiating or other undesirable effects; e.g., a medically prescribed barbiturate for sleeping may be much more potent than intended when taken with alcohol and a tranquilizer.

The practice of mixing prescription drugs appears to be relatively common, and many people take two or more types of minor tranquilizers each day. Another common practice, common among many husbands and wives, is to use each other's tranquilizers, thus negating needed medical supervision.

Even when used as prescribed, it should be recognized that the continual use of minor tranquilizers in heavy dosage can build up tolerance and physiological dependence; abrupt cessation of usage may lead to serious withdrawal symptoms.

*Here we are dealing with prescription drugs, but over-the-counter (OTC) preparations, such as Compōz, Cope, and Nervine are also subject to these dangers.

which results from the toxic effects of over-dosage, and the symptoms associated with withdrawal of the drug from addicted users. We are concerned primarily with the latter. Here the symptoms are more dangerous, severe, and long-lasting than in opiate withdrawal. The patient becomes anxious and apprehensive and manifests coarse tremors of the hands and face; additional symptoms commonly include insomnia, weakness, nausea, vomiting, abdominal cramps, rapid heart rate, elevated blood pressure, and loss of weight. Between the sixteenth hour and the fifth day convulsions may occur. An acute delirious psychosis often develops, which may include symptoms similar to those in delirium tremens.

For individuals used to taking large dosages, the withdrawal symptoms may last for as long as a month, but usually they tend to abate by the end of the first week. Fortunately, the withdrawal symptoms in barbiturate addiction can be minimized by the administration of increasingly smaller doses of the barbiturate itself, or by another drug producing pharmacologically similar effects. The withdrawal program is still a dangerous one, however, especially if barbiturate addiction is complicated by alcoholism or dependence on other drugs.[9]

Although the elimination of psychological dependence on barbiturates may also require psychotherapy or other treatment, this is not so severe a problem as in the case of opiate addiction, where the individual has an overpowering craving for the drug even after the physical dependence has been broken.

The amphetamines and cocaine

In contrast to the barbiturates, which depress or slow down the action of the central nervous system, the amphetamines and cocaine have chemical effects that stimulate or speed up CNS activity.

---

[9]The use of multiple drugs and "polydrug abuse" has become increasingly prevalent.

The amphetamines. The earliest amphetamine to be introduced—Benzedrine, or amphetamine sulfate—was first synthesized in 1927 and became available in drugstores in the early 1930s as an inhalant to relieve stuffy noses. However, the manufacturers soon learned that some customers were chewing the wicks in the inhalers for "kicks." Thus, the stimulating effects of amphetamine sulfate were discovered by the public before the drug was formally prescribed as a stimulant by physicians. In the late 1930s two newer amphetamines were introduced—Dexedrine (dextroamphetamine) and Methedrine (methamphetamine hydrochloride). The latter preparation is a far more potent stimulant of the central nervous system than either Benzedrine or Dexedrine, and hence is considered more dangerous. In fact, its abuse is lethal in an appreciable number of cases.

Initially these preparations were considered to be "wonder pills" that helped people stay alert and awake and function temporarily at a level beyond normal. During World War II military interest was aroused in the stimulating effects of these drugs, and they were used by both allied and German soldiers to ward off fatigue (Jarvik, 1967). Similarly, among civilians, amphetamines came to be widely used by night workers, long-distance truck drivers, students cramming for exams, and athletes striving to improve their performances. It was also discovered that the amphetamines tend to suppress appetite, and they became popular among persons trying to lose weight. In addition, they were often used to counteract the effects of barbiturates or other sleeping pills that had been taken the night before.

Latest available figures indicate that about 8 to 10 billion amphetamine pills are manufactured in the United States every year—enough to give each man, woman, and child about 35 doses apiece. This is a figure far in excess of known medical requirements; it has been estimated that well over a fourth of the pills manufactured each year are diverted into black-market channels.

1. *Causes and effects of amphetamine abuse.* Today the amphetamines, or "pep pills," are used medically for (a) curbing the appetite when weight reduction is desirable,

(b) relieving fatigue and maintaining alertness for sustained periods of time, and (c) alleviating mild feelings of depression. They are also used for individuals suffering from narcolepsy—a disorder in which the subject cannot prevent himself from continually falling asleep during the day—as well as for the treatment of hyperactive children. Curiously enough, the amphetamines have a calming rather than a stimulating effect on most of these youngsters.

Despite their legitimate medical uses, the AMA (1968a) has emphasized that amphetamines are not a magical source of extra mental or physical energy, but rather serve to push the user toward a greater expenditure of his own resources—often to a point of hazardous fatigue. In fact, athletes have damaged their careers by the use of "speed" in trying to improve their stamina and performance (Furlong, 1971). It has also been suggested that amphetamines are much too freely prescribed for weight reduction, in view of their short-term effectiveness and the possible dangers inherent in their abuse. For example, an overweight person may take more of the pills than he is supposed to because he likes their stimulating effects.

As with other drugs, the effects of amphetamines vary with the type, the dosage, the length of time they are taken, and the physical and psychological state of the individual user. Although amphetamines are not considered to be physiologically addictive, the body does build up tolerance to them very rapidly. Thus, habituated users may consume pills by the mouthful several times a day in amounts that would be lethal to nonusers. In some instances, users inject the drug to get faster and more intense results. To get "high" on amphetamines, persons may give themselves from 6 to 200 times the daily medical dosage usually prescribed for dieters. If lesser amphetamines do not provide a sufficient reaction, then Methedrine, or "speed," will produce the desired high. In some instances, amphetamine abusers go on "sprees" lasting several days.

For the person who exceeds prescribed dosages, consumption of amphetamines results in heightened blood pressure, enlarged pupils, unclear or rapid speech, profuse sweating, tremors, excitability, loss of appetite, confu-

---

The cocaine episode in the life of Sigmund Freud

In a lecture to a psychiatric society in 1885, Freud described the effects of ingesting from 50 to 100 mg. of cocaine hydrochloride: he felt a profound sense of elation, greater physical endurance, and increased mental agility. Post reported Freud has having stated:

" 'I take very small doses of it regularly against depression . . . with the most brilliant success. (The effects were) exhilarating and lasting euphoria, which in no way differs from the normal euphoria of a healthy person. . . . You perceive an increase in self-control and possess more vitality and capacity for work. . . .' " (pp. 225–26)

Freud reported that he had no craving for the further use of the drug, even after repeated dosage, nor did he experience unpleasant after-effects such as those that follow "exhilaration brought about by alcohol."

---

sion and sleeplessness. In some instances, the jolt to body physiology from "shooting" Methedrine can raise blood pressure enough to cause immediate death. In addition, the chronic abuse of amphetamines can result in brain damage as well as a wide range of psychopathology, including a disorder known as *amphetamine psychosis*, which investigators consider to be very similar to paranoid schizophrenia.

Suicide, homicide, assault, and various other acts of violence are associated with amphetamine abuse. In the United States, Ellinwood (1971) studied 13 persons who committed homicide under amphetamine intoxication and found that, in most cases, "the events leading to the homicidal act were directly related to amphetamine-induced paranoid thinking, panic, emotional lability, or lowered impulse control" (p. 90). And a study of 100 hospital admissions for amphetamine intoxication revealed that 25 of the subjects had attempted suicide while under the influence of the drug (Nelson, 1969).

2. *Treatment and outcomes.* Withdrawal from the amphetamines is usually painless from a physical viewpoint, since physiological addiction is absent or minimal. In some instances, however, withdrawal on a "cold turkey" basis from the chronic excessive use of amphetamines can result in cramping, nausea, diarrhea, and even convulsions (AMA, 1968a; Kunnes, 1973).

But psychological dependence is another matter, and abrupt abstinence commonly results in feelings of weariness and depression. As one housewife described it:

"I'd go into terrible fits of depression. . . . didn't have anything at all to take. The depression would be accompanied by feelings of panic, but I never knew that this was all withdrawal symptoms. The difference in knowing is that not knowing I was so frightened and didn't know what was happening to me." (Hartmann, Schildkraut, & Watson, 1972, p. 5)

The depression usually reaches its peak in 48 to 72 hours, often remains intense for a day or two, and then tends to lessen gradually over a period of several days. However, mild feelings of depression and lassitude may persist for weeks or even months after the last dose. Where brain damage has occurred, residual effects may also include impaired ability to concentrate, learn, and remember, with resulting social, economic, and personality deterioration.

Cocaine. Like opium, cocaine is a plant product discovered and used in ancient times. As Jarvik (1967) has pointed out:

"The Indians of Peru have chewed coca leaves for centuries and still do, to relieve hunger, fatigue, and the general burdens of a miserable life." (p. 52)

Cocaine has been endorsed by such diverse figures as Sigmund Freud and the legendary Sherlock Holmes, but although its use appears to have increased among young people in the United States, it is not a commonly used drug.

Like opium, cocaine may be ingested by sniffing, swallowing, or injecting. And like the opiates, it precipitates a euphoric state of four to six hours' duration, simultaneous with which the user experiences feelings of peace and contentment. However, this blissful state may be preceded by headache, dizziness, and restlessness. When cocaine is chronically abused, acute toxic psychotic symptoms may occur which are similar to those in acute schizophrenia and encompass frightening visual, auditory, and tactual hallucinations, such as the "cocaine bug" (Post, 1975).

Because of its anesthetic qualities, cocaine is sometimes used as a substitute for morphine. Unlike the opiates, however, cocaine is a cortical stimulant, inducing sleeplessness and excitement, as well as stimulating and accentuating sexual processes. Consequently, individuals with deviant sexual patterns have been known to administer it as an impetus to seduction. Dependence on cocaine also differs from that on opiates, in that tolerance is not increased appreciably with its use, nor is there any physiological dependence.

However, psychological dependence on cocaine, like addiction to opiates, often leads to a centering of behavior around its procurement, concurrent with a loss of social approval and self-respect. The following case illustrates this pattern:

The subject was a strikingly pretty, intelligent woman of 19 who had divorced her husband two years previously. She had married at the age of 16 and stated that she was terribly in love with her husband but that he turned out to be cruel and brutal.

The woman was too ashamed of her marital failure (her parents had violently opposed the marriage and she had left home against their will) to return to her home. She moved away from her husband and got a job as a cocktail waitress in the same bar where her husband had been accustomed to taking her. She was severely depressed, and several of his friends insisted on buying her drinks to cheer her up. This process continued for almost a year, during which she drank excessively but managed to hold her job.

Following this, she met a man in the bar where she worked who introduced her to cocaine, assuring her that it would cheer her up and get rid of her blues. She states that it both "hopped me up and gave me a feeling of peace and contentment." For a period of several months she purchased her supplies of cocaine from this same man until she became ill with appendicitis and was unable to pay the stiff price he asked. Following an appendectomy, she was induced to share his apartment as a means of defraying her expenses and ensuring the supply of cocaine which she had now become heavily dependent on psychologically. She stated that she felt she could not work without it. During this period she had sexual relations with the man although she considered it immoral and had severe guilt feelings about it.

Psychoactive drugs commonly involved in drug abuse

Classification	Drugs	Usage	Medical Usage	Tolerance	Physiological Dependence	Psychological Dependence
Sedatives	Alcohol (ethanol)	Reduce tension Facilitate social interaction "Blot out"	No	Yes	Yes	Yes

	Barbiturates
	  Nembutal (pentobarbital)
	  Seconal (secobarbital)
	  Veronal (barbital)
	  Tuinal (secobarbital and
	    amobarbital)
		Reduce tension
		Induce relaxation and sleep
			Yes	Yes	Yes	Yes

Stimulants	Amphetamines
	  Benzedrine
	    (amphetamine)
	  Dexedrine
	    (dextroamphetamine)
	  Methedrine
	    (methamphetamine)
		Increase feelings of alert-
		  ness and confidence
		Decrease feelings of fatigue
		Stay awake for long periods
			Yes	Yes	No	Yes

	Cocaine (coca)	Decrease feelings of fatigue Increase endurance Stimulate sex drive	No	No (minimal)	No	Yes

Narcotics	Opium and its derivatives
	  Opium
	  Morphine
	  Codeine
	  Heroin
		Alleviate physical pain
		Induce relaxation and
		  pleasant reverie
		Alleviate anxiety and
		  tension
			Yes, except
			heroin
				Yes	Yes	Yes

	Methadone
	  (synthetic narcotic)
		Treatment of
		  heroin dependence
			Yes	Yes	Yes	Yes

Psychedelics and Hallucinogens	Cannabis
	  Marijuana
	  Hashish
	Mescaline (peyote)
	Psilocybin (psychotogenic
	  mushrooms)
	LSD (lysergic acid diethyl-
	  amide-25)
		Induce changes in mood,
		  thought, and behavior
		"Mind expansion"
			No, except
			in research
				No—
				possible
				reverse
				tolerance
				(marijuana)
					No	Yes

Minor Tranquilizers	Librium (chlordiazepoxide
	  hydrochloride)
	Miltown (meprobamate)
	Valium (diazepam)
	Others, e.g., Compoz
	  (scopolamine)
		Alleviate tension and
		  anxiety
		Induce relaxation and
		  sleep
			Yes	Yes	Yes	Yes

In reviewing this list, it is important to note that it is by no means complete; e.g., it does not include many of the new drugs, such as Ritalin, which are designed to produce multiple effects; it does not include the less commonly used volatile hydrocarbons, such as glue, paint thinner, gasoline, cleaning fluid, and nail polish remover, which are highly dangerous when sniffed for their psychoactive effects; and it does not include the major tranquilizers and anti-depressants which are abused, but relatively rarely. We shall deal with the major tranquilizers and antidepressants, as well as the minor tranquilizers, in our discussion of chemotherapy in Chapter 20. It also should be noted that abuse can occur with both prescriptive and nonprescriptive drugs, and with both legal and illegal drugs.

This pattern continued for several months until her "roommate" upped his prices on the cocaine, on the excuse that it was getting more difficult to obtain, and suggested that she might be able to earn enough money to pay for it if she were not so prudish about whom she slept with. At this time the full significance of where her behavior was leading seems to have dawned on her and she came voluntarily to a community clinic for assistance.

Treatment for psychological dependence on cocaine does not differ appreciably from that for other drugs which involve no physiological dependence. Aversion therapy, group techniques, and related procedures may all be utilized. However, as in the case with other such drugs, feelings of tension and depression may have to be dealt with during the immediate withdrawal period.

The major hallucinogens: LSD and related drugs

This classification is composed of drugs whose properties are thought to induce hallucinations. In fact, however, these preparations do not so often "create" sensory images as distort them, so that the individual sees or hears things in different and unusual ways.

The major drugs in this category are LSD (lysergic acid diethylamide), mescaline, and psilocybin. Our present discussion will be restricted largely to LSD because of its unusual hallucinogenic properties and its potentialities for research into brain functioning.

LSD. The most potent of the hallucinogens, the odorless, colorless, and tasteless drug LSD can produce intoxication with an amount smaller than a grain of salt. It is a chemically synthesized substance first discovered by the Swiss chemist Hoffman in 1938.

1. *Effects of LSD.* Hoffman was not aware of the potent hallucinatory qualities of LSD until some five years after his discovery, when he swallowed a small amount. This is his report of the experience:

"Last Friday, April 16, 1943, I was forced to stop my work in the laboratory in the middle of the afternoon and to go home, as I was seized by a peculiar restlessness associated with a sensation of mild dizziness. On arriving home, I lay down and sank into a kind of drunkenness which was not unpleasant and which was characterized by extreme activity of imagination. As I lay in a dazed condition with my eyes closed (I experienced daylight as disagreeably bright) there surged upon me an uninterrupted stream of fantastic images of extraordinary plasticity and vividness and accompanied by an intense, kaleidoscope-like play of colours. This condition gradually passed off after about two hours." (Hoffman, 1971, p. 23)

Hoffman followed up this experience with a series of planned self-observations with LSD, some of which he described as "harrowing." Researchers thought LSD might be useful for the induction and study of hallucinogenic states or "model psychoses," which were thought to be related to schizophrenia. About 1950, LSD was introduced into the United States for purposes of such research as well as to ascertain whether it might have medical or therapeutic uses. As we have noted, however, the "model psychoses" produced by LSD are different from schizophrenia, and despite considerable research, LSD has not proven therapeutically useful.

After taking LSD a person typically goes through about eight hours of changes in sensory perception, lability of emotional experiences, and feelings of depersonalization and detachment. The peak of both physiological and psychological effects usually occurs between the second and fourth hours. Physiological effects include increased heart rate, elevation in blood pressure, augmented muscle tone, and faster and more variable breathing.

As LSD takes effect, the most important psychic manifestation is a tremendous intensification of sensory perception. Objects seem to become clearer, sharper, and brighter, and endowed with dimensions that the subject has never before perceived. Thus he may lose himself in contemplation of a flower, seeing in it colors that he has never seen before, hearing the movements of its petals, and feeling that at last he understands its essential nature. Another phenomenon associated with the drug has been called "humanity identification"—a sensation in which the individual feels himself to be in emphathic concert with all humankind in the experiencing of such universal emotions as love, loneliness, or grief.

In addition to the intensity of the basic perceptual and affective reactions that occur in the early stages of the LSD experience, Katz, Waskow, and Olsson (1968) have pointed to certain contradictory aspects of that experience. These include:

"1. Very strong but opposing emotions occurring approximately at the same time, emotions which may not have a cognitive counterpart;
2. A feeling of being out of control of one's emotions and thoughts;
3. A feeling of detachment from the real world;
4. A feeling of perceptual sharpness, but at the same time perceptions of the outer world as having an unreal quality;
5. The perception of the world and others as 'friendly' but 'suspicious.'" (p. 13)

The LSD "trip" is not always pleasant. It can be extremely harrowing and traumatic, and the distorted objects and sounds, the illusory colors, and the new thoughts can be menacing and terrifying. For example, Rorvik (1970) has cited the case of a young British law student who tried to "continue time" by using a dental drill to bore a hole in his head while under the influence of LSD. In other instances, persons undergoing "bad trips" have set themselves aflame, jumped from high places, and taken other drugs which proved a lethal combination. Of 114 subjects admitted to the Bellevue Hospital in New York City with acute psychoses induced by LSD, 13 percent showed overwhelming fear and another 12 percent experienced uncontrollably violent urges; suicide or homicide had been attempted by approximately 9 percent (Rorvik, 1970). In a study of chronic users of LSD, Blacker and his associates (1968) found that the "bum trip" usually began in a context of ire. For example, one of their subjects reported that he had taken LSD when he was angry with his mother. Initially his trip had been beautiful; then it exploded. He suddenly became very fearful, thought he could hear monsters coming up the stairs, and was convinced that they would come through the door to his room and eat him.

The setting in which LSD is taken appears to be influential in determining its effect, but a favorable milieu alone is no guarantee

Unknown terrors show in the eyes of this young woman who is "stoned" on drugs.

Approximately 1 in 20 consistent users of LSD experience recurrent hallucinatory images which are known as "flashbacks." These images are usually of a negative and frightening nature, as indicated by the following examples reported by Horowitz (1969):

Pt. A: "Now I often see a bright shiny halo around people, especially at the dark edges—sometimes it's rainbow colors—like during the trip."

Pt. B: "Sometimes the sidewalk seems to bend as if it's going downward—even when I'm not on anything—or it just kinda vibrates back and forth."

Pt. C: "I see this giant iguana, all the time, man. Green. In corners. Like under your chair."

Pt. D: "Now I see things—walls, and faces, and caves—probably imprinted on my thalamus from the prehistoric past." (p. 566)

For other patients, experiences were comparable. One 17-year-old youth who had been terror-stricken when he hallucinated a scorpion on the back of his hand during a "bad trip" continued to have flashbacks of the scorpion five weeks later. A 16-year-old youth who had images during a "bad trip" of a human figure being sucked into the vortex of a whirlpool had the same image turn up about three weeks later, and it interrupted whatever he was thinking about 5 or 10 times a day. The flashbacks were frightening, and he could not rid himself of them; consequently he sought professional help.

Among LSD users who experience flashbacks, those who repeatedly use hallucinogens experience the more severe forms. Various causal factors have been implicated in the occurrence of flashbacks, including: (1) neurophysiologic changes in the brain, which disinhibit the retrieval of images from memory storage; (2) a built-in tendency to desensitize oneself to traumatic images experienced during a "bad trip" via the repetition of the images; and (3) the reactivation of primordial images imprinted on the mind, which recalls Jung's concepts of archetypes and the collective unconscious (see page 58).

Fortunately, flashbacks can be worked through in brief psychotherapy, following which they cease to recur.

against adverse reactions. Even a single dose can trigger serious psychological complications. For example, in a study of 52 persons admitted to a New York hospital with LSD-induced psychoses, it was found that 26 had taken the drug only one time, and only 12 of the subjects had shown evidence of serious maladjustment prior to their LSD psychosis (AMA, 1968b). On the other hand, even the same individual may be affected differently by the drug at different times. In fact, the preceding investigators cited cases of persons who had used LSD 100 or more times without apparent difficulty and then suddenly had developed severe, adverse reactions.

An interesting and unusual phenomenon that may occur following the use of LSD is the *flashback*: an involuntary recurrence of perceptual distortions or hallucinations weeks or even months after taking the drug. These experiences appear to be relatively rare among individuals who have taken LSD only once—although they do sometimes occur. On the other hand, as discussed in the illustration on the left, it has been conservatively estimated that about 1 in 20 consistent users experience such flashbacks (Horowitz, 1969). Some persons react with fear to these recurrent images, which "seem to have a will of their own"; extreme anxiety and even psychotic reactions may result. It has been estimated that about 3 percent of persons who use LSD under illegal conditions experience such psychotic reactions.

Some studies have indicated that LSD may cause chromosomal damage and a lowering of immunological defenses to disease, but others have refuted these reports. In any event, the user of LSD does not develop physiological dependence, nor does he build up tolerance requiring increasingly large doses of the drug. However, some chronic users have developed psychological dependence, in the sense that they focus their life around this type of drug experience.

While even the research use of LSD is definitely contraindicated for persons who are maladjusted or under severe emotional stress, the dangers appear to be almost nonexistent for persons who take it under careful supervision in research settings. After a review of available evidence, McWilliams and Tuttle (1973) concluded: "The danger of long-lasting psychological damage is low when the drug is used by emotionally stable individuals in secure, controlled settings . . . indicating the drug's relative safety for continued research" (p. 341).

2. *Use of LSD for self-improvement.* Despite the possibility of adverse reactions, the remarkable effects of LSD were widely publicized during the 1960s, and a number of relatively well-known people experimented with the drug and gave glowing accounts of their "trips." In fact, during this period an "LSD Movement" was under way, based on the conviction that the drug could "expand the mind" and enable one to use talents and realize potentials previously undetected. As a result, a considerable number of people attempted to use LSD as a vehicle for achieving greater personal insight, increased sensitivity, mystic experiences, and better understanding of their place in the universe. This category included a sizeable number of painters, writers, and composers, who attempted to use the drug not only for personal growth but also as a means of creating more original and meaningful works of art.

However, there is no conclusive evidence that LSD enhances creative activity: no recognized works of art have apparently been produced under the influence of the drug or as a consequence of a psychedelic experience. And although several artists have claimed improved creativity stemming from their LSD experiences, objective observers recognize few, if any, refinements (AMA, 1968b). In fact, under the direct influence of LSD, the drawings of one well-known American painter showed progressive deterioration; later, when asked if he felt his LSD experience had improved his creativity, he replied in the negative (Rinkel, 1966).

3. *Treatment and outcomes.* For acute psychoses induced by LSD intoxication, treatment requires hospitalization and is primarily a medical matter. Often the outcome in such cases depends heavily on the personal stability of the individual prior to taking the drug; in some cases prolonged hospitalization may be required.

Fortunately, brief psychotherapy is usually effective in treating psychological dependence on LSD as well as in preventing the recur-rence of flashbacks which may still haunt the individual as a result of a "bad trip." As in the case of trauma experienced in combat or civilian disasters, therapy is aimed at helping the individual work through the painful experience and integrate it into his self-structure.

Mescaline and psilocybin. Two other well-known hallucinogens are mescaline and psilocybin. Mescaline is derived from the small, disclike growths ("mescal buttons") of the top of the peyote cactus; psilocybin is a drug obtained from a variety of "sacred" Mexican mushrooms known as *psilocybe mexicana.*

These drugs have been used for centuries in the ceremonial rites of Indian peoples living in Mexico and in Central and South America. In fact, they were used by the Aztecs for such purposes long before the Spanish invaded the land. Both drugs have mind-altering and hallucinogenic properties, but their principal effect appears to be enabling the individual to see, hear, and otherwise experience events in unaccustomed ways—of transporting him into a realm of "nonordinary reality."

As with LSD, there is no definite evidence that mescaline and psilocybin actually "expand consciousness" or create new ideas; rather, they seem primarily to alter or distort experience.

Marijuana

Although marijuana may be classified as a mild hallucinogen, there are significant differences in the nature, intensity, and duration of its effects as compared with those induced by LSD, mescaline, and other major hallucinogens.

Marijuana comes from the leaves and flowering tops of the hemp plant, *cannabis sativa.* The plant grows in mild climates throughout the world including parts of India, Africa, Mexico, and the United States. In its prepared state, marijuana consists chiefly of the dried green leaves—hence the colloquial name "grass." It is ordinarily smoked in the form of cigarettes ("reefers" or "joints") or in pipes, but it can also be baked into cookies and other foods. In some cultures the leaves are steeped in hot water and the liquid is drunk, much as one might drink tea. Marijuana is related to the stronger drug, hashish, which is derived from the resin exuded by the cannabis plant and made into a gummy powder. Hashish, like marijuana, may be smoked, chewed, or drunk.

Both marijuana and hashish can be traced far back into the history of drug usage. Cannabis was apparently known in ancient China (Blum, 1969; Culliton, 1970), and was listed in the herbal compendiums of the Chinese emperor Shen Nung, written about 2737 B.C.

Until the late 1960s marijuana use in the United States was confined largely to members of lower socioeconomic minority groups and to people in entertainment and related fields. In the late 1960s, however, there was a dramatic increase in its use among youth in our society, and during the early 1970s it was estimated that over half the teen-agers and young adults had experimented with marijuana in social situations, with about 10 percent presumably going from occasional to habitual use. In 1973 an estimated 20 million young people were occasional or habitual users in the United States, and about 7 million pounds of marijuana and hashish were consumed—enough to make over 2 billion cigarettes. In recent years, however, alcohol seems to be increasingly the "drug of choice" for teenagers as well as adults.

Effects of marijuana. The specific effects of marijuana vary greatly, depending on the quality and dosage of the drug, the personality and mood of the user, and the user's past experience with the drug. However, there is considerable consensus among regular users that when marijuana is smoked and inhaled, the individual gets "high." This state is one of mild euphoria distinguished by increased feelings of well-being, heightened perceptual acuity, and pleasant relaxation, often accompanied by a sensation of drifting or floating away. Sensory inputs are enhanced: music sounds fuller, colors look brighter, smells seem richer, and food tastes better. Somehow the world seems to become more meaningful, and even minor events may take on extraordinary profundity. Often there is a stretching out or distortion of the individual's sense of time, so that an event lasting but a few seconds may

seem to cover a much longer span. Short-term memory may also be affected, as when an individual notices he has taken a bite of his sandwich but does not remember doing so. For most users, pleasurable experiences, including sexual intercourse, seem to be greatly enhanced. When smoked, marijuana is rapidly absorbed and its effects appear within seconds to minutes, but seldom last more than 2 to 3 hours. The effects of THC (the synthetically produced drug which appears to be the active ingredient in cannabis) may not be noted for 30 minutes to over 2 hours following oral ingestion.

Marijuana may lead to unpleasant as well as pleasant experiences. For example, if an individual takes the drug while in an unhappy, angry, suspicious, or frightened mood, unsavory events may be magnified. And with high dosages, as well as with certain unstable or susceptible individuals, marijuana can produce extreme euphoria, hilarity, and overtalkativeness; it can also produce intense anxiety and depression as well as delusions, hallucinations, and other psychoticlike behavior. It is of interest to note, however, that in a study reported by Nelson (1969), only 3 hospital admissions for marijuana abuse or intoxication were reported out of 90,733 consecutive admissions, while thousands of admissions and hundreds of deaths were associated with the abuse of alcohol, barbiturates, and amphetamines.

The short-range physiological effects of marijuana include a moderate increase in heart rate, a slowing of reaction time, a slight contraction of pupil size, bloodshot and itchy eyes, a dry mouth, and an increased appetite. Continued use of high dosages tends to produce lethargy and passivity. Here marijuana appears to have a depressant as well as a hallucinogenic effect. However, the effects of long-term and habitual use of the drug are still under investigation, although a number of possible adverse side effects have been related to the prolonged heavy use of marijuana or less frequent use of the more potent hashish (Maugh, 1974).

Marijuana has often been compared to heroin, but the two drugs have little in common with respect to either tolerance or to physiological dependence. Although studies conducted in Eastern countries have found evidence of tolerance to marijuana at high dosage levels over long periods of time, studies in the U.S.—which have involved lower dosages for shorter time periods—have failed to find evidence of tolerance (HEW, 1971). In fact, habitual users often show "reverse tolerance." This may be due in part to the users' having learned the proper method of smoking and to the suggestive influence of anticipated effects. In any event, habitual users rarely feel it necessary to increase their doses to maintain desired effects. In addition, many habitual users of marijuana claim the ability to "turn off" its effects or "come down" from a marijuana "high" if conditions in the situation require it, and a limited amount of research evidence tends to support their claim (Cappell & Pliner, 1973). Nor does marijuana lead to physiological dependence, as heroin does, so discontinuance of the drug is not accompanied by withdrawal symptoms. Marijuana can, however, lead to psychological dependence, in which the individual experiences a strong need for it whenever he feels anxious and tense.

Some key questions concerning marijuana. Aside from alcohol, no drug has triggered as much debate and confusion in our society as marijuana. Many persons, including members of the drug subculture, refuse to see any dangers inherent in its use and even consider it a boon to humanity; other persons see serious dangers in its use and feel that the possession or use of marijuana should be subject to severe legal sanctions.

What are the facts about marijuana? Unfortunately, despite an increasing amount of research, we still do not have adequate answers to a number of pertinent questions.

1. *What are the reasons for using marijuana?* In the late 1960s and early 1970s, the reasons for using marijuana appeared to run the gamut: (a) curiosity, thrill-seeking, and easy euphoria; (b) peer pressure for doing the "in thing" with a given group; (c) desire for self-improvement through gaining new insights and help in realizing one's potential; and (d) and urge to diminish stressful conflicts, insecurities, and anxieties. The last reason was often associated with the discouragement and depression of slum life as well as with the dis-

---

Report of the Indian Hemp Drug Commission: a historical parallel

An interesting parallel may be drawn between contemporary studies of the effects of marijuana and an extensive study initiated by the British government in 1893. The House of Commons, in response to a member's motion, appointed the Indian Hemp Drug Commission to investigate effects of such drugs—which included marijuana. Results of the commission's research were published in 1894 in a 7-volume report, for which data had been gathered in 30 field trips to various cities in India and from interviews with 1193 witnesses (Mikuriya, 1969).

The commission's report was divided into three categories, indicative of the areas in which hemp drugs were popularly believed to have harmful effects:

1. Health. Although hemp drugs were believed to cause dysentery, bronchitis, and asthma, the commission concluded that in moderate dosage, hemp drugs were not physically harmful.

2. Sanity. Although it was also popularly believed that hemp drugs caused insanity, after going over all cases admitted to Indian mental hospitals for the year 1892, the commission concluded that this concept was based on established hospital diagnostic procedures and was fallacious.

3. Crime. After an intensive survey of available evidence, including a review of 81 crimes of violence alleged to have been caused by hemp usage, the commission concluded that there was little or no connection between the use of hemp drugs and crime.

The extent to which these findings are applicable to the question of legalizing marijuana in our own society is speculative, since there is no way of comparing the quality of drugs used, the populations involved, and other relevant variables.

---

illusionment of many youth during the 1960s, including teen-age runaways, who "dropped out" of the mainstream of society and joined drug subcultures.

While these reasons still appear to be operative to some extent as we enter the last half of the 1970s, it is apparent that marijuana has essentially become a direct competitor with alcohol, and the reasons for its use have tended to change accordingly.

2. *Does the use of marijuana have harmful effects?* In the fourth of a series of reports on the use of marijuana, the National Institute of Drug Abuse (1974) summarized the findings of 65 research projects that had been funded by this agency.

The essential thrust of the report was that available research findings did not offer conclusive evidence concerning either the safety or the harmfulness of marijuana. However, the report did point out three areas in which the consequences of marijuana use might be potentially harmful: (a) the weakening of the body's immune mechanisms, (b) a decrease of male sex hormones, and (c) impaired psychomotor performance. The last appeared to be most definitive, indicating that driving under the influence of marijuana has effects similar to those of driving under the influence of alcohol, including impaired reaction time, concentration, and judgment. But until more definitive research findings become available, it seems probable that the controversy concerning the possible hazards of marijuana use is likely to continue.

3. *Does the use of marijuana enhance creativity?* Most investigators have given a definite "no" to this question (Braden, et al., 1974; Yolles, 1969). Although marijuana may induce fantasies that seem creative, at least to the person experiencing them, what actually is produced in terms of writing, painting, or other creative pursuits is usually evaluated as no better—and often worse—than usual. As with the use of LSD and other hallucinogens, an individual may think he has found "the key to the universe"; when he "comes down," however, it is not there.

Conceivably, enhanced feelings, perceptions, and thoughts experienced while under the influence of hallucinogenic drugs can be translated into creative productivity, including new insights into the self, and even self-enhancement. As yet, however, this remains to be proved, and other, less risky, avenues of "mind expansion" are being explored. Humanistic psychologists are particularly interested in exploring nondrug techniques for enhancing awareness, enriching experience, and fostering personal growth; we shall comment further on the "human potential movement" in Chapter 20.

4. *Should marijuana be legalized?* Defenders of marijuana have long argued that the drug is no more dangerous than alcohol—and possibly less so, since it is not appreciably related to violence or crime in the United States. They have pointed out that legalization would provide freer access to a source of pleasure and tension reduction; would ensure a safer product since the federal government could supervise its production, distribution, and sale; and would provide another source of revenue from taxation. In addition, they consider it illogical to sanction the use of drugs that are known to be dangerous, such as alcohol and nicotine-containing tobacco, while making the use of marijuana illegal.

It has also been pointed out that penalties for the possession of small amounts of marijuana—but not for "pushing"—have been reduced by the federal government and most states from a felony to a misdemeanor. In 1973, Oregon removed completely the criminal penalties for the private possession and use of marijuana; the new law provides that persons found in possession of up to 1 ounce of marijuana (enough for about 20 cigarettes) can be charged only with a violation and fined, in effect making the use of marijuana no more criminal than a parking ticket. The long-range results of this experiment remain to be ascertained, but a preliminary study done in 1975 indicated that the use of marijuana had not increased markedly and that its legalization had been well accepted by the public (Skelton, 1975).

The opponents of legalization have taken a variety of stands against it, one being that the use of marijuana leads to the use of "hard" drugs. But even though a high proportion of heroin addicts have also used marijuana, this is not proof of a causal relationship between the two; in fact, an even larger proportion of heroin users have probably used alcohol and other drugs. A second argument has been that the removal of governmental restrictions would inevitably lead to a marked increase in marijuana use, a result that has apparently not occurred so far in Oregon. Perhaps of key importance is the point that the legalization of any drug when we do not have any definitive evidence concerning its long-range effects is taking a major and unnecessary risk.

Until we know more about the possible long-term hazards of marijuana use, it would appear that legalization of this drug does present a certain element of risk. But it seems likely to many observers that if present trends continue, the federal government and most states may follow the pattern set by Oregon, or even possibly legalize marijuana subject to the same or similar restrictions as alcohol. A major step in this direction was taken by Alaska, which in 1975 became the first state to legalize the use of marijuana at home; however, continued prohibitions were maintained against its sale or public use.

Perspectives on drug usage

In his book *The Doors of Perception*, author Aldous Huxley remarked:

"That humanity at large will ever be able to dispense with Artificial Paradises seems very unlikely. Most men and women lead lives at worst so painful, at the best so monotonous, poor and limited that the urge to escape, the longing to transcend themselves if only for a few moments, is and has always been one of the principal appetites of the soul." (1954, p. 62)

Although we may not share Huxley's gloomy view of the human condition, we must admit that drugs are important to many people in our culture. In times of turmoil and stress, drugs are often turned to as a means of alleviating anxiety and of coping with problems.

In many instances, psychoactive drugs appear to serve a useful function—as when tranquilizers are used for alleviating special anxieties, or when moderate amounts of alcohol are used for reducing tension and facilitating social interaction. In fact, Jarvik (1967), speaking of the great advances in psychopharmacology that modern technology is making possible, depicted the following optimistic picture for the future:

". . . drugs may be employed not only to treat pathological conditions (reduce pain, suffering, agitation, and anxiety), but also to enhance the normal state of man—increase pleasure, facilitate learning and memory, reduce jealousy and aggressiveness. Hopefully, such pharmacological developments will come about as an accompaniment of, and not as a substitute for, a more ideal society." (p. 59)

Not only has this optimistic view not materialized, but a note of caution might well accompany it. There always remains the danger that in turning to drugs to escape from unpleasant reality, to resolve problems, and to find euphoria, humankind will be entering a false paradise. Some measure of psychic distress seems an inevitable condition of human existence. At the present time, psychoactive drugs can perhaps best be viewed as two-edged swords that can help us cope with stress and possibly enhance our experience, or can literally wreck our lives.

In this chapter we have reviewed the nature and effects of the major drugs, including alcohol, that are associated with abuse and dependence. We also have examined some of the causal factors involved in such dependence—the characteristics of the drug itself, the physical and psychological makeup of the individual, and the social setting in which the drug is used. Amid the complexities and personal and social implications of drug dependence, two variables appear to be of central importance: (a) the drug-oriented nature of our society, and (b) problems of social control.

Many psychoactive drugs, especially alcohol and tranquilizers, have constructive personal and social uses. However, most of these mind-altering drugs also have potentially harmful effects, particularly if they are abused. Consequently, society feels it necessary to exercise some control over their use; most drugs considered potentially dangerous if abused are legally available only by prescription. However, in the case of certain controversial drugs it is often difficult to exercise effective controls. This is particularly true if large segments of the population simply ignore such controls, as has been the case with marijuana.

One key issue in control is that of which drugs to legalize; a second is whether illicit drug abuse should be dealt with as a crime or as a medical, psychological, and social problem and treated accordingly. Until there is some understanding of and agreement concerning the value of such drugs as well as their hazards, the appropriate use and effective control of psychoactive drugs is likely to continue to pose a major social problem.

13

Organic Brain Syndromes

Injuries, disease, and various chemicals can affect the central nervous system and give rise to abnormal behavior. It has been estimated that more than 20 million people in the United States suffer from such disorders. Fortunately the great majority of cases do not involve serious psychopathology, but even so, mental disorders associated with brain pathology constitute more than a fourth of all first admissions to mental hospitals and clinics.

These disorders may simply involve an impairment of function, or they may be associated with a wide range of psychopathology, depending on (a) the location and extent of neural damage, (b) the premorbid personality of the individual, and (c) the nature of the individual's life situation. There are many cases involving severe brain damage in which mental change is astonishingly slight, whereas in other cases mild brain damage leads to a psychotic reaction. These variations are explained by the fact that the individual reacts to all stress, whether organic or psychological, as a functional unit. A well-integrated person can withstand brain damage or any other stress better than a rigid, immature, or otherwise psychologically handicapped person. Similarly, the individual who has a favorable life situation is likely to have a better prognosis. Since the nervous system is the center for integration of behavior, however, there are limits to the amount of brain damage an individual can tolerate or compensate for without exhibiting impaired functioning.

Brain disorders may be classified as *acute* or *chronic,* the primary consideration being the reversibility of the brain pathology. An acute disorder is likely to be temporary and reversible, whereas a chronic disorder is irreversible because of permanent damage to the nervous system. This classification is not a hard and fast one, because an acute condition may leave some residual damage after the major symptoms have cleared up, while a chronic condition may show some alleviation of symptoms over a sustained period of time. However, a general picture can be given of the two types.

1. *Acute brain disorders* are caused by diffuse impairment of brain function. Such impairment may result from a variety of con-

Disorders Associated with Infection
Disorders with Brain Tumors
Disorders with Head Injury
Disorders with Toxins and Metabolic Disturbances
Psychoses of the Aged

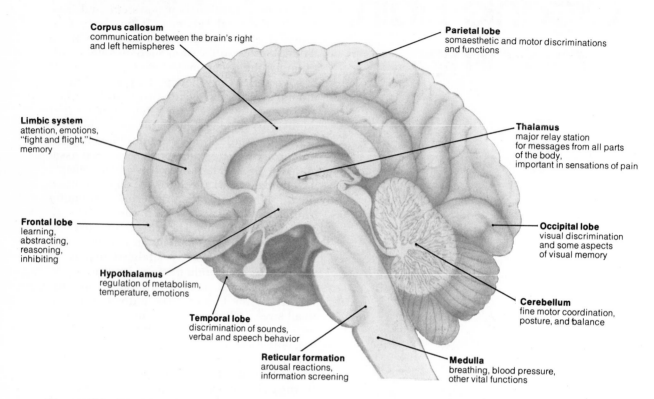

Corpus callosum
communication between the brain's right
and left hemispheres

Parietal lobe
somaesthetic and motor discriminations
and functions

Limbic system
attention, emotions,
"fight and flight,"
memory

Thalamus
major relay station
for messages from all parts
of the body,
important in sensations of pain

Frontal lobe
learning,
abstracting,
reasoning,
inhibiting

Occipital lobe
visual discrimination
and some aspects
of visual memory

Hypothalamus
regulation of metabolism,
temperature, emotions

Cerebellum
fine motor coordination,
posture, and balance

Temporal lobe
discrimination of sounds,
verbal and speech behavior

Reticular formation
arousal reactions,
information screening

Medulla
breathing, blood pressure,
other vital functions

It is very difficult to predict the effects of focused injuries to the brain. Although there is some localization of function (as indicated in this drawing of the right cerebral hemisphere) and damage to a particular area may cause severe impairment of function, the brain's great back-up resources may be able in time to make up for the deficiency. The sheer number of neurons, or nerve cells in the brain—10 to 12 billion—provide a redundancy of capability within each given area, to offset some cell loss. Also, the interaction of all parts of the brain in receiving and transmitting information will often permit an area sharing related information to compensate for loss of function in a damaged area. In addition, the brain has some capability for the repair of damage. The limits of these resources, however, can be reached; and while damage in some areas may lead only to a temporary loss of function, destruction in other areas—as well as extensive damage to any brain area—may result in complete and permanent loss of given functions.

ditions, including high fevers, nutritional deficiencies, and drug intoxication. Symptoms range from mild mood changes to acute delirium. The latter may be complicated by hallucinations, delusions, and other personality disturbances.

The prognosis in acute brain disorders is good; such conditions usually clear up over a short period of time. In some cases, however, the lowering of cortical controls may precipitate a latent psychosis that persists after the immediate brain pathology has cleared up.

2. *Chronic brain disorders* result from injuries, disease, drugs, and a variety of other conditions. The permanent destruction of brain tissue is reflected in some degree of impairment of higher integrative functions. Where the damage is severe, such symptoms typically include:

1. Impairment of orientation—especially for time but often also for place and person

2. Impairment of memory—notably for recent events and less so for events of remote past, with a tendency to confabulate, that is, to "invent" memories to fill in gaps

3. Impairment of learning, comprehension, and judgment—with ideation tending to be concrete and impoverished—and with inability to think on higher conceptual levels and to plan

4. Emotional impairment—with emotional over-reactivity and easy arousal to laughter or tears, or with a blunting of affect

5. Impairment of inner reality and ethical controls—with lowering of behavioral standards and carelessness in personal hygiene and appearance

These symptoms may also occur in acute brain disorders; however, in such cases delirium and hallucinations or stupor are more likely to dominate the clinical picture.

Although there is an attempt on both biological and psychological levels to compensate for damage or loss, the regenerative capacities of the central nervous system are unfortunately limited. Cell bodies and nonmyelinated neural pathways do not have the power of regeneration, which means that their destruction is permanent. However, the central nervous system abounds in back-up apparatus. If a given circuit is knocked out, others may take over, and functions lost as a result of brain damage may often be relearned. The degree of recovery from functional disabilities, even following an irreversible brain lesion, may be relatively complete or limited, and recovery may proceed rapidly or slowly. Since there are limits to both the plasticity and the relearning ability of the brain, extensive brain damage may lead to a permanent loss of function and result in a wide range of physical and psychological symptoms.

In general, the greater the amount of tissue damage, the greater the impairment of function. As we have noted, however, some individuals are able to compensate much better than others for brain pathology. Depending on the severity of symptoms—in either acute or chronic disorders—the clinical picture may be referred to as *mild, moderate,* or *severe.*

In the remainder of this chapter we shall consider some of the more common causes of brain pathology and the related mental disorders that may develop.

Insights into brain functioning as a result of split-brain research

Important insights into the relationship between the brain's right and left hemispheres have been provided by studies of the effects of split-brain surgery. This procedure—which involves dividing the hemispheres by cutting the corpus callosum—is sometimes resorted to in the case of epileptics as a means of controlling their seizures. Apparently the surgery produces no noticeable change in the patient's temperament, intelligence, or personality traits, but it does impede the transmission of sensory messages from one side of the body to the other.

Differences in functioning between the right hemisphere and the left one have been reported by Gazzaniga (1967, 1970) and Sperry, Gazzaniga, and Bogen (1969). For most right-handed people, the left hemisphere controls language, self-awareness, and complex problem-solving functions, while the right hemisphere specializes in perception, spatial orientation, and artistic ability. In a broad sense, the left hemisphere is the logician and the right is the artist. More recent research tends to support these earlier findings (Nebes, 1974; Sussman & MacNeilage, 1975). However, Nebes cautions that this is a tentative way of viewing the function of the two hemispheres; future research will show whether this is an accurate picture of the way the two cerebral hemispheres differ in their specialization.

In this context, several investigators have speculated about the effects of cutting the corpus callosum in infants, agreeing that either hemisphere could probably develop the functions ordinarily handled by both. Thus, in effect, it would be possible to produce two distinct personalities in the same individual.

Disorders Associated with Infection

Mental disorders may appear in connection with brain infections resulting from bacteria or viruses that invade the brain and damage or destroy nerve tissue. Among the major infectious diseases of the brain are cerebral syphilis and encephalitis.

Cerebral syphilis

Syphilitic infection of the brain is associated with three somewhat distinct syndromes—*general paresis, juvenile paresis,* and *meningovascular syphilis.* An understanding of these syndromes can best begin with an understanding of syphilis, an infectious venereal disease that has taken an incalculable toll in human lives and happiness. Unless properly treated, syphilis eventually disables and then kills its victims.

Syphilis appeared with dramatic suddenness several centuries ago and spread within a few years over the known world (Pusey, 1933). Many medical historians contend that syphilis was introduced into Europe by the members of Columbus' crew, who presumably contracted it from the women of the West Indies. In fact, Kemble (1936) has pointed out that Columbus himself may have been infected. During his second voyage, in 1494, Columbus began having attacks of fever, possibly indicating the secondary stage of syphilis. During his third voyage, in 1498, he developed "a severe attack of gout", which was widespread and not confined to one or two of the small joints as gout usually is. During this voyage also, the first signs of mental disorder made their appearance. He began to hear voices and to regard himself as an "ambassador of God." On his last voyage, in 1504, Columbus was so ill that he had to be carried ashore. His whole body was pathologically swollen from the chest downward, his limbs were paralyzed, and his brain affected—all symptoms of the terminal stages of syphilis.

Whatever the origin, syphilis spread like a tornado throughout Europe and became known as *The Great Pox* (Parran, 1937; Pusey, 1933). In 1496 it appeared in Paris and the number of victims became so great that the government passed an emergency decree forbidding a syphilitic to leave his home until completely cured.[1] In Edinburgh during the same year, all afflicted inhabitants were banished to an island near Leith. By 1498 the disease had spread to England. Vasco da Gama and his pioneering Portuguese probably carried the disease around the Cape of Good Hope, and an outbreak occurred in India in 1498, spreading eastward to China by 1505.

The numerous armies of mercenaries and adventurers of that period no doubt contributed to the rapid spread of the disease. Apparently this early strain of syphilis was both extremely contagious and unusually virulent, and attacked its victims with a violence almost unknown today.[2] High fever, delirium, violent headaches, horrible sores, and bone ulcers were typical, even in the early stages of the disease.

During this period there was no name for the disease. Each suffering nation blamed it on some other nation. The Italians called it the *French* or *Spanish disease,* the English called it the *French pox,* and so on. It finally received its specific name when, in 1530, an Italian physician, Fracastorius, wrote a long poem in which the leading character, a shepherd named Syphilis, was stricken with the disease because of an insult to Apollo. The poem became tremendously popular, and *syphilis* became the accepted name for the dread disease.

Although there were many early approaches to treatment, the physicians of those days could offer little help, and it was several hundred years before any major advances were made in the conquest of syphilis. In Chapter 2 we sketched the several steps by

---

[1]A "cure" probably meant the temporary remission or disappearance of symptoms—common during the third stage of syphilis—which the people of that period mistook for recovery.

[2]Undoubtedly the severity of this disease was also due in part to the lack of resistance or partial immunity usually acquired in the case of older diseases.

which the deadly spirochete that causes syphilis was discovered, blood tests developed, and methods of treatment worked out.

Stages of syphilis. The spirochete of syphilis may gain entrance to the body through minute breaks or scratches in the skin, or directly through mucous membranes, such as the lining of the mouth or the genital tract. Even though the mucous membrane is intact, the spirochete can wiggle through it in an hour or so. Syphilis is almost always spread from person to person during sexual intercourse or mouth-genital contact, although in exceptional cases it may be contracted through kissing or from direct contact with open syphilitic sores or lesions. It may also be transmitted from mother to child during fetal development; in this case is it referred to as *congenital syphilis*.

Once they have breached the outer defenses of the body, the spirochetes begin their systematic destruction of internal organs in four fairly well-defined stages.

1. *First stage.* Immediately after the spirochetes gain entrance to the body, they multiply rapidly. From 10 to 20 days later, a sore called a *hard chancre* appears at the point of infection, which usually takes the form either of a pimple that feels hard to the touch or of an open ulcerated sore. In some instances it may be so insignificant that the person is unaware of its existence. Even if untreated, this sore disappears in from 4 to 6 weeks, often leaving the victim with the mistaken notion that it was really only a minor irritation and that he is now cured.

2. *Second stage.* Following the chancre by some 3 to 6 weeks is the appearance of a copper-colored skin rash, which may be mild and transitory or more severe, covering the entire body. This skin eruption may look like measles or smallpox and originally gave rise to the term *Great Pox* to differentiate this disease from *smallpox*. The rash may or may not be accompanied by fever, headaches, indigestion, loss of appetite, loss of hair in spots over the scalp, and other symptoms not usually thought of in connection with syphilis.

3. *Third stage.* This is known as the latent period, for in most cases all symptoms disappear. Again the victim is apt to think he is

---

Some dimensions of the venereal disease problem

In 1974 the World Health Organization reported that venereal disease is increasing throughout the world, and the most common form — gonorrhea — is out of control in many countries.* In fact, the annual incidence of gonorrhea in some countries appears to vary between 5 and 10 percent for the age group 15 to 30. In general, the incidence of venereal disease is twice as high among teen-agers as for the general population.

In the United States there are an estimated million or more Americans with untreated syphilis, with almost 100,000 new cases occurring each year. There are also over two and one-half million new cases of gonorrhea each year, although only about 800,000 are officially reported. In the mid-1970s new cases of syphilis and gonorrhea were occurring at the rate of over 7,000 a day in the U.S. — about 5 new cases per second — with half the victims between 15 and 24 years of age. It has been estimated that in large cities, more than 1 out of 3 high-school students will contract VD before graduation; if present trends continue, the incidence rate is expected to reach 1 out of 2 by the end of this decade.

Since both the syphilitic spirochete and the gonorrhea germ — a coffee-bean-shaped organism — are easily killed by dryness and heat, venereal disease is rarely acquired by any other means than physical contact. The recent marked increase in cases is apparently related to an increased casualness in sexual behavior as well as to the declining use of prophylactic devices since the advent of birth-control pills.

Much more prevalent than syphilis, gonorrhea is commonly considered a relatively mild disease, but it may affect the joints, heart, and other organs. Because gonorrheal infection can cause blindness, the law requires that silver nitrate drops or penicillin be placed in the eyes of all newborn infants. Typical early symptoms of gonorrhea include acute inflammation of the genital and urinary tract, with a discharge of pus. In many cases, however, the symptoms are not pronounced and the victim is unaware of having contracted the disease.

Antibiotics are highly effective in the treatment of both gonorrhea and syphilis, but there are far more untreated than treated cases of VD. Apparently because many people lack information about these disorders, they fail to utilize preventive measures or to seek treatment when infection does occur.

*There are some 13 types of venereal disease transmitted sexually, of which gonorrhea and syphilis have shown the greatest worldwide increase in recent years.

Based on Kaiser Permanente Medical Care Program (1973) and *Los Angeles Times* (Nov. 16, 1974).

---

cured and so either avoid or discontinue treatment. In actuality, however, the germs have gone "underground," having burrowed their way into the bloodstream. Here they multiply and spread throughout the body, attacking various internal organs and, if untreated, causing permanent degeneration. The spirochetes may attack the bone marrow, the spleen, the lymph glands, or any tissue or organ of the body. Blood vessels and nerve cells seem to be favorite targets.

4. *Fourth stage.* In this last stage we see the accumulated damage produced during the latent period. Ten, twenty, and even thirty years after the initial infection, the degenerative work of the spirochete may become apparent in a sudden heart attack, failure of vision (until recent times 15 percent of all blindness in the U.S. was due to syphilis), loss of motor coordination in walking, or mental disturbances. Syphilis is often called the "great imitator" because of the wide range of organic disease symptoms that it may produce. The most frequent and fatal forms of late syphilis are those in which the spirochete invades the walls of heart and blood vessels and the nervous system. It is the latter form with which we are primarily concerned in our study of abnormal psychology.

General paresis. General paresis is a mental disorder caused by the progressive infiltration and destruction of brain tissue by the spirochetes of syphilis. It has also been variously called *general paralysis of the insane, dementia paralytica,* and *paresis.* Approximately 5 percent of untreated syphilitics eventually develop general paresis. The first symptoms usually appear about 10 to 15 years after the primary infection, although the incubation period may be as short as 2 years or as long as 40. Unless the person receives treatment, the outcome is always fatal, death usually occurring within 2 to 3 years after the initial symptoms.

General paresis is associated with a wide range of behavioral and psychological symptoms. During the early phase of this disorder, the individual typically becomes careless and inattentive and makes mistakes in his work. At first he may notice his mistakes but attributes them to being overtired; later he does

not even notice them. Personal habits may show some deterioration, and the once-neat person may become slovenly. Comprehension and judgment suffer, and the individual may show a tendency to evade important problems, or he may react to them with smug indifference. Accompanying these symptoms is a blunting of affect, so that he does not share in the joys, sorrows, or anxieties of loved ones. He seems unable to realize the seriousness of his behavior and may become irritable or resort to ready rationalizations if his behavior is questioned. Overly sentimental behavior is typical and may involve promiscuous sexual patterns.

As the disorder progresses, a number of well-delineated physical symptoms make their appearance. The pupils are irregular in size and the pupillary reflex to light is either sluggish or entirely absent. Typically, speech functions become badly disturbed, with considerable stuttering and slurring of words. A phrase that invariably gives trouble and is of diagnostic significance is "Methodist Episcopal." This may be mispronounced in a number of ways, such as "Meodist Epispal" or "Methdist Pispal." Writing is similarly disturbed, with tremulous lines and the omission or transposition of syllables. Frequently, the individual has a rather vacant, dissipated look, with a silly grin. Where the spirochetes have also damaged neural pathways within the spinal cord, there may be difficulty in motor coordination. Such individuals typically have a shuffling, unsteady walk, referred to as *locomotor ataxia.* In addition, there may be tremors of the face, lips, and fingers and an absence of tendon reflexes, such as the knee jerk. During this period convulsive seizures may also appear.

Paralleling these physical symptoms is a general personality deterioration. The individual is unmannerly, tactless, unconcerned with his appearance, and unethical in his behavior. Memory defects, which may be noticeable in the early phases of the illness, become more obvious. He may be unable to remember what he did just a short time before. He may ask when dinner will be served only a few minutes after he has finished eating it. This memory impairment extends to remote events, and the individual tends to fill in memory losses by

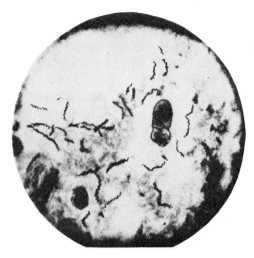

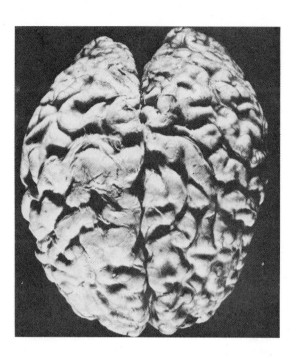

General paresis results when the spirochetes invade the cerebral cortex (left). A postmortem examination typically reveals thickening of the meninges surrounding the brain and atrophy of the convolutions, especially in the frontal and temporal lobes (right).

various fabrications. As his intellectual processes are increasingly impaired, he becomes unable to comprehend the simplest problems and may optimistically squander his money on harebrained schemes or become involved in a variety of antisocial acts.

This entire picture of personality deterioration is usually colored by emotional reactions in the form of either marked euphoria, depression, or apathy. Thus, three categories are commonly used to distinguish clinical types of paretics—*expansive*, *depressed*, and *demented*—although these types are by no means always distinct, and depressed patients frequently change categories by becoming euphoric. As the disease enters the terminal period, the extensive brain damage leads to a similar picture for all three types, in which the patient leads a vegetative life, expresses little interest in anything, becomes inarticulate in speech, and can no longer care for himself. Convulsive seizures usually become common. Finally, a terminal infection or breakdown of bodily functioning leads to death.

The following is a classic example of the expansive type of paretic and well illustrates the euphoria, poorly systematized delusions of grandeur, and ludicrous nature of the plans which these paretics look forward to.

"C. W. flew planes from the United States to North Africa. His route began in Florida, passed through Natal, Ascension Island, and terminated in Dakar. His earlier health record was excellent, save for some 'difficulty' in his early twenties. Now, at 38, he was strong, well liked, and an expert pilot in the ferry command. He had completed a dozen or more trips.

"As he flew his plane eastward on his last journey, C. W. was unusually gay. 'It's a great world,' he sang. 'My rich aunt in Oklahoma is going to leave me $30,000,000.'

"During the periods of relief by his co-pilot, he talked loudly and became chummy with other members of the crew. As a matter of fact, he offered to loan the navigator $50,000. Landing safely in Dakar, his high spirits continued. Then his friends found him buying several 'diamonds' from an Arab street merchant, spending most of his cash for this purpose.

"'Boy,' he exclaimed, 'I got a swell bargain! Six diamonds for $100 cash now and $100 more on my next trip! I sure fooled that Arab; he's never going to collect the rest from me.'

"'How do you know the diamonds are genuine?' he was asked.

From Fetterman, J. L., *Practical Lessons in Psychiatry*, 1949. Courtesy of Charles C Thomas, Publisher, Springfield, Illinois.

Disorders Associated with Infection **465**

" 'I tested them,' he boasted. 'I struck one with a hammer and it proved hard; diamonds are hard.'

"Upon the return journey, C. W. continued the story of his expected wealth and the sum grew with the distance of travel.

" 'It's $40,000,000 I am getting and I expect to share some of it with you guys,' he announced. When his co-pilot received this astounding information with doubt and anxiety, C. W. could not understand it. When the co-pilot asked him to rest, he assured him that his body was perfect, that he didn't need rest. Then he added that he could fly the plane without gas, which he tried to prove by doing some fancy maneuvers in the sky.

" 'Funny,' he said later, 'no one seemed to believe me. Even when I offered them a million each they weren't happy, but looked at each other in such a puzzled way. It made me laugh, how they begged me to rest and how worried they looked when I refused. I was the boss and I showed them.'

"When the plane landed in Brazil by a miracle, C. W. was examined by a physician, forced into another plane and brought to Florida. Upon examination he was talkative, eyes gleaming, exuberant with statements of wealth and power. 'I am now one of the richest men in the world,' he said. 'I'll give you $5,000,000 to start a hospital. My eyes are jewels, diamonds, emeralds,' . . ." (Fetterman, 1949, pp. 267–68)

Frequently, the early signs of general paresis are not recognized by family and friends until an acute episode of some sort occurs. The family of one patient noticed nothing particularly wrong until one day he went to a bar instead of to his office and there became noisy and expansive. Actually, for several months there had been less obvious symptoms, including forgetfulness of business appointments and peculiar color combinations in dress, but no one had noticed anything seriously amiss.

Although much is now known about general paresis, a number of questions still puzzle investigators. Why do only 1 in 20 untreated syphilitics develop general paresis? Why do a higher percentage of whites than blacks develop general paresis after syphilitic infection? Why do far more male than female syphilitics develop general paresis? And why is the relative incidence of general paresis much higher in some countries than in others? Some investigators hold that the syphilitic spirochetes attack the most vulnerable organs of the individual's body and that general paresis develops in persons whose brain tissue has an especially low resistance to syphilis. Other investigators have suggested that different strains of spirochetes may account for many of these differences. But the final answers to these questions are not yet available.

Juvenile paresis. Juvenile paresis results from congenital syphilis and is a condition of general paresis occurring in childhood or adolescence. Although no longer a major problem in the United States, congenital syphilis is still relatively common in certain other countries and contributes to a high infant mortality rate as well as to physical afflictions other than juvenile paresis.

The symptoms in juvenile paresis are similar to those in general paresis and involve a picture of progressive mental and physical deterioration, including progressive impairment of memory, comprehension, and judgment. Motor incoordination, speech disturbances, and convulsions are common. The juvenile paretic usually has no understanding of his condition and is apt to show a relatively simple deterioration without pronounced emotional coloring or marked psychological compensation.

Formerly, syphilis accounted for more than half of all blindness in children at birth. It was also the largest cause of stillbirths and the primary reason for the deaths of many infants during the first weeks of life (Parran, 1937). Although symptoms may appear at any time after birth, ordinarily there are no noticeable symptoms until the child reaches puberty. In some cases, however, retarded physical development, mental retardation, and convulsions make their appearance prior to the onset of the typical paretic syndrome (Bruetsch, 1959). In juvenile paresis, the course of the disorder is longer than in adult paresis, averaging about 5 years between the appearance of initial symptoms and termination in death.

The following is a description of a 15-year-old boy diagnosed as a juvenile paretic.

The patient was referred to the hospital by a school doctor after the boy had become "droopy" in class and began to talk in a rather funny and thick-tongued manner. On admission to the hospital the boy was slightly unsteady in his walk, his pupils were widely dilated and did not show a normal pupillary reflex to light. His emotional mood seemed to alternate from one of depression and apathy to one of mild euphoria. He soiled himself, was careless in his personal appearance, and exposed himself indiscriminately to males and females alike. The following conversation took place during a period of mild euphoria:

Dr.: How are you feeling today, Bob?
Pt.: Jus wonful, jus wonful (silly, fatuous grin).
Dr.: Can you say Methodist Episcopal Church?
Pt.: Mesdus Episfal Chursh.
Dr.: How are your studies progressing at school?
Pt.: Jus fine, jus fine, perfect.

Tragic cases of this kind need not occur if proper safeguards are taken against congenital syphilis.

Historically, Henry VIII of England has often been cited to illustrate the tragic results of congenital syphilis. The first of his wives, Catherine of Aragon, bore four children, all of whom were stillborn or died immediately after birth. A fifth child, a daughter, finally survived to reign later as "Bloody Mary." Mary herself showed many signs of congenital syphilis—her face was prematurely old and scarred; her hair thin and straggling; her head square, with a grotesquely protruding forehead; and her sight extremely bad. Her sudden death at the age of 42 was presumably due to syphilitic complications. Of Henry's six wives, Anne of Cleves, his fourth wife, whose marriage was never consummated, was thought by the medical historian Kemble (1936) to be the only one who might have shown a negative Wassermann (a blood test for syphilis).

Meningovascular syphilis. Meningovascular syphilis differs from general paresis in that the syphilitic damage initially centers in the blood vessels and meninges of the brain rather than in the neural tissue. This form of cerebral syphilis is rare.

The early symptoms in meningovascular syphilis differ from those in general paresis, in that there is rarely any marked deterioration of conduct. Typical are persistent headaches, dizziness, blurring or doubling of vision, lethargy, confusion, and difficulty in concentration. Other symptoms of diagnostic value include disturbed pupillary reactions to light and accentuated knee-jerk reflex. Speech and writing usually are not markedly affected, but convulsive seizures are common.

During the early stages of meningovascular syphilis the actual amount of brain damage is usually less than in general paresis, and the personality deterioration is correspondingly less. In advanced cases the brain damage, symptom picture, and patterns are comparable for the two disorders.

Treatment and outcomes. After penicillin had been developed and found effective in the treatment of syphilis, there was a spectacular drop in the number of cases. Thus during the late 1950s the problem of syphilis was considered solved.

During the period from 1960 to 1970, however, the number of cases of reported syphilis doubled; in 1970, there were an estimated 1 million persons with untreated syphilis in the United States (Ford, 1970; Strage, 1971). This increase has continued into the 1970s with over 100,000 new cases being reported each year, and probably as large or a larger number of unreported cases add to the total.

According to statistics gathered from 102 cities in 1969, the sources of infection in syphilis were, in order of frequency: (a) friend of the opposite sex, 47 percent; (b) stranger of the opposite sex, including prostitutes and casual pickups, 20 percent; (c) homosexual contact, 17 percent; and (d) marital partner, 16 percent (Strage, 1971). Contrary to a widely held popular misconception, it is currently estimated that 5 percent or less of syphilis is spread by prostitutes.

The specific outcomes in cases of paresis receiving medical treatment depend to a large extent on the amount of cerebral damage that has taken place before treatment is started. If the damage is not extensive, the adaptive capacities of the individual—both neurological and psychological—may leave only a small impairment of brain function. Unfortunately, in many cases treatment is not undertaken until the disease has produced extensive and irreparable brain damage. Here about all that can be hoped for is to prevent further inroads of the deadly spirochete. In such cases, the intellectual picture may show considerable improvement, but the patient never approaches his previous level of ability. For treated paretics as a group, the following rough estimates of outcome may be made:

1. Some 20 to 30 percent show good recovery and can resume their former occupation and activities.

2. Another 30 to 40 percent show some improvement, but usually require a transfer to less complex occupational duties as a consequence of residual intellectual or personality impairment.

3. 15 to 25 percent show no improvement.

4. 10 percent die during the course of treatment (or within a 10-year period following the instigation of treatment).

On the other hand, when treatment is started early, approximately 80 percent of general paretics show a sufficient remission of symptoms to return to their original or other type of employment. As with other mental disorders, psychotherapy and sociotherapy may be essential aspects of the total treatment program.

The only fully adequate approach to cerebral syphilis is the prevention of syphilitic infection, or early detection and treatment where infection has taken place. In the United States, facilities are provided for the free diagnosis and treatment of syphilis; most states require examinations before marriage; and public education has been vigorously supported by governmental, educational, and religious agencies. It is also mandatory in all states for physicians to report cases of syphilis to local health authorities. Unfortunately, many people do not seek diagnosis and treatment due to inadequate information or the traditional stigma attached to venereal disease.

In efforts directed toward finding and treating all infected cases, it has become common practice for patients with infectious syphilis to be interviewed for sex contacts. Every effort is then made to locate these individuals and screen them for possible syphilitic infection. For example, a successful search was conducted in a case involving a Sacramento, California, prostitute, named as a contact by an infected male; she, in turn produced a list of 310 male contacts. Although they were chiefly interstate truck drivers scattered over 34 states, Canada, and Mexico, authorities were able to locate them and ask for blood tests (*Los Angeles Times*, 1970). In another case, cited by Strage (1971), an infected homosexual male was able to produce a file of nearly 1000 male contacts together with the details of their sexual acts and preferences.

To improve the efficiency of case-finding, investigators have extended interviews to include not only sex contacts of patients but also friends and acquaintances, whose sexual behavior is assumed to be similar to that of the patient; this is called *cluster testing*.

Although we now have the medical means to eradicate syphilis, it remains a major health problem in our society because its roots are social as well as medical. However, with the cooperation of international and national agencies, better education, and more adequate facilities for diagnosis and treatment, there is every reason to believe that syphilis can eventually be controlled or even eliminated as a public health problem.

Epidemic encephalitis

Epidemic encephalitis was first described in 1917 as an inflammation of the brain caused by a virus. The disease was uncommon prior to an epidemic in Europe and the United States following World War I. It is again relatively rare in Western countries; however, it remains a serious problem in certain parts of Asia and Africa. Although no age group is immune, encephalitis is more common among children and young adults.

Clinical picture. During the acute phase of the disease, symptoms include fever, delirium, and stupor. Typically the individual is lethargic and appears to be sleeping all the time, although he can usually be awakened long enough to answer questions or take nourishment. As a consequence of the lethargy, the condition was once called *encephalis lethargica* and is now popularly known as *sleeping sickness*. Symptoms may also take the form of acute psychomotor excitement, in which the individual becomes restless, agitated, and irritable.

Although some children appear to make a satisfactory recovery, the aftereffects of epidemic encephalitis can be very serious. Previously well-behaved and cheerful children may become restless, aggressive, cruel, and generally unmanageable. They seem to lose their self-control and to be under a continual pressure of restless activity. Often they will state that they do not want to behave as they do, but that they cannot seem to help themselves. Without provocation, they may impulsively engage in destructive, homicidal, sexually aberrant, and other deviant behavior. As a result, such children usually require hospitalization. Other typical symptoms are hypersalivation, motor incoordination, and bizarre posture, such as leaning conspicuously backward or forward when walking. The precise relation of the symptoms to the neurological damage is not known. In children under 5, mental development may be severely retarded, and a child may not attain his normal intellectual status. Jervis (1959) reported that encephalitis accounted for some 5 percent of all institutionalized cases of mental retardation at that time. However, the incidence is much less today. In general, the older the child at the onset of the disease, the less severe the mental impairment.

In cases where the child becomes impulsive, aggressive, and hyperactive, there is residual brain damage that impairs inner controls and the organization of thought processes. The following case illustrates many of the symptoms typically found in severe postencephalitic behavior disorders among children.

"Harold is a boy of fifteen years whose behavior is so unpredictably and dangerously impulsive that his family cannot keep him at home. He must always live in an institution.

"He presents a strange, almost uncannily freakish appearance. He is short and squat in stature and has a short squarish head that is oversized for his body. He walks with an awkward, shambling gait, a little like a monkey. As you watch him, he sidles toward another child in a gingerly, apparently affectionate manner. Suddenly he grasps the child's finger and bends it backward mercilessly; then he slinks impishly away, laughing and chuckling. In a moment he raises his bitten nails to his mouth and stares at the cloudless sky as though abruptly transported, and mutters some incoherent remark about a 'terrible storm coming that will break all the limbs of the trees.' A few minutes later with tears streaming from his eyes he presents an appearance of genuine remorse. He puts his arms around the same child's neck and suddenly chokes the child painfully with a tremendous hug. When a teacher pries him away he tries to bite her hand. He murmurs to the teacher: 'I hurt you, didn't I? Can you whip? Whip me.' Perhaps a while later he may be seen to shuffle stealthily toward the same teacher and whisper to her in a childlike manner: 'I like you.' Then quick as

a flash he may poke his finger into her eye and cry again: 'Can you whip? Whip me.'

". . . The most striking aspects of his behavior are his uncontrolled impulsive cruelties and his perverted craving to suffer pain himself. Like the rest of us, he wants love and affection, but he seeks it in a strange way. He torments and hurts others so they may do the same to him. He appears to derive an erotic pleasure from the pain which he provokes from others in lieu of love. To such injuries he adds those which he inflicts upon himself.

"This is a strange boy indeed. His disordered behavior is the consequence of an inflammatory illness of the brain, encephalitis, which complicated a contagious disease in infancy." (Menninger, 1946, pp. 41–42)

In adults, the aftereffects of epidemic encephalitis are usually not seriously impairing. In some cases, however, residual effects may include one or more of the following: (a) Parkinson's disease—also known as *paralysis agitans* and *shaking palsy*—which is a chronic, progressive disease of the central nervous system; (b) tremors and ocular symptoms, including the loss of the blink reflex, which results in a staring and masklike expression; and (c) impulsive and aggressive behavior, which the individual is aware of but unable to control. In the third instance, the individual has been referred to as "master of what he says" but the "slave of what he does."

Treatment and outcomes. Epidemic encephalitis ordinarily can be arrested by antibiotics that kill the invading virus, and most children and adults make a complete or satisfactory recovery. As we have seen, however, in some children there may be serious residual effects.

In the latter cases, rehabilitation therapy usually includes the use of drugs to diminish hyperactivity and foster increased learning ability and self-control. Educational, psychological, and sociological measures are also usually considered essential aspects of the overall treatment program.

Disorders with Brain Tumors

In the writings of Felix Plater (1536–1614) we find the following rather remarkable account of "A Case of Stupor due to a Tumour in the Brain, Circular like a Gland":

"Caspar Bone Curtius, a noble knight, began to show signs of 'mental alienation' which continued through a period of two years until at last he became quite stupefied, did not act rationally, did not take food unless forced to do so, nor did he go to bed unless compelled, at table he just lay on his arms and went to sleep, he did not speak when questioned even when admonished, and if he did it was useless. Pituita dropped from his nose copiously and frequently: this condition continued for about six months, and finally he died. . . . At the post mortem when the skull was opened and the lobes of the brain separated, a remarkable globular tumor was found on the upper surface of the Corpus Callosum, resembling a gland fleshly, hard and funguslike, about the size of a medium sized apple, invested with its own membranes and having its own veins, lying free and without any connection with the brain itself. . . . This tumour, by its mass, produced pressure on the brain and its vessels, which caused stupor, torpor, and finally death. Some doctors who had seen this case earlier attributed it to sorcery, others just to the humors, but by opening the skull we made clear the abstruse and hidden cause." (1664)

A tumor is a new growth involving an abnormal enlargement of body tissue. Such growths are most apt to occur in the breast, the uterus, the prostate, or the intestinal tract, although they are sometimes found in the central nervous system. In adults, brain tumors occur with the greatest frequency between the ages of 40 and 60.

Some brain tumors are malignant, in that they destroy the brain tissue in which they arise; others are benign in that they are not destructive except by reason of the pressure they exert. Since the skull is a bony, unyielding container, a relatively small tumor in the brain may cause marked pressure and thus may interfere seriously with normal brain functioning.

Clinical picture

The clinical picture that develops in cases of brain tumor is extremely varied and is determined largely by (a) the location, size, and rapidity of growth of the tumor, and (b) the personality and stress tolerance of the individual.

The brain tumor itself may result in both localized and general symptoms. Damage to a particular part of the brain may result in localized disturbances of sensory or motor functions. General symptoms appear when the tumor becomes large enough to result in greatly increased intracranial pressure. Common early symptoms are persistent headache, vomiting, memory impairment, listlessness, depression, and "choked disc"—a phenomenon due to swelling of the optic nerve when cerebrospinal fluid is forced into it by intracranial pressure.

As the tumor progresses and the intracranial pressure increases, there may be clouding of consciousness, disorientation for time and place, carelessness in personal habits, irritability, convulsive seizures, vomiting, sensorimotor losses, hallucinations, apathy, and a general impairment of intellectual functions. Terminal stages are usually similar to other types of severe brain damage, in which the patient is reduced to a vegetative stupor and eventual death.

The range of symptoms that may occur in brain tumor cases was demonstrated by Levin (1949) in an intensive study of 22 cases admitted to the Boston Psychopathic Hospital. These patients ranged in age from 22 to 65 years, the majority falling between the ages of 40 and 60 years. There were 11 males and 11 females. Prior to hospitalization the range of symptoms shown by these patients included:

Symptoms prior to hospitalization	Number of cases
Memory impairment or confusion	13
Depression	9
Seizures	8
Headaches	8
Complaints of visual impairment	6
Drowsiness	6
Irritability	6
Indifference	5
Restlessness	4
Complaint of generalized weakness	4
Loss of sense of responsibility	3
Paranoid ideas	2
Tendency to be combative	2
Euphoria	2
Aphasia	2

The interval between the onset of the symptoms and hospitalization varied from 1 week to 6 years, with an average interval of 17 months. In most cases, symptoms were evident 6 months or more prior to first admission. In this connection, it has been pointed out, however, that minor personality changes and depression often serve to mask the more definitive symptoms of a brain tumor—with the result that diagnosis and treatment are often delayed (Schwab, 1970).

The patient's emotional reaction to the organic damage and to the resulting intellectual impairment may vary. Initially, he may be overly irritable, drowsy, and mildly depressed. As the disorder progresses, however, he may have some insight into the seriousness of his condition and become severely depressed, anxious, and apprehensive. Patients who have less insight into their condition usually react to the brain damage and their failing functions by becoming expansive and euphoric. Such patients seem unconcerned about their illness and may joke and laugh in a most unrestrained and hilarious manner. Such reactions are apparently compensatory and are especially frequent in advanced stages when there is considerable brain damage or pressure.

Serious tumors, especially those with psychological complications, are most common in the frontal, temporal, and parietal lobes. Frontal-lobe tumors often produce subtle peculiarities, such as inability to concentrate, personal carelessness, a loss of inhibitions, and absent-mindedness that later becomes a memory defect. Often, too, the individual becomes silly and prone to punning and general jocularity. In an analysis of 90 patients with frontal-lobe tumors, Dobrokhotova (1968) found three common forms of emotional disorder: (a) the absence of spontaneity; (b) disinhibition and lability of affect—often with euphoria; and (c) forced emotions, which were abruptly expressed and terminated.

Tumors involving the special sensory areas in the brain may result in hallucinations of sight, hearing, taste, and smell. It has been estimated that about half of the patients with brain tumors evidence hallucinations sometime during the course of their illness. Visual hallucinations predominate and may involve dazzling, vividly colored flashes of light, as well as various kinds and sizes of animals and other objects. In temporal-lobe tumors, "Lilliputian hallucinations" are sometimes found, in which the patient sees small figures that he usually knows are not real. Such hallucinations apparently result from irritation of the visual pathways passing through the temporal lobe. Similarly, irritation of the olfactory pathways may result in the perception of peculiar odors, such as rubber burning, for which there is no external stimulus. Auditory hallucinations may include buzzing, ringing, roaring, and occasionally voices and conversations.

Although personality change is so common in brain-tumor cases that it has in the past

Brain tumors can cause a variety of personality alterations. Below is a picture of a meningioma—a tumor of one of the meninges, or coverings of the brain.

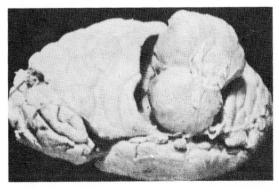

Disorders with Brain Tumors   **471**

been attributed directly to the tumor, we now realize that these symptoms are neither inevitable nor to be thought of as due solely to the tumor. As we have noted, adjustive reactions are typically a function of both the stress situation (including biological, psychosocial, and sociocultural stresses) and the personality of the individual—his personal maturity, stability and level of stress tolerance.

A most dramatic example of the importance of the patient's pre-illness personality in determining the psychological effects of brain pathology is provided in John Gunther's (1949) moving account of his son Johnny's struggle against a malignant brain tumor. Johnny was 16 and in his junior year at preparatory school when the tumor was discovered. During the 14 months that preceded his death, he was subjected to two major operations and a variety of other treatment procedures.

Throughout his ordeal, Johnny never lost his courage, his ambition, his sense of humor, or his mental alertness. Although his strength and general physical condition deteriorated steadily, and he suffered increasing visual impairment, he fought to carry on a normal pattern of activity and to keep up with his studies by being tutored at home. Through tireless and determined effort, he managed to take and pass college entrance examinations—a 6-hour ordeal that followed an hour of standing in line—and to graduate with his class. By this time his physical impairment had become so great that it was a struggle simply to tie his shoelaces or even fasten his belt. At graduation late in May, he could only walk very slowly down the long aisle and grasp the diploma with his weak left hand. Less than a month later, Johnny died.

Treatment and outcomes

Treatment of brain-tumor cases is primarily a medical matter and thus is outside the scope of our present discussion. However, it may be noted that the degree of recovery of the patient in such cases depends both on the size and location of the growth and on the amount of brain tissue that may have to be removed with the tumor. In some cases there seems to be full recovery, while in others there may be a residue of symptoms, such as partial paralysis and a reduction in intellectual level. Where tumors are well advanced and require extensive surgery, the mortality rate is high.

The following case, summarized from a report by Brickner, reveals a postoperative reduction in general intellectual capacity and the overcompensatory reaction of the patient to his changed life situation.

The patient was a man of 40 who had been a successful broker on the New York Stock Exchange. During the operation to remove his tumor, large portions of the frontal lobes of the brain were removed on both sides. As a result the patient's general adjustive capacities—including comprehension, judgment, restraint, memory, and learning capacity—were markedly lowered.

The following excerpt from Brickner's extensive case record on this man will serve to show his impaired intellectual capacity and his grandiose overcompensating reaction.

"**B.:** One thing your illness lost you is the knowledge that you're not perfect.

A.: It's a damned good thing to lose.

B.: Do you really believe in your heart that you are perfect?

A.: Yes. Of course we all have faults. I have faults like everyone else.

B.: Name some of your faults.

A.: I don't think I have any.

B.: You just said you had.

A.: Well, they wouldn't *predominate* on the Exchange.

B.: I mean personal faults.

A.: Yes, I have personal faults. I never give a man an opportunity to do what he wants to do on the Exchange, if I know it.

B.: Is that a fault?

A.: That's being a good broker.

B.: Can you name a personal fault? Do you really believe you're perfect?

A.: You bet I do— pretty near perfect—they don't come much more perfect than I am." (1936, pp. 47–48)

German (1959) found that about 40 percent of all brain tumors were potentially curable; about 20 percent were capable of being arrested for periods of 5 years or more; and the remainder were fatal within a short period of time. Fortunately, however, newer methods of detecting and pinpointing brain tumors and improved treatment procedures have resulted in a marked improvement in outcomes.

Disorders with Head Injury

Since ancient times brain injuries have provided a rich source of material for speculation about mental functions. Hippocrates pointed out that injuries to the head could cause sensory and motor disorders, and Galen included head injuries among the major causes of mental disorders.

Perhaps the most famous historical case is the celebrated American crowbar case reported by Dr. J. M. Harlow in 1868. Since it is of both historical and descriptive significance, it merits a few details:

"The accident occurred in Cavendish, Vt., on the line of the Rutland and Burlington Railroad, at that time being built, on the 13th of September, 1848, and was occasioned by the premature explosion of a blast, when this iron, known to blasters as a tamping iron, and which I now show you, was shot through the face and head.

"The subject of it was Phineas P. Gage, a perfectly healthy, strong and active young man, twenty-five years of age . . . Gage was foreman of a gang of men employed in excavating rock, for the road way. . . .

"The missile entered by its pointed end, the left side of the face, immediately anterior to the angle of the lower jaw, and passing obliquely upwards, and obliquely backwards, emerged in the median line, at the back part of the frontal bone, near the coronal suture. . . . The iron which thus traversed the head, is round and rendered comparatively smooth by use, and is three feet seven inches in length, one and one fourth inches in its largest diameter, and weighs thirteen and one fourth pounds. . . .

"The patient was thrown upon his back by the explosion, and gave a few convulsive motions of the extremities, but spoke in a few minutes. His men (with whom he was a great favorite) took him in their arms and carried him to the road, only a few rods distant, and put him into an ox cart, in which he rode, supported in a sitting posture, fully three quarters of a mile to his hotel. He got out of the cart himself, with a little assistance from his men, and an hour afterwards (with what I could aid him by taking hold of his left arm) walked up a long flight of stairs, and got upon the bed in the room where he was dressed. He seemed perfectly conscious, but was becoming exhausted from the hemorrhage, which by this time, was quite profuse, the blood pouring from the lacerated sinus in the top of his head, and also finding its way into the stomach, which ejected it as often as every fifteen or twenty minutes. He bore his sufferings with firmness, and directed my attention to the hole in his cheek, saying, 'the iron entered there and passed through my head.' " (1868, pp. 330–32)

Sometime later Dr. Harlow made the following report.

"His physical health is good, and I am inclined to say that he has recovered. Has no pain in head, but says it has a queer feeling which he is not able to describe. Applied for his situation as foreman, but is undecided whether to work or travel. His contractors, who regarded him as the most efficient and capable foreman in their employ previous to his injury considered the change in his mind so marked that they could not give him his place again. The equilibrium or balance, so to speak, between his intellectual faculties and animal propensities, seems to have been destroyed. He is fitful, irreverent, indulging at times in the grossest profanity (which was not previously his custom), manifesting but little deference for his fellows, impatient of restraint or advice when it conflicts with his desires, at times pertinaciously obstinate, yet capricious and vacillating, devising many plans of future operations, which are no sooner arranged than they are abandoned in turn for others . . . his mind is radically changed, so decidedly that his friends and acquaintances said he was 'no longer Gage.' " (1868, pp. 339–40)

Head injuries occur frequently, particularly as a result of falls, blows, and automobile and other accidents. It has been estimated that well over a million persons suffer head injuries each year in automobile and industrial accidents; and a sizeable number of cases are the result of bullets or other objects actually penetrating the cranium. Yet relatively few persons with head injuries find their way into mental hospitals, since many head injuries do not involve appreciable damage to the brain. Even when a head injury results in a temporary loss of consciousness, the damage to the brain is usually minor.

Most of us have received a blow on the head at one time or other, and in giving the case

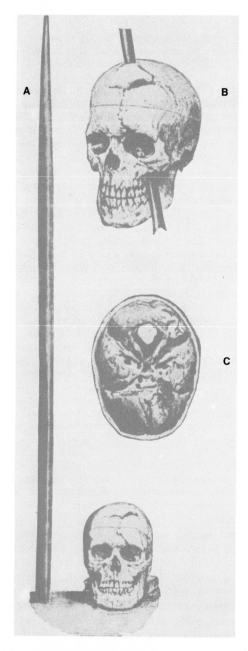

Harlow illustrated his famous crowbar case by these drawings, showing (A) the comparative sizes of the tamping iron and the cranium through which it passed; (B) a view of the cranium showing just where the iron passed through, and also a large section of the skull which was entirely torn away and later replaced; and (C) an upward view from inside the skull, giving the position and relative size of the hole that was made and showing a deposit of new bone partially closing it over.

history of a mental patient, relatives often remember some such incident to which they attribute his difficulties. Patients, too, are apt to search their own childhood for evidence of having fallen on their heads or having been hit on the head. Apparently, blaming the alleged head injury for the difficulties is a convenient method of escaping the "disgrace" of a functional mental disorder and at the same time avoiding any hereditary stigma to the family. Consequently, it should be emphasized that only when the brain injury is severe is it apt to leave any residual handicap.

General symptoms and causal factors

Head injuries usually give rise to immediate acute reactions, the severity of which depends on the degree and type of injury. These acute reactions may then clear up entirely or develop into chronic disorders.

Acute traumatic disorders.[3] Fortunately, the brain is an extraordinarily well-protected organ, but even so, a hard blow on the head may result in a skull fracture in which portions of bone press upon or are driven into the brain tissue. Even without a fracture, the force of the blow may result in small, pinpoint hemorrhages throughout the brain or in the rupturing of larger blood vessels in the brain.

The person rendered unconscious by a head injury usually passes through stages of stupor and confusion on his way to recovering clear consciousness. This recovery of consciousness may be complete in the course of minutes, or it may take hours or days. In rare cases an individual may live for extended periods of time without regaining consciousness. The specific symptoms, of course, depend largely on the nature of the injury.

1. *Cerebral concussion* typically involves a mild head injury that disrupts circulatory and other brain functions and results in a slight clouding or momentary loss of consciousness.

---

[3]The word *trauma* here refers to a physical wound or injury. We have previously used the term to refer to psychological wounds or shocks. This need not be confusing if we remember that stress may be biological or psychological.

On regaining consciousness the individual may be somewhat confused and disoriented, have a loss of memory for the accident, and suffer from a headache. Severe psychological symptoms rarely occur, and the individual usually will recover within a few hours or days. However, a transitory post-concussion syndrome may occur which commonly consists of headache, dizziness, excessive fatigue, and inability to concentrate; partial or total amnesia for the circumstances of the accident usually remains. This simple concussion syndrome is illustrated in the case of a football star who was knocked out in a head-on collision with an opposing player.

The player regained consciousness while being carried off the field but was disoriented and confused, and called signals as if he were still in the game. About an hour after his arrival at the hospital the mental confusion cleared up and he seemed normal except for complaints of a terrible headache and an inability to remember just what happened. For several days thereafter he suffered from headaches, feelings of fatigue, and difficulty in concentrating — but these symptoms were not severe and he shortly rejoined his team.

2. *Cerebral contusion* may occur if the injury to the head is so severe that the brain, normally anchored in a fixed position, is shifted within the skull and is pushed or compressed against the opposite side. In this sudden movement of the brain there may be an actual bruising of its surface against the cranium. Here, in addition to the symptoms that follow a concussion, there may be prolonged unconsciousness for hours or even days, followed by a train of more serious symptoms that may include delirium. When the patient regains clarity of mind, he usually complains of severe headaches, sensitivity to noise and light, and dizziness, nausea, and weakness. Even though these symptoms may, in the main, clear up in a few days or weeks, certain symptoms, such as irritability, may persist for a prolonged period. There may also be an impairment of intellectual and motor functions after the acute symptoms have cleared up.

Cerebral contusion is illustrated by the following case of a flier injured during a crash landing.

When taken to the hospital he was unconscious. Some 8 hours after the accident he returned to consciousness but was confused and mildly delirious. There was a gradual return to clarity over a period of the next 2 days, accompanied by complaints of headache, dizziness, and nausea, especially if he moved. He was also hypersensitive to noise and light. He was able to leave the hospital within a week but complained for several months of headaches and inability to tolerate noise.

3. *Cerebral laceration* is an actual rupture or tearing of the brain tissue. This often occurs in skull-fracture cases when a portion of the bone may be driven into the brain tissue. It may also result from injury by bullets or other objects that penetrate the cranium, or from the internal laceration of the brain, as in cases of severe contusion.

The immediate symptoms of cerebral laceration are similar to those in contusion — unconsciousness followed by confusion or delirium and a gradual return to clarity of mind. In addition to persistent headaches and related symptoms, there may be a residual impairment of intellectual and motor functions. This was illustrated in the crowbar case reported by Dr. Harlow.

During the coma that follows severe cerebral injury — including contusion and laceration — pulse, temperature, and blood pressure are affected and the patient's survival is uncertain. The duration of the coma is determined primarily by the extent of the injury. In severe cases, the patient may be unconscious for days or even weeks. If he survives, the coma is usually followed by delirium, in which he may manifest acute excitement and confusion, disorientation, hallucinations, and generally anxious, restless, and noisy activity. Often he talks incessantly in a disconnected fashion, with no insight into his disturbed condition. Gradually the confusion clears up and he regains contact with reality. Again, the severity and duration of residual symptoms will depend primarily on the nature and extent of the cerebral damage, the premorbid personality of the patient, and the life situation to which he will return.

Some degree of bleeding, or *intracerebral hemorrhage*, occurs in most cases of head injury. In severe head injuries there is usually gross bleeding or hemorrhaging at the site of

Brain trauma and amnesia

Amnesia (loss of memory for previous experience) may result from brain trauma and damage, various labels being applied to designate specific types of memory loss. In *traumatic amnesia* there is a loss of memory for the situation surrounding the trauma; often, brain trauma may also cause some degree of *retrograde amnesia* for events prior to the traumatic incident. Except in extreme cases the memory loss is not extensive and recovery tends to be orderly, with information more remote in time being remembered first and information that immediately preceded or involved the brain trauma being recovered gradually.

Retrograde amnesia resulting from cerebrovascular accidents and other severe types of brain damage may extend farther back in time, so that a person may have no recollection of having gone to school or having married and reared children. Such memory losses may be fully or partially recovered in time, or they may be permanent. In addition, the individual may be subject to *anterograde amnesia* — inability or only partial ability to recall events that occur after the brain damage. Here, new information is not registered and retained in memory storage in a way that facilitates its availability when the individual wishes to retrieve it. A. R. Luria (1972), the Russian neurophysiologist, has poignantly described the case of a brilliant youth who suffered both serious retrograde and anterograde amnesia as a result of a brain wound received in World War II. During the years that followed, he has tried desperately to make a clear and comprehensible world out of the bits and fragments of the past and present that remain of his life. But as Luria has reported, it is a courageous but futile effort to recover the irretrievable; it is "a story that has no ending" (p. 157).

In even more severe cases, the individual may live in a world without continuity, with no coherent memories of past or present, resulting in a loss of his anchorage in time. But as described by Talland (1967), the most severe cases are those who suffer the loss of a sense of self-reference: "Perhaps the ultimate in amnesia is reached when a person correctly performs a required task, instantly forgets that he did so, and believes that the task was actually performed by the person who asked him to undertake it" (p. 49). In behavioristic terms, the individual has become a completely "respondent organism," for he not only fails to see himself as the originator of his actions but tends to remain passive and indifferent until he receives instructions from others. His ability to follow these instructions will depend on whether he can retrieve from his limited memory the essential information for performing the action.

the damage. When the hemorrhaging involves small spots of bleeding—often microscopic sleeves of red cells encircling tiny blood vessels—the condition is referred to as *petechial hemorrhages*. There is some evidence of petechial hemorrhages in most brain injuries, but in fatal cases they are usually multiple or generalized throughout the brain. Professional boxers are likely to suffer such petechial hemorrhaging from repeated blows to the head; they may develop a form of encephalopathy (area or areas of permanently damaged brain tissue) from the accumulated damage of such injuries. Consequently, some former boxers may suffer from impaired memory, inability to concentrate, involuntary movements, and other symptoms—a condition popularly referred to as being "punch-drunk." Johnson (1969) found abnormal EEG's in 10 of 17 retired boxers; and Earl (1966) noted that two former welterweight champions suffered so much brain damage in their professional fights that confinement in mental institutions ended their careers before they reached the age of 30.

Chronic or post-traumatic disorders. Although many patients make a remarkably good recovery, even after severe brain injury, others show various residual *post-concussional* or *post-contusional* symptoms. Common aftereffects of moderate brain injury are chronic headaches, anxiety, irritability, dizziness, easy fatigability, and impaired memory and concentration. Where the brain damage is extensive, the patient's general intellectual level may be markedly reduced, especially where there have been severe frontal-lobe lesions. In addition, various specific neurological and psychologial defects may follow localized brain damage: occipital-lobe lesions may impair vision, parietal-lobe lesions may result in sensory aphasia, and so on. Some 2 to 4 percent of head-injury cases develop posttraumatic epilepsy, usually within 2 years of the head injury but sometimes much later. In general, the longer the period between the injury and the first convulsive seizure, the more likely they are to persist.

In a minority of brain-injury cases—some 2 to 3 percent—there are personality changes, such as those described in the historic case of

Phineas Gage. Among older people and individuals who have suffered extensive damage to the frontal lobes, the symptom picture may be complicated by markedly impaired memory for recent events and by confabulation. This clinical picture is referred to as *Korsakoff's psychosis*.

Treatment and outcomes

Immediate treatment for brain damage is primarily a medical matter and need not concern us here except to note that prompt treatment may prevent further injury or damage—for example, when blood clots must be removed from the brain. In severe cases immediate medical treatment may have to be supplemented by a long-range program of reeducation and rehabilitation.

The great majority of patients suffering from mild concussion recover within a short time. In moderate brain injuries, a sizeable number of patients recover promptly, a somewhat larger number suffer from headaches and other symptoms for prolonged periods, and a few patients develop chronic incapacitating symptoms. In general, an estimated 50 percent of such patients show postconcussional symptoms after 6 months, and about 40 percent after 18 months.

In severe brain-injury cases, the prognosis is less favorable. Some patients have to adjust to lower levels of occupational and social functioning, while others are so impaired intellectually that they can never adjust to conditions outside an institution. Often, however—even in cases where considerable amounts of brain tissue have been destroyed—patients with stable, well-integrated personalities are able to make a satisfactory adjustment. And in many cases there is improvement with time, due largely to reeducation and to the taking over of new functions by intact brain areas.

In general, the following factors indicate a favorable prognosis: (a) a short period of unconciousness or posttraumatic amnesia, (b) nonstrategic location of the brain lesion, (c) a well-integrated premorbid personality, (d) motivation to recover or make the most of residual capacities, (e) a favorable life situato which to return, and (f) an appropriate program of retraining (Brooks, 1974).

Impairment of language and related sensorimotor functions resulting from brain damage

In many cases, brain damage results in fairly specific language and related sensorimotor functions. Among the more common of these are:

Auditory aphasia—Loss of ability to understand spoken words

Expressive aphasia—Loss of ability to speak required words

Nominal aphasia—Loss of ability to recall names of objects

Formulation aphasia—Loss of ability to formulate sentences

Paraphasia—Garbled speech, marked by inappropriate word use, transposed sounds, and ungrammatical sentences

Alexia (dyslexia)—Loss of ability to read (less severe in dyslexia)

Agraphia—Loss of ability to express thoughts in writing

Acalculia—Loss of ability to do simple arithmetic

Apraxia—Loss of ability to perform simple voluntary acts

With reeducation, impaired or lost language and related sensorimotor functions can usually be recovered—either partially or totally.

Various other factors may also have a direct bearing on the outcome of brain injuries. The results of brain damage in infancy, for example, differ from those in adolescence and adulthood, although in both instances the results may range from death to any number of neurological disorders, including epilepsy and mental retardation. Moreover, individuals who are also victims of alcoholism, drug dependence, arteriosclerosis, or any of a wide range of other organic conditions, have an unfavorable outlook. Alcoholics, in particular, are prone to head injuries and other accidents, and do not have good recovery records. Severe emotional conflicts sometimes appear to predispose an individual to accidents and also to delay recovery. Although malingering is thought to be rare in brain-injury cases, monetary compensation may be a factor in the exaggeration and maintenance of symptoms.

Accounts of epileptic seizures are found throughout the recorded history of human beings. They are caused by brain lesions or other pathology which result in a disturbance of the rhythm of electrical discharges of brain cells. Epilepsy affects about 1 person in 100 in the United States—between 2 and 3 million people. Cases occur among all age groups, but more commonly in children and adolescents than adults. In over half the known cases, the age of onset is under 15 years.

Epileptic seizures are infinitely varied in form, but for practical purposes they may be classified into three main types described below. Typical EEG patterns for these three types are contrasted at right with recordings of normal brain waves.

1. Grand mal: "great illness." The most prevalent and spectacular form of epileptic seizure, grand mal, occurs in some 60 percent of the cases. Typically, the seizure is immediately preceded by an aura or warning, such as an unpleasant odor. During an attack the individual loses consciousness and breathing is suspended. His muscles become rigid, jaws clenched, arms extended, and legs outstretched, and he pitches forward or slumps to the ground. With the return of air to the lungs his movements, instead of being rigid (tonic), become jerking (clonic). Muscular spasms begin, the head strikes the ground, the arms repeatedly thrust outward, the legs jerk up and down, the jaws open and close, and the mouth foams. Usually in about a minute the convulsive movements slow, the muscles relax, and the individual gradually returns to normality—in some cases after a deep sleep lasting from a few minutes to several hours. Another, less common, form of convulsive seizure, much like a modified grand-mal attack, is known as *Jacksonian epilepsy;* here, motor disturbances occurring in one region spread over the side in which they originate, and sometimes over the entire body.

2. Petit mal: "small illness." In petit-mal seizures there is usually a diminution, rather than a complete loss, of consciousness. The individual stops whatever he is doing, stares vacantly ahead or toward the floor, and then in a few seconds resumes his previous activity. In some cases, these seizures may occur several times a day; and, unlike grand-mal seizures, they rarely have an advance warning or aura. With onset usually occurring in childhood or adolescence, petit-mal attacks are rare after the age of 20.

3. Psychomotor epilepsy. Psychomotor attacks occur in about 10 percent of child, and 30 percent of adult, epileptics. Attacks usually last from a few seconds to minutes, but in some rare cases they may last considerably longer. Their principal feature is a psychic disturbance, which varies greatly from one individual to another. Despite a lapse or clouding of consciousness, activity continues and the individual appears to be conscious; during his attack he may perform routine tasks or some unusual or antisocial act. A very small percentage of cases may even involve self-mutilation or homicidal assault. The Flemish painter Van Gogh was subject to psychomotor attacks, for which he was later amnesic. On one occasion he cut off one of his ears, wrapped it in a sack, and presented it to a prostitute. In a more serious case, a brain-injured soldier subject to psychomotor epilepsy reported a dream in which he found himself trying to ward off attackers. Actually, he had beaten his 3-year-old daughter to death, but was completely amnesic for the tragic episode.

Fortunately, drug medication and other treatment measures make it possible to prevent seizures in 80 percent or more epileptics. Often treatment procedures also focus on helping the individual cope with personal problems such as feelings of inferiority associated with the affliction. Educational efforts by professional and lay organizations have succeeded in dispelling many misconceptions concerning epilepsy and in helping epileptics live normal lives. For example, epileptics are no longer branded as poor employment risks—on the contrary, they show a relatively low incidence of on-the-job accidents. Also, legal restrictions on the operation of motor vehicles have been changed, so that epileptics are permitted to drive when it is established that they have been free of seizures (with or without medication) for 2 to 3 years. In general, most epileptics make adequate educational, marital, and occupational adjustments.

Based on Batchelor and Campbell (1969), Flor-Henry (1969), Holvey and Talbott (1972), Jasper (1969), Pryse-Phillips (1969), Rodin (1973), Stearman (1973), and Sutherland and Trait (1969).

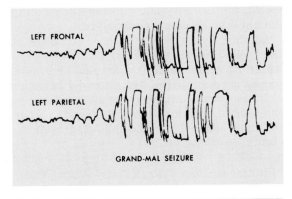

LEFT FRONTAL

LEFT PARIETAL

GRAND-MAL SEIZURE

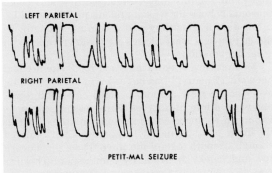

LEFT PARIETAL

RIGHT PARIETAL

PETIT-MAL SEIZURE

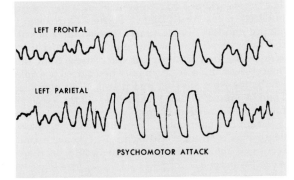

LEFT FRONTAL

LEFT PARIETAL

PSYCHOMOTOR ATTACK

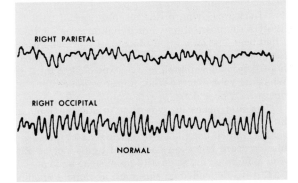

RIGHT PARIETAL

RIGHT OCCIPITAL

NORMAL

Disorders with Toxins and Metabolic Disturbances

Disturbances in cerebral functions may result from several types of toxins and a wide range of metabolic disorders, including nutritive deficiencies, endocrine imbalances, and the stress of surgery or childbirth. Before discussing such disturbances, it is relevant to note that the brain has a protective mechanism—known as the blood-brain barrier (BBB)—which screens the flow of substances from the blood to the central nervous system. While normally denying or restricting entry of harmful substances (for example, keeping 99.5 percent of LSD out of the brain), the BBB also permits ready access to substances essential for health and proper functioning. No other part of the body has a protective mechanism as specialized and efficient. However, a period of oxygen deprivation, as well as the presence of certain toxins, may impair the functioning of the BBB and adversely affect brain functioning, possibly causing brain damage.

Toxic deliria (psychoses)

The most common form of toxic psychosis is delirium accompanying various diseases, such as diphtheria, pneumonia, and uremia. Toxic deliria may also result from extreme exhaustion and from the ingestion of various metals, gases, and drugs. In these disorders there usually is an acute onset of the disturbance with delirium and often coma.

Delirium accompanying disease. The early symptoms of delirium usually consist of restlessness and uneasiness plus an increased sensitivity to noise and light. The individual's sleep may be troubled by frightening dreams. As the delirium progresses, consciousness becomes clouded and the individual becomes confused and disoriented for time and later for place and person. During this phase, attention and concentration are severely diminished, and he is unable to remember or interpret properly what he sees and hears. Often he has visual illusions or hallucinations that may be interwoven with unsystematized delusions.

Although some persons become emotionally elated and euphoric, the typical emotional reaction is fear and apprehension. The fears relate especially to the misinterpretation of sounds, which the individual perceives as threatening to his safety. A footstep may be that of a murderer who is stealthily approaching to kill him. As the delirium becomes more acute, the picture becomes one of increasing confusion, apprehension, and agitation. Often there are periods of drowsiness or coma alternating with the delirium. The degree of the delirium will, of course, depend to a large extent on the severity of the patient's illness— the degree of toxic disturbance. However, persons who have poorly integrated personalities or who are marginally adjusted may become delirious with even mild fever.

Unless the toxic condition is very severe or prolonged, there usually is little or no actual damage to the brain, and the psychopathology is temporary and clears up rapidly.

Exhaustion delirium. Here we find acute confusion or delirium without infection or fever. Although not common, such reactions may occur under conditions of extreme physical exertion. Often there is a combination of physical exhaustion and starvation, as in the case of individuals who become lost in remote forest and desert areas and run out of food and water.

The onset usually is marked by insomnia, mild confusion, some clouding of consciousness, perplexity, vague fears, and fleeting hallucinations and delusions. The individual may see and hear rescuers, or see a lake, or tables loaded with food. Gradually his perceptions of his surroundings become increasingly distorted.

Sometimes the increasing confusion may be punctuated by a period of comparative clarity in which the person finds that he has been wandering in circles. This toxic-exhaustive state may continue for several days or even

weeks, but usually clears up rapidly once the patient is given proper food and rest.

Admiral Byrd's record of his stay alone at the Bolling Advance Weather Base during the Antarctic winter night is a graphic and fascinating account of the thoughts and behavior of a man struggling desperately to survive in the face of cold, loneliness, monoxide poisoning, and exhaustion. The following brief excerpts are of interest.

"The next day, June 1, was a Friday. A black Friday for me. I awakened from a dream of horrors to find that I could hardly move. I realized that all I could reasonably hope for was to prolong my existence for a few days by hoarding my remaining strength; by doing the necessary things very slowly and with great deliberation.

"My first need was warmth and food. The fire had been out 12 hours; I had not eaten in 36. Performing every act in slow motion, I edged out of the bunk and worked into my clothes. Faintness seized me as I touched the floor, and for many minutes I sat in the chair just staring at the candle. Then I gained enough strength to light the stove. The flame burned red and smoky from faulty combustion. This fire was my enemy, but I could not live without it.

"My thirst was the tallest tree in a forest of pain. The tunnel where I cut ice to melt for water was a hundred miles away, but I started out. Soon I slipped and fell. My ice quarry was too far. I licked the tunnel wall until my tongue burned, and then scraped up half a bucket of dirty snow from the floor. It was still a soggy mass when I tried to drink. My hands were shaking and it spilled all over me. Then I vomited all that I had drunk. On the verge of fainting, I crawled up on my bunk to rest.

"Death had confronted me many times. . . . Now death was a stranger sitting in a darkened room, secure in the knowledge that he would be there when I was gone.

"Great waves of fear swept through me and settled deep within. . . .

"Afterwards, lying in the sleeping bag, I tried to analyze the possibilities. For five interminable days I had been lost on a great plateau of pain where all the passes were barred. I had suffered and struggled, hoped and stopped hoping. . . . Now I asked myself, What are your assets? What might be done that has not already been done?

"The first necessity was that to survive I must husband my strength. Second, to avoid further poisoning, I must use the stove sparingly and the gasoline pressure lamp—my one good light—not at all. And to build up my strength I must sleep and eat.

"But if I depended on this routine alone, I should

go mad from the hourly reminders of my own futility. Something more – the will to endure these hardships – was necessary. That must come from deep inside me. But how? By taking control of my thoughts and dwelling only on those which would make for peace. A discordant mind, black with confusion and despair, would finish me off as thoroughly as the cold." (1938, pp. 175–90)

Deliria associated with metals and gases. A variety of metals and gases – such as lead and carbon monoxide – may result in toxic reactions and deliria.

In lead poisoning, early mild symptoms typically include fatigue, weakness, listlessness, and extreme irritability. The disorder is commonest among children, who may vomit, exhibit fear, and cry for no apparent reason. More severe cases are characterized by delirium, along with restlessness, confusion, insomnia, anxiety, hallucinations, tremors, and convulsions.

The inhalation of carbon monoxide in large amounts reduces the blood's capacity to take up oxygen, thus causing anorexemia (impaired functioning of the nerve cells in the brain). Delirium or coma occurs in severe cases.

The delirious state in cases of lead poisoning, as well as carbon monoxide exposure, typically clears up in a matter of hours or days, although, of course, both types of poisoning may result in death. Where cases are severe but nonlethal, common residual symptoms are irritability, lack of emotional control, forgetfulness, confabulation, impaired judgment, and a general lowering of mental capacity. Among children, severe poisoning of either kind may cause convulsive seizures and mental retardation.

Nutritional deficiencies

Nutritional deficiencies have been shown to underlie certain types of psychopathology.

Vitamin and mineral deficiencies. Deficiencies in the vitamin B complex seem to be the type most commonly involved in the production of neuropsychiatric disorders. Perhaps the best known of these deficiencies is beriberi, which once plagued people in the Far East who lived

Peeling paint in old buildings is often the cause of lead poisoning. Even if the lead-based paint has been covered with fresh paint or wallpaper, if the peeling layers can still be pulled off they are a danger to small children.

primarily on a diet of polished rice, deficient in vitamin B_1 (thiamine). "Beriberi" means "I cannot" and is an apt description of the lassitude, weakened muscles, intestinal distress, depression, and lowered "will to do" that follow a deficiency in vitamin B_1.

In an early experiment, Brožek, Guetzkow, and Keys (1946) studied the personality changes in 8 normal young men who were maintained 161 days on a partially restricted intake of B-complex vitamins, followed by 23 days of acute deficiency and 10 days of thiamine supplementation. Little or no evidence of personality change was observed during the period of partial restriction, but consistent and striking deterioration occurred during the acute deficiency, with depression, loss of spontaneity, increased tension, hysteria, hypochondriasis, and increased emotionality. Adding thiamine to the diet produced rapid recovery.

A number of minerals—such as sodium chloride, copper, and calcium—are required for normal brain metabolism. Chronic conditions associated with a low concentration of salt in the blood may lead to a variety of mental symptoms: prominent are lassitude, apathy, apprehension, and depression. Severe dehydration from lack of water may result in apathy, delirium, and stupor.

In addition to the vitamins, minerals, and chemicals we have mentioned, there are many others which—though less directly related to mental symptoms—are essential for bodily health and the maintenance of normal resistance to organic and psychological stress.

Semistarvation. Semistarvation occurs when there is a severe restriction of calorie intake over a prolonged period of time. Throughout human history it has been the commonest type of nutritional deficiency.

A number of observations have been made regarding behavior under conditions of "natural starvation," stemming in the main from famines in the aftermath of wars and from the meager diet of prisoner-of-war and concentration-camp inmates. Observations of advanced stages of semistarvation during famines in Leningrad and other Russian cities during World War II emphasized a number of neurological, physical, and mental changes (Brožek & Grande, 1960). Asthenia was considered the principal mental syndrome, characterized by a slowing of thought processes, impaired ability to concentrate and sustain mental effort, a lowering of higher-level interests and feelings, increased irritability, and apathy with a tendency to daydreaming. Psychotic reactions were rare and occurred mostly in cases where caloric deficiency was complicated by infection, trauma, and related conditions. Writing on the basis of his experience in German POW camps, Leyton (1946) reported similar symptoms and also emphasized a marked reduction in sexual desire, lowered standards of cleanliness, loss of pride in personal appearance, and deterioration of ethical standards.

Unfortunately, many people in the world today still suffer from malnutrition, including vitamin and mineral deficiencies, and it can be readily seen that their condition has serious implications both on individual and social levels. Even in the United States, where food is relatively plentiful, many people suffer the effects of "hidden starvation"—including lowered resistance to both biological and psychological stress—as a consequence of unbalanced and inadequate diets.

Endocrine disturbances

The endocrine glands manufacture hormones, which are essential for normal physiological and psychological functioning. Consequently, underactivity or overactivity of any endocrine gland may markedly affect psychological functioning, in addition to lowering general stress tolerance. Endocrine disturbances may also lead to physical anomalies that, in turn, contribute to adjustive difficulties. For example, pituitary "giants" or "midgets," bearded ladies, extremely fat persons, and other endocrine "freaks" are often subjected to curiosity, ridicule, and similar reactions from others, which make normal personality development and self-acceptance extremely difficult for them.

In the following discussion of thyroid and adrenal dysfunctions—the most common of the endocrine disorders associated with severe psychological disturbances—three points are well worth remembering: (a) endocrine dysfunction may contribute to psychopathology, as well as result from such pathology; (b) malfunction of any gland may have widespread effects on the functioning of other glands and other bodily organs and systems; and (c) glandular dysfunction may vary considerably in degree and its effects may differ widely, depending on the age, sex, and general personality makeup of the individual. It should also be reemphasized that the endocrine system is normally under the general control of the central nervous system.

Thyroid dysfunction. The best understood of the endocrine glands is the thyroid, which regulates bodily metabolism. Either oversecretion or undersecretion of the thyroid hormone *thyroxin* produces definite signs of physical pathology and/or psychopathology. For example, in an intensive study of 17 patients with thyroid dysfunction—10 with hyperthyroidism and 7 with hypothyroidism—Whybrow, Prange, and Treadway (1969) reported that 76 percent manifested profound disruption in psychological functioning. Actual psychotic symptoms occur in about 20 percent of such cases, but they are usually not severe; less than 1 percent of first admissions to mental hospitals involve disorders associated with thyroid dysfunction.

Oversecretion of thyroxin *(hyperthyroidism)* accelerates the metabolic processes and leads to weight loss, tremors, tenseness, insomnia, emotional excitability, and impairment in concentration and other cognitive processes. Where psychotic symptoms do occur, they commonly include intense anxiety, agitation, and transitory delusions and hallucinations. For example, a patient may hear peculiar "clinking" sounds made by the voices of beings from outer space; or he may visualize a pack of wolves preparing to attack him. In occasional cases there is a toxic reaction with delirium, and in other cases the thyroid dysfunction appears to precipitate an underlying schizophrenic or other psychotic pattern.

Pronounced thyroid deficiency in adulthood *(hypothyroidism)*—typically associated with an iodine deficiency—leads to a condition called *myxedema*. Here metabolism is slowed down and the individual typically puts on weight, becomes sluggish in action and

thought, and shows impairment for recent memory, difficulty in concentrating, and other cognitive disturbances. Severe depression appears to be the most common psychotic disturbance associated with hypothyroidism. Whybrow et al. (1969) described a female patient who was seriously depressed, had frequent thoughts of suicide, and became preoccupied with memories of her son who had been killed in an automobile accident some years previously.

"She wished she had been the one killed. She dreamed of digging him from his grave with her bare hands and heard his voice calling her during the day. She felt she had been saved from a previous illness to be punished by her present one." (p. 55)

In general, the impairment in both cognitive and emotional functioning appears more severe in hypothyroidism than in hyperthyroidism. And although treatment of the latter leads to marked improvement, there is evidence that long-standing hypothyroidism may lead to a residual impairment in cognitive functioning (Richter, 1970; Whybrow et al., 1969). Fortunately, present methods of diagnosis are highly efficient, and early treatment has made severe cases of hypothyroidism extremely rare. The relation of hypothyroidism during early life to mental retardation will be discussed in Chapter 14.

Adrenal dysfunction. The adrenals are paired glands consisting of an outer layer called the *adrenal cortex* and an inner core called the *adrenal medulla*. The adrenal cortex secretes steroids that influence secondary sex characteristics as well as steroids that influence stress reactions. The adrenal medulla secretes the hormones adrenaline and noradrenaline (epinephrine and norepinephrine) during strong emotion. In Chapter 4 we noted that such emotional reactions may be useful in emergency situations but that when they are prolonged or become chronic, they can lead to a breakdown in adrenal function. The relation of such a breakdown of function to mental disorders is still uncertain.

Undersecretion or deficiency of the adrenal cortex results in *Addison's disease*—a disorder characterized by a variety of metabolic dis-

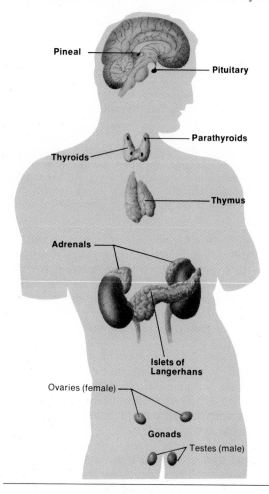

Pineal

Helps regulate body's "biological clock"; may also pace sexual development.

Pituitary

Regulates growth, stimulates activities of other glands.

Dysfunctions

Gigantism—excessive pituitary hormone secretion during growth period, with extreme growth to height of 7 to 9 feet. Intelligence and affect not appreciably modified.

Midgetism—deficient pituitary hormone secretion in early life, preventing normal growth, but body correctly proportioned. Intelligence and affect not appreciably modified.

Acromegaly—excessive pituitary hormone secretion in adulthood, with thickening and elongating of body extremities, especially hands, feet, and jaw.

Thyroids

Influence metabolic rate, growth, and development of intelligence.

Dysfunctions

Cretinism—thyroid deficiency in infancy, with physical and mental dwarfing, heavy features.

Myxedema—thyroid deficiency in adulthood, with overweight, puffed physical features, general sluggishness.

Oversecretion—accelerated metabolic processes, tremors, tenseness, emotional excitability, weight loss. Psychotic symptoms, including delusions and hallucinations, may occur.

---

turbances, including a lowering of blood pressure, body temperature, and basal metabolism and a darkening of the skin. The accompanying mental symptoms typically include lack of vigor, easy fatigability, depressed sexual functions, headaches, irritability, lassitude, and lack of ambition. More severe mental disturbances in Addison's disease are rare and appear to be related to the personality of the patient; however, there is evidence that disturbed brain metabolism plays a dominant role in some psychotic cases.

Oversecretion of the adrenal cortex may lead to a number of rare and dramatic changes in secondary sex characteristics.

An oversecretion of adrenal steroids in the male leads to the development of female characteristics—a condition referred to as *feminism*. An oversecretion of adrenal steroids in the female results in a deepening of voice, shrinking of breast, growth of beard, and other masculine changes—a condition referred to as *virilism*. In children the oversecretion of adrenal steroids accelerates puberty. This condition is referred to as *puberty praecox*, and children subject to it may develop adult stature and reach sexual maturity at a very early age. Although still immature in other areas, such youngsters are usually aggressively interested in sexual matters.

Parathyroids

Regulate calcium and phosphorous metabolism.

Dysfunction

Tetany (due to removal or destruction of parathyroids) — muscular twitches, tremors,cramps, convulsions.

Thymus

May play a role in sexual development and the body's immunity system.

Adrenals

Adrenal medulla secretes adrenaline and noradrenaline, which affect neural functioning and emotion; adrenal cortex secretes steroids (corticoids), which affect body activity and metabolism and influence stress reactions and the development of secondary sex characteristics.

Dysfunctions

Addison's disease — deficiency of deoxycortone from adrenal cortex, with increased fatigability, loss of appetite, anemia, listlessness, irritability, darkening of skin.

Cushing's syndrome — excessive secretion of cortisone, with muscle weakness, reduced sex drive, fatigability, and disfiguring bodily changes.

Feminism — hypersecretion of corticoids in a male, which causes increased estrogen output and development of female characteristics.

Virilism — hypersecretion of corticoids in a female, which causes increased androgen output and the development of male characteristics.

Puberty praecox — hypersecretion of corticoids in a child, which causes early sexual maturity.

Islets of Langerhans

Located in pancreas, secrete insulin, essential for metabolism of carbohydrates.

Dysfunctions

Diabetes — high level of blood sugar resulting from undersecretion of insulin; associated with transitory or chronic nervousness, irritability, anxiety, depression.

Hypoglycemia — low level of blood sugar resulting from oversecretion of insulin; associated with the same emotional effects as described for diabetes.

Gonads

Vital to sexual development and reproduction; the ovaries (female) produce estrogens and progesterone, the testes (male) produce androgens (testosterone).

Dysfunctions

Eunuchism — castration of male before puberty, with development of secondary sex characteristics of female (musculature, bodily proportions, etc.).

Deficiency in development — as a result of insufficient gonadal hormone production during childhood, failure to develop secondary sex characteristics and sex drive.

Menopause or climacteric — marked reduction of gonadal hormone production in females and males, respectively, during middle age. May cause irritability, restlessness, hot flashes (in women), mental depression, and insomnia.

In cases of tumor or abnormal growth of the adrenal cortex, there may be an excessive secretion of cortisone. The resulting clinical picture is referred to as *Cushing's syndrome.* Typical symptoms include muscle weakness, fatigability, reduced sex drive, headache, and a number of disfiguring bodily changes, such as obesity, changes in skin color and texture, and spinal deformity. In some cases there is an excessive growth of body hair. Cushing's syndrome is relatively rare, occurring most often among young women. Reactive emotional disturbances are common among such individuals. The clinical picture not only varies markedly from one patient to another, but often varies in the same patient in the course of the disease.

Treatment for adrenal dysfunction is primarily a medical matter. Cortisone and drugs that suppress corticoid secretions are heavily relied on. In cases of tumor and related conditions, surgery may be indicated. With early detection and treatment the prognosis in adrenal disorders is usually highly favorable. As in other endocrine disorders, however, the psychiatric complications may not subside with the clearing up of the adrenal dysfunction, and additional therapy may be required.

A brief summary of the immediate symptoms associated with the dysfunction of the thyroid, adrenals, and other endocrine glands is shown on pages 484–85.

Postpartum (childbirth) disturbances

It has been estimated that psychotic reactions occur in connection with at least 1 out of every 400 pregnancies, either before or after childbirth. About 10 to 15 percent occur during pregnancy, 60 percent during the first month after childbirth, and the others during the next 8 months. In a study of 100 women who became psychotic from 30 days prior to 90 days after delivery, Melges (1968) found the modal period to be 4 days after delivery.

Clinical picture. Symptoms in postpartum disturbances range from the highly common "blue period"—also referred to as the "maternity blues" or the "disenchantment syndrome"—to severe depression and other psychotic states. Usually postpartum blues are short-lived, lasting no longer than 4 weeks. However, in some cases such mild reactions may progress almost imperceptibly to deep depression, characterized by psychomotor retardation, dejection, self-accusations of sin and unworthiness, and a marked sense of futility. A mother may express a lack of interest in her infant, or have fears that it may be harmed, and/or evidence considerable underlying hostility toward her husband. Such severe depressions constitute a hazard to the lives of both mother and infant, and suicide, infanticide, or both, may occur.

Manic reactions appear to be infrequent following childbirth, but involutional-type depressions with elements of depression, agitation, and suspiciousness may occur. Occasionally, delirious reactions are precipitated by infection, hemorrhage, exhaustion, or toxemia—particularly in marginally adjusted individuals. Here there is a clouding of consciousness, hallucinatory states, and some degree of confusion and disorientation. Formerly toxic-exhaustive psychoses were common following childbirth, but the introduction of antibiotics, improved obstetrical procedures, and antidepressant and related drugs has made these reactions relatively rare.

Causal factors. Except in unusual cases the actual stress of childbirth is not the primary cause of postpartum disturbances. In most cases, stresses associated with pregnancy and adjustments that are attendant on assuming the role of mother serve as precipitating factors in an already unstable person or one particularly vulnerable to this type of stress situation. In fact, psychotic reactions indistinguishable from typical postpartum psychoses occasionally follow the adoption of a child.

In a study of 100 cases of puerperal psychoses, White et al. (1957) emphasized the following factors: (a) unstable marriage; (b) immaturity of patient; (c) long-standing maladjustment of patient; (d) unstable family history; (e) lack of desire for baby on part of wife or husband; (f) extra responsibility, particularly financial, imposed by birth of baby; (g) physical illness of mother or baby, including extreme fatigue resulting from caring for a sick baby; and (h) an unfavorable home situation after delivery, such as poor living conditions.

More recent studies have implicated similar factors, emphasizing that mothers who develop postpartum disturbances experience significantly more insecurity and ambivalence with respect to their marriages and pregnancies than mothers who do not develop such disturbances (Asch & Rubin, 1974; Brown & Shereshefsky, 1972). Many such mothers appear to experience an identity confusion centering around a conflict in their role as mothers, in most cases a repudiation of this role and a "trapped" feeling. Often such a mother experiences strong guilt feelings because she does not enjoy her baby as society expects mothers to do. An immature, nonprotective, and rejecting reaction by the husband to his wife's pregnancy and to his own fatherhood may also markedly augment the stressfulness of the entire situation for the wife. Interestingly enough, the normality or legitimacy of the baby does not appear related to postpartum psychoses.

Treatment and outcomes. Postpartum psychoses tend to be self-limiting, and with the assistance of modern treatment procedures well over 90 percent of these patients recover in a relatively short time. Although in many cases patients have been advised to avoid another pregnancy for 2 or 3 years, such counseling is now carefully weighed in relation to the individual and her life situation. However, follow-up studies have shown that from 25 to 50 percent of such mothers do have a recurrence of psychotic episodes on giving birth to other children (Protheroe, 1969).

At present, preventive measures call primarily for good obstetric care, preparing the mother psychologically for childbirth, and alleviating any undue stresses that the family situation may be placing on her.

Individual discussion with the obstetrician and group discussions in prepartum clinics may help greatly in allaying fears and anxieties and preparing the expectant mother for childbirth and for her role as mother. Similar procedures have proven of value in helping the husband accept and prepare for his role as father, for often a husband may resent the demands made upon him by his wife's pregnancy and the responsibilities associated with becoming a father, as well as feeling displaced by and jealous of the new baby.

Postoperative disturbances

Although observed since at least the sixteenth century, when noted in the writings of Ambroise Paré, psychological disturbances following general surgery are still somewhat of an enigma. In some instances these reactions are of a toxic-delirious type, and in others they involve anxiety, delusions, hallucinations, depression, bizarre behavior, and other psychopathology. Such disturbances appear to result from biological trauma, medication, and psychological stress. Constitutional factors also appear of significance—for example, elderly persons are particularly susceptible to delirious reactions following major surgery.

Postoperative psychoses have been reported by Lunde (1969) for 3 out of 9 heart transplant cases studied. In one case, the disturbance developed gradually several days after the operation, with the individual initially becoming belligerent toward the nurses, and over a period of weeks developing a rather extensive delusional system:

Descriptive data concerning 100 postpartum psychiatric cases

In his study of 100 postpartum psychiatric patients, Melges (1968) reported that his subjects ranged in age from 17 to 46, with a median age of 28. Most were high-school graduates, and a relatively high percentage—21 percent—had graduated from college. The median onset occurred 4 days after the baby's delivery, with 64 percent of the cases showing onset of symptoms within 10 days after delivery. Other findings pertaining to symptoms and causes were as follows:

Major symptoms
Irritability (95 percent)
Confusion (92 percent)
Disorientation for time (90 percent)
Uneasiness (81 percent)
Excitability, restlessness (63 percent)

Chief precipitating cause
Conflict over becoming a mother (observed in 63 percent of the subjects)

Chief predisposing causes
Feelings of ambivalence toward own mother (88 percent)
Knowledge of postpartum psychoses among relatives (23 percent)
Interpersonal conflict (15 percent)

As indicated by the data relating to symptoms and causes, subjects often manifested multiple symptoms, and a case might be attributable to multiple causes. Asch and Rubin (1974) have also reported variations in these typical reactions, including infanticide.

"He accused nurses and various other people of trying to kill him: whenever he did not receive his medication on time ('on time' meaning less than two minutes late or two minutes early), he decided that this was a plot to destroy him. . . .

"Being in reverse isolation, everyone who came into the room looked alike: each wore a gown, a cap, a mask, and gloves. There were literally dozens of people coming in day after day whom the patient could not identify, and he began to put these people into his delusional system. He felt that the masks were being worn so that he could not see the contemptuous, mocking, expressions on their faces. It helped to have the nurses and other people identify themselves each time they came into the room even if it was the third or fourth time that day. It also helped somewhat to provide this patient with newspapers and a TV set." (pp. 119–20)

The patient also was so anxious and disturbed that he suffered from insomnia and went for a week without more than a few hours' sleep, which posed serious problems in treatment.

Lunde noted that in 2 of the 6 cases not manifesting psychoses, interesting personality changes took place. "One man literally decided that the day of his transplant was his new birthday, which he planned to celebrate from then on. He felt he had been born again and was 20 years old" (p. 372). This was a 42-year-old man who received the heart of a 20-year-old. In another case the recipient learned from the press that he had received the heart of a prominent local citizen and stated that "He felt an obligation to live up to the standards set by the man whose heart he had received. He hoped to become more like the donor" (p. 373). Lunde concluded that "as surgery becomes more radical and more vital organs are exchanged, distortions of personality can be expected, since personality and self-image are so closely tied to body image" (pp. 371–72).

Improved surgical techniques combined with the increasing recognition of the need for pre- and post-surgical psychotherapy and family counseling have reduced the number of severe emotional disturbances following organ transplants and other major surgery (Castelnuovo-Tedesco, 1973; Fox & Swazey, 1974; Merrill & Collins, 1974; Tourkow, 1974). However, these operations do pose a variety of psychological and interpersonal problems, and postoperative emotional disturbances still represent a potential and serious complication.

Psychoses of the Aged

"But worse than any loss of limb is the failing mind, which forgets the names of slaves, and cannot recognize the face of the old friend who dined with him last night, nor those of the children whom he has begotten and brought up." (Juvenal)

Such references to mental disturbances experienced by the aged and to the more dramatic aspects of apoplexy are found in the earliest scientific and literary works. Shakespeare's King Lear has been considered an example of senile dementia, and in *Gulliver's Travels* there is a famous passage picturing the progressive physical and mental decline in senility.

The increasing proportion of older people in our population has given rise to a great many psychological, sociological, and medical problems, among them the growing incidence of mental disorders associated with old age.[4] In 1970 an estimated 700,000 older persons in the United States were institutionalized for such disorders; the figure is expected to rise above the million mark by 1980 (Ford, 1970; Jarvik, Yen, & Goldstein, 1974). And these figures say nothing of the many older people about half of whom have mild to severe mental symptoms—who reside in nursing homes; nor does it include the sizeable number of those who are being cared for—or ignored—in the community.

Mental disorders among the aged run the entire gamut. Long-standing neurotic, alcoholic, or drug-dependent patterns may continue into old age, or may make their first appearance during this life period. Depression

---

[4]When we entered the decade of the 1970s there were over 20 million people aged 65 or over in the United States—about 1 person in 10; the number is expected to exceed 30 million by the year 2000 (Neugarten, 1974). In large part, this is due to the increasing life expectancy in our society, which currently exceeds 70 years, and as we continue to conquer killing diseases, a life expectancy of 90 to 100 years may not be far distant. This is in striking contrast to the life expectancy of some 23 years in the days of the Roman Empire.

is a serious problem among large numbers of older citizens, particularly those residing in homes for the aged—including nursing homes—and in mental hospitals (Power & McCarran, 1975). However, the two major psychotic disorders of older people are associated with organic brain pathology—*senile dementia* (associated with cerebral atrophy and degeneration) and *psychosis* with *cerebral arteriosclerosis* (associated with either blocking or ruptures in the cerebral arteries). These two disorders account for about 80 percent of psychotic disorders among older persons, and they will be our primary concern in the present discussion.

Senile dementia

In senile dementia the degenerative brain changes of old age are accompanied by a clinical picture of mental deterioration, which may vary markedly in degree. Slightly more women have this affliction than men, which might be expected in view of the longer life span of women. The average age at first admission to mental hospitals is about 75 for both sexes, although the onset of the disorder may occur at any time from the 60's to the 90's. Since many senile persons are cared for at home before the spouse or family decides on hospitalization, the mean age at onset of the disorder is lower than statistics on first admissions would indicate.

General clinical picture. The onset of senile dementia is usually gradual, involving a slow physical and mental letdown. In some cases the appearance of a physical ailment or some other situational stress is a dividing point, but usually the individual passes into a psychotic state almost imperceptibly, so that it is impossible to date the disorder's onset precisely. The clinical picture may vary markedly from one person to another, depending on the nature and extent of brain degeneration, the premorbid personality of the individual, and the particular stresses in his life situation.

Faulty reactions often begin with the individual's gradual withdrawal into himself, a narrowing of social and other interests, a less-

ening of mental alertness and adaptability, and a lowering of tolerance to new ideas and changes in routine. Often there is a self-centering of thoughts and activities and a preoccupation with the bodily functions of eating, digestion, and excretion. As these various changes—typical in lesser degree of many older people—become more severe, additional symptoms, such as impairment of memory for recent events, untidiness, impaired judgment, agitation, and periods of confusion, make their appearance. Specific symptoms may vary considerably from day to day; thus the clinical picture is by no means uniform until the terminal stages, when the patient is reduced to a vegetative level. There is also, of course, individual variation in the rapidity of progression of the disorder, and in some instances there may be a reversal of psychotic symptomatology and a partial or even good recovery.

Types of senile dementia. Senile reactions have been categorized into five types. It may be emphasized, however, that there is generally a considerable overlapping of symptoms from one type to another.

1. *Simple deterioration.* This is, as the name suggests, a relatively uncomplicated exaggeration of the "normal" changes of old age. The patient gradually loses contact with the environment and develops the typical symptoms of poor memory, tendency to reminisce, intolerance of change, disorientation, restlessness, insomnia, and failure of judgment. This is the most common of the senile psychotic reactions, constituting about 50 percent of the entire group.

The following case—involving an engineer who had retired some 7 years prior to his hospitalization—is typical of simple senile deterioration.

During the past 5 years he had shown a progressive loss of interest in his surroundings and during the last year had become increasingly "childish." His wife and eldest son had brought him to the hospital because they felt they could no longer care for him in their home, particularly because of the grandchildren. They stated that he had become careless in his eating and other personal habits, was restless and prone to wandering about at night, and couldn't seem to remember anything that had happened dur-

In a group of relatively rare diseases of the central nervous system accompanied by progressive mental deterioration — four of which are described below — the clinical pictures may resemble that of senile dementia, except that the disorders characteristically appear in younger persons. Despite considerable research, the etiology of these disorders remains unclarified.

Alzheimer's disease

Named for the German psychiatrist who first described it in 1907, Alzheimer's disease is thought to occur in about the ratio of 1 case for each 25 cases of senile dementia; the true incidence, however, is unknown. Differences from senile dementia are observable chiefly in: (a) the victims' earlier age at onset, usually in the 40's or 50's; (b) rapid progression, with especially severe brain and mental deterioration, often accompanied by tendencies toward overactivity, emotional distress, and agitation; and (c) frequent development of aphasias and apraxias. Typically, death occurs within 2 to 10 years — 4 years on the average. Treatment is limited mainly to routine medical measures and custodial care.

Pick's disease

Even rarer than Alzheimer's disease, Pick's disease (first described by Arnold Pick of Prague in papers published in 1892) is a degenerative disorder of the nervous system, usually having its onset in persons between 45 and 50. Women are apparently more subject to Pick's disease than men, at a ratio of about 3 to 2. Onset is slow and insidious, involving difficulty in thinking, slight memory defects, easy fatigability, and, often, character changes with a lowering of ethical inhibitions. At first there is a rather circumscribed atrophy of the frontal and temporal lobes; as the atrophy becomes more severe, the mental deterioration becomes progressively greater and includes apathy and disorientation as well as impaired judgment and other intellectual functions. The disease usually runs a fatal course within 2 to 7 years. Treatment is limited mainly to routine medical measures and custodial care.

Parkinson's disease

Named after James Parkinson, who described it in 1817, Parkinson's disease rarely occurs before the age of 30, and in the great majority of cases occurs between the ages of 50 and 70. An estimated 1 to 1½ million Americans are so afflicted. The disorder is characterized by rigidity and spontaneous tremors of various muscles, usually beginning in one arm and spreading gradually to the leg on the same side of the body, then to the neck and face, and last to the limbs on the other side. With time, the face becomes rigid and masklike, with speech becoming drawling and indistinct. Often there is a tendency to lean forward in walking, with the result that the individual appears to be running in order to keep from falling forward. Unless the progression of the disease is halted, the patient eventually becomes completely helpless and dependent on others. He may gradually withdraw from social interaction, become apathetic and indifferent, and show a general lessening of intellectual interest, activity, and flexibility. Although the psychological symptoms typically become more pronounced as the disease progresses, intelligence is little affected and these symptoms appear to be primarily a reaction to the affliction. The drug L-dopa, developed during the last decade, offers hope for improvement in about two-thirds of the victims of Parkinson's disease (see p. 491).

Huntington's chorea

Huntington's chorea was first described by the American neurologist George Huntington in 1872. With an incidence rate of about 5 cases per 100,000 persons, the disease usually occurs in individuals between 30 and 50. It is characterized by a chronic, progressive chorea (involuntary, irregular, twitching, jerking movements) with mental deterioration leading to dementia and death within 10 to 20 years. Interestingly enough, behavior deterioration often becomes apparent several years before the neurological manifestations. In a study of 21 cases, Bellamy (1961) found that in 6 patients the first indications of the disease had been behavior problems characterized by such symptoms as violence, depression, confusion, vagrancy, prostitution, paranoid thinking, and suicidal ideas and attempts. The remaining 15 patients — hospitalized with definite neurological signs — had also shown a history of personality changes, extending back 2 to 12 years. By the time of these patients' admission, typical symptoms included depression, hyperactivity, great irritability, poverty of thought and affect, memory failure, and defective attention and judgment. No effective treatment has as yet been developed, although a variety of drugs and surgical procedures may be used to alleviate the symptoms.

Based on Freemon (1973), Holvey and Talbott (1972), Lynch, Harlan, and Dyhrberg (1972), Stang (1970), Van Dellen (1974), and Yahr (1969).

ing the day but was garrulous concerning events of his childhood and middle years.

After admission to the hospital, the patient seemed to deteriorate rapidly. He could rarely remember what had happened a few minutes before, although his memory for remote events of his childhood remained good. When he was visited by his wife and children, he did not recognize them, but mistook them for old friends, nor could he recall anything about the visit a few minutes after they had departed. The following brief conversation with the patient, which took place after he had been in the hospital for 9 months, and about 3 months prior to his death, shows his disorientation for time and person:

Dr.: How are you today, Mr. _____?

Pt.: Oh . . . hello . . . (looks at doctor in rather puzzled way as if trying to make out who he is).

Dr.: Do you know where you are now?

Pt.: Why yes . . . I am at home. I must paint the house this summer. It has needed painting for a long time but it seems like I just keep putting it off.

Dr.: Can you tell me the day today?

Pt.: Isn't today Sunday . . . why, yes, the children are coming over for dinner today. We always have dinner for the whole family on Sunday. My wife was here just a minute ago but I guess she has gone back into the kitchen.

2. *Paranoid reaction.* In this reaction type the memory loss and other manifestations of senile degeneration are usually not so pronounced as in other types of senile reactions. Confusion and other disturbances of consciousness are not common, and often the individual remains oriented for time, place, and person. It is referred to as *paranoid* because the principal characteristic is a gradual formation of delusions, usually of a persecutory nature, which may be accompanied by related hallucinations. For example, the individual may develop the notion that his relatives have turned against him and are trying to rob and kill him. His suspicions are confirmed by the noxious gases he smells in his room, or by the poison he tastes in his food. Fortunately, such delusions are poorly systematized and rarely lead to overt physical attacks on his alleged persecutors. Approximately 30 percent of psychoses associated with senile brain deterioration take a paranoid form.

The following case is typical of this reaction type.

A woman of 74 had been referred to a hospital after the death of her husband because she became un-

Effects of L-dopa therapy

These photographs illustrate the effect L-dopa can have on Parkinson's disease. Before treatment, there is great difficulty even in writing numbers (top). After about three weeks on the drug, there is some improvement (center); and at the end of eight weeks a dramatic improvement can be seen (bottom).

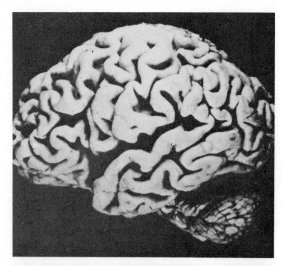

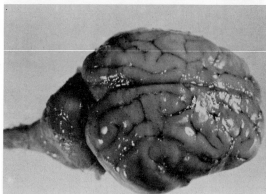

This is the brain (top) of a 79-year-old man who had been hospitalized with a diagnosis of senile dementia; his symptoms included marked confusion, memory defects, especially for recent events, slight aphasia, paranoid ideation, and agitated depression. The cortex shows extensive, diffuse atrophy with a narrowing of the convolutions and a widening of the fissures throughout. Below, for comparison, is a normal brain.

cooperative and was convinced that her relatives were trying to steal the insurance money her husband had left her. In the hospital she complained that the other patients had joined together against her and were trying to steal her belongings. She frequently refused to eat, on the grounds that the food tasted funny and had probably been poisoned. She grew increasingly irritable and disoriented for time and person. She avidly scanned magazines in the ward reading room but could not remember anything she had looked at. The following conversation reveals some of her symptoms:

Dr.: Do you find that magazine interesting?

Pt.: Why do you care? Can't you see I'm busy?

Dr.: Would you mind telling me something about what you are reading?

Pt.: It's none of your business . . . I am reading about my relatives. They want me to die so that they can steal my money.

Dr.: Do you have any evidence of this?

Pt.: Yes, plenty. They poison my food and they have turned the other women against me. They are all out to get my money. They even stole my sweater.

Dr.: Can you tell me what you had for breakfast?

Pt.: . . . (Pause) I didn't eat breakfast . . . it was poisoned and I refused to eat it. They are all against me.

Senile paranoid reactions are largely determined by the pre-psychotic personality of the patient and tend to develop in individuals who have been sensitive and suspicious. Existing personality tendencies are apparently intensified by degenerative brain changes and the stresses accompanying old age.

3. *The presbyophrenic type.* This senile psychosis is characterized by fabrication, a jovial, amiable mood, and marked impairment of memory. Such persons may appear superficially alert and may talk volubly in a rambling, confused manner, filling in gaps in present memory with events that occurred 20 or 30 years before. They usually show a peculiar restlessness or excitability and engage in continual aimless activity; for example, an individual may fold and unfold pieces of cloth as if he were ironing, or he may collect various discarded objects with a great show of importance. This reaction type appears to occur most frequently in individuals who have been lively, assertive, and extrovertive in their younger days; it accounts for less than 10 percent of all senile psychoses.

4. *Depressed and agitated types.* Here the

individual is severely depressed and agitated and usually suffers from hypochondriacal and nihilistic delusions. Often he expresses morbid ideas about cancer, syphilis, and other diseases. Delusions of poverty are also common, and he may feel that he is headed for the poorhouse, that nobody wants him, and that he is a senseless burden on his children and just generally "in the way." In some cases, the person becomes self-accusatory and develops delusions of great sin. In many respects the symptoms resemble those in involutional reactions, and as in other psychotic depressions the possibility of suicide must be guarded against. This type constitutes less than 10 percent of senile reactions.

5. *Delirious and confused types*. In these cases there is a severe mental clouding in which the individual becomes extremely restless, combative, resistive, and incoherent. He recognizes no one and is completely disoriented for time and place. Such delirious states are often precipitated in old people by acute illness or by traumas, such as a broken leg or hip. Although transient delirious episodes often occur in senile dementia, chronic confusion and delirium are uncommon except in terminal states; they account for less than 10 percent of senile reactions.

With appropriate treatment, many persons with senile dementia show some alleviation of symptoms. In general, however, deterioration continues its downward course over a period of months or years. Eventually the patient becomes oblivious of his surroundings, bedridden, and reduced to a vegetative existence. Resistance to disease is lowered, and death usually results from pneumonia or some other infection. We shall elaborate on the treatment and outcomes of senile psychoses shortly.

Psychosis with cerebral arteriosclerosis

Psychoses with cerebral arteriosclerosis are similar to senile psychoses, but there are certain differences in both anatomical and behavioral symptoms.[5] The typical vascular pathology in cerebral arteriosclerosis involves a "hardening" of the arteries of the brain. Large patches of fatty and calcified material known as *senile plaques* accumulate at particular points in the inside layers of the blood vessels and gradually clog the arterial channel. Circulation becomes sluggish or may be blocked altogether by: (a) the accumulation of deposits, leading to a narrowing or blocking of the vessel; (b) *cerebral thrombosis,* in which a blood clot forms at a site where fatty and calcified materials have accumulated and blocks the vessel; or (c) *cerebral embolism,* in which a fragment of hardened material is sloughed off the inside wall of the vessel and carried to a narrow spot where it blocks the flow of blood.

The preceding conditions may result in *cerebrovascular insufficiency* due to impaired circulation in the brain areas supplied by the vessel, or they may result in *intracerebral hemorrhage,* involving a rupture in the vessel with intracranial bleeding. Of course, damage to a large vessel will do more harm than damage to a small one. When the narrowing or eventual blockage is gradual and involves small blood vessels, cerebral nutrition is impaired and there are areas of softening as the brain tissue degenerates. Such areas of softening are found in some 90 percent of patients suffering from arteriosclerotic brain disease.

A sudden blocking or rupture in a small vessel is referred to as a *small stroke* and may result in a variety of transient psychological and physical symptoms, ranging from mental confusion and emotional lability to acute indigestion, changes in handwriting, and unsteadiness in gait. Frequently, individuals suffer a succession of small strokes resulting in cumu-

---

[5]The term *arteriosclerosis* includes a number of diseases of the blood vessels of which atherosclerosis is by far the most common and important. Atherosclerosis involves an arterial lesion characterized by a thickening of the arterial wall and a reduction in blood flow.

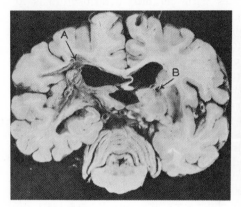 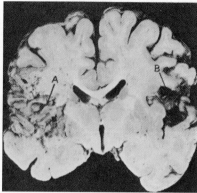 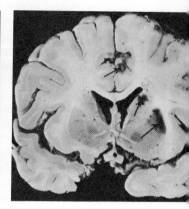

These pictures show cross sections of the brains of persons who suffered from cerebral arteriosclerosis. At the left is a section from the brain of a man who died at 43 after suffering from hypertension and two strokes that had resulted in some paralysis on both sides, emotional lability, and convulsions. The arrows indicate the areas where the cerebrovascular accidents and the specific brain damage occurred.

The center picture is of a section through the frontal lobes of a man who likewise suffered from two strokes; his strokes, however, were separated by an interval of 17 years. The arrow A points to a softening correlated with a recent stroke, which was associated with two months of paralysis on one side; the arrow B points to a cavity resulting from the earlier stroke, which had been associated with aphasia.

Arrows in the picture at right point to scattered emboli in another patient's brain, resulting in many tiny hemorrhages and widespread local damage.

lative brain damage and gradual personality change.

When the blockage or rupture involves a large vessel, the individual suffers a major stroke (*cerebrovascular accident* – CVA). Here there is both focal and generalized impairment of brain function, resulting in coma or an acute confusional state. If the individual survives, his acute symptoms may largely clear up, but typically he will suffer some degree of residual brain damage.

Cerebrovascular accidents kill more than 200,000 Americans each year; about 3 million persons in the United States are handicapped or incapacitated by cerebral arteriosclerosis. The incidence and severity of psychopathology in the latter cases is not known, although it has been estimated that only about 1 case in 6

is causally related to psychotic patterns (Terry & Wisniewski, 1974).

Although cerebral arteriosclerosis may occur in young adulthood or middle age, it usually has its onset in individuals after age 55 with the sex ratio being about equal (Holvey & Talbott, 1972). This disorder appears to be most common among persons on lower socioeconomic levels, but it occurs in all economic groups. The average age of first admission for persons manifesting psychoses associated with cerebral arteriosclerosis is between 70 and 75.

Clinical picture. In about half the cases of psychosis with cerebral arteriosclerosis, symptoms appear suddenly. Here individuals are usually admitted to a medical facility in an acute confusional state resulting from a cerebrovascular accident. Such persons show marked clouding of consciousness, disorientation for time, place, and person, incoherence, and often hemiplegia (paralysis of one side of the body). Convulsive seizures are also relatively common and may precede the acute attack, occur at the same time, or appear at a later point in the illness. In severe cases the patient may die without a clearing of his confusional state.

Acute confusional states may last for days, weeks, or even months, with an eventual remission of the acute symptoms. In these cases, there may be varying degrees of residual brain damage and impairment in physical and mental functions. Often the individual is able to compensate for his brain damage, particularly with the help of special rehabilitative measures designed to alleviate physical handicaps and clear up possible aphasic conditions. Sometimes, however, there is a progressive loss of mental efficiency, accompanied by other psychological symptoms such as emotional lability, irritability, and hypochondriacal concern over bodily functions. In many cases, there appears to be an accentuation—following severe cerebrovascular accidents—of preexisting personality traits of a maladaptive nature.

When the onset of the disorder is gradual, early symptoms may include complaints of weakness, fatigue, dizziness, headache, depression, memory defect, periods of confusion, and lowered efficiency in work. Often there is a slowing up of activity and a loss of zest in living. There may be a considerable delay between the appearance of such symptoms and the hospitalization of the individual.

By the time of hospitalization the clinical picture usually is similar to that in senile dementia. The memory defect has now increased, although it may be somewhat uneven—for example, it may be more severe when the patient is tired or under emotional stress. Emotional lability becomes pronounced, and he may be easily moved to tears or highly irritable, with a tendency to "flare-up" at the slightest provocation. Usually the flare-up is brief and ends with tears and repentance. Increased irritability may be accompanied by suspiciousness and poorly organized delusions of persecution. By this time, there is also a more pronounced impairment of concentration and general intellectual functioning. Interest in the outside world and in others is markedly reduced, as are the individual's initiative and work capacity. Judgment is impaired and in some instances there is a lowering of moral controls. Frequently, there are feelings of depression associated with some insight into failing physical and mental powers. As in cases with an acute onset, there may be marked fluctuations in the clinical picture, but the general course of the disease is in the direction of increasing deterioration and death.

Comparison with the clinical picture in senile dementia. The clinical aspects of senile dementia and psychosis with cerebral arteriosclerosis are so much alike that a differential diagnosis is frequently very difficult to make. In some cases, there is a mixture of the two disorders—a senile reaction may be superimposed on an arteriosclerotic condition or vice versa. However, mixed reactions are not nearly so common as might be expected, and usually one condition or the other predominates.

Among the clinically distinguishing features of these two disorders are: (a) senile dementia is usually gradual and progressive and lasts longer, while psychosis with cerebral arteriosclerosis is more apt to be brought on by a cerebrovascular accident and to run a brief and stormy course ending in death; (b) in senile dementia there is usually more pronounced intellectual impairment, and paranoid patterns are more common; (c) symptoms common in the arteriosclerotic group but less often seen in senile dementia are headaches, dizziness, convulsive seizures, depression, and strong emotional outbursts; and finally (d) the symptoms in cerebral arteriosclerotic reactions typically show more pronounced fluctuations. But although these differences are observable in early and intermediate states, with progressive intellectual deterioration all patients become very much alike.

Causal factors in old-age psychoses

Early investigators seized on brain damage as the only important factor in the causation of both senile dementia and psychosis with cerebral arteriosclerosis. But in recent years, with the increased interest and attention devoted to mental disorders of old age, those early beliefs have undergone considerable revision.

Although cerebral damage alone, when sufficiently extensive, may produce marked mental symptoms, it has become evident that in most cases the organic changes are only one set of interactive factors. In the total clinical picture the prior personality organization of the individual and the stresses in his life situation are also of key importance. And since specific brain pathology, personality makeup, and stress factors vary from person to person, we find a somewhat different causal pattern in each case.

Biological factors. A number of early studies showed a high incidence of senile and arteriosclerotic brain disease in the family backgrounds of elderly psychotics. However, more recent findings, including the study of aging in twins, indicate that it is unrealistic to consider genetic or constitutional factors as *primary* causal agents in these mental disorders. This view, of course, does not exclude their influence on the rapidity of physiological aging.

In recent years the effects of senile and of arteriosclerotic changes in brain metabolism have been strongly emphasized in the causal pattern of old-age psychoses. In cases involving major CVA's, gross disturbances in circulatory and metabolic processes are apparent, and we have noted the confusional states and other symptoms that may result. However, only a small minority of persons who suffer a severe CVA develop a persistent psychotic disorder. In mental disorders having a gradual onset, the role of metabolic factors is even less clear. A diminished flow of blood and lower oxygen consumption accompany senile psychoses, but they are no longer considered of primary etiologic significance (Terry & Wisniewski, 1974). And while prolonged malnutrition, endocrine malfunction, and other metabolic factors are implicated in some cases, they are not ordinarily considered of primary causal significance.

Nor does the extent of brain pathology ordinarily account for the psychotic disorders of old age, a point dramatically demonstrated by Gal (1959), who did a postmortem study of 104 patients ranging in age from 65 to 94 and found a lack of correlation between brain damage and behavior. Extensive cerebral damage was found in some patients who had manifested only mild mental symptoms, while minimal cerebral damage was found in others who had shown severe psychopathology. In general, it appears that psychosocial and sociocultural factors as well as biological factors play an important role in the etiology of psychoses associated with aging.

With progressive cerebral impairment, of course, the degree of residual brain capacity shapes the response in greater measure. This point was well brought out by Ullmann and Gruen in summarizing their findings with 84 patients who had suffered strokes and had shown mild, moderate, or severe degrees of cerebral deficit.

"Patients who have experienced mild strokes with little or no residual mental impairment react to the stress in their own idiosyncratic fashion. Some will integrate the experience successfully; others will become enmeshed in psychopathological maneuvers of varying severity. In patients with moderate or severe brain damage, the situation is quite different. Here the unique features of the stroke are highlighted, the chief of these being that the very organ governing the adaptation to stress is itself impaired. The resulting clinical picture has to be evaluated now, not only in terms of what the experience means to the patient, but also in terms of the capacity the patient has for evaluating the situation." (1961, p. 1009)

Psychosocial factors. It has been said that next to dying, the recognition that we are aging may be the most profound shock we experience in our lifetime. Every day in the United States more than 1000 persons cross the invisible barrier of age 65 and by custom and law are "benched" for the remainder of the game. They are "older persons" or "senior citizens." How these individuals react to their changed status and to the difficult stresses of this age period depends heavily on their personality makeup as well as on the challenges, rewards, and frustrations of their life situation. As important as actual brain changes are, the majority of old-age psychoses depend heavily—and often primarily—on psychosocial and sociocultural factors.

1. *The role of the pre-psychotic personality.* A number of studies have shown that individuals who are handicapped psychologically by undesirable personality traits are especially vulnerable to psychoses and other mental disorders in old age. Obsessive-compulsive trends, rigidity, suspiciousness, seclusiveness, social inadequacy, and poor adaptability to change are some of the traits that have been emphasized in the background of such patients. Even negative attitudes toward growing old, which lead to self-devaluation and a negative self-image, can be serious adjustment handicaps during this period of life.

2. *Stresses characteristic of old age.* An older person faces numerous very real fears and insecurities that are not characteristic of earlier life periods. In fact, the unfavorable environmental circumstances of older people are often more hazardous to mental health than are organic brain changes. Even well-integrated personalities may break down under the combined assault of cerebral changes and severe situational stress.

a) *Retirement and reduced income.* Retirement is often the brand that marks a person as a member of the "old age" group. It can be quite demoralizing if it is forced upon the individual. Repeated studies have shown that most persons of 65 are productive workers and that many would prefer to keep on working when they reach retirement age (Offir, 1974).

Many people depend greatly on their work for status, for self-identity, for satisfying interpersonal relationships, and for meaning in their lives. Retirement often does not meet these needs, and there is a tendency to react with the feeling that one's usefulness and worth are at an end and that one's life is really over—a reaction conducive to rapid physical and mental deterioration.

Retirement usually leads also to a severe reduction in income, which further augments the older person's adjustive burden. In 1970 almost 5 million older Americans were de-scribed as living in poverty, and with the rampant inflation of the 1970s, it is likely that millions of others have suffered the same fate.

b) *Fear of invalidism and death.* The gradual physical deterioration of one's body and the increased possibility of falling prey to some chronic and debilitating disease tend to make one more preoccupied with bodily functions and with the possibility of failing health, symptoms common among older people. Such concern is aggravated when the individual has a history of medical difficulties that are likely to be aggravated by the aging process. Whereas a young person usually expects to make a complete recovery from sickness, many illnesses among older people become chronic and the individual has to adjust to living with them. When chronic illness and failing health lead to pain, invalidism, and dependence on others, the individual faces a difficult life situation.

With aging and physical deterioration, the individual is also confronted with the inescapable fact of his own impending death. Some older people react with equanimity, often stemming from deep religious faith in the meaningfulness of human existence and in the certainty of a life hereafter. Others die as they have lived, with little concern for life or human existence. In fact, they may welcome death as a solution to unsolvable problems and a meaningless life. This is sometimes true also of older people who have lost their friends and loved ones and who feel that they have "outlived their time." However, for many older people the realization that life is drawing to a close is a highly stressful experience.

c) *Isolation and loneliness.* As the individual grows older, he is faced with the inevitable loss of loved ones, friends, and contemporaries. The death of the mate with whom one may have shared many years of close companionship often poses a particularly difficult adjustment problem. This is especially true for women, who in the U.S. tend to outlive their spouses by some 7 years.

Other factors, too, may contribute to social isolation. Children grow up, marry, and move away; impairment of vision or hearing and various chronic ailments may make social interaction difficult; an attitude of self-pity or an inward centering of interest may alienate

One family's adjustment to senility

Mark Jury's grandfather, always an active, respected member of the community he lived in, began to have "spells," times when he became disoriented. Gradually his condition worsened: he was unable to remember who his family was; he believed that red rabbits and other imaginary creatures—chillysmiths and bugeyes, for example, which delighted his granddaughter—lived in the house; he was rude and even obscene. Yet the Jury family chose to keep him at home, ministering to his needs as best they could, even when that meant round-the-clock babysitting for a person who could no longer take care of himself. In spite of the problems, however, there was no resentment on the part of the Jury family. After his grandfather died, Mark Jury said he felt an enormous amount of respect for the old man, who had lived a constructive life and died with as much dignity as possible; he also felt "a tinge of emptiness, a feeling that we would miss the craziness he brought into our lives" (1975, p. 62).

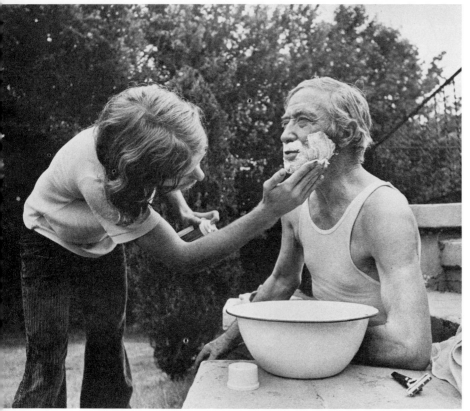

family and friends alike. In many instances, the older person also becomes increasingly rigid and intolerant in his outlook and is unable to make effective use of the opportunities for meaningful social interaction that still remain to him.

Of course, retirement, lowered income, impaired health, and loneliness are not just matters of inability to maintain a particular life style or to interact with loved ones. In a larger view, they involve the inability to contribute productively and to feel oneself a vital and needed part of the human enterprise. In essence, they progressively destroy the older person's links with his world and the meaningfulness of his existence as a human being.

General sociocultural conditions. The significance of sociocultural conditions in senile and arteriosclerotic brain disorders is a matter of considerable speculation, but these conditions do provide the context or "climate" in which aging takes place in our society.[6]

In the United States, the urban rate of first admissions to mental hospitals and related facilities for both senile dementia and psychosis with cerebral arteriosclerosis is approximately twice as high as the rural rate. But we do not know how much this indicates that urban living, with its faster pace, noise, crowds, and other stresses, is more conducive to the development of these disorders—and how much it indicates that more persons are cared for at home in rural areas. The picture is also complicated by the fact that in rural areas the older person enjoys higher social status and is generally able to work productively for a longer period.

In our urban industrial society, the problems of old age have caught us largely unprepared. We have not provided ample conditions for utilizing the experience and wisdom of older people; nor have we provided conditions essential for them to live in reasonable comfort and dignity. In fact, the term "role obsolescence" has been used to refer to society's attitude toward the older person's having outlived his usefulness. And in our youth-oriented culture, many older people come to perceive themselves as obsolete and worthless—and tend to behave accordingly.

Not infrequently children assume a patronizing and protective attitude toward the aging parent, and in other ways tend to deprive him of dignity, responsibility, and a feeling of importance. Many parents are treated as unwanted burdens, and their children may secretly wish that they would die to relieve them of financial and other responsibilities. In a study of older people in France, De Beauvoir (1970) has pointed out that when the French go away for vacations, they sometimes deposit their aged parents in rest homes. Then, on their return home, they "forget" to pick them up, abandoning them like dogs in a kennel. Undoubtedly in the United States, too, many older people are "deposited" in rest or nursing homes to die, even though they may be in relatively good health. The effects of being cast aside simply for "being old" are likely to be devastating.

Treatment and outcomes

Whether or not to hospitalize the aged person who is mentally disordered is often a problem. Individuals manifesting such symptoms as confusion, violent and noisy behavior, depression, antisocial behavior, and disorientation for time, place, and person, usually require institutionalization. However, many investigators regard hospitalization as a last resort, feeling that the sudden change in environment and manner of living is highly stressful for the older person and may lead to a feeling of complete hopelessness. In any event, effective treatment of the mental disorders of later life requires a comprehensive use of medical, psychological, and sociological procedures, as indicated by the needs of the individual.

Medical treatment includes both accurate diagnosis and a wide range of procedures, including surgery, drugs, and dietary changes, designed to ameliorate specific physical disorders and to improve the overall health and well-being of the patient. Anti-psychotic and minor tranquilizing drugs have proven valuable in controlling psychotic symptoms and

[6]A useful source of information concerning the problems of aging in our own and other societies may be found in The Annals of the American Academy of Political and Social Science (Sept. 1974).

alleviating anxiety and tension, but they are not effective in ameliorating the mental deterioration found in advanced cases of senile and arteriosclerotic brain disorders.

There have been favorable reports on the use of group psychotherapy in treating mental disorders associated with old age, but additional research is needed for delineating the most effective psychological treatment procedures for older persons, particularly those suffering from senile and arteriosclerotic brain disorders. In many hospital settings, "token economies" have proven helpful: desired behavior is rewarded by tokens that the patient can exchange for things he wants. A key aspect of such reinforcement procedures is that they parallel the organization of outside society and help counteract tendencies toward progressive institutional dependence and chronicity.

Sociotherapy with older patients is directed toward creating an environment in which the person can function successfully. In a hospital setting or nursing home this includes the provision of comfortable surroundings, together with stimulating activities that encourage the patient to utilize his capacities. Sociotherapy also includes working with the family in an attempt to help them understand the nature of the patient's disorder, to be supportive, and to show that they care. Where the patient is convalescing at home, follow-up visits by the social worker may be of great value in helping both the patient and his family to adjust.

Even seemingly minor innovations in treatment have shown promising results. In an interesting study, for example, Volpe and Kastenbaum (1967) worked with a group of older men who were so physically and psychologically incapacitated that they required around-the-clock nursing care. These men could perform no services for themselves, were agitated and incontinent, and had a record of striking at each other and tearing off their clothes. Some simple amenities were provided on the ward—games, cards, a record player, and a decorated bulletin board; the men were dressed in white shirts and ties; and at 2 P.M. each day they were served beer in 12-ounce bottles with crackers and cheese. Within a month there was a noticeable change in the group's behavior. The amount of medication needed dropped sharply, incontinent and agitated behavior decreased significantly, and social responsivity—as indicated by requests for and participation in parties and dances—markedly increased. The improvement of these men was attributed to their being treated with dignity as responsible individuals, and to the consequent *"expectancies of mutual gratification* on the part of patients and staff members." In essence, the expectations and demand characteristics of the ward had been changed from those of a medical to a social situation; the men were cared for in much the same way as in the era of moral treatment (Chapter 2).

The extent to which meaningful social roles and expectations may help older people cope with the emotional problems of this life period is illustrated by the following case. It involves a professional man who was admitted to a mental hospital for treatment as a result of severe anxiety, indecision, and depression. The rather unusual course of this case follows:

The patient's disorder was apparently precipitated by his retirement from the firm for which he had worked for over 40 years. In the course of his hospitalization, the patient evidenced little improvement until the hospital received a letter from his firm inquiring about his condition. They were experiencing difficulty without him and needed his help. Upon receipt of the news the patient showed marked improvement. He was given a leave of absence and returned to his old job. A follow-up study a year later revealed that he was handling his responsibilities with unimpaired judgment, appeared younger, showed good stamina, and reported regularly to work at the age of 80.

The expectation and reinforcement of "normal" social behaviors can bring about marked behavioral changes in a relatively short time. Kahana and Kahana (1970) found that even such a simple measure as moving aged people from segregated to desegregated wards appeared to be beneficial for both young and old. The younger ones often tried to help the elderly, which provided them with a sense of purpose; their active interest, in turn, increased the elderly individuals' sense of importance. Thus, the prognosis in the psychoses of old age is far from hopeless. Even without complete recovery, many patients can

A stroke poses a serious threat to the victim's life-style, personal relationships, and general ability to cope. The patient's response typically involves feelings of anxiety, depression, helplessness, and often hopelessness. Thus psychotherapy and sociotherapy have become increasingly important aspects of the overall treatment program.

The following phases in group therapy have been described as characteristic for patients who have been transferred from an intensive care unit to a subacute area where they are helped to develop and utilize their capabilities for independent functioning.

Phase 1. Introductory phase. During this phase patients begin to discuss their anxieties about the future, which seems both unknown and uncertain. Commonly they pose such questions as "Will I have another stroke?" "Will I ever be able to walk or use my hands again?" "Is there anything I can do to prevent another stroke?"

Phase 2. Middle phase. As the patients in the group get to know and trust each other and the staff members, they share their "seemingly endless" feelings of anxiety, helplessness, and despair. Often patients express concern about loss of control over their lives and of "getting close to the end."

Phase 3. Termination phase. During this phase patients come to accept their situation and to make the best of their remaining assets. Plans are now made for discharge and resuming their lives with their families and in the community. Often patients "try out" new behavior at home while on weekend passes before their actual discharge from the protective and supportive world of the hospital.

During the entire treatment program, emphasis is also placed on family counseling and involvement in the social aspects of treatment, discharge planning, and rehabilitation.

Based on Oradei and Waite (1974).

return to their homes, and many others can remain in their homes while being treated in community clinics.

Although the outcome in cases of senile and arteriosclerotic brain disorders has traditionally been considered unfavorable, since the cerebral damage and psychopathology seemed irreversible once the psychosis was under way, recent evidence indicates that recovery or improvement is possible in about half of the cases when appropriate treatment is provided. Blau (1970) has pointed out that at the Boston State Hospital, which has an active treatment program for elderly patients and fosters aftercare in the community, almost half of the patients over 60 years of age are discharged within 6 months of their admission.

Interestingly enough, both the greatest number of deaths and the greatest number of improvements among hospitalized elderly psychotics occur during the first year after admission (Goldfarb, 1969). For patients who require continued care in the hospital, about 75 percent die within the first 5 years. In general, the following are considered favorable indicators with respect to outcome: (a) a well-integrated pre-psychotic personality; (b) mild, rather than severe, cerebral pathology; (c) absence of such conditions as severe overweight, hypertension, and alcoholism; (d) average or above-average intelligence, education, and technical competence; and (e) a favorable life situation to which to return.

Increasingly aware of the problems confronting senior citizens, federal, state, and local groups are focusing on all aspects of growing old. Scientists in many areas of the biological and social sciences are investigating the pathological and normal aspects of aging and are exploring—in their respective fields—ways to minimize the aging process. In 1974 the federal government established a special agency, The National Institute on Aging, to foster and coordinate research. Community centers and clinics for assisting older people with retirement and other problems are increasing. Specifically designed housing developments also are being built for the elderly; and a number of older people are experimenting with "communal living." However, it is still too early to assess the long-range impact such approaches will have on dealing with the problems of aging in our society.[7]

While society can do much to improve the status of older people, it is important that older people also help themselves. An encouraging trend here is the growth of such organizations as the National Association of Retired People, which numbers over 5 million members. It provides an impressive array of services for its members as well as fosters legislation to protect the rights and the welfare of older people in our society (Offir, 1974). It does seem important, however, as Neugarten (1974) has pointed out, that senior citizens do not form too strong an age-group identification if they are to create an attractive image of aging, allay the fears of the young about growing old, and eradicate those attitudes toward age that tend to divide our society into age-conscious groups—in essence, if they are to participate in building an "age-irrelevant" society.

At the same time the individual also needs to prepare himself for the problems typical of this life period. He needs to face realistically the fact that he is getting older and plan ahead for an active and useful life in his later years, a life that will take full advantage of the opportunities that are offered to him. Of course, many of the adjustments of old age are highly specific to the situation of the given individual and hence cannot be fully anticipated, but at any age it is important to maintain mental alertness, flexibility, and adaptability while continuing to grow and fulfill one's potential. As Simmons (1960) has put it:

"The secret of success for anyone facing a long life . . . is to find for himself a suitable place in his society in which to age with grace and usefulness, and to participate tactfully and fully up to the very end if at all possible." (p. 63)

In short, old age does pose special problems, but it is by no means incompatible with a meaningful and fulfilling life.

In this chapter we have examined acute and chronic disorders associated with known pathology of the brain or nervous system. Such disorders have a great variety of causes—some of them being syphilitic infection, brain tumors, head injuries, toxic poisoning, metabolic disturbances, and senile brain deterioration—and they may involve mild, moderate, or severe impairment of psychological functioning. In general, brain disorders typically involve such symptoms as impairment of orientation for time, place, and person; emotional shallowness and lability; and impairment of learning, comprehension, and judgment. There are significant differences in the clinical picture from one type of disorder to another, however, and also from one individual to another.

Three interrelated factors are of key importance in determining both the severity of symptoms and the likelihood of successful treatment: (a) the nature and extent of the organic pathology; (b) the personality and stress tolerance of the individual; and (c) his life situation—including the situation to which he returns if he has been hospitalized. As we have observed, the second and third factors are often as important as the first, except in cases of very severe brain damage or deterioration.

---

[7]An interesting discussion of aging in the year 2000, including mental health programs, may be found in *The Gerontologist* (Feb. 1975).

14

Mental Retardation

"Let each become all that he was created capable of being; expand, if possible, to his full growth, and show himself at length in his own shape and stature, be these what they may." (Thomas Carlyle, *Past and Present*, 1843)

Written over a century ago, this statement was selected by the President's Committee on Mental Retardation (1973) as representing the basic theme of its report to the President; it also expresses the basic viewpoint underlying this chapter.

The American Association on Mental Deficiency has defined *mental retardation* as "significantly subaverage general intellectual functioning existing concurrently with deficits in adaptive behavior, and manifested during the developmental period" (AAMD, 1973, p. 11).[1] This definition denotes a level of behavioral performance without reference to causal factors—which may be primarily biological, psychosocial, or sociocultural in nature or a combination of these.

Mental retardation occurs among children throughout the world; in its most severe forms it is a source of great hardship to parents as well as an economic and social burden on the community. The incidence of mental retardation in the United States is estimated to be about 6.5 million persons, or roughly 3 percent of the population. This figure is based on a cutoff point of about IQ 70, which is the cutoff point used by the AAMD. Most states have laws providing that individuals with IQ's below 70 who evidence socially incompetent or disapproved behavior can be classified as mentally retarded and committed to institutions.

The incidence of mental retardation seems to increase markedly at ages 5 to 6, to peak at age 15, and to drop off sharply after that. For the most part, these changes in incidence reflect changes in life demands. During early childhood, individuals with only a mild degree

Levels of Mental Retardation
Mental Retardation Associated with Organic Causes
Mental Retardation Associated with Sociocultural Deprivation
Treatment, Outcomes, and Prevention

---

[1]The American Psychiatric Association (1968) has defined *mental retardation* as "subnormal general intellectual functioning which originates during the developmental period and is associated with impairment of either learning and social adjustment or maturation, or both" (p. 14). While the APA and AAMD definitions are essentially the same, we have used that of the AAMD as being both simpler and more up-to-date.

of intellectual impairment, who constitute the vast majority of mental retardates, appear to be relatively normal. Their subaverage intellectual functioning becomes apparent only when difficulties with schoolwork lead to a diagnostic evaluation. When adequate facilities are available for their education, children in this group can usually master essential school skills and achieve a satisfactory level of socially adaptive behavior. Following the school years, they usually make an acceptable adjustment in the community and thus lose the identity of mental retardates.

Levels of Mental Retardation

The 1973 classification system of the AAMD identifies four levels of mental retardation, ranging from "mild" to "profound."[2] Although this classification is based on the criterion of IQ level, it recognizes that IQ alone does not provide an adequate measure of an individual's adaptive capacity. Thus the individual's level of adaptive behavior—in terms of the degree to which he meets standards of personal independence and social responsibility expected of his cultural and age group—is also of crucial significance in labeling a person as mentally retarded.

1. *Mild mental retardation (IQ 52–68).* As shown in the table on page 507, this group constitutes by far the largest number of those labeled mentally retarded. Persons in this group are considered "educable," and their intellectual levels as adults are comparable to that of the average 8- to 11-year-old child. Their social adjustment often approximates that of the adolescent, although they tend to lack the normal adolescent's imagination, inventiveness, and judgment. Ordinarily they do not show signs of brain pathology or other physical anomalies. Often they require some measure of supervision due to limited ability to foresee the consequences of their actions. With early diagnosis, parental assistance, and special educational programs, the great majority can adjust socially, master simple academic and occupational skills, and become self-supporting citizens.

2. *Moderate mental retardation (IQ 36–51).* Individuals in this group are likely to fall in the educational category of "trainable." In adult life, individuals classified as moderately retarded attain intellectual levels similar to

[2]Formerly both the APA and AAMD classifications of mental retardation included the category of "borderline" retardation (IQ 68–83), but the AAMD classification has dropped this category and simply refers to persons in that IQ range as being of "borderline intelligence."

that of the average 4- to 7-year-old child. While some of the brighter ones can be taught to read and write a little, and some manage to achieve a fair command of spoken language, the rate of learning is relatively slow among members of this group, and the level of conceptualizing extremely limited. Physically, they usually appear clumsy and ungainly, and they suffer from bodily deformities and poor motor coordination. A distinct minority of these children are hostile and aggressive, but typically they present an affable and somewhat vacuous personality picture.

In general, with early diagnosis, parental help, and adequate opportunities for training, most of the moderately retarded can achieve partial independence in daily self-care, acceptable behavior, and economic usefulness in a family or other sheltered environment. Whether or not they require institutionalization usually depends on their general level of adaptive behavior and the nature of their home situation.

3. *Severe mental retardation (IQ 20–35).* Individuals in this group are sometimes referred to as "dependent retarded." Among these individuals, motor and speech development is severely retarded, and sensory defects and motor handicaps are common. These mental retardates can develop limited levels of personal hygiene and self-help skills, which somewhat lessen their dependence, but all their lives they will be dependent on others for care. However, many profit to some extent from training and can perform simple occupational tasks under supervision.

4. *Profound mental retardation (IQ under 20).* The term "life support" mental retardate is sometimes used in referring to individuals in this category. Most of these persons are severely deficient in adaptive behavior and unable to master any but the simplest tasks. Useful speech, if it develops at all, is on a rudimentary level. Severe physical deformities, central nervous system pathology, and retarded growth are typical, and convulsive seizures, mutism, deafness, and other physical anomalies are common. These retardates must remain in custodial care all their lives. However, health and resistance to disease is lowered, and a short life expectancy is usual.

Moderate, severe, and profound cases of mental retardation usually are diagnosed in infancy because of physical malformations, grossly delayed habit training, and other obvious symptoms of abnormality. But although these individuals show a marked impairment of overall intellectual functioning, they may have considerably more ability in some areas than in others. Indeed, in very occasional cases—often referred to as involving "idiot savants"—seriously retarded persons may show a high level of skill in some specific aspect of behavior that does not depend on abstract reasoning. Thus a retardate may be able to remember the serial number on every dollar bill he is shown or has ever seen, or he may be able to tell the day of the week of a given date in any year, without resorting to paper and pencil, or even to making other numerical calculations. In other exceptional cases, a retardate may show considerable talent in art or music. Viscott (1970) provided a detailed case study of a "musical idiot savant"; Hill (1975) cited the case of a retardate with a diagnosed IQ of 54 who could play 11 different musical instruments by ear and possessed outstanding skill in calculating dates. Similarly, Morishima (1975) cited the case of a famous Japanese painter with an assessed IQ of 47. However, such unusual abilities among mental retardates are rare.

In concluding this brief discussion of degrees of mental retardation, it may be noted that a prognosis of potential disability can, to some extent at least, be a self-fulfilling prophecy. All too often an assessment that shows severe limitations in ability is taken as implying that the abilities cannot be changed, so rehabilitative efforts are minimal, which tends to ensure the accuracy of the prognosis.

Relative incidence of mental retardation in the U.S. in four categories

Level of retardation	Approximate incidence
Mild (IQ 52–68)	5,000,000
Moderate (IQ 36–51)	1,100,000
Severe (IQ 20–35)	300,000
Profound (IQ under 20)	100,000

Based in part on Achenbach (1974).

Many retardates can be educated to lead useful, fulfilling lives. Yolanda, who had been an institutionalized "retardate" for 16 years, is now an office assistant with a large corporation and is teaching herself to type. The director of the occupational training center that Yolanda attended maintains that "It doesn't even make any difference whether our students are supposed to be 'educable' or 'trainable' or whatever label someone has slapped on them. All that's important to us is whether they can get and hold a job and take care of themselves. . . . The vast majority make it" (in President's Commission on Mental Retardation Report, 1970).

Mental Retardation Associated with Organic Causes

In the present section we shall consider five categories of biological conditions that may lead to mental retardation, noting some of the possible interrelations between them. Then we shall review some of the major clinical types of mental retardation associated with these organic causes.

1. *Genetic-chromosomal factors.* Mental retardation tends to run in families. This is particularly true of mild retardation, which presumably is heavily influenced by the many genetic factors responsible for variations in intelligence. However, poverty and sociocultural deprivation also tend to run in families, and with early and continued exposure to such conditions, even the inheritance of average intellectual potential may not prevent subaverage intellectual functioning.

As we noted in Chapter 5, genetic factors play a much clearer role in the etiology of relatively rare types of mental retardation such as Down's syndrome. Here, specific genetic defects are responsible for metabolic alterations that adversely affect development of the brain. Genetic defects leading to metabolic alterations may, of course, involve many other developmental anomalies besides mental retardation. In general, mental retardation associated with known genetic-chromosomal defects is moderate to severe in degree.

2. *Infections and toxic agents.* Mental retardation may be associated with a wide range of conditions due to infection. The fetus of a mother with certain virus diseases, such as German measles, may suffer brain damage, as may the fetus of a mother with syphilis. And, as in the case of viral encephalitis, brain damage may result from infections occurring after birth.

A number of toxic agents, such as carbon monoxide and lead, may also cause brain

The basic learning processes of most mental retardates—aside from a minority with serious neurological defects—are not essentially different from those of normal children. However, retardates learn at a slower rate than normal children and are less capable of mastering abstractions and complex concepts. These limitations are especially apparent in learning language and other symbolic skills which require a high level of abstract ability.

Problems which the retardate typically encounters in learning basic academic skills may be summarized as follows:

1. Difficulty in focusing attention. Studies have shown that a retardate's poor learning is often due to the fact that his attention is focused on irrelevant aspects of learning situations. Once he knows what stimulus dimensions are important—for example, attending to form when the shape of the letters is important in learning the alphabet—he may quickly master appropriate discrimination skills and show marked improvement in performance and learning.

2. Deficiency in past learning. Most formal learning requires prior learning. For example, a child on entering school will fall farther and farther behind if he has not previously learned basic verbal, conceptual, and problem-solving skills. Thus a number of programs have been established to help disadvantaged children of preschool age develop basic skills requisite for learning in school.

3. Expectancy of failure—a self-fulfilling prophecy. Because of having experienced more failure in learning attempts than other children, the mentally retarded child tends to begin tasks with a greater expectancy of failure and to engage in avoidance behavior as well. Often the child feels that forces beyond his control determine the outcome of his actions. Thus, if he should succeed in a task, he may not perceive his success as due to his own efforts or ability. He becomes passive, loses his initiative, and begins to rely too much on others. To counteract this tendency, learning experiences must be programmed into manageable components.

These learning difficulties are not exclusive to retardates, but they are common among them and suggest the most suitable paths to be followed in their education. That is, special education classes should be directed at helping retardates discriminate relevant from irrelevant stimuli in learning and problem-solving situations; it should associate new learning with the retardates' present information, needs, and life situations; and it should structure learning tasks in such a sequence that they can be readily mastered by the retardates. Such measures, of course, are useful in all educational settings, but are particularly important in training the mentally retarded.

Based on Bijou (1966), Hagen and Huntsman (1971), Hyatt and Rolnick (1974), Karnes et al. (1970), MacMillan and Keogh (1971), and Tarver and Hallahan (1974).

damage during fetal development or after birth. In some instances, immunological agents, such as antitetanus serum or typhoid vaccine, may lead to brain damage. Similarly, certain drugs taken by the mother during pregnancy may lead to congenital malformations, or an overdose of drugs administered to the infant may result in toxicity and brain damage. In rare cases, brain damage results from incompatibility in blood types between mother and fetus—Rh or ABO system incompatibility. Fortunately, early diagnosis and blood transfusions can now minimize the effects of this disorder.

3. *Prematurity and trauma (physical injury).* Follow-up studies of children born prematurely (weighing less than 1500 grams at birth) have revealed a high incidence of neurological disorders, including mental retardation (Kennedy, 1963; Rothchild, 1967). In fact, very small premature babies are about 10 times more likely to be mentally retarded than normal infants.

Physical injury at birth can also result in retardation. Isaacson (1970) has estimated that 1 baby in 1000 suffers brain damage that will prevent his reaching the intelligence level of a 12-year-old. Although normally the fetus is well protected by its fluid-filled bag, and its skull appears designed to resist delivery stresses, accidents do happen during delivery, as well as after birth. Difficulties in labor due to malposition of the fetus or other complications may irreparably damage the infant's brain. Bleeding within the brain is probably the most common result of such birth trauma. *Anoxia*—lack of sufficient oxygen to the brain stemming from delayed breathing or other causes—is another type of birth trauma that may damage the brain. Anoxia may also occur after birth as a result of cardiac arrest associated with operations, heart attacks, or near drownings.

4. *Ionizing radiation.* In recent years a good deal of scientific attention has been focused on the damaging effects of ionizing radiation on sex cells and other bodily cells and tissues. Radiation may act directly on the fertilized ovum or may produce gene mutations in the sex cells of either or both parents, which, in turn, may lead to defective offspring.

Sources of harmful radiation were once limited primarily to high-energy X rays used for diagnosis and therapy, but the list has grown to include nuclear weapons testing and other radioactive materials to which people may be exposed.

5. *Malnutrition and other biological factors.* As we noted in Chapter 5, deficiencies in proteins and other essential nutrients during early development can result in irreversible physical and mental damage. Protein deficiencies in the mother's diet, as well as in the baby's diet after birth, have been pinpointed as particularly potent causes of lowered intelligence.

A limited number of cases of mental retardation are also associated with other biological agents, such as brain tumors that either damage the brain tissue directly or lead to increased cranial pressure and concomitant brain damage. In some instances of mental retardation—particularly of the severe and profound types—the causes are uncertain or unknown, although extensive brain pathology is evident.

Mental retardation stemming primarily from biological causes can be classified into several recognizable clinical types.

Down's syndrome (mongolism)

Down's syndrome, first described by Langdon Down in 1886, is the most common of the clinical conditions associated with moderate and severe mental retardation. The term *mongolism* has often been used in referring to this syndrome because persons so afflicted frequently have almond-shaped slanting eyes. About 1 in every 600 babies born in the United States is diagnosed as having Down's syndrome, a condition that "has lifelong implications for physical appearance, intellectual achievement and general functioning" (Golden & Davis, 1974, p. 7).

A number of physical features are often found among children with Down's syndrome, but very few of these children have all of the characteristics commonly throught of as typifying this group. In addition to slanting eyes,

In 1800, long before the development of psychotherapy, Jean-Marc Itard attempted to inculcate normal human abilities in a "wild boy" who had been captured by peasants in the forest of Aveyron, France. The boy, who appeared to be between 10 and 12 years old, had been exhibited in a cage for about a year by his captors when Itard rescued him. From an examination of the scars on the boy's body, as well as observation of his personal habits, Itard concluded that he had been abandoned at the age of about 2 or 3.

At first Victor (as Itard named the boy) seemed more animal than human. He was oblivious to other human beings, could not talk, and howled and ate off the ground on all fours like an animal. He evidenced unusual sensory reactions; for example, he did not react if a pistol were fired next to his ear, but he could hear the cracking of a nut or the crackling of underbrush at a great distance. No adverse reaction seemed to result from his going unclothed even in freezing weather. In fact, Victor had a fine velvety skin, despite his years of exposure.

Victor exhibited animal-like behavior in many ways. He had an obstinate habit of smelling any object that was given to him—even objects we consider void of smell. He knew nothing of love and perceived other human beings only as obstacles—in other words, like the wild animals he had known in the forest. He was typically indifferent and uncomplaining but, very occasionally, he showed a kind of frantic rage and became dangerous to those around him. If he had any sense of self-identity, it was apparently more that of an animal than a human.

Philippe Pinel, Itard's teacher, diagnosed Victor's condition as congenital idiocy—concluding that the boy was incapable of profiting from training. But Itard, although only 25 years old and inexperienced in comparison with Pinel, disagreed; in his view, Victor's savage behavior was the result of early and lengthy isolation from other humans. He believed that human contact and intensive training would enable the boy to become a normal person, and, ignoring Pinel's advice, he began his attempt to civilize "the wild boy of Aveyron."

No procedures had yet been formulated that Itard could use in treating Victor; thus he developed a program based on principles which included the following: (a) without human contact a human infant—unlike a lower animal—cannot develop normally; (b) the instinct to imitate is the learning force by which our senses are educated, and this instinct is strongest in early childhood and decreases with age; and (c) in all

human beings, from the most isolated savage to the most educated individual, a constant relationship exists between needs and ideas—the greater the needs, the greater the development of mental capacities to meet them.

In attempting to train Victor, Itard developed methods that have had considerable impact on the subsequent treatment of children with serious learning disabilities. Instructional materials were provided to broaden Victor's discrimination skills in touch, smell, and other sensory modalities, appropriate to his environment; language training was begun through the association of words with the objects Victor wanted; and modeling and imitation were used to reinforce Victor's learning of desired social behaviors.

Initial results were indeed promising. Victor learned to speak a number of words and could write in chalk to express his wants. He also developed affectionate feelings toward his governess.

In June 1801, Itard reported to the Academy of Science in Paris of the rapid progress in the first 9 months of training. But in November 1806, he could only report again on Victor's original savage state and his early rapid progress; for despite significant advances in several areas, Victor had not been made "normal" in the sense of becoming a self-directing and socially adjusted person. Being brought into the proximity of girls, for example, only upset the boy, leaving him restless and depressed, and Itard had to abandon his hope for a normal sexual response as a means of fostering Victor's motivation and socialization.

After devoting $5\frac{1}{2}$ years to the task, Itard gave up the attempt to train "the wild boy of Aveyron." As for Victor, he lived to be 40, but never progressed appreciably beyond the achievements of that first year.

The story of Victor is of absorbing interest to both laymen and scientists. A motion picture that portrays Itard's work with Victor—*The Wild Child*—was produced by François Truffaut. In scientific circles, the lack of conclusive answers will keep psychologists and others puzzling over the question of whether Victor was a congenital mental retardate, a brain-damaged child, a psychotic, or simply a child who had been so deprived of human contact during early critical periods of development that the damage he sustained could never be completely remedied.

Based on Itard (1799; tr. Humphrey & Humphrey, 1932) and Silberstein and Irwin (1962).

This little girl with Down's syndrome is being brought up at home. It is now being realized that institutionalization is not always the answer for babies with mongolism; such children often can develop many capabilities in a loving home environment.

the skin of the eyelids tends to be abnormally thick; the face and nose are often flat and broad, as is the back of the head; and the tongue, which seems too large for the mouth, may show deep fissures. The iris of the eye is frequently speckled. The neck is often short and broad, as are the hands, which tend to have creases across the palms. The fingers are stubby and the little finger is often more noticeably curved than the other fingers. Well over 50 percent of these persons have cataracts, which are not congenital but tend to make their appearance when the child is about 7 or 8 (Falls, 1970). These cataracts aid in diagnoses, but fortunately they rarely become serious enough to warrant surgery. Interestingly enough, there appears to be little, if any, correlation between the number of physical symptoms of Down's syndrome and the degree of mental retardation.

Mongoloids are particularly susceptible to circulatory, gastrointestinal, and respiratory disorders. In approximately 10 percent of the cases there is an associated congenital heart defect, and there is some evidence that Down's syndrome predisposes these children to leukemia (Miller, 1970). However, antibiotics, better medical care, and a more healthful and stimulating environment are increasing the life expectancy of many of the victims of this disorder.

The term *mongolian idiot* was widely used in the past, but it was misleading, inasmuch as most of these children show only moderate mental retardation. Despite their limitations, they are usually able to learn self-help skills, acceptable social behavior, and routine manual skills that enable them to be of assistance in a family or institutional setting. The social adjustment of mongoloid children is often helped by their tendency to be affectionate and relatively docile, although these traits are by no means universal.

Traditionally, the cause of mongolism was assumed to be faulty heredity. A number of early studies demonstrated, however, that more than one case of mongolism in a family was very infrequent, occurring in less than one family in 100. As a consequence, investigators turned to the study of metabolic factors and concluded that mongolism was probably due to some sort of glandular imbalance.

Then, in 1959, the French scientists Lejeune, Turpin, and Gauthier found 47 chromosomes in several mongoloid cases, and research centered on possible chromosomal anomalies in this disorder.

Subsequent studies have shown that about 95 percent of persons with Down's syndrome have 47 chromosomes instead of the normal complement of 46, resulting from a trisomy of chromosome 21 (see the photograph on p. 141). The reason for the trisomy of chromosome 21 is not clear, but the anomaly would appear to result from defective genes leading to some malfunction in the mechanics of the growth process. In the latter context, it may be noted that the risk of Down's syndrome grows significantly with the age of the mother. A woman in her 20's has about 1 chance in 2000 of having a mongoloid baby, whereas the risk for a woman in her 40's is 1 in 50 (Holvey & Talbott, 1972). Thus it would appear that the trisomy of chromosome 21 is influenced by metabolic factors, but it is also possible that the older the mother, the greater the probability of exposure to radiation that may result in gene mutations.

Whatever the cause of the chromosomal anomaly, the end result is distortion in the growth process characteristic of this clinical syndrome.[3] There is no known effective treatment. When parents have had a child with Down's syndrome, they are usually quite concerned about having further children. In such cases genetic counseling may provide some indication of the risk—which may be quite small—of abnormality in additional children.

Both of these sisters were afflicted with PKU, but the youngest one, at the left, was immediately placed on a special diet and the course of the disease was arrested.

Phenylketonuria (PKU)

Phenylketonuria is a rare metabolic disorder, occurring in about 1 in 20,000 births; mental retardates in institutions who suffer from PKU number about 1 in 100 (Schild, 1972).

In PKU the baby appears normal at birth but lacks an enzyme needed to break down phenylalanine, an amino acid found in protein

---

[3]Interestingly enough, McClure et al. (1969) reported a case of autosomal trisomy in an infant chimpanzee who manifested clinical features remarkably similar to those in Down's syndrome among human infants.

foods. When this condition is undetected, the phenylalanine builds up in the blood and leads to brain damage. The disorder usually becomes apparent between 6 and 12 months after birth, although such symptoms as vomiting, a peculiar odor, infantile eczema, and seizures may become apparent during the early weeks of life. Often the first symptoms noticed are signs of mental retardation, which may be moderate to severe, depending on the degree to which the disease has progressed. Motor incoordination and other neurological manifestations relating to the severity of brain damage are also common, and often the eyes, skin, and hair of untreated PKU patients are very pale.

PKU was identified in 1934 when a Norwegian mother sought to learn the reason for her child's mental retardation and peculiar musty odor. She consulted with many physicians to no avail until Dr. Asbjorn Folling found phenylpyruvic acid in the urine and concluded that the child had a disorder of phenylalanine metabolism (Centerwall & Centerwall, 1961).

Most older PKU patients show severe to profound mental retardation, with the median IQ of untreated adult phenylketonurics being about 20. Curiously, however, a number of PKU patients have PKU relatives with less severely affected intelligence. And Perry (1970) has reported the cases of two untreated PKU patients with superior intelligence. These findings have made PKU somewhat of an enigma. It is thought to result from metabolic alterations involving recessive genes, and 1 person in 70 is thought to be a carrier. However, there may be varying degrees of PKU, or possibly another genetic factor may ameliorate the destructive potential of the enzyme defect (Burns, 1972).

Methods for the early detection of PKU have been developed, and dietary and related treatment procedures are utilized. With early detection and treatment—preferably before an infant is 6 months old—the deterioration process can usually be arrested so that levels of intellectual functioning may range from borderline to normal functioning. However, a few children suffer mental retardation despite restricted phenylalanine intake and other treatment measures. For a baby to inherit PKU,

both parents must carry the recessive gene. Thus when one child in a family has PKU, it is important that other children in such families be screened as well.

Cretinism (thyroid deficiency)

Cretinism provides a dramatic illustration of mental retardation resulting from endocrine imbalance. In this condition, the thyroid either has failed to develop properly or has undergone degeneration or injury; in either case, the infant suffers from a deficiency in thyroid secretion. Brain damage resulting from this insufficiency is most marked during the prenatal and early postnatal periods of rapid growth.

In the valleys of central Switzerland and other geographical areas where iodine is deficient in the soil, and therefore in food grown in it, cretinism was once a common affliction. Pregnant women in such areas often gave birth to infants with defective thyroid glands that remained undeveloped or atrophied later. Because cretinism was observed to run in families in such areas it was thought to be a hereditary disorder. In 1891, however, Dr. George Murray published his discovery that the injection of thyroid gland extract was beneficial in cases of *myxedema*—a disorder resulting from thyroid deficiency in adult life and characterized by mental dullness. This discovery, in turn, led to the treatment of cretinism with thyroid gland extract and to the realization that this condition, too, was the result of thyroid deficiency.

Although most cases of cretinism result from lack of iodine in the diet, thyroid deficiency may also occur as the result of birth injuries (involving bleeding into the thyroid) or in connection with infectious diseases such as measles, whooping cough, or diphtheria. The resulting clinical picture will depend on the age at which the thyroid deficiency occurs, as well as on the degree and duration of the deficiency.

Typical descriptions of cretins involve cases in which there has been a severe thyroid deficiency from an early age, often even before

Clinical type	Symptoms	Causes
No. 18 trisomy syndrome	Peculiar pattern of multiple congenital anomalies, the most common being low-set malformed ears, flexion of fingers, small mandible, and heart defects	Autosomal anomaly of chromosome 18
Tay-Sach's disease	Hypertonicity, listlessness, blindness, progressive spastic paralysis, and convulsions (death by the third year)	Disorder of lipoid metabolism, carried by a single recessive gene
Turner's syndrome	Webbing of the neck, increased carrying angle of forearm, and sexual infantilism	Sex chromosome anomaly
Klinefelter's syndrome	Vary from case to case, the only constant finding being the presence of small testes after puberty	Sex chromosome anomaly
Niemann-Pick's disease	Onset usually in infancy, with loss of weight, dehydration, and progressive paralysis	Disorder of lipoid metabolism
Bilirubin encephalopathy	Abnormal levels of bilirubin (a toxic substance released by red cell destruction) in the blood; choreoathetosis frequent	Often, Rh, ABO blood group incompatibility between mother and fetus
Rubella, congenital	Visual difficulties most common, with cataracts and retinal problems often occurring together with deafness and anomalies in the valves and septa of the heart	The mother's contraction of rubella (German measles) during the first few months of her pregnancy

Based on American Psychiatric Association (1968, 1972), Christodorescu et al. (1970), Donoghue, Abbas, and Gal (1970), Holvey and Talbott (1972), Johnson et al. (1970), Nielsen et al. (1970).

birth. Such a cretin has a dwarflike, thick-set body and short, stubby extremities. His height is usually just a little over 3 feet, the shortness accentuated by slightly bent legs and a curvature of the spine. He walks with a shuffling gait that is easily recognizable. His head is large, with abundant black, wiry hair; his eyelids are thick, giving him a sleepy appearance; his skin is dry and thickened and cold to the touch. Other pronounced physical symptoms include a broad, flat nose, large and flappy ears, a protruding abdomen, and failure to mature sexually. The cretin reveals a bland personality, and his thought processes tend to be sluggish. Most cretins fall within the moderate and severe categories of mental retardation, depending on the extent of brain damage. In cases with less pronounced physical

signs of cretinism, the degree of mental retardation is usually less severe.

Early treatment of cretinism with thyroid gland extract is considered essential, and infants not treated until after the first year of life may have permanently impaired intelligence. In long-standing cases, thyroid treatment may have some ameliorating effects, but the damage to the individual's nervous system and general physical development is beyond repair.

As a result of public health measures on both national and international levels with respect to the use of iodized salt and the early detection and correction of thyroid deficiency, severe cases of cretinism have become practically nonexistent in the United States and most, but not all, other countries.

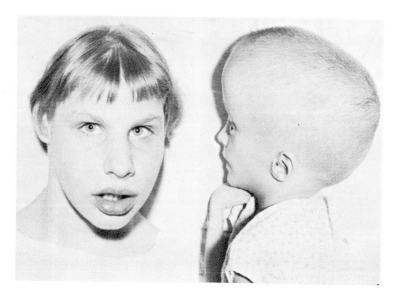

These children show two of the types of mental retardation associated with physiological causes. On the left is a microcephalic girl with the usual cone-shaped skull and receding chin and forehead. On the right is a hydrocephalic boy whose face is of normal size in contrast with the greatly enlarged contours of the skull.

Cranial anomalies

Mental retardation is associated with a number of conditions in which there are relatively gross alterations in head size and shape, and where the causal factors have not been definitely established (Wortis, 1973). In *macrocephaly* ("large-headedness"), for example, there is an increase in the size and weight of the brain, an enlargement of the skull, and visual impairment, convulsions, and other neurological symptoms resulting from the abnormal growth of glia cells that form the supporting structure for brain tissue. Other cranial anomalies include *microcephaly* and *hydrocephalus*, which we shall discuss in more detail.

Microcephaly. The term *microcephaly* means "small-headedness." It refers to a type of mental retardation resulting from impaired development of the brain and a consequent failure of the cranium to attain normal size. In an early study of postmortem examinations of brains of microcephalics, Greenfield and Wolfson (1935) reported that practically all cases examined showed development to have been arrested at the fourth or fifth month of fetal life. Fortunately, this condition is extremely rare.

The most obvious characteristic of the microcephalic is his small head, the circumference of which rarely exceeds 17 inches, as compared with the normal of approximately 22 inches. Penrose (1963) also described microcephalics as being invariably short in stature but having relatively normal musculature and sex organs. Beyond these characteristics, microcephalics differ considerably from each other in appearance, although there is a tendency for the skull to be cone-shaped, with a receding chin and forehead. Microcephalics fall within the moderate, severe, and profound categories of mental retardation, but the majority show little language development and are extremely limited in mental capacity.

Microcephaly may result from a wide range of factors that impair brain development, including intrauterine infections and pelvic irradiation of the mother during the early months of pregnancy (Koch, 1967). A number of cases of microcephaly in Hiroshima and Nagasaki that apparently resulted from atomic bomb explosions during World War II were noted by Miller (1970). The role of genetic factors is not as yet clear. Treatment is ineffective once faulty development has occurred, and, at present, preventive measures focus on the avoidance of infection and radiation during pregnancy.

Hydrocephalus. Hydrocephalus is a relatively rare condition in which the accumulation of an abnormal amount of cerebrospinal fluid within the cranium causes damage to the brain tissues and enlargement of the cranium.

In congenital cases of hydrocephalus, the head is either already enlarged at birth or begins to enlarge soon thereafter, presumably as a result of a disturbance in the formation, absorption, or circulation of the cerebrospinal fluid (Wortis, 1973). The disorder can also develop in infancy or early childhood following the development of a brain tumor, subdural hematoma, meningitis, or other such conditions. Here the condition appears to result from a blockage of the cerebrospinal pathways and an accumulation of fluid in certain brain areas.

The clinical picture in hydrocephalus depends on the extent of neural damage, which, in turn, depends on the age at onset and the duration and severity of the disorder. In chronic cases the chief symptom is the gradual enlargement of the upper part of the head out of all proportion to the face and the rest of the body. The face remains relatively normal, but the protruding skull gives the appearance one might expect in a race of super geniuses. While the expansion of the skull helps minimize destructive pressure on the brain, serious brain damage occurs nonetheless, leading to intellectual impairment and such other effects as convulsions and impairment or loss of sight and hearing. The degree of intellectual impairment varies, being severe or profound in advanced cases.

A good deal of attention has been directed to the surgical treatment of hydrocephalus, and with early diagnosis and treatment this condition can usually be arrested before severe brain damage has occurred (Geisz & Steinhausen, 1974).

Mental Retardation Associated with Sociocultural Deprivation

It was formerly believed that all mental retardation was the result of faulty genes or of other causes of organic brain pathology. In recent years, however, it has become apparent that adverse sociocultural conditions, particularly those involving a deprivation of normal stimulation, may play a primary role in the etiology of mental retardation.[4]

Two subtypes of mental retardation fall in this general category: (a) mental retardation associated with extreme sensory and social deprivation, such as prolonged isolation during the developmental years, as in the case of the wild boy of Aveyron; and (b) cultural-familial retardation, in which the child is not subjected to extreme isolation but rather suffers from an inferior quality of interaction with his cultural environment and with other people. Since the great majority of all mental retardates are cultural-familial, our discussion will focus on this type.

Cultural-familial mental retardation

Children who fall in this category are usually mild mental retardates; they make up the majority of persons labeled as mentally retarded and show no identifiable brain pathology. They are usually not diagnosed as mentally retarded until they enter school and have serious difficulties in their studies.

As a number of investigators have pointed

---

[4]American behavioral scientists have used the terms *psychosocial deprivation, psychosocial disadvantage, cultural-familial retardation,* and *sociocultural deprivation* somewhat interchangeably. We shall use the latter term as a more general category in ordering our present discussion.

out, however, most of these children come from poverty-stricken, unstable, and often disrupted family backgrounds characterized by a lack of intellectual stimulation, an inferior quality of interaction with others, and general environmental deprivation (Braginsky & Braginsky, 1974; Heber, 1970; Tarjan & Eisenberg, 1972).

"They are raised in homes with absent fathers and with physically or emotionally unavailable mothers. During infancy they are not exposed to the same quality and quantity of tactile and kinesthetic stimulations as other children. Often they are left unattended in a crib or on the floor of the dwelling. Although there are noises, odors, and colors in the environment, the stimuli are not as organized as those found in middle-class and upper-class environments. For example, the number of words they hear is limited, with sentences brief and most commands carrying a negative connotation." (Tarjan & Eisenberg, 1972, p. 16)

In fact, three-fourths of the nation's mental retardates come from homes that are socially, economically, and culturally disadvantaged.

As we have noted, these children do not appear very different from other children, and their subaverage intellectual functioning does not usually become apparent until they enter school, where difficulties with their studies lead to a diagnostic evaluation. Since a child's current level of intellectual functioning is based largely on previous learning – and since schoolwork requires complex skills such as being able to control one's attention, follow instructions, and recognize the meaning of a considerable range of words – the child is at a disadvantage from the beginning if his environment has deprived him of the opportunity to learn requisite background skills and be motivated toward further learning. Thus with each succeeding year these children tend to fall farther behind in school performance and relative ratings on intelligence tests, unless remedial measures are undertaken.

A report by the American Psychological Association (1970) has noted:

"Mental retardation is primarily a psychosocial and psychoeducational problem – a deficit in adaptation to the demands and expectations of society evidenced by the individual's relative difficulty in learning, problem solving, adapting to new situations, and abstract thinking." (p. 267)

This statement is not intended to minimize the possible role of adverse biological factors in the total causal pattern; in fact, many of these children do reveal a history of prematurity, inadequate diets, and little or no medical care. But in the great majority of cases of cultural-familial mental retardation, no neurological or physical dysfunction has been demonstrated. Thus efforts to understand mild mental retardation have focused increasingly on the role of environmental factors in either facilitating or impeding intellectual growth.

Assessing cultural-familial retardation

Since mental retardation is defined in terms of both intellectual and social competence, it is essential to assess both of these characteristics before labeling a person as mentally retarded.

Unfortunately, neither of the preceding tasks is an easy one. Errors in the assessment of intelligence can stem from a variety of sources, including: (a) errors in administering tests; (b) personal characteristics of the child, such as motivation to do well on tests; and (c) limitations in the tests themselves, such as cultural bias in content. The latter point has been succinctly stated by Wortis (1972):

"An IQ score, at best, can indicate where an individual stands in intellectual performance compared to others. What others? His nation? His social class? His ethnic group? No intelligence test that has ever been devised can surmount all of these complicating considerations and claim universal validity." (p. 22)

While the assessment of social competence may seem less complicated, especially if it is based on clinical observations and ratings, it is subject to many of the same errors as the measurement of intelligence. Of particular importance are the criteria used by the person or persons doing the assessing. For example, if a child is well adapted socially to life in an urban ghetto but not to the demands of a formal school setting, would he be evaluated as evidencing a high, intermediate, or low level of social competence? Again the conclusions of Wortis concerning the assessment of intelligence would appear to apply.[5]

To label a child as mentally retarded—as significantly subaverage in intellectual and adaptive capability—is an act likely to have profound effects on the child's self-concept, on the reactions of others to him, and on his entire future life. In fact, it may not only be a self-fulfilling prophecy, fueled by the tendency to behave in ways consistent with one's self-concept as well as with others' expectations, but it may lead to institutionalization as well. Obviously it is a label that has profound ethical and social implications. Here one is reminded of the conclusion of Braginsky and Braginsky (1974) that cultural-familial mental retardation is "another of the many myths perpetuated by a society that refuses to recognize its needed social reforms" (p. 30).

"Not everybody's the same"

Eight adolescents who had grown up with the label "retarded" and who had been in special education classes were videotaped in a frank discussion of mental retardation. These quotes were taken from their conversation.

"I think when we were being born, Mother Nature made some mistake and it damaged part of the brain and something didn't turn out right, and it held us back."

"Not everybody's the same."

"To accomplish something takes you twice the effort. . . . To get a C, I would have to work like an A student."

"I wanted to be a social worker. But it would take me 14 or 15 years to do it. So, realistically. . . ."

"You know you are retarded, and everybody calls you it. . . . But you don't want to say it. You know you are within. It chops you down."

"I think parents should tell the kid what is wrong with them. They're going to have to find out sooner or later."

"Sooner is better than later."

"Even though they* may have learning problems, they're human beings just like everybody else, and they deserve basically the same treatment as any other human being."

"You never stop learning. You learn things every day of your life."

"My mother will always see me as a baby, no matter how old I get."

"You have to have the experience of knowing how to live when Mom and Dad aren't around. Because one day they die, too."

"And later on in life, nobody's going to teach you how to be independent and what to do."

"There comes a point when you have to let go . . . when you've got to get them their freedom. Slowly, but surely, they'll get their independence."

*Some of the speakers use "they" in referring to other retarded persons.

We wish to thank the UCLA Mental Retardation and Child Psychiatry Program, its Media Unit, and the Neuropsychiatric Institute (1973) for permission to quote excerpts from the videotape "Experts Discuss: Mental Retardation."

---

[5]A comprehensive discussion of the problems in assessing and labeling the mentally retarded may be found in Mercer (1974) and the American Psychiatric Association (1972).

Treatment, Outcomes, and Prevention

The need is apparent for alleviating adverse environmental conditions and for maximizing the learning and adaptive capacities of the mentally retarded. A number of recent programs have, in fact, demonstrated that significant changes in adaptive capacity are possible through special education and other rehabilitative measures. The degree of change that can be expected is related, of course, to the individual and his level of mental retardation.

Treatment facilities and methods

Fortunately, as we have seen, most mental retardates do not need to be institutionalized. For the 200,000 or more who do, however, state institutions for the mentally retarded are often desperately overcrowded, and in many instances woefully inadequate in terms of the quality of treatment programs offered (Tarjan et al., 1973). In 1970, the President's Commission on Mental Retardation reported that in many instances such facilities were no better than prisoner-of-war camps. Since then some facilities have been greatly improved, but most lack the necessary funds and personnel to provide high-quality rehabilitative programs. Moreover, most private facilities—which are often but not always superior to public ones—are beyond the means of the average family.

For the great majority of mental retardates who do not require institutionalization, educational and training facilities have also been characterized as inadequate. In 1970 an estimated 2 million mentally retarded persons who could use job training and become self-supporting members of their communities were not getting this training. Thus, literally "hundreds of thousands of retarded persons who could be trained and educated to useful work and life in American society are being wasted" (President's Committee on Mental Retardation, 1970). Although conditions may have improved somewhat, it would still appear that the majority of mentally retarded persons in the United States are never reached by services appropriate to their specific needs.

The negative side of this picture has been emphasized here to contrast with what can be done about mental retardation. For example, classes for mild mental retardates, which usually emphasize reading and other basic school subjects, budgeting and money matters, and the development of occupational skills have been notably successful, and have succeeded in helping many mild retardates become independent, productive members of the community. Classes for the moderately and severely retarded usually have more limited objectives, but they emphasize development of self-care and other skills that will enable retardates to function adequately and be of assistance in either a family or institutional setting. In far more cases than had been realized, simple job skills can also be learned by these retardates. For example, Clark, Kivitz, and Rosen (1969) reported on a special project undertaken at the Elwyn Institute in Pennsylvania.

The goal of this program was the successful discharge to independent living in the community of the institutionalized mental retardate. The entire staff was oriented toward rehabilitation; emphasis was placed on the development of practical vocational skills; special programs provided remedial teaching and the learning of socialization skills; and counseling and assessment assured the individualization of training to meet each retardate's needs. As a result of this program, many mentally retarded persons who had been institutionalized for from 2 to 49 years were discharged and obtained skilled or semiskilled jobs in the community while coping successfully with everyday problems. Some married and had families, and none had to be readmitted to the institution. (p. 82)

Subsequent studies have also shown particularly successful results in the occupational training of mild retardates, and with appropriate treatment procedures noticeable improvement in self-help skills and adaptive

Treatment programs for the mentally retarded range from overcrowded state institutions, where the children are often given only custodial care, to programs in which teachers and therapists work with children on an individual basis or in small groups. The picture of the art therapy class shows how the therapist encourages cooperative decision making during the planning and drawing of a mural.

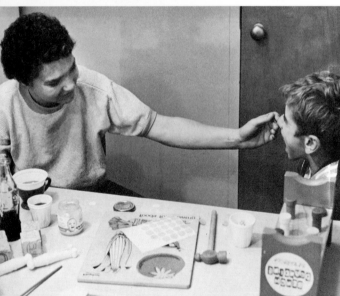

Successful imitation of Dawn's hand-clapping motion earns Randy a new treat.

A boy, Randy, and his therapist, Dawn, shared an exciting experience which is the subject of the following unusual case study by Whalen and Henker.

"Randy is an 11-year-old boy who lives in a state hospital. He is severely retarded; his estimated IQ is 32. Although there are 70 children on his ward, he spends most of his time alone, staring into space or passively watching what is going on around him. He often stands with his arms extended, oscillating his fingers and moving his head from side to side while making bizarre grimaces and clicking sounds with his tongue or teeth. He doesn't speak. He doesn't play. He has neither friends nor enemies among the other children.

"About 11 o'clock each morning Randy can be found stationed by the front door to his ward, eagerly scanning the faces of all who enter. He is waiting for his therapist, Dawn. To those who know and observe Randy, it is remarkable that he seems to know when it is time for his therapy session. He correctly anticipates this event, even though he cannot ask questions or understand explanations, and he certainly has never learned the significance of a clock.

"When Dawn arrives, Randy becomes visibly excited. His mannerisms stop and his smile broadens as his young therapist greets him and escorts him to a special room in another building. She pretends to carry on a conversation with Randy by taking two roles, asking him questions and then answering them for him. Randy's facial expressions and gestures seem to indicate that he is participating, although on a nonverbal level. More importantly, he receives more verbal stimulation in this short period than during the remainder of the day on his overcrowded, understaffed hospital ward.

"While delivering a monologue about the day's events, Dawn prepares for the session. Simple toddlers' toys are pulled out of a cupboard—a 'busy box,' a few blocks, a pounding board, and a hammer. A box of sugared cereal and a carton of chocolate yogurt are opened, and Randy is given a taste of each. Then Dawn announces, loudly, that it is time to go to work. The first item on today's agenda is a review of what Randy learned in the past week. Dawn says, 'Look at me, Randy.' When his attention is secured, she quickly claps her hands and says, 'You do it.' As Randy imitates the simple response, Dawn exclaims, 'Good boy!' and gives Randy a spoonful of yogurt, which is for him a special treat. Dawn then goes through some other activities that, by this time in therapy, are relatively simple for Randy—raise your hand, dial the phone, throw the ball, pound the pegboard. For each task she uses the same sequence of procedures: secure attention, present the training stimulus (a nonverbal demonstration or a verbal direction), elicit the response, and then administer the rewards — praise, physical affection, and food.

"After this warm-up phase, Dawn tries a much harder task, a verbal direction which involves two discriminations. She places a block and a hammer on the table in front of Randy and asks him to hand her the hammer. Randy must choose both the correct object and the correct act. He first picks up the hammer and begins to pound the table. Although he has learned to respond to the direction 'Hand me . . .' and the label, 'Hammer,' he can't yet link the two together. He performs the only response he has ever learned involving a hammer — he pounds the table. Dawn says, 'No,' replaces the hammer, and repeats her verbal request. This time she includes a nonverbal prompt — she holds out her hand. Randy seems to understand the desired act but not the correct object as he places the block in her hand. Again Dawn says 'No' and shakes her head. Next time, she gives Randy more help. She places the hammer on top of the block and holds out her hand as she says, 'Give me the hammer.' With these cues, Randy makes the correct response and Dawn is delighted. Enthusiastic praise and a big hug accompany his food treat.

"Now Dawn settles into the difficult and often tedious job of 'fading the prompts' and teaching Randy to respond to the verbal direction alone, with no gestures or other artificial cues. To achieve this goal she must demand slightly more from Randy on each trial; she must help him less and less. If she prompts too completely or too frequently, he will show no improvement. But if her demands are too great, he may stop responding entirely. She must allow him enough time to practice his new response, but she must change the training task before he becomes too bored or frustrated. In short, multiple therapeutic decisions must be made at each stage of the learning sequence."

The remedial approach described in this situation is widely used in behavior therapy with mental retardates; what is unusual and dramatic about it is that Dawn, the therapist, is also mentally retarded. Both she and Randy resided in the same state institution for mental retardates.

Dawn dressed appropriately and seemed normal in appearance and movement. However, her vocabulary was very limited and her speech poorly articulated — at times being almost unintelligible. Her case history was replete with special-incident reports: she had thrown chairs through windows, run away, and destroyed property.

She also had frequently engaged in physical and verbal assaults on companions as well as on hospital personnel, and her diagnosis of congenital cerebral defect was accompanied by the label "passive aggressive character with psychotic episodes." Though only mildly retarded (her IQ was 60), she was kept from family care placement by her unsuitable social behavior. She had been institutionalized for 11 of her 24 years.

Dawn's therapy sessions with Randy were part of a systematic research study of the "therapeutic pyramid concept" — in which professional therapists prepare moderately retarded adolescents and young adults to teach severely retarded children in simple social behaviors. Behavior therapy techniques are used in the training of "assistants," who use analogous methods with their younger "trainees." The key goal is to facilitate improvement in both assistants and trainees — in other words, to bring about a "double change."

And indeed this double-change phenomenon did occur in the case of Randy and Dawn. Randy learned to imitate gestures, respond to simple verbal requests, and relate to another person. And Dawn, for her part, acquired both occupational and social skills. As an assistant, she learned to arrive at work regularly and on time, assume responsibility, take pride and find satisfaction in her work, earn a salary, and manage her money. She also learned to relate to members of the research staff. In addition, she became uncomfortable about her poor articulation and tendency to "mouth off," and asked for help in improving her behavior. The ultimate consequence of her participation in the pyramid project came in her release from the hospital. She since has been reported adjusting well to her foster home.

As might be expected, research with therapeutic pyramids has shown that the greatest gains are achieved by assistants like Dawn, even though the results have been favorable for trainees as well. Among the assistants, gains have commonly been observed in improving speech skills, developing interpersonal competencies, developing a sense of personal responsibility, and building self-esteem. The success of the initial pyramid project has led to the initiation of similar programs in outpatient clinics, foster-care homes, and special schools.

Based on previously unpublished material by Carol K. Whalen, University of California at Irvine, and Barbara Henker, University of California at Los Angeles. Sources also include Guerney (1969) and Whalen and Henker (1971).

behavior may be achieved even with severe and profound retardates (Rodman & Collins, 1974; Sullivan & Batareh, 1973; Zucker & Altman, 1973).

Although much remains to be learned about the most effective educational and training procedures to use with the mentally retarded—particularly the moderate and severe types—new techniques, materials, and specially trained teachers have produced encouraging results. Operant conditioning methods are being used increasingly to teach a wide variety of skills. Typically, target areas of improvement are mapped out, such as improvement in personal grooming, social behavior, basic academic skills, and simple occupational skills. Within each area, specific skills are divided into simple components that can be learned and reinforced before more complex behaviors are required. Target areas are not selected arbitrarily, of course, but realistically reflect the requirements of the mental retardate's life situation. Training that builds on step-by-step progression and is guided by such realistic considerations can lead to substantial progress even by children previously regarded as uneducable.

One problem that often inflicts great anxiety on parents is whether or not to institutionalize their mentally retarded child. In general, the ones who are institutionalized fall into two groups: (a) those who, in infancy and childhood, manifest severe mental retardation and associated physical impairment, and who enter the institution at an early age, and (b) those who, in adolescence, usually have no physical impairments but show mild mental retardation and fail to adjust socially, eventually requiring institutionalization for delinquent or other acting-out behavior. The families of those in the first group come from all socioeconomic levels, whereas a significantly higher percentage of the families of those in the second group come from lower educational and occupational strata.

Studies suggest that, in general, mentally retarded children are likely to show better emotional and mental development in a reasonably favorable home situation than in an institution (Golden & Davis, 1974). As a consequence of such considerations, institutionalization is not recommended where the child makes a satisfactory adjustment at home and in any special class or training school that he may attend during the day.

The effect of institutionalization on a mentally retarded youth depends heavily, of course, on the institution's facilities as well as on the youth himself. It must be recognized, too, that many mental retardates do not have families in a position to take care of them. For such children, the trend toward community-oriented residential care seems particularly promising (Seidl, 1974). An integral part of such residential care programs, especially for children who have no families, involves the development of foster home placements. Such placements require careful supervision and the education of the foster parents concerning the youth's needs and limitations.

Adolescents and young adults suffering from moderate to mild degrees of mental retardation—both those who are making the transition from institutional to community life and those who reside with their families—appear to benefit from the use of "sheltered workshops" in the community. In such sheltered workshops individuals who cannot compete successfully in modern industry can learn and perform simple occupational tasks under supervision. With the assistance of their families, they may thus find it possible to live reasonably satisfying and constructive adult lives.

New frontiers in prevention

The problem of preventing mental retardation involves the question of genetic factors as well as a wide range of biochemical, neurophysiological, and sociocultural conditions. Inevitably, it is a problem concerned with human development in general.

Until rather recently the most hopeful approach to the prevention of mental retardation has been through routine health measures for pregnant women and the use of diagnostic measures to ensure the early detection and, if possible, correction of pathology. In recent years, however, two new frontiers have opened up in the field of prevention. The first involves work in genetics which has revealed the role of genetic defects in faulty development – as in Tay-Sachs disease – and tests that have been devised to identify parents who have these faulty genes, thus making it possible to provide them with genetic counseling. There are now over 200 clinics in the United States where such counseling is available.

The second frontier in prevention involves the alleviation of sociocultural conditions that deprive children of the necessary stimulation, motivation, and opportunity for normal learning and development. This "new horizon" was well delineated by the late President John F. Kennedy over a decade ago:

"Studies have demonstrated that large numbers of children in urban and rural slums, including preschool children, lack the stimulus necessary for proper development in their intelligence. Even when there is no organic impairment, prolonged neglect and a lack of stimulus and opportunity for learning can result in the failure of young minds to develop. Other studies have shown that, if proper opportunities for learning are provided early enough, many of these deprived children can and will learn and achieve as much as children from more favored neighborhoods. The self-perpetuating intellectual blight should not be allowed to continue." (1963, p. 286)

President Kennedy's report directed the attention of the nation to the tragic and costly problem of mental retardation. It was not until 1970, however, when the President's Committee on Mental Retardation, the American Psychological Association, and other concerned organizations stressed the necessity for a "broad spectrum" approach that real impetus was given to implementing essential measures for the prevention of mental retardation. This broad spectrum approach focused on three "keys to future progress":

1. *Application of existing knowledge.* The provision of more adequate medical and general health care for mother and baby – prior to and during pregnancy, and after birth of the baby – particularly for the socially disadvantaged and other high-risk groups.

2. *Community services.* The provision of community-centered facilities that will provide a coordinated range of diagnostic, health, education, employment, rehabilitation, and related services. This phase of the program includes the training of needed personnel.

3. *Research.* Emphasis on the facilitation and acceleration of research in all phases of the problem: causality, educational procedures, social effects on the family, psychological effects on the individual, and the changing role and functions of state and community agencies.

When fully implemented, this broad spectrum approach should go far toward helping us achieve the 75 percent reduction in the incidence of mental retardation that the President's Committee on Mental Retardation cited as a realistic goal.

In this chapter, we dealt with the major problem of mental retardation in our society. We noted the criteria used in assessing mental retardation, the levels of retardation – from mild to profound – and the fact that the great majority of mental retardates fall in the mild range. We then examined the role of organic factors in the development of several clinical types of mental retardation, and dealt at some length with the role of adverse sociocultural conditions in mental retardation.

In the concluding section of the chapter, we considered approaches to the education and training of mental retardates and emphasized the current view that the great majority of mentally retarded persons can become not only self-respecting but self-supporting members of the community. Finally, we identified two new frontiers in the prevention of mental retardation.

15

Behavior Disorders of Childhood

"An estimated 500,000 American children are afflicted with psychoses and borderline psychotic conditions. Another million suffer from other severe mental disorders. Of the 50 million elementary school children in the United States, it is estimated that between 10 and 12 percent have moderate to severe emotional problems requiring some kind of mental health care. Among the 15 million youngsters in the United States who are being reared in poverty, one out of three has emotional problems that need attention." (NIMH, 1970, p. 7)

Since there is little reason to believe that conditions have improved appreciably since the preceding statement was made, it seems apparent that maladaptive behavior among children constitutes a major problem in our society.

Only in recent years, however, have childhood behavior disorders become the focus of special study. During the nineteenth century, the usual approach was to apply the classification of adult mental disorders to "the insanity of children," with little attempt being made to differentiate between the symptoms and causes of psychopathology in children as opposed to adults. Maladaptive patterns relatively specific to childhood, such as autism and the hyperactive reaction, received virtually no attention at all.

An important step forward came in 1896 with Witmer's founding of the first psychological clinic at the University of Pennsylvania, which provided services for children as well as adolescents and adults. It is of interest to note that of the first two children treated at the clinic, one had a "speech disorder" and the other was a "chronic bad speller." In 1906 Witmer founded a journal, *The Psychological Clinic,* in which he and his students published case reports on a wide range of behavior problems of children. The goal was not to apply a diagnostic label to the child, but to study and understand the child's behavior so that appropriate educational procedures or treatment could be undertaken.

A closely related development was that of the child guidance movement. In 1909 the Juvenile Psychopathic Institute was founded in Chicago under the direction of William Healy, a psychiatrist. This institute fostered the view that the antisocial behavior of chil-

Comparison of Maladaptive Behavior in Childhood and Later Life Periods

Types of Childhood Behavior Disorders

Treatment and Prevention

dren could be modified with psychological methods. As a result of the pioneering work of Healy and Witmer, child guidance clinics were established throughout the United States, and by 1940 had become an accepted feature of the mental health field.

In the last two decades, marked strides have been made in understanding, assessing, and treating the maladaptive behavior patterns of children. But as we shall see, our facilities are woefully inadequate in relation to the magnitude of the task. In the final section of this chapter, we shall give detailed consideration to the problems of both treatment and prevention. First, however, we shall consider the general characteristics of maladaptive behavior in children and describe some of the disorders that are relatively specific to the childhood period.

Comparison of Maladaptive Behavior in Childhood and Later Life Periods

Since personality differentiation, developmental tasks, and typical life stresses differ for childhood, adolescence, and adulthood, we would expect to find some differences in maladaptive behavior patterns for these life periods. For example, schizophrenia and depressive reactions are found in childhood as well as in later life periods, but there are differences in the clinical pictures.[1] In addition, there are certain disorders, ranging from autism and hyperactivity to sleepwalking and bedwetting, that are primarily problems of childhood.

There is no sharp line of demarcation, of course, between the maladaptive behavior patterns of childhood and those of adolescence, nor between those of adolescence and adulthood. Thus although our focus in this chapter will be on the behavior disorders of children, we shall find some inevitable overlapping with those of later life periods. In this context, it is useful to emphasize the basic continuity of an individual's behavior over the years as he attempts to cope with the problems of living. The following comment by Murphy, based on her intensive and long-range studies of children, is directly relevant:

"Seldom do we think of the child as a small human being, carrying on his own struggle to make sense out of life, to meet his own needs, to master the challenges presented by life—but differing from adults especially in the proportion of newness to which he is exposed." (1962, p. 1)

The points outlined below focus on both differences and similarities between maladap-

---

[1]Fish et al. (1968) have attempted a classification of schizophrenic reactions in children under 5, and Poznanski and Zrull (1970) and Ossofsky (1974) have described depressive reactions in infants and children.

tive behavior patterns of childhood and those of later life periods.

1. *The clinical pictures for specific behavior disorders may vary markedly with age.* As we have noted, the clinical pictures in given disorders may vary in childhood from those shown in adolescence and adulthood. For example, while withdrawal and inability to relate to others are characteristic of childhood schizophrenia, delusions and hallucinations are not. Similarly, the suicidal impulses commonly found in adolescent and adult depression are fairly rare in childhood depression.

In children, too, the cognitive behaviors in certain maladaptive patterns may vary considerably from those at other age levels. For example, if a child attempts suicide it may be for the purpose of rejoining a dead parent, a sibling, or a pet. By the very young, suicide may be undertaken without any real understanding that death is final. As Seiden (1970) has put it, "Without the realization that death is final, a child measures his own life's value with a defective yardstick" (p. 29).

2. *Developmental level and degree of dependency markedly influence the clinical picture in childhood disorders.* Since personality differentiation in childhood is not as advanced as in adolescence or adulthood, the child has not as clear-cut a view of himself and his world as he will at a later age. He is not as far along toward self-understanding and the development of a stable sense of identity, and is immature with respect to being guided by inner reality, possibility, and value controls. The immediate moment—since it is less moderated by considerations of the past or future, in the sense of "plans for the future" or an overall averaging of experience—tends to be disproportionately important to him. Thus the child often has more difficulty in coping with stressful events than he may have later when he has a better understanding of himself and his world and can see events in a broader perspective. The child's dependency on others, though serving in some ways as a buffer against stress, also makes him highly vulnerable to rejection and to disappointment and failure.

Because of their inexperience and lack of self-sufficiency, children are more easily upset by seemingly minor problems than the average

Themes of a macabre or frightening nature characterize the drawings of a student who attended a facility for emotionally disturbed children.

adult. However, they typically recover more quickly from their hurts. Thus the emotional disturbances of childhood are likely to be relatively short-lived, undifferentiated, and changeable as compared to those of later life periods.

3. *Underlying emotional problems are commonly masked in childhood.* Often childhood depressive reactions and other emotional problems are "masked." Among young children, for example, irritability, temper tantrums, low frustration tolerance, hyperactivity, and sleep disturbances are common reflections of depression; among older children, "acting out"—through disobedience, running away, and delinquent behavior—may mask an underlying depression (Cytryn & McKnew, 1974; Ossofsky, 1974; Poznanski & Zrull, 1970).

Of course, the masking of emotional problems is by no means restricted to children. Depression may commonly be masked in adolescents by underachievement, delinquency, and running away; it may be similarly masked in adults by inability to sleep, gastrointestinal upsets, and chronic fatigue. But childhood emotional disturbances are typically less differentiated and more changeable, and often no clear pattern of psychopathology emerges even in a child whose behavior is chronically maladaptive.

Types of Childhood Behavior Disorders

The specific childhood disorders we shall discuss in this section are:

Autism (including childhood schizophrenia)
Hyperactive (hyperkinetic) reaction
Unsocialized aggressive reaction
Overanxious and withdrawal reactions
Runaway reaction
Stuttering
Minor "developmental" disorders such as enuresis, sleepwalking, nail-biting, and tics

With the exception of autism, the preceding disorders are less stable than most of the abnormal behavior patterns we have discussed in earlier chapters, and also less resistant to treatment. Often they are referred to simply as *emotional disturbances*, to indicate that the child is not so much "ill" as having problems in living with which he needs assistance. If such assistance is not received, however, the developmental disorders of childhood sometimes merge almost imperceptibly into more serious and chronic disorders during later life.

Autism

The boy is 5 years old. When spoken to, he turns his head away. Sometimes he mumbles unintelligibly. He is neither toilet trained nor able to feed himself. He actively resists being touched. He dislikes sounds. He cannot relate to others, and avoids looking anyone in the eye. He often engages in routine manipulative activities, such as dropping an object, picking it up, and dropping it again. While seated, he often rocks back and forth in a rhythmic motion for hours. Any change in routine is highly upsetting to him. He is in a school for severely psychotic children at UCLA. His diagnosis is childhood autism.

Autism in infancy and childhood was first described by Kanner (1943). It afflicts some 80,000 American children—about 1 child in

2500 — and is about 4 or 5 times more frequent among boys than girls (Schreibman & Koegel, 1975; Treffert, 1970). The children come from all socioeconomic levels, ethnic backgrounds, and family patterns.

Clinical picture. In autism, the child seems apart or aloof from the earliest stages of life; consequently, this disorder is often referred to as "early infantile autism." Mothers remember such babies as never being "cuddly," never reaching out when being picked up, never smiling or looking at them while being fed, and never appearing to notice the comings and goings of other persons. In fact, the autistic child does not evidence any need for affection or contact with anyone, usually not even seeming to know or care who his parents are. As Schreibman and Koegel (1975) have pointed out, "For a loving parent trying to help, this can be crushing" (p. 61).

The absence or severely restricted use of speech is characteristic. If speech is present in an autistic child, it is almost never used to communicate except in the most rudimentary fashion, as by saying "yes" when asked if he wants something to eat, or by the echolalic ("parrotlike") repetition of a few words. Often the autistic child shows an active aversion to auditory stimuli, crying even at the sound of his mother's voice. However, the pattern is not always consistent; autistic children "may at one moment be severely agitated or panicked by a very soft sound while at another time be totally oblivious to loud noise" (Ritvo & Ornitz, 1970, p. 6). Self-stimulation is characteristic of these children, usually taking the form of such repetitive movements as head banging, spinning, and/or rocking, which may continue by the hour. Other bizarre as well as repetitive behavior is typical. This is well described by Gajzago and Prior (1974) in the case of a young autistic boy:

"A was described as a screaming, severely disturbed child who ran around in circles making high-pitched sounds for hours. He also liked to sit in boxes, under mats, and blankets. He habitually piled up all furniture and bedding in the center of the room. At times he was thought deaf though he also showed extreme fear of loud noises. He refused all food except in a bottle, refused to wear clothes, chewed stones and paper, whirled himself, and spun

objects. . . . He played repetitively with the same toys for months, lining things in rows, collected objects such as bottle tops, and insisted on having two of everything, one in each hand. He became extremely upset if interrupted and if the order or arrangement of things were altered." (p. 264)

In contrast to the behavior just described, autistic children are often quite skillful at fitting objects together. Thus, their performance on puzzles or form boards may be average or above. However, even in the manipulation of objects, difficulty with meaning is apparent. For example, when pictures are to be arranged in an order that tells a story, the autistic child shows a marked deficiency in performance.[2]

Many autistic children become preoccupied with and form strong attachments to unusual objects such as rocks, film negatives, or keys. In some instances, the object is so large or bizarre that merely carrying it around interferes with the child's other activities. When his preoccupation with the object is disturbed — for example, by removing it or attempting to substitute something in its place — or when anything familiar in his environment is altered, even slightly, he may have a violent temper tantrum or a crying spell which continues until the familiar sameness is restored. Thus the autistic child is often said to be "obsessed with the maintenance of sameness."

Finally, and of key importance, the autistic child seems to have a blurred and undifferentiated concept of self. He does not perceive himself as the center of his world, and he lacks a central reference point for "anchoring" or integrating his perceptions. Bettelheim (1967, 1974) has referred to this condition as the "absence of I" or "the empty fortress."

In sum, the autistic child typically shows

---

[2]Goodman (1972) has noted that the view that autistic children are potentially of normal intelligence has been questioned by a number of investigators who consider many if not most of these children to be of subnormal intelligence. Some of these children, however, show markedly discrepant abilities. In this context, Goodman described the case of an "autistic-savant" who showed unusual ability at an early age in calendar calculating as well as in other areas, such as naming the capitals of most states and countries. Yet his language development was severely retarded, and he showed the indifference to others and related symptoms characteristic of autistic children.

serious difficulties in four major areas: (a) social attachments and relatedness to others; (b) perceptual-cognitive functioning; (c) language development; and (d) the sense of self, or self-identity. In addition, we noted the bizarre and repetitive activities, the fascination with unusual objects, and the obsessive need to maintain the sameness of his environment.

Because the clinical picture in autism tends to blend almost imperceptibly with that of childhood schizophrenia, a differential diagnosis is often difficult or impossible to make. However, the schizophrenic child typically undergoes a period of seemingly normal development before evidencing withdrawal, thought disturbances, and inappropriate affect, and often he appears concerned and anxious about his relationships with persons and with the world about him. The autistic child, in contrast, is seemingly oblivious to his social environment from the start. As Bettelheim (1969) has stated it, "while the schizophrenic child withdraws from the world, the autistic child fails to ever enter it" (p. 21).

Causal factors. No brain pathology has been delineated in infant or childhood autism, and since it does not run in families, it cannot be attributed directly to a hereditary defect. The possibility remains, however, that defective genes—resulting, for example, from radiation or effects of other mutagens on the mother during pregnancy—may play a key role in the etiological pattern. Thus, while Judd and Mandell (1968) failed to find significant chromosomal abnormalities in a carefully selected group of 11 autistic children, subtler genetic defects cannot be ruled out. In fact, most investigators believe that autism begins with some type of inborn defect that impairs the infant's perceptual-cognitive functioning—his ability to process incoming stimulation and to relate to his world.

In his early studies of childhood autism, Kanner (1943) concluded that an innate disorder in the child is exacerbated by a cold and unresponsive mother, the first factor resulting in social withdrawal and the second tending to maintain the isolation syndrome. However, most investigators have failed to find the parents of autistic children to be "emotional re-

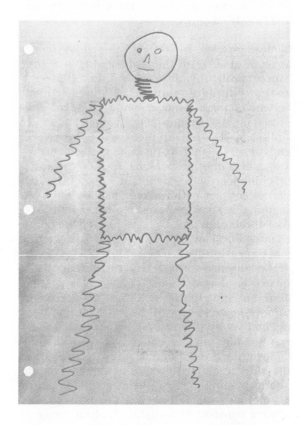

These four pictures were drawn by Joey, a schizophrenic boy who entered the Sonia Shankman Orthogenic School of the University of Chicago at the age of 9. His unusual case history has been reported by Bettelheim (1959).

Joey had been reared by parents in an utterly impersonal way, and he presumably denied his own emotions because they were unbearably painful. Apparently not daring to be human in a world which he felt had rejected him, Joey withdrew into a world of fantasy and perceived himself as a machine that "functioned as if by remote control." This idea is brought out in the drawing above—a self-portrait in which Joey depicts himself as an electrical robot. Bettelheim interpreted this portrait as symbolizing Joey's rejection of human feelings.

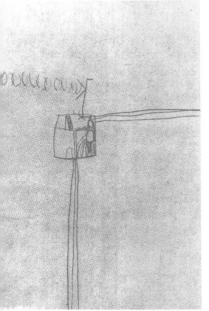  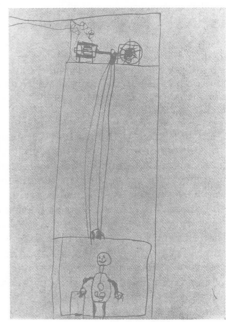

So elaborately constructed and acted out was Joey's mechanical character that: "Entering the dining room, for example, he would string an imaginary wire from his 'energy source'—an imaginary electric outlet—to the table. There he 'insulated' himself with paper napkins and finally plugged himself in. Only then could Joey eat, for he firmly believed that the 'current' ran his ingestive apparatus" (p. 117).

Joey's performance was convincing—so much so that others found themselves responding to him as a mechanical boy rather than as a human being: " . . . one had to look twice to be sure there was neither wire nor outlet nor plug. Children and members of our staff spontaneously avoided stepping on the 'wires' for fear of interrupting what seemed the source of his very life." When his machinery was idle, Joey "would sit so quietly that he would disappear from the focus of the most conscientious observation. Yet in the next moment he might be 'working' and the center of our captivated attention" (p. 117).

In his report on Joey, Bettelheim alluded to the painfully slow process by which Joey was eventually able to establish true relations with other human beings. Three of the drawings (left to right above) depict part of the process. In the earliest of the three, Joey portrays himself "as an electrical 'papoose,' completely enclosed, suspended in empty space and operated by wireless signals." In the next one, he apparently demonstrates increasing self-esteem, for although he is still operated by wireless signals, he is much larger in stature. In the final drawing, Joey depicts "the machine which controls him," but in this one, unlike the previous drawings, "he has acquired hands with which he can manipulate his immediate environment" (p. 119).

When Joey was 12—three years after he had entered the school—". . . he made a float for our Memorial Day parade. It carried the slogan: 'Feelings are more important than anything under the sun.' Feelings, Joey had learned, are what make for humanity; their absence, for a mechanical existence. With this knowledge Joey entered the human condition" (p. 127).

frigerators" (Schreibman & Koegel, 1975; Wolff & Morris, 1971). As Harlow (1969) has somewhat wryly pointed out, it is often extremely difficult to pinpoint cause and effect in studying relationships between mother and child:

"Possibly . . . some children are rendered autistic by maternal neglect and insufficiency, but it is even more likely that many more mothers are rendered autistic because of an inborn inability of their infants to respond affectionately to them in any semblance of an adequate manner." (p. 29)

On the basis of their intensive study of 53 autistic children, Clancy and McBride (1969) have suggested that the usual picture of the autistic child as lacking in language ability and being wholly withdrawn is probably oversimplified. They found that at least some autistic children *do* comprehend language, even though they may not use it to express themselves. These investigators also pointed to the occasional normal commencement of language development, followed by its disappearance as the autistic process becomes manifest. And perhaps even more significantly, they concluded that autistic children are very much aware of—and actively involved with—their environment:

"Autistic children actively seek to arrange the environment on their terms, and so as to exclude certain elements, e.g., intervention from other people, and variety in any aspect of routine. They show a high degree of skill in manipulating people for their ends, and again this skill is usually obvious in the first year of life. In a socially inverted manner the children are as active and resourceful as normal children." (p. 243).

In a more recent study of autistic children, Tinbergen (1974) comes to a somewhat similar conclusion, viewing autism as an approach-avoidant conflict in which the child's natural tendency to explore and relate to the world is overbalanced by aversive experiences and fear—instead of venturing forth into the world, he withdraws into a world he creates for himself. However, his withdrawal is not as haphazard or disorderly as it may seem; rather it involves systematic avoidance of many stimuli and events in the real world, including people.

Clearly, much remains to be learned about the etiology of childhood autism. It would appear, however, that this disorder does begin with an inborn defect or defects in brain functioning, regardless of what other causal factors may subsequently become involved.

Treatment and outcomes. Bettelheim (1967, 1969, 1974), at the Orthogenic School of the University of Chicago, has reported some success in treating autistic children with a program of warm, loving acceptance accompanied by reinforcement procedures. Similarly, Marchant and her associates (1974) in England have reported several successes using a method for introducing "graded change" into the environment of the autistic child, thus tending to shift his behavior from self-defeating to growth-oriented activities.

Similarly, behavior therapy has been used successfully in the elimination of self-injurious behavior and the mastery of the fundamentals of language and social behavior (Bandura, 1969; Lovaas et al., 1973; Lovaas, Schaeffer, & Simmons, 1974). Perhaps the most favorable results are those of Schreibman and Koegel (1975) who reported successful outcomes in the treatment of 10 of 16 autistic children. These investigators relied heavily on the use of parents as therapists in reinforcing normal behavior on the part of their children, and concluded that autism is potentially a "defeatable horror."

Despite such encouraging reports, however, the long-range outcome in the treatment of autism does not appear favorable. Even intensive long-term care in a clinical facility may have minimal results. In general, less than one-fourth of autistic children appear to attain even marginal adjustment in later life. Some idea of the difficulties likely to be encountered in the long-range treatment of autism can be gleaned from an analogy used by Mosher (1971). Suppose that the mother of a child diagnosed as autistic had been spiking his orange juice with LSD since he was a young baby. Then his mother dies and his biochemical condition, which has led to a chaotic view of his world, is corrected. Would the youth be expected to suddenly evidence coping skills and other behaviors comparable to those of children raised without such a handicap?

Thus even in cases with a favorable outcome, the treatment program is usually a long one with due attention to aftercare measures.

The long-range prognosis in childhood schizophrenia appears only slightly more favorable (Bender, 1973; Roff, 1974). The major tranquilizing drugs, so helpful in the treatment of adult patients, have not proved effective with either autistic or schizophrenic children, although they do calm them down. For these childhood disorders, the outcome appears to depend heavily on the severity and duration of the disorder as well as the specific method of treatment.[3]

Hyperactive (hyperkinetic) reaction

Hyperactivity is a common presenting symptom[4] among children seen at child guidance clinics and related facilities. It occurs with the greatest frequency before the age of 8 and tends to become less frequent and of shorter duration thereafter. Typically it disappears or shows marked alleviation by the middle teens. There are an estimated 2 million or more children in the United States who could be labeled as hyperactive—between 5 and 10 percent of elementary schoolchildren (Getze, 1974; Solomon, 1972). The hyperactive syndrome is much more frequent among boys than girls.

Clinical picture. Hyperkinesis—excessive or exaggerated muscular activity—is the key element in a clinical picture that usually also includes some or all of the following:

Short attention span
Easy distractibility
Impulsiveness
Poor motor coordination
Low frustration tolerance

Emotional instability and changeable moods
Hypersensitivity
Lack of inhibition

Hyperkinetic children do not differ in intelligence from comparable groups of normal children; however, they do tend to talk incessantly and to be socially uninhibited and immature. They do not appear to be anxious, although their overactivity, restlessness, and distractibility are often interpreted as indications of anxiety. Usually they do poorly in school, commonly showing specific learning disabilities, such as difficulty in learning to read or in learning other basic school subjects. In fact, hyperactive children pose the majority of behavior problems in the elementary grades.

The following case, involving an 8-year-old girl, reveals a somewhat typical clinical picture:

The subject was referred to a community clinic because of overactive, inattentive, and disruptive behavior. She was a problem to her teacher and to other students because of her hyperactivity and uninhibited behavior. She would impulsively hit other children, knock things off their desks, erase material on the blackboard, damage books and other school property. She seemed to be in perpetual motion—talking, moving about, and darting from one area of the classroom to another. From both parents and teacher she demanded an inordinate amount of attention, and was intensely jealous of other children including her own brother and sister.

Despite her hyperactive behavior, inferior school performance, and other problems, she was considerably above average in intelligence. Nevertheless, she felt "stupid" and had a seriously devaluated self-image. Neurological tests revealed nothing significant. She was labeled as a hyperactive child.

Causal factors. There are no known genetic or chromosomal defects associated with hyperactivity. However, there is a higher-than-average number of premature births among hyperactive children, a substantial number of whom show so-called soft neurological signs, such as perceptual motor coordination deficits. Satterfield et al. (1974) also found a higher-than-average incidence of abnormal EEG's among hyperactive children—22 out of the 120 children tested. Because of such findings, hyperactive children are commonly assumed to be suffering from "minimal brain dysfunction," or MBD. The evidence, however,

---

[3]For this section on autism, the author would like to express his appreciation to a number of investigators whose work was not mentioned in the brief discussion, primarily because of limitations of space. Among these are May and May (1959), Mahler (1952), Rimland (1964, 1971), J. K. Wing (1967), and L. Wing (1971).

[4]*Presenting symptoms* refer to the clinical picture at the time the patient is first seen by professional personnel. *Presenting complaint* and *referral problem* are synonymous terms.

Minimal brain dysfunction (MBD)

In a three-part study sponsored by the U.S. Dept. of Health, Education, and Welfare (Clements, 1966; Paine, 1969; Chalfant & Scheffelin, 1969), children with minimal brain dysfunction (MBD) have been described as

" . . . of near average, average, or above average general intelligence with certain learning and/or behavioral disabilities ranging from mild to severe, which are associated with deviations of function of the central nervous system. These deviations may manifest themselves by various combinations of impairment in perception, conceptualization, language, memory, and control of attention, impulse, or motor function. These aberrations may arise from genetic variations, biochemical irregularities, perinatal brain insults or other illnesses or injuries sustained during the years which are critical for the development and maturation of the central nervous system, or from other unknown organic causes." (Paine, 1969, p. 53)

The ten outstanding characteristics of children with MBD are considered, in order of frequency, to be: (1) hyperactivity, (2) perceptual-motor impairments, (3) emotional lability, (4) general coordination deficits, (5) disorders of attention (short attention span, distractibility, perseveration), (6) impulsivity, (7) disorders of memory and thinking, (8) disorders of speech and hearing, (9) specific learning disabilities (reading, writing, spelling, and arithmetic), and (10) neurological signs, including EEG irregularities.

Although the concept of MBD is widely used, it remains somewhat controversial. Criticism has been directed especially at the practice of inferring that children have MBD simply because they display "typical symptoms" (e.g., poor perceptual-motor coordination, difficulty in learning to read, attention problems, and hyperactivi-

ty) without conducting tests to determine if they actually have a neurological defect. It has also been pointed out that the intellectual, emotional, and behavioral manifestations of minimal brain dysfunction may vary greatly from child to child. For example, children with MBD do not necessarily have reading difficulties, nor are they necessarily hyperactive; in fact, they sometimes evidence a low level of motor activity. In their study on the relationship between MBD and school performance, Edwards, Alley, and Snider (1971) found "no evidence that a diagnosis of MBD, based on a pediatric neurological evaluation . . . is a useful predictor of academic achievement" (p. 134).

On the other hand, the specific "symptoms" of young children with serious learning problems are often so remarkably similar that the concept of a neurological learning disability syndrome can hardly be ruled out. In effect, the "computers" of some children seem to function atypically in the processing of auditory and visual information; and it seems likely in such cases that neurological evaluation would reveal brain dysfunction—or even actual brain damage. Even a clear diagnosis of brain dysfunction or damage may not be particularly useful, of course, unless the precise nature of the disorder can be determined, as well as its significance for behavior, treatment, and outcome. Thus, while the concept of minimal brain dysfunction may be a useful one, there is a strong trend away from using such vague labels (Mayer & Scheffelin, 1975; McGlannan, 1975; Trotter, 1975). Labeling a child as suffering from "minimal brain dysfunction" often provides little specific information, is devaluating to the child, and, in general, "hurts more than it helps."

Based on Bryan (1974), Chalfant and Scheffelin (1969), Clements (1966), Edwards, Alley, and Snider (1971), Lievens (1974), Mayer and Scheffelin (1975), McGlannan (1975), Paine (1969), Trotter (1975), and Tymchuk, Knights, and Hinton (1970).

---

is inadequate for the conclusion that all or even the majority of hyperactive reactions are associated with irregularities or alterations in brain processes. Hyperactivity is a relatively nonspecific symptom in children, and may occur in the anxious, depressed, schizophrenic, and autistic, as well as in those evidencing brain damage or minimal brain dysfunction. The concept of MBD is a controversial one, and is discussed in the illustration above.

Typically, the hyperactive reaction is manifested very early in life. Where it develops in later childhood, family and related stresses are likely to be key factors, leading to anxiety and emotional upset. Currently, the hyperactive syndrome is considered to have multiple causes and multiple effects. Thus labeling a child as "hyperactive" may not indicate much in the way of etiology or appropriate treatment procedures; in addition, such a label may devalue the child in the eyes of his parents as well as playing havoc with his own self-image if he is informed of the diagnosis (Arnold, 1973; Loney, 1974). In general, it would appear that a thorough assessment, including neurological and psychosocial measures, is essential for filling in the clinical picture in the hyperactive reaction and for the formulation of an appropriate treatment program.

Treatment and outcomes. Although the hyperactive syndrome was first described more than 100 years ago, there is some disagreement over the most effective methods of treatment, especially in the use of drugs to calm the hyperactive child.

In general, variations in treatment procedures may be required to meet the needs of individual children. However, behavior modification techniques that feature consistent positive reinforcement and the programming of learning materials and tasks in such a way as to minimize error and maximize immediate feedback are highly effective in the treatment of most hyperactive children. This approach is particularly effective when combined with the use of indicated medication and with the cooperation of parents as change agents in a total treatment program (Feighner & Feighner, 1974; Hewett & Forness, 1974; Johnson & Katz, 1973; O'Dell, 1974).

Interestingly enough, cerebral stimulants, such as the amphetamines, usually have a quieting effect on hyperactive children. Such medication decreases their overactivity and distractibility and at the same time increases their attention and ability to concentrate. As a consequent result, they are often able to function much better at home and at school. In fact, many hyperactive children who have not been acceptable in regular classes are enabled to function and progress in a relatively normal manner. The medication does not appear to affect their intelligence, but rather to help them use their basic capacities more effectively (NIMH, 1971). Although such drugs do not "cure" the hyperactivity, they have been found beneficial in about half to two-thirds of the cases in which medication appears warranted.

Some concern has been expressed, however, about the effects of such drugs, particularly when used in heavy dosage over time. Safer

and Allen (1973) concluded from a longitudinal study of 63 hyperactive children—49 of whom were on medication and 14 of whom were used as controls—that Dexedrine and Ritalin, two of the most commonly used drugs, can have a suppressing effect on normal growth in height and weight. However, in a carefully controlled study, Beck, Langford, MacKay, and Sum (1975) failed to find such effects. Nevertheless, the use of such drugs should be carefully monitored in order to avoid harmful side effects. Caffeine, another cortical stimulant, may also be useful in reducing hyperactivity among many of these children, two cups of coffee per day apparently being suffi-

A number of important questions have been raised concerning the increasing use of drugs in the treatment of certain behavior disorders of children. The principal questions include:

1. Who is being selected for treatment? Few investigators would question the usefulness of amphetamines or related drugs for treating many cases of hyperactivity, but many question the adequacy of assessment procedures used in identifying children who actually need medication. For example, a clear-cut distinction is not always made between the child who appears to need chemotherapy because of minimal brain dysfunction (MBD) and the child whose inattention and restlessness may be the result of hunger, crowded classrooms, irrelevant curriculum content, or anxiety and depression stemming from a pathogenic home situation.

2. Are drugs sometimes being used simply to "keep peace in the classroom"? Those who raise this question point to the possibility that children who manifest bewilderment, anger, restlessness, or lethargy at school may only be showing a normal reaction to educational procedures which fail to spark their interest or meet their needs. To label such children as "sick"—e.g., as evidencing hyperactivity, or some other behavior disorder—and to treat them through medication, these investigators maintain, is to sidestep the difficult and expensive alternative of providing better educational programs. Possibly such an approach also reinforces the notion—all too prevalent in our culture—that if things are not going well, all the individual has to do is take some type of drug.

3. Do the drugs have harmful side effects? Even in the small dosages usually prescribed for children, drugs sometimes have undesirable side effects. In the case of the amphetamines, the side effects appear to be minimal—even being self-correcting to some extent, in that the drug may "speed up" the child if he does not need "slowing down." However, such symptoms as decreased appetite, dizziness, headache, and insomnia have been reported in some cases with other stimulants, such as methylphenidate-hydrochloride (Ritalin). Minor tranquilizers also may have adverse side effects, including lethargy. And even with drugs that seem to produce minimal side effects, the possibility of adverse long-range effects resulting from sustained usage during early growth and development is still being assessed.

The consensus among investigators seems to be that drug therapy for children should be used with extreme caution, and only with those children for whom other alternatives simply do not work, such as the hyperactive child who shows definite indications of MBD and cannot control his behavior without drug therapy. It is also considered important that drug therapy be undertaken only with the informed consent of the parent, as well as the child if he is old enough, and that the child not be given the sole responsibility for taking his medication—a procedure that can lead to drug abuse. At the same time, there is a need to avoid exaggerated public attitudes against the use of drug therapy for children who genuinely need it. Finally, children who do benefit from drug therapy may also need other therapeutic measures for dealing with coexisting problems, such as learning deficiencies and psychological, interpersonal, and family difficulties.

Based on Beck, Langford, Mackay, and Sum (1975), Cole (1975), Eisenberg (1971), Hayes, Panitch, and Barker (1975), Martin and Zaug (1975), and Winsberg, Goldstein, Yepes, and Perel (1975).

cient (Schnackenberg, 1973). But further research is essential before the value of "coffee breaks for hyperactive children" can be adequately assessed.

Even without treatment, hyperactive reactions tend to clear up in the middle teens, although the reason for this change is not clear. However, many children labeled as MBD have a poor prognosis if left untreated, showing a higher-than-average incidence of delinquency and other maladaptive behavior during adolescence and adulthood (Solomon, 1972), possibly due to school failure and the lack of understanding parents. Feighner and Feighner (1974) have described the long-range picture as follows:

"Although the symptom of overactivity usually diminishes with age, many patients will experience an educational and social lag into teenage years and adult life. These continuing handicaps obviously affect a person's ability to make a satisfactory life adjustment in family relationships, vocation, and interpersonal relationships." (p. 462)

Unsocialized aggressive reaction

In his extensive study of the behavior problems of 1500 children seen at the Institute for Juvenile Research, Jenkins (1968) labeled 445 cases as unsocialized aggressive reaction. In many ways similar to the psychopathic personality pattern we have described for adolescents and adults (Chapter 11), this reaction is much more common among boys than girls.

Clinical picture. Although the following case is not necessarily typical of the unsocialized aggressive reaction, it does describe many of the symptoms commonly found in this disorder.

"This 9-year-old, wiry, active boy wore a 'crewcut' with an ever ready, engaging smile. From the beginning of each interview he led things, with careful attention to the responses of the interviewer. In addition to fire-setting he was chronically truant, had vandalized the school, and had set off a fire alarm in school. Speaking about the alarm, he noted, 'This kid dared me to do it and I didn't think it was hooked up.' In the clinic waiting room he got two boys to fight by informing one that the other was saying things about him, and then quickly assumed the role of peacemaker when an adult appeared. He spoke of his love for 'little kids,' and conspicuously held his baby sister in the waiting room, although his mother was unencumbered beside him. In the playroom he chose the activities and frequently seemed to have a program for what he wanted to do that day. This boy was enuretic. His main wish was for 'a gang—for protection.'" (Vandersall & Weiner, 1970, pp. 68–69)

In general, unsocialized aggressive children manifest such characteristics as overt or covert hostility, disobedience, physical and verbal aggressiveness, quarrelsomeness, vengefulness, and destructiveness. Lying, solitary stealing, and temper tantrums are common. Such children tend to be sexually uninhibited and inclined toward sexual aggressiveness. A minority may engage in fire-setting, solitary vandalism, and even homicidal acts. Financially, the damage from acts of vandalism committed each year by such children—particularly vandalism of public-school buildings—runs into the millions of dollars.

Causal factors. There appears to be general agreement among investigators that the family setting of the unsocialized aggressive child is typically characterized by rejection, harsh and inconsistent discipline, and general frustration. Frequently the parents are unstable in their marital relationships, are emotionally disturbed or sociopathic, and provide the child with little in the way of consistent guidance, acceptance, or affection. In a disproportionate number of cases the child lives in a home broken by divorce or separation, and may have a stepparent or series of stepparents. But whether the home is broken or not, the child is overtly rejected—he is unwanted and he knows it.

As we noted in Chapter 11, Wolkind (1974) has used the termed "affectionless psychopathy" to refer to such children who are placed in institutions at an early age. While he found that the symptoms of the antisocial or psychopathic syndrome are commonly found among such institutionalized children, even in relatively good institutional settings, he concluded that the antisocial behavior is heavily influenced by the child's early family life prior to entering the institution. Apparently early anti-

These pictures are of children labeled either "emotionally disturbed" or "behaviorally disordered," and show them interacting with their teachers or counselors. They all attend the Loyola University Guidance Center and Day School in Chicago.

The Guidance Center serves children who have significant difficulty in everyday living in their community but who can continue to attend a regular school and live at home. After an intensive individual diagnostic evaluation, a treatment program is developed that includes both the child and his parents. This program includes a variety of treatment methods such as individual play therapy, group therapy for children or adults, and family therapy.

The Day School serves very emotionally disturbed children who cannot attend regular public school. Each child is studied as an individual and treated accordingly, but the treatment is generally based on the theory that the child has not received or has not been able to accept an optimal amount of love and affection; therefore he needs great amounts of love, but carefully balanced with control. Children in the Day School spend a great deal of their time relating to adults, learning to receive and give affection and slowly learning to control themselves.

social trends on the part of the child may be exacerbated by the trauma of parental rejection and institutionalization, as well as possible effects of the institutional environment.

Treatment and outcomes. The treatment of the unsocialized aggressive child is likely to be ineffective unless some means can be found for modifying the child's life setting. This is difficult where the parents are maladjusted and in conflict between themselves. And often an overburdened parent who is separated or divorced and working simply does not have the time or inclination to learn and practice a more adequate parental role. In some cases the circumstances may call for removal of the child from the home and his placement in a foster home or institution, with the expectation that he later can be returned home if intervening therapy with the parents appears to justify it. Unfortunately, when the child is taken from his home he often interprets this as further rejection—not only by his parents but by society as well. And unless the changed environment offers a warm, kindly, acceptant—and yet consistent and firm—setting, the child is likely to make little progress.

By and large, society tends to take a punitive, rather than rehabilitative, attitude toward the antisocial aggressive youth. Thus, the emphasis is on punishment and on "teaching the child a lesson." Many such individuals are "treated" in indifferent or punitive correctional institutions that actually appear to intensify rather than correct the behavior. Where treatment is unsuccessful, the end product is likely to be a psychopathic personality with a long future of antisocial, aggressive behavior ahead of him. In an intensive longitudinal study of antisocial aggressive behavior in childhood, Robins (1970) found that such behavior is highly predictive of sociopathic behavior in later adolescence and adulthood; similar findings have been reported by Wolkind (1974).

The advent of behavior therapy techniques has, however, made the outlook much brighter for children manifesting unsocialized aggressive reactions. Particularly important is training of the parents in control techniques, so that they function as therapists in reinforcing desirable behavior and modifying environ-

mental conditions that may be reinforcing the maladaptive behavior. The change effected in the parents' overt reactions to the child's positive behavior, as well as to his negative behavior, may finally open up an avenue to a real change in their perception of and feelings toward the child, and to their positive acceptance of him.

Overanxious and withdrawal reactions

Although overanxious and withdrawal reactions are classified separately by the APA, they have so much in common that we shall deal with them under the above general heading. Jenkins (1968) classified 287 of his 1500 cases as reactions of these types, both of which are much more common among boys than girls.

Clinical picture. In general, the overanxious and the withdrawal reactions of childhood appear to share the following characteristics:

> Oversensitivity
> Unrealistic fears
> Shyness and timidity
> Pervasive feelings of inadequacy
> Sleep disturbances
> Fear of school

However, the child labeled as suffering from an overanxious reaction typically attempts to cope with his fears by becoming overdependent on others for help and support, while the child manifesting a withdrawal reaction apparently attempts to minimize his anxiety by turning away from reality and withdrawing into himself.

1. *Overanxious reaction.* The overanxious reaction is characterized by unrealistic fears, oversensitivity, self-consciousness, nightmares, and chronic anxiety. The child lacks self-confidence, is apprehensive in new situations, and tends to be immature for his age. Such children often are described by their parents as prone to be shy, sensitive, nervous, submissive, easily discouraged, worried, and moved to tears. Typically they are overdependent, particularly on their parents. The following case involving "school phobia" illustrates the clinical picture in the overanxious reaction of childhood.

Johnny was a highly sensitive 6-year-old boy who suffered from numerous fears, nightmares, and chronic anxiety. He was terrified of being separated from his mother, even for a brief period. When his mother tried to enroll him in kindergarten, he became so upset when she left the room that the principal arranged for her to remain in the classroom. But after two weeks this had to be discontinued and Johnny had to be withdrawn from kindergarten, since his mother could not leave him even for a few minutes.

Later when his mother attempted to enroll him in the first grade, Johnny manifested the same intense anxiety and unwillingness to be separated from her. At the suggestion of the school counselor, Johnny's mother brought him to a community clinic for assistance with the problem. The therapist who initially saw Johnny and his mother was wearing a white clinic jacket, and this led to a severe panic reaction on Johnny's part. His mother had to hold him to keep him from running away, and he did not settle down until the therapist removed his jacket. Johnny's mother explained that "He is terrified of doctors, and it is almost impossible to get him to a physician even when he is sick."

2. *Withdrawal reaction.* The withdrawal reaction is similar to the overanxious reaction, but here the child attempts to minimize his anxiety by turning inward—in effect detaching himself from a seemingly dangerous and hostile world. The results of this defensive strategy have been described by Jenkins (1969):

"In turning away from objective reality, these children turn away from the normal practice of constantly checking their expectations against experience. With such turning away, their capacity to distinguish fact from fancy tends to deteriorate. They function inefficiently and fail to develop effective patterns of behavior." (p. 70)

Children manifesting the withdrawal reaction tend toward seclusiveness, timidity, and inability to form close interpersonal relationships. Often they appear listless and apathetic and are prone to daydreaming and unrealistic fantasies. The following case is fairly typical:

Tommy was a small, slender, 7-year-old boy from a middle-class family. He was enrolled in the second grade at school but failed to function adequately in the classroom. In referring him to the school counselor, the teacher described him as being withdrawn, shy, oversensitive, and unable to make friends or to participate in classroom activities. During recess he preferred to remain in the classroom and appeared preoccupied with his thoughts and fantasies. He was seriously retarded in reading achievement and other basic school subjects. Psychological assessment showed that he was superior in intelligence but suffered from extreme feelings of inadequacy and a pervasive attitude of "I can't do it."

Causal factors. Various factors have been emphasized as being of etiological significance in both the overanxious and the withdrawal reactions of childhood. The more important of these appear to be:

1. Unusual constitutional sensitivity, easy conditionability by aversive stimuli, and the building up and generalization of "surplus fear reactions."

2. The undermining of the child's feelings of adequacy and security by early illnesses, accidents, or losses that involve pain and discomfort. The traumatic effect of such experiences is often due partly to the child's finding himself in unfamiliar situations, as during hospitalization.

3. The "modeling" effect of an overanxious and protective parent who sensitizes the child to the dangers and threats of his world. Often the parent's overprotectiveness communicates a lack of confidence in the child's ability to cope, thus reinforcing his feelings of inadequacy.

4. The failure of an indifferent or detached parent to provide adequate guidance for the child's development. Although the child is not necessarily rejected by such a parent, neither is he adequately supported in mastering essential competencies and in gaining a positive view of himself. Repeated experiences of failure, stemming from poor learning skills, may lead to subsequent patterns of anxiety or withdrawal in the face of "threatening" situations.

Sometimes a child is made to feel that he must earn his parents' love and respect through outstanding achievement, especially in school. Such a child tends to be overcritical of himself and to feel intensely anxious and devaluated when he perceives himself as failing. Unlike the child who rejoices in his achievements, this child is a "perfectionist who does equally well but is left with a feeling of failure because he thinks he should have done better" (Krebs & Krebs, 1970, p. 40).

5. Inadequate interpersonal patterns, which typically extend beyond the family. The withdrawal reaction, in particular, "occurs in children who have found human contact more frustrating than rewarding" (Jenkins, 1970, p. 141). For the overanxious child, too, interpersonal patterns often appear to be unsatisfactory, although perhaps less aversive on the average than they generally are for the withdrawn child.

The various causal factors that we have been discussing in relation to the overanxious and withdrawal reactions of childhood can obviously occur in differing degrees and combinations. However, all of them are consistent with the view that these disorders result essentially from maladaptive learning.

Treatment and outcomes. Although the overanxious and withdrawal reactions of childhood may continue into adolescence and young adulthood—the first tending toward neurotic avoidance behavior and the latter toward increasingly idiosyncratic thinking and behavior—this is not typically the case. As the child grows and his world widens in school and peer-group activities, he is likely to benefit from such corrective experiences as making friends and succeeding at given tasks. Teachers, who have become more and more aware of the needs of both the overanxious and the shy, withdrawn child—and of ways of helping them—often are able to ensure a child's success experiences and to foster constructive interpersonal relationships. Behavior-therapy procedures, employed in structured group experiences within educational settings, can help speed up and ensure favorable outcomes. Such procedures include desensitization, assertion training, and help with mastering essential competencies.

More formal psychotherapy and behavior therapy, often combined with family therapy, have proven effective in the treatment of children manifesting severe anxiety or withdrawal reactions (Hampe et al., 1973). Montenegro (1968) has described the successful treatment of two young children manifesting pathological separation anxiety. The overall treatment program for one of the youngsters, a 6-year-old boy named Romeo, included the following procedures:

1. Exposure of the child to a graded series of situations involving the actual fear-arousing stimulus—that is, separation from the mother for increasingly longer intervals;

2. The use of food during these separations as an anxiety inhibitor—which might involve taking the child to the hospital cafeteria for something to eat;

3. Instruction of the parents on how to reduce the child's excessive dependence on the mother—for example, through letting him learn to do things for himself.

After ten consecutive sessions, Romeo's separation anxiety was reduced to the point that he could stay home with a competent baby-sitter for an hour, and then increasingly longer. During the summer he was enrolled in a vacation church school, which he enjoyed; and when the new semester began at public school, he entered the first grade and made an adequate adjustment. It may be emphasized that the cooperation of the parents—particularly the mother—was a key factor in the treatment program.

Runaway reaction

Of serious concern in the United States is the estimated million or more boys and girls who run away from home each year. While the average age is about 15, an increasing number are in the 11- to 14-year-old age bracket. Most of these runaways are from white suburbs, and at least half are girls.

Clinical picture. There are many reasons for and "types" of runaways. While the following case is not necessarily typical, it does serve to illustrate this reaction pattern.

Joan, an attractive girl who looked older than her 12 years, came to the attention of juvenile authorities when her parents reported her as a "runaway." Twice before she had run away from home, but no report had been filed. In the first instance she had gone to the home of a girlfriend and returned two days later; in the second she had hitchhiked to another city with an older boy, and returned home about a week later.

Investigation revealed that the girl was having difficulty in her school adjustment and was living in a family situation torn by bickering and dissension. In explaining why she ran away from home, she stated simply that "I just couldn't take it anymore—

all that quarreling and criticism, and no one really cared anyway."

Running away may occur as an isolated incident or as part of a history of "crisis-flight" responses to which some young people and even adults resort in highly stressful situations. Where the pattern tends to become repetitive, runaways are often referred to as "splitters"; in a distinct minority of cases, runaways become "hard road freaks" and adopt a nomadic life-style in which physical aggression, exploitation, and illegal behavior are often essential for survival.

Causal factors. English (1973) has concluded that reasons for running away from home tend to fall into three categories: (a) getting out of a destructive family situation, such as the girl who runs away to avoid sexual advances by her father or stepfather; (b) running away for altruistic reasons, for example, in a desperate effort to draw attention to and change a disturbed family situation; and (c) having a secret, unsharable problem, such as, for girls, being pregnant.

In a study restricted to runaway girls, Homer (1974) distinguished between "run froms," who had usually fought with their parents and run away from home because they were unable to resolve the situation or their anger; and "run tos," who were seeking something outside the home. The "run tos" were typically seekers of pleasure—sex, drugs, liquor, escape from school, and a peer group with similar interests. Usually they stayed with friends or at other "peer-established" facilities. The "run froms" usually ran away from home only once, while the "run tos" were more likely to be repetitive runaways.

At the present time, it would appear that an increasing number of children are "run froms" who are trying to get away from an intolerable home situation. In many instances, for economic or other reasons, they are actually encouraged to leave—and their parents do not want them back. These children are commonly referred to as the "throwaways" (*U.S. News & World Report*, May 12, 1975, pp. 49–50). Most do not feel that they can return to their parents, but very much want a foster home where they will be well-treated and respected.

Treatment and outcomes. Treatment of the child runaway is similar to that for individuals manifesting other disorders of early life. Often family therapy is an essential part of the overall treatment program. In some instances—as in those involving parental abuse, unconcern, or lack of cooperation—juvenile authorities may place the child in a foster home. However, parents are by no means always the primary reason for their child's running away; and a "what-have-we-done-wrong" attitude may lead to unnecessary feelings of guilt.

The majority of runaways are not reported. Of those who are, about 90 percent or more are located by law enforcement officers and, where feasible, returned home. Beginning in late 1974, a toll-free "hot line" was established that informs runaways where the nearest temporary shelter is located and enables them to send messages to their parents if they wish.[5]

Unfortunately, facilities for runaways in our society are seriously limited, usually providing only shelter, and the potential danger exists that such youth may turn to illegal activities. Boys commonly steal to obtain food, and a sizeable number of prostitutes in the large cities are recruited from runaway girls. In our "affluent" society, it would seem that the problem of runaway youth could be dealt with more effectively.

Stuttering

Stuttering is a speech disorder that involves a blocking or repetition of, or sometimes a struggling with, speech sounds. The term *stuttering* is synonymous with the older term *stammering*, which has gradually fallen into disuse. The speaking behavior of the stutterer may vary from mild difficulty with initial syllables of certain words, as in "D-d-d-don't do that," to violent contortions and momentary inability to utter any sound at all. Most stutterers can speak fluently under ordinary circumstances;

---

[5]Two of the nationwide toll-free numbers are 800-621-4000 and 1-800-231-6946. The hotlines do not operate from either Alaska or Hawaii.

Many children, especially teen-agers, run away from home each year. This photograph shows the "runaway bulletin board" in a San Francisco police station.

the blocking tends to occur at moments of important or stressful communication.

Every era has had its quota of these speech sufferers. Some of the more illustrious names on the roster are those of Moses, Aristotle, Vergil, Demosthenes, Charles Lamb, and Clara Barton. In our contemporary world, stuttering has been observed in diverse cultures—among the Bantu of South Africa and the Polynesians of the South Pacific, as well as among members of Oriental and Western societies (Lemert, 1962, 1970).

The actual incidence of stuttering is not known, but it has been estimated that in the Western world some 40 to 50 million children stutter badly; in the United States the figure has been estimated to be between 2 and 3 million (Sheehan, 1970; Steinberg, 1975). Most stuttering begins early in life, the onset occurring before the age of 6 in 90 percent or more of the cases, with the highest incidence occurring between the ages of 2 and 4. More boys than girls stutter, in a ratio of about 4 or 5 to 1.

Clinical picture. The entire performance of the stutterer represents an "internal struggle" to speak. After the momentary disturbance, however, speech becomes smooth and fluent until the next stumbling block. The stutterer's difficulty may vary considerably from one situation to another. Typically, stuttering increases both in severity and frequency in situations where the stutterer feels inferior, self-conscious, or anxious. On the other hand, most stutterers can articulate normally or with minimal difficulty when singing, whispering, adopting some accent or drawl, or when they cannot hear the sound of their own voices. Usually, also, they have little or no difficulty in speaking aloud when they are alone, when addressing animals, or when reading aloud to the tempo of a metronome.

On the basis of his early experiences as a stutterer, and also of his later studies in this field, Sheehan (1970) has pointed out that "for the child or adult who has developed the problem called stuttering, the production of a spoken word can be fraught with dread and difficulty" (p. vii). Certainly one can empathize with the young stutterer in the classroom who is eager to answer a question but fears the humiliation and ridicule his stuttering may elicit. In a world organized around efficient verbal communication, stuttering can be highly stressful and self-devaluating. As Steinberg (1975) has expressed it, "this simple act of social interaction has been transformed into a frightening nightmare" (p. 30).

Causal factors. Stuttering has proved to be a most baffling disorder; attempts to explain it have largely focused on the following factors:

1. *Genetic and neurological factors.* In comparing a large group of children who stuttered with a matched group of nonstutterers, Johnson (1961) found that 9 times as many of the stutterers had siblings or parents—mostly fathers—who also stuttered. In a more recent review of research findings, Sheehan and Costley (1975) concluded that genetic factors do play a significant role in the etiology of stuttering. But these investigators did not rule out the key role of learning in the "familial transmission" of stuttering.

A neurological view that has received considerable emphasis relates stuttering to aberrations in auditory feedback. Since the experimental delay or withholding of auditory feedback greatly reduces or even eliminates severe stuttering, it seems possible that "in certain cases stuttering may be the result of minute physical imperfections in the feedback loop of the hearing mechanism" (Dinnan, McGuiness, & Perrin, 1970, p. 30). However, more recent research in this area has failed to delineate specific aberrations in auditory feedback.

Nor as a group do stutterers evidence brain damage or abnormal brain functioning. Brain damage causes a different type of speech or language disorder called *aphasia*, defined as a loss or impairment of ability to use language because of brain lesions. As we noted in Chapter 13, one common difficulty among aphasics is in finding or "retrieving" from memory the word he wishes to use; the difficulty experienced by the stutterer is in "getting the word out" or pronounced.

2. *Learning and stress.* Currently, most investigators place strong emphasis on the roles of learning and stress as primary causal factors in stuttering.

The potential importance of learning in the development of stuttering was demonstrated some two decades ago by Flanagan, Goldiamond, and Azrin (1959), using operant conditioning procedures. The normally fluent subject received continual electric shock, but blockage of fluent speech turned off the shock for 10 seconds; each additional disfluency in speech that occurred during this 10-second interval further delayed the electroshock. Eventually the subject avoided the aversive stimulation almost entirely by continuous disfluent speech.[6] As Bandura (1969) has pointed out, however, "it is exceedingly improbable that parents of stutterers continuously punish their children's fluent verbal patterns, but respond nonpunitively whenever their children block and stutter" (p. 323).

While it does appear that stuttering develops from the disfluencies that characterize normal speech, particularly during early stages of speech development, the acutal learning processes involved still remain a puzzle. However, the role of stress now appears to offer a possible solution. Most of us have probably experienced blocking of thought and speech in stage fright or in situations where we have had to make unexpected introductions. In these situations it is probably safe to say that we were self-conscious and tense. Defective responses under these conditions are very common. Perhaps we may generalize here and say that any stressful situations that lead to severe feelings of inadequacy, self-consciousness, anxiety, fear, and tension also tend to impair psychomotor coordination and performance—and this may include speech functions. Why stressful situations affect such speech functions far more in some persons than others is not known—although it may relate to the constitutional vulnerability of specific organ systems, including those involved in speech. For example, the child who has been subjected to disruptive factors while learning the difficult motor coordinations needed for speech may be especially vulnerable to later speech difficulties.

---

[6]It may be noted here that MacDonald and Martin (1973) found distinctive differences between stuttering and disfluencies and consider them discrete types of language difficulties.

3. *Role behavior.* Sheehan (1970) and Sheehan and Lyon (1974) have pointed to the potential importance of role behavior—as well as learning and stress—in the development of stuttering. This role behavior may take two different forms, but the eventual result is the same.

In the first form the stutterer plays a "false role," in that he attempts to conceal his stuttering, as by assuming a foreign accent or a regional dialect. Even when this enables him to deceive others about his being a stutterer— at least temporarily—he is likely to experience guilt and doubt. These feelings, in turn, lead him to work even harder at denying his role as a stutterer and concentrating on his false role as a normal speaker. Ironically, however, the stutterer is usually able to be most fluent when he is not trying to keep from stuttering; he has the greatest difficulty when he is trying to avoid disfluent speech. Thus, his false role sooner or later fails in its protective function, confronting him in turn with the view of himself as a stutterer and confirming him in the role of stutterer. In the second form, the individual simply views himself as a stutterer and hence plays that role. "I am a stutterer" becomes a permanent part of his self-concept—a view that is reinforced each time stuttering occurs. And presumably the expectations and reactions of those around him tend to further perpetuate the stuttering role and behavior.

Sheehan makes it clear that accepting the fact that one is a stutterer may have either positive or negative effects. If a person views his stuttering as self-devaluating and a chronic affliction about which he can do nothing, the result is negative. On the other hand, in accepting the fact that he is a stutterer, he has defined his problem. In recognizing his problem however, it is important that he does not feel devaluated or obligated to play the role of a stutterer. Modern therapy places strong emphasis on self-acceptance, but not on self-resignation.

Treatment and outcomes. The following plea for help, written by a high-school youth, reveals the upset that may be caused by stuttering, and the need for effective therapy.

"I have stuttered since childhood, and it is spoiling my whole life. Is there any hope that I can overcome this affliction? Isn't there anything that can be done for boys like me?" (Greene, 1946, p. 120)

Fortunately, since this letter was written marked advances have been achieved. Treatment for stuttering has taken such varied forms as aversive conditioning, desensitization, rhythm exercises, assertion training, hypnosis, social reinforcement of fluency, and the delay of auditory feedback.

These methods fall into two general categories: those involving direct elimination of the stuttering, and those involving acceptance and then elimination. For example, methods such as Demosthenes' speaking with pebbles in his mouth, aversive conditioning, and the delay of auditory feedback fall into the first category. Here, the attempt is to achieve fluency by means of some special technique, with the hope that this fluency will generalize to the individual's life situation. The second approach is based on the view that stuttering is an approach-avoidance conflict generated by certain situations viewed as stressful by the stutterer; as we have noted, this conflict tends to produce a vicious circle in which fear increases the likelihood of stuttering in such situations and the negative feedback in turn reinforces the fear response. The first step here is for the stutterer to accept himself realistically as a person who now stutters but who can be helped. The second step then focuses on achieving speech fluency in stressful situations in which the individual formerly stuttered. Here desensitization, self-assertion, reinforcement, and other therapy approaches may be brought into use. Once fluency is achieved, the vicious circle is broken and positive feedback and reinforcement tend to maintain speech fluency.

Fortunately, about 4 out of 5 cases of stuttering clear up spontaneously (Sheehan & Martyn, 1970). Such recovery ordinarily occurs by the middle or late teens. Even in long-established cases, with appropriate treatment most stutterers can be completely relieved of their symptoms or be greatly helped. The term *appropriate* is important here, because a method that may be effective with one stutterer may be ineffective with another.

Other "developmental" disorders

As in the case of stuttering, the behavior disorders we shall deal with here—enuresis, sleepwalking, nailbiting, and tics—typically involve a single outstanding symptom, rather than a more pervasive maladaptive pattern.

Enuresis. The term *enuresis* refers to the habitual involuntary discharge of urine after the age of 3. It may occur during the day, but is most common at night (bed-wetting). Among older children enuresis often occurs in conjunction with dreams in which a child imagines he is urinating in a toilet, only to awaken and discover that he has wet the bed. Enuresis may vary in frequency, from nightly to occasional instances when the individual is under considerable stress or is unduly tired. Commonly, enuresis occurs from 2 to 5 times a week. The actual incidence of enuresis is unknown, but it has been estimated that some 4 to 5 million children and adolescents in the United States suffer from the inconvenience and embarrassment of this disorder (Turner & Taylor, 1974).

Although enuresis may result from a variety of organic conditions, most investigators have pointed to (a) faulty learning, resulting in the failure to acquire a needed adaptive response—that is, inhibition of reflex bladder emptying; (b) personal immaturity, associated with or stemming from emotional problems; and (c) disturbed family interactions, particularly involving conditions leading to sustained anxiety and/or hostility. In some instances a child may regress to bed-wetting when a new baby enters the family and replaces him as the center of attention; or he may resort to bed-wetting when he feels hostile toward his parents and wants to get even with them, since such behavior annoys and upsets them.

Conditioning procedures, such as using an electrified mattress that rings an alarm at the first few drops of urine, thus awakening the child and eliciting a reflex inhibition of micturition, have proven effective in the treatment of enuresis. Fortunately, the incidence of enuresis tends to decrease significantly with age. Among 6-year-olds, an estimated 16 percent are enuretic, compared with only 3 percent of adolescents and 1 percent or less of young adults (Murphy et al., 1971).

Sleepwalking (somnambulism). Statistics are meager but it would appear that some 5 percent of children experience regular or periodic sleepwalking episodes.

The child usually goes to sleep in a normal manner, but arises during the second or third hour thereafter and carries out some act (Taves, 1969). This walk may take him to another room of the house or even outside, and may involve rather complex activities. He finally returns to bed, and in the morning remembers nothing that has taken place. During the sleepwalking, the child's eyes are partially or fully open, he avoids obstacles, hears when spoken to, and ordinarily responds to commands, such as to return to bed. Shaking the child will usually awaken him, and he will be surprised and perplexed at finding himself in an unexpected place. Such sleepwalking episodes usually last from 15 minutes to a half hour.

The risk of injury during sleepwalking episodes is illustrated by the following case study.

"Last fall, 14-year-old Donald Elliot got up from his bunk in his sleep, looked in the refrigerator, then, still asleep, walked out the back door. It would have been just another sleepwalking episode except that Donald was in a camper-pickup truck traveling 50 miles an hour on the San Diego Freeway. Miraculously, he escaped with cuts and bruises. But his experience, and that of many other sleepwalkers, disproves one of the myths about somnambulism: that people who walk in their sleep don't hurt themselves." (Taves, 1969, p. 41)

The causes of sleepwalking are not fully understood. Kales et al. (1966) have shown that sleepwalking takes place during NREM (nonrapid eye movement) sleep, and hence presumably does not represent the acting out of a dream, as is commonly believed. In general, it would appear that sleepwalking is related to some anxiety-arousing situation that has just occurred or is expected to occur in the near future.

Very little attention has been given to the treatment of sleepwalking. However, Clement (1970) has reported on the treatment of a 7-

year-old boy utilizing behavior therapy, as described on the right. And Nagaraja (1974) has reported the successful treatment of an 8-year-old boy and a 9-year-old girl utilizing a combination of tranquilizers and psychotherapy. But a good deal of additional research is needed before we can generalize concerning the most effective treatment procedures in sleepwalking.

Nail-biting. Probably about a fifth of all children bite their fingernails at one time or other. The incidence appears to be highest among stutterers, children reared in institutions, and children confronted with stressful demands. Although about as many girls as boys bite their nails at early ages, males outnumber females in later age groups, apparently because females are more interested in grooming.

Nail-biting typically occurs in situations associated with anxiety and/or hostility, and appears to be a method of tension reduction that provides the individual with "something to do"; thumb-sucking is probably similarly motivated. It represents a learned maladaptive habit that is reinforced and maintained by its tension-reducing properties.

Little attention has been devoted to the treatment of nail-biting. While mild tranquilizers may prove helpful, it is generally agreed that restraint and bitter-tasting applications have yielded poor results. Behavior therapy should prove effective, but there has been a lack of research evidence on the topic. Of course, initial development of this habit in a child may be checked by helping the child feel more adequate and secure, especially if he is going through some particularly difficult stress period.

Tics. A tic is a persistent, intermittent muscle twitch or spasm, usually limited to a localized muscle group. The term *tic* is used rather broadly to include blinking the eye, twitching the mouth, licking the lips, shrugging the shoulders, twisting the neck, clearing the throat, blowing through the nostrils, grimacing, and many other responses. In some instances, as in clearing the throat, the individual may be aware of the tic when it occurs, but usually he performs the act so habitually that

Treatment of sleepwalking utilizing conditioning procedures

Bobby, a 7-year-old boy, walked in his sleep on an average of four times a week. His mother kept a record, indicating that Bobby's sleepwalking episodes were associated with nightmares, perspiring, and talking in his sleep. During the actual sleepwalking Bobby usually was glassy-eyed and unsteady on his feet. On one occasion he started out the front door. The sleepwalking had commenced about 6 weeks before the boy was brought for therapy, and usually an episode would begin about 45 to 90 minutes after he had gone to bed.

During treatment the therapist learned that just before each sleepwalking episode Bobby usually had a nightmare about being chased by "a big black bug." In his dream Bobby thought "the bug would eat off his legs if it caught him" (Clement, 1970, p. 23). Bobby's sleepwalking episodes usually showed the following sequence: after his nightmare began, he perspired freely, moaned and talked in his sleep, tossed and turned, and finally got up and walked through the house. He was amnesic for the sleepwalking episode when he awakened the next morning.

Assessment data revealed no neurological or other medical problems and indicated that Bobby was of normal intelligence. However, he was found to be "a very anxious, guilt-ridden little boy who avoided performing assertive and aggressive behaviors appropriate to his age and sex" (p. 23). Assertive training and related measures were used but were not effective. The therapist then focused treatment on having Bobby's mother awaken the boy each time he showed signs of an impending episode. Washing Bobby's face with cold water and making sure he was fully awake, the mother would return him to bed, where he was "to hit and tear up a picture of the big black bug." At the start of the treatment program, Bobby had made up several of these drawings.

Eventually, the nightmare was associated with awakening, and Bobby learned to wake up on most occasions when he was having a bad dream. Clement considered the basic behavior therapy model in this case to follow that used in the conditioning treatment for enuresis, where a waking response is elicited by an intense stimulus just as micturition is beginning and becomes associated with and eventually prevents nocturnal bed-wetting.

he does not notice it. In fact, he may not even realize that he has a tic unless someone brings it to his attention. Tics occur most frequently between the ages of 6 and 14.

An adolescent who had wanted very much to be a teacher told the school counselor that he was thinking of giving up his plans. When asked the reason, he explained that several friends told him he had a persistent twitching of the mouth muscles when he answered questions in class. He had been unaware of this muscle twitch, and even after being told about it, could not tell when it took place. However, he became acutely self-conscious, and was reluctant to answer questions or enter into class discussions. As a result, his general level of tension increased, and so did the frequency of the tic – which now became apparent even when he was talking to a friend. Thus, a vicious circle had been established, but proved amenable to treatment by conditioning and self-assertive techniques.

Although tics may have an organic basis, the great majority are psychological in origin – usually stemming from self-consciousness or tension in social situations. Unfortunately, the individual's awareness of the tic often increases his tension in social situations because others can so readily notice it. Tics have been successfully treated by means of drugs, psychotherapy, and conditioning techniques.

Treatment and Prevention

In our discussion of specific childhood disorders, we have noted the wide range of treatment procedures that may be used as well as marked differences in outcomes. On a psychological level, there is an increasing use of behavior therapy, and in this trend we see the decreasing dependence on traditional long-term psychotherapy that has met with limited success. However, short-term psychotherapy, particularly to help children through crisis periods, often plays a crucial role in treatment. We also referred to the importance of sociotherapy in the alleviation of pathogenic family and/or sociocultural conditions that are causing or maintaining the child's behavior problem.

In concluding our review of the behavior disorders of childhood, let us note (a) certain problems that are relatively unique to the treatment of children, and (b) the advent of a new era in the assessment, treatment, and prevention of childhood disorders. As we shall see, this new era is characterized by an increasing emphasis on the "rights of children" and on the social commitment to provide conditions conducive to their optimal development.

Problems associated with the treatment of children

Among the problems that are relatively specific to treating behavior disorders of childhood are these:

1. *The child's inability to seek assistance.* The great majority of emotionally disturbed children who need assistance are not in a position to ask for it themselves, or to transport themselves to and from child guidance clinics. Thus, unlike the adult or the adolescent, who usually can seek help during crisis periods, the child is dependent, primarily on his par-

ents. They must realize when he needs professional help, and take the initiative in seeking it for him. Many children, of course, come to the attention of treatment agencies as a consequence of school referrals, delinquent acts, or parental abuse.

2. *The high incidence of pathogenic family patterns.* The Joint Commission on the Mental Health of Children of the American Orthopsychiatric Association (1968) estimated that 25 percent of the children in our society come from inadequate homes. Even if we assume that conditions have improved since this report was published, there would still appear to be many families that provide an undesirable environment for their children. Since the care of the child is traditionally the responsibility of the parents, and local and state agencies intervene only in extreme cases—usually involving physical abuse—these children are obviously at a disadvantage. Not only are they deprived from the standpoint of environmental influence on their personality development, but they also lack parents who perceive their need for help and who actively seek and participate in treatment programs.

3. *Treatment of the parents as well as the child.* Since most of the behavior disorders specific to childhood appear to grow out of pathogenic family patterns, it usually is essential for the parents, as well as the child, to receive treatment. As we have noted, in some instances the child may be removed from his family setting, or the treatment program may focus on the parents rather than on the child, including the training of parents in the use of shaping and reinforcement procedures. Increasingly, the treatment of children has come to mean family therapy, in which one or both parents as well as the child or siblings participate in all phases of the program. For working parents without spouses and for parents who basically reject the child, treatment may pose a difficult problem. It may also pose a problem for poorer families who lack transportation as well as money. Thus, both parental and economic factors help determine which emotionally disturbed children will receive assistance.

4. *The use of parents as "change agents."* A recent trend has been the use of parents as change agents. In essence, the parents are

This picture of a cruel and aggressive cat and a submissive mouse was drawn by John————, an emotionally disturbed boy who grew up in a broken home in a socially disadvantaged area of Los Angeles. He was admitted to the children's division of a state mental hospital, where he drew the picture. In it, he depicted the world—symbolized by the cat—as a terrifying place. He saw himself as the mouse—helpless and inadequate. After 6 months in the hospital, John showed marked improvement and was admitted to a "Boy's-Town" type of facility which had a controlled, but more natural, environment. At last report, John was making a successful adjustment in his new setting and was continuing to gain needed competencies and self-confidence.

involved in the overall treatment program from the beginning, and are trained in techniques that enable them to help their child. Typically such training focuses on helping the parent understand the nature of the child's behavior disorder and learn the necessary behavior-modification techniques for the nonreinforcement of undesirable behavior and the fostering of adaptive behavior.

Since this is a relatively new approach, a good deal still has to be learned as to how parents can be helped most effectively to help their children. But encouraging results have been obtained to date with parents who care about their children and want to help (Johnson & Katz, 1973; Lexow & Aronson, 1975; O'Dell, 1974).

5. *The problem of placing the child outside the family.* Most communities have juvenile facilities which, day or night, will provide protective care and custody for child victims of unfit homes, abandonment, abuse, neglect,

Problems associated with foster-care placement of children

At any one time, some 400,000 to 500,000 children in the United States are in foster-care facilities; it has been estimated that, if present trends continue, 1 out of 5 children will receive some type of foster care during the course of growing up.

Common reasons for foster-care placement involve neglect, abuse, or desertion of the child by his parents, or the inability of parents to cope with the child's maladaptive behavior. Social service agencies in charge of making foster-care placements attempt to select the best available setting for the child, but the setting may have serious drawbacks, whether the placement is with a foster family or an institution. In a foster family, for example, the child may be treated with relative indifference since he will be leaving soon anyway. This attitude, coupled with the child's own feelings of insecurity and anxiety, may lead to difficulty. Or the foster family may not be able to cope with difficulties associated with a child's emotional problems. In such cases, the result often is "nomadism"—a series of foster-home placements which may have a highly detrimental effect on the child. Institutional placement, on the other hand, may also expose the child to indifferent treatment and deprive him of adequate adult models and relationships.

While foster-care placement often serves an essential and constructive purpose, it would seem desirable to devote more research effort to assessing the nature, effectiveness, and outcomes of the system of foster care in the United States. This is particularly important in view of the large number of children receiving such care.

Based in part on Seidl (1974) and Stone (1970).

and related conditions. Depending on the home situation and the special needs of the child, he will either be returned to his parents or removed from his home. In the latter instance, four types of facilities are commonly relied on: (a) a foster home; (b) a private institution for the care of children; (c) a county or state institution; or (d) the home of relatives. Of course, the quality of the foster home or other placement is a crucial consideration.

It is apparent from the preceding points that much hinges on the availability of treatment facilities for children, and on assuring that children who need assistance receive it. As we turn to a brief consideration of "Child Advocacy Programs," we shall discuss the means of trying to achieve these goals.

Child advocacy programs

In the mid-1970s there were about 60 million children in the United States under 14 years of age. This would indicate that a massive social commitment is needed not only to provide disturbed children with adequate treatment facilities, but also to see that all children grow up in conditions that foster their optimal development.

Unfortunately, however, both treatment and preventive programs in our society are highly inadequate. In 1970, for example, not a single community in the United States provided adequate health services for its children (Lourie et al., 1970). In fact, the National Institute of Mental Health (1970) pointed out that "less than 1 percent of the disturbed youngsters in the United States receive any kind of treatment, and less than half of these receive adequate help" (p. 7). In its final report—*Crisis in Child Mental Health: Challenge for the 1970's*—the Joint Commission on the Mental Health of Children (1970) referred to our lack of commitment to our children and youth as a "national tragedy." The Commission's report concluded:

"Either we permit a fifth of the nation's children to go down the drain—with all that this implies for public disorder and intolerable inhumanity—or we decide, once and for all, that the needs of children have first priority on the nation's resources." (p. 408)

In 1971, a positive step toward dealing with the rights of children and ensuring their access to needed services was taken by the President of the United States when he established the National Center for Child Advocacy.

The objectives of this Center are the implementation and follow-up of the top priorities, or "overriding concerns," that were enumerated at the White House Conference on Children, held in Washington, D.C., in December 1970. The first seven of these priorities bear mention here:

1. The establishment of comprehensive family-oriented health programs, which would include health services, day care, and early childhood education.

2. The development of realistic programs to eliminate racism, which handicaps so many children.

3. The reordering of national priorities, starting with a guaranteed basic family income to provide adequately for the needs of children.

4. Improvement of our system of justice to ensure timely and positive response to the needs of children.

5. Establishment of a national child health care program financed by the federal government to ensure needed and comprehensive care for all children.

6. The development of a system for the early identification of children with special needs, to ensure prompt delivery of appropriate treatment.

7. The establishment of a federal agency for child advocacy in which all ethnic, cultural, racial, and related groups would be fully represented. (Close, 1971, p. 44)

Although conditions appear to be slowly improving, we still have a long way to go in implementing the preceding objectives and assuring adequate health care for children.

In Chapter 21, we shall deal with the goals and programs of government and private organizations directly involved in the movement for comprehensive health care—for all people—and with efforts toward fostering self-actualization and social progress.

In this chapter our focus has been primarily on behavior disorders specific to childhood, including autism, hyperactive reaction, runaway reaction, and other developmental disorders, such as stuttering and enuresis. We excluded from consideration transient situational, neurotic, psychotic, and other mental disorders that occur in other life periods as well as childhood, and that have been covered in preceding chapters.

We noted that it was not until the turn of the century that attention began to be directed toward the study of childhood disorders, and that during the intervening period great strides have been made in understanding and treating them. We have seen that particular emphasis is being placed on the use of behavior modification techniques in treating childhood disorders, and that early detection and correction of faulty behaviors and developmental trends is considered crucial.

We concluded this chapter by noting some of the special problems associated with the treatment of childhood behavior disorders, by commenting on the seeming lack of needed commitment to the welfare of children and youth in our society, and by briefly noting the encouraging trend toward child advocacy programs.

III
Other
Key Areas
of Problem
Behavior

16

Sexual "Deviations"

The development of adult sexual behavior from the undifferentiated potentialities of the infant is a long and complex process, and the resulting patterns are by no means uniform. Moreover, variations are evident in the prevailing attitudes of different cultures toward these patterns. Each society approves or disapproves of certain sexual patterns and labels others as "deviant"; but few patterns, aside from incest, appear to be universally condemned. For example, sharply contrasting attitudes are found for polygamy, prostitution, and homosexuality. In addition, attitudes often change over time within a given culture.

In our own society, there is a widespread challenging of traditional sexual mores, plus a concerted attempt to evaluate the appropriate role of sexual behavior in living. Is monogamous marriage the only "normal" adult pattern? Should premarital and extramarital intercourse be encouraged or at least sanctioned? What avenues of gratification should be open to the person who does not marry? Many sexual patterns formerly considered "perverse" or "immoral" are being examined anew; some are even being redefined as desirable. Mouth-genital contact—considered a "crime against nature" in many states and punishable as a felony—has apparently become relatively acceptable and common in courting and marital behavior. Many people are redefining homosexuality and bisexuality as permissible alternatives to heterosexual relationships. And some subgroups are experimenting with "mate-swapping," communal sex, and group sexual practices.

Thus the question arises as to what range of sexual patterns should be considered permissible, both personally and socially. This question is difficult to answer, in part because taboos against the study of sexual behavior in our society have blocked the accumulation of needed information about differing sexual patterns and their effects on individual and group adjustment.

The first comprehensive field studies were carried out by Kinsey, Pomeroy, and Martin (1948, 1949, 1953), who reported that, in spite of the decades our society has spent trying to suppress all but marital sexual relations, "a not inconsiderable portion of all sexual acts in

Nature and Causes of Sexual Deviations

Human Sexual Inadequacy

Maladaptive and Socially Disapproved Sexual Patterns

Alternative Sexual Patterns

which the human animal engages still fall into the category which the culture rates as 'perverse'" (1949, p. 28). This conclusion seems even more applicable today, in terms of conventional sexual mores. Admittedly, however, we do not know how much the present "sexual revolution" involves actual changes in behavior and how much it simply reflects greater frankness about what has been going on all along.

We shall begin this chapter with a brief discussion of the problem of classifying and explaining the development of deviant sexual behavior; then we shall deal with sexual inadequacy and with several maladaptive sexual patterns; and, finally, we shall consider some alternative—and often controversial—patterns of sexual behavior.

Nature and Causes of Sexual Deviations

The term *sexual deviation,* in its broadest sense, refers to sexual behavior that is different or atypical, that does not follow the prevailing patterns sanctioned by laws or the social mores of the particular society. Since socially sanctioned sexual patterns differ from one culture to another, among subgroups within a given culture, and over time, it is apparent that behavior labeled sexually deviant is not necessarily abnormal or maladaptive in the sense of being inherently detrimental to the individual or to other people. At the same time, certain patterns, such as incest and rape, have been shown to be detrimental, and are so labeled and dealt with by society.

It would appear that in the development and maintenance of maladaptive sexual behavior learning and reinforcement are of key significance. As we shall see, however, other causal factors may also be involved, or may be predominant in the total etiological pattern.

Types of deviant sexual behavior

No satisfactory classification of sexual deviations has as yet been devised. One that has commonly been used is based on: (a) adequacy of sexual behavior in terms of performance and gratification, as in impotence; (b) choice of sex objects, as in incest; (c) mode of gratification, as in rape. While this classification provides useful guidelines, it does not distinguish adequately between sexual patterns that clearly appear to be maladaptive and those that merely fail to conform to established social mores.

To avoid this difficulty, a closely related but broader and more definitive classification of sexual deviations may be used for our purposes.

1. *Maladaptive but not socially disapproved sexual patterns.* This category focuses on sexual inadequacy, broadly referred to as *impotence* in the male and *frigidity* in the female. Such sexual behavior is relatively common and may be highly distressing to the individual and/or the sexual partner as well as detrimental to their personal relationship. But while it is considered maladaptive, it is not subject to social disapproval or sanctions.

2. *Maladaptive and socially disapproved sexual patterns.* Sexual behaviors placed in this category are socially disapproved in terms of choice of sex object, mode of gratification, or both. They are viewed by most people, including mental health personnel, as clearly detrimental to the individual and/or other persons. Included here are such deviant patterns as incest, pedophilia, and rape. The incidence of such sexual behavior is relatively low, and social sanctions against offenders are often severe.

3. *Alternative sexual patterns.* Included here are a variety of sexual behaviors, ranging from premarital and communal sex to homosexuality and prostitution. Although commitment to such patterns is commonly developed on an individual basis, several of the patterns in this category are associated with supportive group structures. Most persons engaging in such behavior consider it an acceptable alternative to sexual patterns approved by traditional social mores.

In the present chapter, we shall follow this threefold classification of sexual deviations, grouping various patterns with reference to their apparent consequences in our society.

Causal factors in deviant sexual behavior

Before discussing specific deviant patterns, it will be useful to review some of the factors commonly involved in the development of such patterns.

Learning and reinforcement. As we have noted, adult sexual behavior is the result of a long process of development, and there is nothing in the undifferentiated sexual potentialities of

the infant guaranteeing that the end result will be a "normal" heterosexual pattern. An almost infinite variety exists in the sexual patterns that an individual can develop.[1]

Our view of ourselves as male or female, the social demands made upon us for playing our expected sexual role, our concept of what sexual behavior is appropriate, and our anticipation of what will be exciting and pleasurable—all these are learned, and they help determine the sexual practices we develop as adults. And through conditioning, almost any object or situation can become sexually stimulating—particularly among preadolescents and adolescents—such as erotic literature, sex scenes in plays and films, pictures of nude or partially nude individuals, and underclothing or other objects intimately associated with members of the opposite sex. Sexual arousal may also accompany strong emotional reactions—such as fear and excitement—especially if associated with the performance of some forbidden act.

With time, however, some stimuli come to be preferred to others, and erotic arousal and gratification are limited to a relatively narrow range of stimuli and behaviors. Thus some individuals may come to prefer plump or thin persons, blondes or brunettes, persons younger or older than themselves, members of their own sex or members of the opposite sex. Some persons may learn to want a considerable amount of sex play prior to actual coitus, or immediate coitus without preliminary sex play; and they may come to find satisfaction in—or be offended by—particular positions, the use of oral or anal techniques, and so on. Social expectations, models, instruction, information, and chance occurrences and reinforcements may all play key roles in this learning process.

Faulty information and lack of interpersonal competencies. Many sexual deviations are associated with faulty information about sexual

---

[1]In hermaphroditism, a rare condition, the individual possesses well-developed genital organs of both sexes. Recent investigators have concluded that hermaphrodites generally identify with the sex-role they are assigned in infancy, and that gender identity is difficult to change after an individual is more than 18 months of age (Lev-Ran, 1974; Money & Ehrhardt, 1972).

behavior. As Kaplan (1975) has pointed out:

"Our sexually repressed society has, until recently, failed to regard sex as a natural function. Thus accurate information about the sexual response has not been freely or widely available. This curtain of ignorance plus the highly emotional attitudes about erotic matters provide a fertile culture medium for the growth of ignorance, myths, and misconceptions. Myths are prevalent about ever-ready male functioning, vaginal orgasms, mutual climax, masturbation, fantasy, frigid women, and so on. A great deal of anxiety and guilt can be generated when there is a discrepancy between real experience and unrealistic expectation. Such misconceptions along with the emotional reactions which accompany them can produce sexual maladjustments and dysfunctions." (p. 14)

Ironically, many sex offenders have rigid ideas about the "sinfulness" of sex, which tends to deny them access to normal sexual outlets and to lead them to the use of deviant and socially disapproved ones.

Often the causal picture is further complicated by a lack of needed interpersonal competencies. In a study of over 800 male sex offenders, including a large percentage of rapists and pedophiles, Cohen and Seghorn (1969) pointed to both inadequate information and the "relative absence of even the most basic social attitudes and values or social skills" (p. 249).

In general, it would appear that a lack of needed information and/or interpersonal competencies provide fertile sources of sexual deviations.

Sexual frustration and other life stress. Sexual behavior depends not only on learning and pleasurable reinforcement but also on opportunities and limitations.

Our society abounds in subtle—and not so subtle—forms of sexual stimulation, yet strong social pressures are exerted to confine sexual behavior to a few patterns under specified conditions. In fact, teen-agers are often expected to refrain from sexual relations entirely, and often from masturbation and petting. The combination of stimulation and frustration can be highly stressful, and may lead to socially disapproved sexual patterns, particularly when inner controls are lowered by alcohol or other drugs. And we have seen that in prisons and other institutions where the sexes

are segregated and denied traditional sexual outlets, the incidence of deviant sexual behavior is usually much higher than in ordinary life situations.

Other stresses may also be associated with deviant sexual behavior. An early study of sex offenders from lower socioeconomic levels led Yalom (1961) to emphasize the extent to which hostility and resentment that develop in a deeply frustrating life situation may be acted out in antisocial sexual offenses, such as rape. Similarly, Hartman and Nicolay (1966) studied 91 expectant fathers apprehended for sexual offenses including exhibitionism, voyeurism, obscene phone calls, pedophilia, and rape or attempted rape. They found that these offenses seemed to be related to the increased stress that the wife's pregnancy had placed upon the husband.

In this context, the concept of multiple sexual outlets, or "total outlet," is relevant. This concept was proposed by Kinsey et al. (1948), who found that the number of outlets among American males varied between two and three, with the particular outlets used depending largely on age and social class but also varying with the strength of the sex drive and the available opportunities for gratification.

The concept of multiple sexual outlets helps explain the observation that many exhibitionists and other sex offenders are married and thus have "normal" sexual outlets in addition to their socially disapproved patterns. It also helps explain how under prolonged frustration individuals may resort to substitutive patterns of a deviant nature.

Provocation by the "victim." In some cases, individuals who commit sex offenses may be "led on" by provocative "victims."

In an early study of the files of the Detroit Police Department, Dunham (1951) reported that the victim was known to the offender in about three-fourths of the cases involving offenses against children, in half of the sexual assault cases, and in one-fourth of the cases of peeping and indecent exposure.

These findings have raised the question of whether the victim may actually encourage the sexual act. Although this seems far-fetched where child victims are concerned, it appears to have some validity with respect to cases involving adolescents and adults. The "victims"—especially in cases of sexual assault and homosexuality—may consciously or unconsciously emit cues that lead to the offender's overt response. Evidence for this hypothesis has been reported by Amir (1971), who, in a study of 646 cases of rape reported to the Philadelphia police department, found 19 percent of them to have been "victim precipitated."

Of course, there is always the possibility that offenders may misinterpret certain behaviors on the part of their victims, such as a woman's scanty attire as being "provocative," when she has no such intent; or she may accept an invitation to a man's apartment, although she does not wish to pursue the relationship beyond a certain point in terms of intimacy. Here the concept of "provocation by the victim" is open to question.

Association with other psychopathology. Many persons arrested for sexual offenses have been found to exhibit other serious maladaptive behaviors. In a pioneering study of 300 typical sex offenders in New Jersey, Brancale, Ellis, and Doorbar (1952) found only 14 percent to be psychologically "normal." The other 86 percent included individuals diagnosed as neurotics, psychotics, mental retardates, brain damaged, and psychopathic personalities. In this context, it is of interest to note Kaplan's (1975) conclusion that *"causality lies on a continuum"* which reaches from relatively minor and transitory conditions to the most profound psychopathology.

Such pathological conditions often involve either inadequate development of or the lowering of inner reality and ethical controls. There also tends to be a somewhat consistent relationship between various categories of psychopathology and particular types of sexually deviant behavior, particularly behavior of a socially disapproved type. For example, neurotics are most likely to be brought to the attention of law-enforcement officers for peeping and exhibitionism, and sociopathic personalities are frequently involved in forcible rape. Such relationships are by no means invariably found, however, and individuals manifesting various types of psychopathology may maintain conventional sexual patterns,

or they may manifest deviations other than those we have mentioned.

In the preceding discussion, we have attempted to outline certain general causal factors commonly associated with deviant sexual patterns. In the discussion of specific patterns that follows, we shall elaborate further on the nature and range of etiological factors.

Human Sexual Inadequacy

As we noted earlier, the first American researchers to break through the barrier of Puritan ethics and its taboos on the study of sexual behavior were Alfred Kinsey and his associates, whose pioneering work *Sexual Behavior in the Human Male* was published in 1948, followed by *Sexual Behavior in the Human Female* in 1953. These studies were in turn followed by the work of William Masters and Virginia Johnson (1966, 1970, 1975) who played a major role in making the investigation of human sexuality and the treatment of sexual inadequacy respectable areas of scientific endeavor.

As a result of more adequate information about human sexual behavior, a growing number of people are coming to realize that they are achieving little or none of their potential for sexual enjoyment and gratification. In essence, they are either being cheated or cheating themselves sexually. Thus the understanding and treatment of human sexual inadequacy has assumed a position of vital importance in our society.

Types of sexual inadequacy

Human sexual inadequacy refers to impairment in the desire for, or ability to achieve, sexual gratification. Such sexual inadequacy may vary markedly in degree and may adversely affect the enjoyment of sex by both partners. The most common forms of sexual inadequacy may be summarized as follows:[2]

1. *Male impotence.* This sexual dysfunction is the inability to achieve or maintain an erection. In *primary impotence*, the male has never been able to attain an erection long enough to have successful sexual relations.

In *secondary impotence*, the male has had a history of at least one ejaculation but is presently unable to produce or maintain an erection. While primary impotence is relatively rare, it has been estimated that secondary impotence has been experienced—at least on a temporary basis—by half or more of the male population.

2. *Male ejaculatory incompetence.* This dysfunction may take either of two forms. In *premature ejaculation* the male is unable to control ejaculation long enough for his partner to achieve satisfaction; in *retarded ejaculation* the male is either unable to trigger an ejaculation or has extreme difficulty in doing so. In milder forms of the latter condition he may eventually achieve an ejaculation by employing fantasy or by means of additional stimulation. Both premature and retarded ejaculation are considered common forms of male sexual inadequacy.

3. *Female orgasmic dysfunction.* This sexual dysfunction may take two somewhat related forms. In *primary orgasmic dysfunction*—commonly referred to as *frigidity*—the female is essentially devoid of sexual feelings and does not respond erotically to sexual stimulation. In *situational orgasmic dysfunction*, the female either cannot achieve an orgasm or can do so only in particular situations, as with a stranger but not with her husband. While frigidity is considered relatively rare, difficulties in achieving orgasm are considered the most common sexual complaint of women.

4. *Vaginismus.* An involuntary spasm of the muscles at the entrance to the vagina that prevents penetration and sexual intercourse is called vaginismus. In some cases, women who suffer from vaginismus are frigid, possibly as a result of conditioned fears associated with a traumatic rape experience; in other cases, however, they are sexually responsive, but are still afflicted with this disorder. This form of sexual inadequacy is relatively rare.

5. *Dyspareunia.* "Dyspareunia" means *painful coitus*; it can occur in either the male or the female. Of these various forms of sexual dysfunction, dyspareunia is the one most likely to have an organic basis, for example, in association with infections or structural pathology of the sex organs. However, it often has

---

[2]Based primarily on Masters and Johnson (1970, 1975) and Kaplan (1974, 1975).

Masters and Johnson, widely known for their studies of sexual response and their therapeutic approach to problems of sexual inadequacy, are pictured counseling a couple at their clinic in St. Louis — the Reproductive Biology Research Foundation. These investigators have concluded from their research efforts (1970) that some 50 percent of American marriages suffer from sexual inadequacy, a factor they consider largely responsible for our high divorce rate. In their view, sexual inadequacy is a form of faulty communication which probably extends to other areas of a couple's relationship as well; consequently, their treatment program is oriented toward improving communication in a marriage and preventing it from being wrecked by ignorance about sex and faulty attitudes toward it.

Stressing the concept that sex is an experience that both partners must enter into without reservation or shame, Masters and Johnson insist that fears or anxieties that either partner may have concerning intercourse — pressures that can turn it into a dreaded "command performance" — must be eliminated. In addition, they treat the married couple as a unit rather than as separate individuals.

Generally, the following steps appear to be basic to the treatment program of Masters and Johnson as well as to that of other prominent sex clinics: (a) a thorough medical examination to rule out the possibility of organic causes of the sexual dysfunction; (b) *sensate focus* — learning to experience pleasure in caressing each other's bodies and genitals while temporarily abstaining from intercourse; and (c) prescribed sexual experiences and therapy sessions. Beyond these basic principles, the formats employed by various major sex clinics may vary considerably.

For the majority of couples participating in Masters and Johnson's treatment program, it appears that a change is effected in attitudes, feelings, and communication, and that sexual relations become an intimate, normal, and desirable experience. Five-year follow-up studies of 510 married couples and 57 unmarried men and women revealed that the program's rate of failure varied markedly with the type of sexual inadequacy — from zero for cases of vaginismus and 2.2 percent for cases of premature ejaculation to 40.6 percent for cases of primary impotence. Overall, the failure rate in treatment was only 20 percent.

a psychological basis, as in the case of women who have a puritanical aversion to sexual intercourse. This form of sexual dysfunction is also rare.

Causal factors of sexual inadequacy

Both sexual desire and genital functioning may be affected by a wide range of organic conditions: injuries to the genitals, disease, fatigue, excessive alcohol consumption, and abuse of certain drugs, including tranquilizers. For males, prolonged or permanent impotence before the age of 60 is rare and almost always due to psychological factors. In fact, according to the findings of Kinsey and his associates only about one-fourth of males become impotent by the age of 70 and even here many cases are due to psychological factors. More recent studies have indicated that men and women in their 80's and 90's are quite capable of enjoying sex (Burros, 1974; Kaplan, 1975; Masters & Johnson, 1975).

Although specific causal factors may vary considerably from one type of sexual dysfunction to another, the following psychosocial factors are commonly found in studies of sexual inadequacy.

1. *Faulty learning.* In some primitive societies older members of the group instruct younger members in sexual techniques before marriage. But in our society, though we recognize that sexual behavior is an important aspect of marriage, the learning of sexual techniques and attitudes is too often left to chance. The result is that many young people start out with faulty expectations and a lack of needed information or harmful misinformation that can impair their sexual adequacy. In fact, Kaplan (1974) has concluded that couples with sexual problems typically practice insensitive, incompetent, and ineffective sexual techniques.

Many females in our society have been subjected to early training that depicted sexual relations as lustful, dirty, and evil. The attitudes and inhibitions thus established can lead to a great deal of anxiety, conflict, and guilt where sexual relations are concerned, whether in or out of marriage. Faulty early conditioning may also have taken the form of indoctrination in the idea that the woman has a primary responsibility to satisfy the man sexually—and therefore to suppress her own needs and feelings. Masters and Johnson (1970) consider such faulty learning to be the primary cause of frigidity in females. In vaginismus a somewhat different conditioning patterning occurs in which the female associates vaginal penetration with prior pain—either physical, psychological, or both—and this defensive reflex comes into operation when penetration is attempted by the sexual partner (Kaplan, 1975).

Although males may also be subjected to early training that emphasizes the evils of sex, such training apparently is a far less important factor in male impotence. However, another type of faulty early conditioning was found by Masters and Johnson (1970) to be a key factor in premature ejaculation in males. Common to the histories of such males was a first sex experience with a prostitute or in a lovers' lane parking place or other situation in which hurried ejaculation was necessary. Apparently, once this pattern was established, the individual had been unable to break the conditioned response. In other instances, initial difficulties in sexual functioning may lead to conditioned anxieties which in turn impair future performance. We shall elaborate on this point in the section that follows.

2. *Feelings of fear, anxiety, and inadequacy.* In a study of 49 adult males with a disorder of sexual potency, Cooper (1969) found anxiety to be a contributing factor in 94 percent of the cases and the primary problem for those whose potency problems had started early. Similarly, Kaplan (1974) has concluded from her studies that "a man who suffers from impotence is often almost unbearably anxious, frustrated, and humiliated by his inability to produce or maintain an erection" (p. 80). Males who suffer from premature ejaculation may also experience acute feelings of inadequacy—and often feelings of guilt as well—stemming from their lack of control and inability to satisfy their sexual partner via intercourse.

Females may also feel fearful and inadequate in sexual relations. A woman may be uncertain about how sexually attractive she is to her partner, and this may lead to anxiety and tension that interfere with her sexual enjoyment. Or she may feel inadequate because she is unable to have an orgasm or does so infrequently. Sometimes a woman who is not climaxing will pretend to have orgasm in order to make her sexual partner feel that his performance is fully adequate. The longer a woman maintains such a pretense, however, the more likely she is to become confused and frustrated; in addition, she is likely to feel resentful toward her partner for being so insensitive to her real feelings and needs. This, in turn, only adds to her sexual problems.

From a more general viewpoint, Masters and Johnson (1975) have concluded that most sexual dysfunctions are due to crippling fears, attitudes, and inhibitions concerning sexual behavior, often based on faulty early learning exacerbated by later aversive experiences.

3. *Interpersonal problems.* Interpersonal problems may cause a number of sexual dysfunctions. Lack of emotional closeness can lead to impotence or frigidity. The individual may be in love with someone else, may find his or her sexual partner physically or psychologically repulsive, or may have hostile and antagonistic feelings as a result of prior misunderstandings, quarrels, and conflicts. Often a one-sided interpersonal relationship—in which one partner does most of the giving and the other most of the receiving—can lead to feelings of insecurity and resentment with resulting impairment in sexual performance (Friedman, 1974; Simon, 1975).

For the female, lack of emotional closeness often appears to result from intercourse with a partner who is a "sexual moron"—rough, unduly hasty, and concerned only with his own gratification. As Kaplan (1974) has pointed out:

"Some persons have as much difficulty giving pleasure as others do in receiving it. These individuals don't provide their partners with enough sexual stimulation because they lack either the knowledge and sensitivity to know what to do, or they are anxious about doing it." (p. 78)

In other instances the individual may be hostile toward and not want to please his or her sexual partner. This seems to occur rather frequently in unhappy and failing marital or

Sexual concerns expressed by some college men and women

In a content analysis of 1000 letters received consecutively by "The Doctor's Bag," a column in the campus newspaper at Michigan State University, Werner (1975) found that 523 (52 percent) contained questions pertaining to sexual matters. Of these, 65 percent related to anatomy and physiology, particularly questions about female anatomy, and 35 percent related to sexual activity. The latter questions focused mainly on sexual intercourse, including oral and anal, but some also concerned petting, masturbation, and homosexuality.

The concerns expressed by female students centered on orgasmic dysfunction, both primary and situational. The following are examples of such concerns:

"I am 20 years old. My boyfriend and I have been having intercourse for a year now, but only on weekends since he goes to another school. I have never had an orgasm from intercourse alone. I have had orgasms as a result of clitoral stimulation during masturbation. My boyfriend never touches my clitoris. Is there something wrong with me? Am I undersexed?" (p. 166)

The sexual concerns expressed by male students centered on sexual dysfunction, particularly involving premature ejaculation and related problems. The following indicate the nature of such concerns:

"During sexual encounters I seem to reach orgasm very fast, always having at least one before intercourse begins . . . They even occur at odd times as when I was giving my girl a back massage. Could it be related to the fact that I never see my girl more than once a month and always feel a high degree of excitement when I do?" (p. 166)

"I cannot ejaculate willfully. The only time I ejaculate is during sleep in the form of a wet dream. This bothers me greatly as I am unable to masturbate and cannot come, even when my girlfriend has oral sex with me." (p. 167)

While Werner is well aware of the danger of generalizing from a limited sample of students who voluntarily reported their problems, he did feel that these letters indicated "the need for sex counseling and education for young people who are sexually active . . ." (p. 164). He also pointed to the unique problems in counseling this population whose members are usually not married. As one writer asked quite simply, "Do you know of anyone who counsels people who are not married?" (p. 166) other intimate relationships in which channels of communication have largely broken down and sex is performed as a sort of habit or duty or simply to gratify one's own sexual needs.

Provided there is no emotional commitment to some other person, many investigators feel that an individual should be able to experience pleasure and orgasm with any personally acceptable partner. However, Switzer (1974) has aptly pointed to a generally agreed-on conclusion: "Orgasm has especially delightful overtones when you're with a person whom you love and when you can abandon yourself" (p. 36).

4. *Changing male-female roles and relationships.* To explain the increase in impotence during the 1970s, a number of investigators have emphasized two phenomena of the past decade: (a) the increasing changes being achieved by the Women's Liberation Movement in our society and (b) the growing awareness of female sexuality (Burros, 1974). These trends have led women to want and expect more from their lives, including their sexual relationships. Women are no longer accepting the Puritan concept of being the passive partner in sex, and many are taking a more aggressive and active role in sexual relations.

While the "liberated woman" seems to "turn on" some men, she also appears to threaten the image many men have of themselves as the supposedly "dominant" partner who takes the initiative in sexual relations. In fact, some men appear to regard women who are sexually assertive and play an active role in sex as "castrating females" (Kaplan, 1974). In addition, such women make many men feel under pressure to perform. As Ginsberg, Frosch, and Shapiro (1972) have expressed it:

"This challenge to manhood is most apparent in a sexually liberated society where women are not merely available but are perceived as demanding satisfaction from masculine performance." (p. 219)

The result may be not only impaired performance but even impotence.

Of course, changing male-female roles in sexual relationships also place greater demands on the female. The expectation of taking an active rather than a passive role may cause the female to make unrealistic demands on her own sexual responsiveness—such as having a highly pleasurable orgasm each time she engages in sexual relations. Such demands are likely to lead to some degree of unfulfilled aspirations, confusion, or self-devaluation, which in turn impairs actual sexual performance. This seems especially true when the female assumes a "spectator's role" and almost literally monitors her own sexual performance—thus depriving it of spontaneity and naturalness.

5. *Homosexuality and other factors.* In some cases the sexual differentiation of individuals has taken a homosexual direction, and their erotic desires have come to be focused on members of their own sex, with corresponding loss of erotic interest in members of the opposite sex. Although most male and female homosexuals seem able to achieve sexual gratification with members of either sex, some homosexuals may be able to achieve gratification only in homosexual relations, particularly during periods in their life when their homosexual commitment is quite strong. Such individuals also may show an impairment in sexual adequacy in homosexual relationships if their commitment to this sexual pattern wanes.

Another condition that may lead to sexual inadequacy is a low sex drive and sexual apathy; sometimes it is difficult to distinguish between such persons and those who are actually impotent or frigid. In Cooper's (1969) study, men whose potency problem developed during later adulthood reported that it came following a progressive decline in sexual interest and performance over months or years. In these cases, anxiety developed only after the potency disorder had become established, and thus appeared to be the result, rather than the cause, of the disorder.

Another possible causal factor in sexual inadequacy is a rejecting and disturbed family background that makes it difficult for the individual to later give and receive affection in intimate interpersonal relationships. And as we noted in earlier chapters, sexual dysfunction is also commonly associated with depression, schizophrenia, and other maladaptive behaviors.

Treatment and outcomes

The treatment of individuals or couples for sexual dysfunctions requires considerable flexibility, depending on the problems of the individual or couple involved. For example, treatment of primary orgasmic dysfunction (frigidity) differs from that of situational orgasmic dysfunction; and that of primary impotence differs from that of premature ejaculation.

The first extensive and systematic report on the treatment of sexual dysfunction is that of Masters and Johnson (1970). While influenced by this approach, a number of recent treatment programs have been introduced with innovative methods of their own, such as that described by Kaplan (1974, 1975). The approach of Masters and Johnson and some recent innovations introduced by other investigators are described in the illustration on page 563.

Despite differences in emphasis and methods in such treatment programs, there seems to be general agreement on the importance of removing crippling misconceptions, inhibitions, and fears, and fostering attitudes toward and participation in sexual behavior as a pleasurable, natural, and meaningful experience.

With competent treatment, some 60 to 100 percent of sexual dysfunctions can be treated successfully, depending in part on the individual or couple and the nature of the problem. For example, Masters and Johnson (1970) and Kaplan (1975) have reported success rates approaching 100 percent in the treatment of premature ejaculation and vaginismus, but the success rates in male impotence and female orgasmic dysfunction are considerably lower. However, the term "competent" should be stressed here, since there are several thousand sex clinics in the United States, and the quality of treatment may range from sophisticated psychotherapy to sheer charlatanism.

Maladaptive and Socially Disapproved Sexual Patterns

The sexual deviations included in this category range from those that are socially disapproved but involve relatively mild social sanctions, such as exhibitionism and voyeurism, to those that are not only socially disapproved but carry severe sanctions, such as pedophilia and rape.

In the present discussion we shall focus on the following patterns: exhibitionism, voyeurism, fetishism, sadism, masochism, incest, pedophilia, and rape. Following our usual format, we shall deal briefly with the clinical picture, causal factors, and treatment and outcomes for each pattern. To keep our discussion of treatment as brief and as meaningful as possible, we shall rely heavily on actual case illustrations.

Exhibitionism

Exhibitionism ("indecent exposure") is the most common sexual offense reported to the police in the United States, Canada, and Europe, accounting for about one-third of all sexual offenses (Rooth, 1974). Curiously enough, it is rare in most other countries. For example, in Argentina only 24 persons were convicted of exhibitionism during a five-year period; in Japan, only about 60 men are convicted of this offense each year. In still other countries, such as Burma and India, it is practically unheard of.

Exhibitionism involves the intentional exposure of the genitals to members of the opposite sex under inappropriate conditions. The exposure may take place in some secluded location, such as a park, or in a more public place, such as a department store, church, theater, or bus. In cities, the exhibitionist often drives by schools or bus stops, exhibits

Obscene phone calls

Each year several hundred thousand obscene, abusive, and threatening phone calls are reported to telephone companies in the United States. But the problem is much more extensive than reports indicate; the police estimate that over twice as many offenses go unreported.

Men typically are the offenders in cases of obscene phone calls, most of which are made to women. Victims commonly include brides whose weddings have recently been reported in the newspaper, or women known to be home alone.

Nadler (1968) has made an extensive study of several cases of obscene phone calls. He found that the causal factors are similar to those in exhibitionism, but obscene phoning is both more aggressive and yet more distant an act. Like the exhibitionist, the obscene caller appears to suffer from pervasive feelings of inadequacy, but the anxiety and hostility he manifests in relating to the opposite sex seems to be greater.

As in the case of exhibitionism, obscene phoning tends to have a compulsive quality, but it apparently involves less sexual excitation. Fortunately, the caller does not tend to be a physical menace, despite the psychological trauma he may inflict on his victims. Regardless of the caller's relative harmlessness, however, society takes a dim view of him; both federal and local laws define his offense as a crime. Information about how to handle obscene (and other abusive) calls has been made available by telephone companies in most cities.

himself while in the car, and then drives rapidly away. In many instances, the exposure is repeated under fairly constant conditions, such as only in churches or buses, or in the same general vicinity and at the same time of day. In one case a youth exhibited himself only at the top of an escalator in a large department store. The kind of sex object too is usually fairly consistent for the individual exhibitionist. For the male offender this ordinarily involves a young or middle-aged female who is not known by the offender.

In some instances exposure of the genitals is accompanied by suggestive gestures or masturbatory activity, but more commonly there is only exposure. Although it is considered relatively rare, a hostile psychopath may accompany exhibitionism with aggressive acts and may knock down or otherwise attack his victim. Despite the rarity of assaultive behavior in these cases, and the fact that most exhibitionists are not the dangerous criminals they are often made out to be in newspaper stories, the exhibitionistic act nevertheless takes place without the viewer's consent and also may upset the viewer; thus, society considers exhibitionism to be a criminal offense.

Exhibitionism is most common during the warm spring and summer months, and most offenders are young adult males. Practically all occupational groups are represented. Among women, the exhibition of the genitals is relatively rare, and when it occurs it is less likely to be reported to the police. Usually exhibitionism by males in public or semipublic places is reported. Occasionally, however, such individuals are encouraged in their activity.

A rather handsome 17-year-old boy had been seating himself beside girls and women in darkened theaters and then exhibiting himself and masturbating. He had been repeatedly successful in obtaining approving collaboration from the "victims" before he finally made the mistake of exposing himself to a policewoman. Out of an estimated 25 to 30 exposures, he was reported on only 3 occasions.

Causal factors. In general, cases of exhibitionism appear to fall into one of three categories:

1. *Exhibitionism associated with personal immaturity.* Witzig (1968) found that about 60 percent of the cases of exhibitionism referred by courts for treatment fall into this category. Here the exhibitionism seems to be based on inadequate information, feelings of shyness and inferiority in approaching the opposite sex, and puritanical attitudes toward masturbation. Commonly, there are strong bonds to an overly possessive mother. Often the exhibitionist states that he struggled against the impulse to expose himself in much the same way that the adolescent may struggle against the impulse to masturbate, but that, as sexual or other tensions increased, he felt compelled to carry out his exhibitionistic activities. And he often feels guilty and remorseful afterward, particularly if he has achieved ejaculation.

Although over half of all exhibitionists are

married, they usually fail to achieve satisfactory sexual and personal relationships with their wives. Witzig (1968) has pointed out that

"These men almost never like to discuss sexual matters with their wives and frequently avoid undressing before them. The idea of living in a nudist colony is a repulsive thought to most exhibitionists, although they are periodically willing to show off their genitals in quite public places." (p. 78)

Many of these offenders state that they married only because of family pressure, and many married at a late age. Thus we are dealing here with an individual who is essentially immature in his sex-role development, even though he may be well educated and competent in other life areas.

Closely related to the exhibitionist's personal immaturity appears to be a second factor: doubts and fears about his masculinity, combined with a strong need to demonstrate masculinity and potency. Apfelberg, Sugar, and Pfeffer (1944), for example, cited the case of an exhibitionist who achieved sexual satisfaction only when he accompanied the exposure of his genitals with a question to his victim as to whether she had ever seen such a large penis. On one occasion the woman, instead of evidencing shock and embarrassment, scornfully assured him that she had. On this occasion, the defendant stated, he received no sexual gratification.

It is worth noting that exhibitionism rarely takes place in a setting conducive to having sexual relations. The exhibitionist attempts to elicit a reaction that confirms his masculinity without entailing the risk of having to perform adequately in sexual intercourse.

In reviewing the role of personal immaturity and sexual ignorance in exhibitionism, it is interesting to note the conclusion of Rooth (1974) that the "sexual revolution" during the last decade in the Western world may have made matters worse: the growing assertiveness of women may make the exhibitionist even more insecure while at the same time he is being bombarded by sexually suggestive material from the "emancipated" mass media, thus increasing his frustration.

2. *Interpersonal stress and acting out.* Another causal factor is suggested by the high incidence of precipitating stress. Often the married exhibitionist appears to be reacting to some conflict or stress situation in his marriage, and his behavior is in the nature of a regression to adolescent masturbatory activity. In such instances, an exhibitionist may state that exhibiting himself during masturbation is more exciting and tension-reducing than utilizing pictures of nude women.

Exhibitionism without genital arousal may take place following a period of intense conflict over some problem—often involving authority figures—with which the individual feels inadequate to cope.

"For example, a Marine who wanted to make a career of the service was having an experience with a superior that made it impossible for him to reenlist. He could not admit to himself that he could be hostile to either the corps or the superior. For the first time in his life, he exposed himself to a girl on the beach. Arrested, he was merely reprimanded and returned to the scene of conflict. A short time later he displayed his genitals to a girl in a parking lot. This time he was placed on probation with the stipulation that he seek treatment, and his enlistment was allowed to terminate in natural sequence. He never repeated the act. He was happily married and seemed to be acting out in this instance a vulgar expression of contempt." (Witzig, 1968, p. 77)

3. *Association with other psychopathology.* Exhibitionism may occur in association with a variety of more pervasive forms of psychopathology. Youths who are severely mentally retarded—both male and female—may be unaware or only partially aware of the socially disapproved nature of their behavior. Some exhibitionists come from the ranks of older men with senile brain deterioration who evidence a lowering of inner reality and ethical controls.

In other cases exhibitionism is associated with sociopathic personality disorders. Such individuals usually have a history of poor school adjustment and erratic work records; often they have had difficulties with authorities as a consequence of other antisocial acts. Their exhibitionism appears to be just one more form of antisocial behavior, in connection with which they may or may not achieve sexual excitation and gratification. In some instances, exhibitionism is associated with manic or schizophrenic reactions. For example, the only woman in a group of offenders studied by Witzig (1968) typically exposed herself prior to the onset of a full-blown psychotic episode.

Treatment and outcomes. Although some exhibitionists deny their guilt, even after conviction, stating that they were merely urinating in an inappropriate place or had forgotten to zip up their slacks, most realize that they have a problem and respond well to group therapy. Successful results with behavior therapy are also commonly reported. Such therapy usually involves aversive conditioning to exhibitionistic acts, desensitization to stresses that may have precipitated given episodes, and fostering more assertive or typical heterosexual patterns.

Aside from psychopathic offenders, who represent a distinct minority, exhibitionists rarely repeat their behavior after treatment. Hence, therapy ordinarily is a sufficient deterrent against further offenses, and imprisonment is not required.

Voyeurism

Voyeurism, scotophilia, and *inspectionalism* are synonymous terms referring to the achievement of sexual pleasure through clandestine peeping. Although children often engage in such behavior, it occurs as a sexual offense primarily among young males. These "peeping Toms," as they are commonly called, usually concentrate on females who are undressing, or on couples engaging in sexual relations. Frequently they masturbate during their peeping activity.

Causal factors. How do people develop this pattern? In the first place, viewing the body of an attractive female seems to be quite stimulating sexually for many males. The saying "He feasted his eyes upon her" attests to the "sexualization" of merely "looking" under certain conditions. In addition, the privacy and mystery that have traditionally surrounded sexual activities have tended to increase curiosity about them.

If a youth with such curiosity feels shy and inadequate in his relations with the other sex, it is not too surprising for him to accept the substitute of peeping. In this way he satisfies his curiosity and to some extent meets his sexual needs without the trauma of actually approaching a female, and thus without the failure and lowered self-status that such an approach might lead to. As a matter of fact, peeping activities often provide important compensatory feelings of power and superiority over the one being looked at, which may contribute materially to the maintenance of this pattern. Also, of course, the suspense and danger associated with conditions of peeping may lead to emotional excitement and a reinforcement of the sexual stimulation.

If a peeper is married, he is rarely well adjusted sexually in his marriage.

A young married college student had an attic apartment which was extremely hot during the summer months. To enable him to attend school, his wife worked; she came home at night tired and irritable and not in the mood for sexual relations. In addition, "the damned springs in the bed squeaked." In order "to obtain some sexual gratification" the youth would peer through his binoculars at the room next door and occasionally saw the young couple there engaged in erotic scenes. This stimulated him greatly, and he thereupon decided to extend his activities to a sorority house. However, during his second venture he was reported and apprehended by the police. This offender was quite immature for his age, rather puritanical in his attitude toward masturbation, and prone to indulge in rich but immature sexual fantasies.

While more permissive laws concerning "adult" movies and magazines have probably removed much of the secrecy from sexual behavior as well as provided an alternative source of gratification for would-be peepers, their actual effect on the incidence of voyeurism is a matter of speculation. For many voyeurs these movies and magazines probably do not provide an adequate substitute for secretly watching the "real life" sexual behavior of an unsuspecting couple.

Although a peeper may become somewhat reckless in his observation of courting couples and thus may be detected and assaulted by his subjects, peeping does not ordinarily have any serious criminal or unalterable antisocial aspects. In fact, many people probably have rather strong inclinations in the same direction, which are well checked by practical con-

Pornography is generally defined as sexually explicit materials—writings, pictures, or movies—whose primary aim is to arouse the viewer sexually. While this definition seems simple enough, it is subject to interpretation; for example, one person may view the painting of a nude woman as pornography while another views it as art. Even judges who officiate in obscenity trials may differ in their opinions concerning the pornographic nature of specific erotic materials.

In recent years a good deal of controversy and concern have focused on the permissive cultural climate in our society, a climate which permits "hard-core" X-rated films, erotic paperbacks, and a wide range of other "pornographic" materials to be marketed openly. Four questions are commonly raised here:

1. Does exposure to pornography lead to undesirable alterations in sexual orientation and to sex crimes?

2. Does exposure to pornography trigger antisocial sexual acts, such as pedophilia or rape?

3. Does exposure to pornography tend to divest sex of meaningful love relationships, so that it becomes an end in itself?

4. Does exposure to pornography threaten the family and moral fabric of our society?

In terms of available evidence, the answer to each of the preceding questions would appear to be "no." For example, rapists and child molesters have reported less exposure to pornography during their formative years than normal curious young males; nor is there any evidence that exposure to pornographic materials alters an individual's orientation in the direction of maladaptive sexual patterns, or that it triggers transient antisocial acts such as pedophilia or rape. In fact, after Denmark legalized pornography, there was a significant reduction in sexual crimes, particularly in offenses against children.

After a thorough assessment of the scientific evidence, the U.S. Commission on Obscenity and Pornography concluded that "If a case is to be made against pornography, it will have to be made on grounds other than demonstrated effects of a damaging personal or social nature" (1970, p. 139). The commission recommended against the censorship of pornographic material for adults who seek it out; the commission did, however, support the view that there should be restricted access to such materials for minors. The latter recommendation was made as a safeguard, even though there was no reliable evidence that such exposure was harmful.

While the recommendations of the commission were applauded by civil-liberty groups, they were condemned by church groups and other organizations who failed to see any merit in pornography and feared the possibility of long-range harm to American morals as well. So the controversy over pornography continued, and, in 1974, the Supreme Court ruled to permit local governments to censor pornography to conform to local views and sensibilities. Whether this decision will end the national controversy on pornography or simply transfer it to the community level remains to be seen.

Based on Goldstein (1974), Goldstein and Kant (with Hartman, 1973), Kutchinsky (1972), Nathan and Harris (1975), and U.S. Commission on Obscenity and Pornography (1970).

siderations and moral attitudes concerning people's rights to privacy.

Treatment and outcomes. The treatment of "peeping Toms" follows the same procedures as those discussed for exhibitionism, and the outcomes are equally favorable. Only in atypical cases—usually involving pervasive psychopathology—is treatment likely to prove difficult or unsuccessful.

Fetishism

In fetishism there is typically a centering of sexual interest on some body part or on an inanimate object, such as an article of clothing. Males are most commonly involved in cases of fetishism—reported cases of female fetishists are extremely rare. The range of fetishistic objects includes breasts, hair, ears, hands, underclothing, shoes, perfume, and similar objects associated with the opposite sex. The mode of using these objects for the achievement of sexual excitation and gratification varies considerably, but it commonly involves kissing, fondling, tasting, or smelling the object.

In order to obtain the required object, the fetishist may commit burglary, theft, or even assault. Probably the articles most commonly stolen by fetishists are women's underthings. One young boy was found to have accumulated over a hundred pairs of panties from a lingerie shop when he was apprehended. In such cases, the excitement and suspense of the criminal act itself typically reinforce the sexual stimulation, and in some cases actually constitute the fetish – the article stolen being of little importance. For example, one youth admitted entering a large number of homes in which the entering itself usually sufficed to induce an orgasm. When it did not, he was able to achieve sexual satisfaction by taking some "token," such as money or jewelry.

Not infrequently, fetishistic behavior consists of masturbation in association with the fetishistic object. Here, of course, it is difficult to draw a line between fetishistic activity and the effort to increase the sexual excitation and satisfaction of masturbation through the use of pictures and other articles associated with the desired sexual object. Utilization of such articles in masturbation is a common practice and not usually considered pathological. However, where antisocial behavior such as breaking and entering is involved, the practice is commonly referred to as fetishistic. For example, Marshall (1974) reported a rather unusual case of a young university student who had a "trouser fetish"; he would steal the trousers of teen-agers which he then used in physical contact during masturbation.

A somewhat different, but not atypical, pattern of fetishism is illustrated by the case of a man whose fetish was women's shoes and legs.

The fetishist in this case was arrested several times for loitering in public places, such as railroad stations and libraries, watching women's legs. Finally he chanced on a novel solution to his problem. Posing as an agent for a hosiery firm, he hired a large room, advertised for models, and took motion pictures of a number of girls walking and seated with their legs displayed to best advantage. He then used these pictures to achieve sexual satisfaction and found that they continued adequate for the purpose. (Adapted from Grant, 1953)

Another atypical type of fetishism involves setting fires. While people who set fires are a mixed group, a sizeable number of fires – including some involving loss of life – are set by fetishists who have come to experience relief of sexual tension from setting and watching a fire burn (Nelson, 1970). Such fires include brush and forest fires, as well as fires in buildings.

Causal factors. In approaching the causal factors in fetishism, we may again note that many stimuli can come to be associated with sexual excitation and gratification. Probably most people are stimulated to some degree by intimate articles of clothing and by perfumes and odors associated with the opposite sex. Thus the first prerequisite in fetishism seems to be a conditioning experience. In some instances this original conditioning may be quite accidental, as when sexual arousal and orgasm – which are reflexive responses – are elicited by a strong emotional experience involving some particular object or part of the body.

The endowment of a formerly neutral stimulus with sexual arousal properties has been demonstrated in an interesting experiment by Rachman (1966), who created a mild fetish under laboratory conditions. A photograph of women's boots was repeatedly shown with slides of sexually stimulating nude females. Subjects came to exhibit sexual arousal – as measured by changes in penile volume – to the boots alone; this response generalized to other types of women's shoes.

In some instances, however, the associations involved in fetishism are not easy to explain. Bergler (1947) cited an unusual case in which a man's sex life was almost completely absorbed by a fetishistic fascination for exhaust pipes of automobiles. Nor would just any exhaust pipe do; it had to be in perfect shape, that is to say, undented and undamaged, and it had to emit softly blowing gases. This became far more attractive to him than sexual behavior with women.

Fetishistic patterns of sexual gratification usually become the preferred patterns only when they are part of a larger picture of maladjustment; the latter typically involves doubts about one's masculinity and potency and fear of rejection and humiliation by members of the opposite sex. By his fetishistic practices and mastery over the inanimate object – which comes to symbolize the desired sexual object—the individual apparently safeguards himself and also compensates somewhat for his feelings of inadequacy.

Treatment and outcomes. When apprehended, fetishists are usually quite embarrassed and penitent about their behavior, but are prone to deny its sexual connotations. In group therapy this process of denial is usually stripped away very rapidly, so that the fetishist has to come to grips with his actual problem. In an early study utilizing a behavior therapy approach, Kushner (1965) reported the successful treatment of a 33-year-old male with a longstanding fetish involving stealing women's panties and masturbating while wearing them. He could achieve orgasm only by means of his fetishistic practice. Initially Kushner utilized electric shock in association with women's panties to eliminate the fetish. Then a desensitization program was undertaken to alleviate the man's fears and anxieties associated with heterosexual relations. This procedure also proved successful and at last report the individual was married and enjoying an active heterosexual life. Later studies utilizing behavior therapy—particularly aversive conditioning—have also reported successful results in the treatment of fetishism (Bandura, 1969; Marshall, 1974; Stekel, 1971).

Sadism

The term *sadism* is derived from the name of the Marquis de Sade (1740–1814), who for sexual purposes inflicted such cruelty on his victims that he was eventually committed as insane. Although the term's meaning has broadened to denote cruelty in general, we shall use it in its restricted sense, to denote achievement of sexual stimulation and gratification through the infliction of pain on a sexual partner. The pain may be inflicted by such means as whipping, biting, and pinching; the act may vary in intensity, from fantasy to severe mutilation and in extreme cases even to murder. Males are ordinarily the offenders, although Krafft-Ebing (1950) has reported a number of cases in which sadists were women. In one unusual case, the wife required her husband to cut himself on the

The paraphernalia in this shop window is sold to some sadists and masochists for their sexual needs.

arm before approaching her sexually. She would then suck the wound and become extremely aroused.

In some cases sadistic activities lead up to or terminate in actual sexual relations; in others, full sexual gratification is obtained from the sadistic practice alone. A sadist may slash a woman with a razor or stick her with a needle, experiencing an orgasm in the process. Showing the peculiar and extreme associations that may occur is the case of a young man who entered a strange woman's apartment, held a chloroformed rag to her face until she lost consciousness, and then branded her on the thigh with a hot iron. She was not molested in any other way. Sometimes sadistic activities are associated with animals or with fetishistic objects instead of other human beings. East (1946) cited the case of a man who stole women's shoes, which he then slashed savagely with a knife. When he was in prison, he was found mutilating photographs that other prisoners kept in their cells by cutting the throats of the women in them. He admitted that he derived full sexual gratification from this procedure.

The following is a more serious case involving sadistic murder:

The offender, Peter Kursten, was 47 years old at the time of his apprehension in Dusseldorf, Germany, for a series of lust murders. He was a skilled laborer, well groomed, modest, and had done nothing that annoyed his fellow workers.

Peter came from a disturbed family background, his father having been an alcoholic who had been sent to prison for having intercourse with Peter's older sister. Peter's own earliest sexual experiences were with animals. When he was about 13 years old, he attempted to have intercourse with a sheep, but the animal would not hold still and he took out a knife and stabbed her. At that moment he had an ejaculation.

As a consequence of this experience, Peter found the sight of gushing blood sexually exciting, and he turned from animals to human females. Often he first choked his victim, but if he did not achieve an orgasm he then stabbed her. Initially he used scissors and a dagger, but later he took to using a hammer or an axe. After he achieved ejaculation, he lost interest in his victim, except in taking measures to cover up his crime.

The offender's sexual crimes extended over a period of some 30 years and involved over 40 victims.

Finally apprehended in 1930, he expressed a sense of injustice at not being like other people who were raised in normal families. (Adapted from Berg, 1954)

The news media have reported more recent cases in which the victims have been mutilated and killed in association with sadistic sexual practices. Included here would be the "horror story" of the sadistic homosexual murders of 27 teen-age boys in Texas during the early 1970s. However, there is a lack of available scientific case material on which to base definitive conclusions concerning the actual clinical picture or the causal factors involved.

Causal factors. The causal factors in sadism appear roughly comparable to those in fetishism.

1. *Experiences in which sexual excitation and possibly orgasm have been associated with the infliction of pain.* Such conditioned associations may occur under a variety of conditions. In their sexual fantasies many children visualize a violent attack by a man on a woman, and such ideas may be strengthened by newspaper articles of sadistic assaults on females. Perhaps more directly relevant are experiences in which an individual's infliction of pain on an animal or another person has given rise to strong emotions and, unintentionally, to sexual excitement. We have noted elsewhere the connection between strong emotional stimulation and sexual stimulation, especially during the adolescent period. Just as in fetishism—where simple conditioning seems to make it possible for almost any object or action to become sexually exciting—conditioning can also be an important factor in the development of sadistic tendencies.

2. *Negative attitudes toward sex and/or fears of impotence.* Sadistic activities may protect an individual with negative attitudes toward sex from the full sexual implications of his behavior, and at the same time may help him express his contempt and punishment of the other person for engaging in sexual relations. Several early investigators have described male sadists as timid, feminine, undersexed individuals, and sadistic behavior as apparently designed to arouse strong emotions in the sex object which, in turn, arouses a great peak of sexual excitement in the sadist and makes orgasm possible. The sadist apparently receives little or no satisfaction if his victim remains passive and unresponsive to the painful stimuli. In fact, he usually wants her to find the pain exciting, and may even insist that she act pleasurably aroused when being stuck with pins, bitten, or otherwise hurt.

For many sexually inadequate and insecure individuals, the infliction of pain is apparently a "safe" means of achieving sexual stimulation. Strong feelings of power and superiority over his victim may for the time shut out underlying feelings of inadequacy and anxiety.

3. *Association with other psychopathology.* In schizophrenia and other severe forms of psychopathology, sadistic sexual behavior and sadistic rituals may result from the lowering of inner controls and the deviation of symbolic processes. Wertham (1949) has cited an extreme case in which a schizophrenic with puritanical attitudes toward sex achieved full sexual gratification by castrating young boys and killing and mutilating young girls. He rationalized his actions as being the only way to save the victims from later immoral behavior. More recent examples of sadistic mutilation and murder associated with deviant sexual and thought processes can be found in the police files of any large city.

Treatment and outcomes. There is little definitive data on the treatment of sadism. However, since erotic fantasies may serve as evocative stimuli for overt sexual deviations, the following case reported by Davison (1968) is of interest.

A 21-year-old male college student's sexual behavior had been limited to masturbatory fantasies of inflicting injuries on women. In treatment, the student was initially instructed to masturbate while looking at pictures of nude women. After such conventional stimuli had acquired sex-arousing value, a second procedure was introduced in which sadistic fantasy was paired with nauseous imagery, such as "steaming urine with reeking fecal boli bobbing on top which he drank." Eventually, the sadistic fantasies were supplanted by normal masturbatory fantasies. Interpreting this counterconditioning as consistent with self-control processes, the student

was encouraged to engage in normal college dating. Prior to his treatment, he stated that he had never been aroused by women and had only twice kissed them. But now he found himself attracted in a normal sexual way to the women he dated. This treatment required only 6 sessions.

Of course, where the individual does not want treatment or where his deviation is associated with severe psychopathology, successful treatment may be more difficult or impossible.

Masochism

The term *masochism* is derived from the name of the Austrian novelist Leopold V. Sacher-Masoch (1836–1895), whose fictional characters dwelt lovingly on the sexual pleasure of pain. As in the case of the term *sadism*, the meaning of *masochism* has been broadened beyond sexual connotations, so that it includes the deriving of pleasure from self-denial, expiatory physical suffering such as that of the religious flagellants, and hardship and suffering in general. We shall restrict our present discussion to the sexual aspects of masochistic behavior. The clinical picture is similar to those in sadistic practices, except that now pain is inflicted on the self instead of on others (Sack & Miller, 1975).

Causal factors. Patterns of masochistic behavior usually come about through conditioned learning: as a result of early experiences, an individual comes to associate pain with sexual pleasure. For example, Gebhard (1965) cited the case of a young adolescent who was having the fractured bones in his arm hurriedly set without an anesthesia. To comfort the boy, the physician's attractive nurse caressed him and held his head against her breast. As a consequence, he experienced a "powerful and curious combination of pain and sexual arousal," which led to masochistic—as well as sadistic—tendencies in his later heterosexual relations.

Such sayings as "being crushed in his arms" or "smothered with kisses" reveal the association commonly made between erotic arousal and pain or discomfort. Thus it is not surprising that "mild sado-masochistic" acts such as biting may occur in an attempt to increase the emotional excitement of the sexual act.[3] However, such behavior does not result in serious physical injury, nor does it serve as a substitute for sexual relations. In actual masochism, however, the individual experiences sexual stimulation and gratification in association with the experience of pain under certain conditions. In his early studies of deviant sexual behavior, for example, East (1946) cited the case of a young woman who frequently cut herself on the arms, legs, and breasts, and inserted pins and needles under her skin. She experienced sexual pleasure from the pain and from seeing the blood from the incisions.

Treatment and outcomes. In dealing with masochism, we are again faced with an almost complete lack of definitive data.

In an interesting treatment program involving three cases of exhibitionism, two of transvestism, and one of masochism, Abel, Levis, and Clancy (1970) utilized the same aversive conditioning techniques. The first step involved making tapes describing each patient's deviant sexual behavior. These tapes were then associated with electric shock; but each shocked run was followed by runs in which the patient could avoid the shock by verbalizing normal sexual behavior in place of the segment of the tape accompanied by shock. In this laboratory situation, deviant sexual responses—as indicated by penile erections to inappropriate stimuli—were inhibited in all subjects, and patient reports indicated that this suppression was generalized to real-life situations. This procedure was successful in suppressing deviant sexual behavior for at least 18 weeks, while yielding evidence of sustained benefits in terms of fostering more socially acceptable and normal sexual outlets. In a more recent study, Larson, Easter, and Ward (1974) described the successful group treatment of 11 masochistic female patients who had not improved in previous treatment. After identifying the behaviors the patients wished to change, these therapists designed

tasks in a hierarchy of five stages in group therapy to help them reach their goals.

Cases of masochism associated with pervasive psychopathology, of course, may prove difficult or impossible to treat successfully.

Incest

Culturally prohibited sexual relations between family members, such as a brother and sister or a parent and child, are called *incestuous*. Although certain societies have approved incestuous relationships—at one time it was the established practice for Egyptian pharaohs to marry their sisters to prevent the royal blood from being "contaminated"—the incest taboo is virtually universal among human societies.[4]

An indication of the very real risks involved in such inbreeding has been provided by Adams and Neel (1967), who compared the offspring of 18 nuclear incest marriages—12 brother-sister and 6 father-daughter—with those of a control group matched for age, intelligence, socioeconomic status, and other relevant characteristics. At the end of 6 months, 5 of the infants of the incestuous marriages had died, 2 were severely retarded mentally and had been institutionalized, 3 showed evidence of borderline intelligence, and 1 had a cleft palate. Only 7 of the 18 infants were considered normal. In contrast, only 2 of the control-group infants were not considered normal—one showing indications of borderline intelligence and the other manifesting a physical defect. Lindzey (1967) concluded that

". . . the consequences of inbreeding are sufficiently strong and deleterious to make it unlikely that a human society would survive over long periods of time if it permitted, or encouraged, a high incidence of incest. In this sense, then, one may say that the incest taboo (whatever other purposes it may serve) is biologically guaranteed." (p. 1055)

A number of investigators have also maintained that the incest taboo also serves to pro-

---

[3]In this context it may be noted that Blanch (1974) has questioned the commonly held view that masochistic sexual behavior is more characteristic of females than males.

[4]An extensive review of the literature on incest which documents its near-universality and cites the various reasons given for its taboo may be found in Devroye (1973) and Schwartzman (1974).

duce greater variability among offspring, and hence to increase the flexibility and long-term adaptability of the population (Schwartzman, 1974).

In our own society incestuous behavior does occur, but its actual incidence is unknown since it takes place in a family setting and only comes to light when reported to law enforcement or other agencies. However, Kinsey et al. (1948, 1953) reported an incidence of 5 cases per 1000 persons in a sample of 12,000 subjects, and Gebhard et al. (1965) found 30 cases per 1000 subjects in a group of 3500 imprisoned sex offenders. In both these studies brother-sister incest was reported as being 5 times more common than the next most common pattern—father-daughter incest. Mother-son incest is thought to be relatively rare.[5] In occasional cases, there may be multiple patterns of incest within the same family.

Causal factors. For an understanding of incestuous behavior, it may be noted that incestuous fantasies and desires are common during the adolescent period, and it is not uncommon for fathers to have such feelings toward their daughters. However, social mores and prohibitions are usually so deeply ingrained that such desires are rarely acted out. Bagley (1969) has suggested that several different causal patterns may be involved where incestuous behavior does occur. The following list represents a slight modification of his schema.

1. *Accidental incest.* When brothers and sisters share the same bedroom during the preadolescent or adolescent period (which is not uncommon among poorer families), they may tend to engage in sexual exploration and experimentation. In some cases older brothers seduce their younger sisters without any apparent understanding of the social prohibitions or possible consequences.

2. *Incest associated with severe psychopathology.* In the case of psychopathic fathers, the incest may simply be part of an indiscriminate pattern of sexual promiscuity; in

other individuals, such as alcoholics and psychotics, the incestuous relations may be associated with the lowering of inner controls.

3. *Incest associated with pedophilia.* Here a father has an intense craving for young children as sex objects, including his own daughters.

4. *Incest associated with a faulty paternal model.* Here a father sets an undesirable example for his son by engaging in incestuous relations with his daughter or daughters, and may encourage his son to do likewise.

5. *Incest associated with family pathology and disturbed marital relations.* Here a family has low morals or is disorganized. In some instances a rejecting, hostile wife may actually foster father-daughter incest.

In general, incestuous fathers who come to the attention of authorities do not have a history of sexual offenses or other criminal behavior, nor do they show a disproportionate incidence of prior hospitalization for mental disorders (Cavillin, 1966). In fact, such fathers tend to restrict their sexual patterns to family members rather than seeking and engaging in extramarital sexual relations. For example, in his intensive study of 12 fathers convicted of incestuous relations with their daughters, Cavillin (1966) reported that only 2 of the 12 had resorted to extramarital relations, despite feeling unloved and rejected by their wives.

Cavillin further reported that the youngest father in the group was 20 and the oldest was 56, and that the average age was 39. The average age of the daughters was 13, the youngest being 3 and the oldest 18. Five of the 12 fathers had had a relationship with more than 1 daughter, usually beginning with the oldest; in 11 of the cases the relationships had gone on for some time—from 3 months to 3 years—before being reported. In all of the cases the fathers were reported by the daughters. In all cases, too, the father felt rejected and threatened by his wife, a pattern also noted by other investigators.

The psychological effect of the incestuous relationship on the daughter appears to depend on her age when the relationship occurs and the anxiety and guilt, if any, she experiences. Most girls studied who were still adolescent expressed feelings of guilt and depression

---

[5]Authorities are more likely to deal with cases of father-daughter than brother-sister incest, since the latter are less likely to be reported.

over this incestuous behavior. Some girls in this situation turn to promiscuity; others run away from home to escape the stressful situation.

Treatment and outcomes. Ordinarily, when an incestuous relationship is broken up, it is by the action of the family members themselves. Many offenses go unreported because, in the case of father-daughter incest, the family may be reluctant to lose the father's economic support. And in cases of brother-sister incest, they may prefer that the brother be admonished and warned, rather than reported and punished. Whatever the circumstances, little occurs in the way of corrective treatment. Nevertheless, the continuation of incestuous patterns over long-range periods is the exception rather than the rule.

Pedophilia

In pedophilia the sex object is a child; the intimacy usually involves manipulation of the child's genitals, or, in the case of a female victim, partial or complete penetration of the vagina. Occasionally the child is induced to manipulate the sex organ of the pedophiliac or to engage in mouth-genital contacts.

Offenders are diverse in terms of the act committed, the intentionality of and general circumstances surrounding the act, and age, education, and developmental history. Most pedophiliacs are men, but women occasionally engage in such practices. The average age of these offenders is about 40 years. Many offenders are or have been married, and many have children of their own. In an early study of 836 pedophiliac offenders in New Jersey, Revitch and Weiss (1962) found that the older offenders tended to seek out immature children, while younger offenders preferred adolescent girls between 12 and 15. Girls outnumbered boys as victims in the ratio of more than 2 to 1.

In most cases of pedophilia the victim is known to the offender, the sexual behavior may continue over a sustained period of time, and usually there is no physical coercion. Although in some cases the offenders may be encouraged or even seduced by their victims,

Swanson (1968) found provocation or active participation by the victim in only 3 of the 25 cases he studied.

Whether or not there is an element of provocation by the victim, the onus is always on the offender, for society's norms relating to pedophilia are explicit. Since pedophiliacs may subject children to highly traumatic emotional experiences as well as physical injury, this is not surprising. An alleged offender is sometimes considered guilty until proven innocent, however, and a number of men have served time in penal institutions because children or their parents interpreted simple affection as attempted intimacy or rape. On the other hand, many cases of sexual assault on children undoubtedly go unreported to spare the child a further ordeal (Sgroi, 1975).

Causal factors. The following causal categories are based on (a) an intensive study of 38 pedophiliac offenders living in a segregated treatment center (Cohen & Seghorn, 1969), and (b) in-depth interviews of a large number of pedophiliacs, some of whom had managed to avoid arrest and others who had been arrested and served time (Rossman, 1973).

1. *The personally immature offender,* who has never been able to establish or maintain satisfactory interpersonal relationships with male or female peers during his adolescent, young adult, or adult life. This was by far the most common type. He is sexually comfortable only with children, and in most cases knows the victim. Usually the act is not impulsive but begins with a type of disarming courtship which eventually leads to sexual play. Either male or female children may be the victims.

2. *The regressed offender,* who during adolescence shows apparently normal development, with good peer relationships and some dating behavior and heterosexual experiences.

"However, throughout this period there exist increasing feelings of masculine inadequacy in sexual and nonsexual activities. And, as he enters adulthood, his social, occupational, and marital adjustment is quite tenuous and marginal. There is frequently a history of an inability to deal with the normal stresses of adult life and alcoholic episodes become increasingly more frequent and result in the breakdown of a relatively stable marital, social, and work adjustment. In almost all instances the pedophilic acts are precipitated by some direct confrontation of his sexual adequacy by an adult female or some threat to his masculine image by a male peer." (Cohen & Seghorn, 1969, p. 251).

The most frequent precipitating event is the offender's discovery that his wife or girlfriend is having an affair with another man. In most of these cases the victim is a female child.

In contrast to the personally immature offender, the regressed offender is not acquainted with his victim, and the act is characteristically impulsive. For example, the offender may be driving a car, see a child, and become overwhelmed by sexual excitation.

3. *The "conditioned" offender.* Included here are individuals who have had their definitive sexual experiences with young boys, often in reformatories; this conditioned behavior continues into adulthood in terms of sexual preference. These individuals are usually callous and exploitive in their sexual behavior, and tend to cruise cheap motion picture theaters and other areas in search of vulnerable children. In many instances, they pick up young hustlers who are available in most large cities. Some of these men are careful about avoiding detection, while others are not and have a history of one or more arrests for such offenses.

4. *The psychopathic offender.* The individuals included here are psychopathic personalities who prey on children in search of new sexual thrills. In some instances, such individuals patronize child prostitutes who are usually available in large cities as well as in some foreign countries.

This category also includes aggressive psychopaths whose behavior is motivated by both aggressive and sexual components:

"The primary aim is aggression, and is expressed in cruel and vicious assaults on the genitalia or by introducing the penis or elongated objects into the victim orally or anally. The sexual excitement increases as an apparent function of the aggression, but the orgasm itself either does not occur or must be reached through masturbation. (Cohen & Seghorn, 1969, p. 251)

Such offenders usually have a history of antisocial behavior and, in general, could be described as hostile, aggressive psychopaths. Ordinarily they select a boy as the object of their aggression. Psychopaths—particularly those who use coercion—are prone to denying their offenses or placing the blame on their victims.

A number of investigators have also pointed to severe psychopathology, in addition to antisocial personality, in pedophiliac offenders. This includes alcoholics, schizophrenics, and older individuals where brain deterioration has led to a weakening of normal inhibitory controls. In fact, pedophilia and exhibitionism are the most common sexual offenses committed by senile and arteriosclreic individuals.

Treatment and outcomes. In most states, pedophilia is punishable by confinement in prison or a mental hospital. For some offenders, imprisonment appears to be the only course to take: although it may do little to modify the behavior of the offender, it does protect society. However, since many pedophiliacs experience genuine remorse and want to change their maladaptive behavior, an increasing number are being screened for treatability and given a choice between imprisonment and treatment in a state mental hospital or other appropriate facility. Here, modern rehabilitative programs—typically utilizing group therapy and, in some instances, behavior modification—are considered highly effective.

Rape

In rape, sexual behavior is usually directed toward a normal sex object but under antisocial conditions.[6] Almost exclusively in reported cases, the male is the offender. Depending on the victim's age, such offenses are referred to as: (a) *statutory rape*, which involves the seduction of a minor; and (b) *forcible rape*, in which the unwilling partner is over 18. It is with the latter type that we are concerned in this section.

Rape has increased more rapidly in the last decade than any other type of violent crime;

---

[6]Here we are referring to heterosexual rape. Statistics on homosexual rapes, particularly among males, are not available, although scattered reports indicate that such incidents do occur.

in 1974 the FBI reported over 55,000 cases of forcible rape. The actual incidence is considered to be 3 to 4 times as high as these figures indicate, since most cases go unreported due to the social stigma involved and the additional trauma the victim is likely to undergo if she reports being raped. Relatively speaking, rape is a young man's crime. Over 60 percent of all arrests are of persons under 25 years of age, with the greatest concentration occurring in the 16-to-24 age range. Surprisingly, almost half of these offenders are married and living with their wives at the time of the crime. As a group, rapists come from the low end of the socioeconomic ladder. Typically they are unskilled workers with low intelligence, low education, and low income.

Rape tends to be a repetitive activity rather than an isolated act, and most rapes are planned events. About 80 percent of rapists commit the act in the neighborhood in which they reside; most rapes take place in an urban, nocturnal setting. However, the specific scene of the rape varies greatly. The act may occur on a lonely street at night, in an automobile in the parking lot of a large shopping center, in the elevators or hallways of buildings, and in other situations where the victim has little chance of assistance. Rapists have also entered apartments or homes by pretending to be deliverymen or repairmen.

About a third or more of all rapes involve more than one offender and are often accompanied by beatings. The remainder are single-offender rapes in which the victim and offender often know each other; the closer the relationship, the more brutal the beating received by the victim is likely to be. When the victim struggles against her attacker, she is also likely to receive more severe injuries or in occasional cases to be killed. However, if she doesn't struggle, society tends to frown on her behavior as encouraging the rapist.

In addition to the physical trauma inflicted on the victim, the psychological trauma may be severe. One especially unfortunate factor in rape is the possibility of unwanted pregnancy. Another is the effect such an incident may have on the victim's marriage or other intimate relationships. The situation is likely to be particularly upsetting to the husband if he has been forced to watch the rape, as is occa-

sionally the case when a victim is raped by the members of a juvenile gang, or if there is some suspicion of the victim having engaged in provocative behavior that encouraged the rapist.

There is no actual data on "victim-precipitated" rape, although this concept has received a good deal of attention from police and social scientists alike. Often it is assumed that the victim is suspect if she has an extensive history of sexual behavior with multiple partners, if she failed to take ordinary precautionary measures, or if she failed to put up a struggle. It is questionable, however, that such information justifies drawing any conclusions about the role of the victim. In any event, about 15 percent of all forcible rapes reported to the police are found upon investigation to be unwarranted; that is, no "forcible" rape attempt or offense actually occurred (Uniform Crime Reports, 1975).

Causal factors. Both sexual and aggressive components are involved in the act of rape—in varying degrees and combinations. On the basis of an intensive study of 27 convicted rapists, Cohen and Seghorn (1969) have suggested the following four distinguishable patterns:

1. *Displaced aggression.* In these cases the act is primarily aggressive.

"The sexual behavior is used to physically harm, to degrade, or to defile the victim in the service of this aggressive intent. The acts are experienced by the offender as the result of an 'uncontrollable impulse' and almost always follow some precipitating, disagreeable event involving a wife, girl friend, or mother. The victim is brutally assaulted, and those parts of the woman's body which usually are sexually exciting frequently become the foci for the offender's violence." (p. 250)

Here sexual excitation is minimal or even absent. The offender must masturbate to achieve an erection, and in many cases he cannot reach an orgasm. Thus the behavior appears to be a release not for intense sexual tensions but for displaced hostility and aggression—particularly since the offender does not usually know his victim.

2. *Compensation.* Here sexual excitation is the key component, and the aggressive fea-

Rape trauma syndrome

Reactions to forcible rape vary greatly, but most victims apparently find the experience highly traumatic. The following represents an integration of data from two major studies, Sutherland and Scherl (1970) and Burgess and Holmstrom (1974), and points up a rather typical psychological trauma syndrome consisting of three phases.

1. Acute reaction
"In the moments, hours, and days immediately following the rape, the victim's acute reactions may take a variety of forms including shock, disbelief, and dismay. She often appears at the police station or the hospital in an agitated, incoherent, and highly volatile state. Frequently she is unable to talk about what has happened to her or to describe the man who has assaulted her. Sometimes the victim will initially appear stable only to break down at the first unexpected reminder of the incident. . . . The Phase One reaction normally resolves within a period of a few days to a few weeks." (Sutherland & Scherl, 1970, p. 504)

During this initial phase, deep concern often centers around telling one's parents or mate about the incident, and about whether they will be understanding or rejecting. Such statements as "They told me this would happen" or "He will never understand" are common. Often the victim expresses self-doubts about her own possible involvement. Unfortunately, however, the attitude of "blame the victim" seems to be deeply ingrained in our society. This attitude tends to complicate the problem of whether or not to bring charges.

2. Outward adjustment
"After the immediate anxiety-arousing issues have been temporarily settled, the patient generally returns to her usual work, school, or home pursuits. . . . [She] announces all is well and says she needs no further help.

"It is our impression that this period of pseudo-adjustment does not represent a final resolution of the traumatic event and the feelings it has aroused. Instead, it seems to contain a heavy measure of denial or suppression. The personal impact of what has happened is ignored in the interest of protecting self and others.

"During this phase the victim must deal with her feelings about the assailant. Anger or resentment are often subdued in the interest of a return to ordinary daily life. The victim may rationalize these feelings by attributing the act to blind chance ('it could have happened to anyone'), to 'sickness' on the part of the assailant, or to an extension of the social struggle of black against white or of poor against rich. In similar fashion and for the same reasons the victim's doubts about her role in the assault are also set aside." (Sutherland & Scherl, 1970, p. 507)

The duration of this second phase was usually brief, and appeared to depend on such factors as the victim's stress tolerance, the way in which she was treated as a rape victim by significant others, and the degree of residual fear and trauma which remained to be worked through. Often the trauma became apparent during the process of reorganization in Phase Three.

3. Integration and resolution
"Phase Three begins when the victim develops an inner sense of depression and of the need to talk. It is during this period that the resolution of the feelings aroused by the rape usually occurs. Concerns which have been dealt with superficially or denied successfully reappear for more comprehensive review. The depression of Phase Three is psychologically normal and occurs for most young women who have been raped.

"There are two major themes which emerge for resolution in this phase. First, the victim must integrate a new view of herself. She must accept the event and come to a realistic appraisal of her degree of complicity in it. Statements such as 'I should have known better than to talk to him . . .' or 'I should never have been out alone' emerge at this time. Second, the victim must resolve her feelings about the assailant and her relationship to him. Her earlier attitude of 'understanding the man's problems' gives way to anger toward him for having 'used her' and anger toward herself for in some way having permitted or tolerated this 'use.' "

Although a specific incident or discovery, such as a diagnosis of pregnancy or need to identify the assailant for police, may precipitate Phase Three, the phase frequently begins with "a more general deterioration . . . of the defenses of Phase Two . . . [with the victim] thinking increasingly about what has happened . . . and functioning progressively less well" (Sutherland & Scherl, 1970, p. 508).

In recent years "hot lines" and other facilities have become available for assisting rape victims. Increasing attention has also been focused on how women can best protect themselves from would-be rapists, as well as on the criminal prosecution of offenders. As Burgess and Holmstrom concluded, rape "is not a private syndrome. It should be a societal concern, and its treatment should be a public charge" (p. 985).

tures are so minimal that if the victim struggles at all, the offender flees.

"In these acts the primary aim is clearly sexual and the aggression is in the service of gratifying the sexual desires. The offender is always in a state of intense sexual excitation and often has an orgasm in the simple pursuit of the victim or upon making some physical contact. The recurrent fantasy in such offenders is that the victims will yield, submit to intercourse, in which he will be especially virile and so pleasing to the victim that she will become enamoured with him and invite him to repeat the sexual acts." (p. 250)

Aside from episodic assaults, these offenders appear to manifest no other antisocial behavior. Typically they are extremely passive and submissive, and almost obsessively concerned with feelings of sexual inadequacy. After an assault they may feel guilty and much concerned about the well-being of the victim.

3. *Sex aggression diffusion.* Here the aggressive and sexual components appear to coexist, so that

". . . the offender is not able to experience . . . sexual desires without a concomitant arousal of aggressive thoughts and feelings. Further, he projects such feelings onto his victim and sees her struggles and protestations as seductive—'Women like to get roughed up; they enjoy a good fight.' Such perceptions are made in the context of very brutal assaults. In offenders where this pattern is present, all object relationships, with both men and women, show this same quality of an eroticization of aggressive behavior." (p. 250)

Such individuals tend to be loud and assertive, and women who come in contact with them may feel both seduced and overwhelmed.

4. *Impulse.* In this pattern, the act of rape is based on impulse and has little to do with either sexual or aggressive feelings.

"The rape is frequently carried out in the context of some other antisocial act such as robbery or theft. . . . The act is opportunistic, narcissistic, and impulsive, and such an offender has a history of predatory, antisocial behavior from his late childhood, preadolescent years." (p. 250)

Although the classification of Cohen and Seghorn was based on a limited sample, it is supported by many earlier as well as later

findings. It does appear appropriate, however, to add one additional category that is implicit in their work as well as that of several other investigators.

5. *Antisocial personality and other pervasive psychopathology.* In an early study of 100 rapists, Kopp (1962) found a high incidence of antisocial or psychopathic personalities, which he described this way:

"This antisocial psychopath is a cold, seemingly unfeeling man who has always taken what he wanted from others without apparent concern for the feelings of his victims or for the consequences of his act. For him, rape is just another instance of aggressive taking, except that in this case he steals sexual satisfaction rather than money or property. When questioned about his offense, he often responds with callous sarcasm, completely devoid of guilt or concern. He may well simply respond with the statement, 'I wanted it so I took it.' The rape fits so well with his character structure and is so typical of his general behavior pattern that he can see nothing wrong with the act, and often goes on to rationalize that his victim probably enjoyed it. He wants no part of therapy unless he sees it as a means of manipulating his way out of incarceration." (p. 66)

Many of the rapists in the *displaced aggression* and *sex aggression diffusion* categories of Cohen and Seghorn would undoubtedly qualify as psychopathic personalities. In any event, persons of this type constitute the largest percent of all rapists.

However, some rapists show other kinds of severe psychopathology. In manic reactions, schizophrenia, and various organic psychoses, for example, the lowering of inner controls may lead to physical assault and occasionally to forcible rape. However, during acute psychotic episodes the individual is likely to be so disorganized as to be capable only of indiscriminate physical assault rather than the coordinated behavior required for forcible rape. In some instances there is a "drunken aggressor," whose behavior may range from clumsy attempts to gain acceptance from a female he mistakenly believes to be available, to pathological violence accompanying an alcoholic lowering of inhibitions. In a study of 77 convicted rapists in New Mexico, for example, Rada (1975) found that 35 percent were alcoholics, and 50 percent were under the influence of alcohol at the time the criminal act was committed.

Treatment and outcomes. As indicated by the illustration on page 581, increasing emphasis is being placed on assisting the victim to deal with the psychological, interpersonal, and legal problems commonly associated with being raped.

Because of the suffering they cause their victims, convicted rapists may be subjected to long prison sentences, particularly if the victim is beaten.[7] The imprisonment seems to have little value, aside from protecting society from further ravages by the offender during the time he's imprisoned. This is particularly true for psychopathic rapists who are not readily amenable to treatment and tend to repeat their criminal behavior. For nonpsychopathic offenders who are personally immature or emotionally disturbed, the outcome of treatment may be more favorable.

Adequate data concerning the use of behavior therapy are not available, but modified aversive procedures may well prove effective. Drugs have proven helpful in reducing sex drive in some individuals who manifest sexually deviant patterns, including pedophilia and rape; in some countries chronic sexual offenders may be given a choice between castration and long imprisonment (Bancroft, Tennent, Loucas, & Cass, 1974; Sturup, 1968; Taus & Susicka, 1973). In fact, during the period from 1950 to 1970, in California 370 defendants chose to be castrated in sex offense cases rather than face long prison terms (*Los Angeles Times*, May 9, 1975). However, this represents a very drastic approach, and the question of its use is complicated by serious ethical and social issues.

---

[7]Of adults arrested for forcible rape, about 75 percent are prosecuted for that offense. Of those prosecuted, about 35 percent are found guilty of rape, and another 15 percent or so are convicted of lesser offenses (Uniform Crime Reports, 1975).

Alternative Sexual Patterns

As we have noted, the sexual patterns or styles in this general category are considered by many to be acceptable alternatives to traditional sexual patterns. Though often subject to social disapproval, there is a lack of conclusive evidence that these patterns are necessarily maladaptive, nor are persons engaging in them ordinarily subjected to legal sanctions—a notable exception being homosexuality. However, legal sanctions with respect to homosexual activities are gradually being removed: California, for example, passed a law in 1975 repealing the century-old state statute that prohibited a variety of sex acts among consenting adults in private, including persons of the same sex.

In our discussion of alternative sexual patterns we shall include masturbation, premarital and marital patterns, prostitution, homosexuality, transvestism, and transsexualism.

Masturbation

Masturbation is defined as self-stimulation of the genitals for sexual gratification. It has been traditionally condemned on religious and moral grounds, as well as for its allegedly harmful physical effects. Everything from physical weakness to impotence, mental deterioration, and insanity have been attributed to it. At one time hospital authorities maintained separate wards for patients whose insanity was presumably due to this practice. Even today many young people are still taught that masturbation is a vile habit that can be prevented with a little self-control.

Many a young person has fought against masturbating and promised not to do it again; then mounting sexual tension led to failure of this resolve. It is difficult to imagine anything more admirably suited to inevitable self-devaluation and personality damage. Often, too, the threat of social disapproval and scorn has been added to an already stressful situation. In one physical education class, for example, an instructor told his students that the effects of masturbation could be detected "by the baggy appearance of the genitals." Through such misinformation, he engendered the widespread fear that others could detect the consequences of such "despicable" behavior. Such fears may not only interfere with an individual's personal and social adjustment but also with his subsequent marital adjustment.

Thus it is worth emphasizing that masturbation as practiced by the average adolescent has no known harmful physiological effects, and is actually considered a normal and healthy sexual outlet for young people. In those instances where masturbation may be considered maladaptive, it is usually part of a larger picture of maladjustment. Children who feel unhappy, lonely, and unwanted may center too much of their activity around masturbatory practices in an attempt to compensate for their frustrations. Occasionally, masturbation may be used as a form of hostile behavior, as in the rather extreme case in which 25 sixth-grade boys masturbated en masse before their female teacher. These boys came from socially disadvantaged homes and their behavior apparently represented a sort of mass protest based on feelings of frustration.

Masturbation may continue into adult life at the expense of normal heterosexual behavior—for example, in the case of an individual who is extremely shy and fearful of the opposite sex; when a person finds his or her spouse unattractive and prefers the more exciting and desirable persons depicted in the fantasies that accompany masturbatory activities; or when the person has strong but inhibited homosexual inclinations and prefers the figures of the same sex in the masturbatory fantasies to heterosexual relations.

Even though masturbation may occur as part of a larger picture of maladjustment, it is ordinarily a normal phase of development that precedes adult heterosexual behavior, and a practice that some persons may revert to under conditions of deprivation. Usually the only undesirable features of masturbation are the worry, guilt, and self-devaluation that may be associated with it.

Premarital and marital patterns

Traditional sexual mores in our society have emphasized abstinence from sexual relations prior to marriage and fidelity to one's spouse following marriage. In recent years, however, these mores have been increasingly challenged—both in theory and in practice.

Premarital sexual relations and cohabitation. Based on their studies, Kinsey et al. (1948, 1953) estimated that 83 percent of males and 50 percent of females had intercourse before marriage. Although the incidence today is not known, the figure is probably higher largely as a result of more "enlightened" views of sexual behavior and the availability of the Pill, which has removed much of the fear formerly associated with premarital sex (Kaplan, 1974, 1975; Masters & Johnson, 1975; Verner & Stewart, 1974).

But although premarital sexual relations may be on the increase, there is no evidence of widespread, indiscriminate sexual activity. Even among persons who no longer consider marriage a prerequisite for sexual relations, emphasis is usually placed on some kind of loving relationship or mutual commitment before sexual involvement. As Sorenson (1973) has pointed out from his extensive surveys of sexual attitudes and behavior among adolescents in America, even though a love affair may last only a week, a month, or a year, it is still considered a special type of event that should enrich one's life if it is to be meaningful and worthwhile.

In this context, it is of interest to note a form of nonmarital relationship which has emerged in our society—*cohabitation*. In cohabitation, the person lives quite openly with a member of the opposite sex on a relatively stable basis—sharing room, board, and bed. Cohabitation has received widespread attention on college campuses; estimates of its incidence among college youth range from 10 to 33 percent, depending on a variety of factors, including the location and type of college (Macklin, 1974).

Although cohabitation may lead to marriage, it is not necessarily a form of "trial marriage." Nor is it equivalent to the expression "shacking up," which implies strong emphasis on sexual relations. Rather it may be described as an "arrangement," or "living together." In this arrangement, the emphasis is on the total relationship as it evolves; sex is only one aspect, although it is assumed that sexual intimacy may grow in importance and meaning as the relationship grows. In essence, cohabitation offers an alternative to the "dating game," and is considered by its advocates as more authentic and meaningful than the transitory interpersonal and sexual relationships often involved in serial dating. It also offers the possibility of a regular sexual partner, which many feel is less hypocritical than dating or even going steady, since it does not maintain a pretense of nonsexual involvement.

It is too early as yet to assess the typical effects of cohabitation on the persons involved, or to determine whether it will lead to happier marriages. In any event, there were well over 900,000 divorces granted in the 12-month period prior to March 1974—an increase of over 200,000 from 1970—and marriages dipped in 1974 in part because an increasing number of young people decided to delay making marital commitments. Thus it is not surprising that a number of investigators think cohabitation should be considered seriously as a transitory step toward eventual marriage or as an alternative pattern to traditional marriage (Macklin, 1974; Thorman, 1973, 1974).

Unconventional marital patterns. In our society, as in many others, extramarital sexual relations have traditionally been regarded as a more serious deviation than premarital relations, subject to correspondingly more severe social and legal sanctions. Adultery has usually been regarded as grounds for separation or divorce and officially it has been rather generally condemned. Yet in the report of Kinsey et al. (1953), extramarital relations at some time during marriage were attributed to 50 percent of men and 27 percent of women. Many investigators believe that such behavior is increasing, especially among women because of the liberating influence of the Pill and other contraceptive devices and women's growing economic independence and freedom.

Whatever its actual incidence, marital infidelity seems to have become for some people a lighthearted and guilt-free activity. Apparently many females as well as males find it quite easy to convince themselves that an extramarital affair is essential for maintaining their mental health, fully enjoying life, or making a marriage tolerable. Moreover, an increasing number of men and women seem willing to accept the loss of sexual exclusivity in their marriage as the price of its permanence. Where spouses were once gripped by feelings of rejection, jealousy, and hostility when learning of such behavior, many now appear relieved that their marriage is suffering "nothing more serious than infidelity."

However, marital infidelity as it has traditionally taken place in our society is no longer the entire picture; for in the last decade a number of alternative marital patterns have emerged that may be subsumed under the general headings of "co-marital sexual agreement" or "permissive matrimony."

It is not our intent in the present context to deal with these alternative marital patterns in detail, since little is known about their actual effects. But while it seems unlikely that marital patterns will return to their traditional mold, there are indications that the sexual "avant-garde"—including those who engage in swinging, group marriage, and so on—is declining in followers and influence. For example, there were an estimated 1 to 1½ million people participating in swinging in 1972, but by 1974 the number had dropped some 20 percent, and the decline seems likely to continue into the late 1970s (*Time*, 1974).

In essence, the question seems to narrow down—in terms of both premarital and marital relationships—to how man-woman relationships will evolve over time in a changing society. Although it is risky to predict the future, it would appear likely that such relationships will avoid depersonalized sex while exploring new depths of interpersonal and sexual intimacy.

Prostitution

Prostitution is defined as the provision of sexual relations in return for money. Technically, there are four types of prostitution, the most common involving heterosexual relations for which the female is paid. There is also heterosexual prostitution for which the male is paid by the female, male homosexual prostitution for which a male provides sexual relations for another male, and female homosexual prostitution for which a female provides sexual relations for another female. The last three types appear to be relatively rare. Hence our focus is on the first type—prostitution involving heterosexual relations for which the female is paid.

Prostitution has flourished throughout history, often being referred to as "the world's oldest profession." In some societies prostitutes are accorded high social status; where prostitution is governmentally regulated, they are accepted much as persons associated with any other social institution. In most segments of our own society, however, prostitution has traditionally been considered evil, and prostitutes have been subjected to legal sanctions and relegated to low social status. There are an estimated 500,000 or more "career" prostitutes in the United States, as well as an equivalent number of persons who serve as part-time prostitutes.

For an indication of the proportion of men in this country who frequent prostitutes, we have only the findings of Kinsey et al. (1948), which, in turn, bear only on the white male population. According to these figures 69 percent of white males had some experience with prostitutes; however, for many men there was only one such experience. The investigators estimated that contact with prostitutes provided less than 5 percent of the total sexual outlet of the population sampled—far lower than in countries where prostitution is governmentally controlled. Packard (1968) reported a decrease in the number of young college males who frequent prostitutes as a consequence of changing sexual mores and the more ready availability of sexual relations with girlfriends.

Since there has been relatively little systematic research on prostitution in the United States, there are many questions for which we lack clear-cut answers. For example, one might ask: (a) Why do men frequent prostitutes? (b) Why and how do women become prostitutes? (c) What sort of relationship do prostitutes have with their clients? (d) What kind of social structure do most prostitutes enter when they become part of "the life"? and (e) What is the outcome for women who make a career of prostitution? Available evidence leads more to conjecture than to hard fact, but it is evident that the answers will vary for different individuals.

Why men frequent prostitutes. Among the reasons commonly reported for men's frequenting of prostitutes are: (a) insufficient opportunity for other types of heterosexual experience, as is often the case with military personnel; (b) desire to discover what such an experience may have to offer, and, in the case of some older men, to have sexual relations with a much younger woman; (c) desire to avoid responsibilities generally associated with sexual relations; (d) difficulty in securing sexual relations with other women—possibly because of timidity or a physical defect; and (e) desire to find a partner willing to engage in deviant sexual practices.

Proportionately it would appear that the largest numbers of males who go to prostitutes are either not married, or are separated or divorced—or are married to wives whom they do not find sexually attractive and hence turn to prostitutes as an alternative and more stimulating source of sexual gratification, which can be had for money but without personal or legal involvement.

Why and how women become prostitutes. Research studies have ascribed widely different motives and characteristics to females who become prostitutes (Gagnon & Simon, 1973). In general, however, it would appear that the main consideration is money—the entry into what appears to be a quick, easy, and unpressured way to make a living. There does not appear to be any systematic process of recruitment, at least in the United States, but rather a process of "enlistment."

Females who do enlist come from all social classes, although the majority appear to come from lower-class or lower-middle-class homes. However, some come from upper-middle and upper-class families and have had every "advantage" in terms of education and material resources. At the other extreme are females from the black ghettos and other poverty-stricken areas who have not been so fortunate and turn to prostitution as the most accessible option for making money and maintaining at least a marginal way of life. In fact, Haggerty (1973) has concluded that "prostitution seems to be a natural 'dumping ground' for uneducated and unemployed women in a male-dominated society" (p. 7). Often prostitutes come from unstable families and have histories of frequent sexual episodes during adolescence. Somewhere along the line they may receive money as well as other presents for their sexual favors, and become interested in the possibility of a career in prostitution.

The inclination to become a prostitute must be implemented by some actual means of entering the profession. In a minority of cases, this may be achieved by entering a house of prostitution or brothel where training is provided. However, an increasing number of women gain entry to "the life" by establishing a dependent relationship with an experienced prostitute or a man who operates as a pimp. All but 1 of the 33 call girls Bryan (1965) studied in the Los Angeles area had personal contact with someone engaged in call-girl activities. In some instances they had been friends; sometimes the contact has started with a homosexual relationship between the two. The initial contact usually determined the type or social level of prostitution at which the woman began. These "social levels" ranged from streetwalking to serving a "select clientele" as a "high-class" call girl.

Once the contact is acquired and the decision made to become a prostitute, the novice typically enters a period of apprenticeship, which may last for several months in the case of call girls. After acquiring the necessary skills and a clientele, she has completed her training period and can go into business for herself.

The prostitute-client relationship. The personality makeup of prostitutes and their relationships with their clients appear to be highly variable.

Although there appears to be a higher-than-average incidence of psychopathology among prostitutes, Jackman, O'Toole, and Geis (1963) have concluded that most prostitutes have normal intelligence and come from an average educational background. Especially as we go up the social scale to the "high-class" call girls, we appear to be dealing in the main with physically attractive, well-educated, and sophisticated young women who believe that prostitution is a perfectly acceptable business venture and preferable to working at some other job. In some instances, of course, they actually do hold other jobs and work as prostitutes in their off-hours; in other cases, their jobs involve entertaining out-of-town businessmen, a responsibility that may or may not include sexual relations.

It has been presumed that the prostitute views her behavior strictly as a matter of business and does not experience orgasm or emotional arousal during a professional contact. However, the relationship appears to vary. For streetwalkers in large cities, who may never expect to see their clients again, the encounter is brief and businesslike; for prostitutes who have repeated contacts with the same client, there may be some emotional involvement. Bryan (1966) found a wide variety of relationships between prostitutes and their clients, ranging from coldness and hostility on the woman's part to friendship and sexual gratification.

The world of prostitution. The world of the prostitute is essentially a subculture with its own values, inhabitants, and required social skills. In general, great value is placed on achieving maximum gains from minimum effort and on cooperating with other working women—although prostitutes often do not like each other. The "johns" (customers) are pictured as basically exploitative, and therefore open to exploitation. And the women tend to view prostitution as an honest occupation—certainly no more dishonest than marrying for money.

As Gagnon and Simon (1973) have pointed out, "The world of the prostitute is primarily composed of other prostitutes, clients, steerers, and procurers, and in some cases pimps; it may include lesbian lovers or madams; and—finally—the police and other agents of law enforcement" (p. 229). Steerers and procurers consist primarily of bellboys, desk clerks, taxi drivers, and other persons who act

Even prostitutes are organizing. Here Margo St. James (center), at the "First Hookers' Convention" in San Francisco, discusses the organization she founded, COYOTE ("call off your old tired ethics").

as "go-betweens" and, of course, receive some monetary or other reward for their services in steering clients to the prostitute.

The social skills required to adapt to the world of prostitution depend on the level of involvement. For example, streetwalkers, bar girls, and call girls need to acquire a much wider range of skills than prostitutes in bordellos where men come to them under some degree of supervision. Many streetwalkers and some bar girls rely heavily on pimps who occupy a despised role in conventional society. Often a prostitute becomes emotionally attached to her pimp, usually because he is the only person she feels she can really trust and with whom she can share her experiences and problems. Possibly in an attempt to maintain his loyalty—or out of a vague sense that the money she earns is somehow "tainted"—she may turn over more of her earnings to him than she is required to.

In the decreasing number of cases where a madam is involved, she essentially serves as the prostitute's employer and supervisor. Hirschi (1962) has described her role as follows:

"The madam . . . hires and fires, makes rules, punishes those who break them, and generally super-

vises the activities of girls on the job. She often keeps lists of customers and girls who may be available if extra help is needed. She may find it necessary to employ accessory personnel such as maids, cooks, bouncers, and spotters. Her contacts with madams in other cities enable her to assist girls in finding new positions. Her problems include those involved in meeting the sometimes rapidly changing tastes of her customers and of working out some sort of stable arrangement with city officials and the police. (p. 39)

In many instances, the world of prostitution is part of the larger world of organized vice. However, the picture appears to vary markedly from one city or region of the country to another.

The outcome of a career in prostitution. The great majority of prostitutes do not spend their entire adult lives in "the life." However, some prostitutes, particularly the older and less attractive ones who have no other source of income, find it very difficult to get out of the profession until they are forced out by age. As Young (1967) has put it, "The older whores will say quite simply: 'There is no way out.' The younger ones will keep their chins up and pretend to themselves they're not like the rest.

Nobody ever went on the game for keeps" (p. 123).

Gagnon and Simon (1973) have pointed out that conditions in the United States make leaving the life of prostitution more difficult than it is in many other countries. For example, in Denmark

"there is no statute against the act of taking pay for a sexual act as long as the female has another occupation. Danish authorities hope that through such a mechanism sufficient ties will be maintained to the conventional community so that the woman may have a past other than one of prostitution when she chooses to leave this career." (p. 233)

In addition, of course, she has some other means of making a living, rather than prostitution.

In the United States, it is often difficult for the prostitute to leave such a life. She usually lacks necessary skills for obtaining needed employment in other areas; in addition, there is the problem of adapting to a new self-concept and to a new value orientation toward sex. Often, too, possible police records may have led to decreasing ties with the regular world and to a close identification and involvement with the world of prostitution. Nevertheless, many prostitutes do eventually marry and attempt to establish a more satisfying life pattern. Obviously serious problems may arise in the process of such a readjustment, including that of dealing with her past—if it is known to her partner—in the new relationship. However, in a study of 22 former prostitutes, Bess and Janus (1974) reported that such a readjustment can be achieved—both on interpersonal and occupational levels.

In any event, despite all the romanticizing of prostitution in movies and other mass media, the world of the prostitute is generally considered a difficult and ultimately unrewarding one (Gagnon & Simon, 1973). As Polly Adler (1953) summed it up in her book about her own experience, "Believe me, whoring is just a slow form of self-destruction."

Homosexuality

Homosexual behavior is sexual behavior directed toward a member of one's own sex; it is generally referred to as "lesbianism" for female relationships. Homosexuality has existed throughout recorded history and among some peoples has been tacitly accepted. The ancient Greek, Roman, Persian, and Moslem civilizations all condoned a measure of homosexuality, and the practice increased as these civilizations declined. In later Greece and Rome, for example, homosexual prostitution existed openly. In fact, it was quite popular for Roman matrons to engage in lesbian activities with their slaves. There is no evidence, however, that homosexuality was an important contributing factor in the decline of these civilizations, as some critics have charged (NAMH, 1971).

In Elizabethan England, an attitude of permissiveness was taken toward homosexuality without apparent harmful effects; in contemporary England, legislation has been passed making it legal for two consenting adults to engage privately in homosexual acts. Most cultures, however, have condemned homosexuality as socially undesirable. In the Netherlands and Denmark, for example, there are no laws against homosexuality, but it is strongly disapproved (Weinberg & Williams, 1974). In our own society, homosexuals—particularly males—are often subject to arrest and imprisonment as well as various forms of social disapproval and discrimination. Nevertheless, homosexuals may be well adjusted, well educated, and highly successful in their occupations. Many have made outstanding contributions in music, drama, and other fields.

Not a few of the notable figures of history—including Alexander the Great, Sappho, Michelangelo, Oscar Wilde, Peter Tchaikovsky, Gertrude Stein, and Virginia Woolf—are thought to have been homosexuals.

Continuum of sexual behavior. Contrary to popular opinion, it is not possible to divide people into two clear-cut groups—homosexuals and heterosexuals. Rather, these labels signify extreme poles on a continuum; in between, we find many individuals whose experiences and desires combine both heterosexual and homosexual components. Kinsey et al. (1948), in one of the first extensive studies of male homosexuals, found that of their white male subjects:

13 percent had reacted erotically to other males without having overt homosexual experiences after the onset of adolescence.

37 percent had had homosexual experience to the point of orgasm after the onset of adolescence.

50 percent of those who remained unmarried to the age of 35 had had overt homosexual experience to the point of orgasm since the onset of adolescence.

18 percent revealed as much of the homosexual as the heterosexual in their histories.

8 percent engaged exclusively in homosexual activities for at least three years between the ages of 16 and 55.

4 percent were exclusively homosexual from adolescence on.

Homosexual relationships were found to be far less common among women and, of those reporting homosexual responses, only about a third had proceeded to the point of orgasm (Kinsey et al., 1953).

Recent investigators have concluded that lesbianism is more common than previous data would indicate, and that homosexuality is on the increase among both males and females. However, the apparent increase may simply reflect our national climate of greater openness toward sex. As Hoover (1973) has pointed out, "No one is sure whether more women are becoming lesbians now or whether they are just more visible" (p. 9).

If we can assume that the number of homosexuals has not changed drastically since Kinsey's studies were made, about 2.6 million men and 1.4 million women in the United States are exclusively homosexual. If we add those who are exclusively homosexual during a period of several years in their lives or who consistently engage in homosexual acts even though they are not exclusively homosexual, the overall figure for men and women would probably approximate some 20 million persons (*APA Monitor*, 1974).

Are homosexuals "sick"? In our society, heterosexuality has been regarded as the "appropriate" mode of sexual behavior, while homosexuality has been regarded as a mental disorder and homosexuals as "sick" persons in need of treatment.

However, research findings indicate that most homosexuals manifest no more evidence of personality maladjustment than would be expected in any matched sample of heterosexuals (Freedman, 1975; Hooker, 1957; Thompson, McCandless & Strickland, 1971; Weinberg & Williams, 1974). Thus the assumption that homosexuality is a mental disorder had been challenged by an increasing number of psychologists and psychiatrists, and, finally, the trustees of the American Psychiatric Association voted to drop homosexuality from the official list of mental disorders in the DSM-II. So while on December 14, 1973, homosexuals were considered mentally disordered sexual deviants, on December 15, 1973, they were no longer so considered. In effect, the millions of "gay" people in our society had undergone an "instant cure" as a result of a vote of the trustees of the American Psychiatric Association.

Since the DSM-II is the official classification of mental disorders followed by psychologists and medical groups in North America, the APA decision is certain to have considerable impact in other countries as well as the United States; it signals a new orientation toward homosexuality as an alternative sexual lifestyle. It does not mean, however, that there is likely to be a marked increase in homosexuality. Rather, it provides each individual with greater freedom for self-determination and self-expression in sexual behavior.

Stereotypes of homosexuals. Various attempts have been made to categorize homosexuals. Such labeling is crude and stereotyped at best and misleading at worst, but it nevertheless does give some idea of the range of homosexual patterns and life-styles, and also of the impact of societal pressures on those who practice homosexuality.

1. The "blatant" homosexual. Here we are dealing with individuals who fit the popular stereotype of the homosexual—the lisping, limp-wristed, swishing caricature of femininity, in the case of the male. His lesbian counterpart, called a "dyke," "stud," or "butch," flaunts her masculinity, even to the point of trying to look like a man. Also included in this category are the "leather boys," who advertise their sadomasochistic homosexuality by wearing leather jackets, chains, and boots. Some transvestites, or "TVs," who enjoy wearing the clothes and often assuming the behavior of the opposite sex, fit in this category, too. However, as we shall see, many transvestites are not homosexuals.

2. *The "desperate" homosexual.* The so-called desperate homosexuals are males who tend to haunt public toilets ("tearooms") or steam baths, apparently driven to homosexual behavior but unable to face the strains of establishing and sustaining a serious homosexual relationship. In his study of the "tearoom trade," Humphreys (1970) referred to such behavior as "impersonal sex in public places" and pointed out that barring unusual developments, "an occasionally whispered 'thanks' at the conclusion of the act constitutes the bulk of even whispered communication" (p. 13).

Of the subjects in Humphreys' study, 54 percent were married. Apparently the "tearoom" is used by many such individuals in an effort, through the anonymity of these contacts, to conceal their homosexuality from their wives—and perhaps even from themselves. Humphreys cited the case of a successful businessman who visited "tearooms" almost daily:

"I guess you might say I'm pretty highly sexed (he chuckled a little), but I really don't think that's why I go to tearooms. That's really not sex. Sex is something I have with my wife in bed. It's not as if I were committing adultery by getting my rocks off—or going down on some guy—in a tearoom. I get a kick out of it. Some of my friends go out for handball. I'd rather cruise the park. Does that sound perverse to you?" (p. 19)

3. *The secret homosexual.* Although members of this group range across all class and racial lines, they tend to come from the middle class and to hold positions that they try to protect by concealing their homosexuality. Often they are married, wear wedding rings, and have wives and employers who never know about their double lives. They are extremely skilled at camouflage and at "passing" as straight. They generally prefer subdued clothes, and maintain a suitably conservative masculine appearance. Since they do not frequent "tearooms" or "gay bars" they may continue their homosexual behavior unsuspected throughout their adult lives. Only a few close friends, their lovers, and occasionally their psychotherapists know about their homosexuality. However, living in continuing fear of detection and possible social sanctions often adds to their adjustive problems.

4. *The situational homosexual.* There are a variety of situations in which individuals engage in homosexual behavior without any deep homosexual commitment. Both males and females may engage in homosexuality in prisons and other institutions, for example, but such individuals usually resume heterosexual behavior on their release. Some prisoners act as homosexual prostitutes. Such individuals may not have homosexual inclinations themselves but may merely engage in homosexual practices for economic advantage.

Davis (1968) has also cited instances of homosexual rape among prisoners in sheriff's vans, detention centers, and prisons. Typically, such assault involves anal intercourse, and apparently it is perpetrated by an individual or a gang who do not consider themselves homosexuals but are attempting to assert dominance and masculinity. Except in penal institutions, however, force appears rare in homosexual activity.

5. *The bisexual.* Individuals who engage in both homosexual and heterosexual practices during a sustained period of their lives are considered "bisexual." Many "desperate homosexuals" would fit into this category, particularly those who are married.

The occurrence of bisexuality is not surprising, since homosexuality is not necessarily an all-or-nothing pattern, and many people have learned to respond sexually in varying degrees to both females and males. For example, Weinberg and Williams (1974) found that about 1 gay male in 5 described himself as falling into one of the following categories: (a) predominantly heterosexual but significantly homosexual; (b) equally homosexual and heterosexual; and (c) predominantly homosexual but significantly heterosexual. As contrasted with men who were exclusively homosexual, bisexual males were found to be more concerned about passing as heterosexuals, have less identification with the gay community, and feel more guilty and anxious about their homosexual behavior. However, these investigators did not find bisexuals to be "marginal men"—to be suffering from psychological problems as a consequence of confusion about their sexual identity or lack of integration into the heterosexual or homosexual worlds. Rather, they seemed quite capable of adapting to this life-style.

In understanding these various stereotypical patterns of homosexuality, it is useful to note the conclusion of Weinberg and Williams (1974) that

" 'homosexual' can refer to a number of things—inclination, activity, status, role, or self-concept—and that a person need not be equally 'homosexual' in all respects. Thus, we find a variety of combinations of being homosexual which include some of these factors and exclude others, for example, hustlers who engage in homosexual activity but deny the self-concept, the married man who has the inclination but does not act on it, and so forth." (p. 208)

Adjusted homosexuals. The majority of homosexuals accept their homosexuality, fulfill responsible social roles, and are often closely associated with the gay community. We have previously pointed to research findings indicating that as a group homosexuals evidence no more personality maladjustment than do heterosexuals. In their extensive study of male homosexuals, for example, Weinberg and Williams (1974) failed to find any major differences in psychological well-being between homosexuals and the male population in general. And although there is little available research data, this finding would appear to apply to lesbians as well, when compared to the general female population (Ohlson, 1975).

Many homosexuals establish intimate and stable relationships with one other person. While these stable relationships are more common among lesbians than male homosexuals, they are by no means exclusive to lesbians. For example, the findings of the Institute for Sex Research cited in Bonnell (1974) indicated that almost one-fifth of gay white males feel that a stable and permanent relationship is the most important consideration in their lives. A minority of such couples enter into a "homosexual marriage," often performed in a church ceremony by a homosexual minister, but generally without benefit of a marriage license.

Similarly, Jensen (1974) found that in the "real" world, as contrasted with controlled environments such as prisons and related institutional facilities,

"female homosexuals often form relatively long-lasting relationships with other female homosexuals with whom they share the same interests. When this relationship includes a common residence and economical cooperation as well as sexual relations, the marital union is established. . . . In these instances, the homosexuals establish permanent unions, which are not uncommon in the homosexual community. Other single homosexuals watch these unions closely, talk about them, sanction their conduct, and envy them, while at the same time hoping their own desire of finding a permanent, satisfying partner will materialize. By way of illustration, when one of the unions was dissolved, all of the subjects in that town were concerned and disappointed. They visited the partner who was mistreated and tried to console her for her loss." (p. 366)

As in the case of male homosexuals, female homosexuals may exchange rings and marital vows in formal ceremonies. However, some homosexuals apparently consider such marriages a phony attempt to emulate the straight world.

In general, it would appear that lesbians place greater emphasis on the quality of their interpersonal relationship and less on its sexual aspects, while male homosexuals tend to place greater emphasis on the sexual aspects of their relationships—in this sense paralleling the male role in the traditional straight society. Interestingly enough, the findings of the Institute for Sex Research "seem to show that Gays and straights for whom sexual variety is an overwhelmingly important part of their lives are more like each other than they are like other Gays and straights" (Bonnell, 1974, p. 4).

In our discussion of the adjusted homosexual, it is relevant to note that special stresses are associated with the gay life-style. In this context, association with the supportive and protective institutions of the gay community appears to be an important aspect of coping with the stresses of a homosexual life-style.

The "gay community." Broadly speaking, the gay community may be described as a geographical area or areas in which the homosexual subculture and its institutions are located. Thus the apartment buildings on certain streets may be rented exclusively to homosexuals; most of the homes in certain areas may be owned by homosexuals; clothing, bookstores, theaters, and other business establishments may cater primarily to homosexual clientele; and a variety of recreational facilities and groups, including ski and travel clubs, may be exclusively homosexual in their membership. In addition there are churches for homosexuals, welfare organizations, service centers, and so on. In essence, the homosexual community constitutes something of a subculture, with unique customs, value systems, communication techniques, and supportive and protective institutions.

The cornerstone of the gay community, however, is the "gay bar"; it also provides the most visible section of the homosexual community in the sense that any person may enter. In major cities, such as Los Angeles, New York, and San Francisco, there are relatively large numbers of such bars; for example, the Los Angeles area has more than 200 gay bars, the majority of which are for male homosexuals. In these bars friends are met, news and gossip exchanged, invitations to parties issued, and warnings about current police activities circulated. The crucial function of the bars, however, is to facilitate making sexual contacts. Typically, these contacts are between strangers, who agree to meet at a certain time and place for sexual purposes. Their relationship is usually transitory, and subsequently each is likely to find a new partner. A central feature of such relationships is the assumption that sexual gratification can be had without obligation or a long-term commitment. When asked what it means to be "gay," one man answered:

"To be gay is to go to the bar, to make the scene, to look, and look, and look, to have a one night stand, to never really love or be loved, and to really know this, and to do this night after night, and year after year." (Hooker, 1962, p. 9)

As we have noted, however, this viewpoint is not characteristic of the majority of homosexuals, but rather of those who find sexual variety of primary importance in their homosexual life-style.

While some steam baths and other facilities cater primarily to homosexuals and may serve as meeting places, they are considered of secondary importance. Weinberg and Williams have summarized the situation:

More and more homosexuals are openly—and even defiantly—proclaiming their sexual preferences, and insisting on their right to be homosexual without harassment.

"Because there are few public locations where homosexuals are able to present their sexual orientations and preferences, the bar emerges as probably the single place that provides the terms and conditions necessary and sufficient for large numbers of homosexuals to congregate in public, engage in leisure-time socializing, and pursue sexual relationships." (1974, p. 29)

As might be expected, there are many kinds of gay bars to serve both general and specific homosexual populations.

In a more general sense, the homosexual community is characterized by overlapping social networks of varying degrees of cohesiveness. There are, for example, loosely knit friendship groups and tightly knit cliques formed of homosexually married couples or of singles who often are heterosexually married. In addition, there are organizations concerned with establishing and protecting the rights of homosexuals; of these, the best known are probably the Mattachine societies for male homosexuals, the first having been founded in Los Angeles in 1950 and named after sixteenth-century Spanish court jesters who wore masks. On the female side are the equally well-known Daughters of Bilitis, whose name is taken from *The Songs of Bilitis*, nineteenth-century lyrics that glorify lesbian love. There are also a number of other organizations and facilities, such as the Gay Community Service Centers, primarily oriented toward helping homosexuals deal with the practical problems associated with the gay life-style.

In general, homosexuals who are affiliated with the gay subculture—as well as most who are not—view homosexuality as an alternative sexual pattern or life-style, and feel entitled to the same rights and protections as any minority group in society.

The question of causal factors. Proportionately there is far more research effort being devoted to trying to explain the development of homosexual than heterosexual life-styles, the latter usually being taken for granted as normal and natural. Thus, it is hardly surprising that many homosexuals feel subjected to discriminative and devaluating scrutiny. Nevertheless, since psychology is concerned with understanding human behavior—including alternative life-styles—it does seem appropriate to comment briefly on possible conditions that may contribute to the development of the homosexual life-style.

While some investigators view biological factors as playing the key role in the development of homosexual behavior, a much larger number stress the importance of psychosocial and more general sociocultural factors. In this context, Money and Ehrhardt (1972) have described sexual differentiation as somewhat like a relay race—except instead of trying to beat other teams, the race is designed to complete a program.

Initially the XX or XY chromosomes pass the baton to the undifferentiated gonad to determine its destiny as ovary or testis. The gonad then differentiates and passes the baton to the hormonal secretion of its cells, and the process of fetal differentiation into the anatomy of a male or female continues. By birth, the first part of the program is completed. After birth, the baton is passed to environmental variables that play a determining role in shaping the individual's gender identity—usually, but not always, in accordance with his genetic sex.

Thus the initial part of the program is filled in by prenatal events, and the final part of the program by postnatal environmental ones, focusing primarily on learning. However, it is quite possible for the prenatal part of the program to markedly influence postnatal sexual differentiation. In any event, translated into actual sexual behavior, the total program may lead to heterosexual, bisexual, or homosexual patterns or life-styles. (Adapted from Money & Ehrhardt, 1972)

1. *Genetic and hormonal factors.* Although Kallmann (1952) reported a 100 percent concordance rate for homosexuality in identical twins as contrasted with only 15 percent for fraternal twins, more recent investigators have not been able to corroborate the view that homosexual tendencies are inherited (Rosenthal, 1970).

Early research also led many investigators to conclude that homosexuality resulted from an abnormal androgen-estrogen ratio. Later studies, however, have failed to support these early findings (Tourney, Petrilli, & Hatfield 1975). Furthermore, even in the occasional instances where hormonal imbalances occur, they may have no causal significance: nonhomosexuals often show similar imbalances; individuals may shift from a homosexual to a heterosexual pattern or vice versa without a change in hormone balance; and treatment with sex hormones to change endocrine balance does not modify the direction of sexual behavior.

Nevertheless, the extensive research of Money and his associates (1969, 1972) provides a convincing demonstration of the effects of too little or too much male hormone during critical stages of fetal development on later sexual differentiation. For example, they cite examples of genetic females exposed to excessive androgen during fetal development. Although raised as girls, their behavior was "masculinized" in various ways as contrasted to the behavior of a control group of girls not exposed to excessive androgens. Presumably if the significant adults in the early postnatal environment of these androgenized girls provided unclear models or communicated unclear messages with respect to male and female sex identity, these girls might be more likely than girls in general to become homosexual. Similarly, genetic males exposed to insufficient prenatal androgen and subjected to an ambivalent postnatal environment concerning sexual identity might be more likely than males in general to become homosexual.

A great deal of research has also been done in the differences in the levels of plasma testosterone in homosexual and nonhomosexual males (Brodie et al., 1974; Kolodny et al., 1971). However, studies have produced widely differing results, and no agreement has been reached on the possible reasons for these differences.

Studies such as those cited above have raised interesting questions about the role of prenatal and postnatal hormonal balance on later sexual behavior, but as yet we lack sufficient evidence on which to base definite conclusions.

2. *Homosexual experiences and their positive reinforcement.* The development of homosexuality is frequently associated with pleasant homosexual experiences during adolescence or early adulthood. In an early study of 79 male homosexuals, East (1946) found early homosexual experiences to be the most common environmental factor. More recent studies have tended to support this finding. In a study of 65 lesbians, for example, Hed-

blom (1973) found that two-thirds engaged in their first homosexual contact before the age of 20 and had been willing and cooperative partners. Forty percent achieved orgasm at the time of their first homosexual experience.

In spite of these findings, it seems doubtful that early homosexual experiences lead to later homosexual life-styles except where they are reinforced by pleasurable repetition and/or meet emotional needs. This kind of emotional support is described in the following excerpt from the case of an adolescent girl who first entered into homosexual behavior in a correctional institution for delinquent girls.

"I have a girl, a simply wonderful girl. . . . I need her. . . . I feel better toward all people. I feel satisfied. Now I have somebody to care for. Now I have somebody I want to make happy and somebody I will work hard for. . . ." (Konopka, 1964, p. 23)

3. *Negative conditioning of heterosexual behavior.* A variety of circumstances may lead to conditioning in which heterosexual behavior becomes an aversive stimulus. For example, where the boy or girl is ridiculed, rebuffed, and humiliated in his effort to approach members of the opposite sex, he may turn toward homosexuality as a safer source of affection and sexual outlet. If a mother catches her son "playing with" a little girl and punishes him for being "bad," she may be subtly telling him that heterosexual behavior is evil. Early sexual relations under unfortunate conditions may have a comparable effect. Konopka (1964) concluded: "Girls who have been raped by their fathers (and they are not rare among delinquent girls) find relationships with men either threatening or disgusting and often turn to other girls for the fulfillment of their emotional need for love" (p. 23).

Similarly, preliminary findings in the study of homosexuals being carried out by the Institute for Sex Research showed that some lesbians shifted from heterosexual to homosexual behavior after disillusionment with their heterosexual partners; conversely, some lesbians shifted to heterosexuality after disillusionment with the gay life (Bonnell, 1974). It was also noted that 35 percent of the gay females and 20 percent of the gay males had previously been married. In fact, the great majority of the subjects in this study had had heterosexual relationships prior to adopting a gay lifestyle.

4. *Family patterns.* In a study of 106 male homosexuals who were undergoing psychoanalysis, Bieber et al. (1962) found a common family pattern involving a dominant, seductive mother and a weak or absent father. Typically the mother, frustrated by an unhappy marital relationship, established a relationship with the son that became seductive and romantic but stopped just short of physical contact. The son, overstimulated sexually, felt anxious and guilty over his incestuous feelings, and the mother, aware of his feelings and fearful of exposing her own incestuous impulses, discouraged overt signs of masculinity. The father, resenting the son as a rival, also made it clear that the son's developing masculinity was offensive. Often the father showed preference for a daughter, and the son, in envy, wished he were a girl. Bieber et al. described the end result as follows:

"By the time the H-son has reached the preadolescent period, he has suffered a diffuse personality disorder. Maternal overanxiety about health and injury, restriction of activities normative for the son's age and potential, interference with assertive behavior, demasculinizing attitudes and interference with sexuality—interpenetrating with paternal rejection, hostility, and lack of support—produce an excessively fearful child, pathologically dependent upon his mother and beset by feelings of inadequacy, impotence, and self-contempt. He is reluctant to participate in boyhood activities thought to be potentially physically injurious—usually grossly overestimated. His peer group responds with humiliating name-calling and often with physical attack which timidity tends to invite among children. His fear and shame of self, made worse by the derisive reactions of other boys, only drive him further away. . . .

"Failure in the peer group, and anxieties about a masculine, heterosexual presentation of self, pave the way for the prehomosexual's initiation into the less threatening atmosphere of homosexual society, its values, and way of life." (pp. 316–17)

Considerable doubt has been cast on the findings of Bieber et al. since the subjects studied were patients in psychoanalysis, the retrospective nature of many of the questions required the subjects to think back over several years for answers, and a high degree of inference was used in interpreting the data. On the other hand, the findings of several later investigators have generally supported the findings of Bieber and his associates (Evans, 1969; Snortum et al., 1969; Stephan, 1973; Thompson, Schwartz, McCandless, & Edwards, 1973). Typically the mothers were close-binding, controlling, and affectionate; the fathers were detached, rejecting, and often hostile. Neither parent fostered a masculine self-image or identity. As children, the male homosexuals in these studies tended to describe themselves as shy, fearful of physical injury, and loners who seldom entered into "rough" competitive sports such as baseball, basketball, or football. In contrast, Siegelman (1974) examined the family constellation described by the preceding investigators among gay and nongay males and found that it did not distinguish among them; rather it was indicative of neuroticism or other psychopathology in both groups.

Although family patterns may create a wide range of adjustment problems and even severe maladjustment, there is insufficient research data to justify the conclusion that the family background of homosexuals as a group is significantly different from that of heterosexuals.

5. *General sociocultural factors.* It would appear that a variety of sociocultural factors, including the specificity of expected role behavior and the severity of social sanctions for deviations, may markedly influence the incidence of homosexual and other unconventional sexual life-styles. For example, Davenport (1965) has described the sexual mores of the Melanesians in the Southwest Pacific. Premarital intercourse is forbidden among them, and both males and females are encouraged to masturbate. In addition, all unmarried males engage in homosexual relations with the full knowledge of the community, but after marriage are expected to assume a heterosexual pattern—a transition they appear to have little difficulty in making. It would also appear that among certain primitive groups living in areas with limited resources, homosexuality has actually been encouraged at one time or another to help control the population of the group; in other instances it has been encouraged among soldiers—as at one time in Greece and in the French Foreign Legion—because it was thought they would fight more fiercely to protect their lovers (Churchill, 1967). In any event, it seems clear that social inhibitions and reinforcements can markedly influence the incidence of homosexuality.

Since research concerning sexual behavior generally and homosexuality in particular has not been greatly encouraged, there are far more questions and hypotheses than conclusive research data about the causal factors in homosexuality. As with other behavior, however, there is evidently a complex interaction of biological, psychosocial, and sociocultural factors in varying degrees and patterns.

Homosexuality and society. Since the problems of homosexuals result in part from the self-devaluation fostered by society, the discrimination directed toward them, and the severe sanctions society often imposes on them, many investigators have urged the legalization of homosexual acts between consenting adults in private. For example, a task force of the National Institute of Mental Health concluded their report as follows:

"We believe that most professionals working in this area—on the basis of their collective research and clinical experience and the present overall knowledge of the subject—are strongly convinced that the extreme approbrium our society has attached to homosexual behavior by way of criminal statutes and restricted employment practices, has done more social harm than good and goes beyond what is necessary for the maintenance of public order and human decency." (Livingood, 1972, pp. 5–6)

As noted earlier, the centuries-old laws against homosexuality in England were repealed by parliament in 1967, making homosexual acts between consenting adults in private none of the law's business. In the United States, Illinois in 1961 was the first state to repeal existing statutes against homosexual acts between consenting adults in private, followed by Connecticut, Oregon, Colorado, Hawaii, Delaware, Ohio, and California in the early and mid-1970s. While the long-range effects of such changes on society remain to be ascertained, there is no evidence to date that they have led to a significant increase in homosexuality or have proven detrimental to the traditional institution of heterosexual marriage.

Whether other states will follow the lead of the preceding ones remains to be seen. However, the elimination of homosexuality as a mental disorder from the official APA classification—making "treatment" unnecessary unless the individual wishes to change his or her sexual orientation—seems to signal a new trend in our views concerning such sexual behavior.

Transvestism and transsexualism

Both transvestism and transsexualism are in a general sense related to but essentially different from male homosexuality and lesbianism, and, proportionately, their incidence is relatively rare. However, it is instructive to briefly examine these patterns as part of our total picture of alternative sexual life-styles.

Transvestism. Transvestism involves the achievement of sexual excitation by dressing as a member of the opposite sex. It is an uncommon condition in which the individual, almost always a male, enjoys excursions into the social role of the other sex. Although a male transvestite, for example, regards himself as a man when dressed as a man, he may have feelings of being a woman when dressed in women's clothing. A medical researcher and transvestite himself for 35 years expressed it this way: "The transvestite finds that he is both a 'he' and a 'she' together—at the same time or alternating from one to the other when opportunity permits or desire compels" (*Los Angeles Times*, September 30, 1973).

Very little is known about transvestism. Most reports are based on studies of single cases, and most of those studied have been in therapy, which may make them an unrepresentative group. However, Buckner (1970) has formulated a description of the "ordinary" transvestite from a survey of 262 transvestites conducted by the magazine *Transvestia*.

"He is probably married (about two thirds are); if he is married he probably has children (about two

Sexual "deviations"

Classification	Pattern	Definition	Societal sanctions against behavior
Maladaptive but not socially disapproved (sexual inadequacy)	Male impotence	Inability to achieve or maintain an erection	None — although may interfere with intimate interpersonal relationships
	Male ejaculatory incompetence	Premature or retarded ejaculation	
	Female organismic dysfunction	Commonly referred to as *frigidity*	
	Vaginismus	Involuntary clamping of vaginal muscles when attempts made to have intercourse	
	Dyspareunia	Intercourse is painful for male or female	
Maladaptive and socially disapproved sexual patterns	Exhibitionism	Public exposure of genitals for sexual gratification	Low
	Voyeurism (peeping)	Clandestine observation of others engaging in sexual activities or in the nude	Low
	Fetishism	Achievement of sexual gratification through the use of objects or through deviant activities	Variable
	Pedophilia	Use of a child as a sex object by an adult	High
	Rape (forcible)	Sexual relations with another person (adult) obtained through force or threat	High
	Incest	Sexual relations between close relatives	High
	Sadism	Achievement of sexual gratification by inflicting pain on others	Variable
	Masochism	Achievement of sexual gratification by having pain inflicted on self	Low to none
Alternative sexual patterns	Masturbation	Self-stimulation of the genitals for sexual gratification	Low to none
	Premarital coitus	Sexual intercourse prior to marriage	Low to none
	Extramarital coitus	Sexual intercourse with partner other than spouse	Low to none
	Promiscuity	Nonselective sexual relations with variety of partners; referred to as *sexual delinquency* in girl under 18	Low
	Prostitution	The practice of engaging in sexual relations for financial gain	Variable
	Homosexuality	Overt sexual activity between members of the same sex.	Variable
	Transvestism	Achievement of sexual excitement by dressing in clothes of the opposite sex	Low
	Transsexualism	Inability to accept one's sex; gender identification with the opposite sex	Low to none

thirds do). Almost all of these transvestites said they were exclusively heterosexual—in fact, the rate of 'homosexuality' was less than the average for the entire population. The transvestic behavior generally consists of privately dressing in the clothes of a woman, at home, in secret. . . . The transvestite generally does not run into trouble with the law. His cross-dressing causes difficulties for very few people besides himself and his wife." (p. 381)

The most extensive studies to date of the personalities of male transvestites are those of Bentler and Prince (1969, 1970) and Bentler, Shearman, and Prince (1970). These investigators obtained replies to a standardized psychological inventory from a large sample of transvestites through the cooperation of a national transvestite organization. The transvestites, in comparison with matched control groups, showed no gross differences on neurotic or psychotic scales. However, they did present themselves as being more controlled in impulse expression, less involved with other individuals, more inhibited in interpersonal relationships, and more dependent.

It would appear that most transvestism can be explained in terms of a simple conditioning model. A male child may receive attention from females in the family who think it is cute for him to dress in feminine attire and hence reinforce this behavior with attention and praise. Such a conditioning process is well portrayed in the case of an adult transvestite studied by Stoller (1967):

"I have pictures of myself dressed as a little girl when I was a small child. My mother thought it was cute. She was right. I was a pretty little girl.

"The highlights of my life as a girl came when I was between the ages of 10 and 17. I had an aunt who was childless and wanted to take me through the steps from childhood to young womanhood. She knew of my desires to be a girl. I would spend every summer at her ranch. The first thing she would do was to give me a pixie haircut, which always turned out pretty good since I would avoid getting a haircut for two months before I went to her ranch. She then would take me into the bedroom and show me all my pretty new things she had bought me. The next day, dressed as a girl, I would accompany her to town and we would shop for a new dress for me. To everyone she met, she would introduce me as her 'niece.'

"This went on every year until I was 13 years old. Then she decided I should start my womanhood. I will never forget that summer. When I arrived I got the same pixie haircut as usual but when we went into the bedroom there laid out on the bed was a girdle, a garter belt and bra, size 32AA, and my first pair of nylons. She then took me over to the new dressing table she had bought me and slid back the top to reveal my very own makeup kit. I was thrilled to death. She said she wanted her 'niece' to start off right and it was about time I started to develop a bust.

"The next morning I was up early to ready myself for the usual shopping trip to town, only this time it was for a pair of high heels and a new dress. I remember I stuffed my bra with cotton, put on my garter belt, and slipped on my nylons with no effort. After all, I became an expert from practice the night before. My aunt applied my lipstick because I was so excited I couldn't get it on straight. Then off to town we went, aunt and 'niece.' What a wonderful day. I shall never forget it." (p. 335)

The adult transvestite who marries faces problems that are well brought out in another case reported by Stoller (1967):

"'We fell in love and as soon as I felt we could we were married. We have been as happy as two people can be and the best part of it is that she knows all about me and not only accepts me as I am but assists in my transformation and then admires me. . . .'

"This is the way the relationship looks at first, when the wife is pleased to see her husband's femininity. She does not know yet that as he becomes a more successful transvestite her enthusiasm will wane. Then he will be hurt that she is no longer interested in his dressing up, his sexual needs, his work. The fighting will start, neither will understand what has happened, and they will divorce." (p. 336)

If a transvestite wishes to change his sexual pattern, aversive conditioning and other behavior therapy procedures appear to be effective (Bandura, 1969; Lambley, 1974). For example, dressing in the clothing of the opposite sex may be paired with an aversive stimulus, such as an electric shock. In addition, the individual may undergo assertion training to foster confidence and adequacy in playing a masculine sexual role. There is no research data on changing the sexual patterns of female transvestites who wish treatment.

Transsexualism. The transsexual is a person who feels trapped in the body of the opposite

James Morris, an English writer and adventurer who climbed Mt. Everest, underwent a sex-change operation. As Jan Morris, she wrote a book, *Conundrum* (1974), about the personal feelings involved and her reasons for changing.

sex. Case histories of transsexuals indicate that their cross-gender identity began in childhood and continued into adulthood (Green, 1974; Money & Ehrhardt, 1972; Sabalis et al., 1974). As we have noted, several investigators have pointed out that gender identity does not automatically correspond to one's physical sex, but in most cases appears to be established early by environmental factors—probably during the first 18 months of life—and is highly resistant to change thereafter.

Efforts to alter gender identity by means of behavior therapy and other psychotherapeutic procedures have generally proven unsuccessful.[8] As a consequence, transsexuals who feel

a complete inability to accept their sex identity have requested surgical sex reassignment in increasing numbers during recent years.

The first transsexual operation is said to have been performed by F. Z. Abraham in the 1930s. While occasional reports of similar operations were forthcoming for the next two decades, it was not until 1953, when Hamburger reported the case of Christine Jorgensen, that surgical sex reassignment became well known. Johns Hopkins Hospital and the University of Minnesota Hospital were among the first in this country to give official support to sex-change surgery; each has since received thousands of requests from individuals for evaluation and management of their cases.

In males, modern surgical procedures accomplish sex conversion through removal of

---

[8]Barlow, Reynolds, and Agras (1973) reported on one of the few instances in which a person diagnosed as a transsexual, in this case a 17-year-old male, was changed successfully by psychotherapy.

male organs and their replacement with an artfully designed vagina that apparently works satisfactorily in many cases, even enabling the individual, now a woman, to achieve orgasm. Weekly injections of sex hormones stimulate breast development, give more feminine texture to the skin, and also lessen beard growth, though electrolysis is usually needed to remove excess hair. Surgery for female transsexuals generally has been less successful, for although surgeons can remove the breasts, ovaries, vagina, and uterus, and can insert a penis constructed from rib cartilage or plastic, the penis does not function normally. Transplants of reproductive organs are not yet possible and the patient will be sterile after surgery.

Various evaluative studies of the outcome of such operations have been reported. One of the best known early studies is that of Benjamin (1966). This investigator questioned 50 transsexuals who had crossed the sex line from male to female. Their ages at the time of surgery ranged from 19 to 58, with an average age of 32. Of these subjects, 44 reported contentment sexually and socially with their new roles as women; 5 complained either about their ability to perform sexually or about their appearance; and 1 was totally dissatisfied with the results. In another study, Pauly (1968) reviewed the postoperative course of 121 male transsexuals who had received sex-reassignment surgery, and found that satisfactory outcomes outnumbered unsatisfactory ones at a ratio of 10 to 1. He also reported previous unsuccessful attempts by psychotherapy to help these patients achieve male-gender identity. Comparable results have been reported in later studies (Green, 1974).

There has been considerable controversy about sex-conversion surgery, however, and many physicians, as well as other professional persons, remain opposed to the operation. Newman and Stoller (1974) have pointed out that occasionally schizophrenics and other mentally disturbed individuals seek sexual reassignment, but that their desire is only transitory. For this and related reasons, it is recommended that those considering sex-reassignment surgery undergo a trial period first during which they receive hormone therapy and live in the new role to get a clearer understanding of the many psychological and social adjustments that will be required.

In this chapter we have dealt with the highly complex and controversial problem of sexual "deviations." In our attempt to classify patterns commonly labeled as deviant—consistent with this book's overall approach to the subject of maladaptive behavior—we have noted that *sexual deviance* is not necessarily to be equated with *maladaptive behavior,* and that societal views of what is deviant are subject to change, a phenomenon that is especially apparent today. In our society, traditional views of sexual behavior are undergoing a reexamination, and many patterns formerly condemned as immoral are being redefined, at least by some, as acceptable. By way of contrast, however, some patterns which received impetus during the "sexual revolution" of the 1960s and early 1970s—such as mate-swapping and swinging—appear to be giving way to a trend toward conventional marital relationships or relatively stable one-to-one nonmarital relationships.

With these considerations in mind, we organized our discussion of sexual "deviations" according to the threefold classification of (a) maladaptive but not socially disapproved sexual patterns, particularly sexual inadequacy, (b) maladaptive and socially disapproved sexual patterns, such as incest and forcible rape, and (c) alternative sexual patterns, such as homosexuality and prostitution. Regarding these last patterns, we dealt with the problems of gender identity and with ethical and other problems associated with attempts to change the sex of an individual through surgery.

In keeping with the theme of this text, our primary emphasis was on maladaptive sexual patterns, but we tried to give as complete and objective a view of alternative sexual patterns as limitations of space permitted.

17

Suicide

References to suicide—to taking one's own life—are found throughout written history.[1] Dido, the founder and queen of Carthage, killed herself because of unrequited love; Zeno, founder of Stoic philosophy, hanged himself at the age of 98 after suffering a minor injury. Attitudes toward suicide varied greatly from one society to another. For example, the early Greeks considered suicide an appropriate solution to many stressful situations, such as dishonor, disappointment in love, and painful conditions in old age. The Romans also considered suicide an acceptable solution to such conditions, but it was forbidden when property rights or interests of the state were involved—as when a slave or soldier deprived the state of his services by killing himself. On the other hand, suicide was condemned by both Judaism and Mohammedanism.

With the advent of Christianity, suicide was denounced as a grievous sin in most of the Western world. Legal attitudes tended to follow those of the church; in early English law suicide was considered a crime, and it was directed that the body of a person who had committed suicide have a stake driven through the heart and be buried at a crossroads. These attitudes toward suicide as morally and legally wrong prevailed throughout the Middle Ages in Western society.

During the Renaissance, however, some philosophers dared to challenge the prevailing views. Merian (1763) concluded that suicide was neither a sin nor a crime but a disease—thus paving the way for consideration of suicide as evidence of emotional disturbance. However, it remained for the French physician Jean Pierre Falret (1794–1870) to deal extensively with the subject of suicide as an indication of mental disorder (Fuller, 1973). In his review of suicide among outstanding historical personalities, Falret (1822) performed what has been called "the first psychological autopsy" when he examined the possibility that Jean Jacques Rousseau had taken his own life.

"In some people the idea of suicide tortures them for months, for a year or even for many years; this

Clinical Picture and Causal Pattern
Suicide Prevention

---

[1]The author is indebted to Farberow (1974) for his historical review of attitudes toward suicide.

The psychological autopsy

In cases where there is serious doubt about whether or not death was self-inflicted, a "psychological autopsy" may be performed. The psychological autopsy focuses on learning as much as possible about the personality makeup, life situation, and state of mind of the deceased, which may indicate the extent to which he contributed to his own death. To obtain this data, interviews are usually arranged with members of the immediate family, relatives, employer, friends, physician, clergy, and other available persons who may be able to supply relevant information. Often, too, personal letters, paintings, literary works, and other sources may be utilized.

In a detailed and incisive psychological autopsy of Lenny Bruce, a well-known entertainer whose death had been officially listed as accidental, Deikel (1974) concluded:

"To what extent did the decedent effect his own demise? There can be no question that the death of Lenny Bruce was a self-administered act." (p. 190)

As one becomes familiar with the personality makeup and life-style of Lenny Bruce and is led through the poignant details of the stressful last years and months of his life, there seems little doubt that the above conclusion is warranted.

In this general context, Deikel cited a comment made by Bruce during a public interview several years before his death — a comment which was considered indicative of the ambivalent perspective in which he viewed himself, and in a sense prophetic of the future:

"Sometimes I look at life in the fun mirror at the carnival. I see myself as a profound, incisive wit, concerned with man's inhumanity to man. Then I stroll to the next mirror and I see a pompous subjective ass whose humor is hardly spiritual. . . . I see traces of Mephistopheles. All my humor is based upon destruction and despair." (Newsweek, Jan. 2, 1961, p. 62)

affliction seems to have taken a long time to sap the existence of the Geneva philosopher. Of a happy temperament but gifted by a high sensitivity, Rousseau becomes afflicted by the miserable state he finds himself in and the somberest of melancholy fills his heart. Apprehensive, faint-hearted, timid, suspicious, he avoids men because he believes they are all perverse, all his enemies. He seeks solitude and soon wishes for death. Let's look at some of his immortal writings to justify our assertion: 'Here am I all alone on earth, without parents, friends or society. Thus the most loving of men has been banished by unanimous agreement. I have been in this painful situation for more than twenty years, it still seems like a dream to me. I have headaches and continual indigestion, the least thing scares me, upsets me and saddens me. . . . Since my body is only an embarrassment, an obstacle to my rest, I shall seek a way to divest myself of it as soon as it will be possible.' " (Cited in Fuller, 1973, p. 60)

Falret then went on to describe the circumstances of Rousseau's death, concluding that "this great writer accomplished his fatal project."

At the present time, suicide ranks among the first ten causes of death in most Western countries (World Health Organization, 1974). In the United States, estimates show that over 200,000 persons attempt suicide each year, and that over 5 million living Americans have made suicide attempts at some time in their lives. Official figures show that some 25,000 successful suicides occur each year, meaning that about every 20 minutes someone in the United States commits suicide. Indeed, the problem may be much more serious than these figures suggest, since many self-inflicted deaths are certified in official records as being attributable to other "more respectable" causes than suicide. Most experts agree that the number of actual suicides is at least twice — and possibly several times — as high as the number officially reported.

Nor can statistics, however accurate, begin to convey the tragedy of suicide in human terms. As we shall see, probably the great majority of persons who commit suicide are actually quite ambivalent about taking their own lives. The irreversible choice is made when they are alone and in a state of severe psychological stress, unable to see their problems objectively or to evaluate alternative courses of action. Thus a basic humanitarian problem in suicide is the seemingly senseless loss of life by an individual who may be ambivalent about living, or who does not really want to die. A second tragic concern arises from the long-lasting distress among significant others that may result from such action. As Shneidman (1969) has put it, "The person who commits suicide puts his psychological skeleton in the survivor's emotional closet. . ." (p. 22).

In our present discussion, we shall focus in turn on some additional aspects of the incidence and clinical picture in suicide, on factors that appear to be of causal significance, and on the problem of treating and preventing potential suicides.[2]

---

[2]In addition to the references cited in the text, the following sources were also consulted: Cohen and Fiedler (1974), Corder et al. (1974), Dizmang et al. (1974), Frederick and Lague (1972), Goodwin (1973), Knott (1973), Parkin (1974), Shore (1975), *U.S. News & World Report* (1974), and Weissman (1974).

Clinical Picture and Causal Pattern

Since the clinical picture and etiology of suicide are so closely interrelated, it is useful to consider these topics under one general heading. This will lead us to a consideration of such questions as Who commits suicide? What are the motives for taking one's own life? What role do significant others play in attempted and actual suicides? What do "suicide notes" reveal about suicide? What general sociocultural variables appear to be relevant to an understanding of suicide?

Who commits suicide?

In the United States, the peak age for suicide attempts is between 24 and 44. Three times as many men as women *commit* suicide, but more women make suicide *attempts*. Most attempts occur in the context of interpersonal discord or other severe life stress. For females, the most commonly used method is drug ingestion, usually barbiturates; males tend to use more lethal methods, particularly firearms, which is probably the reason that successful suicides are higher among men.

While the overall national rate has increased in recent years, the greatest increase in suicide has been in the 15 to 24 age group — for which the rate has almost doubled. An estimated 80,000 young people will attempt suicide in the next 12 months, and some 4,000 will succeed. In fact, suicide now ranks as the second most common cause of death in the 15 to 24 age group, with college students and nonwhites being particularly vulnerable. For example, among black youth the rate is about twice the national average, and among the youth of some Indian groups it is about five times the average (Frederick, 1973).

Other high-risk groups include depressed persons, the elderly (whites), alcoholics, the

In assessing "suicide potentiality," or the probability that a person might carry out his threat to take his own life, the Los Angeles Suicide Prevention Center uses a "lethality scale" consisting of ten categories:

1. Age and sex. The potentiality is greater if the individual is male rather than female, and is over 50 years of age. (The probability of suicide is also increasing for youths.)

2. Symptoms. The potentiality is greater if the individual manifests such symptoms as sleep disturbances, depression, feelings of hopelessness, or alcoholism.

3. Stress. The potentiality is greater if the individual is subject to such stress as the loss of a loved one through death or divorce, the loss of employment, increased responsibilities, or serious illness.

4. Acute vs. chronic aspects. The potentiality is greater when there is a sudden onset of specific symptoms, a recurrent outbreak of similar symptoms, or a recent increase in long-standing maladaptive traits.

5. Suicidal plan. The potentiality is greater in proportion to the lethality of the proposed method, and the organizational clarity and detail of the plan.

6. Resources. The potentiality is greater if the person has no family or friends, or if his family and friends are unwilling to help.

7. Prior suicidal behavior. The potentiality is greater if the individual has evidenced one or more prior attempts

of a lethal nature or has a history of repeated threats and depression.

8. Medical status. The potentiality is greater when there is chronic, debilitating illness or the individual has had many unsuccessful experiences with physicians.

9. Communication aspects. The potentiality is greater if communication between the individual and his relatives has been broken off, and they reject efforts by the individual or others to reestablish communication.

10. Reaction of significant others. Potentiality is greater if a significant other, such as the husband or wife, evidences a defensive, rejecting, punishing attitude, and denies that the individual needs help.

The final suicide potentiality rating is a composite score based on the weighting of each of the ten individual items.

Another interesting approach to the assessment of suicide potentiality involves the use of computers and actuarial methods to predict not only the risk of suicide but also of assaultive and other dangerous behaviors (Greist et al., 1974). Clinicians find this information helpful in making decisions regarding treatment for individuals who are potentially suicidal — e.g., decisions regarding the amount of controls needed or the amount of freedom that can safely be allowed.

Material concerning the lethality scale based on information supplied by the Los Angeles Suicide Prevention Center.

---

separated or divorced, individuals living alone, migrants, people from socially disorganized areas, and certain professionals, such as physicians, dentists, lawyers, and psychologists. Both female physicians and female psychologists commit suicide at a rate about three times that of women in the general population; male physicians have a suicide rate about twice that of men in the general population (Ross, 1974; Schaar, 1974). Among physicians as a group, psychiatrists evidence the highest rate of suicide.

Seiden (1974) has called suicide "the number one cause of unnecessary, premature, and stigmatizing death" in the United States. And in view of the preceding statistics, this statement seems particularly relevant.

Stress factors in suicide

The stress situations associated with suicide are not particularly different from those found in the affective disorders. Thus crises commonly associated with suicide run the gamut from interpersonal disruptions through failure and self-devaluation to loss of meaning and hope. Paykel, Prusoff, and Myers (1975) found that suicide attempters reported 4 times as many aversive events as subjects from the general population, and there was a substantial peaking of such events in the month before the suicide attempt.

1. Interpersonal crises. Interpersonal conflicts and disruptions — such as those associated with marital conflict, separation, divorce, or the loss of loved ones through death — may result in severe stress and suicidal behavior. The following was written by a 19-year-old college student:

Dear Jim:
I've just emptied 40 capsules and put the powder in a glass of water. I'm about to take it. I'm scared and I want to talk to someone but I just don't have anybody to talk to. I feel like I'm completely alone and nobody cares. I know our breakup was my fault but it hurts so bad. Nothing I do seems to turn out right, but nothing. My whole life has fallen apart. Maybe if, but I know.

I've thought about all of the trite phrases about how it will get brighter tomorrow and how suicide is copping out and really isn't a solution and maybe it isn't but I hurt so bad. I just want it to stop. I feel like my back is up against the wall and there is no other way out.

It's getting harder to think and my life is about to end. Tears are rolling down my face and I feel so scared and alone. Oh Jim . . . if you could put your arms around me and hold me close . . . just one last time . . . . J . . . m

Often such interpersonal difficulties include a combination of stressful factors—such as frustration and hostility over feeling rejected, a wish for revenge, and a desire to withdraw from the turmoil of a relationship that is highly conflictful and hurtful but on which the individual feels dependent. In other instances, suicidal behavior may follow the death of a loved one on whom the person felt dependent for emotional support and meaning in life. Widowers in particular are considered a very high-risk group.

2. *Failure and self-devaluation.* Many suicides are associated with feelings of having failed in some important enterprise—often involving occupational aspirations and accomplishments—with resulting feelings of self-devaluation.

James Forrestal had been the Secretary of the Navy and the nation's first Secretary of Defense. In 1949 he took his life by jumping from his sixteenth-floor room at Bethesda Naval Hospital.

Forrestal was described as extremely conscientious, compulsively hard-working, and inclined to make excessive demands on himself; he was highly self-critical and suffered from feelings of inadequacy. Prior to taking his life, he apparently felt increasing pessimism concerning the world situation, and also felt that he had failed to achieve what he had hoped to accomplish in public office. During an episode of self-recrimination and depression, he committed suicide. (Adapted from Rogow, 1969)

A tragic aspect of this case is that James Forrestal was a highly respected man who was admired for his accomplishments in office. In fact, some of his friends thought that his political future might even include the White House.

3. *Inner conflict.* Here the stress situation is characterized by inner conflict and debate in the person's own mind, rather than by interpersonal difficulties or devaluating failures. He may be anxious and confused, struggle with the meaning of life and death, and decide that he does not wish to continue the struggle any longer.

In this context, it is interesting to note the following comment made by Ernest Hemingway to a close friend:

"Hotch, if I can't exist on my own terms, then existence is impossible. Do you understand? That is how I've lived, and that is how I *must* live—or not live." (Hotchner, 1966, p. 297)

This letter was written shortly before Hemingway took his own life after receiving a diagnosis of a terminal illness.

4. *Loss of meaning and hope.* Several investigators have pointed out that of all the feelings associated with suicide, hopelessness is the most predominant (Kovacs, Beck, & Weissman, 1975; Melges & Bowlby, 1969; Minkoff et al., 1973). As long as they see a chance that things will improve, and as long as they see meaning in their lives, most people continue to work toward valued goals. With the loss of hope and meaning, however, an individual may feel that life is futile, that he has no place in "the scheme of things." As a result he may give up trying and take his own life.

The feeling that life has lost its meaning and that there really is no hope often occurs in chronic or terminal illnesses. In a study of surgical patients with malignant neoplasms, Farberow, Shneidman, and Leonard (1963) found that suicide may occur even when the patient has only a few hours or, at most, days to live. Similarly, Abram, Moore, and Westervelt (1971) found the suicide rate among

Suicidal intent

From the standpoint of intent or motivation, suicide appears to be one method of obtaining relief from an aversive life situation. However, since most people undergoing severe stresses do not commit suicide—for example, only a small number of patients who develop terminal cancer take their own lives—the question arises of why an individual uses this method of coping rather than another. This is not an easy question to answer; it involves consideration not only of stress but also of the individual's psychological state at the time of the suicide attempt.

Depression and suicide. It would appear that the majority—about three fourths—of all persons who do commit suicide are depressed at the time of the suicidal act (Leonard, 1974; Zung & Green, 1974). Often the individual is hurt and discouraged and seems to retreat into himself in an attempt to "comprehend" what is happening and to think through a course of action. Unfortunately, as we have seen, during periods of intense stress the individual's ability to think rationally is often impaired. As Farberow and Litman (1970) have expressed it:

"When clinical depression becomes acute, mental myopia is common. That is to say, a depressed person is emotionally incapable of perceiving realistic alternative solutions to a difficult problem. His thinking process is often limited to the point where he can see no other way out of a bad situation other than that of suicide." (p. 85)

One depressed and suicidal young woman described her feelings as "being like a dark fog drifting in and enveloping me, so that I can no longer see or think about anything but darkness and gloom."

In some instances the individual's thinking seems to involve a combination of depression coupled with intense anger and hostility and a desire to seek revenge on other persons. As Weissman, Fox, and Klerman (1973) have described it, "The suicide attempter is usually depressed, hostile, and immersed in a network of interpersonal relations that are frustrating and maladaptive" (p. 454). In still other instances, the individual's thought processes are chaotic, and he is out of contact with reality

Ernest Hemingway shot himself while "cleaning his gun" one morning. Although formally labeled "accidental," his death is considered by many to have been suicide.

chronic dialysis patients to be 400 times that of the general population. Here one is reminded of the haunting lines of Camus' *The Myth of Sisyphus:* "Is one to die voluntarily or to hope in spite of everything?"

Although the preceding categories include most of the key stresses associated with suicidal behavior, the specific stress factors in each category may take many forms. In Chapter 6 we noted the case of the young man who suffered intense guilt feelings for not having saved his wife in the disastrous Cocoanut Grove fire and shortly afterward committed suicide. Similarly, suicide may be associated with severe financial reverses, loss of social status, imprisonment, and other difficult stress situations.

Suicide among college students

Incidence and methods

Ten thousand students in the United States attempt suicide each year, and over 1000 succeed. The incidence of suicide is twice as high among college students as it is among young people in the same age range who are not in college. The greatest incidence of suicidal behavior occurs at the beginning and the end of the school quarter or semester. Approximately three times more female than male students attempt suicide, but the incidence of fatal attempts is considerably higher among males. More than half of those attempting suicide take pills, about one third cut themselves, and the remainder — mostly males — use other methods, such as hanging or gunshot.

Warning signs and threats

A change in a student's mood and behavior is a most significant warning that he may be planning suicide. Characteristically, the student becomes depressed and withdrawn, undergoes a marked decline in self-esteem, and shows deterioration in habits of personal hygiene. This is accompanied by a profound loss of interest in his studies. Often he stops attending classes and remains in his room most of the day. Usually he communicates his distress to at least one other person, often in the form of a veiled suicide warning. A significant number of students who attempt suicide leave suicide notes.

Precipitating factors

When a college student attempts suicide, one of the first explanations to occur to those around him is that he may have been doing poorly in school. However, students who manifest suicidal behavior are, as a group, superior students, and while they tend to expect a great deal of themselves in terms of academic achievement and to exhibit scholastic anxieties; grades, academic competition, and pressure over examinations are not regarded as significant precipitating stresses. Also, while many lose interest in their studies prior to the onset of suicidal behavior and their grades get lower, the loss of interest appears to be associated with depression and withdrawal caused by problems other than academic ones. Moreover, when academic failure does appear to trigger suicidal behavior — in a minority of cases — the actual cause of the behavior is generally considered to be loss of self-esteem and failure to live up to parental expectations, rather than the academic failure itself. For most suicidal students, both male and female, the major precipitating stress appears to be either the failure to establish, or the loss of, a close interpersonal relationship. Often the breakup of a romance is the key precipitating factor. It has also been noted that there are significantly more suicide attempts and suicides by students from families where there has been separation, divorce, or the death of a parent. A particularly important precipitating factor among college males appears to be the existence of a close emotional involvement with the parent that is threatened when the student becomes involved with another person in college and tries to break this "parental knot."

Need for assistance

Although most colleges and universities have mental health facilities to assist distressed students, few suicidal students seek professional help. Thus, it is of vital importance for those around a suicidal student to notice the warning signs and to try to obtain assistance.

Based on Hendin (1975), Miller (1975), Murray (1973), Nelson (1971), Pausnau and Russell (1975), Peck and Schrut (1971), Shneidman, Parker, and Funkhouser (1970), and Stanley and Barter (1970).

when he attempts suicide. This may occur in certain forms of drug intoxication, schizophrenia, psychotic depressions, and states of extreme anxiety and panic.

Degree of intent. The ambivalence that typically accompanies thoughts of suicide finds classic expression in Hamlet's famous soliloquy:

To be, or not to be: that is the question:
Whether 'tis nobler in the mind to suffer
The slings and arrows of outrageous fortune,
Or to take arms against a sea of troubles,
And by opposing end them? To die: to sleep;
No more; and by a sleep to say we end
The heart-ache and the thousand natural shocks
That flesh is heir to, 'tis a consummation
Devoutly to be wish'd. To die, to sleep;
To sleep: perchance to dream: ay; there's the rub;
For in that sleep of death what dreams may come
When we have shuffled off this mortal coil,
Must give us pause. . . .

(*Hamlet,* Act III, scene i)

Recognizing that the vast majority of people who contemplate suicide do not in fact kill themselves, some investigators have focused on analyzing the degree of intent associated with suicidal behavior. Thus Farberow and Litman (1970)—echoing Hamlet—have classified suicidal behavior into three categories: "To be," "Not to be," and "To be or not to be."

The "To be" group involves individuals who do not really wish to die, but rather wish to communicate a dramatic message to others concerning their distress and contemplation of suicide. Their suicide attempts involve minimal drug ingestion, minor wrist slashing, and similar nonlethal methods. They usually arrange matters so that intervention by others is almost inevitable, although sometimes things do go awry. This group is estimated to make up about two thirds of the total suicidal population.

In contrast, the "Not to be" group involves persons who seemingly are intent on dying. They give little or no warning of their intent to kill themselves, and they usually arrange the suicidal situation so that intervention is not possible. Although these persons use a variety of different methods for killing themselves, they generally rely on the more violent and certain means, such as shooting themselves or jumping from high places. It has been estimated that this group makes up only about 3 to 5 percent of the suicidal population.

The "To be or not to be" group constitutes about 30 percent of the suicidal population. It is comprised of persons who are ambivalent about dying and tend to leave the question of death to chance, or, as they commonly view it, to fate. Although loss of a love object, strained interpersonal relationships, financial problems, or feelings of meaninglessness may be present, the individual still entertains some hope of working things out. The methods used are often dangerous but moderately slow acting, such as fairly high drug ingestion, or cutting oneself severely in nonvital parts of the body, thus allowing for the possibility of intervention. The feeling is apparently that, "If I die the conflict is settled, but if I am rescued that is what is meant to be." Often persons in this group lead stormy, stress-filled lives and make repeated suicide attempts. After an unsuccessful attempt, there is usually a marked reduction in emotional turmoil. This reduction is not stable, however, and in a subsequent trial by fate, the verdict may well be death. In a follow-up study of 886 persons making suicidal attempts, Rosen (1970) found the attempts to be serious in 21 percent of the cases and nonserious in 79 percent; at the end of one year, the suicide rate was twice as high among those making serious attempts.

Farberow and Litman's classification is largely descriptive and has little practical value in terms of predicting suicidal behavior. As we indicated, however, the degree of intent does appear predictive of the lethality of the method used—a conclusion strongly supported by the more recent findings of Beck, Beck, and Kovacs (1975). The concept of intent is also a very useful reminder that most people who contemplate suicide retain at least some urge to live. Their hold on life, however tenuous, provides the key to successful suicide prevention programs.

Communication of suicidal intent. Research has clearly demonstrated the tragic fallacy of the opinion that those who threaten to take their lives seldom do so. In fact, such people represent a very high-risk group with respect to suicide. In a cross-cultural study, Rudestam

(1971) conducted extensive interviews with close friends or relatives of 50 consecutive suicides in Stockholm and Los Angeles and found that at least 60 percent of the victims in both cities had made "direct" verbal threats of their intent. An additional 20 percent had made "indirect" threats.

Indirect threats typically include such behaviors as making statements about being better off dead, references to methods of committing suicide and to burial, making a point of saying "If I see you again . . . ," and making dire predictions about something happening to them.

Whether direct or indirect, communication of suicidal intent usually represents "a cry for help." The person is trying to express his distress and ambivalence about taking his life; and, at the same time, he is both warning significant others and soliciting their help. Unfortunately, the message is often not received or is received with skepticism. The latter pattern is particularly apt to occur when the suicidal person has given repeated warnings but has not made an actual suicide attempt. As a consequence, the recipient of the message may state that he did not think it would happen; or that he thought it might happen but only if the person became much more depressed.

As several investigators have pointed out, most people who are contemplating suicide have been reduced to a state of near-hopelessness. But they may feel there is still some hope if they can obtain the understanding and support of significant others. Failing to receive it, they go on to actual suicide.

Emotional content of suicide notes

A number of investigators have analyzed the content of suicide notes in an effort to better understand the motives and feelings of persons who take their own lives. In a pioneering study of 742 suicides, Tuckman, Kleiner, and Lavell (1959) found that 24 percent left notes, usually addressed to relatives or friends. The notes were either mailed or found on the person of the deceased or near the suicide scene.

With few exceptions, the notes were coherent and legible. In terms of emotional content, the suicide notes were categorized into those showing positive, negative, and neutral affects. And, of course, some notes showed combinations of these affective components.

1. *Positive emotional content.* Interestingly enough, 51 percent of the notes in the study by Tuckman et al. (1959) showed positive affect, expressing affection, gratitude, and concern for others. The following is a brief but somewhat typical example.

"Please forgive me and please forget me. I'll always love you. All I have was yours. No one ever did more for me than you, oh please pray for me please." (p. 60)

The following excerpts from a suicide note left by a 30-year-old psychiatrist also show positive affect and concern for others, but discouragement and hopelessness are apparent:

"I'm sorry, but somewhere I lost the road, and in my struggle to find it again, I just got further and further away.

"There should be little sadness, and no searching for who is at fault; for the act and the result are not sad, and no one is at fault." (Shneidman, 1973, p. 379)

Here one is reminded of Darbonne's (1969) description of a suicide note as the "communication of the vanquished" (p. 49).

2. *Negative (hostile) emotional content.* In the study by Tuckman et al. (1959), only 6 percent of the suicide notes were classified as involving pure hostility or negative affect. In most cases the hostility was directed toward others, as in the case of the following note:

"I hate you and all of your family and I hope you never have a piece of mind. I hope I haunt this house as long as you live here and I wish you all the bad luck in the world." (Tuckman et al., 1959, p. 60)

In other cases hostility was directed inward and accompanied by severe self-devaluation, as expressed in the following note.

"I know at last what I have to do. I pray to God to forgive me for all the many sins I have committed and for all the many people I have wronged, I no longer have the strength to go on, what I am about to do might seem wrong to a lot of people, but I don't think so, I have given it plenty of sober consideration." (Tuckman, et al., 1959, p. 60)

3. *Neutral emotional content.* Suicide notes expressing neutral feeling commonly begin with "To whom it may concern," "To the police," or they may not be addressed to anyone. The following is an example.

"To Whom It May Concern,
   "I, Mary Smith, being of sound mind, do this day, make my last will as follows—I bequeath my rings, Diamond and Black Opal to my daughter-in-law, Doris Jones and any other of my personal belongings she might wish. What money I have in my savings account and my checking account goes to my dear father, as he won't have me to help him. To my husband, Ed Smith, I leave my furniture and car.
   "I would like to be buried as close to the grave of John Jones as possible." (Darbonne, 1969, p. 50)

People who leave suicide notes of this type are often older persons who have lost a sense of having a meaningful role in life and wish to "check out" in an orderly way. In the study of Tuckman et al., 25 percent of the suicide notes were classified as neutral.

4. *Mixed emotional content.* The note that follows contains a combination of positive and negative affect.

Dear Daddy:
   Please don't grieve for me or feel that you did something wrong, you didn't. I'll leave this life loving you and remembering the world's greatest father.
   I'm sorry to cause you more heartache but the reason I can't live anymore is because I'm afraid. Afraid of facing my life alone without love. No one ever knew how alone I am. No one ever stood by me when I needed help. No one brushed away the tears I cried for "help" and no one heard.

I love you Daddy,
Jeannie

Eighteen percent of the suicide notes in the study by Tuckman et al. involved a mixture of positive and negative affect.

In a more recent study, Cohen and Fiedler (1974) compared 220 cases of completed suicides who left notes with 813 non-note writers. In contrast to the findings of Tuckman et al.—who reported no differences with respect to such variables as sex, race, and marital sta-

tus—these investigators found that 26 percent of female suicides left notes as contrasted with 19 percent of males. They also found that 40 percent of separated or divorced females left notes as contrasted with approximately 31 percent of single females, 25 percent of married females, and 16 percent of widows. White suicide committers left notes almost three times as often as nonwhite committers. In terms of content, the use of emotional categories corresponded to those reported by Tuckman and his associates—with positive, neutral, mixed, and negative being used in that order of frequency.

With respect to reasons for leaving notes, Cohen and Fiedler (1974) concluded:

"Many note writers seem to be motivated to influence the responses of survivors. The desire to be remembered positively by a survivor may account for the large number of statements expressing positive affect. By statements of love and concern, a note writer may try to reassure both the survivor and himself of the worth of their relationship and his own worth as a person." (pp. 93–94)

However, these investigators, as well as Shneidman (1973), expressed disappointment that suicide notes—written by persons on the brink of life's greatest mystery—failed to contain any "great insights" or "special messages" for the rest of us. As Cohen and Fiedler (1974) expressed it:

"Finally, the large quantity of references to the concrete, mundane features of everyday life is not congruent with the romantic conception of suicide as a grand, dramatic gesture preceded and accompanied by a corresponding state of the psyche into which the suicide note should serve as a kind of window. Perhaps all the drama takes place before the action is decided or it is anticipated in the act itself. Whatever role the dramatic elements may play, the large number of references to the commonplace squares best with the conception of suicide notes as communications tailored to the needs of both the suicide and his survivors as these are perceived by the suicide under the existing circumstances." (pp. 94–95)

General sociocultural factors

Suicide rates vary considerably from one society to another. Hungary, with an annual incidence of 33 per 100,000, has the world's highest rate.[3] Other Western countries with high rates—over 20 per 100,000—include Czechoslovakia, Finland, Austria, and Sweden. The United States has a rate of about 12 per 100,000, which is roughly comparable to that of Canada. In Mexico, New Guinea, and the Philippine Islands the rate drops to less than 1 person per 100,000; and among certain "primitive" groups, such as the aborigines of the Australian western desert, the suicide rate drops to zero—possibly as a result of the strong fear of death among these people (Kidson & Jones, 1968).

Religious taboos concerning suicide as well as the attitudes of a society toward death are apparently important determinants of suicide rates. Both Catholicism and Mohammedanism strongly condemn suicide, and suicide rates in Catholic and Arab countries are correspondingly low. In fact, most societies have developed strong sanctions against suicide, and many still regard it as a crime as well as a sin. Japan is one of the very few major societies in which suicide has been socially approved under certain circumstances—for example, in response to conditions that bring disgrace to the individual or the group. During World War II, large numbers of Japanese villagers were reported to have committed mass suicide when faced with imminent capture by Allied forces. There were also reported instances of group suicide by Japanese military personnel under threat of defeat. In the case of the *Kamikaze,* Japanese pilots who deliberately crashed their planes into American warships during the final stages of hostilities, self-destruction was a way of demonstrating complete personal commitment to the national purpose.

Societal norms cannot wholly explain differences in suicide rates, however, for the incidence of suicide often varies significantly

As a form of public protest in Vietnam, a Buddhist monk turns himself into a burning torch as spectators solemnly watch.

---

[3]Incidence rate is calculated in terms of the number of completed suicides per 100,000 of the living population per year. The figures given are approximations of those reported to the World Health Organization.

among societies with similar cultures and also among different subgroups *within* given societies. For example, it is difficult to account for marked differences in suicide rates between Sweden and the United States, and we have noted differences in our own society with respect to sex, occupation, and age.

In a pioneering study of sociocultural factors in suicide, the French sociologist Émile Durkheim (1897) attempted to relate differences in suicide rates to differences in group cohesiveness. Analyzing records of suicides in different countries and for different historical periods, Durkheim concluded that the greatest barrier against committing suicide in times of personal stress is a sense of involvement and identity with other people. The likelihood of suicide increases, he maintained, among individuals who lack strong group ties (e.g., among single and divorced people as opposed to married ones, among the nonreligious as opposed to those who identify themselves with an organized faith), and it also increases under conditions of normlessness or *anomie*, when traditional group standards and expectations no longer seem to apply (e.g., during periods of economic depression, and after defeat in war). Durkheim termed these two patterns of suicide *egoistic* and *anomic* suicide, respectively. He identified a third pattern of suicide as *altruistic* suicide, in which the individual—far from lacking a sense of group involvement—feels so closely identified with a group that he willingly sacrifices himself for "the greater good." In modern times this pattern has been clearly illustrated not only by the *Kamikaze* but also by Buddhist monks who burned themselves to death as a form of public protest in Vietnam.

Durkheim's theory takes little account of psychosocial factors, other than group cohesion, but it does seem to help explain some of the variations in suicide rates that have been observed. Thus, in our own society, as in those Durkheim studied, suicide rates have tended to increase during economic depressions, to remain constant during periods of domestic stability and prosperity, and to decrease during crises such as war, when people become united in a common purpose.

Durkheim's views also appear relevant to understanding the higher incidence of suicide among subgroups in our society who are subjected to conditions of uncertainty and social disorganization in the absence of strong group ties. In a study sponsored by the National Institute of Mental Health, Hall et al. (1970) found that low-income persons from large urban areas have a high rate of suicidal gestures and attempts. Similarly, suicide rates have been found to be higher than average among people who are "downwardly mobile" (or who fear they may become so) and among groups who are undergoing severe social pressures. For example, in 1932 at the height of "the great depression" in the United States the suicide rate increased from less than 10 to 17.4 per 100,000; and during the early years of severe recession of the mid-1970s, the suicide rate increased to above 12 per 100,000 (NIMH, 1975). Following the same trend of thought, we could point to the environmental pressures that appear to contribute to the high rate of suicide among black youth in our society; and Parkin (1974) has noted the marked increase in suicide among Eskimo teen-agers in Alaska, who appear to find themselves trapped in a sort of "no-man's-land" between past culture and assimilation into the "white world."

A number of investigators, including Havighurst (1969) and Binstock (1974), have suggested that there is an inverse relationship between homicide and suicide in most cultures and ethnic groups. Where homicides are high, the suicide rate tends to be lower, and vice versa. Presumably, where homicide rates are high, frustration and hostility are turned outward against others rather than inward against the self. Further evidence is needed before any definite conclusions can be drawn, but in our society, where violence, homicide, and suicide rates are all high, the proposed inverse relationship is not apparent.

In any event, social forces as well as personal characteristics and life stress appear to be implicated as causal factors in suicidal behavior.

Suicide Prevention

The prevention of suicide is an extremely difficult problem. One complicating factor is that most persons who are depressed and contemplating suicide do not realize that their thinking is highly restricted and irrational and that they are in need of assistance. Less than one third voluntarily seek help; others are brought to the attention of mental health personnel by family members or friends who are concerned because the person appears depressed and/or has made suicide threats. The majority, however, do not receive the assistance they so desperately need. Yet, as we have seen, most persons who attempt suicide give prior warning of their intentions, and if the individual's "cry for help" can be heard in time, it is often possible to successfully intervene.

Currently the main thrust of preventive efforts is on crisis intervention, but efforts are gradually being extended to the broader tasks of alleviating stressful conditions known to be associated with suicidal behavior and of trying to better understand and cope with the suicide problem in "high-risk" groups.

Crisis intervention

The primary objective of crisis intervention is to help the individual cope with an immediate crisis in his life situation. When a serious suicide attempt has just been made, the first step involves emergency medical treatment. Typically such treatment is given through the usual channels for handling medical emergencies—the emergency rooms of general hospitals or clinics. It would appear, however, that only about 10 percent of suicidal attempts are considered of sufficient severity to warrant intensive medical care; the great majority of attempters, after initial treatment, are referred to inpatient or outpatient mental health facilities (Kirstein et al., 1975; Paykel et al., 1974).

When a person contemplating suicide is willing to discuss his problems with someone at a suicide prevention center, it is often possible to avert an actual suicide attempt. The primary objective of such crisis therapy is to help the individual regain his ability to cope with his immediate problems—and to do so as quickly as possible. Emphasis is usually placed on: (a) maintaining contact with the person over a short period of time—usually 1 to 6 contacts; (b) helping the person realize that acute distress is impairing his ability to assess his life situation accurately and to choose among possible alternatives; (c) helping the person see that there are other ways of dealing with his problems that are preferable to suicide; (d) taking a highly directive as well as supportive role—for example, fostering a dependent relationship and telling the person what to do and what not to do; and (e) helping the person see that his distress and emotional turmoil will not be endless. When indicated and feasible, the understanding and emotional support of family members or friends may be elicited; and, of course, frequent use is made of relevant community agencies. Admittedly, however, these are "stopgap" measures rather than complete therapy.

In terms of long-range outcomes, people who have made previous suicide attempts are more likely to kill themselves than those who have not; however, only about 10 percent of suicide attempters who fail kill themselves at a later time (Seiden, 1974; WHO, 1974). As Seiden has expressed it, the suicidal crisis "is not a lifetime characteristic of most suicide attempters. It is rather an acute situation, often a matter of only minutes or hours at the most" (p. 2). Since the suicide rate for previous attempters is much higher than that for the population in general, however, it is apparent that suicide attempters remain a relatively high-risk group who appear to need more assistance, in general, than is likely to be available in short-term crisis intervention.

Farberow (1974) has pointed out that it is important to distinguish between: (a) individuals who have demonstrated relatively stable adjustment but have been overwhelmed by some acute stress—about 35 to 40 percent of persons coming to the attention of hospitals and suicide prevention centers; and (b) indi-

The first of the currently more than 200 professionally organized and operated suicide prevention centers in the United States was established in Los Angeles in 1958. Its founders, Norman L. Farberow and Edwin S. Shneidman, realized the great need for the services such a center could provide while collecting data for a study on suicide on the wards of their local County Hospital. Patients who attempted suicide received adequate treatment for their physical injuries, but little attention was given to their psychological distress. On discharge they often returned to the same environmental stresses which had produced their self-destructive conflicts.

Initially the Suicide Prevention Center searched the medical wards for persons who had attempted suicide and then, on the basis of interview and other assessment data, it helped them find a mental health resource in the community for the kind of treatment they needed. As the SPC became better known, people telephoned for help, and it soon became apparent that the SPC could best serve as a crisis facility. To do so, it has to be accessible and the staff has to be trained in certain basic meanings of suicidal behavior as well as in therapy procedures.

Taking calls for help centers on five steps, which may or may not occur concomitantly. Farberow has enunciated them as follows:

1. Establish a relationship, maintain contact, and obtain information. The worker has to be able to listen nonjudgmentally and to assure the caller of interest, concern, and availability of help with his problems.

2. Identify and clarify the focal problem. Often the caller is so disorganized and confused that he is overwhelmed with all problems, both major and minor, having seemingly lost the ability to determine which is most important.

3. Evaluate the suicide potential. The staff person must determine quickly how close the caller is to acting on his self-destructive impulses, if he has not already done so. He does this by evaluating the information he obtains from the caller against a schedule of crucial items, such as age and sex, suicide plan, and so on. (See "'Lethality Scale' for Assessment of Suicide Potentiality," p. 606.)

4. Assess the individual's strengths and resources. A crisis often presents an opportunity for constructive change. The staff worker attempts to determine the caller's strengths, capabilities, and other resources as he works out a therapeutic plan.

5. Formulate a constructive plan and mobilize the individual's own and other resources. The staff person, together with the caller or significant others, determine the most appropriate course of action for the caller. This may range from involvement of family and friends to referral to a clinic or a social agency or to recommendation of immediate hospitalization.

The emphasis is on crisis intervention and referral, not on long-term therapy, although in recent years therapy groups and other long-range treatment measures have been introduced.

In its organization and operation, the Los Angeles Suicide Prevention Center has provided a prototype for the other suicide prevention centers that have been established throughout the United States.

Based on information supplied by the Los Angeles Suicide Prevention Center.

viduals who have been tenuously adjusted for some time and in whom the current suicidal crisis represents an intensification of ongoing problems—about 60 to 65 percent of suicidal cases. For individuals in the first group, crisis intervention is usually sufficient to help them cope with the immediate stress situation and regain their equilibrium. For individuals in the second group, crisis intervention may also be sufficient to help them deal with the present problem situation, but their life-style of "staggering" from one crisis to another makes them a very high-risk group who need more comprehensive therapy.

During recent years the availability of competent assistance at times of suicidal crisis has been expanded through the establishment of suicide prevention centers. At the present time, there are over 200 such centers in the United States. These centers are geared primarily toward crisis intervention—usually via 24-hour-a-day availability of telephone contact. However, some centers do offer longer term therapy programs, and they can arrange for the referral of suicidal persons to other community agencies and organizations for special types of assistance. Such suicide prevention centers are staffed by a variety of personnel: psychologists, psychiatrists, social workers, clergy, and trained volunteers. Although there was initially some doubt about the wisdom of using nonprofessionals in the important first-contact role, experience has shown that the empathetic concern and peer-type relationships provided by volunteer workers can be highly effective in helping an individual through a suicidal crisis.

It is difficult to evaluate the long-range impact of emergency aid provided by suicide prevention centers, but such facilities seem to have the potential, at least, for significantly reducing suicide rates. The Suicide Prevention Center of Los Angeles (Farberow & Litman, 1970) has reported that in comparison with an estimated suicide rate of 6 percent among persons judged to be high risks for suicide, the rate has been slightly less than 2 percent among approximately 8000 high-risk persons who used their services.

One difficult problem with which suicide prevention centers have to deal is that the majority of persons who are seen do not follow up their initial contact by seeking additional help from the center or other treatment agency. In a follow-up of 53 persons who committed suicide after contact with the Cleveland Suicide Prevention Center, Sawyer, Sudack, and Hall (1972) reported that none had recontacted the center just prior to death. They also found that "the interval between the time of last contact with the Center and the time of death ranged from 30 minutes to 32 months with a median interval of 4 months" (p. 232). Since this report was issued, systematic attempts have been made to expand the services of suicide prevention centers to help them better meet the needs of clients. Thus many centers have introduced long-range aftercare or maintenance therapy programs.

Focus on high-risk groups and other measures

Many investigators have emphasized the need for broadly based preventive programs aimed at alleviating the life problems of people who, on the basis of statistics, fall into high-risk groups with respect to suicide. Few such programs have actually been initiated, but one approach has been to involve older males—a very high-risk group—in social and interpersonal roles that contribute to others as a means of lessening their frequent feelings of isolation and meaninglessness. Among this group, such feelings often stem from forced retirement, financial problems, the death of loved ones, impaired physical health, and being unneeded and unwanted.

Another innovative approach to dealing with persons who are contemplating suicide—and in this sense represent a very high-risk group—was originated by a group of volunteers called the Samaritans, begun in England in 1953 by Reverend Chad Varah. The service extended by the Samaritans is simply that of "befriending." The befriender offers support to the suicidal person with no strings attached. He is available to listen and to help in whatever way he can, expecting nothing—not even gratitude—in return. Since their founding, the Samaritans have spread throughout the British Commonwealth and to many other

Facts about suicide

General

Suicide ranks among the first 10 causes of death in most Western countries, including the United States. Over 200,000 persons attempt suicide each year in the United States, and an estimated 5 million or more Americans have made suicide attempts at some time in their lives. Official figures show that about 25,000 successful suicides occur each year—a rate of about 12 persons per 100,000—although the actual incidence is considered to be at least twice as high as official figures indicate. The incidence of suicide is highest in the spring and summer, and over weekends and during special holidays.

Age and sex

Three times as many men as women commit suicide, but women make more suicide attempts, generally using less lethal means. The peak age for suicide attempts is between 24 and 44, but the peak age for completed suicides is 55 to 64. For both sexes, the incidence of suicide generally increases with age. Over the past several years, however, the incidence of suicide has shown a marked increase among adolescents and young adults.

Marital and occupational status

Suicide rates are higher among divorced persons, followed by the widowed and the single, than among married persons. Among certain professional and occupational groups, also, the rate is higher than average; e.g., it is high for physicians (particularly psychiatrists), lawyers, dentists, and psychologists. It is also high for unskilled laborers and persons with low employment security; and it is disproportionately high among black youth.

General sociocultural factors

The incidence of suicide varies significantly from one society to another as well as among subgroups within a society. In West Germany, Finland, and Hungary, for example, the annual suicide rate is over 20 persons per 100,000, whereas New Guinea and the Philippines have a rate of about 1 per 100,000. Religious beliefs are apparently one significant variable, as suggested by the fact that suicide rates are relatively low in both Catholic and Muslim countries—as they are among religious people generally. The incidence of suicide also varies over time with general sociocultural conditions. Contrary to popular belief, the incidence of suicide tends to decrease during wars, earthquakes, and certain other crises; however, it generally increases during economic depressions and periods of normlessness or social unrest. In the United States, as in other industrialized societies, the suicide rate is significantly greater in urban than in rural areas.

Range of methods used

Every possible method of killing oneself gets tried, including the use of barbiturates and other pills, inhalation of carbon monoxide and other poisonous gases, use of firearms and explosives, hanging, strangulation, suffocation, drowning, cutting and stabbing, jumping from high places, and automobile crashes. Firearms are used in more than 10,000 known suicides each year in the United States.

Differences in methods used by men and women

Among men, the methods used in suicide attempts occur approximately in this order: gunshot, hanging, inhalation of carbon monoxide, drowning, use of barbiturates, jumping, use of other drugs, and cutting and stabbing. Among women, the most common methods are the use of barbiturates, hanging, and gunshot, followed by inhalation of carbon monoxide, use of other drugs, jumping, and cutting and stabbing.

Degree of intent	Most persons who attempt suicide either do not want to kill themselves (approximately two thirds of all who make such attempts) or are ambivalent about the consequences of their act (approximately one third). Only a very small minority—estimated at from 3 to 5 percent—are intent on dying. Investigators have noted that the more violent the method used (such as jumping from high places or the use of firearms or explosives) the more serious the intent. The use of such methods also indicates that, if one attempt fails, another is likely to follow.
Communication of intent	The great majority of persons who eventually attempt suicide make their distress and intentions known beforehand—either by threats or by such other cues as sudden increase in the consumption of alcohol or barbiturates, discussion of the methods of suicide, or a developing depression. Some write suicide notes which, if found in time, may prevent the suicide attempt from succeeding. Contrary to the popular belief that few persons who threaten suicide actually attempt to take their lives, the risk of suicide is very high among such individuals. In fact, the majority of suicide attempts are preceded by direct or indirect threats, predominantly the former.

Intervention

More than 200 Suicide Prevention Centers have been established throughout the United States for the purpose of helping people through suicidal crises. Emotionally disturbed individuals can call such centers around the clock and get help in dealing with their problems, depressions, and self-injurious impulses (see page 616).

The preceding information relates to actual suicidal behavior. However, it would appear that many individuals, while not clearly suicidal in the ordinary sense, also engage in life-threatening behavior. Here, for example, may be those who "drink themselves to death," who are extremely accident-prone as a result of indifference or carelessness, or who otherwise engage in behavior so injurious to mental and physical well-being that it may lead to their death.

Based on Berman (1975), Brown (1975), Browning (1974), Dizmang et al. (1974), Farberow (1974), Kidson and Jones (1968), Ross (1974), Schneidman (1973), Weissman (1974), and World Health Organization (1974).

parts of the world as well, and preliminary findings concerning their effectiveness in suicide prevention seem most promising (Farberow, 1974).

Other measures to broaden the scope of suicide prevention programs include: (a) the use of "psychological autopsies" as described in the illustration on p. 604; (b) assessment of the environments of high-risk groups, often including their work environments; and (c) training of clergy, nurses, police, teachers, and other professional personnel who come in contact with large numbers of people in the community. An important aspect of such training is to be alert for suicidal communications. For example, a parishioner might clasp the hand of the minister after church services and intensely say, "Pray for me." Since such a request is quite normal, the minister who is not alert to suicidal "cries for help" might reply with a simple "Yes, I will" and turn to the next person in line—only to receive the news a few days later that the parishioner has committed suicide.

The preceding approach seems to be one trend toward an "attuned community." As Kalish, Reynolds, and Farberow (1974) have pointed out,

"The person contemplating suicide, the recovered survivor of a suicide attempt, the family members of a publicized suicide, and the volunteers and professionals at a suicide prevention center all share

Marilyn Monroe is just one of the celebrities of the entertainment world who have committed suicide. This picture, taken two weeks before her death, seems to convey a sense of depression and inner turmoil. Her suicide, resulting from an overdose of barbiturates, initiated one of the earliest "psychological autopsies" into the causes of a specific suicide.

one vitally important characteristic: they are functioning in a society that has established norms regarding the meaning of the act of suicide and the act of attempted suicide; with varying degrees of success they have been socialized to live in this society. The study, treatment, and efforts at prevention of suicide inevitably take place within a cultural milieu." (p. 301)

And this cultural milieu can foster suicide, albeit unintentionally, or try to hear and help the individual who communicates a cry for help.

The ethical issues in suicide prevention

In the main we have respected the preservation and fulfillment of human life as a worthwhile value. Thus suicide is generally considered not only tragic but "wrong." However, efforts to prevent suicide also involve problems of ethics. If an individual wishes to take his own life, what obligation—or right—do others have to interfere?

Certainly a persuasive case can be made for the right of a person afflicted with a terminal illness and who suffers chronic and debilitating pain to shorten his agony. But what about the rights of a person who has dependent children, parents, a spouse, or other loved ones who care about him and will be anguished by his death? Here the person's "right to suicide" becomes considerably less apparent, particularly when the person is ambivalent about taking his life, and intervention can help him regain his perspective and see alternative ways of dealing with his distress.

Here we may reemphasize that the great majority of persons who attempt suicide either do not want to die or are ambivalent about taking their lives; and even for the minority who do wish to die, the desire is often a transient one. With improvement in the person's life situation, regaining of hope, and lifting of depression, the suicidal crisis is likely to pass and not recur. As Murphy (1973) has expressed it, "The 'right' to suicide is a 'right' desired only temporarily" (p. 472). Certainly in such cases intervention seems justified.

The dilemma becomes more intense, how-

Ambivalence about taking his life, which is so common in suicidal behavior, was manifested in the behavior of this young man shown clinging to a cable of the Brooklyn Bridge. His indecision about whether to jump or not finally ended after one hour when his guardian and a pastor persuaded him to climb down.

ever, when prevention requires that the individual be hospitalized against his will, when personal items, such as belts and sharp objects, are removed from him, and when medication is forcibly administered to calm him. If suicide is to be prevented in such cases, considerable restriction is needed. And even then such efforts may be fruitless. For example, in a study of hospitalized persons who were persistently suicidal, Watkins, Gilbert, and Bass (1969) reported that "almost one third used methods from which we cannot isolate them — seven head ramming, two asphyxia by aspiration of paper, one asphyxia by food, and three by exsanguination by tearing their blood vessels with their fingers" (p. 1593). Here again, however, as in the case of terminal illness and suffering, we are talking about a distinct minority of suicide cases.

Admittedly the preceding points do not resolve the issue of a "person's basic right to suicide." As in the case of most complex ethical issues, there does not seem to be any simple answer. But unless and until there is suffi-cient evidence to justify this alleged right — as well as the conditions under which this right may be appropriately exercised — it seems the wiser course to encourage existing suicide prevention programs and to foster research into suicidal behavior with the hope of reducing the toll in human life and misery taken each year by suicide in our society.

In this chapter we have dealt with the problem of suicidal behavior. We noted that the great majority of persons who attempt suicide do not want to die or are ambivalent about taking their lives. Often they give advance warning to others of their suicidal concern or intent. We then dealt with the role of interpersonal crises and other causal factors that may enter into suicidal behavior. And finally, we examined the problems and methods of suicide prevention and the ethical issues involved in the concept of a "person's basic right to suicide."

18

Maladaptive Behavior of Groups

With the fantastic pictures of the first landing of astronauts on the moon – and of the earth viewed from the perspective of outer space – the realization was brought home to hundreds of millions of people that our earth itself is a spaceship on which we are the astronauts. Unfortunately, it has also become obvious that our spacecraft is in serious jeopardy. As Dr. H. Brown of the California Institute of Technology has expressed it:

"Our ship has an efficient life-support system which produces our food, purifies our air, and processes our wastes. Our main trouble is that the size of the ship remains constant and the capacity of its processing units increases but very slowly while the population of astronauts increases with frightening rapidity. And not only does the population increase but the per capita volume of waste increases as well. We are poisoning ourselves often to the point of death. We must add to this the unhappy fact that the astronauts of this ship fight with each other and kill each other using weapons which steadily become more powerful and effective." (1967, p. 15)

While we have had a decade to improve conditions since this statement was made, little progress has taken place; in fact, there appears ample reason for continued concern over the future of our spacecraft and of the "astronauts" on it. Thus, in our consideration of what behaviors are maladaptive for human beings, we must broaden our focus from individual and family patterns to larger groups whose structures and behavior can affect us all.

In labeling group behavior as *maladaptive*, we shall utilize the same general criteria we have applied to individual behavior. Thus we shall assume: (a) that human survival and actualization are worthwhile, and (b) that group behavior can be evaluated in terms of its consequences for these objectives. Again we must go beyond a consideration of prevailing social norms, since it is clear that many societies have had norms that turned out to be maladaptive. In addition, many of the patterns of group behavior that we have considered adaptive in the past – such as conquering our natural environment – now raise problems or have clearly become maladaptive in our time. Seemingly, the events on our spacecraft have reached a "critical point" that does not

War and the Threat of War

Prejudice and Discrimination Against Groups

Overpopulation and Ecological Violations

Uncontrolled Social Change

permit us to function in the future as we have in the past—not if we are to survive.

We cannot begin to deal with all maladaptive group behavior in the present chapter. The most we can do is consider some of the key dimensions in a few specific maladaptive patterns that are of crucial importance to all of us; clarify some of the possible consequences of different courses of group action; and note some of the efforts being made to improve the prospects for the human enterprise.

War and the Threat of War

If we look closely at a spaceship produced by modern science and technology, we note that it is designed to achieve certain objectives, that its crew is specified, and that discipline and cooperation are essential to its very existence. But if we look closely at the spaceship Earth, we see some disturbing differences. The crew is hurtling through space with no known goals or reliable navigational guides, and discipline and cooperation are precarious at best. In fact, violent conflict breaks out with alarming frequency, and the threat of global warfare is a continuing menace.

The costs of war

Throughout recorded history, wars have cost dearly in terms of their inevitable accompaniments—death, mutilation, grief, destruction of material resources, privation, and social disorganization. And over the centuries, they have become increasingly costly and ever more destructive. The Civil War in the United States, during a period when the population was far lower than it is today, cost half a million lives. In 1945 the nations of the world concluded a war that had cost 40 million or more lives. The holocaust created by the bomb dropped on Hiroshima in the last week of that war—with estimates of the death toll reaching as high as 200,000 people—has been vividly described:

". . . an explosion filled the sky as though a piece of sun had broken off, a bolt of white-hot terror that twisted steel into unimaginable shapes, melted iron bridges, and incinerated more flesh than has ever been condemned at one time and in one place throughout the history of the human race." (Cousins, 1970, p. 38)

Since World War II, wars have periodically flared up between various countries; the United States has been involved in costly wars in South Korea and in Vietnam. And now several "superpowers" have thermonuclear bombs thousands of times as powerful as the bomb that turned Hiroshima into a scene of epic desolation.

The actual psychological effects of war—on both civilian and military participants—have never been adequately assessed. But certainly its dehumanizing effects must be added to any final cost analysis. With the Vietnam war, for example, the American civilian population became accustomed—if not desensitized—to "body-counts" of enemy dead; to "acceptable losses"; to "preventive warfare"; and to special hospital wards for the mutilated survivors. Those who have actually killed enemy soldiers and/or civilians may react in different ways, but often such experiences are both highly traumatic and brutalizing. For example, one American combat officer in Vietnam could refer to throwing villagers into a ditch and shooting them as "no big deal"; another officer said that "It became necessary to destroy the town to save it." Certainly the experience of regarding other human beings as quarry to be hunted down and destroyed is hardly calculated to prepare human beings to live together cooperatively on our spaceship.

The costs of war also include the diversion of natural resources, productive capacity, trained minds, and dollars to promote death instead of life. Between 1964 and 1970 over $200 billion per year were spent by the countries of the world on arms and armed forces; by the mid-1970s the figure was approaching $250 billion per year. In the decade from 1976 to 1985, the United States alone plans to spend a staggering $1 trillion on military preparedness—in all instances money sorely needed for building a better life for the peoples of the world. Thus war, regardless of the perspective from which we view it, is an extremely costly way of trying to resolve human problems.

The preceding statement is in no way intended to minimize the necessity for national defense in our troubled world or to detract from the heroism of the many brave and dedicated men and women who have sacrificed their lives in warfare to achieve and maintain the freedom we now enjoy in our society. Rather the intent is to suggest that we must

Hiroshima was virtually flattened by the atomic bomb that was dropped on it, ending World War II. Some of the survivors of the blast who seemed unharmed at the time later developed leukemia and died. And even twenty-five years after the holocaust some survivors were still hospitalized; others suffered frequent illnesses or needed periodic blood transfusions.

work out better and more rational means of dealing with our problems if we are to prosper or even survive.

Psychological bases of aggression

Since human beings are the only species—other than ants—that engage in warfare and other acts of collective violence against their own kind, the question has inevitably arisen as to what human characteristics make us prone to this pattern of behavior. If we are ever to achieve peace, we have to come to a better understanding not only of the "international" causes of war but also of the underlying reasons why human beings engage in violent behavior. Among the answers that have been offered are the following.

Aggression as an instinctual part of nature.[1] In addressing his troops during World War II, General George Patton made the following statement:

"Men! This stuff we hear about Americans wanting to stay out of this war—not wanting to fight—is a lot of bullshit. Americans love to fight, traditionally. All real Americans love the sting of clash of battle. . . ."

No doubt leaders of military units have made similar statements to their troops throughout the history of warfare. In fact, General Sherman is reputed to have said, "It is a good thing war is so terrible; otherwise men would love it too much."

Many people other than military leaders have viewed aggression as inherent in human nature. Freud, for example, depicted human beings as essentially predatory animals.

". . . men are not gentle, friendly creatures, wishing for love, who simply defend themselves if they are attacked, but . . . a powerful measure of desire for aggressiveness has to be reckoned with as part of their instinctual endowment. The result is that their neighbor is to them not only a possible helper or sexual object, but also a temptation to them to gratify their aggressiveness . . . to seize his possessions, to humiliate him, to cause him pain, to torture and to kill him. . . .

"Anyone who calls to mind the atrocities of the early migrations, of the invasions of the Huns or by the so-called Mongols under Genghis Khan and Tamurlane, of the sack of Jerusalem by the pious crusaders, even indeed the horrors of the last world-war, will have to bow his head humbly before the truth of this view of man." (1930, pp. 85–86)

According to Freud, the energy that fuels the aggressive instinct in humans gradually accumulates, and if it cannot be discharged in small amounts or in socially constructive ways, it will eventually be discharged in extreme aggression or violence.

Viewing humans in historical perspective, Toynbee (1970) has emphasized the thin veneer that separates civilized human beings from savagery:

"There is a persistent vein of violence and cruelty in human nature. Man has often striven to rid himself of what he recognizes as being a hideous moral blemish, unworthy of human nature's better side. Sometimes man has fancied that he has succeeded in civilizing himself.

"The Romans fancied this when, in the fourth century B.C., they substituted constitutional government for class war. After that, Roman political life was unstained by bloodshed for nearly a quarter of a millennium. But the spell was broken when, in the fateful year 133 B.C., Tiberius Gracchus was lynched—by senators, of all people.

"The Romans were horrified at what they had done. They had violated a taboo against violence that had come to seem to be quite securely established, but their horror did not bring them to their

---

[1]While our discussion will focus on acts involving physical aggression, it may be emphasized that people's integrity can also be violated in other ways, as, for example, by brainwashing or political repression.

senses. During the next 100 years, violence in the Roman world went from bad to worse: violence committed by right against left; by masters against slaves; by citizens against subjects. . . ." (p. 3)

The ethologist Lorenz (1966) has suggested that in the course of evolution from infrahuman forms, we have lost the instinctual controls that protect other animals from members of their own species. He noted that many animals make a great show of aggression toward other members of their species, but that the weaker animal usually withdraws or signals submission. For example, a defeated wolf will bare his throat to the victor, and the stronger animal then will discontinue the attack. But we humans have no such instinctive mechanism.

Thus many investigators view the human race as nature's ultimate word on the subject of the armed predator. And in view of the long chain of violence and cruelty extending from the most ancient times to today's headlines, it is not surprising that aggression has long been perceived as an inherent part of our basic nature—to be held in check but never eliminated completely.

Aggression as a response to frustration. Closely related to the view of aggression as an instinct is the frustration-aggression hypothesis formulated by the psychologists Miller and Dollard (1941). According to this hypothesis, aggression is a logical and expected consequence of frustration, its purpose being to remove or destroy the obstacle to need-gratification.

The frustration-aggression hypothesis has undergone considerable revision over time. One revision views aggressive behavior as based on both an inner readiness to aggress (as a result of frustration) and external cues that provide a target and release the aggressive behavior (Berkowitz, 1965, 1974; Janis et al., 1969). These internal and external forces presumably operate in an additive manner. If one is weak, the other must be strong for aggression to occur. The strength of the inner readiness to aggress depends on factors such as the intensity and arbitrariness of the frustration, while the strength of external cues or releasers depends on conditions such as the anticipated consequences of the aggressive action.

Origins of aggression

There are many biological, psychosocial, and sociocultural conditions which appear capable of resulting in aggression:

1. Biological factors — Many scientists have viewed aggression as generated by instinctual mechanisms under conditions of frustration or threat. Various types of brain pathology, which presumably trigger impulsive aggressive acts, have also received strong emphasis in some cases.

2. Psychosocial factors — Most scientists now accept the view that people can learn aggressive behavior patterns, just as they can learn cooperative ones. Displaced hostility, which may take the form of "scapegoating" (blaming innocent people), has also received its share of attention, as has the role of transient situational factors.

3. Sociocultural factors — Anthropologists and social psychologists have emphasized the differences in aggressive behavior among different societies, which they attribute to social expectations, norms, and reinforcements. Of course, psychosocial and sociocultural factors intermesh in the final outcome as a consequence of learning.

In this context, it is interesting to note the finding of Yager (1975) concerning unnecessary acts of aggression committed by soldiers in Vietnam. He concluded that "Personal violence in combat results from an interaction of individual, group, and situational factors" (p. 257).

The interaction of inner feelings of frustration and external cues was well depicted on a group level in the ghetto riots that erupted in the late 1960s. The frustration component in this case has been described by Clark (1967):

"A central fact emerges from the murky background of the present urban eruptions; a society of affluence has raised the expectations and aspirations of the poor but has bypassed them, thereby increasing their frustration and anger, their bitterness, hostility. . . ." (p. 31)

In this case the external targets were objects symbolizing the white racist society, which was perceived as the source of the frustration; the specific release mechanism was the absence of adequate social controls, with a low level of expectation of punishment for par-

Violence as one way of dealing with certain problems is becoming more prevalent in our society. In this picture an American official punches a Vietnamese man in the face to prevent the man from boarding an overloaded refugee airplane.

ticipants. Presumably many wars could also be explained in terms of this frustration-aggression model.

More recently, however, increasing emphasis has been placed on the seemingly useful but somewhat unclear distinction between "hostile" and "instrumental" aggression (Hartup, 1974; Yager, 1975). The preceding example of ghetto riots would be considered *hostile aggression*, presumably resulting from pent-up frustration over unjust treatment. Such behavior tends to be impulsive, poorly coordinated, and not well designed to remove the source of the frustration. *Instrumental aggression*, on the other hand, represents the use of learned aggressive responses in ways calculated to remove obstacles to goals. While the latter may be accompanied by hostility, it tends to be task oriented and coordinated rather than impulsive. For example, terrorist groups commonly use deliberate violence as a means of achieving political goals.

Aggression as learned coping behavior. While many scientists still emphasize the instinctual tendency of humans to aggress when subjected to frustration, the work of Bandura (1973) and other investigators has shown that aggressive behavior is readily learned through the observation and imitation of aggressive models, and that it can be reinforced and maintained by a variety of rewarding conditions. Preceding frustration is not required.

"In short, people do not have to be angered or emotionally aroused to behave aggressively. A culture can produce highly aggressive people, while keeping frustration at a low level, by valuing aggressive accomplishments, furnishing successful aggressive models, and ensuring that aggressive actions secure rewarding effects." (Bandura, 1973, p. 59)

Children are exposed to three key conditions that influence their level of aggressive potential and/or behavior: their family, their peers, and the broader sociocultural environment. In a 10-year longitudinal study of American children, Eron et al. (1974) emphasized the role of parental models in the child's early development and the way parents may serve as aggressive models by physically punishing the child. The parents' attitudes toward aggression may also have a marked influence on the child. As the child enters adolescence, of course, the attitudes and behaviors of peer-group members become increasingly influential as models of behavior.

In recent years, however, the focus has shifted from the influence of family and peer-group models to the role of the broader socio-cultural environment, particularly the mass media, in the development of aggressive behavior. Violence is standard fare in the television, movies, newspapers, and magazines to which youth are exposed. The extent of this exposure in the case of television is indicated by such facts as (a) approximately 99 percent of families that have young children have television sets; (b) these television sets are turned on for an average of 6 hours per day; and (c) the average child television viewer in our society sees, before age 14, some 12,000 or more violent deaths—as well as a multitude of other cruel and aggressive actions (Buckhout et al., 1971; Murray, 1973). In this context, an official statement issued by the National Commission on the Causes and Prevention of Violence seems particularly pertinent:

"Children begin to absorb the lessons of television before they can read or write. . . . In a fundamental way, television helps to create what children expect of themselves and others, and what constitutes the standards of civilized society. . . .Yet we daily permit our children during their formative years to enter a world . . . of routine demonstrations of killing and maiming." (1969, p. 393)

A number of investigators have pointed out that this exposure of youth to violence in the mass media tends to sensitize them to violence in the world around them, and to foster the acceptance of violence as a means of resolving conflicts (Eron, et al., 1974; Murray, 1973; Shaw, 1974). Perhaps even more important, young people exposed to violent models will learn aggressive actions as a part of their behavior repertoire. Later, under certain conditions, such actions may be brought into operation, particularly if the means for aggres-

---

Some "reasons" for killing enemy soldiers

Despite the horror of war and the long-lasting suffering and waste it causes, the momentum of a war, once undertaken, is sustained by several potent psychological processes.

1. Purpose and meaning. During wartime the individual typically becomes part of an important undertaking in which the stakes are high for him and presumably for his country. For many young people, it is the first time life has taken on real purpose and meaning. In a religious or ideological war, one has a great feeling of self-righteousness, of preserving the truth and right against the forces of evil.

2. Remoteness of the enemy. With modern weapons, most soldiers never see the human beings they are killing; this is particularly true for air force personnel on bombing missions. Face-to-face encounters with the enemy are becoming increasingly rare in modern warfare.

3. Negative image of the enemy. The enemy comes to be seen as wrong, cruel, inferior, and less than human; the soldier rationalizes that killing and mutilating such a being is not cause for guilt. In assessing the lessons learned from the My Lai massacre, Opton (1971) noted a soldier's statement that many men in his company would not think of killing a man: "I mean a white man—a human so to speak."

4. Atrocities committed by the enemy. Witnessed or reported atrocities by the enemy, plus the experience of seeing many of one's buddies killed and mutilated, are seen as justifying ruthlessness on one's own part and may elicit both fear and hostility which, in turn, promote further aggression simply as a matter of survival. In essence, it becomes a matter of "kill or be killed."

5. Habituation effect of killing in wartime. In war, people become habituated to cruelty and killing, to seeing victims in terms of statistics. Dead bodies become objects rather than dead human beings who once had dreams, aspirations, and potential for creative achievement.

Other psychological factors include pressures not to let down one's buddies and pride in doing one's job skillfully and effectively. Some of these factors were dealt with in Chapter 6 in our discussion of combat exhaustion. The end result of all these factors is to provide multiple reinforcements for conformity and participation and a general acceptance of the legitimacy of killing under these circumstances.

sion are available and the reward value of such behavior is likely to be high (Bandura, 1973).

The implications of the above conclusions for civil violence as well as for cruel and inhuman acts committed by soldiers in wartime seem far-reaching. As with other kinds of learned behavior, models help supply the repertoire of responses available to the individual, and the anticipated consequences guide what response he makes at a given time.

Toward preventing war

Despite the incompleteness of our knowledge, much of what we have learned about changing or preventing individual aggression seems relevant to understanding and coping with group violence and war. In addition, considerable progress has been made in understanding, measuring, and forecasting group conflicts. Hopefully, our increasing capacity to understand and predict will prove useful in preventing destructive group conflicts including war.

Preventing group aggression. Although the frustration-aggression and social-learning views of aggression suggest different ways of preventing it, they also tend to complement each other. Thus we would expect that aggression could be lowered or prevented by a combination of the following: (a) reducing the tendency to aggress by reducing the causes of frustration, especially frustration perceived as arbitrary, unfair, and self-devaluating; (b) providing children with constructive rather than violent models, as well as training in constructive ways of dealing with frustration when it does occur; and (c) positively reinforcing constructive behavior while insuring that destructive aggression is surely, swiftly, and fairly punished. Explicitly, the emphasis is on modifying social conditions that lead to aggressive behavior while fostering social conditions that lead to constructive behavior. Implicitly, it means preventive work in devising an environment in which no group feels unfairly shut out from benefits available to other groups, and in which no group thinks that it can meet its needs at the expense of others.

Clearly, aggression is not the only motivation that leads to group conflict and war. Fear, economic pressure, ambition for power, greed, rivalry, and ideological fervor have often been key factors in precipitating wars. Other psychosocial factors, such as misinformation, faulty perceptions of reality, cultural acceptance of war as a means of resolving group conflicts, and rationalizations justifying war have often played tragic roles. And in recent years, the spiraling arms race has contributed its share to war and the threat of war.

Reversing the cycle of aggression and counter-aggression. The typical reaction to aggression is counteraggression, and the typical reaction to fear of aggression is preparation for counteraggression. In both cases there is likely to be an escalation, whether of violence or preparation for violence, with a deterioration in the chances for peace and an increase in the chances of violent conflict. As Janis et al. (1969) have pointed out, "Intergroup hostility between labor and management, between rival political groups, and between rival nations is frequently built up by a series of aggressive and counteraggressive moves" (p. 169).

On the international level, this process has been occurring during the last several decades in a spiraling arms race by the superpowers that has led to ever more deadly destructive capacity. The paradoxical nature of this arms race was pointed out over 30 years ago by Joad (1939):

". . . If, as they maintain, the best way to preserve peace is to prepare for war, it is not altogether clear why all nations should regard the armaments of other nations as a menace to peace. However, they do so regard them, and are accordingly stimulated to increase their armaments to overtop the armaments by which they conceive themselves to be threatened. . . . These increased arms being in their turn regarded as a menace by nation A whose allegedly defensive armaments have provoked them, are used by nation A as a pretext for accumulating yet greater armaments wherewith to defend itself against the menace. Yet these greater armaments are in turn interpreted by neighbouring nations as constituting a menace to themselves and so on. . . ." (p. 69)

With the development of the atom bomb, Winston Churchill saw some hope of resolving

Slightly over 30 years ago, 22 of the most powerful men in Germany's Third Reich were summoned before an international tribunal of judges (two from each of the victorious Big Four powers) to answer for their actions in World War II. One interesting facet of the Nuremberg Trials, as they were called, was the fact that not only military leaders but also cabinet members, industrialists, and persons from other ranks were tried with the men who had actually ordered or done the killing. Another facet was establishment of the principle that the individual is responsible for his acts during wartime even though he is acting under orders.

The principles under which the trials were held were contained in the Charter of Nuremburg, affirmed by the General Assembly of the United Nations in 1945. In 1950, the International Law Commission, containing experts on international law from all the major legal systems in the world, was directed to draw up a formulation of these principles. Its report delineates three kinds of crimes punishable under international law — crimes against peace, war crimes, and crimes against humanity.

Crimes against peace: (a) Planning, preparation, initiation or waging of a war of aggression or a war in violation of international treaties, agreements or assurances; (b) Participation in a common plan or conspiracy for the accomplishment of any of the acts mentioned under (a).

War crimes: Violations of the laws or customs of war which include, but are not limited to, murder, ill-treatment or deportation to slave-labour or for any other purpose of civilian population of or in occupied territory, murder or ill-treatment of prisoners of war, of persons on the seas, killing of hostages, plunder of public or private property, wanton destruction of cities, towns, or villages, or devastation not justified by military necessity.

Crimes against humanity: Murder, extermination, enslavement, deportation and other inhuman acts done against any civilian population, or persecutions on political, racial, or religious grounds.

It was anticipated that these general guidelines would be made more specific as competent domestic and international tribunals heard cases in the future — and, in 1974, the U.N. General Assembly adopted an eight-part definition of aggression by one nation or country against another. The essential nature of this definition is contained in the first article, which states, "Aggression is the use of armed force by a state against the sovereignty, territorial integrity, or political independence of another state, or in any other manner inconsistent with the charter of the United Nations, as set out in this definition." The document then goes on to delineate the specific acts that qualify as "acts of aggression" under international law.

In listing various crimes punishable under international law, it was assumed that the rights involved transcend those of given individuals or states and apply to all humankind.

this paradox when he said that "mankind might be able to maintain a precarious peace through mutual terror."

But the paradox has continued, and it is not proving easy to stop the arms race, to start a rollback in armaments, or to implement the powers of the United Nations Security Council as an international mediating and peace-keeping agency. However, some progress has been made in recent years, including the banning of nuclear weapons tests in the atmosphere, under water, and in outer space. A treaty on the nonproliferation of nuclear weapons has been signed by many countries; however, other countries did not sign, and there continues to be a slow but steady increase in the number of countries possessing such weapons. Similarly, preliminary limitations on strategic arms have been agreed on by some of the superpowers, but real progress toward limiting the development and stockpiling of ever more lethal weapons of mass destruction has yet to be made.

Lawrence (1971) has emphasized the need to work through the United Nations in mobilizing world opinion in the "endeavor to put an end to nuclear armaments — to abolish these weapons wherever they are in existence today and to forbid the making thereafter of all instruments of mass murder" (p. 96). This will not be an easy endeavor, but as York (1970) has concluded, "I am equally sure that unless we nerve ourselves to make the attempt, and make it soon, we are quite simply doomed" (p. 41). The prophetic nature of these statements seems to be underscored by the fact that the "doomsday clock" symbolizing nuclear doom hovering over the world that appears on the cover of the *Bulletin of the Atomic Scientists* was moved from 12 minutes to 9 minutes til "midnight" on Sunday, August 25, 1974. This move was based on the conclusion that the "international nuclear arms race has gathered momentum and is now more than ever beyond control" (p. 4).

Prejudice and Discrimination Against Groups

"We hold these truths to be self-evident, that all men are created equal, that they are endowed by their creator with certain inalienable rights; that among these rights are life, liberty, and the pursuit of happiness."

Declaration of Independence, July 4, 1776

At the time of the writing of the Declaration of Independence, the rights expressed in it pertained only to white male property owners; as time has passed, however, these rights and countless others have come to be interpreted, by law, as belonging to *all* people, of whatever color or sex. But this change did not come quickly; in fact, there is still much to be done to educate people to believe and practice what is a legal reality. Our society has a long history of group prejudice and discrimination. There has been racial prejudice, with cruel discrimination against Indians, blacks, and Mexican-Americans; religious prejudice, with discrimination against Catholics, Jews, and Mormons; and prejudice and discrimination against countless other groups regarded as "different," inferior, or a potential threat, including homosexuals, ex-convicts, older people, and women.[2]

In Chapter 5, we alluded to the damaging effects of racial prejudice and discrimination on an individual's early development as well as to the stressful life situation it creates for its victims in adult life. In the present section, we shall attempt to deal with group prejudice and discrimination in a broader social context, emphasizing its pernicious role in wasted human potential and destructive group divisiveness.

---

[2]As used in the present context *prejudice* refers to any attitude toward other individuals or groups that is based on inadequate and selective sources of information, while *discrimination* refers to overt acts that unjustly deny equal status or opportunity to persons on the basis of their membership in certain groups. Usually, of course, prejudice and discrimination go together.

The scope of the problem

In 1740 the state of South Carolina passed legislation providing that:

"All negroes . . . mulattoes, or mestizos, who are or shall hereafter be in the province, and all their issue and offspring, born or to be born, shall be and they are hereby declared to be and remain forever hereafter absolute slaves. . . ." (Tannenbaum, 1947, pp. 66–67)

Thus blacks were considered simply as property, not as human beings—a practice Hallie (1970) has referred to as "a legal formulation of the essence of cruelty" (p. 298).

The practical implementation of such cruelty is illustrated by the following advertisement that appeared in the *New Orleans Bee:*

"Negroes for sale.—A Negro woman, 24 years of age, and her two children, one eight and the other three years old. Said negroes will be sold separately or together, as desired. The woman is a good seamstress. She will be sold low for cash, or exchanged for groceries.

"For terms, apply to Matthew Bliss and Co., 1 Front Levee." (Tannenbaum, 1947, p. 77)

Although the practice of slavery ended over a hundred years ago, the roots of racism were deeply imbedded in our social fabric and have proven exceedingly difficult to eradicate. Even today, tremendous educational and economic gaps remain and in some cases have increased between black and white people in the United States. It is in this historical perspective that we must view the emerging "black consciousness" and the struggle of the black minority for the rights and opportunities that are technically guaranteed to them by the Constitution.

While blacks have suffered untold hardships and injustices as a result of racial prejudice and discrimination, they have not been alone. Prior to the turn of the twentieth century, for example, the relationship between American Indians and the federal government was "very close to all-out genocide and ethnocide" (Trimble, 1974, p. 1). And even as recently as the early 1970s, we find the following description of the treatment of racial minorities in the United States:

"Afro-Americans, Mexican-Americans (Chicanos), Asian-Americans, and Native-Americans (Indians) have contributed to the development of this nation since its inception. Yet, today, a man of color knows that his color or origin represents agony, suffering, and degradation at the hands of the white man." (Allen et al., 1971, p. 94)

The preceding conclusion was arrived at after a review of the historical evidence and present social situation by a group of "concerned students" representing all skin colors.[3] One of these students expressed his own feelings very poignantly:

"Step into my shoes; wear my skin;
See what I see; feel what I feel
And then you shall know,
Who I am, what I am, and why I am."
Patrick Tamayo
(p. 94)

The actual effects of racial prejudice and discrimination may take many forms, depending on the nature and degree of discrimination and the individuals or groups involved. One thing they have in common, however, is the curtailment of people's rights as human beings, with all that this implies in terms of suffering and wasted potential. And it is small comfort to be told that such discrimination is found in Britain, Nigeria, the Soviet Union, South Africa, and many other countries as well as the United States. Like other forms of cruelty and tyranny, racism debases all those involved—the victims, those who victimize, and those who function as accessories by standing idly by.

Although group prejudice and discrimination have been most obviously directed against racial, ethnic, and religious minorities, many "less visible" groups have also been victims. Older people in the United States are commonly treated as though they were an alien race to which the young and middle-aged are unrelated and will never belong. The physically handicapped are another group that suffer from discrimination. Opportunities for rehabilitation training and gainful employment are severely limited for this sizeable segment of

---

[3]The material they gathered is reprinted in a section called "Out of the Third World Experience" in Buckhout et al., 1971.

The ultimate danger of prejudice

"In Germany, the Nazis first came for the Communists, and I didn't speak up because I was not a Communist. Then they came for the Jews, and I did not speak up because I was not a Jew. Then they came for the trade unionists, and I didn't speak up because I wasn't a trade unionist. Then they came for the Catholics and because I was a Protestant, I didn't speak up. Then they came for ME. . . . By that time there was no one to speak for anyone."

Martin Niemoller (1968)

This confession was made by a prominent Protestant clergyman in Germany. It carries a warning for us all of the consequences of standing idly by while others are victimized by prejudice and discrimination.

our society, particularly for the "disabled disadvantaged," who must deal not only with the problems created by their physical handicaps but also with racial, educational, and related social problems.

In addition there are several million former convicts who are excluded from holding public office as well as from many occupations because of their criminal record—without regard to the nature of their offense or the fact that they have supposedly "paid their debt to society." They must pay taxes but are not permitted to vote, a situation they perceive as "taxation without representation." Gay groups have pointed to the harassment and other forms of discrimination directed against homosexuals in the United States. And we have heard the complaints of the Women's Liberation Movement and witnessed a well-organized campaign to achieve equality for women legally, economically, politically, and socially.

Probably most of us feel "put upon" by computer data banks that invade our privacy; by the ever spiraling burden of inflation and the "money squeeze"; and by a vast, impersonal bureaucracy that seems intent on reducing us to ciphers in a "controlled environment." Thus Lerner (1970) has concluded—perhaps somewhat facetiously—that we are showing signs of becoming a "paranoid" society.

When we broaden our perspective to include a global view, we see widespread examples of racial, political, religious, economic, and other discriminatory practices against particular groups, with all the suffering, resentment, conflict, and possible violence that such discrimination engenders.

Learning and maintenance of group prejudice and discrimination

All forms of group prejudice and discrimination are based on learning, and they are maintained because they are reinforced. However, the specific details vary considerably in different situations.

For purposes of brevity, our present discussion will focus primarily on the learning and maintenance of prejudice and discrimination against other races. But the principles we shall deal with also apply, in varying degrees and combinations, to other forms of group prejudice and discrimination.

Learning and the prejudiced community. Prejudice is a learned attitude; discrimination is a learned response. Both may result from unpleasant experiences with members of the groups involved, but such learning appears rare. In fact, direct contact and shared experience more often work in the other direction.

More commonly, prejudice and discrimination are learned from other people who serve as models and from playing expected roles in social institutions that practice discrimination. This point has been well illustrated by the findings of Coles (1967), who studied children's art in the South and found that it reflected the adult models and culture of the larger society.[4]

"Each of these children has learned to identify himself, somewhat, by his or her skin color—learned so during the first two or three years of life. What they have learned about their skin has been but the beginning of what they will learn. Yet, when they finally know what color they possess and what color they lack, they know something about their future.

---

[4]Interestingly enough, during the decade since this statement was made, many Southern states have made more progress than Northern ones in reducing racial discrimination.

A White Girl

A Black Boy

A White Boy

These drawings were made by a 6-year-old black girl during her first year in an integrated school. The black children are drawn as smaller, less distinct, and less complete than the white children and are not smiling or surrounded by a pleasant scene. These drawings make it clear that even at this age a black child recognizes the prevailing discrepancies in the life space and outlook for black and white children.

A Black Girl

As one little Negro girl in Mississippi said after she had drawn a picture of herself: "That's me, and the Lord made me. When I grow up my momma says I may not like how He made me, but I must always remember that He did it, and it's His idea. So when I draw the Lord He'll be a real big man. He has to be to explain about the way things are.'" (p. 71)

But the more basic question may be raised as to how a prejudiced community gets started in the first place. Attempts to answer this question have included such factors as (a) discomfort or fear in the presence of people who seem different, with a tendency to see and describe them in overly simplified and overly generalized conceptual categories that become stereotypes, accepted and passed on without challenge; (b) the need to enhance the cohesiveness of the group and the self-image of its members by excluding outsiders and considering them as inferior; (c) economic factors, in which there are advantages to the ruling group in exploiting the outsiders, as in the institution of slavery, or in situations in which the outside group is seen as representing an economic threat; (d) the projection of frustrations and hostilities onto minority group members as a form of scapegoating and tension-release for the ruling group; and (e) the operation of psychological defense mechanisms such as rationalization. For example, a slaveholder could rationalize behavior clearly inconsistent with his humanitarian principles by seeing his slaves as childish and irresponsible (thus in need of direction and control) or as less than human (thus to be treated more as animals or objects than as people).

In a given situation, many such factors may combine in the establishment of a prejudiced community. Once such a community comes into being, it tends to be self-perpetuating.

Maintenance of the prejudiced community. As we have seen, we all tend to see our world in accordance with our existing assumptions and to resolve discrepancies by such mechanisms as denial and rationalization. Thus, inaccurate and prejudicial views tend to be perpetuated in our thinking, and the prejudiced person selectively perceives those instances that tend to support his views and ignores the exceptions or interprets them to fit his convictions.

On a group level, the factors that have led to the establishment of the prejudiced community usually operate to maintain it. Where prejudice and discrimination enhance the cohesiveness and self-image of the group, they tend to be reinforced; likewise, where they yield economic or other gains, they are reinforced. Behavior that brings physical and psychological gains is notoriously easy to rationalize as being not only justified but quite logical, natural, and perhaps even righteous. As Hallie (1970) noted, we look at the maiming of others—both psychologically and physically—"with disgust and horror, and yet we find it easy to justify in a hundred expediential and even religious ways" (p. 303).

By all these means, group prejudice and discrimination, both explicit and unrecognized, come to be built in systematic ways into the established institutions and agencies of the community and are then maintained and perpetuated through social norms and sanctions. The final irony occurs when even those who are discriminated against foster the stereotypes of prejudice by accepting the social roles and inferior status accorded them and by coming to believe in the validity of the prejudice and discrimination against them—in essence introjecting and identifying with the values of the "aggressor."

Eliminating group prejudice and discrimination

Throughout history and in most parts of the world, group prejudice and discrimination have been regarded as inevitable and accepted without question. In fact, it would appear that the capacity of societies to mangle people who cannot protect themselves is virtually without limit. Slavery still exists in some parts of the world, and in some countries government policies and even constitutions are frankly and intentionally discriminative. But the blind acceptance of the "inevitability" of prejudice and discrimination is rapidly giving way, and aspirations for equality and a better way of life have spread to even the most isolated peoples on our planet.

In the United States—as a consequence of

both its democratic heritage and its technological and economic resources—this awakening has been strong and the demands for change insistent, particularly with respect to the crucial problem of prejudice and discrimination against racial minorities. Unfortunately, this is proving to be a tremendously difficult problem to solve. As we have seen, the roots of racism go deep into our social fabric and are fed by custom, conflicting economic interests, unrecognized reinforcement for many individuals and groups, difficulties in communicating, and long-accumulated frustration, resentment, and mistrust.

In the present section, we shall confine our discussion to three key approaches to dealing with the problem of racial discrimination: (a) an agreed-upon policy of separatism or segregation; (b) a *de facto* policy of segregation; and (c) a policy fostering an integrated society. Again the principles that emerge offer clues to dealing with other kinds of prejudice and discrimination.

Is separatism the answer? The emerging ethnic consciousness among the black and other minorities in our society has led some of them to reject the idea of joining whites in an integrated society. They feel that they would never really be accepted as full equals by the whites who have so long rejected them and that to integrate would endanger their new-found identity. As a consequence, they have come to share the conviction held by a sizeable number of whites that black people need a period of "autonomy," during which they can develop economic and political power and experience the feelings of adequacy and respect that go with control of their own affairs. In effect, such an approach represents a more-or-less formal and agreed-upon policy of segregation.

Many who have studied the problem over the years take a dim view of separatism as a means of achieving racial equality, comparing it to "getting drunk to cure a hangover."

Is de facto segregation the answer? This approach is essentially a "do-nothing" policy in which existing realities are allowed to continue with no systematic efforts toward separatism or integration.

The Ku Klux Klan is openly—and sometimes violently—anti-Negro, anti-Catholic, and anti-Semitic. The burning cross symbolizes the Klan's "religious purity."

American Indians have suffered the effects of prejudice and discrimination ever since the white people gained control of the country. Some militant Indians are now beginning literally to fight back. One of the most celebrated "battle sites" was Wounded Knee, South Dakota, where this Indian was one of many who held that village for almost four weeks.

The dilemma posed by a policy of inaction was delineated in the Report of the U.S. National Advisory Commission on Civil Disorders (1968): "This is our basic conclusion: Our nation is moving toward two societies, one black, one white—separate and unequal" (p. 1). The report then points out that such a trend could eventually lead to a policy of apartheid, and raises the question, "Is this what we really want?"

This basic issue seems as pertinent today as it did when the report of the National Advisory Commission was issued.

Is integration the answer? If we may assume, at least tentatively, that separatism is not the answer, the question arises as to how we can build an integrated community in which all residents are respected.

Three lines of approach appear to be involved: (a) utilizing intervention programs in infancy and early childhood directed toward preventing the damaging effects of racism on early development; (b) utilizing the mass media, education, and other social institutions to change established attitudes and to foster the view that racism is personally and socially maladaptive; and (c) attempting, through intergroup relationships, improved communication and the delineation of common purposes and goals and ways of implementing them. And while laws cannot abolish prejudice, legislation may prove a useful means of creating social conditions in which the exercise of prejudice and discrimination is likely to prove unrewarding or have aversive consequences, and hence is more likely to be modified or prevented from developing.

During the 1960s and 1970s, many gains have been made in education, in access to the ballot box, in fair employment, in higher-level job opportunities, and in wide acceptance of the urgency of change—not only for racial minorities but also for other groups who have suffered the damaging effects of prejudice and discrimination.

But despite the gains that have been made and many hopeful signs for the future, progress has been agonizingly slow relative to the need and to the hopes of those who for the first time have seen not only "civil rights" but full "social justice" as a right and a possibility. In the United States, as throughout the world, there is a "revolution of rising expectations" among those who see others enjoying affluence and opportunity and no longer accept sickness, poverty, and limited opportunity as their inevitable lot. So long as marked discrepancies in opportunity exist, we can expect dissatisfaction to be strong and vocal among those who feel discriminated against and left behind.

Overpopulation and Ecological Violations

It took hundreds of thousands of years to produce a population of some 250 million human beings by the year A.D. 1, and it took 1600 years for this population to double to 500 million. But the next doubling took only 250 years and the one after that only 75 years. By 1975, the world population exceeded 4 billion, with over 8 billion expected shortly after the end of the twentieth century. In fact, if present trends continue, the world population will reach an estimated 15 billion by the year 2025 and 30 billion by the year 2050 (Kahn, 1970; Molitor, 1974). Thus population growth is following not a linear pattern but rather a geometric one. At this rate, it would be less than a century before there would be 10 people on earth for every one now living.

Actually, scientists are in general agreement that this will not occur—that with presently foreseeable technology and our finite resources, 15 billion people would be difficult or impossible to sustain. The implication is that some time in the next 50 years, the current rate will slow and may be reversed—by circumstances, if not by planning.

We need not peer very far into the future to see that the population explosion will have increasingly important results for the entire fabric of our economic, political, and social life. And accompanying the population problem is the interrelated problem of ecological violations. We are polluting our air, soil, and water at an alarming rate—thus upsetting the balance between us and the environment that is essential for our survival. Since the life-support system of our spacecraft Earth is limited, there are corresponding limits on the number of astronauts that it can accommodate before it will become uninhabitable. Thus the problems of overpopulation and ecological violations that we shall be dealing with in this section are of crucial importance for the quality of human life and even for the very survival of the human species.

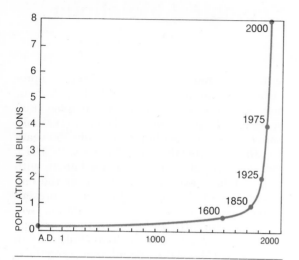

Population growth since A.D. 1

Effects of overpopulation

A number of serious problems stem from overpopulation. In this section we shall deal with two of these: (a) poverty, malnutrition, and starvation, and (b) overcrowding, in terms of both the psychological and social implications. In the next section we shall take up the related problem of ecological imbalance that is resulting from excessive demands on the life-support system of our planet.

Poverty, malnutrition, and starvation. When population outruns available resources, the result is poverty, malnutrition, and frequently starvation. In our own affluent society, we have the potential to provide everyone with adequate nutrition, but we are far from winning the "war on poverty." In 1970 there were over 25 million people in the United States living below the government-set "poverty line,"[5] and some 15 million Americans were actually suffering from hunger and malnutrition (Hollings, 1971a; Pasamanick, 1971). Al-

[5]In 1970, a nonfarm family of four or more persons with an income of less than $3968 per year—slightly over $300 per month—was considered to be living below the "poverty line."

though over half of those below the poverty line were white, the incidence of poverty was proportionately three times greater among blacks than whites; approximately the same ratio held for Mexican-Americans as for blacks. In addition, about one-third of the children under 6 years of age in rural slums and urban ghettos were suffering from growth retardation due to malnutrition (Hollings, 1971b). Our failure to take effective measures to rectify this situation has been referred to by the sociologist Pasamanick as "murderous":

"How much research is necessary to demonstrate that . . . poverty can kill and maim you and degrade your children?" . . . Adequate food intake is not and never was problematic. Where do we stand as a society approaching the third millennium, rich and powerful, but indicted and condemned for killing thousands, maiming hundreds of thousands of children each year in full knowledge of what we have done and continue to do . . . ?" (1971, p. 24)

Yet as we entered the mid-1970s, conditions had not improved appreciably (Reice, 1974), nor were there any signs that they were about to.

From a global viewpoint, as we noted in Chapter 5, the situation is much more foreboding. It was estimated that in the mid-1970s nearly 500 million people were actually starving and another 1.5 billion were suffering from hunger and malnutrition (Abelson, 1975; Canby & Raymer, 1975; Knowles, 1974). In fact, the president of the World Bank estimated that 1 billion persons in the poorer countries of the world—where poverty, disease, and malnutrition are a way of life—face ultimate starvation (McNamara, 1974).

As Brown (1974) has pointed out, however, more efficient methods of transportation and distribution have given starvation a "new image." While some 10,000 people do starve to death each day on our planet, famine is more evenly spread out among the poor peoples of the world. As a result, many manage to live long enough to die of disease and other conditions associated with severe malnutrition and lowered resistance, rather than from starvation per se. But while this "new image" may render news coverage of famines more palatable to the affluent peoples of the world, it does not reduce the ultimate toll in human misery and death for its victims.

Ironically, there seems little doubt that there could be enough food to feed at least three times the world's present population—*if* a concerted effort could be made to develop and use available resources on a global scale (Crosson, 1975; Poleman, 1975; Sanderson, 1975; *Scientific American*, September 1974). And if such an effort is not made, the ultimate cost in political and social instability—as well as human misery and death—is likely to be a high one.

Overcrowding. Experimentation with animals has shown that they experience many pathological effects from overcrowding. In a pioneering study of a baboon colony living in the London Zoo under rather crowded and disorganized conditions, Zuckerman (1932) observed many instances of brutality, bloody fighting, and apparently senseless violence. In some instances, females were torn to pieces; none of the infants survived to maturity. Initially, it was concluded that such behavior stemmed from the violent nature of baboons. But later studies of baboons showed that in their natural African habitat they lived in well-organized and peaceful groups. Their only aggressive behavior was directed toward intruders and predators.

In an interesting series of studies, Calhoun (1962) showed that when a colony of rats were given adequate food and nesting materials but put in a confined area with about twice the normal population density, many forms of abnormal sexual and social behavior appeared. Maternal behavior was so disrupted that few of the young survived. Many of the male rats also showed abnormal behavior; some made indiscriminate sexual advances toward males, females, and juveniles; some showed extreme passivity, moving through the colony like "somnambulists"; and still others "went beserk," attacking others without provocation and in some cases becoming cannibalistic. Even when a few of the healthiest males and females were moved to uncrowded surroundings, they continued to produce smaller than normal litters, and none of their offspring survived to maturity. In a later study that essentially replicated the earlier one, Calhoun and Marsden (1973) reported comparable findings.

Psychological effects of poverty on the adult poor

It is apparent that poverty exacts its toll from the adult poor in terms of such conditions as inferior and crowded living quarters, reduced occupational opportunities, and limited access to recreational pursuits. But as Ireland and Besner (1967) have pointed out, what is not so obvious are the psychological consequences of the life-style of the adult poor: (a) a sense of powerlessness and insecurity, of limited alternatives and little control over their lives or the workings of the larger society; (b) pervasive frustration and isolation, stemming partly from deprivation but also from seeing the affluence around them and being unable to participate in it; and (c) meaninglessness, as a result of feelings of helplessness, isolation, and lack of hope for a better future.

"Constant, fruitless struggle with these conditions is likely to produce estrangement—from society, and from other individuals, even from oneself. The wholeness of life which most of us experience—the conjunction of values, knowledge, and behavior which gives life unity and meaning—is less often felt by the poor. They see life rather as unpatterned and unpredictable, a congeries of events in which they have no part and over which they have no control." (1967, p. 3)

In summary, these investigators concluded that the very poor individual "does not grasp the structure of the world in which he lives, cannot understand his place in it, and never knows what to expect from it" (p. 4).

Despite our awareness of the problem and our efforts to overcome it, "the cities have become more and more the enclave of the poor" (Mydans, 1975, p. 1). And from a broader perspective, hundreds of millions of people on our spaceship live under the most acute physical and psychological deprivation.

In a review of the effects of overcrowding on lower animals, the National Institute of Mental Health (1969) challenged the legend that population explosions among the lemming, an Arctic rodent, are followed by a reckless migration that ends when the animals throw themselves into the sea. In a crowded area being observed by a Swedish scientist, for example, the lemmings did not migrate; rather they went through a period of tension or hysteria, and then they began dying in their holes or other shelters for unexplained rea-

In a field study of the !Kung bushmen of Africa (the ! represents a clicking sound which is part of their language), Draper (1973) noted that their population density is among the lowest in the world—approximately 1 person per 10 miles. Yet the people deliberately established high-density camp settlements. They live in kinship groups of about 30 to 40 people with approximately 188 square feet of space per person (as contrasted with 350 square feet per person set as the desirable standard by the American Health Association). Yet the !Kung appear to experience no harmful effects from the apparent crowding.

Draper considered the !Kung way of life interesting since it presumably preserves or represents the close family and kinship ties that characterized our evolutionary heritage during the age of hunter-gatherers. However, Draper noted that the !Kung have one safety valve if they begin to experience the crowded living conditions as involving interpersonal press or tension; they can move to another kinship camp and thereby escape the interpersonal tensions that may have developed in the present one. She also thought that the distance between camps—15 or more miles—may tend to counteract the possible experience of feeling crowded in a given camp.

Draper concluded, "Whatever may be the ameliorating conditions, it is clear that the !Kung are crowded, yet the absence of presumably stress-related diseases suggests that residential crowding is not necessarily related to social pathology" (p. 303).

sons. Other observers have reported similar findings for lemmings in Alaska and other areas. In summarizing these and other available research studies on lower animals, the report of the NIMH concluded:

". . . there is abundant evidence that among animals, at least, crowded living conditions and their immediate consequence, a greatly increased level of interaction with other members of the population, impose a stress that can lead to abnormal behavior, reproductive failure, sickness, and even death." (p. 20)

It is risky, of course, to assume that conclusions drawn from animal studies will be found to apply on the human level. In fact, we would expect that such stressful conditions would be less disruptive to us, with our great capacity for adaptability, than to species whose normal functioning is largely dependent on built-in mechanisms. On the other hand, it is widely assumed that overcrowding does have profound effects on human beings, and the violence, disorganization, and other pathology associated with congested urban centers are generally thought to be due in part to overcrowding (Trotter, 1974).

Of the little research to date on the effects of overcrowding on human beings, two studies may be cited briefly. In one, a French research team found that when available space in a dwelling was below 10 square meters per person, the incidence of physical and psychological pathology was doubled (Hall, 1966). The second study was of 91 male married Filipinos living in the Samaloc area of Manila (Marsella, Escudero & Gordon, 1970). Many of these men lived in one-room shacks with less than a square meter of space per person; but even the more affluent who lived in larger houses were frequently overcrowded by virtue of the number of persons living in the dwelling. The amount of estimated space per person approximated 5 square meters among lower-class subjects and 16 square meters among upper-class subjects. Under these conditions of overcrowding, three distinct patterns emerged.

1. *Psychosomatic disorders and alienation.* A wide range of psychosomatic symptoms were reported as well as feelings of being lonely and alienated. Since Filipinos seek security through interdependence rather than independence, these symptoms occurring in a crowded house were considered tantamount to complete insecurity.

2. *Arousal, withdrawal, and passivity.* The arousal symptoms seemed to convey feelings of anger, hostility, and general frustration. Since the culture emphasizes "smooth interpersonal relations," withdrawal and apathy were interpreted as attempts to control emotions in socially accepted ways.

3. *Anxiety and eruptive violence.* Many individuals showed a high level of tension and anxiety, apparently related to feelings of alienation and insecurity. Loss of temper and eruptive violence were also common.

In commenting on their findings, the investigators noted that poverty as well as overcrowding may have contributed to the first two patterns. For example, where people live in shacks with barely enough room to lie down to sleep at night, with an almost complete lack of privacy, and with an inevitable future of physical and psychological want, such patterns as alienation, arousal, and withdrawal might reflect the long-continued privation. However, statistical analysis showed that overcrowding in and of itself was still an important variable. And the third pattern—anxiety and eruptive violence—cut across socioeconomic lines and appeared directly due to the overcrowding.

In overviews of recent studies, Lawrence (1974) and Schaar (1975) have cautioned against premature conclusions based on inadequate data, particularly conclusions making dire prognoses of the pathological effects of "overcrowding" on the human level. In a similar overview, however, Trotter (1974) concluded that available findings do support the view that crowding contributes to social problems and pathology. Certainly it would appear that the sheer number of people in a given area will determine many of the adjustive demands made on them. Whether such adjustive demands prove disruptive, however, may depend on a distinction between density and crowding. Density—the number of people per unit area—may not itself be the crux of the problem; rather it may be "interpersonal press" or perception of the situation as being "crowded" that proves disruptive for the individual. In any event, it would appear that some individuals and groups can adjust to much higher population densities than others; but in Western society, the continuing trend toward congregating in large urban centers, coupled with accelerating social change, may prove overstimulating and disruptive for many people, including the more affluent as well as the poor.

Violations of ecological balance

Bengelsdorf (1970) has contrasted the wastefulness of industrial society with the natural ecological balance maintained by nature:

"Unlike industrialized man, nature abhors waste. Miserly nature runs a taut, thrifty spaceship. Every-

thing is reclaimed and recycled. Plants and animals die and are decomposed into reusable molecules that become parts of new plants and animals. And nature recycles its water—from oceans and clouds to rain, to rivers, and back to oceans." (p. 7)

Although our spaceship comes equipped with limited resources and certain built-in laws of geology and biology, the laws of economics are made by people. For example, there is no natural law to the effect that we must burn millions of gallons of gasoline each day in the cities alone or that we must have jetliners with a fuel capacity measured in thousands of gallons. Yet we have long accepted pretty much without question three assumptions about our relationship to our planet: (a) that our environment exists primarily for us to conquer and enjoy; (b) that our planet has infinite resources; and (c) that technological and economic growth are synonymous with "progress" and are worth whatever they cost.

The unfortunate consequences of such attitudes have been nowhere more apparent than in the United States. Each day Americans contribute over a billion pounds of refuse—bottles, paper, cans, discarded automobiles, and so on—to a pollution problem of staggering proportions involving the air, the soil, and the water. Americans have also contributed generously to the "orbiting junkyard" in the stratosphere. In addition, the United States is using up the mineral resources of our planet at an incredible pace. In the last 30 years, Americans have used more nonrenewable fuels, minerals, and other natural resources than were used in the entire world in all previous history. Americans make up less than 6 percent of the world's population, yet use over 40 percent of the world's scarce or nonreplaceable resources. In fact, every baby born in the United States puts roughly 50 times as much stress on the earth's life-support system as a baby born in India. And unfortunately the "energy crisis" has tended to detract attention from the ecological problems.

However, the United States is by no means the only offender. The industrialized nations of the world are not only polluting the air, soil, and water, but are using up the finite resources of our spaceship as if there were no tomorrow. Between 1950 and 1970, for exam-

One of the most tragic cases of industrial pollution occurred in Minamata, Japan, where a petrochemical company fed its wastes, which included manganese, arsenic, mercury, and lead, into the Minamata Bay. The residents of the area, whose diet staple is fish from the Bay, began to suffer a deforming disease of the central nervous system, which was later found to be directly related to metal poisons, particularly mercury poison, in the fish they ate. Even though as many as 10,000 people may have been affected, the petrochemical company has been reluctant to accept any responsibility, and only under pressure has it modified its waste-discharge system.

ple, overfishing and pollution—the latter resulting from the huge amount of wastes that industrialized nations pour into the oceans each day—killed over 40 percent of the marine life in the oceans of the world (Cousteau, 1971), and the statistics would appear to be even more foreboding today. In fact, some species of fish are nearly extinct, and many others are threatened. Unless overfishing and pollution are controlled, all marine life in the oceans may face extinction within a few decades. When we stop to realize that oceans represent some 70 percent of the earth's surface—and that, like the land, their resources are limited—we can readily comprehend the ominous proportion of this ecological problem.

"Ecological illnesses" resulting from pollution of the air have been recognized for some time. We are beginning to realize that noise pollution, too, can adversely affect both our psychological and physiological functioning, ranging from impaired hearing and heart attacks to highly irrational behavior (Berland, 1973; Kiester, 1974). And beyond all these forms of pollution are the dangers arising from the development and stockpiling of ever more powerful weapons of mass destruction and the increasing problem of protection from radioactive and poisonous substances such as strontium-90 and mercury, many of which can get into the food chain. Radioactive wastes created this year from nuclear power reactors will be dangerous for up to a million years, and foolproof methods of storage have yet to be developed. Do we have a right to leave these wastes on our planet for future generations?

Of course, there is no guarantee that the human race will survive. In the long history of the animal world, survival of species is not the general rule. Over two-thirds of the animal species that ever existed are now extinct. Ironically, the dinosaur lasted some 150 million years, while the human race, which has only been around for 3 to 4 million years, is already an endangered species. Yet despite the dawning awareness of the threat to our very survival, we are so far persisting in clearly maladaptive behavior that may well have fatal results.

Coping with overpopulation and ecological problems

The psychologist Leon Rappoport (1971) has somewhat facetiously pointed out that

"The population and pollution problems may cancel each other out over time, since pollution will begin killing off more and more people. Maybe some men will *adapt* in the Darwinian sense, and all the rest will die out. Thus a new type of man may emerge in our species — 'coughing' to be sure."

Famine, pestilence, and war may also solve the overpopulation problem ultimately, if we simply let events run their course.

Assuming that we prefer less painful and costly solutions, it is apparent that we are going to have to come to grips with the problems of food, population, and ecology. And we are going to have to do so soon. In fact, Ehrlich (1970) concluded that the decade of the 1970s represents the last chance for humankind. Although others take a somewhat less gloomy view, there seems to be general agreement among scientists that finding the solutions to these problems cannot be delayed for long. The longer we wait, the fewer will be our options, and the more difficult and expensive it will be to cope with these problems.

From a more encouraging viewpoint, we see an increasing awareness of the problems of population, food, and ecology throughout the world. While some underdeveloped countries still oppose birth control, many, including China and India, have organized programs to control population well under way. The United Nations' 1972 Stockholm conference, with 130 nations in attendance, was the first global meeting to deal with the full range of our planet's environmental problems; and in 1974, the United Nations sponsored a World Population Conference and a World Food Conference. While these conferences can not be described as unqualified successes, they did serve to highlight some of the issues with which the countries of the world must deal, if they are to resolve these problems effectively.

One particularly promising development appears to be the gradual implementation of a global monitoring system for ecological threats such as the seemingly minor but relentless changes taking place in the world's climate. Such a system, utilizing satellites and other technological approaches, will provide information regarding both naturally occurring changes in our environment and the effects of technology on it; this information, in turn, will provide a basis for the formulation of corrective and preventive measures.

In the United States, various corrective measures have already been introduced and encouraged, such as (a) reducing the wasteful consumption of nonrenewable resources and the nonessential use of energy; (b) reducing pollution and recycling of wastes; and (c) family planning and voluntary limitation of family size. In its annual population estimate,

We have been slow to realize that our technology, in giving us unprecedented material conveniences, was also giving us by-products that we did not anticipate or want. In fact, many of our most serious problems today are the unexpected side effects of solutions to previous problems.

the U.S. Bureau of the Census noted in 1975 that population growth has slowed to manageable proportions during the 1970s; if present trends continue, a U.S. population of about 300 million is predicted for the year 2025.

Solving the problems of overpopulation and ecological violations will require the coordinated efforts of political and industrial leaders as well as scientists and the general public. And if the efforts are to succeed, it will require that many of us change our attitudes, broaden our loyalties, and make a personal commitment to helping solve these crucial problems. McNamara (1970, 1974) has elaborated on this point very succinctly:

"There are really no material obstacles to a sane, manageable response to the world's developmental needs. The obstacles lie in the minds of men. We have simply not thought long enough and hard enough about the fundamental problems of the planet. Today we are in fact an inescapable community, united by the forces of communication and interdependence in our new technological order.

"The conclusion is inevitable. We must apply at the world level that same moral responsibility, that same sharing of wealth, that same standard of justice and compassion without which our own national societies would surely fall apart. We can meet this challenge if we have the wisdom and moral

energy to do so. But if we lack these qualities, then I fear we lack the means of survival on this planet." (1970, p. 5)

McNamara went on to point out that if only 6 percent of the sum spent annually on armaments were devoted to developmental aid—or perhaps 2 percent of the increase in real income that the more affluent nations can look forward to in the years ahead—we could make a reasonable beginning in assisting the poor and underdeveloped countries of the world, save literally hundreds of millions of people from starvation, and get within sight of the goal of reducing global population growth to a manageable 1 percent. As Molitor (1974) has expressed it, "We need only the resolve to do the job" (p. 169).

Uncontrolled Social Change

All life involves change. We grow up, shift social roles, face the death of those dear to us, and adjust to numerous other major and minor changes as we go through life. Indeed, our society—as well as the subgroups within it—is constantly changing. Change per se need not cause difficulty. In fact, we are a society that is used to change, and in the main we have regarded it as beneficial.

But though change is a constant companion of human life, cultural change in the past ordinarily took place at a relatively leisurely pace. For example, a century and a half passed between the patenting of the first typewriter in England in 1714 and its appearance on the commercial market. Now new technological innovations are applied and sweep through society with less and less time lag, leading, in turn, to ideas for further innovations. Thus the cycle of technological and social change is both self-perpetuating and self-accelerating. Perhaps the full impact of this point is brought home when we realize that more scientific, technological, and social changes have taken place in the last 75 years than in all preceding history. There are many people living today whose life span encompasses the flight of the first airplane by the Wright brothers, the first transatlantic flight, the development of jet aircraft that can fly faster than sound, and the development of spaceships that have landed men on the moon.

In this final section of the chapter we shall focus on the accelerating pace of technological and social change and the conflicts and maladaptive behavior apparently fostered by social changes that appear to be "too rapid" and inadequately controlled. We shall attempt to view the nature and effects of such change not only in contemporary industrialized society but in the broader perspective of the spaceship Earth.

"Future shock"

A number of investigators have raised the question of whether the human organism is equipped either physiologically or psychologically to cope with the supercharged rate of change in our "manic society" (Bronfenbrenner, 1974; Keniston, 1963; Shackle, 1974; Toffler, 1970). Perhaps no one has expressed it more succinctly than Keniston:

"The human capacity to assimilate such innovation is limited. Men can of course adjust to rapid change—that is, make an accommodation to it and go on living—but truly to assimilate it involves retaining some sense of connection with the past, understanding the relationship of one's position to one's origins and one's destinations, maintaining a sense of control over one's own life in a comprehensible universe undergoing intelligible transformations. This assimilation becomes increasingly difficult in a time like our own." (1963, p. 74)

And it might be added that it seems to have become even more difficult today.

There would appear to be limits to the resilience of the human organism to assimilate change; such limits evidently apply to both the complexity and the rate of change. When these limits are exceeded, the results can be seriously detrimental or even disastrous on both individual and group levels.

Excessive pace and complexity of social change. Toffler (1970) has proposed the term *future shock* to describe the result of social change that has become too fast for people to assimilate; in essence, the future will have arrived too soon.

From the few studies that have been made in the past, such as that of Murphy (1965), it would appear that social change is likely to be particularly stressful when certain conditions are present:

"1. when the tempo is accelerated and especially when major dimensions of change occur within the life span of a single generation,
"2. when [change] involves pervasive reorientation about basic values and assumptions,
"3. when [change] is experienced at the outset of a cycle when few guides and models exist,
"4. when there has been little formal training and preparation in the skills and techniques necessary to accomplish the new tasks,

Paradoxes of our time

The paradox of technology — While modern technology has enabled us to land men on the moon and return them safely to earth, it has not enabled us yet to solve many critical problems on earth, some of which have been caused or exacerbated by technology itself.

The paradox of speed — Our high-speed automobiles are slowed to a crawl during many hours of the day on crowded urban freeways, and high-speed jet travel, involving the crossing of multiple time zones, tends to upset the circadian rhythms, as we noted in Chapter 8.

The paradox of communication — Via communication satellites and mass media, we have developed highly advanced communication facilities and techniques; yet "communication gaps" prevent or distort our understanding of each others' ideas and motives.

The paradox of affluence — The United States is the most affluent nation in the world and in history; yet we have upwards of 25 million people living below the government-set poverty line, are curtailing school programs and urban renewal programs for lack of funds, and are adding each year to an already mammoth national debt.

The paradox of equality — In a society based on the principle of freedom, equality, and justice for all, we find widespread group prejudice and discrimination with limited opportunities and unequal justice for the poor and the "different."

The paradox of child care and education — Although we loudly proclaim our devotion to the well-being of our children, our actions belie our words, as we have seen in Chapter 15. In fact, we spend more on cigarettes, alcohol, and automobiles than we do on our children's education. We also fail to assure them adequate medical, psychological, and related services.

The paradox of defense — The security our costly military defense system should provide is offset by the spiraling arms race, the proliferation of nuclear weapons, and the increase in the number of "superpowers."

The paradox of values — In a society founded on principles which have brought unprecedented well-being and opportunity to a majority of its citizens, we find a sizable number of youth and adults feeling alienated and dehumanized and rejecting an achievement orientation.

Fortunately, steps are under way on a systematic level to resolve these paradoxes. But as yet, they still characterize our time and place in history.

"5. if there are serious ambiguities about what the change is leading to,

"6. if [change] involves new roles or values that are imperfectly integrated into or incompatible with the rest of the sociocultural system,

"7. if [change] involves expectations that are prone to be frustrated given the pre-existing pattern of life, and

"8. if [change] involves expansion rather than substitution and creates a sense of 'overloading.'" (pp. 279–80)

Murphy does not regard this list as all-embracing but offers it simply as a set of parameters or guidelines for assessing the probable stressfulness of particular social changes.

In times of rapid change, cultural mores and social institutions that were accepted yesterday may be rejected today. Margaret Mead (1971) has pointed out that in New Guinea some young people whose parents were cannibals are studying medicine. And the rapidity and complexity of social change with respect to "educational obsolescence" has been well delineated by Glass (1970):

"The obsolescence of education in rapidly developing fields of knowledge has become about equal in rate to the obsolescence of an automobile. In 5 to 7 years it is due for a complete replacement. Consequently, our times, to a degree quite generally unrecognized, demand a major reconstitution of the educational process, which must become one of lifelong renewal." (p. 1041)

Similarly, Toffler (1971) has referred to the increasing obsolescence of family patterns. People who got married in the 1900s could look forward to 30 years together on the average; with the increasing life span, the time has been extended to 50 years. Thus marital partners today are expected to make it together for a much longer period despite the rate and multiplicity of changes around them — in jobs, in sexual patterns, in leisure-time pursuits, in values, life-styles, and so on — all of which tend to make it more difficult for a husband and wife to grow together over the years.

"My own hunch is that most people will try to go blindly through the motions of the traditional marriage, and try to keep the traditional family going, and they'll fail. And the consequence will be a subtle but very significant shift to much more temporary marital arrangements, an intensification of the present pattern of divorce and remarriage . . . to the point at which we accept the idea that marriages are not for life." (p. 35)

Whether or not this particular prediction is borne out, we can readily see that uncontrolled technological and social change can have pervasive effects on individuals, on institutions, and on societies. In the modern world, it has become essential to prepare ourselves to learn, unlearn, and relearn constantly; to expect and accept changing institutions, relationships, and ground rules; and to adapt and readapt at an ever increasing tempo.

Reactions to future shock. We have discussed the effects of life stress on mental and physical disorders, and we have noted that the role of accelerating technological and social change influence the nature and incidence of such disorders. In his own analysis, Toffler (1970) has described the results of future shock as involving a wide range of possible symptoms. For some people, it can lead to a hardening or rigidification of established attitudes—to a reactionary posture. In the face of uncertainty and change, such individuals seemingly guard against the fears generated by novelty and change by simply "putting on blinders" and clinging to the old. Others may react with anxiety, confusion, withdrawal, alienation, or erratic swings in life-style. And for some who keep trying to adapt to changes that come too fast, there may be a breakdown of organized behavior, with irrational violence. Thus Toffler, as well as later investigators such as Lipowski (1974), have concluded that future shock may well be the most important mental health hazard of the future.

We cannot predict all the effects of accelerating social change, but there can be no doubt that every major social institution in western society—family, school, church, military, and government—is going through a period of conflict and crisis. Also, as White (1970) has pointed out, the pressure on world leaders is enormous and increasing. "The pace of change forces us to make decisions faster than we can sort out right from wrong" (p. 521). In this context, Hopkins (1973) has noted:

"One of our great dilemmas, is that all knowledge is about the past, but all decisions are about the future. We speak of learning from the past how to deal with the future, but this concept has limitations in view of the rapidity with which the modern world is changing into the neomodern world. The past is an uncertain guide to the present, which has many unprecedented problems and challenges. And it is an even more uncertain guide to the future . . . ." (p. 254)

Crisis piles on crisis, decisions must be made on inadequate information, and too often the action taken is simply a reaction to the present emergency rather than part of a coherent plan for the future. And always looming in the background, as Symington (1974) warned the United Nations General Assembly, is the fact that "one miscalculation, one sudden terrorist activity, one paranoid leader, could set the spark to a world-wide nuclear holocaust" (p. 9).

Cultures in collision

The phrase *cultures in collision* refers not only to differing value orientations in our own society but also to the ideological conflicts and changes which seem to be the order of the day in our contemporary world.

In the United States, for example, there has been a widespread questioning of traditional social norms and values; in the 1960s and early 1970s we observed the emergence of a "counterculture," with ongoing experimentation in alternative life-styles. Although the term *counterculture* implies a greater gulf between old and new than actually existed, there does seem to be a "new ethic" which emerged from this culture collision.

In essence, however, America is not only a society, a culture, and a way of life; it is also a way of looking at our world and its future. It is a country founded on very idealistic premises—a *dream* for humankind. And not only the younger generation but an increasing number of Americans from all walks of life are questioning the implementation of this dream and are demanding changes more in harmony with its vision.

Nor is the ferment only or even primarily an American phenomenon; nor is it one between the Communist and non-Communist super-

Among wide segments of the population, "patriotism" has come to be seen as a self-righteous chauvinism, a glorying in past exploits, and a rationalization for selfish advancement of one's own country's interests with disregard for the interests of others. In a thought-provoking article, Ralph Nader (1971) has proposed a new kind of patriotism based on the following principles:

1. Patriotism should be rooted in the beliefs and conscience of the individual. If the "consent of the governed" is to have any meaning, it must be based upon the agreement and participation of an informed citizenry.

2. Love of country should include working to improve one's country by taking constructive action against racism, pollution, and other conditions that weaken it and prevent it from attaining its potential or living up to its ideals.

3. Acts that despoil, pollute, desecrate, or otherwise damage our country are unpatriotic. If it is unpatriotic to tear down the flag, it is also unpatriotic to engage in behavior that violates the principles for which the flag stands.

4. A patriotism equated with military exploits and wartime support of one's own country is too limited. Patriotism must also include the duty to advance our ideals toward a better community, country, and world. If patriotism is to have a "manifest destiny," it must be in building a world in which mankind is bound together by the bonds of love and peace.

Implicit in the preceding principles is the concept of patriotism as involving the duty to question and challenge current practices and to dissent from the majority if necessary in order to correct injustice and mistakes. As expressed by a loyal immigrant U.S. citizen, Carl Schurz: "Our country . . . when right, to be kept right. When wrong, to be put right."

powers. In all parts of the world cultures are in collision as old habits are changed and old ideas and institutions are challenged. And throughout the world it is the youth who are most centrally involved in the search for adequate answers to the difficult problems of our time.

In this context, it is interesting to note Toffler's (1975) concept of the "eco-spasm"—his view of the general crisis facing the industrialized world:

"What we are seeing is the general crisis of industrialism—a crisis that transcends the differences between capitalism and Soviet-style communism, a crisis that is simultaneously tearing up our energy base, our value systems, our family structures, our institutions, our communicative modes, our sense of space and time, our epistemology as well as our economy. What is happening, no more, no less, is the breakdown of industrial civilization on the planet and the first fragmentary appearance of a wholly new and dramatically different social order: a super-industrial civilization that will be technological, but no longer industrial." (p. 3)

Whether or not this analysis is accurate, it does serve to point up the magnitude of the problems that confront us in our rapidly changing world.

Coping with accelerating social change

The historian Genovese (1970) has portrayed a rather foreboding picture of the problems created in the United States by inadequately controlled social change:

". . . when the richest nation in world history cannot keep its water and air clean, much less eliminate poverty; when great cities are acknowledged to be ungovernable, not to mention unlivable; when the country is racked with fear, foreboding, and hopelessness—then we had better declare a state of spiritual crisis, for the alternative would be to declare that irrationality, decadence, and disorder constitute our normal and preferred national condition." (p. 25)

While the preceding statement focuses on the negative rather than the positive aspects of the total situation, there have admittedly been a series of crises in the 1970s. Of course, the country has faced and overcome both internal and external crises before, but there seems little historical precedent for the accelerating and inadequately controlled social change and the accompanying value conflicts with which we are now confronted.

It is not our intent—nor would it be feasible or appropriate—to attempt to formulate a simple solution to the many complex and interrelated problems stemming from contemporary social change. However, a few comments do appear in order. For one thing, the solution to the problem of change does not appear to lie in trying to "set the clock back" or in trying to prevent change, but rather in (a) preparing for anticipated change in terms of what to expect and what to do; (b) acquiring the competencies that such change will require; and (c) accelerating the development of an "anticipatory democracy" in which "we the people" can play a responsible role in guiding and controlling social change in ways that will enhance the quality of life.

A second point pertains to the untapped resources of young people. Eisenberg (1970) has expressed it this way: "The energy, idealism, and intelligence of youth are the prime resources of each nation; if these resources are to be wisely spent, our youth must be involved in the mainstream of national life" (p. 1692). In a similar vein, the Panel on Youth of the President's Science Advisory Committee (1973) has suggested that young people be given the opportunity to participate more fully in educational and other social institutions and to assume more responsibility for themselves and others. The evidence indicates that young people acquire the capacity to cope with difficult situations—including rapid social change—when they are provided with the opportunity to assume meaningful and sequential responsibilities in relation to others and to society.

Implicit in the preceding is a third point, namely, that if we are to fulfill our dreams and hopes as a people, we each need to do not only "our thing" but "our part." Lack of concern and commitment to the human enterprise—as well as cynicism and loss of hope—can destroy us just as surely as thermonuclear weapons. We need to remind ourselves that both young and old, in the broader view, are parts of the generation living at this moment in history. The task of preserving human life and improving its quality is laid on us all.

In this chapter we have dealt with maladaptive behavior of groups. In labeling group behavior *maladaptive*, we have utilized the same criteria that we applied throughout to individual behavior: namely, its consequences for the well-being and actualization of the individual and the group. We have briefly described some of the specific problems or maladaptive patterns that must be dealt with if we are to keep our spaceship habitable for humankind. Among these are war and threat of war, group prejudice and discrimination, overpopulation and ecological violations, and uncontrolled social change. We have also noted some of the dimensions that appear relevant to coping with these problems as well as some of the efforts that are currently being made in this direction.

In Part Four, which follows, we shall complete our discussion of abnormal behavior. Chapter 19 deals with the problems of assessing maladaptive behavior and Chapter 20 with contemporary approaches to treatment. In Chapter 21, we shall explore horizons in mental health on both national and international levels, and we shall pursue further a basic theme of the present chapter: the need to develop better ways of preventing maladaptive behavior in order to build a "good future" for human beings on our troubled spacecraft.

IV
Modern
Methods
of Assessment,
Treatment, and
Prevention

19

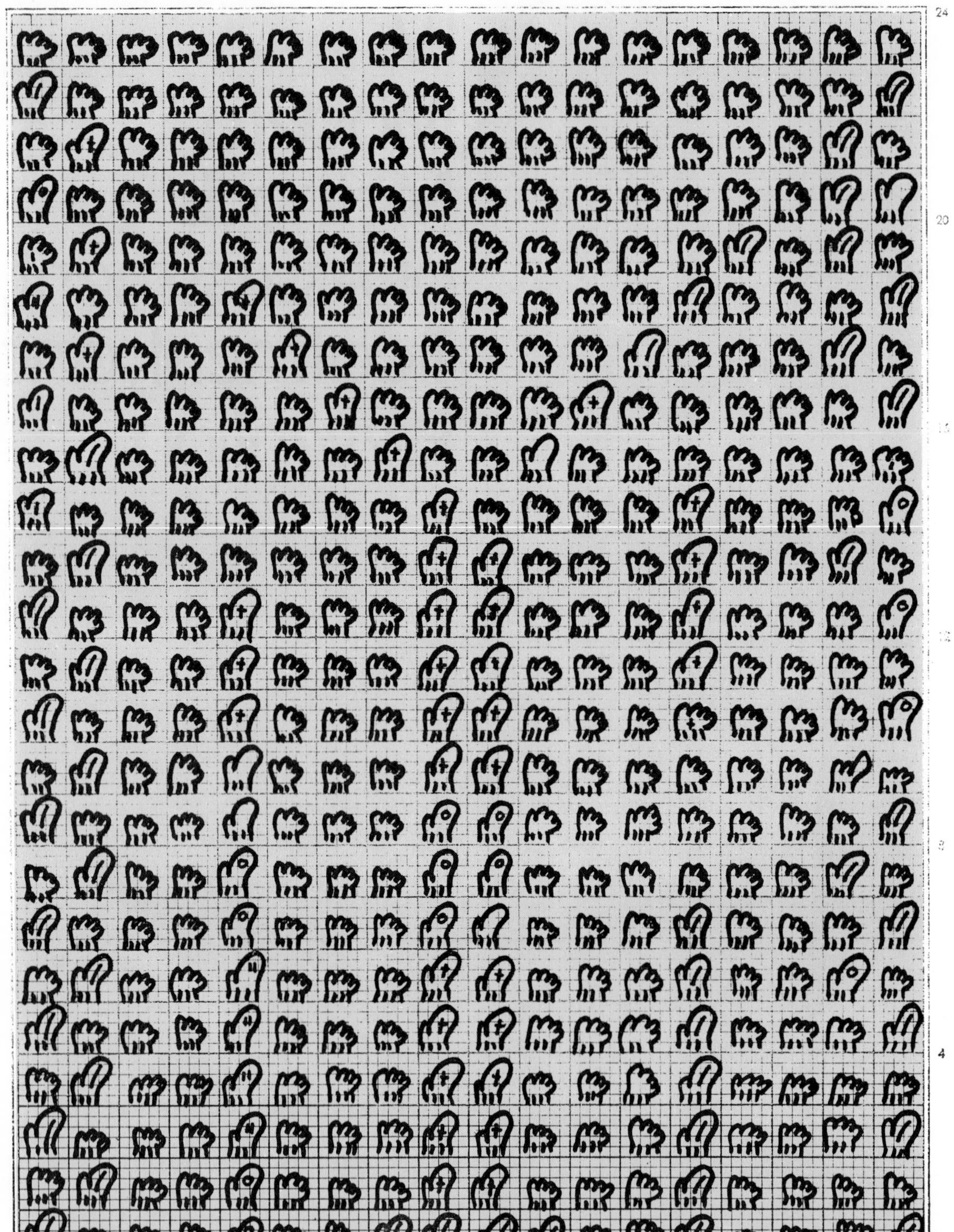

The Problem of Assessment

Clinical assessment is concerned with identifying the nature and severity of maladaptive behavior on the part of the individual or group, and with understanding the conditions that have caused and/or are maintaining the maladaptive behavior.

On an individual level, assessment information provides a working model of the individual and his life situation, which can be used for formulating a sound treatment program. The working model may be relatively comprehensive or limited to identification of the key problems and the specific conditions that are maintaining or exacerbating these problems. In either event, it then provides a basis for making decisions concerning hospitalization, the use of drugs, the role of psychotherapy, the modification of family patterns, and related aspects of possible treatment programs. Where feasible, these decisions are made with the consent and cooperation of the patient, though in cases of severe disorder they may have to be made without his participation.

Decisions about therapy are most likely to be sound if they are based on valid assessment data. Assessment information also provides objective measures that can be compared with measures obtained during and after treatment. This makes it possible to check on the effectiveness of an ongoing treatment program to see if modifications may be indicated; it also enables a comparison of the relative effectiveness of different therapeutic and preventive approaches.

On a group level, assessment information provides a comparable model of group structure and functioning. In assessing the maladaptive behavior of a disturbed family, for example, attention may focus on role behavior, communication patterns, decision-making processes, and other aspects of the family interaction and functioning. Although the focus is on the family as a social system, this does not preclude the clinical assessment of individual family members. Such assessment data, in turn, provide a basis for planning modifications in group organization and behavior, usually with the consent and cooperation of group members.

Initially in this chapter we shall review some of the more commonly used assessment pro-

Interdisciplinary Sources of Assessment Data

Problems in Assessment

Innovative Approaches to Assessment

655

cedures—medical, psychosocial, and group—and show how assessment data are integrated into a coherent clinical picture or model for use in making decisions about treatment. Then we shall note some of the problems and trends in clinical assessment, including the "antitest" revolt, the issues of confidentiality, informed consent, cultural bias, and the use of computers in clinical assessment.

Interdisciplinary Sources of Assessment Data

Since a wide range of factors may play important roles in causing and maintaining maladaptive behavior, assessment typically involves the coordinated use of medical, psychosocial, and sociocultural assessment procedures.

The nature and comprehensiveness of clinical assessments vary, of course, depending on the individual or group under study and the facilities of the treatment agency. Assessment by phone in a suicide prevention center, for example, is quite different from assessment aimed at determining whether a particular hospitalized patient should participate in an encounter group. Clinical assessment usually focuses on the target behaviors and conditions that appear relevant to understanding and treating the particular individual or group. Our attempt here will be to provide a perspective about the collection and use of clinical data, with emphasis on psychosocial assessment.

Medical evaluation

For the medical evaluation, data are collected relevant to the individual's general physical state and any physical pathology that may have a bearing on his maladaptive behavior. Medical data may also be collected concerning adverse physical conditions—such as malnutrition—in given groups or entire societies.

On an individual level, the medical evaluation commonly includes the following:

1. *General physical examination.* The physical examination consists of the kinds of procedures most of us have experienced in getting a "medical checkup." Typically, a medical history is obtained and the major systems of the body are examined.

2. *Neurological examination.* Since brain pathology is involved in some mental disorders, a specialized neurological examination is commonly given in addition to the general medical examination. This may involve the use of electroencephalography to check on brain-wave patterns.

3. *Special diagnostic techniques.* Where EEG's reveal *dysrhythmias* – abnormal brain-wave patterns – or where other data indicate the possibility of brain pathology, a variety of specialized techniques may be used in an attempt to arrive at a precise diagnosis of the nature and extent of the problem.

Medicine and allied sciences are contributing many new procedures of value in assessing conditions that can affect brain functioning. Radioactive isotopes can help locate brain lesions and other types of nervous system disturbances; techniques have been developed for the detection of rare metabolic disorders; and new methods have made it a simple matter to detect the use of heroin and other drugs of dependence. And as we have seen, new techniques have made it increasingly easy to identify genetic and chromosomal abnormalities. These techniques not only make it possible to diagnose conditions such as Down's syndrome in mental retardation, but also permit *preventive assessment.* For example, potential parents may be examined to see if they carry particular genetic aberrations that may adversely affect their offspring.

Psychosocial assessment

Psychological assessment has traditionally focused on the individual, while *sociological* assessment has focused on the individual's life situation. In *psychosocial* assessment these two orientations are combined to provide a realistic picture of the individual in interaction with his environment. This picture includes relevant information concerning the individual's personality makeup, his present and potential level of functioning, and the stresses and resources in his life situation.

A wide range of assessment procedures may be used, among the most important of which are the following.

Interviewing. The interview is probably the oldest method of psychosocial assessment. For centuries, people have assumed that they could "size up" another person by talking with him for a period of time.

In formal assessment, the interview usually involves a face-to-face conversation between two people, conducted in such a way that the clinician can obtain information about various aspects of the life situation, behavior, and personality makeup of the subject. The interview may vary from a simple set of questions designed to gather factual information – as in an *intake* or *case history* interview – to a more complex situation called a *stress interview,* in which questions are asked or tasks assigned under specially contrived, stressful conditions to see how the person functions intellectually and emotionally under difficult conditions. And, of course, there is the *therapeutic interview,* in which both assessment and therapy may take place.

In order to minimize sources of error – such as a possible tendency for the subject to say what he thinks the interviewer wants to hear rather than what he actually thinks or feels – interview assessment is often carefully structured in terms of goals, content to be explored, and the type of relationship the interviewer attempts to establish with the subject. Here, the use of rating scales may help focus and score the interview data. For example, the subject may be rated on a three-point scale with respect to self-esteem, anxiety, and various other characteristics. The structured interview is particularly effective in giving an overall impression of the subject and his life situation and in revealing specific problems or crises – such as marital difficulties, drug dependence, or suicidal fantasies – which may require immediate therapeutic intervention.

Psychological tests. Psychological tests are specialized assessment procedures for ascertaining such characteristics of an individual as intellectual capacity, motive patterns, self-concept, perception of the environment, role behaviors, values, level of anxiety or depression, coping patterns, and general personality integration. Psychological tests are far from perfect tools and often focus on variables within the subject at the expense of important

Behavior observation. Direct observation of a subject's behavior in a clinical or real-life situation, often aided by the use of rating scales

Behavior sample. Assessment data that presumably provide an accurate reflection of the subject's typical behavior

Culture biased. Term applied to assessment criteria that are biased in favor of a given group

Culture fair. Term applied to a test designed to eliminate the effects of ethnic differences in measuring particular traits, such as intelligence

Halo effect. Tendency when rating a specific trait to be influenced by another trait, such as appearance, or by one's overall impression of the subject

Intelligence test. Test used for establishing a subject's level of intellectual capacity

Performance test. Test in which motor rather than verbal responses are emphasized, often requiring perceptual-motor ability

Personality profile. A graphic summary of data from several tests or from subtests of the same test battery or scales that shows the personality configuration of an individual or a group of individuals

Projective test. Technique using neutral or ambiguous stimuli that subject is encouraged to interpret, and from which the subject's personality characteristics can be analyzed

Rating scale. Device for recording the rater's judgment of himself or others on defined traits

Self-report inventory. Procedure in which subject is asked to sort statements in terms of their applicability to him

Test reliability. Consistency with which a test measures a given trait on repeated administrations of the test to given subjects

Test validity. Degree to which a test actually measures what it was designed to measure

Verbal test. Test in which the subject's ability to understand and use words is important in making the required responses

conditions in his life situation. Their value depends heavily on the competence of the clinician who interprets them. In general, however, they are useful diagnostic tools for psychologists in much the same way that biochemical tests, such as the Wassermann, are useful to physicians. In both cases, pathology may be revealed in persons who appear on the surface to be quite normal, or a general impression of "something wrong" can be checked against more precise information.

1. *Intelligence tests.* There is a wide range of intelligence tests from which the clinician can choose. The Wechsler Intelligence Scale for Children (WISC) and the Stanford-Binet Intelligence Scale are widely used in clinical settings for measuring the intellectual capacity of children. Probably the most commonly used test for measuring adult intelligence is the Wechsler Adult Intelligence Scale (WAIS). It includes both verbal and performance material and consists of ten subtests with one alternative subtest. A brief description of two of the subtests—one verbal and one performance—will serve to illustrate the type of functions the WAIS measures:

General information. This subtest consists of questions designed to tap the individual's range of information on material that is ordinarily encountered. For example, the individual is asked to tell how many weeks there are in a year, to name the colors in the American flag, and to tell who wrote *Hamlet*.

Picture completion. This subtest consists of 21 cards showing pictures, each with a part missing. The task for the subject is to indicate what is missing. This test is designed to measure the individual's ability to discriminate between essential and nonessential elements in a situation (Wechsler, 1955, pp. 33–35).

Analysis of scores on the various subtests reveals the individual's present level of intellectual functioning. In addition, the subject's behavior in the test situation may reveal much relevant information, as when he is very apprehensive about not doing well, vacillates in his responses, seeks continual reassurance from the clinician, or is so disturbed that he cannot concentrate on the tasks presented.

2. *Personality tests.* There are a great many tests designed to measure facets of personali-

ty makeup other than intellectual capacity. It is convenient to group these tests into two broad categories—*projective* and *nonprojective*.

a) Projective tests rely on various ambiguous stimuli, such as inkblots, rather than specific test questions and answers. Through his interpretations of ambiguous material, the individual reveals a good deal about his conflicts, motives, intellectual level, coping techniques, and other aspects of his personality makeup. Thus projective tests place greater emphasis on the ways in which learning and self-structure lead the individual to organize and perceive the information presented to him. Prominent among the many projective tests in common usage are the Rorschach Test, the Thematic Apperception Test (TAT), and the Sentence Completion Test.

The Rorschach Test is named after the Swiss psychiatrist Hermann Rorschach, who initiated experimental use of inkblots in personality assessment in 1911. The test utilizes ten inkblot pictures to which the subject responds in succession after being instructed somewhat as follows (Klopfer & Davidson, 1962):

People may see many different things in these inkblot pictures; now tell me what you see, what it makes you think of, what it means to you.

The following excerpts are taken from the responses of a subject to the sample inkblot shown here.

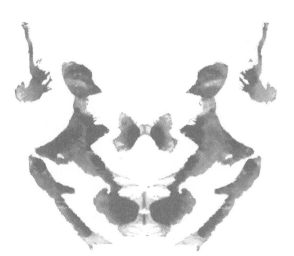

"This looks like two men with genital organs exposed. They have had a terrible fight and blood has splashed up against the wall. They have knives or sharp instruments in their hands and have just cut up a body. They have already taken out the lungs and other organs. The body is dismembered . . . nothing remains but a shell . . . the pelvic region. They were fighting as to who will complete the final dismemberment . . . like two vultures swooping down. . . ."

From this response and other test results, this subject was diagnosed as an antisocial personality with strong hostility.

Interestingly enough, there is evidence that typical responses to this inkblot have changed in the past twenty years, apparently reflecting cultural changes in our society and changing patterns in perception of sexual identity among young people. In the 1950s, most individuals of both sexes described the figures as male, and men who saw the figures as female were judged to be effeminate. Today, however, among individuals of both sexes, especially under age 25, there is an increasing tendency to see feminine figures. This discovery highlights the problem of interpreting the significance of particular test responses in a rapidly changing society and the constant need for checking on the validity of criteria used.

The Thematic Apperception Test (TAT) was introduced in 1935 by its coauthors, Morgan

In the Thematic Apperception Test (TAT), patients tell stories based on a series of drawings such as this one. The TAT is a method of revealing to the trained interpreter some of the dominant personality characteristics of the individual.

Since sentence completion tests are more structured than the Rorschach and most other projective tests, examiners can pinpoint topics they feel should be explored in understanding a subject's personality makeup and problems.

b) Nonprojective personality tests—more structured than the projective ones—typically use the questionnaire, self-inventory, or rating-scale technique of measurement. One of the major clinical nonprojective tests is the Minnesota Multiphasic Personality Inventory, or MMPI, developed by Hathaway and McKinley in 1943. This test consists of over 500 items covering topics from physical condition to moral and social attitudes. Sample items are:

"_____ I sometimes keep on at a thing until others lose their patience with me."
"_____ Bad words, often terrible words, come into my mind and I cannot get rid of them."
"_____ I often feel as if things were not real."
"_____ Someone has it in for me." (1951, p. 28)

The subject checks those items that apply to him. His responses are then compared with the responses that schizophrenics, hysterics, or other types of patients have made; similarities in pattern help in understanding the individual's problem and in planning appropriate treatment. The test also has built-in measures for detecting defensiveness or intentional falsification on the part of the person taking the test.

A second major nonprojective approach is called the Q sort. Here, a large number of statements are prepared concerning various traits, behavior patterns, or situations. For example, there might be statements like: "Is highly tense and anxious most of the time," and "Views sex as evil and strives to inhibit his sexual impulses." The subject is asked to sort these statements into piles graded from "highly typical" of him to "highly untypical." A variety of statistical techniques can then be used to evaluate the results of the sorting.

A third nonprojective approach utilizes the statistical technique of factor analysis in constructing personality tests that measure important and relatively independent personality traits. Here the goal is to measure one trait at a time with maximum precision and objectivity; a personality profile can then be drawn showing the degree to which specific traits are

and Murray of the Harvard Psychological Clinic. It utilizes a series of simple pictures about which the subject is instructed to make up stories. Again the material is sufficiently ambiguous and unstructured so that the individual tends to project his own conflicts and worries into it.

Another projective procedure that has proven useful in personality assessment is the sentence completion test. There are a number of such tests designed for children, adolescents, and adults. The material consists of the beginnings of sentences that the subject is asked to complete, as for example:

1. I wish _____.
2. My mother _____.
3. Sex _____.
4. I hate _____.
5. People _____.

Personality profiles

By combining the test results of many people who show a particular type of maladaptive behavior, it is possible to discover whether they have a characteristic pattern of personality traits that distinguishes them from the general population. For example, this is a composite profile based on the scores of 937 drug addicts serving prison terms. The measures were obtained on the Sixteen Personality Factor Questionnaire. This profile is interpreted as indicating lower-than-average emotional stability (Factor C) and higher-than-average unrealistic thinking (Factor M) and guilt proneness (Factor O).

Since the testing was done entirely on prison inmates, we do not know whether this profile is representative of all drug addicts. Also, it must be borne in mind that such profiles are only descriptive: they indicate a probability of finding certain traits associated with certain behavior but do not tell us whether either one caused the other.

PERSONALITY PROFILE OF DRUG ADDICTS

FACTOR Primary	TRAIT DESCRIPTION for scores on left side of grid	CENTILE RANK 00% 10% 20% 30% 40% 50% 60% 70% 80% 90% 100%	TRAIT DESCRIPTION for scores on right side of grid
A	RESERVED, critical		OUTGOING, warmhearted
B	LESS INTELLIGENT		MORE INTELLIGENT
C	EMOTIONALLY LESS STABLE		EMOTIONALLY STABLE
E	SUBMISSIVE, accommodating		AGGRESSIVE, assertive
F	SERIOUS, quiet		HAPPY-GO-LUCKY, enthusiastic
G	LESS RIGID, casual		STAID, persevering
H	TIMID, shy		VENTURESOME, uninhibited
I	TOUGH-MINDED, realistic		SENSITIVE
L	TRUSTING, adaptable		SUSPICIOUS
M	PRACTICAL, careful		IMAGINATIVE, impractical
N	UNSOPHISTICATED, naïve		SHREWD, sophisticated
O	CONFIDENT, serene		APPREHENSIVE, worrying
Q_1	CONSERVATIVE, traditional		EXPERIMENTING, analytical
Q_2	GROUP ADHERENT		SELF-SUFFICIENT
Q_3	FOLLOWS OWN URGES		CONTROLLED
Q_4	RELAXED		HIGH TENSION LEVEL
Secondary			
Q_I*	INTROVERSION		EXTRAVERSION
Q_{II}*	LOW ANXIETY		HIGH ANXIETY
Q_{III}*	RESPONSIVE EMOTIONALITY		TOUGH POISE
Q_{IV}*	SUBDUED GROUP ADHERENCE		INDEPENDENCE
	LOW NEUROTICISM		HIGH NEUROTICISM

*Roman subscripts denote 'second-order' traits, which are derived from weighted combinations of the first-order trait scores and are broader and more extensive in their effects. (IPAT Personality Profile Series, Copyright 1971, IPAT, Champaign, Illinois. Reproduced by permission.)

Interdisciplinary Sources of Assessment Data   661

characteristic of the given subject and the total pattern they form. The Comrey Personality Scales (1970), measuring key dimensions of personality, is an example of a test battery designed and used in this way.

Many other psychological tests are available for clinical use to reveal the subject's abilities, interests, aptitudes, temperament, anxiety level, self-concept, values, and other facets of his personality makeup. Some in common use are the Sixteen Personality Factor Questionnaire, the Kuder Preference Record, the "F-scale" (of manifest anxiety), and the Kahn Test of Symbol Arrangement. There are also a number of specialized tests such as the Bender Gestalt Test, which tests perception of form and thus may be used to diagnose particular kinds of brain damage.

Direct observation of behavior. The direct observation of the patient's behavior has long been considered an important procedure in psychosocial assessment. In the past, such observations have usually been confined to clinic or hospital settings, and the main purpose has been to find out more about the individual's psychological makeup and level of functioning.

In a hospital setting, for example, a brief description is usually made of the subject's behavior on admission, and periodically more detailed observations are made on the ward. These descriptions include concise notations of relevant information about the subject's personal hygiene, emotional behavior, delusions or hallucinations, motor activity, sexual behavior, aggressive or suicidal tendencies, and so on. To facilitate these observations, rating scales are commonly used that enable the recorder to indicate not only the presence or absence of a trait or behavior but also the prominence of it. The following is an example of such a rating-scale item; the observer is to check the most appropriate alternative.

Sexual behavior:
_____ 1. Sexually assaultive: aggressively approaches males or females with sexual intent.
_____ 2. Sexually soliciting: exposes genitals with sexual intent, makes overt sexual advances to other patients or staff, masturbates openly.
_____ 3. No overt sexual behavior: not preoccupied with discussion of sexual matters.
_____ 4. Avoids sex topics: made uneasy by discussion of sex, becomes disturbed if approached sexually by others.
_____ 5. Excessive prudishness about sex: considers sex filthy, condemns sexual behavior in others, becomes panic-stricken if approached sexually.

Observation of the subject's behavior may be made not only for original assessment purposes but also for later checking on the course or outcome of treatment procedures.

Recently, a good deal of attention has focused on observing the subject's behavior in his real-life setting. For example, a child who has been showing behavior problems may be observed at school, in his peer group, and in his home. Here the purpose is to obtain a sampling of his behavior in ordinary situations in order to understand the problems he is facing, the coping patterns he is using, and the environmental conditions that may be reinforcing his maladaptive behavior. It may turn out that the parents are paying attention to the child only when he engages in undesirable behavior, thus unwittingly reinforcing such behavior even though they are punishing it by scoldings or spankings. Such a "functional analysis of behavior" involves study of both the conditions that precede and stimulate the behavior and the consequences that reinforce it.

In situations where it may not be feasible to observe the subject's behavior in everyday situations—as when he is institutionalized—an entire family may be asked to meet together in the clinic or hospital where their interactions and difficulties can be observed and studied. In other cases a social worker may obtain relevant data in visits to the subject's home, talks with family members and others who are important to the subject, and observation of the stresses and resources in the subject's life situation. Even in cases where considerable data concerning the subject's life situation may be collected in structured interviews or in psychological tests, the collection of supplemental observational data is regarded as desirable.

Extending the use of such data a bit further, the social worker may analyze future situations with which the subject is likely to be confronted. For example, a patient with little education and a history of chronic unemployment might improve sufficiently to leave the institution but be little better off than before unless his treatment has included training in job skills. Thus knowledge of the individual's life situation not only helps in understanding his present maladaptive behavior but is often essential for planning a treatment program that will enable him to meet future challenges in more adaptive ways.

Assessment of groups (social systems)

In group assessment, the focus is on the group as a social system instead of on particular individuals within the group. Here, too, interviewing, testing, observing, and other psychosocial assessment procedures may be used, but the primary concern is with determining social roles, communication patterns, task performance, and other aspects of the group's structure and functioning.

Unfortunately, there are few research findings or guidelines on the assessment of group systems. Hence our discussion will be brief and confined primarily to questions that seem directly relevant to assessing the nature and extent of maladaptive behavior in small groups, such as marital couples and family groups. Most of the questions we shall raise, however, are applicable to larger groups as well as smaller ones.

A number of variables related to group behavior can be explored by means of answers to the following questions:

1. *What are the structural and organizational characteristics of the group?* Here we are concerned with such variables as the social roles available to and enacted by group members, communication patterns in the group, power relationships in the group, norms and values of the group, resources and goals of the group, and the number and characteristics of group members.

2. *What are the functional and task performance characteristics of the group?* This question relates to the playing of roles in the

Assessment of environmental contingencies

Assessment of the environmental contingencies maintaining the maladaptive behavior of a 7-year-old boy has been described by Bijou (1965). The boy had been brought to a clinic by his mother because of overly demanding behavior.

During the first four assessment sessions, the mother was asked to play with her son in the clinic playroom as she would at home. Two observers recorded the behaviors of both mother and son, first using general observations to delineate their overall behavior patterns and then noting the frequency of occurrence of cooperative and demanding behaviors on the part of the child and the mother's reaction to each. This record showed that the mother responded more frequently to the demanding behavior than to the cooperative behavior, leading to the hypothesis that she was reinforcing and maintaining the demanding behavior by her responses.

During the next four sessions, this hypothesis was tested. For two sessions the mother was under instructions to ignore the child except when a flashing red light was turned on. While the light was on, she was to respond to the child in any way that seemed natural to her except that she was limited to only one action or statement. The light remained off when the child made demands but was turned on each time he behaved cooperatively. Under these conditions, the frequency of the child's demands diminished and that of his cooperative behavior increased.

In the final two sessions, the mother was asked to revert to her former way of interacting with the child. The demanding behavior increased again and the cooperative behavior decreased.

This assessment procedure made it possible to formulate an effective treatment program focused on teaching the mother to use her own responses more appropriately at home in guiding her son's behavior.

In recent years new methods have been developed for the direct assessment of interpersonal behavior. Such procedures depend heavily on observation of a subject's "performance samples" in face-to-face communications in small groups.

Pictured here is an innovative group technique called the GAIT (Group Assessment of Interpersonal Traits), developed by Goodman (1972a, 1972b). It can be used for a number of purposes, including screening of would-be encounter-group participants, assessment of individuals seeking to serve as nonprofessional or paraprofessional therapists, and assessment of interpersonal communication deficits in children, teen-agers, and adults (D'Angelli, 1973; Dooley, 1975; Goodman, 1975).

In the GAIT approach all group members rate each other and are rated by staff observers on such characteristics as empathy, acceptance-warmth, degree of openness, and rigidity based on their interaction with each other during a group session. Research has shown a relationship between high scores on certain of these dimensions and effectiveness in working with emotionally disturbed children, as gauged by improvement on the part of the patients (Lindquist & Rappaport, 1973).

GAIT is an example of a small-group approach to the assessment of interpersonal behavior that shows marked promise. It will require further evaluation and refinement before the extent and range of its usefulness can be determined.

group, the actual functioning of communication processes, the handling of conflicts among group members, the decision-making processes of the group, the ways in which the group develops and uses its resources, and the performance of the group in achieving group goals and meeting the needs of group members.

3. *What is the field setting of the group?* Our chief concerns here are with the specific physical and sociocultural environment of the group, the status and role of the group in the larger community or society, the effects of environmental limitations and influences on the group, and the sources of environmental support available to the group.

To answer these questions, a wide range of assessment techniques may be used, including videotaping of interactional patterns to permit more precise analysis, drawing on data from epidemiological studies, and observing "high-risk" groups over a period of time to delineate conditions that may be causing problems.

In preceding chapters we have noted the pathogenic effects of various group conditions on group members as well as on the overall functioning of the group. Accurate answers to the three questions we have reviewed concerning group structure and functioning can be extremely helpful in identifying maladaptive group conditions and behaviors; and such answers can provide a sound basis for formulating treatment programs.

Integration of assessment data

As assessment data are collected, their significance must be interpreted so that they can be integrated into a coherent "working model" for use in planning or changing treatment.

In a clinic or hospital setting, assessment data are usually evaluated in a staff conference attended by members of the interdisciplinary team (perhaps a psychiatrist, a clinical psychologist, a social worker, and other mental health personnel) who are concerned with the decision to be made regarding treatment. By putting together all the information they have gathered, they can see whether the findings complement each other and form a definitive clinical picture or whether there are gaps or discrepancies that necessitate further investigation.

At the time of the original assessment, integration of all the data may lead to agreement on a tentative diagnostic label—such as *schizophrenia* from the APA classification. In the case of marital, family, or larger group assessment, no accepted classification of maladaptive behavior is available and usually a concise summary of the assessment data is made. In any case, the findings of each member of the interdisciplinary team, as well as the recommendations for treatment, are entered in the case record, so that it will always be possible to check back and see why a certain course of therapy was undertaken, how accurate the clinical assessment was, and how valid the treatment decision turned out to be.

New assessment data collected during the course of therapy provide feedback on its effectiveness as well as a basis for making needed modifications in an ongoing treatment program. As we have noted, clinical assessment data are also commonly used in evaluating the final outcome of therapy as well as in comparing the effectiveness of different therapeutic and preventive approaches.

The decisions made on the basis of assessment data may have far-reaching implications for the persons or groups under study. The staff decision may determine whether a depressed person will be hospitalized or remain with his family; whether divorce will be accepted as a solution to an unhappy marriage or a further attempt will be made to salvage the marriage; or whether an accused person will be declared competent to stand trial. Thus a valid decision, based on accurate assessment data, is of far more than theoretical importance.

Problems in Assessment

There have been basic challenges to long-established assessment procedures, particularly to psychological testing. Among the most prominent of these challenges is the *antitest revolt*, which refers to the development of attitudes of suspiciousness and hostility among the general public toward psychological testing. This revolt has been fueled by concern over the invasion of privacy—the right of the client to confidentiality in discussing his problems with mental health professionals—and over the possible misuse of test information. Additional impetus has derived from concern over the cultural bias of many psychological tests, and over the use of such tests for arbitrarily labeling people and assigning them to psychiatric categories—often with damaging consequences to their general well-being, career opportunities, and total life situation.

Confidentiality and informed consent

Psychological tests and other assessment procedures often elicit very personal information. The implicit or explicit agreement of the professional clinician to keep this information confidential is a basic component in the client-professional relationship. In fact, the loss of confidentiality seriously endangers the very relationship on which professional mental health personnel must rely if they are to render effective service.

The problem of safeguarding assessment data initially appears to be a simple one; in the field of law any information supplied by the client to his attorney is held inviolate unless the client consents to its release. In the mental health field, however, it is not so simple. For one thing, it may be advisable to share such information with parents, teachers, or other personnel who will be involved in planning and carrying out treatment. In addition, there are a number of special circumstances in which the disturbed person's right to confidentiality may be abridged, as when there is reason to believe that he may be dangerous to himself or others, or when legal authorities request such information. In fact, under some circumstances, professional mental health personnel are obligated to reveal information to legal authorities and are themselves subject to fine or imprisonment for failure to do so.

Most authorities agree that getting free and informed consent from the client is the safest method of preventing invasion of privacy. It is recommended that before assessment is undertaken, the client should be informed of the limits of confidentiality; then, if he takes part in assessment, his participation is presumably based on free and *informed consent*. This procedure may, of course, restrict his disclosure of information that he feels might be det-

rimental to him—information that might help the therapist in treatment. In addition, informed consent is far from a fail-safe precaution in that the client may not realize how powerful modern assessment procedures can be in revealing information that he might wish to withhold, or even in revealing facets of his personality of which he himself may be unaware.

Another problem is that if such information gets into a computerized data system, it may become available to a wide range of persons and possibly influence the individual's opportunities for employment or promotion on the job and adversely affect many other aspects of his life. In addition, the privilege of withholding consent is not retroactive. Some persons have found that assessment information recorded during high-school or college years has been raised to question their reliability for employment years later. And we are well aware of what usually happens to persons with a history of psychiatric treatment who later seek political office. As Grossman (1971) has pointed out, "There is no predicting the ultimate use and misuse of permanent records of this nature" (p. 97).

Clinical psychologists have been instrumental in getting "privileged communication" laws passed in some states to protect the client's right to privacy concerning information he communicates to licensed psychologists or psychiatrists. But the issue of confidentiality is a complex matter that is far from resolution.

The issue of cultural bias

We have commented before on the detrimental effects of rigid labeling even where the label is an accurate description of the individual's current behavior. When labels are applied on the basis of psychological tests that do not give valid measures, a doubly dangerous situation is created. Where the results of such tests are used to put an individual into a pigeonhole that ever after limits the opportunities open to him, testing is not serving the function for which it was developed and is doing serious harm.

Most psychological tests have been designed

by middle-class psychologists for prediction of performance valued by middle-class people, and many have been standardized on white subjects from predominantly middle or upper socioeconomic levels. It would be expected that persons from other backgrounds might be handicapped in taking such tests and that their scores would not be a fair measure of their potential.

The issue of cultural bias in tests has been of special concern in the movement toward greater equality of opportunity for racial minorities during the last decade. In 1971 the U.S. Supreme Court ruled that employers could not require individuals to pass a standardized intelligence test as a condition of employment unless such a test could be shown to be directly related to job performance. It is widely believed that in the past such tests have, in effect, been used as a means of excluding minority-group individuals from certain jobs where employers have traditionally given preference to whites.

As yet, no completely culture-free psychological test has been developed. Such tests must have content of some kind, and the meaning any content will have for the person being tested depends partly on his previous experience. Even nonverbal psychological tests are not completely free of this dependence on past experience. A great deal of research effort, however, has gone into attempts to develop tests of intelligence and other abilities that are "culture fair." Unfortunately, serious questions remain concerning the actual validity and "bias free" nature of such tests.[1]

Minority groups sometimes charge cultural bias in testing on still other grounds. A test on which a ghetto resident does poorly may, in fact, give an accurate prediction of how he will perform on a job requiring middle-class behavior and attitudes, while failing to reveal many skills and abilities that he does have. Is he therefore to be rejected unless he can be taught to show the middle-class behavior and attitudes? The problem here is in what the objectives of tests should be—whether they should be for screening out those who do not conform to the current accepted mold or for identifying more diverse kinds of talents. Many persons who have been denied equal opportunity in the past see tests as a way of continuing to exclude them, a way of maintaining the status quo.

Criticism of psychological test theory

An even more basic challenge to the use of psychological tests in clinical assessment has stemmed from psychologists' own questioning of the long-accepted assumption that maladjustive behavior can best be understood by looking within the individual at his traits and characteristics. The whole concept of putting a person in a category and giving him a label places the emphasis on internal causation of his behavior. The development of tests to assess these continuing inner characteristics was a logical extension of this concept. Although the contributing influence of the environment was never denied, more or less stable traits within the individual were assumed to account for the consistency in his behavior.

As we have seen, evidence from two sources has been altering this view: (a) the study of groups as social systems has repeatedly shown the extent to which social goals, role requirements, and other group conditions determine the feelings, behavior, and even abilities of individual members, although their behavior may remain consistent so long as their social setting remains the same; (b) the dramatic changes in behavior brought about by changes in reinforcement contingencies have demonstrated how inconstant many supposed "inner characteristics" may be.

Both these developments call into question the concept of entities within the individual. Although they do not demonstrate that internal conditions can be disregarded, their net effect has been to lower clinicians' expectations of what tests will be able to predict. Of the time now allotted to the psychosocial assessment of the individual, a far higher proportion is given to assessment of his transactions with his social environment. Much of the behavior observed does not fit anywhere in the established classification scheme, and the re-

[1] An informative article on cultural bias in the educational uses of tests may be found in Cleary, Humphreys, Kendrick, and Wesman (1975).

sult is a further disenchantment with classification and labeling in general.

Despite admitted problems in theory and practice, however, psychological testing does provide useful—and often essential—information for planning appropriate treatment programs. In addition, such data provide a useful "baseline" against which to evaluate the procedures and outcomes of therapy. Thus it would seem unwise to discard psychological assessment procedures, just as it would be to discard medical ones, in dealing with maladaptive behavior. Rather it would seem more effective to improve the existing procedures of psychological testing and erect safeguards to prevent the misuse of such assessment data.

Innovative Approaches to Assessment

Perhaps the most dramatic innovation in clinical assessment during the last decade has been the increasing sophistication and use of computers in individual assessment. In addition, there has been an increasing reliance on the use of specialized tests to obtain more accurate individual assessment data, as well as a trend toward using models—often with computer assistance—in the assessment of social systems.

Use of computers

Computers are used primarily in three ways in assessment: (a) to gather information directly from the subject; (b) to put together all of the information that has been gathered previously through interviews, tests, and other assessment measures; and (c) to simulate and predict the functioning of social systems. Here we shall deal with the use of computers in individual assessment; in the final section of this chapter, we shall comment on the construction of computer models of social systems.

By comparing the incoming information with data previously stored in its memory banks, the computer can perform a wide range of assessment functions. It can supply a diagnosis, evaluate the risk of certain kinds of behavior, suggest the most appropriate form of treatment, predict the outcome, and print out a summary report concerning the subject.

Over time, the computer builds an increasingly large data base covering many cases, which enables continual refinement of its probability statements. Interestingly enough, the computer is superior to individual clinicians in many of these functions. Goldberg (1970) demonstrated that a computer, programmed with the assessment strategies utilized by 29 clinical psychologists, was more proficient than the individual clinicians in differentiating between neurotic and psychotic individuals on the basis of MMPI profiles. Similarly, Mirabile, Houck, and Glueck (1970) demonstrated that a computer could outperform clinicians in selecting from among three chemotherapy programs for psychotic subjects. In predicting the risk of suicidal or assaultive behavior, the computer appears to be far superior to individual clinicians (Greist et al., 1973; Sletten, Altman, & Ulett, 1971). Computers can also be used to compare a patient's adjustment in the community prior to and after treatment, and to show whether the outcome of treatment was better or worse than the statewide average for a particular disorder (Evenson, Sletten, Hedlund, & Faintich, 1974).

In making predictions for an individual, the computer uses an *actuarial* procedure much like that used by life-insurance companies in predicting risks. Its conclusions are only statements of probability, based on what has happened to a large number of other, supposedly similar, people. For such an approach to work successfully, two conditions are of critical importance: (a) there must be consistent and objective criteria for interpreting test responses and other data; and (b) these criteria must have an adequate statistical base: that is, they must have been derived from information gathered on a large sample of subjects similar to the one being assessed. Both these conditions, in turn, imply a stable world, one that does not change in relevant particulars. To the extent that there has been change in the "real world" since the computer was programmed, its conclusions are subject to possible error.

Use of specialized tests

A number of psychologists have suggested that so-called "all-purpose" tests designed to measure a variety of factors within the same scale or test instrument be discarded. It does not seem productive to attempt to obtain a variety of assessment data or to answer all assessment questions by means of a particular test instrument. In fact, it would seem unrealistic to expect a given test or even a small battery of tests to supply all relevant psychosocial assessment data for a particular patient or subject. Thus as Walker (1974) has pointed out, "an increasing number of well-researched, highly sophisticated, and intensive batteries of tests designed for specific purposes are being developed" (p. 12). By means of these scales, specific questions relevant to the assessment of a given individual can be answered with a high degree of assurance.

Improved assessment of social systems

Since one major trend in modern science is toward increased emphasis on social systems—marital dyads, families, communities, organizations, and even societies—a good deal of research attention is being focused on ways of analyzing such systems. In the course of our discussion, we have already noted some of the forms this attention has taken, such as studying social roles, communication patterns, task performance, and other characteristics of marital, family, and larger groups. These techniques are ways of assessing interpersonal interactions as a basis for making improvements in the functioning of the system.

Another innovative technique that appears to offer great future promise involves the construction of computer models of social systems. Computers then simulate the actual functioning of the system. This not only permits detailed analysis of the system in operation, but also makes it possible to study the effects different changes would have on the overall operation of the system. Simulations of complex social systems are handicapped today by our inadequate knowledge of many of the key variables that affect their functioning. As these variables are better understood, however, computer simulation can become an increasingly accurate replica of "real-world" social processes.[2]

---

[2]A useful sourcebook on innovative approaches to assessment is Kline (1974).

Computer summaries of MMPI information

In a 3-year research and treatment program in delinquency control conducted at the Center for the Study of Crime, Delinquency, and Corrections at Southern Illinois University at Carbondale, delinquent-prone high-school boys were identified and given several kinds of help, including "Big Brother" counselors and different kinds of individual and group therapy. Assessment included the MMPI, responses from which were sent to the Institute of Clinical Analysis in Glendale, California, for computer analysis and report on each subject tested. Computer scoring of a test like the MMPI eliminates the variation that otherwise would occur through differences in the subjective judgments of different scorers. Although MMPI data alone are not definitive, they are useful when combined with other information.

On the basis of all the information collected, precise treatment goals were formulated for each individual. The hypothesis was that if treatment was successful, the individual's MMPI scores on a posttreatment testing would change accordingly.

The computer printouts and graphs shown here summarize the case of a 15-year-old boy who had been referred by school guidance personnel because of problem behaviors, including drug abuse and truancy. At the time of referral, he was characterized as anxious, fearful, self-devaluated, negative in his attitude toward others, and suffering from serious inner conflicts. His MMPI scores were higher than normal for all but one of the clinical scales, and his Multiphasic Index* indicated a high level of overall emotional disturbance.

The primary treatment objectives set for this boy were to reduce his anxiety and help him establish a realistic self-concept. Treatment included individual reality therapy, group counseling for the family, and monetary and social reinforcement contingent on appropriate behaviors or approximations of such behaviors. For example, he was exposed to a variety of social situations and rewarded for participating rather than withdrawing.

Several months later, his scores were in the normal range on all but two of the clinical scales of the MMPI. He showed more confidence in himself, markedly reduced anxiety, and a more positive view of his world, but there still were indications of mild to moderate emotional disturbance (Pooley, 1971).

Several later investigators, including Lachar (1974), have also reported favorably on the accuracy and generalizability of computer interpretations of MMPI test data.

*The Multiphasic Index is an index of basic anxiety that functions like a fever thermometer in indicating the individual's "emotional temperature." It is derived from selected, especially dependable MMPI scores.

Computer summary before treatment

"MI, Emotional Disturbance Index . . . 149. Range 65 to 150. Scores of 90 and up reflect increasing degrees of emotional or personality disorder, i.e., 90 to 99 mild to mod. — 100 to 115 mod. to marked — 116 to 150 marked. . . .

Probability of low disturbance 1%

Probability of moderate disturbance 84%

Probability of marked disturbance 15%

Interpretation . . . The MI, Multiphasic Index, reflects an emotional disorder of marked severity. Responses are inappropriate, unrealistic and self-defeating.

This pattern is usually considered an adolescent maladjustment reaction. It is often associated with delinquency, usually the result of ineptness, misunderstanding, emotional conflicts, or simply following the gang. These persons are over-dependent but act the opposite. They fear close emotional ties because of possible rejection. Their behavior is often irresponsible and their expectations are unrealistic. There is a history of family problems, sexual confusion, poor ego-identification and difficulty with authority. They tend to be non-conforming, unpredictable and impulsive.

Special coping problems . . . Schizoid dissociation or fantasy is strongly indicated. There is evidence suggesting a paranoid trend. There is blocking of deep or positive emotional response, hostile reaction to rejection, and unresolved resentment toward stringent authority surrogates. . . . Investigate suicidal or self-destructive thoughts or plans. Alcohol proneness is indicated. Investigate history concerning excessive drinking."

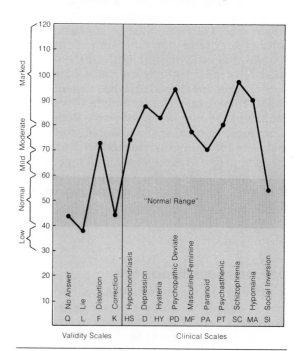

Computer summary after treatment

"MI, Multiphasic Index . . . 96 Mild to moderate elevation

Probability of significant disturbance 36% Two separate and distinct methods of appraising emotional conflict are shown on scores below. Either score may suggest a disorder but clinical significance is greater when both scores are elevated.

MI interpretation . . . The MI, Multiphasic Index, reflects a mild degree of emotional conflict. Resilience or the ability to make satisfactory adjustments is fair to medium.

Summary . . . Significant signs of emotional disorder are revealed. Personality trait or character disorder is the most likely diagnostic classification.

There is little or no call for help which indicates a wish for self-sufficiency. Defenses appear quite adequate. However, good coping ability is probably over-estimated. This suggests more willful intent than tough resilience.

Validity . . . Responses are not polarized in the direction of favorability or unfavorability which indicates the subject presents a reasonably candid picture of himself on the test.

Personality description . . . There is a persistent tendency toward behavior problems . . . rationalization of irresponsible, asocial urges, difficulty with authority, and lack of social conformity. Some lowered morale, worry or self-doubt is admitted. Increased drive reflects a need to meet competitive demands and overcome frustration. . . ."

In the present chapter, we have attempted to gain an overall perspective on clinical assessment. Toward this end we noted the nature and uses of clinical assessment and then dealt briefly with the interdisciplinary sources utilized in collecting relevant assessment data as well as with methods of integrating and interpreting such data. Next we noted some of the problems, such as the antitest revolt, that have surrounded clinical assessment procedures; and we completed the chapter with a brief review of innovative approaches that are leading to advances in clinical assessment. Throughout, we emphasized the trend away from the assessment of individuals to the assessment of individual-environmental interactions, as well as the trend away from the use of assessment data for labeling to its use in treatment and prevention.

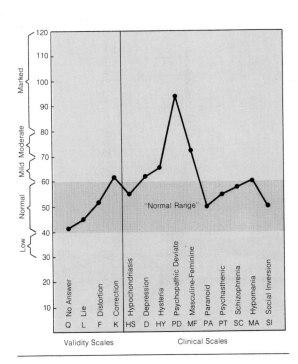

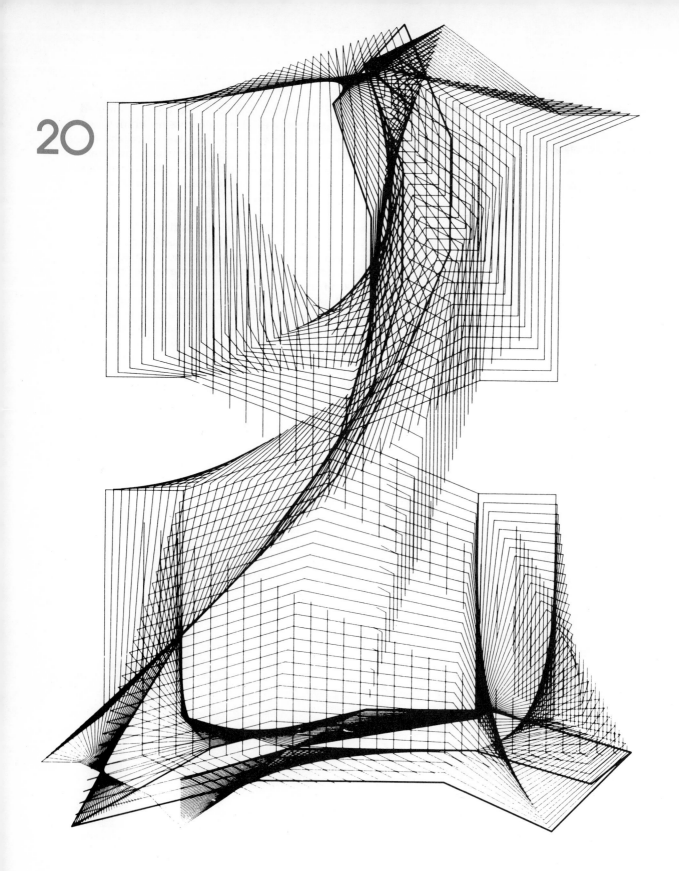

Contemporary Approaches to Therapy

Therapy is directed toward modifying maladaptive behavior and fostering adaptive behavior. There are, of course, a great many other approaches to behavior change, such as formal education, political propaganda, and brainwashing. In therapy, however, the primary goal is to help an individual and/or group achieve more effective coping behavior.

The concept of therapy is not a new one. Throughout recorded history, human beings have tried to help each other with problems of living—including mental disorders—in both informal and formal ways. In Chapter 2 we noted the wide range of procedures that have been advocated for helping the mentally disturbed—from trephining and exorcism to incarceration and torture, from understanding and kindliness to the most extreme cruelty.

In the twentieth century significant advances have been made in the treatment of maladaptive behavior. These include the development, on a biological level, of methods for correcting or alleviating brain pathology and related organic conditions that impair thought, feeling, and action; on a psychosocial level, of a variety of methods for modifying maladaptive behavior, fostering more effective coping techniques, and opening channels for growth; and on a sociocultural level, of methods for correcting or alleviating pathological social conditions and the maladaptive behaviors of entire communities or even societies.

Traditionally the term psychotherapy has been used to refer to the treatment of mental disorders by means of psychological techniques, usually in a patient-therapist relationship, while sociotherapy has focused on helping the patient who has been hospitalized make a successful readjustment to his family and community setting. Since these approaches to therapy have expanded greatly in recent years, we shall use *psychotherapy* as roughly synonymous with *psychosocial approaches to therapy*, and we shall view *sociotherapy* as blending imperceptibly into the more comprehensive *sociocultural approaches to therapy.*

Perhaps our limited knowledge concerning human nature and behavior has made it inevitable that marked differences in viewpoints concerning therapy should have arisen. For

Biological Therapy

Psychosocial Approaches to Therapy

Sociocultural Approaches to Therapy

Current Issues and Trends in Treatment

673

example, some therapists rely primarily on chemotherapy or other biological methods; others rely primarily on behavior therapy or other psychosocial methods. But to be effective, any treatment program should be formulated in relation to the needs and potentialities of the given individual or group. Usually this requires an interdisciplinary approach to therapy.

In the present chapter, we shall examine the major biological, psychosocial, and sociocultural approaches to therapy. Then we shall deal with certain issues and trends that have emerged in recent years. Throughout our discussion, we shall attempt to provide the reader with a broad perspective concerning the goals, procedures, and outcomes of contemporary therapy.

Biological Therapy

Biological approaches to therapy may embrace practically any branch of medicine, depending on the needs of the particular individual. Special diets may be prescribed for those suffering from malnutrition, brain surgery for those with tumors, tranquilizers for agitated individuals, and a number of emergency measures for those suffering from acute drug intoxication. In this section we shall focus on three biological treatment techniques: (a) chemotherapy, (b) electrotherapy, and (c) brain-wave therapy.

Chemotherapy

During the last two decades there has been an extraordinary acceleration in the use of chemicals in the treatment of abnormal behavior, often with dramatic results. This psychopharmacological revolution has come about largely as a result of our expanding knowledge of the role of biochemistry in brain pathology and the development of new drugs for achieving specific therapeutic objectives. In the present context we shall note the major types of drugs used in chemotherapy and attempt to gain a perspective on the advantages and limitations of this therapeutic approach.

Types of drugs used. The most commonly used drugs in chemotherapy fall into three major categories: (a) the antipsychotic drugs, or major tranquilizers, (b) the antianxiety drugs, or minor tranquilizers, and (c) the antidepressant drugs. These drugs are often used in combination, depending on the needs and reactions of the particular individual.

1. *Antipsychotic drugs (major tranquilizers).* For centuries the root of the plant *rauwolfia* (snakeroot) has been used in India for the treatment of mental disorders. In 1943, the *Indian Medical Gazette* reported improvement in manic reactions, schizophrenia, and

other types of psychopathology following the use of *reserpine,* a drug derived from rauwolfia. Reserpine was first used in the United States in the early 1950s, after it was found to have a calming effect on mental patients (Kline, 1954). Early enthusiasm for the drug was tempered, however, by the finding that it may produce low blood pressure, nasal congestion, and other undesirable side effects. Consequently reserpine has now been largely replaced by other major tranquilizing drugs, such as the phenothiazines.

The phenothiazines—also introduced in the early 1950s—have remained the most popular of the major tranquilizing drugs. Two of these drugs, chlorpromazine and trifluoperazine HCl (marketed as Thorazine and Stelazine, respectively), have proven highly successful in calming psychotics manifesting emotional tension, disordered thought processes, and motor hyperactivity. Often the acutely agitated individual calms down within 48 hours after the beginning of treatment, and within two weeks, hallucinations and delusions are usually eliminated or alleviated. Even chronic schizophrenics, as we have noted, may experience some relief of symptoms and take a more active interest in their environment. The phenothiazines are considered relatively safe drugs, but they sometimes have undesirable side effects such as jaundice, drowsiness, and fainting spells. Usually such difficulties clear up with an adjustment in dosage. However, other more subtle complications may arise when phenothiazine drugs are used on an outpatient basis. For example, they do not mix well with alcohol.

Other antipsychotic drugs include the butyrophenones, the thioxanthenes, and the dibenzoxazepines—common trade names being Haldol, Taractan, and Loxitane, respectively. These drugs have effects similar to the phenothiazines and increase the therapist's choice of drugs for meeting the needs of given individuals.

2. *Antianxiety drugs (minor tranquilizers).* Besides the major antipsychotic drugs, a number of minor tranquilizers, or antianxiety drugs, have been introduced in recent years. In fact, such names as Miltown, Librium, and Valium—trade names used for meprobamate, chlordiazepoxide hydrochloride, and diaze-

pam, respectively—have become household words.

Minor tranquilizers are commonly used for reducing tension and anxiety in normal individuals during periods of severe stress as well as in the treatment of neurotic and psychosomatic disorders. Minor tranquilizers may also be used as part of the total treatment program for psychotics and for persons who have formerly been addicted to alcohol or other drugs. Both with normal individuals undergoing crises and with persons being treated for more severe psychopathology, the minor tranquilizers are frequently used in place of barbiturates or other sedatives to help induce relaxation and sleep.

Although the mild tranquilizers are considered to have minimal side effects, they are not without their complications. They commonly produce drowsiness, and when the medication is stopped after prolonged, heavy dosage there may be severe withdrawal symptoms, including insomnia, tremors, hallucinations, and convulsions. In general, these drugs are *contraindicated* (not recommended) for women during pregnancy, for children under 6 years of age, for depressed persons, and for individuals engaged in hazardous occupations that require alertness. As in the case of the major tranquilizers, they should not be used in combination with alcohol.

3. *Antidepressants.* Although the tranquilizing drugs have proven highly beneficial in treating many types of disorders, they are largely ineffective for persons with depressive reactions. In such cases the need is for a "mood elevator"—something that will energize rather than tranquilize. The first drug to be tried for this purpose was *iproniazid,* a drug being tested in the treatment of tuberculosis. It was noted that tubercular patients treated with the drug became euphoric, optimistic, and zestful—often to the extent of not getting enough rest. Tests on depressed patients proved its effectiveness as an antidepressant, but unfortunately it was found to have dangerous side effects—particularly liver toxicity—which prohibited its use.

The discovery of the antidepressant effects of iproniazid, however, led to the study of other monoamine oxidase inhibitors (MAO inhibitors), several of which were found to be effective antidepressants with minimal side effects. Among the more widely used of these have been phenelzine (Nardil) and isocarboxazid (Marplan). Other categories of antidepressants include the tricyclic derivatives, such as Tofranil and Sinequan, and the amitriptyline derivatives, such as Elavil and Triavil.

Because of the effectiveness of the antidepressant drugs, the use of electroconvulsive therapy (ECT) in depression has been greatly reduced. However, the more rapidly acting of the antidepressant drugs must be used with caution because of possible undesirable side effects, including anxiety and agitation; thus ECT is often the preferred method of treatment for severely depressed and possibly suicidal individuals, where it is important to clear up the depression as quickly as possible.

Chemotherapy in perspective. With the advent of modern chemotherapy there has been a reduction in the seriousness and chronicity of many types of psychopathology, particularly the psychoses. Chemotherapy has made it possible for many individuals to function in their family and community setting who would otherwise require hospitalization; it has led to the earlier discharge of those who do require hospitalization and to the greater effectiveness of aftercare programs; and it has made restraints and locked wards largely methods of the past. All in all, chemotherapy not only has outmoded more drastic forms of treatment, but has led to a much more favorable hospital climate for patients and staff alike.

However, there are a number of complications and limitations in the use of chemotherapy. Aside from possible undesirable side effects, the problem of matching drug and dosage to the needs of a given individual is often a difficult one, and it is sometimes necessary to change medication in the course of treatment. In addition, as many investigators have pointed out, tranquilizers and antidepressants tend to alleviate symptoms rather than bring the individual to grips with personal or situational factors that may be reinforcing maladaptive behaviors. Although the reduction in anxiety, disturbed thinking, and other symptoms may tempt therapists to regard a

patient as "recovered," it would appear essential to include psychotherapy and sociotherapy in the total treatment program if such gains are to be maintained or improved on.

Electrotherapy

In this section we shall elaborate briefly on three forms of therapy that involve the influence of electric current on the functioning of the central nervous system. These are: (a) electroconvulsive therapy, (b) electrosleep therapy, and (c) the surgical implantation of microcircuitry.

Electroconvulsive therapy. The groundwork for the development of electroconvulsive therapy (also referred to as electroshock therapy) was laid in 1935, when a Budapest psychiatrist, Von Meduna, observed that there seemed to be a much lower incidence of epilepsy among schizophrenics than in the population as a whole. He also noted that schizophrenic symptoms tended to disappear temporarily following convulsions in those patients who did suffer from epilepsy. Accordingly, he set out to produce epilepticlike convulsions in his schizophrenic patients by chemical means. He first tried administering camphor and oil, but this did not work out well because the convulsions might occur at any time within the next two or three days. He then tried Metrazol, but this drug induced intense fear in the patients and resulted in a high incidence of fatalities. Considered a "barbaric" form of treatment, Metrazol therapy was shortly abandoned.

In 1938 two Italians, Cerletti and Bini, introduced the use of electroshock for the artificial production of convulsive seizures in mental patients. The patient lay on a padded couch with electrodes attached to his head, and an electric current of 70 to 130 volts was administered for a fraction of a second. This shock resulted in convulsions similar to grand-mal seizures of epileptics, after which the patient was unconscious for several minutes. A muscle relaxant was usually administered prior to the electric shock to minimize the intensity of seizure activity and the danger of undesirable side effects such as bone fractures and impaired cardiovascular functioning. Usually a number of shock treatments were given over a period of days and weeks. Electroconvulsive procedures have since been refined to the extent that convulsions are minimal and ECT is considered a relatively safe form of treatment (T. D. Hurwitz, 1974). Although electroconvulsive therapy has not proven effective in the treatment of schizophrenics, it has been found to be highly effective in the treatment of depressives.

But how ECT works is a matter of conjecture. One popular view holds that the electroshock somehow "clears the circuits" in the nervous system, enabling the individual to think more rationally. Some behavior therapists have even suggested that electroconvulsive therapy is so noxious that it acts as a negative reinforcer to "crazy" or depressed behavior, so that the individual changes his behavior to avoid more punishment.

The fact is that ECT is used because it works, even though we do not yet understand *how* it works. But as we have noted, recent advances in chemotherapy have reduced the use of ECT; it is now used chiefly for the rapid alleviation of depression in suicidal individuals.

Electrosleep therapy. Although it has received little attention in the United States, electrosleep, or *cerebral electrotherapy,* has been the subject of extensive research in the U.S.S.R. In this procedure, a soft mask containing electrodes is placed over the upper part of the individual's face. A mild electric current—just enough to cause a slight tingling sensation—is administered. The individual does not lose consciousness or experience convulsions; he may or may not fall asleep during the treatment. Usually, half-hour treatments are administered daily for one or two weeks.

In one of the first studies of electrosleep in the United States, Rosenthal and Wulfsohn (1970) reported favorable preliminary results with a group of more than 40 outpatients suffering from chronic anxiety, depressive states, and associated insomnia.

Unfortunately, later studies have shown less promising results, and the types of disorders for which electrosleep may be appropriate, as well as its long-range effectiveness, remain to be ascertained (Astrup, 1974; Brown, 1975;

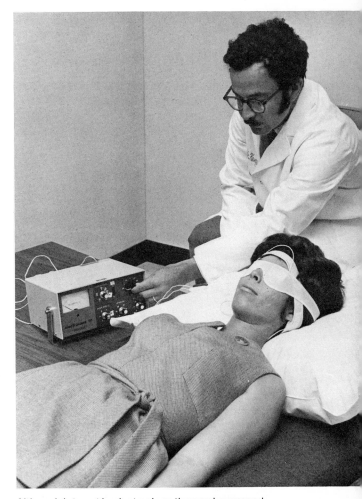

Although interest in electrosleep therapy has waned somewhat in recent years, its possibilities are still being investigated. The battery-operated transistor device shown here passes a low current through the patient's brain.

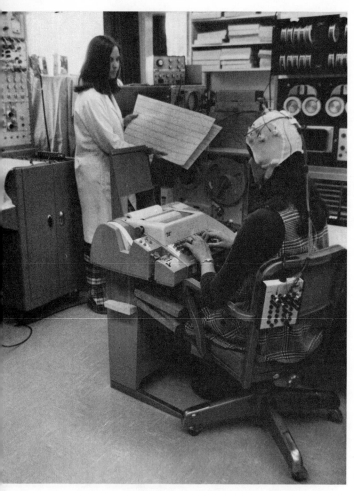

Hearst et al., 1974). However, international efforts to evaluate this form of therapy are being made, and it may well prove to be a useful treatment in and of itself or as an adjunct to a broader treatment program.

Implantation of microcircuitry. One of the new frontiers in brain research involves the electrical stimulation of the brain (ESB) in an attempt to learn more about how various brain areas function. For example, electrical stimulation of the hypothalamus in human beings can produce a whole gamut of emotional responses, from euphoria to terror.

Such findings have led to research in the possibility of surgical implantation of microcircuitry to control some forms of maladaptive behavior that are presumably associated with pathological brain functioning, such as episodic homicidal impulses or chronic suicidal behavior. In fact, it is not beyond the realm of possibility that manic-depressive individuals might one day be able to control extreme mood swings with ESB. However, it may be emphasized that the efficacy of treating most forms of maladaptive behavior by means of the implantation of microcircuitry is not known but seems highly questionable.

In an experimental program at Stanford Research Institute, investigators are attempting to have computers "read" brain waves for instructions. Certain instructions may produce consistent electroencephalograph patterns, so the computer will be able to respond to the patterns each time a different person gives the brain-wave instruction.

Brain-wave therapy

Waking electroencephalograms (EEG's) show a continuous series of brain waves that wax and wane in frequency of occurrence. A number of these brain waves have been identified and labeled in terms of the number of cycles per second and the amplitude of the wave— e.g., alpha, beta, delta, and theta rhythms. The dominance of a given wave pattern appears to be related to specific functions of the brain.

Alpha waves, which have a frequency of 8 to 12 cycles per second and an amplitude of up to 40 microvolts, are associated with an alert state that is devoid of concrete visual imagery and is accompanied by feelings of tranquillity and a lack of tension and anxiety. Alpha waves occur intermittently—the typical individual slipping in and out of alpha from about 5 to 30 times per minute. In contrast, beta waves—which fall into a fast-paced 14 to 28 cycles per second—tend to occur when the individual is attempting to solve a problem or is worrying about something; they are usually accompanied by feelings of tension. Delta waves occur only when the individual is asleep or unconscious and show a frequency of 2 to 3 cycles per second. Theta waves have a frequency of 5 to 7 cycles per second and are particularly prominent in children and young adolescents. The actual functions of both delta and theta waves are still the subject of research.

Most persons are, of course, unaware of their brain-wave patterns and unable to control them consciously. Pioneering studies in the conscious control of alpha waves were conducted in 1958 by Joseph Kamiya. His initial experiments involved placing subjects in a darkened room and monitoring their brain waves. The subjects were instructed to close their eyes and guess whether they were in an alpha or a nonalpha state whenever they heard a bell ring. After each guess they were told whether they were right or wrong. With this type of feedback, the subjects learned in a few sessions to discriminate between alpha and nonalpha states. Even more remarkable, once they had learned to make this discrimination, they could voluntarily switch alpha rhythms on or off. Kamiya (1968) later found he could speed up the process of learning by sounding a feedback tone whenever alpha waves were occurring. Many other investigators using similar biofeedback training (BFT) procedures have obtained comparable results.

In our discussion of psychosomatic disorders, we noted the possible therapeutic value of learning to regulate blood pressure and other functions of the autonomic nervous system. Similar interest has been expressed in the possible therapeutic use of brain-wave control. Investigators have shown that dedicated Zen and Yoga meditators are capable not only of raising and lowering their blood pressure, body temperature, and related functions but also of controlling their brain waves. In fact, Hirai and Kasamatsu (1966) of Tokyo University found a high correlation between brain-wave control and the proficiency rating of Zen masters. During meditation, the EEG of Zen masters showed prominent alpha activity. Those with 20 years or more of Zen practice also showed prolonged patterns of theta activity.

It has been suggested that the use of BFT for the control of brain waves and muscle tension—which has also been referred to as "electronic Yoga"—could be particularly helpful in overcoming chronic anxiety and tension. Townsend, House, and Addario (1975) found biofeedback-mediated relaxation therapy far superior to group therapy in the treatment of chronic anxiety. But despite such promising findings, many questions remain unanswered with respect to BFT. Certainly it is no "miracle cure," and it seems unlikely that learning to deal effectively with life's problems can ever be achieved simply through the control of automatic functions, although such control may help.

An additional form of biological therapy which merits brief mention is acupuncture. Since its relatively recent introduction and testing on a wide scale in the United States, it has been shown to be highly effective in the control of chronic pain (Schneider, 1974). However, its possible usefulness in the treatment of mental disorders remains to be ascertained.

Psychosocial Approaches to Therapy

As Alexander has pointed out, psychotherapy is not far removed from the view of most of us:

". . . Everyone who tries to console a despondent friend, calm down a panicky child in a sense practices psychotherapy. He tries by psychological means to restore the disturbed emotional equilibrium of another person. Even these commonsense, everyday methods are based on the understanding of the nature of the disturbance, although on an intuitive and not a scientific understanding. . . . Methodological psychotherapy to a large degree is nothing but a systematic, conscious application of methods by which we influence our fellow men in our daily life. The most important difference is that intuitive knowledge is replaced by the well established general principles of psychodynamics." (1946, p. 110)

We shall see, however, that these "well established principles" are not always as well grounded scientifically as we might hope.

In general, psychotherapy aims toward (a) changing maladaptive behavior patterns, (b) minimizing or eliminating environmental conditions that may be causing and/or maintaining such behavior, (c) improving interpersonal and other competencies, (d) resolving handicapping or disabling inner conflicts and alleviating personal distress, (e) modifying inaccurate assumptions about oneself and one's world, and (f) fostering a clear-cut sense of one's self-identity and the opening of pathways to a more meaningful and fulfilling existence.

These goals are by no means easy to achieve. Often an individual's distorted environmental perspective and unhealthy self-concept are the end products of faulty parent-child relationships reinforced by many years of life experiences. In other instances, adequate occupational, marital, or social adjust-ment requires major changes in the person's life situation in addition to psychotherapy. It would be too much to expect that the psychotherapist could intervene and in a short period of time undo the entire past history of the individual and prepare him to cope with a difficult life situation in a fully adequate manner.

The psychotherapist does have certain assets on his side, however, the major one being the inner drive of the individual toward integrity and health. Although this inner drive is often obscured in severely disturbed patients, the majority are anxious, unhappy, discouraged, and eager to cooperate in any program that holds hope for improvement. Some degree of cooperation on the part of the individual receiving help is considered essential if psychotherapy is to have much chance of success.

Psychotherapy with severely disturbed individuals usually takes place in a hospital or inpatient clinic setting. The various psychotherapeutic procedures we shall be discussing, however, are by no means confined to inpatients. Most of those who receive psychotherapy for neuroses, alcoholism, or personality disorders do so on an outpatient basis—either in an outpatient clinic or with psychiatrists or clinical psychologists in private practice.

In the discussion that follows, we shall deal with the differing systematic viewpoints, goals, and procedures of the major forms of psychotherapy. The illustration on page 000 provides an overview of some of the key dimensions or characteristics of this rather complex area of study.[1]

Psychoanalytic therapy

As developed by Freud, psychoanalytic therapy is an intensive, long-term procedure for uncovering repressed memories, motives, and conflicts—presumably stemming from problems in early psychosexual development—and helping the individual resolve them in the light of adult reality. It is felt that gaining insight into such repressed material will free the individual from the need to squander his energies on repressive defense mechanisms,

---

[1]A comprehensive but concise description of the major types of psychotherapy may be found in Corsini (1973).

The forms of psychotherapy discussed in this chapter can be classified in a number of ways. Listed below are a few "key dimensions" that will be useful to bear in mind as we examine various approaches to psychotherapy.

1. Individual/group. In individual or one-to-one therapy, the therapist treats one person at a time. The effectiveness of such therapies depends to a great extent on the patient-therapist relationship. In group therapy, several persons are treated at the same time in a group setting. Here the interactions and relationships of the group members to one another are important aspects of therapy. The majority of persons receiving psychological assistance are in some form of group therapy.

2. Cognitive change/behavior change. Some approaches to psychotherapy focus on changes in the patient's values and other assumptions, on the premise that such cognitive change will lead to changed and more effective behavior. Other approaches focus directly on changing given behaviors on the premise that changed behavior will in turn result in cognitive change.

3. Directive/nondirective. Therapists differ widely with respect to the amount of responsibility they place upon the individual being treated as contrasted with the degree to which they themselves direct the course of therapy. In directive therapy, the therapist takes an "active" role, asking questions and offering interpretations; in nondirective therapy, the major responsibility is placed

on the client, and the therapist may simply try to help him clarify and understand his feelings and values.

4. Inner control of behavior/outer control of behavior. In some instances, psychotherapy is aimed at estabishing environmental control of the individual's behavior through principles of reinforcement. In other instances, the primary goal of psychotherapy is to change the individual's value assumptions in such a way as to foster the inner cognitive control of behavior. Of course, external controls may be used as an emergency measure with the expectation that inner controls will eventually be developed and take over.

5. Crisis intervention/personal growth. Crisis intervention therapy is designed to help an individual cope with an immediate stress situation which is approaching or perhaps exceeding the limits of his adjustive capacities. In personal growth oriented therapy, the primary focus is on fostering increased self-understanding, competence, sensory awareness, and other avenues toward the fulfillment of potentialities. Growth-fostering techniques may be used with "normal" individuals as well as the mentally disturbed.

There are some therapists who faithfully adhere to a particular systematic approach, but these are in the minority. The great majority of psychotherapists can best be described as *eclectic* — that is, they attempt to be flexible, utilizing whatever concepts and procedures seem best suited to the needs of a given individual.

---

thus opening the way for better personality integration and more effective living.

Freudian psychoanalysis. Psychoanalytic therapy is not easy to describe, and the problem is complicated by the fact that most people have some more-or-less inaccurate conceptions of psychoanalysis based on cartoons, movies, and television dramas. Perhaps the simplest starting point in our discussion is to describe the four basic techniques of this form of therapy: free association, dream interpretation, analysis of resistance, and analysis of transference. Then we shall note some of the changes that have taken place in psychoanalytic therapy since Freud.

   1. *Free association.* The "basic rule" of

psychoanalysis is that the individual being treated must say whatever comes into his mind, regardless of how personal, painful, or seemingly irrelevant it may be. Usually he sits comfortably in a chair or lies in a relaxed position on a couch and allows his mind to wander freely, giving a running account of his thoughts, feelings, and desires. The therapist usually takes a position behind him, so as not to be a distraction or disrupt the free flow of associations.

   It is important to note that Freud did not view free associations as simply a random matter, but maintained that they are determined like other events. As we have seen, he also thought that the conscious represents a relatively small part of the mind, while the

Hypnosis was known among the ancient Egyptians and other early peoples, but its modern use in psychotherapy dates from the time of Mesmer (see p. 53). Since that time, there have been periodic fluctuations in the popularity of hypnosis in psychotherapy, and differing viewpoints have arisen concerning the exact nature of hypnotic phenomena. In general, hypnosis may be defined as an altered state of consciousness involving extreme suggestibility. Hypnotic induction procedures are designed to bring about a heightened state of selective attention in which the subject "tunes out" irrelevant stimuli and concentrates solely upon the hypnotist's suggestions. The induction of hypnosis and some of the therapeutic uses to which it has been put may be briefly outlined as follows:

1. **Induction of hypnosis.** Hypnosis may be induced by a variety of techniques, most of which involve the following factors: (a) enlisting the cooperation of the subject and allaying any fears of hypnosis; (b) having the subject assume a comfortable position and relax completely; (c) narrowing and focusing the subject's attention, perhaps by having him fix his gaze on some bright object; and (d) directing the subject's activities by means of reinforced suggestions. The latter often involves establishing the assumption that normal bodily reactions have in fact come about at the direction of the hypnotist. For example, the subject may be directed to gaze upward toward an object, and then be told that his eyelids feel slightly heavy. This is a normal reaction to the strain of looking upward, but the subject interprets it as being due to the instructions of the hypnotist; thus the way is paved for the acceptance of additional suggestions.

2. **Recall of buried memories.** Traumatic experiences that have been repressed from consciousness may be recovered under hypnosis. This technique was occasionally used in treating combat-exhaustion cases during World War II. Under hypnosis, the amnesic soldier could relive his battle experience, thus discharging the emotional tensions associated with it and permitting the experience to be assimilated into his self-structure. Civilian shock reactions involving amnesia may be similarly handled.

3. **Age regression.** Closely related to memory recall is hypnotic age regression. The hypnotized subject may be told that he is now a six-year-old child again and will subsequently act, talk, and think very much as he did at the age of six years. Regression to the age just preceding the onset of phobias often brings to light the traumatic experiences that precipitated them. Here again the traumatic experience may be relived in order to desensitize the subject to it.

4. **Dream induction.** Dreams can be induced through hypnosis, although some investigators consider hypnotic dreams to more nearly resemble fantasies than nocturnal dreams. In any event, hypnotic dreams may be used to explore intrapsychic conflicts along the lines of dream analysis worked out by Freud. Perhaps the particular value of such dreams is that the therapist can suggest the theme about which he wants the dreams to center, using them much like projective techniques in exploring the individual's inner conflicts.

5. **Posthypnotic suggestion.** One of the hypnotic phenomena most widely used in psychotherapy is posthypnotic suggestion. Here suggestions made by the therapist during the hypnotic state may be carried over into the waking state, with the subject remaining unaware of their source. For example, the subject may be told that he will no longer have a desire to smoke when he comes out of the hypnotic state. While such suggestions do carry over into the waking state, their duration is usually short. That is, the individual may again experience a desire to smoke in a few hours or a few days. This time factor can be partially compensated for, however, by regular reinforcement of the posthypnotic suggestion in booster sessions.

Some investigators attribute the altered state of consciousness in hypnosis to the subject's strong motivation to meet the demand characteristics of the situation. Barber (1969) has shown that many of the behaviors induced under hypnosis can be replicated in nonhypnotized subjects simply by giving instructions which they are strongly motivated to follow. However, the preponderance of research evidence indicates that behavior induced in hypnotized subjects does differ significantly from that evidenced during simulated hypnosis or role enactment (Diamond, 1974; Fromm & Shor, 1972; Hilgard, 1973, 1974; Miller & Springer, 1974; Nace, Orne, & Hammer, 1974). For example, a number of investigators have offered dramatic evidence that the pain response can be brought almost completely under hypnotic control in many subjects, permitting a degree of pain reduction well beyond that produced in nonhypnotized subjects.

In connection with the use of hypnosis in therapy, it may be pointed out that such drugs as sodium pentothal can be used to produce phenomena similar to those manifested in the hypnotic trance. This form of biological therapy is referred to as *narcoanalysis* or *narcosynthesis*. In Chapter 6 we noted the use of sodium pentothal in the treatment of severe cases of combat exhaustion involving amnesia.

unconscious, like the submerged part of an iceberg, is much the larger portion. The task of the therapist is to identify accurately the materials repressed beneath the surface in the unconscious domain. The therapist then interprets this material to the individual, guiding him toward increased insight into the underlying motives and conflicts of which he has been unaware.

2. *Dream interpretation.* Another important procedure for uncovering unconscious material is dream analysis. When a person is asleep, repressive defenses are lowered and forbidden desires and feelings may find an outlet in dreams. For this reason dreams have been referred to as the "royal road to the unconscious." But some motives are so unacceptable to the individual that even in dreams they are not revealed openly but are expressed in disguised or symbolic form. Thus a dream has two kinds of content: *manifest* content, which is the dream as it appears to the dreamer, and *latent* content, composed of the actual motives that are seeking expression but are so painful or unacceptable that they are disguised.

The process by which the latent content of the dream is transformed into the less painful manifest content is called *dream work.* In dream interpretation, it is the task of the therapist to uncover these disguised meanings by studying the symbols that appear in the manifest content of the dream. For example, a patient's dream of being engulfed in a tidal wave may be interpreted by the therapist as indicating that the patient is going through a major crisis in his life.

3. *Analysis of resistance.* During the process of free association or of associating to dreams, an individual may evidence resistance—an unwillingness or inability to relate certain thoughts, motives, or experiences. For example, he may be talking about an important area in his life and then suddenly switch topics, perhaps stating that "it really isn't that important," or that "it is too absurd to discuss"; or he may give some glib interpretation to his associations. In some instances resistance may be evidenced by coming late to an appointment, or even "forgetting" an appointment altogether. Since resistance prevents painful and threatening material from entering awareness, it must be broken down if the individual is to face his problems and conflicts and deal with them in a realistic manner.

4. *Analysis of transference.* As patient and therapist interact, the relationship between them may become complex and emotionally involved. Often a person carries over and applies to the therapist attitudes and feelings that developed in his relations with significant others in the past, perhaps reacting to the analyst as he did to his mother or father, and feeling the hostility and rejection that he once felt toward his real parent.

By recognizing the transference relationship, the therapist may provide the individual with the experience of having a "good" father. It thus becomes possible for the individual to work though his conflicts in regard to his own father and to overcome feelings of hostility and self-devaluation stemming from his father's rejection. In essence, the pathogenic effects of an undesirable early relationship are counteracted by working through a similar emotional conflict in a therapeutic setting. Since the person's reliving of his own pathogenic past in a sense re-creates his real-life neuroses, this experience is often referred to as a *transference neurosis.*

It is not possible here to consider at length the complexities of transference relationships, but it may be stressed that the patient's attitudes toward the therapist do not always follow simple patterns. Often the patient is ambivalent—distrusting the therapist and feeling hostile toward him as a symbol of authority, but at the same time seeking acceptance and love. In addition, the problems of transference are by no means confined to the patient, for the therapist may also have a mixture of feelings toward the patient. This is known as *countertransference* and must be recognized and handled properly by the therapist. For this reason, it is considered important that the therapist have an understanding of his own motives, conflicts, and "weak spots," and all psychoanalytic therapists have themselves undergone psychoanalysis.

Particularly during the early stages, psychoanalytic therapy is directed toward uncovering unconscious desires and conflicts and helping the person integrate them into the conscious dimension of his personality. However, the new insights achieved by the patient do not automatically generalize to his day-to-day relationships. Thus as the therapy progresses toward its terminal phase, it is increasingly directed toward furthering his emotional reeducation and helping ensure the generalization of new insights and behaviors to his real-life situation.

Psychoanalytic therapy since Freud. Although some psychoanalysts still adhere to standard long-term therapy—which may take years—most analysts have worked out modifications in procedure designed to shorten the time and expense required. Most neo-Freudian therapists place more emphasis on the individual's current interpersonal relationships and life situation and less on his childhood experiences, also playing down Freud's emphasis on repressed sexual desires and conflicts.

Despite such modifications, psychoanalytic therapy is still commonly criticized for being relatively time-consuming and expensive, for being based on a biased model of human nature, for neglecting the patient's immediate problems in the search for underlying causes, and for lacking experimental evidence of its effectiveness. Because it expects the individual to achieve insight and major personality change, it is also limited in its applicability. For example, it is best suited for persons who are average or above in intelligence and who do not suffer from severe psychopathology. However, many individuals do feel that they have profited from psychoanalytic therapy—particularly in terms of greater self-understanding, relief from inner conflict and anxiety, and improved interpersonal relationships.

Behavior therapy

It has been over 50 years since Watson's experiment with little Albert, described in Chapter 3, but it was not until the 1960s that behavior therapy really came into its own. The major reason for the long delay was the dominant position of psychoanalysis in the fields of clinical psychology and psychiatry. In recent years, however, the therapeutic potentialities of behavior-therapy techniques have been strikingly demonstrated in dealing with a wide variety of maladaptive behaviors, and there have been literally thousands of research publications dealing with the systematic application of learning principles to the modification of maladaptive behavior—on group as well as individual levels.

The behavioristic model views the maladjusted person—unless there is brain pathology—as differing from other people only in that (a) he has learned faulty coping patterns that are being maintained by some kind of reinforcement, and/or (b) he has failed to acquire needed competencies for coping with the problems of living. Thus behavior therapy specifies the maladaptive behaviors to be modified and the adaptive behavior to be achieved as well as the specific learning principles or procedures to be utilized. Rather than exploring inner conflicts and attempting cognitive change, behavior therapists attempt to modify behavior directly by manipulating environmental contingencies—that is, by the use of reward and punishment. Their techniques include punishment for maladaptive responses, removal of reinforcers that are maintaining maladaptive behaviors, safe exposure to feared situations, and positive reinforcement for learning new competencies. Behavior-therapy techniques seem especially effective in altering maladaptive behavior when the reinforcement is administered immediately following the desired response, and when the person knows what is expected and why the reinforcement is given. The ultimate goal, of course, is not only to achieve the desired responses but to bring them under the control and self-monitoring of the individual.

We have cited examples of the application of behavior therapy in the chapters on neuroses and other patterns of abnormal behavior. In this section, we shall elaborate briefly on the key techniques of behavior therapy.

Simple extinction. Since learned behavior patterns tend to weaken and disappear over time if they are not reinforced, the simplest way to eliminate a maladaptive pattern is often to remove the reinforcement for it. This is especially true in situations where maladaptive behavior is being reinforced unknowingly by others.

Billy, a 6-year-old first grader, was brought to a psychological clinic by his parents because he "hated school," and his teacher had told them that his showing-off behavior was disrupting the class and making him unpopular. It became apparent in observing Billy and his parents during the initial interview that both his mother and father were noncritical and approving of everything he did. After further assessment, a three-phase program of therapy was undertaken: (a) the parents were helped to discriminate between showing-off behavior and appropriate behavior on Billy's part; (b) the parents were instructed to show a loss of interest and attention when Billy engaged in showing-off behavior while continuing to evidence their approval of appropriate behavior; and (c) Billy's teacher was instructed to ignore Billy, insofar as it was feasible, when he engaged in showing-off behavior and to devote her attention at those times to children who were behaving more appropriately.

Although Billy's showing-off behavior in class increased during the first few days of this therapy program, it diminished markedly thereafter when it was no longer reinforced by his parents and teacher. As his maladaptive behavior diminished, he was better accepted by his classmates, which, in turn, helped reinforce more appropriate behavior patterns and change his negative attitude toward school.

Systematic desensitization. In the preceding section we dealt with the extinction of behavior that is being *positively reinforced*. Behavior that is being *negatively reinforced*—reinforced by the successful avoidance of a painful situation—is harder to deal with. In this case, since the individual becomes anxious and withdraws at the first sign of the painful situation, he never gets a chance to find out whether the aversive consequences he fears are still in operation. In addition, his avoidance is anxiety reducing and hence is itself reinforced.

One commonly used technique for extinguishing negatively reinforced behavior involves eliciting an antagonistic or competing response. Since it is difficult to feel both pleasant and anxious at the same time, the method of desensitization is aimed at teaching the client to emit a response which is inconsistent with anxiety while in the presence (real or imagined) of the anxiety-producing stimulus. The prototype of this approach is the classic experiment of Mary Cover Jones (1924), cited in Chapter 3, in which she successfully elimi-

nated a small boy's conditioned fears of a white rabbit and other furry animals.

The term *systematic desensitization* has been applied to a specific approach developed by Wolpe[2] (1961, 1963, 1969). On the assumption that most neurotic patterns fundamentally are conditioned anxiety responses, Wolpe attempted to train the client to remain calm and relaxed in situations that formerly produced anxiety. Wolpe's approach is elegant in its simplicity, and the carrying out of his method is equally straightforward.

1. *Training in relaxation.* The first step in therapy is training the individual to relax. This is usually done in the first six sessions and consists of having him contract and then gradually relax different muscles until he achieves a state of complete relaxation. The basic technique follows the principles of "progressive relaxation" outlined by Jacobson (1938) and is described in detail by Wolpe (1969). Other techniques that are sometimes used to facilitate complete relaxation include meditation, hypnosis, and drugs.

2. *The construction of hierarchies.* During the early sessions of therapy, time is also spent constructing a hierarchy of the individual's anxieties. This anxiety hierarchy is a list of related stimuli ranked in descending order according to the amount of anxiety they evoke in the client. For example, if a client is overly possessive or jealous of her husband, she describes the situations in which she feels this jealousy. The highest anxiety-producing situation might be observing him at a cocktail party talking intimately with an attractive woman. Further down the list might be hearing him comment favorably about a waitress; and the lowest anxiety-evoking stimulus might be noticing him look casually at a young female hitchhiker. In some instances the anxiety is easier to quantify, as in the case of acrophobia

[2]In an attempt to clarify the confusion in terminology relating to desensitization, Van Egeren (1971) has noted that *reciprocal inhibition* has been applied in classical neurophysiology to momentary, reversible inhibition of one nerve process by another, as in the inhibition of antagonistic skeletal muscles. *Counterconditioning* implies the permanent inhibition of a reaction by means of an incompatible or antagonistic response—as, for example, in the inhibition of anxiety in a fear-arousing situation by the repetitive presentation of food. Wolpe, although referring to his method of desensitization as involving reciprocal inhibition, achieves long-lasting changes in response by means of planned repetition, and thus, in effect, produces counterconditioning.

or of a student's examination anxiety; and, of course, anxiety may focus around more than one theme, as when the client shows a variety of phobias.

3. *Desensitization procedure.* When the client has mastered the relaxation techniques and the therapist has established an appropriate anxiety hierarchy, the actual process of desensitization begins. While the client relaxes completely in a comfortable chair with his eyes closed, the therapist describes a series of scenes to him, directing him to imagine himself experiencing each situation. The first scene presented is a neutral one. If the client remains calm and relaxed, the lowest scene on the hierarchy is presented; then the therapist moves progressively up the hierarchy until the client indicates that he is experiencing anxiety and the scene is terminated. Treatment continues until the client is able to remain in a relaxed state while vividly imagining the scenes that formerly evoked the greatest anxiety.

The usual duration of a desensitization session is 15 to 30 minutes, and the sessions are ordinarily given 2 to 3 times per week. The overall therapy program may, of course, take a number of weeks or even months. Kennedy and Kimura (1974) have shown, however, that even patients who have progressed only 25 to 50 percent of the way through their anxiety hierarchy show significant therapeutic gains, as evidenced by a marked reduction in specific avoidance behaviors when compared with their pretreatment levels.

Several variants of systematic desensitization have been devised. One variation involves the use of a tape recorder to enable a client to carry out the desensitization process at home. Another utilizes group desensitization procedures—as in "marathon" desensitization groups in which the entire program is compressed into a few days of intensive treatment. Perhaps the most important variation is *in vivo* desensitization, in which the client is asked to expose himself in reality to situations to which he has just been desensitized in imagination. This appears to accelerate the desensitization procedure and may be the best method for individuals who do not respond to imagined anxiety-eliciting situations in the same way they do to real-life situations.

Wolpe (1969) has noted three types of problems that may contraindicate desensitization training in certain cases: (a) difficulties in relaxation, (b) misleading or irrelevant hierarchies, and (c) inadequacies of imagery. Desensitization procedures have, however, been used successfully in dealing with a wide range of maladaptive behaviors, including examination anxieties, phobias, anxiety neuroses, and certain cases of impotence and frigidity.

Implosive therapy. Another method of behavior therapy used increasingly in recent years is implosive therapy. Like systematic desensitization, this approach regards neurotic behavior as involving the conditioned avoidance of anxiety-arousing stimuli, and the client is asked to imagine and relive aversive scenes associated with his anxiety.

In this case, rather than trying to banish anxiety from the treatment sessions, the therapist deliberately attempts to elicit a massive flood or "implosion" of anxiety. With repeated exposure in a "safe" setting, the stimulus loses its power to elicit anxiety and the neurotic avoidance behavior is extinguished.

Stampfl and Levis (1967, 1973) who are among the foremost developers of this approach, usually devote the first two or three therapy sessions to ascertaining the nature of the anxiety-arousing stimuli. They described the procedure as follows:

"Once the implosive procedure is begun, every effort is made to encourage the patient to 'lose himself' in the part that he is playing and 'live' the scenes with genuine emotion. . . . The scenes which contain the hypothesized cues are described at first by the therapist. The more involved and dramatic the therapist becomes in describing the scenes, the more realistic the presentation, and the easier it is for the patient to participate. At each stage of the process an attempt is made by the therapist to attain a maximal level of anxiety evocation from the patient. When a high level anxiety is achieved, the patient is held on this level until some sign of spontaneous reduction in the anxiety-inducing value of the cues appears (extinction). The process is repeated, and again, at the first sign of spontaneous reduction of fear, new variations are introduced to elicit an intense anxiety response. This procedure is continued until a significant diminution in anxiety has resulted. . . . Between sessions the patient is instructed to reenact in his imagination the scenes which were presented during the treatment session." (1967, p. 500)

In a report of an actual case, Stampfl (1975) described a young woman who could not swim and was terrified of water–particularly of sinking under the water. Although she knew it was irrational, she was so terrified of water "that she wore a life preserver when she took a bath" (p. 66). She was instructed by the therapist to imagine in minute detail taking a bath without a life preserver in a "bottomless" tub, and slipping under the water. Initially, the patient showed intense anxiety, and the scene was repeated over and over. In addition, she was given a "homework" assignment in which she was asked to imagine herself drowning. Eventually, after imagining the worst and finding that nothing happened, her anxiety diminished; after the fourteenth therapy session, she was able to take baths without feelings of anxiety or apprehension.

As in the case of systematic desensitization, hypnosis or drugs may be used to enhance suggestibility under implosive therapy, and here, too, *in vivo* procedures may be used with individuals who do not imagine scenes realistically. For example, a client with a phobia of airplanes may be instructed to take a short flight on a commercial airliner. This is another means of exposing the client to the anxiety-eliciting stimulus and demonstrating to him that the consequences he had feared do not occur. In a study of patients with agoraphobia (fear of open spaces), Emmelkamp and Wessels (1975) concluded that "prolonged exposure *in vivo* plainly proved to be superior to flooding in the imagination" (p. 7).

Reports on the effectiveness of implosive therapy have generally been quite favorable. In fact, a number of therapists consider implosive therapy superior to systematic desensitization in the treatment of neurotic phobias, since it results in more rapid improvement. However, some investigators have reported unfavorable as well as favorable results with implosive therapy (Emmelkamp & Wessels, 1975; Mealiea, 1967; Wolpe, 1969). This appears to be particularly true of flooding *in vivo*. For example, Emmelkamp and Wessels (1975) found that flooding *in vivo* was terrifying for some clients. In one case, the agoraphobic patient "hid in a cellar out of fear of being sent into the street for 90 minutes by the therapist" (p. 14).

In general, it would appear that while most patients respond favorably to implosive therapy, some do not respond, and a few suffer an exacerbation of their phobias. This finding suggests a need for caution in the use of this method, particularly since it involves procedures that may be highly traumatic.

Aversion therapy. This approach involves the modification of undesirable behavior by the old-fashioned method of punishment. Punishment may involve either the removal of positive reinforcers or the use of aversive stimuli, but the basic idea is to reduce the "temptation value" of stimuli that elicit undesirable behavior. The most commonly used aversive stimulus is electric shock, although drugs may also be used. As we shall see, however, punishment is rarely employed as the sole method of treatment.

Apparently the first formal use of aversion therapy was made by Kantorovich (1930), who administered electric shocks to alcoholics in association with the sight, smell, and taste of alcohol. Since that time aversion therapy has been used in the treatment of a wide range of maladaptive behaviors, including smoking, drinking, overeating, drug dependence, gambling, and various sexual deviations, such as fetishism. Since we have described the use of aversion therapy in the course of our discussion of abnormal behavior patterns, we shall restrict ourselves here to a review of a few brief examples and principles.

A leading exponent of punishment to inhibit maladaptive behavior is Lovaas, who has worked mostly with severely disturbed autistic children. He has found punishment by electric shock to be effective even in extreme cases of self-destructive behavior among such children. In one case a 7-year-old autistic boy, diagnosed as severely retarded, had to be kept in restraints 24 hours a day because he would continually beat his head with his fists or bang it against the walls of his crib, inflicting serious injuries. Though it is difficult to understand why punishment should reduce the frequency of self-destructive behavior, electric shock following such behavior was nevertheless quite effective, bringing about complete inhibition of this maladaptive behavior pattern in a relatively short time (Bucher & Lo-

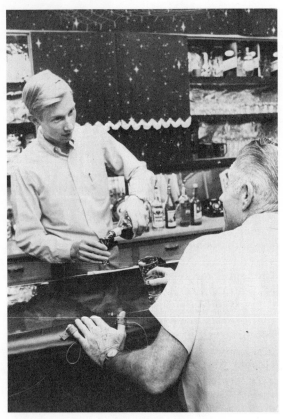

Aversion therapy is commonly used as part of the treatment at alcoholic treatment centers. Each time this man takes a drink, he receives an electric shock.

vaas, 1967). In earlier chapters we have noted that irrational and maladaptive thoughts—obsessions, delusions, and hallucinations—may also be minimized or extinguished by means of electric shock or other aversive control measures. And in Chapter 12 we described the present use and outcomes of aversion therapy—both electroshock and nausea-producing drugs—in the treatment of alcoholism.

A number of investigators have raised the issue of the "intensity dilemma" in aversion therapy. They point out that while aversive procedures depend heavily on the intensity of the noxious stimuli, limitations must be placed on that intensity, for both practical and ethical reasons. The types of punishment used in behavior therapy are also being explored in terms of both ethical and practical considerations (LaVoie, 1974).

Aversion therapy is primarily a way of stopping maladaptive responses for a period of time during which there is an opportunity for changing a life-style by encouraging more adaptive alternative patterns that will prove reinforcing in themselves. This point is particularly important, since otherwise the client may simply refrain from maladaptive responses in "unsafe" therapy situations, where such behavior leads to immediate aversive results, but keep making them in "safe" real-life situations, where there is no fear of immediate discomfort.

The systematic use of positive reinforcement. Systematic programs for the application of behavior therapy are achieving notable success, particularly in institutional settings. Response shaping, modeling, and token economies are among the most widely used of such techniques.

1. *Response shaping.* Positive reinforcement is often used in response shaping; that is, in establishing a response that is not initially in the individual's behavior repertoire. This technique has been used extensively in working with the behavior problems of children. The following case reported by Wolf, Risley, and Mees (1964) is illustrative:

A 3-year-old autistic boy lacked normal verbal and social behavior. He did not eat properly, engaged in self-destructive behavior such as banging his head and scratching his face, and manifested ungovernable tantrums. He had recently had a cataract operation, and required glasses for the development of normal vision. He refused to wear his glasses, however, and broke pair after pair.

The technique of shaping was decided upon to counteract the problem of glasses. Initially, the boy was trained to expect a bit of candy or fruit at the sound of a toy noisemaker. Then training was begun with empty eyeglass frames. First the boy was reinforced with the candy or fruit for picking them up, then for holding them, then for carrying them around, then for bringing the frames closer to his eyes, and then for putting the empty frames on his head at any angle. Through successive approximation, he finally learned to wear his glasses up to twelve hours a day.

2. *Modeling.* Response shaping can be tedious and time-consuming, especially when complex responses are to be learned. Such

Therapy for growth

Interest in therapy as an aid toward self-understanding, fulfillment, and personal growth has been on the rise in recent years. From this trend have developed new approaches to therapy. For example, a group of people at Esalen Institute, a personal growth center, seek to enhance their potential for sensitivity, openness, and sharing at an encounter session (top). Young people seeking the same goal try a different approach at a group session of yoga. Such "therapy" as the latter may seem to involve too many people to accomplish much toward changing maladaptive behavior, but it often increases the individual's awareness of himself and his feelings.

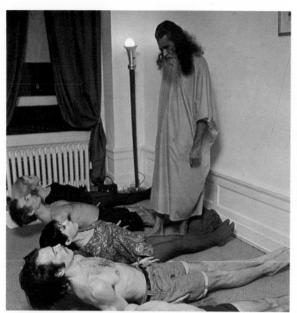

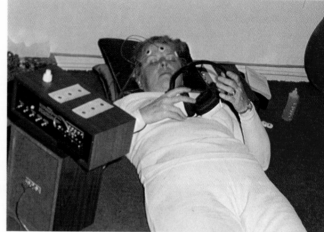

A more exacting form of yoga, under the direction of a trained practitioner, helps people develop a spiritual sense of inner strength and control. From a more modern technological standpoint, biofeedback techniques are used to reach many of the same goals. Minute changes in the body or brain can be monitored and recorded; the person sets a goal for himself — say, a change in brain-wave patterns — and can concentrate his efforts on reaching the goal, constantly monitoring his progress. Biofeedback can be useful not only for altering consciousness but also for changing certain maladaptive behavior patterns, such as asthma attacks that may occur under certain conditions.

Various sorts of sensitivity sessions, such as the one shown on the upper left, are aimed at helping people change maladaptive behavior patterns and increase their interpersonal competencies. Popular right now, especially among women, is assertiveness training, which helps the individual feel more positive about her own feelings and stand up for her rights (top right). Sensitivity sessions are often held for members of certain groups who have similar goals. Shown in the two lower pictures are married couples who want to achieve a better marriage, with more open expression of feelings between each other.

Psychodrama is used both as a therapy tool for patients in mental hospitals as well as by people who want to better understand their own interpersonal actions. The individuals involved assume a real-life encounter and react to it; others in the group—the "audience"—and possibly the therapist then discuss alternative ways of reacting that might be more constructive, and the individuals can act out the situation differently. By actually participating, the individuals can get immediate feedback about their personal interactions and their ability to cope with them.

Participants in nude therapy feel that they can overcome their inhibitions and quickly get beyond superficialities if all physical defenses are done away with.

Behavior contracting is one technique that has been explored in attempts to modify the behavior of disturbed children and adolescents. By definition, such a contract is an agreement—often in writing—governing the exchange of positive reinforcements between two or more persons. Such contracts detail the responsibilities of each party and the privileges to be gained by fulfillment of these responsibilities, as well as sanctions for lack of fulfillment.

In working with emotionally disturbed and disruptive children in the classroom, for example, a contract may be negotiated between the child and teacher in which the child maintains or receives certain privileges so long as he behaves in accordance with the responsibilities set forth by the contract. Usually the principal is also a party to such a contract to ensure the enforcement of certain conditions which the teacher may not be in a position to enforce, such as removing the child from the classroom, for example, if he engages in certain types of misbehavior.

An example of behavior contracting within a family concerns a 16-year-old girl, Candy, who had been admitted to a psychiatric hospital following alleged exhibitionism, drug abuse, truancy from home, and promiscuity (Stuart, 1971). Candy's parents also complained that she was chronically antagonistic in her verbal exchanges with them and was near failing in her schoolwork. Because of the cost of private psychiatric care, they requested that she be made a ward of the juvenile court. They were advised that their allegations would probably not stand up in court; they agreed to let her remain at home under the terms of a behavior contract.

An initial contract, based on unrealistic parental demands, failed when Candy consistently violated its terms by sneaking out at night. A new, more realistic contract between Candy and her parents was then negotiated, and a monitoring form containing a checklist of chores, curfew conditions, and bonus time for each day of the month was provided. Some of the provisions of this contract were:

"In exchange for the privilege of going out at 7:00 p.m. on one weekend evening without having to account for her whereabouts Candy must maintain a weekly average of "B" in the academic ratings of all of her classes and must return home by 11:30 p.m.

"In exchange for the privilege of having Candy complete household chores and maintain her curfew Mr. and Mrs. Bremer agree to pay Candy $1.50 on the morning following days on which the money is earned.

"If Candy is 31 – 60 minutes late she loses the privilege of going out the following day and does forfeit her money for the day." (Stuart, 1971, p. 9)

Behavior contracting proved to be a constructive means of structuring the interaction between Candy and her parents, and Candy's behavior improved steadily. By removing the issues of privileges and responsibilities from the realm of contention, many intrafamilial arguments were avoided, and those that did occur tended to be tempered by the specified options. Through the contract, privileges such as money and free time were established as effective environmental contingencies in fostering desired behavior (p. 11).

---

responses can be acquired much more readily if the subject observes a model and is then reinforced for imitating the model's behavior. As we have noted, modeling and imitation are used in various forms of behavior therapy. For example, in Chapter 7 we noted treatment for snake phobia via modeling. Bandura (1969) found that live modeling combined with instruction and guided participation was the most effective desensitization treatment, resulting in the elimination of snake phobias in over 90 percent of the cases.

Another interesting example of the modeling-imitation-reinforcement paradigm is the program based on the "therapeutic pyramid concept," in which moderately retarded adolescents and young adults are trained, via behavior-therapy techniques, to help professional therapists teach basic verbal and nonverbal skills to severely retarded children (Whalen & Henker, 1971). As described in Chapter 14, the goal of this program is to facilitate improvement in both the assistants and the younger retardates—to bring about a "double change"—and early results have been promising.

3. *Token economies.* Approval and other intangible reinforcers often prove ineffective

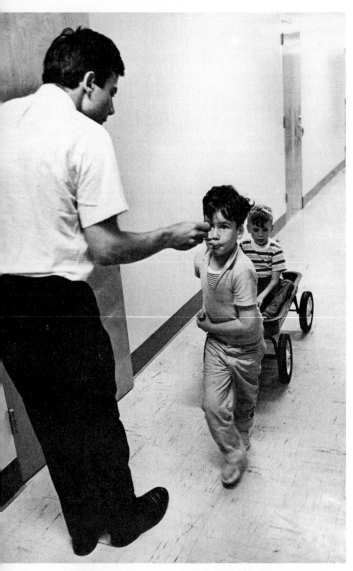

These two autistic boys were enrolled in an intensive behavior-therapy program at the UCLA Neuropsychiatric Institute. Here the boy pulling the wagon is shown receiving immediate positive reinforcement in the form of food for his participation in the activity. Other reinforcement techniques used included punishment and modeling.

in behavior-therapy programs, especially those dealing with severely maladaptive behavior. In such instances, appropriate behaviors may be rewarded with tangible reinforcers in the form of tokens that can later be exchanged for desired objects or privileges. In our discussion of schizophrenia and other maladaptive patterns, we have already noted the use of token economies in establishing certain behaviors. In working with schizophrenics, for example, Ayllon and Azrin (1968) found that using the commissary, listening to records, and going to movies were considered highly desirable activities by most patients. Consequently, these activities were chosen as reinforcers for socially appropriate behavior. To participate in any of them, the patient had to earn a number of tokens by appropriate ward behavior.

Token economies have been used to establish adaptive behaviors ranging from elementary responses such as eating and making one's bed to the daily performance of responsible hospital jobs. In the latter instance, the token economy resembles the outside world where the individual is paid for his work in tokens (money) that he can then exchange for desired objects and activities.

The use of tokens as reinforcers for appropriate behavior has a number of distinct advantages: (a) the number of tokens earned by the patient can be equated with the amount of desired behavior that he manifests; (b) tokens are not readily subject to satiation and hence tend to maintain their incentive value; (c) tokens can reduce the delay that often occurs between appropriate performance and reinforcement; (d) the number of tokens earned and the way in which they are "spent" are largely up to the patient, and (e) tokens tend to bridge the gap between the institutional environment and the demands and rewards encountered in the outside world.

The ultimate goal in token economies, as in other programs of extrinsic reinforcement, is not only to achieve desired responses but to bring such responses to a level where their adaptive consequences will be reinforcing in their own right—thus enabling natural rather than artificial reward contingencies to maintain the desired behavior. For example, extrinsic reinforcers may be used initially to help children overcome reading difficulties, but once the child becomes proficient in reading skills, these skills will presumably provide their own intrinsic reinforcement.

Assertive training. Assertive training has been used as a method of desensitization as well as a means of developing more effective coping techniques. It appears particularly useful in helping individuals who have difficulties in interpersonal situations because of conditioned anxiety responses that prevent them from "speaking up" for what they consider to be appropriate and right. Such inhibition may lead to continual inner turmoil, particularly if the individual feels strongly about the situation. Assertive training may also be indicated in cases where an individual consistently allows other people to take advantage of him or maneuver him into situations which he finds uncomfortable.

The expression of assertive behavior—first by role-playing in the therapy setting and then by practice in real-life situations—is guided by the therapist. Often attention is focused on developing more effective interpersonal skills; in some instances, the client is taught to use techniques of "gamesmanship" or "lifemanship" in situations where he seems at a disadvantage. For example, he may learn to ask the other person such questions as "Is anything wrong? You don't seem to be your usual self today." Such questions put the focus on the other person without indicating an aggressive or hostile intent on the part of the speaker. Of course, situations calling for affectionate or other positive responses may also elicit intense or inappropriate anxiety. In any event, each act of assertion inhibits the anxiety associated with given interpersonal situations, and therefore weakens the maladaptive anxiety response patterns. At the same time, it tends to foster more adaptive interpersonal behaviors.

Although assertive training is a highly useful therapeutic procedure in certain types of situations, it does have limitations. For example, Wolpe (1969) has pointed out that it is largely irrelevant for phobias involving nonpersonal stimuli. It may also be of little use in some types of interpersonal situations; for instance, if a person is rejected by some individual who is important to him, assertive behav-

ior may tend to aggravate rather than resolve the problem. However, in interpersonal situations where maladaptive anxiety can be traced to lack of self-assertiveness, this type of therapy appears particularly effective.

Evaluation of behavior therapy. As compared with psychoanalytic and other interview psychotherapies, behavior therapy appears to have three distinct advantages. First is the precision of the treatment approach. The target behaviors to be modified are specified, the methods to be used are clearly delineated, and the results can be readily evaluated. Second is the economy of time, cost, and personnel. Behavior therapy usually gets results in a short period of time, leading to faster relief of personal distress for the individual, as well as financial savings. In addition, more people can be treated by a given therapist. Third is the dependence on explicit principles of learning. Since the interpersonal skills of the therapist play a relatively minor role, the training of therapists is easier and shorter. This also makes it possible for behavior-therapy methods to be mastered and used by paraprofessionals.

The effectiveness of behavior therapy must be evaluated in terms of the type of behavior being treated as well as the specific methods used. Like other forms of psychotherapy, behavior therapy has proven relatively unsuccessful in the treatment of such patterns as childhood autism, schizophrenia, and severe depression, although considerable improvement is often shown in such cases. Similarly, different kinds of behavior therapy vary in their effectiveness for particular problems: desensitization seems most useful in treating conditioned avoidance responses, aversive techniques in establishing impulse control, and modeling combined with positive reinforcement in the acquisition of complex responses. But although behavior therapy is not a "cure-all," it has proven effective in the treatment of a wide range of maladaptive behaviors, typical reports indicating a success rate of well over 50 percent and sometimes as high as 90 percent, depending largely on the type of maladaptive pattern being treated.[3]

---

[3] A comprehensive review and critique of behavior therapy techniques may be found in Russel (1974).

Humanistic-existential therapies

"For this is the journey that men make: to find themselves. If they fail in this, it doesn't matter much what else they find." James Michener (1949, p. 488)

The humanistic and existential viewpoints and therapies have emerged as a "third force" in psychology during the last two decades. To a large extent, they have developed in reaction to the psychoanalytic and behavioristic viewpoints, which many feel do not accurately take into account either the existential problems or the full potentialities of contemporary men and women. In a society dominated by computerized technology and mass bureaucracy, proponents of the humanistic-existential therapies see psychopathology as stemming in many cases from problems of alienation, depersonalization, loneliness, and the lack of a meaningful and fulfilling existence, which are not met either by delving into forgotten memories or by correcting specific responses.

The humanistic-existential therapies follow some variant of the general viewpoints spelled out in Chapter 3. They are based on the assumption that we have the freedom to control our own behavior—that we can reflect upon our problems, make choices, and take positive action. Whereas behavior therapists see themselves as "behavioral engineers," responsible for changing specific behaviors by appropriate modifications in the environment, humanistic-existential therapists feel that the client must take most of the responsibility for the success of therapy, with the therapist serving as counselor, guide, and facilitator. The basic theme is well expressed in the above quotation from James Michener's early novel, *The Fires of Spring*.

Client-centered therapy. The client-centered therapy of Carl Rogers (1951, 1961, 1966) has been by far the most widely used humanistic approach to therapy. Viewing humans as essentially good and rational, this approach recognizes that the individual may be hampered in achieving his inherent potentialities for growth by evading experiences that threaten his self-concept. This process of self-defense ultimately leads to an incongruence between the individual's conscious experience and his actual "gut" reactions and hence results in lowered integration, impaired personal relationships, and maladjustment.

The primary objective of Rogerian therapy is to resolve this incongruence—to help the client become able and willing to be *himself*. To this end, a psychological climate is established in which the client can feel unconditionally accepted, understood, and valued as a person. This frees him to explore his real feelings and thoughts and to accept them as part of himself. As his self-concept becomes more congruent with his experiencing, he becomes more self-accepting, more open to experience, and a better integrated person.

The therapist's task is not to direct the course of therapy by asking questions or giving answers. Rather, he restates in his own words what the client has been saying and helps clarify the client's true feelings about it. The therapist does not offer interpretations, nor does he attempt to lead the client beyond the boundaries of his or her current awareness. The following excerpt from a counselor's second interview with a young woman will serve to illustrate these techniques of reflection and clarification. Even though it was recorded when client-centered therapy was in its infancy, it still seems relevant today:

Alice: "I was thinking about this business of standards. I somehow developed a sort of a knack, I guess, of—well—habit—of trying to make people feel at ease around me, or to make things go along smoothly. . . .
Counselor: In other words, what you did was always in the direction of trying to keep things smooth and to make other people feel better and to smooth the situation.
Alice: Yes. I think that's what it was. Now the reason why I did it probably was—I mean, not that I was a good little Samaritan going around making other people happy, but that was probably the role that felt easiest for me to play. I'd been doing it around home so much. I just didn't stand up for my own convictions, until I don't know whether I have any convictions to stand up for.
Counselor: You feel that for a long time you've been playing the role of kind of smoothing out the frictions or differences or what not. . . .
Alice: M-hm.
Counselor: Rather than having any opinion or reaction of your own in the situation. Is that it?

Alice: That's it. Or that I haven't been really honestly being myself, or actually knowing what my real self is, and that I've been just playing a sort of false role. Whatever role no one else was playing, and that needed to be played at the time, I'd try to fill it in." (Rogers, 1951, pp. 152–53)

The idea that "the doctor knows best" is notably missing from this form of therapy; the therapist does not offer advice, resort to moral exhortation, or suggest "right" ways of behaving. Instead, he restricts himself to reflecting and clarifying the patient's feelings and attitudes in such a way as to promote self-understanding, positive action, and personal growth.

Existential therapy. Existential therapy can best be understood in terms of certain fundamental concepts on which it rests—concepts stemming from the existential model that we reviewed in Chapter 3.

First of all, this approach to therapy emphasizes the importance of existence itself, of the human situation as experienced by the individual. Second, the existentialists are deeply concerned about the predicament of humankind, the breakdown of traditional faith, the alienation and depersonalization of the individual in contemporary society, and the lack of meaning in the lives of many people. Third, existential therapists see the individual as having a high degree of freedom and thus as capable of doing something about his predicament. Unlike other living creatures, human beings have the ability to be aware of, reflect on, and question their existence. And fourth, they consider that the individual's freedom confronts him with the responsibility for *being*—for deciding what kind of person to become, for establishing his own values, and for actualizing his potentialities as a human being.

Existential therapists do not follow any rigidly prescribed procedures, but emphasize the uniqueness of the individual and his "way-of-being-in-the-world." They stress the importance of *confrontation*—challenging the individual directly with questions concerning the meaning and purpose of his existence—and the *encounter*—the complex relationship that is established between two interacting human beings in the therapeutic situation. In contrast

to behavior therapy, existential therapy calls for the therapist to share himself—his feelings, his values, and his existence—and not to let the client respond to him as anything other than he really is (Havens, 1974; May, 1969). For example, the existential therapist might respond to the statement, "I hate you just like I hated my father," by saying "I am not your father, I am me, and you have to deal with me as Dr. S., not as your father." The focus is on the here and now—on what the individual is choosing to do, and therefore be, at this moment. This sense of immediacy, of the urgency of experience, is the touchstone of existential therapy and sets the stage for clarifying and choosing alternative ways of being.

The existential approach is illustrated by the treatment of Hilda, a 29-year-old woman whose case was diagnosed as "chronic undifferentiated schizophrenia." This was the third time she had been hospitalized for mental illness.

"Prior to this current hospitalization she had been unemployed; had 'floated around and almost starved.' Her relationships with females were negative and hostile; with men, always rather 'shady, mistress types of things.' She expressed feelings of failure, inadequacy, anger and dread. She was loud, boisterous, brutally frank and blistering to anyone who 'crossed' her. . . .

"The questions that interested me most were: What was her world? What was she to herself? . . . . I knew that I would have to encounter her where she was before she would be able to accept me as a helping person, who was—in essence—criticizing her way of being. My 'treatment goal' was, therefore, to encounter her in her own world, which seemed to be constructed upon a series of negative reflections which made unauthentic being in the world the only existence possible for her. . . .

"We then began to explore, in earnest, 'the world of Hilda,' as she termed it, and I followed where she led. She proved to be unsure of where she had been or where she was. As she grew more and more related to me, I began to ask her: 'Where are you?' It was not very long before she stopped saying 'in the nuttery . . .'; and started telling me things which made me wonder if she were not trying to give me something; trying to tell me about Hilda. She began to disorganize but could write:

"'I'm glad I'm young in heart. You're at this time my strongest contact with reality. You are it. This "epistle" represents my "search for reality." Ha, ha. Let's call it that: one fool's search. . . .'

"Finally, she evaluated my relationship to her:

"'. . . I wanted to give you my illness . . . but you don't want it. You want me to just lose it and work it out of my system . . . Keep watching the light up there above San Francisco like a beacon! Guide me, please guide me out of this . . . I'm mesmerized today. . . . Now I'm going ashore, the bridge will be my vehicle. . . .'

"Shortly after this 'prophecy,' she became so disorganized that I could not read her writings, nor follow her arguments. However, I tried, spending time with her almost every day. She was put on an increased dosage of Thorazine but still managed to get to group meetings and to our interviews. Even in her disorganization, she clung to her relationship with me, and managed to write:

"'. . . I must listen when you talk, I'm not always there. . . .'

"She had encountered me, perhaps long before I became fully aware of it. The idea of love—love without purpose—was emerging from deep within her. On 800 milligrams of tranquilizer, she gradually became less disorganized. With a burst of unbelievable energy, she began to plan for a 'future'; took hospital jobs, as she said, 'fighting to stay awake.'

"When the patients on her ward elected her president of the government group, she got up and ran out of the room, crying violently. I felt that I had lost; she had recoiled from letting herself be liked. But she returned to the room, accepting the role of president.

"She was in the midst of turning from her futureless, pseudo-world of distortions to the world of possibility, in which one could find hope and meaning; in which one could establish an authentic relationship!

"One of the last things she wrote, before she gave up writing, was a poem which began:

Glorious night all is right

No time for flight too tired to fight . . .

and ended:

I'm awake I'm awake

A happy wake for a former fake. . . .

"Hilda remained on leave for one year, received her discharge and managed extremely well for approximately another year. She experienced a slight relapse and was rehospitalized elsewhere for about three months. After this, she once again returned to the community." (Curry, 1962, pp. 129–35)

Gestalt therapy. The term *gestalt* means "whole," and gestalt therapy emphasizes the unity of mind and body—placing strong emphasis on the integration of thought, feeling, and action. One of the newer and more innovative approaches, gestalt therapy was developed by Frederick Perls (1967, 1969).

Though gestalt therapy is commonly used in a group setting, the emphasis is on the individual. The therapist works intensively with one individual at a time, attempting to help him perceive those aspects of himself and of his world that are "blocked out." To increase awareness of self and of areas of avoidance, the individual may be asked to act out fantasies concerning his feelings and conflicts or to act out one part of the conflict in one chair and then switch chairs to take the part of the "adversary." This technique of working through unresolved conflicts is called "taking care of unfinished business." We all go through life, according to Perls, with unfinished or unresolved traumas and conflicts. We carry the excess baggage of these unfinished situations into new relationships and tend to act out our tensions in our relations with other people. If we are able to complete our past unfinished business, we shall then have much less psychological tension to cope with and be more realistically aware of ourselves and our world.

The individual is completely on his own in the therapeutic process, even though he may be expressing himself in front of the group. Denied the use of his usual techniques for avoiding self-awareness, he is brought to an "impasse," in which he must confront his feelings and conflicts. According to Perls, "In the safe emergency of the therapeutic situation, the neurotic discovers that the world does not fall to pieces if he gets angry, sexy, joyous, mournful" (1967, p. 311). Thus he finds that he can, after all, get beyond the impasse on his own.

In Perls' approach to therapy, a good deal of emphasis is placed on dreams:

". . . all the different parts of the dream are fragments of our personalities. Since our aim is to make every one of us a wholesome person, which means a unified person, without conflicts, what we have to do is put the different fragments of the dream together. We have to *re-own* these projected, fragmented parts of our personality, and *re-own* the hidden potential that appears in the dream." (1967, p. 67)

In the following dialog, taken from the transcript of a "dreamwork seminar," Perls (Fritz) helps a young woman (Linda) discover the meaning of her dream:

Linda: I dreamed that I watch . . . a lake . . . drying up, and there is a small island in the middle of the lake, and a circle of . . . porpoises—they're like porpoises except that they can stand up, so they're like porpoises that are like people, and they're in a circle, sort of like a religious ceremony, and it's very sad—I feel very sad because they can breathe, they are sort of dancing around the circle, but the water, their element, is drying up. So it's like a dying—like watching a race of people, or a race of creatures, dying. And they are mostly females, but a few of them have a small male organ, so there are a few males there, but they won't live long enough to reproduce, and their element is drying up. And there is one that is sitting over here near me and I'm talking to this porpoise and he has prickles on his tummy, sort of like a porcupine, and they don't seem to be a part of him. And I think that there's one good point about the water drying up, I think—well, at least at the bottom, when all the water dries up, there will probably be some sort of treasure there, because at the bottom of the lake there should be things that have fallen in, like coins or something, but I look carefully and all that I can find is an old license plate . . . That's the dream.

Fritz: Will you please play the license plate.

L: I am an old license plate, thrown in the bottom of a lake. I have no use because I'm no value—although I'm not rusted—I'm outdated, so I can't be used as a license plate . . . and I'm just thrown on the rubbish heap. That's what I did with a license plate, I threw it on a rubbish heap.

F: Well, how do you feel about this?

L: (quietly) I don't like it. I don't like being a license plate—useless.

F: Could you talk about this. That was such a long dream until you come to find the license plate, I'm sure this must be of great importance.

L: (sighs) Useless. Outdated . . . The use of a license plate is to allow—give a car permission to go . . . and I can't give anyone permission to do anything because I'm outdated . . . In California, they just paste a little—you buy a sticker—and stick it on the car on the old license plate. (faint attempt at humor) So maybe someone could put me on their car and stick this sticker on me, I don't know . . .

F: Okeh, now play the lake.

L: I'm a lake . . . I'm drying up, and disappearing, soaking into the earth . . . (with a touch of surprise) *dying* . . . But when I soak into the earth, I become a part of the earth—so maybe I water the surrounding area, so . . . even in the lake, even in my bed, flowers can grow (sighs) . . . New life can grow . . . from me (cries). . .

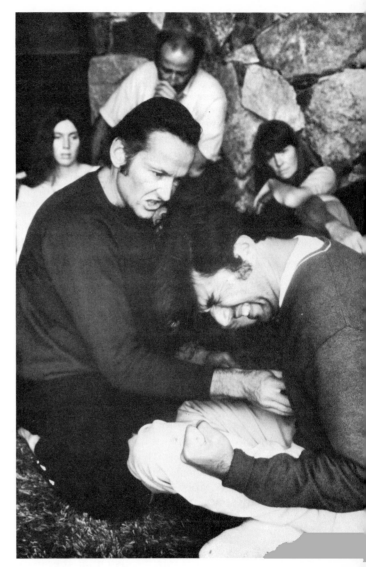

At a gestalt therapy session at Esalen, in Big Sur, California, the leader (left) encourages a member to express his pent-up feelings of anger.

F: You get the existential message?

L: Yes. (sadly, but with conviction) I can paint—I can create—I can create beauty. I can no longer reproduce, I'm like the porpoise . . . but I . . . I'm . . . I . . . keep wanting to say I'm *food* . . . I . . . as water becomes . . . I water the earth, and give life—growing things, the water—they need both the earth and water, and the . . . and the air and the sun, but as the water from the lake, I can play a part in something, and producing—feeding.

F: You see the contrast: On the surface, you find something, some artifact—the license plate, the artificial you—but then when you go deeper, you find the apparent death of the lake is actually fertility . . .

L: And I don't need a license plate, or a permission, a license in order to . . .

F: (gently) Nature doesn't need a license plate to grow. You don't have to be useless, if you are organismically creative, which means if you are involved.

L: And I don't need permission to be creative . . . Thank you. (Perls, 1969, 81–82)

In gestalt therapy sessions, the focus is on the more obvious elements of the person's behavior. Such sessions are often called "gestalt awareness training," since the therapeutic results of the experience stem from the process of becoming more aware of one's total self and one's environment. Gestalt therapy has become a widely used form of therapy, perhaps because it blends many of the strong points of psychoanalysis (working through intrapsychic conflicts), behaviorism (the focus on overt behavior), and the humanistic-existential orientation (the importance of self-awareness and personal growth).[4]

Other humanistic-existential therapies. Two other forms of therapy that may be roughly classified as humanistic-existential therapies merit consideration.

1. *Rational-emotive therapy (EMT).* This approach stems from the work of Ellis (1958, 1973, 1975), who has pointed out that in our society we learn many beliefs during early life that tend to be continually reinforced through a sort of self-dialog. For example, an individual may continually tell himself that: "It is necessary to be loved and approved by everyone"; "One should be thoroughly adequate and competent in everything he does"; or "It

is catastrophic when things are not as one would like them to be." Such "mistaken ideas" inevitably lead to faulty emotional responses and to ineffective and self-defeating behavior.

The task of psychotherapy thus becomes one of unmasking the client's self-defeating ideas and verbalizations, helping him understand their role in causing and maintaining his difficulties, and helping him change his faulty assumptions and verbalize more constructive ones to himself. Thus rational therapy places heavy emphasis on cognitive change designed to help the individual deal effectively with his irrational *shoulds*, *oughts*, and *musts*, to grow as a person, and to live a creative, emotionally satisfying, and fulfilling life.

2. *Reality therapy.* As formulated by Glasser (1965; Glasser & Zunin, 1973), reality therapy assumes that in early life the individual develops a basic sense of right and wrong that provides the basis for his later values. Difficulties arise when the individual's actual behavior is in conflict with this basic sense of right and wrong.

Therapy focuses on helping the client clarify his basic values and evaluate his current behavior and future plans in relation to these values. Presumably there is little difficulty in helping the client delineate a clear set of values; these are often influenced by the values of the therapist, who in this form of therapy is considered to function as a moral agent and model. However, difficulties may arise in helping the individual learn to live responsibly; that is, in accordance with his values. The latter task is achieved largely by helping him perceive the aversive consequences of living irresponsibly and the sense of personal fulfillment that results from clarifying and living in accordance with one's basic values.

Favorable results with a wide range of patients have been reported for both rational-emotive and reality therapy. Of particular interest is Glasser's (1967) report of successful results with reality therapy in dealing with delinquents, and the report of its successful application on a group basis in helping the wives of military personnel through the crisis of widowhood (Glasser & Zunin, 1973).

---

[4]An extensive discussion of the principles and procedures of gestalt therapy may be found in Kempler (1973).

Evaluation of the humanistic-existential therapies. The humanistic-existential therapies have been criticized for their lack of a highly systematized model of human behavior, their lack of agreed-upon therapeutic procedures, and their vagueness about what is supposed to happen between client and therapist. It is these very features, however, that are seen by many proponents of this general approach as contributing to its strength and vitality. There is no systematized model of human behavior, because the individual cannot be reduced to an abstraction, and any attempt at doing so only results in diminishing his status. Similarly, because of the uniqueness of each person, it is impossible to suggest what techniques should be used with all, or even most, individuals.

In any event, many of the humanistic-existential concepts—the uniqueness of the individual, his untapped potentialities, his present predicament, his quest for meaning and fulfillment, his conflict between being and nonbeing, and his existential anxiety—have had a major impact on our contemporary views of psychotherapy.

Interpersonal therapy: marital and family therapy, transactional analysis

In Chapter 3 we noted the emphasis of the interpersonal viewpoint on the role of faulty communications, interactions, and relationships in maladaptive behavior. This viewpoint has had an important impact on other approaches to therapy—particularly on the behavioristic and humanistic-existential therapies. For example, in behavior therapy we have seen the emphasis on modifying social reinforcements that may be maintaining maladaptive responses; in humanistic-existential therapy we have seen the concern with such problems as lack of acceptance, relatedness, and love in the individual's life.

In many cases, however, disordered interpersonal relationships are at the very center of an individual's problems. Such cases require therapeutic techniques that focus on relationships rather than individuals. In this section we shall explore the growing fields of marital and family therapy and then examine in some detail the popular interpersonal technique of transactional analysis.

Marital therapy. The large numbers of people seeking assistance with problems centering around their marriage situation have made this a growing field of therapy. Typically the partners are seen together, and therapy focuses on clarifying and improving the interactions and relationships between them.

Attempts to achieve this goal include a wide range of concepts and procedures. Most therapists emphasize mutual need gratification, social role expectations, communication patterns, and similar interpersonal factors. Not surprisingly, happily married couples tend to differ from unhappily married couples in that they talk more to each other, keep channels of communication open, make more use of nonverbal techniques of communication, and show more sensitivity to each other's feelings and needs. Faulty role expectations often play havoc with marital adjustment. For example, Paul (1971) cited the case of a couple who came for marital therapy when the 39-year-old husband was about to divorce his wife to marry a much younger woman. During therapy he broke into sobs of grief as he recalled the death of his Aunt Anna, who had always accepted him as he was and created an atmosphere of peace and contentment. In reviewing this incident, the husband realized that his girlfriend represented his life-long search for another Aunt Anna. This led to a reconciliation with his wife, who was now more understanding of his needs, feelings, and role expectations.

One of the difficulties in marital therapy is the intense emotional involvement of the marital partners, which makes it difficult for them to perceive and accept the realities of their relationship. Often, wives can see clearly what is "wrong" with their husbands but not with themselves, while husbands usually have remarkable "insight" into their wives' flaws but not their own. To help correct this problem, videotape recordings have been used increasingly to recapture crucial moments of intense interaction between the marital partners. Watching these tapes then fosters fuller awareness of the nature of their interactions. Thus the husband may realize for the first time that he tries to dominate rather than listen to his wife and consider her needs and expectations; or a wife may realize that she is continually nagging and undermining her husband's feelings of worth and esteem. The following statement was made by a young wife after viewing a videotape playback of the couple's first therapy session:

"See! There it is—loud and clear! As usual you didn't let me express *my* feelings or opinions, you just interrupted me with your own. You're always *telling* me what I think without *asking* me what I think. And I can see what I have been doing in response—withdrawing into silence. I feel like, what's the use of talking."

This insight was shared by the husband, and the couple was able to work out a much more satisfactory marital relationship within a few months.

Other relatively new and innovative approaches to marital therapy include training marital partners to use Rogerian nondirective techniques in helping each other clarify their feelings and interactions. Behavior therapy has been used to bring about desired changes in the marital relationship by teaching the spouses to reinforce desired behavior and to withdraw reinforcement for undesirable behavior. Finally, Eisler et al. (1974) utilized a combination of videotape playbacks and assertive training to assist three passive-avoidant husbands improve their marital relationships.

In one case, for example, a 45-year-old high-school teacher responded passively and ineffectively to a highly critical wife. In contrast to the videotaped interactions of husband and wife made at the beginning of therapy, the videotapes made at the termination of therapy showed such positive results as improved communication, an increased frequency of expressions of affection and approval, and a marked increase in the amount of smiling in their interactions. Both spouses stated that their posttreatment marital adjustment seemed more satisfying.

Family therapy. Therapy for the family group overlaps with marital therapy but has somewhat different roots. While marital therapy developed in response to the large number of clients who came for assistance with marital problems, family therapy had its roots in the finding that many people who showed marked improvement in therapy—often in institutional settings—had a relapse upon their return home. It soon became apparent that many of these people came from disturbed family settings that required modification if they were to maintain their gains.

A pioneer in the field of family therapy has described the problem as follows:

"Psychopathology in the individual is a product of the way he deals with his intimate relations, the way they deal with him, and the way other family members involve him in their relations with each other. Further, the appearance of symptomatic behavior in an individual is necessary for the continued function of a particular family system. Therefore changes in the individual can occur only if the family system changes. . . ." (Haley, 1962, p. 70)

This viewpoint led to an important concept in the field of psychotherapy, namely, that the problem of the "identified patient" is often only a symptom of a larger family problem. A careful study of the family of a disturbed child may reveal that the child is merely reflecting the pathology of the family unit. If the child is seen alone in therapy, he may be able to work out some of his problems; but when he goes back home, he will have to face the same pathological circumstances that led to his problems in the first place. As a result, most family therapists share the view that the family—and not simply the designated person—should be directly involved in therapy.

Perhaps the most widely used approach to family therapy is the "conjoint family therapy" of Satir (1967). Her emphasis is on improving faulty communications, interactions, and relationships among family members and fostering a family system that better meets the needs of family members. The following example shows Satir's emphasis in family therapy upon the problem of faulty communication.

Husband: She never comes up to me and kisses me. I am always the one to make the overtures.
Therapist: Is this the way you see yourself behaving with your husband?
Wife: Yes, I would say he is the demonstrative one. I didn't know he wanted me to make the overtures.

Sports fans have long since become accustomed to closeups, split-screen images, and instant replay in viewing football games and other sports on TV. Now individuals in psychotherapy—whether in an effort to deal with some immediate problem of adjustment or to find pathways for personal growth—are learning to see themselves in a different perspective as a consequence of the use of these same techniques.

In transactional analysis, for example, a husband and wife may see very clearly on instant replay how they are interacting in a child-parent type of relationship; an al-

coholic may see tapes of his behavior when he was admitted to a community clinic for detoxification; or a person in an encounter group, such as the group shown here, may see the "smug, know-it-all look" on her face and understand why the other members of the group have been giving her negative feedback about this aspect of her behavior.

In short, the use of video playback techniques in psychotherapy is opening up exciting avenues for personal change and growth.

Th: Have you told your wife that you would like this from her—more open demonstration of affection?

H: Well, no you'd think she'd know.

W: No, how would I know? You always said you didn't like aggressive women.

H: I don't, I don't like *dominating* women.

W: Well, I thought you meant women who make the overtures. How am I to know what you want?

Th: You'd have a better idea if he had been able to *tell* you. (Satir, 1967, pp. 72–73)

At the other extreme of the continuum with regard to methods, but still concerned with

faulty relationships, are the behavioristically oriented therapists. For example, Huff (1969) has suggested that the task of the therapist involves reducing the aversive value of the family for the identified patient as well as that of the patient for other family members. "The therapist does this by actively manipulating the *relationship* between members so that the relationship changes to a more positively reinforcing and reciprocal one" (p. 26). N. Hurwitz (1974) has elaborated on the role of the family therapist as an intermediary whose functions include "interpreter, clarifier, emissary, go-

There are a number of specialized therapeutic techniques for use with children, which may be used either in conjunction with family therapy or in individual treatment programs. Among these is *play therapy*, in which children are encouraged to express themselves spontaneously. Provided with a "family" of dolls, this four-year-old is able to structure the family situation in ways that reflect his feelings about his parents and siblings and his place in the family.

between, messenger, catalyst, mediator, arbitrator, negotiator, and referee" (p. 145). These role demands are most exacting, and are commonly shared by cotherapists, one male and one female.

As in the case of marital therapy, videotape recordings have been increasingly used in family therapy to enhance awareness of interactive patterns. Another innovation in family therapy has been the use of workshops in which several families remain together for a certain period of time, usually over a weekend. A pioneer in this area, Stoller (1967), described a workshop experience as follows:

"Families come to the workshop with ready-made relationships, but they have not learned to talk about them. As initial shyness and family chauvinism wear off, the interplay begins. . . .

"There are rules: Regardless of which family they belong to, group members are expected to respond to each other directly, and to express their perceptions as clearly as possible. As families get to know one another, they become aware of the implicit contractual arrangements which determine their behavior. The workshop . . . is a microcosm of the difficulties

that families encounter at home; experimenting with new and more fruitful ways of dealing with these problems is a major goal of the session." (p. 33)

Since this observation was made, such workshops have become an accepted procedure in family therapy.

Transactional analysis. Eric Berne (1964, 1972) developed an innovative technique of interpersonal therapy based on the notion that our personalities are composed of three "ego states"—Child, Adult, and Parent—which correspond very roughly to Freud's id, ego, and superego. Our Parent is that part of our behavior which we have incorporated from our own parents or from other parental models whom we have inadvertently learned to emulate. Statements such as "You shouldn't eat so much" or "Put on a sweater if you're going outside in the cold" are examples of our Parent talking. Such statements may be appropriate when spoken to a child, but if they are used with a spouse, it may well be that the speaker is playing too active a Parent role. Our Child is that part of us which is a carry-over from our childhood feelings. "I'll eat as much as I want, and don't always yell at me!" is an example of the Child responding to the first Parent above. A Child response to the second command might be simply to break down and cry—behavior possibly appropriate for a real child, but not for a mature adult. Finally, the Adult in each of us is that part of us which processes information rationally and appropriately for the present unique set of circumstances. An Adult response to the Parent's sweater command might be, "I really don't think it is cold enough for a sweater."

In transactional analysis, the therapist analyzes the interactions among group members (often married couples) and helps the participants understand the ego states in which they are communicating with each other. As long as each participant reacts to the other in the way that he is being addressed, e.g., as a Child to a Parent, the transactions may continue indefinitely. Many couples find out that they have been having "complementary" transactions for years, but that they have always been communicating as mother to son or father to daughter. However, when one party decides to discontinue playing Child to the spouse's Parent, the game ceases, and conflicts develop that must be worked out. Since analysis is done in a group setting, other members are encouraged to participate; the method of their participation often invites analysis of how they, in turn, communicate with other people.

Berne characterized many of our social interactions as "games"—not because they are played "for fun," but because they are played according to a set of unspoken rules. In *Games People Play* (1964), he described a number of these, most of which are deadly serious and highly destructive in their effects.

1. *Why Don't You—Yes But (YDYB).* This is considered the prototype game in transactional analysis and involves what is commonly referred to as "gamesmanship" or "one-up-manship." The game is perpetrated by A who adopts a docile stance toward B (the victim) and presents some personal problem in such a way that B is induced to offer advice—e.g., to adopt a counterstance of Therapist. Once the advice has been offered, A responds by saying "Yes, but . . . ," and proceeds to add additional informa-

tion about his problem that renders B's advice erroneous or irrelevant. At this point B may come back with an alternative solution, still believing that A is sincere in offering him the Therapist role. A again follows the same procedure and "shoots" B down again. This game may go on for several rounds until B finally realizes he has been defeated and is forced to assume a self-effacing stance, perhaps acknowledging that A "sure has a tough problem." In this game, A has perpetrated a transactional role reversal in which he achieves competitive satisfaction at B's expense. A has, so to speak, "put B down."

2. *Wooden Leg.* This game involves the adoption of a "sick" role—much like that in conversion hysteria. In essence, the individual asks "What do you expect from a person with a 'wooden leg'?" e.g., a personality deficiency, physical deformity, or slum background. As we have seen, our society relaxes its demands on persons who are "sick"—who are temporarily or permanently incapable of meeting usual social standards of performance by virtue of some serious misfortune or handicap. It is a "helpless" game played by the Child who wants sympathy but does not not really want to get better. The payoff is, "Oh yes, I understand; don't worry, we'll take care of you and give you whatever comfort you need." Of course, this kind of game is maladaptive in that the individual—whether or not he has an actual handicap—avoids acquiring the competencies and sense of responsibility needed for independence and self-direction.

3. *Now I've Got You, You Son of a Bitch (NIGYSOB).* This game involves an aggressive payoff in which the perpetrator adopts a self-effacing stance that invites competitive exploitation from his victim. Since there is presumably "a little larceny in all of us," the victim unwisely accepts the proffered role and initiates a program of exploitation. The perpetrator plays along for a while, but at a certain point suddenly reverses his stance and reveals the exploitation; with an appropriate show of anger and indignation, he assumes his justly deserved aggressive position of NIGYSOB. The victim, in turn, is forced into the apologetic and devaluating role of guilty self-effacement.

By analyzing the "games" we play, transactional analysis makes us aware of our basic coping patterns and their consequences in terms of our interpersonal relationships and life adjustment. In holding up a mirror so that we can see our behavior for what it really is, transactional analysis reveals how we often unthinkingly manipulate and harm other people as well as ourselves. And as a form of therapy, it holds out the possibility of eliminating the subterfuge and deceit with which we deal with one another and of achieving more authentic, meaningful, and satisfying interpersonal relationships and life styles.

In concluding our discussion of interpersonal therapy, it may be emphasized that in the latter half of the twentieth century we are confronted with serious problems in human relations as well as technological change. Although we still lack much needed research data concerning the effectiveness of these therapies, it is interesting to note the increasing emphasis on interpersonal relationships rather than individual "deviance." We shall see a continuation and extension of this orientation when we discuss encounter groups and the human potential movement.

Group therapy and the encounter group

Treatment of patients in groups received a good deal of impetus in the military during World War II, when psychotherapists were in short supply. It was found to be effective in dealing with a variety of problems, and group therapy rapidly became an important therapeutic approach in civilian life. In fact, all the major systematic approaches to psychotherapy that we have discussed—psychoanalysis, behaviorism, and so on—have been applied in group as well as individual settings.

Traditional group psychotherapy. Group therapy has traditionally involved a relatively small group of patients in a clinic or hospital setting, using a variety of procedures depending upon the age, needs, and potentialities of the patients and the orientation of the therapists. The degree of structure and of patient participation in the group process varies in different types of groups.

Didactic group therapy consists of the presentation of more or less formal lectures and visual materials to patients as a group. For example, a group of alcoholic patients may be shown a film depicting the detrimental effects of excessive drinking on the human body, with a group discussion afterwards. While this approach by itself has not proven

effective in combating alcoholism, it is often a useful adjunct to other forms of group therapy.

Psychodrama is an interesting form of group therapy based on role-playing techniques. The patient, assisted by staff members or other patients, is encouraged to act out problem situations in a theaterlike setting. This technique frees the individual to express his anxieties and hostilities or relive traumatic experiences in a situation which simulates real life but is more sheltered. The goal is to help the patient achieve emotional catharsis, increased understanding, and improved interpersonal competencies. This form of therapy, developed initially by Moreno (1959), has proved beneficial for the patients who make up the audience as well as for those who participate on the stage (Sundberg & Tyler, 1962; Yablonsky, 1975).

It may be noted that group therapy may also be completely unstructured, as in activity groups where children with emotional problems are allowed to act out their aggressions without interference.

Encounter-group therapy. In the '60s and '70s the entire field of group therapy has been changed by the advent of encounter groups, and it seems appropriate to end our discussion of psychotherapy with an account of this increasingly popular form of group therapy. Some encounter groups stem from the sensitivity training or T-groups started over 20 years ago at the National Training Laboratories in Bethel, Maine; others stem from patterns developed at the Esalen Institute in California, Synanon, and similar "growth centers."

Some encounter groups are directed toward helping normal individuals learn more about how their feelings and behavior affect themselves and others, while other groups are directed primarily toward the treatment of personal problems and hence tend to be an extension of traditional group therapy. It is these therapeutically oriented encounter groups with which we are presently concerned, although many of the aspects of group process described here are characteristic of both types of groups.

1. *Format and goals.* There has always been a great deal of flexibility and experimentation in encounter groups, and a variety of formats have emerged. Thus there are leaderless groups of drug addicts, marathon groups in which the participants are conventionally clad and marathons in the nude, and encounter groups involving the confrontation of members of conflicting groups in the community.

Usually the encounter group consists of some 6 to 12 participants with one or two group leaders; the physical setting is relatively bare, permitting maximum freedom of movement and activity. Specific goals in encounter-group therapy vary considerably, depending on the nature and orientation of the group. However, the focus is on providing an intensive group experience that helps members work through emotional problems and achieve more effective coping techniques. The group situation, with its intensive give-and-take, is much closer to social reality than is traditional individual therapy; in fact, it typically goes beyond conventional social reality in terms of the honesty and frankness it demands in interpersonal interactions.

The encounter-group leader — more appropriately described as a leader-participant since his function is not highly directive — is usually responsible for screening group members and for scheduling meetings. He is also responsible for establishing a climate of "psychological safety" in which each member feels safe to drop his façade, to express his feelings, and to try out new ways of interacting with others. He may also serve as a model by expressing his own feelings openly and honestly and accepting expressions of hostility or other negative feelings directed toward him without becoming defensive. He encourages group members to give descriptive feedback (such as "it made me uncomfortable when you said that") rather than evaluative feedback (such as "you are really obnoxious"). It is also the responsibility of the group leader to see that confrontations among group members are resolved in a constructive way, and in general to serve as a resource person when the group needs guidance or comes to an impasse.

2. *Group process.* The emphasis in encounter groups is on the removal of masks, the free and honest expression of feelings, and the resolution of confrontations and other interactions that emerge within the group. This in

Types of intensive group experience

There are a number of different types of groups designed to provide intensive group experiences. Some are oriented primarily toward therapy and others toward personal growth. Some of the more common may be summarized as follows:

1. Sensitivity training groups. Also referred to as T-groups, these groups initially focused on the development of human relations skills but have since become much broader in scope.

2. Encounter groups. This category includes a variety of groups which may focus on the modification of maladaptive behavior or on fostering increased effectiveness and growth of essentially normal persons.

3. Awareness groups. These groups usually focus on sensory awareness, body awareness, and body movement, utilizing awareness training, nonverbal expression, spontaneous dance, and related activities.

4. Creativity groups or workshops. These groups focus on individual spontaneity, expression, and creativity, often through painting and other art media.

5. Therapy groups. These groups focus on the treatment of patients in small group settings and may utilize a variety of procedures depending upon the needs of the patients and orientation of the therapist or therapists. They may overlap with encounter groups oriented toward therapy.

There are also a number of other forms of intensive group experience including *team building groups,* which are widely used in industry to facilitate the attainment of production and related goals as well as providing opportunities for improved human relations, leadership training, and personal growth. The *Synanon group* or *"game,"* developed originally for the treatment of drug addiction, may also be considered under the general rubric of encounter groups, as may groups engaged in gestalt therapy or transactional analysis.

Group therapy ranges from relatively structured group sessions held for therapeutic purposes, such as the one shown in the photo at top, to larger, more informal groups, motivated by the desire for a more fulfilling life based on self-understanding and a sense of communion with others (center). Exercises such as the one showing the woman being passed along above the heads of the other people are designed to foster feelings of cooperation and trust.

turn requires prompt and honest feedback, both negative and positive, from other group members. Usually a good deal of support and affection develops within the group, especially for members who are experiencing periods of crisis.

Nonverbal techniques may be used as "warming-up" exercises to facilitate awareness and group interaction. Such techniques include *eyeball-to-eyeball*, in which two participants gaze into each other's eyes for 60 to 90 seconds; the *blind mill*, in which all of the group members walk around with their eyes closed, learning how to communicate by touch; and *trusting exercises*, in which participants take turns being lifted and passed around the circle formed by other group members. Partial or total disrobing has also been used, and is reported to enhance feelings of spontaneity and confidence rather than eliciting sexual excitement.

Verbal techniques also may be used to facilitate group interaction, to provide feedback, and to focus on personal problems. One method is to have a member occupy the "hot seat" while the others provide feedback about their reactions to him and his behavior. A variation of this technique is called *positive and negative bombardment*, in which the members are instructed to say only negative or positive things about the person on the "hot seat," with the proviso that they must be sincere. This may help the member gain a remarkably different impression of himself than he had before. Here we are reminded of the words of the poet Robert Burns:

O wad some Pow'r the giftie gie us
To see oursels as ithers see us!

Most encounter-group therapists consider such warming-up exercises as useful in getting people to "open up" and to develop feelings of trust and mutual support. Other therapists consider any type of structured technique to be "gimmicky" and counterproductive and prefer to allow group interaction to take its natural course. So far, there is no conclusive evidence as to which approach works best.

Encounter group experiences may be intensified by the use of the *marathon* format in which the group meets for a live-in weekend with only a brief break for sleep. The "opening-up" process appears to be hastened by the continuous contact as well as the lowering of inhibitions that accompanies fatigue. Presumably the participants are too tired to play games, and there is more immediacy, openness, and honesty of expression. This approach also helps members focus on the immediate group experience—on the here and now rather than the past or future. Thus the marathon encounter group has been called a "pressure cooker" because of the emotional tension it builds up and the reduced amount of time apparently required to achieve therapeutic goals.

3. *Termination and reentry.* The term *reentry* refers to the return of group members from the new climate of the encounter group to the everyday world. It is often difficult for the individual to return to the mundane patterns of everyday life, where his new understandings and ways of behaving may not be readily accepted. For example, there is considerable risk in being completely open with others and giving honest feedback in family, work, or social groups.

As yet there is no simple strategy for overcoming the reentry problem. Some group leaders utilize a final session of the group for "reflections," during which participants share their feelings about the group experience and how it may carry over into their lives. In some cases, follow-up sessions are scheduled. Of course, for many encounter groups there is no set termination date. For example, encounter groups for alcoholics and drug addicts may be more or less continuous, with the membership changing over time as new members enter the group and old ones leave it.

Evaluation of encounter-group therapy. Although we shall not attempt to assess the advantages and pitfalls of encounter groups, a few comments seem in order. The potency of this approach is indicated by the fact that a group of strangers can learn, in a relatively short period of time, to function with a high degree of honesty, trust, and supportiveness. Participants frequently attest that the intensive group experience has had a profound influence on their lives. A typical reaction upon termination of the group is "I feel I

Just what is it that goes on in an encounter group? On the basis of his extensive work with such groups, Rogers (1970) has delineated a pattern of events which is typical of the group process. An adaptation of his analysis is presented below.

1. Milling around. As the group leader makes it clear that group members have unusual freedom but also responsibility for the direction of the group, there tends to be an initial period of confusion, frustration, awkward silences, and "cocktail-party talk"—polite surface interaction intermixed with questions about the group.

2. Resistance to personal expression or exploration. Initially, members tend to portray only their "public selves"; only fearfully and gradually do they begin to reveal aspects of the private self.

3. Description of negative feelings. Interestingly enough, the first expression of feelings concerning the here-and-now interaction in the group tends to involve negative feelings directed toward the group leader or other group members.

4. Expression and exploration of personally meaningful material. Despite the resistance to revealing one's private self, the voicing of critical or angry feelings, and the initial confusion, the event most likely to occur next is for some member to take the gamble of revealing some significant aspect of himself—perhaps a seemingly hopeless problem of communication between himself and his wife. Apparently this member has come to realize that this is in effect "his" group, and he can help shape its direction; apparently also the fact that negative feelings have been expressed in the group without catastrophic results tends to foster a climate of trust.

5. The expression of immediate interpersonal feelings in the group. Although this may occur at any point in the group process, it involves the explicit expression of feelings, positive or negative, experienced at the moment by one member toward another. Each of these immediate expressions of feeling is usually explored in the increasing climate of trust which is developing in the group.

6. Development of a healing capacity in the group and the beginning of change. One fascinating aspect of the intensive group experience is the manner in which some group members evidence a spontaneous capability for responding to the pain and suffering of others in a therapeutic way—thus paving the way for change. This healing capacity may extend beyond the regular group sessions, as when a few members remain after the session is over to offer support and therapeutic assistance to a member they sense is experiencing serious difficulties.

7. Dropping of façades, confrontations, and feedback. As the group sessions continue, many things are occurring simultaneously and it is difficult to organize them into any coherent pattern: the various threads and stages overlap and interweave. As time goes on, the group finds it increasingly unacceptable for any member to hide behind a mask or façade, refusing to reveal himself to the group as he really is. In a general sense, the group *demands* that each individual be his true self.

This may result in a direct confrontation, often negative in tone, between two group members. In this type of *basic encounter* with other group members, individuals come into more direct, honest, and closer contact than is customary in ordinary life. This is likely to provide the individual with a good deal of totally new feedback concerning himself and his effects on others.

8. Expression of positive feelings and behavior change. Rogers states that "an inevitable part of the group process seems to be that when feelings are expressed and can be accepted in a relationship, then a great deal of closeness and positive feeling results. Thus as the sessions proceed, an increasing feeling of warmth and group spirit and trust is built up, not out of positive attitudes only but out of a realness which includes both positive and negative feelings" (pp. 34–35). He concludes that while there are certain risks inherent in the intensive encounter group experience, there is also great therapeutic potential.

know each of you better and feel closer to you than to most people I have known or worked with for years."

On the other hand, professionals have pointed with concern to the lack of scientific data concerning the actual effects of encounter-group therapy, the lack of adequate screening of group members, and the lack of adequate training of many group leaders. They point to the possibilities of short-term change and subsequent discouragement after reentry into the world of reality, of the aggravation of personal problems that are brought out but not adequately resolved in the group, and of the development of sexual involvements among group members which may jeopardize their marriages. Similarly, one hears references to "encounter freaks" who wander like lost souls from one encounter group to another, always seeking intimacy and belonging that they never really capture.

A particularly relevant study of "encounter group casualties" is summarized on the right. Since these casualties were "ordinary" college students, the question arises about what might be expected in a setting where all the members are there because they have been judged to be "emotionally disturbed."

Perhaps any potential adverse effects of encounter group therapy can be minimized by ensuring the qualifications of group leaders, by more careful screening of participants, and by following the other guidelines established by the American Psychological Association (1973).[5]

Encounter group "casualties"

Encounter groups encourage, support, and frequently pressure members toward increased awareness of feelings, interpersonal patterns, and potential for change. The result is often a more positive self-concept, increased competency, and the opening of pathways toward personal growth. Unfortunately, failure in the face of group pressure can be a crushing experience, confirming and intensifying an individual's negative self-evaluation.

In a study of 16 "encounter group casualties," Yalom and Lieberman (1971) found that 3 of the subjects had psychotic experiences during or shortly after the termination of the group experience. Apparently these casualties were unable to handle the input overload—the intensive emotional stimulation, feedback about unrecognized aspects of self, and pressure to "open up"—at a time when their need was for support of their tenuous inner control. The other subjects were referred to as casualties because they became more psychologically depressed or evidenced more maladaptive effects persisting through the time of a follow-up interview 8 months later.

The major tragedy uncovered by this study was the suicide of a student shortly after the second meeting of his group. This suicide was not considered an encounter group casualty, because the person had a long history of emotional difficulties and his suicide could not necessarily be attributed to his group experience. Nevertheless, his suicide note vividly illustrates the extreme difficulty that a vulnerable person can have in an encounter group:

"I felt great pain that I could not stop any other way. It would have been helpful if there had been anyone to understand and care about my pain, but there wasn't. People did not believe me when I told them about my problems or pain or else that it was just self pity; or if there had been someone to share my feelings with, but all they said was that I was hiding myself, not showing my true feelings, talking to myself. They kept saying this no matter how hard I tried to reach them. This is what I mean when I say they do not understand or care about my pain; they just discredited it or ignored it and I was left alone with it. I ask that anyone who asks about me see this; it is my only last request." (p. 19)

---

[5]A comprehensive description of encounter groups and their advantages and limitations may be found in Schutz (1973) and Croghan (1974).

Sociocultural Approaches to Therapy

Sociocultural approaches to therapy typically involve the modification of the individual's life situation in order to provide a more supportive or therapeutic environment. Such modification can take many forms, some of which we have already mentioned. It may involve changing parental behavior that is reinforcing and maintaining a child's maladaptive behavior; it may involve foster-home care for children who are abused by their parents; it may involve the hospitalization of an emotionally disturbed child or adult; or it may involve the placement of criminal offenders in a "correctional" or penal institution. In this section we shall be concerned with the role of the mental hospital, community mental health services, and the therapeutic modification of communities and larger social systems.

Institutionalization and aftercare

As we have seen, it is sometimes necessary to remove persons — children, adolescents, adults, and the aged — from their family and community settings and place them in mental hospitals or inpatient clinics for treatment. Typically the sequence of events involves (a) admission to the hospital, (b) assessment and treatment, and (c) discharge and aftercare. Assessment procedures were discussed in Chapter 19; here we shall focus on treatment procedures and aftercare.

The mental hospital as a therapeutic community. Any of the traditional forms of therapy that we have been discussing may, of course, be used in the hospital setting. In more and more mental hospitals, however, these techniques are being supplemented by an effort to make the hospital environment itself a *thera-*

peutic community. That is, all the ongoing activities of the hospital are brought into the total treatment program, and the environment, or *milieu,* is a crucial aspect of therapy. The aim is to get patients back into their family and community settings as soon as possible.

In the therapeutic community, as few restraints as possible are placed on the freedom of the patient, and the orientation is toward encouraging patients to take responsibility for their behavior as well as to participate actively in their treatment programs. Open wards permit patients the use of grounds and premises. Self-government programs confer "citizenship" on them, giving them responsibility for managing their own affairs and those of the ward. All hospital personnel are oriented toward treating the patients as human beings who merit consideration and courtesy. A number of studies have shown the beneficial effects of such staff attitudes on everyone concerned, staff and patients alike.

The interaction among patients — whether in encounter groups, social events, or other activities — is planned in such a way as to be of therapeutic benefit. In fact, it is becoming apparent that often the most beneficial aspects of the therapeutic community are the interactions among the patients themselves. Differences in social roles and backgrounds may make empathy between staff and patients difficult, but fellow patients have "been there" — they have had similar problems and breakdowns and have experienced the anxiety and humiliation of being labeled "mentally ill" and hospitalized. Thus constructive and helping relationships frequently develop among patients in a warm, encouraging milieu.

As we have seen, a highly successful method for helping chronic patients take increased responsibility for their behavior has been the use of token economies as part of the total milieu approach. Such programs are effective both in shaping various socially desirable behaviors and in helping bridge the gap between the hospital environment and the world outside.

It may be emphasized that the ultimate goal of hospitalization is to enable the patient to resume his place in society. There is always the danger that the mental hospital may become a permanent refuge from the world, either because it offers total escape from the demands of everyday living or because it encourages patients to settle into a chronic "sick" role. To avoid this, hospital staffs try to establish close ties with the family and community and to maintain a "recovery-expectant" attitude. Between 70 and 85 percent of patients labeled as psychotic and admitted to mental hospitals can now be discharged within a few weeks, or at most months, and with adequate aftercare the readmission rate can be markedly reduced.

Provisions for aftercare. Even where hospitalization or other institutional approaches have modified maladaptive behavior and perhaps fostered needed occupational, interpersonal, and related skills, the readjustment of the individual in his community setting may still be a very difficult one. We have noted that up to 45 percent of schizophrenic patients are readmitted within a year after their discharge. Adequate aftercare programs can help smooth the transition from institutional to community life and markedly reduce the number of relapses.

The last decade has seen an emerging trend toward the establishment of *day hospitals* and *halfway houses.* Since the founding of the first day hospital in Moscow in 1932, there has been a marked growth in this type of facility in Europe and more recently in the United States (Silverman & Val, 1975). Currently the day hospital is designed for two key functions: (a) to provide an alternative to full-time inpatient care, and (b) to act as a transitional center between full-time hospitalization and return to the community. The latter function is also served by halfway houses, which provide needed aftercare and help former patients function adequately in the community. Typically such halfway houses are not run by professional mental health personnel, but by the residents themselves.

In a pilot program with a group of newly released mental patients, Fairweather and his colleagues (1969) demonstrated that these patients could function in the community in a patient-run halfway house. Initially a member of the research staff coordinated the daily operations of the lodge, but he was shortly replaced by a lay person. The patients were given full responsibility for operating the lodge, for

The hospitalization syndrome

Although individuals differ markedly in their response to hospitalization, we have noted that some who reside in large mental hospitals over long periods of time tend to adopt a passive role and become "colonized," losing the self-confidence and motivation required for reentering the outside world. In fact, a sizeable number of chronic patients become adept at manipulating their symptoms and making themselves appear "sicker" than they are in order to avoid the possibility of discharge from the sheltered hospital environment. This pattern is not ordinarily considered to be the result of hospitalization alone, but rather is attributed to an interaction between the patient and the hospital milieu. The following are some of the steps which have been delineated in the development of this hospitalization, or, as it is also called, *social breakdown,* syndrome.

1. Deficiency in self-concept. A precondition for the development of the social breakdown syndrome is the presence of severe self-devaluation and inner confusion concerning social roles and responsibilities.

2. Social labeling. During an acute crisis period in the person's life he has probably been labeled as psychotic and perhaps even dangerous to himself or others and involuntarily sent to a mental hospital, legally certified as incompetent and lacking in self-control.

3. Induction into the "sick" role. Admission procedures, diagnostic labeling, and treatment by staff members and other patients all too often initiate the individual into the role of a "sick" person — helpless, passive, and requiring care and external control.

4. Atrophy of work and social skills. In institutions that serve primarily as "storage bins" for the emotionally disturbed, basic work and social skills may atrophy through disuse. And during prolonged hospitalization, technological changes in the outside world may contribute to the obsolescence of one's work skills.

5. Development of the chronic sick role. Eventually the confused and devaluated patient becomes a full member of the sick community in which passive dependence and "crazy" behavior are not only common but expected. Now he has been "colonized" — he has learned and adopted the chronic sick role.

In spite of the current emphasis on short-term hospitalization and intensive aftercare, there is still a "hard core" of chronic patients who remain relatively untouched by these new procedures. However, the staffs of large mental hospitals are becoming more aware of this problem of chronicity and are introducing various corrective procedures for remotivation and resocialization, as well as stressing a recovery-expectant attitude.

There are a number of procedures which have proved of therapeutic value, particularly in hospital settings, but which are usually considered aids or adjuncts to the total therapy program rather than as systematic approaches to psychotherapy.

1. Bibliotherapy. Books, pamphlets, and other reading material are often of value in helping the patient realize that others have problems similar to his and in increasing his self-understanding and motivation to improve. Specific reading materials are usually selected in terms of the needs and intellectual abilities of the patient. Related to this type of therapy is the practice of providing patients or prison inmates with the opportunity to take extension or correspondence courses for credit, and in some instances to attend educational institutions.

2. Audio-visual aids. Videotape playbacks of excerpts from marital, encounter group, and other forms of therapy are often extremely helpful in reviewing and integrating critical events and processes in therapy sessions. In addition, there are many fine films dealing with alcoholism, drug abuse, and other maladaptive patterns which can be utilized in overall treatment programs.

3. Occupational therapy. This may involve constructive work which contributes to the operation of the hospital or clinic, formal training in actual job skills, or the supervision of the patient in a therapeutic role in helping other patients — often with the expectation that the patient may later become a paraprofessional.

4. Social events. Many mental hospitals and clinics have a regular schedule of social events including dances, teas, and "cocktail hours." In some instances patients may operate a closed-circuit television program featuring items of interest to patients. In addition, theatrical productions may be put on by patients. Such social events help the patients feel less isolated and more involved in their environment.

5. Athletics. Regularly scheduled athletic events for patient participation may include softball, basketball, and other team sports. Where facilities are available, a physical conditioning program may be worked out to meet individual needs.

6. Music therapy. Patients are commonly provided the opportunity for both listening to music and playing an instrument — often as part of a musical group. Traditional music and folk singing have been found especially effective in fostering patient interest and group cohesiveness.

7. Art therapy. Painting, clay sculpturing, and other art media may facilitate the communication of feelings and assist in the resolution of inner conflicts, as may creative writing of prose or poetry. In addition, patients commonly experience a sense of pride and accomplishment in their creative productions. In some instances, art exhibitions are held and prizes awarded, and there may be competition between different hospital or clinic facilities in such exhibitions.

regulating each other's behavior, for earning money, and for purchasing and preparing food.

Forty months after their discharge, a comparison was made of these ex-patients and a comparable group of 75 patients who had been discharged at the same time but had not had the halfway house experience. Whereas most members of the halfway house were able to hold income-producing jobs, to manage their daily lives, and to adjust in the outside world, the majority of those who had not had the halfway house experience were unable to adjust to life on the outside.

Similar halfway houses have been established for alcoholics and drug addicts and other persons attempting to make an adjustment in the

community after institutionalization. Such establishments may be said to be specialized in the sense that all residents share similar backgrounds and problems, and this seems to contribute to their effectiveness.

One of the chief problems of halfway houses is that of gaining the acceptance and support of community residents. As Denner (1974) has pointed out, this requires the initiation of educational and other social measures directed toward increasing community understanding, acceptance, and tolerance of troubled people who may differ somewhat from community norms. That such an approach is not necessarily unrealistic, however, is demonstrated in the example of Gheel — "the town that cares" — which we discussed in Chapter 2 (Aring, 1975).

Community mental health services

As the trend toward treatment in the family and community setting — rather than in large state mental hospitals — has gathered impetus, we have seen the development of community mental health facilities throughout the country. Where such facilities are available to provide immediate assistance to the individual or the family, many crises can be rapidly alleviated. Thus the family is not disrupted, nor does the individual have to be sent to a distant institution and, later, face the problem of return to family and community.

An interesting illustration of this trend is found in the study of Langsley (1968) and his co-workers who tried intercepting certain patients at the point of hospital entry and returning them to their homes instead for a type of family crisis treatment under the supervision of trained therapists. These individuals, selected on a random basis, exhibited a wide range of mental disorders including schizophrenia and severe depression. Most of them were successfully treated at home with the participation of family members. Only about 20 percent of the first 75 eventually entered a mental hospital during a 6-month period. And those eventually hospitalized spent only a third as much time in the hospital as did a control group not treated at home before hospitalization.

As Denner (1974) has pointed out, however, returning "madness" to the community is not without its problems. The family must be willing to participate in therapy, and the home must provide a supportive environment and not one that reinforces and maintains the maladaptive behavior. Qualified therapists must be available in the community, and the resistance of family members as well as neighbors to having a "mentally ill" person in their midst must be overcome. However, this approach tends to shift the criterion for hospitalization from the severity of the individual's symptoms to the degree of family support and the availability of therapeutic supervision outside the hospital setting.

Community mental health centers. In 1963 President Kennedy sent a message to Congress calling for "a bold new approach" to mental disorders. From this message came the Community Mental Health Centers Act providing federal assistance to communities for constructing such centers. Since that time, over 400 mental health centers have been built, providing services for millions of Americans in their home communities. These centers offer at least five types of services to local residents and institutions: (a) *inpatient care* for persons requiring short-term hospitalization; (b) *partial hospitalization*, with day hospitalization for patients able to return home evenings, or night hospitalization for patients able to work but in need of further care; (c) *outpatient therapy* permitting patients to live at home and go about their daily activities; (d) *emergency care* with psychiatric services around the clock; and (e) *consultation and education* for members of the community. These services are provided without discrimination for all who need them — young or old, well-to-do or indigent.

These community mental health centers are highly flexible and have a number of advantages. For example, the emotionally disturbed individual need no longer face the choice between being admitted to a distant hospital or receiving no treatment at all. If his disturbance is severe he can enter the center's inpatient facility for short-term hospitalization; if he can remain on the job or in his family with supportive care, he can enter partial hospitalization; and if outpatient therapy is sufficient for his needs, he can obtain it at the center. In addition, such community centers usually utilize an interdisciplinary approach to therapy, involving psychiatrists, psychologists, social workers, nurses, and other mental health personnel. Finally, such centers have many resources at their disposal, thus enabling the individual to obtain most or all of the needed services at one agency instead of traveling around the city from one place to another.

"Free clinics" and other community service agencies. During the early part of the "hippie" movement in the 1960s, many young people developed serious psychological and physical problems, often associated with the heavy use of psychedelic and other drugs. Yet because of their rejection of the "Establishment," they were reluctant to utilize the usual private and public mental health facilities.

In response to the need for free, anonymous treatment facilities, the Haight-Ashbury and Berkeley Free Clinics were organized and staffed by volunteer physicians, psychiatrists, psychologists, and other health personnel. Clients were not charged for treatment; no information was given out to parents or relatives; and no questions were asked about drug usage, sexual behavior, or truancy. This freedom from being "hassled" appeared to have a constructive effect on these young people, whose problems were associated with feeling oppressed by a society they perceived as being hypercritical and "uptight." Since the establishment of the free clinics in San Francisco, many similar clinics have opened throughout the country, and the range of services they offer has been greatly expanded; while focusing on the needs of youth, they offer assistance to clients of all ages.

In addition, the last decade has seen the development of a wide spectrum of community service agencies in which imaginative and concerned members of the community are attempting to cope with the interrelated problems of unemployment, delinquency, crime, family disorganization, and mental health. Included here, for example, are community youth centers for "hard to reach" teen-agers in poverty areas. These youth centers provide such services as job counseling, remedial education, drug programs staffed by ex-addicts, "rap sessions" for dealing with personal problems, leadership training, and home counseling for the youths and their families. Prominent among these agencies also are community coordinating councils concerned with delineating the problems in their areas, improving the quality of family life, fostering community involvement, and developing needed facilities.

While some of these service agencies receive minimal governmental support, many do not; rather such agencies supplement the more formally organized and federally assisted community mental health centers.

Modifying larger social systems

It is now being recognized that not only the immediate family but larger groups and institutions in the society may behave in maladaptive ways and/or may be pathogenic for the individuals within them. Thus there has been increasing concern not only with providing community-based facilities for treating individuals and families but also with approaches to modifying maladaptive conditions in organizations, institutions, and larger social systems.

One approach to therapeutic intervention with larger groups originated in a project of the Connecticut Interracial Commission begun in 1946 under the direction of the psychologist Kurt Lewin. Lewin and his colleagues arranged a series of discussion groups in which black and white leaders could get together to air their differences. Because of Lewin's long-standing interest in group processes, he also appointed observers to be present at the meetings and record their comments on the group interaction. The conferees insisted that they too be allowed to participate in the postmortem sessions, and found the feedback both informative and exciting, particularly when it focused on their own behavior. The experience of these groups led to the establishment of the National Training Laboratories in Bethel, Maine, now known as the NTL Institute for Applied Behavioral Science.

The NTL combines research in basic group processes with offering practical help to various groups and individuals through intensive group experiences, particularly sensitivity training. T-groups, as they are called, have been directed especially toward men and women in business, government, and civic organizations and toward professional people who are directly involved in supervising, helping, or dealing with people in special ways—such as business executives, physicians, clergy, youth leaders, teachers, lawyers, police officers, psychologists, and social workers. "Labs" held each year for selected groups incorporate sensitivity training with lectures on organizational functioning and growth, the study of relationships between as well as within groups, and related supplementary experiences.

A second approach to therapeutic intervention on larger group levels started about the same time as sensitivity training, and involves the establishment of psychological consulting firms for helping organizations in the selection and training of personnel, in the resolution of organizational problems, and in the correction of maladaptive group functioning. In some instances, the consulting firm undertakes a "performance contract" in which it guarantees to produce certain results and is paid for its services in proportion to its success in meeting these objectives.

A third and more recent approach involves the application of community psychology to the development of the "competent community."

"Conceptually, the competent community is one that utilizes, develops, or otherwise obtains resources, including of course the fuller development of the resources of the human beings in the community itself. . . . It is not the presence of problems but the manner in which they are coped with that is all important." (Iscoe, 1974, pp. 608–9)

This is a relatively new field, however, and as yet there has been little research concerning therapeutic intervention in communities and larger social systems. But in pursuing this approach the following questions appear relevant: (a) What are the problems and resources of the system? (b) What changes are essential for achieving coping objectives? (c) What means are available and realistic for achieving these changes? and (d) What can be done to ensure the cooperation and participation of group members in carrying out desired changes? These questions may be applied to the system as a whole or to malfunctioning subsystems within the larger social system.

As we move from the family to larger social systems, the problems of therapeutic intervention become much more complex. A change in one subsystem to correct a glaring problem may have far-reaching consequences on the entire system that the planners have not fully anticipated; in some cases changes that seem adaptive in the short run may prove to be maladaptive in the longer perspective. For example, health measures in underdeveloped countries, which seem intuitively to be a highly desirable undertaking, may bring about greater misery than before if the resulting reduction in the death rate is not accompanied by a reduction in the birth rate and provision of a more adequate food supply. Thus there has been an increasing recognition that the needed solutions to problems of social systems may be "counterintuitive"—counter to what we would expect intuitively. Yet only as we anticipate the joint effects of many variables can we make accurate predictions.

As we saw in Chapter 19, one modern technique that is helping social scientists "rehearse" the effects of particular interventions or combinations of interventions is computer simulation. When sufficient information concerning key variables in the situation is available, this approach has proven highly accurate and useful. Unfortunately, such information is not always available, and far-reaching actions are often taken on the basis of woefully insufficient information.

Current Issues and Trends in Treatment

In this chapter we have described a variety of treatment orientations and procedures and commented on some of the current trends in the field of therapy. We shall close by briefly examining some of the issues and trends that are on the "growing edge" of this field, including: (a) crisis intervention, (b) the use of paraprofessionals, (c) the problem of evaluating "success" in psychotherapy, (d) the issue of values, and (e) the human potential movement.

Crisis intervention

Crisis intervention has emerged as a response to a widespread need for immediate help for individuals and families confronted with highly stressful situations. Often such people are in a state of acute turmoil and feel overwhelmed and incapable of dealing with the stress by themselves. In such instances they do not have time to wait for the customary initial therapy appointment, nor are they usually in a position to continue therapy over a sustained period. They need immediate assistance.

To meet this need, two modes of therapeutic intervention have been developed: (a) short-term crisis therapy involving face-to-face discussion, and (b) the telephone "hot line." These forms of crisis intervention are usually handled either by professional mental health personnel or by paraprofessionals.

Short-term crisis therapy. The sole concern of short-term crisis therapy is the current problem with which the individual or family is having difficulty. In essence, the therapist tries to provide as much help as he can or as the client will accept.

Although the treatment of medical problems may involve crisis intervention, we are concerned here with personal or family problems of an emotional nature. In such crisis situations the therapist is usually very active, helping clarify the problem, suggesting plans of action, providing reassurance, and otherwise giving needed information and support. Strong emphasis is usually placed on mobilizing the support of other family members. Often this enables the person to avoid hospitalization and disruption of family life. Crisis intervention may also involve bringing other mental health or medical personnel into the treatment picture.

Most individuals and families who need short-term crisis therapy do not continue in treatment for more than one to six sessions. Often, in fact, they come to the therapist or clinic for an "emotional Band-Aid," and after receiving needed guidance and support do not return.

The "hot line." As we noted in Chapter 17, the Suicide Prevention Center in Los Angeles has opened up a whole new approach to dealing with people in crises. All major cities in the United States and most smaller ones have developed some form of telephone hot line to help individuals undergoing periods of deep stress. While the threat of suicide is the most dramatic example, the range of problems that people call about is virtually unlimited—from breaking up with someone to being on a bad drug trip. In addition, there are specific hot lines in various communities for rape victims and for runaways who need assistance.

As with other crisis intervention, the person on the other end of the hot line is confronted with the problem of rapidly assessing "what's wrong" and "how bad it is." But even if his assessment is accurate and he does everything within his power to help the individual—within the confines imposed by the telephone—the caller may become extremely upset while talking about his problem and hang up without leaving his name, telephone number, or address. This can be a deeply disturbing experience for the therapist—particularly if, for example, the caller has announced that he has just swallowed a lethal dose of sleeping pills. Even in less severe cases, it often happens that the hot-line therapist never learns whether the caller ever solved his problem. Of course,

College students, like this girl, and other volunteer workers can do a great deal to augment the programs of mental hospitals and other institutions. One important function is simply to provide companionship and social interaction for patients who might otherwise have only minimal contact with overworked staff members.

in other instances personal contact may be made with the caller, as when he comes in for counseling.

Crisis intervention is probably the most discouraging for the therapist of any treatment approach that we have discussed. Despite the high frustration level of this work, however, crisis intervention therapists fill a crucial need in the mental health field—particularly for the young people who make up the majority of their clients. For thousands of individuals in desperate trouble an invaluable social support is provided by the fact that there is somewhere they can go for immediate help or someone they can call who will listen to their problems and try to help them. Thus it is not surprising that we are witnessing the proliferation of crisis intervention services and telephone hot lines.

The use of paraprofessionals

While many professionals in the field of mental health believe that only extensively trained and experienced personnel are qualified to undertake the complex task of therapeutic intervention, it has become increasingly clear that there are simply not enough professional personnel to do the job. As a consequence, there has been increased interest in the possibility of training nonprofessionals in therapy procedures. As Halleck (1971) has expressed it, "there are many relatively uneducated but otherwise intelligent and sensitive persons in all strata of our society who could and would make excellent therapists if they were properly trained" (p. 100). In addition, programs have been instituted to train and make more effective use of nurses, clergy, police officers, and other professional personnel. And, of course, student volunteers provide another reservoir of human resources for community service as paraprofessionals.

Currently there would appear to be three primary nontraditional sources of mental health workers.

1. *Community college trainees.* The junior or community college may offer a two-year program leading to an Associate of Arts (AA) degree with specialized training in some mental health area; or it may provide opportunities for the upgrading and extension of skills on the part of hospital attendants, nurses, police officers, and other personnel already working in this area or related fields. Other colleges and universities have established four-year programs along similar lines. Such programs are roughly analogous to the training of paramedical personnel.

2. *Lay volunteers.* The use of lay volunteers in working with mental patients goes back many years, but until recently this approach has not been subjected to systematic study and evaluation. The contribution such lay volunteers can make is well illustrated in a study by Katkin and his colleagues (1971). They utilized female volunteers who functioned primarily in a supportive role in providing posthospital therapy for mental patients. In comparison with a control group of patients who had a recidivism rate of 34 percent within a one-year period, the recidivism rate in the experimental group was only 11 percent. Yet the program did not involve extensive training, but relied primarily on supervision the volunteers received while working with the patients. After reporting positive results in a similar training program, Nicoletti and Flater (1975) concluded that the utilization of volunteers is not a panacea but that it is a vital contributor to meeting the increasing demands in the mental health area.

3. *Former patients.* Perhaps the most creative and exciting work being done in implementing mental health resources is the use of former mental patients, prison inmates, delinquents, drug addicts, or other previously disturbed individuals to treat those with similar problems. We have also commented on the use of actual patients who are progressing favorably in helping those who are more seriously disturbed and the "pyramid approach" in which the less severely mentally retarded assist in the training of more severely retarded individuals. And as we have seen (Chapter 14), these "therapists" often get as much benefit from giving therapy as their trainees do from receiving it.

This approach has sometimes been described as "the blind leading the blind," but it would appear that there is much to be said for the understanding and therapeutic potential of someone who has "been there."

In essence, we appear to be creating a new breed of therapist who will ordinarily be a resident of the community in which he serves, who will have lived much the same kind of life as his clients, and who will understand and be able to communicate with them because he "speaks their language."

Evaluation of "success" in psychotherapy

In recent years there has been a good deal of questioning of the value of psychotherapy. Despite the fact that hundreds of thousands of people undergo some form of psychotherapy each year, we have surprisingly little scientific data to show how often such therapeutic intervention is successful. While attempts have been made to assess and compare the outcomes of various forms of therapy, the wide variations among therapists, patients, goals, procedures, and definitions of success have made it virtually impossible to reach any valid conclusions. Some investigators have questioned whether any form of psychotherapy is effective; others have concluded that while the participants may undergo a profound experience, the outcomes are at best uncertain.

What are some of the problems involved in evaluating the success of psychotherapy? Attempts at evaluation generally depend on one or more of the following sources of information: (a) the therapist's impression of changes that have occurred, (b) the patient's reports of change, (c) reports from the patient's family or friends, (d) comparison of pre- and post-treatment personality test scores, and (e) measures of change in selected overt behaviors.

Unfortunately, each of these sources has

serious limitations. Since the therapist quite naturally wants to see himself as competent and successsful, he is not the best judge of his own effectiveness. Furthermore, he can inflate his improvement rate by consciously or unconsciously encouraging difficult patients to discontinue therapy with him. It has also been somewhat facetiously remarked that the therapist often thinks the patient is getting better because he is getting used to the patient's symptoms. The patient, too, is an unreliable source concerning the outcomes of therapy. He may not only want to think that he is getting better but may report that he is being helped in an attempt to please the therapist. Family and relatives may also tend to see the improvement they had hoped for, although they often seem to be more realistic than the therapist or patient in their long-term evaluations. Psychological tests may show change but are likely to focus on certain measures in which the therapist is interested. Such tests are not necessarily valid predictors of how the client will behave in real-life situations, nor do they give any indication of whether changes are likely to be enduring.

Changes in selected behaviors appear to be the safest measure of outcome, but even this criterion is subject to limitations, for changes in the therapy situation may not generalize to other life situations. In addition, the changes selected reflect the goals of the individual therapist. For example, one therapist may consider therapy "successful" if a patient becomes more manageable on the ward; another, if an individual becomes a more growth-oriented and self-directing person.

To complicate matters further, such terms as "recovery," "marked improvement," and "fair improvement" are open to considerable differences in interpretation, and there is always the possibility that spontaneous improvement or "regression toward the mean" — which in essence means a change in the direction of less deviant behavior — will be attributed to the particular form of treatment used. In spite of these difficulties, however, it is possible to study the effectiveness of various treatment approaches separately — determining what procedures work best with various types of individuals. In the course of our discussion of abnormal behavior patterns we have men-

tioned a number of such studies, most of which have demonstrated positive outcomes from psychotherapy.

In this context, it is relevant to ask what happens to people who do not obtain formal treatment. In view of the many ways that people can help each other, it is not surprising that there may be considerable improvement without therapeutic intervention. Some forms of psychopathology, such as manic-depressive reactions and some types of schizophrenia, appear to run a fairly predictable course even without treatment; and there are many instances in which neurotics and other disturbed persons improve over time for reasons that are not apparent.

But even if many emotionally disturbed individuals do improve over time without psychotherapy, it seems clear that psychotherapy can often accelerate such improvement or ensure desired behavior change that might not otherwise occur. Thus we can summarize by saying that the experience of psychotherapy usually appears to have a beneficial effect. But the issue of evaluation remains a vital one — both ethically and practically — if psychologists and other mental health personnel are to intervene in other persons' lives.

The issue of values

Many persons — both inside and outside the mental health professions — have come to see psychotherapy primarily as an attempt to get people adjusted to a "sick" society, rather than encouraging them to work toward its improvement. As a consequence, psychotherapy has often been considered the guardian of the status quo. Such charges, of course, bring us back to the question we raised in Chapter 1: What do we mean by "abnormal"? Our answer to that question can only be made in the light of our values.

Critics charge that the mental health profession is geared to help middle-class individuals who come from relatively favorable environmental conditions, rather than those who have been thwarted and emotionally crippled by adverse economic and social conditions. As Sager (1968) has expressed it:

"The social conditions of the ghetto, the intertwisted network of social agencies that decide the fate of its residents, combine to repel or overwhelm us. Confrontation with the dead-end plight of a family or with the desperate inability of an individual to extricate himself from his crushing environment forces us to realize that our therapeutic task, when performed in keeping with the models we were taught, is equally hopeless." (p. 421)

In a broader perspective, of course, we are concerned with the complex and controversial issue of the role of values in science. For psychotherapy is not a system of ethics but a set of tools to be used at the discretion of the therapist. Thus mental health professionals are confronted with the same kind of question that confronts scientists in general. Should the physical scientist who helps develop thermonuclear weapons be morally concerned about how they are used? Similarly, should the psychologist or behavioral scientist who develops powerful techniques of behavior control be concerned about how they are used?

Many psychologists and other scientists try to sidestep this issue by insisting that science is value free—that it is concerned only with gathering "facts," not with how they are applied. But each time therapists decide that one behavior should be eliminated or substituted for another, they are making a value choice. And the increasing social awareness of today's mental health professionals has brought into sharp focus ethical questions concerning their roles as therapists and value models as well as their roles as agents for maintaining the status quo or fostering social change. For therapy takes place in a context that involves the values of the therapist, the client, and the society in which they live. There are strong pressures on the therapist—from parents, schools, courts, and other social institutions—to help people adjust to "the world as it is." At the same time there are many counterpressures, particularly from young people who are seeking support in their attempts to become authentic persons rather than blind conformists.

The dilemma in which contemporary therapists often find themselves is well illustrated by the following case example.

A 15-year-old high-school sophomore is sent to a therapist because her parents have discovered that she has been having sexual intercourse with her boyfriend. The girl tells the therapist that she thoroughly enjoys such relations and feels no guilt or remorse over her behavior, even though her parents strongly disapprove. In addition, she reports that she is acutely aware of the danger of becoming pregnant and is very careful to take contraceptive measures.

What is the role of the therapist? Should he encourage her to conform to the mores of society and postpone the gratification of her sexual needs until she is older and more mature? Or, if he believes that what she is doing is not harmful to others, even though it is contrary to parental and social norms, should he help her and her parents adjust to the pattern of sexual behavior she has chosen?

It becomes apparent that there are diametrically opposed ways of dealing with the same problems in therapy. Society must enforce conformity to certain norms if it is to maintain its organization and survive. But how does one distinguish between those norms that are relevant and valid and those that are irrelevant and outmoded? It is often up to individual therapists to decide what path to take, and this requires value decisions on their part concerning what is best for the individual and for the larger society. Thus mental health professionals find themselves confronted with the problem of "controlling the controller"; that is, of developing ethical standards and societal safeguards to prevent misuse of the techniques they have developed for modifying individual and group behavior.

The human potential movement

In the last decade, we have seen a great deal of experimentation with procedures designed to increase the self-understanding and awareness of essentially normal people and help them find pathways to enriched experience and to more meaningful human relationships. The basic idea underlying this "human potential movement" is that average people actually utilize only a fraction of the creativity, feeling, and experiencing of which they are capable. The primary objective is to help individuals learn to become more spontaneous and creative, drop their façades and be more authentic in their interactions with others, and try out new ways of feeling, communicating, and being.

A wide range of techniques for achieving these objectives are being explored – including exercises in relaxation and sensory awareness; nude sensitivity training; Tai-Chi (meditation in movement); dance therapy; body massage; transcendental meditation; seminars on love and sex; the celebration of life as a religious experience; Zen Buddhism, Yoga, and related topics; gestalt therapy workshops; assertiveness training; transactional analysis; and encounter groups. Usually there is no fixed format, but group interaction tends to be emphasized; most of our conventional ideas about thinking, feeling, and relating to each other come under scrutiny; and considerable freedom is provided for exploring new pathways in experiencing and personal growth.

The human potential movement is but one aspect of the growing concern with creating a healthier society. With its emphasis on fostering greater self-understanding, increased sensory awareness, enriched emotional experiencing, and more intimate and fulfilling personal relationships, it may well represent a counterforce to dehumanization in our age of impersonal mass bureaucracy.

Just as we look on Cro-Magnons as extremely primitive in their personal, emotional, and social development, so may people of centuries hence look back at us as extremely primitive in terms of the actualization of our human potentialities. In any event, the human potential movement, together with the growing social consciousness of mental health personnel, appears to augur well for the future. Whether these trends will have sufficient strength and impact to counteract the negative forces in our society remains to be seen. But they do appear to be providing momentum in a constructive direction.

In this chapter we have discussed a wide range of approaches to therapy – biological, psychosocial, and sociocultural – examining both standard techniques and new developments. We have noted the general trend toward an interdisciplinary approach to treatment, and we have also commented on more specific trends. Among the latter were the increasing emphasis on the use of behavior therapy in modifying specific maladaptive behaviors and on the humanistic-existential therapies in fostering self-understanding and personal growth. We have also noted the new emphasis on interpersonal and encounter-group therapies as well as the increasing concern with modifying pathological social conditions that foster the development and maintenance of maladaptive behavior. And in the closing sections we have glanced briefly at some of the issues and trends of concern in the field of therapy today. In our final chapter, which now follows, we shall take up the problems of preventing mental disorders, fostering comprehensive health, and building a good future for humankind. These are problems that pose a challenge for all of us who share the dream of a better society in a better world.

Action for Mental Health and a Better World

"Some men look at the way things are and say why. I dream things that never were and say why not."

Robert F. Kennedy (1968)

As modern psychology, psychiatry, and allied fields have become established and sophisticated sciences, they have directed their efforts toward preventing as well as assessing and treating abnormal behavior. Just as medical science developed vaccines and antitoxins for treating smallpox, diphtheria, and polio, so the contemporary social sciences are attempting to formulate and apply principles that can help us prevent maladaptive behavior and foster a better world for all people. Such efforts are taking place on international as well as national, state, and local levels, and by governmental, professional, and voluntary citizen groups.

What we have said in earlier chapters concerning the causation of abnormal behavior has, of course, direct implications for its prevention. We know that metabolic deficiencies as well as sociocultural deprivation underlie certain types of mental retardation, and it has become possible to detect and correct many of these conditions before the individual's development is seriously arrested.

Likewise, genetic counseling may aid prospective parents who would probably bear children with genetic defects. Unfortunately, we still lack sufficient knowledge about the causes of the functional psychoses and other forms of maladaptive behavior to be equally positive and specific in preventing them. However, as our understanding of maladaptive behavior is continually augmented by new scientific findings, we are becoming increasingly capable of preventing the unhappiness and waste of human potentials that mental disorders inevitably exact.

In this, our final chapter, we shall examine the nature of preventive measures that can be taken to deter maladaptive behavior; discuss the scope of organized efforts for mental health both in the United States and throughout the world; and finally suggest some of the contributions that the individual can make to prevent mental disorders and help build a good future for all who travel on the spaceship Earth.

Perspectives on Prevention
Organized Efforts for Mental Health
Horizons in Mental Health

Perspectives on Prevention

In the prevention of mental disorders we are concerned with two key tasks: seeking out and eradicating the causes of mental disorders, and establishing conditions that foster positive mental health. Preventive measures thus run the gamut from programs directed toward known and specific causal agents to programs aimed at more general social advances.

In our present discussion we shall utilize the concepts of primary, secondary, and tertiary prevention, which we introduced briefly in Chapter 6 in connection with military psychology and psychiatry (see page 199).

Primary prevention

Primary prevention includes all measures designed to foster healthy development and effective coping behavior—on biological, psychosocial, and sociocultural levels.

1. *Physical health measures.* Preventive physical health measures begin with help in family planning and include both prenatal and postnatal care. A good deal of current emphasis is being placed on guidance in family planning—how many children to have, when to have them in relation to marital and other family conditions, and even whether to have children at all. Such guidance may include genetic counseling, in which a variety of new tests for diagnosing genetic defects may be administered to potential parents to assess their risk of having defective children.

Breakthroughs in genetic research have also made it possible to detect and often alleviate genetic defects before the baby is born; when *in utero* treatment is not feasible, such information provides the parents with the choice of having an abortion rather than a seriously defective baby. Continued progress in genetic research may make it possible to correct faulty genes, thus providing humankind with fantastic new power to prevent hereditary pathology. But while this would help ensure a healthy beginning in life, it would not minimize the crucial importance of adequate prenatal and postnatal care—including medical supervision to ensure adequate nutrition for the expectant mother, obstetric care at the time of delivery, and follow-up postnatal care.

2. *Psychosocial health measures.* Our definition of *normality* as "optimal development and functioning" implies opportunities for learning needed competencies—physical, intellectual, emotional, and social. As we have seen, failure to develop the skills required for effective problem solving, for handling emotions constructively, and for establishing satisfying interpersonal relationships places the individual at a serious disadvantage in coping with life problems.

A second crucial psychosocial health measure involves acquiring an accurate frame of reference—in terms of reality, possibility, and value assumptions. We have seen repeatedly that when an individual's assumptions about himself or his world are inaccurate, his behavior is likely to be maladaptive. Likewise, inability to find satisfying values that foster a meaningful and fulfilling life constitutes a fertile source of maladjustment and mental disorders.

Psychosocial health measures also ordinarily require preparation of the individual for the types of problems he is likely to encounter during given life stages. For example, pregnancy and childbirth usually have a great deal of emotional significance to both parents and may disturb family equilibrium or exacerbate an already disturbed marital situation. Thus family planning may involve psychosocial as well as physical health considerations. Similarly, the individual needs to be prepared adequately for other developmental tasks characteristic of given life periods, including old age.

3. *General sociocultural measures.* With our growing realization of the importance of pathological social conditions in producing maladaptive behavior, increased attention is being focused on broad sociocultural measures that will foster the healthy development and effective functioning of all members of the group.

This trend is reflected in a wide spectrum of social measures ranging from public education and social security to economic planning and social legislation directed toward ensuring adequate health care for all citizens. Such sociocultural measures must, of course, take into consideration the future stresses and health problems we are likely to encounter in our rapidly changing society.

As the National Institute of Mental Health has summarized the matter, "In the final analysis, the mental health of each citizen is affected by the maturity and health of our society—from the smallest unit to the largest" (1969, p. 120).

Secondary prevention

Secondary prevention emphasizes the early detection and prompt treatment of maladaptive behavior in the individual's family and community setting. Thus it is concerned with the incidence and scope of maladaptive behavior in specific populations, with the early detection of such behavior, with the variety and availability of mental health facilities, and with crisis intervention.

Science has found that most contagious physical diseases can be brought under control once their distribution and modes of communication are discovered via epidemiological studies. In Chapter 13, for example, we noted the application of the epidemiological approach to the early detection and eradication of syphilis in a major urban area. Epidemiological studies are also helping investigators obtain information concerning the incidence and distribution of various maladaptive behaviors in our society. For example, such studies have shown that high-school dropouts, recently divorced or widowed people, the physically disabled, and elderly persons living alone are high-risk groups for various disorders.

Epidemiological studies tell us what to look for and where to look; the next step is to deal with these trouble spots. Since 1950 we have witnessed a marked increase in the variety and availability of mental health facilities in

To help them develop a sense of self-identity, these children in an experimental kindergarten class draw and cut out life-size figures of themselves.

the United States. The new comprehensive community mental health centers are of particular significance, since they mark a distinct trend way from the traditional state mental hospital approach. As we have seen, such centers are designed to provide both inpatient and outpatient treatment, partial hospitalization on either a day or a night basis, and emergency services 24 hours a day—in essence, to provide individuals and families with the type of care they need when they need it and close to home. Further, the community mental health center makes it possible to elicit the active participation of members of the community in planning the treatment programs that will best meet the needs of its particular population and in serving as nonprofessional volunteers.

We have dealt with the nature of life crises and crisis intervention in earlier chapters and need not go into detail again here. However, it may be emphasized that such crises may confront individuals of all ages, as well as family groups, communities, and even entire societies. A common problem of children receiving assistance at community mental health centers involves transient situational reactions to special stresses or crises. Similarly, we have noted the trauma that divorce can bring to a family, or that racial conflict can bring to a community.

Emergency services for a wide range of emotional problems are increasingly available not only in the community mental health centers and the psychiatric wards of general hospitals but also via the "hot lines" described in earlier chapters. These telephone services bring help to many troubled people who would never present themselves at a mental health facility. Callers seek help with a wide range of problems including personal relationships, drugs, sex, family conflicts, legal questions, loneliness, and abortion.

It is not possible, of course, to prevent crises altogether, nor would we wish to avoid all stress and challenge. Successful mastery of challenges and crises is needed for individual and group growth. On the other hand, failure to deal adequately with crises can lead to the breakdown of individual or group functioning. Thus crisis intervention must be considered a crucial aspect of secondary prevention.

Tertiary prevention

Despite crisis intervention and other secondary preventive measures, some persons do require hospitalization for emotional disorders. Tertiary prevention involves prompt and intensive inpatient treatment for such disorders. Its aim is to prevent the disorder from becoming chronic and to enable the individual to return home as soon as possible.

In many cases, intensive inpatient treatment can be given in the local community mental health center or in a nearby general hospital. But even where the individual requires treatment in a state mental hospital—which is usually a considerable distance from his home—the emphasis is on brief hospitalization and long-range follow-up care. Such follow-up care becomes the primary responsibility of community mental health facilities and personnel as well as of the person's family and of the community as a whole. It seeks to ensure that the individual will be helped to make an adequate readjustment and return to full participation in his home and community setting with a minimum of delay and difficulty.

Even in a society as affluent as ours, the comprehensive preventive approach that we have outlined—involving primary, secondary, and tertiary prevention—places a heavy strain on our resources. However, the alternative would be even more costly in both financial and human terms. Fortunately, as we noted in Chapter 3, there is a strong trend in our society toward the comprehensive public health concept—the goal advanced by the World Health Organization of "a sound mind, in a sound body, in a sound society."

Organized Efforts for Mental Health

With increasing public awareness of the magnitude and severity of our contemporary mental health problem, a large number of governmental, professional, and lay organizations have joined in a concerted attack on mental disorders — a broad-based attack directed toward better understanding, more effective treatment, and long-range prevention. This trend is apparent not only in our society but also in many other countries. And international as well as national and local organizations and measures are involved.

Governmental, professional, and lay organizations

Traditionally, dealing with mental disorders has been primarily the responsibility of state and local agencies. During World War II, however, the extent of mental disorders in the United States was brought to public attention when a large number of young men — 2 out of every 7 recruits — were rejected for military service for psychiatric reasons. This discovery, in turn, led to a variety of organized measures for coping with the mental health problem.

The government and mental health. Aware of the need for more research, training, and services in the field of mental health, Congress in 1946 passed its first comprehensive mental health bill, the National Mental Health Act, which laid the basis for the federal government's present mental health program.

The 1946 bill provided for the establishment of a National Institute of Mental Health (NIMH) in or near Washington, D.C., to serve as a central research and training center and headquarters for the administration of a grant-in-aid program. The grant-in-aid feature was designed to foster research and training else-where in the nation and to help state and local communities expand and improve their own mental health services. New powers were conferred on NIMH in 1956, when Congress, under Title V of the Health Amendments Act, authorized the Institute to provide "mental health project grants" for experimental studies, pilot projects, surveys, and general research having to do with the understanding, assessing, treating, and aftercare of mental disorders.

As a result of recent organizational changes, the NIMH is now one of three Institutes under the newly formed Alcohol, Drug Abuse, and Mental Health Administration. A partial diagram of the rather confusing hierarchy of governmental agencies concerned with health problems is shown in the illustration on page 726. Suffice it to point out here that the NIMH: (a) conducts and supports research on the biological, psychosocial, and sociocultural aspects of mental disorders; (b) supports the training of professional and paraprofessional personnel in the mental health field; (c) assists communities in planning, establishing, and maintaining more effective mental health programs; and (d) provides information on mental health to the public and to the scientific community. Its two companion institutes — the National Institute on Alcohol Abuse and Alcoholism and the National Institute on Drug Abuse — perform comparable functions in their respective fields.

A central concept in the federal government's mental health program, as we have seen, is that of comprehensive care in the community. This concept was first implemented by legislation in 1963 that outlined a national program for mental health and a related program to combat mental retardation. The next milestone came in 1967 with the Report of the National Commission on Community Mental Health Services, which further emphasized the concept of mental health as a community affair and supplied additional guidelines for the community mental health movement. It led to the passage two years later of the Community Mental Health Centers Act, which provided for the construction and staffing of community mental health centers throughout the nation. Since 1970 we have seen the advent of a number of new programs, including the establishment of a National

Department of Health, Education, and Welfare (HEW)

Public Health Service (USPHS)

National Institutes of Health (NIH)[1]

Alcohol, Drug Abuse, and Mental Health Administration (ADAMHA)

National Institute on Alcohol Abuse and Alcoholism (NIAAA)

National Institute on Drug Abuse (NIDA)

National Institute of Mental Health (NIMH)

[1]The NIH is divided into 11 institutes. There are separate institutes on cancer, environmental health sciences, aging, and other areas focusing on physical disorders.

Center for Child Advocacy, the Office of Juvenile Justice and Delinquency Prevention, and the National Institute on Aging.

Although the federal government provides leadership and financial aid, the states and localities actually plan and run most programs. In addition, the states establish, maintain, and supervise their own mental hospitals and clinics. A number of states have also pioneered, through their own legislation, in the development of community mental health centers, rehabilitation services in the community for ex-patients, and facilities for dealing with alcoholism, drug abuse, and other special mental health problems. A significant trend has been in the development of state "Community Mental Health Services Acts," by which states provide grants-in-aid to localities for the development and expansion of local mental health services. Usually the programs also provide consultant services to schools, courts, and welfare agencies.

Through the combination of federal grants and state funds, a wide range of vital mental health facilities and activities has been made possible, including financing of badly needed basic research in the field of mental disorders.

Professional organizations and mental health. There are a number of professional organiza-

tions in the mental health field. Some of the most influential of these are listed in the chart on pages 728–29.

One of the most important functions of these organizations is to set and maintain high professional and ethical standards within their special areas. This function may include: (a) establishing and reviewing training qualifications for professional and paraprofessional personnel; (b) setting standards and procedures for accreditation of undergraduate and graduate training programs; (c) setting standards for accreditation of clinic, hospital, or other service operations and carrying out inspections to see that the standards are followed; and (d) investigating reported cases of unethical or unprofessional conduct, and taking disciplinary action where necessary.

A second key function of these professional organizations involves communication and information exchange within their fields via meetings, symposia, workshops, refresher courses, and related activities. In addition, all such organizations sponsor programs of public education as a means of advancing the interests of their professions, drawing attention to mental health needs, and attracting students to careers in their professional fields.

A third key function of professional organizations, which is receiving increasing attention, is that of applying their insights and methods to contemporary social problems. The tenor of this approach was established by the theme of the 1969 convention of the American Psychological Association which was "Psychology and the Problems of Society." In his presidential address to the convention, George A. Miller stated, "We must somehow incorporate our hard-won knowledge more effectively into the vast social changes that we all know are coming" (1969, p. 1063). Similarly, the 1970 convention of the American Orthopsychiatric Association, whose membership includes psychologists, psychiatrists, and social workers, gave top priority to its Council on Social Issues. And in his presidential address to the American Psychiatric Association in 1970, Raymond Waggoner urged the need for psychiatrists to be concerned about various social problems such as racism, overpopulation, social commitment, and the "search for a future":

"In sum, I plead for a psychiatry that is involved with fundamental social goals. I plead for a psychiatry that will eschew isolation altogether and assume its proper role in advancing the total health of our nation. I plead for a psychiatry that is at once concerned with individual liberty and communal responsibility. And I ask of psychiatrists that they be not only pragmatists but also dreamers with a vision of the future." (p. 8)

In the 1970s we have seen the growing involvement of professional mental health organizations in social problems and issues. In 1974, for example, the Board of Trustees of the American Psychiatric Association endorsed the United Nations program for a decade of action to combat racism and racial discrimination and directed that efforts be made to implement this program as it applies to conditions in the United States. Similarly, in 1975 the Council of Representatives of the American Psychological Association approved a resolution condemning the General Conference of UNESCO for excluding Israel from the European Regional Group of that organization. In addition, the major professional organizations have taken strong stands on human rights, including the establishment of equal opportunities for women and the provision of adequate health services for all people.

Composed as they are of qualified personnel, professional mental health organizations are in a unique position to serve as consultants on mental health problems and programs not only on the national level but also on state and local levels. Increasingly, they are establishing closer liaison with one another as well as with both governmental and voluntary agencies concerned with mental health.

Role of voluntary mental health organizations and agencies. While professional mental health personnel and organizations can give expert technical advice in regard to mental health needs and programs, real progress in helping plan and implement these programs must come from an informed and concerned citizenry. In fact, it has been repeatedly stated that it has been nonprofessionals who have blazed the trail in the mental health field.

Prominent among the many voluntary mental health agencies is the National Association for Mental Health (NAMH). It was founded in

One of the most successful community health organizations is the Los Angeles Free Clinic, open to all residents of the community. Not only does it provide free psychological counseling, as shown here, but it also provides medical and dental services, a "sex information helpline," and a "convict hotline" to work with prison parolees. Its Switchboard/Hotline handles 50,000 calls a year for crisis, information, and referral.

Professional organizations concerned with mental health

American Psychological Association (APA)

An association of professionally trained psychologists. Its purpose is to advance psychology as a science, as a profession, and as a means of promoting human welfare. It has over 30 divisions concerned with various special areas within psychology, and it establishes and monitors standards for the training and practice of psychologists in mental health areas.

American Psychiatric Association (APA)

An association of physicians with training in psychiatry. Its purpose is to further the study of the nature, treatment, and prevention of mental disorders; to help set, improve, and maintain standards of practice and service in mental hospitals, clinics, general hospital psychiatric units, and institutions for the mentally retarded; to further psychiatric research and education; and to foster enlightened views with regard to the social and legal aspects of psychopathology and the role of psychiatry in fostering human welfare.

American Medical Association (AMA)

An association of physicians who are members of constituent state medical associations. In addition to its myriad other functions, it is concerned with mental disorders as a general health problem and with fostering research, education, and legislation to advance comprehensive health efforts in the United States.

American Psychoanalytic Association (APA)

An association of analytically trained psychiatrists. It sets standards for the training of psychoanalysts, fosters research, and is concerned with the alleviation of social problems.

American Sociological Association (ASA)

An association of sociologists, social scientists, and other professional persons interested in research, teaching, and application of sociology. Its sections on Social Psychology, Medical Sociology, and Criminology have special pertinence to mental health.

National Association of Social Workers (NASW)

An association of professionally trained social workers, organized to promote the quality and effectiveness of social work and to foster mental health. It establishes and monitors standards for training and practice, encourages research, and interprets the role of social work in the community.

American Nurses Association (ANA) and National League for Nursing (NLN)

An association of registered nurses concerned with high standards of professional practice. Two of its clinical committee groups (one on Psychiatric Nursing Practice and one on Maternal and Child Health Nursing) have special mental health concerns. A Coordinating Council unites its program with that of the National League for Nursing, a voluntary organization of professional, semi-professional, and lay persons and of institutions and organizations; the National League is the principal standard-setting group in the nursing field.

American Occupational Therapy Association (AOTA)

A society of registered occupational therapists administering medically supervised activities to physically or mentally ill persons. It maintains standards of education and training, makes surveys and recommendations on request, and works with its state association in the preparation and certification of occupational therapy volunteer assistants.

National Rehabilitation Association (NRA)

An association of physicians, counselors, therapists, and others (including organizations) concerned with rehabilitation of the physically and mentally handicapped. Reviews existing services and makes recommendations for improved rehabilitation programs.

American Orthopsychiatric Association (AOA)

An organization of psychiatrists, psychologists, social workers, sociologists, and members of other disciplines working in a collaborative approach to the study and treatment of human behavior, primarily in clinical settings. The AOA encourages research and is directly concerned with fostering human welfare.

National Council for Family Relations (NCFR)	Primarily composed of and directed toward practitioners serving couples and families through counseling, therapy, education, and community service. The NCFR fosters research and the application of its findings to practice.
American Association on Mental Deficiency (AAMD)	An interdisciplinary association of physicians, educators, administrators, social workers, psychologists, psychiatrists, and others interested in assisting the mentally retarded. It works with the American Psychiatric Association in setting standards for hospitals and schools for the mentally retarded.
Council for Exceptional Children (CEC)	Made up largely of professional workers in fields dealing with mentally retarded, physically handicapped, and emotionally disturbed children. Fosters research and its applications, education, and social legislation relating to exceptional children.
Group for the Advancement of Psychiatry (GAP)	An invitational association of limited membership (approximately 185 psychiatrists at any one time). Members are organized into small committees for the purpose of studying and reporting on various aspects of psychiatry and on the applications of current knowledge. Its influential, action-directed reports are often developed through consultation and collaboration with experts from many other disciplines.
American Association for the Advancement of Science (AAAS)	Composed of scientists from many disciplines. Its objectives include furthering the work and mutual cooperation of scientists, improving the effectiveness of science and its contribution to human welfare, and increasing understanding and appreciation of the importance and promise of scientific methods in human progress.

Most of these organizations sponsor national conventions, workshops, symposia, and public educational programs and publish journals in their respective areas. They are also concerned with broad social problems as well as with the special problems in their professional areas.

1950 by the merger of the National Committee for Mental Hygiene, the National Mental Health Foundation, and the Psychiatric Foundation; and it was further expanded in 1962 by amalgamation with the National Organization for Mentally Ill Children. Through its national governing body and some 1000 local affiliates, the NAMH works for the improvement of services in community clinics and mental hospitals; it helps recruit, train, and place volunteers for service in treatment and aftercare programs; and it works for enlightened mental health legislation and provision of needed facilities and personnel. It also carries on special educational programs aimed at helping people understand mental disorders and fostering positive mental health.

With a program and organization similar to that of the NAMH, the National Association for Retarded Children (NARC) works to reduce the incidence of mental retardation, to seek community and residential treatment centers and services for the retarded, and to carry on a program of education aimed at better public understanding of the retardate and greater support for legislation on the retardate's behalf. The NARC also fosters scientific research into mental retardation, the recruitment and training of volunteer workers, and programs of community action. On the local level, it is especially interested in forming groups of parents of retarded children in order to help such parents better understand, accept, and deal with their children's limited capabilities.

These and other voluntary health organizations, such as Alcoholics Anonymous, are particularly American in their development of extensive programs of research, service, and training of volunteers financed by public donations. To succeed in their objectives, of course, they need the backing of a wide constituency of knowledgeable and involved citizens.

International efforts for mental health

Mental health is a major problem not only in the United States but in the rest of the world as well. Indeed, many of the unfavorable conditions in this country with regard to the causes and treatment of mental disorders are greatly magnified in developing countries throughout the world.

It was the knowledge of this great unmet need that served to bring about the formation of several international organizations at the end of World War II. We shall briefly review here the World Health Organization and the United Nations Educational, Scientific, and Cultural Organization (both agencies of the United Nations), as well as the World Federation for Mental Health.

The World Health Organization (WHO). It is the general function of the World Health Organization to formulate recommendations concerning physical and mental health to be carried out by member states of the United Nations. The Canadian psychiatrist Brock Chisholm, the first Director-General, said: "The desperate need of the human race at this most precarious stage of its development is for understanding of man and for the development of methods by which he can learn to live in peace with his kind" (1948, p. 543). Chisholm then called for study of the psychological conditions that stand in the way of the physical and mental health of human beings.

A WHO Expert Committee on Mental Health had its first meeting in 1949 to formulate the principles that should govern the activities of WHO in the mental health field. In view of the very great needs and the shortage of professional personnel and facilities throughout the world, the Committee considered that it would be impossible to provide adequate facilities for therapy for mental disorders within the foreseeable future. As a consequence, the Committee placed its first emphasis on the study and eradication of physical diseases like malaria, syphilis, and cardiovascular diseases, and on improving the general physical health and welfare of the people of the world, while developing and applying mental health resources as rapidly as conditions permitted.

This committee, which has a rotating membership, has conducted studies and issued reports on a variety of mental disorders, on pathological social conditions, and on the development of community mental health facilities. It has made mental health consultants available to member states and has provided training grants and contributed to conferences and workshops both local and worldwide in scope.

WHO has headquarters in Geneva and regional offices for Africa, the Americas, Southeast Asia, Europe, the Eastern Mediterranean, and the Western Pacific. Hence its activities extend into areas with diverse physical environments, types of social organization, and mental health facilities. In its work, WHO does not try to impose a predetermined plan on this diversity; rather it works toward identifying the basic needs of each country or region and then delineating the most useful efforts to be made. In helping member states through consultation or other assistance, WHO also strives to make its services available over a period of several years to ensure continuity and success for the programs that are undertaken. Since its inception, WHO has made many significant contributions to the fostering of physical and mental health among the peoples of the world.

The United Nations Educational, Scientific, and Cultural Organization (UNESCO). The constitution of UNESCO (1945) contains a statement that seems to strike many people with the force of a spiritual conversion: "Since wars begin in the minds of men, it is in the minds of men that the defenses of peace must be constructed." By promoting collaboration among nations through educational, cultural, and scientific channels, UNESCO attempts to foster peace and respect for human rights and fundamental freedoms for all.

There were 135 UN member countries belonging to UNESCO in 1975. In general, UNESCO programs are divided into three main areas: (a) *international intellectual cooperation* aimed at the communication of information and the exchange of ideas among member countries; (b) *operational assistance* through the provision of specialists to advise governments in the planning of educational and other projects and to provide day-by-day assistance in their implementation; and (c) *promotion of peace* through increased knowledge of international problems, emphasis on human rights, and mutual understanding among peoples. On many problems UNESCO works cooperatively with other agencies—sometimes as instigator or catalyst, sometimes as consultant, sometimes as one of several cooperating groups. For example, the use of satellites for educational and mental health purposes was initially arranged by UNESCO.

UNESCO is also working to provide better opportunities for young people to participate actively in the social, economic, and cultural life of their own countries and of the world. It also helps in the training of scientists and technicians, as well as in developing scientific research in developing countries. Thus on many fronts UNESCO is working for the progress of education, culture, and research and for the intellectual and moral unity of humankind in a peaceful world.

The World Federation for Mental Health. The World Federation for Mental Health was established in 1948 at an international congress of nongovernmental organizations and individuals concerned with mental health. Its purpose is to further cooperation at the international level between governmental and nongovernmental mental health agencies, and its membership now extends to more than 50 countries. The Federation has been granted consultative status by both WHO and UNESCO, and it assists the UN agencies by collecting information on mental health conditions all over the world.

We have now seen something of the maze of local, national, and international measures for mental health. It is the first time in history that mental health problems have been viewed as having discoverable causes and as being amenable to treatment and prevention by scientific means, and it is also the first time that a systematic attack has been waged against these problems on a worldwide level. Many people now believe the statement Julian Huxley (1959) made nearly two decades ago, that through the advances of modern science and technology "human life could gradually be transformed from a competitive struggle against blind fate into a great collective enterprise, consciously undertaken . . . for greater fulfillment through the better realization of human potentialities" (p. 409).

Limitations in mental health efforts

In contrast to the potential we now see and to the progress that has been achieved during the last half century in the understanding, treatment, and prevention of mental disorders is the inescapable fact that many limitations still exist. Even in our own country, minimal mental health standards are far from being met, and often the standards themselves are open to question. In fact, the organization and delivery of mental health services in the United States is today lagging behind that of Israel, Sweden, and various other countries.

Limitations in personnel. There is a serious inadequacy in the number of professional and paraprofessional personnel to deal with the mental health problems of the more than 200 million people in our country. For example, in 1975 there were only about 26,000 psychiatrists and 24,000 clinical psychologists in the United States, with comparable shortages of personnel in social work, psychiatric nursing, child care, and other mental health fields. The personnel shortage is particularly acute among those working with emotionally disturbed children.

The ratio is even more inadequate in most of the developing countries. For example, India, with an enormous population, still has only a handful of professionally trained mental health personnel; other developing countries have comparable or even more severe shortages of personnel.

Limitations in facilities. Despite the dramatic reduction in the number of patients in mental hospitals, many of the buildings still used to house mental patients are badly deteriorated and obsolete. Furthermore, the construction of the new community mental health centers required as a result of the shift toward local treatment has lagged badly; this, of course, affects the delivery of services to both young people and adults. Thus the recognized need for early detection and correction of behavior disorders before they become more severe and disabling is not being adequately met in most American communities. And, of course, facilities in the developing countries are practically nonexistent or at best woefully inadequate.

Limitations in research. In relation to the magnitude and social importance of mental disorders in our society, research in the area of mental health is very inadequately financed. In fact, we spend over 100 times as much money on alcohol as on research in mental health. And in the developing countries, very little research is being carried on. Yet it is apparent that a key factor in the effectiveness of the mental health movement is the research upon which its concepts and procedures are based.

In general, our mental health programs suffer from serious limitations in personnel, facilities, research, and finances. Of course, as the federal government's programs for better general health care for all citizens gather momentum, it seems likely that these limitations will gradually be corrected. Ultimately, however, mental health is inextricably tied to the values and priorities that we choose in building the world of the future.

Horizons in Mental Health

The question has arisen as to whether we or any other technologically advanced nation can achieve mental health in isolation from the rest of the world, however great our efforts. Mental disorders, wars, international tensions, racism, poverty, and similar problems are interrelated. What happens to the rest of the world affects us also, both directly and indirectly. The possibility of nuclear war breeds anxiety about the future in the minds of most of us, and our military defenses against perceived threats from other parts of the world absorb vast funds and energy that otherwise might be turned to health, education, and a better quality of life for our citizens at home.

It would appear that every measure undertaken to reduce international conflict and improve the condition of humankind makes its contribution to our own nation's programs for social progress and mental health. Without slackening our efforts at home, we shall probably find it increasingly essential to participate in international measures toward reducing group tensions and promoting mental health and a better world for people to live in. These measures will require understanding and moral commitment from concerned citizens.

Toward a "good future"

As we saw in Chapter 18, our present task, speaking broadly, is to learn to plan for the effective running of our spaceship before it is too late. This will require planning on community, national, and international levels.

To some people in our society, social planning seems contrary to the American way of life and the ideal of individual freedom. Yet as the NIMH (1969) has emphasized, "Social planning does not imply authoritarian control; a planned society does not mean a closed society. Techniques are now emerging to guarantee that planning will enhance, not diminish, the power and influence of individuals in controlling their destinies and achieving their personal goals. 'Advocacy planning' and 'participatory democracy' provide for the inclusion of all interested groups and individuals in the planning and decision-making process" (p. 117). In fact, to be planless in our complex, interdependent, and rapidly changing world is to invite—and perhaps ensure—disaster.

The "futurists." As Shepherd (1971) pointed out, "Man may be headed for extinction, like the dinosaur." He added, however, "Unlike the dinosaur, man has options" (p. 15).

Recently a growing number of scientists and organizations have become involved in delineating what our options are—in delineating various possible futures for our own country and for humankind. In June 1975, more than 2000 men and women—scientists, industrialists, and distinguished scholars from various fields—met in Washington, D.C., at the second assembly of the World Future Society to pool their ideas as to where the world may be heading and what options are open to us. On a more permanent basis, various scientific groups have been set up by the federal government, by the military, by major universities, and by private foundations. These groups are composed of scientists from diverse fields and devote full time to considering the range of future alternatives open to us and the possible consequences of given alternatives. As we have already seen, the use of computers to simulate changes in social systems and to ascertain both the short-term and long-term consequences of the changes on the total system is receiving increasing emphasis.

Although these futurists are not comparable to psychotherapists on an individual or small-group level, they do provide somewhat the same functions in the society in helping people recognize the alternatives available to them and visualize the probable consequences of different choices. Perhaps the chief message of the futurists is that we are not trapped by some absurd fate but can and must choose our own destiny. Thus it is essential that we carefully explore and weigh all the alternatives. It has even been suggested, somewhat

Is an engineered society the answer?

Considerable controversy has been stirred by B. F. Skinner's book *Beyond Freedom and Dignity* (1971). In it, Skinner argues that our values of freedom and dignity not only have been based on false assumptions about choice and free will but are endangering our survival. In his view, we must give up these values because they are preventing us from engineering an environment that will make us behave as we should. He envisions a society in which all people behave for the good of others because the reinforcements induce them to, and since the most effective reinforcements are positive rather than negative ones, he expects a safer, more pleasant situation for all concerned under such a system.*

Many questions are raised by this proposal. There is the practical question of who would do the controlling and decide what was good for the society. There is the moral question of whether some should decide what others should do and have enough power to manipulate them into doing it. There is the reality question of whether, in fact, all relevant interpersonal behavior *could* be controlled by such an engineered society—and how it would be possible to ensure against error on the part of the controllers and provide for necessary changes in the system in the light of changing environmental conditions. There is the philosophical question of how, if freedom is an illusion, we could change our direction by decision and planning: how could we do on a social level what we lack the autonomy to do as individuals? And if we could, there is the existential question of what it would do to people's sense of self-worth and experience of meaning to see themselves as objects manipulated for their own good, with no possibility of controlling their own destiny.

Although it is clear that consequences do guide behavior and that social inducements and pressures strongly influence what we do, the basic behavioristic assumptions of determinism and environmental control are by no means accepted by all, as we have seen. One immediate effect of Skinner's proposal was pressure in Congress to cut off public funds for research that might lead to such control of the individual by society. Again it would appear that people accustomed to democratic values do not take readily to the notion of external regimentation even "for their own good."

*An informative discussion of Skinner's views about the application of behavioristic principles to the building of an engineered society may be found in Day (1975), Skinner (1974, 1975), and Szasz (1975).

facetiously, that various types of future worlds be portrayed on television, allowing the public to vote on the future of their choice.

Sounding a more somber note, many scientists and others are seriously worried about the possibility that some elite minority may someday plan and exercise control over the rest of us, using the very techniques provided by behavioral scientists. We have been forewarned of this possibility by such frightening "utopias" as those depicted in Huxley's *Brave New World* (1932), Orwell's *1984* (1949), and Skinner's *Walden Two* (1948). Skinner went on to argue in *Beyond Freedom and Dignity* (1971) that freedom is not only illusory but actually a dangerous goal to seek and that the use of powerful behavior control techniques in an engineered society is our best hope.

It will be no easy task to ensure that science is used to enlarge rather than restrict our lives. Recognizing the overriding need to safeguard our society against the misuse of behavioral controls, scientists are becoming increasingly concerned with the value orientations upon which choices among alternative "futures" will be based.

The enduring problem of values. We are all concerned not only with *whether* the human race will survive but also with *how*—with the quality of life that will be possible. It will not be enough to preserve human life for a future world of "unsanity" or lockstep regimentation or bare subsistence. As we consciously take the future into our own hands, it is critical that we first consider the entire range of options open to us and then make wise value judgments in choosing among these alternatives.

Thus again we are confronted with the question of *Why?* Why these goals rather than other goals? Why these means rather than other means? The answers to these questions involve value judgments. Although science can specify the conditions that will foster passivity, creativity, or other personality traits, it is our values that determine the kind of children we want to rear, the kind of lives we want to live, and the type of world we want to live in.

Where we lack values for making choices, are confused about our values, or put our faith in false values, the results are likely to be destructive and maladaptive. Although it would be both arrogant and premature to attempt a formulation of values to be used as guides in making our choices, it would appear that we are likely to have to come to grips with the following tentative value assumptions as minimal essentials:

1. A belief in the worth of the individual and of human survival
2. A belief that personal growth and social progress are possible and worthwhile
3. A belief in equal justice and in providing opportunities for all persons to fulfill their potentialities
4. A belief in the value of the "truth" that we try to approach by means of scientific inquiry
5. A belief in the maxim "love one another" and other basic ethical tenets of the world's religious philosophies
6. A belief in the right and responsibility of all people to have a voice in decisions that will affect their lives
7. A belief in humankind as a functional part of the universe with potentialities for evolution that can be fulfilled
8. A belief in the responsibility of all individuals for carrying forward the progress made by preceding generations and for contributing to the creation of a good future for all who travel on the spaceship Earth

These value assumptions are not universally accepted, and, being assumptions, they are not subject to proof. They are suggested here simply as guidelines that may merit consideration by a generation of youth who are seeking a new ethic that can match the impact of science on society. If we have no faith in the worth or growth potential of the individual, in the possibility or value of social progress, or in the potentiality of a meaningful role in the universe for humankind, then these value assumptions will be useless. However, people do not easily adopt the doctrine of despair so vividly portrayed by Shakespeare, that life is

"a tale
Told by an idiot, full of sound and fury,
Signifying nothing." (*Macbeth*, Act V, Scene v)

As we embark upon the great adventure of shaping the future, let us hope that we will learn to change what needs to be changed while preserving what is valid of our heritage from the past. For it has taken many thousands of years to achieve the imperfect level of freedom and opportunity that we have reached in our society. As Haskins (1968) has pointed out, we must be continually aware of the danger that "in embracing new and experimental courses on myriad fronts of movement with the ardor that we must, we do not at the same time discard long-tested values and long-tried adaptive courses, which, if they are lost, will only have, one day, to be rewon—and probably at enormous cost."

In any event, this book can go no further toward a value orientation. Beyond this point, we will each be confronted with the challenge of exploring the world of values and making our own value judgments and choices.

The individual's contribution

> "Each man can make a difference, and each man should try."
>
> John F. Kennedy

When students become aware of the tremendous scope of the mental health problem both nationally and internationally and the woefully inadequate facilities for coping with it, they often ask, "What can I do?" This is not an idle question, for much of the progress that has been achieved in the treatment of mental disorders has resulted from the work of concerned citizens rather than professional mental health personnel. Thus it seems appropriate to suggest for interested students a few of the lines of action that they can profitably take where valuable contributions can be made.

Many opportunities in mental health work are open to trained personnel, both professional and paraprofessional. Social work, clinical psychology, psychiatry, and other mental health occupations are rewarding in terms of personal fulfillment. And as we have seen there is a shortage of trained personnel in the mental health field. In addition, there are many occupations, ranging from law enforcement to teaching and the ministry, that can and do play key roles in the mental health and well-being of people. Training in all of these

fields usually offers individuals opportunities to work in community clinics and related facilities, to gain experience in understanding the needs and problems of people in distress, and to become familiar with community resources.

Citizens can find many ways to be of direct service if they are familiar with national and international resources and programs and invest the effort necessary to become cognizant of their community's special needs and problems. Whatever their roles in life—student, teacher, police officer, lawyer, homemaker, business executive, or trade-unionist—their interests are directly at stake. For although the mental health of a nation may be manifested in many ways—in its purposes, courage, moral responsibility, scientific and cultural achievements, and quality of daily life—its health and resources derive ultimately from the individuals within it. In a participatory democracy, it is they who plan and implement its goals.

Besides accepting some measure of responsibility for the mental health of others through the quality of one's own interpersonal relationships, there are several other constructive courses of action open to each citizen, including: (a) serving as a volunteer in a mental hospital, community mental health center, or youth service organization; (b) supporting realistic measures for ensuring comprehensive health services for all age groups; and (c) working toward improved public education, responsible government, the alleviation of group prejudice, and the establishment of a more sane and harmonious world.

All of us are concerned with mental health for personal as well as altruistic reasons, for we want to overcome the harassing problems of contemporary living and find our share of happiness in a meaningful and fulfilling life. To do so, we may sometimes need the courage to admit that our problems are too much for us. When existence seems futile or the going becomes too difficult, it may help to remind ourselves of the following basic facts, which have been emphasized in the course of the present text.

1. From time to time each of us has serious difficulties in coping with the problems of living.

2. During such crisis periods, we may need psychological and related assistance.

3. Such difficulties are not a disgrace; they can happen to anyone if the stress is sufficiently severe.

4. The early detection and correction of maladaptive behavior is of great importance in preventing the development of more severe or chronic conditions.

5. Preventive measures—primary, secondary, and tertiary—are the most effective long-range approach to the solution of both individual and group mental health problems.

To recognize these facts is essential because statistics show that almost all of us will have to deal with severely maladaptive behavior or mental disorder in ourselves or those close to us in the course of our lives. The interdependence among us and the loss to us all, individually and collectively, when any one of us fails to achieve his or her potential are eloquently expressed in the famous lines of John Donne (1624):

"No man is an island, entire of itself; every man is a piece of the continent, a part of the main. If a clod be washed away by the sea, Europe is the less, as well as if a promontory were, as well as if a manor of thy friends or of thine own were: any man's death diminishes me, because I am involved in mankind, and therefore never send to know for whom the bell tolls; it tolls for thee."

Glossary

Abnormal. Maladaptive behavior detrimental to the individual and/or the group.

Abreaction. Expression of pent-up emotions.

Acting-out. Defense mechanism in which individual reduces anxiety, hostility, or other unpleasant emotions by permitting their expression in overt behavior.

Activation (arousal). Energy mobilization required for organism to pursue its goals and meet its needs.

Actualization strivings. Strivings toward growth and fulfillment.

Actuarial approach. Application of probability statistics to human behavior, as in insurance.

Acute. A disorder of sudden onset and relatively short duration.

Acute alcoholic hallucinosis. State of alcoholic intoxication characterized by auditory hallucinations.

Adaptability. Flexibility in meeting changed circumstances or demands.

Addison's disease. Disease of the adrenal glands characterized by an anemic, emaciated condition and a brownish coloration of the skin.

Adequacy feelings. Feeling of being confident or capable.

Adjustive behavior. Behavior by which the individual attempts to deal with stress and meet his needs, including efforts to maintain harmonious relationships with the environment.

Adjustment. Outcome of the individual's efforts to deal with stress and meet his needs.

Adrenal cortex. Outer layer of the adrenal glands; secretes the adrenal steroids and other hormones.

Adrenal glands. Endocrine glands located at the upper end of the kidneys; consist of inner adrenal medulla and outer adrenal cortex.

Adrenaline. Hormone secreted by the adrenal medulla during strong emotion; causes such bodily changes as an increase in blood sugar and a rise in blood pressure. Also called *epinephrine.*

Affect. Experience of emotion or feeling.

Affective disorder. Psychosis and related thought disturbances characterized by severe disturbances of feeling.

Aftercare. Follow-up therapy after release from a hospital.

Age regression. Inducing a hypnotized subject to evidence behavior of an earlier life period.

Aggression. Behavior aimed at hurting or destroying someone or something.

Agitated depression. Type of psychotic depressive reaction characterized by both severely depressed mood and hyperactivity.

Agitation. Marked restlessness and psychomotor excitement.

Agoraphobia. Morbid fear of large, open places.

Alarm reaction. First stage of the general-adaption-syndrome, characterized by the mobilization of defenses to cope with a stressful situation.

Alcoholic deterioration. Personality deterioration, including impaired judgment, associated with alcoholism.

Alcoholic intoxication. State reached when alcohol content of blood is 0.1 percent or above.

Alcoholism. Dependence on alcohol to the extent that it seriously interferes with life adjustment.

Algophobia. Irrational fear of pain.

Alienation. Lack or loss of relationships to others.

Alpha waves. Brain waves having a frequency of 8 to 12 cycles per second and accompanied by a state of wakeful relaxation.

Alzheimer's disease. A presenile dementia.

Ambivalence. Simultaneous existence of contradictory emotional attitudes toward the same person, e.g., love and hate.

Ambulatory schizophrenic. Mild schizophrenic who is not hospitalized and continues to live and function in the community.

Amnesia. Total or partial loss of memory.

Amphetamine. One type of drug that produces a psychologically stimulating and energizing effect.

Anal stage. In psychoanalytic theory, stage of psychosexual development in which behavior is presumably focused on anal pleasure and activities.

Analgesia. Insensitivity to pain without loss of consciousness.

Analytic psychology. The school or system of psychology developed by Carl Jung.

Androgen. Hormones associated with the development and maintenance of male characteristics.

Anesthesia. Loss or impairment of sensitivity (usually to touch but often applied to sensitivity to pain and other senses as well).

Anomie. State of disregulation of social norms and values.

Anorexia nervosa. Loss or severe diminishment of appetite.

Anoxia. Lack of sufficient oxygen.

Antabuse. Drug used in the treatment of alcoholism.

Anterograde amnesia. Loss of memory for events following trauma or shock.

Antianxiety drugs. Drugs which are used primarily for alleviating anxiety.

Antidepressant drugs. Drugs which are used primarily to elevate mood and relieve depression.

Antisocial (psychopathic) personality. Personality disorder involving a marked lack of ethical or moral development.

Anxiety. Generalized feelings of fear and apprehension.

Anxiety attack. Acute episode of intense anxiety.

Anxiety hierarchy. Ranking of anxiety-eliciting situations utilized in systematic desensitization therapy.

Anxiety neurosis. Type of neurosis characterized by chronic anxiety and apprehension.

Aphasia. Loss or impairment of ability to communicate and understand language symbols—involving loss of power of expression by speech, writing, or signs, or loss of ability to comprehend written or spoken language—resulting from brain injury or disease.

Approach-avoidance conflict. Type of stress situation involving both positive and negative features.

Apraxia. Loss of ability to perform purposeful movements.

Arousal. See **Activation.**

Ateriosclerosis. Degenerative thickening and hardening of the walls of the arteries, occurring usually in old age.

Assertive training. Behavior therapy technique for helping individuals become more self-assertive in interpersonal relationships.

Astasia-abasia. Inability to stand or walk without the legs wobbling about and collapsing, although the person has normal control of legs while sitting or lying down; no associated organic pathology.

Asthma. A respiratory disorder.

Ataxia. Muscular incoordination, particularly of the arms and legs. See **Locomotor ataxia.**

Atrophy. Wasting away or shrinking of a bodily organ.

Attitude. A consistent, learned, emotionalized predisposition to respond in a particular way to a given object, person, or situation.

Aura. Subjective sensations, such as a peculiar odor, preceding an epileptic seizure.

Autism. Disorder beginning in infancy characterized by inability of child to relate to others or form normal self-concept.

Automation. The use of machines to control machines.

Autonomic nervous system. The section of the nervous system that regulates the internal organs; consists primarily of ganglia connected with the brain stem and spinal cord and may be subdivided into the sympathetic and parasympathetic systems.

Autonomic reactivity. Individual's characteristic degree of emotional reactivity to stress.

Autonomy. Self-reliance; the sense of being an individual in one's own right.

Autosome. Any chromosome other than those determining sex.

Aversion therapy. Form of behavior therapy in which punishment or aversive stimulation is used to eliminate undesired responses.

Aversive conditioning. Use of noxious stimuli to punish unwanted behavior.

Aversive stimulus. A stimulus that elicits psychic or physical pain.

Avoidance conditioning. Form of conditioning in which the subject learns to behave in a certain way in order to avoid an unpleasant stimulus.

"Bad trip." An unpleasant or traumatic experience while under the influence of a hallucinogenic drug, such as LSD.

Barbiturate. Type of commonly used synthetic sedative drug.

Bedlam. Popular corruption of the name of the early London asylum of St. Mary of Bethlehem.

Behavior control. Shaping and manipulation of behavior by drugs, persuasion, and other techniques.

Behavior modification. See **Behavior therapy.**

Behavior therapy. Therapeutic procedures based primarily on application of principles of respondent and operant conditioning.

Behavioral contract. A contract, often between family members, stipulating privileges and responsibilities.

Behavioral sciences. The various interrelated disciplines, including psychology, sociology, and anthropology, that focus on human behavior.

Behaviorism. School of psychology which formerly restricted itself primarily to study of overt behavior.

Benign. Of a mild, self-limiting, nature; not malignant.

Bestiality. Sexual relations with animals.

Beta waves. Brain waves having a frequency of 18 to 30 cycles per second and associated with problem solving and feelings of tension.

Biochemical disorders. Disorders involving disturbances in metabolic processes.

Biofeedback. Feedback information concerning blood pressure and other bodily processes under control of the autonomic nervous system.

Biogenic amines. Chemicals that serve as neurotransmitters or modulators.

Biological clocks. The 24-hour rhythmic fluctuations in metabolic processes of plants and animals. Also called *circadian cycles.*

Bisexual. A person sexually attracted to both females and males.

Blocking. Involuntary inhibition of recall, ideation, or communication (including sudden stoppage of speech).

Body image. A person's image of his or her body in terms of attractiveness and other characteristics.

Brain pathology. Diseased or disordered condition of the brain.

Brainwashing. Extreme form of thought modification and control.

Brain waves. Minute oscillations of electrical potential given off by neurons in the cerebral cortex and measured by the electroencephalograph.

Brain-wave therapy. The attempt to use alpha or other brain waves for psychotherapeutic purposes.

Butch. Slang term for *lesbian,* particularly one who assumes a masculine appearance.

Cardiovascular. Pertaining to the heart and blood vessels.

Case study. Assessment information on a specific individual.

Castrating. Refers to any source of injury to or deprivation of the genitals, or more broadly, to a threat to the masculinity or feminity of the individual.

Catalepsy. A condition in which the muscles are waxy and semirigid, tending to maintain the limbs in any position in which they are placed.

Catatonic schizophrenia. Type of schizophrenia characterized by periods of extreme excitement and extreme withdrawal.

Catharsis. Discharge of emotional tension associated with repressed traumatic material, e.g., by "talking it out."

Central nervous system (CNS). The brain and spinal cord.

Cerebral arteriosclerosis. Hardening of the arteries in the brain.

Cerebral concussion. Mild head injury that disrupts brain functions.

Cerebral contusion. Brain damage resulting from head injury severe enough to shift brain and compress it against skull.

Cerebral cortex. The surface layers of the cerebrum.

Cerebral hemorrhage. Bleeding into brain tissue from a ruptured blood vessel.

Cerebral laceration. Tearing of brain tissue associated with severe head injury.

Cerebral syphilis. Syphilitic infection of the brain.

Cerebral thrombosis. The formation of a clot or thrombus in the vascular system of the brain.

Cerebrovascular accident (CVA). Blockage or rupture of large blood vessel in brain leading to both focal and generalized impairment of brain function. Also called *stroke*.

Cerebrum. Main part of brain; divided into left and right hemispheres.

Character disorder. See **Antisocial personality.**

Chemotherapy. Use of drugs in treatment of mental disorders.

Child advocacy. Movement or agencies concerned with protecting rights and ensuring well-being of children.

Chlorpromazine. One of the major tranquilizing drugs.

Chorea. A pathological condition characterized by jerky, irregular, involuntary movements. See also **Huntington's chorea.**

Chromosomes. Chainlike structures within cell nucleus that contain genes.

Chronic. Referring to relatively permanent maladaptive pattern or condition.

Circadian rhythms. Regular biological cycle of sleep and activity characteristic of each species.

Civil commitment. Procedure whereby an individual certified as mentally disordered can be hospitalized, either voluntarily or against his will.

Classical (respondent) conditioning. Basic form of learning in which a previously neutral stimulus comes to elicit a given response.

Claustrophobia. Irrational fear of small enclosed places.

Client-centered psychotherapy. A nondirective approach to psychotherapy developed chiefly by Carl Rogers and based on his personality theory.

Climacteric. The life period associated with the menopause in women and various related glandular and bodily changes in men.

Clinical picture. Diagnostic picture formed by observation of patient's behavior or by all available assessment data.

Clinical psychology. Field of psychology concerned with the understanding, assessment, treatment, and prevention of maladaptive behavior.

Cocaine. A stimulating and pain-reducing psychoactive drug.

Cognitive dissonance. Condition existing when new information is contradictory to one's assumptions.

Cognitive map. See **Frame of reference.**

Cognitive process (cognition). Mental processes, including perception, memory, and reasoning, by which one acquires knowledge, solves problems, and makes plans.

Cohabitation. A male and female living together without being married.

Coitus. Sexual intercourse.

Collective unconscious. Term used by Carl Jung to refer to that portion of the unconscious which he considered common to all humanity.

Coma. Profound stupor with unconsciousness.

Community mental health. Application of psychosocial and sociocultural principles to the improvement of given environments.

Community psychology. Use of community resources in dealing with maladaptive behavior. It tends to be more concerned with community intervention rather than with personal or individual change.

Compensation. Type of ego-defense mechanism in which an undesirable trait is covered up by exaggerating a desirable trait.

Complex. Group of emotionally toned attitudes, desires, or memories which are partially or totally repressed.

Compulsion. An irrational and repetitive impulse to perform some act.

Computer assessment. Use of computers to obtain or interpret assessment data.

Computer model. Use of computer to simulate group functioning.

Conceived values. The individual's conception of the ideal values.

Concept. General idea based on similarities among different objects, events, etc.

Concordance. Similarity in diagnosis or other traits in a twin pair.

Concussion. See **Cerebral concussion.**

Conditioned reinforcer. A reinforcer that derives its value from basic unconditioned reinforcers.

Conditioning. See **Classical conditioning** and **Operant conditioning.**

Confabulation. The filling in of memory gaps with false and often irrelevant details.

Confidentiality. Commitment on part of professional person to keep information he obtains from a client confidential.

Conflict. Simultaneous arousal of opposing impulses, desires, or motives.

Congenital. Existing at birth or before birth but not necessarily hereditary.

Conscience. The functioning of an individual's system of moral values in the approval or disapproval of his own thoughts and actions. Equivalent to Freudian concept of superego.

Consciousness. Awareness of inner and/or outer environment.

Constitution. The relatively constant biological makeup of the individual, resulting from the interaction of heredity and environment.

Contingency. Relationship, usually causal, between two events in which one is usually followed by the other.

Continuous reinforcement. Reward or reinforcement given regularly after each correct response.

Control group. A group of subjects compared with experimental group in assessing effects of independent variables.

Convulsion. Pathological, involuntary, muscular contractions.

Corpus callosum. Nerve fibers that connect the two hemisphere of the brain.

Correlational studies. Studies dealing with the extent to which two or more variables co-vary.

Corticovisceral control mechanisms. Brain mechanisms that regulate autonomic and other bodily functions.

Counseling psychology. Field of psychology that focuses on helping persons with problems pertaining to education, marriage, or occupation.

Counterconditioning. Relearning by using particular stimulus to establish a new (and generally more adaptive) response.

Counterculture. Subculture in conflict with established culture in a given society.

Countertransference. Arousal by the client of feelings of transference on the part of the analyst during the course of psychoanalytic therapy.

Covert. Concealed, disguised, not directly observable.

Crazy. Mentally disordered (term not used in scientific circles)

Cretinism. Condition arising from thyroid deficiency in early life and marked by mental retardation and distinctive physical characteristics.

Criminal responsibility. Legal question of whether an individual should be permitted to use insanity as a defense after having committed some criminal act.

Crisis. Stress situation which approaches or exceeds adaptive capacities of individual or group.

Crisis intervention. Various methods for rendering therapeutic assistance to an individual or group during a period of crisis.

Critical period. Period of development during which organism most needs certain inputs or is most ready for acquisition of a given response.

Cultural bias. Use of assessment criteria which are biased in favor of a given group.

Cultural-familial mental retardation. Mental retardation resulting from lack of needed environmental stimulation, with no evidence of brain pathology.

Culture-free test. Test designed to eliminate the effects of cultural differences on performance.

Cushing's syndrome. An endocrine disorder resulting from oversecretion of *cortisone* and marked by mood swings, irritability, and other mental symptoms.

Cyclothymic (affective) personality. Personality type characterized by extreme mood swings—alternating periods of depression and elation.

Day hospital. A community-based mental hospital where the patients are treated during the day, returning to their homes at night.

Decompensation. Ego or personality disorganization under excessive stress.

Defense mechanism. See **Ego-defense mechanism.**

Defense-oriented reaction. Reaction involving one's feelings of adequacy and worth rather than objective handling of the stress situation.

Deficiency motivation. Motivation directed primarily toward maintaining or restoring physiological or psychological equilibrium rather than toward personal growth.

Delinquency. Antisocial or illegal behavior by a minor.

Delirium. State of mental confusion characterized by clouding of consciousness, disorientation, restlessness, excitement, and often hallucinations.

Delirium tremens. Acute delirium associated with prolonged alcoholism; characterized by intense anxiety, tremors, and hallucinations.

Delusion. Firm belief opposed to reality but maintained in spite of strong evidence to the contrary.

Delusion of persecution. False belief that one is being mistreated or interfered with by one's enemies. Often found in schizophrenia.

Delusion system. An internally coherent, systematized pattern of delusions.

Dementia. Severe mental disorder involving impairment of mental ability; not congenital.

Dementia praecox. Older term for schizophrenia.

Denial of reality. Ego-defense mechanism by means of which the individual protects himself from unpleasant aspects of reality by refusing to perceive them.

Deoxyribonucleic acid (DNA). Principal component of the genes.

Dependent variable. In an experiment, the factor which the hypothesis predicts will change with changes in the independent variable.

Depersonalization. Loss of sense of personal identity, often with a feeling of being something or someone else.

Depression. Emotional state characterized by extreme dejection, gloomy ruminations, feelings of worthlessness, loss of hope, and often of apprehension.

Depressive neurosis. Neurotic reaction characterized by persistent dejection and discouragement.

Depressive stupor. Extreme degree of depression characterized by marked psychomotor underactivity.

Desensitization. Therapeutic process by means of which reactions to traumatic experiences are reduced in intensity by repeatedly exposing the individual to them in mild form, either in reality or in fantasy.

Detoxification. Treatment directed toward ridding the body of alcohol or other drugs.

Deterrence. The premise that punishment for criminal offenses will deter that criminal and others from future criminal acts.

Developmental task. A competency that is considered essential to master during a particular life period, e. g., learning to talk during infancy.

Deviant behavior. Behavior which deviates markedly from the average or norm.

Diagnosis. Determination of the nature and extent of a specific disorder.

Didactic group therapy. Group therapy consisting of more or less formal group lectures and discussions.

Directive therapy. Type of therapeutic approach in which the therapist supplies direct answers to problems and takes much of the responsibility for the progression of therapy.

Discrimination learning. Learning to interpret and respond differently to two or more similar stimuli.

Diseases of adaptation. Stomach ulcers and other disease conditions resulting from the stresses of life.

Disintegration. Loss of organization or integration in any organized system.

Disorganization. Severely impaired integration.

Disorientation. Mental confusion with respect to time, place, or person.

Displacement. Ego-defense mechanism in which an emotional attitude or symbolic meaning is transferred from one object or concept to another.

Dissociation. Separation or "isolation" of mental processes in such a way that they become split off from the main personality or lose their normal thought-affect relationships.

Dissociative reaction. Psychoneurotic reaction characterized by amnesia, fugue, somnambulism, or multiple personality.

Dizygotic (fraternal) twins. Twins that develop from two separate eggs.

DNA. Deoxyribonucleic acid, principal component of genes.

Dominant gene. A gene whose hereditary characteristics prevail in the offspring.

Double-approach conflict. Type of conflict in which individual is confronted with choosing between two or more desirable alternatives.

Double-avoidant conflict. Type of conflict in which individual is confronted with choosing between two or more aversive alternatives.

Double-bind. Situation in which an individual will be disapproved for performing a given act and equally disapproved if he does not perform it.

Down's syndrome (mongolism). Form of mental retardation associated with chromosomal anomalies.

Dream analysis. Psychoanalytic technique involving the interpretation of the patient's dreams.

Drive. Internal conditions directing organism toward a specific goal, usually involving biological rather than psychological motives.

Drug abuse. Use of a drug to extent that it interferes with health and/or occupational or social adjustment.

Drug addiction (dependence). Physiological and/or psychological dependence on a drug.

Drug therapy. See **Chemotherapy.**

DSM-II. Current diagnostic manual of the American Psychiatric Association.

Dual personality. See **Multiple personality.**

Dwarfism. A condition of arrested growth and very short stature.

Dyad. A two-person group.

Dysfunction. Impairment or disturbance in the functioning of an organ.

Dyslexia. Impairment of the ability to read.

Dyspareunia. Painful coitus in male or female.

Dysrhythmia. Disturbance in rhythm.

Dyssocial personality. Behavior pattern characterized by criminal values but good ego strength.

Echolalia. Meaningless repetition of words by an individual, usually of whatever is said to him.

Echopraxia. Repetition of another person's actions or gestures.

Ecology. Relation or interaction between organisms and their physical environment.

Economy, principle of. Theory that the individual meets stress in the simplest way possible.

Eco-spasm. Term used by Toffler to refer to the breakdown of industrial civilization on Earth, accompanied by the initial fragmentary appearance of a new type of civilization.

Ego. In psychoanalytic theory, the rational subsystem of the personality which mediates between id and superego demands and reality. More generally, the individual's self-concept.

Ego-defense mechanism (reaction). Type of reaction designed to maintain the individual's feelings of adequacy and worth rather than to cope directly with the stress situation; usually unconscious and reality distorting.

Ego-ideal (self-ideal). The person or "self" the individual thinks he could and should be.

Ego involvement. Perception of a situation in terms of its importance to the individual.

Egocentric. Preoccupied with one's own concerns and relatively insensitive to the concerns of others.

Ejaculatory incompetence. A male's inability to ejaculate.

Electra complex. In psychoanalytic theory, an excessive emotional attachment (love) of a daughter for her father.

Electroconvulsive therapy (ECT). Use of electricity to produce convulsions and unconsciousness; also called *electroshock therapy*.

Electroencephalogram (EEG). A recording of the brain waves by an electroencephalograph.

Electrotherapy. Methods of therapy which involve the influence of electric current on the central nervous system.

Embolism. Lodgment of a blood clot in a blood vessel too small to permit its passage.

Emotion. A strong feeling accompanied by physiological changes.

Emotional insulation. Ego-defense mechanism in which the individual reduces the tensions of need and anxiety by withdrawing into a shell of passivity.

Empathy. Ability to understand and to some extent share the state of mind of another person.

Encephalitis. Inflammation of the brain.

Encounter. Term applied to the interaction between client and therapist (in existential therapy) or between patients (in encounter-group therapy).

Encounter group. Small group designed to provide an intensive interpersonal experience focusing on feelings and group interactions; used in therapy or to promote personal growth.

Endocrine glands. Ductless glands which secrete hormones directly into the lymph or blood stream.

Endogenous factors. Factors originating within the organism that affect behavior.

Energizer. Drug which has a stimulating effect.

Engram. Hypothesized physiological change in nervous system thought to be responsible for memory.

Entrophy. Deterioration and eventual disintegration or death of a living system.

Enuresis. Bed-wetting; involuntary discharge of urine.

Environmental psychology. Field of psychology focusing on the effects of environmental setting on an individual's feelings and behavior.

Enzyme. Catalyst regulating metabolic activities.

Epidemiology. Study of the distribution of physical or mental disorders in a population.

Epilepsy. Group of disorders varying from momentary lapses of consciousness to generalized convulsions.

Epinephrine. Hormone secreted by the adrenal medulla; also called **adrenalin.**

Equilibrium. Steady state; balance.

Erotic. Pertaining to sexual stimulation and gratification.

Escape learning. Conditioned response in which the subject learns to terminate or escape an aversive stimulus.

Essence. Existential term referring to the fact that one's existence is given but what is made of it is up to the individual and becomes his essence.

Essential hypertension. High blood pressure, presumably of a psychological or emotional origin.

Estrogens. Female hormones produced by the ovaries.

Ethnic group. Group of people who are treated as distinctive in terms of culture and group patterns.

Ethnocentrism. Belief that one's own country and race are superior to other countries and races.

Etiology. Causation; the systematic study of the causes of disorders.

Eugenics. The application of methods of selective breeding of human beings with the intent of improving the species.

Euphoria. Exaggerated feeling of well-being and contentment.

Exacerbate. Intensify.

Excitation. Process whereby activity is elicited in a nerve.

Exhibitionism. Public display or exposure of genitals for conscious or unconscious purpose of sexual excitement and pleasure.

Existential anxiety. Anxiety concerning one's ability to find a satisfying and fulfilling way of life.

Existential neurosis. Disorder characterized by feelings of alienation, meaninglessness, and apathy.

Existential therapy. Therapy based on existential concepts, emphasizing the development of a sense of self-direction and meaning in one's existence.

Existentialism. A view of human beings that emphasizes the individual's responsibility for becoming the kind of person he should be.

Exogenous. Originating from or due to external causes.

Expanded consciousness. Sensation caused by psychedelic drugs or meditation in which individual feels his mind is opened to new types of experience.

Experimental method. Rigorous scientific procedure by which hypotheses are tested.

Experimental neurosis. Neurotic behavior produced in animals by inescapable conflicts and other types of stress.

Extinction. Gradual disappearance of conditioned response when it is no longer reinforced.

Extrapunitive. Characterized by a tendency to evaluate the source of frustrations as external and to direct hostility outward.

Extraversion. Personality type oriented toward the outer world of people and things rather than concepts and intellectual concerns.

Fabrication. Relating imaginary events as if they were true without intent to deceive; confabulation.

Familial. Pertaining to characteristics which tend to run in families and have a higher incidence in certain families than in the general population.

Family therapy. Form of interpersonal therapy focusing on relationships within the family.

Fantasy. Daydream; also, an ego-defense mechanism by means of which the individual escapes from the world of reality and gratifies his desires in fantasy achievements.

Feedback. Knowledge of results of one's behavior; used in judging appropriateness of one's responses and making corrections where indicated.

Fetishism. Maladaptive sexual deviation in which an individual achieves sexual gratification by means of some inanimate object or part of the body.

Fetus. Embryo after the sixth week following conception.

Field properties. Characteristics of the environment surrounding a living system.

Fixation. Unreasonable or exaggerated attachment to some person or arresting of emotional development on a childhood or adolescent level.

Fixed-interval schedule. Schedule of reinforcement based on fixed period of time after previous reinforced response.

Fixed-ratio schedule. Schedule of reinforcement based on reinforcement after fixed number of nonreinforced responses.

Flashback. The recurrence of a drug experience, usually in a negative manner, without further ingestion of the drug.

Flight of ideas. Rapid succession of ideas without logical association or continuity.

Flooding. Anxiety-eliciting technique used in implosive therapy.

Folie à deux. A psychotic interpersonal relationship involving two people; e.g., husband and wife both become psychotic with similar symptomatology.

Follow-up study. Research procedure in which individuals are studied over a period of time or are recontacted at a later time after initial study.

Forensic psychiatry. Branch of psychiatry dealing with legal problems raised by mental disorders.

Frame of reference. The reality, ethical, and possibility assumptions which form the individual's "cognitive map" for interpreting and coping with his world.

Fraternal twins. Dizygotic twins; fertilized by separate germ cells, thus not having same genetic inheritance. May be of the same or opposite sex.

Fraudulent interpersonal contract. Violation of rules or norms governing healthy interpersonal relationships.

Free association. Psychoanalytic procedure for probing the unconscious in which individual gives a running account of his every thought and feeling.

Free-floating anxiety. Anxiety not referable to any specific situation or cause.

Frigidity. Inability to experience sexual pleasure or orgasm on the part of the female.

Frontal lobe. Portion of the brain active in reasoning and other higher thought processes.

Frustration. Thwarting of a need or desire.

Fugue. Dissociative reaction in which the individual leaves his present life situation and establishes a somewhat different mode of life in another locale. Although he is amnesic for his past life, his other abilities are unimpaired and he appears normal to those around him.

Functional psychoses. Severe mental disorders attributed primarily to psychological stress.

Furor. Transitory outbursts of excitement or anger during which the individual may be quite dangerous.

Future shock. Condition brought about when social change proceeds so rapidly that the individual cannot cope with it adequately.

Gay. Synonym for "homosexual."

Gender identity. Individual's identification as being male or female.

General-adaptation-syndrome. Reaction of the individual to excessive stress; consists of the alarm reaction, the stage of resistance, and the stage of exhaustion.

General paresis. Mental disorder associated with syphilis of the brain.

General systems theory. A comprehensive theoretical model embracing all living systems.

Generalization. Tendency of a response that has been conditioned to one stimulus to become associated with other similar stimuli.

Generalized reinforcer. Reinforcer such as money which may influence a wide range of stimuli and behaviors.

Genes. Ultramicroscopic areas of DNA which are responsible for transmission of hereditary traits.

Genetic code. Means by which DNA controls the sequence and structure of proteins manufactured within each cell and also makes exact duplicates of itself.

Genetic counseling. Counseling prospective parents concerning the probability of their having defective offspring as a result of genetic defects.

Genetics. Science of heredity.

Genital stage. In psychoanalytic theory, the final stage of psychosexual development involving shift from autoeroticism to heterosexual interest.

Genitalia. Organs of reproduction, especially the external organs.

Genotype. Genetic characteristics inherited by an individual.

Geriatrics. Science of the diseases and treatment of the aged.

Germ cells. Reproductive cells (female ovum and male sperm) which unite to produce a new individual.

Gerontology. Science dealing with the study of old age.

Gestalt psychology. School of psychology which emphasizes patterns rather than elements or connections, taking the view that the whole is more than the sum of its parts.

Gestalt therapy. Type of psychotherapy emphasizing the wholeness of the person and integration of thought, feeling, and action.

Gigantism. Abnormally tall stature resulting from hyperfunctioning of the pituitary.

Gonads. The sex glands.

Grand mal epilepsy. Type of epilepsy characterized by generalized convulsive seizures.

Grief work. Necessary period of mourning for an individual to assimilate his loss into his self-structure and view it as an event of the past.

Group therapy. Psychotherapy with two or more individuals at the same time.

Guilt. Feelings of culpability arising from behavior or desires contrary to one's ethical principles. Involves both self-devaluation and apprehension growing out of fears of punishment.

Habit. Any product of learning, whether it is a customary or transitory mode of response.

Habituation. Process whereby an individual's response to the same stimulus lessens with repeated presentations.

Halfway house. Facility which provides aftercare following institutionalization, seeking to ease the individual's adjustment to the community.

Hallucination. Sense perception for which there is no appropriate external stimulus.

Hallucinogens. Drugs or chemicals capable of producing hallucinations.

Hashish. The strongest drug derived from the hemp plant; a relative of marijuana.

Hebephrenic schizophrenia. Type of schizophrenia characterized by severe personality decompensation or disintegration.

Hemophobia. Pathological fear of blood. Also called *hematophobia.*

Hemiplegia. Paralysis of one lateral half of the body.

Heredity. Genetic transmission of characteristics from parents to their children.

Hermaphroditism. Anatomical sexual abnormality in which an individual has well-developed sex organs of both sexes.

Heterosexuality. Sexual interest in a member of the opposite sex.

Hierarchy of needs. The concept that needs arrange themselves in a hierarchy in terms of importance or "prepotence," from the most basic biological needs to those psychological needs concerned with self-actualization.

High-risk group. Group showing great vulnerability to physical or mental disorders.

Holistic. A systematic approach to science involving the study of the whole or total configuration; the view of human beings as unified psychobiological organisms inextricably immersed in a physical and sociocultural environment.

Homeostasis. Tendency of organisms to maintain conditions making possible a constant level of physiological functioning.

Homosexuality. Sexual preference for member of one's own sex.

Hormones. Chemicals released by the endocrine glands that regulate activity in various bodily organs.

Hostility. Emotional reaction or drive toward the destruction or damage of an object interpreted as a source of frustration or threat.

Humanistic-existential therapy. Type of psychotherapy emphasizing personal growth and self-direction.

Human potential movement. Movement concerned with enrichment of experience, increased sensory awareness, and fulfillment of human potentials.

Huntington's chorea. Incurable disease, presumably of hereditary origin, which is manifested in jerking, twitching movements and mental deterioration.

Hydrocephalus. Organic condition associated with brain damage and mental retardation.

Hydrotherapy. Use of hot or cold baths, ice packs, etc., in treatment.

Hyper-. Prefix meaning increased.

Hyperkinetic (hyperactive) reaction. Disorder of childhood characterized by overactivity, restlessness, and distractibility.

Hypertension. High blood pressure.

Hyperventilation. Rapid and deep breathing associated with intense anxiety.

Hypesthesia. Partial loss of sensitivity.

Hypnosis. Trancelike mental state induced in a cooperative subject by suggestion.

Hypnotherapy. Use of hypnosis in psychotherapy.

Hypnotic regression. Process by which a subject is brought to relive, under hypnosis, early forgotten or repressed experiences.

Hypo-. Prefix meaning *decreased.*

Hypochondriacal delusions. Delusions concerning various horrible disease conditions, such as the belief that one's brain is turning to dust.

Hypochondriacal neurosis. Condition dominated by preoccupation with bodily processes and fear of presumed diseases.

Hypomania. Mildest form of manic reaction, characterized by moderate psychomotor overactivity.

Hypothalamus. Key structure at the base of the brain; important in emotion and motivation.

Hypothesis. Statement or proposition, usually based on observation, which is tested in an experiment; may be denied or supported by experimental results but never conclusively proved.

Hysteria. Older term used to include conversion and dissociative neurotic reactions; involves the appearance of symptoms of organic illness in the absence of any related organic pathology.

Hysterical neurosis. Disorder characterized by involuntary psychogenic loss of motor or sensory function.

Hysterical personality. Personality pattern characterized by excitability, emotional instability, and self-dramatization.

Id. In psychoanalytic terminology, the reservoir of instinctual drives; the most inaccessible and primitive stratum of the mind.

Identical twins. Monozygotic twins; developed from a single fertilized egg.

Identification. Ego-defense mechanism in which the individual identifies himself with some person or institution, usually of an illustrious nature.

Ideology. System of beliefs.

Idiot. Older term referring to severe and profound degrees of mental retardation (IQ below 24).

Idiot savant. A mental retardate who can perform unusual mental feats, usually involving music or manipulation of numbers.

Illusion. Misinterpretation of sensory data; false perception.

Implosive therapy. Type of behavior therapy in which desensitization is achieved by eliciting a massive "flood" or implosion of anxiety.

Impotence. Inability of male to achieve orgasm.

Impulse. Tendency to action.

Incentive. External inducement to behave in a certain way.

Incest. Sexual relations between close relatives such as father and daughter or brother and sister.

Independent variable. Factor whose effects are being examined in an experiment; it is manipulated in some way while the other variables are held constant.

Index case. In a genetic study, the individual who evidences the trait in which the investigator is interested. Same as *proband.*

Inferiority complex. Strong feelings of inadequacy and insecurity which color an individual's entire adjustive efforts.

Infantile autism. See **Autism.**

Inhibition. Conscious restraint of impulse or desire.

Innate. Inborn.

Inner controls. Reality, value, and possibility assumptions which serve to inhibit dangerous or undesirable behavior; could also apply to conditioned avoidance reactions.

In patient. Hospitalized mental patient.

Insanity. Legal term for mental disorder, implying lack of responsibility for one's acts and inability to manage one's affairs.

Insight. Clinically, the individual's understanding of his illness or of the motivations underlying his behavior; in general psychology, the sudden grasp or understanding of meaningful relationships in a situation.

Insight therapy. Type of psychotherapy focusing on helping the patient achieve greater self-understanding with respect to his motives, values, coping patterns, and so on.

Insomnia. Difficulty in sleeping.

Instinct. Inborn tendency to particular behavior patterns under certain conditions in absence of learning; characteristic of species.

Instrumental act. Act directed toward achieving specific goals and meeting needs.

Instrumental (operant) conditioning. Type of conditioning in which the subject is reinforced for making a predetermined response, such as pressing a lever.

Integration. Organization of parts (psychological, biological functions) to make a functional whole.

Integrative properties. Tendency of living systems to maintain their organization and functional integrity.

Integrity. Quality of being unified and honest with self and others.

Intellectualization. Ego-defense mechanism by which the individual achieves some measure of insulation from emotional hurt by cutting off or distorting the emotional charge which normally accompanies hurtful situations.

Intelligence. Pertaining to ability to learn, reason, and adapt.

Intelligence quotient (IQ). Measurement of intelligence expressed as a number or position on a scale. Comparable to term *intellectual level.*

Interdisciplinary (multidisciplinary) approach. Integration of various scientific disciplines in understanding, assessing, treating, and preventing mental disorders.

Intermittent reinforcement. Reinforcement given intermittently rather than after every response.

Interpersonal accommodation. A reciprocal process of give and take meant to promote satisfactory interpersonal relationships.

Intrapsychic conflict. Psychoanalytic concept referring to conflict between id, ego, and superego.

Introjection. Incorporation of qualities or values of another person or group into one's own ego structure with a tendency to identify with them and to be affected by what happens to them.

Intromission. Insertion of the penis into the vagina or anus.

Intropunitive. Responding to frustration by tending to blame oneself.

Introspection. Observing (and often reporting on) one's inner experiencing.

Introversion. Direction of interest toward one's inner world of experience and toward concepts rather than external events and objects.

In vivo. Taking place in a real-life situation as opposed to the therapeutic or laboratory setting.

Involutional melancholia (involutional psychotic reaction). Depressive psychotic reaction characterized by depression, agitation, and apprehension.

Ionizing radiation. Form of radiation; major cause of gene mutations.

Isolation. Ego-defense mechanism by means of which contradictory attitudes or feelings which normally accompany particular attitudes are kept apart, thus preventing conflict or hurt.

Juvenile delinquency. Legally prohibited behavior committed by minors.

Juvenile paresis. General paresis in children, usually of congenital origin.

Klinefelter's syndrome. Type of mental retardation associated with sex chromosome anomaly.

Korsakoff's psychosis. Psychosis usually associated with chronic alcoholism and characterized by disorientation, gross memory defects, and confabulation.

Labeling. Assigning an individual to a particular diagnostic category, such as schizophrenia.

Lability. Instability, particularly with regard to affect.

Latent. Inactive or dormant.

Latent content. In psychoanalytic theory, repressed wishes indirectly expressed in the manifest content of dreams.

Latent learning. Learning that becomes evident only after an incentive is introduced.

Law of effect. Principle that responses that have rewarding consequences are strengthened and those that have aversive consequences are weakened or eliminated.

Learning. Modification of behavior as a consequence of experience.

Lesbian. Female homosexual.

Lesion. Destruction of a portion of the brain.

Lethality scale. Criteria used to assess the likelihood of an individual's committing suicide.

Level of aspiration. Standard by which the individual judges success or failure of his behavior.

Libido. In general psychoanalytic terminology, the instinctual drives of the id. In a narrow sense, the drive for sexual gratification.

Life crisis. Stress situation that approaches or exceeds the individual's adjustive capacity.

Life history method. Technique of psychological observation in which the development of particular forms of behavior is traced by means of records of the subject's past or present behavior.

Life-style. The general pattern of assumptions, motives, cognitive styles, and coping techniques that characterize the behavior of a given individual and give it consistency.

Lobotomy. Drastic form of psychosurgery rarely used at present. It involves cutting the nerve fibers that connect the frontal lobes to the thalamus.

Locomotor ataxia. Muscular incoordination usually resulting from syphilitic damage to the spinal-cord pathways.

Logic-tight compartments. Form of intellectualization in which contradictory desires or attitudes are "sealed off" in separate areas of consciousness.

Lunacy. Legal term roughly synonymous with insanity.

Lycanthropy. The delusion of being a wolf.

Lysergic acid diethylamide-25 (LSD). A potent hallucinogen.

Macrocephalic. Having an abnormally large cranium.

Madness. Nontechnical synonym for mental illness.

Maintaining cause. Environmental reinforcers or contingencies that tend to maintain maladaptive behavior.

Maintenance strivings. Strivings directed toward maintenance of physiological and psychological equilibrium and integration.

Major tranquilizers. Antipsychotic drugs, such as the phenothiazenes.

Maladaptive (abnormal) behavior. Behavior which is detrimental to well-being of the individual and/or group.

Maladjustment. A more or less enduring failure of adjustment; lack of harmony with self or environment.

Malinger. To fake illness or disability symptoms consciously.

-mania. Suffix denoting a compulsive or morbid preoccupation with some impulse or activity; e.g., compulsive stealing is called kleptomania.

Manic-depressive psychoses. Group of psychotic disorders characterized by prolonged periods of excitement and overactivity (mania) or by periods of depression and underactivity (depression) or by alternation of the two.

Manifest content. In psychoanalytic theory, the apparent meaning of a dream; masks the latent content.

Mannerism. Recurring stereotyped gesture, posture, or movement.

Marathon encounter group. Intensive group experience lasting for 2 or more days with only brief breaks for sleep.

Marijuana. Drug derived from the plant *cannabis indica;* often used in cigarettes called "reefers" or "joints."

Marital schism. Marriage characterized by severe chronic discord which threatens continuation of marital relationship.

Marital skew. Marriage maintained at expense of distorted relationship.

Marital therapy. Therapy directed toward improving communication and interaction between marital partners.

Masked deprivation. Rejection of child by mother; does not involve separation.

Masked disorder. "Masking" of underlying depression or other emotional disturbance by delinquent behavior or other patterns seemingly unrelated to the basic disturbance.

Masochism. Sexual deviation in which an individual obtains sexual gratification from having pain inflicted upon him.

Mass hysteria. Group outbreak of hysterical reactions.

Masturbation. Self-stimulation of genitals for sexual gratification.

Maternal deprivation. Lack of adequate care and stimulation by the mother or surrogate.

Maturation. Process of development and body change resulting from heredity rather than learning.

Megalomania. Delusions of grandeur.

Melancholia. Mental disorder characterized by severe depression.

Meninges. Membranes which envelop the brain and spinal cord.

Mental age (MA). A scale unit indicating level of intelligence in relation to chronological age.

Mental deficiency. Synonym for mental retardation; the latter term is now preferred.

Mental disease. Mental disorder associated with an organic disease of the nervous system.

Mental disorder. Entire range of abnormal behavior patterns.

Mental illness. Once used synonymously with mental disorder but now ordinarily restricted to psychoses.

Mental retardation. Below-normal intelligence, usually meaning an IQ below 68.

Mescaline. One of the hallucinogenic drugs.

Mesmerism. Theories of "animal magnetism" (hypnosis) formulated by Anton Mesmer.

Methadone. An orally administered narcotic which kills the craving for heroin and paves way for rehabilitation of heroin addicts.

Microcephaly. Form of mental retardation characterized by abnormally small cranium and retarded development of brain.

Migraine headache. Type of psychosomatic disorder characterized by recurrent headaches, usually on one side of head only, and associated with emotional tension.

Milieu. The immediate environment, physical or social or both; sometimes used to include the internal state of an organism.

Minimal brain dysfunction (MBD). Controversial term referring to various "soft" neurological signs presumably indicative of malfunctioning of brain.

Minor tranquilizers. Antianxiety drugs such as the meprobramates.

Model. An analogy that helps a scientist order his findings and see important relationships among them.

Model psychoses. Psychoticlike states produced by various hallucinogenic drugs such as LSD.

Modeling. Form of learning in which individual learns by watching someone else (the model) perform the desired response.

Modus operandi. Manner or mode of behavior; a criminal's typical pattern of performing his crimes.

Mongolism. See **Down's syndrome.**

Monozygotic twins. Identical twins, developed from one fertilized egg.

Moral nihilism. Doctrine which denies any objective or real ground for moral beliefs, and holds that the individual is not bound by obligation to others or society.

Moral therapy. Therapy based on provision of kindness, understanding, and favorable environment; prevalent during early part of 19th century.

Morbid. Unhealthy, pathological.

Morita therapy. Treatment of neuroses involving deprivation of external stimulation and other procedures.

Moron. Term formerly used to refer to mild degrees of mental retardation.

Morphine. Addictive opiate drug.

Motivation. Often used as a synonym for drive or activation; implies that the organism's actions are partly determined in direction and strength by its own inner nature.

Motivational selectivity. Influence of motives on perception and other cognitive processes.

Motive. Internal condition which directs action toward some goal; term usually used to include both the drive and the goal to which it is directed.

Multiple personality. Type of dissociative reaction characterized by the development of two or more relatively independent personality systems in the same individual.

Mutant gene. Gene that has undergone some change in structure.

Mutation. Change in the composition of a gene, usually causing harmful or abnormal characteristics to appear in the offspring.

Mutism. Refusal or inability to speak.

Myxedema. Disorder due to thyroid deficiency in adult life, characterized by mental dullness.

Narcissism. Self-love.

Narcolepsy. Abnormal reaction characterized by transient, compulsive states of sleepiness.

Narcotherapy (narcoanalysis, narcosynthesis). Psychotherapy carried on while the patient is in a sleeplike state of relaxation induced by a drug such as sodium pentothal.

Narcotic drugs. Drugs such as morphine which lead to physiological dependence and increased tolerance.

Need. Biological or psychological condition whose gratification is necessary for the maintenance of homeostasis or for self-actualization.

Negativism. Form of aggressive withdrawal which involves refusing to cooperate or obey commands, or doing the exact opposite of what has been requested.

Neologism. A new word; commonly coined by persons labeled as schizophrenic.

Neonate. Newborn infant.

Neoplasm. Tumor.

Nervous breakdown. Refers broadly to lowered integration and inability to deal adequately with one's life situation.

Neurasthenic neurosis. Neurotic disorder characterized by complaints of chronic weakness, easy fatigability, and lack of enthusiasm.

Neurology. Field concerned with study of brain and nervous system and disorders thereof.

Neuron. Individual nerve cell.

Neurosis. Emotional disturbance characterized by exaggerated use of avoidance behavior and defense mechanisms against anxiety.

Neurosyphilis. Syphilis affecting the central nervous system.

Neurotic nucleus. Basic personality characteristics underlying neurotic disorders.

Neurotic paradox. Failure of neurotic patterns to extinguish despite their self-defeating nature.

Neurotransmitters. Chemical substances which transmit information from one neuron to another.

Night hospital. Mental hospital in which an individual may receive treatment during all or part of the night while carrying on his usual occupation in the daytime.

Nihilistic delusion. Fixed belief that everything is unreal.

Nomadism. Withdrawal reaction in which the individual continually attempts to escape frustration by moving from place to place or job to job.

Nondirective therapy. An approach to psychotherapy in which the therapist refrains from advice or direction of the therapy. See also **Client-centered psychotherapy.**

Norepinephrine. Hormone secreted by adrenal medulla. Also called *noradrenalin.*

Norm. Standard based on measurement of a large group of persons; used for comparing the scores of an individual with those of others in a defined group.

Normal. Conforming to the usual or norm. Healthy.

Normal distribution. Tendency for most members of a population to cluster around a central point or average with respect to a given trait, with the rest spreading out to the two extremes.

NREM sleep. Stages of sleep not characterized by the rapid eye movements that accompany dreaming.

Obsession. Persistent idea or thought which the individual recognizes as irrational but cannot get rid of.

Obsessive-compulsive neurosis. Disorder characterized by persistent intrusion of unwanted desires, thoughts, or actions.

Obsessive-compulsive personality. Personality disorder characterized by excessive concern with conformity and adherence to ethical values.

Occipital lobe. Portion of cerebrum concerned with visual function.

Occupational therapy. Use of occupational training or activity in psychotherapy.

Oedipus complex. Desire for sexual relations with parent of opposite sex, specifically that of a boy for his mother.

Olfactory hallucinations. Hallucinations involving the sense of smell, as of poison gas.

Operant conditioning. Form of learning in which the correct response is reinforced and becomes more likely to occur.

Operational definition. Defining a concept on the basis of a set of operations that can be observed and measured.

Opium. Narcotic drug which leads to physiological dependence and the building up of tolerance; derivatives are morphine, heroin, paregoric, and codeine.

Oral stage. First stage of psychosexual development in Freudian theory, in which mouth or oral activities are primary source of pleasure.

Organic brain syndromes. Mental disorders associated with organic brain pathology.

Organic viewpoint. Concept that all mental disorders have an organic basis.

Orgasm. Peak sexual tension followed by relaxation.

Outcome research. Studies of effectiveness of psychotherapy.

Outpatient. An ambulatory patient who visits a hospital clinic for examination and treatment, as distinct from a hospitalized patient.

Ovaries. Female gonads.

Overanxious reaction. Disorder of childhood characterized by chronic anxiety, unrealistic fears, sleep disturbances, and exaggerated autonomic responses.

Overarousal. Excessive physiological mobilization or response to a stimulus.

Overloading. Subjecting organism to excessive stress, e.g., forcing the organism to handle or "process" an excessive amount of information.

Overprotection. Shielding a child to the extent that he becomes too dependent on the parent.

Overt behavior. Activities which can be observed by an outsider.

Ovum. Female gamete or germ cell.

Panic. Severe personality disorganization involving intense anxiety and usually either paralyzed immobility or blind flight.

Paradigm. A model or pattern; in research, a basic design specifying concepts considered legitimate and procedures to be used in the collection and interpretation of data.

Paranoia. Psychosis characterized by a systematized delusional system.

Paranoid personality. Individual showing behavior characterized by projection (as a defense mechanism), suspiciousness, envy, extreme jealousy, and stubbornness.

Paranoid schizophrenia. Type of schizophrenia in which delusions and hallucinations are usually prominent.

Paranoid state. Transient psychotic disorder in which the main element is a delusion, usually persecutory or grandiose in nature.

Paraphasia. Garbled speech.

Paraprofessional. Individual who has been trained in mental health services, but not at the professional level.

Parasympathetic nervous system. Division of the autonomic nervous system that controls most of the basic metabolic functions essential for life.

Paresthesia. Exceptional sensations, such as tingling.

Paresis. See **General paresis.**

Parkinson's disease (Paralysis agitans). Progressive disease characterized by a masklike, expressionless face and various neurological symptoms.

Partial reinforcement. Intermittent reinforcement of a response.

Passive-aggressive personality. Personality pattern characterized by passively expressed aggressiveness.

Pathogenic. Pertaining to conditions which lead to pathology.

Pathological intoxication. Severe cerebral and behavioral disturbance in an individual whose tolerance to alcohol is extremely low.

Pathology. Abnormal physical or mental condition.

Pederasty. Sexual intercourse between males via the anus.

Pedophilia. Sexual deviation in which an adult engages in or desires sexual relations with a child.

Peer group. Social group of equivalent age and status.

Perception. Interpretation of sensory input.

Perceptual filtering. Processes involved in selective attention to aspects of the great mass of incoming stimuli which continually impinge on organism.

Peripheral nervous system. Nerve fibers passing between the central nervous system and the sense organs, muscles, and glands.

Perseveration. Persistent continuation of a line of thought or activity once it is under way. Clinically, inappropriate repetition.

Personality. The unique pattern of traits which characterizes the individual.

Personality disorder. See **Psychopathic personality.**

Perversion. Deviation from normal.

Petit mal. Relatively mild form of epilepsy involving a temporary partial lapse of consciousness.

Phallic stage. In psychoanalytic theory, the stage of psychosexual development during which genital exploration and manipulation occur.

Phallic symbol. Any object which resembles the erect male sex organ.

Phenomenological. Referring to the immediate perceiving and experiencing of the environment by the individual.

Phenylketonuria (PKU). Type of mental retardation resulting from a metabolic deficiency.

Phobia. Irrational fear; the individual may realize its irrationality but nevertheless be unable to dispel it.

Phobic neurosis. Disorder characterized by intense fear of an object or situation which the individual consciously realizes poses no real danger to him.

Physiological dependence. Type of drug dependence involving withdrawal symptoms when drug is discontinued.

Pick's disease. Form of presenile dementia.

Pineal gland. Small gland at the base of the brain which helps regulate body's biological clock and may also pace sexual development.

Pituitary gland. Endocrine gland associated directly with growth.

Placebo. An inactive drug administered in such a way that individual thinks he is receiving an active medication.

Play therapy. Use of play activities in psychotherapy with children. The counterpart for adults is recreational therapy.

Pleasure principle. In psychoanalysis, the demand that an instinctual need be immediately gratified regardless of reality.

Positive reinforcer. A reinforcer that increases the probability of recurrence of a given response.

Posthypnotic amnesia. Subject's lack of memory for the period during which he was hypnotized.

Posthypnotic suggestion. Suggestion given during hypnosis to be carried out by the subject after he is brought out of hypnosis.

Postpartum disturbances. Emotional disturbances associated with childbirth.

Posttraumatic disorders. Residual symptoms following traumatic experience.

Precipitating cause. The particular stress which triggers a disorder.

Predisposing cause. Factor which lowers the individual's stress tolerance and paves the way for the appearance of a disorder.

Predisposition. Likelihood that an individual will develop certain symptoms under given stress conditions.

Prejudice. Emotionally toned conception favorable or unfavorable to some person, group, or idea.

Premature ejaculation. Inability of male to inhibit ejaculation long enough to satisfy his partner.

Prematurity. Birth of an infant before the end of normal period of pregnancy.

Premorbid. Existing prior to onset of mental disorder.

Prenatal. Before birth.

Presenile dementia. Senile brain deterioration occurring at an early age and accompanied by mental disorder.

Pressure. Demand made on an organism.

Primary cause. Cause without which a disorder would not have occurred.

Primary impotence. Form of impotence in which male has never been able to sustain an erection long enough to have successful intercourse.

Primary orgasmic dysfunction. Inability on the part of a woman to have an orgasm.

Primary prevention. Establishing conditions designed to prevent occurrence of mental disorders.

Primary process. The gratification of an instinctual id demand by means of imagery or fantasy; a psychoanalytic concept.

Primary reaction tendencies. Constitutional tendencies apparent in infancy, such as sensitivity and activity level.

Privileged communication. Freedom from the obligation to report to the authorities information concerning legal guilt revealed by a client or patient.

Proband. In a genetic study, the individual who evidences the same trait in which the investigator is interested. Same as *index case.*

Process-reactive. Dimensions of schizophrenia referring to gradual or acute onset of symptoms.

Prognosis. Prediction as to the probable course and outcome of a disorder.

Programmed learning. Method of instruction or learning in which the student is guided through the subject matter step by step.

Projection. Ego-defense mechanism in which individual attributes his own unacceptable desires and impulses to others.

Projective technique. Any psychological technique for the diagnosis of personality organization utilizing relatively unstructured stimuli which reveal the individual's basic attitudes, conflicts, and so on.

Prostitution. Sexual intercourse for financial gain.

Pseudo-community. Delusional social environment developed by a paranoiac.

Pseudo-mutuality. Relationship among family members that appears to be mutual, understanding, and open, but in fact is not.

Psilocybin. Psychoactive drug derived from a mushroom.

Psychedelic drugs. "Mind expanding" drugs, such as LSD, which often result in hallucinations.

Psychiatric nursing. Field of nursing primarily concerned with mental disorders.

Psychiatrist. Medical doctor who specializes in the diagnosis and treatment of mental disorders.

Psychiatry. Field of medicine concerned with understanding, assessing, treating, and preventing mental disorders.

Psychic pain. Synonym for *anxiety.*

Psychic trauma. Stressful psychological experience of a severely traumatic nature.

Psychoactive drug. Any drug that markedly affects psychological functioning.

Psychoanalysis. Theoretical model and therapeutic approach developed by Freud.

Psychodrama. Psychotherapeutic technique in which the acting of various roles is a cardinal part.

Psychogenic. Of psychological origin: originating in the psychological functioning of the individual.

Psychological autopsy. An analytical procedure used to determine whether or not death was self-inflicted.

Psychological need. Need emerging out of environmental interactions, e.g., the need for social approval.

Psychological test. Standardized procedure designed to measure the subject's performance on a specified task.

Psychomotor. Involving both psychological and physical activity.

Psychomotor epilepsy. State of disturbed consciousness in which the individual may perform various actions, sometimes of a homicidal nature, for which he is later amnesic.

Psychomotor retardation. Slowing down of psychological and motor functions.

Psychopathic (antisocial) personality. Sociopathic disorder characterized by lack of moral development and inability to show loyalty to other persons or groups.

Psychopathology. Mental disorder.

Psychopharmacological drugs. Drugs used in treatment of mental disorders.

Psychophysiologic disorders. See **Psychosomatic disorders.**

Psychosexual development. Freudian view of development as involving a succession of stages, each characterized by a dominant mode of achieving libidinal pleasure.

Psychosis. Severe personality disorder involving loss of contact with reality and usually characterized by delusions and hallucinations. Hospitalization is ordinarily required.

Psychosocial. Pertaining to personality makeup or characteristics of the individual and to interpersonal interactions and relations which influence the individual's development and/or behavior.

Psychosocial deprivation. Lack of needed stimulation and interaction during early life.

Psychosomatic (psychophysiologic) disorders. Physical symptoms, which may involve actual tissue damage, resulting from continued emotional mobilization under stress; usually involve single organ system under autonomic nervous system innervation.

Psychosurgery. Brain surgery used in treatment of functional mental disorders. Also broadly used to refer to any form of brain surgery used to correct brain pathology resulting in a mental disorder.

Psychotherapy. Treatment of mental disorders by psychological methods.

Puberty. Stage of physical development when reproduction first becomes possible.

Punishment. Application of aversive stimulation in response to behavior considered undesirable.

Q-sort test. A personality inventory in which subject, or someone evaluating him, sorts a number of statements into piles according to their applicability to the subject.

Racism. Prejudice and discrimination directed toward individuals or groups because of their racial background.

Random sample. Sample drawn in such a way that each member of population has equal chance of being selected; hopefully representative of population from which drawn.

Rape. To force sexual relations upon another person.

Rapport. Interpersonal relationship characterized by a spirit of cooperation, confidence, and harmony.

Rating scale. Device for evaluating oneself or someone else in regard to specific traits.

Rational-emotive therapy. Form of psychotherapy focusing on cognitive and emotional restructuring to foster adaptive behavior.

Rational psychotherapy. Form of psychotherapy which encourages patient to substitute rational for irrational assumptions in his inner dialogue with himself.

Rationalization. Ego-defense mechanism in which the individual thinks up "good" reasons to justify his actions.

Reaction formation. Ego-defense mechanism in which individual's conscious attitudes and overt behavior are opposite to his repressed unconscious wishes.

Reality assumptions. Assumptions which relate to the gratification of needs in the light of environmental possibilities, limitations, and dangers.

Reality principle. Awareness of the demands of the environment and adjustment of behavior to meet these demands.

Reality testing. Behavior aimed at testing or exploring the nature of the individual's social and physical environment; often used more specifically to refer to the testing of the limits of permissiveness of his social environment.

Reality therapy. Form of therapy based on assumption that emotional difficulties arise when an individual violates his basic sense of right and wrong.

Recessive gene. Gene which is effective only when paired with an identical gene.

Recidivism. A shift back to one's original behavior (often delinquent or criminal) after a period of treatment or rehabilitation.

Reciprocal inhibition. Technique of desensitization used in behavior therapy in which responses antagonistic to anxiety are paired with anxiety-eliciting stimuli.

Recompensation. Increase in integration or inner organization. Opposite of *decompensation*.

Reentry. Return from the openness of an encounter group to the real world, which is presumably less open and honest.

Referral. Sending or recommending an individual and/or family for psychiatric assessment and/or treatment.

Regression. Ego-defense mechanism in which the individual retreats to the use of less mature responses in attempting to cope with stress and maintain ego integrity.

Rehabilitation. Use of reeducation rather than punishment in dealing with criminal offenders.

Reinforcement. In classical conditioning, the process of following the conditioned stimulus with the unconditioned stimulus; in operant conditioning, the rewarding of desired responses.

Rejection. Lack of acceptance of another person, usually referring to such treatment of a child by his parents.

Reliability. Degree to which a test or measuring device produces the same result each time it is used to measure the same thing.

REM sleep. Stage of sleep involving rapid eye movements (REM), associated with dreaming.

Remission. Marked improvement or recovery appearing in the course of a mental illness; may or may not be permanent.

Representative sample. Small group selected in such a way as to be representative of the larger group from which it is drawn.

Repression. Ego-defense mechanism by means of which dangerous desires and intolerable memories are kept out of consciousness.

Reserpine. One of the early antipsychotic drugs, now largely supplanted by newer drugs.

Resistance. Tendency to maintain symptoms and resist treatment or uncovering of repressed material.

Resistance to extinction. Tendency of a conditioned response to persist despite lack of reinforcement.

Respondent conditioning. See **Classical conditioning.**

Reticular activating system (RAS). Fibers going from the reticular formation to higher brain centers and presumably functioning as a general arousal system.

Reticular formation. Neural nuclei and fibers in the brain stem which apparently play an important role in arousing and alerting the organism and in controlling attention.

Retrograde amnesia. Loss of memory for events during a circumscribed period prior to brain injury or damage.

Retrospective study. Research approach which attempts to retrace earlier events in the life of the subject.

Reverse tolerance. Situation in which a decreased amount of some psychoactive drug brings about the effects formerly achieved by a larger dose.

Rigid control. Coping patterns involving reliance upon inner restraints, such as inhibition, suppression, repression, and reaction formation.

Rigidity. Tendency to follow established coping patterns, with failure to see alternatives or extreme difficulty in changing one's established patterns.

Role. See **Social role.**

Role distortion. Violation of expected role behavior in an undesirable way.

Role obsolescence. Condition occurring when the ascribed social role of a given individual is no longer of importance to the social group.

Role playing. Form of psychotherapy in which the individual acts out a social role other than his own or tries out a new role for himself.

Rorschach test. Projective personality test making use of inkblots to elicit assessment data from the subject.

Sadism. Sexual deviation in which sexual gratification is obtained by the infliction of pain upon others.

St. Vitus' dance. Hysterical chorea of common occurrence during the Middle Ages.

Sample. Group upon which measurements are taken; should normally be representative of the population about which an inference is to be made.

Scapegoating. Displacement of aggression onto some object, person, or group other than the source of frustration.

Schedule of reinforcement. Program of rewards for requisite behavior.

Schizo-affective psychosis. Disorder characterized by schizophrenic symptoms in conjunction with pronounced depression or elation.

Schizoid personality. Personality pattern characterized by shyness, oversensitivity, seclusiveness, and eccentricity.

Schizophrenia. Psychosis characterized by the breakdown of integrated personality functioning, withdrawal from reality, emotional blunting and distortion, and disturbances in thought and behavior.

Secondary cause. Factor which contributes to a mental illness but which in and of itself would not have produced it, as distinct from the *primary cause.*

Secondary gain. Indirect benefit from neurotic or other symptoms.

Secondary impotence. Condition in which male is capable of successful intercourse but manifests impotence 25 percent or more of the time.

Secondary prevention. Preventive techniques focusing on early detection and correction of maladaptive patterns within context of individual's present life situation.

Secondary process. Reality-oriented rational processes of the ego.

Secondary reinforcer. Reinforcement provided by a stimulus that has gained reward value by being paired with a primary reinforcing stimulus.

Security. Maintenance of conditions necessary to need gratification.

Sedative. Drug used to reduce tension and induce relaxation and sleep.

Self (ego). The integrating core of the personality which mediates between needs and reality.

Self-acceptance. Being satisfied with one's attributes and qualities while remaining aware of one's limitations.

Self-actualization. Fulfillment of one's potentialities as a human being.

Self-concept. The individual's sense of his own identity, worth, capabilities, and limitations.

Self-devaluation. Lowered feelings of worth and self-esteem.

Self-differentiation. Degree to which the individual achieves a sense of unique identity apart from the group.

Self-direction. Basing one's behavior on inner assumptions rather than external contingencies.

Self-esteem. Feeling of personal worth.

Self-evaluation. Way in which the individual views himself— his worth, adequacy, etc.

Self-fulfillment. Living a meaningful, actualizing, and fulfilling life.

Self-ideal. See **Ego-ideal.**

Self-identity. Individual's delineation and awareness of his continuing identity as a person.

Self-recrimination. Self-condemnation and blame.

Self-reinforcement. Reward of self for desired or appropriate behavior.

Self-theory. Personality theory which utilizes the self-concept as the integrating core of personality organization and functioning.

Self-worth. The individual's evaluation of himself.

Senile. Pertaining to old age.

Senile dementia. A form of psychosis caused in part by deteriorative brain changes due to aging.

Sensate focus training. Training to derive pleasure from touching one's partner and being touched by him or her; used in sexual therapy to enhance sexual feelings and help overcome sexual inadequacy.

Sensitivity training group (T-group). One type of small group designed to provide intensive group experience and foster self-understanding and personal growth.

Sensory awareness. Openness to new ways of experiencing and feeling.

Sensory deprivation. Restriction of sensory stimulation below the level required for normal functioning of the central nervous system.

Sentence-completion test. Form of projective technique utilizing incomplete sentences which the subject is to complete.

Separation anxiety. Intense fear experienced when individual is separated from someone on whom he feels dependent.

Sequelae. Symptoms remaining as the aftermath of a disorder.

Sexual deviate. Individual who manifests nonconforming sexual behavior, often of a pathological nature.

Sexual inadequacy. Inability or impaired ability to experience or give sexual gratification.

Shaping. Form of instrumental conditioning used in training animals; at first, all responses resembling the desired one are reinforced, then only the closest approximations, until finally the desired response is attained.

Sheltered workshops. Workshops where mentally retarded or otherwise handicapped individuals can engage in constructive work in the community.

"Shock" reaction. Transient personality decompensation in the face of sudden acute stress.

Shock therapy. Use of electroshock or related methods in treating mental disorders.

Siblings. Offspring of the same parents.

Sick role. Protected role provided by society via medical model for individual suffering from severe physical or mental disorder.

Situational stress reaction (acute). Superficial maladjustment to newly experienced life situations which are especially difficult or trying.

Situational orgasmic dysfunction. Inability of a woman to have an orgasm with a particular person or in a particular situation.

Situational test. Test which measures performance in a simulated life situation.

Social exchange. Model of interpersonal relationships based on the premise that such relationships are formed for mutual need gratification.

Social norms. Group standards concerning behaviors viewed as acceptable or unacceptable.

Social pathology. Abnormal patterns of social organization, attitudes, or behavior; undesirable social conditions which tend to produce individual pathology.

Social role. Behavior expected of individual occupying given position in group.

Social sanction. Punishment by group for violation of social norms.

"Social" self. The façade the individual displays to others as contrasted with his private self.

Social worker. Person in mental health field with a master's degree in social work (MSW) plus supervised training in clinical or social service agencies.

Sociocultural. Pertaining to broad social conditions which influence the development and/or behavior of individuals and groups.

Socioeconomic status. Position on social and economic scale in community; determined largely by income and occupational level.

Sociogenic. Having its roots in sociocultural conditions or causes.

Sociopathic disorder. Lack of social responsibility and inability to conform to prevailing social norms even when such norms are adaptive.

Sociotherapy. Treatment of interpersonal aspects of the individual's life situation.

Sodium pentothal. Barbiturate drug sometimes used in psychotherapy to produce a state of relaxation and suggestibility.

Sodomy. Sexual intercourse via the anus.

Somatic. Pertaining to the body.

Somatic weakness. Special vulnerability of given organ systems to stress.

Somatotype. Physique or build of a person, as assessed by various theories relating temperament to physical characteristics.

Somnambulism. Sleepwalking.

Spasm. Intense, involuntary, usually painful contraction of a muscle or group of muscles.

Spasticity. Marked hypertonicity or continual overcontraction of muscles, causing stiffness, awkwardness, and motor incoordination.

Special vulnerability. Low tolerance for specific types of stress.

Sperm. Male gamete or germ cell.

Split-brain research. Research associated with split-brain surgery, which markedly impedes transmission of information from one cerebral hemisphere to the other.

Spontaneous recovery (remission). Recovery of a mental patient without treatment or with minimal treatment.

S-R psychologists. Psychologists who emphasize the role of stimulus-response (S-R) connections in learning. Also called *associationists*.

Stage of exhaustion. Third and final stage in the general-adaptation-syndrome, in which the organism is no longer able to resist continuing stress; may result in death.

Stage of resistance. Second stage of the general-adaptation-syndrome.

Standardization. Procedure for establishing the reliability and validity of a test.

Startle reaction. Sudden involuntary motor reaction to intense unexpected stimuli; may result from mild stimuli if person is hypersensitive.

Statutory rape. Sexual intercourse with a minor.

Stereotype. A generalized notion of how people of a given race, religion, or other group will appear, think, feel, or act.

Stereotypy. Persistent and inappropriate repetition of phrases, gestures, or acts.

Stimulants. Drugs that tend to increase feelings of alertness, reduce feelings of fatigue, and enable individual to stay awake over sustained periods of time.

Stimulus generalization. The spread of a conditioned response to some stimulus similar to, but not identical with, the conditioned stimulus.

Stress. Any adjustive demand that requires coping behavior on part of individual or group.

Stress-decompensation model. View of abnormal behavior which emphasizes progressive disorganization of behavior under excessive stress.

Stress interview. Interview of a subject under simulated stress conditions.

Stress tolerance (frustration tolerance). Nature, degree, and duration of stress which an individual can tolerate without undergoing serious personality decompensation.

Stroke. See **Cerebrovascular accident.**

Stupor. Condition of lethargy and unresponsiveness, with partial or complete unconsciousness.

Stuttering. Speech disorder characterized by a blocking or repetition of initial sounds of words.

Sublimation. Ego-defense mechanism by means of which frustrated sexual energy is partially channeled into substitutive activities.

Substitution. Acceptance of substitute goals or satisfactions in place of those originally sought after or desired.

Successive approximation. See **Shaping.**

Suicide. Taking one's own life.

Superego. Conscience; ethical or moral dimensions (attitudes) of personality.

Suppression. Conscious forcing of desires or thoughts out of consciousness; conscious inhibition of desires or impulses.

Surrogate. Substitute parental figure.

Survey methods. Procedures for obtaining opinions or other data concerning a given population.

Swinging. Mate swapping and other group sex practices.

Symbol. Image, object, or activity that is used to represent something else.

Symbolism. Representation of one idea or object by another.

Sympathetic division. Division of the autonomic nervous system which is active in emergency conditions of extreme cold, violent effort, and emotions.

Symptom. An observable manifestation of a physical or mental disorder.

Syncope. Temporary loss of consciousness resulting from cerebral anemia.

Syndrome. Group or pattern of symptoms which occur together in a disorder and represent the typical picture of the disorder.

Syphilophobia. Morbid fear of syphilis.

System. An assemblage of interdependent parts, living or nonliving.

Systematic desensitization. A behavior therapy technique for eliminating maladaptive anxiety responses.

Tachycardia. Rapid pulse.

Tactual hallucinations. Hallucinations involving the sense of touch, such as feeling cockroaches crawling over one's body.

Tarantism. Type of hysterical dancing occurring in epidemic form during the Middle Ages.

Task-oriented reaction. Realistic rather than ego-defensive approach to stress.

Tay-Sachs disease. Genetic disorder of lipoid metabolism usually resulting in death by age 3.

Telepathy. Communication from one person to another without use of any known sense organs.

Temporal lobe. Portion of cerebrum located in front of occipital lobe and separated from frontal and parietal lobes by the fissure of Sylvius.

Tension. Condition arising out of the mobilization of psychobiological resources to meet a threat; physically, involves an increase in muscle tonus and other emergency changes; psychologically, is characterized by feelings of strain, uneasiness, and anxiety.

Tertiary prevention. Preventive techniques focusing on short-term hospitalization and intensive aftercare when an emotional breakdown has occurred, with aim of returning individual to his family and community setting as soon as possible.

Testes. Male reproductive glands or gonads.

Testosterone. Male sex hormone.

Therapeutic. Pertaining to treatment or healing.

Therapeutic community. The hospital environment used for therapeutic purposes.

Therapy. Treatment; application of various treatment techniques.

Theta wave. Brain wave having a frequency of only 5 to 7 cycles per second.

Threat. Real or imagined danger to individual or group.

Thymus. Gland of uncertain function located in neck and upper thorax; usually atrophies in human adults.

Thyroids. Endocrine glands located in neck which influence body metabolism, rate of physical growth, and development of intelligence.

Thyroxin. Hormone secreted by the thyroid glands.

Tic. Intermittent twitching or jerking, usually of facial muscles.

Token economy. Reinforcement technique often used in hospital or institutional settings in which individuals are rewarded for socially constructive behavior with tokens that can then be exchanged for desired objects or activities.

Tolerance. Physiological condition in which increased dosage of an addictive drug is needed to obtain effects previously produced by smaller dose.

Tonic. Pertaining to muscle tension or contraction; muscle tone.

Toxic. Poisonous.

Toxic deliria (psychoses). Severe disturbances in cerebral functions resulting from toxins.

Trait. Characteristic of individual which can be observed or measured.

Trance. Sleeplike state in which the range of consciousness is limited and voluntary activities are suspended; a deep hypnotic state.

Tranquilizers. Drugs used for antipsychotic purposes and/or reduction of anxiety and tension. See also **Major tranquilizers, Minor tranquilizers.**

Transactional analysis. Form of interpersonal therapy based on interaction of "Child," "Adult," and "Parent" ego states.

Transference. Process whereby client projects attitudes and emotions applicable to another significant person onto the therapist; emphasized in psychoanalytic therapy.

Transient situational disorder. Temporary mental disorder developing under conditions of overwhelming stress, as in military combat or civilian catastrophes.

Transsexualism. Identification of oneself with members of opposite sex, as opposed to acceptance of one's sexual identity.

Transvestism. Persistent desire to dress in clothing of the opposite sex, often accompanied by sexual excitement.

Trauma. Severe psychological or physiological stress resulting in injury or wound.

Traumatic. Pertaining to a wound or injury.

Traumatic neurosis. See "Shock" reaction.

Tremor. Repeated fine spastic movement.

Turner's syndrome. Form of mental retardation associated with sex chromosome anomaly.

Ulcer. Open sore in mucosa lining of the stomach.

Unconscious. Lack of awareness; as used by Freud, psychological material that has been repressed. Also, loss of consciousness.

Unconscious motivation. Motivation for an individual's behavior of which he is unaware.

Underarousal. Inadequate physiological response to a given stimulus.

Undoing. Ego-defense mechanism by means of which the individual performs activities designed to atone for his misdeeds, thereby, in a sense, "undoing" them.

Unsocialized aggressive reaction. Behavior disorder of childhood.

Vaginismus. An involuntary muscle spasm at the entrance to the vagina that prevents penetration and sexual intercourse.

Validity. Extent to which a measuring instrument actually measures what it purports to measure.

Values. Assumptions concerning good and bad, right and wrong.

Variable. A characteristic or property that may assume any one of a set of different qualities.

Vasomotor. Pertaining to the walls of the blood vessels.

Vegetative. Withdrawn or deteriorated to the point where the individual leads a passive, vegetablelike existence.

Verbigeration. Prolonged and monotonous repetition of meaningless words and phrases.

Vertigo. Dizziness.

Vicarious living. Attempt to evade efforts toward self-fulfillment by repressing one's own individuality and identifying with some hero or ideal.

Vicious circle. Chain reaction in which individual resorts to an unhealthy defensive reaction in trying to solve his problems, which only serves to complicate them and make them harder to solve.

Virilism. Accentuation of masculine secondary sex characteristics, especially in a woman or young boy, caused by overactivity of the adrenal cortex.

Viscera. Internal organs.

Visual hallucinations. Hallucinations involving sense of sight.

Voyeurism. Achievement of sexual pleasure through clandestine "peeping," usually watching other persons disrobe and/or engage in sexual activities.

Wassermann test. Serum test used in the diagnosis of syphilis.

Waxy flexibility. Condition in which a patient will maintain the position in which his limbs are placed for an unusually long period of time.

Withdrawal. Intellectual, emotional, or physical retreat.

Withdrawal symptoms. Wide range of symptoms evidenced by addicts when the drug on which they are physiologically dependent is not available.

Word salad. Jumbled or incoherent use of words by psychotic or disoriented individuals.

Working through. Confronting and dealing with a problem situation until satisfactory adjustments are achieved and established.

Worry. Persistent concern about past behavior or about anticipated dangers in the present or future.

X chromosome. Sex-determining chromosome; all female gametes contain X chromosomes, and if fertilized ovum has also received an X chromosome from its father it will be female.

XYY syndrome. A chromosomal anomaly in males (presence

of an extra Y chromosome) possibly related to aggressive behavior.

Y chromosome. Sex-determining chromosome found in half of the total number of male gametes; uniting with X chromosome always provided by female produces a male offspring.

Zygote. Fertilized egg cell formed by union of male and female gametes.

Acknowledgments and References

The reference list includes not only the sources from which the author has drawn material, but also acknowledgments of the permission granted by authors and publishers to quote directly from their works.

Journal abbreviations

ACTA PSYCHIATR. SCANDIN. — *Acta Psychiatrica Scandinavica*
AIR UNIVER. QUART. REV. — *Air University Quarterly Review*
AMER. J. MED. SCI. — *American Journal of Medical Science*
AMER. J. MENT. DEF. — *American Journal of Mental Deficiency*
AMER. J. NURS. — *American Journal of Nursing*
AMER. J. OCCUPA. THER. — *American Journal of Occupational Therapy*
AMER. J. ORTHOPSYCHIAT. — *American Journal of Orthopsychiatry*
AMER. J. PSYCHIAT. — *American Journal of Psychiatry*
AMER. J. PSYCHOTHER. — *American Journal of Psychotherapy*
AMER. PSYCHOLOGIST — *American Psychologist*
AMER. SCIEN. — *American Scientist*
ANN. N.Y. ACAD. SCI. — *Annals of the New York Academy of Science*
ANN. AMER. ACAD. POLIT. SOC. SCI. — *Annals of the American Academy of Political and Social Science*
ANNU. REV. PSYCHOL. — *Annual Review of Psychology*
ARCH. GEN. PSYCHIAT. — *Archives of General Psychiatry*
ARCH. INT. MED. — *Archives of Internal Medicine*
ARCH. NEUROL. PSYCHIAT. — *Archives of Neurology and Psychiatry*
BEHAV. RES. THER. — *Behavior Research and Therapy*
BEHAV. SCI. — *Behavioral Science*
BEHAV. TODAY — *Behavior Today*
BRIT. J. EDUC. PSYCHOL. — *British Journal of Educational Psychology*
BRIT. J. MED. PSYCHOL. — *British Journal of Medical Psychology*
BRIT. J. OPHTHALMOL. — *British Journal of Ophthalmology*
BRIT. J. PSYCHIAT. — *British Journal of Psychiatry*
BRIT. MED. J. — *British Medical Journal*
BULL. MENNINGER CLIN. — *Bulletin of the Menninger Clinic*
CHARACT. & PERS. — *Character and Personality*
CHILD DEVELOP. — *Child Development*
COMM. MENT. HLTH. J. — *Community Mental Health Journal*
DEVELOP. MED. CHILD NEUROL. — *Developmental Medicine & Child Neurology*
DEVELOP. PSYCHOL. — *Developmental Psychology*
DIS. NERV. SYS. — *Diseases of the Nervous System*
GEN. PSYCHIAT. — *General Psychiatry*
GROUP PSYCHOTHER. — *Group Psychotherapy*

HARVARD ED. REV. — *Harvard Educational Review*
HUMAN DEVELOP. — *Human Development*
INTER. J. GROUP PSYCHOTHER. — *International Journal of Group Psychotherapy*
INTER. J. PSYCHIAT. — *International Journal of Psychiatry*
INTER. J. PSYCHOANAL. — *International Journal of Psychoanalysis*
J. ABNORM. PSYCHOL. — *Journal of Abnormal Psychology*
J. ABNORM. SOC. PSYCHOL. — *Journal of Abnormal and Social Psychology*
JAMA — *Journal of the American Medical Association*
J. AMER. ACAD. CHILD PSYCHIAT. — *Journal of the American Academy of Child Psychiatry*
J. APPL. BEH. ANAL. — *Journal of Applied Behavior Analysis*
J. BEHAV. RES. EXP. PSYCHIAT. — *Journal of Behavior Research and Experimental Psychiatry*
J. BEHAV. THER. EXP. PSYCHIAT. — *Journal of Behavior Therapy and Experimental Psychiatry*
J. CHILD. PSYCHOL. PSYCHIAT. — *Journal of Child Psychology and Psychiatry.*
J. CLIN. PSYCHOL. — *Journal of Clinical Psychology*
J. CLIN. PSYCHOPATH. — *Journal of Clinical Psychopathology*
J. COMPAR. PHYSIOL. PSYCHOL. — *Journal of Comparative and Physiological Psychology*
J. CONS. CLIN. PSYCHOL. — *Journal of Consulting and Clinical Psychology*
J. COUNS. PSYCHOL. — *Journal of Counseling Psychology*
J. CRIM. LAW, CRIMINOL., POLICE SCI. — *Journal of Criminal Law, Criminology, and Police Science*
J. CRIM. PSYCHOPATH. PSYCHOTHER. — *Journal of Criminal Psychopathology and Psychotherapy*
J. EXPER. ANAL. BEHAV. — *Journal of Experimental Analysis of Behavior*
J. EXPER. CHILD PSYCHOL. — *Journal of Experimental Child Psychology*
J. EXPER. PSYCHOL. — *Journal of Experimental Psychology*
J. EXPER. RES. PERSON. — *Journal of Experimental Research in Personality*
J. GEN. PSYCHOL. — *Journal of General Psychology*
J. GENET. PSYCHOL. — *Journal of Genetic Psychology*
J. GERIAT. PSYCHOL. — *Journal of Geriatric Psychology*
J. HLTH. SOC. BEHAV. — *Journal of Health and Social Behavior*
J. LEARN. DIS. — *Journal of Learning Disabilities*
J. MARR. FAM. — *Journal of Marriage and the Family*
J. MENT. SCI. — *Journal of Mental Science*
J. NERV. MENT. DIS. — *Journal of Nervous and Mental Disease*
J. PERSONAL. — *Journal of Personality*
J. PERS. SOC. PSYCHOL. — *Journal of Personal and Social Psychology*
J. PSYCHIAT. — *Journal of Psychiatry*

J. PSYCHIAT. RES. — *Journal of Psychiatric Research*
J. PSYCHOL. — *Journal of Psychology*
J. PSYCHOSOM. MED. — *Journal of Psychosomatic Medicine*
J. PSYCHOSOM. RES. — *Journal of Psychosomatic Research*
J. SOC. PSYCHOL. — *Journal of Social Psychology*
J. SPEC. ED. — *Journal of Special Education*
J. SPEECH HEAR. DIS. — *Journal of Speech and Hearing Disorders*
J. SPEECH HEAR. RES. — *Journal of Speech and Hearing Research*
MENT. HLTH. DIG. — *Mental Health Digest*
MENT. HLTH. PROG. REP. — *Mental Health Program Reports*
MENT. HYG. — *Mental Hygiene*
MONOGR. SOC. RES. CHILD DEVELOP. — *Monographs of the Society for Research in Child Development*
N.C. MED. J. — *North Carolina Medical Journal*
NEW ENGL. J. MED. — *New England Journal of Medicine*
N.Y. ST. J. MED. — *New York State Journal of Medicine*
PSYCHIAT. DIG. — *Psychiatry Digest*
PSYCHIAT. QUART. — *Psychiatric Quarterly*
PSYCHIAT. SOC. SCI. REV. — *Psychiatry and Social Science Review*
PSYCHOANAL. QUART. — *Psychoanalytic Quarterly*
PSYCHOANAL. REV. — *Psychoanalytic Review*
PSYCHOL. BULL. — *Psychology Bulletin*
PSYCHOL. REC. — *Psychological Record*
PSYCH. REP. — *Psychological Reports*
PSYCH. REV. — *Psychological Review*
PSYCHOSOM. MED. — *Psychosomatic Medicine*
PSYCH. TODAY — *Psychology Today*
PUBL. MASS. MED. SOC. — *Publication of the Massachusetts Medical Society*
QUART. J. STUD. ALCHOL. — *Quarterly Journal of Studies in Alcoholism*
SAT. REV. — *Saturday Review*
SCI. J. — *Science Journal*
SCI. NEWS — *Science News*
SCI. NEWSLETTER — *Science Newsletter*
SCI. TECH. — *Science and Technology*
SCIENTIF. AMER. — *Scientific American*
SOC. PSYCHIAT. — *Social Psychiatry*
SOCIOL. QUART. — *Sociological Quarterly*
WORLD MENT. HLTH. — *World Mental Health*

Preface

APA TASK FORCE ON ISSUES OF SEXUAL BIAS IN GRADUATE EDUCATION. Guidelines for nonsexist use of language. *Amer. Psychologist*, June 1975, 30(6), 282–84.

1. Abnormal Behavior in Our Times

AMERICAN PSYCHIATRIC ASSOCIATION. *Diagnostic and statistical manual of mental disorders*. Washington, D.C.: APA, 1968.
AMERICAN PSYCHOLOGICAL ASSOCIATION. *Ethical standards of psychologists*. Washington, D.C.: APA, 1963.
BLUEMEL, C. S. *War, politics, and industry*. Denver: World Press, 1948.
BORN, W. Great artists who suffered from mental disorders. *Ciba Symposia*, 1946, **7**, 225–33.
CLEARY, T. A., HUMPHREYS, L. G., KENDRICK, S. A., & WESMAN, A. Educational uses of tests with disadvantaged students. *Amer. Psychologist*, Jan. 1975, 30(1), 15–41.

EDWARDS, J. Sinners in the hands of an angry God. *The works of President Edwards in eight volumes* (Vol. 7). Worcester: Isiah Thomas, 1809.
JAHODA, M. *Current concepts of positive mental health*. New York: Basic Books, 1958.
KAPLAN, A. A philosophical discussion of normality. *Arch. Gen. Psychiat.*, 1967, **17**, 325–30.
LANGER, E. J., & ABELSON, R. P. A patient by any other name . . .: clinician group difference in labeling bias. *J. Cons. Clin. Psychol.* Feb. 1974, 42(1), 4–9.
LOMBROSO, C. *Man of genius*. New York: Scribner's, 1891.
MARKS, J. *Genius and disaster*. New York: Greenberg, 1925.
MARTINDALE, C. Father's absence, psychopathology, & poetic eminence. *Psych. Rep.*, Dec. 1972, 31(3), 843–47.
MENNINGER, K. *The human mind* (3rd ed.). New York: Knopf, 1945.
NATIONAL INSTITUTE OF MENTAL HEALTH. Cited in *Psychiatric News*, 1969, 4(2), 19.
RABKIN, J. G. Opinions about mental illness: a review of the literature. *Psychol. Bull.*, Mar. 1972, **77**(3), 153–71.
ROBINSON, E. A. "Richard Cory" is reprinted by permission of Charles Scribner's Sons from *The Children of the Night* by Edwin Arlington Robinson (1897).
SCHMIDT, F. L., & HUNTER, J. E. Racial and ethnic bias in psychological tests: divergent implications of two definitions of test bias. *Amer. Psychologist*, Jan. 1974, 29(1), 1–8.
SEWELL, W. S. (Ed.). *Famous personalities*. Philadelphia: Blakiston, 1943.
ULLMANN, L. P., & KRASNER, L. *Psychological approach to abnormal behavior*. Englewood Cliffs, N.J.: Prentice-Hall, 1969.
UNITED STATES DEPARTMENT OF HEALTH, EDUCATION AND WELFARE. National health survey. *Roche Report*, 1971, 1(9), 2.
WHITWELL, J. R. *Historical notes on psychiatry*. London: H. K. Lewis, 1936.
WORLD HEALTH ORGANIZATION. Wide research needed to solve the problem of mental health. *World Ment. Hlth.*, 1960, **12.**
ZILBOORG, G., & HENRY, G. W. *A history of medical psychology*. New York: Norton, 1941.

2. Historical Background and the Organic Viewpoint

ARING, C. D. The Gheel experience: eternal spirit of the chainless mind! *JAMA*, 1974, **230**(7), 998–1001.
ARING, C. D. Science and the citizen. *Scientif. Amer.*, Jan. 1975, **232**(1), 48–49; 52–53.
BELGIAN CONSULATE. Los Angeles, California. Personal communication, Jan. 2, 1975.
BENNETT, A. E. Mad doctors. *J. Nerv. Ment. Dis.*, 1947, **106**, 11–18.
BROMBERG, W. *The mind of man*. New York: Harper, 1937.
BROWNE, E. G. *Arabian medicine*. New York: Macmillan, 1921.
CAMPBELL, D. *Arabian medicine and its influence on the Middle Ages*. New York: Dutton, 1926.
CASTIGLIONI, A. *Adventures of the mind*. New York: Knopf, 1946.
COCKAYNE, T. O. *Leechdoms, wort cunning, and star craft of early England*. London: Longman, Green, Longman, Roberts & Green, 1864–1886.
DEUTSCH, A. *The mentally ill in America*. New York: Columbia University Press, 1946.
GLOYNE, H. F. Tarantism. *American Imago*, 1950, **7**, 29–42.

GUTHRIE, D. J. *A history of medicine.* Philadelphia: Lippincott, 1946.

KARNOSH, L. J. (with collaboration of Zucker, E. M.). *Handbook of psychiatry.* St. Louis: C. V. Mosby, 1945. Reprinted by permission.

LEWIS, N. D. C. *A short history of psychiatric achievement.* New York: Norton, 1941.

LOWREY, L. G. *Psychiatry for social workers.* New York: Columbia University Press, 1946.

MENNINGER, R. W. The history of psychiatry. *Dis. Nerv. Sys.,* 1944, **5,** 52–55.

MORA, G. Paracelsus' psychiatry. *Amer. J. Psychiat.,* 1967, **124,** 803–14.

PLATO. *The laws* (Vol. 5). G. Burges (Tr.). London: George Bell & Sons, n. d.

POLVAN, N. Historical aspects of mental ills in Middle East discussed. *Roche Reports,* 1969, **6**(12), 3.

RABKIN, J. G. Opinions about mental illness: a review of the literature. *Psychol. Bull.,* Mar. 1972, **77**(3), 153–71.

REES, T. P. Back to moral treatment and community care. *J. Ment. Scien.,* 1957, **103,** 303–13. In H. B. Adams, "Mental illness" or interpersonal behavior? *Amer. Psychologist,* 1964, **19,** 191–97.

ROSEN, G. Emotion and sensibility in ages of anxiety. *Amer. J. Psychiat.,* 1967, **124,** 771–84.

RUSSELL, W. L. A psychopathic department of an American general hospital in 1808. *Amer. J. Psychiat.,* 1941, **98,** 229–37.

SELLING, L. S. *Men against madness.* New York: Garden City Books, 1943.

SIGERIST, H. E. *Civilization and disease.* Ithaca, N.Y.: Cornell University Press, 1943.

STONE, S. Psychiatry through the ages. *J. Abnorm. Soc. Psychol.,* 1937, **32,** 131–60.

TOURNEY, G. A history of therapeutic fashions in psychiatry, 1800–1966. *Amer. J. Psychiat.,* 1967, **124,** 784–96.

TSENG, W. S. The development of psychiatric concepts in traditional Chinese medicine. *Arch. Gen. Psychiat.,* Oct. 1973, **29**(4), 569–75.

WHITE, A. D. *A history of the warfare of science with theology in Christendom.* New York: Appleton, 1896.

WHITE, R. W. Abnormalities of behavior. *Annu. Rev. Psychol.,* 1959, **10,** 265–86.

WHITWELL, J. R. *Historical notes on psychiatry.* London: H. K. Lewis, 1936.

ZILBOORG, G., & HENRY, G. W. *A history of medical psychology.* New York: Norton, 1941.

3. Psychosocial and Sociocultural Viewpoints

BANDURA, A. *Principles of behavior modification.* New York: Holt, Rinehart & Winston, 1969.

BANDURA, A. Behavior theory and the models of man. *Amer. Psychologist,* Dec. 1974, **29**(12), 859–69.

BENEDICT, R. Anthropology and the abnormal. *J. Gen. Psychol.,* 1934, **10,** 59–82.

BERNE, E. *Games people play: the psychology of human relationships.* New York: Grove Press, 1964.

BERNE, E. *What do you say after you say hello?* New York: Grove Press, 1972.

BERTALANFFY, L. VON. The world of science and the world of value. In J. F. T. Bugental (Ed.), *Challenges of humanistic psychology.* New York: McGraw-Hill, 1967.

BERTALANFFY, L. VON. General systems theory. In W. Buckley (Ed.), *Modern systems research for the behavioral scientist.* Chicago: Aldine, 1968.

BROWN, J. F., & MENNINGER, K. A. *Psychodynamics of abnormal behavior.* New York: McGraw-Hill, 1940.

BUCKLEY, W. (Ed.) *Modern systems research for the behavioral scientist.* Chicago: Aldine, 1968.

DRAGUNS, J. G., & PHILLIPS, L. *Culture and psychopathology: the quest for a relationship.* Morristown, N.J.: General Learning Press, 1972.

FARIS, R. E. L., & DUNHAM, H. W. *Mental disorders in urban areas.* Chicago: University of Chicago Press, 1939. (Reprinted, 1965.)

GILLULY, R. H. A new look at the meaning of reality. *Sci. News,* 1971, **99,** 335–37.

GORDON, J. S. Who is mad? Who is sane? The radical psychiatry of R. D. Laing. *Atlantic,* 1971, **227**(1), 50–66.

HOMANS, G. C. *Social behavior: its elementary forms.* New York: Harcourt Brace Jovanovich, 1961.

ISAACS, W., THOMAS, J., & GOLDIAMOND, I. Application of operant conditioning to reinstate verbal behavior in psychotics. *J. Speech Hear. Dis.,* 1960, **25,** 8–12.

JACO, E. G. *The social epidemiology of mental disorders.* New York: Russell Sage Foundation, 1960.

JAMES, W. *The principles of psychology* (Vols. 1 & 2). New York: Holt, 1890.

JONES, M. C. A laboratory study of fear: the case of Peter. *Pedagogical Seminary,* 1924, **31,** 308–15.

KOESTLER, A. *The invisible writing.* New York: Macmillan, 1954.

LAING, R. D. *The politics of experience.* New York: Ballantine, 1967.

LASZLO, E. *The systems view of the world.* New York: Braziller, 1972.

LENNARD, H. L., & BERNSTEIN, A. *Patterns in human interaction.* San Francisco: Jossey-Bass, 1969.

LEVY, L., & ROWITZ, L. Mapping out schizophrenia. *Human Behavior,* May 1974, **3**(5), 39–40.

LOVAAS, O. I., FRIETAG, G., GOLD, V. J., & KASSORLA, I. C. Experimental studies in childhood schizophrenia. *J. Exper. Child. Psychol.,* 1965, **2,** 67–84.

MALINOWSKI, B. *Sex and repression in savage society.* New York: Humanities, 1927.

MASLOW, A. H. *Toward a psychology of being.* New York: Van Nostrand, 1962.

MASLOW, A. H. Toward a humanistic biology. *Amer. Psychologist,* 1969, **24**(8), 734–35.

MEAD, G. H. *Mind, self, and society: from the standpoint of a social behaviorist.* Chicago: University of Chicago Press, 1934.

MILLER, J. G. Living systems: basic concepts. *Behav. Sci.,* 1965, **10,** 193–237. [a]

MILLER, J. G. Living systems. Structure and process. *Behav. Sci.,* 1965, **10,** 337–79. [b]

MORRIS, M. G. Psychological miscarriage: an end to mother love. *Trans-action,* 1966, **3**(2), 8–13.

PAVLOV, I. P. *Lectures on conditioned reflexes* (Vol. 2). W. H. Gantt (Ed. & tr.). New York: International Publ., 1941.

SELLING, L. S. *Men against madness.* New York: Garden City Books, 1943.

SKINNER, B. F. *Walden two.* New York: Macmillan, 1948.

SKINNER, B. F. *Science and human behavior.* New York: Macmillan, 1953.

SKINNER, B. F. *Beyond freedom and dignity*. New York: Knopf, 1971.

SKINNER, B. F. *About behaviorism*. New York: Knopf, 1974.

SMITH, M. B. The revolution in mental health care—a "bold new approach"? *Trans-action*, 1968, **5**(5), 19–23.

SULLIVAN, H. S. *The interpersonal theory of psychiatry*. H. S. Perry & M. L. Gawel (Eds.). New York: Norton, 1953.

THIBAUT, J. W., & KELLEY, H. H. *The social psychology of groups*. New York: Wiley, 1959.

THORNDIKE, E. L. *The psychology of learning*. New York: Teachers College, 1913.

WAHLER, R. G. Behavior therapy for oppositional children: love is not enough. Paper presented at Eastern Psychological Assn. meeting, Washington, D.C., April 1968.

WATSON, J. B., & RAYNER, R. Conditioned emotional reactions. *J. Exper. Psychol.*, 1920, **3**, 1–14.

WOLPE, J. Conditioned inhibition of craving in drug addiction. *Behav. Res. Ther.*, 1965, **2**, 285–88.

4. Personality Development and Adjustment: An Overview

ARONSON, E. The rationalizing animal. *Psych. Today*, May 1973, **6**(12), 46–50, 52.

AVERILL, J. R. Personal control over aversive stimuli and its relationship to stress. *Psychol. Bull.*, Oct. 1973, **80**(4), 286–303.

BANDURA, A. *Aggression: a social learning analysis*. Englewood Cliffs, N.J.: Prentice-Hall, 1973.

BARD, M. The price of survival for cancer victims. *Trans-action*, 1966, **3**(3), 10–14.

BERGER, R. J. Morpheus descending. *Psych. Today*, 1970, **4**(1), 33–36.

BERKOWITZ, L. Some determinants of impulsive aggression. *Psych. Rev.*, Mar. 1974, **81**(2), 165–76.

BETTELHEIM, B. Individual and mass behavior in extreme situations. *J. Abnorm. Soc. Psychol.*, 1943, **38**, 417–52.

BLUESTONE, H., & MC GAHEE, C. L. Reaction to extreme stress. *Amer. J. Psychiat.*, 1962, **119**, 393–96.

BOMBARD, A. *The voyage of the Hérétique*. New York: Simon and Schuster, 1954.

CANTRIL, H. A fresh look at the human design. In J. F. T. Bugental (Ed.), *Challenges of humanistic psychology*. New York: McGraw-Hill, 1967.

COCHRANE, R., & ROBERTSON, A. The life events inventory: a measure of the relative severity of psycho-social stressors. *J. Psychosom. Res.*, Mar. 1973, **17**(2), 135–40.

COLEMAN, J. C. Life stress and maladaptive behavior. *Amer. J. Occupa. Ther.*, May–June 1973, **27**(4), 169–80.

COLEMAN, J. C., & HAMMEN, C. L. *Contemporary psychology and effective behavior*. Glenview, Ill.: Scott, Foresman, 1974.

DEMENT, W. Effects of dream deprivation. *Science*, 1960, **131**, 1705–7.

DEMENT, W. Paper presented at meeting of American Academy of Psychoanalysis. New York, Dec. 7–9, 1963.

ERDELYI, M. H. A new look at the new look: perceptual defense and vigilance. *Psych. Rev.*, Jan. 1974, **81**(1), 1–25.

ERICKSON, M. H. Experimental demonstrations of the psychopathology of everyday life. *The Psychoanalytic Quarterly*, 1939, **8**, 342–45. Reprinted by permission.

FENZ, W. D., & EPSTEIN, S. Stress: in the air. *Psych. Today*, 1969, **3**(4), 27–28; 58–59.

FRIEDMAN, P. Some aspects of concentration camp psychology.

Amer. J. Psychiat., 1949, **105**, 601–5.

FROMM, E. *The sane society*. New York: Holt, Rinehart, & Winston, 1955.

GESELL, A. Human infancy and the embryology of behavior. In A. Weider (Ed.), *Contributions toward medical psychology*. New York: Ronald, 1953.

GLESER, G., & SACKS, M. Ego defenses and reaction to stress: a validation study of the Defense Mechanisms Inventory. *J. of Cons. Clin. Psychol.*, Apr. 1973, **40**(2), 181–87.

GOTTSCHALK, L. A., HAER, J. L., & BATES, D. E. Effect of sensory overload on psychological state: changes in social alienation—personal disorganization and cognitive-intellectual impairment. *Arch. Gen. Psychiat.*, 1972, **27**(4), 451–56.

HAMBURG, D. A., & ADAMS, J. E. A perspective on coping behavior. *Arch. Gen. Psychiat.*, 1967, **17**, 277–84.

HARLOW, H. F., & HARLOW, M. K. Learning to love. *Amer. Scien.*, 1966, **54**, 244–72.

HAURI, P., CHERNIK, D., HAWKINS, D., & MENDELS, J. Sleep of depressed patients in remission. *Arch. Gen. Psychiat.*, Sept. 1974, **31**(3), 386–91.

HAYTHORN, W. W., & ALTMAN, I. Together in isolation. *Trans-action*, 1967, **4**(3), 18–22.

HEBB, D. O. The American revolution. *Amer. Psychologist*, 1960, **15**, 735–45.

HOLMES, D. S. Investigations of repression: differential recall of material experimentally or naturally associated with ego threat. *Psychol. Bull.*, Oct. 1974, **81**(10), 632–53.

HOLMES, T. H., & RAHE, R. H. The social readjustment rating scale. *J. Psychosom. Res.*, Apr. 1967, **11**(2), 213–18.

HOLMES, T. S., & HOLMES, T. H. Short-term intrusions into the life style routine. *J. Psychosom. Res.*, June 1970, **14**(2), 121–32.

HUNT, J. MC V. *Intelligence and experience*. New York: Ronald Press, 1961.

HUXLEY, A. Human potentialities. In R. E. Farson (Ed.), *Science and human affairs*. Palo Alto, Calif.: Science and Behavior Books, 1965.

HUXLEY, J. *Evolution in action*. New York: Harper & Row, 1953.

JACOBSON, B., & KALES, A. Deep sleep needed for best health. *University of California Bulletin*, 1967, **15**, 168.

KATZ, J. L., WEINER, H., GALLAGHER, T., & HELLMAN, L. Stress, distress, and ego defenses. *Arch. Gen. Psychiat.*, 1970, **23**, 131–42.

KEYS, A., BROŽEK, J., HENSCHEL, A., MICKELSON, O., & TAYLOR, H. L. *The biology of human starvation*. Minneapolis: University of Minnesota Press, 1950.

LANGSLEY, D. G. Crisis intervention. *Amer. J. Psychiat.*, Dec. 1972, **129**(6), 110–12.

LAZARUS, R. S. *Psychological stress and the coping process*. New York: McGraw-Hill, 1966.

MASLOW, A. H. Toward a humanistic biology. *Amer. Psychologist*, 1969, **24**(8), 734–35.

MASLOW, A. H. (Ed.). *Motivation and personality*. New York: Harper & Row, 1954, 1970.

MASLOW, A. H. *Farther reaches of human nature*. Escalen Institute Book Publishing Program, New York: Viking Press, 1971.

MASSERMAN, J. H. *Principles of dynamic psychiatry* (2nd ed.). Philadelphia: W. B. Saunders Company, 1961.

MEAD, M. *Male and female*. New York: Morrow, 1949.

MECHANIC, D. *Students under stress*. New York: Free Press, 1962.

MILLER, J. G. Living systems: Basic concepts. *Behav. Sci.*, 1965, **10**, 193–237.

NARDINI, J. E. Survival factors in American prisoners of war of the Japanese. *Amer. J. Psychiat.*, 1952, **109**, 241–48.

NARDINI, J. E. Psychiatric concepts of prisoners of war confinement. The William C. Porter Lecture – 1961. *Military Medicine*, 1962, **127**, 299–307.

PIAGET, J. *Genetic epistemology.* New York: Columbia University Press, 1970.

POPKIN, M. K., STILLNER, V., OSBORN, L. W., PIERCE, C. M., & SHURLEY, J. T. Novel behaviors in an extreme environment. *Amer. J. Psychiat.*, June 1974, **131**(6), 651–54.

ROHRER, J. H. Interpersonal relations in isolated small groups. In B. E. Flaherty (Ed.), *Psychophysiological aspects of space flight.* New York: Columbia University Press, 1961.

SARGENT, D. A. In Loss of identity in prison. *Sci. News*, June 16, 1973, **103**(24), 390.

SEARS, R. R., MACCOBY, E. E., & LEVIN, H. *Patterns of child rearing.* New York: Harper & Row, 1957.

SELYE, H. *The stress of life.* New York: McGraw-Hill, 1956.

SELYE, H. Stress. *Psych. Today*, 1969, **3**(4), 24–26.

SKEELS, H. M. Adult status of children with contrasting early life experiences. *Monogr. Soc. Res. Child Develop.*, 1966, **31**(3).

SOMMERSCHIELD, H., & REYHER, J. Posthypnotic conflict, repression, and psychopathology. *J. Abnorm. Psychol.*, Oct. 1973, **82**(2), 278–90.

SONNENBORN, T. M. The new genetics. *Sci. Tech.*, 1962, **1**(9), 66–74.

TEILHARD DE CHARDIN, P. *The phenomenon of man.* New York: Harper & Row, 1961.

UHLENHUTH, E. H., & PAYKEL, E. S. Symptom intensity and life events. *Arch. Gen. Psychiat.*, Apr. 1973, **28**(4), 473–77.

U.S. NEWS & WORLD REPORT. How the POW's fought back. May 14, 1973, **74**(20), 46–52; 110–15.

WEISS, P. A., & TAYLOR, A. C. Shuffled cells can reconstruct same organs. *Sci. Newsletter*, 1960, **78**, 263.

WHITE, W. A. Medical philosophy from the viewpoint of a psychiatrist. *Psychiatry*, 1947, **10**(1–2), 77–98; 191–210.

WHYBROW, P. C., & MENDELS, J. Toward a biology of depression: some suggestions from neurophysiology. *Amer. J. Psychiat.*, 1969, **125**(11), 45–54.

WILSON, E. B. *The cell in development and heredity* (3rd ed.). New York: Macmillan, 1925.

WYATT, R. J., FRAM, D. H., KUPFER, D., & SNYDER, F. Total prolonged drug-induced REM sleep suppression in anxious-depressed subjects. *Arch. Gen. Psychiat.*, 1971, **24**(2), 145–55.

5. Causes of Abnormal Behavior

ADELSON, E. The dream hunters. *Family Health*, Aug. 1974, **6**(8), 34–37.

ALEXANDER, J. F. Defensive and supportive communications in normal and deviant families. *J. Couns. Clin. Psychol.*, Apr. 1973, **40**(2), 223–31.

ANTHONY, J. E. A clinical evaluation of children with psychotic parents. *Amer. J. Psychiat.*, 1969, **126**(2), 177–84.

ANTROBUS, J. In E. Adelson, The dream hunters. *Family Health*, Aug. 1974, **6**(8), 34–37.

ASKEN, M. J. Psychoemotional aspects of mastectomy: a review of recent literature. *Amer. J. Psychiat.*, Jan. 1975, **132**(1), 56–59.

BANDURA, A., ROSS, D., & ROSS, S. A. Imitation of film-mediated aggressive models. *J. Abnorm. Soc. Psychol.*, 1963, **66**, 3–11.

BASOWITZ, H., KORCHIN, S. J., PERSKY, H., & GRINKER, R. R. *Anxiety and stress.* New York: McGraw-Hill, 1955.

BATESON, G. Minimal requirements for a theory of schizophrenia. *Arch. Gen. Psychiat.*, 1960, **2**, 477–91.

BEACH, F. A., & JAYNES, J. Effects of early experience upon the behavior of animals. *Psychol. Bull.*, 1954, **51**, 239–63.

BECKER, E. Toward a comprehensive theory of depression. *J. Nerv. Ment. Dis.*, 1962, **135**, 26–35.

BECKER, W. C. Consequences of different kinds of parental discipline. In M. L. Hoffman & L. W. Hoffman (Eds.), *Review of child development research* (Vol. 1). New York: Russell Sage Foundation, 1964.

BEHAR, M. Prevalence of malnutrition among preschool children of developing countries. In N. W. Scrimshaw & J. E. Gordon (Eds.), *Malnutrition, learning, and behavior.* Cambridge, Mass.: M.I.T. Press, 1968.

BERES, D., & OBERS, S. J. The effects of extreme deprivation in infancy on psychic structure in adolescence. In R. S. Eissler et al. (Eds.), *The psychoanalytic study of the child.* Vol. 5. New York: International University Press, 1950.

BERGSMA, D. (Ed.). *Medical genetics today* (National Foundation Series). Baltimore: Johns Hopkins University Press, 1974.

BLADESLEE, A. L. Nutritional time bomb. *Today's Health*, 1967, **45**(6), 7.

BLAU, A., SLAFF, B., EASTON, K., WELKOWITZ, J., SPRINGARN, J., & COHEN, J. The psychogenic etiology of premature births. *Psychosom. Med.*, 1963, **25**, 201–11.

BOWLBY, J. Separation anxiety. *Inter. J. Psychoanal.*, 1960, **41**, 89–93.

BOWLBY, J. Separation: anxiety and anger. *Psychology of attachment and loss series* (Vol. 3). New York: Basic Books, 1973.

BRENNER, M. H. *Mental illness and the economy.* Cambridge, Mass.: Harvard University Press, 1973.

BRONFENBRENNER, U. The origins of alienation. *Scientif. Amer.*, Aug. 1974, **231**(2), 53, 57, 60–61.

BROWN, L. R. Global food insecurity. *The Futurist*, Apr. 1974, **8**(2), 56–64.

BUCK, V. E. *Working under pressure.* New York: Crane, Russak, 1972.

BULLARD, D. M., GLASER, H. H., HEAGARTY, M. C., & PIVCHEK, E. C. Failure to thrive in the neglected child. *Amer. J. Orthopsychiat.*, 1967, **37**, 680–90.

CAINE, L. *Widow.* New York: Morrow, 1974.

CALHOUN, J. B. Population density and social pathology. *Scientif. Amer.*, Feb. 1962, **206**(2), 139–46; 148.

CALHOUN, J. B., & MARSDEN, H. Not with a bang but with a whimper. *Sci. News*, Feb. 3, 1973, **103**(5), 73.

CARSON, R. C. *Interaction concepts of personality.* New York: Aldine, 1969.

CHAPNICK, P. Creeping up on eugenics. *The Sciences*, May 1973, **13**(4), 6–10.

CHESS, S., THOMAS, A., & BIRCH, H. G. *Your child is a person.* New York: Viking, 1965.

COLEMAN, J. C., & HAMMEN, C. L. *Contemporary psychology and effective behavior.* Glenview, Ill.: Scott, Foresman, 1974.

COMMITTEE 17. Council of the Environmental Mutagen Society: environmental mutagenic hazards. *Science*, Feb. 14, 1975, **187**(4176), 503–14.

COOPERSMITH, S. *The antecedents of self-esteem.* San Francisco: Freeman, 1967.

CORTÉS, J. B., & GATTI, F. M. Physique and propensity. *Psych. Today,* 1970, 4(5), 42–44; 82; 84.

CREASY, M. R., & CROLLA, J. A. Prenatal mortality of trisomy 21 (Down's syndrome). *Lancet,* Mar. 23, 1974, 1(7856), 473–74.

DAMON, A., & POLEDNAK, A. P. Physique and serum pepsinogen. *Human Biology,* 1967, 39(4), 355–67.

DAVENPORT, R. K., ROGERS, C. M., & RUMBAUGH, D. M. Long-term cognitive deficits in chimpanzees associated with early impoverished rearing. *Develop. Psychol.,* Nov. 1973, 9(3), 343–47.

DAVIDSON, M. A., MC INNES, R. G., & PARNELL, R. W. The distribution of personality traits in seven-year-old children. *Brit. J. Educ. Psychol.,* 1957, 27, 48–61.

DENENBERG, V., ROSENBERG, K., HALTMEYER, G., & WHIMBEY, A. Programming life histories: effects of stress in ontogeny upon emotional reactivity. *Merrill-Palmer Quarterly,* 1970, 15, 109–16.

DENNIS, W. Spaulding's experiment on the flight of birds repeated with another species. *J. Compar. Physiol. Psychol.,* 1941, 31, 337–48.

DENNIS, W. Causes of retardation among institutional children: Iran. *J. Genet. Psychol.,* 1960, 96, 47–59.

DEUR, J. I., & PARKE, R. D. Effects of inconsistent punishment on aggression in children. *Develop. Psychol.,* 1970, 2, 403–11.

DEWHURST, K., OLIVER, J. E., & MC KNIGHT, A. L. Sociopathic consequences of Huntington's disease. *Psychiat. Dig.,* Feb. 1971, 32(2), 38.

DOBBING, J. Growth of the brain. *Sci. J.,* 1967, 3(5), 81–86.

DOBZHANSKY, T. The present evolution of man. *Scientif. Amer.,* 1960, 203(3), 206–17.

DOBZHANSKY, T. Genetics and the diversity of behavior. *Amer. Psychologist,* June 1972, 27(6), 523–30.

DURANT, W., & DURANT, A. *Rousseau and revolution.* New York: Simon & Schuster, 1967.

EARL, H. G. 10,000 children battered and starved: hundreds die. *Today's Health,* 1965, 43(9), 24–31.

EISENBERG, L. Student unrest: sources and consequences. *Science,* Mar. 27, 1970, 167(3926), 1688–92.

ELDRICH, H. The American dream: a happy home. *Behav. Today,* Apr. 1, 1974, 5(14), 90–91.

ERON, L. D., HUESMANN, L. R., LEFKOWITZ, M. M., & WALDER, L. O. How learning conditions in early childhood—including mass media—relate to aggression in late adolescence. *Amer. J. Orthopsychiat.,* Apr. 1974, 44(3), 412–23.

FLYNN, W. R. Frontier justice: a contribution to the theory of child battery. *Amer. J. Psychiat.,* 1970, 127(3), 375–79.

GARDNER, J. W. The abused child. *McCalls,* Sept. 1967, 94, 97; 143.

GARTNER, A., & RIESSMAN, F. Is there a new work ethic? *Amer. J. Orthopsychiat.,* July 1974, 44(4), 563–67.

GELVEN, M. Guilt and human meaning. *Humanitas,* Feb. 1973, 9(1), 69–81.

GIL, D. G. Unraveling child abuse. *Amer. J. Psychiat.,* Apr. 1975, 45(3), 346–50.

GLUECK, S., & GLUECK, E. *Family environment and delinquency.* Boston: Houghton Mifflin, 1962.

GLUECK, S., & GLUECK, E. *Non-delinquents in perspective.* Cambridge: Harvard University Press, 1968.

GREEN, A. H., GAINES, R. W., & SANDGRUND, A. Child abuse: pathological syndrome of family interaction. *Amer. J. Psy-*

chiat., Aug. 1974, 131(8), 882–86.

HARLOW, H. F. *Learning to love.* San Francisco: Albion, 1973.

HARLOW, H. F., & HARLOW, M. Learning to love. *Amer. Scien.,* 1966, 54, 244–72.

HARLOW, H. F., & SUOMI, S. J. Nature of love—simplified. *Amer. Psychologist,* 1970, 25(1), 161–68.

HARMELING, P. C. Therapeutic theater of Alaska Eskimos. *Group Psychother.,* 1950, 3, 74–76.

HARMETZ, A. Medical breakthrough: curing a deadly defect before the baby is born. *Today's Health,* Dec. 1974, 52(12), 14–17; 60–62.

HARVEY, C. D., & BAHR, H. M. Widowhood, morale, and affiliation. *J. Marr. Fam.,* Feb. 1974, 36(1), 97–106.

HELFER, R. E., & KEMPE, C. H. (Eds.). *The battered child.* Chicago: University of Chicago, 1968.

HERRICK, C. J. *Evolution of human nature.* Austin: University of Texas Press, 1956.

HERSHER, L., MOORE, U., RICHMOND, J. B., & BLAUVELT, H. The effects of maternal deprivation during the nursing period on the behavior of young goats. *Amer. Psychologist,* 1962, 17, 307.

HETHERINGTON, E. M. Girls without fathers. *Psych. Today,* Feb. 1973, 6(9), 47; 49–52.

HOLMES, T. H., & RAHE, R. H. The social readjustment rating scale. *J. Psychosom. Res.,* Apr. 1967, 11(2), 213–18.

HOLMES, T. S., & HOLMES, T. H. Short-term intrusions into the life-style routine. *J. Psychosom. Res.,* June 1970, 14(2), 121–32.

HURLEY, J. R. Parental acceptance-rejection and children's intelligence. *Merrill-Palmer Quart.,* 1965, 11(1), 19–32.

HURLOCK, E. B. *Developmental psychology* (3rd ed.). New York: McGraw-Hill, 1968.

INSELF, P. M., & MOOS, R. H. Psychological environments: expanding the scope of human ecology. *Amer. Psychologist,* Mar. 1974, 29(3), 179–88.

JARVIK, L. F., YEN, F. S., & GOLDSTEIN, F. Chromosomes and mental status. *Arch. Gen. Psychiat.,* Feb. 1974, 30(2), 186–90.

JENKINS, R. L. Psychiatric syndromes in children and their relation to family background. *Amer. J. Orthopsychiat.,* 1966, 36, 450–57.

JENKINS, R. L. The varieties of children's behavioral problems and family dynamics. *Amer. J. Psychiat.,* 1968, 124, 1440–45.

JOINT COMMISSION ON MENTAL HEALTH OF CHILDREN. *Crisis in child mental health: challenge for the 1970's.* New York: Harper & Row, 1970.

KADUSHIN, A. Reversibility of trauma: a follow-up study of children adopted when older. *Social Work,* 1967, 12(4), 22–23.

KAGAN, J. In B. Pratt (Ed.), Kagan counters Freud, Piaget theories on early childhood deprivation effects. *APA Monitor,* 1973, 4(2), 1; 7.

KAISER FOUNDATION HEALTH PLAN, INC. *Planning for health.* Summer 1970, 1–2.

KALLMANN, F. J. *Heredity in health and mental disorder.* New York: Norton, 1953.

KALLMANN, F. J. The uses of genetics in psychiatry. *J. Ment. Scien.,* 1958, 104, 542–49.

KAPLAN, B. J. Malnutrition and mental deficiency. *Psychol. Bull.,* Nov. 1972, 78(5), 321–34.

KNOWLES, J. In A. Rossiter (Ed.), Planet grows crowded. *Los Angeles Evening Outlook,* Mar. 30, 1974, 5.

LAING, R. D., & ESTERSON, A. *Sanity, madness, and the family.* London: Tavistock, 1964.

LANDY, D., & SIGALL, H. Beauty is talent: task evaluation as a function of the performer's physical attractiveness. *J. Pers. Soc. Psychol.,* Mar. 1974, **29**(3), 299–304.

LANGNER, T. S., GERSTEN, J. C., GREENE, E. L., EISENBERG, J. G., HERSON, J. H., & MCCARTHY, E. D. Treatment of psychological disorders among urban children. *J. Cons. Clin. Psychol.,* Apr. 1974, **42**(2), 170–79.

LANGNER, T. S., & MICHAEL, S. T. *Life stress and mental health* (Vol. 20). New York: Free Press, 1963.

LAPPÉ, M. Genetic knowledge and the concept of health. *The Hastings Center Report,* Institute of Society, Ethics and the Life Sciences, Sept. 1973, **3**(4), 1–3.

LEFKOWITZ, M. M., HUESMANN, L. R., WALDER, L. O., ERON, L. D. Developing and predicting aggression. *Sci. News,* Jan. 1973, **103**(3), 40.

LESSAC, M., & SOLOMON, R. L. Effects of early isolation on the later adaptive behavior of beagles. *Develop. Psychol.,* 1969, **1**(1), 14–25.

LEVITAN, M., & MONTAGUE, A. *Textbook of human genetics.* New York: Oxford University Press, 1971.

LEVY, D. M. Maternal overprotection. In N. D. C. Lewis & B. L. Pacella (Eds.), *Modern trends in child psychiatry.* New York: International University Press, 1945.

LOPER, M. L. Trauma of child beating. *Los Angeles Times,* Oct. 12, 1970, IV, 1, 11.

LOYD, G. F. Finally, facts on malnutrition in the United States. *Today's Health,* 1969, **47**(9), 32–33.

LYNCH, H. T., HARLAN, W. L., & DYHRBERG, J. S. Subjective perspective of a family with Huntington's chorea. *Arch. Gen. Psychiat.,* July 1972, **27**(1), 67–72.

MILLER, R. W. Delayed radiation effects in atomic-bomb survivors. *Science,* 1969, **166**(3905), 569–73.

MINDE, K. K., HACKETT, J. D., KILLOU, D., & SILVER, S. How they grow up: 41 physically handicapped children and their families. *Amer. J. Psychiat.,* June 1972, **128**(12), 104–10.

NATIONAL INSTITUTE OF MENTAL HEALTH. *The mental health of urban America.* Washington, D.C.: Public Hlth. Serv. Publ. No. 1906, 1969.

NELSON, H. Sleep: it's the kind you get—not how much. *Los Angeles Times,* Apr. 3, 1967, II, 6.

NELSON, H. How to be successfully fired. *Behav. Today,* Apr. 29, 1974, **5**(17), 118–19. [a]

NELSON, H. Search for carriers of rare disease slated. *Los Angeles Times,* Part 2, Mar. 6, 1974, 1–2. [b]

PEMBERTON, D. A., & BENADY, D. R. Consciously rejected children. *Brit. J. Psychiat.,* Nov. 1973, **123**(576), 575–78.

POLLACK, J. H. Five frequent mistakes of parents. *Today's Health,* 1968, **46**(5), 14–15; 26–29.

POZNANSKI, E. O. Children with excessive fears. *Amer. J. Orthopsychiat.,* Apr. 1973, **43**(3), 428–38.

PRINGLE, M. L. K. *Deprivation and education.* New York: Humanities Press, 1965.

PROVENCE, S., & LIPTON, R. C. *Infants in institutions.* New York: International University Press, 1962.

REICE, S. Editorial. *Family Health,* Apr. 1974, **6**(4), 4.

REISEN, A. H. The development of visual perception in men and chimpanzee. *Science,* 1947, **106**, 107–8.

RIBBLE, M. A. Infantile experience in relation to personality development. In J. McV. Hunt (Ed.), *Personality and the behavior disorders* (Vol. 2). New York: Ronald, 1944. Pp. 621–51.

RIBBLE, M. A. Anxiety in infants and its disorganizing effects. In N. D. C. Lewis & B. L. Pacella (Eds.), *Modern trends in child psychiatry.* New York: International University Press, 1945.

ROBINS, L. N. The adult development of the antisocial child. *Seminars in Psychiatry,* Nov. 1970, **2**(4), 420–34.

ROBINSON, S., & WINNIK, H. Z. Severe psychotic disturbances following crash diet weight loss. *Arch. Gen. Psychiat.,* Oct. 1973, **29**(4), 559–62.

RUTTER, M. Maternal deprivation reconsidered. *J. Psychosom. Res.,* Aug. 1972, **16**(4), 241–50.

SANDERSON, F. H. The great food fumble. *Science,* May 9, 1975, **188**(4188), 503–9.

SATIR, V. *Conjoint family therapy.* (Rev. ed.). Palo Alto, Calif.: Science and Behavior Books, 1967.

SCRIMSHAW, N. S. Early malnutrition and central nervous system function. *Merrill-Palmer Quart.,* 1969, **15**, 375–88.

SEAMAN, M. Antidote for alienation. *Trans-action,* 1966, **3**(4), 35–39.

SEARS, R. R. Relation of early socialization experiences to aggression in middle childhood. *J. Abnorm. Soc. Psychol.,* 1961, **63**, 466–92.

SEARS, R. R., MACCOBY, E. E., & LEVIN, H. *Patterns of child rearing.* New York: Harper & Row, 1957.

SELYE, H. *The stress of life.* New York: McGraw-Hill, 1956.

SELYE, H. Stress. *Psych. Today,* 1969, **3**(4), 24–26.

SERGOVICH, F., VALENTINE, G. H., CHEN, A. T., KINCH, R., & SMOUT, M. Chromosomal aberrations in 2159 consecutive newborn babies. *New Engl. J. Med.,* 1969, **280**(16), 851–54.

SHAW, C. R., & SCHELKUN, R. F. Suicidal behavior in children. *Psychiatry,* 1965, **28**, 157–68.

SHELDON, W. H. (with the collaboration of C. W. Dupertuis & E. McDermott). *Atlas of men.* New York: Harper & Row, 1954.

SOLOMON, J. Sea of drugs. *The Sciences,* May 1973, **13**(4), 23–28.

SONTAG, L. W., STEELE, W. G., & LEWIS, M. The fetal and maternal cardiac response to environmental stress. *Human Develop.,* 1969, **12**, 1–9.

SPENCER, S. M. The disease we've overlooked. *Family Health,* Jan. 1973, **5**(1), 38; 40; 42–43.

STEINMETZ, S. K., & STRAUS, M. A. The family as cradle of violence. *Society,* Sept./Oct. 1973, **10**(6), 50–56.

STIERLIN, H. A family perspective on adolescent runaways. *Ment. Hlth. Dig.,* Oct. 1973, **5**(10), 1–4.

TERR, L. A family study of child abuse. *Amer. J. Psychiat.,* 1970, **127**, 665–71.

TIME. On being an American parent. Dec. 15, 1967, **90**(24), 30–31.

TIZARD, B., & REES, J. The effect of early institutional rearing on the behavior problems and affectional relationships of four-year-old children. *J. Child Psychol. Psychiat.,* Jan. 1975, **16**(1), 61–73.

TOFFLER, A. *Future shock.* New York: Random House, 1970.

TRAUB, E. Quote from "What can happen if you're an overprotective parent" by E. Traub. *Today's Health* (April 1974), **52**(4), 40–43; 67–69, published by the American Medical Association.

U.S. NEWS & WORLD REPORT. Rising problems of single parents. July 16, 1973, **73**(3), 32.

U.S. NEWS & WORLD REPORT. Surge in easy divorces and the problems they bring. Apr. 22, 1974, **76**(16), 43.

WALTERS, B. My favorite interviews. *Newsweek,* May 6, 1974, **83**(18), 59. Poem from "Appraisal" in *City of the Heart,*

Robert J. Smithdas (Copyright © 1966 by Robert J. Smithdas, published by Taplinger Publishing Company, New York). Reprinted by permission.

WATZLAWICK, P., BEAVIN, J., & JACKSON, D. D. *Pragmatics of human communication.* New York: Norton, 1967.

WINICK, C. The beige epoch: depolarization of sex roles in America. *Ann. Amer. Acad. Polit. Soc. Sci.*, 1968, **376**, 18–24.

WOLFE, T. *Look homeward angel.* New York: Scribners, 1929.

WOLKIND, S. N. The components of "affectionless psychotherapy" in institutionalized children. *J. Child Psychol. Psychiat.*, July 1974, **15**(3), 215–20.

WOLKIND, S. N., & RUTTER, M. Children who have been "in care": an epidemiological study. *J. Child Psychol. Psychiat.*, June 1973, **14**(2), 97–105.

6. Transient Situational Disorders

ADLER, A. Neuropsychiatric complications in victims of Boston's Cocoanut Grove disaster. *JAMA*, 1943, **123**, 1098–1101.

ALLERTON, W. S. Psychiatric casualties in Vietnam. *Roche Medical Image and Commentary*, 1970, **12**(8), 27.

ARCHIBALD, H. C., & TUDDENHAM, R. D. Persistent stress reaction after combat. *Arch. Gen. Psychiat.*, 1965, **12**(5), 475–81.

BARTEMEIER, L. H., KUBIE, L. S., MENNINGER, K. A., ROMANO, J., & WHITEHORN, J. C. Combat exhaustion. *Journal of Nervous and Mental Disease*, 1946, **104**, 385–89; 489–25. Published by The Williams & Wilkins Co. Copyright 1946 and reprinted by permission of The Smith Ely Jelliffe Trust.

BELL, E., JR. The basis of effective military psychiatry. *Dis. Nerv. System*, 1958, **19**, 283–88.

BETTELHEIM, B. Individual and mass behavior in extreme situations. *J. Abnorm. Soc. Psychol.*, 1943, **38**, 417–52.

BETTELHEIM, B. *The informed heart.* New York: Free Press, 1960.

BLOCH, H. S. Army clinical psychiatry in the combat zone—1967–1968. Reprinted from *The American Journal of Psychiatry*, volume **126**, pages 289–98, 1969. Copyright, 1969, the American Psychiatric Association.

BORUS, J. F. Incidence of maladjustment in Vietnam returnees. *Arch. Gen. Psychiat.*, Apr. 1974, **30**(4), 554–57.

BOURNE, P. G. Military psychiatry and the Vietnam experience. *Amer. J. Psychiat.*, 1970, **127**(4), 481–88.

CHAMBERS, R. E. Discussion of "Survival factors. . . ." *Amer. J. Psychiat.*, 1952, **109**, 247–48.

CHODOFF, P. The German concentration camp as a psychological stress. *Arch. Gen. Psychiat.*, 1970, **22**(1), 78–87.

DEFAZIO, V. J., RUSTIN, S., & DIAMOND, A. Symptom development in Vietnam era veterans. *Amer. J. Orthopsychiat.*, Jan. 1975, **45**(1), 158–63.

EITINGER, L. Pathology of the concentration camp syndrome. *Arch. Gen. Psychiat.*, 1961, **5**, 371–79.

EITINGER, L. Concentration camp survivors in the postwar world. *Amer. J. Orthopsychiat.*, 1962, **32**, 367–75.

EITINGER, L. *Concentration camp survivors in Norway and Israel.* New York: Humanities Press, 1964.

EITINGER, L. Psychosomatic problems in concentration camp survivors. *J. Psychosom. Res.*, 1969, **13**, 183–90.

EITINGER, L. A follow-up study of the Norwegian concentration camp survivors: Mortality and morbidity. *Israel Annals of Psychiatry and Related Disciplines*, Sept. 1973, **11**, 199–210.

FARBER, I. E., HARLOW, H. F., & WEST, L. J. Brainwashing, conditioning, and DDD (debility, dependency and dread). *Sociometry*, 1956, **19**, 271–85.

FORREST, D. V. Psychiatric casualties in Vietnam. *Roche Medical Image and Commentary*, Oct. 1970, **12**(8), 27.

FRANKL, V. E. *Man's search for meaning* (Rev. ed.). Boston: Beacon Press, 1963.

FRIEDMAN, P. The effects of imprisonment. *Acta Medica Orientalia, Jerusalem*, 1948, 163–67.

FRIEDMAN, P., & LINN, L. Some psychiatric notes on the Andrea Doria disaster. *Amer. J. Psychiat.*, 1957, **114**, 426–32.

GOLDSMITH, W., & CRETEKES, C. Unhappy odysseys: psychiatric hospitalization among Vietnam returnees. *Amer. J. Psychiat.*, 1969, **20**, 78–83.

GRINKER, R. R. An essay on schizophrenia and science. *Arch. Gen. Psychiat.*, 1969, **20**, 1–24.

GRINKER, R. R., & SPIEGEL, J. P. *War neuroses.* Philadelphia: Blakiston, 1945.

HAFNER, H. Psychological disturbances following prolonged persecution. *Soc. Psychiat.*, 1968, **3**(3), 80–88.

HAUSMAN, W., & RIOCH, D. M. Military psychiatry. *Arch. Gen. Psychiat.*, 1967, **16**, 727–39.

HAYTHORN, W. W., & ALTMAN, I. Together in isolation. *Transaction*, 1967, **4**(3), 18–22.

HINKLE, L. E., JR., & WOLFF, H. G. Communist interrogation and indoctrination of "enemies of the states." *Arch. Neurol. Psychiat.*, 1956, **76**, 115–74.

HOROWITZ, M. J. Psychic trauma. *Arch. Gen. Psychiat.*, 1969, **20**, 552–59.

HUNTER, E. *Brain-washing in Red China.* New York: Vanguard, 1954.

KARPE, R., & SCHNAP, I. Nostopathy—a study of pathogenic homecoming. *Amer. J. Psychiat.*, 1952, **109**, 46–51.

KEISER, L. *The traumatic neurosis.* Philadelphia: Lippincott, 1968.

KINKEAD, E. *In every war but one.* New York: Norton, 1959.

KUSHNER, F. H. All of us bear the scars. *U.S. News & World Report*, Apr. 16, 1973, **74**(16), 41.

LEOPOLD, R. L., & DILLON, H. Psychoanatomy of a disaster: a long term study of post-traumatic neuroses in survivors of a marine explosion. *Amer. J. Psychiat.*, 1963, **119**, 913–21.

LIFTON, R. J. Home by ship: reaction patterns of American prisoners of war repatriated from North Korea. *Amer. J. Psychiat.*, 1954, **110**, 732–39.

LIFTON, R. J. *Thought reform and the psychology of totalism: a study of "brainwashing" in China.* New York: Norton, 1961.

LIFTON, R. J. The "Gook syndrome" and "numbed warfare." *Sat. Rev.*, Dec. 1972, **55**(47), 66–72.

LINDEMANN, E. Symptomatology and management of acute grief. *Amer. J. Psychiat.*, 1944, **101**, 141–48.

LUDWIG, A. O., & RANSON, S. W. A statistical follow-up of treatment of combat-induced psychiatric casualties. I and II. *Military Surgeon*, 1947, **100**, 51–62; 169–75.

MC DAVID, J. W., & HARARI, H. *Social psychology: individuals, groups, societies.* New York: Harper & Row, 1968.

MENNINGER, W. C. *Psychiatry in a troubled world.* New York: Macmillan, 1948.

MODLIN, H. C. The postaccident anxiety syndrome: psychosocial aspects. *Amer. J. Psychiat.*, 1967, **123**, 1008–21.

NARDINI, J. E. Survival factors in American prisoners of war of the Japanese. Reprinted from *The American Journal of Psychiatry*, volume **109**, pages 241–48, 1952. Copyright

1952, the American Psychiatric Association.

NARDINI, J. E. Psychiatric concepts of prisoners of war confinement. The William C. Porter Lecture—1961. *Military Medicine*, 1962, **127**, 299–307.

OKURA, K. P. Mobilizing in response to a major disaster. *Comm. Ment. Hlth. J.*, Summer 1975, 2(2), 136–44.

ORWELL, G. *1984*. New York: Harcourt, 1949.

POLNER, M. Vietnam War stories. *Transaction*, 1968, **6**(1), 8–20. Quote published by permission of Transaction, Inc., from *Transaction*, Vol. 6, #1. Copyright © 1968, by Transaction, Inc.

POPKIN, M. K., STILLNER, V., OSBORN, L. W., PIERCE, C. M., & SHURLEY, J. T. Novel behaviors in an extreme environment. *Amer. J. Psychiat.*, June 1974, **131**(6), 651–54.

QUARANTELLI, E. L., & DYNES, R. R. When disaster strikes. *Psych. Today*, Feb. 1972, **5**(9), 66–70.

RIOS, P. Quote from The Vietnam casualties are prisoners of war—for life, by Pete Rios from *The Chicago Daily News* (June 3, 1973). Reprinted by permission.

SATLOFF, A. Psychiatry and the nuclear submarine. *Amer. J. Psychiat.*, 1967, **124**(4), 547–51.

SAUL, L. J. Psychological factors in combat fatigue. *Psychosom. Med.*, 1945, **7**, 257–72.

SCHAAR, K. Is the Vietnam veteran getting enough psychological help? *APA Monitor*, May 1974, **5**(5), 1; 5.

SCHANCHE, D. A. The emotional aftermath of "the largest tornado ever." *Today's Health*, Aug. 1974, **52**(8), 16–19; 61; 63–64.

SCHEIN, E. H., SCHNEIER, I., & BARKER, C. H. *Coercive persuasion*. New York: Norton, 1961.

SEGAL, H. A. Initial psychiatric findings of recently repatriated prisoners of war. *Amer. J. Psychiat.*, 1954, **111**, 358–63.

SERXNER, J. An experience in submarine psychiatry. *Amer. J. Psychiat.*, 1968, **125**(1), 25–30.

SIGAL, J. J., SILVER, D., RAKOFF, V., & ELLIN, B. Some second-generation effects of survival of the Nazi persecution. *Amer. J. Orthopsychiat.*, Apr. 1973, **43**(3), 320–27.

SOBEL, MAJ. R. Anxiety-depressive reactions after prolonged combat experience—the old sergeant syndrome. *Bull. U.S. Army Med. Dept., Combat Psychiat. Suppl.*, Nov. 1949, 137–46.

STERN, R. L. Diary of a war neurosis. *Journal of Nervous and Mental Disease*, 1947, **106**, 583–86. Published by the Williams & Wilkins Co. Copyright 1947 and reprinted by permission of The Smith Ely Jelliffe Trust.

STRANGE, R. E., & BROWN, D. E., JR. Home from the wars. *Amer. J. Psychiat.*, 1970, **127**(4), 488–92.

STRASSMAN, H. D., THALER, M. B., & SCHEIN, E. H. A prisoner of war syndrome: apathy as a reaction to severe stress. *Amer. J. Psychiat.*, 1956, **112**, 998–1003.

TUOHY, W. Drugs fight shell shock in Vietnam. *Los Angeles Times*, July 30, 1967, F, 12–13.

TUOHY, W. Combat fatigue: U.S. lessens its toll in Vietnam. *Los Angeles Times*, Dec. 1, 1968, A, 1.

UHLENHUTH, E. Free therapy said helpful to Chicago train wreck victims. *Psychiatric News*, Feb. 7, 1973, **8**(3), 1; 27.

VAN PUTTEN, T., & EMORY, W. H. Traumatic neuroses in Vietnam returnees. *Arch. Gen. Psychiat.*, Nov. 1973, **29**(5), 695–98.

WARNES, H. The traumatic syndrome. *Ment. Hlth. Dig.*, Mar. 1973, **5**(3), 33–34.

WATZLAWICK, P., BEAVIN, J., & JACKSON, D. D. *Pragmatics of human communication*. New York: Norton, 1967.

WEST, L. J. Psychiatric aspects of training for honorable survival as a prisoner of war. *Amer. J. Psychiat.*, 1958, **115**, 329–36.

WHITE, GEN. T. D. The inevitable climb to space. *Air Univer. Quart. Rev.*, 1958–1959, **10**(4).

WILBUR, R. S. In S. Auerbach (Ed.), POWs found to be much sicker than they looked upon release. *Los Angeles Times*, June 2, 1973, Part I, p. 4.

WILLIAMS, A. H. A psychiatric study of Indian soldiers in the Arakan. *Brit. J. Med. Psychol.*, 1950, **23**, 130–81.

WOLFF, H. G. Stressors as a cause of disease in man. In J. M. Tanner (Ed.), *Stress and psychiatric disorder*. London: Oxford, 1960.

7. Neuroses

ABSE, D. W. Hysteria. In S. Arieti (Ed.), *American handbook of psychiatry* (Vol. 1). New York: Basic Books, 1959, Pp. 272–92.

ADAMS, P. L. Family characteristics of obsessive children. *Amer. J. Psychiat.*, May 1972, **128**(11), 98–101.

ALARCON, R. D. Hysteria and hysterical personality: How come one without the other? *Psychiat. Quart.*, 1973, **47**(2), 258–75.

BANDURA, A. *Principles of behavior modification*. New York: Holt, Rinehart & Winston, 1969.

BANDURA, A. *Aggression: a social learning analysis*. Englewood Cliffs, N.J.: Prentice-Hall, 1973.

BANDURA, A., BLANCHARD, E. B., & RITTER, B. Relative efficacy of desensitization and modeling approaches for inducing behavioral, affective, and attitudinal changes. *J. Pers. Soc. Psychol.*, 1969, **13**, 173–79.

BEARD, G. M. *A practical treatise on nervous exhaustion (neurasthenia), its symptoms, nature, sequences, treatment* (5th ed.). New York: E. B. Treat, 1905.

BECK, A. T., LAUDE, R., & BOHNERT, M. Ideational components of anxiety neurosis. *Arch. Gen. Psychiat.*, Sept. 1974, **31**(3), 319–25.

BIANCHI, G. N. Patterns of hypochondriasis: a principle components analysis. *Brit. J. Psychiat.*, May 1973, **122**(570), 541–48.

BLANCHARD, E. B., & YOUNG, L. D. Clinical applications of biofeedback training: a review. *Arch. Gen. Psychiat.*, May 1974, **30**(5), 573–89.

BROWN, W. L. Psycho-iconography of the office neurotic. *Clinical Symposia*, 1957, **9**(5), 173–75.

BUTTON, J. H., & REIVICH, R. S. Obsession of infanticide. A review of 42 cases. Reprinted from *Archives of General Psychiatry*, Aug. 1972, **27**(2), 235–40. Copyright 1972, American Medical Association.

CARR, A. T. Compulsive neurosis: two psychophysiological studies. *Bulletin of the British Psychological Society*, 1971, **24**, 256–57.

CARR, A. T. Compulsive neurosis: a review of the literature. *Psychol. Bull.*, May 1974, **81**(5), 311–18.

CHADOFF, P. The diagnosis of hysteria: an overview. *Amer. J. Psychiat.*, Oct. 1974, **131**(10), 1073–78.

COHEN, D. B. On the etiology of neurosis. *J. Abnorm. Psychol.*, Oct. 1974, **83**(5), 473–79.

COOKERLY, J. R. The outcome of the six major forms of marriage counseling compared: a pilot study. *J. Marr. Fam.*, Nov. 1973, **35**(4), 608–11.

COVI, L., LIPMAN, R. S., DEROGATIS, L. R., SMITH, J. E., III, & PATTI-

SON, J. H. Drugs and group psychotherapy in neurotic depression. *Amer. J. Psychiat.*, Feb. 1974, **131**(2), 191–97.

DOWNING, R. W., & RICKELS, K. Mixed anxiety-depression: fact or myth? *Arch. Gen. Psychiat.*, Mar. 1974, **30**(3), 312–17.

EIDUSON, B. T. The two classes of information in psychiatry. *Arch. Gen. Psychiat.*, 1968, **18**, 405–19.

ELIOT, T. S. *The cocktail party.* 1950. Reprinted by permission of Harcourt Brace Jovanovich, Inc., and Faber and Faber Ltd.

ENGELHARDT, D. M. Pharmacologic basis for use of psychotropic drugs: an overview. *N.Y. St. J. Med.*, Feb. 1974, **74**(2), 360–66.

FRANKEL, A. S. Treatment of a multisymptomatic phobic by a self-directed, self-reinforced imagery technique: a case study. Reprinted from the *Journal of Abnormal Psychology,* 1970, Vol. **76**, pp. 496–99, "Treatment of a Multisymptomatic Phobic by a Self-Directed, Self-Reinforced Imagery Technique" by A. S. Frankel, by permission of the American Psychological Association.

GIBSON, H. B. Morita therapy and behavior therapy. *Behav. Res. Ther.*, Nov. 1974, **12**(4), 347–55.

GOODWIN, D. W., GUZE, S. B., & ROBBINS, E. Follow-up studies in obsessional neurosis. *Arch. Gen. Psychiat.*, 1969, **20**, 182–87.

GRABER, D. Megavitamins, molecules, and minds. *Human Behavior,* May 1973, **2**(5), 8–15.

HALLECK, S. L. Hysterical personality traits. Reprinted from *Archives of General Psychiatry,* 1967, **16**, 750–57. Copyright 1967, American Medical Association.

HALPERN, H. J. Hysterical amblyopia. *Bull. U.S. Army Med. Dept.*, 1944, No. 72, 84–87.

HAMMER, H. Astasia-abasia: a report of two cases at West Point. *Amer. J. Psychiat.*, 1967, **124**(5), 671–74.

HEARST, E. D., CLONINGER, C. R., CREWS, E. L., & CADORET, R. J. Electrosleep therapy. *Arch. Gen. Psychiat.*, Apr. 1974, **30**(4), 463–66.

HODGSON, R. J., & RACHMAN, S. The effects of contamination and washing in obsessional patients. *Behav. Res. Ther.*, May 1972, **10**(2), 111–17.

HURVITZ, N. The family therapist as intermediary. *The Family Coordinator*, Apr. 1974, **23**(2), 145–58.

IRONSIDE, R., & BATCHELOR, I. R. C. The ocular manifestations of hysteria in relation to flying. *Brit. J. Ophthalmol.*, 1945, **29**, 88–98.

JENKINS, R. L. Psychiatric syndromes in children and their relation to family background. *Amer. J. Orthopsychiat.*, 1966, **36**, 450–57.

JENKINS, R. L. The varieties of children's behavioral problems and family dynamics. *Amer. J. Psychiat.*, 1968, **124**(10), 1440–45.

JENKINS, R. L. Classification of behavior problems of children. *Amer. J. Psychiat.*, 1969, **125**(8), 1032–39.

JONES, M. C. A laboratory study of fear: the case of Peter. *Pedagogical Seminary*, 1924, **31**, 308–15.

KAUFMANN, W. *Without guilt and justice: from decidophobia to autonomy.* New York: Peter H. Wyden, 1973.

KENYON, F. E. Hypochondriasis: a survey of some historical, clinical, and social aspects. *Inter. J. Psychiat.*, 1966, **2**, 308–25.

KERCKHOFF, A. C., & BACK, K. W. The bug. *Psych. Today,* 1969, **3**(1), 46–49.

KIDSON, M. A., & JONES, I. H. Psychiatric disorders among aborigines of the Australian Western Desert. *Arch. Gen. Psychiat.*, 1968, **19**, 413–17.

KIERSCH, T. A. Amnesia: a clinical study of ninety-eight cases. *Amer. J. Psychiat.*, 1962, **119**, 57–60.

KLINE, N. S. Drug treatment of phobic disorders. *Amer. J. Psychiat.*, 1967, **123**(11), 1447–50.

KNOFF, W. A history of the concept of neurosis, with a memoir of William Cullen. *Amer. J. Psychiat.*, 1970, **127**(1), 80–84.

KORA, T., & OHARA, K. Morita therapy. *Psych. Today,* Mar. 1973, **6**(10), 63–68.

KRAINES, S. H. *The therapy of the neuroses and psychoses* (3rd ed.). Philadelphia: Lea & Febiger, 1948. Reprinted by permission.

LADER, M., & MATHEWS, A. Physiological changes during spontaneous panic attacks. *J. Psychosom. Res.*, 1970, **14**(4), 377–82.

LANCASTER, E., & POLING, J. *Final face of Eve.* New York: McGraw-Hill, 1958.

LEWIS, W. C. Hysteria: the consultant's dilemma. *Arch. Gen. Psychiat.*, Feb. 1974, **30**(2), 145–51.

LIEBSON, I. Conversion reaction: a learning theory approach. *Behav. Res. Ther.*, 1969, **7**, 217–18.

LIPTON, S. Dissociated personality: a case report. *Psychiatric Quarterly*, 1943, **17**, 35–36. Permission granted by *Psychiatric Quarterly.*

LONDON, P. The end of ideology in behavior modification. *Amer. Psychologist,* Oct. 1972, **27**(10), 913–20.

MADDI, S. R. The existential neurosis. *J. Abnorm. Psychol.*, 1967, **72**, 311–25.

MALMO, R. B. Emotions and muscle tension: the story of Anne. *Psych. Today,* Mar. 1970, **3**(10), 64–67; 83.

MARKS, I. M. Agoraphobic syndrome (phobic anxiety state). *Arch. Gen. Psychiat.*, 1970, **23**(6), 538–53.

MASSERMAN, J. H. *Principles of dynamic psychiatry* (2nd ed.). Philadelphia: W. B. Saunders Company, 1961. Reproduced by permission of the author and publisher.

MATHER, M. D. The treatment of an obsessive-compulsive patient by discrimination learning and reinforcement of decision-making. *Behav. Res. Ther.*, 1970, **8**(3), 315–18.

MELVILLE, K. Changing the family game. *The Sciences*, Apr. 1973, **13**(3), 17–19.

MENNINGER, K. A. *The human mind* (3rd ed.). New York: Knopf, 1945. From pages 139–140 in *The Human Mind*, by Karl Menninger. Copyright 1930, 1937, 1945 and renewed 1958, 1965 by Karl Menninger. Reprinted by permission of Alfred A. Knopf, Inc.

MUCHA, T. F., & REINHARDT, R. F. Conversion reactions in student aviators. *Amer. J. Psychiat.*, **127**, 1970, 493–97.

MURPHY, G. *Personality.* New York: Harper & Row, 1947.

NEMIAH, J. C. Obsessive-compulsive reaction. In A. M. Freedman & H. I. Kaplan (Eds.), *Comprehensive textbook of psychiatry.* Baltimore: Williams & Wilkins, 1967.

O'NEILL, M., & KEMPLER, B. Approach and avoidance responses of the hysterical personality to sexual stimuli. *J. Abnorm. Psychol.*, 1969, **74**, 300–305.

PARRY-JONES, W., SANTER-WESTSTRATE, H. G., & CRAWLEY, R. C. Behavior therapy in a case of hysterical blindness. *Behav. Res. Ther.*, 1970, **8**(1), 79–85.

PAUL, G. L. Outcome of systematic desensitization. II. In C. M. Franks (Ed.), *Assessment and status of the behavior therapies.* New York: McGraw-Hill, 1968. Pp. 105–59.

POLLIN, W., ALLEN, M. G., HOFFER, A., STABENAU, J. R., & HRUBEC, Z. Psychopathology in 15,909 pairs of veteran twins. *Amer. J. Psychiat.*, 1969, **126**, 597–609.

PORTNOY, I. The anxiety states. In S. Arieti (Ed.), *American handbook of psychiatry* (Vol. 1). New York: Basic Books, 1959. Pp. 307–23.

PRUSOFF, B., & KLERMAN, G. L. Differentiating depressed from anxious neurotic outpatients. *Arch. Gen. Psychiat.*, Mar. 1974, **30**(3), 302–9.

RACHMAN, S., MARKS, I. M., & HODGSON, R. The treatment of obsessive-compulsive neurotics by modeling and flooding *in vivo. Behav. Res. Ther.*, Nov. 1973, **11**(4), 463–72.

RASKIN, M., JOHNSON, G., & RONDESTVEDT, J. W. Chronic anxiety treated by feedback-induced muscle relaxation. *Arch. Gen. Psychiat.*, Feb. 1973, **28**(2), 263–67.

RAZANI, J. Treatment of phobias by systematic desensitization. *Arch. Gen. Psychiat.*, Mar. 1974, **30**(3), 291–93.

ROSENTHAL, S. H., & WULFSOHN, N. L. Electrosleep—a clinical trial. *Amer. J. Psychiat.*, 1970, **127**(4), 533–34.

SALZMAN, L. Obsessions and phobias. *Inter. J. Psychiat.*, 1968, **6**, 451–68.

SLAVNEY, P. R., & MCHUGH, P. R. The hysterical personality. *Arch. Gen. Psychiat.*, Mar. 1974, **30**(3), 325–29.

SOLOMON, P., LEIDERMAN, P. H., MENDELSON, J., & WEXLER, D. Sensory deprivation. *Amer. J. Psychiat.*, 1957, **114**, 357–63.

STEELE, J. The hysteria and psychasthenia constructs as an alternative to manifest anxiety and conflict-free ego functions. *J. Abnorm. Psychol.*, 1969, **74**, 79–85.

STERN, R. S., LIPSEDGE, M. S., & MARKS, I. M. Obsessive ruminations: a controlled trial of thought-stopping technique. *Behav. Res. Ther.*, Nov. 1973, **11**(4), 659–62.

TEMPLER, D. I., & LESTER, D. Conversion disorders: a review of research findings. *Comprehensive Psychiatry*, July/Aug. 1974, **15**(4), 285–94.

THEODOR, L. H., & MANDELCORN, M. S. Hysterical blindness: a case report and study using a modern psychophysical technique. *J. Abnorm. Psychol.*, Dec. 1973, **82**(3), 552–53.

THIGPEN, C. H., & CLECKLEY, H. M. A case of multiple personality. *J. Abnorm. Soc. Psychol.*, 1954, **49**, 135–51.

THIGPEN, C. H., & CLECKLEY, H. M. *Three Faces of Eve.* New York: McGraw-Hill, 1957.

TROTTER, R. J. Will vitamins replace the psychiatrist's couch? *Sci. News*, July 28, 1973, **104**(4), 59–60.

VERBEEK, E. Hysteria. *Psychiatria clinica*, 1973, **6**(2), 104–20.

VOLKAN, V. Regriefing therapy. *Behav. Today*, June 18, 1973, **4**(25), 2.

WEISS, E., & ENGLISH, O. S. *Psychosomatic medicine.* Philadelphia: W. B. Saunders, 1943.

WOLPE, J. *Psychotherapy by reciprocal inhibition.* Stanford: Stanford University Press, 1958.

WOLPE, J. For phobia: a hair of the hound. *Psych. Today*, 1969, **3**, 34–37.

8. Psychosomatic Disorders

ABRAMSON, E. E. A review of behavioral approaches to weight control. *Behav. Res. Ther.*, Nov., 1973, **11**(4), 547–56.

ALEXANDER, F. *Psychosomatic medicine.* New York: Norton, 1950.

ARAUJO, G. D., VAN ARSDEL, P. P., JR., HOLMES, T. H., & DUDLEY, D. L. Life change, coping ability and chronic asthma. *J. Psychosom. Res.*, Dec. 1973, **17**(5), 359–63.

ASTOR, G. From sitting on top of the world to sitting in a wheelchair. *Today's Health*, Mar. 1973, **51**(3), 20–26.

BACHRACH, A. J., ERWIN, W. J., & MOHR, J. P. The control of eating behavior in an anorexic by operant conditioning techniques. In L. P. Ullmann & L. Krasner (Eds.), *Case studies in behavior modification*, New York: Holt, Rinehart & Winston, 1965. Pp. 153–63.

BASEDOW, H. *The Australian aboriginal.* London: Adelaide, 1927.

BLANCHARD, E. B., & YOUNG, L. D. Self-control of cardiac functioning: a promise as yet unfulfilled. *Psychol. Bull.*, Mar. 1973, **79**(3), 145–63.

BLANCHARD, E. B., & YOUNG, L. D. Clinical applications of biofeedback training: a review of evidence. *Arch. Gen. Psychiat.*, May 1974, **30**(5), 573–89.

BLEEKER, E. Many asthma attacks psychological. *Sci. News*, 1968, **93**(17), 406.

BRADY, J. V. Personal communication to F. L. Ruch & P. G. Zimbardo, 1970. In F. L. Ruch & P. G. Zimbardo, *Psychology and life* (8th ed.). Glenview, Ill.: Scott, Foresman, 1971. P. 48.

BRADY, J. V., PORTER, R. W., CONRAD, D. G., & MASON, J. W. Avoidance behavior and the development of gastroduodenal ulcers. *J. Exper. Anal. Behav.*, 1958, **1**, 69–73.

BRESLER, D. Personal correspondence with author re ongoing acupuncture research project at UCLA, funded by NIMH, 1975.

BROWN, B. B. *New mind, new body bio-feedback: new directions for the mind.* New York: Harper & Row, 1974.

BROWN, D. G. Stress as a precipitant factor of eczema. *J. Psychosom. Res.*, Aug. 1972, **16**(5), 321–27.

BROWN, G. W. Life-events and psychiatric illness: some thoughts on methodology and causality. *J. Psychosom. Res.*, Aug. 1972, **16**(5), 311–20.

BUDZYNSKI, T. In M. Schneider, Some cheering news about a very painful subject. *The Sciences*, May 1974, **14**(4), 6–12.

BULATOV, P. K. The higher nervous activity in persons suffering from bronchial asthma. In Problems of interrelationship between psyche and soma in psychoneurology and general medicine. *Institute Bechtereva*, 1963, 317–28. *Inter. J. Psychiat.*, Sept. 1967, p. 245.

CAILLIET, R. *Low back pain syndrome* (2nd ed.). Philadelphia: F. A. Davis Co., 1968.

CANNON, W. B. "Voodoo" death. *American Anthropologist*, 1942, **44**(2), 169–81.

CRISP, A. H. Premorbid factors in adult disorders of weight, with particular reference to primary anorexia nervosa (weight phobia). *J. Psychosom. Med.*, 1970, **14**(1), 1–22.

CROWN, S., & CROWN, J. M. Personality in early rheumatoid disease. *J. Psychosom. Res.*, July 1973, **17**(3), 189–96.

DAVIS, M. H., SAUNDERS, D. R., CREER, T. L., & CHAI, H. Relaxation training facilitated by biofeedback apparatus as a supplemental treatment in bronchial asthma. *J. Psychosom. Res.*, Mar. 1973, **17**(2), 121–28.

DAY, G. The psychosomatic approach to pulmonary tuberculosis. *Lancet*, May 12, 1951, p. 6663.

DUNBAR, F. *Psychosomatic diagnosis.* New York: Harper & Row, 1943.

DUNBAR, F. *Emotions and bodily changes* (4th ed.). New York: Columbia University Press, 1954.

EDWARDS, C. C. What you can do to combat high blood pressure. *Family Health*, Nov. 1973, **5**(11), 24–26.

ELLIS, E. F. Asthma—the demon that thrives on myths. *Today's Health*, 1970, **48**(6), 63–64.

FARIS, R. E. L., & DUNHAM, H. W. *Mental disorders in urban areas.* Chicago: University of Chicago Press, 1939.

FISCHER, H. K., & DLIN, B. M. Psychogenic determination of time of illness or death by anniversary reactions and emotional deadlines. *Psychosomatics,* May/June 1972, **13**(3), 170–73.

FRIED, J. J. Biofeedback: teaching your body to heal itself. *Family Health,* Feb. 1974, **6**(2), 18–21; 31.

GRAHAM, D. T. Some research on psychophysiologic specificity and its relation to psychosomatic disease. In R. Roessler & N. S. Greenfield (Eds.), *Physiological correlates of psychological disorder.* Madison: University of Wisconsin Press, 1962. Pp. 221–38.

GREGORY, I., & ROSEN, E. *Abnormal psychology.* Philadelphia: W. B. Saunders, 1965.

GWYNNE, P. Acupuncture update. *Today's Health,* Jan. 1974, **52**(1), 16–19; 66.

HALBERSTAM, M. Can you make yourself sick? A doctor's report on psychosomatic illness. *Today's Health,* Dec. 1972, **50**(12), 24–29.

HALL, S. M., HALL, R. G., BORDEN, B. T., & HANSON, R. W. Follow-up strategies in the behavioral treatment of overweight. *Behav. Res. Ther.,* June 1975, **13**(2/3), 167–72.

HALMI, K. A., POWERS, P., & CUNNINGHAM, S. Treatment of anorexia nervosa with behavior modification. *Arch. Gen. Psychiat.,* Jan. 1975, **32**(1), 93–96.

HEARST, E. D., CLONINGER, C. R., CREWS, E. L., & CADORET, R. J. Electrosleep therapy: a double-blind trial. *Arch. Gen. Psychiat.,* Apr. 1974, **30**(4), 463–66.

HINKLE, L. E., & WOLFF, H. G. Health and social environment. In A. Leighton, J. Calusen, & R. Wilson (Eds.), *Exploration in social psychiatry.* Garden City, N.Y.: Basic Books, 1957. Pp. 105–37.

HOKANSON, J. E., & BURGESS, M. The effects of three types of aggression on vascular process. *J. Abnorm. Soc. Psychol.,* 1962, **64**, 446–49.

HORAN, J. J., BAKER, S. B., HOFFMAN, A. M., & SHUTE, R. Weight loss through variations in the coverant control paradigm. *J. Cons. Clin. Psychol.,* Feb. 1975, **43**(1), 68–72.

IKEMI, Y., AGO, Y., NAKAGAWA, S., MORI, S., TAKAHASHI, N., SUEMATSU, H., SUGITA, M., & MATSUBARA, H. Psychosomatic mechanism under social changes in Japan. *J. Psychosom. Res.,* Feb. 1974, **18**(1), 15–24.

JACOBS, M. A., SPILKEN, A. Z., NORMAN, M. M., & ANDERSON, L. S. Life stress and respiratory illness. *Psychosom. Med.,* 1970, **32**, 233.

JACOBS, M. A., SPILKEN, A. Z., NORMAN, M. M., & ANDERSON, L. S. Patterns of maladaptive and respiratory illness. *J. Psychosom. Res.,* 1971, **15**(1), 63–72.

JENKINS, C. D. Behavior that triggers heart attacks. *Sci. News,* June 22, 1974, **105**(25), 402.

KAHN, A. U., STAERK, M., & BONK, C. Role of counterconditioning in the treatment of asthma. *J. Psychosom. Res.,* Dec. 1973, **17**(5 & 6), 389–92.

KAHN, R. L. Stress: from 9 to 5. *Psych. Today,* 1969, **3**(4), 34–38.

KIDSON, M. A. Personality and hypertension. *J. Psychosom. Res.,* Jan. 1973, **17**(1), 35–41.

KIDSON, M. A., & JONES, I. Psychiatric disorders among aborigines of the Australian Western Desert. *Arch. Gen. Psychiat.,* 1968, **19**(4), 413–17.

KNAPP, P. H. The asthmatic and his environment. *J. Nerv. Ment. Dis.,* 1969, **149**(2), 133–51.

KUSHNER, M. The operant control of intractable sneezing. In C. D. Spielberger (Ed.), *Contributions to general psychology: selected readings for introductory psychology.* New York: Ronald Press, 1968.

LANG, P. Autonomic control. *Psych. Today,* 1970, **4**(5), 37–41.

LANG, P. J., STROUFE, L. A., & HASTINGS, J. E. Effects of feedback and instructional set on the control of cardiac-rate variability. *J. Exp. Psychol.,* 1967, **75**, 425–31.

LEBEDEV, B. A. Corticovisceral psychosomatics. *Inter. J. Psychiat.,* 1967, **4**(3), 241–46.

LEON, G. R., & CHAMBERLAIN, K. Comparison of daily eating habits and emotional states of overweight persons. *J. Cons. Clin. Psychol.,* Aug. 1973, **41**(1), 108–15.

LEONARD, A. G. *The lower Niger and its tribes.* London: Barnes & Noble, 1906.

LIEBMAN, R., MINUCHIN, S., & BAKER, L. An integrated treatment program for anorexia nervosa. *Amer. J. Psychiat.,* Apr. 1974, **131**(4), 432–36.

LILJEFORS, I., & RAHE, R. H. An identical twin study of psychosocial factors in coronary heart disease in Sweden. *Psychosom. Med.,* Sept./Oct. 1970, **32**(5), 523–42.

LIPTON, E. L., STEINSCHNEIDER, A., & RICHMOND, J. B. Psychophysiologic disorders in children. In L. W. Hoffman & M. L. Hoffman (Eds.), *Review of child development research.* Russell Sage Foundation, 1966. Pp. 169–220.

LUKEMAN, D. Conditioning methods of treating childhood asthma. *J. Child Psychol. Psychiat.,* Apr. 1975, **16**(2), 165–68.

MASON, E. E., & ITO, C. Gastric bypass. *Annals of Surgery,* 1969, **170**, 329–39.

MATARAZZO, R.G., MATARAZZO, J.D., & SASLOW, G. The relationship between medical and psychiatric symptoms. *J. Abnorm. Soc. Psychol.,* 1961, **62**(1), 55.

MAYER, J. Fat babies grow into fat people. *Family Health,* Mar. 1973, **5**(3), 24–27.

MAYS, J. A. High blood pressure, soul food. *Los Angeles Times,* Jan. 16, 1974, II, 7.

MILLER, J. P. Relax! The brain machines are here. *Human Behavior,* Aug. 1974, **3**(8), 16–23.

MILLER, N. E. Learning of visceral and glandular responses. *Science,* Jan. 31, 1969, **163**(3866), 434–45.

MILLER, N. E. Applications of learning and biofeedback to psychiatry and medicine. In A. M. Freedman, H. I. Kaplan, & B. J. Sadock (Eds.), *Comprehensive textbook of psychiatry* (2nd ed.). Baltimore: Williams & Wilkins, 1975.

MURASE, T., & JOHNSON, F. Naikan, Morita, and western psychotherapy. *Arch. Gen. Psychiat.,* July 1974, **31**(1), 121–28.

MURATA, S. New help for the headache that won't go away. *Family Health,* Feb. 1973, **5**(2), 29–31; 55–56.

NECHELES, H. A blood factor in peptic ulcers. *The Sciences,* 1970, **10**(9), 15–16.

NELSON, H. High blood pressure found in third of adults in survey. *Los Angeles Times,* March 27, 1973, II, 1; 3.

OLDS, S. Say it with a stomach ache. *Today's Health,* 1970, **48**(11), 41–43; 88.

PARKES, C. M., BENJAMIN, B., & FITZGERALD, R. G. Broken heart: a statistical study of increased mortality among widowers. *Brit. Med. J.,* Mar. 22, 1969, **1**, 740–43.

PASAMANICK, B. Prevalence and distribution of psychosomatic conditions in an urban population according to social class. *Psychosom. Med.,* 1962, **24**, 352–56.

PAYNE, R. L. Recent life changes and the reporting of psychological states. *J. Psychosom. Res.,* Feb. 1975, **19**(1), 99–103.

PENICK, S., FILION, R., FOX, S., & STUNKARD, A. J. Behavior modification in the treatment of obesity. *Psychosom. Med.,* 1971, **33**(1), 49–55.

PHILIPP, R. L., WILDE, G. J. S., & DAY, J. H. Suggestion and relaxation in asthmatics. *J. Psychosom. Res.*, June 1972, **16**(3), 193–204.

RAHE, R. H., & HOLMES, T. H. Life crisis and major health change. *Psychosom. Med.*, 1966, **28**, 774.

RAHE, R. H., & LIND, E. Psychosocial factors and sudden cardiac death. *J. Psychosom. Res.*, 1971, **15**(1), 19–24.

RAU, J. H., & GREEN, R. S. Compulsive eating: a neurophysiologic approach to certain eating disorders. *Comprehensive Psychiatry*, May-June 1975, **16**(3), 223–32.

RAWITCH, R. Oscar winner dies on day he predicted. *Los Angeles Times*, July 5, 1973, II, 2.

REES, L. The importance of psychological, allergic and infective factors in childhood asthma. *J. Psychosom. Res.*, 1964, **7**, 253–62.

RENNIE, T. A. C., & SROLE, L. Social class prevalence and distribution of psychosomatic conditions in an urban population. *Psychosom. Med.*, 1956, **18**, 449–56.

ROBINSON, H., KIRK, R. F., JR., FRYE, R. F., & ROBERTSON, J. T. A psychological study of patients with rheumatoid arthritis and other painful diseases. *J. Psychosom. Res.*, Feb. 1972, **16**(1), 53–56.

ROMO, M., SILTANEN, P., THEORELL, T., & RAHE, R. H. Work behavior, time urgency, and life dissatisfactions in subjects with myocardial infarction: a cross-cultural study. *J. Psychosom. Res.*, Feb. 1974, **18**(1), 1–8.

ROSENTHAL, S. H. Electrosleep: a double-bind clinical study. *Biological Psychiatry*, Apr. 1972, **4**(2), 179–85.

SCHACHTER, S. Eat, eat. *Psych. Today*, 1971, 4(11), 44–47; 78–79.

SCHWAB, J. J. Comprehensive medicine and the concurrence of physical and mental illness. *Psychosomatics*, 1970, **11**(6), 591–95.

SCHWAB, J. J., MC GINNIS, N. H., NORRIS, L. B., & SCHWAB, R. B. Psychosomatic medicine and the contemporary social scene. *Amer. J. Psychiat.*, 1970, **126**(11), 108–18.

SCIENCE NEWS. Hypertension and hypnotism. Oct. 6, 1973, **104**(14), 217.

SEE, C. Anorexia nervosa is starvation by choice. *Today's Health*, May 1975, **53**(5), 46–50.

SENAY, E. C., & REDLICH, F. C. Cultural and social factors in neuroses and psychosomatic illnesses. *Social Psychiatry*, 1968, 3(3), 89–97.

SHELLEY, W. B., & EDSON, L. There's more to skin problems than meets the eye. *Family Health*, Dec. 1973, 5(12), 26–27; 53.

SHOEMAKER, J. E., & TASTO, D. L. The effects of muscle relaxation on blood pressure of essential hypertensives. *Behav. Res. Ther.*, Feb. 1975, **13**(1), 29–43.

STEIN, J. *Neurosis in contemporary society: process and treatment.* Belmont, Calif.: Brooks/Cole, 1970.

STERNBACH, R. A. Psychosomatic diseases. In G. D. Shean (Ed.), *Studies in abnormal behavior.* Chicago: Rand McNally, 1971. Pp. 136–54.

STUART, R. B. A three-dimensional program for the treatment of obesity. *Behav. Res. Ther.*, 1971, **9**, 177–86.

SUBACK-SHARPE, G. What acupuncture can – and cannot – do. *Family Health*, Sept. 1973, 5(9), 18–21; 51–52.

SZYRNSKI, V. Anorexia nervosa and psychotherapy. *Amer. J. Psychother.*, Oct. 1973, **27**(4), 492–505.

TASTO, D. L., & HINKLE, J. E. Muscle relaxation treatment for tension headaches. *Behav. Res. Ther.*, Aug. 1973, **11**(3), 247–49.

THIEL, H., PARKER, D., & BRUCE, T. A. Stress factors and the risk of myocardial infarction. *J. Psychosom. Res.*, Jan. 1973, **17**(1), 43–57.

TIME. From Shocks to stop sneezes. *Time*, (June 17, 1966) p. 72. Reprinted by permission from *Time*, The Weekly Newsmagazine; Copyright Time Inc.

TURNBULL, J. W. Asthma conceived as a learned response. *J. Psychosom. Res.*, 1962, **6**, 59–70.

WARREN, W. A study of anorexia nervosa in young girls. *J. Child Psychol. Psychiat.*, 1968, 9(1), 27–40.

WATSON, A. A. Death by cursing – a problem for forensic psychiatry. *Medicine, Science and the Law*, July 1973, **13**(3), 192–94.

WEISMAN, A. Psychosocial death. *Psych. Today*, Nov. 1972, **6**(6), 77–78; 83–84; 86.

WEITZMAN, E. D., & LUCE, G. Biological rhythms: indices of pain, adrenal hormones, sleep, and sleep reversal. In NIMH, *Behavioral sciences and mental health.* Washington, D.C.: Govt. Printing Office, 1970.

WOLF, S., & WOLFF, H. G. *Human gastric functions.* New York: Oxford University Press, 1947.

WOLFF, H. G. *Headache and other head pain.* Cambridge: Oxford University Press, 1948.

WOLFF, H. G. Life stress and cardiovascular disorders. *Circulation*, 1950, **1**, 187–203.

WOLFF, H. G. Life stress and bodily disease. In A. Weider (Ed.), *Contributions toward medical psychology* (Vol. 1). New York: Ronald Press, 1953.

WOLPE, J. For phobia: a hair of the hound. *Psych. Today*, 1969, 3(1), 34–37.

9. Schizophrenia and Paranoia

ALLEN, M. G. Psychiatry in the United States and the USSR: a comparison. *Amer. J. Psychiat.*, Dec. 1973, **130**(12), 1333–37.

ANTHONY, E. J. The developmental precursors of adult schizophrenia. In D. Rosenthal & S. Kety (Eds.), *The transmission of schizophrenia.* Elmsford, N.Y.: Pergamon, 1968.

ARIETI, S. An overview of schizophrenia from a predominantly psychological approach. *Amer. J. Psychiat.*, Mar. 1974, **131**(3), 241–49.

AYLLON, T., & AZRIN, N. H. The measurement and reinforcement of behavior of psychotics. *J. Exper. Anal. Behav.*, 1965, **8**, 357–84.

BANDURA, A. *Principles of behavior modification.* New York: Holt, Rinehart & Winston, 1969.

BANNISTER, D. Schizophrenia: carnival mirror of coherence. *Psych. Today*, 1971, 4(8), 66–69; 84.

BATESON, G. Cultural problems posed by a study of schizophrenic process. In A. Auerback (Ed.), *Schizophrenia: an integrated approach.* New York: Ronald Press, 1959.

BATESON, G. Minimal requirements for a theory of schizophrenia. *Arch. Gen. Psychiat.*, 1960, **2**, 477–91.

BENDER, L. The life course of children with schizophrenia. *Amer. J. Psychiat.*, July 1973, **130**(7), 783–86.

BETTELHEIM, B. *Truants from life: the rehabilitation of emotionally disturbed children.* New York: Free Press, 1955.

BLEULER, M. The offspring of schizophrenics. *Schizophrenia Bulletin*, NIMH, Spring 1974, **8**, 93–107.

BORN, W. Artistic behavior of the mentally deranged; and Great Artists who suffered from mental disorders. *Ciba Symposia*, 1946, **8**, 207–16; 225–32.

BOWEN, M. Family relationships in schizophrenia. In A. Auerback (Ed.), *Schizophrenia: an integrated approach.* New York: Ronald Press, 1959.

BOWEN, M. A family concept of schizophrenia. In D. D. Jackson (Ed.), *The etiology of schizophrenia.* New York: Basic Books, 1960.

BOWERS, M., JR. The onset of psychosis—A diary account. *Psychiatry,* 1965, **28**, 346–58. Permission granted by author and The William Alanson White Psychiatric Foundation.

BRODEY, W. M. Some family operations and schizophrenia. *Arch. Gen. Psychiat.,* 1959, **1**, 379–402.

BROEN, W. E., JR. *Schizophrenia: research and theory.* New York: Academic Press, 1968.

BROWN, G. W. Life-events and psychiatric illness: some thoughts on methodology and causality. *J. Psychosom. Res.,* Aug. 1972, **16**(5), 311–20.

BUBER, M. Distance and relation. *Psychiatry,* 1957, **20**, 97–104.

CAFFEY, E. M., GALBRECHT, C. R., & KLETT, C. J. Brief hospitalization and aftercare in the treatment of schizophrenia. *Arch. Gen. Psychiat.,* 1971, **21**(1), 81–86.

CAMERON, N. Paranoid conditions and paranoia. In S. Arieti (Ed.), *American handbook of psychiatry.* New York: Basic Books, 1959.

CAMERON, N., & MARGARET, A. Experimental studies in thinking. I. Scattered speech in the responses of normal subjects to incomplete sentences. *J. Exper. Psychol.,* 1949, **39**(5), 617–27.

CAMERON, N., & MARGARET, A. *Behavior pathology.* Boston: Houghton Mifflin, 1951.

CARLSON, C. G., HERSEN, M., & EISLER, R. M. Token economy programs in the treatment of hospitalized adult psychiatric patients. *Ment. Hlth. Dig.,* Dec. 1972, **4**(12), 21–27.

CAROTHERS, J. C. The African mind in health and disease. In *A study in ethnopsychiatry.* Geneva: World Health Organization, 1953, No. 17.

CAROTHERS, J. C. Culture, psychiatry, and the written word. *Psychiatry,* 1959, **22**, 307–20.

CARPENTER, W. T., STRAUSS, J. S., & BARTKO, J. J. Flexible system for the diagnosis of schizophrenia: report from the WHO International Pilot Study of Schizophrenia. *Science,* Dec. 21, 1973, **182**(4118), 1275–77.

COHEN, S. M., ALLEN, M. G., POLLIN, W., & HRUBEC, Z. Relationship of schizo-affective psychosis to manic depressive psychosis and schizophrenia. *Arch. Gen. Psychiat.,* June 1972, **26**(6), 539–46.

COPELAND, J. Aspects of mental illness in West African students. *Soc. Psychiat.,* 1968, **3**(1), 7–13.

CROWLEY, T. J. Token programs in an acute psychiatric hospital. *Amer. J. Psychiat.,* May 1975, **132**(5), 523–28.

CURRY, A. E. The world of a schizophrenic woman. Reprinted from *The Psychoanalytic Review,* Vol. **49**, No. 1, 1962, through the courtesy of the Editors and the Publisher, National Psychological Association for Psychoanalysis, New York, N.Y.

DEARING, G. P. Russians support genetic basis for schizophrenia. *Psychiatric News,* 1969, **4**(8), 18.

DIAMOND, B. L. Sirhan B. Sirhan: a conversation with T. George Harris. *Psych. Today,* 1969, **3**(4), 48–56.

DRIEMEN, P. M., & MINARD, J. Preleave planning: effect upon rehabilitation. *Arch. Gen. Psychiat.,* 1971, **24**(1), 87–90.

EISENBERG, L. The interaction of biological and experiential factors in schizophrenia. In D. Rosenthal & S. S. Kety (Eds.), *The transmission of schizophrenia.* Elmsford, N.Y.: Perga-

mon Press, 1968. Pp. 403–9.

ELLINWOOD, E. H., SUDILOVSKY, A., & NELSON, L. M. Evolving behavior in the clinical and experimental amphetamine (model) psychosis. *Amer. J. Psychiat.,* Oct. 1973, **130**(10), 1088–93.

ENDERS, L. J., & FLINN, D. E. Clinical problems in aviation medicine: Schizophrenic reaction, paranoid type. *Aerospace Medicine,* 1962, **33**, 730–32. Reprinted by permission.

FEINSILVER, D. Communication in families of schizophrenic patients. *Arch. Gen. Psychiat.,* 1970, **22**(2), 143–48.

FENZ, W. D., & VELNER, J. Physiological concomitants of behavior indexes in schizophrenia. *J. Abnorm. Psychol.,* 1970, **76**(1), 27–35.

FIELD, M. J. *Search for security: an ethnopsychiatric study of rural Ghana.* Evanston: Northwestern University Press, 1960.

FLECK, S. Family dynamics and origin of schizophrenia. *Psychosomatic Medicine,* 1960, **22**, 337–39.

FORGUS, R. H., & DE WOLFE, A. S. Coding of cognitive input in delusional patients. *J. Abnorm. Psychol.,* June 1974, **83**(3), 278–84.

FREEMAN, T. On the psychopathology of schizophrenia. *J. Ment. Sci.,* 1960, **106**, 925–37.

GALTON, F. *Inquiries into human faculty and its development.* London: Macmillan, 1883.

GOLDSTEIN, M. J., JUDD, L. K., RODNICK, E. H., & LA POLLA, A. Psychophysiological and behavioral effects of phenothiazine administration in acute schizophrenics as a function of premorbid states. *J. Psychiat. Res.,* 1969, **6**, 271–87.

GOLDSTEIN, M. J., RODNICK, E. H., & JUDD, L. K. Cited in Schizoid therapy. *Newsweek,* June 7, 1971, 77–78.

GOTTESMAN, I. I., & SHIELDS, J. *Schizophrenia and genetics.* New York: Academic Press, 1972.

GRALNICK, A. Folie a deux—the psychosis of association: a review of 103 cases and the entire English literature, with case presentations. *Psychiat. Quart.,* 1942, **14**, 230–63.

GRANT, V. W. Paranoid dynamics: a case study. Reprinted from *The American Journal of Psychiatry,* volume **113**, pages 143–48, 1956. Copyright 1956, the American Psychiatric Association.

GREEN, H. *I never promised you a rose garden.* New York: Holt, Rinehart & Winston, 1964.

GRINSPOON, L., EWALT, J. R., & SHADER, R. Psychotherapy and pharmacotherapy in chronic schizophrenia. *Amer. J. Psychiat.,* 1968, **124**(12), 1645–52.

GROSS, G., & HUBER, G. Zur prognose der schizophenier. *Psychiatria Clinica,* 1973, **6**(1), 1–16.

GRUNEBAUM, H., & PERLMAN, M. S. Paranoia and naivete. *Arch. Gen. Psychiat.,* Jan. 1973, **28**(1), 30–32.

GRUZELIER, J. H., LYKKEN, D. T., & VENABLES, P. H. Schizophrenia and arousal revisited. *Arch. Gen. Psychiat.,* May 1972, **26**(5), 427–32.

HAWK, A. B., CARPENTER, W. T., & STRAUSS, J. S. Diagnostic criteria and five-year outcome in schizophrenia. *Arch. Gen. Psychiat.,* Mar. 1975, **32**(3), 343–47.

HEATH, R. G. GUSCHWAN, A. F., & COFFEY, J. W. Relation of taraxein to schizophrenia. *Dis. Nerv. Sys.,* June 1970, **31**(6), 391–95.

HEATH, R. G., KRUPP, I. M., BYERS, L. W., & LILJEKVIST, J. I. Schizophrenia as an immunologic disorder. *Arch. Gen. Psychiat.,* 1967, **16**(1), 1–33.

HEATH, R. G., MARTENS, S., LEACH, B. E., COHEN, M., & ANGEL, C. Effect on behavior in humans with the administration of taraxein. *Amer. J. Psychiat.*, 1957, **114**, 14–24.

HEATH, R. G., MARTENS, S., LEACH, B. E., COHEN, M., & FEIGLEY, C. A. Behavioral changes in nonpsychotic volunteers following the administration of taraxein, the substance obtained from serum of schizophrenic patients. *Amer. J. Psychiat.*, 1958, **114**, 917–20.

HESTON, L. Psychiatric disorders in foster home reared children of schizophrenic mothers. *Brit. J. Psychiat.*, 1966, **112**, 819–25.

HESTON, L. L. The genetics of schizophrenic disease. *Science*, 1970, **167**, 249–56.

HIMWICH, H. E. Study backs biochemical etiology in schizophrenia. *Psychiatric News*, 1970, **5**(10), 15.

HOFFMAN, J. L. Psychotic visitors to government offices in the national capital. *Amer. J. Psychiat.*, 1943, **99**, 571–75.

HOGARTY, G. E., & GOLDBERG, S. C. Drug and sociotherapy in the aftercare of schizophrenic patients: one-year relapse rates. *Arch. Gen. Psychiat.*, Jan. 1973, **28**(1), 54–64.

HOGARTY, G. E., GOLDBERG, S. C., SCHOOLER, N. R., & ULRICH, R. F. Drug and sociotherapy in the aftercare of schizophrenic patients: two-year relapse rates. *Arch. Gen. Psychiat.*, Nov. 1974, **31**(5), 603–8.

HORWITT, M. K. Fact and artifact in the biology of schizophrenia. *Science*, 1956, **124**(3), 429–30.

JACOB, T. Family interaction in disturbed and normal families: a methodological and substantive review. *Psychol. Bull.*, Jan. 1975, **82**(1), 33–65.

KALLMANN, F. J. *Heredity in health and mental disorder.* New York: Norton, 1953.

KALLMANN, F. J. The use of genetics in psychiatry. *J. Ment. Sci.*, 1958, **104**, 542–49.

KAUFMAN, I., FRANK, T., HEIMS, L., HERRICK, J., REISER, D., & WILLER, L. Treatment implications of a new classification of parents of schizophrenic children. *Amer. J. Psychiat.*, 1960, **116**, 920–24.

KETY, S. S. From rationalization to reason. *Amer. J. Psychiat.*, Sept. 1974, **131**(9), 957–63.

KINZIE, J. D., & BOLTON, J. M. Psychiatry with the aborigines of West Malaysia. *Amer. J. Psychiat.*, July 1973, **130**(7), 769–73.

KRINGLEN, E. *Heredity and environment in the functional psychosis: an epidemiological-clinical twin study.* Oslo: Universitsforlaget, 1967.

KURIANSKY, J. B., DEMING, W. E., & GURLAND, B. J. On trends in the diagnosis of schizophrenia. *Amer. J. Psychiat.*, Apr. 1974, **131**(4), 402–7.

LAING, R. D. Schizophrenic split. *Time*, Feb. 3, 1967, 56.

LAING, R. D. *The divided self.* New York: Pantheon, 1969.

LAING, R. D. Quoted in J. S. Gordon, Who is mad? Who is sane? R. D. Laing: in search of a new psychiatry. *Atlantic*, 1971, **227**(1), 50–66.

LAING, R. D., & ESTERSON, A. *Sanity, madness, and the family.* London: Tavistock, 1964.

LEMERT, E. M. Paranoia and the dynamics of exclusion. *Sociometry*, 1962, **25**, 2–25.

LEVY, L., & ROWITZ, L. *The ecology of mental disorders.* New York: Behavioral Publications, 1972.

LEWINSON, T. S. Dynamic disturbances in the handwriting of psychotics; with reference to schizophrenic, paranoid, and manic-depressive psychoses. Reprinted from *The American Journal of Psychiatry*, volume **97**, pages 102–35, 1940.

LIDZ, T. The family, language, and the transmission of schizophrenia. In D. Rosenthal & S. S. Kety (Eds.), *The transmission of schizophrenia.* Elmsford, N.Y.: Pergamon Press, 1968. Pp. 175–84.

LIDZ, T. The influence of family studies on the treatment of schizophrenia. *Psychiatry*, Aug. 1969, **32**(3), 237–51.

LIDZ, T. *The origin and treatment of schizophrenoid disorders.* New York: Basic Books, 1973.

LIDZ, T., CORNELISON, A. R., FLECK, S., & TERRY, D. Intrafamilial environment of the schizophrenic patient. I. The father. *Psychiatry*, 1957, **20**, 329–42.

LIDZ, T., CORNELISON, A. R., TERRY, D., & FLECK, S. Irrationality as a family tradition. *Arch. Neurol. Psychiat.*, 1958, **79**, 305–16.

LIDZ, T., FLECK, S., ALANEN, Y. O., & CORNELISON, A. R. Schizophrenic patients and their siblings. *Psychiatry*, 1963, **26**, 1–18.

MANDELL, A. J., SEGAL, D. S., KUCZENSKI, R. T., & KNAPP, S. The search for the schizococcus. *Psych. Today*, Oct. 1972, **6**(5), 68–72.

MC GHIE, A., & CHAPMAN, J. Disorders of attention and perception in early schizophrenia. *British Journal of Medical Psychology*, 1961, **34**, 103–16. Reprinted by permission of the authors and the British Psychological Society.

MENNINGER, K. Diagnosis and treatment of schizophrenia. Reprinted with permission from the *Bulletin of the Menninger Clinic*, vol. **12**, 101–04, copyright 1948 by The Menninger Foundation.

MILLER, C. Worlds that fail. *Trans-action*, 1966, **4**(2), 36–41.

MILNER, K. O. The environment as a factor in the aetiology of criminal paranoia. *J. Ment. Sci.*, 1949, **95**, 124–32.

MORRISON, J. R. Catatonia: retarded and excited types. *Arch. Gen. Psychiat.*, Jan. 1973, **28**(1), 39–41.

MORRISON, J. R. Catatonia: prediction of outcome. *Comprehensive Psychiatry*, July/Aug. 1974, **15**(4), 317–24.

MURPHY, H. B. Cultural factors in the genesis of schizophrenia. In D. Rosenthal & S. S. Kety (Eds.), *The transmission of schizophrenia.* Elmsford, N.Y.: Pergamon Press, 1968. Pp. 137–52.

PAUL, G. L. Chronic mental patients: current status – future directions. *Psychol. Bull.*, 1969, **71**, 81–94.

PAVLOV, I. P. *Conditioned reflexes and psychiatry.* (Trans. & ed. W. H. Gant.) New York: Inter. Publ., 1941.

RATNAVALE, D. N. Psychiatry in Shanghai, China: observations in 1973. *Amer. J. Psychiat.*, Oct. 1973, **130**(10), 1082–87.

RIEDER, R. O. The offspring of schizophrenic parents: a review. *J. Nerv. Ment. Dis.*, Sept. 1973, **157**(3), 179–90.

RIEDER, R. O., ROSENTHAL, D., WENDER, P., & BLUMENTHAL, H. The offspring of schizophrenics: fetal and neonatal deaths. *Arch. Gen. Psychiat.*, Feb. 1975, **32**(2), 200–211.

ROFF, J. D. Adolescent schizophrenia: variables related to differences in long-term adult outcome. *J. Cons. Clin. Psychol.*, Apr. 1974, **42**(2), 180–83.

ROLF, J. E., & HARIG, P. T. Etiological research in schizophrenia and the rationale for primary intervention. *Amer. J. Orthopsychiat.*, July 1974, **44**(4), 538–54.

ROSEN, H., & KIENE, H. E. Paranoia and paranoiac reaction types. *Diseases of the Nervous System*, 1946, **7**, 330–37. Reprinted by permission of the Physicians Postgraduate Press.

ROSENTHAL, D. *Genetic theory and abnormal behavior.* New York: McGraw-Hill, 1970.

ROSENTHAL, D., WENDER, P. H., KETY, S. S., WELNER, J., & SCHULSINGER, F. The adopted-away offspring of schizophrenics. *Amer. J. Psychiat.*, Sept. 1971, **128**(3), 307–11.

SACKS, M. H., CARPENTER, W. T., & STRAUSS, J. S. Recovery from delusions: three phases documented by patient's interpretation of research procedures. *Arch. Gen. Psychiat.*, Jan. 1974, **30**(1), 117–20.

SARVIS, M. A. Paranoid reactions: perceptual distortion as an etiological agent. *Arch. Gen. Psychiat.*, 1962, **6**, 157–62.

SCHWARTZ, D. A. A re-view of the "paranoid" concept. *Gen. Psychiat.*, 1963, **8**, 349–61.

SCHWARTZ, J., & BELLACK, A. S. A comparison of a token economy with standard inpatient treatment. *J. Cons. Clin. Psychol.*, Feb. 1975, **43**(1), 107–8.

SHAKOW, D. On doing research in schizophrenia. *Arch. Gen. Psychiat.*, 1969, **20**(6), 618–42.

SINGER, M., & WYNNE, L. C. Differentiating characteristics of the parents of childhood schizophrenics, childhood neurotics and young adult schizophrenics. *Amer. J. Psychiat.*, 1963, **120**, 234–43.

SINGER, M., & WYNNE, L. C. Thought disorder and family relations of schizophrenics. III. Methodology using projective techniques. *Arch. Gen. Psychiat.*, 1965, **12**, 182–200. [a]

SINGER, M., & WYNNE, L. C. Thought disorder and family relations of schizophrenics. IV. Results and implications. *Arch. Gen. Psychiat.*, 1965, **12**, 201–12. [b]

SOBEL, D. E. Infant mortality and malformations in children of schizophrenic women. *Psychiatric Quart.*, 1961, **35**, 60–64.

SOMMER, R., & OSMOND, H. The schizophrenic no-society. *Psychiatry*, 1962, **25**, 244–55.

SONI, S. D., & ROCKLEY, G. J. Socio-cultural substrates of folie à deux. *Brit. J. Psychiat.*, Sept. 1974, **125**(9), 230–35.

STABENAU, J. R., TUPIN, J., WERNER, M., & POLLIN, W. A comparative study of families of schizophrenics, delinquents, and normals. *Psychiatry*, 1965, **28**, 45–59.

STEPHENS, J. H., ASTRUP, C., & MANGRUM, J. C. Prognostic factors in recovered and deteriorated schizophrenics. *Amer. J. Psychiat.*, 1966, **122**(10), 1116–21.

STRAKER, M. Schizophrenia and psychiatric diagnosis. *Amer. J. Psychiat.*, June 6, 1974, **131**(6), 693–94.

STRAUSS, J. S. Hallucinations and delusions as points on continua function. *Arch. Gen. Psychiat.*, 1969, **21**(5), 581–86.

SWANSON, D. W., BOHNERT, P. J., & SMITH, J. A. *The paranoid.* Boston: Little, Brown, 1970.

TANNA, V. L. Paranoid states: a selected review. *Comprehensive Psychiatry*, Nov./Dec. 1974, **15**(6), 453–70.

TORREY, E. F. Is schizophrenia universal? An open question. *Schizophrenia Bulletin*, Winter 1973, **7**, 53–59.

TSUANG, M. T., FOWLER, R. C., CADORET, R. J., & MONNELLY, E. Schizophrenia among first-degree relatives of paranoid and nonparanoid schizophrenics. *Comprehensive Psychiatry*, July/Aug. 1974, **15**(4), 295–302.

TURNER, R., DOPKEEN, L., & LABRECHE, G. Marital status and schizophrenia: a study of incidence and outcome. *J. Abnorm. Psychol.*, 1970, **76**(1), 110–16.

WENDER, P. H. In R. Cancro, Genetics of schizophrenia: some misconceptions clarified. *Roche Report, Frontiers of Psychiatry*, Jan. 1, 1972, **2**(4), 1–2; 8.

WENDER, P. H., ROSENTHAL, D., KETY, S. S., SCHULSINGER, F., & WELNER, J. Cross-fostering: a research strategy for clarifying the role of genetic and experiential factors in the etiology of schizophrenia. *Arch. Gen. Psychiat.*, Jan. 1974, **30**(1), 121–28.

WILSON, J. R. *The mind.* New York: Time-Life Inc., 1969.

WINKLER, R. C. Management of chronic psychiatric patients by a token reinforcement system. *J. Appl. Beh. Anal.*, Spring 1970, **3**(1), 47–55.

WINKLER, R. C. A reply to Fethke's comment on "the relevance of economic theory and technology to token reinforcement systems." *Behav. Res. Ther.*, May 1973, **11**(2), 223–24.

WYNNE, L. C., RYCKOFF, I. M., DAY, J., & HIRSCH, S. I. Pseudo-mutuality in the family relations of schizophrenia. *Psychiatry*, 1958, **21**, 205–20.

YARDEN, P. E. Observations on suicide in chronic schizophrenics. *Comprehensive Psychiatry*, July/Aug. 1974, **15**(4), 325–33.

YERBURY, E. C., & NEWELL, N. Genetic and environmental factors in psychoses of children. *Amer. J. Psychiat.*, 1943, **100**, 599–605.

YOLLES, S. F. Quote from "Unraveling the mystery of schizophrenia" by S. F. Yolles from *Today's Health* (April 1967), **45**, 42; 82–84, published by the American Medical Association.

ZIFERSTEIN, I. Speaking prose without knowing it. *Inter. J. Psychiat.*, 1968, **6**(5), 366–70.

10. Major Affective Disorders

ABRAMS, R., & TAYLOR, M. A. Unipolar mania: a preliminary report. *Arch. Gen. Psychiat.*, Apr. 1974, **30**(4), 441–43.

AKISKAL, H. S., & MCKINNEY, W. T., JR., Overview of recent research in depression: integration of ten conceptual models into a comprehensive clinical frame. *Arch. Gen. Psychiat.*, Mar. 1975, **32**(3), 285–305.

ALLEN, M. G., COHEN, S., POLLIN, W., & GREENSPAN, S. I. Affective illness in veteran twins: a diagnostic review. *Amer. J. Psychiat.*, Nov. 1974, **131**(11), 1234–39.

AMERICAN PSYCHIATRIC ASSOCIATION. *Diagnostic and statistical manual of mental disorders* (2nd ed.). Washington, D.C.: APA, 1968.

ARIETI, S. Manic-depressive psychosis. In S. Arieti (Ed.), *American handbook of psychiatry.* New York: Basic Books, 1959. Pp. 419–54.

BAGLEY, C. Occupational class and symptoms of depression. *Social Science and Medicine*, May 1973, **7**(5), 327–40.

BECK, A. T. Cognition, affect, and psychopathology. *Arch. Gen. Psychiat.*, June 1971, **24**(6), 495–500.

BECKER, J. *Depression: theory and research.* New York: Halstead Press, 1974.

BECKER, J., & ALTROCCHI, J. Peer conformity and achievement in female manic-depressives. *J. Abnorm. Psychol.*, 1968, **73**(6), 585–89.

BIBRING, E. The mechanisma of depression. In P. Greenacre (Ed.), *Affective disorders.* New York: International University Press, 1953.

BRATFOS, O., & HAUG, J. O. The course of manic-depressive psychosis: a follow-up investigation of 215 patients. *Acta Psychiatr. Scandin.*, 1968, **44**(1), 89–112.

BRISCOE, C. W., & SMITH, J. B. Depression and marital turmoil. *Arch. Gen. Psychiat.*, Dec. 1973, **29**(6), 811–17.

BRISCOE, C. W., SMITH, J. B., ROBINS, E., MARTEN, S., & GASKIN, F. Divorce and psychiatric illness. *Arch. Gen. Psychiat.*, July 1973, **29**(1), 119–25.

BROWN, B. Depression roundup. *Behav. Today*, Apr. 29, 1974, **5**(17), 117.

BROWN, G. W. Life-events and psychiatric illness: some thoughts on methodology and causality. *J. Psychosom. Res.*, Aug. 1972, **16**(5), 311–20.

BUNNEY, W. E., JR., MURPHY, D. L., GOODWIN, F. K., & BORGE, G. F.

The "switch process" in manic-depressive illness: a systematic study of sequential behavioral changes. *Arch. Gen. Psychiat.*, Sept. 1972, **27**(3), 295–302.

BUNNEY, W. E., JR., PAUL, M. I., & CRAMER, H. Biological trigger of "switch" from depression to mania may be CAMP. *Roche Reports*, 1971, **1**(6), 1–2, 8. Reprinted by permission of Dr. W. E. Bunney, Jr., and Dr. M. I. Paul.

CAINE, L. *Widow*. New York: Morrow, 1974.

CARLSON, G., & GOODWIN, F. K. The stages of mania: a longitudinal analysis of the manic episode. *Arch. Gen. Psychiat.*, Feb. 1973, **28**(2), 221–28.

CAROTHERS, J. C. A study of mental derangement in Africans, and an attempt to explain its peculiarities, more especially in relation to the African attitude of life. *J. Ment. Sci.*, 1947, **93**, 548–97.

CAROTHERS, J. C. Frontal lobe function and the African. *J. Ment. Sci.*, 1951, **97**, 12–48.

CAROTHERS, J. C. The African mind in health and disease. In *A study in ethnopsychiatry*. Geneva: World Health Organization, 1953, No. 17.

CAROTHERS, J. C. Culture, psychiatry, and the written word. *Psychiatry*, 1959, **22**, 307–20.

CHODOFF, P. The depressive personality: a critical review. *Arch. Gen. Psychiat.*, Nov. 1972, **27**(2), 666–73.

COLE, J. O. Depression. *Amer. J. Psychiat.*, Feb. 1974, **131**(2), 204–5.

ENGEL, G. L. Anxiety and depression withdrawal: the primary affects of unpleasure. *Inter. J. Psychoanal.*, 1962, **43**, 89–97.

ENGLISH, O., & FINCH, S. M. *Introduction to psychiatry*. New York: Norton, 1954.

FERSTER, C. B. A functional analysis of depression. *Amer. Psychologist*, Oct. 1973, **28**(10), 857–70.

FIELD, M. J. *Search for security: An ethnopsychiatric study of rural Ghana*. Evanston: Northwestern University Press, 1960.

GOLDSMITH, W., & CRETEKOS, C. Unhappy Odysseys: Psychiatric hospitalization among Vietnam returnees. *Arch. Gen. Psychiat.*, 1969, **20**, 78–83.

GOODWIN, F. K., & BUNNEY, W. E. A psychobiological approach to affective illness. *Psychiatric Annals*, Feb. 1973, **3**(2), 19–53.

GREGORY, I. *Psychiatry, biological and social*. Philadelphia: W. B. Saunders, 1961.

GRINKER, R. An essay on schizophrenia and science. *Arch. Gen. Psychiat.*, 1969, **20**(1), 1–24.

HARE, E. H. The changing content of psychiatric illness. *J. Psychosom. Res.*, Aug. 1974, **18**(4), 283–89.

HARTMANN, E. Longitudinal studies of sleep and dream patterns in manic-depressive patients. *Arch. Gen. Psychiat.*, 1968, **19**, 312–29.

HAURI, P. Depression. *Behav. Today*, Apr. 29, 1974, **5**(17), 123.

HAURI, P., CHERNIK, D., HAWKINS, D., & MENDELS, J. Sleep of depressed patients in remission. *Arch. Gen. Psychiat.*, Sept. 1974, **31**(3), 386–91.

HELZER, J. E., & WINOKUR, G. A family interview study of male manic depressives. *Arch. Gen. Psychiat.*, July 1974, **31**(1), 73–77.

HENDERSON, D., & GILLESPIE, R. D. *A textbook of psychiatry for students and practitioners*. New York: Oxford University Press, 1950.

HILL, D. Depression: disease, reactions, or posture? *Amer. J. Psychiat.*, 1968, **125**(4), 445–57.

HIROTO, D. S., & SELIGMAN, M. E. P. Generality of learned helplessness in man. *J. Pers. Soc. Psychol.* Feb. 1975, **31**(2), 311–27.

HURWITZ, T. D. Electroconvulsive therapy: a review. *Comprehensive Psychiatry*, July/Aug. 1974, **15**(4), 303–14.

IANZITO, B. M., CADORET, R. J., & PUGH, D. D. Thought disorder in depression. *Amer. J. Psychiat.*, June 1974, **131**(6), 703–6.

JACO, E. G. *The social epidemiology of mental disorders*. New York: Russell Sage Foundation, 1960.

JANOWSKY, D. S., EL-YOUSEF, M. K., & DAVIS, J. M. Interpersonal maneuvers of manic patients. *Amer. J. Psychiat.*, Mar. 1974, **131**(3), 250–55.

JANOWSKY, D. S., LEFF, M., & EPSTEIN, R. Playing the manic game. *Arch. Gen. Psychiat.*, 1970, **22**, 252–61.

JENNER, F. A., GJESSING, L. R., COX, J. R., DAVIES-JONES, A., & HULLIN, R. P. A manic-depressive psychotic with a 48 hour cycle. *Brit. J. Psychiat.*, 1967, **113**(501), 859–910.

JOHNSON, G. Antidepressant effect of lithium. *Comprehensive Psychiatry*, Jan./Feb. 1974, **15**(1), 43–47.

JOHNSON, W. B. Euphoric and depressed moods in normal subjects. I. *Charact. & Pers.*, 1937, **6**, 212–16.

KALLMANN, F. J. The use of genetics in psychiatry. *J. Ment. Sci.*, 1958, **104**, 542–49.

KARNOSH, L. J. (with collaboration of Zucker, E. M.). *Handbook of psychiatry*. St. Louis: Mosby, 1945. Reprinted by permission of the C. V. Mosby Co.

KIDSON, M., & JONES, I. Psychiatric disorders among aborigines of the Australian Western Desert. *Arch. Gen. Psychiat.*, 1968, **19**, 413–22.

KILLIAN, L. M., & BLOOMBERG, S. "The patient's narrative" from Rebirth in a therapeutic community: a case study. *Psychiatry*, Feb. 1975, **38**(1), 39–54. Copyright 1975 The William Alanson White Psychiatric Foundation, Inc. Reprinted by permission of the author and The William Alanson White Psychiatric Foundation, Inc.

KRAEPELIN, E. *Clinical psychiatry* (6th ed.). New York: Macmillan, 1937. Originally published 1899.

LAZARUS, A. P. Learning theory in the treatment of depression. *Behav. Res. Ther.*, 1968, **8**, 83–89.

LEFF, M. J., ROATCH, J. F., & BUNNEY, W. E., JR. Environmental factors preceding the onset of severe depressions. *Psychiatry*, 1970, **33**(3), 298–311.

LEHMANN, H. E. Clinical perspectives on anti-depressant therapy. *Amer. J. Psychiat.*, May 1968, **124**(11, Suppl.), 12–21.

LEWINSOHN, P. M. A behavioral approach to depression. In R. J. Friedman & M. M. Katz (Eds.), *The psychology of depression: contemporary theory and research*. New York: Halstead Press, 1974.

LEWINSOHN, P. M., & GRAF, M. Pleasant activities and depression. *J. Cons. Clin. Psychol.*, Oct. 1973, **41**(2), 261–68.

LIBERMAN, R. P., & RASKIN, D. E. Depression: a behavioral formulation. Reprinted from *Archives of General Psychiatry*, June 1971, **24**(6), 515–23. Copyright 1971, American Medical Association.

LIBET, J. M., & LEWINSOHN, P. M. Concept of social skill with special reference to the behavior of depressed persons. *J. Cons. Clin. Psychol.*, Apr. 1973, **40**(2), 304–12.

LIPTON, M. A. Affective disorders: Progress but some unresolved questions remain. *Amer. J. Psychiat.*, 1970, **127**(3), 357–58.

LORR, M., & KLETT, C. J. Cross-cultural comparison of psychotic syndromes. *J. Abnorm. Psychol.*, 1968, **74**(4), 531–43.

MASSERMAN, J. H. *Principles of dynamic psychiatry*. Philadelphia: W. B. Saunders Company, 1961.

MEYER, A. *Collected papers of Adolf Meyer* (4 vols.). Baltimore: Johns Hopkins Press, 1948–1952.

OSSOFSKY, H. J. Endogenous depression in infancy and childhood. *Comprehensive Psychiatry*, Jan./Feb. 1974, **15**(1), 19–25.

PAYKEL, E. S., MYERS, J., DIENELT, M., KLERMAN, G., LINDENTHAL, J., & PEPPER, M. Life events and depression. *Arch. Gen. Psychiat.*, 1969, **21**, 753–60.

PETO, A. Body image and depression. *Inter. J. Psychoanal.*, 1972, **53**(2), 259–63.

POZNANSKI, E., & ZRULL, J. P. Childhood depression. *Arch. Gen. Psychiat.*, 1970, **23**(1), 8–15.

PRIEN, R. F., KLETT, C. J., & CAFFEY, E. M. Lithium carbonate and imipramine in prevention of affective episodes. *Arch. Gen. Psychiat.*, Sept. 1973, **29**(3), 420–25.

RASKIN, A. A guide for drug use in depressive disorders. *Amer. J. Psychiat.*, Feb. 1974, **131**(2), 181–85.

REICH, L. H., DAVIES, R. K., & HIMMELHOCH, J. M. Excessive alcohol use in manic-depressive illness. *Amer. J. Psychiat.*, Jan. 1974, **131**(1), 83–86.

REICH, T., CLAYTON, P. J., & WINOKUR, G. Family history studies: the genetics of mania. *Amer. J. Psychiat.*, 1969, **125**(10), 1358–69.

RENNIE, T. A. C., & FOWLER, J. B. Prognosis in manic-depressive psychoses. *Amer. J. Psychiat.*, 1942, **98**, 801–14.

ROSENTHAL, S. H. The involutional depressive syndrome. *Amer. J. Psychiat.*, 1968, **124**(11, Suppl.), 21–34.

SCHANCHE, D. A. If you're way, way down—or up too high . . . . *Today's Health*, May 1974, **52**(5), 39–41; 65–67.

SCHOU, M. Cited in Rewarding study of depression. *Sci. News*, 1974, **105**(17), 270.

SELIGMAN, M. E. P. Fall into hopelessness. *Psych. Today*, June 1973, **7**(1), 43–47; 48.

SETHI, B. B., NATHAWAT, S. S., & GAPTA, S. C. Depression in India. *J. Soc. Psychol.*, Oct. 1973, **91**(1), 3–13.

SLATER, E. T. O. Genetics in psychiatry. *J. Ment. Sci.*, 1944, **90**, 17–35.

TAIT, C. D., & BURNS, G. C. Involutional illnesses: a survey of 379 patients, including follow-up study of 114. *Amer. J. Psychiat.*, 1951, **108**, 27–36.

TAYLOR, M., & ABRAMS, R. Manic states: a genetic study of early and late onset affective disorders. *Arch. Gen. Psychiat.*, May 1973, **28**(5), 656–58.

TITLEY, W. B. Prepsychotic personality of involutional melancholia. *Arch. Neurol. Psychiat.*, 1936, **36**, 19–33.

ULLMANN, L. P., & KRASNER, L. *Psychological approach to abnormal behavior*. Englewood Cliffs, N.J.: Prentice-Hall, 1969.

WEISS, J. M. Cited in Depressing situations. *Sci. News*, Apr. 6, 1974, **105**(14), 224.

WINOKUR, G. Depression in the menopause. *Amer. J. Psychiat.*, Jan. 1973, **130**(1), 92–93.

ZUNG, W. W. K. A cross-cultural survey of symptoms in depression. *Amer. J. Psychiat.*, 1969, **126**(1), 116–21.

11. Sociopathic Disorders, Delinquency, and Crime

ALEXANDER, S. Under the rock. *Newsweek*, July 8, 1974, **84**(2), 35.

ALSOP, J. Cosa Nostra bigger than president's attack on it. *Los Angeles Times*, April 25, 1969, II, 10.

ARIEF, A. J., & BOWIE, C. G. Some psychiatric aspects of shoplifting. *J. Clin. Psychopath.*, 1947, **7**, 565–76.

BACON, M. K., CHILD, I. L., & BARRY, H., III. A cross-cultural study of correlates of crime. *J. Abnorm. Soc. Psychol.*, 1963, **66**, 291–300.

BANDURA, A. *Principles of behavior modification*. New York: Holt, Rinehart & Winston, 1969.

BANDURA, A. *Aggression: a social learning analysis*. Englewood Cliffs, N.J.: Prentice-Hall, 1973.

BANDURA, A., & WALTERS, R. H. *Social learning and personality development*. New York: Holt, Rinehart & Winston, 1963.

BLAKE, G. Community treatment plan aids delinquents. Five year experiment. *Los Angeles Times*, Jan. 26, 1967, I, 6.

BLUEMEL, C. S. *War, politics, and insanity*. Denver: World Press, 1948. Reprinted by permission of the heirs of Dr. Bluemel.

BOLEN, D. W., & BOYD, W. H. Gambling and the gambler. *Arch. Gen. Psychiat.*, 1968, **18**(5), 617–30.

BORKOVEC, T. D. Autonomic reactivity to sensory stimulation in psychopathic, neurotic, and normal juvenile delinquents. *J. Cons. Clin. Psychol.*, 1970, **35**, 217–22.

BOYD, W. H., & BOLEN, D. W. The compulsive gambler and spouse in group psychotherapy. *Inter. J. Group Psychother.*, 1970, **20**, 77–90.

BURKS, H. L., & HARRISON, S. I. Aggressive behavior as a means of avoiding depression. *Amer. J. Orthopsychiat.*, 1962, **32**, 416–22.

BUSS, A. H. *Psychopathology*. New York: Wiley, 1966.

CALDWELL, A. B., BOLEN, D. W., & BOYD, W. H. Pathologic gamblers not necessarily obsessive. *Roche Report: Frontiers of Psychiatry*, Oct. 15, 1972, **2**(17), 3.

CAMPAGNA, A. F., & HARTER, S. Moral judgment in sociopathic and normal children. *J. Pers. Soc. Psychol.*, Feb. 1975, **31**(2), 199–205.

CAPUTO, D. V., & MANDELL, W. Consequences of low birth weight. *Develop. Psychol.*, 1970, **3**(3), 363–83.

CHESNO, F. A., & KILMANN, P. R. Effects of stimulation on sociopathic avoidance learning. *J. Abnorm. Psychol.*, Apr. 1975, **84**(2), 144–50.

CLARKE, J. The precipitation of juvenile delinquency. *J. Ment. Sci.*, 1961, **107**, 1033–34.

CLIMENT, C. E., ROLLINS, A., ERVIN, F. R., & PLUTCHIK, R. Epidemiological studies of women prisoners, I: medical and psychiatric variables related to violent behavior. *Amer. J. Psychiat.*, Sept. 1973, **130**(9), 985–90.

CLONINGER, C. R., & GUZE, S. Psychiatric illness and female criminality: the role of sociopathy and hysteria in the antisocial woman. *Amer. J. Psychiat.*, 1970, **127**(3), 303–11.

COHEN, J., & HANSEL, M. *Risk and gambling: a study of subjective probability*. New York: Philosophical Library, 1956.

COLEMAN, J. C. Life stress and maladaptive behavior. *Amer. J. Occupa. Ther.*, May/June 1973, **27**(4), 169–80.

CRESSEY, D. R. *Theft of the nation: the structure and operations of organized crime in America*. New York: Harper & Row, 1969.

CRICHTON, R. *The great imposter*. New York: Random House, 1959. Summarized from *The Great Imposter*, by Robert Crichton. © Copyright 1959 by Robert Crichton. Used by permission of Random House, Inc.

DAVIDSON, W. S., & SEIDMAN, E. Studies of behavior modification and juvenile delinquency: a review, methodological critique, and social perspective. *Psychol. Bull.*, Dec. 1974, **81**(12), 998–1011.

DEVEREAUX, G. Psychodynamics of Mohave gambling. *American Imago*, 1950, **7**, 55–56.

DOLESCHAL, E., & KLAPMUTS, N. New criminology. *Behav. Today*, Jan. 21, 1974, **5**(3), 18–19.

ELKIND, D. Middle-class delinquency. *Mental Hygiene*, 1967, **51**, 80–84.

EYSENCK, H. J. *Behaviour therapy and the neuroses*. London: Pergamon Press, 1960.

FELDMAN, R., & WEISFELD, G. An interdisciplinary study of crime. *Crime and Delinquency*. Apr. 1973, **19**(2), 150–62.

FENZ, W. D. Heart rate responses to a stressor: a comparison between primary and secondary psychopaths and normal controls. *J. Exper. Res. Person.*, 1971, **5**(1), 7–13.

FINE, R. H., & FISHMAN, J. J. Institutionalized girl delinquents. *Dis. Nerv. Sys.*, 1968, **29**(1), 17–27.

FINKELSTEIN, B. Offenses with no apparent motive. *Dis. Nerv. Sys.*, 1968, **29**(5), 310–14.

GANZER, V. J., & SARASON, I. G. Variables associated with recidivism among juvenile delinquents. *J. Cons. Clin. Psychol.*, Feb. 1973, **40**(1), 1–5.

GINSBURG, B. E. Cited in E. Kiester, Jr., Violence in America: the latest theories and research. *Today's Health*, Jan. 1974, **52**(1), 52–53.

GLUECK, S., & GLUECK, E. T. Delinquency prediction method reported highly accurate. *Roche Reports*, 1969, **6**(15), 3.

GOLDFARB, R. L. Americans prisons: self-defeating concrete. *Psych. Today*, Jan. 1974, **7**(8), 20; 22; 24; 85; 88–89.

GREENACRE, P. Conscience in the psychopath. *Amer. J. Orthopsychiat.*, 1945, **15**, 495–509.

GREENBERG, H., & BLANK, H. R. Murder and self-destruction by a twelve-year-old boy. *Adolescence*, 1970, **5**(20), 391–96.

GREER, S. Study of parental loss in neurotics and sociopaths. *Arch. Gen. Psychiat.*, Aug. 1964, **11**(2), 177–80.

GROUP FOR THE ADVANCEMENT OF PSYCHIATRY (GAP). *Misuses of psychiatry in the criminal courts: competency to stand trial*. New York: GAP Publications Office, 1974.

GUTHRIE, P. D. California copes with change. *Los Angeles Times*, May 25, 1975, IV, 3.

GUZE, S. B., GOODWIN, D. W., & CRANE, J. B. Criminality and psychiatric disorders. *Arch. Gen. Psychiat.*, 1969, **20**, 592–97.

HANEY, B., & GOLD, M. The juvenile delinquent nobody knows. *Psychol. Today*, Sept. 1973, **7**(4), 48–52; 55.

HARE, R. D. Psychopathy, autonomic functioning and the orienting response. *J. Abnorm. Psychol.*, 1968, **73**(Monogr. Suppl. 3, part 2), 1–24.

HARE, R. D. From *Psychopathy: theory and research* by Robert D. Hare. New York: Wiley, 1970. Copyright © 1970, by John Wiley & Sons, Inc. Reprinted by permission of John Wiley & Sons, Inc.

HAZLETT, B. Juvenile gangs: violence and fatal assaults on increase. *Los Angeles Times*, Apr. 14, 1974, II, 1; 3.

HEAVER, W. L. A study of forty male psychopathic personalities before, during, and after hospitalization. *Amer. J. Psychiat.*, 1943, **100**, 342–46.

HENLEY, A. Muggers of the mind. *Today's Health*, 1971, **49**(2), 39–41; 71.

HOLDEN, C. Prisons: faith in "rehabilitation" is suffering a collapse. *Science*, May 23, 1975, **188**(4190), 815–17.

HOOVER, J. E. The story of crime in U.S. *U.S. News & World Report*, Oct. 7, 1968, 61–68.

HORTON, P. C., LOUY, J. W., & COPPOLILLO, H. P. Personality disorder and transitional relatedness. *Arch. Gen. Psychiat.*, May 1974, **30**(5), 618–22.

HOWARD, J. W., JR. Law enforcement in an urban society. *Amer. Psychologist*, Apr. 1974, **29**(4), 223–32.

JACOBS, P. A., BRUNTON, M., & MELVILLE, M. M. Aggressive behavior, mental sub-normality, and the XYY male. *Nature*, 1965, **208**, 1351–52.

JARVIK, L. F., KLODIN, V., & MATSUYAMA, S. S. Human aggression and the extra Y chromosome: fact or fantasy? *Amer. Psychologist*, Aug. 1973, **28**(8), 674–82.

JENKINS, R. L. Classification of behavior problems of children. *Amer. J. Psychiat.*, 1969, **125**, 1032–39.

KIESTER, E., JR. Explosive youngsters: what to do about them. *Today's Health*, Jan. 1974, **52**(1), 49–53; 64–65.

KIRKHAM, G. L. What a professor learned when he became a "cop" by George L. Kirkham. *U.S. News & World Report*, Apr. 22, 1974, **76**(16), 70–72. Reprinted by permission.

KLEIN, M. W. Impressions of juvenile gang members. *Adolescence*, 1968, **3**(9), 53–78.

KONOPKA, G. Adolescent delinquent girls. *Children*, 1964, **11**(1), 21–26.

KONOPKA, G. Rehabilitation of the delinquent girl. *Adolescence*, 1967, **2**(5), 69–82. Reprinted by permission of Libra Publishers, Inc.

LANGNER, T. S., GERSTEN, J. C., GREENE, E. L., EISENBERG, J. G., HERSON, J. H., & MC CARTHY, E. D. Treatment of psychological disorders among urban children. *J. Cons. Clin. Psychol.*, Apr. 1974, **42**(2), 70–79.

LAW ENFORCEMENT ASSISTANCE ADMINISTRATION (LEAA). Cited in From FBI chief: "War against organized crime is being won." *U.S. News & World Report*, Apr. 8, 1974, **76**(14), 50–51.[a]

LAW ENFORCEMENT ASSISTANCE ADMINISTRATION (LEAA). LEAA drops research support; behavior modification under fire. *APA Monitor*, Apr. 1974, **5**(4), 1; 4.[b]

LEFKOWITZ, M. M., HUESMANN, L. R., WALDER, L. O., & ERON, L. D. Developing and predicting aggression. *Sci. News*, Jan. 20, 1973, **103**(3), 40.

LIFE. The kid with the bad eye. 1951, **30**(5), 17–21.

LIVINGSTON, J. Compulsive gamblers: a culture of losers. *Psych. Today*, Mar. 1974, 51–55.

LOMBROSO-FERRERO, G. *Criminal man*. New York: Putnam's, 1911.

LYKKEN, D. T. A study of anxiety in the sociopathic personality. *J. Abnorm. Soc. Psychol.*, July 1957, **55**(1), 6–10.

MAC DONALD, J. M. A psychiatric study of check offenders. *Amer. J. Psychiat.*, 1959, **116**, 438–42.

MC CANDLESS, B. R., PARSONS, W. S., & ROBERTS, A. Perceived opportunity, delinquency, race, and body build among delinquent youth. *J. Cons. Clin. Psychol.*, 1972, **38**(2), 281–87.

MC CORD, W., & MC CORD, J. *The psychopath: an essay on the criminal mind*. New York: Van Nostrand Reinhold, 1964.

MC GEE, R. A. What's past is prologue. *Ann. Amer. Acad. Polit. Soc. Sci.*, 1969, **381**, 1–10.

MC NEIL, E. B. *The quiet furies*. Englewood Cliffs, N.J.: Prentice-Hall, 1967.

MELGES, F. T., & BOWLBY, J. Types of hopelessness in psychopathological process. *Arch. Gen. Psychiat.*, 1969, **20**, 690–99.

MELVILLE, K. Capital punishment. *The Sciences*, May 1973, **13**(4), 20–22.

MENNINGER, K. *The crime of punishment*. New York: Viking Press, 1968.

MURPHY, P. V. Crime and its causes – a need for social change. *Los Angeles Times*, Dec. 13, 1970, H, 1–2.

ODELL, B. Accelerated entry into the opportunity structure: a sociologically-based treatment for delinquent youth. *Sociol-*

ogy & Social Research, Apr. 1974, **58**(3), 312–17.

OSTROW, R. J. Soaring crime rate is severe setback: Saxbe warns U.S. *Los Angeles Times*, Aug. 28, 1974, I, 1; 12.

PATTERSON, G. Cited in Kiester, E., Jr., Explosive youngsters: what to do about them. *Today's Health*, Jan. 1974, **52**(1), 48–53; 64–65.

PEMBERTON, D. A., & BENADY, D. R. Consciously rejected children. *Brit. J. Psychiat.*, Nov. 1973, **123**(576), 575–78.

POLK, K. Urban and nonurban delinquency. *Behav. Today*, Sept. 30, 1974, **5**(35), 253.

PRESIDENT'S COMMISSION ON LAW ENFORCEMENT & THE ADMINISTRATION OF JUSTICE. Katzenbach, N. D. (Chairman), *The challenge of crime in a free society*. Washington, D.C.: U.S. Government Printing Office, 1967.

QUAY, H. C. Psychopathic personality as pathological stimulation seeking. *Amer. J. Psychiat.*, 1965, **122**(2), 180–83.

ROBERTS, A. H., ERIKSON, R. V., RIDDLE, M., & BACON, J. G. Demographic variables, base rates, and personality characteristics associated with recidivism in male delinquents. *J. Cons. Clin. Psychol.*, Dec. 1974, **42**(6), 833–41.

ROSTEN, R. A. Some personality characteristics of compulsive gamblers. Unpublished dissertation, UCLA, 1961.

SAXBE, W. Cited in Ostrow, R. J. Soaring crime rate is severe setback: Saxbe warns U.S. *Los Angeles Times*, Aug. 28, 1974, I, 1; 12.

SCHARFMAN, M., & CLARK, R. W. Delinquent adolescent girls: residential treatment in a municipal hospital setting. *Arch. Gen. Psychiat.*, 1967, **17**(4), 441–47.

SCHMAUK, F. J. Punishment, arousal, and avoidance learning in sociopaths. *J. Abnorm. Psychol.*, Dec. 1970, **76**(3), 325–35.

SCHWARTZ, B. The effect in Philadelphia of Pennsylvania's increased penalties for rape and attempted rape. *J. Crim. Law, Criminol. Police Sci.*, 1968, **59**(4), 509–15.

SCHWARTZ, H. Danger ahead in get-tough policy. *Los Angeles Times*, May 25, 1975, IV, 5.

SHAFFER, J. W., TOWNS, W., SCHMIDT, C. W., JR., FISHER, R. S., & ZLOTOWITZ, H. I. Social adjustment profiles of fatally injured drivers. *Arch. Gen. Psychiat.*, Apr. 1974, **30**(4), 508–11.

SHAINBERG, D. Motivations of adolescent military offenders. *Adolescence*, 1967, **2**(6), 244–54.

SHERROD, B. *Dallas Times Herald*, n.d. Quoted in D. Bolen & W. H. Boyd, Gambling and the gambler. *Arch. Gen. Psychiat.*, 1968, **18**(5), 617–30.

SILBER, D. E. Controversy concerning the criminal justice system and its implications for the role of mental health workers. *Amer. Psychologist*, Apr. 1974, **29**(4), 239–44.

SILVERMAN, H. Determinism, choice, responsibility, and the psychologist's role as an expert witness. *Amer. Psychologist*, 1969, **24**(1), 5–9.

SINGER, M. Delinquency and family disciplinary configurations: an elaboration of the superego Lacunae concept. *Arch. Gen. Psychiat.*, Dec. 1974, **31**(6), 795–98.

SMALL, J. G. The organic dimensions of crime. *Arch. Gen. Psychiat.*, 1966, **55**(1), 82–89.

SMITH, R. L. Strange tales of medical imposters. *Today's Health*, 1968, **46**(10), 44–47; 69–70.

SOLOMON, J. Why gamble? A psychological profile of pathology. *The Sciences*, July/Aug. 1972, **12**(6), 20–21.

STOJANOVICH, K. Antisocial and dyssocial. *Arch. Gen. Psychiat.*, 1969, **21**(5), 561–67.

STRINE, G. Compulsive gamblers pursue elusive dollar forever. *Los Angeles Times*, Mar. 30, 1971, III, 1; 6.

SUTHERLAND, E. H., & CRESSEY, D. R. *Principles of criminology*

(7th ed.). Philadelphia: Lippincott, 1966.

SUTKER, P. B., & MOAN, C. E. A psychosocial description of penitentiary inmates. *Arch. Gen. Psychiat.*, Nov. 1973, **29**(5), 663–67.

TIME. Young man with a gun. Jan. 22, 1951, 19–20.

TIME. Billy's last words. Dec. 22, 1952.

TROTTER, S. Patuxent: "therapeutic" prison faces test. *APA Monitor*, May 1975, **6**(5), 1; 4; 12.

ULMAR, G. Adolescent girls who steal. *Psychiat. Dig.*, 1971, **32**(2), 27–28.

UNIFORM CRIME REPORTS. Federal Bureau of Investigation. U.S. Dept. of Justice. Washington, D.C.: U.S. Government Printing Office, 1975.

U. S. NEWS & WORLD REPORT. Crime: a high price tag that everybody pays. Dec. 16, 1974, **78**(25), 32.

WOLKIND, S. N. The components of "affectionless psychopathy" in institutionalized children. *J. Child Psychol. Psychiat.*, July 1974, **15**(3), 215–20.

YABLONSKY, L. *The violent gang*. New York: Macmillan, 1962.

ZIMBARDO, P. G. A field experiment in autoshaping. In C. Ward (Ed.), *Vandalism*. London: Architectural Press, 1973.

12. Alcoholism and Drug Abuse

ABELSON, P. H. Death from heroin. *Science*, 1970, **168**, 1289.

AL-ANON. *Al-Anon—family treatment tool in alcoholism*. New York: Al-Anon Family Group Headquarters, Inc., 1971.

AMERICAN MEDICAL ASSOCIATION, Department of Mental Health. The crutch that cripples: drug dependence. Part I. *Today's Health*, 1968, **46**(9), 11–12; 70–72. [a]

AMERICAN MEDICAL ASSOCIATION, Department of Mental Health. The crutch that cripples: drug dependence. Part II. *Today's Health*, 1968, **46**(10), 12–15; 73–75. [b]

AMERICAN MEDICAL ASSOCIATION, Committee on Alcoholism and Drug Dependency. *The illness called alcoholism*. Chicago: AMA, 1969.

AMERICAN PSYCHIATRIC ASSOCIATION. Position Statement on Barbiturates. *Amer. J. Psychiat.*, June 1974, **131**(6), 743.

BALES, R. F. Cultural differences in rates of alcoholism. *Quart. J. Stud. Alcohol.*, 1946, **6**, 480–99.

BANDURA, A. *Principles of behavior modification*. New York: Holt, Rinehart & Winston, 1969.

BASSIN, A. Psychology in action. *Amer. Psychologist*, June 1975, **30**(6), 695–96.

BAYH, B. Cited in Barbiturate abuse held U.S. epidemic. *Los Angeles Times*, Dec. 5, 1972, I, 1; 9.

BAZELL, R. J. Drug abuse: methadone becomes the solution and the problem. *Science*, Feb. 23, 1973, **179**(4075), 772–75.

BENGELSDORF, I. S. Alcohol, morphine addictions believed chemically similar. *Los Angeles Times*, Mar. 5, 1970, II, 7.

BERZINS, J. I., ROSS, W. F., ENGLISH, G. E., & HALEY, J. V. Subgroups among opiate addicts: a typological investigation. *J. Abnorm. Psychol.*, Feb. 1974, **83**(1), 65–73.

BLACKER, K. H., JONES, R. T., STONE, G. C., & PFEFFERBAUM, D. Chronic users of LSD: the "acidheads." *Amer. J. Psychiat.*, 1968, **125**(3), 97–107.

BLUM, R. *Society and drugs* (Vol. 1). San Francisco: Jossey-Bass, 1969.

BOEHM, G. At last—a nonaddicting substitute for morphine? *Today's Health*, 1968, **46**(4), 69–72.

BRADEN, W., STILLMAN, R. C., & WYATT, R. J. Effects of marijuana on contingent negative variation and reaction times. *Arch. Gen. Psychiat.*, Oct. 1974, **31**(4), 537–41.

774   Acknowledgments and References

BREKHMAN, I. I., & SAM, Y. A. Psychoactive preparations used by paleoasiatic peoples. *Roche Report,* 1967, **4**(8), 3.

CALLNER, D. A. Behavioral treatment approaches to drug abuse: a critical review of the research. *Psychol. Bull.,* Mar. 1975, **82**(2), 143–64.

CAPPELL, H. D., & PLINER, P. L. Volitional control of marijuana intoxication: a study of the ability to "come down" on command. *J. Abnorm. Psychol.,* Dec. 1973, **82**(3), 428–34.

CHAFETZ, M. E. A new day of hope for alcoholics. *Amer. J. Psychiat.,* 1971, **127**(2), 118–19.

CHINLUND, S. The female addict. *Sci. News,* 1969, **95**(14), 578.

CLAESON, L. E., & MALM, U. Electro-aversion therapy of chronic alcoholism. *Behav. Res. Ther.,* 1973, **11**(4), 663–65.

COMMISSION OF INQUIRY INTO THE NON-MEDICAL USE OF DRUGS. *Interim report.* Ottawa, Canada: Crown, 1970.

CULLITON, B. J. Pot facing stringent scientific examination. *Sci. News,* Jan. 24, 1970, **97**(4), 102–5.

CURLEE, J. Alcoholism and the "empty nest." *Bull. Menninger Clin.,* 1969, **33**(3), 165–71.

DAVIDSON, W. S. Studies of aversive conditioning for alcoholics: a critical review of theory and research methodology. *Psychol. Bull.,* Sept. 1974, **81**(9), 571–81.

DOLE, V. P., & NYSWANDER, M. The miracle of methadone in the narcotics jungle. *Roche Report,* 1967, **4**(11), 1–2; 8; 11.

DOLE, V. P., NYSWANDER, M., & WARNER, A. Successful treatment of 750 criminal addicts. *JAMA,* 1968, **206**, 2709–11.

DOLE, V. P., & ROBINSON, J. W. Methadone treatment of randomly selected criminal addicts. *New Engl. J. Med.,* 1969, **280**(25), 1372–75.

DUPONT, R. L. Cited in Return of the hard drug menace. *U.S. News & World Report,* June 30, 1975, **78**(26), 29.

ELLINWOOD, E. H. Assault and homicide associated with amphetamine abuse. *Amer. J. Psychiat.,* 1971, **127**(9), 90–95.

ELLISON, B. Robert Young's toughest role. *Today's Health,* 1971, **49**(5), 25–27; 59–60.

ERDMANN, G. W. Personal correspondence with the author, 1975.

FURLONG, W. B. How "speed" kills athletic careers. *Today's Health,* Feb. 1971, **49**(2), 30–33; 62; 64; 66.

GEARING, F. R. Methadone project called success after five years. *Psychiatric News,* 1970, **5**(12), 18.

GILBERT, J. G., & LOMBARDI, D. N. Personality characteristics of young male narcotic addicts. *J. Couns. Psychol.,* 1967, **31**, 536–38.

GOLDSTEIN, A., ET AL. Researchers isolate opiate receptor. *Behav. Today,* Mar. 4, 1974, **5**(9), 1.

GOODWIN, D. W., SCHULSINGER, F., HERMANSEN, L., GUZE, S. B., & WINOKUR, G. Alcohol problems in adoptees raised apart from alcoholic biological parents. *Arch. Gen. Psychiat.,* Feb. 1973, **28**(2), 238–43.

GOODWIN, D. W., SCHULSINGER, F., MOLLER, N., HERMANSEN, L., WINOKUR, G., & GUZE, S. B. Drinking problems in adopted and nonadopted sons of alcoholics. *Arch. Gen. Psychiat.,* Aug. 1974, **31**(2), 164–69.

GREENE, M. H., BROWN, B. S., & DUPONT, R. L. Controlling the abuse of illicit methadone in Washington, D.C. *Arch. Gen. Psychiat.,* Feb. 1975, **32**(2), 221–26.

GREENE, M. H., & DUPONT, R. L. Heroin addiction trends. *Amer. J. Psychiat.,* May 1974, **131**(5), 545–50.

GUNTHER, M. Female alcoholism: the drinker in the pantry. *Today's Health,* June 1975, **53**(6), 14–19.

HABER, J. Robert Young: Welby has the right Rx for life. *Los Angeles Times Calendar,* Feb. 21, 1971, 13; 27.

HARTMANN, E. L., SCHILDKRAUT, J. J., & WATSON, R. Depression, altered sleep pattern follow amphetamine withdrawal. *Roche Report. Frontiers of Psychiatry,* Mar. 1, 1972, **2**(5), 5–6.

HAZLETT, B. Two who played with death – and lost the game. *Los Angeles Times,* Mar. 2, 1971, II, 1; 5.

HEKIMIAN, L. J., & GERSHON, S. Characteristics of drug abusers admitted to a psychiatric hospital. *JAMA,* 1968, **205**(3), 125–30.

HEW. Physical damage of pot yet unproven, says HEW. *Psychiatric News,* 1971, **6**(7), 3.

HOFFMAN, A. LSD discoverer disputes "chance" factor in finding. *Psychiatric News,* 1971, **6**(8), 23–26.

HOROWITZ, M. J. Flashbacks: recurrent intrusive images after the use of LSD. *Amer. J. Psychiat.,* 1969, **126**(4), 147–51.

HORTON, D. The functions of alcohol in primitive societies: a cross-cultural study. *Quart. J. Stud. Alcohol.,* 1943, **4**, 199–320.

HUXLEY, A. *The doors of perception and heaven and hell.* New York: Harper & Row, 1954.

JARVIK, M. E. The psychopharmacological revolution. *Psych. Today,* 1967, **1**(1), 51–58.

JELLINEK, E. M. Phases of alcohol addiction. *Quart. J. Stud. Alcohol.,* 1952, **13**, 673–78.

JELLINEK, E. M. Phases of alcohol addiction. In G. D. Shean (Ed.), *Studies in abnormal behavior.* Chicago: Rand McNally, 1971. Pp. 86–98.

JONES, M. C. Personality correlates and antecedents of drinking patterns in adult males. *J. Cons. Clin. Psychol.,* 1968, **32**(1), 2–12.

JONES, M. C. Personality antecedents and correlates of drinking patterns in women. *J. Cons. Clin. Psychol.,* 1971, **36**(1), 61–69.

KATZ, M. M., WASKOW, E. E., & OLSSON, J. Characteristics of the psychological state produced by LSD. *J. Abnorm. Psychol.,* 1968, **73**(1), 1–14.

KING, L. J., MURPHY, G., ROBINS, L., & DARVISH, H. Alcohol abuse: a crucial factor in the social problems of Negro men. *Amer. J. Psychiat.,* 1969, **125**(12), 96–104.

KUNNES, R. Double dealing in dope. *Human Behavior,* Oct. 1973, **2**(10), 22–27.

LEVITT, L. P. *Illinois State Plan for the Prevention, Treatment, and Control of Alcohol Abuse and Alcoholism* (Vol. 1). Objectives – Plan of Action – Basic Data. Department of Mental Health and Developmental Disabilities, State of Illinois. Apr. 1, 1974, 1–364.

LOS ANGELES POLICE DEPARTMENT. *Youth and narcotics.* Reprinted by Los Angeles City School District, 1952, 3–4.

MAUGH, T. H., II. Marijuana: the grass may no longer be greener. *Science,* Aug. 23, 1974, **185**(4152), 683–85.

MCCLELLAND, D. C., DAVIS, W. N., KALIN, R., & WANNER, E. *The drinking man.* New York: The Free Press, 1972.

MCWILLIAMS, S. A., & TUTTLE, R. J. Long-term psychological effects of LSD. *Psychol. Bull.,* June 1973, **79**(6), 341–51.

MIKURIYA, T. H. On smoking pot. *Trans-action,* 1969, **7**(2), 8; 10.

NATIONAL INSTITUTE ON ALCOHOL ABUSE AND ALCOHOLISM. The economic costs of alcohol misuse. *Alcohol World,* Winter 1974/1975, 19–20.

NATIONAL INSTITUTE ON DRUG ABUSE. *Marijuana and health, 3rd annual report to Congress from the Secretary of Health, Education, and Welfare.* Washington, D.C.: U.S. Government Printing Office, 1974.

Acknowledgments and References   **775**

NELSON, H. Study compares drug dangers. *Los Angeles Times,* Oct. 6, 1969, I, 3; 25.

PERT, C. B., & SNYDER, S. H. Opiate receptor: demonstration in nervous tissue. *Science,* Mar. 9, 1973, **179**(4077), 1011–14.

PLINER, P. L., & CAPPELL, H. D. Modification of affective consequences of alcohol: a comparison of social and solitary drinking. *J. Abnorm. Psychol.* Aug. 1974, **83**(4), 418–25.

POST, R. M. Cocaine psychoses: a continuum model. *Amer. J. Psychiat.,* Mar. 1975, **132**(3), 225–31.

PRATT, B. Studies reveal alcoholism differs in males and females. *APA Monitor,* July 1972, **3**(7), 1.

RINKEL, M. Psychedelic drugs. *Amer. J. Psychiat.,* June 1966, **122**(6), 1415–16.

ROE, A., BURKS, B. S., & MITTELMANN, B. Adult adjustment of foster children of alcoholic and psychotic parentage and the influence of the foster home. *Memorial Section on Alcohol Studies,* No. 3., New Haven: Yale University Press, 1945.

ROEDER, F., ET AL. Cited in Brain surgery for addiction. *Sci. News,* Feb. 16, 1974, **105**(7), 106.

RORVIK, D. M. Do drugs lead to violence? *Look,* Apr. 7, 1970, 58–61.

ROSE, A., & BURKS, B. Roundup of current research: is the child really the father of the man? *Trans-action,* 1968, **5**(6), 6.

SCHAEFER, H. H. Accepted theories disproven. *Sci. News,* 1971, **99**(11), 182.

SEIXAS, F. A., & CADORET, R. What is the alcoholic man? *New York Academy of Sciences,* Apr. 15, 1974, **223**, 13–14.

SIEGLER, M., OSMOND, H., & NEWELL, S. Models of alcoholism. *Quart. J. Stud. Alcohol.,* 1968, **29**(3–A), 571–91.

SKELTON, G. Oregonians stand behind new law on marijuana. *Los Angeles Times,* Feb. 10, 1975, I, 16–17.

SOBELL, M. B., & SOBELL, L. C. Alcoholics treated by individualized behavior therapy: one year treatment outcome. *Behav. Res. Ther.,* Nov. 1973, **11**(4), 599–618.

TAVEL, M. E. A new look at an old syndrome: delirium tremens. *Arch. Int. Med.,* 1962, **109**, 129–34.

THORNTON, W. E., & THORNTON, B. P. Narcotic poisoning: a review of the literature. *Amer. J. Psychiat.,* Aug. 1974, **131**(8), 867–69.

TIME. Alcoholism: new victims, new treatment. Apr. 22, 1974, **103**(16), 75–81.

U.S. DEPARTMENT OF HEALTH, EDUCATION, AND WELFARE (HEW). *Alcohol and health.* Morris E. Chafetz, Chairman of the Task Force. Washington, D.C.: U.S. Government Printing Office, 1974.

U.S. NEWS & WORLD REPORT. School-age drunks—a fresh worry. Apr. 14, 1975, **78**(15), 40.

WESTERMEYER, J. Use of alcohol and opium by the Meo of Laos. *Amer. J. Psychiat.,* Feb. 1971, **127**(8), 1019–23.

WESTERMEYER, J. Opium dens: a social resource for addicts in Laos. *Arch. Gen. Psychiat.,* Aug. 1974, **31**(2), 237–40.

WIKLER, A. Dynamics of drug dependence: implications of a conditioning theory for research and treatment. *Arch. Gen. Psychiat.,* May 1973, **28**(5), 611–16.

WILSNACK, S. C. Feminity by the bottle. *Psych. Today,* Apr. 1973, **6**(11), 39–43; 96. [a]

WILSNACK, S.C. Sex role identity in female alcoholism. *J. Abnorm. Psychol.,* Oct. 1973, **82**(2), 253–61. [b]

WILSON, J. Q. The return of heroin. *Commentary,* Apr. 1975, **49**(4), 46–50.

WINOKUR, G., REICH, T., RIMMER, J., & PITTS, F. N., JR. Alcoholism. III: diagnosis and familial psychiatric illness in 259 alcoholic probands. *Arch. Gen. Psychiat.,* 1970, **23**(2), 104–11.

WOODRUFF, R. A., GUZE, S. B., CLAYTON, P. J., & CARR, D. Alcoholism and depression. *Arch. Gen. Psychiat.,* Jan. 1973, **28**(1), 97–100.

YOLLES, S. Cited in Pop drugs: the high as a way of life. *Time,* Sept. 26, 1969, **94**(13), 74.

13. Organic Brain Syndromes

ANNALS OF THE AMERICAN ACADEMY OF POLITICAL AND SOCIAL SCIENCE. Political consequences of aging. Sept. 1974, **415**.

ASCH, S. S., & RUBIN, L. J. Postpartum reactions: some unrecognized variations. *Amer. J. Psychiat.,* Aug. 1974, **131**(8), 870–74.

BATCHELOR, I., & CAMPBELL, R. *Henderson and Gillespie's textbook of psychiatry for students and practitioners* (10th ed.). New York: Oxford University Press, 1969.

BELLAMY, W. E., JR. Huntington's chorea. *N.C. Med. J.,* 1961, **22**, 409–12.

BLAU, D. The course of psychiatric hospitalization in the aged. *J. Geriat. Psychol.,* 1970, **3**(2), 210–23.

BRICKNER, R. M. *The intellectual functions of the frontal lobes.* New York: Macmillan, 1936.

BROOKS, D. N. Recognition, memory, and head injury. *Journal of Neurology, Neurosurgery, & Psychiatry,* July 1974, **37**(7), 794–801.

BROWN, W. A., & SHERESHEFSKY, P. Seven women: a prospective study of postpartum psychiatric disorders. *Psychiatry,* May 1972, **35**(2), 139–59.

BROŽEK, J., & GRANDE, F. Abnormalities of neural function in the presence of inadequate nutrition. In J. Field (Ed.), *Handbook of physiology. Section I: Neurophysiology* (Vol. 3). Baltimore, Md.: Williams & Wilkins, 1960.

BROŽEK, J., GUETZKOW, H., & KEYS, A. A study of personality of normal young men maintained on restricted intakes of vitamins of the B complex. *Psychosom. Med.,* 1946, **8**, 98–109.

BRUETSCH, W. L. Neurosyphilitic conditions. In S. Arieti (Ed.), *American handbook of psychiatry* (Vol. 2). New York: Basic Books, 1959.

BYRD, R. E. *Alone.* New York: Putnam, 1938. Reprinted by permission of G. P. Putnam's Sons from *Alone* by Admiral Richard E. Byrd. Copyright 1938 by Richard E. Byrd. Copyright renewed 1966 by Marie A. Byrd.

CASTELNUOVO-TEDESCO, P. Organ transplant, body image, psychosis. *Psychoanal. Quart.,* July 1973, **42**(3), 349–63.

DE BEAUVOIR, S. The terrors of old age. *Newsweek,* Feb. 9, 1970, p. 54.

DOBROKHOTOVA, T. A. On the pathology of the emotional sphere in tumorous lesion of the frontal lobes of the brain. *Zhurnal Nevropatologii i Psikhiartrii,* 1968, **68**(3), 418–22.

EARL, H. G. Head injury: the big killer. *Today's Health,* 1966, **44**(12), 19–21.

FETTERMAN, J. L. *Practical lessons in psychiatry.* Springfield, Ill.: Charles C Thomas, 1949.

FLOR-HENRY, P. Temporal lobe epilepsy: etiological factors. *Amer. J. Psychiat.,* 1969, **126**(3), 400–403.

FORD, A. B. Casualties of our time. *Science,* 1970, **167**(3196), 256–63.

FOX, R. C., & SWAZEY, J. P. *The courage to fail: a social view of organ transplants and dialysis.* Chicago, Ill.: University of Chicago Press, 1974.

FREEMON, F. R. Pretesting for Huntington's chorea. *The Hastings Center Report,* Sept. 1973, **3**(4), 13.

GAL, P. Mental disorders of advanced years. *Geriatrics*, 1959, **14**, 224–28.

GAZZANIGA, M. S. The split brain in man. *Scientif. Amer.*, 1967, **217**(2), 24–29.

GAZZANIGA, M. S. *The bisected brain*. New York: Appleton-Century-Crofts, 1970.

GERMAN, W. J. Initial symptomatology in brain tumors. *Connecticut Medicine*, 1959, **23**, 636–37.

GOLDFARB, A. I. Predicting mortality in the institutionalized aged. *Arch. Gen. Psychiat.*, 1969, **21**, 172–76.

GUNTHER, J. *Death be not proud*. New York: Harper, 1949.

HARLOW, J. M. Recovery from the passage of an iron bar through the head. *Publ. Mass. Med. Soc.*, 1868, **2**, 327.

HOLVEY, D. N., & TALBOTT, J. H. (Eds.). *The Merck manual of diagnosis and therapy* (12th ed.). Rahway, N.J.: Merck, Sharp, & Dohme Research Laboratories, 1972.

JARVIK, L. F., YEN, F. S., & GOLDSTEIN, F. Chromosomes and mental status. *Arch. Gen. Psychiat.*, Feb. 1974, **30**(2), 186–90.

JASPER, H. (Ed.). *Basic mechanisms of the epilepsies*. Boston: Little, Brown, 1969.

JERVIS, G. A. The mental deficiencies. In S. Arieti (Ed.), *American handbook of psychiatry* (Vol. 2). New York: Basic Books, 1959.

JOHNSON, J. The EEG in the traumatic encephalography of boxers. *Psychiatrica Clinica*, 1969, **2**(4), 204–11.

JURY, M. The nobility in our Gramp's decision to die. *Today's Health*, Jan. 1975, 18–23; 62.

KAHANA, B., & KAHANA, E. Changes in mental status of elderly patients in age-integrated and age-segregated hospital milieus. *J. Abnorm. Psychol.*, 1970, **75**, 177–81.

KAISER PERMANENTE MEDICAL CARE PROGRAM. *Planning for health*. Los Angeles: Kaiser Foundation Health Plan, Inc., 1973.

KEMBLE, J. *Idols and invalids*. New York: Doubleday, 1936.

LEVIN, S. Brain tumors in mental hospital patients. *Amer. J. Psychiat.*, 1949, **105**, 897–900.

LEYTON, G. B. The effects of slow starvation. *Lancet*, 1946, **251**, 73–79.

LOS ANGELES TIMES. Prostitute's diary aids in syphilis hunt. Apr. 1, 1970, III, 16.

LOS ANGELES TIMES. Venereal disease rise called alarming by U.N. Nov. 16, 1974, I, 2.

LUNDE, D. T. Psychiatric complications of heart transplant. *Amer. J. Psychiat.*, 1969, **126**(3), 117–21.

LURIA, A. R. *The man with a shattered world: the history of a brain wound* (L. Solotaroff, trans.). New York: Basic Books, 1972.

LYNCH, H. T., HARLAN, W. L., & DYHRBERG, J. S. Subjective perspective of a family with Huntington's chorea: implications for family counseling. *Arch. Gen. Psychiat.*, July 1972, **27**(1), 67–72.

MELGES, F. T. Postpartum psychiatric syndromes. *Psychosom. Med.*, 1968, **30**, 95–108.

MENNINGER, K. *The human mind*. New York: Knopf, 1946. From pages 41–42; 139–40 in *The Human Mind*, by Karl Menninger. Copyright 1930, 1937, 1945 and renewed 1958, 1965 by Karl Menninger. Reprinted by permission of Alfred A. Knopf, Inc.

MERRILL, R. H., & COLLINS, J. L. Acute psychosis in chronic renal failure: case reports. *Military Medicine*, Aug. 1974, **139**(8), 622–24.

NEBES, R. D. Hemispheric specialization in commissuroto-

mized man. *Psychol. Bull.*, Jan. 1974, **81**(1), 1–14.

NEUGARTEN, B. L. Age groups in American society and the rise of the young-old. *The Annals of the American Academy of Political and Social Science*, Sept. 1974, **415**, 187–98.

OFFIR, C. Old people's revolt—"At 65, work becomes a four-letter word." *Psych. Today*, Mar. 1974, **7**(10), 40.

ORADEI, D. M., & WAITE, N. S. Group psychotherapy with stroke patients during the immediate recovery phase. *Amer. J. Orthopsychiat.*, Apr. 1974, **44**(3), 386–95.

PARRAN, T. *Shadow on the land*. New York: Reynal & Hitchcock, 1937.

PLATER, F. *Praxeos medical Tomi tres*. (Basil 1656), *Histories and Observations*. London: Culpeper and Cole, 1664.

POWER, C. A., & MCCARRAN, L. I. Treatment of depression in persons residing in homes for the aged. *The Gerontologist*, Apr. 1975, **15**(2), 132–35.

PROTHEROE, C. Puerperal psychoses: a long term study. *Brit. J. Psychiat.*, 1969, **115**(518), 9–30.

PRYSE-PHILLIPS, W. *Epilepsy*. London: Bristol-Wright, 1969.

PUSEY, W. A. *The history and epidemiology of syphilis*. Springfield, Ill.: Charles C Thomas, 1933.

RICHTER, C. P. *The role of biological clocks in mental and physical health*. Washington, D.C.: U.S. Public Health Service, 1970.

RODIN, E. A. Psychomotor epilepsy and aggressive behavior. *Arch. Gen. Psychiat.*, Feb. 1973, **28**(2), 210–13.

SCHWAB, J. J. Comprehensive medicine and the concurrence of physical and mental illness. *Psychosomatics*, 1970, **11**(6), 591–95.

SIMMONS, L. Aging in preindustrial societies. In C. Tibbits (Ed.), *Handbook of social gerontology*. Chicago: University of Chicago Press, 1960.

SPERRY, R. W., GAZZANIGA, M. S., & BOGEN, J. E. Interhemispheric relationships: the neocortical commissures—syndromes of hemispheric disconnection. *Handbook of Clinical Neurology* (Vol. 1). New York: Wiley, 1969.

STANG, R. R. The etiology of Parkinson's disease. *Dis. Nerv. Sys.*, 1970, **31**(6), 381–90.

STEARMAN, M. B. Cited in Controlling epilepsy by biofeedback. *Sci. News*, Sept. 1, 1973, **104**(9), 132–33.

STRAGE, M. VD: the clock is ticking. *Today's Health*, 1971, **49**(4), 16–18; 69–71.

SUSSMAN, H. M., & MACNEILAGE, P. F. Studies of hemispheric specialization for speech production. *Brain & Language*, Apr. 1975, **2**(2), 131–51.

SUTHERLAND, J. M., & TRAIT, H. *The epilepsies: modern diagnosis and treatment*. Edinburgh: Livingstone, 1969.

TALLAND, G. Amnesia: a world without continuity. *Psych. Today*, 1967, **1**(1), 43–50.

TERRY, R., & WISNIEWSKI, H. Sans teeth, sans eyes, sans taste, sans everything. *Behav. Today*, Mar. 25, 1974, **5**(12), 84. Summary of paper delivered at the American Association for the Advancement of Science, San Francisco, Mar. 1974.

TOURKOW, L. P. Psychic consequences of loss and replacement of body parts. *Journal of the American Psychoanalytic Association*, 1974, **22**(1), 170–81.

ULLMANN, M., & GRUEN, A. Behavioral changes in patients with strokes. *Amer. J. Psychiat.*, 1961, **117**, 1004–9.

VAN DELLEN, T. R. Alzheimer's outlook is far from bright. *Chicago Tribune*, Aug. 23, 1974, I, 12.

VOLPE, A., & KASTENBAUM, R. TLC. *Amer. J. Nurs.* 1967, **67**, 100–103.

WHITE, M. A., PROUT, C. T., FIXSEN, C., & FOUNDEUR, M. Obstetrician's role in postpartum mental illness. *JAMA*, 1957, **165,** 138–43.

WHYBROW, P. C., PRANGE, A. J., & TREADWAY, C. R. Mental changes accompanying thyroid gland dysfunction. *Arch. Gen. Psychiat.*, 1969, **20,** 48–63.

YAHR, M. D. Progress in Parkinson's disease. *The Sciences*, 1969, **9**(7), 20–23.

14. Mental Retardation

ACHENBACH, T. M. *Developmental psychopathology.* New York: Ronald Press, 1974.

AMERICAN ASSOCIATION ON MENTAL DEFICIENCY. *Manual on terminology and classification in mental retardation* (Rev. ed.). H. J. Grossman (Ed.). Special Publication Series No. 2, 1973, 11+. Washington, D.C., 1973.

AMERICAN PSYCHIATRIC ASSOCIATION. *Diagnostic and statistical manual of mental disorders* (2nd ed.). Washington, D.C.: APA, 1968.

AMERICAN PSYCHIATRIC ASSOCIATION. Classification of mental retardation. Supplement to the *Amer. J. Psychiat.*, May 1972, **128**(11), 1–45.

AMERICAN PSYCHOLOGICAL ASSOCIATION. Psychology and mental retardation. *Amer. Psychologist*, 1970, **25,** 267–68.

BIJOU, S. W. A functional analysis of retarded development. In N. R. Ellis (Ed.), *International review of research in mental retardation.* (Vol. 1). New York: Academic Press, 1966.

BRAGINSKY, B. M., & BRAGINSKY, D. D. The mentally retarded: society's Hansels and Gretals. *Psych. Today*, Mar. 1974, **7**(10), 18; 20–21; 24; 26; 28–30.

BURNS, G. W. *The science of genetics.* New York: Macmillan, 1972.

CENTERWALL, W. R., & CENTERWALL, S. A. Phenylketonuria (Folling's disease): the story of its discovery. *Journal of the History of Medicine*, 1961, **16,** 292–96.

CHRISTODORESCU, D., COLLINS, S., ZELLINGHER, R., & TAUTU, C. Psychiatric disturbances in Turner's syndrome: report of three cases. *Psychiatrica Clinica*, 1970, **3**(2), 114–24.

CLARK, G. R., KIVITZ, M. S., & ROSEN, M. Program for mentally retarded. *Sci. News*, 1969, **96,** 82.

DONOGHUE, E. C., ABBAS, K. A., & GAL, E. The medical assessment of mentally retarded children in hospital. *Brit. J. Psychiat.*, 1970, **117**(540), 531–32.

FALLS, H. F. Ocular changes in Down's syndrome help in diagnosis. *Roche Report*, 1970, **7**(16), 5.

GEISZ, D., & STEINHAUSEN, H. On the "psychological development of children with hydrocephalus." (German) *Praxis der Kinderpsychologie und Kinderpsychiatrie*, May-June 1974, **23**(4), 113–18.

GOLDEN, D. A., & DAVIS, J. G. Counseling parents after the birth of an infant with Down's syndrome. *Children Today*, Mar.-Apr. 1974, **3**(2), 7–11.

GREENFIELD, J. C., & WOLFSON, J. M. Microcephalia vera. *Arch. Neurol. Psychiat.*, 1935, **33,** 1296–1316.

GUERNEY, B. G., JR. (Ed.). *Psychotherapeutic agents: new roles for nonprofessionals, parents, and teachers.* New York: Holt, Rinehart & Winston, 1969.

HAGAN, J. W., & HUNTSMAN, N. J. Selective attention in mental retardation. *Develop. Psychol.*, 1971, **5**(1), 151–60.

HEBER, R. *Epidemiology of mental retardation.* Springfield, Ill.: Charles C Thomas, 1970.

HILL, A. L. Investigation of calendar calculating by an idiot savant. *Amer. J. Psychiat.*, May 1975, **132**(5), 557–59.

HOLVEY, D. N., & TALBOTT, J. H. (EDS.). *The Merck manual of diagnosis and therapy* (12th ed.). Rahway, N.J.: Merck, Sharp, & Dohme Research Laboratories, 1972.

HYATT, R., & ROLNICK, N. (EDS.). *Teaching the mentally handicapped child.* New York: Behavioral Publications, 1974.

ISAACSON, R. L. When brains are damaged. *Psych. Today*, 1970, **3**(4), 38–42.

ITARD, J. *The wild boy of Aveyron.* Paris, 1799. G. Humphrey & M. Humphrey (Tr.). New York: Century, 1932.

JOHNSON, H. R., MYHRE, S. A., RIWALCABA, R. H. A., THULINE, H. C., & KELLEY, V. C. Effects of testosterone on body image and behavior in Klinefelter's syndrome: a pilot study. *Develop. Med. Child Neurol.*, 1970, **12**(4), 454–60.

KARNES, M. B., TESKA, J. A., & HODGINS, A. S. The effects of four programs of classroom intervention on the intellectual and language development of 4-year-old disadvantaged children. *Amer. J. Orthopsychiat.*, 1970, **40,** 58–76.

KENNEDY, J. F. Message from the President of the United States relative to mental illness and mental retardation. *Amer. Psychologist*, 1963, **18,** 280–89.

KOCH, R. The multidisciplinary approach to mental retardation. In A. A. Baumeister (Ed.), *Mental retardation: appraisal, education, and rehabilitation.* Chicago: Aldine, 1967,.

MACMILLAN, D. L., & KEOGH, B. K. Normal and retarded children's expectancy for failure. *Develop. Psychol.*, 1971, **4**(3), 343–48.

MCCLURE, H. M., BELDEN, K. M., PIEPER, W. A., & JACKSON, C. B. Autosomal trisomy in a chimpanzee: resemblance to Down's syndrome. *Science*, 1969, **165**(3897), 1010–12.

MERCER, J. R. *Labeling the mentally retarded: clinical and social system perspective on mental retardation.* Berkeley, Calif.: University of California Press, 1973.

MILLER, R. Does Down's syndrome predispose children to leukemia? *Roche Report*, 1970, **7**(16), 5.

MORISHIMA, A. His spirit raises the ante for retardates. *Psych. Today*, June 1975, **9**(1), 72–73.

NIELSEN, J., BJARNASON, S., FRIEDRICH, U., FROLAND, A., HANSEN, V. H., & SORENSEN, A. Klinefelter's syndrome in children. *J. Child Psychol. Psychiat.*, 1970, **11**(2), 109–20.

PENROSE, L. S. *Biology of mental defect* (3rd ed.). New York: Grune & Stratton, 1963.

PERRY, T. The enigma of PKU. *The Sciences*, 1970, **10**(8), 12–16.

PRESIDENT'S COMMITTEE ON MENTAL RETARDATION. *The decisive decade.* Washington, D.C.: U.S. Government Printing Office, 1970.

PRESIDENT'S COMMITTEE ON MENTAL RETARDATION. *The goal is freedom.* DHEW Publication No. (OHD) 74-21001. Washington, D.C.: U.S. Government Printing Office, 1973.

RODMAN, D. H., & COLLINS, M. J. A community residence program; an alternative to institutional living for the mentally retarded. *Training School Bulletin*, May 1974, **71**(1), 41–48.

ROTHCHILD, B. F. Incubator isolation as a possible contributing factor to the high incidence of emotional disturbance among prematurely born persons. *J. Genet. Psychol.*, 1967, **110**(2), 287–304.

SCHILD, S. Parents of children with PKU. *Children Today*, July/Aug. 1972, **1**(4), 20–22.

SEIDL, F. W. Community oriented residential care: the state of the art. *Child Care Quarterly*, Fall 1974, **3**(3), 150–63.

SILBERSTEIN, R. M., & IRWIN, H. Jean-Marc-Gaspard Itard and the savage of Aveyron: an unsolved diagnostic problem in child psychiatry. *J. Amer. Acad. Child Psychiat.*, 1962, **1**(2), 314–22.

SULLIVAN, J. P., & BATAREH, G. J. Educational therapy with the severely retarded. *The Training School Bulletin*, May 1973, **70**(1), 5–9.

TARJAN, G., & EISENBERG, L. Some thoughts on the classification of mental retardation in the United States of America. *Amer. J. Psychiat.*, May 1972 Supplement, **128**(11), 14–18.

TARJAN, G., WRIGHT, S. W., EYMAN, R. K., & KEERAN, C. V. Natural history of mental retardation: some aspects of epidemiology. *Amer. J. Ment. Def.*, Oct. 1973, **77**(4), 369–79.

TARVER, S. G., & HALLAHAN, D. P. Attention deficits in children with learning disabilities: a review. *J. Learn. Dis.*, Nov. 1974, **7**(9), 560–69.

VISCOTT, D. S. A musical idiot savant. *Psychiatry*, 1970, **33**(4), 494–515.

WHALEN, C. K., & HENKER, B. A. Pyramid therapy in a hospital for the retarded. *Amer. J. Ment. Def.*, 1971, **75**(4), 414–34.

WORTIS, J. Comments on the ICD classification of mental retardation. *Amer. J. Psychiat.*, May 1972 Supplement, **128**(11), 21–24.

WORTIS, J. (Ed.). *Mental retardation and developmental disabilities: an annual review* (Vol. 5). New York: Brunner/Mazel, 1973.

ZUCKER, S. H., AND ALTMAN, R. An on-the-job training program for adolescent trainable retardates. *Training School Bulletin*, Aug. 1973, **70**(2), 106–10.

15. Behavior Disorders of Childhood

ARNOLD, L. E. Is this label necessary? *Journal of School Health*, Oct. 1973, **43**(8), 510–14.

BANDURA, A. *Principles of behavior modification.* New York: Holt, Rinehart & Winston, 1969.

BECK, L., LANGFORD, W. S., MACKAY, M., & SUM, G. Childhood chemotherapy and later drug abuse and growth curve: a follow-up study of 30 adolescents. *Amer. J. Psychiat.*, Apr. 1975, **132**(4), 436–38.

BENDER, L. The life course of children with schizophrenia. *Amer. J. Psychiat.*, July 1973, **130**(7), 783–86.

BETTELHEIM, B. Joey: a "mechanical boy." *Scientif. American*, 1959, **200**, 116–27. From "Joey: A 'Mechanical Boy' " by Bruno Bettelheim. Copyright © March 1959 by Scientific American, Inc. All rights reserved.

BETTELHEIM, B. *The empty fortress.* New York: Free Press, 1967.

BETTELHEIM, B. Laurie. *Psych. Today*, 1969, **2**(12), 24–25; 60.

BETTELHEIM, B. *A home for the heart.* New York: Alfred A. Knopf, 1974.

BRYAN, T. H. Learning disabilities: a new stereotype. *J. Learn. Dis.*, May 1974, **7**(5), 46–51.

CHALFANT, J. C., & SCHEFFELIN, M. A. *Central processing dysfunctions in children: a review of research.* INNDS monogr. no. 9. Washington, D.C.: U.S. Government Printing Office, 1969.

CLANCY, H., & MCBRIDE, G. The autistic process and its treatment. *J. Child Psychol. Psychiat.*, 1969, **10**(4), 233–44.

CLEMENT, P. Elimination of sleepwalking in a seven-year-old boy. *J. Cons. Clin. Psychol.*, 1970, **34**(1), 22–26.

CLEMENTS, S.D. *Minimal brain dysfunction in children—terminology and identification.* Washington, D.C.: HEW, 1966.

CLOSE, K. Selecting priorities at the White House Conference on Children. *Children*, 1971, **18**(2), 42–48.

COLE, S. O. Hyperkinetic children: the use of stimulant drugs evaluated. *Amer. J. Orthopsychiat.*, Jan. 1975, **45**(1), 28–37.

CYTRYN, L., & MCKNEW, D. H., JR. Factors influencing the changing clinical expression of the depressive process in children. *Amer. J. Psychiat.*, Aug. 1974, **131**(8), 879–81.

DINNAN, J. A., MC GUINESS, E., & PERRIN, L. Auditory feedback—stutterers versus nonstutterers. *J. Learn. Dis.*, 1970, **3**(4), 30–34.

EDWARDS, R. P., ALLEY, G. R., & SNIDER, W. Academic achievement and minimal brain dysfunction. *J. Learn. Dis.*, 1971, **4**(3), 134–38.

EISENBERG, L. Principles of drug therapy in child psychiatry with special reference to stimulant drugs. *Amer. J. Orthopsychiat.*, 1971, **4**(3), 371–79.

ENGLISH, C. J. Leaving home: a typology of runaways. *Society*, July/Aug. 1973, **10**(5), 22–24.

FEIGHNER, A. C., & FEIGHNER, J. P. Multimodality treatment of the hyperkinetic child. *Amer. J. Psychiat.*, Apr. 1974, **131**(4), 459–63.

FISH, B., SHAPIRO, T., CAMPBELL, M., & WILE, R. A classification of schizophrenic children under five years. *Amer. J. Psychiat.*, 1968, **124**(10), 109–17.

FLANAGAN, B., GOLDIAMOND, I., & AZRIN, N. H. Instatement of stuttering in normally fluent individuals through operant procedures. *Science*, 1959, **130**, 979–81.

GAJZAGO, C., & PRIOR, M. Two cases of "recovery" in Kanner syndrome. *Arch. Gen. Psychiat.*, Aug. 1974, **31**(2), 264–68.

GETZE, G. Brain impairment found in 5 to 10% of school children. *Los Angeles Times*, Jan. 30, 1974, II, 1; 8.

GOODMAN, J. A case study of an "autistic-savant": mental function in the psychotic child with markedly discrepant abilities. *J. Child Psychol. Psychiat.*, Oct. 1972, **13**(4), 267–78.

GREENE, J. S. Hope for the stutterer. *Hygeia*, 1946, **24**(2), 120–21.

HAMPE, E., NOBLE, H., MILLER, L. C., & BARRETT, C. L. Phobic children one and two years posttreatment. *J. Abnorm. Psychol.*, Dec. 1973, **82**(3), 446–53.

HARLOW, H. A brief look at autistic children. *Psychiat. Soc. Sci. Rev.*, 1969, **3**(1), 27–29.

HAYES, T. A., PANITCH, M. L., & BARKER, E. Imipramine dosage in children: a comment on "Imipramine and electrocardiographic abnormalities in hyperactive children." *Amer. J. Psychiat.*, May 1975, **132**(5), 546–47.

HEWETT, F. M., & FORNESS, S. R. *Education of exceptional learners.* Boston: Allyn & Bacon, 1974.

HOMER, L. E. The anatomy of a runaway. *Human Behavior*, Apr. 1974, **3**(4), 37.

JENKINS, R. L. The varieties of children's behavioral problems and family dynamics. *Amer. J. Psychiat.*, 1968, **124**(10), 134–39.

JENKINS R. L. Classification of behavior problems of children. *Amer. J. Psychiat.*, 1969, **125**(8), 68–75.

JENKINS, R. L. Diagnostic classification in child psychiatry. *Amer. J. Psychiat.*, 1970, **127**(5), 140–41.

JOHNSON, C. A., & KATZ, R. C. Using parents as change agents for their children: a review. *J. Child Psychol. Psychiat.*, July 1973, **14**(3), 181–200.

JOHNSON, W. *Stuttering and what you can do about it.* Minneapolis: University of Minnesota Press, 1961.

JOINT COMMISSION ON THE MENTAL HEALTH OF CHILDREN. Position statement: statement of the American Orthopsychiatric

Association on the work of the Joint Commission on the Mental Health of Children. *Amer. J. Orthopsychiat.*, 1968, **38**(3), 402–9.

JOINT COMMISSION ON THE MENTAL HEALTH OF CHILDREN. *Crisis in child mental health: challenge for the 1970's.* New York: Harper & Row, 1970.

JUDD, L., & MANDELL, A. Chromosome studies in early infantile autism. *Arch. Gen. Psychiat.*, 1968, **18**(4), 450–57.

KALES, A., PAULSON, M. J., JACOBSON, A., & KALES, J. Somnambulism: psychophysiological correlates. *Arch. Gen. Psychiat.*, 1966, **14**(6), 595–604.

KANNER, L. Autistic disturbances of affective content. *Nervous Child*, 1943, **2**, 217–40.

KREBS, M., & KREBS, R. Are you raising a perfectionist? *Today's Health*, 1970, **48**(8), 39–41.

LEMERT, E. M. Stuttering and social structure in two Pacific societies. *J. Speech Hear. Dis.*, 1962, **27**, 3–10.

LEMERT, E. M. Sociological perspective. In J. Sheehan (Ed.), *Stuttering: research and therapy.* New York: Harper & Row, 1970.

LEXOW, G. A., & ARONSON, S. S. Health advocacy: a need, a concept, a model. *Children Today*, Jan./Feb. 1975, **4**(1), 2–6; 36.

LIEVENS, P. The organic psychosyndrome of early childhood and its effects on learning. *J. Learn. Dis.*, Dec. 1974, **7**(10), 626–31.

LONEY, J. The intellectual functioning of hyperactive elementary school boys: a cross-sectional investigation. *Amer. J. Orthopsychiat.*, Oct. 1974, **44**(5), 754–62.

LOURIE, R., STUBBLEFIELD, R., HIRSCHBERG, C., & PUGH, D. Psychiatrists clarify Joint Commission report on children. *Roche Report*, 1970, **7**(13), 1–3; 11.

LOVAAS, O. I., KOEGEL, R., SIMMON, J. Q., & LONG, J. S. Some generalization and follow-up measures on autistic children in behavior therapy. *J. Appl. Beh. Anal.*, Spring 1973, **6**(1), 131–66.

LOVAAS, O. I., SCHAEFFER, B., & SIMMONS, J. Q. In O. I. Lovaas & B. D. Bucker (Eds.), *Perspectives in behavior modification with deviant children.* Englewood Cliffs, N.J.: Prentice-Hall, 1974.

MACDONALD, J. D., & MARTIN, R. R. Stuttering and disfluency as two reliable and unambiguous response classes. *J. Speech Hear. Res.*, Dec. 1973, **16**(4), 691–99.

MAHLER, M. S. Autistic and symbiotic processes. *Psychoanalytic Studies of Children*, 1952, **7**(286).

MARCHANT, R., HOWLIN, P., YULE, W., & RUTTER, M. Graded change in the treatment of the behavior of autistic children. *J. Child Psychol. Psychiat.*, July 1974, **15**(3), 221–27.

MARTIN, G. I., & ZAUG, P. J. Electrocardiographic monitoring of enuretic children receiving therapeutic doses of imipramine. *Amer. J. Psychiat.*, May 1975, **132**(5), 540–42.

MAY, J. M., & MAY, M. A. The treatment and education of the atypical, autistic child in a residential school situation. *Amer. J. Ment. Def.*, Nov. 1959, **64**(6), 435–43.

MAYER, C. L., & SCHEFFELIN, M. State-wide planning for special education in California. *J. Learn. Dis.*, Apr. 1975, **8**(4), 50–54.

MC GLANNAN, F. K. Learning disabilities: the decade ahead. *J. Learn. Dis.*, Feb. 1975, **8**(2), 56–59.

MONTENEGRO, H. Severe separation anxiety in two preschool children: successfully treated by reciprocal inhibition. *J. Child Psychol. Psychiat.*, 1968, **9**(2), 93–103.

MOSHER, L. R. New treatment systems for schizophrenia. *Schizophrenia*, 1971, **3**(2), 87–93.

MURPHY, L. *The widening world of childhood.* New York: Basic Books, 1962.

MURPHY, S., NICHOLS, J., EDDY, R., & UMPHRESS, A. Behavioral characteristics of adolescent enuretics. *Adolescence*, 1971, **6**(21), 1–18.

NAGARAJA, J. Somnambulism in children: clinical communication. *Child Psychiatry Quarterly*, Jan. 1974, **7**(1), 18–19.

NATIONAL INSTITUTE OF MENTAL HEALTH, United States Department of Health, Education, and Welfare. Mental Health Publication No. 5027. Washington, D.C.: U.S. Government Printing Office, 1970.

NATIONAL INSTITUTE OF MENTAL HEALTH. Amphetamines approved for children. *Sci. News*, 1971, **99**(4), 240.

O'DELL, S. Training parents in behavior modification: a review. *Psychol. Bull.*, July 1974, **81**(7), 418–33.

OSSOFSKY, H. J. Endogenous depression in infancy and childhood. *Comprehensive Psychiatry*, Jan./Feb. 1974, **15**(1), 19–25.

PAINE, R. S. *Minimal brain dysfunction.* National Project on Learning Disabilities. Public Health Service Publication No. 2015. Washington, D.C.: U.S. Government Printing Office, 1969.

POZNANSKI, E., & ZRULL, J. Childhood depression. *Arch. Gen. Psychiat.*, 1970, **23**(1), 8–15.

RIMLAND, B. *Infantile autism: the syndrome and its implications for a neural theory of behavior.* New York: Appleton-Century-Crofts, 1964.

RIMLAND, B. The differentiation of childhood psychoses: an analysis of checklists for 2,218 psychotic children. *Journal of Autism and Child Schizophrenia*, Apr./June 1971, **1**, 161–74.

RITVO, E., & ORNITZ, E. A new look at childhood autism points to CNS disease. *Roche Report*, 1970, **7**(18), 6–8.

ROBINS, L. N. The adult development of the antisocial child. *Seminars in Psychiatry*, Nov. 1970, **2**(4), 420–34.

ROFF, J. D. Adolescent schizophrenia: variables related to differences in long-term adult outcome. *J. Cons. Clin. Psychol.*, Apr. 1974, **42**(2), 180–83.

SAFER, D. J., & ALLEN, R. P. Stimulant drugs said to suppress height, weight. *Psychiatric News*, May 2, 1973, **8**(9), 9.

SATTERFIELD, J. H., CANTWELL, D. P., SAUL, R. E., & YUSIN, A. Intelligence, academic achievement, and EEG abnormalities in hyperactive children. *Amer. J. Psychiat.*, Apr. 1974, **131**(4), 391–95.

SCHNACKENBERG, R. C. Caffeine as a substitute for Schedule II stimulants in hyperkinetic children. *Amer. J. Psychiat.*, July 1973, **130**(7), 796–98.

SCHREIBMAN, L., & KOEGEL, R. L. Autism: a defeatable horror. *Psych. Today*, Mar. 1975, **8**(10), 61–67.

SEIDEN, R. Child suicide. *The Sciences*, 1970, **10**(9), 28–32.

SEIDL, F. W. Community oriented residential care: the state of the art. *Child Care Quarterly*, Fall 1974, **3**(3), 150–63.

SHEEHAN, J. G. (Ed.). *Stuttering: research and therapy.* New York: Harper & Row, 1970.

SHEEHAN, J. G., & COSTLEY, M. S. A reexamination of the role of heredity in stuttering. *J. Speech Hear. Dis.*, In press, 1975, **40**.

SHEEHAN, J. G., & LYON, M. A. Role perception in stuttering. *Journal of Communication Disorders*, 1974, **7**(2), 113–26.

SHEEHAN, J. G., & MARTYN, M. Stuttering and its disappearance. *J. Speech Hear. Dis.*, 1970, **13**(2), 279–89.

SMALL, I., SMALL, J., ALIG, V., & MOORE, D. Passive-aggressive personality disorder: a search for a syndrome. *Amer. J. Psy-*

chiat., 1970, **126**(7), 973–83.

SOLOMON, J. Thursday's child. *The Sciences*, June 1972, **12**, 6–9; 26–29.

STEINBERG, H. Helping the stutterer. *Family Health*, May 1975, **7**(5), 30–33; 64.

STONE, H. *Foster care in question: a national reassessment by twenty-one experts.* New York: Child Welfare League of America, 1970.

TAVES, I. Is there a sleepwalker in the house? *Today's Health*, 1969, **47**(5), 41; 76.

TINBERGEN, N. Ethology and stress disease. *Science*, July 5, 1974, **185**(4145), 20–27.

TREFFERT, D. A. Epidemiology of infantile autism. *Arch. Gen. Psychiat.*, 1970, **22**, 431–38.

TROTTER, S. Labeling: it hurts more than it helps. *APA Monitor*, Jan. 1975, **6**(1), 5.

TURNER, R. K., & TAYLOR, P. D. Conditioning treatment of nocturnal enuresis in adults: preliminary findings. *Behav. Res. Ther.*, Feb. 1974, **12**(1), 41–52.

TYMCHUK, A. J., KNIGHTS, R. M., & HINTON, G. G. The behavioral significance of differing EEG abnormalities in children with learning and/or behavior problems. *J. Learn. Dis.*, 1970, **3**(11), 547–52.

U.S. NEWS & WORLD REPORT. More kids on the road—now it's the "throwaways." May 12, 1975, **78**(19), 49–50.

VANDERSALL, T. A., & WEINER, J. M. Children who set fires. *Arch. Gen. Psychiat.*, 1970, **22**(1), 63–71.

WING, J. K. Diagnosis, epidemiology, aetiology. In J. K. Wing (Ed.), *Early childhood autism.* Elmsford, N.Y.: Pergamon Press, 1967.

WING, L. *Autistic children.* Secaucus, N.J.: Citadel Press, 1974.

WINSBERG, B. G., GOLDSTEIN, S., YEPES, L. E., & PEREL, J. M. Imipramine and electrocardiographic abnormalities in hyperactive children. *Amer. J. Psychiat.*, May 1975, **132**(5), 542–45.

WOLFF, W. M., & MORRIS, L. A. Intellectual personality characteristics of parents of autistic children. *J. Abnorm. Psychol.*, 1971, **77**(2), 155–61.

WOLKIND, S. N. The components of "affectionless psychopathy" in institutionalized children. *J. Child Psychol. Psychiat.*, July 1974, **15**(3), 215–20.

16. Sexual "Deviations"

ABEL, G. G., LEVIS, D. J., & CLANCY, J. Aversion therapy applied to taped sequences of deviant behavior in exhibitionism and other sexual deviations: a preliminary report. *J. Behav. Res. Exp. Psychiat.*, 1970, **1**(1), 59–66.

ADAMS, M. S., & NEEL, J. V. Children of incest. *Pediatrics*, 1967, **40**, 55–62.

ADLER, P. *A house is not a home.* New York: Holt, Rinehart & Winston, 1953.

AMIR, M. *Patterns in forcible rape.* Chicago: University of Chicago Press, 1971.

APA MONITOR. Homosexuality dropped as mental disorder. Feb. 1974, **5**(2), 1; 9.

APFELBERG, B., SUGAR, C., & PFEFFER, A. Z. A psychiatric study of 250 sex offenders. *Amer. J. Psychiat.*, 1944, **100**, 762–70.

BAGLEY, C. Incest behavior and incest taboo. *Social Problems*, 1969, **16**(4), 505–19.

BANCROFT, J., TENNENT, G., LOUCAS, K., & CASS, J. The control of deviant sexual behavior by drugs: 1. Behavioural changes following estrogens and anti-androgens. *Brit. J. Psychiat.*, Sept. 1974, **125**(9), 310–15.

BANDURA, A. *Principles of behavior modification.* New York: Holt, Rinehart & Winston, 1969.

BARLOW, D. H., REYNOLDS, E. J., & AGRAS, W. S. Gender identity change in a transsexual. *Arch. Gen. Psychiat.*, Apr. 1973, **28**(4), 569–76.

BENJAMIN, H. *The transsexual phenomenon.* New York: Julian Press, 1966.

BENTLER, P. M., & PRINCE, C. Personality characteristics of male transvestites. III. *J. Abnorm. Psychol.*, 1969, **74**(2), 140–43.

BENTLER, P. M., & PRINCE, C. Psychiatric symptomology in transvestites. *J. Clin. Psychol.*, 1970, **26**(4), 434–35.

BENTLER, P. M., SHEARMAN, R. W., & PRINCE, C. Personality characteristics of male transvestites. *J. Clin. Psychol.*, 1970, **126**(3), 287–91.

BERG, A. *The sadist.* O. Illner & G. Godwin (trans.). New York: Medical Press of New York, 1954.

BERGLER, E. Analysis of an unusual case of fetishism. *Bull. Menninger Clin.*, 1947, **2**, 67–75.

BESS, B. E., & JANUS, S. S. Factors in successful renunciation of prostitution. Paper delivered at 1974 Annual Convention of American Psychiatric Association, Preliminary Program, Detroit, Mich., May 6–10, 1974.

BIEBER, I., DAIN, H., DINCE, P., DRELLECH, M., GRAND, H., GRUNDLACH, R., KREMER, M., RITKIN, A., WILBUR, C., & BIEBER, T. Quote from *Homosexuality: a psychoanalytic study*, by Irving Bieber et al., © 1962 by the Society of Medical Psychoanalysts, Basic Books, Inc., Publishers, New York.

BLANCH, A. The problem of feminine masochism: an approach through theory and literature. *Cornell Journal of Social Relations*, Spring 1974, **9**(1), 1–15.

BONNELL, C. Preliminary results reported. New Kinsey study may scrap some myths. *The Advocate*, Dec. 18, 1974, 4.

BRANCALE, R., ELLIS, A., & DOORBAR, R. Psychiatric and psychological investigations of convicted sex offenders: a summary report. *Amer. J. Psychiat.*, 1952, **109**, 17–21.

BRODIE, H. K. H., GARTRELL, N., DOERING, C., & RHUE, T. Plasma testosterone levels in heterosexual and homosexual men. *Amer. J. Psychiat.*, Jan. 1974, **131**(1), 82–83.

BRYAN, J. H. Apprenticeships in prostitution. *Social Problems*, 1965, **12**, 287–97.

BRYAN, J. H. Occupational ideologies and individual attitudes of call girls. *Social Problems*, 1966, **13**, 441–50.

BUCKNER, H. T. The transvestic career path. *Psychiatry*, 1970, **33**(3), 381–89.

BURGESS, A. W., & HOLMSTROM, L. L. Rape trauma syndrome. *Amer. J. Psychiat.*, Sept. 1974, **131**(9), 981–86.

BURROS, W. M. The growing burden of impotence. *Family Health*, May 1974, **6**(5), 18–21.

CAVALLIN, H. Incestuous fathers: a clinical report. *Amer. J. Psychiat.*, 1966, **122**(10), 1132–38.

CHURCHILL, W. *Homosexual behavior among males: a cross-cultural and cross-species investigation.* New York: Hawthorne, 1967.

COHEN, M., & SEGHORN, T. Sociometric study of the sex offender. *Journal of Abnormal Psychology*, 1969, **74**(2), 249–55. Copyright 1969 by the American Psychological Association and reproduced by permission.

COOPER, A. J. A clinical study of "coital anxiety" in male potency disorders. *J. Psychosom. Res.*, 1969, **13**(2), 143–47.

DAVENPORT, W. Sexual patterns and their regulation in a society of the Southwest Pacific. In F. Beach (Ed.), *Sex and behavior*. New York: Wiley, 1965.

DAVIS, A. J. Sexual assault in the Philadelphia prisons and sheriff's vans. *Trans-action*, 1968, **6**(2), 28–35.

DAVISON, G. C. Elimination of a sadistic fantasy by a client-controlled counterconditioning technique: a case study. *J. Abnorm. Psychol.*, 1968, **73**, 84–90.

DEVROYE, A. Incest: bibliographical review (French). *Acta Psychiatrica Belgica*, Nov. 1973, **73**(6), 661–712.

DUNHAM, H. W. *Crucial issues in the treatment and control of sexual deviation in the community*. Lansing, Mich.: State Dept. of Mental Hlth., 1951.

EAST, W. N. Sexual offenders. *J. Nerv. Ment. Dis.*, 1946, **103**, 626–66.

EVANS, R. B. Childhood parental relationships of homosexual men. *J. Cons. Clin. Psychol.*, 1969, **33**(2), 129–35.

FREEDMAN, M. *Personal definition and psychological function*. New York: Harper & Row, 1975.

FRIEDMAN, J. H. Woman's role in male impotence. *Medical Aspects of Human Sexuality*, June 1974, **8**(6), 8–23.

GAGNON, J. H., & SIMON, W. *Sexual conduct; the social sources of human sexuality*. Chicago: Aldine, 1973.

GEBHARD, P. H. Situational factors affecting human sexual behavior. In F. Beach (Ed.), *Sex and behavior*. New York: Wiley, 1965.

GEBHARD, P. H., GAGNON, J. H., POMEROY, W. B., & CHRISTENSON, C. V. *Sex offenders: an analysis of types*. New York: Harper & Row, 1965.

GINSBERG, G. L., FROSCH, W. A., & SHAPIRO, T. The new impotence. *Arch. Gen. Psychiat.*, Mar. 1972, **26**(3), 218–20.

GOLDSTEIN, M. J. Pornography, sex deviancy: an exaggerated link. *The Los Angeles Times*, Oct. 23, 1974, II, 7.

GOLDSTEIN, M. J., & KANT, H. S. (with collaboration of Hartman, J. J.). *Pornography and sexual deviance*. Berkeley, Calif.: University of California Press, 1973.

GRANT, V. W. A case study of fetishism. *J. Abnorm. Soc. Psychol.*, 1953, **48**, 142–49.

GREEN, R. *Sexual identity conflict in children and adults*. New York: Basic Books, 1974.

HAGGERTY, S. The oldest profession. *Los Angeles Times*, June 19, 1973, II, 7.

HARTMAN, A. A., & NICOLAY, R. C. Sexual deviant behavior in expectant fathers. *J. Abnorm. Psychol.*, 1966, **71**(3), 232–34.

HEDBLOM, J. H. Dimensions of lesbian experience. *Archives of Sexual Behavior*, Dec. 1973, **2**(4), 329–41.

HIRSCHI, T. The professional prostitute. *Berkeley Journal of Sociology*, 1962, **7**, 37–41; 47–48.

HOOKER, E. The adjustment of the male overt homosexual. *Journal of Projective Techniques*, 1957, **21**, 18–31.

HOOKER, E. The homosexual community. In *Proceedings of the XIV International Congress of Applied Psychology* (Vol. II). *Personality research*. Copenhagen: Munksgaard, 1962.

HOOVER, E. L. Lesbianism: reflections of a "straight" woman. *Human Behavior*, Oct. 1973, **2**(10), 9.

HUMPHREYS, L. Tearoom trade: impersonal sex in public places. *Trans-action*, 1970, **7**(3), 10–25.

JACKMAN, N. R., O'TOOLE, R., & GEIS, G. The self-image of the prostitute. *Sociol. Quart.*, 1963, **4**(2), 150–61.

JENSEN, M. S. Role differentiation in female homosexual quasi-marital unions. *J. Marr. Fam.*, May 1974, **36**(2), 360–67.

KALLMANN, F. J. Twin and sibship study of overt male homosexuality. *American Journal of Human Genetics*, June 1952, **4**(2), 136–46.

KAPLAN, H. S. No-nonsense therapy for six sexual malfunctions. *Psych. Today*, Oct. 1974, **8**(5), 76–80; 83–84; 86.

KAPLAN, H. S. *The illustrated manual of sex therapy*. New York: Quadrangle/The New York Times Book Company, 1975.

KINSEY, A. C., POMEROY, W. B., & MARTIN, C. E. *Sexual behavior in the human male*. Philadelphia: W. B. Saunders, 1948.

KINSEY, A. C., POMEROY, W. B., & MARTIN, C. E. Concepts of normality and abnormality in sexual behavior. In P. H. Hoch & J. Zubin (Eds.), *Psychosexual development in health and disease*. New York: Grune & Stratton, 1949. Pp. 11–32.

KINSEY, A. C., POMEROY, W. B., & MARTIN, C. E. *Sexual behavior in the human female*. Philadelphia: W. B. Saunders, 1953.

KOLODNY, R. C., MASTERS, W. H., HENDRYS, J., & TORO, G. Plasma testosterone and the semen analysis in male homosexuals. *New Engl. J. Med.*, Nov. 18, 1971, **285**(21), 1170–74.

KONOPKA, G. Adolescent delinquent girls. *Children*, 1964, **11**(1), 21–26.

KOPP, S. B. The character structure of sex offenders. *Amer. J. Psychother.*, 1962, **16**, 64–70.

KRAFFT-EBING, R. V. *Psychopathica sexualis*. New York: Pioneer Publications, 1950.

KUSHNER, M. The reduction of a long-standing fetish by means of aversive conditioning. In L. P. Ullmann & L. Krasner (Eds.), *Case studies in behavior modification*. New York: Holt, Rinehart & Winston, 1965. Pp. 239–42.

KUTCHINSKY, B. The effect of easy availability of pornography on the incidence of sex crimes: the Danish experience. Institute of Criminal Science. University of Copenhagen, 1972.

LAMBLY, P. Treatment of transvestism and subsequent coital problems. *J. Behav. Ther. Exp. Psychiat.*, July 1974, **5**(1), 101–2.

LARSON, D., EASTER, P., & WARD, B. A group treatment for masochistic patients. *Hospital & Community Psychiatry*, Aug. 1974, **25**(8), 525–28.

LEV-RAN, A. Gender role differentiation in hermaphrodites. *Archives of Sexual Behavior*, Sept. 1974, **3**(5), 391–424.

LINDZEY, G. Some remarks concerning incest, the incest taboo, and psychoanalytic theory. *Amer. Psychologist*, 1967, **22**(12), 1051–59.

LIVINGOOD, J. M. (ED.). *National Institute of Mental Health Task Force on Homosexuality: final report and background papers*. Rockville, Md.: National Institute of Mental Health, 1972.

LOS ANGELES TIMES. A transvestite's plea for understanding and tolerance. Sept. 30, 1973, IV, 7.

LOS ANGELES TIMES. Deadline nears for 2 to be castrated or go to jail. May 9, 1975, I, 3; 33.

MACKLIN, E. D. Cohabitation in college: going very steady. *Psych. Today*, Nov. 1974, **8**(6), 53–56; 57–59.

MARSHALL, W. L. A combined treatment approach to the reduction of multiple fetish-related behaviors. *J. Cons. Clin. Psychol.*, Aug. 1974, **42**(4), 613–16.

MASTERS, W. H., & JOHNSON, V. E. *Human sexual response*. Boston: Little, Brown, 1966.

MASTERS, W. H., & JOHNSON, V. E. *Human sexual inadequacy*. Boston: Little, Brown, 1970.

MASTERS, W. H., & JOHNSON, V. E. *The pleasure bond: a new look at sexuality and commitment*. Boston: Little, Brown, 1975.

MONEY, J., & ALEXANDER, D. Psychosexual development and absence of homosexuality in males with precocious puberty. *J. Nerv. Ment. Dis.*, 1969, **148**(2), 111–23.

MONEY, J., & EHRHARDT, A. A. *Man & woman, boy & girl: differentiation and dimorphism of gender identity.* Baltimore: Johns Hopkins University Press, 1972.

NADLER, R. P. Approach to psychodynamics of obscene telephone calls. *N.Y. St. J. Med.* 1968, **68**(1), 521–26.

NAMH. NAMH supports repeal of homosexual status. *Psychiatric News*, 1971, **6**(3), 1.

NATHAN, P. E., & HARRIS, S. L. *Psychopathology and society.* McGraw-Hill, 1975.

NELSON, H. People who set fires not all the same type, expert says. *Los Angeles Times.* Sept. 29, 1970, II, 3; 27.

NEWMAN, L. E., & STOLLER, R. J. Nontranssexual men who seek sex reassignment. *Amer. J. Psychiat.*, Apr. 1974, **131**(4), 437–41.

OHLSON, E. L. In R. Cole & S. G. Lewis, Studies challenge myths on gay men, women. *The Advocate*, Jan. 1, 1975, 3; 10.

PACKARD, V. *The sexual wilderness.* New York: David McKay, 1968.

PAULY, I. B. The current status of the change of sex operation. *J. Nerv. Ment. Dis.*, 1968, **147**(5), 460–71.

RACHMAN, S. Sexual fetishism: an experimental analogue. *Psychol. Rec.*, 1966, **16**, 293–96.

RADA, R. T. Alcoholism and forcible rape. *Amer. J. Psychiat.*, Apr. 1975, **132**(4), 444–46.

REVITCH, E., & WEISS, R. G. The pedophiliac offender. *Dis. Nerv. Sys.*, 1962, **23**, 73–78.

ROOTH, G. Exhibitionists around the world. *Human Behavior*, May 1974, 3(5), 61.

ROSENTHAL, D. Genetic theory and abnormal behavior. New York: McGraw-Hill, 1970.

ROSSMAN, P. The pederasts. *Society*, Mar./Apr. 1973, **10**(3), 28–32; 34–35.

SABALIS, R. F., FRANCES, A., APPENZELLER, S. N., & MOSELEY, W. B. The three sisters: transsexual male siblings. *Amer. J. Psychiat.*, Aug. 1974, **131**(8), 907–9.

SACK, R. L., & MILLER, W. Masochism: a clinical and theoretical overview. *Psychiatry*, Aug. 1975, **38**(3), 244–57.

SCHWARTZMAN, J. The individual, incest, and exogamy. *Psychiatry*, May 1974, **37**, 171–80.

SGROI, S. M. Sexual molestation of children. *Children Today*, May-June 1975, 4(3), 18–21; 44.

SIEGELMAN, M. Parental background of male homosexuals and heterosexuals. *Archives of Sexual Behavior*, Jan. 1974, **3**, 3–18.

SIMON, W. Male sexuality: the secret of satisfaction. *Today's Health*, Apr. 1975, **53**(4), 32–34; 50–52.

SNORTUM, J. R., MARSHALL, J. E., GILLESPIE, J. E., MC LAUGHLIN, J. P., & MOSBERG, L. Family dynamics and homosexuality. *Psych. Rep.*, 1969, **24**(3), 763–70.

SORENSON, R. C. *Adolescent sexuality in contemporary America: the Sorenson report.* New York: World Publishing Co., 1973.

STEKEL, W. *Sexual aberrations: the phenomena of fetishism in relation to sex* (2 vols.). New York: Liveright, 1971.

STEPHAN, W. G. Parental relationships and early social experiences of activist male homosexuals and male heterosexuals. *J. Abnorm. Psychol.*, 1973, **82**(3), 506–13.

STOLLER, R. J. Transvestites' women. Reprinted from *The American Journal of Psychiatry*, volume 124, pages 333–339, 1967. Copyright 1967, the American Psychiatric Association.

STURUP, G. K. Treatment of sexual offenders in Herstedvester, Denmark: the rapists. *Acta Psychiatr. Scandin.*, 1968, 44(Suppl. 204), 1–62.

SUTHERLAND, S., & SCHERL, D. J. Quote from Patterns of response among victims of rape, by Sandra Sutherland Fox and Donald J. Scherl. *American Journal of Orthopsychiatry*, April 1970, **40**(3), 503–11. Copyright 1970, the American Orthopsychiatric Association, Inc. Reproduced by permission.

SWANSON, D. W. Adult sexual abuse of children: the man and circumstances. *Dis. Nerv. Sys.*, 1968, **29**(10), 677–83.

SWITZER, E. Female sexuality. *Family Health*, Mar. 1974, **6**(3), 34–36; 38.

TAUŠ, L. & SUŠICKÁ, L. Five-year observation of five sexual deviants after therapeutic intervention. *Ceskoslovenská Psychiatrie*, Feb. 1973, **69**(1), 51–55.

THOMPSON, N. L., JR., & MCCANDLESS, B. R., & STRICKLAND, B. R. Personal adjustment of male and female homosexuals and heterosexuals. *J. Abnorm. Psychol.*, 1971, **78**(2), 237–40.

THOMPSON, N. L., JR., SCHWARTZ, D. M., MCCANDLESS, B. R., & EDWARDS, D. A. Parent-child relationships and sexual identity in male and female homosexuals and heterosexuals. *J. Cons. Clin. Psychol.*, Aug. 1973, **41**(1), 120–27.

THORMAN, G. Cohabitation: a report on the married-unmarried life style. *The Futurist*, Dec. 1973, **7**(6), 250–53.

THORMAN, G. Living together unmarried. *The Humanist*, Mar./Apr. 1974, **34**(2), 15–18.

TIME. Avant-garde retreat? Nov. 25, 1974, **104**(22), 100; 103.

TOURNEY, G., PETRILLI, A. J., & HATFIELD, L. N. Hormonal relationships in homosexual men. *Amer. J. Psychiat.*, Mar. 1975, **132**(3), 288–90.

UNIFORM CRIME REPORTS. *Federal Bureau of Investigation. U.S. Dept. of Justice.* Washington, D.C.: U.S. Government Printing Office, 1975.

U.S. COMMISSION ON OBSCENITY AND PORNOGRAPHY. *The Report of the Commission on Obscenity and Pornography.* Washington, D.C.: Government Printing Office, 1970.

VENER, A. M., & STEWART, C. S. Adolescent sexual behavior in middle America revisted: 1970–1973. *J. Marr. Fam.*, Nov. 1974, **36**(4), 728–35.

WEINBERG, M., & WILLIAMS, C. J. *Male homosexuals: their problems and adaptations in three societies.* New York: Oxford University Press, 1974.

WERNER, A. Sexual dysfunction in college men and women. Quoted from *The American Journal of Psychiatry*, Feb. 1975, **132**(2), 164–65. Copyright 1975, the American Psychiatric Association.

WERTHAM, F. *The show of violence.* New York: Doubleday, 1949.

WITZIG, J. S. The group treatment of male exhibitionists. *Amer. J. Psychiat.*, 1968, **125**, 75–81.

YALOM, I. D. Group therapy of incarcerated sexual deviants. *J. Nerv. Ment. Dis.*, 1961, **132**, 158–70.

YOUNG, W. Prostitution. In J. H. Gagnon & W. Simon (Eds.), *Sexual deviance.* New York: Harper & Row, 1967.

17. Suicide

ABRAM, H. S., MOORE, G. L., & WESTERVELT, F. B., JR. Suicidal behavior in chronic dialysis patients. *Amer. J. Psychiat.*, Mar. 1971, **127**(9), 119–21.

BECK, A. T., BECK, R., & KOVACS, M. Classification of suicidal behaviors: I. Qualifying intent and medical lethality. *Amer. J. Psychiat.*, Mar. 1975, **132**(3), 285–87.

BERMAN, A. L. The epidemiology of life-threatening events.

Suicide, Summer 1975, 5(2), 67–77.

BINSTOCK, J. Choosing to die: the decline of aggression and the rise of suicide. *The Futurist*, Apr. 1974, 8(2), 68–71.

BROWN, J. H. Reporting of suicide: Canadian statistics. *Suicide*, Spring 1975, 5(1), 21–28.

BROWNING, C. H. Epidemiology of suicide: firearms. *Comprehensive Psychiatry*, Nov./Dec. 1974, 15(6), 549–53.

COHEN, S. L., & FIEDLER, J. E. Quote from "Content analysis of multiple messages in suicide notes" by Stuart L. Cohen and J. E. Fiedler from *Life-Threatening Behavior*, Summer 1974, 4(2), 75–95. © Human Sciences Press, 72 Fifth Avenue, New York, N.Y. 10011, 1974.

CORDER, B. F., SHORR, W., & CORDER, R. F. A study of social and psychological characteristics of adolescent suicide attempters in an urban disadvantaged area. *Adolescence*, Spring 1974, 9(33), 1–6.

DARBONNE, A. R. Suicide and age: a suicide note analysis. *J. Cons. Clin. Psychol.*, 1969, 33, 46–50.

DEIKEL, S. M. The life and death of Lenny Bruce: a psychological autopsy. *Life-Threatening Behavior*, Fall 1974, 4(3), 176–92.

DIZMANG, L. H., WATSON, J., MAY, P. A., & BOPP, J. Adolescent suicide at an Indian reservation. *Amer. J. Orthopsychiat.*, Jan. 1974, 44(1), 43–49.

DURKHEIM, E. *Suicide: a study in sociology*. Trans. J. A. Spaulding & G. Simpson. Ed. G. Simpson. New York: Free Press, 1951. Originally published 1897.

FALRET, J. P. *De l'hypocondrie et du suicide*. Paris: Caroullebois, Libraire de la Société de Médecine, 1822.

FARBEROW, N. L. *Suicide*. Morristown, N.J.: General Learning Press, 1974.

FARBEROW, N. L., & LITMAN, R. E. A comprehensive suicide prevention program. Suicide Prevention Center of Los Angeles, 1958–1969. Unpublished final report DHEW NIMH Grants No. MH 14946 & MH 00128. Los Angeles, 1970.

FARBEROW, N. L., SHNEIDMAN, E. S., & LEONARD, C. Suicide among general medical and surgical hospital patients with malignant neoplasms. Veterans Administration, Dept. of Medicine and Surgery, *Medical Bulletin* MB–9, Feb. 25, 1963, 1–11.

FREDERICK, C. J. *Suicide, homicide, and alcoholism among American Indians* (U.S. Dept. of Health, Education, & Welfare Publication No. (ADM) 74-42). Washington, D.C.: U.S. Government Printing Office, 1973.

FREDERICK, C. J., & LAGUE, L. *Dealing with the crises of suicide* (Public Affairs Pamphlet 406A). New York: Public Affairs Committee, Inc.

FULLER, M. From Suicide past and present: A note on Jean Pierre Falret, by Marielle Fuller. *Life-Threatening Behavior*, Spring 1973, 3(1), 58–65. © Human Sciences Press, 72 Fifth Avenue, New York, N.Y. 10011, 1973.

GOODWIN, D. W. Alcohol in suicide and homicide. *Quart. J. Stud. Alcohol.*, Mar. 1973, 31(1, Part A), 144–56.

GRIEST, J. H., GUSTAFSON, D. H., STAUSS, F. F., ROWSE, G. L., LAUGHREN, T. P., & CHILES, J. A. Suicide risk prediction: a new approach. *Life-Threatening Behavior*, Winter 1974, 4(4), 212–23.

HALL, J. C., BLISS, M., SMITH, K., & BRADLEY, A. Suicide gestures, attempts found high among poor. *Psychiatric News*, July 1, 1970, 20.

HAVIGHURST, R. J. Suicide and education. In E. S. Shneidman (Ed.), *On the nature of suicide*. San Francisco: Jossey-Bass, 1969.

HENDIN, H. Student suicide: death as a life-style. *J. Nerv. Ment. Dis.*, Mar. 1975, 160(3), 204–19.

HOTCHNER, A. E. *Papa Hemingway*. New York: Random House, 1966.

KALISH, R. A., REYNOLDS, D. K., & FARBEROW, N. L. Community attitudes toward suicide. *Comm. Ment. Hlth. J.*, Fall 1974, 10(3), 301–8.

KIDSON, M., & JONES, I. Psychiatric disorders among aborigines of the Australian Western Desert. *Arch. Gen. Psychiat.*, 1968, 19, 413–22.

KIRSTEIN, L., PRUSOFF, B., WEISSMAN, M., & DRESSLER, D. M. Utilization review of treatment for suicide attempters. *Amer. J. Psychiat.*, Jan. 1975, 132(1), 22–27.

KNOTT, J. E. Campus suicide in America. *Omega: Journal of Death & Dying*, Spring 1973, 4(1), 65–71.

KOVACS, M., BECK, A. T., & WEISSMAN, A. Hopelessness: an indicator of suicidal risk. *Suicide*, Summer 1975, 5(2), 95–103.

LEONARD, C. V. Depression and suicidality. *J. Cons. Clin. Psychol.*, Feb. 1974, 42(1), 98–104.

MELGES, F. T., & BOWLBY, J. Types of hopelessness in psychopathological process. *Arch. Gen. Psychiat.*, June 1969, 20(6), 690–99.

MERIAN. Sur la creinte de la mort, sur la mepris de la mort, sur le suicide: memoire. *Histoire de l'Academie Royale des Sciences et Belles-Lettres de Berlin*, 1763, XIX: 385, 392, 403.

MILLER, J. P. Suicide and adolescence. *Adolescence*, Spring 1975, 10(37), 11–24.

MINKOFF, K., BERGMAN, E., BECK, A. T., & BECK, R. Hopelessness, depression, and attempted suicide. *Amer. J. Psychiat.*, Apr. 1973, 130(4), 455–59.

MURPHY, G. E. Suicide and the right to die. *Amer. J. Psychiat.*, Apr. 1973, 130(4), 472–73.

MURRAY, D. C. Suicidal and depressive feelings among college students. *Psych. Rep.*, Aug. 1973, 33(1), 175–81.

NATIONAL INSTITUTE OF MENTAL HEALTH. Rising suicide rate linked to economy. *Los Angeles Times*, Apr. 20, 1975, VIII, 2; 5.

NELSON, H. County suicide rate up sharply among young. *Los Angeles Times*, Jan. 26, 1971, II, 1.

PARKIN, M. Suicide and culture in Fairbanks: a comparison of three cultural groups in a small city of interior Alaska. *Psychiatry*, Feb. 1974, 37(1), 60–67.

PAUSNAU, R. O., & RUSSELL, A. T. Psychiatric resident suicide: an analysis of five cases. *Amer. J. Psychiat.*, Apr. 1975, 132(4), 402–6.

PAYKEL, E. S., HALLOWELL, C., DRESSLER, D. M., SHAPIRO, D. L., & WEISSMAN, M. M. Treatment of suicide attempters. *Arch. Gen. Psychiat.*, Oct. 1974, 31(4), 487–91.

PAYKEL, E. S., PRUSOFF, B. A., & MYERS, J. K. Suicide attempts and recent life events. *Arch. Gen. Psychiat.*, Mar. 1975, 32(3), 327–33.

PECK, M. A., & SCHRUT, A. Suicidal behavior among college students. *HSMHA Health Reports*, Feb. 1971, 86(2), 149–56.

ROGOW, A. A. Private illness and public policy: the cases of James Forrestal and John Winant. *Amer. J. Psychiat.*, 1969, 125(8), 1093–97.

ROSEN, D. H. The serious suicide attempt: epidemiological and follow-up study of 886 patients. *Amer. J. Psychiat.*, 1970, 127(6), 64–70.

ROSS, M. This doctor will self-destruct . . . *Human Behavior*, Feb. 1974, 3(2), 54.

RUDESTAM, K. E. Stockholm and Los Angeles: a cross-cultural study of the communication of suicidal intent. *J. Cons. Clin.*

Psychol., 1971, **36**(1), 82–90.

SAWYER, J. B., SUDAK, H. S., & HALL, S. R. A follow-up study of 53 suicides known to a suicide prevention center. *Life-Threatening Behavior*, Winter 1972, **2**(4), 227–38.

SCHAAR, K. Suicide rate high among women psychologists. *APA Monitor*, July 1974, **5**(7), 1; 10.

SEIDEN, R. H. Suicide: preventable death. *Public Affairs Report*, Aug. 1974, **15**(4), 1–5.

SHNEIDMAN, E. S. Fifty-eight years. In E. S. Shneidman (Ed.), *On the nature of suicide*. San Francisco: Jossey-Bass, 1969. Pp. 1–30.

SHNEIDMAN, E. S. Suicide notes reconsidered. *Psychiatry*, Nov. 1973, **36**(4), 379–94. Copyright 1973, The William Alanson White Psychiatric Foundation, Inc. Reprinted by permission of the author and The William Alanson White Psychiatric Foundation, Inc.

SHNEIDMAN, E. S., PARKER, E., & FUNKHOUSER, G. R. You and death. *Psych. Today*, 1970, **4**(3), 67–72.

SHORE, J. H. American Indian suicide—fact and fantasy. *Psychiatry*, Feb. 1975, **38**(1), 86–91.

STANLEY, E. J., & BARTER, J. T. Adolescent suicidal behavior. *Amer. J. Orthopsychiat.*, 1970, **40**(1), 87–96.

TUCKMAN, J., KLEINER, R., & LAVELL, M. Emotional content of suicide notes. Reprinted from *The American Journal of Psychiatry*, volume **116**, pages 59–63, 1959. Copyright 1959, the American Psychiatric Association.

U.S. NEWS & WORLD REPORT. Upsurge in suicides—and in ways to prevent them. July 1, 1974, **77**(1), 47–48.

WATKINS, C., GILBERT, J. E., & BASS, W. The persistent suicidal patient. *Amer. J. Psychiat.*, 1969, **125**, 1590–93.

WEISSMAN, M. M. The epidemiology of suicide attempts, 1960–1971. *Arch. Gen. Psychiat.*, June 1974, **30**(6), 737–46.

WEISSMAN, M. M., FOX, K., & KLERMAN, G. L. Hostility and depression associated with suicide attempts. *Amer. J. Psychiat.*, Apr. 1973, **130**(4), 450–55.

WORLD HEALTH ORGANIZATION. In W. Tuohy, World health agency zeroes in on suicide. *Los Angeles Times*, Oct. 25, 1974, VI, 1–3.

ZUNG, W. W. K., & GREEN, R. L., JR. Seasonal variations of suicide and depression. *Gen. Psychiat.*, Jan. 1974, **30**(1), 89–91.

18. Maladaptive Behavior of Groups

ABELSON, P. H. The world's disparate food supplies. *Science*, Jan. 24, 1975, **187**(4173), 217.

ALLEN, L. S., ET AL. Out of the third world experience. In R. Buckhout et al. (Eds.), *Toward social change*. New York: Harper & Row, 1971. Pp. 94–96.

BANDURA, A. *Aggression: a social learning analysis*. Englewood Cliffs, N.J.: Prentice-Hall, 1973.

BENGELSDORF, I. S. Dear student: our spaceship earth's in trouble; so are we. *Los Angeles Times*, Apr. 16, 1970, II, 7.

BERKOWITZ, L. The concept of aggressive drive: some additional considerations. In L. Berkowitz (Ed.), *Advances in experimental social psychology* (Vol. 2). New York: Academic Press, 1965.

BERKOWITZ, L. Some determinants of impulsive aggression: role of mediated associations with reinforcements for aggression. *Psych. Rev.*, Mar. 1974, **81**(2), 165–76.

BERLAND, T. Getting the message about noise . . . loudly and clearly. *Today's Health*, May 1973, **51**(5), 68–69.

BRONFENBRENNER, U. The origins of alienation. *Scientif.*

Amer., Aug. 1974, **231**(2), 53–57; 60–61.

BROWN, H. Where wonder is taking us: Caltech and the world of science. *Los Angeles Times*, Dec. 10, 1967, 5.

BROWN, L. R. Global food insecurity. *The Futurist*, Apr. 1974, **8**(2), 56–64.

BUCKHOUT, R., & 81 CONCERNED BERKELEY STUDENTS. (Eds.) *Toward social change*. New York: Harper & Row, 1971. Four line poem by Patrick Tamayo. Copyright © 1971 by Harper & Row, Publishers, Inc. Reprinted by permission of the publishers.

BULLETIN OF THE ATOMIC SCIENTISTS. Editorial: we re-set the clock. 1974, **30**(7), 4–5.

CALHOUN, J. B. Population density and social pathology. *Scientif. Amer.*, 1962, **206**(2), 139–50.

CALHOUN, J. B., & MARSDEN, H. Cited in Not with a bang but with a whimper. *Sci. News*, Feb. 3, 1973, **103**(5), 73.

CANBY, T. Y., & RAYMER, S. Can the world feed its people? *National Geographic Mazagine*, July 1975, **148**(1), 2–31.

CLARK, K. B. Explosion in the ghetto. *Psych. Today*, 1967, **1**(5), 31–38; 62–64.

COLES, R. *Children of crisis: a study of courage and fear*. Boston: Little, Brown, 1967.

COUSINS, N. Hiroshima. *Look*, Aug. 11, 1970, pp. 38, 43–45. Reprinted by permission of Norman Cousins.

COUSTEAU, J. Cited in Issue of the year: the environment. *Time*, Jan. 4, 1971, 21–22.

CROSSON, P. R. Institutional obstacles to expansion of world food production. *Science*, May 9, 1975, **188**(4188), 519–24.

DRAPER, P. Crowding among hunter-gatherers: the !Kung bushmen. *Science*, Oct. 19, 1973, **182**(4109), 301–3.

EHRLICH, P. People pollution. *Audubon*, 1970, **72**(5), 4–9.

EISENBERG, L. Student unrest: sources and consequences. *Science*, 1970, **167**(3926), 1688–92.

ERON, L. D., HUESMANN, L. R., LEFKOWITZ, M. M., & WALDER, L. O. How learning conditions in early childhood—including mass media—relate to aggression in late adolescence. *Amer. J. Orthopsychiat.*, Apr. 1974, **44**(3), 412–23.

FREUD, S. *Civilization and its discontents*. London: Hogarth, 1930.

GENOVESE, E. D. A massive breakdown. *Newsweek*, July 6, 1970, 25–27.

GLASS, B. Educational obsolescence. *Science*, 1970, **170**(3962), 1041.

HALL, E. T. *The hidden dimension*. New York: Doubleday, 1966.

HALLIE, P. P. Sadean and institutional cruelty. In F. Korten, S. Cook & J. Lacey (Eds.), *Psychology and the problems of society*. Washington, D.C.: American Psychological Association, 1970. Pp. 295–303.

HARTUP, W. W. Aggression in childhood: developmental perspectives. *Amer. Psychologist*, May 1974, **29**(5), 336–41.

HOLLINGS, E. Hunger survey finds retarded growth in slum-area children. *Los Angeles Times*, March 11, 1971, I, 5. [a]

HOLLINGS, E. Hunger survey finds retarded growth in slum-area children. *Los Angeles Times*, March 25, 1971, I, 1; 23. [b]

HOPKINS, F. S. The postulated future, the invented future and an ameliorated world. *The Futurist*, Dec. 1973, **7**(6), 254–58.

IRELAND, L. M., & BESNER, A. Low-income outlook on life. In L. M. Ireland (Ed.), *Low-income life styles*. Washington, D.C.: U.S. Government Printing Office, 1967. Pp. 1–12.

JANIS, I. L., MAHL, G. R., KAGAN, J., & HOLT, R. *Personality: dy-*

namics, development, and assessment. New York: Harcourt Brace Jovanovich, Inc., 1969.

JOAD, C. E. M. *Why war?* Harmondsworth: Penguin Special, 1939.

KAHN, H. The Malthusian score. *Time,* 1970, **96**(8), 1.

KENISTON, K. Social change and youth in America. In E. H. Erikson (Ed.), *Youth: change and challenge.* New York: Basic Books, 1963.

KIESTER, E. Noise, noise, noise! *Family Health,* Jan. 1974, **6**(1), 20–21; 48; 50; 52.

KNOWLES, J. In A. Rossiter (Ed.), Planet grows crowded. *Los Angeles Evening Outlook,* Mar. 30, 1974, 5.

LAWRENCE, D. Can nuclear weapons be abolished? *U.S. News and World Report,* Sept. 27, 1971, 96.

LAWRENCE, J. E. S. Science and sentiment: overview of research on crowding and human behavior. *Psychol. Bull.,* Oct. 1974, **81**(10), 712–20.

LERNER, M. Life, liberty, and the pursuit of paranoia. *Los Angeles Times,* July 2, 1970, II, 7.

LIPOWSKI, Z. J. Sensory overloads, information overloads and behavior. *Psychotherapy and Psychosomatics,* 1974, **23**(1), 264–70.

LORENZ, K. *On aggression.* New York: Harcourt Brace Jovanovich, Inc., 1966.

MARSELLA, A. J., ESCUDERO, M., & GORDON, P. The effects of dwelling density on mental disorders in Filipino men. *J. Hlth. Soc. Behav.,* 1970, **11**(4), 288–93.

MC NAMARA, R. S. Cited in McNamara paints grim picture of world plight. *Los Angeles Times,* Sept. 22, 1970, I, 5.

MC NAMARA, R. S. Cited in One billion face not deprivation but death. *Los Angeles Times,* Oct. 9, 1974, II, 5.

MEAD, M. Family future. *Trans-action,* 1971, **8**(1), 50–53.

MILLER, N. E., & DOLLARD, J. *Social learning and imitation.* New Haven, Conn.: Yale University Press, 1941.

MOLITOR, G. T. T. The coming world struggle for food. *The Futurist,* Aug. 1974, **8**(4), 169–78.

MURPHY, J. M. Social science concepts and cross-cultural methods for psychiatric research. In J. M. Murphy & A. H. Leighton (Eds.), *Approaches to cross-cultural psychiatry.* New York: Cornell University Press, 1965. Pp. 251–84.

MURRAY, J. P. Television and violence: implications of the Surgeon General's research program. *Amer. Psychologist,* June 1973, **28**(6), 472–78.

MYDANS, S. Plight of cities tied to social problems. *Los Angeles Times,* July 13, 1975, IV, 1; 6.

NADER, R. We need a new kind of patriotism. *Life,* 1971, **71**(2), 4.

NATIONAL COMMISSION ON THE CAUSES AND PREVENTION OF VIOLENCE. *Violence and the media.* Staff Report (Vol. 9). Washington, D.C.: U.S. Government Printing Office, 1969.

NATIONAL INSTITUTE OF MENTAL HEALTH. *The mental health of urban America.* Washington, D.C.: U.S. Government Printing Office, 1969.

NIEMOLLER, M. Speech given in 1966. Cited in B. Mandelbaum (Ed.), *Choose life.* New York: Random House, 1968.

OPTON, E. Lessons of My Lai. In R. Buckhout et al. (Eds.), *Toward social change.* New York: Harper & Row, 1971. Pp. 176–86.

PASAMANICK, B. Inaction on hunger called "murderous." *Psychiatric News,* 1971, **6**(7), 1; 24.

POLEMAN, T. T. World food: a perspective. *Science,* May 9, 1975, **188**(4188), 510–18.

RAPPOPORT, L. Personal communication with the author, 1971.

REICE, S. Editorial. *Family Health,* Apr. 1974, **6**(4), 4.

SANDERSON, F. H. The great food fumble. *Science,* May 9, 1975, **188**(4188), 503–9.

SCHAAR, K. Crowding: what's bad for rats may be ok for humans. *APA Monitor,* Jan. 1975, **6**(1), 7.

SCIENTIFIC AMERICAN. *The human population.* Sept. 1974, **231**(3).

SHACKLE, G. L. S. Decision: the human predicament. *Ann. Amer. Acad. Polit. Soc. Sci.,* Mar. 1974, **412**, 1–10.

SHAW, D. Violent movies create violent kids. *Today's Health,* Oct. 1974, **52**(10), 10–11; 62–63; 65.

SYMINGTON, S. In S. Shannon (Ed.), Symington warns U.N. of 'nuclear holocaust.' *Los Angeles Times,* Oct. 22, 1974, I, 9.

TANNENBAUM, F. *Slave and citizen: the Negro in America.* New York: Knopf, 1947.

TOFFLER, A. *Future shock.* New York: Random House, 1970.

TOFFLER, A. Is the family obsolete? *Look,* Jan. 26, 1971, 35.

TOFFLER, A. *The eco-spasm report: Why our economy is running out of control.* New York: Bantam Books, 1975.

TOYNBEE, A. Human savagery cuts thin veneer. *Los Angeles Times,* Sept. 6, 1970, C, 3.

TRIMBLE, J. E. The unsettled ashes of General Armstrong Custer: genocide, slavery, oppression and land rip-offs of native persons by foreign governments. *Society for the Psychological Study of Social Issues Newsletter,* May 1974, No. 136, 1; 14–17.

TROTTER, R. J. Cities, crowding, & crime. *Sci. News,* Nov. 2, 1974, **106**(18), 282–83.

U.S. NATIONAL ADVISORY COMMISSION ON CIVIL DISORDERS. *Report.* Washington, D.C.: U.S. Government Printing Office, 1968.

WHITE, T. *The making of the president: 1968.* New York: Pocket Books, 1970.

YAGER, J. Personal violence in infantry combat. *Arch. Gen. Psychiat.,* Feb. 1975, **32**(2), 257–61.

YORK, H. F. We *can* reverse the arms race. *Life,* 1970, **69**(24), 40–41.

ZUCKERMAN, S. *The social life of monkeys and apes.* London: Kegan Paul, 1932.

19. The Problem of Assessment

BIJOU, S. W. Experimental studies of child behavior, normal and deviant. In L. Krasner & L. P. Ullmann (Eds.), *Research in behavior modification: new developments and implications.* New York: Holt, Rinehart & Winston, 1965. Pp. 56–81.

CLEARY, T. A., HUMPHREYS, L. G., KENDRICK, S. A., & WESMAN, A. Educational uses of tests with disadvantaged students. *Amer. Psychologist,* Jan. 1975, **30**(1), 15–41.

COMREY, A. *Comrey personality scales.* San Diego: Educational Industrial Testing Service, 1970.

D'ANGELLI, A. Group composition using interpersonal skills: an analogue study of the effects of members' interpersonal skills on peer ratings and group cohesiveness. *J. Couns. Psychol.,* Nov. 1973, **20**(6), 531–43.

DOOLEY, D. Assessing nonprofessional mental health workers with the GAIT: an evaluation of peer ratings. *American Journal of Community Psychology,* June 1975, **3**(2), 99–110.

EVENSON, R. C., SLETTEN, I. W., HEDLUND, J. L., & FAINTICH, D. M. CAPS: an automated evaluation system. *Amer. J. Psychiat.,* May 1974, **131**(5), 531–34.

GOLDBERG, L. R. Man versus model of man. *Psychol. Bull.*, 1970, **73**(6), 422–32.

GOODMAN, G. *Companionship therapy: studies in structured intimacy.* San Francisco: Jossey-Bass, 1972. [a]

GOODMAN, G. Systematic selection of psychotherapeutic talent: the group assessment of interpersonal traits. In S. E. Golann & C. Eisdorfer (Eds.), *Handbook of community mental health.* New York: Appleton-Century-Crofts, 1972. [b]

GOODMAN, G. Personal correspondence with the author, at UCLA, 1975.

GREIST, J. H., GUSTAFSON, D. H., STAUSS, F. F., ROWSE, G. L., LAUGHREN, T. P., & CHILES, J. A. A computer interview for suicide-risk prediction. *Amer. J. Psychiat.*, Dec. 1973, **130**(12), 1327–32.

GROSSMAN, M. Insurance reports as a threat to confidentiality. *Amer. J. Psychiat.*, 1971, **128**(1), 96–100.

HATHAWAY, S. R., & MCKINLEY, J. C. *The Minnesota multiphasic personality inventory* (Rev. ed.). New York: Psychological Corporation, 1951.

KLINE, P. (ED.). *New approaches in psychological measurements.* New York: Wiley, 1974.

KLOPFER, B., & DAVIDSON, H. *The Rorschach technique: an introductory manual.* New York: Harcourt Brace Jovanovich, Inc., 1962.

LACHAR, D. Accuracy and generalizability of an automated MMPI interpretation system. *J. Cons. Clin. Psychol.*, Apr. 1974, **42**(2), 267–73.

LINDQUIST, C. U., & RAPPAPORT, J. Selection of college student therapeutic agents: further analysis of the "Group assessment of interpersonal traits: technique." *J. Cons. Clin. Psychol.*, 1973, **41**(2), 316.

MERCER, J. R. A policy statement on assessment procedures and the rights of children. *Harvard Ed. Rev.*, Feb. 1974, **44**(1), 125–41.

MIRABILE, C. S., HOUCK, J., & GLUECK, B. C., JR. Computer beats clinician in prognosis contest. *Psychiatric News*, 1970, **5**(18).

PANEL ON YOUTH. *Youth, transition to adulthood.* Report of the Panel on Youth of the President's Science Advisory Committee, June 1973.

POOLEY, R. *An experiment in delinquency prevention and control.* Carbondale: Southern Illinois University, 1971. From "An Experiment in Delinquency Prevention and Control" by Richard Pooley. Analysis developed by the Institute of Clinical Analysis in Glendale, California (MMPI–ICA Report). Reprinted by permission.

SLETTEN, I. W., ALTMAN, H., & ULETT, G. A. Routine diagnosis by computer. *Amer. J. Psychiat.*, 1971, **127**, 1147–52.

WALKER, C. E. Training in clinical psychology: the future? *The Clinical Psychologist*, Winter 1974, **27**(2), 12–13.

WECHSLER, D. *Manual for the Wechsler Adult Intelligence Scale.* New York: Psychological Corporation, 1955.

20. Contemporary Approaches to Therapy

AGUILERA, D. C., & MESSICK, J. M. *Crisis intervention: theory and methodology.* St. Louis, Mo.: Mosby, 1974.

ALEXANDER, F. Individual psychotherapy. *Psychosom. Med.*, 1946, **8**, 110–15.

AMERICAN PSYCHOLOGICAL ASSOCIATION. Guidelines for psychologists conducting growth groups. *Amer. Psychologist*, Oct. 1973, **28**(10), 933.

ARING, C. D. Gheel: the town that cares. *Family Health*, Apr. 1975, **7**(4), 54–55; 58; 60.

ASTRUP, C. A follow-up study of electrosleep. *Biological Psychiatry*, Feb. 1974, **8**(1), 115–17.

AYLLON, T., & AZRIN, N. H. *The token economy: a motivational system for therapy and rehabilitation.* New York: Appleton-Century-Crofts, 1968.

BANDURA, A. *Principles of behavior modification.* New York: Holt, Rinehart & Winston, 1969.

BARBER, T. X. *Hypnosis: a scientific approach.* New York: Van Nostrand Reinhold, 1969.

BERNE, E. *Games people play.* New York: Grove Press, 1964.

BERNE, E. *What do you say after you say hello?* New York: Grove Press, 1972.

BROWN, C. C. Electroanesthesia and electrosleep. *Amer. Psychologist*, Mar. 1975, **30**(3), 402–10.

BUCHER, B., & LOVAAS, O. I. Use of aversive stimulation in behavior modification. In M. R. Jones (Ed.), *Miami symposium on the prediction of behavior 1967: Aversive stimulation.* Coral Gables: University of Miami Press, 1968. Pp. 77–145.

CORSINI, R. J. (ED.). *Current psychotherapies.* Itasca, Ill.: Peacock Publishers, 1973.

CROGHAN, L. M. Encounter groups and the necessity for ethical guidelines. *J. Clin. Psychol.*, Oct. 1974, **30**(4), 438–45.

CURRY, A. E. The world of a schizophrenic woman. Reprinted from *The Psychoanalytic Review*, Vol. **49**, No. 1, 1962, through the courtesy of the Editors and the Publisher, National Psychological Association for Psychoanalysis, New York, N.Y.

DENNER, B. Returning madness to an accepting community. *Comm. Ment. Hlth. J.*, 1974, **10**(2), 163–72.

DIAMOND, M. J. Modification of hypnotizability: a review. *Psychol. Bull.*, Mar. 1974, **81**(3), 180–98.

EISLER, R. M., MILLER, P. M., HERSEN, M., & ALFORD, H. Effects of assertive training on marital interaction. *Arch. Gen. Psychiat.*, May 1974, **30**(5), 643–49.

ELLIS, A. Rational psychotherapy. *J. Gen. Psychol.*, 1958, **59**, 35–49.

ELLIS, A. Rational-emotive therapy. In R. J. Corsini (Ed.), *Current psychotherapies.* Itasca, Ill.: Peacock Publishers, 1973.

ELLIS, A. Creative job and happiness: the humanistic way. *The Humanist*, Jan.-Feb. 1975, **35**(1), 11–13.

EMMELKAMP, P. M. G., & WESSELS, H. Flooding in imagination vs. flooding *in vivo*: a comparison with agoraphobics. *Behav. Res. Ther.*, Feb. 1975, **13**(1), 7–15.

ERICKSON, R. C. Outcome studies in mental hospitals: a review. *Psychol. Bull.*, July 1975, **82**(4), 519–40.

FAIRWEATHER, G. W., SANDERS, D. H., MAYNARD, H., & CRESSLER, D. L. *Community life for the mentally ill: an alternative to institutional care.* Chicago: Aldine, 1969.

FROMM, E., & SHOR, R. E. *Hypnosis: research developments and perspectives.* Chicago: Aldine, 1972.

GLASSER, W. *Reality therapy.* New York: Harper & Row, 1965.

GLASSER, W. Reality therapy—a new approach. In O. H. Mowrer (Ed.), *Morality and mental health.* New York: Rand McNally, 1967. Pp. 126–34.

GLASSER, W., & ZUNIN, L. N. Reality therapy. In R. Corsini (Ed.), *Current psychotherapies.* Itasca, Ill.: Peacock Publishers, 1973.

HALEY, J. Whither family therapy. *Family Process*, 1962, **1**, 69–100.

HALLECK, S. Therapy is the handmaiden of the status quo.

Psych. Today, 1971, **4**(11), 30–32; 98–100.

HAVENS, L. L. The existential use of the self. *Amer. J. Psychiat.,* Jan. 1974, **131**(1), 1–10.

HEARST, E. D., CLONINGER, C. R., CREWS, E. L., & CADORET, R. J. Electrosleep therapy: a double-blind trial. *Arch. Gen. Psychiat.,* Apr. 1974, **30**(4), 463–66.

HILGARD, E. R. The domain of hypnosis: with some comments on alternative paradigms. *Amer. Psychologist,* Nov. 1973, **28**(11), 972–82.

HILGARD, E. R. Weapon against pain: hypnosis is no mirage. *Psych. Today,* Nov. 1974, **8**(6), 120–22; 126; 128.

HIRAI, T., & KASAMATSU, A. An electroencephalographic study of the Zen meditation. *Folia Psychiatrica et Neurologica Japonica,* 1966, **20,** 315–36.

HUFF, F. W. A learning theory approach to family therapy. *The Family Coordinator,* 1969, **18**(1), 22–26.

HURWITZ, N. The family therapist as intermediary. *The Family Coordinator,* Apr. 1974, **23**(2), 145–58.

HURWITZ, T. D. Electroconvulsive therapy: a review. *Comprehensive Psychiatry,* July/Aug., 1974, **15**(4), 303–14.

ISCOE, I. Community psychology and the competent community. *Amer. Psychologist,* Aug. 1974, **29**(8), 607–13.

JACOBSON, E. *Progressive relaxation.* Chicago: University of Chicago Press, 1938.

JONES, M. C. A laboratory study of fear: the case of Peter. *Pedagogical Seminary,* 1924, **31,** 308–15.

KAMIYA, J. Conscious control of brain waves. *Psych. Today,* 1968, **1**(11), 56–60.

KANTOROVICH, F. An attempt at associative reflex therapy in alcoholism. *Psychological Abstracts,* 1930, **4282.**

KATKIN, S., GINSBURG, M., RIFKIN, M., & SCOTT, J. Effectiveness of female volunteers in the treatment of outpatients. *J. Couns. Psychol.,* 1971, **18**(2), 97–100.

KEMPLER, W. Gestalt therapy. In R. Corsini (Ed.), *Current Psychotherapies.* Itasca, Ill.: Peacock Publishers, 1973.

KENNEDY, T. D., & KIMURA, H. K. Transfer, behavioral improvement, and anxiety reduction in systematic desensitization. *J. Cons. Clin. Psychol.,* Oct. 1974, **42**(5), 720–28.

KLINE, N. S. Use of *Rauwolfia serpentina* in neuropsychiatric conditions. *Ann. N.Y. Acad. Sci.,* 1954, **54,** 107–32.

LANGSLEY, D. Treatment goes home. *Sci. News,* 1968, **94**(6), 133.

LAVOIE, J. C. Type of punishment as a determinant of resistance to deviation. *Develop. Psychol.,* Mar. 1974, **10**(2), 181–89.

MAY, R. *Love and will.* New York: Norton, 1969.

MEALIEA, W. L., JR. The comparative effectiveness of systematic desensitization and implosive therapy in the elimination of snake phobia. Unpublished doctoral dissertation, University of Missouri, 1967.

MICHENER, J. A. *The fires of spring.* New York: Random House, 1949.

MILLER, R. R., & SPRINGER, A. D. Implications of recovery from experimental amnesia. *Psych. Rev.,* Sept. 1974, **81**(5), 470–73.

MORENO, J. L. Psychodrama. In S. Arieti et al. (Eds.), *American handbook of psychiatry* (Vol. 2). New York: Basic Books, 1959.

NACE, E. P., ORNE, M. T., & HAMMER, A. G. Posthypnotic amnesia as an active psychic process. *Arch. Gen. Psychiat.,* Aug. 1974, **31**(2), 257–60.

NICOLETTI, J., & FLATER, L. A community-oriented program for training and using volunteers. *Comm. Ment. Hlth. J.,* Apr.

1975, **11**(1), 58–63.

PAUL, N. The family as patient. *Time,* May 31. 1971, 60.

PERLS, F. S. Group vs. individual therapy. *ETC: A Review of General Semantics,* 1967, **34,** 306–12.

PERLS, F. S. *Gestalt therapy verbatim.* Lafayette, California: Real People Press, 1969. Reprinted by permission.

ROGERS, C. R. *Client-centered therapy.* Boston: Houghton Mifflin, 1951. Reprinted by permission of Houghton Mifflin Company and Constable & Company Limited.

ROGERS, C. R. *On becoming a person: a client's view of psychotherapy.* Boston: Houghton Mifflin, 1961.

ROGERS, C. R. Client-centered therapy. In S. Arieti et al. (Eds.), *American handbook of psychiatry* (Vol. 3). New York: Basic Books, 1966.

ROGERS, C. R. *Carl Rogers on encounter groups.* New York: Harper & Row, 1970.

ROSENTHAL, S. H., & WULFSOHN, N. L. Electrosleep—a clinical trial. *Amer. J. Psychiat.* 1970, **127**(4), 175–76.

RUSSEL, E. W. The power of behavior control: a critique of behavior modification methods. Special Monograph Supplement. *J. Clin. Psychol.,* Apr. 1974, **30**(2), 111–36.

SACERDOTE, P. Hypnosis in cancer patients. *American Journal of Clinical Hypnosis,* 1966, **9,** 100–8.

SAGER, C. J. The group psychotherapist: bulwark against alienation. *American Journal of Group Psychotherapy,* 1968, **18,** 419–31.

SATIR, V. *Conjoint family therapy* (Rev. ed.). Palo Alto: Science and Behavior Books, 1967.

SCHNEIDER, M. J. Some cheering news about a very painful subject. *The Sciences,* May 1974, **14**(4), 6–12.

SCHUTZ, W. C. Encounter. In R. Corsini (Ed.), *Current psychotherapies.* Itasca, Ill.: Peacock Publishers, 1973, 401–43.

SILVERMAN, W. H., & VAL, E. Day hospital in the context of a community mental health program. *Comm. Ment. Hlth. J.,* Spring 1975, **11**(1), 82–90.

STAMPFL, T. G. Implosive therapy: staring down your nightmares. *Psych. Today,* Feb. 1975, **8**(9), 66–68; 72–73.

STAMPFL, T. G., & LEVIS, D. J. Essentials of implosive therapy: a learning-theory-based psychodynamic behavioral therapy. *J. Abnorm. Psychol.,* 1967, **72,** 496–503.

STAMPFL, T. G., & LEVIS, D. J. *Implosive therapy: theory and technique.* Morristown, N.J.: General Learning Press, 1973.

STOLLER, F. H. The long weekend. *Psych. Today,* 1967, **1,** 28–33.

STUART, R. B. Behavioral contracting within the families of delinquents. *Journal of Behavior Therapy and Experimental Psychiatry,* 1971, **2,** 1–11. Copyright 1971, Pergamon Press.

SUNDBERG, N. D., & TYLER, L. E. *Clinical psychology.* New York: Appleton-Century-Crofts, 1962.

TOWNSEND, R. E., HOUSE, J. F., & ADDARIO, D. A comparison of biofeedback-mediated relaxation and group therapy in the treatment of chronic anxiety. *Amer. J. Psychiat.,* June 1975, **132**(6), 598–601.

ULLMAN, L. P., AND KRASNER, L. *A psychological approach to abnormal behavior.* Englewood Cliffs, N.J.: Prentice-Hall, 1975.

VAN EGEREN, L. F. Psychophysiologic aspects of systematic desensitization. *Behav. Res. Ther.,* 1971, **9**(1), 65–77.

WHALEN, C. K., & HENKER, B. A. Pyramid therapy in a hospital for the retarded. *Amer. J. Ment. Def.,* 1971, **75**(4), 414–34.

WOLF, M., RISLEY, T., & MEES, H. Application of operant conditioning procedures to the behavior problems of an autistic child. *Behavior Research and Therapy*, 1964, **1,** 305–12. Permission granted by Maxwell International Microforms Corporation.

WOLPE, J. The systematic desensitization treatment of neuroses. *J. Nerv. Ment. Dis.*, 1961, **132,** 189–203.

WOLPE, J. Quantitative relationships in the systematic desensitization of phobias. *Amer. J. Psychiat.*, 1963, **119,** 1062.

WOLPE, J. *The practice of behavior therapy.* New York: Pergamon, 1969.

YABLONSKY, L. Psychodrama lives. *Human Behavior*, Feb. 1975, 4(2), 24–29.

YALOM, I. D., & LIEBERMAN, M. A. A study of encounter group casualties. *Arch. Gen. Psychiat.*, 1971, **25,** 16–30.

21. Action for Mental Health and a Better World

CHISHOLM, B. The future of psychiatry. *Amer. J. Psychiat.*, 1948, **104,** 543.

DAY, W. F. A defense of Skinner's behaviorism: comments on Professor Szasz's review. *The Humanist*, Mar./Apr. 1975, **35**(2), 29; 31–32.

DONNE, J. Meditation XVII. *Devotions upon emergent occasions.* London, 1624.

HASKINS, C. P. *Report to the president, 1966–1967.* Washington, D.C.: Carnegie Institute, 1968.

HUXLEY, A. *Brave new world.* New York: Harper & Row, 1932.

HUXLEY, J. The future of man. *Bulletin of the Atomic Scientists*, 1959, **15,** 402–9.

KENNEDY, R. F. Quoted in Kennedy, E. M. A tribute to his brother. *Vital Speeches*, 1968, 34(18).

MC HALE, J. Forecasting and futures research. *Society*, July/Aug. 1975, **12**(5), 22–28.

MILLER, G. A. Psychology as a means of promoting human welfare. *Amer. Psychologist*, Dec. 1969, **24**(12), 1063–75.

NATIONAL INSTITUTE OF MENTAL HEALTH. *The mental health of urban America.* Washington, D.C.: U.S. Government Printing Office, 1969.

ORWELL, G. *1984.* New York: Harcourt Brace Jovanovich, Inc., 1949.

RAIFFA, H. A multinational institute explores global problems. *The Futurist*, June 1975, **9**(3), 147–49.

SHEPHERD, J. Rebirth, *Look*, 1971, **35**(1), 15.

SKINNER, B. F. *Walden two.* New York: Macmillan, 1948.

SKINNER, B. F. *Beyond freedom and dignity.* New York: Knopf, 1971.

SKINNER, B. F. *About behaviorism.* New York: Knopf, 1974.

SKINNER, B. F. The steep and thorny way to a science of behavior. *Amer. Psychologist*, Jan. 1975, **30**(1), 42–49.

SZASZ, T. S. A critique of Skinner's behaviorism. *The Humanist*, Mar./Apr. 1975, **35**(2), 26; 30–31.

UNESCO. *Constitution.* Paris: UNESCO, 1945.

WAGGONER, R. W. The presidential address: cultural dissonance and psychiatry. *Amer. J. Psychiat.*, 1970, **127**(1), 1–8.

Picture Credits

Cover (detail) and front endsheets (entire painting): "Road With Cypress and Star," oil on canvas by Vincent van Gogh, 1890. The Rijksmuseum Kröller-Müller, Otterlo, The Netherlands

Contributions toward medical psychology, edited by Arthur Weider. Copyright 1953 The Ronald Press Company, New York

278 Harper Brothers Memorial

280 U.S. Army Photo, Walter Reed Army Institute

282 Odette Mennesson-Rigaud/Photo Researchers

287 From "The Control of Eating Behavior in an Anorexia by Operant Conditioning Techniques" by Arthur J. Bachrach, William J. Erwin and Jay P. Mohr, from *Case Studies in Behavior Modification* edited by Leonard P. Ullmann and Leonard Krasner. Copyright © 1965 by Holt, Rinehart and Winston, Inc.

290 "Strange Visitor in My Garden." Courtesy of *Psychiatric News,* painting by Wayne Attaway

293 © Copyright 1946, CIBA Pharmaceutical Company, from *CIBA Symposia.*

298 From "Flexible System for the Diagnosis of Schizophrenia: Report from the WHO International Pilot Study of Schizophrenia" by W. T. Carpenter, J. S. Strauss, & J. J. Bartko, *Science,* Dec. 21, 1973, 182(4118), 1275–77, Table 2. Copyright 1973 by the American Association for the Advancement of Science. Reprinted by permission.

299 Jerry Cooke © 1955

302 Wide World

303 Wide World

305 From J. Plokker's *Art from the Mentally Disturbed,* courtesy of Mouton & Company, n.v. Publishers, THE HAGUE

329 Jerry Cooke © 1955

338 "Femme aux seins nus" by Guillaume. Courtesy the Collection de la Compagnie de l'Art Brut

344 Ken Heyman

345 Jerry Cooke © 1955

351 Adapted from Carlson, G. A., & Goodwin, F. K. The stages of mania: a longitudinal analysis of the manic episode. Reprinted from the *Archives of General Psychiatry,* Feb. 1973, 28(2), 221–28. Copyright 1973, American Medical Association

357 From Taylor, M. A., & Abrams, R. The phenomenology of mania. Reprinted from the *Archives of General Psychiatry,* October 1973, 29(4), 520–27. Copyright 1973, American Medical Association

360 Paul Fusco/Magnum

364 "Liz at Bailey's Mistake"/Christian Sunde

368 "El Preso" by Juan Genoves. Photograph courtesy of Marlborough Gallery, New York

372–73 Courtesy of Dr. C. Fraser

384 Elliot Erwitt/Magnum

390 Allan Grant

394 Charles Gatewood

406 Cornell Capa/Magnum (top); Paul Sequeira (bottom)

409 UPI

412 Photo by Dr. Peter Witt, Division of Research, North Carolina Department of Mental Health, Raleigh, N.C.

415 Charles Gatewood

416 From "The Effects of Alcohol," *Time,* April 22, 1974, 77. Chart entitled "Alcohol Levels in the Blood," by L. A. Greenberg adapted and reprinted by permission from *Time,* The Weekly Newsmagazine; Copyright Time Inc.

422 Photos courtesy of George W. Erdmann

437 Bob Combs/Rapho-Photo Researchers

441 Charles Gatewood

443 Leo Choplin/Black Star

451 Robert Foothorop/Jeroboam, Inc.

458 Drawing by an epileptic. Courtesy of Angela T. Folson, Ph.D., Neuropsychologist, V.A. Hospital, Danville, Illinois

465 F. Jahnel, "Pathologische Anatomie der progressiven Paralyse," in O. Bumke, *Handbuch der Geisteskrankheiten,* Vol. 11, copyright 1930. Reprinted by permission of Springer-Verlag (left); H. H. Merritt, R. D. Adams & H. C. Solomon, *Neurosyphilis.* New York: Oxford University Press, 1946. Reprinted by permission (right)

471 From Boyd's *Pathology for the Surgeon,* 8th Edition, by William Anderson, © 1967, W. B. Saunders Company

474 American Psychiatric Association

479 Diagrams from Louis P. Thorpe, Barney Katz, & Robert T. Lewis, *The Psychology of Abnormal Behavior: A Dynamic Approach* (2nd ed.). Copyright © 1961 The Ronald Press Company, New York.

481 Bruce Davidson/Magnum

492 N. Malamud, *Atlas of Neuropathology,* University of California Press, 1957. Originally published by the University of California Press; reprinted by permission of The Regents of the University of California (top); Arnold Ryan Chalfant and Charles Reynolds (bottom)

494 N. Malamud, *Atlas of Neuropathology,* University of California Press, 1957. Originally published by the University of California Press; reprinted by permission of The Regents of the University of California

498–99 Photos by Mark and Dan Jury, copyright 1975 by Mark and Dan Jury

504 "Femme, enfant et oiseaux" by Carlo. Courtesy the Collection de la Compagnie de l'Art Brut

508 Courtesy of The President's Committee on Mental Retardation; photo Gary Fine

512 Howard Bennett

513 Courtesy of the National Association for Retarded Children, Inc.

516 Courtesy of Dixon State School, Dixon, Illinois

520 Burk Uzzle/Magnum (top); Linda Schwartz (center); Stephen Deutch (bottom)

522 Courtesy of Carol K. Whalen, University of California at Irvine and Barbara Henker, University of California at Los Angeles

526 "Odalisque" by Jacqueline. Courtesy the Collection de la Compagnie de l'Art Brut

532–33 Courtesy of Dr. Bruno Bettelheim

540 Bob Natkin

545 Larry Keenan, Jr./Nest

551 Courtesy of John Harris, Children's Division, Camarillo State Mental Hospital, Camarillo, California

556 "Femmes et Oiseaux" by Miguel Hernandez. Courtesy the Collection de la Compagnie de l'Art Brut

563 Bob Levin/Black Star

573 Sepp Seitz/Magnum

588 UPI

593 Virginia Hamilton

600 Bruno de Hamel (left); Jerry Bauer (right)

600–601 George W. Gardner

602 "The Shriek," lithograph, printed in black by Edvard Munch, 1896. $20^{5}/_{8}'' \times 15^{13}/_{16}''$. Collection, The Museum of Modern Art, New York. Mathew T. Mellon Fund

608 Karsh, Ottowa/Woodfin Camp and Associates

613 Wide World

616 Courtesy of The Los Angeles Suicide Prevention Center

620 Allan Grant

621 T. Cowell/Black Star

622 "Angulo 18°" by Juan Genoves. Photograph courtesy of Marlborough Gallery, New York

625 U.S. Department of Defense

628 UPI

635 From *Children of Crisis: A Study of Courage and Fear* by Robert Coles. Copyright 1964, 1965, 1966, 1967 by Robert Coles. By permission of Atlantic-Little, Brown and Company in association with the Atlantic Monthly Press

637 Leif Skoogfors

638 UPI

644 W. Eugene Smith/Magnum

646 The New York Times

652–53 Ron Mesaros: "Muscle Beach," 1968

654 Untitled by Bradford Croston

659 Courtesy Hans Huber, Publishers, Berne

660 Reprinted by permission of the publishers from *Thematic Apperception Test* by Henry A. Murray, Harvard University Press. Copyright 1943 by The President

and Fellows of Harvard College; copyright renewed 1971 by Henry A. Murray

664 Courtesy of Dr. Gerald Goodman, University of California at Los Angeles

670–71 From "An Experiment in Delinquency Prevention and Control" by Richard Pooley. Analysis developed by the Institute of Clinical Analysis in Glendale, California (MMPI-ICA Report). Reprinted by permission

672 Courtesy of Eric McKinley, ERDA

677 Courtesy of the University of Texas Medical School at San Antonio

678 Liane Enkelis/Jeroboam, Inc.

688 Curt Gunther/Camera 5

690 Allan Grant

695 Arthur Schatz, Time Magazine, © Time Inc.

699 James H. Karales/Peter Arnold

700 Tom Medcalf

704 Courtesy of the National Institute of Mental Health (top); Ken Regan/Camera 5 (center); Bob Nadler/DPI (bottom)

715 Michael Semak

720 NASA

723 Eve Arnold/Magnum

727 Courtesy of the Los Angeles Free Clinic, photo by Herb Krashin

Color Section (beginning opposite page 144)
  i Lizabeth Corlett/DPI (top left, top right); Jeanne Heiberg/Peter Arnold (bottom)
  ii Wide World (top left); Burt Glinn/Magnum (top right); Elliot Erwitt/Magnum (bottom)
  iii John Launois/Black Star (top); Tom Tracy/Alpha from FPG (bottom)
  iv John Launois/Black Star (top); Paul S. Conklin (center); Arnold Zann (bottom)

Color Section (beginning opposite page 304)
  i Courtesy of Al Vercoutere, Camarillo State Hospital, Camarillo, California
  ii "Afternoon at Home" by Louis Wain. Victoria and Albert Museum, Crown Copyright (left); Guttmann/Maclay Collection, Institute of Psychiatry, London (top right)
  iii Guttmann/Maclay Collection, Institute of Psychiatry, London
  iv–viii Courtesy of Al Vercoutere, Camarillo State Hospital, Camarillo, California

Color Section (beginning opposite page 688)
  i C. R. Tony Fletcher (top); C. Ray Moore/Shostal Associates (bottom)
  ii Steve Shapiro/Black Star (top); Clinton S. Bond/BBM Associates (center, bottom)
  iii Alex Webb/Magnum (top); Gordon Menzie/Photophile (center); Ellis Herwig/Stock, Boston (bottom left, bottom right)
  iv Steve McCarroll/Photophile (top); Geoffrey Gove/Rapho-Photo Researchers (center); Michael Mattei/Camera 5 (bottom)

Name Index

Abbas, K. A., 515
Abel, G. C., 576
Abelson, P. H., 438, 640
Abelson, R. P., 12
Abram, H. S., 607–8
Abrams, R., 349, 357
Abramson, E. E., 285
Abse, D. W., 242
Achenbach, T. M., 507
Adams, J. E., 123
Adams, M. S., 576
Adams, P. L., 256
Addario, D., 679
Adelson, E., 151
Adler, A., 58, 200
Adler, P., 589
Ago, Y., 283
Agras, W. S., 600
Akiskal, H. S., 342, 349, 350, 352
Alanen, Y. O., 318
Alarcon, R. D., 241
Alexander, D., 595
Alexander, F., 279, 680
Alexander, J. F., 162
Alexander, S., 403, 407
Alford, H., 698
Alig, V., 375
Allen, L. S., 633
Allen, M. G., 256, 309, 328, 349
Allen, R. P., 537
Allerton, W. S., 187, 196
Alley, G. R., 536
Allport, G., 66
Alsop, J., 401
Altman, H., 669
Altman, I., 99, 215
Altman, R., 524
Altrocchi, J., 352
Amir, M., 561
Anderson, L. S., 269
Angel, C., 312
Anthony, E. J., 318–19
Anthony, J. E., 165
Antrobus, J., 151
Apfelberg, B., 569
Appenzeller, S. N., 600
Araujo, G. D., 278
Archibald, H. C., 197
Arief, A. J., 399
Arieti, S., 316, 353
Aring, C. D., 41, 711
Arnold, E. L., 537
Aronson, E., 102
Aronson, S. S., 551
Asch, S. S., 486, 487
Astor, G., 279
Astrup, C., 328, 677
Averill, J. R., 114

Ayllon, T., 329, 690
Azrin, N. H., 329, 546, 690

Bachrach, A. J., 287
Back, K. W., 240
Bacon, J. G., 395
Bacon, M. K., 389
Bagley, C., 352, 577
Bahr, H. M., 172
Baker, L., 287
Baker, S. B., 285
Bales, R. F., 428
Bancroft, J., 583
Bandura, A., 61, 63, 66, 120, 164, 231, 242, 257, 263, 328, 381, 388, 389, 391, 393, 424, 426, 534, 546, 573, 599, 628, 630, 689
Bannister, D., 319
Barber, T. X., 682
Bard, M., 103
Barker, C. H., 211
Barker, E., 538
Barlow, D. H., 600
Barrett, C. L., 543
Bartemeier, L. H., 187
Barter, J. T., 609
Bartko, J. J., 298
Basedow, H., 282
Basowitz, H., 151
Bass, W., 621
Bassin, A., 430
Batareh, G. H., 524
Batchelor, I. R. C., 238, 478
Bates, D. E., 99
Bateson, G., 162, 319
Bayh, B., 444
Bazell, R. J., 436
Beach, F. A., 156
Beard, G. M., 253
Beavin, J., 162, 211
Beck, A. T., 223, 342, 350, 352, 607, 610
Beck, L., 538
Beck, R., 607, 610
Becker, E., 172
Becker, J., 352
Becker, W. C., 158
Behar, M., 150
Belden, K. M., 513
Belgium Consulate, 41
Bell, E., Jr., 187, 194
Bellack, A. S., 329
Bellamy, W. E., Jr., 490
Benady, D. R., 157, 389
Bender, L., 327, 535
Benedict, R., 76, 78
Bengelsdorf, I. S., 414, 643
Benjamin, B., 279

Benjamin, H., 601
Bennett, A. E., 40
Bentler, P. M., 599
Beres, D., 153
Berg, A., 574
Berger, R. J., 97, 100
Bergler, E., 572
Bergman, E., 607
Bergsma, D., 142, 144
Berkowitz, L., 120, 627
Berland, T., 645
Berman, A. L., 619
Berne, E., 74, 700–701
Bernstein, A., 80
Berry, H., III, 389
Bertalanffy, L. Von, 81
Berzins, J. I., 440
Besner, A., 641
Bess, B., 589
Bettelheim, B., 128, 129, 208, 316, 531, 532–33, 534
Bianchi, G. N., 249
Bibring, E., 354
Bieber, I., 596
Bieber, T., 596
Bijou, S. W., 502, 663
Binstock, J., 614
Birch, H. G., 149, 163
Bjarnason, S., 515
Blacker, K. H., 451
Bladeselee, A. L., 149
Blake, G., 394
Blanch, A., 576
Blanchard, E. B., 231, 260, 288
Blank, H. R., 388
Blau, A., 147
Blau, D., 502
Blauvelt, H., 156
Bleeker, E., 281
Bleuler, M., 292, 312
Bliss, M., 614
Bloch, H. S., 187, 189, 192, 195, 196
Bloomberg, S., 361
Bluemel, C. S., 5, 373, 375
Bluestone, H., 127
Blum, R., 454
Blumenthal, H., 313
Boehm, G., 436
Bogen, J. E., 461
Bohnert, M., 223
Bohnert, P. J., 333, 334, 336
Bolen, D. W., 383, 384, 385
Bolton, J. M., 325
Bombard, A., 99, 235
Bonk, C., 286
Bonnell, C., 592, 595–96
Bopp, J., 605

Borge, G. F., 347, 348
Borkovec, T. D., 379
Born, W., 5, 293
Borus, J. F., 195
Bourne, P. G., 187
Bowen, M., 319
Bowers, M., 297–99
Bowie, C. G., 399
Bowlby, J., 155, 381, 607
Boyd, W. H., 383, 384, 385
Braden, W., 456
Bradley, A., 614
Brady, J. V., 280
Braginsky, B. M., 518, 519
Braginsky, D. D., 518, 519
Brancale, R., 561
Bratfos, O., 360
Brekhman, I. L., 435
Brenner, M. H., 179
Bresler, D., 285
Brickner, R. M., 472
Briscoe, C. W., 353, 367
Brodey, W. M., 319
Brodie, H. K. H., 595
Broen, W. E., Jr., 313
Bromberg, W., 36
Bronfenbrenner, U., 167, 178, 647
Brooks, D. N., 477
Brown, B., 340, 359
Brown, B. B., 288
Brown, B. S., 442
Brown, C. C., 677
Brown, D. E., Jr., 198–99, 213
Brown, D. G., 273
Brown, G. W., 279, 325, 353
Brown, H., 623
Brown, J. F., 54
Brown, J. H., 619
Brown, L. R., 150, 640
Brown, W. A., 486
Brown, W. L., 224
Browne, E. G., 31
Browning, C. H., 619
Brožek, J., 99, 482
Bruce, L., 604
Bruce, T. A., 274
Bruetsch, W. L., 466
Brunton, M., 398
Bryan, J. H., 587
Bryan, T. H., 536
Buber, M., 319–20
Bucher, B., 687–88
Buck, V. E., 176
Buckley, W., 81
Buckner, H. T., 597
Buckout, R., 629, 633
Budzynski, T., 288
Bulatov, P. K., 276

Subject Index

stress, 210, 211

Community, and aftercare, 710–11, 724; and suicide prevention, 617, 619–20

Community reinforcement approach, 432

Community treatment facilities, 22, 46, 80, 708, 711–12, 723–24, 730, 731–32; for the aged, 502; for alcoholics, 429, 432, 433, 434, 710; for criminals, 404, 411; for delinquency, 394–95; for drug users, 442–43, 710; at Gheel, 41, 711; for mental retardates, 520, 524, 525, 729; for psychotics, 327, 329–30, 361, 709, 711

Compensation, 128, 129, 131, 580, 582, 584

Competencies, 680, 681, 684; and abnormal behavior, 136, 140, 161; assessing, 518–19; and development, 91, 92, 94, 95, 102–3, 104, 109, 722; and neuroses, 257, 261; and psychoses, 321, 330; and psychosomatic disorders, 275, 278

Competent community, 713

Competition, 175–76, 218, 441

Complexity and pace of modern living, 177

Comprehension, and brain disorders, 461, 464, 466, 472

Comprey Personality Scales, 662

Compromise reactions, 122

Compulsions, 232, 233, 234, 235–37, 387, 568 (See Obsessive-compulsive neurosis)

Computers, and change, 733; use of, in assessment, 666, 668–69, 670–71, 713

Concentration camp survivors, 206, 208, 211, 213, 257, 283, 482

Concentration difficulties, 448, 537; and brain disorders, 467, 471, 475, 476, 480, 482, 483, 495; in neuroses, 220, 254; in psychoses, 294, 340, 367; and situational stress, 197, 199, 208

Concordance rates, and schizophrenia, 309

Concussion, 474–75, 476, 477

Conditioning, 59–62, 281; of autonomic nervous system, 281, 679; in brainwashing, 210; in neuroses, 222, 228, 257; and psychosomatic disorders, 276, 281 (See also Behavior therapy)

Confidentiality, and assessment, 19, 665–66

Conflict, 5, 105, 109, 111, 112–13, 121, 569, 664, 680, 681, 683, 694; experimentally induced, 59–60, 258–59; group (See War); in neuroses, 236, 238, 245–46, 248, 258; and rapid change, 647, 648, 649; sexual, 175, 225, 229, 287, 317, 321, 336, 420, 560, 564; sources of, 174–76; in suicide, 607; and unrealistic demands, 159, 160; in values, 94, 129, 173–75, 647, 648, 649, 651

Conformity, 14, 70–71, 88, 173

Confrontation groups, 68, 693

Confusion (See Disorientation)

Congenital syphilis, 463, 466

Conjugal visits, 409

Conquering hero fantasy, 123

Conscience, 55, 90, 93, 157, 160, 374; and depression, 255; inadequate development of, 370, 377–78, 380; and psy-

choses, 321, 352, 363

Conscious, 56, 57, 681, 684

Consciousness, 204, 681, 682; and brain injury, 473, 474–75; clouding of, 470, 474–75, 479, 480, 491, 495; hysterical reactions, 238, 244, 246, 255

Conscious personality, 246

Constitution (See Biological factors)

Controlling behavior of others, by neurotics, 250–51, 253

Contusion, 475, 476

Conversion reaction, 219, 236–44, 255, 260, 263

Convulsions, and brain disorders, 464, 466, 467, 470, 481, 485, 494, 495; and drug usage, 448, 675; and mental retardates, 507, 515, 516, 517

Coping, and decompensation, 131–33; and psychoses, 321, 352; and psychosomatic disorders, 277–79, 284; with stress, 11, 113, 115, 117 (See also Stress reactions)

Corticovisceral control mechanism, 276–77, 284

Cortisone, 485

Counterconditioning, 685

Countertransference, 683

Cranial anomalies, 516–17

Creativity, 66, 108, 265, 718; encounter groups for, 703; using drugs to enhance, 453, 456

Cretinism, 484, 514–15

Crime, 5, 177, 369, 371, 396–411, 579–80; and body build, 144, 145, 397; and discrimination against ex-convicts, 634; and drugs, 389, 399, 436, 438, 441, 447, 455, 456; and faulty family relations, 163; milestones in dealing with, 410; organized, 401, 403; and war, 626, 631

Crisis intervention, 116, 615–17, 619, 620, 681, 714–15, 724

Crisis situations, in the seventies, 650–51; and transient situational stress, 115, 162

Critical periods, in learning, 95–96

Criticism, 226, 334, 335, 341

Cross-cultural studies, 76–79, 80, 83, 400

Cross-tolerance, 439

Crucial phase of alcoholism, 421, 423

Crying spells, and combat fatigue, 187, 189, 196; and depression, 362; as a stress reaction, 104, 122, 124; and transient situational stress, 187, 189, 196, 209

Cultural-familial mental retardation, 517–20

Cultural relativism, 14–15, 79

Culture, and aggression, 628–29; and alcoholism, 428; in collision, 649–50; and drug usage, 440–41, 457; and psychoanalysis, 58; and psychopathology, 71, 76–80; and sexual practices, 557, 558; and suicide, 614 (See also Society, Sociocultural factors)

Culture bias, and assessment, 19, 518, 658, 665, 666–68

Culture fair, 658, 667

Curiosity, and maintenance, 101–2

Cushing's syndrome, 485

Cyclothymic personality, 374

Cynicism, 178

Cynophobia, 261

Dancing mania, 31–32, 240

Daydreaming, 123, 374, 482, 542

"DDD" syndrome, 208

Death, 103, 147, 497; due to stress, 131, 132, 208, 211, 282–83; and existential model, 71; feelings of, in neuroses, 220–21, 255; and psychoses, 346–47, 353, 355; as stress, 109, 112, 114–15, 167–68, 172, 200, 201, 202, 353, 364, 393, 497, 607, 617; through voodoo, 282–83

Death (destructive) instinct, 55, 57

Death marches, 210, 211

Decision making, 220, 225, 228, 352, 367, 649, 664

Decompensation, 132–33, 137–38, 185, 401; in schizophrenia, 292, 294, 295, 297, 300, 312, 330, 337; in transient situational disorders, 185–213

Defense mechanisms, 56, 57, 67, 91, 296; in alcoholism, 421–22, 423, 426; neurotic, 219; phobia as, 227–32; psychotic, 296, 321, 324, 335–36, 354–56; against stress, 118, 120, 122–31, 132, 136, 174

Deficiency motivation, 106

Dehumanization, 3, 5, 18, 70, 406, 407, 625, 648, 719

Dehydration, 437, 441, 482, 515

Dejection, 187, 188, 254, 255

Delayed combat reactions, 192

Delinquency, 5, 369, 386–95, 396, 399, 530, 539, 544, 595; and body build, 144, 145; and faulty family relationships, 162, 163, 168; incidence of, 386–87, 396–97; and mental retardation, 387, 524; milestones in dealing with, 410; and schizophrenia, 316; and therapy, 670–71, 696

Delirious and confused senile dementia, 493

Delirious mania, 343

Delirium, and alcoholism, 419–20; and brain disorders, 244, 460, 461, 462, 468, 475, 479–81, 493; and drug withdrawal, 437, 446; and psychoses, 296

Delirium tremens, 419–20, 423, 429, 446

Delusional systems, in paranoia, 330–33, 336, 337

Delusions, 8, 132; and brain disorders, 465–66, 480, 483, 484, 487, 491, 493, 495; drug induced, 443, 454; and involutional melancholia, 362, 363, 365; in manic-depressive psychoses, 343, 346; in paranoia, 330, 331, 332, 333; in schizophrenia, 291, 294–95, 296, 297, 298, 300, 307, 308, 310, 312, 318, 321, 327, 529, 675; stages of recovery from, 327; therapy for, 675; types of, 296

Demands, educational, occupational, and family, 176; unrealistic, 158–59, 222, 689

Demara, F. W., 376–77

Dementia paralytica, 464

Dementia praecox, 292 (See Schizophrenia)

Demonology, abnormal behavior as, 26–27, 30, 31–37, 49, 59

Emotional insulation, 126–27, 128, 321, 401
Emotional mobilization, 117–18, 151, 193, 281 (See also Psychosomatic disorders)
Emotions, 151; and alcohol, 417, 418–19; and brain disorders, 461, 464, 466, 471, 482, 483, 484, 493, 494, 495; and drugs, 436, 447, 450, 451; and psychopathic personality, 377–78
Employment, 639; and alcoholism, 414–15, 418, 422, 423, 429, 434; and delinquency, 392; dissatisfaction with, 177, 179, 205, 250, 283; loss of, 127, 179, 221, 606; and psychosomatic disorders, 280, 283
Encounter groups, 22, 69, 656, 664, 702–7, 710, 719; for gambling, 385; for neuroses, 261, 262
Endocrine dysfunctions, 269, 482–86, 496, 514, 594–95
Endogenous hallucinogen, search for, 312
Endomorphic body type, 145
Enuresis, 530, 539, 548, 553
Environment, 680; assessment of, 663, 664; characteristics of, 177; and development, 86–87, 147, 153–69, 178; and retardation, 517–19, 520
Epidemic encephalitis, 468–69
Epidemiological studies, 79, 83, 723
Epilepsy, 476, 477, 478, 676
Eskimos, 78, 171, 428, 614
Estrogens, 363, 485
Ethics, and suicide prevention, 620–21; and therapy, 23, 717–18, 726 (See also Moral standards)
Eunuchism, 485
Euphoria, and brain disorders, 465, 467, 471, 480; from drugs, 436, 439, 447, 454, 455, 457
Excitation and inhibition processes, 119, 313, 349–50
Ex-convicts, and discrimination, 634
Exhaustion and disintegration phase, 131, 132, 138
Exhaustion delirium, 480
Exhibitionism, 560, 561, 567–70, 571, 579, 598, 689
Existential anxiety, 71–72, 180, 257
Existential model, 52, 70–72, 73, 83, 103; and psychopathology, 72, 136–37, 140, 256, 257, 324; and therapy, 261, 692–97
Existential neurosis, 219, 255, 256, 260, 265
Exorcism, for abnormal behavior, 26–27, 33–34, 673
Expectancy, of treatment, 198
Experimental neurosis, 59–60, 258–59
Expert witnesses, psychologists and psychiatrists as, 410
Exploitation of others, 369, 371, 579, 701
Explosive personality, 374
Extended family, 170
Extinction, 62, 65, 230, 286, 684–85, 686
Extramarital relations, 175, 577, 585, 598

Factor analysis, 661–62
Failure, 111, 114, 127, 171, 542, 546; and

neuroses, 222, 223, 237, 255; and psychoses, 333, 334, 335, 336, 346, 347, 353, 356, 365; and suicide, 606, 607
"Failure to thrive" syndrome, 154
Family, alcoholism in, 424–25, 426–27, 433; assessment of, 663–64, 665, 669; and communication difficulties, 75, 197; and crime, 399; demands of, 158–59, 161, 177; and development, 152–69; and disturbed children, 532, 534, 539, 541, 543–44; in the future, 170, 468–69; and mental retardation, 512, 514, 517–18; pathogenic, 165–69, 316–20, 334, 352, 378–80, 389, 391, 399, 566, 670; planning, 645–46, 722; and psychoses, 316–20, 334, 352; and sexual deviations, 566, 577–79, 596
Family therapy, 655, 670, 698–700; for alcoholism, 429, 432; for childhood disorders, 543, 544, 551; postoperative psychoses, 488; for psychosomatic disorders, 286; for schizophrenia, 329, 330; after a stroke, 502
Fantasy, 56, 58, 123, 128, 456, 542; in neuroses, 222, 223, 225, 233, 234–35, 255; in psychoses, 305, 306, 308, 317, 321; in psychosomatic disorders, 279; in sexual deviations, 575, 582, 584
Father, and abnormal behavior, 138, 162, 163; and alcoholism, 424; in antisocial personalities, 380; and childbirth disturbances, 486, 487; in delinquency, 389, 391; and deprivation, 518; and manic-depressive reactions, 349; and sexual deviations, 577–78, 595, 596
Fatigue, 105, 117, 140, 151, 174, 374; and alcoholism, 418; amphetamines for, 446–47, 449; and brain disorders, 475, 476, 485, 495; in combat, POW, and civilian stress situations, 197, 198, 199, 202, 205; in neuroses, 251–54, 255; in psychoses, 342, 486
Faulty communications, 160, 161–62; and schizophrenia, 319; sexual inadequacy as, 263
Faulty development, 94, 136, 222 (See also Biological factors, Parent-child relationships, Interpersonal factors, Psychological factors, Psychosocial factors, Sociocultural factors)
Faulty discipline, and abnormal development, 159–61; and antisocial behavior, 379–80, 389, 391, 399; and childhood disorders, 539
Faulty learning, 64, 66, 136, 140, 548, 685; and antisocial behavior, 379–80, 383–84, 389–91, 411; and neuroses, 217, 222, 228–29, 257, 265; and paranoia, 334–36; and psychosomatic disorders, 278, 284; and schizophrenia, 320–24; and sexual deviation, 559, 564, 565, 572, 574, 575, 595, 599
Fear, 116, 120, 160, 174, 402, 480, 487, 581, 629; in alcoholism, 419–20, 423; and childhood disorders, 541, 546; in combat and shock reactions, 192, 193, 198, 203, 204, 208, 210; death from, 282–83; and old age, 496–97; reduction and elimination of, 229–31; and sexual deviation, 562, 563, 564–65, 567, 573, 574, 575, 584, 591, 596

Fearfulness vs. positive action, 174
Feedback, 113, 122, 138–39, 699, 703, 705, 706
Females, and alcoholism, 415–16, 418, 425; and antisocial personality, 370; and childhood disorders, 531, 544; and crime, 396–97, 400; and delinquency, 387, 389, 391, 393, 395; discrimination against, 178, 632, 634; and drug usage, 438, 440; and neuroses, 227, 249, 254; and paresis, 466; and promiscuity, 391; and psychoses, 340, 362, 489, 490; and psychosomatic disorders, 270; and sexual deviations, 562, 564–65, 566, 569, 576, 578, 585, 586–89, 590; and sexual revolution, 566, 569; and suicide, 605, 606, 609, 612, 618
Feminism, 484, 485
Fetishism, 571–73, 574, 598, 687
Fever, and brain damage, 460, 468, 480
Field properties of living systems, 82
Filtering, in autistics, 531–32; in schizophrenics, 293–94, 299, 305, 308, 321
Flashbacks and LSD, 452, 453
Flexibility, lack of, and brain disorders, 489, 497, 503; and neuroses, 218, 232
"Flight into reality," 354–55, 367
Folie à deux, 318
Former patients, in mental health work, 522–23, 709–10, 712, 716
Foster homes, 523, 524, 541, 544, 551–52, 708
Frame of reference, 90, 91, 92, 96, 118, 261, 722; faulty, 140, 160, 161, 174, 275; and psychoses, 321, 336
Fraudulent interpersonal contracts, 170
Free association, 25, 55, 57, 681, 683
Freedom, in existential view, 70–71, 136, 140
Free-floating anxiety (See Anxiety neurosis)
Frigidity, 241, 559, 562, 564, 565, 566, 567, 598, 686
Frontal lobe, 460, 471, 472, 476, 477, 490, 494
Frustration, 109, 111, 112, 120, 127, 171–72, 641; and aggression, 392, 627–28, 630; and eczema, 278; and neuroses, 224; and prejudice, 636, 637; and sexual deviation, 560, 564, 565, 569, 584; and suicide, 607, 614
Frustration-aggression hypothesis, 627–28
Frustration tolerance (See Stress tolerance)
"F-scale," 662
Fugue states, 244, 245–46, 248, 255
Fulfillment, 15, 58, 66, 67, 70, 72, 91, 94, 136–37; lack of, in neuroses, 218, 224, 256
Functional psychoses, 16, 291–367 (See also Psychoses)
"Future shock," 3–4, 180, 647–49

Gage, P., 473, 474
Galen, 30, 33, 269, 271, 435, 473
Gamblers Anonymous, 384, 385–86
Gambling, 369, 382–86, 401, 411
Games, in relationships, 74–75, 700–702
"Gangplank fever," 242

Gangs (See Peer groups)
Gastrointestinal disorders, and neuroses, 228, 239, 258; and psychosomatic disorders, 268, 269, 283; and transient situational disorders, 197, 213
Gay community, 591, 592–94
Gene mutagens, 142, 510, 513, 532
Gender identity, 594–95, 600–601
General adaptation syndrome, 351
Generalization, in conditioning, 62, 63
General paresis, 47–48, 81, 462, 464–66, 467
General systems approach, 81–83, 177
Genetic code, 86, 89
Genetics and heredity, and alcoholism, 424–25; and childhood disorders, 532, 546; counseling, 513, 525, 657, 722; and crime, 397–98; and development, 86, 93; and faulty development, 89, 139–44, 146, 147, 149; and homosexuality, 594–95; and manic-depressive reactions, 349; and mental retardation, 508, 510, 512–14, 515, 524; and neuroses, 256–57; and old-age psychoses, 496; and predisposition to mental illness, 143–44, 152; and psychosomatic disorders, 275; and schizophrenia, 309–11
Genital stage of development, 56
Genitourinary disorders, 239, 269
German measles, 508, 515
Gestalt therapy, 261, 694–96, 703, 719
Gheel colony, 40–41, 711
Ghetto life, 179, 587, 627, 628, 640; and alcoholism and drug usage, 432, 441; delinquency and crime in, 380–81, 387, 395, 399, 400; and psychoses, 325–26; and psychosomatic disorders, 283–84; and retardation, 517–19, 525, 640 (See also Poverty)
Gigantism, 482, 484
Goals, and antisocial personality, 370; and coping with stress, 111, 120, 122, 160, 195; and development, 104, 108, 171; and neuroses, 222; and psychoses, 334, 335; and psychosomatic disorders, 274, 278
Goering, H., 373, 375
Gonads, 484, 485
Gonorrhea, 462
Government, and mental health, 725–26, 732
Grandeur, delusions of, 296, 300, 310, 312, 321, 330, 331, 333, 340, 342, 357, 465–66
Grand mal, 478, 676
Grief, and trauma, 201; -work, 124
Group Assessment of Interpersonal Traits (GAIT), 664
Group cohesiveness, and prejudice, 636; and suicide, 614
Group for the Advancement of Psychiatry (GAP), 729
Groups, assessment of, 655, 663–64, 669, 671; conflict between, 624–32; identification with, 173, 178, 392–93; norms of, 90, 623; overpopulation and ecology, 639–46; pathology of, 18, 132, 168, 380, 387, 390, 392–93, 623–51; prejudice against, 632–39; uncontrolled social change, 647–51; and war, 624–32

(See also Peer groups)
Group therapy, 22, 285, 408, 410, 679 681, 702–7, 712–13; and the aged, 501, 502; for alcoholism, 430, 432–33; for drug dependency, 442, 450; for psychoses, 328, 336, 359; for sexual deviates, 570, 573, 579
Growth (See Personal growth)
Growth motivation, 106
Guilt, 8–9, 56, 57, 421, 433, 608; coping with, 115. 160. 172, 174; delusions of, 296; lack of, 369, 371, 373, 381, 388, 405; in neurotics, 228–29, 233, 234–35, 243, 246, 248, 253, 255; in psychotics, 296, 341, 342, 346, 347, 352, 355, 356, 358, 362, 366, 367, 486; and sexual deviation, 564, 568, 577–78, 582, 584, 596; and suicide, 201, 608; in transient situational disorders, 192, 194, 198, 201, 202, 203, 210
Gustatory hallucinations, 296

Halfway houses, for alcoholics, 428, 432, 433, 434, 710; after hospitalization, 709–11
Hallucinations, 104, 132, 137; in alcoholism, 419–20; in brain disorders, 460, 461, 470, 471, 475, 480, 481, 483, 484, 486, 487, 490; drug induced, 437, 443, 448, 450, 452, 453, 454, 675; in manic-depressive reactions, 340, 341, 343, 346; in paranoia, 330, 332; in schizophrenia, 291, 293, 295–96, 297, 300, 306, 307, 308, 310, 312, 321, 327, 529, 675; therapy for, 675; and transient situational disorders, 209; types of, 296
Hallucinogens, 435, 450–53, 456
Halo effect, 658
Hashish, 449, 454
Headaches, 538; and brain disorders, 462, 470, 471, 475, 476, 477, 485, 495; and neuroses, 228, 239; and psychosomatic disorders, 268, 269, 270, 271, 272, 273, 281, 285, 286, 288, 289; and situational stress, 207, 209, 213
Head injury, and brain damage, 473–79
Health care movement, 553, 721–32
Health problems (See Physical illness)
Hearing impairment, and mental retardation, 507, 517
Heart disease, 147, 213, 222, 223, 343, 415; and psychosomatic disorders, 270, 274, 277, 283, 288, 289; and severe stress, 118, 152, 176, 213
Heart palpitations, 197, 220, 222, 226
Hebephrenic schizophrenia, 305–6, 307, 308. 325, 337, 358
Helplessness, 381, 399, 502, 641; learned-, 354; and psychoses, 317, 354, 359
Hematophobia, 227
Hemic and lymphatic disorders, 269
Heredity (See Genetics and heredity)
Hermaphroditism, 559
Heroin, 389, 413, 414, 436–43, 449, 454–55
Hierarchy of needs, 106
High blood pressure (See Hypertension)
Hippocrates, 27–28, 29, 30, 236, 346, 473
Hiroshima, 142, 516, 624, 625, 626
Histrionic personality, 241, 374

Holistic reactions, 119
Homeostasis, 97, 104, 108–9, 277
Homicide, 396, 398, 400, 405, 539, 614; and alcoholism, 414, 417; by delinquents, 387, 390, 393, 394, 395; and drugs, 447, 451; by psychotics, 341, 399, 400; and sexual deviation, 574
Homosexuality, 225, 258, 467, 468, 557, 559, 561, 565, 566, 583, 584, 589–97, 598, 634; and paranoia, 336; in prison, 404, 409, 560, 579, 591
Hope, need for, 103–4, 172, 211, 213, 422, 610, 611, 620
Hopelessness, 104, 105, 117, 127, 210, 381, 392, 399, 500, 511, 641; and death, 283; and neuroses, 250, 251, 254; and POW camps, 257, 283; and psychoses, 346, 347, 354, 359, 362, 365, 366; and suicide, 606, 607–8, 611
Hormone imbalance, and homosexuality, 594–95
Hormone therapy, 485–86, 514, 515, 601
Hospitalization, 708–9, 724; to prevent suicides, 360, 363; for psychoses, 291, 292, 308, 325, 326–27, 330, 337, 360, 361, 363, 366; syndrome, 709 (See also Institutions)
Hostile aggression, 628
Hostility, and abnormal development, 147, 158, 171, 627, 629, 636; and alcoholism and drug usage, 417, 418–19, 440; in childhood disorders, 539–41, 548, 549; and development, 120, 121, 126, 128; and mental retardation, 509; in neuroses, 222, 225, 234, 235, 253, 254, 255; in personality disorders, 370, 371, 374, 381, 389, 399, 659; in psychoses, 321, 332, 333, 341, 352, 355; in psychosomatic disorders, 270, 271, 272; and sex deviations, 560, 565, 568, 579, 580, 584, 587, 596; and suicide, 607, 608, 611, 614; in therapy, 683; and transient situational disorders, 208, 209, 211, 213
Hot lines, 544, 581, 714–15, 724
Humanistic-existential therapies, 692–97, 719
Humanistic model, 52, 66–70, 83, 136, 257, 456
Humanitarian approach to mental illness, 37–46
"Humanity identification," 450
Human nature, and aggression, 626–27; behavioristic view of, 65–66, 67; psychoanalytic view of, 57–59, 67, 626; humanistic view of, 66, 67–69; existential view of, 70–72
Human potential movement, 456, 692, 696, 718–19, 731
Hunger, 97–99, 106, 208, 285 (See also Deprivation, food)
Huntington's chorea, 142, 143, 144, 490
Hydrocephalus, 516–17
Hygiene, deterioration of, 209, 461, 464, 467, 470, 471, 482, 609
Hyperactivity, 147; and brain disorders, 468–69, 490; in children, 447, 527, 528, 530, 535–39, 553; in psychoses, 304, 339, 341, 342, 343, 350, 357, 367, 378
Hypersensitivity, 174, 187, 193, 203, 220, 226, 374, 418, 535, 541, 542

490, 492, 495; and chronic situational stress, 205, 212, 213; in children, 530; and combat reaction, 87, 193, 197, 202; in neuroses, 257; in psychoses, 306, 342, 343, 362

Isocarboxazid, 676

Isolation, 172, 197, 423, 426, 641; and brainwashing, 210, 211; as a defense mechanism, 127, 128, 209, 279; effect of, 104, 154, 209, 214, 235, 517; and old age, 497–98; and suicide, 617

"Italian School of Criminology," 397

Jacksonian epilepsy, 478

Job dissatisfaction, 177, 179, 205, 250, 283

Judgment, impairment of, and alcoholism, 416, 418; in brain disorders, 461, 464, 466, 472, 481, 489, 490, 495, 501; and personality disorders, 375, 379; in psychoses, 308, 340, 341, 343

Juvenile paresis, 462, 466–67

Juvenile status offenders, 395

Kahn Test of Symbol Arrangement, 662

Key stresses, 115–16

Killing, during war, 194, 198, 629

Klinefelter's syndrome, 515

Korean War, 185, 186, 187, 196, 197, 200, 208, 210–11, 625

Korsakoff's psychosis, 420, 477

Kuder Preference Record, 662

Labeling, effects of, 19, 20–21, 665, 666, 667, 709

La Bicêtre hospital, 39–40, 42

Language development, and brain disorders, 460, 461, 477; and childhood disorders, 531, 532, 534, 536; and deprivation, 153; and mental retardation, 507, 509, 511, 516, 518, 522–23

Latency stage of development, 56

Latent schizophrenia, 308

Law of effect, 61

L-dopa therapy, 490, 491

Leadership, 101, 108, 187, 195–96

Lead poisoning, 481, 508

"Learned helplessness," 354

Learning, aggression as, 164, 627, 628–30; in autonomic nervous system, 275, 281, 679; in behavioristic model, 59–66; and brain disorders, 460, 461, 472, 535–36, 538, 539; and development, 91, 96, 106, 128–29, 136; and disturbed children, 527, 535–39, 546; and environment, 153, 517–18, 525; faulty (See Faulty learning); and mental retardation, 506–7, 509, 517–18; and prejudice, 634–36

Legal system and crime, 398, 403, 405, 407, 410

Lesbianism, 587, 589, 590, 592, 593, 595, 597

Lethality scale of suicide potentiality, 606, 616

Level of aspiration, 108, 121

Libido, 55, 57

Librium, 449, 675

Life change units (LCU), 117, 274, 279, 352

Life instinct, 55

Life span, 148, 488

Life stress, 274, 275, 325, 375 (See also Life change units)

Life style, 90, 108, 146; and neuroses, 218, 226, 227, 257, 261, 263, 264, 265

Limbic system, 460

Lithium salts and lithium therapy, 350, 359

Locomotor ataxia, 464

Loneliness, 157, 160, 173, 235, 692; existential, 172; in old age, 497, 500; and psychoses, 340; and psychosomatic disorders, 274; and space flights, 214

"Long eye" syndrome, 104, 209, 283

Losses, and stress, 171–72, 200, 364, 366

Love, 103, 104, 169; ability to give and receive, 153, 157, 170, 371, 531, 532, 534; and development, 103, 148, 153, 165, 166; and psychoses, 316–17, 319, 330

Loyalty, to group, 188, 195, 210

Lycanthropy, 32–33

Lysergic acid diethylamide (LSD), 152, 310, 311, 414, 449, 450–53, 456, 479

Macrocephaly, 516

Mainlining, 436

Maintenance strivings, 96–104, 106, 109

Maintenance therapy, 617

Maladaptive family structures (See Pathogenic families)

Males, and alcoholism, 415–16, 418, 425, 432; and antisocial personality, 370, 378; and childhood disorders, 531, 535, 539, 541, 545; and crime and delinquency, 387, 393, 395, 396–97, 398, 400; and drug usage, 439–40, 456; and gambling, 384–85; impotency, 558, 559, 562, 563, 564, 565, 566, 567, 598, 686; and neuroses, 227, 249, 254; and paresis, 466; and psychoses, 340, 362, 489, 490; and psychosomatic disorders, 270; and sexual deviations, 562, 564, 568, 570, 571, 573, 578, 579–80, 585, 589, 590, 597; and suicide, 605, 606, 609, 612, 617, 618; XYY anomaly in, 397–98

Malingering, 240, 243, 249, 477

Malnutrition, 640–41; among alcoholics, 418, 420, 423; and brain disorders, 481–82, 496; in drug users, 438; in POW camps, 208, 213, 482; and retardation, 149–50, 460, 510, 518

Manic activity, 27, 30, 437

Manic-depressive reactions, 60, 100, 291, 339, 340–61, 399, 569–70; causal factors in, 349–59; sleep patterns of, 100, 351–52, 359; treatment of, 359–61, 675–76, 678, 717; types of, 341–49

Mannerisms, and schizophrenia, 306, 310

Marathon groups, 686, 703, 705

Marijuana, 413, 414, 418, 435, 439, 453–57

Marital instability, 169–70

Marital interactions, destructive, 317–19

Marital schism, 318

Marital skew, 318

Marital status, and crime, 400; and psy-

choses, 313, 358; and sexual deviations, 560, 569, 570, 577, 578, 580, 586, 591, 592, 597, 599; and suicide, 605–6, 618

Marriage, 614, 618; and alcoholism, 418, 423, 427; assessment of, 663, 665, 669; changing role of, 170, 585, 648–49; demands of, 169–70, 176; and depressive reactions, 357; and neuroses, 225–26, 234, 245, 251–53; therapy for, 563, 697–98, 701, 710; unconventional patterns of, 557, 584–85, 601

"Masked deprivation," 153–55, 156

Masking of emotional problems, 530

"Mask of insanity," 324

Masochism, 575–76, 598

Mass madness, 31–33, 240

Mass media, 629–30, 238, 648

Masturbation, 159, 175, 236, 305, 387, 560, 565, 568, 570, 572, 575, 579, 580, 583–84, 596, 598

Maternal deprivation, effects of, 95–96, 152–55

Maturation, 95–96

Maturity, trends toward, 92–93

Meaning, in existential view, 71, 72, 180, 255, 256, 693; loss of, and suicide, 607–8, 610, 612, 617; need for, 103–4, 172, 174, 500, 503, 641; and neuroses, 255, 256, 257

Medical evaluation, 656–57

Medical model of abnormal behavior, 47–49, 51, 54, 59, 136

Medulla, 460

Melancholia, 28, 30

Memory impairment, and alcohol, 420, 421; and brain disorders, 460, 461, 464, 466, 470, 471, 472, 475, 476, 477, 483, 489, 490, 491, 492, 495; and drugs, 444; and MBD, 536; and psychoses, 346; and situational stress, 209

Meningitis, 517

Meningovascular syphilis, 467

Menopause, 363, 485

Mental health, 721–37; early concern for, 45–46; and the future, 732–37; and governmental aid, 725–26; international efforts for, 730–31; limitations on programs of, 731–32; organizations promoting, 725–29; personnel in, 21–22, 664–65, 709, 711, 712, 725, 726; preventive measures for, 722–24; role of citizen and, 727, 729, 736–37

Mental retardation, 505–25; biological factors in, 142, 146, 147, 483, 508–17; and brain disorders, 466, 469, 477, 481; broad spectrum approach to, 525; causes of, 508, 510, 721; classification of, 506–7; cultural-familial, 517–19; delinquency and crime, 387, 399, 524; and deprivation, 95–96, 150, 153, 154, 516–20; incidence of, 505, 507, 518; and sexual deviations, 561, 569, 576; types of, 510, 512–18; treatment and prevention of, 514, 515, 517, 520–25, 689, 716, 725, 729

Meprobamates, 435, 449

Mescaline, 152, 310, 311, 449, 450, 453

Mesmer and mesmerism, 53, 54, 682

Mesomorphic body type, 145

Metabolic disturbances, 657; and brain

depressive reactions, 349; and neuroses, 256; and schizophrenia, 143, 309
Type A people, and psychosomatic disorders, 277, 289

Ulcers (See Peptic ulcers)
Unconscious, Adler's collective-, 58; and brain injury, 475; and motivation, 106–7; and psychoanalytic model, 54, 56, 57, 683; and stress reactions, 119–20
Undoing, 127, 128
Unemployment, as stress, 127, 179, 221
Unhappiness, and neuroses, 218, 260, 265; and psychosomatic disorders, 279
Unipolar reactions of manic-depression, 340
United Nations, 631, 645, 649, 727, 730–31
UNESCO, 727, 730–31
U.S. Department of Health, Education, and Welfare, 147, 429
Unpredictability, and combat fatigue, 193–94
Unrealistic demands, 158–59, 222, 689
Unreality, feelings of, 228, 362
Unsocialized aggressive reaction, 530, 539–41
Upper class, and mental retardation, 518
Urban areas, 640, 642; and crime delinquency, 393, 396, 399, 642; and psychoses, 79, 326, 358, 500; and suicide, 614, 618 (See also Ghetto life)

Vaginismus, 562, 563, 564, 567, 598
Validity of tests, 518, 658, 667
Valium, 449, 675
Value assumptions, 90, 91, 92, 93, 162, 172, 722, 735–36
Values, conflicts in, 94, 129, 173–75, 648; and delinquency, 165, 392; and the future, 733, 735–36; loss of, 4, 178, 180, 210; in models, 67, 69, 70–71, 72, 103, 172; need for, 87, 90–94, 103–4. 722, 735–36; and neuroses, 256, 257, 261; in pathogenic family patterns, 165, 379–80; and psychotherapy, 681, 696, 717–18; and rapid change, 647, 648, 649, 651; and reality therapy, 696
Vandalism, 131, 373, 539
Venereal disease, 462–63, 467–68
Verbal tests, 658
Videotapes, in therapy, 697–98, 699, 700, 710
Vietnam conflict, 185, 186, 187, 189, 190–91, 194, 196, 198–99, 200, 205, 212, 357, 624, 627
Violence, 3, 5, 151, 177, 614, 627, 642, 649; and antisocial personality, 370; causes of, 625–30; and crime, 398, 401, 403, 405, 407; and delinquency, 388, 393; and models, 57, 68, 626 (See also Aggression, Crime, War)
Violent behavior, and alcoholism, 414, 417, 418–19; and antisocial personality, 370; in brain disorders, 393, 490, 500; and drugs, 441, 447, 455, 456; in psychoses, 341, 343, 447
Viral encephalitis, 508

Virilism, 484, 485
Visceral disorders (See Psychosomatic disorders)
Visceral symptoms, in neurotic reactions, 237, 238, 239, 242, 250, 255
Vision, and alcohol, 417; and brain disorders, 460, 467, 471, 472; and conversion reactions, 237, 238, 242; and mental retardation, 515, 516, 517; and syphilis, 464, 467
Visual hallucinations, 296, 300, 310, 343, 357, 448, 450–51, 452, 453, 454, 471
Vitamin deficiencies, 481–82
Voice masking, 547
Volunteers in mental health work, 617, 716, 724, 727, 729, 736
Voodoo, 282–83
Voyeurism, 560, 561, 567, 570–71, 598
Vulnerabilities, 94, 114, 218, 233; and abnormal development, 144, 147, 149, 151; in alcoholics, 425; and combat reactions, 185, 195; in manic-depressives, 349, 352; in neurotics, 218, 219, 233, 256, 256–57; and psychosomatic disorders, 276, 277–79, 284; in schizophrenia, 143–44, 309, 311, 313, 320; and trauma, 192, 194, 203

War, 177, 624–32, 650, 732; and models, 57, 68, 626; prevention of, 630–32; reactions to, 185–200, 207–13, 236–38; and responsibility for crimes, 631; and suicide, 613, 614, 618
War goals, acceptability of, and stress, 194, 198
Warmth and affection, and development, 146, 153
Wassermann, A. von, 48, 467
Wechsler Adult Intelligence Scale (WAIS), 658
Wechsler Intelligence Scale for Children (WISC), 658
Weyer, J., 36–37, 46
Widowed, and suicide, 607, 617, 618, 723
"Will-to-meaning," 71
Windigo psychosis, 78–79
"Wintering over" reactions, 209, 214
Witchcraft, 34–37, 43
Withdrawal, 121–22, 128, 609, 649; from alcohol, 429; in chemotherapy, 675; in childhood disorders, 532, 534, 541, 542–43; from drugs, 436–37, 441–42, 445, 450, 455; in old-age psychosis, 489; in schizophrenia, 292, 297, 300, 304–5, 306, 308, 310, 324, 532; in transient situational stress disorders, 202, 208, 210
Work responsibilities, and psychosomatic disorders, 274, 280, 283
World Health Organization, 16, 463, 724, 730, 731
World War I, 236, 238
World War II, 624, 725; and combat reactions, 185, 186–87, 188–89, 192, 194, 196, 197; and conversion reactions, 238; and Kamikaze, 613; 614; and prisoner-of-war camps, 206–8, 210, 213, 482
Worry, 174, 374, 541, 584; and psychoses, 342, 362; and ulcers, 270

Worth, 114, 125, 128, 137, 393, 612, 735; lack of, and psychoses, 336, 346, 347, 356, 365, 366; need for, 103, 128–29, 131; and neuroses, 250; and old-age psychoses, 497, 500
Writing, and brain disorders, 464; of schizophrenics, 298–99, 303, 315
Wundt, W., 51

XYY Chromosomal type, and criminality, 397–98

Yoga, 679, 719
Youth, and antisocial personality, 370, 382; and crime, 396–97, 400, 409; and delinquency, 386–95; and responsibility, 167, 651; and therapy, 712, 715
Youth-oriented culture, 146, 500

Zen, 679, 719
"Zombie reactions," and POW's, 211
Zoophobia, 227

Classification of Abnormal Behavior Patterns

(Diagnostic nomenclature of the American Psychiatric Association*)

I
Mental Retardation

Borderline mental retardation

Mild mental retardation

Moderate mental retardation

Severe mental retardation

Profound mental retardation

Where known, the associated physical condition should be specified: e.g., following infection, chromosomal abnormality, prematurity, or psychosocial (environmental) deprivation.

II
Organic Brain Syndromes

Senile and pre-senile dementia

Alcoholic psychosis

Psychosis associated with intracranial infection

Psychosis associated with other cerebral condition (e.g., arteriosclerosis, brain trauma, intracranial neoplasm)

Psychosis associated with other physical condition (e.g., endocrine disorder, metabolic or nutritional disorder, systemic infection, drug or poison intoxication, childbirth)

This category includes both acute and chronic brain syndromes as well as psychotic and nonpsychotic brain syndromes (e.g., the latter includes mental disturbances associated with intracranial infection and related pathology but less severe than psychosis).

III
Psychoses Not Attributed to Physical Conditions Listed Previously

Schizophrenia
    Simple type
    Hebephrenic type
    Catatonic type
    Paranoid type
    Acute schizophrenic episode

This category also includes latent type, residual type, schizo-affective type, childhood type, and chronic undifferentiated type schizophrenia.

Major affective disorders (affective psychoses)
    Involutional melancholia
    Manic-depressive illness, manic type
    Manic-depressive illness, depressed type
    Manic-depressive illness, circular type
    Other major affective disorder

Paranoid states
    Paranoia
    Involutional paranoid state
    Other paranoid state

Other psychoses
    This category includes psychotic depressive reaction, reactive confusion, acute paranoid reaction, and unspecified reactive psychosis.

IV
Neuroses

Anxiety neurosis

Hysterical neurosis
    Conversion type
    Dissociative type

Phobic neurosis

Obsessive compulsive neurosis

Depressive neurosis

Neurasthenic neurosis (neurasthenia)

Depersonalization neurosis

Hypochondriacal neurosis

Other neurosis

V
Personality Disorders and Certain Other Nonpsychotic Mental Disorders

Personality disorders
    This category includes paranoid personality, cyclothymic personality, schizoid personality, explosive personality, obsessive-compulsive personality, hysterical personality, asthenic personality, antisocial personality, passive-aggressive personality, and inadequate personality.

Sexual deviations
    Sexual orientation disturbance (homosexuality)[1]
    Fetishism
    Pedophilia
    Transvestitism
    Exhibitionism
    Voyeurism
    Sadism
    Masochism
    Other unspecified deviation

Alcoholism
    Episodic excessive drinking
    Habitual excessive drinking
    Alcohol addiction
    Other (and unspecified) alcoholism

Drug dependence
    Opium, opium alkaloids, and their derivatives
    Synthetic analgesics with morphine-like effect
    Barbiturates
    Other hypnotics and sedatives or "tranquilizers"
    Cocaine
    Hashish, marihuana
    Psycho-stimulants
    Hallucinogens
    Other drug dependence

[1]This category is reserved for individuals whose sexual interests are directed primarily toward members of the same sex and who either wish to change their sexual orientation or are disturbed by it. This category does not include homosexuality per se, which is considered an acceptable alternative sexual pattern and does not constitute a mental disorder.